AN INTRODUCTION
TO THE
HISTORY OF SOCIOLOGY

EDITED BY HARRY ELMER BARNES

AN INTRODUCTION

TO THE

HISTORY OF SOCIOLOGY

THE UNIVERSITY OF CHICAGO PRESS
CHICAGO · ILLINOIS

THE UNIVERSITY OF CHICAGO PRESS, CHICAGO 37
The University of Toronto Press, Toronto 5, Canada

Copyright 1948 by The University of Chicago. All rights reserved
Published 1948. Sixth Impression 1961. Composed and printed by
THE UNIVERSITY OF CHICAGO PRESS, *Chicago, Illinois, U.S.A.*

To the Memory of
ALBION WOODBURY SMALL

PREFACE

THIS collaborative work on the history of sociology is presented as a comprehensive summary and critical appraisal of the growth of sociological thought from the ancient Near East to our own day, with the main emphasis on the systematic sociologists from Comte to Sorokin. An effort has been made to indicate what social philosophers and sociologists have said about the origins of human society, the ways of group life, the development and expression of social interests, the modes of social discipline and social control, and the main causes of both cultural lag and social progress.

The book both covers the development of the concepts and subject matter of sociology and provides the reader with a panorama of the ideas and problems with which social philosophy and sociology have wrestled for the last three thousand years. Hence it embodies many a practical and illuminating analysis of the chief processes and problems of social existence and group life, as well as furnishes a discriminating and critical anthology of the formal doctrines of the leading social philosophers and sociologists. We have sought to steer away from a mere musty and antiquarian review of esoteric lore and have tried to bring out as vividly as possible the manner in which the chief writers on the subject have handled the main issues involved in group behavior and social organization down through the years. While the sociological systems dealt with are cogently elucidated, it is also made clear how these systems of social thought usually grew out of the conditions and problems of the time and were regarded, in one way or another, as a solution of the social questions and crises of the era and culture of the writers. The sociological theories are thus traced directly back and related to the life and times of each of the writers considered.

Our survey of the development of sociological thought begins with a brief review of the ideas of the sages and prophets of antiquity on the origins and purposes of social life and then passes on to a consideration of the Greek ideas of the good life, the ideal society, and the perfect state. The Roman adaptations and variations of these Greek theories are next

vii

summarized. Then the rise of the Christian philosophy of life and social goals is presented, along with a consideration of the medieval view of the role of church and state in organized society. Turning next to modern times, we examine the social theories associated with the rise of the national state, the right of revolution, and the growth of representative government, such as the "divine-right" theory, the doctrine of a social contract, the notion of secular absolutism, and the conception of popular sovereignty.

Well down into the eighteenth century, all these problems of associated life were dealt with by what we term "social philosophy," which covered social organization, political life, legal concepts, economic activities, ethical problems, and the like. During the late eighteenth century and the first third of the nineteenth, this larger, enveloping matrix of social philosophy gradually differentiated into sociology and the special social sciences, sociology emerging as the basic and normative social science in the writings of Saint-Simon, Comte, and Spencer. A larger body of material which threw light on social life and an increasing interest in the historical and inductive approach to social problems were the main factors accounting for the rise of sociology and the special social sciences, a process which is examined with some thoroughness. But the main portion of this work is reserved for a consideration of systematic sociological writing which begins with Auguste Comte. There was plenty of sociological thinking before Comte, but no sociological systems.

In analyzing the systematic writings of the outstanding sociologists, primary stress has been placed upon emphasizing the basic conceptions and contributions of the author rather than upon seeking out each fugitive detail, thus avoiding the mistake of losing sight of the forest of essentials in a wandering quest for the trees of triviality. Aside from the chapters written by the editor, it can be said that each author has almost invariably possessed some special knowledge and competence with respect to the sociologist treated, and, in some instances, the author is the foremost authority in the world on the person whose doctrines are analyzed. Special emphasis is laid on the public significance of the system and doctrines of the sociologists studied, indicating their bearing upon political policy and social reform. The editor has carried throughout his chapters a definite scheme of presentation and analysis in accordance with this purpose, but he has not forced his collaborators to conform to any preconceived plan of exposition, believing that the systems themselves will naturally suggest the most suitable pattern of presentation. It is believed, however, that a reasonable degree of uniformity and consistency of treatment has been attained—at least as much as the very nature of the project would permit, without artificiality and unnatural rigidity.

The history of systematic sociology really gets under way with the analysis of the eminent pioneers in systematization: Comte, Spencer, Morgan, Sumner, Ward, and Gumplowicz. The more important contributions of each of these authors to the clarification of the province of sociology and to its content and purpose are pointed out at some length. For the most part, their systems represented, in one way or another, the impact of evolutionary doctrine on social thinking. The highly contrasting conceptions of these writers as to the possibilities of social planning are made clear—Comte, Morgan, and Ward believing that the main purpose of sociology is to facilitate planned progress, while Spencer, Sumner, and Gumplowicz held that the great practical service of sociology is to warn against the futility and danger of the notion that man can facilitate and hasten social progress through deliberate action.

After the pioneers are adequately expounded and appraised, we pass on to consider the leading sociologists, grouped by country and language. Within each national group the treatment is personal and individual rather than based upon schools of thought. This method of presentation has been chosen for several reasons. In the first place, nearly every history of sociological thought in the English language, with the exception of the second volume of the editor's work with Howard Becker, presents sociological thinking as organized about special schools of interest rather than as elucidating individual systems. Moreover, the Barnes and Becker volume aims more at a comprehensive review of all social thought in each country than at an extended exposition of the few outstanding systems of sociology. More important than anything else, however, is the fact that this work is primarily a history of systematic sociology, and the only practical way of setting forth and critically appraising sociological systems is to deal with one systematizer at a time, indicating, of course, his relations to, or dependence upon, other systematizers. The treatment of the systematic sociologists in each country is, however, prefaced by a brief survey of the various schools of sociological writing in that country. In the case of some countries, notably Italy and England, the systematic sociologists have been very few, so we have had to rest content mainly with a sampling of characteristic types of sociological thought in these nations.

The analysis of sociological systems following the era of pioneers leads off with a consideration of the sociologists who wrote in the German language, and these authors are treated more completely and thoroughly than in any other work in English. Novicow and Kovalevsky are selected as representative of the Russian sociologists. The more important sociological writings in France, Italy, Spain, England, and the United States are reviewed at some length, and Cornejo is presented as the most important and productive of the systematic Latin-American sociologists.

It can safely and modestly be asserted that this book comprises the most comprehensive summary of systematic sociological writing in any language. It brings the history of sociological thought down to the era and stage where systematization was gradually but rather completely replaced by specialization in some more restricted field of description and analysis. This work thus ends logically at a highly appropriate point of termination. It is not likely that there will be many more attempts to create systems of sociology; hence these volumes may reasonably be regarded as the definitive summation and appraisal of this type of intellectual enterprise in the field of social thought. In other words, the era of systematic sociology has come approximately to an end; and our book describes its background, origin, development, and mature products. Sociological writing from this time onward promises to be mainly specialized forms of social theory; and what has already been accomplished in this type of work has been reviewed in the book which Professor Becker and the editor helped to write on *Contemporary Social Theory.*

The main purpose of this volume is, naturally, to bring together a critical summary of systematic sociological writing; but the by-products may have even greater practical value, namely, the bearing of systematic sociology upon the clarification and solution of some of our chief public problems and the manifestation of the various ways in which leading social thinkers have approached the critical issues of their day. Not only will the reader who goes through these pages attain a competent grasp upon the growth of systematic sociological thought; he should also secure a far wider and more penetrating understanding of the problems of the last century, which have thrown us, in our generation, into the most acute crisis in the history of the human race—one in which a new social order is to be fashioned, either by deliberate planning or by revolution born of ignorance and evasion. Readers will gain acquaintance with the main questions which have been raised about social origins and relations, the problems of group life and interests which sociologists have discussed, the solutions that they have offered, the techniques that they have employed, and the manner in which time and place have affected social situations and the methods utilized in analyzing them.

Hence the perusal of this book will not only extend the reader's horizon and knowledge with respect to systematic sociology but should also improve his capacity to comprehend social problems and the sociological analysis thereof, thus enabling him to operate more effectively as an intelligent citizen of the republic. It has been the contention of sociologists from Auguste Comte and Lester F. Ward to Sorokin that the chief justification of sociology is the guidance it can furnish to public officials and private citizens relative to building a better social order. It has been maintained by such writers that only by heeding the teachings of sociology can a sound social system be constructed and perpetuated. If there is any considerable modicum of truth in this assertion, then these volumes should have great practical utility in our critical era, for here are to be found all the main doctrines of all the chief sociologists bearing upon questions of public import.

If the editor may be permitted a personal word, this project brings to an end his labors in the history of social theory, to which he has devoted, in one field or another, some eleven volumes. It is hoped that this book may be deemed a fitting conclusion. If some disagree widely with the methods and procedure followed, it may be observed that the field is open to other books, and the best proof that this enterprise does not complete the task is to produce a better book. It is a source of personal gratification that this work is being published by the University of Chicago Press, for it was just thirty years ago that Dean Small published in the September, 1917, issue of the *American Journal of Sociology* the editor's first contribution to the history of social thought. The editor also wishes to express here his thanks to Howard Becker for invaluable suggestions as to competent authors.

HARRY ELMER BARNES

COOPERSTOWN, NEW YORK
August 1, 1947

TABLE OF CONTENTS

PART I. HISTORICAL INTRODUCTION: SOCIOLOGY BEFORE COMTE

I. ANCIENT AND MEDIEVAL SOCIAL PHILOSOPHY 3
Harry Elmer Barnes

II. SOCIAL THOUGHT IN EARLY MODERN TIMES 29
Harry Elmer Barnes

PART II. THE PIONEERS OF SOCIOLOGY

III. THE SOCIAL AND POLITICAL PHILOSOPHY OF AUGUSTE COMTE: POSITIVIST UTOPIA AND THE RELIGION OF HUMANITY 81
Harry Elmer Barnes

IV. HERBERT SPENCER AND THE EVOLUTIONARY DEFENSE OF INDIVIDUALISM 110
Harry Elmer Barnes

V. LEWIS HENRY MORGAN: PIONEER IN THE THEORY OF SOCIAL EVOLUTION 138
Leslie A. White

VI. WILLIAM GRAHAM SUMNER: SPENCERIANISM IN AMERICAN DRESS . 155
Harry Elmer Barnes

VII. LESTER FRANK WARD: THE RECONSTRUCTION OF SOCIETY BY SOCIAL SCIENCE 173
Harry Elmer Barnes

VIII. THE SOCIAL PHILOSOPHY OF LUDWIG GUMPLOWICZ: THE STRUGGLES OF RACES AND SOCIAL GROUPS 191
Harry Elmer Barnes

PART III. LEADING SOCIOLOGISTS IN GERMANIC COUNTRIES

INTRODUCTORY NOTE: LEADING SOCIOLOGICAL TRENDS AND SOCIOLOGISTS IN GERMANIC COUNTRIES 209

IX. THE PSYCHOSOCIOLOGICAL THOUGHT OF WILHELM WUNDT . . 216
Alexander Goldenweiser

X. THE SOCIOLOGICAL SYSTEM OF FERDINAND TÖNNIES: "COMMUNITY" AND "SOCIETY" 227
Rudolf Heberle

XI. THE SOCIOLOGY OF GEORG SIMMEL: THE FORMS OF SOCIAL INTER-
ACTION 249
    Rudolf Heberle

XII. THE SYSTEMATIC SOCIOLOGY OF LEOPOLD VON WIESE: THE ORIGIN
AND STRUCTURE OF INTERHUMAN RELATIONS 274
    J. Milton Yinger

XIII. MAX WEBER'S SOCIOLOGICAL ANALYSIS OF CAPITALISM AND MODERN
INSTITUTIONS 287
    Talcott Parsons

XIV. THE SOCIOLOGY OF RELIGION OF ERNST TROELTSCH 309
    J. Milton Yinger

XV. THE SOCIAL AND ECONOMIC PHILOSOPHY OF WERNER SOMBART:
THE SOCIOLOGY OF CAPITALISM 316
    F. X. Sutton

XVI. THE SOCIOLOGICAL DOCTRINES OF FRANZ OPPENHEIMER: AN
AGRARIAN PHILOSOPHY OF HISTORY AND SOCIAL REFORM . . . 332
    Paul Honigsheim

XVII. ALFRED WEBER'S CONCEPTION OF HISTORICOCULTURAL SOCIOLOGY . 353
    Sigmund Neumann

XVIII. THE SOCIOLOGICAL THEORIES OF HANS FREYER: SOCIOLOGY AS A
NATIONALISTIC PROGRAM OF SOCIAL ACTION 362
    Ernest Manheim

XIX. GUSTAV RATZENHOFER: SOCIOLOGICAL POSITIVISM AND THE THEORY
OF SOCIAL INTERESTS 374
    Robert Schmid

XX. THE UNIVERSALISTIC THEORY OF SOCIETY OF OTHMAR SPANN AND
HIS SCHOOL 385
    Bartholomew Landheer

XXI. THE SOCIAL AND POLITICAL THEORIES OF LUDWIG STEIN: A PHI-
LOSOPHY OF SOCIAL PROGRESS AND POLITICAL REFORM 400
    Harry Elmer Barnes

PART IV. CONTINENTAL EUROPEAN SOCIOLOGY IN
NON-GERMANIC COUNTRIES

XXII. THE SOCIOLOGICAL DOCTRINES OF JACQUES NOVICOW: A SOCI-
OLOGICAL CRITICISM OF WAR AND MILITARISM 419
    Harry Elmer Barnes

XXIII. THE SOCIOLOGICAL THEORIES OF MAKSIM M. KOVALEVSKY . . 441
    N. S. Timasheff

INTRODUCTORY NOTE: MAIN TENDENCIES IN FRENCH SOCIOLOGY 458

XXIV. THE SOCIOLOGICAL THEORIES OF ALFRED FOUILLÉE 461
  Augustin Guyau (Translated and Adapted by *Arthur Julius Nelson*)

XXV. THE SOCIAL AND POLITICAL THEORY OF GABRIEL TARDE 471
  Harry Elmer Barnes

XXVI. THE PSYCHOSOCIOLOGICAL THEORIES OF GUSTAVE LE BON . . . 481
  Harry Elmer Barnes

XXVII. THE SOCIOLOGISM OF ÉMILE DURKHEIM AND HIS SCHOOL . . . 499
  Emile Benoit-Smullyan

XXVIII. THE DOCTRINES OF GUILLAUME DE GREEF: SYNDICALISM AND SOCIAL REFORM IN THE GUISE OF A CLASSIFICATORY SOCIOLOGY . . . 538
  Dorothy W. Douglas

XXIX. REPRESENTATIVE ITALIAN CONTRIBUTIONS TO SOCIOLOGY: PARETO, LORIA, VACCARO, GINI, AND SIGHELE 553
  W. Rex Crawford

XXX. ADOLFO POSADA: THE "LESTER F. WARD" OF SPANISH SOCIOLOGY . 585
  Rex D. Hopper

PART V. ENGLISH SOCIOLOGISTS SINCE HERBERT SPENCER

INTRODUCTORY NOTE: ENGLISH SOCIOLOGY SINCE SPENCER 603

XXXI. THE SUPRARATIONAL SOCIAL PHILOSOPHY OF BENJAMIN KIDD . . 606
  Harry Elmer Barnes

XXXII. LEONARD TRELAWNEY HOBHOUSE: EVOLUTIONARY PHILOSOPHY IN THE SERVICE OF DEMOCRACY AND SOCIAL REFORM 614
  Harry Elmer Barnes

XXXIII. EDWARD ALEXANDER WESTERMARCK AND THE APPLICATION OF ETHNOGRAPHIC METHODS TO MARRIAGE AND MORALS 654
  C. Wright Mills

XXXIV. ROBERT BRIFFAULT AND THE REHABILITATION OF THE MATRIARCHAL THEORY 668
  Huntington Cairns

XXXV. PATRICK GEDDES, VICTOR BRANFORD, AND APPLIED SOCIOLOGY IN ENGLAND: THE SOCIAL SURVEY, REGIONALISM, AND URBAN PLANNING 677
  Lewis Mumford

XXXVI. GRAHAM WALLAS AND THE SOCIOPSYCHOLOGICAL BASIS OF POLITICS AND SOCIAL RECONSTRUCTION 696
  Harry Elmer Barnes

XXXVII. ARNOLD JOSEPH TOYNBEE: OROSIUS AND AUGUSTINE IN MODERN DRESS 717
  Harry Elmer Barnes

PART VI. SOCIOLOGICAL THEORY IN AMERICA

Introductory Note: The General Character of American Sociology . . 739

XXXVIII. The Sociological Theories of Franklin Henry Giddings: Con-
         sciousness of Kind, Pluralistic Behavior, and Statistical
         Method 744
            Clarence H. Northcott

XXXIX. Albion Woodbury Small: Promoter of American Sociology
       and Expositor of Social Interests 766
          Harry Elmer Barnes

XL. William Isaac Thomas: The Fusion of Psychological and
    Cultural Sociology 793
       Harry Elmer Barnes

XLI. The Social and Political Theories of J. H. W. Stuckenberg . 805
        Harry Elmer Barnes

XLII. The Sociological Theories of Edward Alsworth Ross . . . 819
         William L. Kolb

XLIII. Charles Horton Cooley: Pioneer in Psychosociology . . . 833
          Richard Dewey

XLIV. Charles Abram Ellwood: Founder of Scientific Psychological
      Sociology 853
         Harry Elmer Barnes

XLV. The Sociological Theories of Edward Cary Hayes 869
        Harry Elmer Barnes

XLVI. The Sociological Ideas of Pitirim Alexandrovitch Sorokin:
      "Integralist" Sociology 884
         Hans Speier

XLVII. The Systematic Sociology of Mariano H. Cornejo 902
          L. L. Bernard

INDEX

Index 933

PART 1

HISTORICAL INTRODUCTION

SOCIOLOGY BEFORE COMTE

CHAPTER I

ANCIENT AND MEDIEVAL SOCIAL PHILOSOPHY

Harry Elmer Barnes

I. SOCIAL THINKING IN THE ANCIENT ORIENT

THE social philosophy of ancient and medieval writers must be gleaned from a large mass of philosophical, theological, economic, political, and legal doctrines, for, as might be expected, there was no strict differentiation between social philosophy, on the one hand, and religious, moral, economic, and political theories, on the other hand. Nor is there to be found in many cases any serious attempt to build up a definite or well-balanced system of social philosophy.

At the same time, the recognition of these facts furnishes no adequate justification for refusing to go back of Comte for the sources of sociological thought. It is hoped that even this brief survey of the pre-Comtian period will substantiate the truth of the statement that, from the time of the Egyptian social prophets onward, thinkers were approaching, and to a certain extent successfully formulating, the chief problems of sociology. Indeed, as Professor A. W. Small pointed out, only the most mediocre writer can be adequately described merely by classifying him as sociologist, historian, economist, or political scientist.[1]* The aim and purpose of the writer constitute the most reliable basis for estimating his contributions to social science. One is, therefore, justified in seeking the origins of sociological thought as far back in the past as a conscious attempt can be discovered on the part of any writer to record or to explain the fundamental problems of social relationships, organization, and development.

In any attempt, however cursory, to trace the development of sociological thought, it is necessary to keep in mind the fundamental truth, so well expressed by Professor Giddings and Professor Small, namely, that the doctrines of any writer lose much of their significance if their relation to the prevailing social environment is not pointed out and

---

* For the greater convenience of the reader, the footnotes in this book are grouped at the end of each chapter.

the purposes of the work clearly indicated. While in this survey the treatment of these important phases of the general topic must, like the summary of doctrines, be extremely condensed, an attempt will be made to indicate the general conditions out of which the sociological thinking of each period developed.

Anything like a systematic discussion of social phenomena began with the Greeks. The writers of oriental antiquity were prevented by the general conditions of their social environment from offering any strikingly original generalizations concerning the origin and nature of social institutions. An agrarian economy, caste, superstition, an inflexible religious system, and sumptuary legislation, begotten of the passion of the antique mind for homogeneity, tended to give social institutions a fixity and sanctity which discouraged any extensive speculation as to their origin, nature, or possible means of improvement. When social institutions were "frozen" by a tyrannical customary code and upheld by an inscrutable Providence, there could be no "science" of society. Consequently, in oriental antiquity most of the thinking upon social problems consisted in formulating justifications of the existence of the given social regime, these mainly centering about the sanctions of a unique revealed religion or the superior wisdom of ancestors.

Fundamental moral and social precepts and ideals of social justice are to be found in the works of the Egyptian scribes; valuable bits of applied and descriptive sociology may be gleaned from the Babylonian records, particularly from the Code of Hammurabi; much of sociological interest may be found in the ancient books of India; the Hebrew legal codes and prophetic teachings are replete with sociological and anthropological interest; and most of the Chinese religious and moral doctrines come from a more remote antiquity than those of the great philosophers of Greece; but the first coherent analysis of social phenomena and processes, so far as extant records furnish the basis for judgment, originated with the Greek philosophers of the post-Socratic period.

The outstanding traits of ancient oriental social thought may safely be characterized somewhat as follows: the social thinking was informal, sporadic, and unorganized rather than systematic or the product of deliberate study. It was highly personal and individual in origin and expression, and not the outgrowth of schools or types of social thought or of conscious social analysis. The individual rather than the group was

the center of most social thinking. Social theory was pre-eminently practical and utilitarian, devoted to supplying advice and admonition concerning everyday life. It was decidedly hortatory and emotional in attitude and intent. Such social thinking as related to groups rather than to
individuals was concerned mainly with so-called "primary" groups,
such as the clan, the neighborhood, and the village. But law and government received some attention. The trend of the social thinking was
conservative and traditional, mainly retrospective in outlook. There
was no conception of social progress, and such social change as was
envisaged was believed to be brought about by supernatural forces,
which were held to be the source of all social causation. Professor
Joyce O. Hertzler thus summarizes the outstanding contributions of
ancient oriental social thinking to our understanding of social processes
and problems:

> Among a considerable array of specific contributions, those following must be
> specifically mentioned. We have examined in the preceding chapters much mate-
> rial indicating the development of social consciousness; the recognition of the
> difficulties arising out of personal contacts in group life; a devotion to thought
> about man's relationship to man in groups; a discussion of human and social
> values and philosophies of life; much thought about social control, especially the
> regulative institutions, such as the state, family, and property; some treatment of
> certain aspects of social organization; some worry about codes governing almost
> every aspect of group life; much thought about the importance and nature of man's
> social duties and obligations, with special reference to moral codes and social
> proprieties; some thought on the preparation for group life, especially education,
> its theory and technique, but including other means of inculcating institutional
> lore; the nature of human nature; occasional thought in the form of deft, though
> partial, social criticism and prophecy; and some treatment of social differentiation,
> especially the phenomena of class relations and social inequalities.[2]

II. SOCIAL PHILOSOPHY AMONG THE GREEKS

While it is impossible to account for Greek originality and freedom
of thought entirely upon the basis of the surrounding conditions, it is
nevertheless true that the characteristic trends in the sociological thinking of the Greeks can be traced back to the social environment.[3]

In the first place, there was rarely any extensive or highly centralized
political organization, bringing together in one unified state many different peoples. This allowed the tribal spirit of localism and provincialism
to have free play, and this spirit pervaded most of Greek thinking upon
social phenomena. With the exception of the Stoics, the contrast between
Greek and barbarian stands out clearly in most of the important Greek

studies of social institutions. But if the Greek city-state fostered a rather narrow local conceit, it also rendered possible a high degree of like-mindedness on the part of the citizens. This led to that group self-consciousness which lay at the basis of those utopian or idealistic theories of society that appeared in the *Republic* of Plato and the *Politics* of Aristotle.

Again, the freedom and liberty of the Athenian city-state and the absence of a coercive state religion made for that critical philosophy which first appeared on any considerable scale among the Attic Greeks. Despite the pretensions of Athens to commercial empire, Greek civilization was based primarily upon an agricultural economy, which, through its routine and repetition, encouraged a static outlook upon the social process. Consequently, one is not surprised to find Aristotle setting up stability as the most perfect test of the excellence of a state. Despite their intellectual activity, there was little inductive study of social phenomena among the Greeks. Aristotle furnishes the only notable exception to this statement. The Greeks despised the humble and commonplace methods of natural science and preferred the freer and wider ranges of a priori generalizaton. The possibilities of deductive thinking about the social process were, accordingly, exhausted by the Greeks. It was not until natural science had established inductive methods in social science that the *Republic* and the *Laws* of Plato and the *Politics* of Aristotle were surpassed as analyses of social phenomena by the works of Comte, Quételet, Spencer, and Ward.

The period of Greek thought before Plato has left no voluminous textual remains, but, from the sources available, several interesting suggestions and developments may be discovered. Hesiod (eighth century B.C.) outlined the culture ages from the conventional viewpoint of a descent from a "Golden Age" and voiced his protest against existing social and economic conditions. Anaximander (610–546 B.C.) antedated John Fiske by twenty-four centuries in his discussion of the prolongation of human infancy in its relation to human society. Theognis (*ca.* 550 B.C.) clearly expounded the principles of eugenics as applied to the human race. Aeschylus (525–456 B.C.) anticipated Lucretius by more than four centuries in his highly interesting account of the general evolution of civilization. Herodotus (*ca.* 485–425 B.C.), by his acute observations and striking descriptions of the manners, customs, and physical characteristics of foreign peoples, justly earned the title of the first great "descriptive sociologist." The Sophists advanced the conception of a primordial state of nature and a subsequent social, or at least governmental, contract. Hippocrates (*ca.* 460–380 B.C.), in his work on *Airs, Waters, and Places,* presented the first serious analysis of the influence of physical environment upon human society. He described the effect of climate and topography upon the peoples of Europe and Asia in regard to physical characteristics and political institutions with a sweep and detail not equaled again until the time of ibn-Khaldun and Bodin. He believed that the peoples of warm climates were clever but weak and wicked. Those of cold climates were strong but stupid. The inhabitants of temperate climates, especially the Greeks, combined the good qualities of the others without their weaknesses. They were strong, brave, and wise. Hippocrates' work constituted the point of departure for most treatments of the influence of physical environment on society until the time of Karl Ritter. Finally, Socrates (471–399 B.C.) presented the doctrine of a law of nature, as contrasted with human law, and attempted to reduce ethics to a body of well-reasoned knowledge.

Plato (427–347 B.C.) in his search for an adequate definition of justice, was led into making an analysis of society and of the state. He outlined the organic theory of society and believed that not only the economic but also the ethical basis of society is embodied in the functional division of labor. In this respect his *Republic* contributed what is probably the most satisfactory analysis of the economic foundations of society to be found in the works of any writer of antiquity.[4]

Plato recognized the existence and importance of the social mind, though he wrongly believed it to be merely the sum of the individual minds in the social group. Adopting the premise that man can control his own social relations and that concerted volition is the inevitable result of similar external surroundings, he constructed one of the most nearly complete of the utopian plans for an ideal society of which history bears any record.[5] It is interesting to note that, aside from its communistic aspects, this utopia of Plato provided for the first comprehensive scheme of eugenics in the history of social or biological philosophy. Plato's theory that the élite should govern society stimulated later aristocratic political theory and has been embraced by the Fascist and "managerial" philosophers in our own day.

Especially interesting was Plato's contribution to historical sociology in his *Laws.* With almost the perspective of a nineteenth-century evolutionist, he discerned something of the true nature of social evolution and of the time required for its consummation, and he presented his own theories on the subject, which were exceedingly accurate for one possessed of only his scanty data.[6] Finally, in decided contrast to his predecessors and to many of his successors, Plato tried to comprehend and analyze society as a unity and in its entirety.

Aristotle (384–322 B.C.), the most influential of all Greek writers on social philosophy, both on account of the profundity of his insight into social processes and because of his pontifical relationship to medieval thought, made many advances over Plato in his investigation of the basis of political and social relationships. In the first place, Aristotle's *Politics* introduced to some extent the inductive method of studying social phenomena, while Plato had relied almost entirely upon the far less scientific deductive mode of approach. But probably more important than this was Aristotle's direct and clean-cut assertion that man is by nature a social being.[7] This dictum, had it been heeded by later writers, would have precluded the possibility of such erroneous interpretations of society as that of an original social contract, which was based upon the doctrine of the origin of society in conscious self-interest. As a deduction from this dogma of man's inherent sociability, Aristotle pointed out the necessity of social relations for the complete development of the human personality, and he made plain the abnormality of the nonsocial being.

Aristotle presented an explanation of social evolution in terms of the social instinct, the expansion of man's social nature, and the widening scope of the desire for, and need of, society.[8] In this respect, he made a considerable advance over Plato, who had adopted the utilitarian and economic interpretation, almost to the exclusion of the instinctive element. Although Aristotle's interpretation of society was more inclusive and well-balanced, it fell far short of the thoroughness of Plato's in its analysis of the economic foundations of society.

In his criticism of Plato's communistic scheme, Aristotle advanced arguments against communism, which, for completeness, were unequaled until contemporary times.[9] But his own project for an ideal commonwealth was not any more satisfactory than that of Plato, for both plans were permeated with the Greek ideals of exclusiveness, provincialism, and localism and with the notion that social stability is the end most to be sought in the institutions of society and that society is prior to the individual in importance.

The subjective basis of organized society Aristotle believed to be embodied in friendship, in the analysis of which he anticipated Professor Giddings' theory of the "consciousness of kind."[10]

Aristotle also gave a more complete statement than did Plato of the analogy between the individual organism and society and of the influence of physical environment upon society. In his theory of the effect of physical surroundings on man and society, Aristotle revived and adapted the theories of Hippocrates, so as to furnish a geographical basis for the alleged superiority of the Greeks. He held that, by their intermediate geographical situation, the Greeks were able to combine the superior mental attainments of southern peoples with the greater bravery of the northerners and, at the same time, to escape the fickleness of the inhabitants of warm regions and the stupidity of the people of the north. The common ancient and medieval doctrine of the general cultural superiority of the inhabitants of the temperate climates was, in all probability, only a statement of observed facts. The detailed explanation, however, was hardly as satisfactory, being based upon the fantastic astrological doctrine of planetary influences on man and the equally grotesque Greek physical philosophy, with its physiological chemistry founded on the theory of the four elements and the four humors.[11]

The distinctive sociological contributions of the Stoic and the Epicurean social philosophies are not difficult to account for on the basis of the conditions of the time. The swallowing-up of the Greek city-states in the imperial system of Alexander and the disorder which followed the disintegration of his empire led naturally, on the one hand, to the cosmopolitan serenity and resignation of the Stoics and, on the other, to the individualistic and materialistic doctrines of the Epicureans, who valued society and the state solely for their aid in securing a superior degree of personal detachment, convenience, and safety.

The Stoics, who represented the school of philosophy which was founded by Zeno (ca. 350–ca. 260 B.C.) in the latter half of the fourth century B.C. and lasted on until the close of the western Roman Empire, interpreted society in terms of rational thought.[12] They held, with Aristotle, that all men must be social, both for the development of their own personalities and for the proper discharge of their duties toward their fellow-beings. Their conception of society was far broader than that of the other schools of Greek philosophy, to whom the world was either Greek or barbarian. The cosmopolitan Stoic conception of world society and world citizenship did much to develop the idea of the essential brotherhood of mankind, at least the brotherhood of the élite. Especially important in their ethical doctrines was the Stoic emphasis upon the law of nature as the proper guide for moral conduct.

The Epicureans, founded by Epicurus (342–270 B.C.), presented a conception of society diametrically opposed to that held by the Stoics, maintaining that society has its only rational basis in conscious self-interest.[13] This led to the deliberate institution of social relations, in order to escape the evils and inconveniences of a presocial and isolated condition. This theory, it will easily be perceived, was based on a fallacious, intellectualistic conception of society. It opened the way for the later development of the doctrine of the presocial state of nature and the foundation of social relations in a contract based upon the perception of the utility of such an arrangement. With the possible exception of the Sophists and Plato, Epicurus was the first to envisage an original social contract, though it was more after the nature of a governmental, than of a social, contract. As contrasted with the cosmopolitan and idealistic Stoics, the Epicureans were, thus, individualists and evolutionary materialists, though they were by no means advocates of sensuality, as is often asserted.

Polybius (203–121 B.C.), the Greek student of Roman history, is usually overlooked by students of the history of social philosophy, but he is, nevertheless, one of the most important figures in the early development of that subject. His conception of social evolution was, in the main, accurate. He explained the aggregation and association of primitive men as resulting from a sense of weakness and a perception of likeness. Government, he believed, arose in force and was rendered permanent by the reflective action of the social mind, as it gradually perceived more clearly the utility of political relations. This was the argument advanced by Hume, nineteen centuries later, in his assault upon the doctrine of a social contract.[14]

Polybius also made an important contribution in explaining the origin of morality and justice as due to group approval or disapproval of social practices and modes of conduct.[15] In this way he suggested a line of treatment exploited in modern times by writers like Bagehot and Sumner. Polybius also set forth the first clear statement of the theory of reflective sympathy, later developed by Spinoza, Hume, and Adam Smith.[16] Again, he was the first writer on political science who proposed to secure liberty and governmental stability through a system of checks and balances in political organization. Finally, Polybius presented one of the clearest statements of the popular classical conception of the cyclical nature of the historical process—a view taken up by Machiavelli and more recently revived by Le Bon, Gumplowicz, and Spengler.[17]

III. SOCIAL PHILOSOPHY AMONG THE ROMANS

Polybius was the last great Greek social philosopher. The minds of the Romans were of a legal and practical character, little given to constructive speculative philosophy. Their contribution was to adapt Greek social philosophy to Roman conditions and to promote political organization and legal development, not to formulate original theories of the state and society. The Romans, in building up a world empire, came into contact with many different legal codes; and this stimulating "contact of cultures" led to the formulation of theories of the origin and nature of law in general.

While the Romans contributed little to social philosophy in the way of original theories, it is to the Roman followers of the later Greek schools of philosophy that one must look for the most nearly complete statements of such doctrines as have been preserved, for most of the Greek writings of this period have been lost.

The chief Roman representative of the Epicurean school was the great philosophic poet, Lucretius (99–55 B.C.), the most original mind that Rome produced.[18] Acknowledging with pride his obligations to Epicurus, he is entitled, by his sketch of the course of human and social development, to rank as the first great evolutionary sociologist. Combining the current written and oral accounts of the customs of primitive peoples with the previous theories of poets and philosophers, Lucretius produced a theory of social evolution which was infinitely superior, in most aspects, to anything presented by any other writer down to the period of late eighteenth-century social philosophy. The struggle for existence; the survival of the fittest; the mode of life among primitive peoples; the origin of language, fire, industry, religion, domestic relations, and the arts of pleasure; the sequence of the culture ages; and the development of commercial relations are set forth in his great poem,

On the Nature of Things, with a clearness, accuracy, and modernity which preclude the possibility of entire conjecture or of a mere reading into his writings of later ideas which did not occur to him.[19]

But, powerful a thinker as was Lucretius, he had little immediate influence upon posterity, Horace being the only later Roman writer who was deeply affected by Epicurean principles. The Epicurean theories were too rationalistic and dynamic for the Roman mind to approve and were even more repugnant to the Christian writers, owing to their denunciation of *religio* as the chief cause of human misery. So it is to Cicero, a would-be eclectic with strong Stoic leanings, and to Seneca, an avowed Stoic, that one must turn for an exposition of the political and social philosophy generally accepted by the Romans.

Cicero (106–43 B.C.) followed Plato in attempting to describe an ideal commonwealth, but he did not feel the need of constructing a plan for a utopian society, since he thought that the Roman commonwealth possessed all the essential characteristics of the perfect state. He accepted Aristotle's dictum of the natural sociability of man rather than the Epicurean doctrine that society results from a sense of weakness in isolation and a perception of the utility of association. But he did emphasize the advantages of associated life, while denying that they furnish the fundamental explanation of society.[20] He also agreed with Aristotle as to the value of friendship and like-mindedness as a psychological basis of human association. From the Stoics he derived his doctrine of the brotherhood of man, and from Polybius he appropriated the theories regarding the classification and cycles of government and the value of checks and balances. In short, it was his summing-up of the various contemporary theories in a coherent body of social thought that constituted Cicero's main achievement.

Seneca (3 B.C.—A.D. 65) was the next systematic social philosopher after Cicero among the Romans. Seneca's chief contribution to social philosophy was his revival of the ancient Greek conception of the primitive period of society as a "golden age." This was followed by the origin of the conventional institutions of society as a remedy for the evils which crept in and brought the golden age to an end. In the age of "golden innocence" mankind lived without coercive authority, gladly obeying the wise and without any social distinctions based on property or caste. The main reason for the breakdown of this simple primitive arrangement was the origin of private property. People then became dissatisfied with common ownership, and the resulting lust after wealth and authority rendered necessary the institution of political authority to curb these growing evil propensities.[21]

The chief importance of this doctrine is not its enunciation by Seneca but its later adoption by the Christian Fathers. They identified the golden age with the state of man before the "Fall" and thus reinforced the already extremely retrospective character of Christian social philosophy, which rendered impossible any dynamic conception of human progress.

The Stoic doctrines relative to society and politics reached their highest development among the Romans in the writings of Epictetus (about A.D. 90) and the Emperor Marcus Aurelius (A.D. 121–80). In fact, the loss of most of the Greek originals has made these two writers our main sources for the Stoic interpretation of society.

Another philosophic development in the Roman period that had important consequences for the history of sociology was Neo-Platonism, which found its main representative in Plotinus (A.D. 204–70), with its renunciation of the world of sense-perception and its tendencies toward unlimited credulity and bitter hostility to rationalism and skepticism. Neo-Platonism furnished the general intellectual setting adopted by patristic and medieval theology. It militated strongly against any trend toward a rational conception of social processes and institutions. Neo-Platonism, the conception of a former golden age, and the eschatological view of society, which was drawn as much from Persian religions and the pagan mysteries as from Christian texts, all combined to make up the otherworldly and antirational intellectual environment in which Christian theology and social philosophy flourished.[22]

Julius Caesar, in his *Commentaries* on the Gallic wars, and Tacitus, in his description of the early Germans in the *Germania,* presented studies in descriptive sociology and comparative ethnology which were hardly surpassed until the modern studies of primitive-culture areas by trained ethnologists. As is the case with the writings of Herodotus, recent critical historical investigations have tended to confirm, rather than to discredit, the main contentions of both Caesar and Tacitus.

In Roman times the familiar classical theory of the wisdom and physical weakness of southern peoples, the ferocity and stupidity of those of northern climes, and the general superiority of those inhabiting intermediate or temperate areas was carried along by Vitruvius, the chief

Roman authority on architecture; Galen, the leading physician of the Roman period; and Vegetius, an authority on military methods. They interpreted this doctrine to prove the superiority of the Romans, as Hippocrates and Aristotle had exploited it to buttress the notion of Greek ascendency.

Finally, there must be noted the important conception developed by the Roman lawyers regarding the origin and nature of political authority. It is the opinion of recent and reliable authorities that, from the second to the sixth centuries A.D., there was but one legal theory of the origin of political authority, namely, that it had its foundation in the consent of the people. However remote from popular consent might be the method by which the emperor at any time arose to power, the theory remained the same. That this conception had a very great influence upon the later development of the theory of a social, and especially of a governmental, contract and upon the idea of popular sovereignty is beyond doubt. Another important allied Roman legal doctrine was that of the absolute nature of secular authority. It was held that the power of the state transcends that of any other group in society. In later times this was interpreted to mean that the state is superior to the church. Of significance also was the Roman legal theory that our personal rights and civil liberties must be protected by constitutions and laws.

IV. THE SOCIAL PHILOSOPHY OF EARLY AND PATRISTIC CHRISTIANITY

The views of the founders of Christianity in regard to the nature of society were not fundamentally different from that of the Stoics, namely, the brotherhood of man in the spirit of God. The Christians were, however, more universal and democratic in their doctrine, since the Stoics had in reality meant the brotherhood of the wise or of those who could participate through their reason in the divine *logos*. Christianity tended to break down this distinction between the wise and the ignorant and to emphasize the possibility of universal human brotherhood through the medium of faith and belief rather than through the exercise of reason.

The social doctrines of Jesus were embodied in the highly idealistic and plastic exhortations to brotherly love, human service, and the recognition of human brotherhood.[23] They were not reduced, or intended to be reduced, to any rigid scheme of dogma or ritual and were, on that account, all the more valuable and adjustable to changing conditions. It was inevitable, however, that, when the attempt was made to put these lofty ideals into operation on a large scale in secular society and to perfect an ecclesiastical organization, they would, when not entirely forgotten, be compressed within narrow bounds of dogmatic interpretation and ritualistic expression. From such restrictions they have not yet escaped, and, throughout the greater part of the history of Christendom, ecclesiastical organizations have been perverted from a means to an end into an end in themselves.

The first, and perhaps the greatest, figure in this development was Paul. He proclaimed the doctrine of love, the organic nature of society, and the necessity of civil government to repress evil. But, at the same time, he was busy instructing the "brethren" in matters of creed and organization, and he instituted that greatest of Christian rites, the Eucharist.[24] Paul initiated the movement, which was carried on by the Fathers until, by the fifth century A.D., the doctrines of Jesus had been transformed from a few plastic ideals into that rigid, dogmatic, ritualistic, and eschatological system of creed and organization known as "medieval Christianity."

Yet the modern writer must not fail to recognize the very great importance and significance of the Roman Catholic church in medieval life, despite its dogmas and intellectual rigidity. Through its elaborate sacramental system it provided the primitive European mind with an effective instrument for meeting the dangers, mysteries, crises, and perplexities of human existence.

The Christian Fathers, as a source of religious dogma and authority hardly second to the Holy Scriptures, are most important in the history of social philosophy. Although their doctrines cover some six centuries, nevertheless their social ideas possess sufficient coherence to allow the patristic period to be discussed as a unity.

The fundamental doctrines of the Fathers upon the origin, nature, and objectives of society may be summarized under the following propositions:[25] (1) Mankind is by nature social, society thus being a natural product, in agreement with the ideas of Aristotle and the Stoics. (2) Seneca's "golden" state of nature, without coercive government, was identified with the state of man in Eden before the "Fall" of man. (3) Civil government was rendered necessary by that "Fall," as a remedy for the crimes and vices of mankind. (4) While government was thus rendered essential by the "Fall," nevertheless it is a divine institution devised to curb further evil, the political rulers derive their power from God and are the agents of God, and political rebellion is a sin. (5) Whatever practical value social institutions may have in rendering more endurable this earthly life, their service in this respect is only fleeting and, at best, immeasurably less important than preparation for the institutions of the heavenly kingdom. (6) Social reform or progress was thus regarded as relatively unimportant, and it was held that one might better endure serious social inconveniences than jeopardize his salvation by dissipating his energy in attempting to improve earthly conditions. (7) The theory that the poor are a part of the divine order, to promote the spiritual welfare of almsgivers, dominated the ideals and methods of charity and relief until the English Poor Law of 1603.

The eschatological approach to life and society, with its relative disregard of earthly values and institutions, found its highest development in Augustine's *City of God* (written 413–26). Here the doctrine was set forth with great vigor, and the main criterion for measuring the excellence of human institutions was the aid or hindrance which they offered to the attainment of heavenly salvation.

V. MEDIEVAL SOCIAL PHILOSOPHY

The social philosophy of the medieval period grew naturally out of the elements which were fused in the development of medieval civilization. From the Romans there came the conception, most clearly expressed by Seneca, of the conventional or artificial nature of political institutions, as a result of the descent from a primitive golden age and a resulting governmental contract; and the doctrines of the lawyers, upholding the ideas of secular absolutism, popular sovereignty, and popular consent as the basis of imperial power. From Christianity came the notion of the "Fall" of man, which harmonized well with the pagan conception of the descent from a golden age; the doctrine of the divine character of political authority; and the dogma of the autonomy of the spiritual life. The new states of northern Europe contributed the notion that political authority is but the delegated authority of the whole community, thus agreeing with, and giving added emphasis to, the legal theory of the Roman lawyers in regard to popular sovereignty. The basic Christian conception of the brotherhood of man and the organic unity of Christendom, together with the sharp differentiation of classes in the medieval period into ecclesiastics, nobles, burghers, and laborers, tended to revive the Platonic view of the organic unity of society, based upon the functional division of labor. The revival of Aristotle by the Scholastics in the later Middle Ages reintroduced Aristotle's emphasis upon the natural sociability of man and led to the final harmony and synthesis of social philosophy in the medieval period. This maintained that, while society is a natural product, government is equally necessary and natural in order to give stability to society. These are the chief tendencies in medieval social philosophy.[26] Attention may now be turned to the individual presentations of these doctrines and to a consideration of their variation in different periods. There were few advances in social philosophy from the sixth to the ninth century. While the term "Middle Ages," in the old sense, has now been relegated to the field of rhetoric, there can be little doubt of the reality of the term "Dark Ages," when applied to the intellectual life of the period between the beginning of the barbarian "invasions" and the intellectual revival of the ninth century, represented by such men as Agobard of Lyons, Rhabanus Maurus, Hincmar of Reims, and Johannes Scotus Erigena.

So far as there was any interest in the subject of social and political philosophy, the views of the Fathers were adopted without question in the encyclopedic compilations of the time; the chief authority of the period being Isidore of Seville (d. 636), who was a transitional figure between the patristic period and the Dark Ages.

The chief practical political problem was the division of power between state and church. The Fathers had prepared the ground for this struggle by their acceptance of the doctrine of Paul and Peter that government is a divine institution. But the church was also divine, and hence arose the problem of deciding the primacy of two institutions, each with divine and, therefore, infinite powers. The situation was further complicated because the church entered into the feudal system as a great landholder, while the secular rulers aspired to invest churchmen with the symbols of spiritual, as well as secular, authority. The adjustment of the relations between these "two powers"—secular and spiritual—absorbed the writers of this period and later culminated in the extreme theocratic view of the state as presented in the *Polycraticus* of John of Salisbury and in the spirited defense of secular authority by Pierre Dubois and Marsiglio of Padua.[27]

Even the intellectual awakening of the ninth century contributed little new to social and political theory. The writers accepted the common tradition of a primitive state of nature, full of disorder and inconveniences, to remedy which political authority was instituted.[28]

In the eleventh and twelfth centuries, however, there were interesting developments. The revival of Roman law brought with it the theories of popular sovereignty and secular absolutism, and the canon-law doctrine strengthened the patristic conception of a primitive golden age followed by the "Fall," which rendered political organization essential for the preservation of order.

The fiery priest, Manegold of Lautenbach (d. after 1085), in his defense of Gregory VII, clearly enunciated the principle of a governmental compact as the basis of political authority, apparently for the first time in the history of western Europe, though his statement was only a definite formulation of the general theory of the time.[29] Tyranny was defined as the breaking of the original contract by which the ruler was appointed, and it constituted a valid basis for rebellion.

The theocratic doctrine of the state received its fullest exposition in the *Polycraticus* of John of Salisbury (1115–80), an English churchman who had studied under Abélard. The inferiority of the prince to the priest was emphasized at great length, tyranny was defined, and tyrannicide was justified. The ruler or prince was, however, acknowledged to be essential to society, in order to restrain human wickedness.

In addition to these views, John outlined the most detailed analogy between the individual organism and the state that had yet been produced. He suggested that in society we find groups or classes that correspond to the soul, mind, heart, and the other organs in the individual person. The prince is the head of the body politic, the priesthood the soul, the senate the heart, the judges and administrators the sense organs, the soldiers and functionaries the hands, the financial officers the stomach and intestines, and the peasantry the feet.[30]

This notion had been anticipated by Plato and Aristotle. Aquinas elaborated the organic analogy, and it received an even more thorough statement by Marsiglio of Padua and Nicholas of Cusa. It was given special relevance and plausibility by virtue of its compatibility with the medieval system of estates—the ruling princes, the higher clergy, nobility, burghers, peasants, and so on. The functional character of this medieval conception of society has been admirably summarized by Professor J. H. Randall:

> The fundamental note in medieval civilization is the complete harmony between the individual and the social. Society is a great hierarchy of ascending orders, in which every man has his God-appointed function and recognized obligations, and at the same time his rights and privileges. Each man is a member of some estate or group, and each estate is an essential organ of the whole, discharging a function at once peculiar to itself and necessary to the full life of Christendom. Only through his participation in this group life can the individual attain his own ends, and conversely, only with the aid of every individual and every group can society afford the appropriate setting for the fullest life of its individual members. All men exist in and for each other, and are bound to each other by an intricate network of mutual obligations.[31]

This functional view of society, in more realistic fashion, has gained popularity in our day with certain liberal economists like R. H. Tawney, and especially with the Guild Socialists.

The mature period of Scholastic political and social philosophy began in the thirteenth century, with the work of Albertus Magnus (1206–1280). It had its origin in the desire to give the Christian viewpoint a systematic philosophical expression, for which purpose the logic and philosophy of Aristotle were admirably adapted. Albertus incorporated the *Politics* of Aristotle in his commentary upon political problems and opened the way for the work of his greater pupil, Thomas Aquinas (1225–74). The latter's *De regimine principum* was one of the most suggestive and systematic of the treatises on social and political philosophy that appeared during medieval times.[32]

As a Scholastic philosopher, Aquinas naturally accepted the dictum of Aristotle regarding the inherent sociability of man. Adopting Aristotle's analysis of political origins, he held that civil society comprehends three ideas: first, that man is by nature social; second, that in society there is a community of purpose and interests, since only through social relations can man realize his own best interests; and, third, that a superior power is necessary to direct society for the common good and to enable the ruler to utilize his greater talents for the benefit of the community. The state had its origin in the natural patriarchal rule of the heads of families. But, in order to create extensive and efficient political organization, it was necessary to delegate this power to a common superior through a governmental compact.

Aquinas proceeded to prove his true Scholastic spirit by blending with this primarily Aristotelian theory the dogma of the church that political authority comes ultimately from God alone, though he may delegate it through the medium of the people. With this goes its corollary that political power is inferior to spiritual power. Departing from Aristotle again, Aquinas denied that the city-state is the ideal political organization and took a step in the direction of Machiavelli by declaring his preference for a province made up of several cities. He also followed John of Salisbury in outlining the organic analogy in the state.

Aquinas' theories regarding the influence of climate upon society and culture embodied the tradition common to classical times, as handed down in the works of Aristotle and Vegetius, with some original comments by himself. It was the usual tradition of the superiority of the peoples of the "middle zones" or temperate climate, now exploited, however, to exalt Christian Europe.

Dante (1265–1321) set forth his political theories in a plan for a universal European monarchy, co-ordinate in authority with the church. This project was designed to put an end to international strife, so that "society might realize its function of unhampered exercise of the intellectual faculties of man in speculation and action."[33] With his co-ordination of state and church, Dante stood in his doctrines midway between John of Salisbury, on the one hand, and the secular absolutism of Pierre Dubois and Marsiglio of Padua, on the other. These last two writers defended the superiority of the state. Dante's book was an epitaph of the political past rather than a prophecy of the future. Protestantism broke up the universal church, while nationalism disrupted both imperial conceptions and the ideals of international order.

In his popular work, *The Banquet,* Dante presented an interesting interpretation of the social process of imitation, thus anticipating Gabriel Tarde. In discussing how fame and notoriety develop, he illustrated the way in which imitation proceeds in a geometric ratio and is refracted by its media.

VI. SOCIAL PHILOSOPHY DURING THE TRANSITION FROM MEDIEVAL TO MODERN TIMES

The marked changes in European society between 1300 and 1600 produced comparable and parallel developments in political theory. Christian supernaturalism, feudalism, imperial ideals, and the struggle between church and state had dominated the medieval period. The growth of monarchies, the increased power of the state, and the origins of representative government brought in new and warmly debated issues after 1300.

Characteristic of the early modern attack on the medieval synthesis was the criticism of the prevailing medieval doctrine of the superiority of the church over the state. Even Dante's notion of the co-ordinate powers and functions of a universal church and empire was viewed with doubt.

The rise of Roman law with the teaching of Irnerius at Bologna (beginning about 1085) revived and encouraged the doctrine of the supremacy of the state over the church and over all other social institutions.[34] The experts in Roman law lined up with kings and emperors in defense of the pretensions of the secular monarchs. Roman law had declared that the power of the state is absolute and can override the opposition of any group within the state. Two of the most notable representatives of Roman legal theory in politics in this age were Pierre Dubois and Marsiglio of Padua.

Pierre Dubois (1255–1321), in his *De recuperatione terre sancte,* defended Philip the Fair in his struggle with Pope Boniface VIII. He warned the Pope not to meddle with temporal affairs, since such interference in the past had cost the Christians the possession of the Holy Land. He outlined a comprehensive program of social reform, in which, among other enlightened suggestions, he advocated a reconstruction of the French government; the reform of law and the expediting of justice; more practical and efficient education—including education for selected classes of women; the confiscation of church property; the revamping of the French army; and international arbitration to settle disputes between nations. He has been hailed by not a few modern scholars as the chief social radical of the Middle Ages. Professor W. I. Brandt and others have, however, thought him interesting primarily as a man who brought together most of the novel political and social ideas of his age without producing much original thought of his own.[35]

Marsiglio of Padua (1270–1342), in his *Defensor pacis,* one of the most important political treatises produced during the late medieval period, attacked the Catholic church with something of the spirit and modernity of the Deists and Voltaire. He offered a powerful criticism of the basic Catholic doctrine of the primacy of Peter. He declared that priests are merely the ministers of salvation, and he denied that they possess the power of forgiving sins or any right to interfere in temporal matters.[36]

In his strictly social and political philosophy Marsiglio was somewhat less original.[37] He accounted for the origin of society on a purely utilitarian basis. Society is essential to mankind, in order that we may carry on those co-operative activities necessary to group existence and human comfort. But unregulated society is likely to degenerate into disorder. Hence civil government is indispensable. Ultimate political authority is merely delegated by the people, in whose hands sovereign power always reposes. Marsiglio was the first notable defender of popular sovereignty and representative government—two of the leading dogmas of modern politics. Marsiglio also emphasized the organic unity and functional character of society by outlining the organic analogy in comprehensive fashion. The six estates or professions were made to correspond to the systems of organs in the individual organism. Further, by his separation of politics from theology, Marsiglio took a step toward Machiavelli's separation of politics from ethics.

Nicholas of Cusa (1401–64), in his *De concordantia catholica,* presented the most elaborate development of the functional analogy between the individual organism and the state that had yet appeared. He also introduced the conception of political pathology and, reviving the Platonic phrase, characterized the ruler as physician-in-chief to the sick state. He must prescribe for its ills according to the best advice of political philosophers, past and present.[38] In the more strictly political aspects of his theories, Nicholas emphasized the notion of popular consent as the basis of political authority and outlined an original scheme of representative government.

Aeneas Sylvius (1405–64), in his *De ortu et auctoritate imperii Romani,* advanced the clearest distinction between the social and the governmental contracts that is to be found in the writings of early modern authors. According to his notion, people originally lived in a state of nature. This proved warlike and unsatisfactory, so they agreed to establish orderly social relations through a social contract. Then they found it necessary to institute a government and to set forth the limitations thereupon by means of a governmental contract.[39]

The outstanding political writer of the period conventionally known as the "Renaissance" was Niccolò Machiavelli (1469–1527). He advanced

beyond Plato and Aristotle in separating ethics from politics and proceeded to make one of the most acute analyses of human nature to be
found in the history of early modern social philosophy. A perfect child of
the "conspirital society" that formed his political environment, he frankly
based his analysis of society upon the premise of man's self-interest and
the insatiability of human desire. He further maintained that personal
prestige and material prosperity are amply sufficient to satisfy these desires, in so far as they can be quenched. There was no theology in his
political theory.[40]

In his *Prince* and his *Discourses*—the latter is the less well-known,
but by far the more profound, work—he logically deduced from these
realistic views of human nature the methods that are to be followed by
a successful ruler of a monarchy and of a republic, respectively.

The *Prince* was the keenest sociological study of leadership and political pragmatism that had yet been made. Machiavelli took the position
that the end—success—justifies the means used and that whatever works
well is right. He thus effectively separated political theory from the
ethical elements that had colored it for centuries. In the *Discourses* he
outlined with equal candor the policies that should be followed by the
government of a successful and expanding republic. It was in this work
that he dealt most thoroughly with the problems of social relationships
and political processes. Further, there was a germinal conception of
social dynamics in his criticism of the ideal of social stability and provincialism, as expressed by Plato and Aristotle. He frankly held that a
state must either expand and develop or decay. Finally, Machiavelli
took social philosophy out of the realm of abstract speculation and
made a real start toward putting it on the firm foundation of historical
induction.

Despite these contributions, Machiavelli's analysis of society was not
synthetic or well balanced. His works were more after the fashion of
handbooks of political methods for the use of a self-seeking despot or
an imperialistic republic than systematic social and political theory.
They have, however, enjoyed great popularity and have exerted a very
wide influence upon rulers and practical politics.

The inroads made by the national monarchs upon feudalism and the
growth of the absolutistic national state led to appropriate justifications
of secular absolutism in political writings. This trend was evident in
the writings of Pierre Dubois and Marsiglio of Padua, but it received

a fuller and more resolute statement in the *Six Books concerning the Commonwealth* by the distinguished French publicist, Jean Bodin (1530–96).

Bodin approached nearer to a comprehensive exposition of the social process than any other writer had done since the time of Aristotle. He traced the genesis of society from an original family, which expanded and dispersed but was in time reunited through the operation of the social instinct and a growing perception of the utility of co-operative activity. Society, according to Bodin, is essentially a comprehensive union of lesser constituent groups, organized for the purpose of carrying on trade, worship, and similar activities. But, while society itself had this peaceful origin, the state and sovereign power developed out of force through the conquest of one group by another—an anticipation of social Darwinism.[41]

It is not difficult to discern the similarity between Bodin's conception of the origin of the state and that set forth by Hume and Ferguson and later developed by Gumplowicz and his school. His definition of sovereignty as the "supreme power in a state unrestrained by law" was a starting-point of modern political science. In his doctrine of the single-family origin of society he followed Aristotle and anticipated Blackstone and Maine. His theory of the group basis of civil society gave Althusius the suggestions which he developed to that extreme which is characteristic of the modern writings of Gumplowicz, Gierke, and their many followers. In co-ordinating ethics and politics, Bodin paved the way for Grotius; and his suggestions as to the influence of sympathy in society were in line with the later developments of this doctrine by Spinoza, Hume, Ferguson, Adam Smith, and Sutherland. By assuming a lawless state of primitive freedom, he gave an impetus to that old tradition which received its fullest elaboration a century later in the writings of the social-contract school, with its assumption of an unregulated state of nature.

In his work on historical interpretation, *A Method for Easily Understanding History,* Bodin presented one of the first attempts at a philosophy of history, a line of investigation cultivated earlier by ibn-Khaldun and later exploited by Vico, Voltaire, Turgot, Herder, Condorcet, Hegel, Comte, and Buckle.

Finally, Bodin's analysis of the influence of physical environment upon society and politics was the most comprehensive and systematic that had yet appeared, though not so original as is usually affirmed. He derived his ideas here from tradition and from astrology and the Hippocratic doctrine of the four humors. From these sources he produced the most elaborate discussion up to that time of the effect of climate upon mankind. But it amounted to the same old notion that the people of the south are wise but weak, those of the north fierce but stupid, and those of the middle climates both strong and wise. But, this time, the doctrine was used to vindicate the political and cultural leadership of France rather than of Greece or Italy. In other words, it was, as before, no more than a rationalization of patriotic pride.[42]

It is perhaps typical of the process whereby medieval civilization was disrupted by the intrusion of elements from without, to find that the first writer to possess the modern dynamic ideas of progress and the unity of the social process was the Muslim historian and statesman, ibn-Khaldun (1332–1406). At the outset, in his *Prolegomena to Universal History,* which was the systematic exposition of his theoretical views, he drew a sharp distinction between the popular episodical history and history as he conceived of it—namely, as a science tracing the origin and development of civilization.[43] Man, he maintained, is by nature social, since his wants are so varied and extensive that they can be supplied only through co-operative effort. But the conflict of desires produces quarrels and leads to the necessity for instituting government to insure order and stability. With almost the emphasis of Professor Giddings, he insisted upon the necessity of homogeneity for the existence of a stable state. His analysis of the tribal society of the Arabs was probably unsurpassed as a study of this period of human society until the time of L. H. Morgan. Again, his analysis of the influence of physical environment upon society was more thorough than any other study of this subject until the time of Bodin, if not until that of Montesquieu.

But the most important of the innovations of this interesting writer was his grasp of the unity and continuity of the historical process. In sharp contrast to the static conceptions of the prevailing Christian historiography, he grasped the fundamental conception that the stages of civilization are always in a constant process of change, like the life of the individual. He pointed out clearly the co-operation of psychic and environmental factors in this process of historical development. All in all, Khaldun, rather than Vico, has the best claim to the honor of having founded the philosophy of history, and his view of the factors involved in the historical process was sounder and more modern than that of the Italian of three centuries later.

NOTES

1. A. W. Small, *The Cameralists* (Chicago, 1909), chap. i; and *The Meaning of Social Science* (Chicago, 1910), *passim*.

2. J. O. Hertzler, *The Social Thought of the Ancient Civilizations* (New York, 1936), pp. 340–41. By permission of the McGraw-Hill Book Co.

3. This scanty survey of the social environment of Greek social philosophy may be supplemented by A. E. Zimmern, *The Greek Commonwealth* (Oxford, 1924); G. W. Botsford and E. G. Sihler, *Hellenic Civilization* (New York, 1915), pp. 210–54, 303–48, 423–526, 657–708; and F. S. Marvin, *The Living Past* (Oxford, 1917), chap. iv.

4. *Republic*, in Benjamin Jowett's *Dialogues of Plato*, ii. 369; iv. 433. The best account of Greek political and social thought in English is contained in Ernest Barker, *Greek Political Theory* (2 vols.; New York, 1918).

5. *Republic* iii. 412–17; v. 458–62; see John Wild, *Plato's Theory of Man* (Cambridge, Mass., 1946).

6. *Laws* (Jowett) iii. 676–84.

7. *Politics* (Jowett) i. 2.

8. *Ibid.* i. 1–2.

9. *Ibid.* ii. 2–7.

10. *Nichomachean Ethics,* trans. Peters, viii. 1. 9, 14; ix. 12.

11. Cf. Franklin Thomas, *The Environmental Basis of Society* (New York, 1925), pp. 16 ff.

12. Eduard Zeller, *Stoics, Epicureans, and Sceptics* (New York, 1892), pp. 311–40; G. L. Scherger, *The Evolution of Modern Liberty* (New York, 1904), pp. 18–22; Ludwig Stein, *Die soziale Frage im Lichte der Philosophie* (Stuttgart, 1923), pp. 171 ff.; and the extracts given in C. M. Bakewell, *A Source-Book of Ancient Philosophy* (New York, 1907), pp. 269–89. For a new compilation of the extant writings of Epicurus, Epictetus, Lucretius, and Marcus Aurelius see W. J. Oates, *The Stoic and Epicurean Philosophers* (New York, 1940).

13. The significant passages from Epicurus are preserved in Diogenes Laertius, *Lives and Opinions of Eminent Philosophers* x. 3. 33–35; see also Oates, *op. cit.,* pp. 3–69.

14. Polybius, *History of Rome,* trans. Schuckburgh, vi. 5–6; see also the selections in F. W. Coker, *Readings in Political Philosophy* (New York, 1914), pp. 106–17.

15. *History of Rome* vi. 5–6.

16. *Ibid.*

17. Cf. J. B. Bury, *The Ancient Greek Historians* (New York, 1909), pp. 205 ff., 248.

18. On Lucretius see the commentary of Gustave Masson, *Lucretius, Epicurean and Poet* (2 vols.; New York, 1907–9); and Oates, *op. cit.,* pp. 69–219.

19. Lucretius *De rerum natura,* trans. Munro ("Bohn's Library"), v. 325 ff., 778 ff.

20. *De officiis,* trans. Edmonds ("Bohn's Library"), i. 17, 44; *De republica,* trans. Yonge ("Bohn's Library"), i. 25, 26. For the effect of Cicero's opinion on this point on medieval political theory cf. Otto Gierke, *Political Theories of the Middle Ages,* trans. F. W. Maitland (Cambridge, 1900), n. 306.

21. *Epistularum moralium ad Lucilium,* ed. Haase, xiv. 2; *The Epistles of Lucius Annaeus Seneca,* trans. Morell (2 vols.; London, 1786), ii. 115–36, Letter XC.

22. Cf. Adolf Harnack, *History of Dogma* (7 vols.; London, 1895–1900), I, Appendix, 336 ff.; and T. Whittaker, *The Neo-Platonists* (Cambridge, 1910); for selections from Plotinus see Bakewell, *op. cit.,* pp. 340–93.

23. Shailer Mathews, *The Social Teachings of Jesus* (New York, 1910), pp. 16, 115, 151; and G. B. Stevens, *The Teachings of Jesus* (New York, 1911), pp. 117–18. For opinions and alignment of authorities upon the much-discussed problem of whether the Kingdom of God was an earthly social conception or an eschatological fantasy see Nathaniel Schmidt, *The Prophet of Nazareth* (New York, 1907), pp. 32, 296 ff.; and Stevens, *op. cit.*, pp. 65, 166.

24. A. J. Carlyle, *History of Medieval Political Theory* (5 vols.; Edinburgh, 1903–28), I, 89–90, 97–98; and F. C. Conybeare, *Myth, Magic, and Morals* (Watts, 1909), chaps. i, xiv. For up-to-date interpretations of Paul see F. A. Spencer, *Beyond Damascus* (New York, 1934); and Irwin Edman, *The Mind of Paul* (New York, 1935).

25. Justin Martyr, "First Apology," in *Ante-Nicene Fathers*, Vol. I, chap. xvii; Irenaeus, "Against Heresies," *ibid.*, Vol. I, Book V, chap. xxiv, sec. i; Lactantius, "Divine Institutes," *ibid.*, Vol. VII, Book VI, chap. x; "The Workmanship of God," *ibid.*, Vol. VII, chap. iv.; Tertullian, "Scorpiace," *ibid.*, Vol. III, chap. xiv; "Apology," Vol. III, chap. xxiv; Athanasius, "Against the Heathen," in *Nicene and Post-Nicene Fathers*, Vol. X, Book I, chap. xxviii; Augustine, "On the Good of Marriage," *ibid.*, Vol. III, sec. i; "The City of God," *ibid.*, Vol. II, Book V, chap. xix; Book XIX, chaps. v, xv; Jerome, letter quoted in J. H. Robinson, *Readings in European History* (New York, 1904), I, 86–87; Gregory the Great, "Pastoral Rule," in *Nicene and Post-Nicene Fathers*, Vol. XII, Book I, chap. iii; Isidore of Seville *Etymologies* xv. 2; Carlyle, *op. cit.*, Vol. I, chaps. viii-xv; Gierke, *op. cit.*, nn. 16–18, 137.

26. These diverse sources of medieval political theory are admirably summarized by A. J. Carlyle, "The Sources of Medieval Political Theory," in the *American Historical Review*, October, 1913, pp. 1–12; and more elaborately analyzed in his *History of Medieval Political Theory*, Vol. I, *passim*, and Vol. III, Introd.; see also Ernest Barker, in F. C. Hearnshaw, *The Social and Political Ideas of Some Great Medieval Thinkers* (New York, 1923), chap. i. For political and social thought in medieval and early modern times see Hearnshaw, *op. cit.*; and his *The Social and Political Ideas of Some Great Thinkers of the Renaissance and Reformation* (New York, 1925); C. H. McIlwain, *The Growth of Political Thought in the West* (Macmillan, 1932); Bede Jarrett, *Social Theories of the Middle Ages* (Boston, 1926); W. A. Dunning, *Political Theories, Ancient and Medieval* (New York, 1902); and R. G. Gettell, *History of Political Thought* (New York, 1924).

27. For this period see J. M. Littlejohn, *The Political Theory of the Schoolmen and Grotius* (privately printed, 1895), Part I, pp. 11–48; though somewhat diffuse, this work is the most complete exposition in English of the Scholastic political and social theory.

28. Cf. Carlyle, *History of Medieval Political Theory*, I, 211–12; and Littlejohn, *op. cit.*, pp. 26–33.

29. Carlyle, "The Sources of Medieval Political Theory," *op. cit.*, p. 8; and *History of Medieval Political Theory*, III, 160–69.

30. Carlyle, *History of Medieval Political Theory*, III, 126 f., 136 ff.; Gierke, *op. cit.*, p. 24 and n. 76; Hearnshaw, *The Social and Political Ideas of Some Great Medieval Thinkers*, chap. iii; and Littlejohn, *op. cit.*, pp. 42–47. There is an abridged English edition of the *Polycraticus*, edited by Professor John Dickinson (New York, 1927). It must be borne in mind that these medieval analogies were purely anthropomorphic and not genetically related to the later biological analogies.

What was, perhaps, an even more extreme statement of the ecclesiastical claim for the primacy of the church over the civil power was embodied in the *Summa de potestate ecclesiastica* of Augustinus Triumphus, written in the fourteenth century, during the papal "captivity" at Avignon. However, this had little practical significance, for, as Professor Dunning has well remarked, the papal pretensions increased about in proportion to the decline of the actual powers of the papacy.

31. J. H. Randall, Jr., *The Making of the Modern Mind* (Boston, 1926), pp. 58–59. By permission of the Houghton Mifflin Co.

32. *De regimine principum* i. 1; Littlejohn, *op. cit.*, pp. 69–74, 84–87, 104–8; and Crahay, *La Politique de Saint Thomas d'Aquin* (Brussels, 1896), chaps. i–ii; see also the selections given by Coker, *op. cit.*, pp. 123–35, particularly pp. 129–33.

33. *De monarchia*, ed. and trans. Henry; cf. Littlejohn, *op. cit.*, pp. 219–28; and Hearnshaw, *The Social and Political Ideas of Some Great Medieval Thinkers*, chap. v.

34. P. G. Vinogradoff, *Roman Law in Mediaeval Europe* (New York, 1910).

35. F. M. Powicke, "Pierre Dubois, a Medieval Radical," in *Historical Essays of Owens College*, ed. Tout and Tait (Manchester, 1902), pp. 169–91; Hearnshaw, *The Social and Political Ideas of Some Great Medieval Thinkers*, chap. vi; and W. I. Brandt, "Pierre Dubois, Modern or Medieval?" *American Historical Review*, April, 1930.

36. Cf. selections from the *Defensor pacis*, given in Robinson, *op. cit.*, I, 495–97; and Gierke, *op. cit.*, p. 51 and n. 182.

37. *Defensor pacis* i; see selections in Coker, *op. cit.*, pp. 160–67; Littlejohn, *op. cit.*, p. 230; Hearnshaw, *The Social and Political Ideas of Some Great Medieval Thinkers*, chap. vii; and Gierke, *op. cit.*, pp. 47 f. and nn. 155, 170, 267.

38. Gierke, *op. cit.*, p. 24, n. 79; and Hearnshaw, *The Social and Political Ideas of Some Great Thinkers of the Renaissance and Reformation*, chap. ii.

39. *De ortu* 1–2; Gierke, *op. cit.*, n. 306; and Dunning, *op. cit.*, pp. 282–83.

40. On Machiavelli, see Hearnshaw, *The Social and Political Ideals of Some Great Thinkers of the Renaissance and Reformation*, chap. iv.

41. Jean Bodin, *The Six Books of a Commonweale*, English trans. by Richard Knolles (London, 1606), pp. 47 ff., 262 ff.

42. Thomas, *op. cit.*, pp. 48 ff.

43. Nathaniel Schmidt, *Ibn Khaldun* (New York, 1930).

CHAPTER II

SOCIAL THOUGHT IN EARLY MODERN TIMES

Harry Elmer Barnes

I. THE COURSE OF SOCIAL PHILOSOPHY DURING THE GENERAL
DOMINATION OF THE DOCTRINE OF A SOCIAL CONTRACT

THE great popularity, from 1600 to 1800, of the social-contract theory
of the origin of organized society is not difficult to account for in
the light of the political and social environment. The late A. J. Carlyle
has emphasized the general acceptance of the doctrine of a governmental compact throughout the medieval period, and it has already
been pointed out that Aeneas Sylvius apparently made the important
distinction between the governmental compact and the more fundamental social contract. Professor Giddings insisted that the social-contract
theory grows naturally out of a society in which political relations have
been based on parliamentary procedure and sound legal foundations
and where there is a considerable degree of homogeneity in the population. The fact that the first definite instances of the enunciation of the
social-contract theory may be assigned to churchmen, who had been
under the sway of the well-established legal systems of the Catholic
church and the Church of England, lends plausibility to this theory.
Again, Professor D. G. Ritchie has pointed out the prevalence of many
actual contractual associations in the seventeenth century, such as the
Mayflower Compact, the Solemn League and Covenant, and the "Associations" of the Commonwealth period. He has also indicated the cogency
of the contract doctrine to those writers who were seriously concerned
with establishing the basis and justification of political liberty.[1]

Finally, it needs to be noted that the contract theory bore a definite
relation to the economic and political conditions of the period. The
growth of commerce and capital had made possible the existence of
strong national states and had also emphasized the importance of contracts in the sphere of economic activities. The origin and justification
of these powerful new political organizations offered an impressive

challenge to social and political philosophers, and the doctrine of a social contract was the most important early modern answer to this problem.

It should always be borne in mind that the majority of the exponents of the social-contract theory did not advance this theory as a literal historical account of the origin of the state but set it forth as a logical explanation of its existence. Many eager critics have made undeserved capital out of a misunderstanding of this important aspect of the contract theory, though Hume showed that its logical foundations were as weak as its historical basis.

The increased numbers, power, and ambition of the new middle class produced by the commercial revolution brought them into conflict with the absolute monarchs, who tried to tax and restrict the trade of the merchants in an arbitrary manner. In order to justify bourgeois resistance, the theory of natural rights, the social contract, and the right of revolution were most convenient and appropriate. Such notions had great practical political value in this period.

The work of the English churchman, Richard Hooker (1552-1600), was almost as suggestive as that of Bodin.[2] While his treatise, *The Laws of an Ecclesiastical Polity* (1594-1600), dealt primarily with the defense of the Anglican church, he devoted a portion of the first book to a general discussion of society and government.

Hooker emphasized the fact that government originates in the consent of the governed and must be administered according to law. He thus agreed with the previous doctrines of a governmental compact and popular sovereignty. This doctrine of a contract as the origin of government was, as we have seen, an old one. It had appeared in the writings of the Sophists, of Epicurus, Lucretius, the Roman lawyers, Manegold of Lautenbach, Aquinas, Marsiglio, William of Ockham, Nicholas of Cusa, and the monarchomachs of the sixteenth century, such as Hotman, Languet, Duplessis-Mornay, Knox, and Buchanan. But no previous writer, with the exception of Aeneas Sylvius, had advanced the doctrine of a social contract, namely, the idea that society itself arose out of a deliberate determination of men to escape from the evils of a presocial condition.

Hooker explicitly states this doctrine of social origins through a social contract, and it seems certain that he may be accorded the rather questionable honor of having first expounded the theory in an extended fashion.[3] Hooker did not, however, go so far as Hobbes and claim that men in the state of nature were antisocial. He agreed with Aristotle on this point, but he asserted that sociability had to be supplemented by a covenant which embodies the rules according to which associated life is to be guided and restrained.

Another churchman of this time, the Spanish Jesuit, Francisco Suárez (1548–1617), in his *Tractatus de legibus ac deo legislatore* (1612), expanded the doctrines of Aquinas by devoting especial attention to the function of law as the regulating principle in human association. To Suárez, man was almost a "legal animal," so minutely did he analyze his dependence upon law. It was in this respect that he made his chief advance beyond Aristotle and Aquinas, for he accepted their dictum that man is by nature social.[4] Suárez was also one of the founders of international law and perhaps the first to distinguish clearly between natural law and international law.

Another important element in the work of Suárez was his harmonizing of the doctrine of popular sovereignty with the theory that monarchy is the best type of government. While the supreme power resides in the people, they may alienate it from themselves and confer it upon the ruler by an act of popular will. Once this power is delegated, it is irrevocable, except in the case of tyranny on the part of the monarch. In dealing with tyranny, the delegated leaders of a commonwealth may legitimately depose a monarch, but Suárez denied the right of any individual to slay a tyrant, no matter how base or oppressive the rule of the latter. These political doctrines were contained in his *Defensio fidei catholicae,* a reply to the divine-right doctrine of James I.[5]

Suárez's contemporary and fellow-Jesuit, the Spanish writer, Juan de Mariana (1536–1624), offered an interesting interpretation of the early history of human society in his *De rege et regis institutione* (1605). In the beginning, said he, men had lived like animals, without authority and guided only by instinct. But they were free from the greed and artificial immoralities of civilization. Man, however, had greater wants than other animals; his offspring was less rapid in reaching maturity; and he was less adequately protected from natural dangers and external enemies by his natural endowment. Therefore, to live in safety from hostile attacks, men had to set up group life and submit to the authority of some capable leader who was able to direct the resulting political society for the general welfare.[6]

Mariana's somewhat sentimental picture of the state of nature more closely approached that set forth by Rousseau in his famous second *Discourse* than the views of any other writer of the period. While believing in the natural sociability of man, Mariana clearly implied the existence of a social contract in his theory of civic origins. He also set forth a theory of the influence of the prolongation of infancy upon social life which was directly in line with that elaborated in recent times by John Fiske.

The German jurist, Johannes Althusius (1557–1638), was long regarded as the first Continental writer to elaborate the doctrine of a social contract. His chief expositor, Otto von Gierke, thus interpreted his views. Gierke and Figgis, his English disciple, also regarded Althusius as the founder of political pluralism and of the doctrine of the federal state. There is some basis for such an opinion of Althusius in the first edition of his *Politica methodice digesta;* but Professor Carl J. Friedrich, editor of the latest text of this work, points out that Althusius' mature theory of social and political origins was biological rather than political or legalistic. He held that politics is the science that explains how human beings live together. This process of living together he defined as "symbiosis." The origins of society and the state are not to be sought in any contract but are natural sociobiological phenomena or processes. Society and the state are not the products of conscious deliberation but of a biological drive to close association, in which the community absorbs—"devours"—the individual and the state absorbs the community. He was thus more a forerunner of contemporary totalitarianism than of federalism.[7]

The famous Dutch scholar and statesman, Hugo Grotius (1583–1645), may, for all practical purposes, be regarded as the founder of international law, though Dubois, Gentili, Hooker, and Suárez had earlier made valuable suggestions. He is most noted for his systematic work in this field, which was embodied mainly in the famous *De jure belli et pacis.* In his "Prolegomena" to this work he advanced important doctrines regarding the origin and foundation of social institutions. While he interpreted society, in its most general sense, as being the natural expression of human nature with its "appetite for society," he was convinced, on the other hand, that the state had its origin in a contract. In his work on international law, Grotius endeavored to promote that like-mindedness in regard to the essentials of international policy which Professors Giddings and Tenney have insisted is the indispensable basis of any possible hope for the future peace of mankind. While Grotius' work on international law was an innovation, his confusing and inconsistent theory of sovereignty and his denial of popular sovereignty are considered retrogressive.

The *Patriarcha* of Robert Filmer (d. 1653) was an attack upon the doctrine of the contractual origin of government. While Filmer appealed to reason rather than to authority and made a good case against the contract doctrine, his own substitute, namely, patriarchal authority bestowed upon Adam by God, was even less valid than the contract doctrine. Because he put the case on the grounds of nature rather than of theology, Filmer's notion marks a transition from theological arguments to the use of natural law and utilitarian conceptions in support of the divine right of kings.

Among the chief contributions of the Commonwealth period to social and political philosophy were the individualizing of the conception of a social contract, by assuming that every citizen must be a party to the contract; the appeal to the law of nature to establish the rights of men; and the specific formulation of the doctrine of popular sovereignty and the right of revolution. It was the contribution of John Milton (1608–74) to work these doctrines into a philosophical statement and to promulgate them with sufficient coherence to secure their recognition.[8]

There was one conspicuous democratic development in seventeenth-century England, namely, the rise of the so-called "Levelers" during the period of the Commonwealth. They were made up of real democrats, both within the army and outside, and were led by John Lilburne, who deserves a prominent rank among the leading apostles of democracy.

The Levelers boldly proclaimed the sovereignty of the people and held that Parliament should be the servant rather than the master of the mass of Englishmen. They demanded universal manhood suffrage, excluding only those who were servants or paupers, annual sessions of Parliament, and equal electoral districts. They also espoused a number of other democratic proposals, such as abolition of imprisonment for debt, elimination of monopolies and sinecures, abolition of tithes, and reform of the criminal law. In this program they anticipated some of the policies and demands of the Chartists just two centuries later. The Levelers certainly constitute the most significant democratic development before the days of the Jacksonian Democrats in the United States and the Chartists in England.[9]

Despite the previous developments of the social-contract doctrine, it remained for the English philosopher, Thomas Hobbes (1588–1679), to give that conception its first classic statement. Going far beyond any of the previous writers in the detail and "remorseless logic" with which he analyzed the situation, he assumed the existence of a presocial state of nature, which was "a state of war of all men against all men" and in which the life of man was "poor, nasty, brutish, and short."[10] He flatly denied the dictum of Aristotle that man is by nature social and maintained that all society is for either gain or glory and that any permanent social grouping must originate in the mutual fear which men have toward one another.[11] He was as realistic as Machiavelli in his analysis of human nature and believed with the latter that all human activity springs from man's insatiable desires.[12]

Hobbes held that, to escape the miseries of the turbulent and unregulated state of nature, men agreed to unite into a civil society for their mutual protection. In doing so, they made an inalienable transfer of their individual powers to the general governing agent or sovereign.[13] Hobbes did not, however, hold that either the state of nature or the contract was necessarily true in a literal historic sense. Hobbes's analysis was psychological, and he has been correctly called the "father of social psychology." It was the irrevocable nature of the social contract and the conception of the unlimited sovereign power of the ruler which distinguished the doctrines of Hobbes from those of the majority of the other members of the contract school.

Besides this voluntary contract, Hobbes contended that there might be another type of civic origins based upon force, when a conqueror compelled submission on pain of death.[14] In this latter version Hobbes was in line with the vital principle of the school represented by Gumplowicz. Hobbes's conception of the nature and attributes of sovereignty was an important contribution, but he confused the state and the government and erroneously ascribed sovereign power to the latter.

The German statesman and philosopher, Samuel von Pufendorf (1632–94), attempted a reconciliation of the doctrines of Grotius and Hobbes in his *De jure naturae et gentium*. His ethics were primarily those of Grotius, while his political doctrines were mainly Hobbesian. He held that the social instinct in man can account for the existence of the family and lesser social groups but that a social and a governmental contract were necessary to bring into being the state and government. While Pufendorf began his analysis of the state of nature with the assumption that it was a state of peace, he ended with about the same conclusion as that arrived at by Hobbes.

Pufendorf's conception of the contract was threefold. First, there was a social contract, which embodied the agreement to unite in social life; then a vote was taken to determine the form of government desired; and, finally, the arrangement was ended by a governmental contract between the rulers and the governed, regulating the principles and limits of political administration. Pufendorf thus united more clearly than had Hooker the related concepts of a social and a governmental contract.[15] His conception of sovereignty was as confusing as that of Grotius, for, while defining it as supreme power in the state, he held that it must also be limited to what a sane man would term "just action."

The Jewish philosopher, Baruch Spinoza (1632–77), was, in his political theory, a member of the contract school. He agreed with Hobbes as to the existence of a presocial state of nature which was one of general war and universal enmity.[16] Society, he maintained, had a purely utilitarian basis in the advantages of mutual aid and the division of labor.[17] To render this advantageous association secure, however, it was necessary that its utilitarian basis be supplemented by a contract to give it a legal foundation and to guarantee to each citizen the natural rights which he possessed as an individual prior to the contract. He claimed that the contract was rendered valid only by the superior advantages which it offered and that the sovereign was such only so long as he could maintain his authority. This justification of rebellion Spinoza considered to be the only sure guaranty of just rule and individual liberty.[18] Spinoza was mainly interested in using the contract as a buttress for liberty, while Hobbes had been chiefly concerned in utilizing it to justify royal absolutism.

In his *Ethics* Spinoza gave a clear statement to the theory of reflective sympathy, earlier hinted at by Aristotle and Polybius; later revived and developed by Hutcheson, Hume, Adam Smith, and Alexander Sutherland; and, in our day, occupying a prominent position in Professor Giddings' system of sociology.

The *Patriarcha* of Filmer called forth two better-known works in refutation of its thesis. The first was Algernon Sidney's (1622–83) *Dis-*

courses concerning Government. Sidney criticized Filmer's work in detail, proclaimed that the origin of government is to be found in the consent of the governed, and declared himself for the indefeasible sovereignty of the people. Of all English writers in the seventeenth century, Sidney was, perhaps, the most effective assailant of absolute monarchy and was a martyr to this cause. He favored a mixed government, combining elements of monarchy, aristocracy, and democracy.[19]

The second refutation of the *Patriarcha* constituted the first of John Locke's (1632-1704) *Two Treatises of Government.* But the *Second Treatise* was far more epoch-making in its doctrines, for Locke here set forth his important conception of the social contract and his justification of revolution.

In his views on the state of nature, Locke differed radically from Hobbes, Spinoza, and even Pufendorf, in that he denied that it was by any means a condition of general war and disorder. It was not even a presocial state but was, rather, a prepolitical situation, in which every man had the right to execute the laws of nature.

The very social nature of man, Locke contended, would prevent the state of nature from being one of isolation and unsociability. The most serious deficiency in the state of nature was the lack of an impartial judge who could settle all disputes in an equitable manner and take the power of executing the laws from the hands of each individual.[20] The chief and immediate cause of man's leaving the state of nature was the increase of private property and the desire to use and preserve it in safety.[21] This emphasis upon the security of property might have been expected from the apologist of the bourgeois revolution of 1688. Locke held that the chief purpose of government and law is to protect property.

Locke made the most direct claim of any writer of the contract school for the historicity of the social contract as the means of instituting civil society, and he maintained that it must be assumed to lie at the basis of all the states then in existence.[22]

He differentiated clearly between society, in general, as created by the social contract, and the government, to which society delegates the functions of political control. By so doing he was able to show how government may be dissolved without destroying civil society itself.[23] This dissolution of the government, or revolution, is justifiable whenever the terms or purposes of the social contract are violated by those in power. The majority of the citizens are the only group qualified to judge when the infractions have become sufficient to warrant revolution.[24] Locke thus laid the theoretical foundation for the American and French revolutions, as well as justifying the English revolution of 1688.

The ingenious and romantic Rousseau (1712-78) was the last of the classical contract school.[25] In his earlier writings Rousseau took the position, in opposition to Hobbes, that the condition of man in the state of nature was almost ideal in its rude simplicity and that the state of war was unknown in those idyllic days. Man reached perfection in the age of ancient patriarchs. The development of civilization, while bringing increasing enlightenment, had only contributed to the physical and moral degeneration of the race and to the growth of inequality, corruption, and tyranny.

In his later writings, especially his *Social Contract,* Rousseau abandoned his earlier praise of the natural state of man and took practically the same position as Locke, namely, that, while this condition was not one of war, its uncertainties and inconveniences rendered the institution of civil society imperative. The only way in which civil society could be set up and unified power and general protection secured was through the medium of a social contract. This contract gave rise to the state or civil community and not to the government. Rousseau thus distinguished between the state and government, making sovereign power the prerogative of the state and governmental power purely delegated. His definition of sovereignty as the absolute power of the state, growing out of an expression of the general will, was probably his chief contribution to political philosophy.

Rousseau's notion of popular sovereignty became the doctrinal bulwark of democratic theory. He went on to insist that every governmental issue must be submitted to a popular vote and held that all citizens must obey every measure which has received the approval of a majority of the voters. Rousseau also maintained that voters should register their opinions and elect their candidates in districts based on population and geographical areas. He thus helped to upset the vocational representation of medieval and early modern Europe—representation by estates and interests—and encouraged the trend toward territorial representative units, based on population.

While the importance of Rousseau's conception of popular sovereignty is generally conceded, historians now tend to ascribe less significance to Rousseau's dogmas as direct causal influences in the French

Revolution than was formerly the case. Few men have been further removed from the temperament of the practical revolutionist than Rousseau was.

Finally, Rousseau's important contributions to educational theory in his *Émile* should be mentioned. Here he laid special emphasis upon the value of a spontaneous development of the whole personality rather than upon formal discipline or the mere acquisition of knowledge. He also helped to infuse a democratic tendency into education by declaring it to be the right of every child to have an adequate education, a position even more warmly defended by Helvétius.

Further on, we shall present the criticisms of the social-contract theory by Hume, Ferguson, Burke, and others. Suffice it to say here that among them they completely discredited the doctrine on both psychological and historical grounds.

II. THE RISE OF A THEORY OF PROGRESS

One of the more conspicuous results of the rise of science and the growth of rationalism between 1500 and 1800 was the gradual appearance of an idea of progress. It is a significant fact that more than 99 per cent of man's existence upon the planet was passed through without any consciousness of the actual progress of human culture. Human progress down to the seventeenth century was natural and spontaneous and was in no sense the result of any collective effort to realize a conscious goal of racial and cultural advancement.

The ancient Jews, holding to the doctrine of the "Fall" of man, logically believed that perfection was to be found in the past rather than to be sought in the future. The classical writers shared to some degree a comparable notion, namely, the dogma of a decline from a golden age. Even more popular with the Greeks and Romans was the conception of the cyclical nature of human development. Culture would rise to a certain point and then decline to a level comparable to that which had existed at the beginning. Then the process would start all over again, and the cycle would be repeated. The Christians took over the Jewish notion of the "Fall" of man and combined it with the pagan view of the decline from a golden age. Man could never expect any utopia here on earth. The state of blessedness is to be attained only in the world to come. The Last Judgment and the end of things earthly was, according to the Christian view as stated in the Book of Revelation, to be preceded by unusually horrible and devastating earthly occurrences.

Gradually, however, there arose the conviction that better things might be in store for humanity here on this earth. Back in the thirteenth century Roger Bacon had had a vision of what applied science might do for man. Montaigne had a glimmering of a new idea when he suggested that human learning should be concerned with human happiness here on earth rather than with the salvation of the soul in the life to come. Francis Bacon and Descartes united in decrying the authority of the past. Bacon had contended that the moderns were superior to the ancients and suggested that utopia might be secured through applying science to human problems.

The doctrine of progress, as it is conventionally understood, began, however, with men like Bernard de Fontenelle (1657–1757).[26] In his *Dialogues of the Dead* (1683) Fontenelle hardly went beyond the contention that the ancients were no better than the moderns; but five years later, in his *Digression on the Ancients and the Moderns,* he took a more positive attitude. He held that the ancients and the moderns are essentially alike in a biological sense, there being no progress in this respect. In the fine arts, which are chiefly a spontaneous expression of the human spirit, there seems to be no law of progress. The ancient peoples achieved great things here, but the best modern works in art, poetry, and oratory equal the most perfect ancient examples. On the other hand, in science and industry we find an altogether different story. In these fields development is cumulative. There has been vast progress here since antiquity, and even greater things may be looked for in the future. Moreover, Fontenelle agreed with Francis Bacon that unreasoning admiration for the ancients is a major obstacle to progress. It is doubtful if anybody, even in our own day, has more successfully stated the general principles involved in the problem of what we call "progress" than did Fontenelle.

Charles Perrault (1628–1703) was a contemporary of Fontenelle and expressed very much the same views in his *Parallel of the Ancients and Moderns* (1688–96). But he was so much impressed by what he regarded as the perfection of culture in his own generation that he was not much concerned with future progress—if, indeed, he would have conceded that anything could be better than his own age.

A more dynamic attitude toward future progress was taken by the Abbé de Saint-Pierre (1658–1753). He contended that progress is real and that the achievements of his own age were more notable than those of the era of Plato and Aristotle. He was particularly interested in social progress and believed in the desirability of an academy of political science to guide social advance. He placed great faith in the power of a wise government and was a forerunner of Helvétius and the Utilitarians.

Claude Adrien Helvétius (1715–71) was the foremost of the French social optimists of this period. He believed thoroughly in the possibility of human perfection and thought it could be effectively achieved through universal enlightenment and rational education. He had faith in the equality of men and held that existing inequalities can be eliminated through education.

In the first half of the eighteenth century the Italian, Giovanni Battista Vico (1668–1744), a philosopher of history, worked out a conception of progress in his *La Scienza nuova*. He held that human progress does not take place directly or in a straight line. Rather, it takes the form of a spiral. There may seem to be cycles of development, but they never go back to the original starting-point. Each turn is on a higher level than the preceding.

A little later, in France, a more realistic historical theory of progress was expounded by Anne Robert Jacques Turgot (1729–81), himself an eminent contributor to the philosophy of history. He laid great stress upon the continuity of history and the cumulative nature of progress. He contended that the more complex the civilization, the more rapid is human progress. Hence, cultural advance was very slow in primitive times but has been greatly accelerated in the modern epoch. Even more optimistic was the distinguished writer of the French Revolutionary period, the Marquis de Condorcet, author of *A Sketch of the Intellectual Progress of Mankind*. He not only stated his belief in the reality of progress but presumed to divide the history of civilization into ten periods, each representing a definite stage in the development of human civilization. Nine of these periods had already been passed through, and the French Revolution and modern science were leading us to the brink of the tenth, which would produce an era of happiness and well-being the like of which had never before been known.

There were other men who contributed variously to the notion of progress. The German philosopher, Herder, attempted to work out laws of progress based on the collaboration of nature and God. Immanuel Kant sought to prove the reality of moral progress. The English publicist, William Godwin (1756–1836), believed that perfection might be obtained through the abolition of the state and property and the indoctrination of rationality through private instruction. Henri de Saint-Simon (1760–1825) followed the line of the Abbé de Saint-Pierre in holding that a basic social science must be provided to guide human progress. These notions culminated in the historical philosophy and sociology of Auguste Comte (1798–1857). He worked out a comprehensive panorama of the "laws" governing intellectual progress and formulated an expansive philosophy of history, embodying the division of the past into a large number of periods and subperiods, each characterized by some phase of cultural advance.

III. UTOPIAS, SOCIAL AND REVOLUTIONARY DOCTRINES
AFFECTING THE LOWER CLASSES

The doctrines set forth between 1600 and 1800 justifying revolution that we have discussed above were concerned primarily with the transformation of political institutions and affected mainly the upper-class landowners and the middle-class merchants. But there were many writers between 1500 and 1800 who recognized that political progress means little unless accompanied by comparable social and economic changes. Others saw clearly that no type of social reform is adequate unless it touches the life of the masses of agricultural and industrial workers. They asserted that the doctrine of the equality of man must go deeper than mere beautiful political phrases and must apply to the economic and social status of the various members of society. Some of these proposals for social change took the form of "utopias," or pictures of ideal society, envisaging novel principles not yet adopted in the civilizations of the writers.[27] Locke and other apologists for the rising bourgeois system had contended that the chief purpose of society, government, and law is to protect private property. The radical utopians of this period took the opposite view and held that the ideal society must limit or even, in the opinion of some of these writers, do away with private property altogether.

Programs and movements for social reform date back in their origins almost to the dawn of written history. Oppression of certain classes existed in the first historical societies, and it is not surprising that some of the earliest Egyptian literature reflects the growth of discontent among the subject groups. As Professor E. R. A. Seligman once pointed out, the desire to improve the social environment has been a dynamic impulse encouraging the evolution of economic and social doctrines, though it is quite true that theories which have once been the harbingers of progress may later be utilized as a bulwark of the existing order.

While proposals for the betterment of social conditions have appeared in all ages, they have been most numerous after great social and economic revolutions that have altered the status of existing classes and have brought an unusual amount of misery to those whose condition was most seriously affected by the transition. As Professor Robert Flint expressed it: "It is in their times of sorest depression that nations usually indulge most in dreams of a better future and that their imaginations produce most freely social ideals and utopias."

The growth of wealth and class differentiation in antiquity; the development of Athens into a commercial empire; the growth of the plutocracy in the Roman Republic; the disintegration of Roman society in the fourth and fifth centuries A.D.; the breakdown of feudalism and the origin of the national states; the rise of the *bourgeoisie* following the commercial revolution; and that greatest of all social and economic revolutions, the industrial revolution of the late eighteenth and nineteenth centuries—these are well-known examples of social and economic transformations that brought social upsets and human misery in their train and stimulated the formulation of numerous programs of social reform, written by those who were distressed over the social suffering that ensued. We are here concerned with the transformations, confusion, and misery caused by the breakdown of the medieval system and the origins of modern industry, commerce, and agricultural methods following the close of the Middle Ages.

The first and the most famous of modern utopias was the work of an English scholar and official, Sir Thomas More (1478–1535). More wrote during the Tudor period, when English society, particularly among the lower classes, was feeling the impact of the breakdown of the manorial system and the rise of large-scale sheep-farming. The suppression of the English monasteries by Henry VIII also increased the general misery of the time. In the opening section of his *Utopia* More presents us with a vivid picture of the disorder and suffering of the time.

In order to suggest a remedy for these sorry conditions, More portrayed an ideal society on the fanciful island of Amaurote. Here wealth was to be divided equally, so as to put an end to that avarice and covetousness which More, like Plato, regarded as the root of all human evils. The whole society on the island was to be a well-organized community, based upon co-operative principles. Altruism would prevail, and each person would have in his mind the interests of all others. Everybody was to engage in agriculture and, in addition, to learn some useful trade. The government was to be a combination of aristocracy and the force of public opinion. More did not believe that many laws would be required, since equality and the co-operative principle would automatically bring to an end most of those evil desires and acts which require legislative restraint.

Francis Bacon, as has been noted, advocated the betterment of human society through the application of natural science. His ideal society, described in *The New Atlantis,* was located on an island off the coast of South America. Its central feature was the House of Solomon, where the scientists gathered and worked. They also sent out travelers to visit the rest of the world and to gather in new scientific knowledge. This was to be applied to increasing the happiness and welfare of the population. All superstition was to be rooted out, and social improvements were to be assured through the knowledge acquired by the scientists.

Much more radical were the proposals embodied in *The City of the Sun,* written by an Italian friar, Tommaso Campanella (1568–1639). He maintained that society is based upon the threefold principles of power, love, and intelligence; and he contended that there can be no perfect social system unless this trinity receives due recognition in the organs of social control and political administration. Campanella argued for the complete abolition of all slavery, for the dignity and importance of labor, and for the elimination of the leisure class. Everybody was to work, but he believed that a short day would suffice to produce all the required necessities of life. He favored communism in property. He held that the home and the family are the chief foundation of the property instinct. Hence, property cannot be done away with so long as the individual home is maintained. Community of wives and children he believed to be essential to the elimination of the acquisitive tendency.

The utopia of James Harrington (1611–77), an English publicist, had a much more aristocratic cast. In his *Oceana* he held that society must be organized on psychological principles, so as to make certain the leadership of the intellectually élite. Furthermore, political organization must be so arranged as to secure the predominant influence of the landholding classes, which, he believed, constitute the intellectual aristocracy. He sponsored the equal division of landed property and a wide use of the elective principle in government.

The *Télémaque* of François Fénelon (1651–1715) was a long and fanciful pedagogical novel, which utilized a picture of life in the simple Homeric society in order to inculcate ideals suitable for the education of a modern prince. It endeavored to teach sound principles of government at wide variance with the tyranny and exploitation that then prevailed under the French Bourbons. His ideal government was that of a benevolent monarchy, devoted to peace, economy, social justice, and the development of agriculture. He developed his political doctrines further in his *Tables de Chaulnes*. Among the novel principles that Fénelon suggested was the education of women, to which he devoted an entire book.

The beginning of true social radicalism is to be discerned in *The Code of Nature,* a detailed communistic utopia, written in 1755 by a Frenchman named Morelly, about whose life little is known. He advocated a new social system, based upon the rights of the masses and the laws of nature rather than upon something handed down from above by benevolent autocrats. He took man in a state of nature and primitive society as his standard of comparison. Here, without either property or political force, Morelly pictured man as inherently good. The purpose of government and human institutions should be to preserve this inherent human goodness and social equality. Therefore, he advocated the abolition of private property and the establishment of social equality. His notion of communism was not mere equality of property but actual communal ownership of goods by all members of society. He laid special stress upon the social distribution of the products of industry. He attacked the doctrine of innate ideas and contended that there is no natural idea or instinct of property. Hence there will be no great difficulty in putting an end to the institution of private property. As a form of government, Morelly proposed what he designated as "democracy" but what was really benevolent rule by patriarchs.

Contemporary with Morelly and holding much the same ideas was the Abbé Gabriel Bonnet de Mably (1709–85), especially in his treatise on *Legislation*. He attempted to reconcile the selfish and social tendencies in man by holding that, while self-interest furnishes the basic drive in human activity, true happiness can be found only in social life. Man originally lived in a state of relative perfection but fell from this happy estate into misery because of the rise of private property and the quarrels which this promoted. The underlying cause of human suffering and social evils has been the accumulation and the unequal distribution of wealth. The rise of money helped along this degradation of man and society. Mably held that we cannot suddenly return to perfection by establishing pure communism. We must start by restricting property rights and holdings. We can then work gradually toward communism. The governmental system through which he proposed to achieve this result was about what we should call a "conservative republic."

During the French Revolution a notable movement toward social radicalism was led by François Babeuf (1760–97). He took seriously the "Equality" slogan of the French Revolution and insisted that any equality of real significance must be social and economic, as well as political. These principles he embodied in his *Manifesto of the Equals,* in which he held that, in primitive society, economic and social equality were the rule, and he said that society and government should preserve this equality. To Babeuf they seemed to be defending and perpetuating inequality. He, therefore, advocated communism in property and equality of individual status. He was especially bitter against private property in land. He warmly supported the doctrine of democracy as a form of government. Though Babeuf himself was guillotined, his doctrines cropped up again in the Revolution of 1848 and in the Paris Commune of 1871.

IV. SOCIAL PHILOSOPHY DURING THE PERIOD OF ITS GRADUAL TRANSITION INTO SOCIOLOGY

A. THE CULTURAL BACKGROUND

Around the beginning of the eighteenth century a new era seemed to be dawning in social philosophy. The old a priori speculation and interpretation of society in purely subjective terms was gradually abandoned, though there was a temporary recrudescence in the writings of

Rousseau. Vico presented a theory of progress and a new attitude in studying primitive society. Berkeley and the social reformers reflected the influence of Newtonian natural science. Montesquieu produced the first great objective and descriptive treatise on sociology. Voltaire partially crushed obscurantism. Fontenelle, Turgot, Kant, and Condorcet were the first conspicuous advocates of the doctrines of continuity in history and of the possibility of infinite human progress. Along with Herder and others, they gave an impetus to the philosophy of history. Hume presented the first important psychological interpretation of society, annihilated the social contract, and suggested a naturalistic study of religion as a form of human behavior.

Ferguson and Herder combined the objective and subjective methods of analyzing the social process. Economic influences were studied in detail by the Physiocrats, Adam Smith, and the Classical Economists. The French Revolution emphasized, perhaps to excess, the doctrine of the amenability of social processes to rational and artificial direction. The scientific historical approach to the study of social institutions was manifested in the works of Eichhorn, Savigny, Niebuhr, Ranke, and Guizot. Finally, Saint-Simon classified the sciences and pointed out the need of a synthetic science of society to furnish a reliable guide for reconstructing the social order. The various lines of approach to the interpretation of social processes which were to converge in sociology were, thus, all in process of development during the eighteenth century and the first quarter of the nineteenth. When one reflects upon the situation, it appears neither strange nor miraculous that Comte was able, after 1820, to conceive of, and partially formulate, the laws of a synthetic system of sociology. At best, he only skilfully combined interpretations which were current in his time.

The environmental origins of social philosophy during the period of its transition into sociology are not difficult to discover.[28] The older tendencies, centering about the creation of the national state, furnished the center of orientation for the doctrines of the Mercantilists and the Cameralists, whose influence lasted well into the eighteenth century. The reaction against their excessive emphasis upon the paramount importance of the state and upon the necessity of extensive state activity found expression in the laissez faire doctrines of the Physiocrats and the English Classical Economists.

Natural science, which received its highest expression in Newton, reacted powerfully upon eighteenth-century political and social philosophy. If Galileo and Newton had been able to interpret the physical universe in terms of such simple formulas as the laws of "falling bodies" and "inverse squares," it seemed probable to many social philosophers that equally simple formulas could be found to explain and control social and political phenomena. This idea was a foundation of the prevalent eighteenth-century doctrine that a few "self-evident dictates of pure reason" are adequate to interpret and to adjust social and political relations. It also provided the basic philosophy which buttressed the laissez faire tenets of the Physiocrats and Adam Smith.

The critical spirit of the eighteenth century, which found its ablest representatives in Voltaire, the Encyclopedists, Hume, and Paine, can be traced to a number of sources. Bacon and Descartes, in the previous century, had proclaimed the futility of dependence upon the past. The natural science contributed to a general spirit of skepticism and curiosity. The extensive geographical discoveries and explorations extended the contact of cultures, which is the most potent agency in awakening a criticism of social institutions. The Deists emphasized the necessity of introducing reason into religion, the very possibility of which had been denied by Luther. All these forces and tendencies gave rise to that destructive criticism of old theories and institutions which was necessary to clear the ground for a new synthetic and dynamic study of society.

Montaigne, and Shaftesbury, Pope, and other Deists, attacked the depressing theological view of the inherent depravity and hopeless wickedness of man and made possible a conception of man as a worthy subject for scientific analysis, thus justifying the social sciences.

The critical spirit, the Deistic conception of the reasonable decency of man, and the dynamic type of mind created by the further developments of science, commerce, and industry opened the way to the idea of the future progress of the race, so admirably expressed by Fontenelle, Turgot, Condorcet, and Godwin.

The industrial revolution, the greatest transformation in the history of humanity, broke down the foundations of the previous social system even more completely than the commercial revolution had destroyed the medieval order. Out of the confusion, as an aid in solving the newly created social problems, there came a further development and differentiation of the special social sciences. The necessity of providing a synthetic and systematic science of society, to criticize the validity of the multitude of schemes presented to reconstruct the disintegrating social order, brought into being sociology in its present connotation.

B. GEOGRAPHICAL AND BIOLOGICAL INTERPRETATIONS OF SOCIETY

We have already called attention to the theories offered by Hippocrates, Aristotle, Vegetius, Aquinas, and Bodin relative to the influence of physical factors, especially climate, upon mankind and human society. In the period after 1700 the idea was developed far more completely, and the chief exponent of this interpretation of social and political processes was the French publicist, Charles de Secondat, baron de Montesquieu (1689–1755), author of the famous *The Spirit of Laws* (1748).[29] Montesquieu's notions on the effect of climate on mankind were drawn in part from the English physician and publicist, John Arbuthnot, who, in 1733, wrote an *Essay on the Effects of Air on Human Bodies*. Montesquieu's wide use of examples from the Moslem East was helped along by reading Jean Chardin's *Travels into Persia and the East Indies*.

The purpose of *The Spirit of Laws* was to lay down the fundamental principles of legislation. These Montesquieu found to be: (1) the close adaptation of institutions and legislation to the character of the peoples for whom they are intended, and (2) the harmonious interaction of the various institutions, laws, and other devices for insuring social control which are applied by any group. Such a view led him to investigate the factors which produce the diverse physical and cultural characteristics to be observed among the various peoples of the world. He upheld the notion that the main cause of the diversities among human types and cultures is geographical influences, especially climate. By examining the effects of geographical factors on men, one could understand the traits of the different peoples of the world and thus be in a position to determine the appropriate laws and institutions for each type of man.

Montesquieu frankly abandoned the conventional view that there is some absolutely best state, economic order, religion, form of family, or moral code, and he fully adopted the comparative approach. That institution is "best" which is best adapted to the conditions of the people for whom it is intended. Climate and other geographical factors have created the various types of man, and it is the function of the wise legis-

lator to discover and recognize these types and their traits and to legis-
late accordingly.

To illustrate: Montesquieu maintained that a despotism is best adapted
to peoples dwelling in warm climates, a limited monarchy to those in
temperate climates, and a republic to dwellers in cold areas. Moham-
medanism is eminently suited to those living in the tropics, Catholicism
to those in intermediate climates, and Protestantism to those in colder
zones. Polygamy is particularly practical for the tropics, whereas monogamy is preferable in temperate and cold regions. Drinking should be
tabooed in the warm climates, because no stimulus is needed to produce
vivacity; but heavy drinking may be tolerated in cold areas because of
the need of internal heat, of a stimulation of the senses, and of an
encouragement of playfulness among the "phlegmatic peoples of the
north."

Montesquieu's emphasis on the importance of geographical factors
in shaping social institutions gave an impetus to anthropogeography.
Many writers on history, politics, and economics adopted Montesquieu's
views in whole or in part. Count Buffon held that racial differences are
due chiefly to differences in the geographical habitat of the races. The
German philosopher, Herder, generally agreed with Montesquieu as
to the effects of geographical environment on man, though he laid
rather more stress on organic and psychic forces than did Montesquieu.
He contended that, while Montesquieu's notions regarding climatic influences on man were most suggestive, they must be accepted with careful scrutiny and due discrimination. But he conceded that geographic
factors have much to do with shaping national character. Adam Ferguson
accepted Montesquieu's ideas with some qualification in his *History
of Civil Society*. Montesquieu's notions were critically examined by
Charles Comte in his *Treatise on Legislation*. Much new scientific material on climatic influences was provided by the travels, researches, and
writings of the great German explorer and naturalist, Alexander von
Humboldt, who got away from pure theory and gathered data in the
field in scientific fashion. Such work made possible the publication in
1818 of Karl Ritter's *Die Erdkunde im Verhältnis zur Natur und
zur Geschichte der Menschen,* the first truly scientific work on anthropogeography.

Changes in population levels have naturally aroused the interest of
observers of social conditions. We have already shown that population

problems have been discussed by writers for thousands of years. A scholar in the field of population questions, Charles E. Stangeland, has actually written a good-sized book on the many theories of population growth that were set forth before the time of Malthus, with whom many people believe that the discussion of population problems began. We have no space here for the discussion of historical curiosities in the field of population theory, so we shall limit ourselves to a summary of the notions of Thomas Robert Malthus (1776–1834).[30]

In 1798 appeared the first edition of Malthus' *Essay on Population,* which was destined to have a remarkable influence on economic and social discussions for more than a century. The substance of Malthus' argument was as follows: (1) population tends to increase at a geometric ratio (1, 2, 4, 8, 16, and so on), while the food supply cannot possibly be made to increase at more than an arithmetic ratio (1, 2, 3, 4, and so on); and (2), as a result, population tends always to press upon the underlying means of subsistence.

Malthus saw two kinds of checks to the tendency of population to outrun its food supply—(1) positive: war, pestilence, and starvation; and (2) negative: postponement of marriage to a later age and what he described as "moral restraint." Malthus sincerely believed that a considerable part of the population in the England of his day could hardly escape a life of poverty and misery. He feared that, for the immediate future at least, any increase in the means of subsistence would tend to encourage a more than corresponding increase in the population.

Malthus issued later and more complete editions of his famous work on population. Though he did not alter his basic ideas, as contained in the original edition of his book, later versions did modify certain important details. In the later and more complete statements of his doctrines, Malthus tended to lay less stress upon the alleged precise ratio between the increase of human numbers and the means of subsistence. He was more inclined to emphasize the general tendencies implied in these ratios. He also was willing to admit that many factors, in addition to the pressure of population on the means of subsistence, help to determine the growth of numbers in any given population. Finally, he became rather more optimistic, in that he believed that his proposed negative or preventive checks on population growth were actually beginning to work and were rendering unnecessary the more harsh and drastic conditions involved in the positive checks.

Malthus has been vigorously defended and bitterly criticized in the years which have elapsed since his "law" of population was enunciated. Both his defenders and his critics have usually lacked historical perspective. For conditions as they existed in 1798, Malthus was reasonably sound in his doctrines; but scientific and technological changes in the interval since his day have made Malthusian principles, in large part, an intellectual curiosity in our era.

The two or three "industrial revolutions" have completely altered the situation relating to the food supply. The first industrial revolution gave us the reaper, binder, thresher, and other mechanical methods of carrying on agriculture, the elements of scientific fertilization, and the beginnings of efficient methods of storing and preserving foods. The second industrial revolution carried the process further by providing the tractor, gang-plow, reaping and threshing combine, ultra-scientific soil-testing and fertilization, scientific canning and refrigeration to aid in food preservation, and other comparable advances. So important are these results that Professor O. W. Willcox estimates that we could produce all the food needed in the United States by the scientific cultivation of one-fifth of the land now under cultivation and with the use of only one-fifth of the farm labor now employed. Even more dramatic and portentous for the future is the onset of the third industrial revolution, which offers the prospect of synthetic chemical production of foods in laboratories and factories remote from the farms and with no discernible limit to food production. There are social considerations justifying population limitation, but we can now produce food enough today to support any reasonable or probable population under normal conditions.

Malthus' *Essay* stimulated further interest in population problems. In his *Dissertations on Man* (1806), Dr. Thomas Jarrold denied that economic factors, such as the pressure of population on the means of subsistence, bring about a decline in the birth rate. Like Gini, in our day, he attributed any decline in the birth rate to some occult physiological influence which reduces both fecundity and fertility. In his book on *Current Evils in Ireland* (1828), Michael T. Sadler tried to combine the physiological and economic explanations of birth-rate trends. He held that human hardship and privation tend to increase fecundity, while a state of plenty leads to a decrease. The greater the density of population, all other things being equal, the greater the prosperity and the lower the fecundity. Hence, whenever population becomes dense, the birth rate automatically drops and the population is reduced.

In the eighteenth century there were a number of psychological interpretations of social processes and institutions which were far more realistic and valuable than the dubious hypothesis of a social contract. We shall now present some of the outstanding contributions to this field of social theory.

The work of the brilliant Irish prelate, George Berkeley (1684–1753), was as important for sociology as for philosophy.[31] In his *Sermon on Passive Obedience,* which was largely devoted to a criticism of Locke's theory of revolution, he did not commit himself to the belief in a social contract but held that if such a process be assumed, then its terms must be binding in perpetuity. He assumed the natural sociability of man and the necessity of government to regulate society; from these premises he concluded that obedience to established authority must be regarded as a law of nature.

More important than this bit of reactionary political theory is his generally neglected essay on *The Principles of Moral Attraction,* which is one of the most suggestive essays in the whole history of social philosophy. This was probably the first attempt to interpret social processes in terms of the Newtonian laws of mechanics. Assuming that the social instinct is analogous to the principle of gravitation in the physical world, Berkeley worked out in an ingenious manner the ways in which this socializing force operates to create the various social processes and institutions.

As masses attract each other more strongly when they are closer together in space, so the attraction of different individuals in society for each other increases in proportion to the degree of resemblance which they bear to each other. Again, as the tendency toward sociability and co-operation is the centripetal force in society, so human selfishness and individualistic traits are the centrifugal force, and a stable society can exist only when the former is in excess of the latter. The similarity between these conceptions and certain vital portions of the sociological systems of Herbert Spencer and Professor Giddings is readily apparent.

However, suggestive as Berkeley may have been, there can be little doubt that the contributions of David Hume (1711–76) to social philosophy are the most important that any Englishman advanced before the time of Ferguson and Adam Smith. As Montesquieu had been the herald of descriptive sociology, so Hume came nearer to modern psychological sociology than any other man of this age.[32]

In the first place, he totally destroyed both the historical and the philosophical foundations of the doctrine of a social contract. That Rousseau and others later dared to advance this theory is either a serious reflection upon their intelligence or an indication of their ignorance of Hume's destructive criticism.

Society, according to Hume, has its origin in instinct and not in intelligent self-interest. Man is by nature a social being; the state of nature is only a creation of the imagination in a priori philosophy; and the social-contract theory assumes the impossible condition of knowledge prior to experience—knowledge of the benefits of society before society had ever existed.

As a substitute for this rejected contract doctrine, Hume offered a psychological interpretation of society of the utmost importance. Society originates in the sex instinct, which is the ultimate social fact. This gives rise to the family, which is held together by that sympathy which always springs up among those who are alike and dwell in contiguity. Spontaneous sympathetic bonds are soon supported by custom and habit, which gradually make the group conscious of the advantages of association. This genetic family and community group expands and is at first held together by the influence of sympathy and mutual aid. But human selfishness renders this sympathetic basis of association inadequate, and efficient social control can then be found only in the institution of government. Government originates in force and then develops authority and stability from a growing sense of common interests on the part of the group. The social process thus starts in instinct, develops through feeling and emotion, and, finally, comes under the control of the intellect.

Especially important in Hume's psychological interpretation of society was his emphasis upon sympathy as the chief factor in social assimilation and upon imitation as the basis of "type-conforming" groups. His analysis of imitation as the force which reduces social groups to cultural homogeneity was an attack upon the environmental theories of Montesquieu and was a direct anticipation of Bagehot and Tarde. In addition, Hume was probably the first writer to develop a truly psychological interpretation of religion, which he treated simply as a form of human behavior. Finally, his emphasis upon utility as the criterion by which to estimate the desirability of any institution was the starting-point for the social philosophy and ethics of the English Utilitarians.

A more thorough treatment than Hume's of the social significance of sympathy was contained in Adam Smith's *Theory of Moral Sentiments* (1759).[33] Smith held that no man can be so selfish that he is not interested in the welfare of others. That one weeps over the grief of others is a fact too obvious to take the trouble of proving. Yet, since one cannot experience the feelings of others, this sense of mutual sorrow must arise from one's imagining one's self in the place of the suffering person and as being subject to the same emotions. This changing places with the sufferer, then, Smith asserted to be the only source of fellow-feeling for the sorrow of others.

Not only is this a general reaction; it extends to particular parts of the individual organism. If one is about to be injured or has been injured in a certain part of his body, the observers are immediately afflicted with a sense of shuddering or of pain in a similar part of their own anatomy. Not only pain and sorrow but also pleasurable emotions produce a similar feeling in the mind of the spectator, who puts himself, through the power of imagination, in the place of the person observed. Although "pity" is the term generally used to describe fellow-feeling for a person afflicted with sorrow or pain, Smith consistently employed the term "sympathy," since it may be applied to fellow-feeling for both pleasant and unpleasant emotions. Sight or knowledge of affliction will stir up this fellow-feeling, and in many cases simply the expression of the face which conveys the impression of a certain emotion may set up a comparable one in the spectator.

The social-contract theory represented a form of rationalism in social thought. Rationalism was carried along further in the eighteenth century in the eulogy of pure reason as a dominant social force. The two outstanding exponents of this rationalistic social psychology were the Abbé Sieyès and William Godwin.

An enthusiastic manifesto of rationalistic social theory appeared in the works of Count Joseph Emanuel Sieyès (1748–1836), usually known as the Abbé Sieyès, a French writer of the Revolutionary period and author of *What Is the Third Estate?* When one has worked out in his mind the type of government and society that is desirable, it is possible to set up such a system if adequate popular support can be enlisted for it. In short, institutions do not have to be allowed to change slowly, while old abuses persist. They can be altered to suit the needs of the time and made to produce speedily the results desired by wise men. Such a view justified revolution, if desirable reforms could not be obtained in any other way. This doctrine was a threat to vested monarchical and aristocratic interests, which rested chiefly on tradition, inertia, and the superstition that what is must continue to be.

William Godwin's *Enquiry concerning Political Justice* created considerable excitement when it appeared in 1793. Godwin believed that all human misery is the direct result of the restraining and warping influences of coercive human institutions and that government, at its best, is an evil. He advised the abolition of government, of strict marriage regulations, and of all social groups larger than the parish and declared for the equal distribution of property. Godwin was, on the other hand, emphatic in his praise of the noncoercive and spontaneous forms of society and of co-operative activity. He held that the growing influence of pure reason would be the means by which the ultimate perfection of the human race could be attained. His rosy hopes for the future of mankind were only exceeded by those expressed by Condorcet.

The transition from rationalism to utilitarianism was brought about in the writings of Jeremy Bentham (1748–1842), who first attained prominence through his *Fragment on Government,* published in 1776. This was a relentless attack upon Blackstone's complacent social and political philosophy. While it was in part the rending-asunder of a straw man that Bentham had erected, this work is important in social philosophy for its acute differentiation between natural and political society, its detailed criticism and rejection of the theory of a social contract and natural rights, and its justification of any form of government by the test of its utility. As his slogan for utilitarian ethics and practical reform Bentham adopted the phrase, earlier used by Hutcheson, Beccaria, and Priestley, "the greatest happiness of the greater number"; and his psychology was the simple hedonism or "felicific calculus" which assumes that man is motivated and controlled by the desire to secure pleasurable, and to avoid painful, experiences.[34]

This intellectualistic social psychology of Bentham had an enormous influence on social thought. It was the basis of the so-called "psychological economics," from Stanley Jevons to John Bates Clark, which was not overthrown until the days of Veblen, Wesley Mitchell, and Max Weber. It furnished the foundations of political psychology from Bentham to Bryce, finally punctured by Graham Wallas' *Human Nature in Politics* and Walter Lippmann's *A Preface to Politics*. It deeply influenced the thinking of early sociologists like Spencer and Ward but was ultimately upset by Sumner's *Folkways,* which stressed the importance of custom, habit, and other irrational factors in social behavior.

Bentham produced epoch-making contributions to criminal-law reform, prison reform, the reconstruction of the system of poor relief, the establishment of a public health system, the encouragement of public education, the recommendation of general thrift and savings banks, the reform of local government, colonial self-government, and the like. He is said to have carried in his pockets model constitutions for the leading countries of his time. Constructive legislation in England in the nineteenth century owed far more to Bentham than to any other person.

D. THE HISTORICAL APPROACH TO THE STUDY OF SOCIETY

During this period there were many very interesting advances in the interpretation of social evolution beyond the crudities of the social-contract theory.[35] Some of these have been casually mentioned in connection with the rise of the theory of progress. Perhaps the first of the important historical treatments of human society after the treatise of Bodin was the work of the Italian historian, jurist, and philosopher, Giovanni Battista Vico. His stimulating book, *La Scienza nuova,* is frequently regarded as the starting-point of historical philology, ethnology, and the modern idea of historical progress and is often, but erroneously, described as the first treatise on sociology.

Vico rejected the notion of a social contract and expressed his belief in the natural sociability of man and the necessity of social relationships to produce the well-rounded human personality. He regarded religion as the most vital cohesive principle of society and thus foreshadowed the doctrines of Hegel and Kidd. By making highly original studies in the mental life of primitive man he opened the way for the modern schools of comparative philology, mythology, and religion. He offered a theory of progress which stated that development does not take place in a straight line or through identical recurring cycles but, rather, in a sort of spiral movement, in which every turn is a degree higher and more mature than its predecessor. By discussing the relativity of the excellence of social institutions, as adapted to different external conditions, he led up to Montesquieu's elaborate discussion of this subject.

According to Vico, the essence of historical development consists of the creations and alterations in the collective mind—changes in the character of the "human spirit"—from age to age. Like so many later philosophers of history, he also postulated three major stages of historical development—the divine, the heroic, and the human. The divine period was characterized by the dominion of the feelings and raw emotions in the world of the spirit and by theocracy in the realm of politics. The heroic period displayed the powers of poetic imagination in the collective mentality and gave rise to aristocracy in politics. The third period manifested positive knowledge in the collective mentality and produced political freedom, embodied in constitutional monarchies and republics. As we made plain above, Vico believed that these triadic cycles repeat themselves, but never on the same level. There is a gradual spiral advance in the culture of mankind. Vico's ideas were in harmony with romanticism in many ways, especially his notion of changes in the character of the collective spirit of mankind and his idea of the potency of God in history.

Montesquieu was not only an important contributor to early anthropogeographical ideas but also stimulated the historical study of human society. He emphasized the great variety of forces which promote social evolution, especially geographical and commercial factors. He and his disciples best reflected the reaction of the commercial revolution upon the history of human society. Montesquieu's ideas relative to the social background of history were contained in his *Spirit of Laws,* but his specific contribution to history was his *Causes of the Greatness and Decadence of the Romans* (1734). This proved the profundity of his approach to history, for here he set forth a comprehensive synthesis of the causes of the rise and decline of Roman civilization which anticipated most of the conclusions of historians since his day. He foreshadowed recent specialists in holding that the main reason for the collapse of the Roman Empire was that it grew too large and unwieldy for its rudimentary economy to support.

Montesquieu inspired a number of distinguished historians and historical sociologists. Among the more notable were Arnold Heeren, the able historian of the institutions and commerce of antiquity, and Adam Ferguson, the first real historical sociologist.

Johann Gottfried Herder (1744–1803) is important chiefly as one of the founders of the philosophy of history. His most notable work, *Ideas for the Philosophy of the History of Humanity,* was a composite of many current doctrines. It combined Rousseau's exaggerated enthusiasm for the state of nature and freedom from authority, Voltaire's conception of the reality and permanence of national character, Montesquieu's doctrine of the relation between national character and the physical environment, and the mystical conception, later elaborated by Hegel, of the gradual development of humanity toward a state of freedom. Herder had an evolutionary outlook, and he is credited with being the "father of the historical sense" in Germany: "Every civilization buds, flowers and fades according to natural laws of growth." His special emphasis upon the uniqueness of national character and the organic unity of cultural evolution put him in direct line with the Romanticists and stimulated the trend toward nationalistic sentiment in historical writing.

Immanuel Kant (1724–1804) conceived of history as the record of the unfolding of the plan of nature. This plan is the perfect development of all the latent capacities of man. Kant claimed that the motive power in this process of development is the struggle within the individual and society between the forces of communism and competition. Consequently, this process will move ahead most rapidly in that country which allows the greatest freedom and scope for this struggle and yet provides for individual liberty, protection, and the equitable administration of law.

Such a condition, Kant asserted, cannot be attained until the external relations between societies have been put on a firm, stable, and peaceful basis and the resources of the nations have been set free from war to undertake the great program of progress and enlightenment. The only way to arrive at such a condition of international peace is to establish a universal federation of nations. Looking back over history, Kant thought that he could see in its events evidence of the gradual working-out of this very plan of federation and peace. Kant was an optimist and believed that progress is constantly going on, and he explained the sharp criticisms of conditions in his day as simply manifestations of a more refined moral conscience.

An extremely abstract conception of the philosophy of history appeared in the *Characteristics of the Present Age* by another German philosopher, Johann Gottlieb Fichte (1762–1814). For Fichte, the motive of progress is the quest for human perfection. When there is nothing else left to strive for, we can still strive to create God, a task which we need never fear we shall finish.

Fichte believed that the historical scheme of things, as designed by God, embraces five epochs: (1) the age of innocence, in which reason manifested itself only crudely in the form of blind instinct; (2) the age of authority, demanding the subordination of reason to passive obedience; (3) the age of indifference to truth, thus involving the complete rejection of reason; (4) the age of science, in which truth is revered above all other things and we become conscious of reason; and (5) the age of art, when humanity becomes free and beautifies itself as befitting the image of Absolute Reason.

In his *Addresses to the German Nation* (1807), Fichte held that the hope of the future lay with the German peoples. They are, said Fichte, an *Urfolk,* or unmixed race, possessing "hidden and inexhaustible springs of spiritual life and power." The Romance peoples are a *Mischvolk,* or a product of race mixture. Consequently, they bloomed prematurely in civilization and even in Fichte's day were, so he thought, on the high road to decadence. It is no wonder that Fichte's doctrine was a strong stimulant to the growth of nationalism in Germany.

Most famous of all the Germanic philosophies of history in this period was that of the pontifical dialectician, Georg Wilhelm Friedrich Hegel (1770–1831). Hegel's *Philosophy of History* was a highly subjective work—a record of the unfolding of the self-consciousness of freedom in the human spirit. Like that of Fichte, Hegel's philosophy had a strong nationalistic impulse. It implied that the Germans of the post-Reformation period were invested by God with the mission of bringing the blessings of freedom to mankind.

Though the analysis just given reveals the general pattern of Hegel's theory of history, progress itself comes as the result of conflict and synthesis. A movement or idea—thesis—gets under way. Then its opposite—antithesis—makes it appearance. Out of the clash between the two, there comes an ultimate synthesis, which marks a further step toward truth. The synthesis then becomes another thesis, and the process goes on.

This Hegelian dialectic of progress had much influence on later historical thought, particularly through its partial adoption by Karl Marx and its exploitation by Marx in the service of a materialistic philosophy of history. Hegel stimulated other important work in historical research, especially the magisterial studies of Greek philosophy by Eduard Zeller and the investigation of Christian origins by Ferdinand Christian Baur. While Hegel's historical influence was felt in a double direction— Marxism and nationalism—it is the latter influence which is more prominent today. The celebration in 1931 of the centenary of his death was almost wholly nationalist.

Hegel also revolutionized the development of social thought by repudiating the artificial and intellectualistic notions of the philosophers of the Enlightenment and insisting that social institutions, government, religion, and the like are the natural products of an evolutionary development. The followers of Hegel founded the social sciences and launched the critical study of legal and religious origins.

The contributions of the Scotch philosopher, Adam Ferguson (1723–1816), to the development of historical sociology have not been sufficiently acknowledged.[36] French and German writers, like Comte, Gumplowicz, and Ludwig Stein, have recognized his importance in this field, but English and American students of the subject have until recently minimized or entirely overlooked the genuine worth of his work.

That Ferguson was moving in the right direction may be seen in the fact that he combined the descriptive and historical method of Montesquieu with the psychological and critical procedure of Hume. His treatment was thus both descriptive and analytical. He rejected all a priori methods, as well as the ideas of a state of nature and a social contract. He insisted on studying society as it is, and from such study he found that the primary social fact is the inherent sociability of the human species, arising from instinct and supported by utility.

The dynamic element was emphasized in the work of Ferguson, who ridiculed the ideas of Aristotle and Hobbes that social stability and peace are the chief goal of society. He laid so much stress upon the value of competition and conflict in social development that Ludwig Gumplowicz has claimed him as the first great apostle of the "group-struggle" theory of social development. His *History of Civil Society* was the most valuable and complete study of political and social origins prior to the writings of Auguste Comte and Gumplowicz.

Important contributions to social thinking came from several different groups of students of the economic factors and processes in social life. The chief trend in German and Austrian economic thought in the middle of the eighteenth century, in so far as it was related to the development of sociological thinking, is to be found in the writings of the Cameralists, of whom Johann Heinrich von Justi (1717–68) and Joseph von Sonnenfels (1733–1817) were the most important.

The Cameralists were a group of technological writers rather than social philosophers. Like the English Mercantilists, they were mainly concerned with providing the national treasury with ample means to maintain its domestic policy and to defend itself against enemies from without. Their chief significance in the development of sociological thought lies in the fact that they furnish an excellent example of a group whose writings were sharply oriented and co-ordinated by the specific purpose which they had in mind. Since the problem of foreign trade in Germanic states was far less important than in England at that date, the German philosophy of extensive state intervention naturally turned toward domestic economic and political problems. This brought up the question of the technique of social improvement by means of public planning, which gave a sociological cast to the whole movement.

An American sociologist, Professor Albion W. Small, has well summarized the sociological significance of the Cameralists.[37] As he points out, cameralism frankly subordinated everything else to control by the state for the purpose of improving national existence. It was an attempt to select and adopt those policies and practices which would help most directly to make the ruler and his people secure at home and to strengthen them against other rulers abroad. It was soon perceived that this program was not merely a matter of material factors but also involved the systematic training and education of the people.

The founders of economic liberalism—the revolt against mercantilism —were the group of French writers in the middle of the eighteenth century known as the "Physiocrats," so named from the work of one of their adherents, Du Pont de Nemours, entitled *Physiocracy, or the Natural Constitution of That Form of Government Most Advantageous to the Human Race* (1767).[38] They derived their basic doctrine from the English Deists and the French *philosophes,* to the effect that social, political, and economic phenomena are governed by the same natural laws that Newton and his associates believed they had proved to rule the physical universe.

The Physiocrats were convinced that the improvement of all human institutions could best be realized by letting them freely adjust themselves to this natural order, a situation which they believed would most certainly be brought about by a regime of unlimited competition. If man refrained from legislation and from any attempt to control economic processes by artificial means, then God and his natural order would have full sway. One reason for human unhappiness and misery, so they said, was the existence of a large number of archaic and restrictive laws which, being statutory and unnatural, were holding back the free dominion of natural law over the affairs of men.

Accordingly, the Physiocrats vigorously advocated the immediate and total abolition of all restrictive legislation and the introduction of an era of laissez faire individualism. They contended that the only desirable functions of the state are the protection of life and property, the enforcement of contracts, the erection of public buildings and other public works, and the promotion of education, so that man might grasp more completely the principles of natural law. Extensive social legislation was regarded as dangerous, since it would surely impede the operation of those beneficent natural principles upon which these advocates placed their chief reliance. The Physiocrats contributed doctrines of less significance in their interpretation of social progress in terms of increasing the net product of agriculture and their scheme of reform in public finance, which centered about the notion of a single tax on land.

The general notions of the Physiocrats concerning individualism and the inactivity of the state received the support of the distinguished French economist and statesman, Turgot, and intrigued the first great systematic writer on political economy, the Scotch philosopher, Adam Smith (1723–90). The chief significance of Adam Smith for the history of economic thought is that he embodied the laissez faire thesis in a notable work, *An Inquiry into the Nature and Causes of the Wealth of Nations* (1776).[39] This received so wide a circulation and attracted so extensive a following for Smith's doctrines that the eminent historian, H. T. Buckle, nearly a century later, regarded this book as the most influential and beneficial one ever written.

Despite his general acceptance of the Physiocratic position as to the proper functions of the state, Smith abandoned to a considerable degree their excessive laudation of agriculture and emphasized the prime value, to a state, of commerce and manufacturing. Especially did he revive the Platonic doctrine of the importance of the division of labor and expert specialization in increasing productivity. His emphasis upon the part played by labor in production paved the way for the later views of Ricardo and the Socialists with respect to the "labor theory of value." His advocacy of free trade, on the ground of the advantages of an international division of labor, was one of the most forceful arguments ever advanced for commercial freedom.

Smith died before the industrial revolution had fully developed even in England, and there is good evidence for believing that he did not even foresee the complete course of this transformation, much less stand out as a conscious apologist of the new capitalist class. But his doctrines were of a sort that fitted in admirably with the popular policy of noninterference with business. The capitalist manufacturers favored this policy, in order that they, if not their employees, might enjoy the alleged "blessings of the perfect freedom of contract." Smith's notions were, therefore, expanded and exploited by the middle class and by sympathetic economists like James Mill, to provide authoritative theoretical foundations for opposition to all social legislation designed to advance the interests of the industrial proletariat.

The most extensive development of the concepts of Adam Smith naturally took place in England, where he had written and where that commercialism which was most congenial to his views was the furthest advanced, but he was honored by reverent disciples in every important European country and in the United States. His most distinguished English disciples, the so-called "Classical Economists," were Thomas Robert Malthus (1766–1834), David Ricardo (1772–1823), James Mill (1733–1836), John Ramsay McCulloch (1789–1864), and Nassau William Senior (1790–1864). The Classical Economists gave systematic expression to the laissez faire dogmas and assumed to found them on "iron laws" of economics. They thus implied that social and economic reforms usually violate both natural laws and economic logic.[40]

F. SOCIOLOGICAL ELEMENTS IN POLITICAL THOUGHT

Of all the writers in the field of political theory in the eighteenth century, one of the most impressive to present-day readers is Montesquieu. He was one of the founders of "rational politics." A member of the French nobility, he was educated for the magistracy, in which he served for many years. Early attracted to the comparative study of human institutions, his first publication was a series of satirical compositions known as *The Persian Letters* (1721).[41] In these he ironically criticized contemporary European society from the standpoint of imaginary travelers. Through the fiction of two Persians traveling in Europe and writing of French society to their friends and relatives back home, he was able to make a witty and spicy attack upon the whole French social system. This clever satire was widely read even in the court circles.

Like Montaigne, to whom we may reasonably compare him in spirit, Montesquieu was fascinated by Plutarch and by the Romans generally. He thought that their history offered a complete historical laboratory for the study of human institutions. In 1734 he published the results of his years of reflection on Roman life under the title *The Greatness and Decadence of the Romans*. Fourteen years later there appeared what is incomparably his greatest work, *The Spirit of Laws*.

Montesquieu differed from most of his contemporary social thinkers in that he did not produce a mechanical solution for social difficulties, nor did he usually bring his findings to the support of any social reform. He developed the "comparative" study of institutions to a very high point. Instead of applying himself to a particular situation, he ranged up and down the known fields of information about social groups, customs, and laws, seeking out the underlying spirit. In addition to feeding his interest through books, he traveled extensively, visiting nearly every country in Europe. Montesquieu distilled his carefully accumulated facts into *The Spirit of Laws*. Very few dogmatic generalizations found their way into this work. Perhaps the distinguishing feature of the book is the number of practical suggestions offered to lawmakers. On the other hand, he made no proposal of drastic reform, and even his admiration for the British constitution, which he misunderstood, did not lead him to advocate its adoption in France.

It was his underlying idea, as we have noted, that laws, customs, and institutions are the product of geographical factors, particularly climatic conditions, and that what might admirably serve one people would be quite unsuitable for another. On this ground he rejected the British system for France, arguing that his country was better served by a more "Gothic" form of government. Yet, despite his own distrust of formulas, his belief that the British government was designedly divided into three departments—the executive, the legislative, and the judicial, operating under a system of checks and balances—had a momentous influence on the makers of the American Constitution.

The fundamental contribution of the political philosopher and orator, Edmund Burke (1729–97), was his eloquent and commanding statement of the corporate unity of society.[42] He ruthlessly criticized the a priori and rationalistic political philosophy of his time and declared that the creation of governments is not a matter of pure reason but of historic growth and long political experience. Burke's view of history, however, was not dynamic; history to him was chiefly an instrument for defending existing institutions and combating social change. While accepting a modified version of the contractual basis of society, he maintained that this contract was universal in scope and binding in perpetuity, and he bitterly assailed the interpretation which justified revolution and led to the French Revolution.

Burke's heated criticism of the French Revolution was effectively answered by Tom Paine (1737–1809) in his *Rights of Man* and his *Dissertation on the First Principles of Government*. According to Paine, man is by nature social, owing to his social instinct and the necessity of co-operative activities. The state of nature was not presocial, but one in which men possessed the natural rights of liberty and equality. This condition had to be abandoned and governmental authority established because of human weaknesses, which made unregulated existence intolerable. Government was created by a contract between the members of society and not between the governed and the governors. Man did not give up his natural rights when government was established but merely added civil rights to them. Paine recognized that social relations, institutions, customs, co-operation, and the like are more important to the individual than government, and he regarded the latter as, at best, artificial and a necessary evil. His criticism of monarchy was an admirable antidote to the doctrines of Bossuet, and he was one of the most ardent advocates of democracy and popular sovereignty in the late eighteenth century. Especially important was his doctrine that the minority must be protected by constitutional checks on absolute majority rule.

The generally reactionary character of the political philosophy of the Romanticist writers on politics and law, such as Burke, Louis de Bonald, Joseph de Maistre, Ludwig von Haller, Herder, Fichte, Friedrich von Schelling, Hegel, and Friedrich Karl von Savigny, has led many to overlook the vital sociological note in these writings. They rejected the ideas of the rationalistic writers of the Enlightenment, who had expounded intellectualistic interpretations of the origin of society and the state as artificial products of conscious choice and deliberation. The Romanticists insisted that social institutions, government, religion, and the like are the natural outgrowth of an organic evolutionary development. This encouraged giving more attention to the social and cultural foundations of all human institutions—a trend of a distinctly sociological nature.

G. NEW CONTRIBUTIONS TO LEGAL THEORY

Much more accurate and illuminating than the application of natural law, with which we are familiar, but of much less practical import for applied jurisprudence and legal processes at the time, was the rise of comparative jurisprudence in the work of Montesquieu and others.[43] It represented, in a rough way, the extension of the conception of the common law to the race as a whole. Just as the common law represented a pooling of the experiences of the various communities in a nation, so law as a whole was a product of the experiences of the many races and nations on the planet. Great interest was taken in comparing the legal codes of diverse peoples, in pointing out their differences and similarities, and in trying to deduce legal principles of broad general application. No other school of law at the time was so civilizing. No man who thoroughly appreciated the great variety of legal concepts and practices among the peoples of the world could well be arrogant concerning the laws of his particular country.

A somewhat more precise application of this approach to law led to the origins of the historical school of jurisprudence. Montesquieu had been concerned with the laws of all peoples. The historical jurists were mainly interested in the evolution of the law within the boundaries of their particular state. Most of them regarded law as an organic outgrowth of the culture of the nation. Of these early historical jurists, perhaps the best known was Burke. Adam Ferguson combined the historical and comparative approaches to law, a procedure that has become increasingly popular from his day to our own. It has served to lessen provincialism and patriotic conceit in jurisprudence.

Rationalism had a decisive but by no means uniform influence upon legal evolution. John Locke tended toward rationalism in philosophy, but he laid special stress upon the law of nature. Many later rationalists departed widely from this precedent. They were prone to stress the deliberate character of sound law and to regard it as the dictates of reason applied to specific social problems. In the opinion of this school, public legislation is the only valid type of law. There was also a tendency to lay stress upon the responsibility of law to insure to every man a right to enjoy life, liberty, and property. It was natural that this group should be in favor of the codification of law, while the historical school was opposed to such a notion. The latter held that an artificial product of reason might be codified but that a living, growing achievement, such as a historical system of law, could not be.

The famous English jurist, William Blackstone (1723–80), ably unified many legal tendencies in his *Commentaries on the Laws of England* (1765–69). He combined Locke's rationalism and Montesquieu's comparative point of view. By giving due attention to both common-law principles and legal evolution, he brought together common-law jurisprudence and the historical approach. In laying stress on the supremacy of parliamentary statutes, he laid the basis for the later analytical jurisprudence of Austin and his successors. His *Commentaries* —the first complete summation and survey of English jurisprudence and legal principles—are notable for their notion that the history of law is a phase of the history of ideas, for their admirable literary quality, and for their comprehensiveness. They had vast influence upon legal thinking in England and America.

In the course of his legal writing, Blackstone made important observations on social and political theory. In discussing the origin of society and government, he refused to accept the doctrine of a state of nature and a subsequent social contract as historic facts. Nevertheless, he claimed that it was man's weakness in isolation that was the primary motive for association and that contractual relations must be implied as the philosophic foundations of society and government. Like Sir Henry Maine, he considered that the original social group was the patriarchal family, and he held that larger societies are but reunited offshoots of the original family that had once dispersed because it had become too large for a single habitation. Blackstone's view of the attributes of sovereignty as supreme, irresistible, absolute, and uncontrolled power in the state greatly resembles the definition of Professor John William Burgess, and it is generally agreed that Burgess' theory stands in a direct line of descent from Blackstone.

It was but a short step from the rationalistic school of law to the Utilitarian—both relied primarily upon human reason; both were interested in reform. Utilitarian jurisprudence was merely a further development and refinement of the rationalistic doctrine. What its chief exponent, Jeremy Bentham, did was to hold that rational jurisprudence must also be a science of social reform, designed in every part to increase the happiness of the largest possible number of men. There was still in it, however, a strong strain of individualism. Bentham believed that every man is the best judge of his own happiness. Hence there should be no restrictions on the acts of anyone except those necessary to secure equal freedom for others. Bentham especially eulogized the importance of freedom of contract. He came closer than others of his day, however, to the notion of law as an adjunct to, or even an instrument of, social engineering.

Friedrich Karl von Savigny (1779–1861) was the true founder of historical jurisprudence. He emphasized the necessity of observing the principle of historical development in the formation of law, maintaining that it evolves unconsciously out of the genius of a people. As a living organic thing, it cannot be codified. In his memorable controversy with Thibaut in 1814, Savigny vigorously opposed the proposal to prepare a code of law for Germany. Like Burke, then, his grasp of history was more apparent than real, and both were equally blind to the practical value of new legislation and a systematic legal code. That a later generation has upheld the judgment of Thibaut is proved by the production of the magnificent German Imperial Code, which was framed between 1874 and 1900.

The most important practical product of legal cogitation during this era was the codification of French law that began in 1793, as a result of revolutionary enthusiasm, and ended in the magnificent *Code Napoléon*. Legal codifications in other European countries followed in the nineteenth century.

One of the worst survivals of barbarism in Europe in the eighteenth century lay in criminal law. Men were still subjected to torture during the process of trial in many countries. Sentences were severe and punishments extremely brutal. The death sentence was often imposed for such a trivial offense as petty theft. Corporal punishment, including branding and mutilation, was still usual. Debtors were commonly imprisoned. Prisons were reserved chiefly for debtors and those accused of crime prior to trial. These prisons were mostly filthy, uncomfortable, and brutally administered.

The barbarous criminal law was attacked by Voltaire and Montesquieu in the middle of the eighteenth century. The latter's *Persian Letters,* especially, satirized the European criminal law of this period. But the most influential reformer in the field of criminal law was the Italian nobleman, Cesare di Beccaria (1738–94). His *Essay on Crimes and Punishments* (1764) was probably the most effective book ever written in the whole history of criminal-law reform. He argued that the prevention of crime is more important than punishment and that capital punishment should be abandoned. Indeed, with the exception of the recent application of psychology and psychiatry to crime, Beccaria suggested most of the essentials of criminological progress that have been achieved in the nearly two centuries since his work was published.

Beccaria's ideas deeply influenced the reform of the criminal codes of the American states after 1776, the new criminal code of Revolutionary France, and the reform of the British criminal code by Bentham, Romilly, Buxton, Mackintosh, and Peel in the first half of the nineteenth century. In 1800 there were about two hundred capital offenses in the British criminal code. By 1861 they had been reduced to three: treason, murder, and piracy. Torture was gradually abolished in European criminal procedure, and fair trials were provided for accused persons. Imprisonment for debt was slowly outlawed. It did not disappear even in the United States, however, until the Jacksonian period, when it was wiped out by the rising tide of democratic enthusiasm.

H. THE RISE OF ANTHROPOLOGY AND ETHNOLOGY

Anthropology, which studies man's physical nature and cultural achievements, came into being during this period.[44] The investigation of man's physical characteristics was forwarded by the anatomical studies of Andreas Vesalius (1514–64) and his successors. Carolus Linnaeus (1707–78), while he still held to the uniqueness of man in possessing a soul, linked mankind to the rest of the animal world in his system of classification, listing man as *Homo sapiens Linnaeus,* of the order of primates, and divided into four species, white, yellow, red, and black.

Johann Friedrich Blumenbach (1752–1840), of Göttingen, founded physical anthropology. He combed the museums for skulls and other physical remains of man and approached physical anthropology and anatomy from the comparative point of view. He amplified and rendered more precise the classification of the human races suggested by Linnaeus. He founded scientific craniology by his concept of the *norma verticalis,* or the shape of the skull as seen from above. Peter Camper (1722–89), a Dutch anatomist and naturalist, advanced the study of craniology by his description of the facial angle and jaw projection.

Even more important was the work of Anders Retzius (1769–1860), of Stockholm, who rendered more scientific Blumenbach's concept of the *norma verticalis.* Retzius devised what is known as the "cephalic index," namely, the ratio of the breadth of the skull to its length as expressed in a percentage. The narrow-skulled type he called "dolichocephalic," and the broad-skulled, "brachycephalic." He adopted from Camper the idea of the facial angle and took over from Friedrich Tiedemann (1781–1861) methods of determining comparative skull capacity. He thus systematized physical anthropology in its earlier stages of development, from which it was carried further by Quatrefages, Broca, Topinard, Virchow, and their successors. A dynamic orientation was given to physical anthropology by the evolutionary biology of Jean Lamarck (1744–1829). From that time onward, anthropology could begin to measure up to the definition of Robert Ranulf Marett as "the whole history of man as fired and pervaded by the idea of evolution."

The expansion of Europe, explorations, and colonization brought Europeans into contact with the most diverse cultures, from the more advanced peoples of the Moslem Near East, India, and China to the most primitive of native peoples. This led to the cultivation of comparative ethnology, religion, and ethics. The prevailing notions of primitive culture were rescued from the mysticism of the "state-of-nature" philosophy and placed upon the substantial basis of concrete descriptions of actual primitive life. To some writers, such as Adam Ferguson, this suggested the idea of the evolution of culture and institutions, though little progress was made here until the days of Sir John Lubbock, Herbert Spencer, and Lewis Henry Morgan.

An extensive literature reflected this growing knowledge of, and interest in, comparative ethnology. We can mention only a few representative examples. The travel literature was well represented by the *Travels into Persia and the East Indies* of Jean Chardin (1643–1715), from which Montesquieu derived most of his ideas of oriental life and customs, polygyny, and despotic forms of governments. Books written

by historians of the discoveries and colonization added much to knowledge in comparative ethnology. Such were Oviedo y Valdés' (1478–1557)
Natural History of the Indies; the *Da Asia* of Joao de Barros (1496–
1570), which dealt with Portuguese conquests in Brazil and the East
Indies; the works of Bartolomé de Las Casas (1474–1566) on the Indians
of the New World; Bernal Díaz del Castillo's (1492–1581) *True History
of the Conquest of New Spain;* the *General History of Explorations* by
Antoine Prévost d'Exiles (1697–1763); the *General History and Description of New France* by François Xavier de Charlevoix (1682–1761);
Richard Hakluyt's *The Principal Navigations, Voyages, and Discoveries
of the English Nation* (1588); and William Robertson's *History of
America.*

The nearest approach to real comparative ethnology in such writings
was embodied in the *Customs of the American Savages Compared with
the Customs of Early Times* by Joseph François Lafitau (1681–1746).
The general cultural and philosophical impact of overseas contacts on
European thought was best expressed in *The Philosophical and Political
History of the Settlements and Trade of Europeans in the East and
West Indies* by Guillaume Thomas Raynal (1713–96).

When the doctrine of evolution was enunciated in the nineteenth
century, the interest in comparative ethnology was given a new and
more dynamic turn. What this led to will be described later on, when
we discuss such writers as Morgan, Spencer, Sumner, Westermarck,
and Briffault.

V. THE INDUSTRIAL REVOLUTION, PLANS FOR SOCIAL REFORM,
AND THE RISE OF SOCIOLOGY

The industrial revolution was one of the most sweeping social transformations which had thus far taken place in the history of human
society. It tangled and tore the whole web of social life in the Western
world and forced extensive readjustments to meet the new conditions
of living. The misery and suffering which resulted led to a large number
and variety of proposals for social and economic reconstruction. Nothing
which had previously taken place had given so tremendous an impulse
to the humanitarian movement. These programs of social reform, and
the proposals of a social science to guide them, began as the result of the
disintegrating influence of the commercial revolution. By the time of

Saint-Simon we have a full reflection of the effects of the industrial revolution.

For the most part, these plans of social reform and reconstruction rested more upon profound sympathy with the unfortunate classes than upon any scientific conception of society and the proper methods of securing social reform. In due time, however, many students of the social problems of the age became convinced that, if social reform was not to be wasteful and misguided, it would have to rest upon a "science of society," which would indicate the nature of, and the limitations upon, social betterment. A. W. Small, in his *Origins of Sociology,* has clearly indicated the interrelationship between these early social-reform movements and the rise of sociology.[45]

The brilliant Abbé Charles Castel de Saint-Pierre seems to have been the first to suggest clearly that man's future lies in his own hands. He embodied his theory of progress in his *Observations on the Continual Progress of Universal Reason* (1737). His predecessors were interested chiefly in showing that there had been some progress since antiquity. The Abbé was more concerned with the idea that man might plan a better future and work directly to achieve this end. In his *Discourse on the Polysynodie* (1718) he anticipated Turgot, Saint-Simon, and Auguste Comte by declaring that we must depend primarily upon social science and an academy of experts to aid us in planning for a happier future. He is also well known for a specific contribution to the betterment of the race, namely, a comprehensive plan for perpetual peace through arbitration, published in three volumes in 1713–17. He regarded war, along with religious superstition and political despotism, as the main obstacles to progress.

The French economist, Turgot, the friend and defender of the Physiocrats, produced an interesting and original interpretation of progress and historical development. In his two discourses, delivered at the Sorbonne in 1750 on the *Advantages to the Human Race from the Establishment of Christianity* and on the *Successive Advances of the Human Mind,* he set forth in clear and unmistakable language the doctrine of continuity in history, the cumulative nature of evolution and progress, and the causal sequence between the different periods of history. He also, doubtless, furnished Comte with the suggestions which grew into the latter's law of the three stages of intellectual progress. While he viewed progress as primarily a matter of intellectual improvement, his conception of continuity in cultural development and of the essential unity of the historic process was a brilliant contribution. Like Saint-Pierre, Turgot believed that we must put informed intelligence to work if progress is to be made more speedy and certain. He definitely implied that scholars could work out a broad science of social progress to guide man in planning for the future.

The Marquis de Condorcet (1743–94) is representative of that group who looked upon the French Revolution as the climax of a long period of preparation for a new era of civilization. Comte pronounced him as much the best student of "social dynamics" in the eighteenth century, as Montesquieu had been of "social statics." His *A Sketch of the Intellectual Progress of Mankind* (1793) was one of the most optimistic and original of the writings of the period. His review of the previous stages of history led him to believe that civilization was rapidly advancing and that the French Revolution might be regarded as the culmination of this process. He developed a theory of historical progress which was far in advance of the earlier doctrines of Vico or Turgot and was expressed mainly in terms of the increase of knowledge and the growth of scientific achievement.

Condorcet's hope for the future of humanity was not less optimistic than his interpretation of the past. He made many remarkably accurate, as well as some extravagant, predictions as to what science would be able to accomplish for the race. He was, thus, one of the first writers to combine the scientific and the utopian theories of society. All in all, his work is most refreshing in contrast to that depressing conception of the descent from a "golden age" which was first expressed by Hesiod and had deeply influenced European thought from that time to the nineteenth century, especially after the classical conception had been reinforced by the Hebrew myth of a primal Paradise, which had come into the current of western European thought with the introduction of Christianity.

Count Henri de Saint-Simon (1760–1825) anticipated the main theoretical positions in the sociological system of Auguste Comte. If one substituted the word "sociology" for the term *science politique,* used by Saint-Simon with practically the same connotation that Comte gave to "sociology," then Saint-Simon may be said to have formulated Comte's chief theses, though even he himself only collected and systematized the doctrines current at the time.

After a critical examination of his works, Franck Allengry enumerates the following as the fundamental doctrines advanced by Saint-Simon: (1) Science must be distinguished from art in all departments of knowledge. (2) The sciences must be classified in the order of their increasing complexity, and a new science—*la science politique*—should be put at the head of the hierarchy. (3) This *science politique* must be based on the solid inductions of history and observation and must be animated by the conception of development and progress. (4) The general law of progress is that formulated by Turgot and Bourdin, namely, the law of the three stages of the psychological evolution of the race: the conjuctural, the "miconjectural," and the positive. (5) All sociological theories of progress must be founded upon this fundamental law. (6) The practical conditions of social life, and not supernatural sanctions, must be made the basis of the new morality, and the happiness of the race must be realized through a transformation of the present social order rather than in heaven. (7) This transformation requires a new industrial organization, a new social and political system, and a union of Europe in a new fraternity, *Le nouveau christianisme.*

One who is familiar with Comte's system need not be told that all that remained was for him to expand and to systematize the outlines laid down by Saint-Simon, and the the best critics agree that such was the primary contribution of Comte to sociology.

In his program of social reform, Saint-Simon proposed to organize society under the control of industrial experts, who were to direct production with a view to bringing plenty to all mankind. The industrial experts, in turn, were to be instructed by a select group of social scientists, who would apply themselves to discovering new truths and to inculcating both the new information and all that was worthy in the old. In this idea, Saint-Simon may be regarded as founder of technocracy and of the "managerial" social philosophy set forth in our day by James Burnham and others.

Auguste Comte (1798–1857) worked over and systematized some of the leading tendencies in social science in the eighteenth and early nineteenth centuries, in order to create a comprehensive system of sociology. His indebtedness to Saint-Simon for many of his leading ideas is obvious. Other influences may be discerned along with those of Saint-Simon. From Hume, Kant, and Gall he derived his chief doctrines as to causation and positivism in method. Comte's peculiar view of history as a combination of the inevitable and the providential may be traced to the opinions of Hume, Herder, and Turgot on historical determinism and to the emphasis of Bossuet, Vico, and De Maistre on the providential element in history. Saint-Pierre, Montesquieu, Turgot, Condorcet, and Saint-Simon had pointed out the need of a broad and fundamental science of society to act as a guide for political theory and practice. Finally, Montesquieu had introduced the modern conception of social law, Condorcet had elaborated the theory of progress, and Saint-Simon had insisted upon the necessity of transforming the social order.

There was, thus, little that was original in the theoretical content of Comte's system of sociology; his main contribution was to integrate and to give a comprehensive and systematic form to some of the most important of the social theories which were current in his time. In some ways, Comte was behind the scientific achievements of his age and failed to absorb some of the most important developments and innovations of the period, which have since entered into the shaping of sociological thought. At the same time, Comte cannot be denied a certain degree of genius, for there have been few minds which have been able to grasp in a more penetrating or comprehensive manner the unity of human society or to appreciate better the vast number of factors which are involved in its organization and development.

This cursory enumeration of the chief tendencies in the study of social phenomena in the eighteenth and nineteenth centuries gives one a basis for testing the validity of the assertion of Professor Small that sociology did not have its origin in isolation from the special social sciences and that the latter had faced and partially solved some of the important problems of sociology. It also throws light on the apparently contrary thesis of Professor Giddings that a new type of approach to the study of social phenomena, which was definitely sociological, began in a systematic way with Auguste Comte and developed directly through the writings of Spencer, Ward, and the sociologists of the present generation.

The reconciliation of these conflicting views of the matter is to be found in their respective opinions of the nature of sociology. If one accepts Professor Small's contention that sociology is the philosophical synthesis of the results of the special social sciences, then his view of the origin of sociology may be regarded as valid. On the other hand, if one agrees with Professor Giddings that sociology is the elemental and basic social science, characterized by the investigation of society in its broadest and most fundamental aspects, then one must concede that the formal differentiation of sociology as a distinct social science began with the systematization of earlier doctrines by Auguste Comte.

If, as Professors Ellwood and Vincent contended, both views are tenable and mutually complementary, then the conflict of opinions is more apparent than real, and one may seek the origin and development of sociology in the last century, both in the works of avowed sociologists and in the increasing tendency of the special social sciences to adopt the broader sociological method of approach to their problems.

On the whole, this last solution of the controversy seems the more accurate and satisfactory. The fundamental fact to be insisted upon is that the essence, if not the name, of sociology was an inevitable result of the necessity of providing an adequate science of society and an equally natural product of a more comprehensive method of analyzing social phenomena. It was not the fortuitous invention of the mind of a single man or the precarious product of a single age.

It so happened that, about the time that the general social, economic, and intellectual setting in western Europe and the advances in positive knowledge and scientific methods first made possible such a thing as a science of society, Auguste Comte, an enthusiastic thinker, with a genius for assimilation and systematization, appeared upon the scene and gave a name and a systematic expression to an already potent and dynamic tendency. That sociology would, have come into existence in its present nature and strength, though perhaps under a different name, even if there had been no Auguste Comte, is quite conceivable to one who has read the previous works of Vico, Montesquieu, Turgot, Hume, Ferguson, Adam Smith, Herder, Condorcet, and Saint-Simon or who has investigated the development of social science since 1850.

NOTES

1. "Contributions to the History of the Social Contract Theory," *Political Science Quarterly*, 1891, pp. 665–67.

2. N. Sykes, in F. J. C. Hearnshaw, *The Social and Political Ideas of Some Great Thinkers of the Sixteenth and Seventeenth Centuries* (New York, 1926), pp. 63–89. On sixteenth-century political thought see J. W. Allen, *European Political Thought in the Sixteenth Century* (New York, 1928).

3. Richard Hooker, *The Laws of an Ecclesiastical Polity*, Book I, chap. x; cf. also Allen, *op. cit.*

4. *Tractatus de legibus ac deo legislatore* (1612), Book I, "On Law in General."

5. Cf. J. M. Littlejohn, *The Political Theory of the Schoolmen and Grotius* (privately printed, 1895), pp. 262–96; W. A. Dunning, *A History of Political Theories from Luther to Montesquieu* (New York, 1905), pp. 133–49; and Hearnshaw, *op. cit.,* chap. iv.

6. Juan de Mariana, *De rege et regis institutione* (1605 ed.), chap. i, "Homo natura est animal sociabile." Cf. John Laures, *The Political Economy of Juan de Mariana* (New York, 1928).

7. For the most up-to-date treatment of Althusius see the Introduction to C. J. Friedrich, *Politica methodice digesta of Johannes Althusius* (Cambridge, 1932). On Grotius' contributions to social thought see Albert Salomon, "Hugo Grotius and the Social Sciences," *Political Science Quarterly,* LXII, No. 1 (March, 1947), 62–81.

8. G. P. Gooch, *English Democratic Ideas in the Seventeenth Century* (New York, 1907), pp. 177–83, 241–45, 314–19.

9. T. C. Pease, *The Leveller Movement* (American Historical Association, 1917).

10. Thomas Hobbes, *Philosophical Rudiments concerning Government and Society,* ed. Molesworth, chap. i, secs. 11–12; *Leviathan,* chap. xiii.

11. *Philosophical Rudiments,* chap. i, sec. 2.

12. *Leviathan,* chap. xl.

13. *Ibid.,* chap. xvii.

14. *Ibid.*

15. Samuel von Pufendorf, *The Law of Nature and of Nations,* trans. Basil Kennett and annotated by Barbeyrac (London, 1729), Book I, chap. ii, pp. 102 ff.; Book VII, chap. i, pp. 629 ff.

16. Baruch Spinoza, *A Theological-political Treatise,* trans. Elwes (1887), chap. xvi.

17. *Ibid.,* chaps. v, xvi; *A Political Treatise,* trans. Elwes (1887), chap. ii, sec. 15.

18. *Theological-political Treatise,* chap. xvi. Cf. R. A. Duff, *Spinoza's Political and Ethical Philosophy* (Glasgow, 1903).

19. Algernon Sidney, *Discourses concerning Government* (3d ed.; London, 1751), chap. ii, sec. v, particularly pp. 75 ff.

20. John Locke, *Two Treatises of Government,* ed. Morley (1884), Book II, chap. ii, secs. 6–7; chap. iii, sec. 19; chap. vii, secs. 77, 87.

21. *Ibid.,* chap. ix, secs. 123–24, 127; chap. xi, secs. 135, 138.

22. *Ibid.,* chap. viii, *passim.*

23. *Ibid.,* chap. xix, secs. 211–21.

24. *Ibid.,* chap. xix, sec. 240.

25. G. D. H. Cole (ed.), *Rousseau's Social Contract and Discourses* (New York, 1914).

26. On the theory of progress see J. B. Bury, *The Idea of Progress* (New York, 1932); and F. J. Teggart (ed.), *The Idea of Progress: A Collection of Reading* (Berkeley, Calif., 1925).

27. On the utopian writings of this period see W. B. Guthrie, *Socialism before the French Revolution* (New York, 1907), and Jessica Peixotto, *The French Revolution and Modern French Socialism* (New York, 1901).

28. See H. E. Barnes, *History of Western Civilization* (2 vols.; New York, 1935), Vol. II, Parts I–II.

29. Franklin Thomas, *The Environmental Basis of Society* (New York, 1925), pp. 58 ff.

30. W. S. Thompson, *Population: A Study in Malthusianism* (New York, 1915).

31. Berkeley's *Works,* ed. Frazer (4 vols., 1901), IV, 111–18, 186–90.

32. David Hume, *A Treatise of Human Nature,* ed. Green and Grose (1874), II, 111 ff., 140, 155, 183, 259–73; *Essays, Moral, Political, and Literary,* ed. Green and Grose (1874), Vol. I, Part I, Essay V; Part II, Essay XII. On Hume, Ferguson, and Adam Smith, see Gladys Bryson, *Man and Society: The Scottish Inquiry of the Seventeenth Century* (Princeton, N.J., 1945).

33. Adam Smith's major works, *The Theory of Moral Sentiments* and the *Wealth of Nations,* are available in numerous editions. The notes recovered from his lectures delivered at the University of Glasgow have been edited by Edward Cannan under the title, *Lectures on Justice, Police, Revenue, and Arms* (Oxford, 1896). On Sieyès, Godwin, and rationalistic social thought, see W. A. Dunning, *A History of Political Theories from*

Rousseau to Spencer (New York, 1920), chap. iii, and pp. 362–64; and H. N. Brailsford, *Shelley, Godwin, and Their Circle* (New York, 1915).

34. Wesley C. Mitchell, "Bentham's Felicific Calculus," *Political Science Quarterly,* June, 1918; on Bentham and his followers, see Elie Halévy, *The Growth of Philosophical Radicalism* (New York, 1928).

35. On this section see H. E. Barnes, *A History of Historical Writing* (Norman, Okla., 1937), chaps. vii–viii.

36. W. C. Lehmann, *Adam Ferguson and the Beginnings of Modern Sociology* (New York, 1930).

37. A. W. Small, *The Cameralists* (Chicago, 1909).

38. Henry Higgs, *The Physiocrats* (New York, 1897).

39. A. W. Small, *Adam Smith and Modern Sociology* (Chicago, 1907); and Eli Ginzberg, *The House of Adam Smith* (New York, 1934).

40. Charles Gide and Charles Rist, *History of Economic Doctrines* (New York, 1915), Book I.

41. W. A. Dunning, *A History of Political Theories from Luther to Montesquieu, A History of Political Theories from Rousseau to Spencer;* and C. E. Vaughan, *Studies in a History of Political Philosophy before and after Rousseau* (2 vols.; New York, 1925).

42. Edmund Burke, *Works* (12 vols.; Boston, 1884), Vols. III–IV, esp. III, 358–60. On Burke see J. MacCunn, *The Political Philosophy of Burke* (London, 1913); and A. K. Rogers, "The Social Philosophy of Burke," *American Journal of Sociology,* July 1912.

43. On legal developments in this period see Fritz Berolzheimer, *The World's Legal Philosophies* (New York, 1912), chap. v.

44. A. C. Haddon, *A History of Anthropology* (New York, 1910); and R. H. Lowie, *A History of Ethnological Thought* (New York, 1939).

45. On this section see A. W. Small, *Origins of Sociology* (Chicago, 1924), *passim,* esp. chap. i; and Dunning, *Political Theories from Rousseau to Spencer,* chaps. iii, ix.

PART II

THE PIONEERS OF SOCIOLOGY

CHAPTER III

THE SOCIAL AND POLITICAL PHILOSOPHY OF AUGUSTE COMTE: POSITIVIST UTOPIA AND THE RELIGION OF HUMANITY

Harry Elmer Barnes

I. LIFE AND WORKS OF AUGUSTE COMTE

WE HAVE provided in the foregoing chapters a comprehensive background for understanding the rise of sociology. But we might profitably discuss here in an introductory paragraph the main factors motivating the sociological pioneers. In every case it was a combination of the ameliorative motive and interest in social evolution. All were primarily concerned about the relation of sociology to the question of social progress and social justice. Comte and Ward thought that social science could promote social justice and speed up social progress through preaching the gospel of social or artificial guidance of social evolution. The great lesson which the social sciences have to teach seemed to them to be that the social process could and should be controlled by the social mind, well stocked with reliable social science. Spencer, Sumner, and Gumplowicz were just as heartily interested in the relation of social science to social progress as were Comte and Ward, but they took exactly the opposite position with respect to social control over the evolution of society. They believed that the great conclusion of social science is that man should keep his hands off the process of social change and let the latter be controlled by the automatic workings of natural evolutionary laws. But all six of the pioneers were agreed that the main justification of sociology is to be found in the generalizations that it can offer with respect to social change and social reform. Morgan was more directly interested in the forces, factors, and stages of social evolution than he was in social reform, but he was not unconcerned about the latter, and his sympathies were decidedly in favor of the school of thought represented by Comte and Ward.

81

While no single member of the so-called "organismic school" of sociologists, such as Lilienfeld, Schäffle, Worms, *et al.,* would merit a chapter in this section on sociological pioneers, a chapter on the whole group would have been included here had these writers not been summarized in Barnes and Becker, *Social Thought from Lore to Science* (I, 677 ff.). Further, Comte's and Spencer's ideas on this subject and Fouillée's and Hobhouse's qualifications of the doctrine are included in this volume.

It is over one hundred years since Auguste Comte published the famous prospectus of his comprehensive social philosophy under the title of *A Program of Scientific Work Required for the Reorganization of Society.*[1] In the century and a quarter which have passed, many one-sided philosophies of society have been proposed and many incomplete schemes of social reform propounded. Many writers in recent years, such as L. T. Hobhouse and C. A. Ellwood, have, however, tended to revert to the position of Comte and hold that we must have a broad philosophy of society. This must include a consideration of biological, psychological, and historical factors and a program of social reform which would provide for improvement in both technical efficiency and social morale. Further, there has also developed a widespread distrust of the "pure" democracy of the last century. There is a growing feeling that we must endeavor, more and more, to place in positions of political and social power that intellectual aristocracy in which Comte placed his faith to provide desirable leadership in the reconstruction of European society. In the light of the above facts, a brief analysis of the political and social philosophy of Comte may have practical, as well as historical, interest to students of philosophy and social science.

Auguste Comte was born in Montpellier in 1789 and received his higher education at the Ecole polytechnique. During six years of his young manhood he was a close friend and ardent disciple of the progressive French thinker, Count Henri de Saint-Simon.[2] In 1824 there came a sharp break which led Comte into a somewhat ungracious depreciation of his former master. They differed chiefly in the degree to which they placed confidence in the revolutionary philosophy and tendencies of the times, Comte being inclined to take a more conservative position than his teacher.

Comte's earliest work of importance was the prospectus of his social philosophy, mentioned above.[3] In 1826 he presented in lectures the first formal exposition of the principles of his Positivist philosophy in his own home, where he was honored by the attendance of such distinguished men as the German scientist, Alexander von Humboldt.

Comte's first great work—the *Cours de philosophie positive*—appeared between the years 1830 and 1842. From 1836 until 1846 he was an examiner for the Ecole polytechnique. After his dismissal from this position, he was supported chiefly by contributions from his disciples and admirers. His friendship with Clotilde de Vaux (1845–46) doubtless contributed strongly to Comte's eulogy of women, which appeared particularly in his *Polity*. He founded the Positivist Society in 1848. Comte's last and most important work—the *Système de politique positive* ("Principles of a Positive Polity")—appeared between 1851 and 1854. He died in 1857.

In the first of his chief works—the *Philosophy*—Comte worked out in more detail than in his earlier sketches and essays his main theoretical positions. These include the hierarchy of the sciences; the necessity for, and the nature of, sociology, with its two main divisions of social statics and social dynamics; and the law of the three stages of intellectual progress, with ample historical illustrations and confirmation. The *Polity* was a detailed expansion of his theoretical doctrines and their practical application to the construction of a "Positive" or scientifically designed commonwealth. While many are inclined to maintain that the *Philosophy* contains all Comte's important contributions to sociology, such is far from the case. Though the *Polity* is verbose, prolix, involved, and repetitious, nearly all Comte's chief postulates are developed in it with far greater maturity and richness of detail than in the *Philosophy*.[4]

II. COMTE'S GENERAL CONTRIBUTIONS TO SOCIAL THEORY

It is generally conceded by the foremost students of Comte's social philosophy that his chief contribution lay in his remarkable capacity for synthesis and organization rather than in the development of new and original social doctrines. He derived much from writers on social philosophy, from Aristotle to Saint-Simon. From Aristotle he obtained his fundamental notion as to the basis of social organization, namely, the distribution of functions and the combination of efforts. From Hume, Kant, and Gall he received his conceptions of positivism in method and his physical psychology. From Hume, Kant, and Turgot he obtained his views of historical determinism, and from Bossuet, Vico, and De Maistre his somewhat inconsistent doctrine of a providential order in history. From Turgot, Condorcet, Bourdin, and Saint-Simon he derived his famous law of the three stages in the intellectual development of mankind.

From Saint-Pierre, Montesquieu, Condorcet, and Saint-Simon he secured his conception of sociology as the basic and directive science, which must form the foundation of the art of politics. Each had made special contributions to this subject. Montesquieu had introduced the conception of law in the social process, stressing particularly the influence of the physical environment. Condorcet had emphasized the conception of progress and the role of science therein. Saint-Pierre and Saint-Simon had insisted upon the necessity of providing a science of society sufficiently comprehensive to guide social and industrial reorganization. It was the significant achievement of Comte to work out an elaborate synthesis of these progressive contributions of the thought of the previous century and to indicate the bearing of this new social science upon the problems of European society in the nineteenth century.[5]

Comte's outstanding doctrines, namely, the classification of the hierarchy of the sciences with sociology at the head; the division of this subject into social statics and dynamics; the law of the three stages of universal social progress; and the conception of the organic nature of society, with its corollary of society as a developing organism, have been so often repeated in résumés of sociological theory that they have become commonplaces. Even a cursory reading of Comte's major works, however, is bound to impress the reader with the fact that he had much more to offer than can be intelligently summarized under the above headings. There are few problems in social theory or cultural history upon which he did not touch.[6]

Comte's fundamental methodological position is that, if human knowledge is to be extended in the future, it must be accomplished through the application of the positive or scientific method of observation, experimentation, and comparison. Sociological investigation must follow this general procedure, with the qualification that, when the comparative method has been applied to the study of consecutive stages of human society, a fourth method, the historical, will have been provided. From this we may expect extensive and illuminating results. Nothing fruitful can be hoped for from the metaphysicians. Comte's strictures upon their methods and results are particularly vigorous and, to many, equally convincing.

Comte constructed a hierarchy of the sciences, beginning with mathematics and passing through astronomy, physics, chemistry, and biology to the new science of sociology, which was to complete the series. The fundamental theoretical foundations of this classification were: first, that each science depends upon those below it in the series; second, that, as one advances through the series, the subjects become more specific, complex, and less amenable to scientific measurement and prediction; and, finally, that the difficulties of sociology are due to the greater complexity of the phenomena with which it deals and the lack of adequate measurement of these phenomena rather than to any generic difference in the desirable methodology.

While Comte did not elaborate to any great extent the organic conception of society, still he may be said to have offered the suggestions for the later school of so-called "Organicists," and he is notable for holding that the organic doctrine was no mere analogy but a reality. It is the individual who is an abstraction rather than the social organism. Comte summed up in the following manner the organismic doctrines as set forth in his *Philosophy:* Society is a collective organism, as contrasted to the individual organism or plant, and possesses the primary organic attribute of the *consensus universel*. There is to be seen both in the organism and in society a harmony of structure and function, working toward a common end through action and reaction among its parts and upon the environment. This harmonious development reaches its highest stage in human society, which is the final step in organic evolution. He anticipated Herbert Spencer by holding that social progress is characterized by an increasing specialization of functions and a corresponding tendency toward a more perfect adaptation of organs. Finally, social disturbances are maladies of the social organism and are the proper subject matter of social pathology.[7]

In the *Polity* Comte elaborated the similarity between the individual and the social organism. In the family may be found the social cell; in the social forces may be discerned the social tissues; in the state (city) may be discovered the social organs; and in the various nations are to be detected the social analogues of the system of organs in biology. The great difference between the individual organism and the social organism lies in the fact that the character of the former is essentially immutable, while the latter is capable of immense improvement, if guided according to scientific principles. Another distinction is that the social organism allows a far wider distribution of functions, combined with a higher degree of co-ordination of organs.

Comte defined sociology specifically as the science of social order and progress and, in a more general way, as the science of social phenomena. It is closely related to biology, the subject matter of the latter being organization and life, while that of sociology is order and progress.

Comte divides sociology into two major departments—social statics, or *théorie générale de l'ordre spontané des sociétés humaines,* and social dynamics, or *théorie générale du progrès naturel de l'humanité.* He finds that the underlying basis of social order is the principle which he attributes to Aristotle, though it probably belongs more rightfully to Plato, namely, the distribution of functions and the combination of efforts. The former takes shape in the specialization and division of labor in society, and the latter is realized through the institution of government.

The governing principle of social progress is to be found in the law of the three stages of intellectual advance.[8] Through each of these stages —the theological, metaphysical, and scientific—must pass the proper development and education of the individual, the various realms of human knowledge, and the general process of social evolution. None of these stages can be eliminated, though intelligent direction may hasten the process, or lack of wisdom retard it. Each stage is the necessary antecedent of the following one, and any period is as perfect as the conditions of the time will permit. All institutions are, thus, relative in their degree of excellence, and none can hope to attain to absolute perfection.

Objectively considered, progress may be regarded as consisting in man's increasing control over the environment. Again, progress may be broken up into three constituent parts—intellectual, material, and moral. Intellectual progress is to be found in the law of the three stages of mental evolution; material progress in "an analogous progression in human activity which in its first stage is Conquest, then Defense; and lastly Industry." Moral progress "shows that man's social nature follows the same course; that it finds satisfaction, first in the Family, then in the State, and lastly in the Race."[9] In promoting progress the desires and emotions are the driving forces, and the intellectual factors are the guiding and restraining agencies.

While Comte's philosophy of history has been criticized by many for being too one-sided and merely stressing intellectual factors, most of these critics have overlooked those passages in the *Polity* in which he foreshadows Spencer and Giddings by describing the three great stages of human progress as the "Military-theological," the "Critical-metaphysical," and the "Industrial-scientific."[10]

Comte laid great stress upon the family as the fundamental social institution and upon religion as one of the most important regulative agencies in society. While somewhat utilitarian in his attitude toward the social application of religion, his exposition of the principles of the Positivist creed is developed in great detail in the *Polity*. His attitude with respect to the basic importance of the family and religion, appreciated by Ward, has been revived with a more scientific analysis and application by Professor Charles A. Ellwood.

Finally, as Lester F. Ward so clearly pointed out, Comte held that the great practical value of sociology is to be found in its application to scientific social reform. In his most elaborate work, the *Polity,* he developed at great length what he believed might be the ultimate type of social organization, if society is wise enough to study and apply the science which investigates the laws of its organization and progress.

III. COMTE'S SOCIAL AND POLITICAL PHILOSOPHY

A. SOCIOLOGY AND POLITICAL SCIENCE

Comte makes no clear distinction between political science and sociology. Indeed, he seems to regard sociology as the perfected political science of the future. At the same time, he clearly differentiates sociology from the older political philosophy, dominated by metaphysical methods and concepts. Sociology has nothing in common with the old a priori method that characterized the earlier political philosophy. It must be based on the assured scientific procedure of observation, experimentation, and comparison. It is doubtful whether Comte believed it possible that there could be a science of the state distinct from the general science of society. At any rate, his political theory is inextricably connected with his psychology, theology, ethics, and economics, which are included within his sociology.

Comte denied that the special social sciences are true sciences. He held that society must be studied as a whole by a unitary science—sociology. Political science, to Comte, was that part of his sociology which was concerned with the history of the state and the theory and practice of its organization. He rarely, if ever, treated these subjects in isolation but dealt with each as a phase of social evolution and organization as a whole.

B. THE NATURE OF THE STATE

Comte's ideas concerning the nature of the state and its distinction from society, nation, and government are vague and uncertain. Comte was too much interested in the ultimate Positivist society of the future to devote much attention to any elaborate discussion of the theoretical foundations of the contemporary national bourgeois state. This was, at best, merely a transitional form of social organization: "Between the city, uniting man and his dwelling place, and the full development of the Great Being around a fitting centre, a number of intermediate forms of association may be found, under the general name of states. But all of these forms, differing only in extent and permanence, may be neglected as undefined."[11] Comte's general attitude would have made it hard for him to conceive clearly such an entity as society politically organized, as distinct in practice, at least, from its material and spiritual aspects. His own theory of society was so all-inclusive, with its mixture of family ethics, theological dogmas, and economic arrangements with politics, that it was not favorable to clearly formulated concepts in the political realm.

The only point on which he may be said to be unmistakably clear is his dogma that there can be no fixed social relations of any permanence without a political organization, that is, a government. The first principle of positive political theory, he says, is that "society without a government is no less impossible than a government without society. In the smallest as well as in the largest associations, the Positive theory of a polity never loses sight of these two correlative ideas, without which theories would lead us astray, and society would end in anarchy."[12] When, however, Comte begins to discuss the governmental arrangements in his society, he immediately introduces conceptions quite foreign to orthodox notions of governmental organizations. Such are his advocacy of increasing governmental rectitude through the influence of family morality and of intrusting its encouragement and surveillance to the priests of the religion of humanity. In short, it seems that Comte regarded the state as the agency which should direct the general material activities of society. While this is the most frequent connotation of the term "state" as employed by Comte, he often uses it in sense identical with the nation or with society in general.

Upon the question as to what constitutes the fundamental attributes of the state, Comte is a little more clear. In fact, he quite agrees with what are now considered the indispensable attributes of any state or political society, namely, population, territory, a sovereign power, and a governmental organization. His insistence upon the indispensability of government has been pointed out above. Finally, in his unequivocal statement of the necessity of adequate social control in any stable society and the recognition that political organization ultimately rests upon force, Comte makes it plain that he discerned the need of a sovereign power to create and maintain a permanent political society.

Comte also anticipated the modern trends in political science by stressing the importance of the psychological and economic factors in the state. He sums up his position on these points very briefly in the following passage: "When Property, Family, and Language, have found a suitable Territory, and have reached the point at which they combine any given population under the same, at least the same spiritual, government, there a possible nucleus of the Great Being has been formed. Such a community, or city, be it ultimately large or small, is a true organ of Humanity."[13] This passage is an admirable example of how Comte was wont to introduce into political thought highly visionary and figurative ethical and theological concepts.

C. THE GENESIS OF SOCIAL AND POLITICAL INSTITUTIONS

1. *Philosophical analysis of principles.*—Comte treated the subject of the origin of society, state, and government in both an analytical and a historical manner. In his analytical treatment he based his procedure on the Aristotelian dogma of the inherent sociability of mankind. He declared that the notion of a state of nature is mere metaphysical nonsense and the allied contract theory of political origins untenable. Man, he held, prevailed over the other animals because of his superior sociability, and in the development of this important social nature the prolongation of human infancy was perhaps the most important factor. Here Comte anticipated John Fiske's notion.

The unit of society, according to Comte, is not the individual but the family. The great function of the family in history has been to create the basic social and psychic traits which ultimately produce the state. The growth and perfection of language was the main factor making it possible for the state to develop from the family:[14]

A *society*, therefore, can no more be decomposed into *individuals* than a geometric surface can be resolved into lines, or a line into points. The simplest association, that is, the family, sometimes reduced to its original couple, constitutes the true unit of society. From it flow the more complex groups, such as classes and cities.[15]

During the whole continuance of the education of the race, the principal end of the Domestic Order is gradually to form the Political Order. It is from this latter, finally, that the critical influence originates, whereby the family affections are raised up to their high social office, and prevented from degenerating into collective selfishness.[16]

While society in a psychological sense is ultimately based upon the social instinct, grounded in sympathy, and expressed mainly in the family, the wider and more highly developed forms of social organization, as exemplified by society and the state, are founded upon the Aristotelian principle of the distribution of functions and the combination of efforts. It is this co-operative distribution of functions which marks off political society from domestic association, which is based upon sympathy.

The great point of superiority of the social organism over the individual organism is that it allows a higher degree of distribution of functions, co-ordinated with a more perfect adaptation of organs. The perfect distribution of functions and co-ordination of organs in society is the ultimate goal of social evolution. It is in a study of the relation between these two principles that one may discover the true relation between society and government. The reason for this is that too much specialization, while it leads to the development of great skill and a high degree of interest in narrow fields, is likely to result in the disintegration of society through a loss of the conception of the unity of the whole and of the mutual relations between the individual and society. It is the function of government to co-ordinate human activities and to guard against dangerous extremes of specialization while, at the same time, conserving its beneficial administrative effects.

In proportion as the distribution of functions is fully realized in society, there results a natural and spontaneous process of subordination, the principle being that those in any occupation come under the direction of the class which has control over their general type of functions, i.e., the next class above them in the hierarchy of industrial differentiation. Government tends naturally to arise out of the controlling and directing forces which are centered, at first, in the smaller and functional groups of society. In the past, war has been the chief factor in unifying into one central agency this previously scattered political power. Industry is, however, more and more coming to be the source of social discipline and governmental control. The habits of command and of obedience already formed in industry have only to be extended to public spheres, to produce a power in the state capable of controlling the divergencies, and regulating the convergencies of the individuals within it.[17]

This material basis of government, in the principles of the division of labor, combination of efforts, and superiority and subordination, harmonizes with the psychic characteristics of humanity, which lead some to command and others to obey. While it is necessary to recognize the almost universal desire to command, it is no less essential to observe that most people find it more agreeable to throw the burden of expert guidance upon others.

But one must go beyond this fundamental analytical basis of the state, in the distribution of functions and the combination of efforts, to construct a complete system of political philosophy. With this Aristotelian axiom must be combined the Hobbesian notion of force as the ultimate foundation upon which governmental organization rests: "Social science would remain forever in the cloud-land of metaphysics, if we hesitated to adopt the principle of Force as the basis of Government. Combining this Hobbesian doctrine with that of Aristotle, that society consists in the combination of efforts and the distribution of functions, we get the axioms of a sound political philosophy."[18]

To the doctrine of Aristotle and Hobbes, however, must further be added the more specific notions of Comte himself. He finds that, along with the requirements just named, there is needed an efficient general regulating power or system of social control: "Close study, therefore, shows that there are three things necessary for all political power, besides the basis of material Force: an Intellectual guidance, a Moral sanction, and lastly a Social control."[19]

This regulative power is to be found in the religion of Humanity and should be administered by the priests of that cult. There are, thus, in the perfect state three grades of society: the family based on feeling or affection; the state or city based on action; and the church, based primarily on intelligence but, in reality, synthesizing all three. These grades of society correspond to, and have their foundation in, the three fundamental functions of man's cerebral system—feeling, action, and intellect—which Comte took over from Gall's phrenology and made the basis of his psychology and much of his social science.

This final element, the church, with its universal surveillance and guidance of all social activities, will make possible the dissolution of the great tyrannical states and the perfection of the social organism without any danger of anarchy or license. In the place of the conventional political state, as it now exists, there will be a group of cities united by the common religious tutelage provided by the worship of Humanity as administered by its priests. Such political entities are, after all, as large as any which could be created without taking the risk of tyranny or dictatorship. Comte thus tended partially to revive the localism and municipal character of the utopias of Plato and Aristotle and, to a certain degree, anticipated Le Play and modern regionalism:

The foundation of a universal Church will enable the gradual reduction of these huge and temporary agglomerations of men to that natural limit, where the State can exist without tyranny..... No combination of men can be durable, if this is not really voluntary; and in considering the normal form of the State we must get rid of all artificial and violent bonds of union, and retain only those which are spontaneous and free. Long experience has proved that the City, in its full completeness and extent of surrounding country, is the largest body politic which can exist without becoming oppressive..... But besides this, the Positive Faith, with its calm grasp over human life as a whole, will be sufficient to unite the various Cities in the moral communion of the Church, without requiring the help of the State to supplement the task with its mere material unity.

Thus the final creation of a religious society whereby the great organism is completed, fulfills all the three wants of the political society. The intellectual guidance, the moral sanction, and the social regulation which government requires to modify its material nature, are all supplied by a Church, when it has gained a distinct existence of its own.[20]

2. *The historical evolution of social and political institutions.*—In treating the origin of society and the state from a historical point of view, Comte reminds one of Hegel's account of the successive migrations of the *Weltgeist* until it finally settled among the German people.[21] Comte ranges over the history of humanity and traces the stages through which the race has passed in its preparation for the final goal of its evolution—the Positivist society. One difference between Hegel and Comte is that Comte presented a much more accurate interpretation of the facts of history than did Hegel. When viewed in the light of his time, he was by no means so devoid of historical information as some recent historical

critics seem to indicate. He seems to have been acquainted with Gibbon, Hallam, and Guizot, for instance, and he grasped the significance of many fundamental movements in history, particularly economic trends, which escaped many later and more erudite political historians. A comprehensive grasp of the vital factors at work in history is as essential to a true conception of historical development as is a detailed knowledge of the "objective facts of history." Judged by this criterion, Comte was no less of a real historian than many of the extremely careful and critical political historians of the nineteenth century.

It is beyond the scope of this chapter to present in detail Comte's philosophy of history. All that will be attempted is a brief statement of his fundamental principles and a summary of the portions of his work dealing with the evolution of social and political institutions.

Comte's philosophy of history is based on as ingenious a system of triads as characterized the work of Vico.[22] In the first place, social evolution, like social organization, is a product of the tripartite functions of man's cerebral system—feeling, action, and intellect. Feeling or emotion, which is the basis of morality, passes through three stages in which man's social nature finds satisfaction: first, in the family, then in the state, and, finally, in the race. Or, as he puts it in other words, altruism in antiquity is domestic and civic, in the Middle Ages it is collective, and in the Positive period it is universal. Still another way of describing this phase of evolution is to say that the sympathetic instincts of humanity advance through the stages of attachment, veneration, and benevolence. There is a close relationship between these different aspects of moral evolution, since fetishism, which founded the family, also developed the feeling of attachment; polytheism, which founded the state, fostered veneration; and monotheism, with its universality, favored the sentiment of benevolence.

Man's activational evolution proceeds through the stages of conquest, defense, and industry. Finally, the evolution of the intellect follows the famous three stages—the theological, metaphysical, and Positive or scientific. In this process emotion is the dynamic power, action the agent of progress, and intellect the guiding force. Comte did not, therefore, as many writers would seem to indicate, base his philosophy of history exclusively on the single element of intellectual evolution. Even the law of the three stages of intellectual progress aimed at a larger synthesis, which would include material and spiritual factors, though the religious element played a predominant part in his scheme. Comte's periods of intellectual development, in broad outline, were the theological, divided into fetishism, polytheism, and monotheism; the metaphysical stage, or the period of the "Western revolution" from 1300 to 1800; and the beginnings of the Positive period from 1800 onward. Each of these periods was further subdivided.

In the period of fetishism, or what would now be called "animism," the family or private society was instituted and with it that fixity of residence which made the later development of the state possible. In the first polytheistic period, that of theocratic or conservative polytheism (i.e., the period of the great oriental empires), the main political contribution was the founding of the city (i.e., the state) and the development of the institution of landed property. Its great defect was the attempt to found a church before civic life had been perfected. Another unifying and disciplinary feature of this period was the wide development of the caste system. In the next period, that of intellectual polytheism (i.e., the Greek age), there were no important political contributions except in a negative sense. The service of the Greeks was intellectual and was rendered by freeing humanity from theocratic influences. National solidarity was impaired by the attacks of the Greeks upon property and upon caste without providing other unifying influences, and their political life was mainly the rule of demagogues. If the Greeks made any political contribution at all, it was in repelling the Persian advance.

In the Roman period, or the age of social monotheism, there were several phases of political progress. The most important was the development of the conception of "Fatherland," which Comte defines as "the permanent seat of all those moral and intellectual impressions, by whose unbroken influence the individual destiny is moulded.[23] . . . . Nothing is so well adapted to consolidate social ties as their habitual consolidation around a material seat, which is equally appropriate to relations of Continuity as to those of Solidarity."[24] The world is thus indebted to Rome for the first definite step taken toward sociocracy. Roman law also tended toward sociocracy, since, to a considerable degree, it substituted social sanctions for supernatural sanctions in the administration of the law. Finally, when Roman warfare was transformed from conquest into defense, it naturally transformed slavery into serfdom and the Empire into a small-state system. This opened the way for the development of feudalism, the germs of which are to be found in the cession of Roman territory to barbarian chieftains.

The next period was that of the defensive monotheism, or the Catholic-feudal transition. It was the period of the establishment of the church, comparable to the foundation of family and state in earlier periods: "The distinguishing feature of medieval civilization was the two-fold nature of the aims in view and the combination of two heterogeneous elements for its attainment."[25] The general purpose of the period was to systematize life, and this, the work of the church, failed for the most part. The special purpose of the age was the emancipation of women and laborers, the work mainly of feudalism, and this was, to a large degree, successful. Since the religion of this period was universal and political power local, there then began the indispensable separation of church and state. At the same time, warfare was finally transformed from aggression to defense. Mariolatry, with its idealization of woman, was an advance toward sociolatry, or the worship of humanity. Great steps in advance were taken with the separation of employers from employed, the rise of the guild corporations, and the emancipation of the serfs.

But, despite these important contributions, it was not possible for this period of defensive monotheism to inaugurate the Positivist regime. Another period, that of the "Western revolution" had to intervene. This corresponds to the metaphysical period of mental development. The eight main forces operating to bring about this revolution were: the influence of women; scientific advances; modern industrial improvements; the growth of art; the development of the state; the decay of the church; the work of the legists; and, finally, the negative contributions of the metaphysicians.

In this period industry became consolidated, as employers and employed united in their mutual interest against the other classes. Government, in turn, began to patronize industry because it recognized that its development was essential to furnishing the income needed to maintain military activities. This reacted upon the rulers by making them responsible administrators of the public wealth. This dual process marked the real entry of industry into Western politics as the chief aim of the modern polity. Civilization, hitherto military, now became progressively industrial in character. The whole period, and particularly that of the French Revolution, was one of disintegration and of preparation for positivism.

In the program of the next, or Positive, period, Comte conceded that important beginnings had already been made before his day. Condorcet had supplied the philosophic foundations of sociology. De Maistre renewed the veneration for the best elements in the Middle Ages. Scientific advances had been made by Lamarck, Bichat, Broussais, Cabanis, and Gall. Comte discovered the two fundamental laws of sociology, and his sociological system, which was too intellectualistic in the *Philosophy*, was well rounded on its emotional side by his friendship with Clotilde de Vaux and appeared in a more complete form in the *Polity*. On the intellectual side, then, everything was ready for the institution of the Positivist system, and, appropriately enough, at just this time the *coup d'état* of 1851 had revived the institution of dictatorship, which was the great preliminary step in the political field preparatory to the inauguration of Positivism. Comte himself stood ready to assume the office of supreme pontiff of the new religion.

Psychology and history had thus conspired, through man's fundamental makeup and the struggles of ages, to render the Positivist system as inevitable as it was desirable. In this last stage of social evolution, "Family, State, and Church are finally to be distinguished and harmonized, or fixed in their proper organic relations to each other, so as to preclude forever their warfare or intrusion upon each other's provinces."[26]

D. FORMS OF THE STATE AND THE GOVERNMENT

As to the forms of the state and the government, while Comte was familiar with the conventional Aristotelian classification, it was regarded by him as of minor importance and of superficial significance. To him there were only two fundamental types of society, state, and government—theocracy and sociocracy. The former was the government of theologically oriented priests, in which the temporal power was subordinated to the spiritual. The latter was the condition to be reached in the Positivist state, where spiritual and temporal power were to be separated and properly co-ordinated and in which social organization was to be based on the principles of Comte's sociology. It has been the problem of the greater part of human history to bring about the transformation of theocracy into sociocracy.

E. SOVEREIGNTY

In a system of social control like that proposed by Comte, in which authority was to be divided into moral, material, and intellectual power, each to be enforced by separate organs, and in which the latter, while the most important, was to be administered through persuasion and suggestion, it is easy to see that there was little place for any such concept as that of political sovereignty in its conventional modern meaning. Probably the directors of material activities, that is, the leaders of the employer class, came the nearest to having sovereign power of any of Comte's proposed governing agencies; at least, they were to possess the functions of ordinary civil government. So far as he discusses the problem of sovereignty, he seems to mean by it the possession of political authority.[27]

The nearest Comte gets to a positive theory of sovereignty is his approbation of Hobbes's doctrine that government has an important basis in force. He says, in speaking of popular sovereignty, that the Positive theory on this point separates the elements of truth from those of error in metaphysical doctrine. He here accepts two different conceptions of popular sovereignty: one a political connotation, applicable in special cases, and the other a moral interpretation, suitable in all cases. By the "political" aspect he means that the voice of the people should be appealed to in instances which concern the practical interests of the whole community and are intelligible to the masses, such as declarations of war and the decisions of the law courts. On the other hand, it would be manifestly absurd to have the whole people decide on questions of particular interest requiring special and trained judgment. The moral aspect of popular sovereignty consists in the proposition that the efforts of the whole of society should be centered on the common good, that is, should seek to establish "the preponderance of social feeling over all personal interests."[28]

F. THE POSITIVIST SCHEME OF SOCIAL RECONSTRUCTION

It is difficult to grasp the full meaning and significance of Comte's plan of social organization without a preliminary statement of the historical background of Comte's doctrines. He was witnessing the disintegration of the old social order, as a result of the French and the industrial revolutions, and was keenly conscious of the evils of the new, though still transitional, society. Quite in contrast to Say, Bastiat, and other French optimists, Comte joined with Sismondi in condemning the new capitalistic order. His indictment of the new bourgeois age is well stated by Lucien Lévy-Bruhl:

> Comte saw the bourgoisie at work during Louis Phillippe's reign, and he passes severe judgment upon it. Its political conceptions, he says, refer not to the aim and exercise of power, but especially to its possessions. It regards the revolution as terminated by the establishment of the parliamentary regime, whereas this is only an "equivocal halting-place." A complete social reorganization is not less feared by this middle class than by the old upper classes. Although filled with the critical spirit of the eighteenth century, even under a Republican form it would prolong a system of theological hypocrisy by means of which the respectful submission of the masses is insured, while no strict duty is imposed upon the leaders. This is hard upon the proletariat, whose condition is far from improving. It "establishes dungeons for those who ask for bread." It believes that these millions of men will be able to remain indefinitely "encamped" in modern society without being properly settled in it with definite and respected rights. The capital which it holds in its hands, after having been an instrument of emancipation, has become one of oppression. It is thus that, by a paradox difficult to uphold, the invention of machinery, which *a priori*, one would be led to believe, would soften the condition of the proletariat, has, on the contrary, been a new cause of suffering to them, and has made their lot a doubly hard one. Here, in brief, we have a formidable indictment against the middle classes, and in particular against the political economy which has nourished them.[29]

Yet the problem was not one of capitalism, as such, or its abolition. It was not the industrial or financial technique of the new industrial order which was at fault, but the failure to develop a new industrial and social morality which could exert proper control and discipline over the modern industrial system:

> That there should be powerful industrial masters is only an evil if they use their power to oppress the men who depend upon them. It is a good thing, on the contrary, if these masters know and fulfill their duties. It is of little consequence to popular interests in whose hands capital is accumulated, so long as the use of it is made beneficial to the social masses.
>
> But modern society has not yet got its system of morality. Industrial relations which have become immensely developed in it are abandoned to a dangerous empiricism, instead of being systematized according to moral laws. War, more or less openly declared, alone regulates the relations between capital and labour.[30]

What was needed, then, was a new industrial and social morality, to be inculcated through the Positive educational system. This would be far more effective than state-socialistic schemes and paternalistic legislation. Comte's scheme of social reconstruction was, thus, one which rested more on a moral than on a political or economic basis. The socialization of the modern order "depends far more upon moral than upon political measures. The latter can undoubtedly prevent the accumulation of riches in a small number of hands, at the risk of paralyzing industrial activity. But these tyrannical proceedings would be far less efficacious than the universal reproof inflicted by Positive ethics upon a selfish use of the riches possessed."[31] "Everything then depends upon the common moral education, which itself depends upon the establishment of a spiritual power. The superiority of the Positive doctrine lies in the fact that it has restored this power."[32] "Once common education is established, under the direction of the spiritual power, the tyranny of the capitalist class would be no more to be feared. Rich men would consider themselves as the moral guardians of the public capital. It is not here a question of charity. Those who possess will have the 'duty' of securing, first, education and then work for all."[33]

In turning, now, to a more detailed consideration of Comte's scheme for a new social dispensation, it must be borne in mind that his chief aim was to develop a new social morality, believing, as he did, that this would be the only force adequate to solve the problems of modern industrialism.

Comte's theory of social reconstruction, like his doctrines of social organization and his philosophy of history, rested ultimately upon the threefold division of the human personality into feeling, action and intelligence. In the first place, one should turn to his analysis of the social forces. They are (1) material force, based on action and expressed in number and wealth; (2) intellectual force, founded on speculation and manifested in conception and expression; and (3) moral force, based on affection and expressed in command prompted by character and obedience prompted by the heart. It is the supreme task of social organization, as well as its chief difficulty, to combine these forces in the right proportion without the undue predominance of anyone.

In the state one finds that the fundamental social classes are founded on this same general principle: "In the smallest cities capable of separate existence, we find these classes: the Priests who guide our speculation; the Women who inspire our highest affections; and the practical Leaders who direct our activity, be it in war or in industry."[34] The agency needed to connect and harmonize these three basic social classes is to be found in the mass of the people or the proletariat, "for they are united to the affectionate sex by domestic ties; to the Priesthood through the medium of the education and advice which it gives them; and to the practical Leaders through common action and the protection afforded them."[35]

Every social class, except the women, should be arranged on an hierarchical basis according to the principle of social importance and specialization of function: "Our ultimate state will exhibit a classification of society more distinct than any we know in all sides of human life. From High Priest of Humanity down to the humblest laborer, society will show the same principle at work distributing ranks: generality of view decreasing as independence of life increases."[36]

The directive power, or what might perhaps be called the "function" of government, in Comte's society was to be centered in the priests of the Positive religion and in the leaders of industry. The temporal and military power of the past was to give way to the principle of *capacité industrielle,* as applied to material control, and *capacité positive,* as applied to intellectual direction and moral surveillance.

The most important class in the Positivist society was to be the priesthood, or those distinguished by positive capacity. At the outset, it should be understood that Comte's priests were not theologians but sociologists. They were to be the scientific directors of society, selected for their special talent and their close acquaintance with those sociological principles upon which enlightened social policy depends. They were to interpret to man the religious, or, rather, the sociological, doctrines of Positivism, of which the principle was love; the basis, order; and the end, progress. Aside from special training, the priesthood must be eminent for the qualities of courage, perseverance, and prudence.

Of the organization of the Positive priesthood, which Comte describes in the most minute detail, only the most general outline can be given here. It suffices to say that there were to be some twenty thousand priests for western Europe, presided over by a High Priest of Humanity, with his headquarters at Paris. He was to be assisted by seven national chief priests, and this number was to be increased to forty-nine at the final regeneration of the world and its conversion to Positivism. The remainder of the priesthood were to be local priests and vicars attached to the local temples, which were to be distributed in the proportion of one to every ten thousand families. The priests were to be paid a fixed salary, so low as to preclude pecuniary reasons for desiring service in the profession.

It is rather difficult to say just what Comte considered the fundamental function of the priesthood, as he enumerates in various places several "supreme duties" of this class. It seems, however, that he regarded their duties, in general, as comprising the following: They were, above all, to be the systematic directors of education. They were to judge of the ability of each member of society and try, as far as possible, by means of suggestion and personal opinion, to have him placed in society according to his merits and capacities. This, Comte admits, is a rather difficult task, since one can hardly judge of the capacity of an individual until his career is well advanced, but the priesthood should do its best to arrive at a correct preliminary estimate. Again, the priests should foster the feeling of continuity between different generations and of solidarity between the different social classes by teaching men their relation to nature, to the past, and to other men. Then the priests should be the moral censors of the community, using the force of their opinion to keep men aware of their social duties and obligations and to warn them in case of deviation. Finally, they should be the fountain-spring of useful scientific knowledge and social advice. In short, the priests should constitute the ideal aristocracy of intellect, being not unlike the philosopher-kings for whom Plato had longed. In terms of our day, they would be the "brain trust" of government.

The Positivist priests would not, however, aspire to possess an iota of temporal power. It was the mixture of spiritual and temporal power which was the great defect of antiquity, and it was the great contribution of Christianity that it had separated the two. The powers of the priesthood were, instead, to be employed in the following extra-legal ways: In the first place, they were to exercise their influence through the medium of their teaching and preaching. Then they were to give a proper direction to public opinion. Again, they might express their formal condemnation of any act. Finally, they were to have a most important advisory function in all affairs of civic life. They might suggest action by the "secular arm of the law" but must never undertake such action on their own responsibility and initiative. It seems that Comte, like Jefferson before him, relied upon the assumption that the people would sufficiently admire and respect superior intellectual ability and moral integrity to insure willing submission to the guidance of the priesthood—a noble theory, but something which history has shown thus far to be very difficult to assure in practice.

The material or industrial power, as well as the actual functions of civil government, were to be divided among the employer class, subdivided into bankers, merchants, manufacturers, and agriculturists, each arranged on a hierarchical principle and all possessing *"capacité industrielle."* As the most influential and least numerous of the employer class, the bankers were to possess the most authority. The general principle of concentration of power among the employers was that there should be a single manager for as large a field of industry as one man could personally direct. While the employers would have the legal right to fix their incomes at any figure they might deem desirable, still they would be checked from excessive greed by their greater need and desire for public esteem. Moreover, it was a function of the Positivist priests to make the wealthy realize their social responsibility.

In this manner Comte hoped to assure both industrial efficiency and social justice. In their relations to their employees the leaders of industry would always keep in mind the two following principles: "that everyone at all times shall be the entire owner of everything of which he has the constant and exclusive use" and "that every industrious citizen shall be secured in the means of fully developing his domestic life."[37] As to the transmission of wealth and industrial functions, each individual would have the right to nominate his successor seven years before the date of his expected retirement and to submit this nomination to the approval of public opinion. Free testamentary disposition of wealth was to be allowed in all cases.

In the matter of moral authority in the Positivist society, Comte held that domestic morality should be guided by the women and the public morality safeguarded by the priesthood. The moral influence of woman was to be insured by the Positivist rule of indissoluble monogamous marriage and perpetual widowhood.

With respect to foreign relations in the Positivist society, Comte held that such problems would be largely eliminated upon the adoption of the Positivist religion, with its universal priesthood and its tendency to dissolve the greater nations into a host of nontyrannical city-states.

In treating individual liberty and the principles of state interference, Comte erected no constitutional barriers to tyranny. The individual had to rely upon the probability that the moral exhortations of the priesthood would be heeded by the governing class. Again, the individual had no private sphere of rights which was free in any sense from invasion by some agency of the directing power of society. Duties, rather than rights, were the central feature of Comte's political philosophy. In fact, the individual, as such, was all but ignored, and attention was centered upon the social organism. Even universal suffrage and parliamentary government were condemned. Thus Comte solved the problem of the reconciliation of sovereignty and liberty by failing to provide for any assurance of either.

In this way Comte proposed for the foundations of the state a rather curious combination of religious and intellectual idealism with benevolent, though partly nonpolitical, paternalism. This, more than anything else, separates the doctrines of Comte from those of his successor in the field of sociology—Herbert Spencer.

G. PUBLIC OPINION AND SOCIAL CONTROL

Comte laid considerable stress upon the value of public opinion as an effective agent of social control. He held that it is almost the sole guaranty of public morality, and he maintained that without an intelligently organized public opinion there could be little hope of any extended reform and reconstruction of social institutions. The requisite conditions, he says, for the proper organization of public opinion are "first, the establishment of fixed principles of social action; secondly, their adoption by the public and its consent to their application in special cases; and, lastly, a recognized organ to lay down the principles and to apply them to the conduct of daily life."[38] The workingmen's clubs, which were then flourishing in the first flush of enthusiastic beginnings (i.e., during the Revolution of 1848), Comte looked upon as likely to be one of the chief instrumentalities in getting rules of social conduct adopted by the public.

To be effective, however, public opinion must have an able and recognized organ of expression, for its spontaneous formulation and direct enunciation by the people are rarely possible or effective. Once more, Positivism could come to the rescue, with all the needed apparatus for an effective expression of public opinion. Its doctrines supplied the proper rules of social conduct. The proletariat furnished the necessary dynamic power. The priest-philosopher-sociologists of the Comtian regime offered an unrivaled organ for the intelligent expression of public opinion. All three requisite conditions for a healthy public opinion were in existence, but not yet in a proper relation to each other. The indispensable step which was needed was a "firm alliance between philosophers and proletaries."[39]

Finally, according to Comte, the influence of public opinion will probably become even greater in the future: "All views of the future condition of society, the views of practical men as well as of philosophic thinkers, agree in the belief that the principal feature of the State to which we are tending will be the increased influence which Public Opinion is destined to exercise."[40] When it has become the great regulator of society, it will eliminate revolutions and violent disputes by "substituting peaceable definition of duties."[41]

It is perfectly obvious that in a society like that designed by Comte, with its hierarchical arrangement of governmental agents and its hereditary transmission of them, there could be no such institution as the modern political party. The nearest thing that could be possible would be a group of agitators attempting to direct public opinion in some definite manner.

H. THE NATURE OF SOCIAL AND POLITICAL PROGRESS

In regard to the nature of social evolution and the laws governing its progress, Comte was about midway between the positions of Spencer and Ward, though the latter regarded him as the founder of the principle of "social telesis." Comte held, on the one hand, that the general tendencies of social evolution and the fundamental direction of progress were subject to invariable laws and confined to certain fixed stages which could not be seriously altered by human interference. At the same time, he maintained that social development might be modified and considerably hastened by the intelligent co-operation of mankind, based upon an understanding of the great laws of social evolution, that is, of Comte's philosophy of history.

All schemes of social reform, to be successful, must be in harmony with the general march of civilization and not too far ahead of the conditions of the time. It is the function of social science to gather together all the relevant facts concerning the course of social evolution in the past, so that the political and social policy of the present may accord with what seem to be the universal laws of development. While society need not passively revere the laws of social evolution but may hasten progress by intelligent action, still nothing could be more foolish than to imagine that social systems can be reconstructed in a day by drawing up a new constitution.

Comte defended his own proposals by contending that they were not his own arbitrary propositions but a statement of the lessons of history and social science as to the evolution and future state of society. Some of the more significant of Comte's remarks on the above problem are the following:

It appears, therefore, from the preceding remarks that the elementary march of civilization is unquestionably subject to a natural and invariable law which overrules all special human divergencies.....

Political science should exclusively employ itself in coordinating all the special facts relative to the progress of civilization and in reducing these to the smallest possible number of general facts, the connection of which ought to manifest the natural law of this progress, leaving for a subsequent appreciation the various causes which can modify its rapidity.....

But society does not and cannot progress in this way [i.e., by making constitutions for social reform as in the French Revolution]. The pretention of constructing off-hand in a few months, or even years, a social system, in its complete and definite shape is an extravagant chimera absolutely incompatible with the weakness of the human intellect.

A sound political system can never aim at impelling the human race, since this is moved by its proper impulse, in accordance with a law as necessary as, though more easily modified than, that of gravitation. But it does seek to facilitate human progress by enlightening it.....

There is a great difference between obeying the progress of civilization blindly and obeying it intelligently. The changes it demands take place as much in the first as in the second case; but they are longer delayed, and, above all, are only accomplished after having produced social perturbations more or less serious, according to the nature and importance of these changes. Now the disturbances of every sort, which thus arise in the body politic, may be, in great part, avoided by adopting measures based on an exact knowledge of the changes which tend to produce themselves.....

Now in order to attain this end, it is manifestly indispensable that we should know as precisely as possible, the actual tendency of civilization, so as to bring our political conduct into harmony with it.[42]

I. THE SOCIAL ENVIRONMENT AND SOCIAL AND POLITICAL THEORY

That there is a very intimate relation between the type of social and political system and the social theory of the period was one of the fundamental theses of Comte's philosophy of history. Scientific views of society could hardly be expected in the theological period. Comte states this very clearly in the following passage: "Short as is our life, and feeble as is our reason we cannot emancipate ourselves from the influence of our environment. Even the wildest dreamers reflect in their dreams the contemporary social state."[43] His best review of this point is to be found in his history of the attempts to found a scientific science of society before his own day. The bearing of the social and political ideas of his time upon Comte's writings is evident throughout his works.

J. SUMMARY OF COMTE'S SOCIAL IDEAS

Comte's sociology has been called by some writers a "prolegomenon" to the subject. Similarly, it would not be inaccurate to declare that the same relationship exists between his theory of society and the state and that of most later sociologists. The main doctrines of Comte along political and social lines which suggest subsequent developments are the following: (1) the sociological view of the state and the thesis that political activities and institutions must be studied in their wider social setting and relationships; (2) the organic theory of the society and state, later developed by Spencer, Schäffle, Lilienfeld, Fouillée, De Roberty, Worms, and others; (3) the more universal sociological doctrine that the state is not an artificial product of a rational perception of its utility but a natural product of social necessity and historic growth; (4) the theory that the only rational limits of state activity are to be determined by a study of sociological principles and not by an appeal to "natural" laws; (5) a proper recognition of the all-important function of the broader social and extra-legal methods of social control—a line which has been exploited by such writers as Professors Ross, Cooley, Giddings, and Sumner; (6) a recognition of the necessary interrelationship of measures for social amelioration, the fundamental characteristics of human nature, and the principles of sociology—a matter to which sociologists are constantly calling the attention of the social economists and philanthropists; (7) a synthetic view of the historic process through which the present social and political organization has been reached, particularly suggestive for its emphasis upon the transition of society and the state from a military to an industrial basis—a view made much of by Spencer and later writers.

Comte's immediate influence was not great, and his devoted followers were few. Except for Maximilien Littré and Comte's French disciples and Frederic Harrison and his group in England, the Positive social philosophy was not enthusiastically adopted.[44] Only a few years after the publication of the *Polity,* Darwinism made its appearance. This, together with Spencerian evolution, turned sociology either into the social

Darwinism of Gumplowicz and his school or into the much less significant field of biological analogies developed by Schäffle, Lilienfeld,
Worms, and others. Spencerian sociology lent its great prestige to the
defense of laissez faire and to the denunciation of "social telesis." French
sociology after Comte developed chiefly in the more restricted fields of
methodology, social anthropology, and social psychology.

Sociology in America was, for the first generation, based either on
Spencerianism, as with Giddings; upon the German *Klassenkampf*
doctrines, as with Small and his school; or upon the French social
psychology, as with Ross. Only Lester F. Ward took Comte seriously,
and Ward diverged so widely from Comte in his system of social
philosophy that most of his readers forgot his tribute to the Frenchman.
Finally, the well-nigh complete bourgeois domination of Western society
tended to discourage the cultivation of the doctrines of a writer so critical
of unregulated capitalism as Comte.

Whether doctrines akin to those of Comte will have any considerable
vogue in the construction of future plans of social reorganization is a
problem of prophecy and not of the history of social theory, but it seems
safe to say that no less comprehensive scheme will be adequate to the
reorganization of the social order.

Recent intellectual and social developments bearing some resemblance
to fundamental ideas of Comte have been the humanistic conception of
religion set forth by John H. Dietrich, Charles Francis Potter, and
others; the technocracy movement, which would hand economic life
over to industrial engineers; the idea that the élite should govern, which
Novicow, Mosca, and Pareto espoused and which has been adopted in
rather vulgar and insincere fashion by the Fascists; and the conception
of a managerial society, as set forth by James Burnham and others.

NOTES

1. See the brief article on this matter in the *American Journal of Sociology,* January, 1922,
pp. 510–13. For more bibliographic detail on Comte and his writings, see H. E. Barnes
and Howard Becker, *Social Thought from Lore to Science* (2 vols.; Boston, 1938), I,
xlii–xlvi.

2. See W. H. Schoff, "A Neglected Chapter in the Life of Comte," *Annals of the American Academy of Political and Social Science,* VIII, (1896), 491–508.

3. For a list of Comte's works see Maurice Defourny, *La Sociologie positiviste d'Auguste
Comte* (Louvain, 1902), pp. 19–22.

4. This point has been especially stressed by Comte himself and by G. H. Lewes and
Frederic Harrison. For a vigorous attack on the value of the *Polity* see *Annals of the American Academy of Political and Social Science,* VIII, (1896), 506.

5. Franck Alengry, *La Sociologie chez Auguste Comte* (Paris, 1900), pp. 389 ff., 435–76; Defourny, *op. cit.*, pp. 350–54; Henri Michel, *L'Idée de l'état* (Paris, 1896), pp. 451–58. For studies of Comte's thought see Littré, *Auguste Comte et la philosophie positive* (Paris, 1863); Depuy, *Le Positivisme d'Auguste Comte* (Paris, 1911); Lucien Lévy-Bruhl, *The Philosophy of Auguste Comte* (New York, 1903); G. H. Lewes, *Comte's Philosophy of the Sciences* (London, 1853); Edward Caird, *The Social Philosophy and Religion of Comte* (Glasgow, 1885); A. Roux, *La Pensée d'Auguste Comte* (Paris, 1920); and Herman Gruber, *Comte der Begründer des Positivismus* (Freiburg, 1889).

6. An excellent attempt to estimate Comte's contribution to social science has been made in French by Defourny, *op. cit.*, and Alengry, *op. cit.* A more special treatment of his political theories is attempted by Fezensac, *Le Système politique d'Auguste Comte;* and by L. Chiappini, *Les Idées politiques d'Auguste Comte* (Paris, 1913). In Germany we have Heinrich Waestig, *Auguste Comte und seine Bedeutung für Socialwissenschaft* (1894). For one of the latest treatments see McQuilkin DeGrange, *The Curve of Societal Movement* (Hanover, 1930).

7. Cf. F. W. Coker, *Organismic Theories of the State* (New York, 1910), pp. 123–24; cf. also L. T. Hobhouse, *Social Evolution and Political Theory* (New York, 1913), p. 204.

8. Harriet Martineau, *The Positive Philosophy of Comte*, I, 1–3, and III, *passim;* see also L. T. Hobhouse in *Sociological Review*, I, 262–79. Comte possessed almost as great a love for triads as did Vico. Thus he finds three stages of intellectual progress, three divisions of cerebral functions, three types of social forces, three grades of society, three social classes, three stages of religion, and three classes of regulating power in society.

9. *Polity*, IV, 157.

10. *Philosophie positive*, IV, 17 ff., 578–87; *Polity*, III, 44–45 and *passim*. Cf. W. A. Dunning, *Political Theories from Rousseau to Spencer* (New York, 1920), pp. 393–94: "Whatever addition it may receive, and whatever corrections it may require, this analysis of social evolution will continue to be regarded as one of the greatest achievements of the human intellect." For a recent scholarly treatment see Alexander Marcuse, *Die Geschichts-Philosophie Auguste Comtes* (Berlin, 1932). A. W. Benn, with undue enthusiasm, declares it the best sketch of universal history ever written (*Modern Philosophy* [New York, 1913], p. 156).

11. *Polity*, II, 241.

12. *Ibid.*, p. 224; cf. also *Philosophie positive*, IV, 485–95.

13. *Polity*, II, 241.

14. *Ibid.*, pp. 153, 183; cf. also *Philosophie positive*, IV, 447–69.

15. *Polity*, II, 153.

16. *Ibid.*, p. 183.

17. *Ibid.*, p. 246.

18. *Ibid.*, p. 247.

19. *Ibid.*, p. 249.

20. *Ibid.*, p. 251. This independence of the church is possible only when its realm of domination is more extensive than that of the political group (*ibid.*, pp. 252–53).

21. Cf. Friedrich Dittman, "Die Geschichtsphilosophie Comtes und Hegels, ein Vergleich," *Vierteljahrsschrift für wissenschaftliche Philosophie*, XXXVIII, 281–312; XXXIX, 38–81.

22. One should look for Comte's philosophy of history not exclusively in the last volumes of his *Philosophy* but in the third volume of his *Polity*, for he himself tells the reader (*Polity*, III, 5) that his complete theory is to be found only in that volume. For Comte's most compact summary of his philosophy of history see the *Polity*, III, 421–22; see also Marcuse, *op. cit.*

23. *Polity*, III, 305–6.

24. *Ibid.*, p. 307.

25. *Ibid.*, p. 353.

26. Caird, *op. cit.*, p. 35. For Robert Flint's rather unsympathetic treatment of Comte's philosophy of history see his *History of the Philosophy of History in France* (London, 1894), pp. 575–615.

27. On Comte's views of sovereignty see René Millet, *La Souveraineté d'après Auguste Comte* (Paris, 1905).

28. *Polity,* I, 106–10.

29. *The Philosophy of Auguste Comte,* pp. 320–21.

30. *Ibid.,* pp. 328–29.

31. *Ibid.,* p. 329.

32. *Ibid.,* p. 331.

33. *Ibid.,* p. 329.

34. *Polity,* II, 291.

35. *Ibid.,* p. 292.

36. *Ibid.,* p. 266. There are here certain anticipations of the modern sociopolitical theory of the functional reorganization of the state (cf. F. Pecant, "Auguste Comte et Durkheim," *Revue de métaphysique et de morale,* October–December, 1921, pp. 64 ff.). For an exposition of Comte's social program see H. D. Hutton, *Comte's Theory of Man's Future* (London, 1877).

37. *Polity,* II, 334–35.

38. *Ibid.,* p. 112.

39. *Ibid.,* pp. 117–20.

40. *Ibid.,* p. 110.

41. *Ibid.,* p. 120.

42. *Ibid.,* IV, 536, 558–60. For Ward's appreciation of Comte's anticipation of the doctrine of social telesis see *Dynamic Sociology* (2 vols.; New York, 1883), I, 137.

43. *Philosophie positive,* II, 11; cited by L. M. Bristol in *Social Adaptation* (Cambridge, 1915), p. 12.

44. Cf. J. E. McGee, *A Crusade for Humanity: The History of Organized Positivism in England* (London, 1931).

CHAPTER IV

HERBERT SPENCER AND THE EVOLUTIONARY DEFENSE OF INDIVIDUALISM

Harry Elmer Barnes

I. GENERAL NATURE OF SPENCER'S PHILOSOPHICAL AND SOCIOLOGICAL SYSTEM

A. LIFE AND WORKS

COMTE'S work in the field of sociology was taken up and greatly amplified by the philosopher who, better than anyone else, summed up the main currents of nineteenth-century social thought, Herbert Spencer (1820–1903). This does not mean that Spencer regarded Comte as his scientific precursor. In fact, quite the opposite was the case, for Spencer published his first sociological treatise, *Social Statics,* before he had any detailed knowledge of Comte's ideas, and it seems that in many respects the similarity between the two writers was accidental. On the other hand, it is hard to agree entirely with Spencer in his attempt to prove his complete independence of Comte and his fundamental divergence from the views of the latter.[1] Rather, it would be almost as accurate to accept the verdict of Henri Michel: "It does not follow that the *Principles of Sociology* can actually be regarded as an original book by anyone who has read the *Opuscules* [i.e., the early essays] of Comte. All the leading ideas, and even the method, of Spencer are to be seen in the *Opuscules.* Comte traced the outlines: Spencer only filled them in."[2]

A child of feeble health, Spencer was taught at home and never received any public education. In this aspect of home training he resembled his famous contemporary, John Stuart Mill. His failure to follow a university career doubtless tended to contribute strongly to the refusal of formal academic circles in England to take a lively interest in Spencer's teachings; and his lack of a properly socialized existence in early life certainly had not a little to do with his individualistic tendencies as an adult. Aside from these more strictly personal elements,

Spencer's nonconformist inheritance from his family and his reaction against the radical revolutionary doctrines of his youth are matters which must be taken into consideration when attempting to get an insight into the sources of his philosophic tendencies and an understanding of his intellectual predispositions.[3]

Spencer early acquired a taste for mechanics, and in 1837 he became chief engineer of the London and Birmingham Railroad. He resigned from this position in 1848 to become subeditor of the *Economist;* and during the four years that he served in this capacity he produced (1850) his first important contribution to sociology, *Social Statics.* During the next eight years he developed the basic principles of his system of synthetic philosophy and published them in the *First Principles* in 1863. No one can understand Spencer's philosophy if he has not read this work, any more than one can appreciate Comte's fundamental ideas if one has not read his early essays.

In this volume Spencer disposed of metaphysical theology by relegating it to the realm of the ultimately unknowable; he outlined his theory of universal evolution; and he indicated the main lines of its application to the totality of human knowledge. He did not, as has frequently been asserted, attempt to apply the theories of Darwin to a restatement of science and philosophy. Rather, he applied to this field his own theory of evolution, which had been formulated prior to, and independent of, that of Darwin and was built upon a thoroughly distinct, though compatible, set of fundamental propositions.[4]

B. SPENCER'S PHILOSOPHY OF SOCIETY

This is not the place to attempt to pass final judgment upon the merits of Spencer's system as a whole. It certainly suggested the general line of approach to modern scientific knowledge, which seems, on the whole, essentially correct, namely, the evolutionary viewpoint, however much of Spencer's particular view of evolution may fail to bear the test of later and more specialized inductive and quantitative studies. Again, it is quite safe to say that his system represents one of the most impressive products of a single human mind since the time of Aristotle. Further, there can be little doubt that, for innate mental productivity, Spencer is quite unequaled among modern writers. It requires a remarkable man, for instance, to produce Wundt's treatises on psychology, in which the author seems to have had a good acquaintance with every important work on his special subject. But, though such a work may be infinitely more valuable from a scientific point of view, it requires less genius to produce it than it did for Spencer to create the *Principles of Psychology* from the recesses of his own mind, after having read less formal psychology than the average elementary-school teacher in an American public school.

In short, whatever in Spencer's system may be destroyed by subsequent scientific progress—and it seems that much of it has even now passed into the realm of rhetoric—still he may claim the distinguished honor of having placed nearly all the phases of scientific study upon the road to further progress by making their guiding principle the concept of evolution. The late William Graham Sumner has well stated the significance of Spencer's establishment of the evolutionary principle in social science:

> Mr. Spencer addressed himself at the outset of his literary career to topics of sociology. In the pursuit of those topics he found himself forced to seek constantly more fundamental and wider philosophical doctrines. He came at last to the fundamental principles of the evolution philosophy. He then extended, tested, confirmed, and corrected these principles by inductions from other sciences, and so finally turned again to sociology, armed with the scientific method which he had acquired. To win a powerful and correct method is, as we all know, to win more than half the battle. When so much is secure, the question of making the discoveries, solving the problems, eliminating the errors, and testing the results, is only a question of time and of strength to collect and master the data.[5]

The natural and social sciences were thus rescued from the retrospective and obscurantic tendencies with which they had been struggling more or less hopelessly ever since patristic theology had shackled induction and empiricism by reliance upon ecclesiastical authority and justification by faith and by opposition to the discovery of any scientific facts subversive of the tenets of accepted "truth."[6]

As Spencer's whole system of social science was built upon his general laws of evolution, it is essential to understand the fundamental propositions involved in his doctrines on this point. This is incomparably more important in Spencer's sociology than his development of the organic analogy, though most expositors and critics of his sociology have dwelt mainly upon the latter.

Spencer's laws of universal evolution are found in their complete development in the second part of his *First Principles*. In the first place, he finds three fundamental truths or propositions. Of these, the basic one is the law of the persistence of force, which means the existence and persistence of some ultimate cause which transcends knowledge. The two other principles are the indestructibility of matter and the continuity of motion, both being derived from the principle of the persistence of force. There are, in turn, four secondary propositions. The first is the persistence of the relations among forces, or the uniformity of law. The second is the transformation and equivalence of forces, namely, that force is never lost but is merely transformed. The third is the law that everything moves along the line of least resistance or of greatest attraction. The fourth and final law is that of the rhythm or alternation of motion.

To render this system complete, some law must be found which will govern the combination of these different factors in the evolutionary process. This need is supplied by the law that, with the integration of matter, motion is dissipated and, with the differentiation of matter, motion is absorbed. As a result, the process of evolution is characterized by a passage from an incoherent homogeneity to a coherent and co-ordinated heterogeneity. From these foundations, Spencer summarizes his complete law of universal evolution as follows: "Evolution is an integration of matter and a concomitant dissipation of motion during which the matter passes from a relatively indefinite, incoherent homogeneity to a relatively coherent heterogeneity and during which the retained motion undergoes a parallel transformation."

When we add to this basic foundation of his evolutionary system such important corollaries as the instability of the homogeneous, due to the incidence of unlike forces; the spread of differentiating factors in a geometrical ratio; the tendency of differentiated parts to become segregated through a clustering of like units; and the final limit of all the processes of evolution in an ultimate equilibrium, Spencer's system of evolution stands complete in outline. As the reverse of evolution stands dissolution, in which the achievements of evolution are undone through a reversal of the stages in the process.[7]

Spencer briefly applied this evolutionary formula to all phenomena in the remaining portion of his *First Principles,* and the application to social processes therein to be found is the vital portion of Spencer's sociological system. The detailed expansion of this preliminary outline found in the *First Principles* constitutes Spencer's system of "Synthetic Philosophy."

Spencer's formal treatment of sociology, aside from the outline of his system in the *First Principles,* is to be found in the *Study of Sociology* —a sort of prolegomenon to the subject and still an indispensable introduction—and in the three large volumes of the *Principles of Sociology.* While Spencer gave an excellent summary of his whole philosophical system, he failed to present a succinct digest of his sociological theory. Professor Giddings attempted to supply this need and performed the task in a manner satisfactory to Spencer. His lucid and comprehensive summary follows:

Societies are organisms or they are super-organic aggregates.

Between societies and environing bodies, as between other finite aggregates in nature, there is an equilibration of energy. There is an equilibration between society and society, between one social group and another, between one social class and another.

Equilibration between society and society, between societies and their environment, takes the form of a struggle for existence among societies. Conflict becomes an habitual activity of society.

In this struggle for existence fear of the living and of the dead arises. Fear of the living, supplementing conflict, becomes the root of political control. Fear of the dead becomes the root of religious control.

Organized and directed by political and religious control, habitual conflict becomes militarism. Militarism moulds character and conduct and social organization into fitness for habitual warfare.

Militarism combines small social groups into larger ones, these into larger and yet larger ones. It achieves social integration. This process widens the area within which an increasingly large proportion of the population is habitually at peace and industrially employed.

Habitual peace and industry mould character, conduct, and social organization into fitness for peaceful, friendly, sympathetic life.

In the peaceful type of society coercion diminishes, spontaneity and individual initiative increase. Social organization becomes plastic, and individuals moving freely from place to place change their social relations without destroying social cohesion, the elements of which are sympathy and knowledge in place of primitive force.

The change from militarism to industrialism depends upon the extent of the equilibration of energy between any given society and its neighboring societies, between the societies of any given race and those of other races, between society in general and its physical environment. Peaceful industrialism cannot finally be established until the equilibrium of nations and of races is established.

In society, as in other finite aggregates, the extent of the differentiation and the total complexity of all the evolutionary processes depend upon the rate at which integration proceeds. The slower the rate the more complete and satisfactory is the evolution.[8]

Better known than Spencer's interpretation of society in terms of the laws of evolution, though not so vitally connected with his system, is his development of the analogy between society and an organism. This analogy was by no means original with Spencer, as it is to be found in Plato, Aristotle, Paul, and many of the early Christian Fathers. It was common throughout the Middle Ages and had later been considerably elaborated, among others by Comte, Krause, and Ahrens. It was reserved for Spencer, however, to present the first systematic development of the theory.[9]

Spencer enumerates six fundamental similarities between society and an organism. First, both differ from inorganic matter through an augmentation of mass and visible growth during the greater part of their existence. Second, as both increase in size, they increase in complexity of structure. Third, progressive differentiation of structure in both is accompanied by a like differentiation of functions. Fourth, evolution establishes in both society and animal organisms not only differences, but definitely related differences, of such a character as to make both possible. Fifth, the analogy between society and an organism is still more evident when it is recognized that, conversely, every organism is a society. Finally, in both society and the organism the life of the aggregate may be destroyed, but the units will continue to live on for a time.

On the other hand, there are three important differences to be noted between society and the organism. In the first place, whereas in the individual organism the component parts form a concrete whole and the living units are bound together in close contact, in the social organism the component parts form a discrete whole and the living units are free and more or less dispersed. Again, and even more fundamental, whereas in the individual organism there is such a differentiation of functions that some parts become the seat of feeling and thought and others are practically insensitive, in the social organism no such differentiation exists; there is no social mind or sensorium apart from the individuals that make up the society. As a result of this second difference, there is to be observed the third distinction, namely, that, while in the organism the units exist for the good of the whole, in society the whole exists for the good of the members.[10]

Another important phase of Spencer's biological interpretation of society was his famous theory of population trends, first set forth in 1852. He maintained that there is a fundamental antagonism between "individuation" and "genesis." As civilization became more complex, an ever larger portion of the available physiological energy of the race is exhausted in the activities associated with personal development and expression. Hence less energy remains available for reproductive interests and activities. In short, advanced and mature civilizations seem to be unfavorable to high fecundity. This doctrine was an implied criticism of Malthusianism. Adopted by Henry C. Carey in the United States, it was exploited to counteract the pessimism of the social philosophy of Malthus and the Classical Economists.

These two fundamental theories of society—the evolutionary and the organic—comprise the major theoretical contributions of Spencer to sociology. His remaining voluminous works on sociology are primarily descriptive, though in many cases they present a keen analysis of social processes.

Just how Spencer's sociological system will rank in the future, when more refined statistical and ethnological studies permit the general body of sociological theory to assume something like a final form, it is difficult to say. It seems safe to hold that, as a physical interpretation of society, his system will remain, in general outline, the final statement of the subject. The organic analogy will doubtless be accepted as an interesting bit of figurative description but will be discarded as possessing little value as an explanation of social processes. How much will remain of his historical sociology can hardly be estimated at present. Already the researches of the more critical ethnologists, like Professor Ehrenreich in Germany, Professors Durkheim, Hubert, and Mauss in France, Professors Rivers and Marett in England, and Professor Boas and his disciples in America, have challenged in drastic fashion the almost mechanical evolutionary systems of the classical school of anthropology, of which Spencer was one of the most thoroughgoing exponents. One can no longer hold with Professor T. N. Carver that not to have read Spencer's *Principles of Sociology* imposes a handicap greater than would result from the neglect of any other treatise.[11] Still it will probably be accurate to say that, viewed from the standpoint of the historical development of sociology, Spencer's contribution was one of the most far-reaching in its influence that has yet been made. Professor A. W. Small has admirably summarized the significance of Spencer's position, particularly as set forth in the *Principles of Sociology*:

Spencer's scheme is an attempt to give name, and place, and importance to the meaning factors in human association. It is not a system of speculative conceptions.

It is an attempt to represent in language the literal facts of society in the relations in which they actually occur in real life. It is a device by means of which, in proportion as it is adapted to its purpose, we should be able more truly, more comprehensively, and more profoundly to understand, for instance, the life of the people of the United States, than we could without the aid of such description. The fair test is, not to ask whether this scheme leaves nothing in the way of social exposition to be desired, but whether it lays bare more of essential truth about society than is visible without such an interpretation; not whether there is a remainder to be explained, but whether more appears in the confusion of everyday life than is discovered before it is seen in terms of these symbols. Judged by this test the Spencerian scheme is certainly an approach to truth.[12]

II. SPENCER'S LEADING SOCIAL AND POLITICAL THEORIES

A. THE RELATION OF SOCIOLOGY TO POLITICAL SCIENCE AND THE STUDY OF THE STATE

As regards the relation of sociology to political science, Spencer differed from Comte in holding that the special social sciences are distinct, but co-ordinated, branches of sociology and that, as such, they are legitimate bodies of science. However, his differentiation between the scope of sociology and that of the special social sciences was not clearly worked out. His summary of the relation of sociology to political science and of the legitimate treatment of political problems by sociology, as presented in his chapter on "The Scope of Sociology" in the *Study of Sociology,* covered completely the field now generally allotted to political science, though with a distinctly sociological orientation. He says here:

Sociology has next to describe and explain the rise and development of that political organization which in several ways regulates affairs, which combines the actions of individuals for purposes of tribal or national offence or defense; and which restrains them in certain of their dealings with one another, as also in certain of their dealings with themselves. It has to trace the relations of this coordinating and controlling apparatus, to the area occupied, to the amount and distribution of population, and to the means of communication. It has to show the differences of form which this agency presents in different social types, nomadic and settled, militant and industrial. It has to describe the changing relations between this regulating structure which is unproductive, and those structures which carry on production. It has also to set forth the connexions between, and the reciprocal influences of, the institutions carrying on civil government, and other governmental institutions simultaneously developing the ecclesiastical and the ceremonial. And then it has to take account of those modifications which persistent political restraints are ever working in the character of the social units, as well as the modifications worked by the reaction of these changed characters on the political organization.[13]

This is an excellent outline of what might constitute a sociological survey, if not a complete sociological theory, of the state. Spencer's fulfilment of this task in the section of his *Principles of Sociology* dealing with "Political Institutions" and in numerous essays and parts of other works was doubtless one of the most extensive treatments of political problems that any sociologist, with the possible exception of Gumplowicz and Ratzenhofer, has attempted.

Spencer seems to have distinguished in a fairly definite manner between the concepts of society and of state, though he makes no attempt at a formal treatment of this somewhat academic subject. He unquestionably regards the state as society, politically organized. He conceives of the state as that conscious organization of co-operative activity in a society which concerns the group as a whole. "Political organization," he says, "is to be understood as that part of social organization which consciously carries on directive and restraining functions for public ends."[14]

Thus, Spencer does not make the state coextensive with society or a further refinement of society but simply regards it as society when organized as a political unit. Society, as a whole, is supported by two types of co-operation: spontaneous private co-operation, which is concerned with matters that do not affect the group as a unit except in indirect ways; and the "consciously devised" co-operation which deals with the public activities of the group as a totality. It is only the latter that directly creates and supports the state.

He does not, however, distinguish so clearly between the state and the government—something that is hard for an Englishman to do, since in England legal sovereignty and the lawmaking power reside in the same body. At the same time, it seems reasonably clear that Spencer would have defined government as the particular form which the political organization may assume at any time or place, in other words, the correct notion of the government as the mechanism of administration. Speaking in terms of the organic analogy, the state is the system which has for its function the regulation of the social organism; the organs which perform this function are known as the "government." As to the distinction between the terms "state" and "nation," it seems that Spencer used the word "nation" as meaning the state in its objective political and geographic aspects—the conventional use of the term, though not the connotation given to it by the strict terminology of political science.

Spencer agrees with the usual conception as to what constitutes the fundamental attributes of the state, so far as territory, population, and governmental organization are concerned, but he balks at the notion of an unlimited sovereign authority. To an arch-individualist like Spencer, the conception of an irresistible power in society, against which the individual had no legal right of resistance, was most repugnant. Hobbes, Bentham, and Austin are as scathingly attacked by Spencer as Blackstone was by Bentham: "Analyze his assumption, and the doctrine of Austin proves to have no better basis than that of Hobbes. In the absence of admitted divine descent or appointment, neither single-headed ruler nor many-headed ruler can produce such credentials as the claim to unlimited sovereignty implies."[15]

Natural or, perhaps better, individual rights rather than sovereignty were the cornerstone of Spencer's political theory. But individual rights, as conceived by Spencer, are neither those which are assumed by metaphysical ethics nor those artificial rights conferred by a governmental agent. They are those indispensable rights which must be guaranteed to an individual so that society may exist and function properly. Such a doctrine of natural rights is perfectly valid and is not, as Ernest Barker intimates, entirely incompatible with the doctrine of a social organism. It is chiefly the excessive extent of these natural rights insisted upon by Spencer which may be called in question rather than the theoretical aspects of the problem.

C. THE FOUNDATIONS AND JUSTIFICATION OF POLITICAL AUTHORITY

The question of the origin of the state and the government Spencer treats both analytically and historically. In both senses the immediate basis of political control and that which has made its existence possible through the ages is the "fear of the living," in the same way that the "fear of the dead" is the foundation of religious control.[16] Of course, this fundamental distinction is not perfect, for in some cases political control is furthered by the fear of the dead, as when a chief is believed to be able to control the ghosts of his ancestors; and, likewise, the fear of the existing ecclesiastical hierarchy is an important element in effective religious control. But, in general, this must be admitted to be a valid principle of differentiation.

In an analytical sense the state and the government arise because society cannot function adequately without them. A society is not established by the mere physical contiguity of a mass of individuals. It is constituted only when there is an organized system of co-operation among these units. The state and government not only supply one of the two great types of co-operation, that which controls the group as a whole in relation to public ends, but they also promote the development of private co-operation. They eliminate the conflict among individuals and increase the size of the group in which co-operation may exist. The larger the group, the greater the amount of division of labor and specialization that is possible. In like manner, legal rights and their enforcement find their philosophical justification in the fact that only under political protection can society continue its existence and function properly. Speaking in terms of the organic analogy, the explanation of the state is identical in principle, since in any perfected organism there must be a potent regulating system in order to insure the proper functioning of the sustaining and distributing systems.

The structure of government, similarly, is easily amenable to analysis. There is a natural triune structure, due to the inherent differences in mankind. Whether one examines a primitive tribe or a modern state, the organization for governmental purposes falls into three classes: (1) the *leader;* (2) the small minority of able and distinguished men, i.e., the *consulting body;* (3) the vast mass of inexperienced and mediocre citizens, who simply listen to, and agree with or dissent from, the acts and opinions of the leader and the council, i.e., the *representative body.* Despotism, oligarchy, and democracy simply reflect the undue prominence of one of these three components of government. The great force lying behind political power and the particular structures through which it is manifested is "the feeling of the community." This is based, to a certain degree, upon the reaction of the community to present problems, but it depends to a far greater extent upon the social heritage which is crystallized into custom and tradition. Political organization is simply the public agency for applying this "feeling of the community." This unconscious fear of the dead (the "dead hand"), which is the psychological content of custom, thus aids the fear of the living in maintaining political control. This notion Spencer sums up in the following manner:

We are familiar with the thought of the "dead hand" as controlling the doings of the living in the use made of property; but the effect of the "dead hand" in ordering life at large through the established political system is immeasurably greater. That which, from hour to hour in every country, governed despotically or otherwise, produces the obedience making political action possible, is the accumulated and organized sentiment felt towards inherited institutions made sacred by tradition.[17]

D. THE HISTORICAL EVOLUTION OF SOCIAL AND POLITICAL INSTITUTIONS

Spencer's account of the historical evolution of social and political organization is very elaborate, but his conclusions are open to the same degree of skepticism as is his generalized account of the evolution of institutions. His method was one—that of the classical anthropologists —which is now abandoned by most scholarly and critical ethnologists at the present time. From his voluminous *Descriptive Sociology* he would gather together illustrative material bearing upon the evolution of any particular institution, regardless of the relation of that particular practice to the whole cultural complex of the social groups from which the information was drawn or of the different stages of culture which contributed evidence in support of his thesis. The Shoshonean Indians and the Italian cities at the time of the Renaissance might thus be offered as supporting evidence for a particular process or "stage" in social evolution. The mass of material offered to the reader, its seeming comprehensiveness, as apparently drawn from all parts of the world and from all ages, and the incomparable logical skill with which Spencer marshaled his evidence, all tended for years to make Spencer's historical sociology the *sine qua non* of the subject.[18]

The application of more refined methods in ethnology and the cumulative evidence from intensive original investigation of cultural areas by competent ethnologists have, however, tended to call in question many of Spencer's generalizations. Aside from his faulty methodology, the general assumptions of the classical school of anthropology, of which he was a prominent member, regarding the universality of cultural traits and the orderly progress of institutional evolution have been seriously challenged by later investigations. It is now rather generally conceded by ethnologists that it requires about four specialists competently to investigate any particular cultural area, to say nothing of attempting to survey the whole course of social evolution. An accurate historical sociology can be written only in that distant future when reliable monographs by specialists have summarized what ethnologists and cultural historians have discovered regarding particular areas and special periods. Nevertheless, it is doubtful whether anyone could have reached better logical conclusions by the use of Spencer's methods, and the healthy skepticism which one may entertain regarding his conclusions should not prevent one from having the highest respect for the constructive logic and the brilliant fertility of imagination displayed in Spencer's history of society.

Spencer's main conclusions regarding the evolution of social and political organization may be summarized about as follows: At the outset, society may be assumed to have existed as undifferentiated and unorganized hordes. The beginning of public authority and political organization was the temporary submission of the group to a leader in time of war. The natural prowess of this leader in war was often supplemented by his supposed power to control ghosts and obtain their aid, thus bringing a supernatural sanction to his rule.

In due course of time, with the increasing complexity of society, the more frequent periods of warfare, and the better organization of military activity, this temporary war leader evolved into the chief or king, who held his power for life. In turn, the difficulties and disorder which occurred at the death of a leader and during the period of the choice of a successor tended to establish the principle of hereditary leadership. In this manner stability and permanence of leadership were provided for. Along with this development of the ruler went the parallel evolution of the consultative and representative bodies. At first merely spontaneous bodies meeting in times of necessity, they later evolved into formal senates and assemblies.

The processes of integration and differentiation are exhibited in the development of political organization, as well as in evolution in general. The long period of military activity which characterized the earlier stages of political evolution brought about the consolidation of the petty primitive groups and their respective territory. Because the best-organized groups tended to win in the intergroup struggle, the integration of society and the extension of the range of power of the successful state was a cumulative process. Along with the integration of political authority, both in the scope of its application and in the expansion of the area of control, there went a corresponding increase in differentiation and co-ordination. The differentiation in society, which begins in the family, is extended through the periods of conquest that characterize early political progress, until it has created the classes of wealthy rulers, ordinary freemen, serfs, and slaves. As political power becomes concentrated in a definite ruling class and is increased in scope and applied over a larger territory, it has to be delegated in order to be administered with efficiency. All the vast machinery of modern government, with its ministeries; its local governing agencies; its judicial, revenue, and military systems, is but the further differentiation and co-ordination of the earlier fundamental organs of government, manifested in the simple triune structure of chief, council, and assembly.

The state, at first, centers all its attention upon military organization, conquest, and territorial aggrandizement; but, as time goes on, its concern is turned more and more toward the development of industry. From this moment onward, the process of political evolution becomes a transformation of the military state into the industrial state. This process is still under way. The purely industrial state, however, is not the final goal of social evolution. The ultimate stage to be hoped for is one in which the resources of a developed industrialism may be turned toward the perfection of human character in the higher and more truly socialized aspects of moral conduct, thus bringing into being the ethical state.

Despite his elaborate treatment of the origin and development of the different branches of political organization, Spencer nowhere gives a clear picture of the evolution of the state and sovereign power as a related whole, and this failure doubtless contributed in a large degree to making Spencer unable to grasp and concede the real significance of the state.

E. FORMS OF THE STATE AND THE GOVERNMENT

In his treatment of the forms of the state, Spencer discards for political analysis the conventional classification of states and devotes his attention to a classification based upon the end toward which organized political society functions. Spencer finds that political society has functioned for two specific ends in the course of history—military aggression and industrial development. Comte had suggested such a differentiation, though he had more accurately interpolated a critical and revolutionary period between the primarily military and the primarily industrial eras. These two periods, while sharply differentiated in principle, tend to overlap in a historical sense. The present era, while beginning to be primarily industrial, still contains only too many survivals from the military regime.[19] Nevertheless, close analysis reveals the fact that each of these systems is characterized by a definite set of principles and produces a type of character in its citizens which is almost diametrically opposed to that which is found in the other.

In the militant type of society, unified action is necessary, and all must take their part in this activity. All the energies of the society are devoted to the furthering of military efficiency, since those who cannot fight are busily engaged in providing supplies for the warrior class. The individual is thus completely subordinated to society through the despotic governmental organization which is essential to produce this highly specialized adjustment of society to military activity.

To secure a proper administration of this despotic control over a large area and a considerable population, there must be a thorough regimentation of society, extending from the ruler to the humblest subject. The regulation administered by this despotic and bureaucratic system is both positive and negative. This system of regimentation develops a rigidity in society, owing to the enforced specialization, which makes it difficult for the individual to change his place in society. In fact, the position of the individual in the military era is merely one of status. In order to secure economic independence, so valuable in time of war, the society pursues a vigorous policy of protectionism. Since success in war is the supreme aim of society, bravery and strength are made the chief moral qualities toward which the ambitious individual may aspire. A selfish patriotism that regards the triumph of the particular group or nation as the chief end of social activity is the dominating sentiment in the militant state. The deadening influence of bureaucratic officialdom lessens individual initiative, fosters the belief that universal governmental activity is indispensable, and blinds society to the conception of the evolutionary factors in progress and social evolution.

The industrial type of society is not to be distinguished from the militant solely by the amount of industry which is being carried on, as militant states may be very industrious. Neither can it be completely characterized by having as its chief end the development of industry, for socialistic and communistic states also pretend to aim at this goal. Rather, the industrial type of society is one which combines the goal of industrial development with absolute freedom of individual initiative within the limits of order and equity. In the industrial type of society there is no longer any all-pervading compulsory political activity; the small amount of such discipline that is retained is designed merely to prevent unnecessary interference with individual initiative and freedom. For this type of society a representative, and not a despotic, government is required, and the function of such a government is to administer justice or, in other words, to see that each member of society gets a reward which is directly proportionate to, and resultant upon, his efforts.

The government, instead of being both positively and negatively regulative, as in the militant state, is now only negatively regulative. The position of the individual changes from one of status to one of contract. Individual activity and voluntary co-operation are encouraged. Society in the industrial regime is plastic and easily adaptable to change. Finally, since there is no longer any need of economic self-sufficiency, the rigid protectionist policy must break down, and the economic barriers of nationality tend gradually to be dissolved. A regional form of government, or a federation of governments, may be looked forward to as the goal of political organization. As to the reaction of the industrial era upon the traits of society, patriotism tends to become more refined, society loses its faith in the infallible efficacy of governmental interference, and individuality becomes stronger, more self-assertive, and mutually respectful of rights. Though industrialism is still only very imperfectly realized, it should not be assumed to be the final goal of social evolution. A new era, primarily devoted to the development of man's ethical nature, may be hoped for after the industrial regime has been perfected. The final or ultimate form of social and political organization, then, is the ethical state.

Spencer does not devote any considerable space to the question of the forms of government. His detailed account of the evolution of "political forms" is mainly concerned with an analysis of the development of what are usually known as the "departments" of government. Spencer claims, however, that a close relation exists between these departments of government and the different forms of government, for he revives the old classical doctrine that monarchy is a government characterized by the undue predominance of the single leader; oligarchy a type in which the council is abnormally prominent; and democracy that in which the representative factor has become disproportionately powerful. Though Spencer grants the existence of these three types of government, he really believes that there are only two pure forms—monarchy and representative government, meaning by the latter, democracy.

Between these two extremes, which are based upon the contradictory assumptions that society should obey the will of one individual and that its members should be governed by their own wills, there are a number of different grades of mixed governments. While these mixed forms of government are absurd from the standpoint of logic, they are good enough in practice, as their incongruities agree with those of a society in transition from the rigid military state to the plastic industrial state: "Nevertheless, though these mixed governments, combining as they do two mutually destructive hypotheses, are utterly irrational in principle, they must of necessity exist, so long as they are in harmony with the mixed constitution of the partially adapted man."[20]

Democracy, Spencer defines as "a political organization modelled in accordance with the law of equal freedom."[21] Or, again, he describes it as "a system which, by making the nation at large a deliberative body, and reducing the legislative assembly to an executive, carries self-government to the fullest extent compatible with the existence of a ruling power."[22]

While granting that monarchy and despotism had their historical function, Spencer was wholly in favor of democracy in any society in which the citizens have reached a sufficiently high level of moral and intellectual development to be intrusted with the administration of this type of government. Not every society is fitted for the maintenance of a democratic government. Conduct has to be ruled either by internal or by external restraint; hence, among those people whose moral sense has not been sufficiently developed to furnish an adequate internal restraint, a democracy is out of place and a more coercive type is needed. Not only must there be a high moral sense among the citizens to make democracy practicable, but there must also be a sufficient degree of intelligence and a high enough estimation of the value of freedom to make the citizens alert in detecting infringements upon their liberty and capable in use of the franchise. When such conditions exist, democracy is the ideal type of government. In no case should one put faith in a particular type of government as such. The best is out of place and likely to fail except among a people whose national character fits them by experience for such a form:

Anyone who looks through these facts and facts akin to them for the truth they imply may see that forms of government are valuable only where they are products of national character. No cunningly devised political arrangements will of themselves do anything. No amount of knowledge respecting the uses of such arrangements will suffice. Nothing will suffice but the emotional nature to which such arrangements are adapted—a nature which during social progress has evolved the arrangements.[23]

F. SOVEREIGNTY, LIBERTY, AND THE SOCIOLOGICAL THEORY OF POLITICAL RIGHTS

For the doctrine of legal sovereignty Spencer had little respect. The whole conception was repugnant to his mind. Consequently, he avoided any attempt to trace its origin or to define its attributes. His main concern was to dispute the tenets of the upholders of the doctrine and to establish logical and historical grounds for justifying limitations upon sovereignty.

Spencer was willing to admit that there is such a thing as what Dicey calls "political sovereignty," but he claimed that some higher justification of submission to authority must be discovered. To this quest he devotes the last essay in *Man versus the State,* which he entitles "The Great Political Superstition," meaning by this the doctrine of the sovereignty of the legislature, which had supplanted the outgrown doctrine of the sovereignty of the monarch. In order to find theoretical justification for the submission of the minority to the majority, Spencer formulated the hypothetical question as to just what type of agreement to co-operate the majority of the citizens would enter into with a considerable degree of unanimity. This reminds one of Rousseau's famous problem of establishing political authority and at the same time preserving the liberty of the individual.

Spencer finds, in answer to his query, that practically all would agree to co-operate in defending their territory against external aggression and in protecting their persons and property against internal violence and fraud. To this extent, then, the submission of the minority is valid and legitimate; beyond this point such submission is unjust and illegitimate.

A hypothetical contract thus replaces the old doctrine of an actual contract as the solution of the problem of reconciling liberty and authority. When one remembers that few of the classical writers of the contract school, with the possible exception of Locke, believed in the actual historicity of the social contract, Spencer's solution does not seem to differ greatly in principle from theirs, however different may have been his deductions from that principle.

As to the vital question of the origin of the basic rights of the individual, Spencer claims, in opposition to Bentham and to recent political scientists in general, that they are not historically derived from governmental action but are really antecedent to government. They are those indispensable modes of individual freedom which have been found by ages of experience to be essential to any normal and continuous social life. They existed by sheer social necessity before any legal enactment, and the only role government has played has been to codify and enforce these rights which previously existed in custom and usage.

Such a doctrine of natural or individual rights, however erroneous may be its historical justification, is not logically inconsistent with the doctrine of the social organism. Spencer's theory of natural rights as the product of social experience rather than as derived from a priori rationalization is valid. The most cogent criticism of his theory is that what he assumed to be derived from the experience of the race was quite frequently the outgrowth of his fertile imagination concerning what the experience of the race ought to have been.

G. THE PROPER AND LEGITIMATE SCOPE OF STATE ACTIVITY

With the possible exception of his dogma that sound social reform could not be expected to flow from direct legislative measures, the most famous item in Spencer's political theory was his analysis of the legitimate sphere of state activity. As one eminent sociologist observed, Spencer was so busy throughout his life attempting to formulate a doctrine of what the state should not do that he failed to develop any coherent positive theory of the state. Spencer's well-known vigorous opposition to extensive state activity or positive remedial social legislation seems to have been based upon two main factors: (1) the dogmas of automatic social evolution that were current in the middle and third quarter of the nineteenth century and (2) the traits of his neurotic constitution which made the authority of the state abhorrent to him.

The idea that social development and the proper working of the social process is an automatic and spontaneous affair had been accepted long before the time of Spencer. In its earliest modern form it grew out of the reaction of Newtonian cosmic mechanics upon the social science of the eighteenth century. The English Deists and the French *philosophes* developed the notion that social institutions are governed by the same "natural laws" that Newton had shown to dominate the physical universe. Their assumption was taken up and incorporated in social science by the French Physiocrats and the Classical Economists, the latter employing it as a philosophic defense of the new capitalistic system produced by the industrial revolution. Though this conception was shown to be unsound early in the nineteenth century by Rae, Hodgkin, and Sismondi, it prevailed very generally throughout the century.

With the development of the evolutionary hypothesis, a new "naturalism" was provided. It was believed that the highly organized types of animal life had developed from lower forms in an automatic and independent manner. It was easy to postulate a direct analogy between organic and social evolution and to contend that social evolution is a wholly spontaneous process which artificial human interference could in no way hasten but might fatally obstruct or divert. It was Spencer, more than any other writer, who popularized this view of social development as an argument against state activity—a position which Lester F. Ward, Leonard T. Hobhouse, Ludwig Stein, and Albion W. Small have seriously challenged.

Spencer seems to have derived from some source what the modern dynamic psychologists would designate as an extreme "anti-authority complex." Coupled with what is known regarding his early life, especially his early domination by male relatives, and his confirmed neurotic tendencies, his persistent and ever growing resentment against the extension of governmental activity probably was personally motivated by a subconscious neurotic reaction. It must also be remembered that Spencer came from a dissenting family and was reared in that atmosphere. It seems, on the whole, that his attitude toward government must have had a deep-rooted emotional foundation, since it diverged materially from some of the vital premises of his general philosophy. This inconsistency was constantly causing him trouble and entailed considerable labor in patching up a reconciliation between his political individualism and his sociological principles.

Be this as it may, his attitude in respect to the question of state activity may quite well have been suggested, and it certainly was abundantly nourished, by the political conditions of his lifetime. The revolutionary ideas of the early nineteenth century, with their doctrines of the efficacy of hasty and violent political reform, and the great volume of proposed remedial legislation designed to solve the problems caused by the disorganization of the older social control by the industrial revolution were admirably adapted to awaken sentiments like those entertained by Spencer and to prevent them from becoming dormant.[24]

Spencer published his first essay on this subject, entitled "The Proper Sphere of Government," in 1842, and eight years later there appeared his first substantial treatise, *Social Statics*. The fundamental principle of this work is Spencer's law of equal freedom, which is but a revival of Rousseau's definition of liberty. He contends that each individual is to enjoy as perfect a degree of freedom as is compatible with the equal privilege of other individuals. In this work Spencer states his famous theory of the state as a joint-stock company for the mutual protection of individuals and presents his catalogue of activities from which the state should refrain, with a detailed analysis of his views in support of his position. This list of interdicted or tabooed activities include the following, some of which are rather startling: commercial regulation, state religious establishments, charitable activities tending to interfere with natural selection, state education, state colonization, sanitary measures, regulation and coining of money, postal service, provision of lighthouses, and improvements of harbors. The real duty of the state is to administer justice, which consists theoretically in maintaining the law of equal freedom and practically in protecting the life and property of the citizens from internal robbery and fraud and from external invasion.

In the *Study of Sociology* (1873) Spencer repeats his fundamental notions regarding political laissez faire, especially in the justly famous opening chapter on "Our Need of a Social Science" and in the equally excellent chapter on "The Political Bias." In one passage in his *Study of Sociology*,[25] Spencer anticipates the view of Sumner regarding the "forgotten man" as the one who bears most of the financial burden of state activity and gets the least benefit from this legislation. His political theories, expressed in the *Principles of Sociology*, are mainly historical and analytical and, with the exception of the contrasts between militant and industrial society, deal only incidentally with the question of the legitimate scope of state activity. Between 1850 and 1884, when he published his *Man versus the State*, Spencer contributed a large number of articles on the subject of noninterference. These have been, for the most part, gathered together in the third volume of his *Essays, Scientific,*

Political, and Speculative (1891). Perhaps the most important among them is his "Specialized Administration" (1871), issued in answer to Professor Huxley's attack on Spencerian doctrines in his essay on "Administrative Nihilism" (1870). By the doctrine of "specialized administration" Spencer means the relinquishment by the government of its function of positive regulation of human activities and the perfection of its negatively regulating function. He also published a telling diatribe against socialism under the title "From Freedom to Bondage"; and the second essay in his *Man versus the State,* "The Coming Slavery," is also mainly devoted to a refutation of socialistic propositions.

Finally, in *Man versus the State* and in *Justice,* one may look for Spencer's last word on the subject. In the former he inveighs against the socialistic tendencies of the age and the attempted extension of family ethics into the field of state activity. He attempts a refutation of the contemporary dogma of the sovereignty of Parliament as the representative of the majority. His final doctrine regarding the proper sphere of government, as here stated, is that it should be limited to the provision of safety from physical assault, the freedom and enforcement of contracts, and the protection of the individual from foreign aggression, in other words, to be concerned purely with negative regulations. In the Postscript to the final edition of *Man versus the State,* he admits that he is fully aware that his theory of state activity is far in advance of his age and that it will not be adopted for generations to come, but he justifies his devotion to the cause on the ground that society must have an ideal to guide it toward realization.

Spencer has been roundly criticized by many writers, notably by D. G. Ritchie, for the inconsistency between his doctrine of the social organism and his inference that, with the further evolution of society, the regulating structure of government will gradually disintegrate. That there is a discrepancy here which even Spencer's ingenuity was never quite able to explain away cannot be denied, but the logical completion of the organic doctrine, with its assertion that the function of government must become more and more all-inclusive, is hardly satisfactory. With a type of society in which intellect guides legislation, as was assumed by Comte and later by Ward, progress might be hoped for through an extension of state activity; but, in view of the present general level of intelligence and moral character of the usual run of the governmental officers in modern political systems, many thinkers would rather trust to the efficacy of voluntary organization. It seems that this was essentially Spencer's view.

As to the activity of the state in international matters, it has already been pointed out that Spencer believed that the state should protect its citizens from the aggression of invaders. Spencer was not a believer in the doctrine of passive submission. He did, however, strongly advocate the principle of nonaggression. He believed in the principle of international arbitration and prophesied that, in time, this would be the universal mode of settling international disputes. He looked forward, in the distant future, to a general dissolution of strict national lines and the institution of a universal government or a federation of governments. Spencer followed up his belief in international arbitration by personal activity in promoting a peace society that worked for international conciliation, and he tells in his *Autobiography* of the injury to his health caused by his exertions in this field of effort.

Spencer was also a vigorous critic of the new capitalistic imperialism which developed in England and in the world generally, following the seventies. In one of his latest articles, entitled "Imperialism and Slavery," Spencer criticized British policy in the Boer War as based wholly on the principle of superior force, which he alleged to be the dominating principle of the new imperialism. He further asserted that imperialism inevitably leads to militarism, destroys democracy both at home and abroad, and vastly increases the burdens of taxation. He thus came very near to the position taken by the neoliberals, Hobhouse and Hobson, differing chiefly in not complaining that the expenditures for imperialism reduced desirable appropriations for social legislation at home.

In conclusion, it seems that whatever one may think of Spencer's doctrine of the legitimate field of state activity, no thoughtful person can easily dissent from the assumptions which produced at least half of his opposition to state interference: (1) the present low level of political morality; (2) the general lack of intelligence or, at least, of special competence on the part of the agents of government; (3) the failure of the electorate to exercise any considerable degree of wisdom in the choice of these agents; and (4) the present perversion of the attitude toward government as an end in itself rather than as a means toward an end. He held that these shortcomings all combine to make our governmental machinery miserably incompetent to deal with the complex problems of modern civilization. The improvement of this condition can be effected in but two ways: a decrease in the activity of government or an increase in its efficiency. The latter is held by most contemporary writers to be by all odds preferable, but Spencer considered it so remote a possibility that he chose to put his trust in the former. That he had some valid grounds for his attitude is distressingly apparent.

H. PROGRESS, SOCIAL REFORM, AND STATE ACTIVITY

Spencer's writings on the subject of social reform are about as prolific and spirited as those dealing with the proper field of state activity. In fact, ᵗhese questions are but different sides of the same problem. As the foundation of his doctrine concerning state activity was equal freedom, natural rights, and negative regulation, so in regard to social reform his central dictum was that results are not proportional to appliances.

Spencer did not deny the need of political reform or the tendency of all governmental structure to become conservative and to resist change. In his *Principles of Sociology* Spencer gives an illuminating discussion of how political organization, like all other social institutions, tends to resist change. It was not the need of reform that he questioned; it was, rather, the efficacy of the methods and principles of reform then proposed.

What Spencer desired to emphasize was that it is futile to expect that any measure directly designed to remedy a certain situation could be successful unless it took into consideration the general cultural complex of which the particular defect was a part and allowed for the interdependence of social forces and institutions. Writers have accused Spencer of dealing with "straight men" and formulating a "political arithmetic," but, in this field of social reform at least, he was sufficiently conscious of the actual conditions which confront the social reformer. His classic statement of this principle is contained in the following paragraph from the *Study of Sociology:*

You see that this wrought-iron plate is not quite flat; it sticks up a little here toward the left—"cockles," as we say. How shall we flatten it? Obviously, you reply, by hitting down on the part that is prominent. Well, here is a hammer, and I give the plate a blow as you advise. Harder, you say. Still no effect. Another stroke: well, there is one, and another, and another. The prominence remains, you see: the evil is as great as ever—greater, indeed. But this is not all. Look at the warp which the plate has got near the opposite edge. Where it was flat before it is now curved. A pretty bungle we have made of it. Instead of curing the original defect, we have produced a second. Had we asked an artisan practised in "planishing," as it is called, he would have told us that no good was to be done, but only mischief, by hitting down on the projecting part. He would have taught us how to give variously—directed and specially—adjusted blows with a hammer elsewhere: so attacking the evil not by direct but by indirect actions. The required process is less simple than you thought. Even a sheet of metal is not to be successfully dealt with after those common-sense methods in which you have so much confidence. What, then, shall we say about a society? "Do you think I am easier to be played on than a pipe?" asks Hamlet. Is humanity more readily straightened than an iron plate?[26]

Nevertheless, Spencer was not a complete and unqualified advocate of laissez faire. What he was trying to combat was the all too prevalent tendency to repose complete trust in the efficacy of legislation as a cure-all for social ills. As a spirited advocate of the opposite school, he naturally went too far. What he wanted to impress upon society was the necessarily small part which an individual or even a generation can hope to achieve in changing the direction of social evolution. He did not desire to discourage either individual or collective effort toward reform, provided that it recognized the necessary social limitations upon the scope or results of such action. He sums up this position well in the following paragraph:

Thus while admitting that for the fanatic some wild anticipation is needful as a stimulus, and recognizing the usefulness of his delusion as adapted to his particular nature and his particular function, the man of the higher type must be content with greatly moderated expectations, while he perseveres with undiminished efforts. He has to see how comparatively little can be done, and yet find it worth while to do that little: so uniting philanthropic energy with philosophic calm.[27]

Few would today uphold so extreme a policy of laissez faire as Spencer sanctioned or wait so patiently for the impersonal laws of evolution to work out a program of reform as he assumed to be willing to do. Yet we cannot well doubt the wisdom of his advice to beware of the doctrine of the possibility of manufacturing progress by legislation that is not based on the widest possible knowledge of the sociological principles involved. This is the lesson which sociologists are still trying to impress upon well-meaning, but ill-informed, philanthropists.[28]

I. EXTRA-LEGAL ASPECTS OF POLITICAL ORGANIZATION

Spencer offered numerous reflections regarding the extra-legal aspects of political activity and organization. It has already been pointed out that he rightly conceived of public opinion, or "the feeling of the community," as the vital force behind governmental activity which gives it vigor and effectiveness and that he believed that no form of government can succeed unless it is in accord with the public sentiments of the time. His analysis of the overwhelming part which custom and tradition play in formulating public opinion has also been described. As to political parties, Spencer held that their influence is mainly negative. They usually merely becloud the real issues in any political situation by their bias in one direction or the other.

On the general subject of the extra-legal forms of social control, it may be said that Spencer rendered a real service to political and social thought in correlating political organization with general social organization and in showing how hopeless it was for political reformers to attempt any political change or reform without looking at the state in its relation to society and taking into consideration the basic dependence of political activity upon social forces and interests. In this regard he performed the main service which sociologists have to offer to political theory and practice. The significance of this view has been well stated by Professor Small in what he designates as the central notion of the Spencerian philosophy: "The members of society, from the very earliest stages, arrange themselves in somewhat permanent forms; these forms are rearranged in adaptation to varying needs; the forms are related, both as cause and effect, to the individuals who make up the society; they are thus factors that may never be left out of account in attempts to understand real life."[29]

J. SUMMARY OF SPENCER'S SOCIAL AND POLITICAL THEORIES

Spencer's salient social and political doctrines, then, may be summarized as follows: (1) he revived the contract (agreement) doctrine to account philosophically for the justification of political authority; (2) he put forward a strong sociological statement of individualistic political philosophy, in which the state was completely subordinated to the individual and was regarded simply as an agent for securing a greater degree of freedom for the individual than was possible without its "negative interference" with human conduct; (3) he denied the possibility of securing social progress by direct remedial legislation (at least of the type he was familiar with) and asserted that society must wait for the automatic working of the general laws of evolution to bring about permanent progress; (4) he set forth one of the most elaborate expositions ever devised of the organismic theory of society; (5) he developed a philosophy of political evolution based upon the purpose for which organized society functions, finding these purposes to have been, first, military expansion, then industrial development, and, finally, ethical improvement; (6) finally, Spencer made the important contribution of correlating the state with society in the attempt to estimate its position and functions in the wider social process.

In short, Spencer approached public problems from the broad viewpoint of the sociologist, however inconsistent and inadequate at times may have been his application of the principles of his social philosophy to the solution of those problems.

NOTES

1. See Spencer's *Essays, Scientific, Political, and Speculative* (New York, 1891), pp. 118–49, essay entitled "Some Reasons for Dissenting from the Philosophy of M. Comte."

2. Henri Michel, *L'Idée de l'état* (Paris, 1896), p. 462 (author's translation); see also Eugene de Roberty, *Auguste Comte et Herbert Spencer* (Paris, 1904).

3. For a brief statement of the sources of Spencer's doctrines see Ernest Barker, *Political Thought in England from Herbert Spencer to the Present Day* (New York, 1915), pp. 86–90. For his own account of his early years see his *Autobiography* (2 vols.; New York, 1904), I, 48–142. For more bibliographic detail on Spencer, see H. E. Barnes and Howard Becker, *Social Thought from Lore to Science* (2 vols.; Boston, 1938), I, xlix–li.

4. See A. G. Keller, *Societal Evolution* (New York, 1931), pp. 12 ff. *The First Principles* was followed by the *Principles of Biology* (1864–67), the *Principles of Psychology* (1872), the *Study of Sociology* (1873), the *Principles of Sociology* (1876–96), the *Principles of Ethics* (1879–93), and *Man versus the State* (1884). In addition to these systematic works, Spencer published a large number of articles which were collected in numerous volumes of essays. For a complete list of Spencer's works see the article entitled "Spencer" in the eleventh edition of the *Encyclopaedia Britannica;* and in W. H. Hudson, *An Introduction to the Philosophy of Herbert Spencer* (New York, 1894), Appendix, pp. 231–34.

Spencer produced this mass of material under conditions far from conducive to its speedy and efficient execution. He was a chronic neurasthenic during the entire period of the development of his sociological system, and his pecuniary resources were not always sufficient to keep his plan in a normal state of progress. The Preface to the third volume of his *Principles of Sociology,* published in 1896, which completed the work to which he had devoted practically a lifetime, sums up the difficulties of the writer and expresses his satisfaction at his final success.

5. William Graham Sumner, *The Forgotten Man and Other Essays* (New Haven, 1918), p. 401.

6. Four good works dealing with Spencer's philosophical system are: Hudson, *op. cit.;* Josiah Royce, *Herbert Spencer: An Estimate and Review* (New York, 1904); Hector Macpherson, *Spencer and Spencerism* (New York, 1900); and H. Elliott, *Herbert Spencer* (New York, 1916). An authorized and approved digest of his system as a whole is to be found in F. H. Collins, *An Epitome of the Synthetic Philosophy* (New York, 1889). Finally, no one should consider himself thoroughly acquainted with Spencer unless he has read his *Autobiography,* which appeared posthumously in two volumes in 1904, and David Duncan's *Life and Letters of Herbert Spencer* (2 vols.; New York, 1908).

7. For Spencer's summary of his system see his Preface to Collins, *op. cit.,* pp. viii–xi; cf. also Robert Mackintosh, *From Comte to Benjamin Kidd* (London, 1899), chaps. viii–ix.

8. Franklin H. Giddings, *Sociology: A Lecture* (New York, 1908), pp. 29–30.

9. *The Social Organism* (1860); *Specialized Administration* (1871); *Principles of Sociology,* Vol. I, Part I. Citations from the *Principles of Sociology* are from the New York edition of 1896.

10. *Principles of Sociology,* Vol. I, Part II, chaps. ii–ix, particularly chap. ii. More detailed analysis of Spencer's organic theory of society are to be found in F. W. Coker, *Organismic Theories of the State* (New York, 1910), pp. 124–39; and Ezra T. Towne, *Die Auffassung der Gesellschaft als Organismus, ihre Entwickelung und ihre Modifikationen* (Halle, 1903), pp. 41–48.

11. See his review of the work in F. G. Peabody, *A Readers' Guide to Social Ethics and Allied Subjects,* p. 29.

12. A. W. Small, *General Sociology,* p. 130. For estimates of Spencer's importance for sociology see F. H. Giddings, *Principles of Sociology* (New York, 1896), Book I, chap. i, and his adaptations of Spencer's doctrines in all his works; Ward, *Dynamic Sociology,* I, 139–219; Small, *op. cit.,* pp. 109–53; E. A. Ross, *Foundations of Sociology* (New York, 1905), pp. 42–47; and, above all, Leopold von Wiese, *Zur Grundlegung der Gesellschafts-lehre: Eine kritische Untersuchung von Herbert Spencer's System der synthetischen Philosophie* (Jena, 1906).

13. *Principles of Sociology,* Vol. I, sec. 210, p. 438; cf. also *Study of Sociology,* chap. i. Among the best analyses of certain phases of Spencer's political theories are D. G. Ritchie, *Principles of State Interference* (London, 1891); Barker, *op. cit.,* chap. iv; and Coker, *op. cit.,* pp. 124–39.

14. *Principles of Sociology,* II, 247.

15. *Man versus the State* (with the abridged and revised *Social Statics* [New York, 1892]), pp. 380–81. As Ritchie points out, part of Spencer's confusion with respect to the problem of sovereignty was due to his tendency to personify the abstract philosophical concept.

16. *Principles of Sociology,* I, 437.

17. *Ibid.,* II, 317.

18. For Spencer's own description of his method see his *Autobiography,* Vol. II, chap. xlvii, esp. pp. 325–27.

19. *Principles of Sociology,* II, 568–605 ff.

20. *Social Statics* (abridged edition with *Man versus the State* [New York, 1892]), pp. 248–49.

21. *Ibid.,* p. 105.

22. *Ibid.,* p. 248.

23. *Study of Sociology* (New York, 1876), p. 275; cf. also *Principles of Sociology,* II, 230–43.

24. For Spencer's own account of the development of his political theories see his *Autobiography,* II, 431–36. This seems to be somewhat of a "rationalization after the fact."

25. *Op. cit.,* pp. 285–86.

26. *Ibid.,* pp. 270–71.

27. *Ibid.,* p. 403.

28. For Spencer's account of his ambitious plan to make a study of the effect of so-called "reform legislation" during the whole period of medieval and modern English history see in *Various Fragments* (New York, 1898), pp. 136–40, an essay entitled "Record of Legislation."

29. *General Sociology,* p. 153.

CHAPTER V

LEWIS HENRY MORGAN: PIONEER IN THE THEORY OF SOCIAL EVOLUTION

Leslie A. White, University of Michigan

I. MORGAN'S LIFE AND WRITINGS

IF IT was Herbert Spencer who was mainly responsible for introducing the concept of evolution into social thought, in general, in the nineteenth century, it was an American ethnologist and sociologist, Lewis Henry Morgan, who applied the notion of evolution to social development and constructed the most impressive system of institutional evolution produced in that century.

"Morgan was undoubtedly the greatest sociologist of the past century," declared the distinguished British ethnologist, Alfred C. Haddon.[1] Judgments may well differ as to who was *the* greatest sociologist of the nineteenth century; but there can be no doubt that Morgan was one of the greatest.

Lewis Henry Morgan was born on a farm near the village of Aurora, New York, on November 21, 1818. He was educated at Cayuga Academy, in Aurora, and at Union College, from which he was graduated in 1840. After studying law at Aurora, he went to Rochester, New York, in 1844 to practice. He married, settled in Rochester, and lived there for the rest of his life. Morgan took an active part in the intellectual life of Rochester of his day and was for many years the guiding spirit in the Pundit Club, which had its first meeting in his home. Many of his contributions to science were first read in manuscript before this club. Morgan was active also in civic matters, serving one term in the Assembly and one term in the Senate of the state of New York. Partly through his legal practice but largely through investments in mining and business enterprises in northern Michigan, Morgan accumulated a considerable fortune, which enabled him eventually to give up his legal practice and to devote himself wholly to his scientific labors.

Morgan's first notable work was the *League of the Ho-de-no-sau-nee*

138

or Iroquois (1851) the "first scientific account of an Indian tribe ever given to the world."[2] In 1868 his classic, *The American Beaver and His Works,* appeared. Two years later, the Smithsonian Institution published his monumental *Systems of Consanguinity and Affinity of the Human Family.* This work may be regarded, in some respects at least, as Morgan's most original and brilliant achievement.[3] But it is his *Ancient Society* (1877) for which Morgan is most widely known. This work, which grew out of his *Systems of Consanguinity,* has been translated into many of the languages of Europe and into Chinese and Japanese and has exerted an influence upon sociological thought that was as profound as it was widespread. Morgan's last work, *Houses and House-Life of the American Aborigines,* appeared in 1881, shortly before his death.

Contrary to a notion that has gained currency in recent decades, Morgan was no mere "armchair philosopher." He did a great deal of field work in a day when investigations in the field were dangerous as well as arduous. In addition to his field work among the Iroquois of New York, Morgan made several long field trips to Kansas and Nebraska territories, to the Rocky Mountains, to Hudson's Bay Territory, and to New Mexico—and made them in a day when hostile tribes still waged war against the whites and when railroads had extended westward hardly as far as the Missouri River.

Although Morgan never taught at a university or held a position with any scientific institution, he nevertheless exerted considerable influence in scientific and educational circles. He was active in the American Association for the Advancement of Science for many years, serving as its president in 1880. He received an honorary LL.D degree from Union College in 1873 and was elected to the National Academy of Sciences in 1875. His death came on December 17, 1881.[4]

II. MORGAN AS SOCIAL EVOLUTIONIST

Morgan was truly a pioneer in social science. He began his work at a time when the Christian cosmogony was accepted without question by virtually everyone. As a young man, Morgan accepted the account of creation in Genesis, just as Darwin had done. But by the time he had come to write *Ancient Society,* Morgan had placed himself squarely against the biblical account of man's origin. Although *Ancient Society* was dedicated to a Presbyterian minister and although God is alluded

to in the last paragraph of the book, Morgan specifically repudiated
the then current theological explanation of savage cultures, which held
that they are the result of degradation after the Fall of Man. This theory,
Morgan asserted,

came in as a corollary from the Mosaic cosmogony, and was acquiesced in from a
supposed necessity which no longer exists..... The views herein [i.e., in *Ancient
Society*] presented contravene, as I am aware, an assumption which has for centuries been generally accepted..... It [the degradation theory] was never a scientific proposition supported by facts. It is refuted.....[5]

Thus Morgan, like Darwin, was obliged to oppose Christian theology
in order to establish the views of science. Likewise, both Morgan and
Darwin broke with the old and ushered in the new. Morgan did for
sociology what Darwin did for biology—introduced and established
as a fundamental concept the theory of evolution. And, if anything,
Morgan's achievement is even greater than Darwin's, for Morgan was
able to show *why* cultures evolve, as well as to describe the ways in
which the development came about. Darwin was able to show how
evolution occurs as a consequence of organic variations, but he was not
able to explain how and why the variations appeared in the first place.

It is in his theory of social, or cultural, evolution, then, that we find
Morgan's greatest contribution to sociological thought. To be sure, the
idea of social evolution did not originate with Morgan; many writers
before him had dealt with this concept in one manner or another. But
it is in Morgan that we find, for the first time, a sound, naturalistic
theory, one that is adequate to the needs and requirements of modern
science. The gist of his theory may be briefly put: Culture advances as
the technological means of man's control over his habitat, particularly
over his means of subsistence, are enlarged and improved; "....the
great epochs of human progress have been identified, more or less
directly, with the enlargement of the sources of subsistence."[6] Man is
an animal who "at the outset" lived as a mere beast. But, because of
articulate speech with which to communicate ideas from one individual
to another and from one generation to the next, man has been able to
elevate himself from the brute level and to advance himself from
savagery to civilization. Tools and weapons are the principal means by
which man increases his control over nature and "enlarges his sources
of subsistence." The bow and arrow "must have given a powerful
upward influence to ancient society."[7] The discovery of metals, espe-

cially iron, and their uses contributed immeasurably to cultural advance.[8] The domestication of animals not only enlarged man's sources of subsistence but "supplemented human muscle with animal power, contributing a new factor of the highest value . . . . the production of iron gave the plow with an iron point, and a better spade and axe. Out of these, and the previous horticulture, came field agriculture; and with it, for the first time, unlimited subsistence,"[9]—i.e., unlimited resources for culture-building. As technology advanced, social institutions changed. The profound change from subsistence upon wild foods to intensive agriculture produced a correspondingly radical change in society: the institutions of tribal society gave way to the institutions of civil society; the clan and tribe were replaced by the political state.

We have here a simple, sound theory of cultural evolution. Man lives by exploiting the resources of nature by technological means. Social institutions are society's ways of organizing itself to wield and use its technology. As the technology advances, social institutions must change also. It is clear, of course, that this theory is applicable to the present as well as to the past. If a social revolution, a change from tribe to state and empire, resulted from the transition from a wild-food technology to intensive agriculture, what social consequences may be expected from the technological revolution of the present power age or the future age of atomic energy?

Although Morgan sets forth this theory of cultural evolution clearly and succinctly in Part I of *Ancient Society*, he does not employ it consistently throughout this work. He speaks of social institutions as developing from a "few primary germs of thought" that were originally "implanted in man's mind." Parts II, III, and IV of *Ancient Society* are concerned with the "growth of the idea of" government, the family, and property, respectively. One frequently gets the impression that the evolution of social institutions (the "growth of primary germs of thought") takes place independently of technological advance, which results from "inventions and discoveries," or, at most, that social evolution and technological evolution run along parallel but independent lines.[10] Morgan does, indeed, speak of "two independent lines of investigation." But it should be noted that he says independent lines of investigation, not independent lines of development. Thus it might appear that Morgan had two theories of social evolution: one in which technology was the determinant; the other in which ideas inherent in man's mind just grew and expressed themselves in social institutions.

We shall not attempt to explain at this time why Morgan expressed his philosophy of evolution as he did. It seems likely that his "primary germs of thought," lodged originally in "man's mind" and subsequently growing from age to age was a concept borrowed from the prevailing psychology of his day.[11] But, apart from a few lapses, as, for example, when he explains the polygamy of the Mormons as "a relic of savagism not yet eradicated from the human brain,"[12] Morgan shows that the growth of social institutions is dependent upon, or even an expression of, technological advances. This interpretation runs through the entire book but is especially evident in Morgan's account of the transition from tribal society to civil society. Morgan's statement of the theory of the technological determination of social evolution is, perhaps, not so explicit, pointed, and emphatic as it might be, and his demonstration of this theory is frequently obscured by his psychology of the "germs of thought." But we must not forget that Morgan was a pioneer; he invented this theory. To demand philosophic purity and perfect refinement of expression of him is, of course, unreasonable; it is enough that he formulated this most basic theory of social science, gave it to us, and showed us how to use it.[13]

III. MORGAN'S THEORY OF THE EVOLUTION OF THE FAMILY

Holding a prominent place in Morgan's theory of cultural evolution is his special theory of the evolution of the family. According to Morgan, the original condition of human society was that of a "horde living in promiscuity." Out of this emerged the Consanguine family, which was the first stage in the evolution of the family. The Consanguine family was "founded upon the intermarriage of brothers and sisters in a group." Next came the Punaluan family, which prohibited marriage between brothers and sisters but constituted "group marriage"— a group of brothers possessed their wives in common, or a group of sisters possessed their husbands in common. In the Syndyasmian family, which came next, we have "the pairing of a male with a female under the form of marriage, but without exclusive cohabitation. It was the germ of the Monogamian Family."[14] The Patriarchal family appeared next and, finally, the Monogamian family, "founded upon marriage between single pairs, with an exclusive cohabitation." Thus Morgan distinguished five stages in the evolution of the family. It will be noted that the course of development assumed by Morgan had a definite direction: from promiscuous and unregulated unions in the original horde through "group marriage," which was progressively reduced by customary restrictions until monogamy was attained.

A vigorous, and sometimes bitter, debate upon the subject of the origin and evolution of the family followed the publication of *Systems of Consanguinity* and *Ancient Society*. It has not become extinguished even yet.[15] But the consensus is that Morgan's theory is untenable. The discovery that monogamy is customary among the most primitive of peoples; the failure to establish Morgan's theory by any method other than Morgan's; and, above all, the modern studies of monkeys and apes, which show fairly conclusively that the family form, as a sociological consequence of physiological processes, is universal among primates (of the Old World at least) have overthrown Morgan's theory once and for all. Morgan formulated his theory of the evolution of the family in his attempt to explain the various systems of kinship terminology which he had discovered. His various family forms were essentially devices to explain systems of kinship nomenclature. It was something like the physicists' creation of "luminiferous ether" to account for the transmission of light from the sun to the planets. Once the Consanguine and other forms of the family had been invented to explain relationship terms, the indisputable fact of the kinship systems made the forms of the family seem plausible. But Morgan did more than reason in a circle; he had the testimony of men who had lived among the Hawaiians which, he believed, established the actual existence of the Punaluan family among the Polynesians.[16] His theory was tested and indorsed by two intelligent and educated men who were intimately acquainted with the aborigines of Australia.[17] Thus he had reason for confidence in his theory.[18] Today we can explain kinship nomenclatures in another way, we know more about primitive peoples, and we know something of the physiology of sex among primates, all of which renders Morgan's theory obsolete. It was a bold and brilliant achievement, like the Ptolemaic system of astronomy or the theory of luminiferous ether. But, like these theories, Morgan's has had to give way to a better one.

IV. KINSHIP AND THE CLASSIFICATORY SYSTEM OF RELATIONSHIPS

In the discovery of systems of kinship we find one of Morgan's most brilliant achievements. Before Morgan's day, a few men here and there had noted that many primitive peoples do not observe the same rules in the designation of kindred that we do. But these differences were merely noted as "strange customs" or dismissed as "heathen practices." It was Morgan who first recognized that the customs of primitive peoples in this respect were indeed systems, governed by definite rules, and not mere savage caprice or vagary; it was he who first formulated, as an objective for science, the problem of kinship nomenclatures; and it was he who laid the foundation upon which our modern studies of kinship systems rest.

Although Morgan failed to see that kinship in human society is primarily and essentially a social phenomenon and only secondarily and incidentally a biological matter,[19] he did discover and appreciate the fact that relationship terms are sociological devices employed in the regulation of social life. A relationship term is the designation of an individual or a class of individuals that is socially significant. Every society of human beings is divided into social classes or groups, which, with reference to any individual in the society, are designated with kinship terms such as "uncle," "sister," "mother-in-law," etc. One's behavior toward one's fellows varies, depending upon the category of relationship in which the person stands. Since the categories are labeled with kinship terms, a close functional relationship obtains between kinship nomenclature and social organization and behavior.[20] These are the views and postulates upon which a modern school of social anthropologists bases much of its work.[21] They were discovered, elucidated, and established by Morgan many decades ago.[22]

V. "SOCIETAS" AND "CIVITAS": THE TRANSITION FROM
KINSHIP TO CIVIL SOCIETY

Morgan surveyed the entire span of human history and saw that, with reference to social organization, it is divisible into two great categories: "ancient society" (or "primitive society," as we tend to call it today) and modern, civil society. He called the first type of society *societas,* the second *civitas.*[23] Morgan's distinction of these two great types of human society and his description of each constitute one of his greatest contributions to sociological thought.[24]

Ancient society, the *societas,* was founded upon "persons and upon relationships purely personal." Civil society, the *civitas,* was founded upon territory and upon property. Thus, in primitive society a person's status and role in social life were determined by his personal relationship to other members of the society. And, since in almost all instances all members of a *societas* regard themselves as related to one another, a person's role in primitive society is determined and regulated by ties of *kinship,* as well as by merely personal ties. A *societas* is thus a community of kindred. In a *civitas,* on the other hand, a person's status and role are determined by his place of residence—deme, township, state, etc.—and by his relationship to property. The relationship between persons is thus impersonal. The members of a *societas* are kinsfolk, the members of a *civitas* are citizens. The clan[25] and tribe are the characteristic units of ancient society. The political state is the form characteristic of the *civitas.*

Ancient society is democratic, and all men are free and equal.[26] In civil society there are class distinctions:[27] masters and slaves; lords, vassals, and serfs; kings and subjects; or the rich and the poor.

VI. PROPERTY AND INHERITANCE IN RELATION TO SOCIAL EVOLUTION

Bearing directly upon the differences between these two great types of society is Morgan's treatment of property. This subject is dealt with in various places in *Ancient Society,* but particularly in the fourth and last part of this work, which is devoted to the "Growth of the Idea of Property." This part, although relatively brief—less than a quarter as long as the part devoted to the family and less than one-tenth as long as the part on government—nevertheless contains some of Morgan's most significant contributions to modern sociology and the science of culture.

Peoples with crude and simple cultures have little property, and the problem of inheritance at death is an insignificant one. In many instances the few articles owned by the deceased are either buried with him or destroyed, or they may be divided among his close relatives and friends. But, as culture advances and property accumulates, the problem of inheritance becomes important. The course of social evolution has been profoundly influenced, according to Morgan, by the accumulation of property and by the exigencies of inheritance at death.

The "first great rule of inheritance," according to Morgan, decreed that the effects of a deceased person were to be inherited by the members of his clan, or "gens." "Practically they were appropriated by the nearest of kin; but the principle was general, that the property should remain in the gens of the decedent and be distributed among its members." The second rule limited the heirs to agnates of the deceased, excluding other clansmen, or "gentiles." The third rule restricted heirs to children (unless, of course, there were none), excluding agnates. It was the accumulation of property and the desire of men to bequeath it to their sons that caused a change of descent through females to descent through males, Morgan believed. He points out that the rule prohibiting marriage within the gens among the Greeks was occasionally relaxed in the case of heiresses: marriage within the gens being permitted in such cases in order to keep the property from passing outside the gens. Morgan speaks of the family as a "property-making organization" as William F. Ogburn has, in dealing with the family in Colonial America.[28] Property, "as it increased in variety and amount, exercised a steady and constantly augmenting influence in the direction of monogamy." Thus we note a close relationship between "the growth of the idea of the family" and the "growth of the idea of property." As the family narrowed itself down from the Consanguine family ("group marriage") to monogamy, the body of legitimate heirs of a decedent contracted from the gens as a whole to his own children. And it was property that, to a great extent, determined the course of social or family evolution. As Morgan once put it: "Property became sufficiently powerful in its influence to touch the organic structure of society."[29]

Whatever modification of Morgan's formulations might be necessary or desirable today, his general thesis is as sound and as important as ever: property and the customs of inheritance have exerted a profound influence upon the course of social evolution, affecting directly the form of family, marriage, and divorce and influencing indirectly other aspects of society. An exhaustive sociological study of the influence of property and inheritance upon such things as polygamy, primogeniture, crime, celibacy of a portion of the clergy, divorce, etc., in our own culture for the last fifteen hundred years would be most illuminating.

It is property, its quantity and variety, and its method of tenure and inheritance, Morgan argues, that determine whether a society will have privileged classes or not. Among primitive peoples property is relatively insignificant quantitatively and, apart from "articles purely personal," is owned and consumed in common. This does not mean, of course, that an agricultural tribe had only one big field and no individual fields or gardens, nor does it mean that all food within a tribe was stored in one big warehouse from which it was served in a tribal community mess hall. It means that land and other natural resources were communally *owned,* although individual rights to the use of a plot of ground might exist. There was no private property in land and other natural resources; there was no buying and selling of real estate. Everyone in the tribe had free and unrestricted access to the resources of nature, to the means of life. Herein lay the freedom of primitive society, of the *societas.* Community of effort in production prevailed, as a rule, in situations where it could be carried on effectively. In consumption, the members of a household which in primitive society frequently includes a number of families, were fed from common stores. And between households—who were, of course, groups of kindred—there was often such exchange of goods, especially in times of shortage, that, as many investigators since Morgan have put it, "a whole village (or community) must be without food before a single family can starve." Therein lay the equality of primitive society. Thus, "communism in living," as described by Morgan in *Houses and House-Life,* was the basic principle of society among primitive peoples. The freedom and equality which character-ize primitive society are but social expressions of the customs relating to the tenure, exchange, and consumption of property.

But with advances in culture came changes in customs relating to property and, as further consequences, changes in the organization of society. "Systematical cultivation of the earth tended to identify the family with the soil." The right to cultivate a portion of the land held in common by the tribe passed into ownership in severalty. Commerce grew with the accumulation of wealth through agriculture and manu-facture. With the development of money, everything came to be bought and sold, men as well as land. Private property became established. The constitution of society was transformed as a consequence. Instead of the liberty, equality, and fraternity of the *societas,* there was inequality, class divisions, aristocracy, and slavery. "Property and office were the foundations upon which aristocracy planted itself." The "growth of the idea of property .... introduced human slavery as an instrument in its production; and after the experience of several thousand years, it caused the abolition of slavery upon the discovery that a freeman was a better property-making machine."[30] The transition from democratic gentile society to aristocratic society is seen by Morgan from still another angle:

.... From the increased abundance of subsistence through field agriculture, nations began to develop, numbering many thousands under one government, where before they would be reckoned by a few thousands. The localization of tribes in fixed areas and in fortified cities, with the increase of the numbers of people, intensified the struggle for the possession of the most desirable territories. It tended to advance the art of war, and to increase the rewards of individual prowess. These changes of condition and of the plan of life .... [were] to overthrow gentile and establish political society.[31]

As property has been the great factor in bringing about the transition from primitive society, so has it been the instrument which has formed and shaped the institutions of civil society. "Government and laws are instituted with primary reference to .... the creation, protection, and enjoyment" of property.[32] "It is impossible to overestimate the influence of property in the civilization of mankind,"[33] Morgan declares. The "idea of property," which was so feeble "in the mind of the savage," has grown until it has become the "master passion of civilized man."

Morgan's view of the consequences of this master-passion is set forth in a striking passage:

Since the advent of civilization, the outgrowth of property has been so immense, its forms so diversified, its uses so expanding and its management so intelligent in the interests of its owners, that it has become, on the part of the people, an unmanageable power. The human mind stands bewildered in the presence of its own creation. The time will come, nevertheless, when human intelligence will rise to the mastery over property, and define the relations of the state to the property it protects, as well as the obligations and the limits of the rights of its owners. The interests of society are paramount to individual interests, and the two must be brought into just and harmonious relations. A mere property career is not the final destiny of mankind, if progress is to be the law of the future as it has been of the past. The time which has passed away since civilization began is but a fragment of the past duration of man's existence; and but a fragment of the ages yet to come. The dissolution of society bids fair to become the termination of a career of which property is the end and aim; because such a career contains the elements of self-destruction. Democracy in government, brotherhood in society, equality in rights and privileges, and universal education, foreshadow the next higher plane of society to which experience, intelligence and knowledge are steadily tending. It will be a revival, in a higher form, of the liberty, equality and fraternity of the ancient gentes.[34]

In *Ancient Society*, Morgan has little specifically to say about social classes in modern society, although he declares the question of aristocracy *versus* democracy is one of the "great problems" of modern society, and adds: "As a question between equal rights and unequal rights, between equal laws and unequal laws, between the rights of wealth, of rank and of official position, and the power of justice and intelligence, there can be little doubt of the ultimate result."[35]

But, in his European *Travel Journal,* Morgan discusses the condition of society in Italy, Austria, Germany, France, and England at some length. His comments upon English society are especially interesting. He observes that the aristocracy proper is an obsolete and relatively impotent class. Their place has been taken by "a Plutocracy .... consisting of the great merchants, great manufacturers and great bankers of the Kingdom who are now the governing power, the true ruling aristocracy of the land."[36] He comments upon a meeting of working men in Hyde Park as follows:

These meetings will gradually organise a public sentiment against the existing order of things..... The merchants, capitalists, and middling men keep clear of these meetings because their sympathies are on the other side..... When the time comes, if it ever does, the working men will have to rise upon the merchants and traders as well as the aristocrats and push them out of the way in one body.[37]

VII. AN EVALUATION OF MORGAN'S POSITION IN SOCIOLOGY AND ANTHROPOLOGY[38]

Morgan's eminence and influence were great during his lifetime and for a decade or two thereafter; but he has suffered an eclipse since the turn of the century. The forces of antievolutionism, which fought Darwinism so vigorously, entrenched themselves upon the sociological field after being driven from the field of biology. In America the attack upon Morgan and social evolutionism has been led chiefly by the anthropologist, Franz Boas, and his disciples. One of the latter has gone so far as to declare that the idea of social evolution is "the most inane, sterile, and pernicious theory ever conceived in the history of science."[39] Alexander Goldenweiser has written "critiques" of evolutionism again and again, in which he describes "the downfall of evolutionism." But, if, on the one hand, Morgan has been attacked, on the other hand, he has been ignored. Franz Boas does not even mention Morgan's name in his essay, "The History of Anthropology,"[40] although he discusses the evolutionist school and mentions other evolutionists by name. Radcliffe-Brown does not list Morgan in the bibliography of his long article on "The Social Organization of Australian Tribes,"[41] although it contains 188 references to over a hundred titles by fifty-odd authors, despite the fact that Morgan was the first ethnologist of repute to write on Australian social organization.[42] Indeed, it might fairly be said that it was Morgan, aided by his disciples, Lorimer Fison and A. W. Howitt, whom he taught and guided by correspondence,[43] who founded the science of Australian ethnology. Radcliffe-Brown mentions Morgan in the text of his article only to oppose him.

Morgan has been so grossly misrepresented by some of his critics that it is difficult to believe that they have even read his works. Paul Radin has asserted that "to all Boas' disciples Morgan has since remained anathema and unread."[44] Morgan's biographer, Bernhard J. Stern, has declared that "Morgan nowhere in his books uses the word 'evolution.' "[45] Ralph Linton has made the same charge.[46] The fact is that "evolution" appears on the *very first page* of the Kerr edition of *Ancient Society* and twice in the first four pages of the Holt edition. It is found here and there in subsequent pages of *Ancient Society* and in other books and articles by Morgan. Lowie, Stern, and Linton have pictured Morgan as a man who was never able to free himself from his theological upbringing and accept the philosophy of modern science in general or of Darwinism in particular. Nothing could be further from the truth, as the present writer has demonstrated.[47] Morgan was a staunch champion of science throughout his entire adult life. The high-water mark of misrepresentation was perhaps reached recently by A. R. Radcliffe-Brown, who made the remarkable "discovery" that Morgan was not even a *social* evolutionist but merely a *petit bourgeois* with a simple faith in progress, measured by the provincial standards of his home town, Rochester, New York![48]

Ancient Society came to the attention of Karl Marx, who regarded it as a great work and was much impressed with it. He planned to write a book dealing with Morgan's contributions but was prevented from doing so by his death. The book was eventually written by Frederich Engels, Marx's lifelong friend and co-worker, under the title, *Der Ursprung der Familie, des Privateigenthums und des Staats* (1884).[49] *Ancient Society* became a Marxist classic. This fact has unquestionably had much to do with the change in attitude toward Morgan that has taken place since his day.

No one, of course, would maintain today that Morgan's work was complete, perfect, and final. He had his shortcomings and made mistakes, as many another pioneer in science has. But he was more than a mere pioneer, for he made many contributions of enduring value. His general theory of cultural evolution is perfectly sound today and is as indispensable to sociology as Darwinism is to biology. Culture evolves as the technological means of exploiting the resources of nature are enlarged and improved. Morgan's distinction between primitive society, characterized by communal ownership of the resources of nature and by liberty, equality, and fraternity in social life, and modern civil society, resting upon private ownership of the resources of nature and characterized by aristocracy and plutocracy instead of democracy, is tremendously illuminating. His discovery of kinship systems and their sociological significance laid the basis and showed the way for a modern school of social anthropologists. In some respects modern sociologists and anthropologists have not advanced beyond positions attained by Morgan. Few have gone beyond Morgan in his treatment of the role of property in social evolution and in social life generally. Some have even receded.[50] Few, if any, sociologists or social anthropologists have exploited Morgan's study of house architecture as an expression of social life and organization. Thus, while portions of Morgan's work are obsolete today (his theory of the evolution of the family, for example), much of it is perfectly sound and amazingly "modern." And his thesis of an evolutionary development of culture, repudiated or ignored by so many today, is the most basic concept of social science. Sociologists and social anthropologists would do well not merely to "go back to Morgan" but to return to him, so that they may again go *forward* along the broad highway that he laid out for us long ago.

NOTES

1. *History of Anthropology* (London, 1910), p. 133. Haddon, M.A., Sc.D., F.R.S., was Fellow of Christ's College and University Reader in Ethnology at Cambridge University.

2. J. W. Powell, "Sketch of Lewis H. Morgan," *Popular Science Monthly*, XVIII (1880), 115. As recently as 1922, Alexander Goldenweiser, who had himself done field work among the Iroquois, wrote: "The best general treatise on the Iroquois still remains Lewis H. Morgan's 'The League of the Iroquois,' " (*Early Civilization* [New York, 1922], p. 418)

3. An eminent British anthropologist, the late W. H. R. Rivers, pays this tribute to *Systems of Consanguinity:* "I do not know of any discovery in the whole range of science which can be more certainly put to the credit of one man than that of the classificatory system of relationship by Lewis Morgan. By this I mean, not merely that he was the first to point out clearly the existence of this mode of denoting relationship, but that it was he who collected the vast mass of materials by which the essential characters of the system were demonstrated, and it was he who was the first to recognize the great theoretical importance of his new discovery" (*Kinship and Social Organization* [London, 1914], pp. 4–5; see also p. 93).

4. For biographical accounts of Morgan see, in addition to articles in encyclopedias and dictionaries of biography, (1) the aforementioned sketch by J. W. Powell, written during Morgan's lifetime; (2) Bernhard J. Stern, *Lewis Henry Morgan: Social Evolutionist* (Chicago, 1931), which, however, contains numerous errors and distortions; and (3) Rochester Historical Society ("Publication Fund Series," Vol. II [Rochester, N.Y., 1923]),

which contains a number of sketches of Morgan's life and work, some of them written by men who knew Morgan personally.

5. *Ancient Society* (New York, 1877), pp. 7–8, 506. All page references to *Ancient Society* used in this chapter are taken from the first edition, by Henry Holt & Co., not from the later edition by C. H. Kerr & Co.

6. *Ibid.*, p. 19.

7. *Ibid.*, p. 22.

8. *Ibid.*, pp. 43, 535, 539.

9. *Ibid.*, p. 26.

10. *Ibid.*, p. 4.

11. Adolph Bastian, a contemporary of Morgan, frequently gave expression to this view (see L. Gumplowicz, *The Outlines of Sociology*, English trans. [Philadelphia, 1899], pp. 38–39, 46, 47). Immanuel Kant, too, spoke of the unfolding of "germs implanted by nature" (*The Idea of a Universal History*, trans. Thomas De Quincey [Hanover, 1927], p. 13). Henry Sumner Maine discusses forms of moral restraint "unfolded out of" certain "germs" (*Ancient Law* [3d American ed.; New York, 1888], p. 116).

12. *Ancient Society*, p. 61.

13. See Leslie A. White, "Energy and the Evolution of Culture," *American Anthropologist*, XLV (1943), 335–56, for a modern formulation of Morgan's theory of cultural development.

14. *Ancient Society*, p. 28.

15. See Gerrit S. Miller, Jr., "Some Elements of Sexual Behavior in Primates and Their Possible Influence on the Beginnings of Human Social Development," (*Journal of Mammalogy*, Vol. IX [1928]); B. Malinowski, *Sex and Repression in Savage Society* (New York, 1927); and R. H. Lowie, *The Family as a Social Unit* ("Papers of the Michigan Academy of Arts and Sciences," Vol. XVIII [1932]), pp. 53–69.

16. Morgan, *Ancient Society*, p. 427.

17. See Lorimer Fison and A. W. Howitt, *Kamilaroi and Kurnai* (Sydney, 1880).

18. Cf. Leslie A. White (ed.), *Pioneers in American Anthropology* (2 vols.; Albuquerque, N.M., 1940), which depicts the support and encouragement which Morgan received from an able and erudite scholar who was to become one of America's most distinguished anthropologists and documentary historians, Adolph F. Bandelier.

19. Many social anthropologists, even today, think of kinship as something biological, as is indicated by their use of such terms as "fictitious kinship" to designate the sociological phenomenon of kinship.

20. In 1909 A. L. Kroeber challenged this thesis in "Classificatory Systems of Relationship," *Journal of the Royal Anthropological Institute*, Vol. XXXIX. Kroeber's position has received some support from other students; but, after more than a half-century of testing, the sociological interpretation of kinship terms still stands (see R. H. Lowie, "Relationship Terms," *Encyclopaedia Britannica* [14th ed.]).

21. Social anthropologists do not always acknowledge their indebtedness to Morgan, however. A. R. Radcliffe-Brown, one of the foremost students of kinship in recent years, occasionally refers to Morgan to criticize or oppose him (see, e.g., "The Social Organization of Australian Tribes," *Oceania*, I (1931), 426; "Kinship Terminologies in California," *American Anthropologist*, XXXVII [1935], 530–35, in which recognition of Morgan's contributions is conspicuously lacking; and "The Study of Kinship Systems," *Journal of the Royal Anthropological Institute*, LXXI [1941], 1–18). In only one instance, so far as I am aware has he taken cognizance of Morgan's part in founding the science of kinship ("Some Problems of Bantu Sociology," *Bantu Studies* [Johannesburg, 1922], I, 40).

22. "To Morgan we owe a discovery and analysis of classificatory kinship terminologies, with all that they mean, and that is really a vast aspect of primitive sociology" (B. Malinowski, in his Introd. to H. Ian Hogbin, *Law and Order in Polynesia* [London, 1934], p. xlv).

23. R. H. Lowie (*Primitive Society* [New York, 1920], p. 391, and *History of Ethnological Theory* [New York, 1937], p. 50) and Stern (*op. cit.*, p. 138) have pointed

out that Maine formulated a like distinction sixteen years before Morgan; and they give one the impression ("a distinction adopted by Morgan . . . . [Lowie, *History of Ethnological Theory*, p. 50]) that Morgan merely developed Maine's idea. It is true that, in 1861, Maine distinguished between blood tie and local contiguity as bases of political organization (*op. cit.*, pp. 124–26). Morgan, however, emphasized the property basis of civil society as well as territorial boundaries, whereas Maine did not. Morgan's use and development of this idea are distinctly his own.

24. "Indeed we may agree with Morgan that the passage from lower forms of civilization to higher forms such as our own was essentially a passage from society based on kinship to the state based on political organization" (Radcliffe-Brown, "Some Problems of Bantu Sociology," pp. 40–41).

25. Morgan used the word "gens," of Greek derivation, instead of the Gaelic "clan." We employ the latter term, as it is more widely used and understood.

26. This is not wholly and absolutely true. There are minor and insignificant exceptions to this, as to many another generalization in science. But, by and large, it holds.

27. In primitive society we find distinctions which rest upon such things as the exclusive right of one group in a tribe to certain titles or crests. But this does not constitute a *class* division as the term is here used. By "class division" we mean that one group in society is supported by the labor of another group.

28. "The Family and Its Functions," *Recent Social Trends* (New York, 1933).

29. *Ancient Society*, p. 389.

30. *Ibid.*, p. 505.

31. *Ibid.*, p. 540.

32. *Ibid.*, p. 505. "Government, institutions and laws are simply contrivances for the creation and protection of property," observes Morgan (Leslie A. White [ed.], *Extracts from the European Travel Journal of Lewis H. Morgan* ["Rochester Historical Society Publications," Vol. XVI (Rochester, N.Y., 1937)], p. 269).

33. *Ancient Society*, p. 505.

34. *Ibid.*, p. 552. This noble passage has inspired and impressed many. The distinguished German sociologist, Ferdinand Tönnies, quoted it more than once (see "The Problems of Social Structure," *Proceedings of the Congress of Arts and Sciences at St. Louis, 1904* [Boston and New York, 1906], V, 839).

35. *Ancient Society* p. 551.

36. *Extracts from the European Travel Journal*, pp. 263–64.

37. *Ibid.*, p. 376.

38. See also Lowie's appraisal of Morgan, "Lewis H. Morgan in Historical Perspective," in R. H. Lowie (ed.), *Essays in Anthropology* (Berkeley, 1936); and *History of Ethnological Theory*, chap. vi.

39. Berthold Laufer in his review of Lowie's *Culture and Ethnology* (*American Anthropologist*, XX [1918], 90).

40. *Science*, XX (1904), 513–24.

41. *Oceania*, Vol. I, Nos. 1–4 (1930–31).

42. Morgan wrote the following on Australia: "Australian Kinship, from Original Memoranda of Rev. Lorimer Fison," *Proceedings of the American Academy of Arts and Sciences*, Vol. VIII (1872); "Organization of Society upon the Basis of Sex," *Ancient Society*, Part II, chap. i; and Introd. to Fison and Howitt, *op. cit.*

43. They dedicated their book, *Kamilaroi and Kurnai*, to Morgan.

44. "The Mind of Primitive Man," *New Republic*, XCVIII (1939), 303.

45. *Op. cit.*, p 23.

46. In an essay entitled "Error in Anthropology" (in Joseph Jastrow [ed.], *The Story of Human Error* [New York, 1936], p. 313, which was, perhaps, not the most fortunate place in which to make such a claim).

47. "Morgan's Attitude Toward Religion and Science," *American Anthropologist*, XLVI (1944), 218–30. Lowie's contribution to this conception of Morgan, which was not cited in the essay just mentioned, is to be found in *History of Ethnological Theory*, p. 54.

48. "On Social Structure," *Journal of the Royal Anthropological Institute,* LXX (1940), 11.

49. English translation by E. Untermann (Chicago, 1902); also an English translation, containing Engels' prefaces to the 1st and 4th eds. (New York, 1942).

50. Professor R. H. Lowie has, in his chapter on "Property" (chap. ix), in *Primitive Society,* made a heroic effort to obscure the distinction which Morgan drew between the communal tenure of property (or natural resources) in primitive society and the institution of private property in modern society. This chapter in Lowie's book was singled out for special praise by Edward Sapir in his review of *Primitive Society (Freeman,* Vol. I, June 30, 1920).

CHAPTER VI

WILLIAM GRAHAM SUMNER: SPENCERIANISM
IN AMERICAN DRESS

Harry Elmer Barnes

I. GENERAL CHARACTERISTICS OF SUMNER'S SOCIOLOGICAL THOUGHT

AMONG the sociologists of America there is little doubt that the late William Graham Sumner (1840–1910) of Yale University was the most vigorous and striking personality. Because Sumner was probably the most inspiring and popular teacher that either Yale University or American social science has ever produced, his direct contact with thousands of students was more important for the development of sociology in the United States than his own published works upon the subject. Consequently, in even a brief introduction to his contributions to sociology, an attempt to interpret his personality and methods, as revealed in his writings and in written and oral estimates of former students at Yale, is more essential than it would be in the case of most American sociologists.

Despite the fact that Sumner frequently emphasized the necessity for an objective point of view in social science and decried any attempt upon the part of a sociologist to moralize,[1] it is impossible for a reader to emerge from a protracted examination of Sumner's economic, political, and sociological writings without becoming convinced that Sumner was primarily a preacher, in the true sense of that term.

Trained originally for the ministry and serving for a short time as an ordained curate of the Episcopal church, Sumner tells his readers[2] that he left the ministry because he wanted to be able to turn his attention to political, economic, and social questions rather than to the preparation of sermons on theological subjects. It is hard to escape the conviction that he turned his professorial career in these more fertile fields into an intellectual ministry which has been unexcelled for its success, influence, and inspiration by that of any other American teacher.

Sumner was as subtle in his preaching as Jefferson was in his political epistolography, for he constantly disclaimed any attempt to do more than set forth concrete facts in a candid manner. Yet his *What Social Classes Owe to Each Other* is, above all, an exhortation to independent thought and action, self-reliance, and individual initiative; and the element of the preacher is not entirely absent even in *Folkways*. If one adds to this initial zeal the influence of a commanding personality; wide learning; a splendid, if not entirely accurate or consistent, dogmatism; and a mastery of incisive English, which makes his essays models of terse nineteenth-century critical prose, it is not difficult to understand Sumner's reputation as a teacher or his dominating influence at Yale.

Sumner's writings are intensely dogmatic, and he was an uncompromising foe of all the unscientific sentimentality which permeated so much of the quasi-sociological writings and movements of Sumner's generation. His basic message to his students and readers in this respect has been concisely epitomized by one of his leading students as "Don't be a damn fool!"

Sumner's dogmatism, however, was not entirely logical or consistent. For example, he stated that he did not believe in either metaphysics or psychology and that he had always tried to prevent sociology from being infected by either. Nevertheless, he frequently indulged in a rather elementary type of metaphysics of his own, and his *Folkways* is unquestionably the most important objective treatment of a very essential portion of social psychology that has ever been written.

As Professor Albion Woodbury Small remarked, Sumner's position in the development of sociology in the United States has not been definitely determined. While it is true that, as Professor A. G. Keller asserts, Sumner was always primarily a sociologist in method and point of view, there can be no doubt that he built up his academic and literary reputation chiefly in the fields of economics and political science as an exceedingly vigorous advocate of "hard money," free trade, and laissez faire. Again, while Sumner may claim a definite priority over any other American teacher in introducing a serious course in sociology into the university curriculum, he never published a systematic exposition of sociology, and his great monograph, *Folkways,* did not appear until three years before his death. These circumstances doubtless account for the fact that few persons who have not been Yale students or who have not been intimately acquainted with Sumner's academic work are aware that Sumner may accurately be classed as a sociologist. One need not be surprised that Professor Small was "shocked" in 1907 by the proposal of Sumner as president of the American Sociological Society. The extent of Sumner's interest and activity in sociology was not fully apparent until Professor Keller completed Sumner's projected work in four volumes, *The Science of Society* (1927–28). For the most part, however, this is an amplification of the methods and content of the earlier *Folkways*.[3] It has been ably digested and summarized in Professor Keller's *Man's Rough Road* (1932).

Sumner's own published works on sociology, aside from several brief essays, were almost entirely limited to his *Folkways*. Of this work it is not inaccurate to say that it is unsurpassed as a sociological achievement by any single volume in any language and that it has made the sociological treatment of usages, manners, customs, mores, and morals essentially a completed task.

So far as one can judge from his essays and lectures upon sociology, from his autobiographical sketches, and from Professor Keller's comments, Sumner's sociological views were colored by his economic and political predispositions and were inspired by the general attitudes and methods of Darwin, Spencer, and Julius Lippert. An evolutionary view of social life and development, a slight predilection for the use of biological concepts, and a firm conviction of the pre-eminent value of ethnography as the "data" and, to a large extent, the substance of sociology are the dominant features of Sumner's sociological thought. He seems to have been little influenced by, or acquainted with, the contemporary systematic sociological literature of America or Europe; and Professor Keller states that he even had little respect for such works. The doctrinal resemblance of Sumner's work to that of Spencer is to be seen in his political individualism, his reliance primarily on the ethnographic method, and his opposition to war and imperialism. The most extended expression of Sumner's views on the nature of the social sciences are to be found in Part VII of the third volume of his posthumous *Science of Society*.

It seems that Sumner's position in American sociology may be at least tentatively summarized as follows: He was the first teacher of sociology in the country from the standpoint of both time and ability; his *Folkways* is one of the finest treatments of a special field of sociology that has yet appeared; his sociological writings were primarily concrete and descriptive rather than abstract and theoretical; and his views regarding social initiative or "collective telesis," to adopt Ward's terminology, were exceedingly biased and archaic, being almost a *reductio ad absurdum* of the laissez faire individualistic position.

No extended analysis of Sumner's *Folkways* can be attempted within the scope of the present chapter, but it is essential that its fundamental conceptions be pointed out. As the subtitle of his work indicated, it is "a study of the sociological importance of usages, manners, customs, mores, and morals." The work is essentially an attempt to explain the origin, nature, value, and persistence of certain of the most important and characteristic group habits. Briefly, Sumner's theory of the folkways is that, guided in a general way by the instincts which he inherited from his animal ancestors and by the psychophysical capacity to distinguish pain from pleasure, man has gradually built up, by a process of trial and error, certain types of group conduct which have been found by experience to be conducive to the successful outcome of the struggle for existence. These group habits or folkways operate primarily on a subconscious or habitual level. They acquire greater power as time passes, through the force of tradition, habit, and religious sanction.

When the folkways reach the stage at which they are raised to the level of conscious reflection and are regarded as adapted to securing the continued welfare and prosperity of the group, they thereby become transformed into mores.[4] The mores, supported by group authority, are the chief agency through which societal selection operates. The mores determine what shall be regarded as right or wrong modes of conduct in any group, morality thus being not absolute and universal but relative and local. The question of the evolution of the mores and the ability of society consciously to change them was discussed by Sumner in many passages of his works, and he made it plain that he did not believe that members of any group are competent to discuss and criticize the validity of their own mores, much less to change them by predetermined action.[5] The following selected and rearranged quotations from the *Folkways* epitomize Sumner's theoretical position with respect to the mores:

Men in groups are under life conditions; they have needs which are similar under the state of the life conditions; the relations of the needs to the conditions are interests under the heads of hunger, love, vanity, and fear; efforts of numbers at the same time to satisfy interests produce mass phenomena which are folkways by virtue of uniformity, repetition, and wide concurrence. The folkways are attended by pleasure or pain according as they are well fitted for the purpose. Pain forces reflection and observation of some relation between acts and welfare.

At this point the prevailing world philosophy suggests explanations and inferences, which become entangled with judgments of expediency. However, the folkways take on a philosophy of right living and life policy for welfare. When the elements of truth and right are developed into doctrines of welfare, the folkways are raised to another plane. They then become capable of producing inferences, developing into new forms, and extending their constructive influence over men and society. Then we call them the mores.

The mores are the folkways, including the philosophical and ethical generalizations as to societal welfare which are suggested by them, and inherent in them, as they grow. They are the ways of doing things which are current in a society to satisfy human needs and desires, together with the faiths, notions, codes, and standards of well living which inhere in those ways, having a genetic connection with them. By virtue of the latter element the mores are traits in the specific character of a society or a period. They pervade and control the ways of thinking in all the exigencies of life, returning from the world of abstractions to the world of action, to give guidance and to win revivification.

At every turn we find new evidence that the mores can make anything right. What they do is that they cover a usage in dress, language, behavior, manners, etc., with the mantle of current custom, and give it regulation and limits within which it becomes unquestionable. The limit is generally a limit of toleration. The mores set the limits or define the disapproval.

The most important fact about the mores is their dominion over the individual. Arising he knows not whence or how, they meet his opening mind in earliest childhood, give him his outfit of ideas, faiths, and tastes, and lead him into prescribed mental processes. They bring to him codes of action, standards, and rules of ethics. They have a model of the man-as-he-should-be to which they mould him, in spite of himself and without his knowledge. If he submits and consents, he is taken up and may attain great social success. If he resists and dissents, he is thrown out and may be trodden underfoot.

The mores are therefore an engine of social selection. Their coercion of the individual is the mode in which they operate the selection. It is vain to imagine that a "scientific man" can divest himself of prejudice or previous opinion, and put himself in an attitude of neutral independence towards the mores. He might as well try to get out of gravity or the pressure of the atmosphere. The most learned scholar reveals all the philistinism and prejudice of the man-on-the-curbstone when the mores are in discussion. The most elaborate discussion only consists in revolving on one's own axis. When the statesmen and social philosophers stand ready to undertake any manipulation of institutions and mores, and proceed upon the assumption that they can obtain data upon which to proceed with confidence in that undertaking, as an architect or engineer would obtain data and apply his devices to a task in his art, a fallacy is included which is radical and mischievous beyond measure.[6]

In addition to his notion of the mores, the other fundamental conception in Sumner's sociological theory was the assumption that social, as well as organic, evolution is almost entirely an automatic, spontaneous process which cannot be extensively altered by social effort. In the light of Sumner's admitted obligation to Spencer, it seems reasonable to suppose that Sumner's view of social development either was directly derived from the latter or was strengthened by Spencer's vigorous exposition of this doctrine, particularly in his *Study of Sociology*. The following passage is the best summary of Sumner's views on the subject of the automatic evolution of society and the futility of social initiative:

If this poor old world is as bad as they say, one more reflection may check the zeal of the headlong reformer. It is at any rate a tough old world. It had taken its trend and curvature and all its twists and tangles from a long course of formation. All its wry and crooked gnarls and knobs are therefore stiff and stubborn. If we puny men by our arts can do anything at all to straighten them, it will be only by modifying the tendencies of some of the forces at work, so that, after a sufficient time, their action may be changed a little, and slowly the lines of movement may be modified. This effort, however, can at most be only slight, and it will take a long time. In the meantime, spontaneous forces will be at work, compared with which our efforts are like those of a man trying to deflect a river, and these forces will have changed the whole problem before our interferences have time to make themselves felt.

The great stream of time and earthly things will sweep on just the same in spite of us. It bears with it now all the errors and follies of the past, the wreckage of all the philosophies, the fragments of all the civilizations, the wisdom of all the abandoned ethical systems, the debris of all the institutions, and the penalties of all the mistakes. It is only in imagination that we stand by and look at and criticize it and plan to change it. Everyone of us is a child of his age and cannot get out of it. He is in the stream and is swept along with it. All his sciences and philosophy come to him out of it. Therefore the tide will not be changed by us. It will swallow up both us and our experiments. It will absorb the efforts at change and take them into itself as new but trivial components, and the great movement of tradition and work will go unchanged by our fads and schemes.

The things which will change it are the great discoveries and inventions, the new reactions inside the social organism, and the changes in the earth itself on account of changes in the cosmical forces. These causes will make of it just what, in fidelity to them, it ought to be. The men will be carried along with it and be made by it. The utmost they can do by their cleverness will be to note and record their course as they are carried along, which is what we do now, and is that which leads us to the vain fancy that we can make or guide the movement. That is why it is the greatest folly of which a man can be capable, to sit down with a slate and pencil to plan out a new social world.[7]

It would be interesting to know to what extent Sumner's rather vehement support of laissez faire was derived from his reading of Spencer and how far it was the outcome of his practical experience in American municipal politics, early in his career. At any rate, Sumner's dogmatic opposition to the doctrine that social reform can be effected through the agency of political machinery may be pardoned, as it would be a rare individual who could emerge with any other viewpoint from the simultaneous influence of Spencer's *Study of Sociology* and three years' experience in American city politics.[8]

II. SPECIFIC CONTRIBUTIONS TO SOCIAL AND POLITICAL THEORY

A. THE NATURE OF THE STATE

Though a professor of political science, Sumner never published any systematic treatment of political theory.[9] His reputation as a contributor to social and political theory rests upon a clear and vigorous elaboration of certain specific topics, chiefly the differentiation between democratic and republican government, a defense of laissez faire, and a condemnation of imperialism.

Sumner's conception of the state was extremely practical and matter of fact. He had little patience with the transcendental theories of writers like Hegel, who regarded the state as "perfected rationality" or an "ethical person." He says, in summarizing his analysis of the validity of the dogma that the state is an ethical person:

> It appears, therefore, that the assertion that we ought to conceive of the state as an ethical person does not rest upon any such solid analysis of the facts of life and the nature of the state as would make it a useful and fruitful proposition for further study of social phenomena, but that it is a product of the phrase-mill. It is one of those mischievous dicta which seem to say something profound; but, upon examination, prove to say nothing which will bear analysis.[10]

Sumner held that the state, as an abstraction, is nothing more than "all-of-us." In actual practice, "it is only a little group of men chosen in a very haphazard way by the majority of us to perform certain services for all of us."[11]

B. FORMS OF GOVERNMENT

Sumner was also opposed to the dogmatic statement that any type of government is absolutely the "best" under all circumstances. Like Montesquieu, he made a strong plea for the recognition of the principle of relativity in the excellence of political institutions. The "best" government for any particular people is simply that type which is best adapted to the general social, economic, and intellectual conditions which prevail: "We must abandon all hope of finding an absolutely 'best' system of government. If we study human nature and human history, we find that civil institutions are only 'better' and 'best' relatively to the people for whom they exist, and that they can be so called only as they are more closely adjusted to the circumstances of the nation in question."[12]

Though Sumner denied that there could be any absolutely or universally "best" government, there was, nevertheless, no doubt in his own mind as to what type of government was best adapted to the United States of his day. He was an uncompromising advocate of a conservative constitutional republic, based upon a sound system of representation. Such a government he defined, following Alexander Hamilton, as a "form of self-government in which the authority of the state is conferred for limited terms upon officers designated by election."[13] Sumner's political tenets were founded upon a curious, if interesting, combination of a Hamiltonian admiration of an aristocracy of talent; the ardent Jeffersonian defense of individualism, laissez faire, and free trade; and the conservative Republican advocacy of "hard money."

Sumner laid great stress upon the necessity of clearly differentiating between a "pure" democracy and a representative republic. Democracy is based upon the principle of equality and involves the direct participation of the people in every act of the government. The aim of a republic, on the other hand, is not equality but the securing and guaranteeing of civil liberty. Sumner held that democracy is an error in principle, in so far as it rests upon the assumption of the inherent equality of mankind. He said on this point that "the assertion that all men are equal is perhaps the purest falsehood in dogma which was ever put into human language; five minutes' observation of facts will show that men are unequal through a very wide range of variation."[14]

From this error of democracy in principle and as a result of its non-adaptability to the government of a large area, Sumner held that the attempt to preserve the ideals and practices of "pure" democracy in the federal and state governments of the United States was a dangerous anachronism and a menace to civil liberty and effective administration. With admirable clarity Sumner points out the fact that a "pure" democracy is fitted only for the administration of small local units, such as rural townships. The United States has completely outgrown the possibility of successfully employing this type of a democratic system in the federal or state governments. In adopting the necessary system of representation, we have carried over the extremely dangerous dogma of the older rural democratic local government that all men are equally fit to hold office and that officeholding is the legitimate privilege of every person. This general disregard of the necessity for expert guidance and for special talent in the holding of public office is the chief defect of our political system. Its other main imperfection is its impotence in the face of plutocratic and partisan interests.

If our political system is to be successful in the future, it must restore a proper estimation of the value of real statesmanship, purify the principle of representation, and improve the civil service in opposition to the antiquated dogmas and practices of pure democracy. None of these indispensable prerequisites of a successful republican system can be expected, however, without an intelligent and politically educated electorate.

C. THE PROBLEM OF SOCIAL REFORM THROUGH STATE ACTIVITY

There can be no doubt that Professor Sumner's reputation as a political theorist rests primarily upon his defense of laissez faire and his advocacy of a restriction of the functions of the state. He was easily the most able and tireless exponent in this country of the individualistic social philosophy which writers like Wilhelm von Humboldt and Spencer had upheld in Europe. Sumner's arguments in favor of laissez faire center around three main propositions: (1) that it is morally wrong to extend state activities, inasmuch as the burdens are not distributed in accordance with the benefits received; (2) that the state is proved by history to be incompetent as compared with private enterprise, and, moreover, when it extends its activities, it neglects its proper function of maintaining order and preserving liberty; and (3) that, since social evolution is primarily a product of nonvolitional forces, the interference of the state in an attempt to accelerate the process of evolution cannot fail to be mischievous and an impediment to progress.[15]

The fundamental purpose for which states exist, according to Sumner, is to secure and preserve civil liberty. Civil liberty he defines as "the careful adjustment by which the rights of individuals and the state are reconciled with one another to allow the greatest possible development of all and of each in harmony and peace."[16] In other words, the problem of state activity can be expressed in the abstract as follows: "Can we get from the state security for individuals to pursue happiness in and under it and yet not have the state itself become a burden and hindrance only a little better than the evil which it wards off?"[17] In practice this problem reduces itself to the simple question: "What ought Some-of-us do for Others-of-us?"[18]

It is in his answer to this practical question that Sumner makes his most original and distinctive defense of the principle of laissez faire, which he renders in his picturesque terminology as "mind your own business!"[19] Nearly all examples of an extension of state activity involve an agreement between A and B, who are "the ignorant social doctors," as to what C, who is the "Forgotten Man," shall do for D, who represents the class that has failed in the struggle for existence. The Forgotten Men make up that great self-respecting middle class in society. Being industrious, independent, and unobtrusive, this class attracts little attention, but, in reality, it is incomparably the most important of all social classes in its contribution to every phase of civilization.[20]

While this middle class never asks for any assistance from the government for itself, it invariably has to defray a disproportionate share of the expense of every extension of state activity: "It's the 'Forgotten Man' who is threatened by every extension of the paternal theory of government. It is he who must work and pay. When, therefore, the statesmen and social philosophers sit down to think what the State can or ought to do, they really mean to decide what the Forgotten Man shall do."[21]

The expense which is inherent in every extension of state activity always falls upon the middle class, but this class gets little or no benefit from these added burdens and tends to be crushed or diminished by them. Inasmuch as this class is, beyond all comparison, the most important element in the population, any extension of state action tends to menace the most valuable group in society for the benefit of those whose very need of assistance marks them off as inferior.[22]

It is important to note that Sumner does not defend laissez faire from a purely metaphysical individualistic standpoint but maintains that, from the strictly sociological point of view, a curtailment of state activity is indispensable. Sumner's answer to his famous question, "What do social classes owe to each other?" is that the sole duty of one class to another in society is to maintain an attitude of good will and mutual respect toward the other and to strive to bring about liberty and security, so that every class may improve its opportunities. Under no circumstances should one social class attempt to redistribute the achievements or products of the other classes.

In extending its activity into new and questionable fields, the state, Sumner holds, is losing its grip upon its primary function of providing "peace, order, and security." The extra-legal powers which have been usurped by party leaders and labor organizations have already vitiated the ability of the state to give security to the populace, and this practically means a revival of the "private war," so common in primitive society. Paternalistic legislation also provides a means for insidious and corrupt plutocratic interests to give themselves legal security in carrying on their exploitation of society.

History has never proved the state to be as competent as private enterprise, and the government of the United States has never shown a degree of intelligence and efficiency at all comparable to that exhibited by our private enterprise. As we have no reason to believe that the capacity of the state is likely to be improved, the only alternative is to restrict as much as possible the functions of the state and to leave the greatest possible opportunity for the development of the more competent private enterprise and personal initiative. The most urgent necessity in regard to the state is not to increase the sphere of its activity but to improve the performance of its legitimate functions.

Sumner's last argument in favor of laissez faire involves the question of the possibility and desirability of achieving the improvement of society by direct state action, in other words, the problem of the amenability of social evolution to artificial acceleration. Sumner's theory on this point is a combination of the ideas of Burke and the Romanticists on the historical development of institutions and the impossibility of making a sudden break with the past with Spencer's conception of the automatic and nonvolitional nature of social evolution. The attempt to reform social conditions by direct legislative action, he believed, is foredoomed to failure because of the spontaneous nature of social evolution and the impossibility of taking into account all the factors involved in any particular case: "Social improvement is not won by direct effort. It is secondary, and results from physical or economic improvements. That is why schemes of direct social amelioration always have an arbitrary, sentimental, and artificial character, while true social advance must be a product and a growth."[23]

The conviction that social improvement can be effected by direct action, then, is but one of those schemes for lifting one's self by one's bootstraps which have been discredited by natural science but have found a last intrenchment in social science.

In the place of Ward's term "attractive legislation," Sumner coins that of "speculative legislation" to designate all schemes to alter the existing social order by direct legislative action. After the manner of Burke, he declares that all "speculative legislation" is opposed to the fundamental principles of the Anglo-American legal and political systems, which are marked by "slow and careful growth, historic continuity, and aversion to all dogmatism and abstractionism."[24] The very complexity of social conditions prevents "speculative legislation" from achieving the desired results: "It is a characteristic of speculative legislation that it very generally produces the exact opposite of the result it was hoped to get from it. The reason is because the elements of any social problem which we do not know so far surpass in number and importance those which we do know that our solutions have far greater chance to be wrong than to be right."[25]

Another important reason for distrusting the efficacy of direct legislative action for social reform is to be found in the fact that, even if the plans for reform were perfectly scientific as theoretical abstractions, they would be likely to fail in their practical application. They would have to be put into operation, not by the learned reformers, but by the incompetent and avaricious machine politicians who constitute our body of public officials.[26]

In view of all these important objections to an extension of state activity, Sumner maintained that it was not only a matter of theoretical importance but also a patriotic and civic duty for all intelligent men to resist any increase of state interference. It is even futile to hope that politicians can make such changes in the social order as will retain the useful elements in the past and secure the benefits of innovations. It is a mere waste of time to reflect what the state might accomplish if politicians could attain real wisdom and integrity, for it is generally agreed that they never can do so. In short, Sumner advocated a greater efficiency in the exercise of the legitimate or "police" functions of the state and maintained that progress must come through the gradual and unconscious operation of social, economic, and intellectual forces.[27]

D. SOVEREIGNTY, LIBERTY, AND POLITICAL RIGHTS

Sumner's discussion of the problems of sovereignty, liberty, and rights is not particularly important or entirely consistent, though in certain points it is suggestive. He was not inclined to assign much importance to the concept of sovereignty. "Sovereignty is the most abstract and metaphysical term in political philosophy." It is undefinable and hence abused by all writers on political science. In another reference to the subject, however, he apparently regards sovereignty as identical with ultimate political power in a state and holds that the location of this power in a society is the criterion for classifying states.

In regard to liberty, Sumner is particularly insistent that there is no real liberty apart from law and political authority. Sumner distinguishes three different types or conceptions of liberty: anarchistic, personal, and civil. The anarchistic view of liberty, which was prominent in the earlier writings of Rousseau, maintains that man is free from all social responsibility. According to this fallacious view of liberty, no member of modern society can be said to possess liberty, unless it be the tramp. Personal liberty simply means a freedom from artificial impediments in the struggle for existence. Civil liberty is "a status created for the individual by laws and institutions, the effect of which is that each man is guaranteed the use of all his own powers exclusively for his own welfare."[28] As has already been pointed out, Sumner held that it is the chief purpose of the state to produce and preserve civil liberty.

Sumner was not entirely consistent in his discussion of political rights. In one reference to the subject he denied that the conception of natural rights possesses any validity whatever. In another analysis of the subject he held that the conception possessed a very considerable value and stated that "natural rights, as opposed to chartered rights, means that every man must, in the view of social order and obligation, be regarded as free and independent, until some necessity had been established for restraining him."[29] In his latest treatment of the subject Sumner reached what may be called a distinctly sociological conception of rights, namely, that they are "rules of the game of social competition which are current now and here." To be effective, they must be "recognized in laws and provided for by institutions."

E. IMPERIALISM AND EXPANSIONISM

Not only was Sumner an ardent advocate of laissez faire in domestic or internal policies, but he also vigorously criticized the imperialistic tendencies in the United States which took form about 1896 and culminated in the Spanish-American War and the conquest of several Spanish colonies. In both cases his fundamental argument was the same.

Imperialism, like paternalistic legislation, imposes upon the population burdens which quite outweigh the benefits which are forthcoming. The increased expenses of government are thrown upon the middle class, and imperialistic administration necessitates a curtailment of liberty and the adoption of militaristic measures which seriously threaten the existence of free republican government and industrial democracy.[30] Sumner's attack on imperialism was an effective answer to Benjamin Kidd and to Sumner's American contemporary, Franklin H. Giddings, who, in his *Democracy and Empire,* was ardently defending the new American imperialism.

Sumner made no attempt to dogmatize as to the exact size of the state whch is most desirable, but he laid down the general proposition that in every case there is a maximum size of the political unit which is most advantageous under the given circumstances. In each instance it is the task of the best statesmanship to determine the size which is most expedient. The tendency of the statesmanship of the nineteenth century to make nationality, in its ethnic sense, the test of the expedient size of the state has been proved fallacious. Sweden and Norway are homogeneous as regards nationality but have not been able to form a compact political unity, while Austria-Hungary, though extremely heterogeneous from the standpoint of nationality, was welded into a fairly coherent and stable political unit.

If territorial expansion proceeds beyond this expedient size, though it may enhance the prestige of the ruler or governing classes, it does not give added strength to the state. Under the present international system of unrestricted travel and enterprise, new territory acquired by a state means merely an increase in its burdens and liabilities and brings no adequate return. Not since the abolition of the old mercantilistic colonial system has additional territory proved an asset to a state.

More serious than the financial liabilities which are bound to be incurred by an imperialistic policy is the reaction of imperialistic ideas and practices upon the politics of the state. The whole imperialistic complex is fundamentally opposed to republicanism and industrialism. It invariably creates an attitude of political arrogance and chauvinism. When conquered territories are populated by peoples widely different in culture from the conquering state, they must either be admitted into the state to participate in government or be ruled as subjects. In the first case, corruption or disintegration is likely to take place, while the second alternative involves a sacrifice of republican principles. Imperialism invariably creates militarism, which is at all points opposed to industrial republicanism. It favors plutocracy by diverting the attention of the people from the sinister acts of corrupt interests at home. If persisted in, imperialism is bound to transform the United States into an empire and to render our republic merely a transitional form. Finally, only a person of defective intelligence would maintain that the accomplishments of the United States in war are better calculated to inspire patriotism than its achievements in peaceful pursuits.[31]

Sumner riddles some of the stock arguments which are usually adduced in favor of imperialism. He argues that no state is fitted to judge when another is adapted for self-government or to decide what constitutes a stable government in another state. On such grounds a conquest of the United States might be justified from the standpoint of certain other nations. Again, it is a very dangerous fallacy to claim that a nation must conquer adjoining territory to protect its present dominions. It was claimed that the United States must have Hawaii to protect California; according to this doctrine, the conquest of the Philippines would render necessary the acquisition of China, Japan, and the East Indies to protect the Philippines. "Of course this means that, on the doctrine, we must take the whole earth in order to be safe on any part of it, and the fallacy stands exposed."[32] Had Sumner lived to December 7, 1941, and Pearl Harbor, he would have seen the complete and tragic vindication of his prophecies as to the logical and final outcome of American imperialism. The following extracts admirably summarize the main arguments of Sumner against imperialism:

> Any extension will not make us more secure where we are, but will force us to take new measures to secure our new acquisitions. The preservation of acquisitions will force us to reorganize our internal resources, so as to make it possible to prepare them in advance and to mobilize them with promptitude. This will lessen liberty and require discipline. It will increase taxation and all the pressure of government. It will divert the national energy from the provision of self-maintenance and comfort for the people, and will necessitate stronger and more elaborate governmental machinery. All this will be disastrous to republican institutions and democracy. Moreover, all extension puts a new strain on the internal cohesion of the pre-existing mass, threatening a new cleavage within. If we had never taken Texas and northern Mexico we should never have had secession.[33]

> The issue [involved in imperialism] is nothing less than whether to go on and maintain our political system or to discard it for the European military and monarchial tradition. It must be a complete transformation of the former to try

to carry on under it two groups of political societies, one on a higher, the other on a lower plane, unequal in rights and powers; the former ruling the latter perhaps by military force.[34]

It is well for Sumner's complacency and peace of mind that he did not survive into the days of the New Deal and the second World War. The extensive social legislation of the New Deal and our participation in a great imperialistic war would have outraged every fiber of Sumner's being.[35] Even more vehement would have been his reaction to President Truman's proposal in March, 1947, that the United States become a sort of twentieth-century Byzantine empire.

F. SUMMARY OF SUMNER'S CONTRIBUTIONS TO SOCIAL THOUGHT

In summary, one may reasonably observe (1) that Sumner took over both Darwinian and Spencerian evolutionism and embodied them in his social thinking; (2) that he followed Spencer in holding that social evolution is inherently an automatic process, with which social effort should not interfere; (3) that he applied more comprehensively than any other American sociologist the ethnographic and comparative methods of the European anthropologists and ethnographers; (4) that he produced the outstanding sociological analysis of the origin and nature of moral codes and social customs; (5) that he formulated the most forceful American statement of the evolutionary basis of individualism and laissez faire; (6) that his arguments are the most impressive American critique of the conception of social planning and governmental activity; and (7) that he was the outstanding American sociological opponent of militarism and imperialism, comparable in this way to L. T. Hobhouse in England.[36]

NOTES

1. Cf. his *What Social Classes Owe to Each Other* (New York, 1883), p. 155 (hereafter cited as *"Social Classes"*).

2. Cf. "A Sketch of William Graham Sumner," *Popular Science Monthly*, June, 1889, pp. 261–68; reprinted in *The Challenge of Facts and Other Essays* (New Haven, 1914). For the most satisfactory accounts of Sumner as a personality and the salient facts of his life and academic career see H. E. Starr, *William Graham Sumner* (New Haven, 1925); and A. G. Keller, *Reminiscences of William Graham Sumner* (New Haven, 1933).

3. Volume I deals with the nature and evolution of the mores, industrial evolution and economic institutions, and political institutions and ideas; Vol. II treats of religion and religious mores; Vol. III handles marriage, the family, and sex mores generally; Vol. IV is an extended and valuable case book, illustrating the ethnographic method as applied to sociology.

4. W. G. Sumner, *Folkways: A Study of the Sociological Importance of Usages, Manners, Customs, Mores, and Morals* (Boston, 1907), pp. 2–4, 28–29, 30, 33–34, 59, 521–22; see also *The Science of Society* (4 vols.; New Haven, 1927–28), Vol. I, Part I.

5. *Folkways,* pp. 97–98. Sumner's disciple and successor at Yale, Professor A. G. Keller, has extended his master's discussion of the mores with respect to automatic evolution and conscious alteration in *Societal Evolution* (New York, 1915; new ed., 1931), chaps. iv–vi.

6. Pp. 30, 33–34, 59, 97–98, 173–74, 521–22. By permission of Ginn & Co.

7. "The Absurd Attempt To Make the World Over," written in 1894 and reprinted in *War and Other Essays,* pp. 208–10. This statement, written a decade after the appearance of the *Social Classes,* and the opinion expressed more than ten years later in *Folkways,* which was quoted above, constitute a definite answer to Professor Small's query (*American Journal of Sociology,* May, 1916, p. 733) as to whether Sumner ever changed his views regarding the efficacy of social effort and initiative. By permission of the Yale University Press.

8. Sumner was an alderman in New Haven from 1873 to 1876. Sumner's works which form the basis of the analysis of his social and political theory are, in addition to *Folkways* and *The Science of Society,* his *What Social Classes Owe to Each Other,* and his collected essays. The latter are contained in the following volumes:

a) *Collected Essays in Political and Social Science* (New York, 1885). This contains the following essays which deal with political theory: "The Theory and Practice of Elections" (pp. 98–139); "Presidential Elections and Civil Service Reform" (pp. 140–59).

b) *War and Other Essays* (New Haven, 1913). The pertinent selections in this are: "Sociology" (pp. 167–92); "The Absurd Attempt To Make the World Over" (pp. 195–210); "State Interference" (pp. 213–26); "The Fallacy of Territorial Expansion" (pp. 285–93); "The Predominant Issue" (pp. 337–52).

c) *Earth Hunger and Other Essays* (New Haven, 1913). Particularly valuable are the following: "Rights" (pp. 79–83); "Equality" (pp. 87–89); "Liberty" (pp. 109–203); "Fantasies and Facts" (pp. 207–79); "Democracy" (pp. 283–333).

d) *The Challenge of Facts and Other Essays* (New Haven, 1914). Especially to be noted are "Legislation by Clamor" (pp. 185–90); "The Shifting of Responsibility" (pp. 193–98); "The State as an Ethical Person" (pp. 201–4); "The New Social Issue" (pp. 207–12); "Speculative Legislation" (pp. 215–19); "Republican Government" (pp. 223–40); "Democracy and Responsible Government" (pp. 243–86); "Advancing Political and Social Organization in the United States" (pp. 289–344); "Introductory Lecture to Courses in Political and Social Science" (pp. 391–403).

e) *The Forgotten Man and Other Essays* (New Haven, 1918), containing also a bibliography of Sumner's works and an index to the last four volumes of essays. A list of Sumner's published books and articles is also to be found in *War and Other Essays,* pp. 377–81.

f) *Selected Essays of William Graham Sumner* (New Haven, 1924). This is a judicious selection of essays taken from the preceding five volumes. It is the most representative brief anthology of Sumnerian thought.

g) The latest selection and anthology is *Essays of William Graham Sumner* (2 vols.; New Haven, 1934).

9. The nearest approach to a comprehensive statement of his political theory is to be found in *Collected Essays in Political and Social Science,* pp. 98 ff.; see also *The Science of Society,* Vol. I, chaps. xvi–xx. For his general social theory the best anthology is the *Selected Essays of William Graham Sumner.*

No sociologist save Comte has ever been blessed or cursed by such reverent discipleship as has Sumner. A Sumner Club has been maintained at Yale from 1914 to the present day. It published an interesting bulletin on Sumner's ways and thoughts. Recently, Professor M. R. Davie has edited a symposium on the relation of Sumner's thought to current problems, *Sumner Today* (New Haven, 1940).

10. *The Challenge of Facts,* p. 203.

11. *Social Classes,* p. 9; see also *The Science of Society,* Vol. I, chaps. xvi, xx. It is obvious that Sumner's view of the state as a practical institution is identical with the conception of government as held by the best political scientists.

12. *The Challenge of Facts,* p. 244.

13. *Ibid.,* p. 226.

14. *Earth Hunger*, p. 88. Were Sumner alive, his views on Bolshevism would not be likely to lack the characteristic Sumnerian vigor (see *Sumner Today*, p. 111).

15. *Social Classes, passim; War and Other Essays*, pp. 208–10, 224–25; *Earth Hunger*, p. 299. It is of fundamental importance to note that none of Sumner's arguments for non-interference is based upon the conventional individualistic tenets.

16. *The Challenge of Facts*, p. 239. In this rather vague and equivocal definition, Sumner barely escapes bringing forth a product of the "phrase mill," as he liked to call the source of all rhetorical or metaphysical definitions. For Sumner's most mature discussion of liberty see *The Science of Society*, I, 622 ff.

17. *War and Other Essays*, p. 128.

18. *Social Classes*, p. 12.

19. *Ibid.*, p. 120.

20. *Ibid.*, pp. 126, 148–49.

21. *Ibid.*, p. 150.

22. *Ibid.*, pp. 148–51. This vital point in Sumner's political theory is analyzed and criticized by Professor F. H. Giddings, *Democracy and Empire* (New York, 1900), pp 110–21. Sumner's attitude is, of course, the argument that Guizot employed in defending the French middle class during the assault upon its financial power in the Restoration period. Showing how Rome had fallen, not because of immorality or paganism but on account of the extinction of the middle class by unjust taxation, Guizot tried to make it clear that France was inviting a similar fate by weakening the *bourgeoisie*.

23. *Social Classes*, pp. 160–61; cf. also *War and Other Essays*, pp. 208–10; and *Earth Hunger*, pp. 283 ff.

24. *The Challenge of Facts*, p. 215.

25. *Ibid.*, p. 219; cf. also Spencer, *The Study of Sociology*, pp. 270–71.

26. *Earth Hunger*, p. 287. These arguments against large-scale state activity, which have just been enumerated, embody Sumner's main theoretical contributions to the subject. For minor considerations and questions of detail see *Earth Hunger*, pp. 283–87, 300–301. It is, of course, well known that the specific curtailment of state action in which Sumner was most interested was an abolition of the system of protective tariffs in the United States.

27. *Social Classes*, pp. 162, 167; *Earth Hunger*, pp. 304–5; *War and Other Essays*, pp. 208–10. There is no evidence that Sumner ever changed his views regarding the futility of attempting to accelerate social evolution by legislative effort. His successor, Professor A. G. Keller, has discussed this problem further, and argues that any artificial acceleration of evolution in society must be achieved indirectly through an improvement of the "mores of self-maintenance" (*Societal Evolution*, esp. chap. v).

28. *Social Classes*, p. 34; see also *The Science of Society*, I, 622 ff.

29. *Earth Hunger*, pp. 223. For Sumner's most complete discussion of natural rights see *The Science of Society*, I, 600–606.

30. *War and Other Essays*, pp. 285 ff.

31. *Ibid.*, p. 334. Sumner's remarkable discussion of the part that war has played in social processes and social evolution, as well as his accurate prediction that European "defensive" preparedness for war would ultimately lead to a general European conflict, is contained in his *War and Other Essays*, chap. i.

32. *Ibid.*, p. 351.

33. *Ibid.*, p. 292.

34. *Ibid.*, p. 246; cf. also the nearly identical arguments advanced by L. T. Hobhouse, *Democracy and Reaction* (London, 1905), chaps. ii and viii. The arguments of Sumner are criticized by Giddings, *op. cit.*, pp. 269–90. While Giddings' criticism is by no means as effective as in the case of his analysis of Sumner's doctrines on state interference, chaps. i, xvii, and xx of Professor Giddings' work constitute the most vigorous defense of imperialism yet contributed by an American sociologist.

35. See the recent volume *Sumner Today, passim*.

36. For a fine summary of Sumner's social theory see L. L. Bernard, "The Social Science Theories of William Graham Sumner," *Social Forces*, XIX (1940), 153–75.

CHAPTER VII

LESTER FRANK WARD: THE RECONSTRUCTION
OF SOCIETY BY SOCIAL SCIENCE

Harry Elmer Barnes

I. GENERAL CHARACTERISTICS OF WARD'S SOCIOLOGICAL SYSTEM

AMONG American writers it can be said that Lester F. Ward (1841–1913) produced the most impressive and comprehensive system of sociology and was also the earliest systematic American sociologist. His *Dynamic Sociology,* which many critics consider his *magnum opus,* appeared in 1883, about midway between the publication of the first and last volumes of Spencer's *Principles of Sociology.* In addition to many articles in periodicals, Ward's sociological system was embodied in six considerable volumes.[1]

Whatever may be the estimate of the future regarding the place of Ward in the history óf sociology, it is certain that no other sociologist approached the subject equipped with a body of scientific knowledge which equaled that possessed by Ward. Herbert Spencer's *Synthetic Philosophy* may display more acute reasoning powers and a greater talent for the logical marshaling of evidence, but his scientific knowledge was not at all comparable to that possessed by Ward.

Ward's formal scientific career was that of government expert in paleobotany, to which he made contributions only second in importance to his work in sociology.[2] Ward's predilection for introducing his botanical terminology into his sociology often gives the latter as strange, technical, and repellent a tone as is to be found in the writings of the extreme "Organicists." Some of his scientific terms, however, such as "sympodical development," "synergy," "creative synthesis," "gynaecocracy," and "social telesis," are rather ingenious and have been fairly widely absorbed into conventional sociological thought and expression. A complete exposition of Ward's sociological system is manifestly impossible within the scope of the present work. Attention will be confined to his cardinal contributions.

As to the subject matter of sociology, Ward says: "My thesis is that the subject matter of sociology is human achievement. It is not what men are but what they do. It is not the structure but the function."[3] Since nearly all the earlier sociologists had been chiefly concerned with an analysis of social structure, Ward's point of approach was novel and epoch-making. The divisions of sociology are two—pure and applied. Pure sociology is theoretical and seeks to establish the principles of the science. Applied sociology is practical and points out the possible applications of pure sociology to social betterment. It "deals with artificial means of accelerating spontaneous processes of nature."[4]

Ward divides the body of his sociological system, accordingly, into "genesis" and "telesis." The former treats of the origin and spontaneous development of social structures and functions and the latter deals with the conscious improvement of society. In the department of social genesis, Ward's most important contributions may be summarized under the following headings: sympodial development, creative synthesis, synergy, the law of parsimony, the functions and biological origin of mind, social statics and dynamics, and the classification of the social forces.

The natural or genetic development of society is "sympodial." By this, Ward means that type of development found in certain plants in which the trunk, after developing to a certain extent, gives off a branch or sympode, which, from that point onward, virtually becomes the trunk, until it is, in turn, displaced by another sympode. The doctrine of "creative synthesis," which Ward adopted from the German psychologist, Wilhelm Wundt, he explains as denoting that "each combination is something more than the mere sum of its component factors."[5] Every synthesis of nature is, like the chemical compound, a new creation. This is probably the most useful of the contributions of Ward's pure science to his sociology. "Synergy," a word derived in part from botany and in part from Hegelian dialectic, is defined as "the systematic and organic working together of the antithetical forces of nature."[6] This is one of the basic conceptions underlying the theory of the spontaneous development of society. Finally, the "law of parsimony," which is the basic law of social mechanics, is described as the tendency of natural forces to work along the line of least resistance or greatest attraction.[7] The identity of this with Spencer's principle of motion along the line of least resistance is obvious.

With his characteristic daring and confidence, Ward describes the origin of life and the biological basis of mind. Life originated through the process of "zoism," which was a creative synthesis taking the form of the recompounding of the highest known chemical properties.[8] The mind is also a creative product of "zoism." It originated in the fact of "awareness," and its irreducible element is the capacity of detecting and differentiating painful and pleasurable stimuli coming from the environment.[9] Feeling and desire, which had an earlier origin than the intellect, are the dynamic and impelling forces of mind; intellect, which is a later and higher product, is the directive faculty.[10]

Ward considered his distinction between social statics and social dynamics and his discussion of the nature of each of these to be one of his most important theoretical contributions. Social statics deals with social equilibration and the establishment of a social order—the building-up of social structures.[11] The development of the social order is a "struggle for structure" rather than a struggle for existence. The best structures survive. In the growth of social structures social synergy is the most important principle. It is the force which creates all structures and explains all organization. Through this principle of synergy there is brought about the collaboration of the antithetical forces of nature in the following sequence of processes: collision, conflict, antagonism, opposition, antithesis, competition, interaction, compromise, collaboration, co-operation, and organization.

Synergy, in the development of the social order, takes place mainly through the process that Ward calls "social karyokinesis." This is the social analogue of fertilization in the biological field and is manifested in the contact, amalgamation, and assimilation of different social groups. All the stages enumerated in the above sequence are exemplified in this process, which ends in the production of a homogeneous nation. Ward here follows the theory of Ratzenhofer and Gumplowicz regarding the "struggle of races and social groups" as the main factor in state-building.

Social dynamics deals with social progress or the changes in the structure of society.[12] In social dynamics there are three fundamental principles—difference of potential, innovation, and conation. The difference of potential is manifested in the crossings of cultures which take place through social assimilation and amalgamation. Progress comes from a fusion of unlike elements. Innovation, which is the social analogue of the sport or mutation in the organic world, is the product of psychic exuberance. Conation, or social effort, is that application of social energy from which achievement results. This achievement takes the form of the satisfaction of desire, the preservation of life, and the modification of the environment.

Ward classifies the social forces as ontogenetic or preservative, phylogenetic or reproductive, and sociogenetic or spiritual.[13] It is in connection with his discussion of the phylogenetic forces that Ward develops his famous theory of "gynaecocracy," according to which he holds that the female sex was the original sex in nature and was the most important until it was subordinated by the social restraints imposed upon it after man discovered his relation to the child.[14]

In his exposition of the principle of social telesis, Ward lays down the fundamental proposition that energy must be controlled if evolution is to result. There are two possible methods of control: the unconscious control of nature manifested in *genesis* and the conscious direction by mind involved in *telesis*.[15] The conscious method of control by mind is manifestly superior to the unconscious control of nature. Nature is wasteful in providing an immense mass of raw materials and leaving them to be improved very slowly through natural selection. The tendency of mind is to economize through foresight and the adjustment of means to ends. This control of the dynamic forces of nature and society through the adjustment of means to ends is what Ward designates as "telesis."

In this process of conscious or telic control of the social forces, the development of the state was the most important step ever taken by man or society.[16] Nevertheless, though the state is the chief agent through which the conscious control of the social process is and will be carried on, society cannot perfect this conscious control through any agency until there is developed an adequate and sufficiently diffused knowledge of the nature and the operation of the social forces. Therefore, the provision of a system of education which will make possible the universal diffusion of this essential knowledge is the indispensable prerequisite to the complete development of collective or social telesis.[17]

In conclusion, one may safely say that Ward's outstanding contributions to sociology were his grasp of the relation between cosmic and social evolution and his doctrine of the superiority of the conscious to the unconscious control of the social process. In neither of these respects has he been surpassed by any other sociologist.[18] Of these two cardinal contributions the latter is by far the more important, for the obvious reason that the former is at best but picturesque and eloquent guesswork and must always be so until the range of human knowledge is greatly extended. The latter, however, is perhaps the most important single contribution of sociology to human thought, and Ward's significance rests mainly upon the fact that his presentation of this conception has been the most effective that sociology has so far produced. Professor F. H. Giddings has summed up this aspect of Ward's system with characteristic clarity:

> Throughout all Ward's work there runs one dominating and organizing thought. Human Society, as we who live now know it, is not the passive product of unconscious forces. It lies within the domain of cosmic law, but so does the mind of man: and this mind of man has knowingly, artfully, adapted and readapted its social environment, and with reflective intelligence has begun to shape it into an instrument wherewith to fulfill man's will. With forecasting wisdom man will perfect it, until it shall be at once adequate and adaptable to all its uses. This he will do not by creative impulse evolving in a void, but constructive intelligence shaping the substantial stuff of verified scientific knowledge. Wherefore, scientific knowledge must be made the possession of mankind. Education must not merely train the mind. It must also equip and store with knowledge.
>
> This great thought Dr. Ward apprehended, expressed, explained, illuminated, drove home to the mind of all who read his pages, as no other writer, ancient or modern, has never done. It is his enduring and cogent contribution to sociology.[19]

II. SPECIFIC CONTRIBUTIONS TO SOCIAL AND POLITICAL THEORY

A. THE RELATION OF SOCIOLOGY TO POLITICAL SCIENCE

The conception which Ward holds of the relation of sociology to political science is apparent from his view of the general relation between sociology and the special social sciences. The special social sciences furnish the data which the more comprehensive social science—sociology—co-ordinates and uses as the basis of its generalizations. But sociology is more than the mere sum of the special social sciences. It is the true creative synthesis and, like a chemical compound, is a new product and of a higher order than the constituent units. Political science, as a special social science, furnishes the data for the generalizations which sociology offers upon political problems. Ward's famous and authoritative statement of the nature of sociology and its relation to the special social sciences is worth quoting:

> It is not quite enough to say that it is a synthesis of them [the special social sciences] all. It is the new compound which their synthesis creates. It is not any of them and it is not all of them. It is that science which they spontaneously generate. It is a genetic product, the last term in the genesis of science. The special social sciences are the units of aggregation that organically combine to create

sociology, but they lose their individuality as completely as do chemical units, and the resultant product is wholly unlike them and is of a higher order. All this is true of any of the complex sciences, but sociology, standing at the head of the entire series, is enriched by all the truths of nature and embraces all truth. It is the *scientia scientiarum*.[19a]

B. GENERAL DEFINITIONS AND CONCEPTS

Ward's distinctions, if they may be called such, between the terms "society," "state," "government," and "nation" are very vague and unsatisfactory. He certainly did little to clarify the terminology of political science. He does not employ any of the above terms in a consistent or uniform manner, nor does he in any place define any of them in an exact sense.

"Society" is used as the generic term for associated life and also to describe advanced forms of human associations. That he did not regard the distinction between the terms "state," "government," and "nation" as fundamental is apparent from the following passage: "If anyone objects to the use of the word government, there is no reason why the word nation or state may not be substituted. The name is not essential."

However careless Ward may have been in his use of terms to describe the fundamental political organization of society, he was not in the least equivocal in regard to its importance.[20] He invariably insists that the state or the government is the most important social institution. He repeatedly emphasized the value of the organic analogy which represents the state as the brain of the social organism. The following paragraph, which is almost Hegelian in spirit, best summarized Ward's conception of the state:

We thus see that the state, though genetic in its origin, is telic in its method; that it has but one purpose, function, or mission, that of securing the welfare of society; that its mode of operation is that of preventing the anti-social action of individuals: that in doing this it increases the freedom of human action so long as it is not anti-social; that the state is therefore essentially moral and ethical; that its own acts must necessarily be ethical; that being a natural product it must in a large sense be representative; that in point of fact it is always as good as society will permit it to be; that while thus far in the history of society the state has rarely performed acts that tend to advance mankind, it has always been the condition to all achievement, making possible all the social, industrial, artistic, literary, and scientific activities that go on within the state and under its protection. There is no other institution with which the state may be compared, and yet, in view of all this, it is the most important of all human institutions.[21]

Ward did not enter into any formal discussion of the problem of sovereignty. He defines liberty as "the power to act in obedience to desire."[22] The love of liberty has thus been instinctive and universal in mankind. In theory, government is the necessary foe of liberty. In fact, however, government, by checking license, has prevented man from losing more liberty than it has taken away. The restraint of absolute liberty by government has made possible the development of man's intellectual powers, so that ultimately he may be restored to the possession of his complete original liberty, but not a liberty which is based upon ignorance. The liberty of the future will be one that is founded upon an intelligent comprehension of man's relations to society and will not require crude artificial restraints to prevent its enjoyment from threatening the disintegration of society.

Ward relates his interpretation of political parties very definitely to his theory of social mechanics. The fundamental principle underlying his sociological interpretation of the struggles between different political parties is that of "social synergy." Party antagonism, in reality, brings about a co-operation between seemingly antithetical forces and secures their working together toward an end of which they are unconscious:

> The vigorous interaction of the two forces, which looks so much like antagonism, strife, and struggle, transforms force into energy and energy into power, and builds political and social structures. And after they are constructed, the same influences transform them, and it is this that constitutes social progress. Political institutions —the laws of every country—are the product of this political synergy, the crystallized action of legislative bodies created by political parties.[23]

In the same way, therefore, that the struggle between races and groups creates society and the state, the struggle between political parties within the state transforms the state and produces political progress. Moral, rather than technical, questions are best adapted for political issues. The progressive and liberal parties, which are characterized by the advocacy of an extension of governmental activity, are the real friends of individualism and liberty. The "coming slavery," to use Spencer's term, has already arrived, says Ward, in the form of the plutocratic, laissez faire control of society and political organization by the conservative capitalistic parties. The progressive parties, which stand for collective action, are the force which is attempting to secure emancipation from this slavery and exploitation.

C. THE ORIGIN OF SOCIETY AND THE STATE, AND THE STAGES OF POLITICAL EVOLUTION

While Professor Small remarked with accuracy that Ward modified his sociological thought but little between the publication of his *Dynamic*

Sociology and his death, this is decidedly not the case with his theory of the origin of the state.

The theory which he advanced in the *Dynamic Sociology* was quaint and curious, being virtually a combination of Hobbes's view of a pre-social state of nature with Rousseau's conception of the origin of the state through an artifice of the most powerful individuals.[24] In the first place, Ward here envisages four broad stages of social development. The first was the solitary or "autarchic" stage, in which man lived in solitude and as far from a social state as was in keeping with the possibility of propagating and rearing his kind. The earliest condition of man was thus presocial, if not antisocial. The second stage in social evolution was the "anarchic," or that of the "constrained aggregate." Social groups had expanded through natural or genetic increase, but, being without government, they lived in a "state of utmost liberty and utmost license." The third stage he designates as the "national" or "politarchic" stage, which was distinguished by the origin of a crude form of government. The wars which took place between these first national groups led to the formation of larger political societies and will ultimately lead to the development of the fourth or final stage in social evolution. This ultimate stage, which he designates as the "cosmopolitan" or "pantarchic," will come when social integration has produced the world state.

In his specific account of the origin of the state in the *Dynamic Sociology,* Ward starts with the utterly untenable theory of the antisocial nature of primitive man. He denies the validity of the Aristotelian tradition regarding the sociability of man. Since the passions of primitive man were intense and the means of satisfying them limited, the condition of life must have been one of conflict, and orderly society could not have been possible until the development of political control and protection. The origin of society and government must have been coeval. But mankind did not find its way out of this state of primitive anarchy through the social contract. The people as a whole never sought government; government always created itself. Government was initiated by a few especially ambitious individuals who were possessed of superior sagacity and who desired social power and position. They disguised their real intentions by claiming to intervene to protect the weak and oppressed: "The plan must have consisted in speciously claiming as the real object the protection of the injured and the punishment of the injuring. This, as the sagacity of the founders of government foresaw, would secure them adherents and confirm their authority."[25] Owing to this insidious and oppressive origin of political authority, man has ever since that time been trying to escape from the burdens which government has imposed. But the many evils that have accompanied the development of government are not the result of the application of the principle of political control; they are a consequence of the perversions of sound and wise government by mankind.

During the interval between the appearance of his *Dynamic Sociology* and the publication of the *Pure Sociology,* Ward became acquainted with the now generally accepted theory of Ferguson, Spencer, Bagehot, Gumplowicz, and Ratzenhofer, to the effect that the state, as it is defined by political science, originated through the processes of group conflict, amalgamation, and assimilation. This doctrine Ward accepted with great enthusiasm. He says of it: "It furnishes the first scientific, or in the least satisfactory, theory that has been advanced as to the origin and true constitution of the state, so that, after grasping this principle in its entirety, all the old notions about the state become rubbish, and any work on the nature of the state that does not recognize and start from this standpoint is superficial and practically worthless."[26]

D. THE FORMS OF GOVERNMENT

As a general classification of the forms of government, Ward proposes the terms "autocracies," "aristocracies," and "democracies." Within the general classification of democracy, Ward distinguishes three distinct variations: "physiocracy," "plutocracy," and "sociocracy." Physiocracy is that type of government which developed in western Europe as a result of the teaching of the Physiocrats and Adam Smith and of such individualistic writers as Wilhelm von Humboldt and Spencer. It is that sort of laissez faire government that is based upon honest but wrongheaded individualistic political philosophy.

Plutocracy is that perversion of physiocracy that resulted when, in the early nineteenth century, the corrupt and selfish vested interests of capitalism exploited the individualistic political philosophy for the purpose of maintaining themselves in their position of ascendancy. The exponents of this theory make a wide use of the individualistic appeal for governmental inactivity and utilize the deep-seated prejudice of the masses against government, so that they may be allowed to continue their exploitation of society. This perversion of individualism, which originated a century ago, is still the current form of contemporary political theory and organization.

Sociocracy is the next logical stage in political evolution. It is, in reality, the ideal democracy from which the current partisanship, ignorance, hypocrisy, and stupidity have been eliminated. In short, it is administration of the government by society for the public interest, and not the present exploitation of society for the benefit of a particular party or group of interests. Sociocracy does not lay stress primarily upon the external form of government but "goes to the substance, and denotes that, in whatever manner organized, it is the duty of society to act consciously and intelligently, as becomes an enlightened age, in the direction of guarding its own interests and working out its own destiny."[27] Under a sociocratic form of government "society would inquire in a business way without fear, favor, or bias, into everything that concerned its welfare, and if it found obstacles it would remove them, and if it found opportunities it would improve them. In a word, society would do under the same circumstances just what an intelligent individual would do. It would further in all possible ways its own interests."[28]

E. THE FUNCTIONS OF THE STATE

In his theories regarding the function and sphere of state activity, Ward was the most vigorous and consistent opponent of Spencerian and Sumnerian laissez faire individualism among the strictly sociological writers of his time.[29] In fact, Ward's treatment of this subject is the most satisfactory and important division of his social and political theories. While no writer has been more scathing in his condemnation of the defects and evils in contemporary political systems, Ward always distinguished carefully between the institution of government and its perversions. For the latter he had unlimited contempt, but he never lost his faith in the efficacy of the government as an agent of social reform, if it could be put on a scientific basis and purged of its corruption and stupidity.

Ward enumerates four chief functions of government: the restraint, protection, accommodation, and amelioration of society.[30] The first of these has never been a legitimate function; the second will be necessary so long as men do not refrain from injuring their fellows; the third is, and always will be, an indispensable function of government; while the fourth, which is the most important of all, has been scarcely put into action at all.

The restraint of the citizens by the government is not conducted in the interests of the community but is designed to allow the ruling classes to proceed with their exploitation. How long it will be before society divests the government of this function will depend upon the rapidity of the growth of social intelligence and enlightenment. By the "protective" function of government Ward means the "police" function, which is concerned with the prevention of fraud and violence. This cannot be dispensed with until the fraudulent and violent elements in society are eliminated by the general advance of enlightenment and intelligence. The function of accommodation, however, is never likely to be outgrown:

> Man is neither ubiquitous, omniscient, nor omnipotent; hence he needs agents to transact business in localities where he cannot be; to acquire skill and dexterity in subjects with which everyone cannot afford time to acquaint himself; and to perform duties by means of organization which individuals, acting independently, would not possess the strength to perform. In short, society needs and must always have an organized agency to represent it.[31]

In carrying on its restraining, protecting, and accommodating functions, government has not directly promoted progress. But, while possessing no directly progressive element, it has been the indispensable prerequisite of all progress. Government can directly improve the condition of society in a conscious or telic manner if the legislators will only become social scientists. There can be no scientific government, no important development of the ameliorative function of government, until legislators have gained a knowledge of the nature and means of controlling the social forces, in the same way that the natural scientist discovers the physical laws of nature and applies this knowledge in controlling natural laws and adapting them to the service of technology.[32]

Ward's whole defense of government as the most effective instrument of society in promoting progress rests primarily upon his above-mentioned distinction between honest and intelligent government and its past and present perversions. As to origins, the extant governments almost universally arose in exploitation. They were established by, and have been conducted in the interest of, those who desired to govern and exploit. A rationally constituted government should be instituted by, and conducted for the benefit of, those desiring to be governed. Again, whereas in our actual governments the people look up to the government as their master and the government regards the citizens in the light of subjects, in a rational political system the officers of government would be viewed as public servants and would be compelled, upon pain of removal, to perform their stipulated duties. In a model government the social distance which separates the governing and the governed would be eliminated. The people would recognize that they are the source of political authority and that the government is merely their agent. Governments are at present analogous to large stock companies conducted in the interest of the officers and not for the profit of the stockholders. Progress toward the perfection of government must first come "in the direction of acquainting every member of society with the special nature of the institution, and awakening him to a more vivid conception of his personal interest in its management."

In his essay on "False Notions of Government,"[33] Ward points out the unfortunate results which have come about as a result of the failure to distinguish between the true principles and the actual practices of government. The deep-seated popular distrust of government was very beneficial in the earlier periods of despotism, but the recent democratization of government has removed the need for this suspicious and wrongheaded attitude toward political control and direction, and its persistence is detrimental. It keeps good men from entering public life; it perverts the notion of the true purpose of government; it intensifies party strife by emphasizing the aspect of spoil; it makes government worse by encouraging the politician to live up to his unsavory reputation; and, finally, it deprives government of much of its usefulness by weakening its protective function.

These "false notions of government" must be removed. The people must be made to grasp the correct conception of government and take the proper steps to remove its abuses and use it for their own ends. Accordingly, Ward severely criticizes as obstructionists those "Misarchists," of whom the most conspicuous examples among sociologists have been Herbert Spencer, W. G. Sumner, and Jacques Novicow, for their strenuous attempts to perpetuate this "pernicious view of government." The exploitation of society by organized wealth requires the intervention of government at present, just as the exploitation by individuals, tyrants, nobles, and lawless characters created a need for the origin of the protective function of government.

F. THE STATE, EDUCATION, AND SOCIAL REFORM

The basic principles of Ward's sociology are nowhere better displayed than in his doctrines regarding the solution of social problems and maladjustment through the agency of governmental activity—in other words, his treatment of government as the chief instrument in collective or social telesis.

That the government must be the seat of control of the social process is evident from the fact that it alone can be viewed as the social analogue of the brain in the individual organism. The present stupidity of the personnel and activities of governments is the basis of the familiar argument that government can never give evidence of any creditable degree of intelligence. When the general level of social intelligence is raised, there is every reason to believe that the knowledge of those in control of the government will be proportionately improved.[34]

In his *Psychic Factors of Civilization*,[35] Ward summarizes what he regards as the indispensable prerequisites for the successful operation of social or collective telesis through the instrumentality of government. The legislators must either be social scientists or work in co-operation with sociologists. The prevalent confusing legislative methods must be eliminated. This can best be brought about by an extension of the use of the committee system and by conferring upon the executive the power to participate in legislation. Finally, there must be a greater use of statistics as the data upon which all scientific lawmaking must be based.[36]

Like Comte, to whom he was much indebted for many of his political theories and much of his political terminology, Ward placed his chief reliance on sociology as the source of the information which is essential for any extensive development of scientific government. Ward's legislators, like the priests of the Positivist regime, were to be trained sociologists. Hence the diffusion of a knowledge of fundamental sociological principles must precede the scientific development and application of governmental activity in behalf of social reform. The legislators must be thoroughly acquainted with the nature of, and the method of controlling, the social forces. In current jargon, Ward was an ardent supporter of government through a "brain trust" and the great sociological forerunner of the "social-planning" program. Unfortunately, however, says Ward, sociological knowledge itself is as yet in a very imperfect and undeveloped stage. In 1903, according to Ward, it was in practically the same stage of development that physics and chemistry were in during the fifteenth century. This indispensable sociological knowledge must be imparted by an improved system of education.

Ward takes as his point of departure in discussing the social function of education the thesis that the social forces can be directed into safe and useful channels only if their nature and the means of their control are understood. Education should thus be valued in proportion "as it gives to its possessor correct views of life, of his relations to society, and to nature." The educational system which embraces this useful type of information should be carried on by the state and should be universal. The whole sociological problem and significance of education he sums up in the following characteristic paragraph:

> It is the question whether the social system shall always be left to nature, always be genetic and spontaneous, and be allowed to drift listlessly on, intrusted to the by no means always progressive influences which have developed it and brought it to its present condition, or whether it shall be regarded as a proper subject of art, treated as other natural products have been treated by human intelligence, and made as much superior to nature, in this only proper sense of the word, as other artificial productions are superior to natural ones.[37]

When this revised and universal system of education is put into effect, government, which will be sociocratic in form, can be conducted on truly scientific principles, and it will then be in a position to promote progress by the indirect or telic method of "social invention" and "attractive legislation." True social invention "consists in making such adjustments as will induce men to act in the manner most advantageous to society." These adjustments must take the form of "attractive legislation," which will replace the wrongheaded and repressive legislation of the present day.

This principle of "attractive legislation" Ward explains in the following manner: The "desire, passions, and propensities of men" are the great impelling forces of society. They have vast potentialities for both good and evil. Repressive legislation, which constitutes the vast majority of modern laws, simply curbs this energy without deriving any benefit from it. Attractive legislation would not aim to check or restrain this vital energy of society but, instead, would divert it from harmful forms of expression and would direct it into constructive channels. In terms of the new dynamic psychology, it would provide a rational method of *sublimating* social energy.

The scientific statesmanship of the future must attempt to guide and utilize social forces and energy in the same manner that the applied scientists of today control and utilize the physical energy of nature. Ward's best summary of the fundamental characteristics of the political regime based upon the principles of attractive legislation and collective telesis is contained in the following paragraphs, which are, at the same time, a fairly adequate summary of his whole social philosophy:

> As a scientific investigator, the legislator would then set for himself the task of devising means to render harmless those forces now seen to be working evil results, and to render useful those now running to waste. Not only would the present prohibitive legislation, which seeks to accomplish its ends by direct, or brute method, be rapidly supplanted by attractive legislation accomplishing its purposes by the indirect, or intellectual, method, and thus fulfilling the protective functions of government at a saving of enormous loss through the friction of opposition, but the accommodative function would now be in condition to advance toward the position of a truly ameliorative one.
>
> Society, possessed for the first time of a completely integrated consciousness, could at last proceed to map out a field of independent operation for the systematic realization of its own interests, in the same manner that an intelligent and keen-witted individual pursues his life-purposes. Not only would protection and accommodation be secured without loss of liberty and at the least possible cost to society, but directly progressive measures would be adopted looking to the organization of human happiness.
>
> Fully realizing the character and mode of operation of the truly progressive agencies of society, government would not simply foster and protect these, but would increase and intensify them and their influence. No longer doubting that progress, upon the whole, must be in proportion to the degree and universality of intelligence, no effort or expense would be spared to impart to every citizen an equal and adequate amount of useful knowledge.[38]

Ward's prophetic vein was not entirely exhausted by this eloquent picture of the scientific legislation of the future. He even dared to predict that, in the still more remote future, with the perfection of the intellect and the completeness of knowledge, the state and government may disappear. This seems to be a denial, however, of Ward's statement mentioned above, to the effect that society would never outgrow the need for the accommodating function of government.

III. SUMMARY APPRAISAL OF WARD'S SOCIAL THOUGHT

In summarizing Lester F. Ward's contributions to social thought, it is fair to say: (1) that Ward made the most impressive effort by a sociologist to link up the concepts of natural and social science; (2) that he was the first notable sociologist of post-Darwinian days to emphasize the difference between biological and social evolution and to contend that the latter can be brought under social and mental control; (3) that he clearly distinguished between the genetic method of organic evolution and the telic processes of social development; (4) that he forecast the growing trend toward state interference and governmental planning and urged that these be guided by realistic social education; (5) that he was, thus, the father of the "social-studies" movement, in so far as this is related to public advancement and social progress; (6) that he anticipated by several generations the current social emphasis in education; and (7) that he stressed the fact that the data and laws of social science are chiefly useful in promoting social betterment and finding a short cut to utopia, which can otherwise be reached only by the slow and wasteful methods of naturalistic evolution.[39]

NOTES

1. *Dynamic Sociology* (2 vols.; New York, 1883); *The Psychic Factors of Civilization* (Boston, 1893); *The Outlines of Sociology* (New York, 1898); *Pure Sociology* (New York, 1903); *Applied Sociology* (Boston, 1904). His *Pure Sociology* appeared in a reduced and clarified form in J. Q. Dealey and L. F. Ward, *Textbook of Sociology* (New York, 1905). Ward's minor works and notices of his major contributions are brought together in his "mental autobiography," *Glimpses of the Cosmos* (8 vols.; New York, 1913).

Of these works, *Dynamic Sociology* is the best extended exposition of his whole social philosophy, a briefer and clearer presentation of which is to be found in the second part of his *Outlines of Sociology*. *Pure Sociology* is the authoritative exposition of his sociological system, which, again, is more clearly presented in Dealey and Ward's *Textbook of Sociology*. His social psychology is best brought together in *Psychic Factors of Civilization*, while his *Applied Sociology* is the classic exposition of his conception of social telesis.

His *Pure Sociology* is reviewed by H. H. Bawden in *American Journal of Sociology*, IX, (1903–4), 408–15; is criticized in detail by A. W. Small, *American Journal of Sociology*, IX (1903–4), 404–7, 567–75, 703–7; and is critically analyzed by J. M. Gillette in *American Journal of Sociology*, XX (1914–15), 31–67.

Estimations of Ward's significance for sociology by eminent sociologists appear in *American Journal of Sociology*, X (1904–5), 643–53; XIX (1913–14), 61–78; XXI (1915–16), 748–58, 824.

The most complete treatment of Ward as man, scientist, and sociologist is the enthusiastic book by Samuel Chugerman, *Lester F. Ward: The American Aristotle* (New York, 1939). There is a well-selected anthology of Ward's sociological writings in Clement Wood, *The Substance of the Sociology of Lester F. Ward* (New York, 1930). For biographical details see E. P. Cape, *Lester F. Ward: A Personal Sketch* (New York, 1930).

2. His academic career was limited to lectures at several university summer-school sessions and six years (1906–12) as professor of sociology at Brown University. For the formative experiences in Ward's life see B. J. Stern, *Young Ward's Diary* (New York, 1935).

3. *Pure Sociology*, p. 15.

4. *Ibid.*, pp. 3, 431.

5. *Ibid.*, p. 79.

6. *Ibid.*, p. 171.

7. *Ibid.*, p. 161.

8. *Ibid.*, pp. 115–19.

9. *Ibid.*, pp. 119–35.

10. *Ibid.*, pp. 97, 99 ff., 124 ff., 142, 467 ff.

11. *Ibid.*, pp. 175 ff.

12. *Ibid.*, pp. 221 ff.

13. *Ibid.*, p. 261.

14. *Ibid.*, pp. 296 ff., 336–41, 345.

15. *Ibid.*, pp. 463 ff.

16. *Ibid.*, p. 551.

17. *Ibid.*, pp. 573–75; *Dynamic Sociology*, Vol. II, chap. xiv; *Applied Sociology, passim*. With this outline of Ward's sociology based upon his *Pure Sociology* compare his own summary in the Preface of his *Dynamic Sociology*.

18. Cf. A. W. Small, *American Journal of Sociology*, XXI (1915–16), 752; F. H. Giddings, *American Journal of Sociology*, XIX (1913–14), 67–68.

19. Giddings, *loc. cit.* It is hardly necessary to point out that this is essentially a contradiction of Spencer's thesis and that it constitutes the chief difference between the social philosophy of the two men who were to sociology what Niebuhr and Ranke were to history and Turgot and Adam Smith to economics.

19a. *Pure Sociology*, p. 91.

20. *Psychic Factors of Civilization*, p. 297. Cf. *Pure Sociology*, p. 188, where, in opposition to the conventional view, he argues that the institution of government by society required and produced the state.

21. *Pure Sociology*, p. 555.

22. *Dynamic Sociology*, II, 233.

23. Ward, "The Sociology of Political Parties," *American Journal of Sociology*, XIV (January, 1908), 440–41.

24. As expressed in Rousseau's famous *Second Discourse*. For Ward's own frank admission of the archaic and erroneous nature of his earliest theory of the state see his "Sociology and the State," *American Journal of Sociology*, XVI (March, 1910), 679–80.

25. *Dynamic Sociology*, II, 224. This tendency of the few to dominate in political control has been scientifically analyzed by F. H. Giddings, who designates it as the principle of "protocracy" (see his *Responsible State* [Boston, 1918], pp. 19 ff.).

26. Ward, *American Journal of Sociology*, VII (1901–2), 762; cf. also *ibid.*, XV (1909–10), 679–80; *Pure Sociology*, pp. 204 ff. As Ward agrees entirely with Gumplowicz and Ratzenhofer upon the subject of the origin of the state, it will not be necessary to repeat his version of their doctrine. In addition to the reference to *Pure Sociology*, Ward's interpretation of the Gumplowicz-Ratzenhofer theory of the origin of the state is best summarized in *American Journal of Sociology*, X (1904–5), 643–53; and *Publications of the American Economic Association* (3d ser., 1904), V, No. 2, 187 ff. The criticisms which can be directed against this group-struggle origin of the state are best formulated by J. Novicow in his *La Critique de Darwinisme social* (Paris, 1910); and E. C. Hayes, *An Introduction to the Study of Sociology* (Philadelphia, 1915), pp. 538 ff.

27. *The Psychic Factors of Civilization*, p. 311, introductory note.

28. *Ibid.*, p. 327.

29. See, in particular, his "Professor Sumner's Social Classes," in *Glimpses of the Cosmos*, III, 301–5; and "The Political Ethics of Herbert Spencer," *ibid.*, V, 38–66.

30. *Dynamic Sociology*, II, 212, 217, 231.

31. *Ibid.*, pp. 241–42.

32. *Ibid.*, pp. 245–50; *Pure Sociology*, pp. 568–69; *Outlines of Sociology*, pp. 187–89; *Psychic Factors of Civilization*, pp. 309–12. Ward, then, essentially adopted the doctrine of Plato and Comte that perfect government could come only when society and government were controlled and directed by sociologists.

33. *Dynamic Sociology*, II, 243.

34. *Outlines of Sociology*, pp. 187–89, 268–76; *Pure Sociology*, p. 565; and *Psychic Factors of Civilization*, p. 297.

35. Pp. 309–12.

36. Cf. Ward's article on "The Way to Scientific Law-making" (1877), reprinted in *Glimpses of the Cosmos*, II, 168–71. This is one of the earliest and clearest statements of the value of statistics in scientific legislation and antedated by five years Jevons' classic exposition of this subject in his *The State in Relation to Labor* (London, 1882); cf. also Graham Wallas, *Human Nature in Politics* (Boston, 1909), pp. 121 ff., 132 ff.

37. *Dynamic Sociology*, II, 632–33; cf. also *Applied Sociology, passim.* Ward's best brief statement of the sociological significance of education is to be found in his address, "Education and Progress," in *Glimpses of the Cosmos*, VI, 333–40. See also E. P. Kimball, *Sociology and Education* (New York, 1932).

38. *Dynamic Sociology*, II, 249–50.

39. For further authoritative material on Ward's significance in social science see J. Q. Dealey, "Lester Frank Ward," in H. W. Odum (ed.), *American Masters of Social Science* (New York, 1927), chap. iii.

CHAPTER VIII

THE SOCIAL PHILOSOPHY OF LUDWIG GUMPLOWICZ
THE STRUGGLES OF RACES AND
SOCIAL GROUPS

HARRY ELMER BARNES

I. GENERAL NATURE OF THE SOCIOLOGICAL SYSTEM
OF LUDWIG GUMPLOWICZ

ONE of the pioneers in the development of sociological theory and the leader of the so-called "conflict school" was the Austrian publicist and sociologist, Ludwig Gumplowicz (1838–1909),[1] a prolific writer and a man possessed of wide, if not wholly critical, learning. No other sociologist, with the possible exception of Lester F. Ward, has been more impressed with the finality of his own doctrines; and one cannot escape the conviction that many, if not most, of the propositions which he submitted as being supported by "blind natural law" or as manifestations of "inevitable tendencies of the cosmic process" were merely the opinions of Gumplowicz upon the particular problem under consideration. Yet, despite his dogmatism, Gumplowicz must be accorded the credit of having first intensively explored one of the most fertile fields of sociological investigation. His thorough analysis of the social process, viewed as the interaction of conflicting groups, is one of the most fundamental notions yet brought forward by sociology and constitutes a contribution of the greatest permanent value. In addition to his specific interpretation of the nature of the social process, Gumplowicz was, perhaps, the first avowed sociologist to emphasize the importance of the general sociological concept of association and socialization as a developmental process—a line of sociological thought which has been greatly expanded by Gumplowicz' fellow-countryman, General Gustav Ratzenhofer, and by Professor Albion W. Small, a leading disciple of the latter.

191

Sociology, according to Gumplowicz, is the science of the interrelation of social groups. It is the function of sociology to demonstrate that social phenomena are amenable to measurement and can be reduced to verifiable laws: "The function of sociology consists in showing that universal laws apply to social phenomena; in pointing out the peculiar effects produced by them in the social domain; and finally in formulating the special social laws."[2]

Gumplowicz gives a narrow interpretation to the nature of social phenomena, describing them as those which appear "through the operation of groups and aggregates of men on one another."[3] Accordingly, the social process throughout history has consisted in the relations and reciprocal actions between heterogeneous social groups. Social laws, in turn, become the laws of the interaction and development of syngenetic social groups. Gumplowicz' whole system of sociology was thus limited and somewhat distorted by his presuppositions; but it cannot be denied that he fearlessly developed his deductions from the assumed premises with Hobbesian logic and clarity.

Gumplowicz' sociological system has long been regarded as the classic example of the influence of a writer's social and political environment upon his theory. The almost unique ethnic and cultural diversity and the continual struggle of national groups and social classes in Austria-Hungary, as well as the control of political authority by a minority in both states of the Dual Monarchy, unquestionably colored, if not entirely determined, the main lines of his whole sociological system, based, as it was, upon the premises of ethnic diversity, group and class conflict, the political sovereignty of a ruling minority, and the problems of national emancipation, cultural assimilation, and ethnic amalgamation. It is highly important that this should be kept in mind in estimating the validity of regarding Gumplowicz' propositions as sociological laws of universal applicability.

Aside from his excessive emphasis upon social groups and their conflict as the unit of sociological investigation, the two most noteworthy propositions in the sociological system of Gumplowicz were his denial of the importance of the individual and his refusal to admit the existence of verifiable human progress for humanity as a whole. No other sociologist—not even Tarde, Durkheim, Sighele, Le Bon, or Trotter—went to such an extreme as Gumplowicz did in minimizing the importance of the individual and in magnifying the extent of the domination exerted by the group over the individual. In a passage which has become threadbare through citation he said: "The individual simply plays the part of the prism which receives the rays, dissolves them according to fixed laws, and lets them pass out again in a predetermined direction and with a predetermined color."[4] Despite the fact that the group completely prevails over the individual in giving the latter his life-patterns and habits of thought and obedience, groups, at least public groups, are, in turn, at the mercy of aggressive leaders. As he put it in his *Sozialphilosophie im Umriss:*

It seems that the simple fact of aggregation brings out the sheeplike character of human beings, for wherever we observe the great assemblies, whether in public meetings or in parliament, whether we have to do with shareholders' meetings, corporate meetings, or university convocations, we everywhere find that the majority is content to accept the leadership of single individuals, acting no longer in accordance with its own convictions, but enslaved by the phrases employed by the leaders.[4a]

It is obvious that this view is essentially similar to that held about the behavior of crowds and parliaments by Le Bon and Sighele, whose opinions will be analyzed later on in this book.

Even further from general acceptance among sociologists is Gumplowicz' denial of any substantial progress of humanity as a totality. While recognizing social and cultural advances in particular periods and in specific societies, he questioned the existence of any permanent improvement of human society as a whole and held that the historic process is the record of the rise and fall of countless successive civilizations, following a cyclical course of growth and decline. Thus, Gumplowicz not only rejected the doctrine of Turgot, Condorcet, Godwin, Comte, and Ward regarding the possibility of indefinite progress but also even refused to accept the rather timid contention of Vico that progress took the course of a spiral. With Machiavelli and Le Bon, he fell back upon the theory of the cyclical nature of the movement of history, which was common in classical times and was then best expressed by Polybius.

Gumplowicz' general sociological theories lead directly to his analysis of social and political institutions. He applied his doctrine of group conflict to an interpretation of the nature, development, and functioning of the state and regarded it as adequate to explain every phase of political action and theory.[5]

A. THE RELATION OF SOCIOLOGY TO POLITICAL SCIENCE

Gumplowicz' conception of the relation of sociology to the special social sciences is clear and logical: "Being the science of human society and social laws, sociology is obviously the basis of all the special social sciences treating parts of human society, or of particular manifestations of associated life."[6] Sociological investigations have first made possible a scientific study of political institutions, since only by being based upon the laws of social development and social processes, which have been revealed by sociology, can the analysis of political phenomena assume a scientific character.

B. THE NATURE OF THE STATE

Gumplowicz' theory of the nature of the state is strictly in accord with his general sociological doctrines and is distinctly a sociological conception of the state. "The state," he holds, "is a social phenomenon consisting of social elements behaving according to social laws."[7] At the same time, the state must be carefully differentiated from society. The term "society" may be applied to the ensemble of conflicting interest-groups within any organized unit of mankind, but the term "folk" is better suited to the description of such a cultural unity. In a more accurate sense, a society is a "group centering about some one or more common interests."[8] The state, on the other hand, is a portion of mankind organized and controlled by a sovereign minority:

> If nothing but the universal and essential characteristics of every state were incorporated in the definition, an agreement could easily be reached, for there are but two. First, there are certain institutions directed to securing the sovereignty of some over others; secondly, the sovereignty is always exercised by a minority. A state, therefore, is the organized control of the minority over the majority. This is the only true and universal definition; it is apt in every case.[9]

The state, according to the conception held by Gumplowicz, is far from an "ethical being." It has never been founded to preserve justice or to improve the general welfare. The sole motive in the formation of all states has been the desire to establish sovereignty for the purpose of exploitation. The concern of the highly developed states with justice and welfare is but incidental to their original and fundamental motive and purpose, namely, exploitation. Again, questions of morality cannot be intelligently considered in a discussion of the nature and actions of states. The state is an inevitable product of "blind natural laws" operating upon heterogeneous social groups. Hence it is a natural phenomenon. It is not "above morality" but, rather, has no more relation to ethical considerations than an earthquake or a tornado.

C. THE ORIGIN AND DEVELOPMENT OF STATES, VIEWED AS THE PRODUCT OF THE CONFLICT OF GROUPS AND THEIR PROGRESSIVE AMALGAMATION

It is through his theory of the origin and development of the state that Gumplowicz has made his most important contribution to social and political theory. While few would agree with the details of his doctrine or with his sweeping generalizations regarding the universality of the origin of states wholly through conquest and conflict, it is generally admitted that the account of political origins which he sets forth with great vigor and clarity is the most satisfactory and fundamental explanation of the origin of the state that has yet been produced. It probably goes further toward clearing up the problem of political origins than any other single theory, and it has gained such general acceptance among sociologists that it may almost be considered as the sociological theory of the origin of the state.[10]

For the sake of orientation in further analysis, the theory of Gumplowicz regarding political origins may be briefly summarized as follows: Mankind must be assumed to have had a polygenetic origin, resulting in the existence of many different and heterogeneous social groups. These groups were led into conflict with one another through the natural and inevitable tendency of all individuals and groups to seek to improve their economic status and to increase the means of satisfying their desires. The earliest conquests of one group by another normally resulted in the extermination of the conquered; but, sooner or later, slaughter was commuted into physical and political subjection, and there arose the institutions of political sovereignty and the state. The first crude and elementary political society was soon complicated by the origin of various social, economic, and religious classes, each called into existence to supply some definite need in society. The process of conflict, which originally took the shape of intergroup conquests, accordingly became transformed into a conflict between the different classes within the state. This process led to a general amalgamation and assimilation of the diverse elements within the state and the gradual political emancipation of the masses. When carried to completion, a folk state or nation—the supreme product of social evolution—was fully created. Attention may now be turned to a brief analysis of the main stages and processes involved in this interpretation of the origin and development of the state.[11]

Quite in contrast with the procedure of Ward, who boldly analyzed the conditions existing in the period before the "chaos," Gumplowicz maintains that the sociologist cannot discover the ultimate origin of society but must content himself with assuming the existence of the social groups required to create the social process. He does not consistently hold to this position, however, but attempts to defend so extreme a view of polygenism that he practically succeeds in constructing a *reductio ad absurdum* of the polygenist position. In short, he holds that the "prehistoric" period was characterized by the origin and differentiation of heterogeneous social groups, while the historic era has witnessed their integration, amalgamation, and assimilation. There is some evidence, however, that Gumplowicz modified his extreme polygenetic doctrines toward the close of his life, as a result of a visit paid to him by Lester F. Ward in 1903. He conceded at that time that the human race may have had a single origin and then been differentiated into numerous groups.

Throughout the period of associated human life there have been certain forces making for group unity and solidarity, which, as a totality, can be described by the general term "syngenism." This he defines as "that phenomenon which consists in the fact that invariably in associated modes of life, definite groups of men, feeling themselves closely bound together by common interests, endeavor to function as a single element in the struggle for domination."[12] It is a complex of physical, economic, moral, and cultural forces, combined in different proportions in various periods and in diverse social groups. In the earliest groups consanguinity was the strongest social bond, but, as society developed, the economic and psychic forces became increasingly important.

Gumplowicz, then, assumes at the outset of social and political development a large number of small social groups or hordes, each united by consanguinity and identity of economic interests and living in sexual promiscuity and equality of social position. The origin of the matriarchate, and, later, the patriarchate provided a crude type of organization for these groups. This preliminary period of social evolution was broken down by the origin of war and intergroup conflict, and thus was initiated that eternal process of social struggle which can never have an end. In external relations states have continually attempted to effect further conquests, and within each expanding political society there has been a ceaseless contest going on between an ever increasing number of competing interest-groups and classes. The fundamental motive of group conquest throughout history has been the desire for an improvement of economic well-being:

> The motive force in the establishment of primitive political relations was economic, as has been seen; higher material welfare was sought. But this force never fails; the innermost nature of man keeps it in ceaseless operation, promoting the development of the state as it laid its foundation. Investigate the cause of any political revolution, and the result will prove that social progress is always produced by economic causes. Indeed, it cannot be otherwise, since man's material need is the prime motive of his conduct.[13]

In the earliest period of group conflict the conquered were exterminated, but in the course of time there was instituted that fundamental transformation in social evolution whereby a general massacre was commuted into slavery and economic exploitation. In this process of the superimposition of one social group upon another and the subjection and exploitation of the weaker is to be found the origin of sovereignty and the state. No state, Gumplowicz contends, has ever arisen except through the conquest of one group and ethnic stock by another. The state is invariably a composite of heterogeneous racial and social elements. "No state has arisen without original ethnical heterogeneity; its unity is the product of social development."[14] Political relations in the early states conformed to the economic foundations of the new compound society. The sovereign minority exploited the conquered majority, and the first states were, thus, a twofold organization: on the one hand, of sovereignty and, on the other, of enforced labor:

> Thus nature laid the foundations of ethnically composite states in human necessities and sentiments. Human labor being necessary, sympathy with kindred and tribe and deadly hatred of strangers led to foreign wars. So conquest and the satisfaction of needs through the labor of the conquered, essentially the same though differing in form, is the great theme of human history from prehistoric times to the latest plan for a Congo state.[15]

The minority of conquerors were able, in the first instance, to overcome, and later exploit, the conquered majority because of superior unity and discipline, for unity and discipline are the chief sources of the strength of all social groups.

As soon as the first political relations were established through group conquest, resulting in the exploitation of a subject majority by a sovereign minority, the process of social conflict became transformed from external strife between groups or states into a struggle between classes within the state. This intra-group conflict, in addition to its fundamental economic motive, was also stimulated by the "necessity for satisfying ambition, love of glory, the interests of a dynasty, and various other ideals; and the life and death struggle between hordes anthropologically different becomes a contest between social groups, classes, estates, and political parties."[16] The earliest class conflict was the struggle for adjustment between the sovereign and the subject classes. This relatively simple process was soon interrupted, however, by the development of a class of foreign merchants, whose appearance marked the beginning of that extremely important element in every population, the middle class or the *bourgeoisie*. In response to the growing needs of the developing state, there grew up out of these primary or original classes of rulers, merchants, and exploited masses such secondary or derived classes as the priesthood, professional classes, and artisans: "The phenomenon of class-building can be referred to a universal law: each want produces its own means of satisfaction. In so far as a class is able to satisfy a social want it is indispensable."[17]

The social process, in so far as it was confined to the internal affairs of the state, now became a complex and involved struggle between the various classes for the control of the policy of the state, in order to advance their respective interests: "The struggle between social groups, the component parts of the state, is as inexorable as that between hordes or states. The only motive is self-interest.....The social struggle consists in establishing appropriate institutions for increasing the power of one social group at the expense of others."[18]

The struggle of groups and classes within the state has provided the dynamic core of history. In ancient times the plebeians battled against the patricians. In the Middle Ages kings contended against churchmen, nobles and burghers against kings, and the peasantry against both. In early modern times the kings and *bourgeoisie* united to crush out feudalism, but soon the middle class was opposing the absolute monarchs with the aid of the proletariat. Finally, the workers rose against the middle class and sought to set up democracy and socialism.

To carry on this conflict of classes within the state, appropriate organs were necessary. Participation in legislation was found to be the most effective mode of social and political conflict. This explains the long struggle of the third and fourth estates to secure the right of participating in the legislative function of the state, as well as the tenacity of the ruling classes in their attempt to exclude others from this privilege. In all cases the basis and measure of political power has been the ability to control human labor and its products. The ruling caste, composed of the original conquerors, kept its control over the labor of the masses through the aid of the habit of obedience and allegiance. The middle class obtained its political power from its control over material goods, for which it could demand labor or its equivalent. The priestly class was able to secure political authority through its control over the minds of men and hence over their services. The exploited masses, whose services constituted the basis of all political power, were excluded from exercising any civic rights until after a long and difficult struggle for political emancipation.

In the process of participating in legislation and carrying on class conflict within the state, political parties came to be the most popular organs after the rise of representative government. Gumplowicz was one of the first sociologists to conceive of the political party as an "interest-group," which is the outstanding sociological contribution to the theory of political parties. He held that, the greater the number of mutual interests which any party can muster, the stronger and more enduring will be the party. Usually, common material interests constitute the strongest party bond, but uniform traditions and beliefs also solidify party organization and activity. As we pointed out earlier, Gumplowicz believed that party assemblies and conventions are completely dominated by alert leaders. He thus anticipated Robert Michels' idea of the inevitably oligarchical nature of political parties, and Professor Giddings' notion of "protocracy."

The first concessions granted by the ruling caste gave rise to the notion of rights among the lower classes. The middle class was the first to make the appeal to "universal human rights, to freedom and equality." It pretended to be interested in advancing the interests of the masses and thus gained their support. While the masses were not rewarded to the extent of the promises made by the middle class, they gained experience in the methods of carrying on the struggle for political emancipation, and, sooner or later, they succeeded in securing admission to the exercise of political functions and to a share in political authority. The process of political emancipation was greatly hastened and facilitated when the ruling caste was threatened by enemies from without and needed to conciliate its subjects in order to secure loyalty and unity. Political rights are not metaphysical entities, says Gumplowicz, but merely the "regulations built up for the existence of unlike elements side by side and reduced by practice to rules and principles."[19] They are only the legal statement of the actual relations which exist in any political society at any time. Hence there can be no basis for any doctrine of inherent or metaphysical "natural rights":

> The premise of "inalienable human rights" rests upon the most unreasonable self-deification of man and overestimation of the value of human life, and upon complete misconception of the only possible basis of the existence of the state.[20] . . . . Rights are not founded upon justice. On the contrary, justice is created only by the actual rights as they exist in the state. . . . . It is the simple abstraction of political rights, and it stands and falls with them.[21]

Parallel with this process of political and economic development and continually interacting with and upon it are the psychic and physical processes of social unification. Assimilation, or the psychic process, proceeds most rapidly. The first step is the adoption of the language of the conquerors. Next follows the acceptance of their religion, manners, and customs, and a cultural unity is formed. Finally, there comes the physical process of intermarriage or amalgamation, and an ethnic unity is produced. This unified and homogeneous social group constitutes a "folk state" or nation—the final outcome of social and political evolution.

The generalized account of political and social evolution which has been summarized above is, in reality, oversimplified, for a large and highly developed state is rarely or never the product of a single conquest but is normally the compound result of many processes of conquest and of partial or complete assimilation and amalgamation. A unified folk state seldom remains such for any considerable period of time, for, as Gumplowicz contends in common with Machiavelli, Treitschke, and others, a state has an inevitable tendency to expand or decline. New conquests bring in another set of heterogeneous elements, and the process outlined above must begin anew. No limit can be set to the extent of the possible or desirable expansion of a state. The natural tendency is for a state to increase until its strength fails from external resistance or internal disruption. As was pointed out above, Gumplowicz maintains that ethical considerations have no relation to the conduct of states in a process of expansion. The state is a product of nature and is ruled and guided by the laws of nature and thus is not amenable to ethical judgment. This is, of course, but the reappearance of the old Machiavellian doctrine, slightly embellished with a dash of pseudo-Darwinian sociology.

D. STATE ACTIVITY AND SOCIAL PROGRESS

Gumplowicz' pessimistic denial of social progress and his doctrine of social determinism have already been analyzed. It is obvious that such a conception leaves no possibility for any such thing as social initiative; and, though Gumplowicz adopted most of the Marxian premises, he accepted none of the socialistic deductions regarding the possibility of a transformation of society and the state by collective action. Society and the state are products of natural forces which are independent of all human direction. They develop through the action of "blind natural laws" that mankind is powerless to alter. Further, his conception of the cyclical nature of social development rules out any such notion as the indefinite perfectibility of man and society through an increase in knowledge and the development of "collective telesis." Both society and the individual must be resigned to their fate, for they are powerless to avert it. In fact, Gumplowicz maintains that the chief practical value of his sociology is that it will prevent the waste of human energy in futile utopian schemes of social reform. There is reason to believe, however, that Ward's above-mentioned visit to Gumplowicz in 1903 had some influence in inducing Gumplowicz to admit the possibility of some degree of successful social guidance of institutional development and of competent government planning.[22]

III. THE INFLUENCE AND HISTORICAL SIGNIFICANCE OF GUMPLOWICZ' INTERPRETATION OF SOCIAL EVOLUTION

In estimating the significance of Gumplowicz for the history of sociology and political science and for the development of militarism and racial egoism in recent European history, it is necessary to differentiate those elements in his system which are of permanent value from those which have now been rejected, even by writers belonging to his particular group among sociologists.

While few authoritative students of anthropology would today accept Gumplowicz' extreme doctrine of the polygenetic origin of the several branches of the human race, it is generally agreed that his chief contribution to sociology has consisted in his systematic elaboration of what has come to be accepted as the sociological theory of the origin of the state and political sovereignty, though most commentators would grant that he underestimated the pacific and co-operative factors which played at least some part in that process. His other significant and enduring contribution was his analysis of political activity within the state as a process of ceaseless struggle and continuous adjustment and readjustment between groups and classes which have their constituent principle in a common interest or policy. His revival and elucidation of the concept of the political party as an interest-group was a significant phase in the analysis of what has probably been the most fertile notion elaborated by political science in the last fifty years. When properly recognized and embodied in law and parliamentary practice, it will probably do more than anything else to give intelligence, rationale, and directness to party government. This notion has been accepted and expanded by French publicists, such as Duguit, Durkheim, and Benoist and especially by the Austrian sociologist, Ratzenhofer. The latter's system has been interpreted to American readers through its critical exposition and analysis by Professor Albion W. Small and has been applied to the analysis of the operation of the American government by A. F. Bentley in what is undoubtedly the most valuable contribution made by an American writer to the analysis of the more fundamental processes of government since Calhoun published his *Disquisition on Government*.[23]

Unfortunately, the disastrous aspects of the doctrines of Gumplowicz are no less numerous and apparent. He was the most extreme advocate, among sociologists of any recognized standing, of the unqualified applicability of a misconstrued and perverted Darwinian biology to the interpretation of social processes, and he was an equally ardent supporter of political fatalism or the futility of human legislative activity in the face of the operation of the "blind natural laws" that set at naught the deeds of man. His representation of war as the main agency in political development and the only reliable arbiter of the pretensions of national *Kultur* was eagerly pounced upon by militarists, even less scientific and objective than Gumplowicz, such as Moltke and Bernhardi in Germany,

J. A. Cramb and Lord Roberts in England, Déroulède in France, and Mahan in America, to furnish a plausible pseudo-scientific cloak for the advancement of their national, class, and party interests. The importance of this type of theory in the creation of the state of mind that precipitated the tragedies of 1914 and 1939 is now generally recognized, and Gumplowicz must bear his share of the burden of responsibility. Further, his frequent assertion that the state is above all considerations and obligations of morality, like a natural phenomenon, was a congenial doctrine expanded by the exponents of *Machtpolitik* and *Realpolitik*, both in Germany and elsewhere.

IV. THE PROGRESS IN THE THEORY OF GROUP CONFLICT
SINCE GUMPLOWICZ

Probably the best criticism that can be made of the system of Gumplowicz is to examine it in the light of the doctrines of those members of the so-called "conflict school" who have written since Gumplowicz set forth his theories in the *Rassenkampf* and the *Grundriss*. Not another leading theorist of this school accepts his bald parallelism between biological and social evolution or approves of his notion that the struggle of races, states, and social groups must continue without termination or mitigation. All either contend that conflict is gradually transformed from the crude and elementary physical plane to a higher level of competition, or they maintain that conflict ultimately ends in adaptation and co-operation. Loria, Vaccaro, and Oppenheimer have emphasized the tendency of the primordial physical struggle between groups to become transformed into an economic conflict.[24] Novicow has held that a study of social evolution reveals the fact that the primitive physical contest is progressively commuted through the alliance and federation of groups and the substitution of intellectual competition for physical conflict.[25] This field of psychic struggles and adjustments has been explored with the greatest acumen by Tarde and Sighele.[26] According to De Greef, social evolution is a process of gradual substitution of contract and consent for the brute force of more primitive times.[27] Spencer and Tarde, but more especially Vaccaro, have built up systems of sociology based upon the thesis that conflict ultimately terminates in an equilibrium or in adaptation.[28] Finally, Ratzenhofer and Small have insisted that conflict is continually tempered by socialization and transformed into co-operation and that the "conquest state" of early days is superseded by the "culture state" of the modern age.[29]

Therefore, even the adherents of the "conflict" theory are generally agreed that the transformation of conflict into alliance and co-operation seems to be the outcome of social evolution, and they would apparently support the notion that war must be followed by an ultimate international adjustment, which will, in time, suppress the recrudescence of the crude process of physical warfare.

NOTES

1. Professor in the University of Graz after 1882. Brief sketches of Gumplowicz' life and sociological writings are to be found in the *American Journal of Sociology*, XV (November, 1909), 405–13.

2. *The Outlines of Sociology*, trans. F. W. Moore (Philadelphia, 1899), pp. 82–83.

3. *Ibid.*, p. 83.

4. *Ibid.*, p. 157. Cf. also the following: "The greatest error of the individualistic psychology is the supposition that man thinks. . . . . This is an error. He is not self-made mentally any more than he is physically. His mind and thoughts are the product of his social medium, of the social element whence he arose, in which he lives" (*ibid.*, pp. 156, 760). Or again: "On the altar of her method of study, sociology sacrifices man. He, the lord of creation, the author of historical events as the historians think, he who as monarch or as minister guides according to his will the destiny of peoples . . . . sinks away, in sociology, to a meaningless cipher. In complete contradiction to the portrayals of the historians, even the mightiest statesman is from the point of view of the sociologist only a blind tool in the invisible but all-powerful hand of his social group, which itself in turn only follows an irresistible law of nature" (*Soziologie und Politik* [Leipzig, 1892], p. 54; cited and translated by Professor G. L. Burr, *American Historical Review*, January, 1917, p. 269 and note).

The selection of Gumplowicz by historians and political scientists as an illustration of the sociological view of human individualty and freedom is entirely analogous to a choice of Froude and Lamartine by sociologists as samples of historical methodology and accuracy. Sociologists, such as Spencer, Novicow, and W. G. Sumner, have not been lacking who have defended the extreme individualistic point of view, and those alarmed by the exaggerations of Gumplowicz can gain a great deal of satisfaction and reassurance from a study of the works of Professor C. H. Cooley, who has undoubtedly given the world one of the best interpretations of the interrelation of the individual and society that has been presented by any writer, sociological or psychological. Even the extreme doctrine of Gumplowicz, however, is probably as near to the truth as the opposite views of Fichte, whose spirit inspired, in part, the founders of modern scientific historiography.

4a. *Sozialphilosophie im Umriss* (Graz, 1910), p. 124.

5. Gumplowicz' writings on sociology and political theory are voluminous. No other sociologist has contributed so extensively to political and legal theory. His fundamental theories, centering about the conflict of groups and classes, are brought out in a dozen volumes and many essays published between 1875 and 1910, and they form the specific content of no less than seven separate books. As he added nothing except in the way of amplification, to the doctrines expressed in his earliest works, the rather monotonous repetition and reiteration of the same principles tend more to weary than to convince the reader. The earliest statement of his "group-conflict" theory appeared in his *Rasse und Staat* (Vienna, 1875). This doctrine received its first systematic presentation in *Der Rassen-*

kampf (Innsbruck, 1883). The theory was further amplified and systematized and made a part of a coherent body of sociological theory in the *Grundriss der Sociologie* (Vienna, 1885), translated as *The Outlines of Sociology,* which work constitutes the best statement of his sociological doctrines. His sociological theory was applied to political institutions, but without any important changes or additions, in *Soziologie und Politik,* and *Die soziologische Staatsidee* (Innsbruck, 1902). His whole sociological system was summed up conveniently in *Sozialphilosophie im Umriss,* published posthumously in 1910. Aside from the works mentioned, Gumplowicz' chief publications were *Philosophisches Staatsrecht* (1877); *Verwaltungslehre* (1882); *Das österreichische Staatsrecht* (1891), *Rechtstaat und Socialismus* (1881); *Soziologische Aussätze* (1899); *Geschichte der Staatstheorien* (1905); *Das allgemeine Staatsrecht* (1907).

    6. *Outlines of Sociology,* p. 90.

    7. *Ibid.,* p. 116.

    8. *Ibid.,* pp. 136–38.

    9. *Ibid.,* p. 118; cf. *La Lutte des races* (French translation of revised edition of *Der Rassenkampf,* by Charles Baye [Paris, 1893]), pp. 218, 222–23.

    10. An enthusiastic defense of this theory by Lester F. Ward is to be found in *American Journal of Sociology,* VIII (May, 1902), 762. Its limitations are pointed out by F. H. Giddings, *Principles of Sociology,* p. 316; and E. C. Hayes, *An Introduction to the Study of Sociology* (Philadelphia, 1915), pp. 538 ff. It is bitterly criticized and entirely rejected by Jacques Novicow in *War and Its Alleged Benefits* (New York, 1911), and *La Critique du Darwinisme social* (Paris, 1910). Most sociologists and historians, however, reject his deductions rather than the essentials of his theory of political origins.

    11. The analysis which follows is based upon Gumplowicz' most extensive treatment of the origin of the state as found in Book IV of *Der Rassenkampf* and Part III of the *Grundriss.* Somewhat condensed versions of the same theory are to be found in *Soziologie und Politik,* pp. 72–78; *Die soziologische Staatsidee,* pp. 88–134; and *Sozialphilosophie im Umriss,* pp. 58–68.

    12. "Le phénomène consistant en ce que toujours, dans la vie sociale, certains groupes d'hommes, sentant qu'ils sont étroitement reliés entre eux, cherchent à agir comme un seul facteur dans la lutte pour la domination" (*La Lutte des races,* pp. 241–42).

    13. *Outlines of Sociology,* p. 123. Though an ardent supporter of the Marxian doctrine of the economic interpretation of history, Gumplowicz rejected the socialistic dogma of state activity as the chief factor in social reform.

    14. *Ibid.,* p. 119. In another part of his work Gumplowicz rather grudgingly admits that it is conceivable that a state may, in extremely rare instances, have originated through the peaceful division of labor and the differentiation of classes; but he maintains that, even in such cases, its later history as a conflict of divergent interests would be the same as though it had originated in group conflict (*ibid.,* p. 136).

    15. *Ibid.,* p. 121.

    16. *Ibid.,* pp. 123–24.

    17. *Ibid.,* p. 132.

    18. *Ibid.,* p. 145; cf. also pp. 125, 132, 144–46.

    19. *Ibid.,* p. 178.

    20. *Ibid.,* p. 180.

    21. *Ibid.,* p. 181.

    22. *La Lutte des races,* pp. 350–52. See *American Journal of Sociology,* XI (March, 1905), 647–51, for an interesting account of a conversation between Gumplowicz and Ward, in which the former apparently made some concessions to the latter's conception of social progress and "collective telesis."

    23. A. F. Bentley, *The Process of Government* (Chicago, 1908).

    24. A. Loria, *The Economic Foundations of Society* (New York, 1899); M. A. Vaccaro, *Les Bases sociologiques du droit et de l'état* (Paris, 1898); F. Oppenheimer, *The State* (Indianapolis, 1914).

25. J. Novicow, *Les Luttes entre sociétés humaines* (Paris, 1893); *La Fédération de l'Europe* (Paris, 1901).

26. G. Tarde, *L'Opposition universelle* (Paris, 1897), and *Social Laws* (New York, 1907); S. Sighele, *Psychologie des sectes* (Paris, 1898).

27. G. de Greef, *Introduction à la sociologie* (2 vols.; Paris, 1911).

28. H. Spencer, *First Principles*, Part II; G. Tarde, *La Logique sociale* (Paris, 1895); Vaccaro, *op. cit.*, especially Introd., pp. v–vii, and 78 ff. It is to be regretted that L. M. Bristol, in his helpful book on *Social Adaptation* (Cambridge, 1915), failed to include a discussion of Vaccaro, who has done more than any other sociologist to develop the notion of "adaptation" as a sociological process.

29. G. Ratzenhofer, *Wesen und Zweck der Politik* (3 vols.; Leipzig, 1893), and *Die sociologische Erkenntnis* (Leipzig, 1898); and A. W. Small, *General Sociology* (Chicago, 1905), pp. 190 ff.

PART III

LEADING SOCIOLOGISTS IN
GERMANIC COUNTRIES

INTRODUCTORY NOTE

LEADING SOCIOLOGICAL TRENDS AND SOCIOLOGISTS IN GERMANIC COUNTRIES*

WHILE there have been more eminent sociologists in Germany and Austria than in any other country except the United States, few of them have been trained as sociologists or have taught sociology in Germanic universities. And the opposition to sociology in respectable university circles has been much more marked than in the United States —almost as notable as in England. Most Germanic sociologists have been trained as philosophers, economists, jurists, anthropologists, or historians—even as theologians. And they have usually held chairs in one of the above subjects rather than in sociology proper. The numerous and notable Germanic contributions to sociology have thus been made in the face of much professional opposition and in spite of many academic handicaps.

One of the more fundamental methodological discussions in Germanic sociological literature was that which turned upon the question of whether the methods of natural science could be applied to the social sciences. Among those who returned a negative answer, the leader was the philosopher, Wilhelm Dilthey (1833–1911), whose main ideas were embodied in his *Einleitung in die Geisteswissenschaften.* He held that the ultimate units of the physical sciences are physical, while those of the social sciences are psychic; hence different methods of approach must be adopted for each field. The subjective social sciences cannot be studied by the abstract and conceptual methodology of the natural sciences. This position was attacked by the philosopher, Wilhelm Windelband, and by the logician, Heinrich Rickert (1863–1936), who set forth his notions in his *Die Grenzen der naturwissenschaftlichen Begriffsbildung.* They held that social science may fruitfully and legitimately use the methods of natural science, but they excepted history from the

*By the editor.

209

social sciences in this respect, holding that history must deal with the unique and individual aspects of social phenomena and cannot legitimately deduce generalized laws of historical development—a position attacked by the English historian Arnold Toynbee. The controversy has been carried further by Theodor Litt in his *Individuum und Gemeinschaft* and by F. W. Jerusalem in his *Die Gesetzmässigkeit des sozialen Lebens.* Litt inclines to the view that the social sciences have a unique methodology, while Jerusalem holds that sociology is a legitimate field for testing scientific methods in the social sciences.

German writers took the lead in creating the science of anthropogeography, which studies the relations between man, society, and the physical environment. The subject was founded in its modern form by the great geographer, Karl Ritter (1779–1859), in his famous *Erdkunde,* and was carried along by Oskar Peschel (1826–75) and Friedrich Ratzel (1844–1904). Peschel's chief work was his *Neue Probleme der vergleichenden Erdkunde.* Peschel was especially interested in the relation between geographic factors and historical developments and cultural distributions. He substituted a morphological approach for the philosophical trend of Ritter. Originally trained as a biologist, Ratzel was concerned with a reconciliation between the principles of biological evolution and the operation of geographical influence on mankind. His *Anthropogeographie* marked the culmination of generalized anthropogeography both in Germany and in the Western world. Ratzel was particularly interested in the geographical basis of history, which he believed to reside in the principles of migration and isolation, as conditioned by geographic influences. The trend away from universal generalization toward an analytical and regional approach to anthropogeography was first effectively set forth in Germany by Ferdinand von Richthofen (1833–1905) in his *Vorlesungen über allgemeine Siedlungs- und Verkehrsgeographie,* at the turn of the century.

The biological sociology of Germanic writers was based on differing applications of the Darwinian hypothesis to social processes. The idea of the analogy between the biological organism and social units and processes was worked out with great elaborateness by the Russo-German scholar, Paul von Lilienfeld (1829–1903), in his *Gedanken über die Socialwissenschaft der Zukunft,* and by the philosopher and social economist, Albert Schäffle (1831–1903), in his *Bau und Leben des Sozialen Körpers.* In a modified and discriminating fashion the doctrine of the social organism was revived by Franz Oppenheimer as the frame of reference for his notions of social reform.

The thesis of the so-called "social Darwinism," namely, that war and the struggle of races is analogous to the struggle for existence in biological evolution, was defended with great brilliance and enthusiasm by the Austro-Polish sociologist and jurist, Ludwig Gumplowicz (1838–1909), in his *Der Rassenkampf,* in which he attributed the origins of the state and the growth of social structures to the impact of war and the struggle of social groups. His disciple, Gustav Ratzenhofer (1842–1904), agreed with Gumplowicz but extended his activity to a study of how the struggle of interests within the state modifies political institutions and constitutes the essence of the social process. His principal work was the *Wesen und Zweck der Politik,* widely popularized in the United States by Albion W. Small. The social Darwinism of Gumplowicz was attacked at the time of the first World War by the physiologist, G. F. Nicolai, in his *Biology of War.*

A more comprehensive application of the Darwinian principles to social analysis appeared in the anthropometry and social selectionism of Alfred Otto Ammon (1842–1916) and Wilhelm Schallmayer (1857——), both of whom made an honest effort to work out a theory of social evolution in terms of the principles of heredity, selection, variation, the struggle for existence, and the survival of the fittest. Ammon's main work was *Die Gesellschaftsordnung und ihre natürlichen Grundlagen,* while that of Schallmayer was entitled *Vererbung und Auslese im Lebenslauf der Völker.* This kind of work, envisaging also the possibilities of eugenics, marks the highest development of biological sociology in Germany—or elsewhere.

Sharply conditioned also by evolutionism were the ethnographic contributions made to sociology in Germany. Probably the most influential of the ethnographers who applied the evolutionary principle to society and culture was Julius Lippert (1839–1909), whose principal work was *Kulturgeschichte der Menschheit in ihrem organischen Aufbau,* probably the most important single book of the older evolutionary school, with the sole exception of Morgan's *Ancient Society.* It exerted a great influence even outside Germany, for instance, upon Sumner and Keller in the United States. Very significant also was the folk psychology of the great psychologist, Wilhelm Wundt (1832–1920), best summarized in his *Elemente de Völkerpsychologie* and especially notable for its reconstruction of primitive mentality and its theory of the evolution of culture. Franz Müller-Lyer (1857–1916) made much of the ethnographic methods in his various works on social institutions and the evolution of culture. Very fruitful for sociology was the earlier work of Wundt's disciple, Alfred Vierkandt (1867——), *Naturvölker und Kulturvölker,* which vastly improved the comparative approach to the study of cultures, as used by the earlier ethnographers. The final culmination of ethnosociology in Germany is the monumental work of Richard Thurnwald (1869——) on *Die menschliche Gesellschaft in ihren ethnosoziologischen Grundlagen,* which assembles a vast body of material and applies a discriminating method of ethnographic analysis and comparison, avoiding the extremes of the older evolutionism.

While social psychology has not been so extensively cultivated by Germans as it has been by French, Italian, British, and American writers, a number of scholars have given their attention to this subject. They have carried the subject far beyond the old folk psychology of Bastian, Lazarus, and Steinthal. Wundt put folk psychology on a more scientific basis, having at his disposal the rigorous psychological methods and the vast psychological knowledge which he had developed in his laboratory at Leipzig. Ferdinand Tönnies presented a profound study of public opinion, which he analyzed more discriminatingly than most other writers on the subject, in his *Kritik der öffentlichen Meinung.* In his *Individuum und Gemeinschaft,* Litt arrived at views similar to those of C. H. Cooley relative to the relations between society and the individual personality. A somewhat comparable attitude is taken by Hans Stoltenberg (1888——) in his *Soziopsychologie* and *Psychosoziologie.* Especially useful is Stoltenberg's distinction between social psychology, which, he holds, is mainly concerned with the group conditioning of individual behavior and personality, and psychosociology, a department of sociology in which the emphasis is placed on the psychological factors affecting group life rather than human personalities. In his *Experimentelle Massenpsychologie,* Walter Moede has made an especially rigorous study of the impact of social groups upon individual behavior.

The relation of sociology to history has been discussed by many German writers. Paul Barth (1858–1922), in his famous *Die Philosophie der Geschichte als Soziologie,* argued that sociology in its genetic aspects is essentially an expanded and enriched history. He opposed Windelband and Rickert by holding that natural-science methods are applicable to the field of history. Ernst Troeltsch (1865–1923) was one of the most successful of Germanic scholars in demonstrating what a broad cultural and institutional history can contribute to sociological knowledge and understanding. He set forth his theoretical views in his *Der Historismus und seine Probleme,* in which he agreed with Dilthey that natural-science methods cannot be applied to the social sciences and with Rickert with respect to the unique and individual character of historical materials. But far and away the most important work of any German scholar on the relation between history and sociology is that of Alfred Weber, the younger brother of Max Weber. In his *Kulturgeschichte als Kultursoziologie* he attempted not only a generalized and theoretical summation of *Kulturgeschichte* but also a synthesis of idealism and historical materialism. Comparative *Sittengeschichte* has been cultivated by Wundt, Max Weber, Troeltsch, and Vierkandt.

The chief German contributions to general sociology will be presented at length in the pages which follow, and we need do no more than characterize them briefly. General sociology in Germany was founded by Ferdinand Tönnies (1855–1936), famed for his classic distinction between community (*Gemeinschaft*) and society (*Gesellschaft.*) He also distinguished between pure, applied, and empirical sociology; analyzed the structure of social groups; and contributed the leading Germanic study of public opinion. Georg Simmel (1858–1918) was, perhaps, the most completely analytical of the Germanic sociologists. He is especially noted for his conception of sociology as the science of the nature and interaction of social structures, and for his very careful study of the formation and persistence of social groupings. Simmel's disciple, Leopold von Wiese (1876——), has carried further Simmel's study of social processes and regards sociology as the science of interhuman relationships and of the social structures that grow out of these relationships. He is the leading systematizer among recent German sociologists. Vierkandt turned from his early interest in folk psychology to sociology, in which he has shown varied interests and talents. He espouses the views of Simmel and Von Wiese as to the central theme of sociology, namely, the study of social structures and interhuman relationships. He has stressed the motives that bring about these relationships and inclines to accept McDougall's notion of instincts as the most important contribution to this problem. In his *Die Stetigkeit im Kulturwandel,* he presented a masterly study of social change and cultural lag, anticipating by more than two decades the contributions of Ogburn to this subject.

The foremost critic of Simmel and his followers is the Austrian social philosopher, Othmar Spann (1878——), the exponent of what is known as philosophical "universalism" in social theory, in distinction from the particularistic theories which are based on the principles of natural science. These notions are developed especially in his *Gesellschaftslehre* and *Gesellschafts-Geistes*. Spann lays great stress upon the importance of the group and of the totality of society and the state in a manner reminiscent of Plato. While much of his writing is abstract and metaphysical, Spann's theories emerge as a philosophical defense of a benign totalitarianism, and they have been popular with Fascist ideologists.

One of the most influential and often quoted of German sociologists was Max Weber (1864-1920), best known for his study of the relation of early Protestantism to the rise of capitalism and its ideals. This led him into remarkable comparative studies of the nature of Eastern religions and Christianity and of their relation to the capitalistic spirit. Weber stressed the fact that sociology must be an abstract science of social processes, structures, and types and must refrain from expressing value judgments and other forms of subjectivism. Nor can sociology legitimately attempt to solve social problems or suggest programs of social reform. While he devoted less attention to methodology and was less thorough in his analysis of causes, Werner Sombart (1863-1941), in his *Der moderne Kapitalismus,* gave us the most complete study ever written of the rise, nature, and mutations of the capitalistic system and its accompanying mentality. Agrarian society and economics rather than capitalism claimed the attention of Franz Oppenheimer (1864-1943), whose sociological system combines a number of different strains—the social-organism doctrine of Schäffle; Gumplowicz' and Ratzenhofer's notions of the struggle of social groups and interests; and the ethnographic studies of social and economic origins, among others. In treating of the nature of sociology, Oppenheimer contends that it must be a general science of the social process, relying primarily upon social psychology, history, and economics. Oppenheimer finds the key to social evolution and social problems in the relative ratio of landholding, as between a large number of small peasant proprietors and a limited and aristocratic landed gentry, with essential peasant servility in the latter case.

Several of the Germanic sociologists have been especially interested in social reform. Among these have been Schäffle, Ammon, and Oppenheimer, already mentioned. Particularly optimistic was Ludwig Stein (1859–1930), who emphasized the dogma of social progress and outlined a program of social reform in his *Die soziale Frage im Lichte der Philosophie* and combated Spengler's pessimism in his *Evolution and Optimism*. Hans Freyer (1887——), after further extending the historical implications of Tönnies' concept of community and society, developed the idea that sociology should provide the theoretical basis of a program of national rehabilitation. His notions proved congenial to the outlook of National Socialism, and Freyer joined with Sombart in allegiance to the Nazi regime in Germany. Since the war he has, not illogically, lined up with the Russians in Leipzig.

Germanic sociologists, like those in other countries, reflect the ideas and influences in their social environment. A scientific effort to discover and elucidate the environmental basis of social theories has inspired what is known as "the sociology of knowledge," first set forth in comprehensive fashion by Max Scheler in the mid-1920's, and by Karl Mannheim, a decade later, in his *Ideology and Utopia*.

We may now turn to a more detailed consideration of leading German sociologists. Others might make a somewhat different selection, but it surely would differ only in minor details. It can hardly be denied that the names which follow are the outstanding representatives of German sociological trends. Some attention would have been given to Mannheim and the sociology of knowledge had not the subject been thoroughly covered in chapter iv of Barnes and Becker's *Contemporary Social Theory*. Those who lament the fact that Vierkandt is not included may be referred to chapter ii of Theodore Abel's *Systematic Sociology in Germany*.[1]

NOTE

1. For an excellent bibliographic summary of Germanic sociology see Louis Wirth, "Modern German Conceptions of Sociology," *American Journal of Sociology*, XXXII (November, 1926), 461–70. For a list of the main treatments of Germanic sociology, see Barnes and Becker, *Social Thought from Lore to Science* (Boston, 1938), II, xii–xiv.

CHAPTER IX

THE PSYCHOSOCIOLOGICAL THOUGHT
OF WILHELM WUNDT

ALEXANDER GOLDENWEISER

I. WUNDT'S CAREER AND WRITINGS

INTERNATIONALLY acclaimed as one of the founders of experimental psychology, Wilhelm Wundt (1832–1920), the sociologist, has remained relatively unknown among sociologists in English-speaking lands. Also he has on occasion been misunderstood. In the course of an extraordinarily long scientific career, Wundt has contributed, as scholar and original thinker, to the entire range of the theoretical, and to several of the experimental, sciences, starting with physiology and ending with philosophy. At the age of twenty-five, Wundt became associated with the University of Heidelberg, where he lectured in the summer of 1857 on experimental physiology. In the winter of 1859–60 he lectured on physical anthropology; in the summer of the same year, on ethnography; in the summer of 1862, on psychology; in the summer of 1867, on the philosophical results of nature study; and in the winter of 1873–74, on cosmology. Thus, by the time he reached the age of forty-two, he had already encompassed in his lectures almost the entire range of subjects within which was to lie the contributions of his lifetime.

Having accepted a chair in philosophy at Zurich in 1874, he lectured the following summer on logic and scientific methodology, as well as for the first time on folk psychology. The enormous work in ten volumes which was to grow out of these initial courses did not begin to appear until a quarter of a century later—the first volume in 1900, when Wundt was sixty-eight, and the tenth and last in 1920, when he was almost totally blind.

Wundt remained only one year in Zurich, to proceed from there to a chair in philosophy at the University of Leipzig, where he was to remain for forty-five years. Here he lectured on philosophy, psychology, logic, ethics, methodology and folk psychology, delivering his last lecture on July 17, 1917.

As a lecturer, Wundt, whose books are not always easy to read, was luminous and popular—some thought excessively so. His lecture hall attracted audiences as enormous as were those of Kuno Fischer at Heidelberg or those of Simmel or Du Bois-Reymond in Berlin.

Here, in Leipzig, he founded the *Philosophische Studien* (20 vols.; 1883–1903), to be followed by the *Psychologische Studien,* of which ten volumes appeared between 1906 and 1918. Long before his death, Wundt was to find himself in the position of being one of the leading scientific thinkers of the age. His works were translated into twelve languages: Bulgarian, English, French, Greek, Dutch, Japanese, Italian, Lithuanian, Russian, Spanish, Czech, and Hungarian. It seems reasonable to state that, in all probability, Wundt was the last human being of whom it can accurately be said, as of Aristotle and Leibniz, that he substantially mastered the whole range of human knowledge.

It is curious that a man of such learning and penetration should have fallen into the common human error of misunderstanding himself. It seems obvious to anyone familiar with Wundt's career that he represented a typical case of a closet philosopher, a lone surveyor, from a distance, of human thought. Yet in the Preface of his autobiographical book, *Erlebtes und Erkanntes,* written in August, 1920, just before his death, we find him saying that, if asked to name the factor that had proved most potent in his life—if not at all times, at least at the culminating points of his career—he would mention his participation in the concerns of state and society. "This factor has introduced me to life, repeatedly it has exerted a powerful influence upon me, and once more it has come near me when my life was nearing its end." Yet where is the evidence of Wundt's telling participation in the political events of his day or of his many days?

When he was still connected with the University of Heidelberg, Wundt had enjoyed a stimulating apprenticeship with Helmholtz. Now, at Leipzig, inspired by the new vistas opened for psychology by Gustav Theodor Fechner and Ernst Henrich Weber, he established his Psychologisches Institut, which for many years became the mecca of aspiring psychologists. To Leipzig can be traced the experimental trend in American psychology: G. Stanley Hall, Edward B. Titchener, and James McKeen Cattell, all studied here. Titchener, who built up the

Cornell psychology department, was the chief American translator and interpreter of Wundt's work.

It is, therefore, particularly regrettable that the only biographical sketch of Wundt widely read in the United States should have been that contained in G. Stanley Hall's *Founders of Modern Psychology*. At least in the case of Wundt, Hall, who studied under Wundt, seems to have been prejudiced and somewhat misinformed. In his autobiography, *Erlebtes und Erkanntes,* Wundt charges that Hall's account was "invented from beginning to end" (*von Anfang bis zum Ende erfunden*). Hall states, for example, that Wundt had been engaged by Helmholtz to assist him in his mathematical calculations and that the association was soon broken on account of Wundt's insufficient training in mathematics. When referring to this alleged incident, Wundt, a little peeved, has the following to relate: "When I told of this to a German mathematician, namely that Helmholtz was supposed to have kept an assistant for the purpose of preparing his mathematical computations, he broke out into Homeric laughter. This absurd notion is as incompatible with Helmholtz's character as it is with the originality of this great mathematician."

II. FUNDAMENTAL CONCEPTS

Wundt's sociological thought articulates so closely with his psychological system that the one cannot be understood without the other.[1] By contrast with the intellectualism of the English associationists, Wundt placed will, or conation, at the center of his psychological interpretations. It is the will that is the primal seed of the psyche, as well as its integrating or synthesizing element. The integrative aspect of the psychic process is emphasized by Wundt throughout all the phases of his *Physiological Psychology* and his *General Psychology*. The guiding concept here is "apperception," which is juxtaposed to the "perception" of the associationists. Whereas the concept of perception laid stress on the element of experience as affecting the mind, apperception adds to this the receptive and molding role of the mind itself, based on its pre-existing organization. The same external facts or events are perceived differently in accordance with the nature, former experience, or momentary state of the apperceiving mind. There is in apperception a constructive or creative element. Something new appears which was neither present before the perception took place nor given in the perception as such.

This is the simplest and basic example of what Wundt calls "creative synthesis" (schöpferische Synthese).[2] He proceeds to trace this type of function through the entire range of mental life.

This leads Wundt to consider the concept of causality in application to the psychological process. To pave the way for this analysis, he introduces the concept of "psychic actuality" (psychische Aktualität). He points out that all ultimate interpretations of natural phenomena are, and must be, made in terms of a stable substratum, which is, of course, hypothetical. These interpretations, including the causal ones, must therefore be conceptual. Not so in the psychic domain. Here the real is the experienced—no substratum beyond that experience would have any meaning. In consequence, causal linkages on this level can be referred only to such experienced contents. As these psychic contents or processes are presented to the subject in image-like (anschaulich) form, the causality here must also be imagistic, not conceptual.[3] Wundt retains the term "causality" when dealing with psychic processes, but with a meaning different from, in fact opposite to, that which it carries in the physical sciences. In the latter, action and reaction are equal and opposite: a cause is equal to its effect and vice versa. In the psychic domain there is a transmutation and a growth (in accordance with the principle of the "growth of psychic energy") :[4] the effect, as it were, is greater than the cause.

This contrast between psychic causality and physical causality in Wundt's system is especially interesting in view of Wundt's adherence to the principle of psychophysical parallelism. Physical things cause physical things; psychic things cause psychic things (the "causality," to repeat, being different in the two instances). But there is no causal link between physical things and psychic events, neither in the one nor in the other direction. Here there is merely parallelism: parallel to the chain of physical causality runs a chain of psychic causality.[5]

In application to more involved psychic complexes, in their individual and social settings, the principle of creative synthesis expresses itself in two further principles: the "mutation of motives" (Wandlung der Motive) and "heterogeneity of ends" (Heterogenie der Zwecke). Social forms may remain the same, but the psychological motivation constantly changes, or pre-existing forms or organizations are subsequently devoted to new purposes. In the psychosocial domain new wine is constantly being poured into old bottles, or new bottles are provided for old wine.[6]

III. THE ESSENTIALS OF FOLK PSYCHOLOGY

Equipped with these concepts, Wundt approached the problems of folk psychology. Here we find him once more breaking definitely with his precursors, the English associationists and their intellectual cousins, the classical evolutionists. He shifts the emphasis from the intellectual to the emotional and intuitive domain. The reaction of man's mind to nature, we read, does not take the form of an "association of ideas" or that of thought in the narrow sense. On the contrary, there is a direct intuitive response—what Wundt calls a "mythological apperception." To illustrate: the lightning is not brought into association with a snake, nor is there a rational conclusion that it must be a snake. Instead, the lightning is simply apperceived as a snake. Again, Wundt breaks through the individualism of the classical evolutionists, prefacing his concrete investigation of primitive culture by an elaborate theoretical discussion of the relation of the individual to society. He shows here that the psychological life of the individual is so constantly determined by, and so closely interwoven with, his social setting that one cannot be understood without the other. Not that Wundt accepts a social mind or soul; but he insists on the functional relationship between the component individuals of a group, a relationship unconscious, to be sure, but also all-persuasive, so that its separate threads simply cannot be disentangled from the resulting psychological whole.[7]

Of the entire range of culture, three aspects are especially subject to group penetration: language, myth (including religion), and custom (*Sprache, Mythus und Sitte*). Upon analysis of these terms, it will be seen that almost the whole of the cultural content is included, excepting only material culture and its adhering arts. Wundt's enormous work on folk psychology, *Die Völkerpsychologie,* is an attempt to demonstrate in the concrete the principles formulated in these prefatory remarks. The first two volumes are devoted to an analytical examination of an enormous amount of material dealing with primitive languages. This is followed by a volume which was originally conceived as an introduction to the section on religion and myth but was separated in subsequent editions into a distinct treatise on art, a sort of history of human imagination. Then came three volumes on myth and religion, followed by two volumes on social organization, one volume on law, and a final volume on culture and history.[8]

While Wundt does not wholly escape the pitfalls of evolutionary construction, his evolutionism is more critical, more sophisticated, as it were, than that of the classical school. Nowhere does he apply the principle of unilinearity, always leaving room for alternative chains of development. The constant emphasis, moreover, on the interplay of motives and purposes, on the transmutation of psychic values, results in a picture both more complex and more nearly corresponding to historical reality than that achieved by the English evolutionists. Wundt held that the folk-psychology material which he gathered and analyzed in his work was not merely valuable in itself but also contributed a prime source to be explored by the individual psychologist. The foundations of individual psychology must, of course, be known and understood by him who deals with folk-psychology material; but the individual psychologist also finds his own source material enriched by the facts which can be disclosed only by the folk-psychology approach.[9]

In the final volume of the *Völkerspsychologie* (*Kultur und Geschichte*) Wundt summarizes the results of his study and supplements them by a theoretical discussion of the concept of law in history, a subject already broached in certain sections of the third volume of his *Logic* (*Die Logik der Geisteswissenschaften*). In contrast to the approach of the evolutionists, Wundt claims that the regularities discovered here belong to psychology, not to history. The principles derived from the generalizations of psychology, it is true, are applicable to history. It disports itself, as it were, within a field delimited by psychological possibilities. As a heuristic principle, Wundt uses here the concept of "singular law" (*singulares Gesetz*), a term applied to those instances in which a psychological principle is exemplified by a particular historical event or series. But the historical series, as such, is and must be singular and unique.[10]

In a briefer work, *The Elements of Folk Psychology*, Wundt undertakes an analysis of cultural development from a different angle. Whereas in the *Völkerpsychologie* he was mainly intent on following trends of development, *The Elements of Folk Psychology* is devoted to a generalized description of cultural eras which succeed one another in the history of culture.

Wundt divides the history of human culture and the evolution of the *Zeitgeist* into four main stages: (1) the period of primitive man;

(2) the period of totemism; (3) the period of gods and heroes; and (4) the period of humanity.

By the "period of primitive man" Wundt meant truly primitive culture, more rudimentary than that possessed by any existing primitive peoples. Therefore, his description of the psychology of primitive man had to be chiefly an exercise in psychological reconstruction. As such, it was probably the ablest presentation ever executed by a scholar. The totemic period is literally named, being based on the assumption of universal gentile society and an accompanying totemic complex. Though some of the basic assumptions as to gentile society and totemism are unsupported by the facts, Wundt's treatment of the so-called "kinship" period of social evolution possesses remarkable psychological insight. The age of heroes emerged when the human hero replaced the deified animal of the totemic stage. The gods were introduced through rationalizing experience and crises. During this age of gods and heroes, the state, property, economic and social classes, and the concept of the individual personality made their appearance. Religion took on moral implications and became an important social force. It was, thus, an era of remarkable cultural and institutional progress. The stage of humanity comes in with the rise and fall of great world empires and the subsequent development of a sense of mutual interdependence, humanity, and brotherhood. Wundt's views of this era are reminiscent of Comte's notions of the final stage of social evolution. Though unsound in many details, Wundt's scheme of social evolution was clear and precise, and this accounts in large part for its wide popularity and its acceptance in many circles.[11]

NOTES

1. Wundt's literary output was enormous. Only his principal works can be given here: *Logik* (3d ed.; 3 vols.; Stuttgart, 1906–8); *Grundzüge der physiologischen Psychologie* (5th ed.; 3 vols.; Leipzig, 1908–11; Eng. trans. 2d ed.); *Grundriss der Psychologie* (3d ed.; Leipzig, 1907; Eng. trans., 1st ed.); *System der Philosophie* (2 vols.; Stuttgart, 1889); *Einleitung in der Philosophie* (Leipzig, 1901); *Vorlesungen über die Menschen- und Tierseele* (4th ed.; Leipzig, 1906; Eng. trans., 2d ed.); *Ethik* (4th ed.; 3 vols.; Stuttgart, 1912); *Kleine Schriften* (2 vols.; Leipzig, 1910). His most important work for sociology is the *Völkerpsychologie* (2d ed.; 10 vols.; Leipzig, 1910–20 [4th ed., Leipzig, 1927]), comprising: Vols. I–II, *Language;* Vol. III, *Art;* Vols. IV, V, and VI, *Myth and Religion;* Vols. VII–VIII, *Society;* Vol. IX, *Law;* Vol. X, *Culture and History;* and *Elemente der Völkerpsychologie* (Leipzig, 1912; Eng. trans.), *The Elements of Folk Psychology* [1916]). Wundt's autobiography, *Erlebtes und Erkanntes* (Leipzig, 1919), mentioned in the text, is very impersonal but gives a fine picture of a long and rich period of German thought.

A little book by Wundt's daughter, Eleanore, who was his faithful companion and secretary for many years, *Wilhelm Wundt's Werke* (Leipzig, 1927), gives a complete list of Wundt's writings.

2. "A perception [we read] is never a mere sum of the sensations into which it can be decomposed; what gives the perception its significance is a synthesis of the sensations. We could never derive the harmonious tone quality from a mere sum of sounds, not the flat or corporeal appearance of an object from a sum of space sensations. These syntheses are specific experiences, no less so than is a single color or a separate sound" (*Logik* [3d ed.], Vol. III: *Die Logic der Geisteswissenschaften*, p. 272 (writer's translation). Note the obvious relationship to William James's conception of mental integration, as well as to the concepts of the Gestalt psychologists).

3. Wundt adds significantly: ".... in this actualistic causality [*aktuelle Kausalität*] of psychology the decisive logical motive of the causal concept appears in purer form than it does in the substantial causality of the study of nature. For that motive consists primarily in a linkage of thought of experienced events. In the natural sciences, on the other hand, with their objective orientation, the aim is to establish causal linkages in a form independent of the subject. This necessitates the introduction of an objective base for natural causality. Thus the concept of substantial determination is ushered in" (*Logik*, III, 260–61 [the writer's translation]).

4. This principle, as well as Wundt's idea of the nonequivalence of cause and effect in psychic causality, has been attacked with considerable force by Max Weber.

5. This should not be confused with the metaphysical theory of psychophysical parallelism, also designated as pan-psychism, which holds that all psychic processes have physical correlates and (N.B.!) vice versa and that the linkage between the two is that of parallelism, not causality. Wundt, in his capacity of psychologist, speaks not as a philosopher but as a natural scientist. Psychophysical parallelism to him means that *whenever* evidence indicates the occurrence of physical processes in conjunction with psychic ones or of psychic processes with physical ones, the relation between the two series of processes is one of parallelism, whereas within each series causal linkages obtain.

In view of the fact that Wundt's position here has often been misunderstood and as, moreover, the presence of a metaphysical (that is, nonexperiential) postulate would be fatal to the scientific status of his theory, a direct quotation seems in place. Writes Wundt: "If, on the contrary, the principle [of parallelism] is accepted empirically ...., then it merely signifies that psychic processes cannot be derived from physical ones nor physical from psychic ones in the same causal sense in which we strive to derive physical processes from other physical ones and psychic processes from other psychic ones, but that all we may assume here is a regular co-existence of certain links of the two causal series. Such co-existence does, of course, not preclude the presence on the physical side of certain phenomena to which no psychic ones correspond *nor on the psychic side of certain phenomena with reference to which no accompanying physical ones can be either demonstrated or conjectured, with any degree of probability"* (*Logik*, III, 254 [translation and italics the author's]).

That the principle of parallelism, even in this limited sense, may prove inadequate, especially as a substitute for causality between the physical and the psychic, is another matter. This point is both too complex and too technical for inclusion here. At present, one or two references will have to suffice (see Heinrich Rickert, "Psychophysische Causalität und psychophysischer Parallelismus," *Philosophische Abhandlungen* [*Christoph Sigwart zu seinem siebzigsten Geburtstage gewidmet*] [1900], pp. 59–87; Ludwig Busse, "Die Wechselwirkung zwischen Leib und Seele und das Gesetz der Erhaltung der Energie" [*Philosophische Abhandlungen*, pp. 89–126]; and Christoph Sigwart, *Logik* [Eng. trans., London, 1895], Vol. II, chap. v).

In conjunction with this separation of psychic causality from physical causality, Wundt draws a sharp distinction between the psychic and the physical and the concepts referring to the two realms. "Our thinking," he says, "is built upon the impressions derived from the sense organs, our will upon the supply of innervation-energy stored up in the nervous system. The principle of equivalence [between the physical and the psychical] does not extend beyond this external side of psychic life. All those relations of psychic elements which constitute their worth for our psychic life are subject to psychical causality; also, the physical and psychic elements, representing two closed systems of causal interrelations, are not only different but incommensurable" (*Physiologische Psychologie* [5th ed.], III, 316 [writer's translation]). In the physical domain, values are magnitudes (*Grössenwerthe*); in the psychic domain, magnitudes are values (*Werthgrössen*).

6. It must be stressed here that Wundt's concept of "ends" or "purposes" has nothing mystical about it. His teleology is not at all like the "design" of the theologians—or of the philosophers. "The 'end' is merely that result of preceding conditions to which a certain value has been attributed, and the result is conceived as telic on account of that value element. From this valuational standpoint the conditions become the 'means' and, in so far as they have figured as contributory emotional or intellectual factors, they become the 'motives' of the teleological occurrence" (*Logik*, III, 281). Thus the interpretation through "ends" and that through "motives" are merely forward- and backward-looking conceptualizations of the same affair. The situation, however, is further complicated by the circumstance that motives fluctuate and ends become transmuted. Wundt's position here is that, with the rise of scientific ideology, a relative steadiness of ends or purposes may be attained, but, even so, only within the limits of a restricted cultural epoch. As one epoch or era passes into the next, a transmutation of both ends and motives becomes inevitable. It follows that the cultural eras are characterized by different sets of motives and purposes. (These deep and far-reaching reflections were set down by Wundt one year before his death, when he was eighty-seven and almost blind [see *Völkerpsychologie*, Vol. X: *Kultur und Geschichte*, pp. 152–62]).

7. To understand Wundt's position here it is important to read his extensive controversy with Lazarus and Steinthal, editors of the *Zeitschrift für Völkerpsychologie und Sprachwissenschaft*, the first volume of which appeared in 1860. Whereas these two students sided with the then rising concept of a folk soul or group mind, Wundt insisted that no minds are conceivable except those of individuals and that, from a psychological standpoint, the group was a functional, not an existential, entity. After reflecting on the metaphysical notion of a nonexperiential folk soul, Wundt has this to say: "We can only use here the actualistic concept of the soul [*aktueller Seelenbegriff*] as the sum-total of psychic processes. Only from this standpoint can we determine the relation of the concepts 'individual soul' and 'folk soul,' as well as the relation of the individual to the group. While it is true that the latter presupposes its component individuals, it does not follow that it represents a mere addition and enhancement of the traits and activities of individuals. What the group contributes here is the combination and interaction of individuals, thus making possible individual contributions belonging specifically to group life" (*Völkerpsychologie* [4th ed.], Vol. I: *Die Sprache*, p. 20; cf. also Lazarus and Steinthal, "Einleitende Gedanken über Völkerpsychologie," *Zeitschrift für Völkerpsychologie und Sprachwissenschaft*, I, 1–73; Wundt, "Ziele und Wege der Völkerpsychologie," *Philosophische Studien*, IV, 1 ff.; and Steinthal, "Begriff der Völkerpsychologie," *Zeitschrift für Völkerpsychologie und Sprachwissenschaft*, XVII, 333 ff.).

8. It is interesting to note that two other European thinkers had contributed to the philosophy of culture history while Wundt was thinking out his own—Karl Marx and Herbert Spencer. Of the three, Marx anchored his entire culture-historical thought in the socioeconomic case, whereas the spiritual aspects of culture, as "epiphenomenal" and noncausal, received at his hand the scantiest of treatment; Spencer and Wundt, on the contrary, left out the socioeconomico-technological level almost completely (except that Spencer presented an altogether one-sided picture of "industrial institutions" by contrasting them with military ones); Spencer also left out art (as did Marx), whereas Wundt devoted a whole volume to it. Nor can these discrepancies in the contents of the three systems be explained away by pointing out that Marx wrote as an economist, Spencer as a sociologist, and Wundt as a psychologist, for each of the three was laboring—avowedly so—upon a culture-historical philosophy. I need scarcely add that all three would have benefited by

including what they had omitted and permitting it to play freely upon the rest of their material.

9. "Psychology needs the folk-psychological material comprised in certain social sciences not less urgently than the latter require a psychological foundation. As soon as psychology begins to exploit the sources which pour in upon it from the different spheres of psychic life, the contributions of psychology itself to the interpretation of individual facts, contributions derived from the broader contemplation of psychic life, will no longer remain unrecognized. For in one respect, at least, the most refined practical tact and the richest life-wisdom cannot come up to the achievements of scientific psychology, in so far, namely, as the latter is capable of utilizing the standpoints derived from the analysis of the simpler mental processes for an interpretation of the involved phenomena of social life. So long as they ignore these guides furnished by scientific psychology, the historian, linguist, and mythologist must operate with complex concepts. Only when a bridge has been built to span the gap between the individual mind and the psychic aspects of the social process does it become possible, by retracing one's steps, to apply folk-psychological conclusions to the investigation of those formations of the individual consciousness which elude the methods of the scientific psychologist" (*Völkerpsychologie* [4th ed.], Vol. I: *Die Sprache*, p. 29 [writer's translation]). To this we may well add that, barring a few highly specialized fields, this mutually fructifying relationship between individual and social psychology still remains a desideratum.

10. The concept of *singular law* is illumined in the following important passage, which begins with a distinction between "principles" and "laws": "Principles are of universal application, in so far as they are rooted in general conditions operative at all times and places. Laws, on the contrary, can only possess a relative generality, in so far as they are always dependent on specific conditions. The generality of a law is the more restricted the greater the conflux of conditions comprised in the law. The limit of this series can therefore be designated as a *singular law* (or better: singular lawfulness) which expresses the following: in a given series of events and conditions each link is categorically and causally determined by pre-existing and accompanying circumstances; on account of the complexity of the conditions, however, the entire series, in this particular form, is singular: it has never occurred before, nor may it be expected to recur in the future. The most general conditions, again, which obtain everywhere and always in the historical domain, and to which correspond certain principles which everywhere control historic happenings, are the universally valid motives of human behavior. It would therefore be more correct to designate the so-called historic principles as psychological principles applied to history" (*Logik* [3d ed.], III, 429–30).

Cf. the relevant remarks by John Dewey on the nature of sequential events: "By the nature of the case, causality, however it be defined, consists in the sequential order itself, and not in a last term which as such is irrelevant to causality, although it may, of course, be in addition an initial term in another sequential order. The view held—or implied—by some 'mechanists,' which treats an initial term as if it had an inherent generative force which it somehow emits and bestows upon its successors, is all of a piece with the view held by teleologists which implies that an end brings about its own antecedents. *Both isolate an event from the history in which it belongs and in which it has its character.* Both make a fictitiously isolated position in a temporal order a mark of true reality, one theory selecting initial place and the other final place. But, in fact, causality is another name for the sequential order itself; and since this is an order of a history having a beginning and an end, there is nothing more absurd than setting causality over against either initiation or finality" (*Experience and Nature* [New York, 1925], pp. 99–100). The conclusion is that "initiation" and "finality" (or, with Wundt, "motive" and "purpose") are merely ways of looking at causal or sequential events. (These remarks by Dewey, though illuminating in the context of this discussion of Wundt, may themselves prove more than questionable from another angle, a subject that cannot be pursued here.)

11. It may well be doubted whether Wundt, writing today rather than a generation ago, would have gone as far as he did in this hopefully prognosticatory section of his

book. Considerable light on the problems brought to the fore by Wundt's penetrating analysis can be gained from an examination of the various issues of *L'Année sociologique* (1898–1908), in which Emile Durkheim and his disciples, Hubert and Mauss, engaged in frequent discussion and recrimination with Wundt. The strictly psychological mode of approach adopted by the German scholar received little sympathy from this school of French sociologists, who attempted to construct a system of concepts as objective as those of physical science. Nevertheless, in so far as these sociologists stressed the significance of social determinants in psychology, a background was created for many points of contact between their position and that of Wundt.

Among Wundt's sociological followers, Alfred Vierkandt deserves special mention. His *Naturvölker und Kulturvölker* (Leipzig, 1896) and *Die Stetigkeit im Kulturwandel* (Leipzig, 1908), although not distinguished by originality, represent interesting applications of Wundtian principles.

CHAPTER X

THE SOCIOLOGICAL SYSTEM OF FERDINAND TÖNNIES: "COMMUNITY" AND "SOCIETY"*

RUDOLF HEBERLE, *Louisiana State University*

I. MAIN FACTS CONCERNING TÖNNIES' LIFE AND ACADEMIC CAREER

FERDINAND TÖNNIES was born in 1855 on a farm in Eiderstedt on the west coast of Schleswig-Holstein. Originally Dutch settlers, his paternal ancestors had been farmers in those parts for over two hundred years. The Tönnies were one of the leading families in this Frisian region, where serfdom had never developed and where many elements of the ancient Germanic rural community had been preserved. His mother came from a rural family in the east of Holstein, which had given to the country many Lutheran pastors and professional men of distinction.

In 1864 the family moved to the small town of Husum. Here the young Tönnies formed a friendship with the much older poet, Theodor Storm, which became one of the important influences in his life.[1] He was graduated from the Gymnasium in 1872, and, not yet seventeen years of age, he began to study classical philology and philosophy at the University of Jena and later at Leipzig, Bonn, Berlin, and Tübingen, where he received the degree of Doctor of Philosophy in 1877. From then on, Tönnies, following his genuine intellectual interest, devoted himself to social philosophy and the social sciences. The influence of the philological training is, however, quite conspicuous even in his later writings.

Among those who, during these student years, left the most lasting imprint on Tönnies' mind were his countryman, Friedrich Paulsen, noted philosopher; Adolph Wagner, the economist; and Wilhelm

* Revised and supplemented reprint from *American Sociological Review*, Vol. II, No. 1 (February, 1937). This article was originally written in German. For the translation, the author is indebted to Mrs. Frank D. Graham, of Princeton. He assumes, however, full responsibility for the present form of the essay.

Wundt, the sociopsychologist.[2] Wagner, with his idea of an increasing regulation of social life by the state, influenced Tönnies' thinking in the direction of state socialism. Wundt's theorem of *Zweckwille* and *Triebwille* obviously left its mark on his thought.

As early as 1877, Tönnies had become interested in Thomas Hobbes, the most outspoken advocate of state omnipotence.[3] His Hobbes studies led him to comprehensive reading in the fields of political philosophy and natural law, as well as in the more recent social sciences. He acquired a thorough knowledge of the German, English, and—to a lesser extent— the French literature. In these years of private studies his main object became the understanding of the true meaning both of the rational school of natural law and of the opposing historical and romantic theories. To him it appeared that "all irrational and less rational forms of thought . . . . were never simply unreasonable but that they had their peculiar meaning which finally was a derivation from human will."[4] The social theories became to him sociological data in themselves, expressions of social volition and reflections of actual social conditions. It became clear to him that ideas like communism and socialism were to be regarded not as mere phantasms, as thought-out utopias, but as forms of actual social life. The existence of primitive communism had, he believed, been proved by recent ethnological studies, and Tönnies began to conceive of the history of mankind as a movement from original simple communism through various stages of individualism and finally to state and international socialism.[5] These ideas were presented in 1887 in his now famous book, *Gemeinschaft und Gesellschaft*.

Six years earlier Tönnies had become a lecturer (*Privatdozent*) at the University of Kiel, with which he remained affiliated until his dismissal by the National Socialists in 1933. Although Tönnies' connection with the University of Kiel lasted through more than half a century, he always remained in a sense an outsider. Only for eight years, six of which were war years, when the universities were almost deserted, did Tönnies hold the rank of a full professor. While this limited his influence on the younger generation, it gave him leisure for work and liberty to travel, which he did extensively and with great pleasure.[6]

Though conservative in temperament, Tönnies took part in virtually all the more important progressive movements of his time. His special sympathy belonged to the two branches of the organized labor movement—the consumers' co-operatives and the labor unions. In them he saw the beginnings from which a better society might develop.

Tönnies was one of the founders of the German Sociological Society and was its president for many years; he also was an honorary member of the American Sociological Society. His professional contacts and personal friendships with the prominent men and women of his time were numerous and covered a wide range of scholars, writers, artists, and statesmen. While his life lacks any dramatic aspects, it was, never-theless, a rich, intensive life in close contact with the historical processes of the period.

Tönnies died in 1936, over eighty years old, one of the last scholars in our time who could be said to possess a truly universal erudition in the humanities and the cultural and social sciences.

II. TÖNNIES' CHIEF WRITINGS

The works of Ferdinand Tönnies cover so many topics and such wide fields of sociology, social philosophy, economics, and politics that, at first glance, it seems almost impossible in a short essay to do justice to the lifework of a man who, at his death, had surpassed the biblical age by a decade. The task, however, is made lighter by the fact that the focus of Tönnies' scheme of thought lies in the concepts which first appeared in *Gemeinschaft und Gesellschaft*. On this theory Tönnies' international reputation rests. In vigor of thought and beauty of style, *Gemeinschaft und Gesellschaft* has hardly been surpassed by any of the numerous later writings of the author. Here, already, the social-psychological foundations and the fundamental sociological categories of Tönnies' scheme are well and truly laid.

In a large part of his later work Tönnies has "applied" the funda-mental concepts of *Gemeinschaft und Gesellschaft*[7] to special phenomena of social life, as, e.g., morals and folkways[8] or public opinion.[9] The broader public knows Tönnies merely as the author of *Gemeinschaft und Gesellschaft,* but it would be unjust to identify his scientific life-work with the theorem of that book and its application, for, on the one hand, his sociological system was fully developed only in later years and, on the other, his achievements in the social sciences reach far beyond the narrower field of theoretical sociology.

Tönnies' sociological system as a whole was for many years known only to his personal students. It has, indeed, never been published in adequate form but only in some short essays and in the *Einführung in die Soziologie,* a book of his maturer years which did not attain to the classic form of the *Gemeinschaft und Gesellschaft.* The *Einführung,* nevertheless, is quite indispensable to the understanding of Tönnies' theory and, because of its easy style, will be found to be very useful in the teaching of sociology.

Tönnies' interest in sociological problems was stirred by his studies of Thomas Hobbes's philosophy of law and theory of the state and, as we shall see, his own sociology cannot be rightly understood or fully appreciated unless these early studies are kept in mind. In his book on Hobbes and in numerous later papers on problems more or less closely related to Hobbes's philosophy, Tönnies has made valuable contributions to the theory of the modern state and to the philosophy of law. These deserve recognition quite apart from Tönnies' purely sociological writings.

The third and least-known phase of Tönnies' work is that of the empirical investigations to which a considerable part of his lifework was devoted. Among these studies the following may be mentioned here: the surveys of the socioeconomic situation of longshoremen and seamen in Hamburg and other ports, which Tönnies was asked to undertake after a big strike in Hamburg;[10] a study of the relationship between certain moral phenomena and socioeconomic conditions in Schleswig-Holstein;[11] a series of papers on criminality in Schleswig-Holstein,[12] based upon material collected in the chief prisons of the province; a study on suicide [13] in Schleswig-Holstein; a paper on cyclical changes in marriage rates and in the proportion of male to female births in relation to certain economic data,[14] unhappily published during the first year of World War I. This was one of the first German contributions to the empirical study of business cycles. For these investigations he had developed a method of correlation of his own invention.[15]

III. LEADING PHASES OF TÖNNIES' SOCIOLOGICAL THEORY

A. SOCIOLOGICAL THEORY AND RESEARCH; THE THREE SPHERES OF SOCIOLOGY

It was detrimental to the appreciation of Tönnies in America that these studies attracted scarcely any attention there and that, at the time when *Gemeinschaft und Gesellschaft* gained a broader public in Germany, there was among American sociologists little interest in what they held to be "armchair sociology." And yet Tönnies, believing firmly in the possibility of "exact" methods in the social sciences, never thought of sociological theory as being an end in itself or as independent of research. Tönnies distinguishes three disciplines of sociology,[16] distinct in their epistemological aspects and in the methods essential to each:

1. Pure or theoretical (*reine, theoretische*) sociology
2. Applied (*angewandte*) sociology
3. Empirical (*empirische*) sociology or sociography

This division relates to sociology in the narrower sense. Besides this, Tönnies asserted the validity of a wider concept of sociology, which had come to general recognition outside of Germany and which included social biology, demography, and social psychology.

Tönnies' idea of "pure" sociology corresponds approximately to "general sociology"[17] in the meaning which has now become rather generally accepted. It is a logical system of concepts of "normal" or ideal types (in the meaning of Max Weber) of *soziale Wesenheiten* ("social entities") in a static condition. Such a system of concepts is a necessary means to the description and understanding of empirical social phenomena.[18]

The "application" of these "pure" concepts to the analysis and explanation of concrete historical societies (*Kulturen*) and to historical processes of social evolution is the field of *angewandte Soziologie*.[19] Here the original meaning of sociology as a scientific philosophy of history, as conceived by Lorenz Stein and A. Comte, is restored. Tönnies planned a comprehensive treatise on the evolution of modern society, which he intended to be the complement to *Gemeinschaft und Gesellschaft*. He published some papers on the subject of *Progress and Evolution in Society*[20] and, a half year before his death, the first volume of the larger work was published under the title *Geist der Neuzeit*. The difference beween *reine* and *angewandte* sociology is not only that between a static and a dynamic theory of society but also, and primarily, that between a constructive and a deductive approach. In *angewandte* sociology empirical data are to be systematized and interpreted according to the principle of evolution from "Gemeinschaft" toward "Gesellschaft."[21]

The sociographic study of present social conditions and processes, or *empirische Soziologie,* can proceed by inductive or empirical methods,[22] since in this field almost any data required are available or can be made available. But, of course, even in these empirical studies the concepts of pure sociology will be used in order to select and organize the "facts."[23] This concept of *Soziographie* corresponds approximately to the more recent type of American social surveys and ecological studies as a scientific representation of sociologically relevant facts in concrete communities or groups. This threefold system of sociology, in the special sense, can be said to combine in an organic unity the main approaches to the subject of society which have led to the development of different and apparently irreconcilable schools of sociological thought.[24]

B. GEMEINSCHAFT AND GESELLSCHAFT

The core of Tönnies' system lies in the doctrine of human relationships or social entities (*soziale Wesenheiten*). This doctrine is based on the distinction between the two "fundamental concepts" *Gemeinschaft* and *Gesellschaft.* The historical importance of this theorem for the social sciences lies in the synthesis of the rational and the Romantic conceptions of society. The two concepts of social life which, since the days of Aristotle, have been the principal subject of discussion among social philosophers are held to be one-sided pictures of the reality of social life. The essential contribution is not the mere construction of two antithetic concepts (we shall see that they are not at all meant to be strictly antithetical) but the clear conceptual differentiation of two fundamental patterns, representing opposite potentialities of concrete social formations, and, furthermore, the recognition that the difference between the two schools of social philosophy is due to the fact that their proponents have each taken only one of the two spheres into their conception of the whole of social reality.

It is true that we find the inception of this recognition with Hobbes in the distinction between natural and political commonwealths. But the clear formulation in the concepts of *Gemeinschaft* and *Gesellschaft* was possible only after the Romantic theory of state and society had prepared the way; the knowledge of the social life of primitive peoples, which, during the nineteenth century, was attained through cultural anthropology, comparative philology, and the studies of comparative law, was also a prerequisite.

It is impossible within the limits of this chapter to trace in detail the influence on Tönnies of German natural-rights philosophers and thinkers of the Romantic school and, above all, of English and American scholars (e.g., Morgan, *Ancient Society*). In *Gemeinschaft und Gesellschaft* Tönnies has especially acknowledged the decisive stimulus which he received from Sir Henry Maine's antithesis of status and contract.[25]

The distinction between *Gemeinschaft* and *Gesellschaft* as fundamental concepts of social groups recalls the distinction between organic and mechanical social entities (even Tönnies occasionally employs these pictures, but only as analogies) or between those relationships which have grown naturally out of sympathetic sentiments and those which have been set up consciously and for a definite purpose.

The essential points in Tönnies' theory, however, are as follows:

1. All social relationships are to be regarded as creations of the human will. They exist as social facts only through the will of individuals to associate.

2. This will and, along with it, the inner relationship of the associated individuals with one another can be of very varied character: a group or relationship can be willed either because it is desired to attain through it a definite end (with complete indifference toward, or even antipathy against, partners, e.g., a business co-operation), or because, from sympathy with the partners, it is felt that the relationship is valuable in itself (e.g., friendship). Tönnies designates the two types of will as *Wesenwille* and *Kürwille*. *Kürwille*[26] means the rational will which distinguishes between end and means (the concept corresponds fairly exactly to Max Weber's concept of the *zweckrationale* behavior). *Wesenwille* means any process of willing which springs from the temper and character of an individual, whether it has its origin in inclination, in habit, or in conviction.[27]

3. The *Wesenwille*, therefore, is by no means necessarily irrational. On the contrary, one can distinguish rather between degrees of rationality of the *Wesenwille* and of the "communities" which derive therefrom. The scale runs from those in which the instinctive sympathy of biologically related individuals determines the individual will to those which are based solely on a relationship arising out of common adherence to certain values (e.g., blood-relationship, neighborliness, friendship; family, community, guild). The wholly mental forms (stages) of *Gemeinschaft*[28] come nearest to the *gesellschaftlichen* relationships, which are always purely mental.[29]

The two categories of *Gemeinschaft* and *Gesellschaft* stand in a complicated relationship to each other which is not always understood by critics. The objection has been raised[30] that these concepts represent, on the one hand, antithetical conceptional categories and, on the other hand, stages of historical development and that they also are mere classificatory concepts. The last of these is certainly not Tönnies' meaning. Though he sometimes designates the family or the village as a *Gemeinschaft* and the city or the state as a *Gesellschaft,* this is only as a paradigm. To him *Gemeinschaft* and *Gesellschaft* are pure concepts of ideal types which do not exist as such in the empirical world. They cannot, therefore, be applied as classificatory concepts. Rather, they are to be regarded as traits, which, in empirical social entities, are found in varying proportions. If one should, for example, define the family as a *Gemeinschaft,* the road to sociological understanding would thereby be barred; it is the peculiar task of the sociologist to find out to what extent a family in a concrete situation (e.g., a wage-earner's family in a great city) corresponds more to the type of *Gesellschaft* than does a family in another situation (e.g., on a farm).[31] If one takes the concepts in this sense, it will be possible to apply them to historical phenomena without doing violence to the logic of the system.

A peculiar difficulty lies in the fact that the two categories are not strictly antithetical, inasmuch as a purely *gesellschaftliche* empirical condition of social life is, for Tönnies, inconceivable; for, since man in his behavior is never motivated alone by intellect and reason but, whatever the stage of social development, by inclinations and emotions, that is to say, fundamentally by *Wesenwillen* and only partially by *Kürwillen,* all empirical "associations" must have a *Gemeinschafts,* or "community," basis.[32]

C. THEORETICAL (PURE) SOCIOLOGY; SOCIAL GROUPS

The social entities are classified as (1) social relations (*Verhältnisse*); (2) social collectives (*Samtschaften*); and (3) social corporations (*Körperschaften*). These social entities are to be conceptually distinguished from natural and psychic relations. Natural relation by common blood does not, per se, constitute a social relation. A social relation springs from a psychic relation "in the measure in which the latter is felt not only as such but is also willed to exist and persist"—and in so far as certain common and mutual rights and duties of the participants are derived from it (e.g., courtship developing into marriage).

A social relation, thus, is thought of as something "valid"—not only by the participants but, if it is not a secret relation, by other persons. These, however, can refuse to recognize the validity, e.g., if parents refuse to recognize the engagement of their daughter. A complex of social relations between more than two persons is called a "social circle" (*sozialer Kreis*), e.g., a circle of friends. This is the link between social relation and social collective (*Samtschaft*).

Under collective, or *Samtschaft,* we are to understand a group of individuals who, because of common natural or psychic traits, are regarded as units (race or language groups); social *Samtschaften* are such natural or psychic groups, in so far as they are recognized by the associated individuals themselves as units, to which their assent is given and which they will to persist. A people would be the best example of a *Samtschaft* resting on natural and psychic common characteristics; the political party may be considered as an example of a purely psychic or mental *Samtschaft.*

"Corporations"—social bodies or social unions—are to be distinguished from the two former categories inasmuch as they possess an organization, that is, that definite persons can perform definite functions, which are regarded by the members of the corporation, and even by outsiders, as the acts of the corporation. The corporation is thought of as a person, which possesses a rational will to which it can give validity through its organs or functionaries. Thus the idea of social entity comes to full expression in the concept of the corporation.

A corporation may be based on a social *Samtschaft,* as the church rests in the community of believers, or it may originate from a social *Samtschaft,* as the party machine from the mass of those who feel that they are bound together by similar political ends.

All three categories of *soziale Wesenheiten* can be willed predominantly by *Wesenwillen* or by *Kürwillen* and therefore predominantly correspond to the type of *Gemeinschaft* or *Gesellschaft,* as the case may be.

While, as a rule, in social philosophy a "superindividual" character is attributed only to corporations, in which case the concept of the juristic person is usually employed, it is an essential feature of Tönnies' theory that even the "social relation" is conceived as a creature of the will of the partners, which exists in their consciousness as something objective, toward which the partners recognize that they have definite obligations, and from which they acquire certain rights. Thus, one may say: "My friendship to X binds me to do or refrain from doing this or that." When social relations are legally sanctioned as, for instance, in marriage or the relation of employer and employee, the identity, in principle, of their mode of existence with the corporations becomes obvious.

And with that we define the point at which the objects of sociology and social psychology diverge. Sociology deals with types of social relationship, not with the typical psychic attitudes of the persons related.

The state, as the most important corporation, has been the object of philosophical and sociological speculations and theories ever since antiquity. Tönnies considers the so-called *Allgemeine Staatslehre* as a part of sociology,[33] so far as it deals with the *Sein* and not with the *Sollen*, i.e., with really existing states and not with ideals of the state. Several of his most important writings are concerned with problems of the theory of the state, and, during the first World War, Tönnies wrote an excellent comparative study of the English and the German state.[34]

D. SOCIAL NORMS AND VALUES

It is the criterion of the social life of human beings, as distinguished from the mere living-together in groups, such as occurs also among animals, that it is subject to a normative order; for this reason the theory of social norms and social values—from which these norms derive their meaning—is the necessary complement to the theory of social entities. Tönnies was always particularly interested in the theory of social norms, and therefore we find it more systematically developed in his work than is the theory of social values.[35]

In this paper only the elementary features of Tönnies' theory of norms can be presented. Social norms are defined as all commandments and inhibitions, of general validity to individuals linked together in a social entity, which regulate the conduct of those individuals toward one another and toward outsiders. These regulations gain validity by the agreement (consent)—expressed or tacit—of the individuals; they may be norms autonomous or heteronomous; and they may be followed from conviction of their rightness or merely in order to avoid the detrimental consequences of disobedience.

Tönnies distinguishes (1) three classes of norms: order, law, and morality, and (2) the following kinds of social will, by which the norms (as objects of will) are created:[36] (*a*) *gemeinschaftliche* forms of social will: (i) unanimity, or concord, as the general trait of all common willing, which, based upon relations formerly described as of "community" type, appears to be natural and necessary per se, (ii) custom, based upon habits in common, (iii) religion, based upon faith in supernatural commanding powers; (*b*) *gesellschaftliche* forms of social will:

(i) convention, (ii) legislation, (iii) public opinion (based upon common interests).

"Order" is the most general complex of norms, primarily based upon either concord or convention. It might be said that it comprises those norms which are valid through the normative power of facts.

Law is the complex of norms, which, according to their idea, are to be interpreted and enforced by judicial decision. Law is created either by custom or by formal and intentional "legislation."

Morality is the complex of those norms the interpretation and application of which are thought of as the function of an imaginary judge (God or conscience). The norms of morality are sanctioned more or less either by religion or by public opinion.

All these distinctions, however, are of purely conceptual character; in reality, transitions exist between the various types of norms, and each category contains elements of the others. The systems of norms of the various social entities are composed of norms of order, law, and morality.[37]

Tönnies' concept of custom is defined in a manner slightly different from the usual concept: for him custom is not the original unity (or common origin) of all norms, out of which law and morality develop at a higher level of culture. And, again, custom is not a definite body of norms. It is the will of a social entity rooted in common habits, by which definite norms attain content and validity.

The distinction between customary law and law by legislation is not identical with the distinction between codified law and unwritten law, for even customary law is liable to become codified and sanctioned by legislation. But, in order to regulate constantly arising new conditions, the modern state has to establish laws which are sanctioned by no "sacred" customs but only by their being generally reasonable or by their serving certain interests, as, for example, most rules of modern transportation and traffic law.

Thus the systematic theory of law, in so far as law is factually effective and can, therefore, be studied by empirical methods, forms an essential part of pure sociology. But for Tönnies even those ideas of the origins of law and of laws valid under all conditions of human society which form the theory of "natural law" become essential subjects of sociological theory because of their great importance in political respects. Tönnies has added to the well-known rationalistic theory of natural law—of

which he considers Hobbes to be the classic philosopher—the principles
of a modern "community-law of nature."

By resuming Aristotle's idea of man as a being by nature destined
to live in communities, the concept of a legal order based upon natural
altruism and not on conflicting interests restrained by reason could be
constructed. In every social relationship based upon mutual sympathy
and upon the feeling of duty arising from it, there would lie hidden the
bud of a system of law, which could be called "natural law of community."[38] This system of law would, in every one of its institutions,
express the principles of solidarity within the community and of the
immediate interdependence of rights and duties. It would especially
presuppose common property in land and in other means of production of primary importance, and even common use of these.[39] This type
of law, being motivated only by the common good of the people, would
not permit of any disparity between law and morality. These ideas and
their explication, especially with regard to the legal status of wage-
earners as given in the *Einführung*,[40] have attained a high degree of
actuality in spite of their perversion by the National Socialist regime;
they might also be interesting to American social reformers, since they
furnish arguments against an individualistic philosophy of law, which
is likely to bar the way to social reform. Law, in so far as it results
from legislation by democratic procedure, is, according to Tönnies,
an emanation of public opinion.

E. TÖNNIES' THEORY OF PUBLIC OPINION

The phenomenon of public opinion was especially attractive to
Tönnies, who, after more than a decade of theoretical and historical
studies, published in 1922 a comprehensive work on this subject. The
Kritik der öffentlichen Meinung[41] contains in the first book the theory
of Public Opinion; in the second book, empirical "applications" and
observations on the characteristics, contents, and functions of public
opinion; the third book deals with public opinion on social problems
and public opinion concerning the first World War. The present discussion has to be restricted to the theoretical part. Tönnies himself
summarizes his theoretical contributions as follows:

1. *The* Public Opinion of a country or nation, or the Public Opinion in the
   strict sense, is distinguished conceptually as an expression of group will from
   the popular notion of public opinion as a conglomeration of various diverse
   and contradictory views.

2. The Public Opinion as the politically valid opinion is distinguished conceptually from local or apolitical public opinions.

3. This Public Opinion can be of a more or less fixed, fluid, or gaseous condition of aggregation, depending on the issues involved.

4. In conformity with Giddings' distinction between popular beliefs and "genuine public opinion," Tönnies distinguishes both public opinion and *the* Public Opinion from popular sentiment and feelings—Public Opinion is, by contrast, a product of critical, i.e., intellectual, thinking.[42]

These distinctions are, of course, intended only for strictly conceptual, critical, and dialectic thinking.

All social phenomena, according to Tönnies, can be properly understood only by an inquiry into the notions which people themselves have of them. Language offers a first clue. Tönnies, therefore, in an instructive etymological discussion, traces the relation of individual and collective opinion to the basic forms of will and to belief and knowledge. He shows that, while opinions are dependent on sentiments and interests are conditioned by the situations in which individuals and groups are living, the holding of an opinion presupposes a mental decision and determination.

Since like conditions and like interests tend to result in like opinions,[43] there will be in a complex society many such public opinions, representing the essentially unanimous thought of various social collectives. In this sense, *a* public opinion is found in small towns, as well as in occupational or other groups.[44] This "unarticulated" public opinion is to be conceptually distinguished from *the* Public Opinion of an entire nation. This latter concept refers to the collective will, not merely a point of view, of the political body or community. *The* Public Opinion, in this specific sense, deserves its name in a threefold sense: first, with regard to its subject, which is the politically conscious public of a nation; second, in so far as it is opinion publicly expressed; third, in so far as it refers to public affairs.[45] The popular notion of public opinion is vague, not distinguishing sharply between the clamor of many and often disharmonious voices of public opinions and the collective will of a people which is thought to be as unified as the will of a person.[46] It is in this articulate or specific sense that *the* Public Opinion, as a political power, is often contrasted to the power of governments and parliaments, to which it is thought to be superordinated.[47]

Empirically, in modern society, this Public Opinion tends to be actually the opinion and political will of the propertied, urban, and educated upper classes. It is, however, presented to the less wealthy, the rural, and the uneducated classes with the claim of authority, as the correct opinion which every respectable citizen and loyal patriot is expected to share. As a means of social control, Public Opinion takes in modern society the place which was occupied by religion in medieval communities, although its claims are based on intellectual, i.e., critical, scientific thought, unlike religion, which is based on faith and belief in the inconceivable, the miraculous.

Not only this intellectual basis but also the fact that Public Opinion can be "made" to suit the aims of groups in control of the means of expression and communication of ideas make it essentially a phenomenon of rational group will. Doubt or deviation from Public Opinion is, however, considered and treated very much like religious heresy.

It should be noted that Tönnies' treatment of Public Opinion differs in two respects from that of many other authors on the subject. His conceptual distinction of *the* Public Opinion from *a* public opinion and public opinions in general enables him to point out the essentially rationalistic or intellectual nature of *the* Public Opinion, while others have been more impressed with the emotional aspects of public opinion. For the same reason, Tönnies emphasizes the tendency of Public Opinion to assume the characteristic of a doctrine, while the popular notion is rather that of the wavering, chameleon-like nature of public opinion.

The link between pure and applied sociology is furnished by the theory of *soziale Bezugsgebilde,* i.e., of those systems of activities of economic, political, and spiritual or moral character "in which social will finds its fields of action."[48] This part of Tönnies' sociological system may be said to be the least developed. Here a general sociology of religion or of art and similar theories would find their place within the system.

F. APPLIED OR SPECIAL SOCIOLOGY—TÖNNIES AND MARX

Tönnies shows that, in the course of social evolution, *kürwillige* attitudes and *gesellschaftliche* social entities and norms arise pre-eminently from trade, from the modern state, and from science. As to the question which of the three spheres of economics, politics, and culture, into which we are accustomed—under the necessity of analytical abstraction —to divide the unity of social life, should be given the leading role in social evolution or, rather, the highest degree of variability, Tönnies commits himself to the economic interpretation of history or, as he preferred to say, to a realistic interpretation of social evolution.[49] In this regard, Tönnies stood perhaps less under the influence of Karl Marx than in accord with seventeenth- and eighteenth-century social theory in England and France. In Germany this tradition had been interrupted by the philosophic school of idealism and, being restored by Karl Marx, was adopted as a slogan in political conflict, thereby losing credit with the great public. While Marx attributes to technological conditions an important role among the "forces of production," thereby relying largely upon an extra-economic factor for the explanation of social evolution, Tönnies conceives capitalism as an outgrowth of trade, in particular of large-scale and foreign trade, which is not limited to the simple exchange of goods for money and of money for goods but whose function consists in the profitable use of money as "capital." The infiltration of this kind of trade into the realms of industrial and agricultural production, in the shape of the plantation economy, home industry, the sweatshop, and the factory, tends to burst all the old traditional "community" conditions of economic life.[50]

And yet Tönnies, being vitally interested in questions of theological and philosophical doctrine, has certainly not underestimated the importance of ideas in social life. For him, the economic (realistic) interpretation of history was a useful device of analysis but not the last word in wisdom. However, he held the opinion that only those ideas which, regardless of their "rightness," had actual validity and significance in society because they express the real or assumed interests of influential social groups could, in fact, exert their sway on social life. Therefore, he expected social reforms to result not from propagation of ethical social doctrines but from appeal to the well-understood group interests of the parties involved in social conflicts. For the same reason Tönnies disapproved of the opinion, chiefly shared by political reactionaries, that the faults of the modern social system were due to the heretical doctrines of individualistic social philosophy. He considered these theories rather as attempts at an understanding and justification of the modern social order. That Thomas Hobbes should have recognized the radically new principle of the modern state as opposed to all earlier "communal" forms of political bodies and should have undertaken to make it conceivable by the doctrine of a social covenant, Tönnies appreciated as the sociologically significant feature of Hobbes's theory of the state and of the rationalistic doctrine of social contract in general; for the modern omnipotent centralistic state, independent as it was in principle of any ethnic basis, could, in fact, be understood only by a rationalistic construction, and the principle of sovereignty could be justified only by some such fictional devices of thought. The modern state is, in this regard, distinct from both the antique *polis* (representing, in principle, a "community") and from the feudalistic and *ständischen* medieval realms. Tönnies conceives the state as a revolutionary force, which tends to weaken and even to destroy most of the older community elements of the social order and which establishes a new "associational" order in its place.

G. POLITICAL ATTITUDE AND PERSONAL EXPERIENCE

Tönnies has been blamed for the bias which his theory implied. He has been called a pessimist and even a romantic. Against such criticism —brought, at first, by his elderly friend, Harald Höffding, the famous Danish philosopher, and only recently by L. von Wiese—Tönnies would defend himself by explaining that his intention was simply to describe the irreversible course of social evolution which he occasionally compared to the life-cycle of human beings. Nobody could say whether youth or old age was "better," and there was no sense in putting the question in this fashion. And yet it could not be denied that youth, in certain respects, was preferable to age and that, in other respects, old age had its own advantages. Thus Tönnies' verdict on the development of scientific thinking and its victory over theology and metaphysics— a victory he welcomed—was absolutely positive. He had been a supporter of the movement for the establishment of "ethical culture," independent of religion in its narrower sense. He considered the modern state, although he labeled it an "associational" group, all but an evil; on the other hand, he believed the solution of many social problems arising from the evolution of modern capitalism to be possible through a combination, in some way, of the efforts of co-operative and trade-union movements with those of state socialism.[51] Tönnies was, however, a man of firm judgment and, on many things, he held rather fixed opinions. Thus it cannot be denied that antipathy toward many features of capitalism and industrial society crops out quite obviously in his writings. But, if he had written on feudal society, he would not have failed to condemn in no less cogent fashion certain features of precapitalistic society. There was, however, no reason for such criticism in *Gemeinschaft und Gesellschaft,* since this book was intended as a critique of the present and not of the past.

The strong and far-reaching influence[52] of this chief book of Tönnies was due not only to the fact that in it was attained a synthesis of the strivings of social philosophy and political theory since more than three centuries, but also to the enthusiasm of a vigorous thinker whose theories sprang not from mere intellectual interest but from intensive experience. Tönnies had himself gone through the process of assimilation from a social background predominated by "community" values and norms to a social milieu of essentially "associational" type, when, as a young man, he had left a countryside of farms and small towns for the world of big cities. He had, morever, in those political changes and social conflicts which occurred during his childhood and youth, observed with vigilant eyes the full unfolding of the modern state and of the capitalistic middle-class (*bürgerliche*) society in Germany. In his native Eiderstedt he had observed the influence of the capitalistic commercial spirit on the life and character of a society of cattle-grazing farmers. But he had also seen how Eiderstedt, on the incorporation of the duchies of Schleswig and Holstein into Prussia, had lost considerable remnants of self-government preserved under the Danish regime and had been converted from a semi-medieval political community into a mere administrative district within a modern state. During his early manhood there occurred the first big strikes of labor and the attacks of Bismarck on the Socialist labor movement. When Tönnies took sides with the laborers, he was motivated not merely by his sociological theory. Having an extraordinary facility in making contacts with plain people and gaining their confidence, he had, quite early, acquired a comprehensive knowledge of the conditions of life of the working-class people and of "what was on the worker's mind." He was, however, concerned not only about the well-being of the laboring class but also about the future of the whole nation. Like his friend and teacher, Adolf Wagner, and the other so-called *Kathedersozialisten,* he was convinced that social peace could be guaranteed for the future only by radical social reforms.[53] A peaceful condition of group life appeared to him so obviously to be the end and meaning of any social order, that, even in pure sociology, he would admit as its essential subject only the peaceful relations between men.[54] He therefore condemned any kind of social revolution, since he believed that a sudden and doctrinaire recasting of existing institutions would not lead to better conditions but, rather, would give rise to new and unforeseen social evils.[55] On the other hand, he held his own science justified and necessary, just because of the existing conflicts and tensions in modern society. Tönnies wrote in 1926:

> It is the recent gigantic change in the fundamental conditions of social life, a change that, for the last hundred years, has been increasingly endangering the very existence of society—it is the Social Problem which proves unquestionably the necessity for and the importance of the new science of sociology. In it the cultural sciences find the same systematic completion that Biology intends to give the descriptive natural sciences. Necessity decides. The Labor Movement has been, from its beginning to the present day, an important stimulant for the thinking about the relations and antagonisms of the social classes. . . . .

Sociology, he said, was the science of the statesman—if not of the statesman of today, then inevitably of the statesman of the day after tomorrow. In the Preface to the *Einführung* we read, however, that the future of nations would be shaped by politicians and diplomats only within comparatively narrow limits. The essential factor was, rather, the general conditions of life, the well-being or the ill-feeling which would influence the willing and not-willing of the broad masses of a nation; these, however, were the working people, together with the intellectually farsighted, experienced, and thinking elements, so far as the latter are earnestly and persistently devoted to the improvement of the conditions of the people. It was generally known how wide and deep were the divergencies of opinions in this regard and that there were but few people who were willing and also able to think and to strive, not for the benefit of a certain class or rank but for the future life and welfare of their nation and (just for the sake of their nation) of all humanity. Sociology would be best justified if it helped to increase the number of these friends of the people and of humanity at large and if it contributed to a strengthening and deepening of their knowledge.

The following are the main sociological writings of Tönnies, together with a selected list of leading commentaries thereon:

I. WORKS OF TÖNNIES

Gemeinschaft und Gesellschaft (1887), 8th ed. Leipzig, 1935.
Fundamental Concepts of Sociology: Gemeinschaft und Gesellschaft. Translated and supplemented by CHARLES P. LOOMIS. New York, 1940.
Thomas Hobbes, Leben und Lehre (1896). 3d ed. Stuttgart, 1925.

Die Entwicklung der sozialen Frage (1907). 4th ed. Berlin, 1926.

"Das Wesen der Soziologie" (Vortrag in der Gehe-Stiftung), *Neue Zeit- und Streit-fragen*, Vol. IV (1907).

"Entwicklung der Soziologie in Deutschland im 19. Jahrhundert," *Entwicklung der deutschen Volkswirtschaftslehre im 19. Jahrhundert: Festgabe für Gustav Schmoller.* Leipzig, 1908.

Die Sitte. Frankfurt am Main, 1909.

Der englische Staat und der deutsche Staat. Berlin, 1917.

Marx Leben und Lehre. Berlin, 1921.

Kritik der öffentlichen Meinung. Berlin, 1922.

"Zweck und Mittel im sozialen Leben," *Hauptprobleme der Soziologie: Erinner-ungsgabe für Max Weber.* München and Leipzig, 1923.

"Die Einteilung der Soziologie." *Zeitschrift für die gesamte Staatswissenschaft*, Vol. LXXIX (1925); also published in *Atti del 5. congresso internazionale di filosofia.* Naples, 1925.

Fortschritt und soziale Entwicklung: Geschichtsphilosophische Ansichten. Karls-ruhe, 1926.

"The Concept of Law and Human Progress." Translated by KARL J. ARNDT and C. L. FOLSE in *Social Forces*, Vol. XIX, No. 1 (1940).

Soziologische Studien und Kritiken, Vols. I (Jena, 1925); II (Jena, 1926); III (Jena, 1929).

Einführung in die Soziologie. Stuttgart, 1931.

Inledning till Sociologien. Translated by E. BOSSE. Oslo, 1932.

"Eigentum," "Moderne Familie," "Gemeinschaft und Gesellschaft," "Stände und Klassen," articles in *Handwörterbuch der Soziologie.* Stuttgart, 1931.

Geist der Neuzeit. Leipzig, 1935.

"Mein Verhältnis zur Soziologie," in R. THURNWALD (ed.), *Soziologie von heute: Ein Symposion der Zeitschrift für Völkerpsychologie und Soziologie.* Leipzig, 1932.

"Philosophical Terminology," *Mind: Quarterly Review of Psychology and Philosophy*, Vols. VIII (new ser., 1899) and IX (1900).

"The Problems of Social Structure," *Congress of Arts and Science: Universal Exposition.* St. Louis, 1904.

II. CRITICISMS AND EXPOSITIONS

STOLTENBERG, H. L. *Ein Führer durch F. Tönnies "Gemeinschaft und Gesellschaft."*

ROSENBAUM, EDUARD. "Ferdinand Tönnies' Work," *Schmoller's Jahrbuch für Gesetzgebung*, XXXVIII (1914), 14.

WIRTH, LOUIS. "The Sociology of Ferdinand Tönnies," *American Journal of Sociology*, Vol. XXXII (1926).

LEEMAN's V. *Ferdinand Tönnies en de duitsche sociologie.* Brugge, 1932. *F. Tönnies et la sociologie contemporaine en Allemagne.* Paris, 1933.

HEBERLE, R. "Ferdinand Tönnies," *Internationales Handwörterbuch des Gewerkschaftswesens.* Berlin, 1932.

JAHN, GEORG. *Ferdinand Tönnies.* Leipzig, 1935.

FREYER, HANS. "Ferdinand Tönnies und die deutsche Soziologie," *Weltwirtschaftliches Archiv*, Vol. XLIV (1936).

SALOMON, ALBERT. "In Memoriam Ferdinand Tönnies (1855–1936)," *Social Research*, Vol. III (1936).

For the most comprehensive bibliography see: Brencke, Else, "Verzeichnis der Schriften von Ferdinand Tönnies aus den Jahren 1875 bis 1935," *Reine und angewandte Soziologie: Eine Festgabe für Ferdinand Tönnes zu seinem achtzigsten Geburtstage*. Leipzig, 1936.

JURKAT, ERNST. "Die Soziologie von Ferdinand Tönnies," *Geistige Arbeit*, November, 1936.

Kölner Vierteljahrshefte für Soziologie, Vol. V, Heft 1/2 (1925). Contains several articles dedicated to Tönnies on account of his seventieth birthday.

ERNST JURKAT (ed.). *Reine und angewandte Soziologie: Eine Festgabe für Ferdinand Tönnies zu seinem 80. Geburtstage*. Leipzig, 1936.

PARSONS, TALCOTT. *The Structure of Social Action*. 1937.

ZIMMERMAN, CARLE C. *The Changing Community*. New York, 1938.

NOTES

1. Heinrich Meyer, "Theodor Storm und Ferdinand Tönnies," *Monatshefte für deutschen Unterricht*, Vol. XXXII (Madison, Wis., December, 1940). This publication of the correspondence between Storm and Tönnies in the years 1872–88 contains valuable biographical information.

2. See H. E. Barnes and Becker, *Social Thought from Lore to Science* (Boston, 1938), II, 881.

3. "Mein Verhältnis zur Soziologie," in R. Thurnwald (ed.), *Soziologie von heute: Ein Symposion der Zeitschrift für Völkerpsychologie und Soziologie* (Leipzig, 1932), p. 103.

4. *Ibid*. (Translation by R. Heberle.)

5. *Ibid.*, p. 104.

6. In 1904 Tönnies visited his intimate friend, Professor Kuno Francke, head of the German Department at Harvard, and read a paper at the Congress of Arts and Sciences held in connection with the Exposition at St. Louis. Following that time he developed an intense interest and comprehensive knowledge of American life and affairs.

7. *Gemeinschaft* can be translated by "community," *Gesellschaft* by "society," or in some cases more adequately by "association." In order to avoid any misunderstandings and to emphasize that these terms designate the specific concepts of Tönnies, the German words have been retained throughout this paper.

8. *Die Sitte* (Frankfurt, 1909).

9. *Kritik der öffentlichen Meinung* (Berlin, 1922).

10. "Hafenarbeiter und Seeleute in Hamburg vor dem Strike [sic] 1896–97," *Archiv für Sozialwissenschaft und Sozialpolitik*, Vol. X (1897); "Der Hamburger Strike von 1896–97," *ibid.*; and "Die Ostseehäfen Flensburg, Kiel, Lübeck," in "Die Lage der in der Seeschifffahrt beschäftigten Arbeiter," *Schriften des Vereins für Sozialpolitik*, Vol. CIV (1903).

11. "Studie zur schleswig-holsteinischen Agrarstatistik," *Archiv für Sozialwissenschaft und Sozialpolitik*, Vol. XXX (1910).

12. "Verbrechertum in Schleswig-Holstein," *ibid.*, Vols. LII (1924) and LVIII (1927); "Die schwere Kriminalität von Männern in Schleswig-Holstein in den Jahren 1899–1914 in Verbindung mit Dr. E. Jurkat," *Zeitschrift für Völkerpsychologie und Soziologie*, Vol. V (1929); "Ortsherkunft von Verbrechern in Schleswig-Holstein," *Deutsches statistisches Zentralblatt*, Vol. XXI (1929); *Uneheliche und verwaiste Verbrecher* ("Kriminal statistische Abhandlungen," Heft 14 [Leipzig, 1930]).

13. "Der Selbstmord in Schleswig-Holstein: Eine statistisch-soziologische Studie," *Veröffentlichungen der schl. holst. Universitäts-Gesellschaft* (Breslau, 1927); "Der Selbstmord in Schleswig-Holstein," *Nordelbingen,* Vol. VIII (1930).

14. "Die Gesetzmässigkeit in der Bewegung der Bevölkerung," *Archiv für Sozialwissenschaft und Sozialpolitik,* Vol. XXXIX, No. 1 (1914), and No. 3 (1915).

15. "Eine neue Methode der Vergleiche statistischer Reihen," *Schmoller's Jahrbuch,* Vol. XXX (1909); see also H. Striefler, "Zur Methode der Rangkorrelation nach Tönnies," *Deutsches statistisches Zentralblatt,* Vol. XXIII, No. 5 (1931).

16. Ferdinand Tönnies, "Die Einteilung der Soziologie," *Zeitschrift für die gesamte Staatswissenschaft,* Vol. LXXIX (1925).

17. With Tönnies the term *generelle Soziologie,* however, has a different meaning: it comprises all disciplines pertaining to human society, whereas *spezielle Soziologie,* or sociology in the proper sense, is confined to the study of "social entities" and excludes, for instance, social psychology and social biology.

18. In "Wege und Ziele der Soziologie," the presidential address at the first conference of the German Sociological Society, Tönnies said that sociology was fundamentally a philosophical science: "....As such Sociology is mainly concerned with concepts.....It has to formulate these concepts, i.e., make them ready for use, ... so as to hang upon them like on nails or to seize as with clamps, the facts of experience. In this realm. it is not so much its task to perceive facts but to construct the handiest, the most useful implements for their perception: a task of supreme importance, which is, frequently to their own disadvantage, not much appreciated by the mere empiricist" (*Soziologische Studien und Kritiken,* II [Jena, 1926], 131).

19. "As long as Pure Sociology is not established as a fairly solid system of concepts and theories, Applied Sociology should only be regarded as an attempt to apply certain concepts and theories which are, perhaps provisionally only, accepted for the interpretation of historical developments. Applied Sociology will always be in touch with what has gained a certain amount of importance under the name of Philosophy of History.....A task which is closer to Applied Sociology insofar as it wishes to be more scientific than Philosophy of History, is the study of separate periods of culture, of cultures themselves, in their development and decline..... With the aid of sociological terminology and theory, Applied Sociology could follow the course of the European .... development in its fundamental phases up to the present hour. Thus it will end up with the inquiry into present day social life, a research that should be as thorough as possible. However, a third part of Special Sociology makes this research its task; a part which by its method is to be distinguished both from Pure as from Applied Sociology. Its method is .... the empirical, i.e., the inductive method. Therefore, we call it Empirical Sociology or Sociography" (*Einführung in die Soziologie* [Stuttgart, 1931], pp. 317, 319–21). (Author's translation.)

20. *Fortschritt und soziale Entwicklung: Geschichtsphilosophische Ansichten* (Karlsruhe, 1926).

21. Cf. the quotation in n. 19.

22. Statistics will be employed as much as possible. Tönnies liked to explain his idea of *Soziographie* by comparison with the older type of German *Statistik,* of which he considered *Soziographie* to be an improved renovation.

23. See R. Heberle, "Soziographie," *Handwörterbuch der Soziologie* (Stuttgart, 1931). Here Tönnies' concept of *Soziographie* is criticized, and the subject is more strictly defined.

24. Tönnies shows especially the possibility of combining "formal" sociology with historical sociology.

25. Tönnies gives a short enumeration of the sources of his theory in "Mein Verhältnis zur Soziologie," in Thurnwald (ed.), *op. cit.*

26. *Küren* means "to choose."

27. It is obvious that the idea of *Wesenwille* is derived from Schopenhauer's *bewusstloser Wille.*

28. For the concept of *Gemeinschaft* see Tönnies. *Studien und Kritiken,* II. 271.

29. Thus the concept of *Wesenwille* corresponds approximately to Max Weber's types of emotional-affectual, traditional, and *wertrationales* behavior.

30. Cf. Theodor Geiger, *Die Gestalten der Gesellung* (Karlsruhe, 1922), pp. iii, 22.

31. An individual *gemeinschaftliche* relation (e.g., a love-match) can change into a *gesellschaftliche* relation (if the marriage is preserved only for reasons of respectability).

32. Certainly, Tönnies does not distinguish between the categorical relation of the members of a group to the whole and their personal relation to one another. For example, a joint stock company as a social form remains also a *Gesellschaft,* if the stockholders or, at all events, the active elements among them are personal friends or even connected by kinship. This distinction has been elaborated by Max Graf Solms, *Gestalt und Gerüst der Menschenwelt* (Karlsruhe, 1929).

33. The differentiation between sociology and political science does not go so far in Germany as it does in the United States.

34. *Der englische und der deutsche Staat* (Berlin, 1917).

35. This theory has been elaborated very ably by E. Jurkat, *Das soziologische Wertproblem* (dissertation, Kiel, 1930).

36. "Einteilung der Soziologie," *Studien und Kritiken,* II, 438.

37. *Ibid.,* pp. 438 ff.

38. *Einführung in die Soziologie,* p. 218.

39. *Ibid.,* p. 220.

40. Pp. 217 ff.

41. Also, "Macht und Wert der öffentlichen Meinung," *Dioskuren: Jahrbuch für Geisteswissenschaften,* ed. Walter Strich, II (1923), 72–99.

42. *Kritik,* pp. vi–vii.

43. *Ibid.,* p. 27.

44. *Ibid.,* p. 130.

45. *Ibid.,* p. 131; "Macht und Wert," p. 82.

46. "Macht und Wert," p. 83.

47. *Ibid.,* p. 73.

48. "Einteilung," p. 441; *Einführung,* Book V.

49. *Einführung,* pp. 270 ff.

50. The explanation in detail of these ideas was reserved for the above-mentioned treatise on the evolution of modern society.

51. "Vorrede zu *Gemeinschaft und Gesellschaft"* (3d ed., 1919); reprinted in *Studien und Kritiken,* I, 58 ff.

52. This influence cannot be discussed here. It reaches far beyond Germany; more or less obvious symptoms of Tönnies' influence are to be traced in Austria and southeastern Europe, in Scandinavia, and even in Japan and China. It may only be mentioned that Sombart and Max Weber both accepted the concepts of *Gemeinschaft* and *Gesellschaft.* Spengler's *Untergang des Abendlandes* is supposed to have been influenced largely by Tönnies' ideas, although Tönnies is never quoted. In the United States, Tönnies' ideas have been recognized recently by an increasing number of sociologists, of whom only a few can be mentioned here: H. Becker, E. F. Eubank, R. M. MacIver, T. Parsons, Carle C. Zimmerman, and Charles P. Loomis, the translator of *Gemeinschaft und Gesellschaft.*

53. Cf. *Die Entwicklung der sozialen Frage bis zum Weltkrieg* (Berlin, 1926).

54. Compare the criticism by Wiese and the reply by Tönnies in *Soziologie von heute.*

55. *Einführung,* p. ix.

CHAPTER XI

THE SOCIOLOGY OF GEORG SIMMEL: THE FORMS OF SOCIAL INTERACTION

Rudolf Heberle, *Louisiana State University*

I. SIMMEL'S LIFE AND CHIEF WRITINGS

GEORG SIMMEL (1858–1918) belongs to the generation of European scholars who, at the end of the nineteenth century, broke with the "classical tradition" in sociology and originated a renaissance of sociological theory and research. Born in Berlin of Jewish parentage, he became a lecturer in philosophy (*Privatdozent*) at the age of twenty-seven at the University of Berlin, in which position he remained until 1914, when he was called to Strassburg as a professor of philosophy. He taught there under the adverse conditions of wartime until he died in the fall of 1918.

Simmel was primarily a philosopher, whose interests were not at all confined to the problems of society; in fact, his sociological essays form only part of his lifework. He had a strong interest in history, in the fine arts, and in literature. Perhaps the most adequate characterization of his work as a whole would be to say that it represents a philosophy of contemporary culture.[1] It is in this context that his sociological work has to be appraised—as *one* among several approaches. Simmel rose soon to international reputation as a sociologist; several of his studies were published almost simultaneously in German, English, and French. This accessibility of his sociological work is partly responsible for the fact that he was probably better known in his time in the United States than most of the other leading German sociologists of his generation.

II. SIMMEL'S CONCEPTION OF THE SCOPE AND METHOD OF SOCIOLOGY

To represent within the framework of a single chapter the sociological work of Georg Simmel involves some difficulty which arises from the peculiarity of his work. Simmel himself admits that he did not develop a system. His sociological work consists of a series of essays on subjects not systematically related but selected because of their importance for the study of forms of social interaction. This was the aspect of social life which Simmel considered to be the specifically sociological problem. His essays, therefore, represent a highly personal choice of subjects, and, moreover, their content is the highly personal work of a brilliant, analytical mind. Their attractiveness and their value is largely conditioned by the form of presentation; the mere skeleton of basic ideas and concepts would be a very dry and unimaginative affair if deprived of the brilliancy of illustration, the striking analogies and differentiations, and the often surprising indication of structural similarities between apparently very disparate phenomena. Even in Spykman's able condensation of Simmel's essays, much of their intellectual and aesthetic qualities is lost. Therefore, no attempt will be made here to present in a comprehensive summary the contents of Simmel's writings. For this purpose the reader may be referred to Spykman's book and to the numerous papers by Simmel which are available in English translations. Instead, this chapter deals, rather, with the methodological principles of Simmel's sociological work. Only by way of illustration will some of the main theorems be discussed. This procedure is, in fact, congenial to Simmel's own style of work.

Simmel is generally considered to be the founder of the so-called "formal school" in sociology. This is certainly an adequate designation of his main contribution to the development of sociology. How far this was an original idea is problematic.[2] The essence of Simmel's position is that sociology, in the strict sense, or "pure" sociology, in distinction from the other social sciences which deal with special fields of human social life, has, as its specific object of cognition, the forms of social interaction that occur in all those spheres of social life and really constitute the essence of society.

Such phenomena as superordination and subordination, the specialization of functions, the phenomena of conflict and competition, the formation of parties, and the like can be studied as such, irrespective, in principle, of the fields (economic, political, religious, etc.) which form the "content" of the action of those groups in which they occur; for— and this is the empirical justification for this concept of form—the same pattern of interaction occurs in connection with quite different aims or purposes, while, on the other hand, the same aims or purposes can be realized through quite different forms of social interaction. This circumstance permits the isolation by abstraction of the various forms of interaction of the different kinds of combinations of men as such, for the purpose of analytic and comparative inquiry.[3] In these "forms" of association and dissociation we have the phenomenon of society as such, in pure essence, separated theoretically from all its particular contents.

When Simmel first presented his ideas, he found that sociology was widely conceived of as a comprehensive study of all social facts and that, since everything in human life has a social relevance, sociology would be "the science of everything human"—except for those subjects reserved for the sciences of external nature.[4] This position would, according to Simmel, mean merely a dumping of all existing sciences dealing with social phenomena "into one great pot," or it would reduce sociology to a mere method of investigation, a directive principle which can be applied in the most varied and diverse fields of science, without itself constituting a science.[5]

This concept of sociology lacks a definite object of cognition (*Erkenntnisobjekt*). In a similar way psychology has been considered as a solution of the problems of all the sciences; and yet psychology, as a science, is concerned solely "with the functions of the mind as such" and is separated from "the special sciences which from particular points of view investigate the particular contents of perceptive knowledge."[6] "Just as psychology as a science does not deal with everything conditioned by consciousness, so sociology does not necessarily include everything that belongs in a society or that is conditioned by its existence."[7] New sciences, Simmel points out, arise if the inquisitive mind is focused on certain aspects of the chaos of existence which can be isolated by a process of abstraction. Thus mathematics deals with the formal and numerical aspects of physical bodies, while chemistry and physics deal with the qualitative aspects of substances of those bodies. Since economics, politics, law, and the "cultural sciences" deal with the contents or the substance of society, sociology, it appears, would deal with the social as such, that is, with society in its essence. Hence the conception of the isolability of the "forms" of social interaction furnishes the basis for the abstraction of a new object of cognition. Pure sociology thus becomes a sort of geometry of social interaction.[8]

Before entering on a further discussion of this position, some of Simmel's arguments in its defense have to be presented. One objection to the very notion of a science of society is that society is an abstraction, that only the individuals are real. Simmel, however, points out that the concept of the "individual" is also an abstraction. "Society" or human groups appear just as real, if one looks at human existence from a per-spective[9] where the single individual disappears. What is really decisive is the cognitive intention (*Erkenntnisabsicht*): "the special ends of cognition determine whether immediately manifest or experienced reality shall be inquired into with regard to a personal or a collective object."[10]

> Any science selects from the totality of immediately experienced phenomena one series or one aspect under guidance of a certain concept; sociology thus is justified in dissecting the individual "Existenzen" and bringing them together again accord-ing to its own concept by thus asking: according to what "laws" do human beings move, in so far as they form, by interaction, groups, and in so far as they are deter-mined by this existence in groups?[11]

Although the primary motivation for this construction of the object of cognition of pure sociology is epistemological, Simmel is, of course, aware that a living science could develop only around significant prob-lems. He considers, however, the systematic study of the pure forms of society as of fundamental importance. In a critical comment on his-torical materialism he suggests that the "real substance of the historical process" might be found in the change of sociological forms, as such, with the economic system being merely one of several "superstructures" conditioned by the basic interrelations of human beings.[12]

While Simmel limits the field of sociology proper in this way, he does not want to see sociology restricted to the organized and "perma-nent" interrelations only. Besides the state, the family, the guilds and classes, and other "permanent" associations, there exists an indefinite variety of seemingly less important forms of relations and types of interaction which "by filling in the spaces between those, so to speak, official formations bring really into existence the society that we know."[13]

Simmel's new concept of pure sociology is also directed against the identification, quite common at his time, of sociology with philosophy of history. In contrast to the latter, which always involves metaphysical, aesthetic, or religious interpretations of history, sociology "restricts itself entirely to the realm of phenomena and their immediate psychological explanation."[14] On the other hand, he thought that sociology, by sepa-rating out the phenomena of socialization, might lead to the discovery of "historical laws" within one special field, whereas the nonspecialized historical studies had failed to reveal such laws for the historical processes as a whole.[15] Two other concepts of sociology have to be distinguished from this concept of pure sociology:

1. In so far as economic, political, or other cultural phenomena and historical processes can be studied as phenomena of group life, as results of interaction between individuals, that is, under application of the sociological *method,* such studies might be labeled "sociology," though in a vague and inaccurate sense. However, by way of abstraction, a complex of problems can be lifted from such studies which Simmel considers as sociological in a rather specific sense. These problems are all related to the elaboration of those *general* characteristics of the realities of life which result from the fact that life occurs within the framework of social groups. The attempt to discern a general, socially conditioned "law" of historical evolution, such as Tönnies', Durkheim's or Comte's, would belong here. And so would the inquiry into the conditions of the power and value of groups and of collective action, as contrasted to power and value of individuals and their action. Simmel refers to these problems as "general sociology."[16]

2. Any empirical science is framed by two philosophical disciplines: its epistemology and its metaphysics. Sociology, in so far as it deals with fundamental categories of social life, serves as an epistemological foundation for the special social sciences.[17] On the other hand, there are other questions which go beyond the scope of these necessarily fragmentary special sciences. All those questions of the signficance and meaning of economic, political, etc., phenomena and processes and the final question of whether the meaning and purpose of human existence are embodied in the individual or in the association—these are questions of interpretation, which cannot be solved by empirical studies. Nor is the discussion of such questions independent of personal value-judgments. Simmel suggests that this discipline be called "philosophical sociology."[18] His main work, however, is devoted to pure sociology."

When Simmel in his *Grundfragen* wanted to exemplify his idea of pure sociology, he included a paper originally read at the first congress of the German Sociological Society in 1910, entitled "The Sociology of Social Entertainment."[19] It may, therefore, be summarized here for the same purpose, namely, that of conveying an idea of Simmel's approach and procedure and the kind of insights at which he arrives.

"Social gatherings" or sociables—or *Geselligkeit*—are a manifestation of the social urge as such. Since such social gatherings, in their true form, are not motivated by any special concrete purpose, as are all other types of associations, they represent, in a playful way, the essence of all social life. Their relation to the concreteness of society resembles the relation existing between a work of art and reality.

The relations of the individuals in social gatherings are regulated by a peculiarly ambiguous principle of a quasi-ethical nature: on the one hand, everything referring to, or reminiscent of, the roles played by the participants in their working-day life (e.g., their rank and occupation) has to be ignored; on the other hand, the most intimate and personal qualities of the individuals are also barred from entering into the relations. Every participant will use restraint in expression of his personality and of his impulses and will avoid engaging in too personal and intimate psychic relations. The participants come together "merely as human beings," and yet they refrain from letting the whole of their personality enter into the interaction process. This polarity of the behavior pattern is the essence of "tact." Furthermore, social gatherings are the artistic stylization or play-form of real society: sociable "games" and other forms of entertainment imitate societal processes of competition, conflict, and co-operation. "Flirting" is the play-form of erotics, and "conversation" becomes an end in itself, whereas, in "real society," talking serves the purpose of conveying certain "contents"—here, in social gatherings, one talks for entertainment; and, while the conversation is the better, the more interesting and significant its subject, the subject matter does not constitute its purpose. It can, therefore, be changed quickly and will never be taken seriously. Finally, social entertainment also symbolizes the ethical forces of society. The integration of the individual into the social whole, on the one side, and the enrichment of the individual by the pleasure, prestige, and other compensations received, which is the very essence of the ethical function of society, on the other side, are also found in *Geselligkeit*—in abstract form, free from all concrete ends or purposes.

However, "all *Geselligkeit* is merely a *symbol* of life, as it is reflected in the flow of an easygoing happiness-bestowing game or play, and yet it is a symbol of *life;* the picture of life is modified only as far as the distance requires, just like the most subjective and phantastic art, that renounces all copying of reality, is still nourished by a profound and faithful relation to reality—otherwise, its effect will be empty and insincere. Thus, if conviviality severs all ties connecting it with the realities of life, it changes from a play to a vain playing with meaningless forms."[20] This phenomenon of decadence can be observed in the autumn of the *ancien régime* and similar periods.

Social entertainment is, in its true form, a stylization of society; it is a game in which one behaves "as if" everybody was everybody else's equal and friendly companion. This is no more a deception than art and play, with their deviations from reality, can be considered lies. Only when such gatherings become mere means for the promotion of aims of other than a mere sociable quality or for the concealment of such purposes does the element of lie and deception enter and the true meaning of the forms of polite sociability become corrupted. Simmel concludes:

> These forms of entertainment would not mean relief and pleasant relaxation from the ever-present burdens of life for so many serious people, if they were merely devices of escape, merely a momentary avoidance of life's seriousness. This may often be actually the case, but the liberation and relief which are enjoyed precisely by the more serious personalities is due to the fact that the being together and the interaction through which life in all its gravity is realized can here be enjoyed in the form of an artful play—in sublimation and dilution.....[21]

III. THE LEADING CONTRIBUTIONS OF SIMMEL TO SOCIOLOGICAL THEORY

A. THE NATURE OF SOCIETY

Society is, for Simmel, essentially psychic interaction between human beings[22] both as individuals and as group members. Society is really not a substance but a process, a happening (*Geschehen*), or "something functional," something that human beings do and experience. One should perhaps, avoid the term "society" and, instead, use the term "association" to denote the true nature of social reality.[23] However, not all psychic interaction constitutes a process of association, e.g., not the mere exchange of glances between two individuals who pass each other on the street.[24] Such are "border phenomena," which, by repetition and intensification, may assume the character of social processes. The criterion seems to be that in association processes the individuals become "linked together" by "mutual influence and determination." One will, therefore, have to assume that between a mere being together and a perfect association there is a continuous range of more or less intensive mutual influencing. Even the large, interindividual groups (organizations), with which the idea of society is usually identified, are to Simmel "nothing but solidifications of direct interactions between individuals."[25] However, social relations, in the perfect sense, are not only psychic but *moral* relations.

This involves the following two main principles: (1) In the case of any kind of interaction in which one party loses all human significance for the other, any relationship in which one party considers the other merely as a means for an end which is not related to this other party, or where an attitude of complete indifference of the one party to the other is existent, such relations are not *social* relations at all, in the strict sense of the term. No association exists in such cases, just as it does not exist between the carpenter and his bench. (2) "Society can be regarded as a system of relations of morally, legally, conventionally, and in many other ways, entitled and obliged beings,"[26] or association involves reciprocity of rights and duties.

This principle is of consequence in the analysis of relations of power, domination, and authority. To speak of "compulsion" in social relations is usually incorrect, since such interaction involves in most cases a measure of voluntary decision and action on the part of the "compelled" individuals.

In the *Philosophy of Money,* Simmel points out[27] that even the modern state can seldom really compel citizens, it can merely induce them into certain actions because of fear of punishment. Only in matters of taxation can the state use direct compulsion, in so far as monetary wealth can be seized by force. Simmel elaborated this idea again in "Superordination and Subordination" and pointed out that this is one reason why despotic regimes tend to favor the substitution of money taxes for contributions in kind or in services. Consequently, any kind of domination is possible only in so far as and as long as a minimum of consent is existent among the dominated—even if such consent merely takes the form of avoidance of the greater evil of disobedience.[28]

It should also be noted that this concept of social interaction excluded the man-object relations, as such, from the realm of sociology; they constitute objects of sociology only in so far as they involve relations between persons.

The same functionalistic approach, which dissolves all social phenomena into complexes of relationships, is apparent in the treatment of social types likes "the stranger,"[29] or "the poor."[30]

From Simmel's point of view, processes that seem to cause dissociation are as important in the life of groups as are the associating processes. There are no completely harmonious groups; and, if such a group could be found, it would not show any life.[31] A certain amount of conflict is, for example, an organic element in marriage relations. The attitude of opposition is often the only means by which antagonistic individuals can tolerate being together in the same association.[32] Of course, conflict relations cannot, by themselves, result in social forms but only in connection with associating forces—both together constitute the concrete living unity of a group.[33] However, the function and effect of conflict vary with the structure of the relationship, and it requires a casuistic[34] analysis to understand these variations. Opposition, competition, jealousy, envy—all such conflict phenomena vary with the basis and degree of likeness and integration in the groups.[35]

There exists a definite correlation between the structure of any social group and the amount of antagonisms permissible among its members.[36] Here, as in many cases, Simmel shows the ambiguous nature of social constellations: "The same centripetal structure of the group makes it either more resistant against dangers arising from antagonism among its members or weakens its ability to resist—depending upon the additional conditions." Among the large groups, those that are highly organized will stand a greater degree of friction and partition than the more mechanical conglomerations.[37] However, in so far as conflicts, in societies of the less elaborately organized type, can more easily be localized, the group as a whole will be less sensitive. On the whole, the larger group will have more reserves of uniting energies. The modern state, for example, can tolerate the strife of political parties and can even utilize these antagonisms for its very equilibrium and development, while the Greek city-states were destroyed, torn to pieces by the internal party struggles.[38]

The same principle can be observed in the effect of intergroup conflict on the solidarity of the conflicting groups; it may compel factions to unite, or it may lead to a complete seccession of minorities already discontented with the course of action pursued by the majority. Simmel seems to have been deeply impressed by this ambiguity of social situations, which is one reason why accurate prediction of social events is so difficult. He refers to it on many occasions.

In spite of Simmel's functional concept of society, the notion of "form" is largely identical with what may be more properly called "structure." His excellent study of the determination of the character groups by the number of members[39] shows this very clearly. Among the structural problems discussed by Simmel, that of superordination and subordination deserves special consideration because of the basic importance of the phenomenon.[40]

Three main types of domination and authority are distinguished: (1) domination by a single person, (2) domination by a group of several persons, and (3) subordination to an impersonal objective principle. The value of the treatment lies, however, not in this classification but in the execution of a minute analysis of specific situations under each of these main types.

Simmel assumes that an inverse relation exists between the extent to which each individual enters into the group with his personality and the extent to which a single ruler can dominate the group modified by the size and homogeneity of the group.[41] While an absolutely rigid authoritarian rule is intolerable in a family group in which every member participates with almost his entire personality, it becomes possible and tolerable in a very large group into which every individual enters only with a small "quantum" of his "personality."[42]

Rule by a body of several persons, while it can be as "absolute" and as "hard" as monocracy, is likely to be more objective and impersonal.[43]

One of the main cases of subordination to an objective principle is the so-called "rule of law"; the others are those forms of authority which are derived from the position of the ruling person in a kinship or household group (patriarchate, matriarchate, patrimonial rule, etc.).

Simmel assumes that the development of subordination proceeds from personal rule to impersonal authority: as in the intellectual field the trend is from subordination under society (i.e., the authority of prevailing opinion) to subordination under objective (scientific) truth. Thus in the political field the ruler himself is finally subordinated to the objective principle of a social order by which his own will is bound.

This evolutionary trend can be traced in the family, in the state, and also in the economic system. In the relations between employer and employees the same evolution occurs to the extent that both parties become subordinated to the objective principle of contract, especially if the contract is based on a collective agreement between an employers' association and a labor union.[44]

Simmel, although he is aware of the possible advantages for the subordinated individuals of the personal elements in authority, thinks that, in general, depersonalization of authority relations makes subordination more tolerable and less humiliating. In connection with this idea he offers some observations on the alternation of superordination and subordination by limitation of terms of office and other devices, which should be interesting to the student of democratic institutions.[45]

Simmel then discusses the selection of the best-fitted individuals for positions of authority. He points out that a perfect correspondence of personal qualifications and social position is, in principle, impossible because of the always existing surplus of qualified individuals.[46] The development of a bureaucracy with elaborate specialization of positions and the detailing of functions of authority to experts tend to minimize the required personality standards for most positions of authority. On the other hand, the highest offices in the modern states would require extraordinary personal qualifications if the officeholder were chosen strictly on account of his relative personal ability, as compared with those of other minor functionaries. The difficulty arising from the scarcity of such highly qualified individuals is often mitigated by the adaptability of men to new and larger tasks; in other cases the device of conveying an objective dignity of office, which is not based on personal qualification, is resorted to.

Since the questions "What contributes to the integration or disintegration of groups?" and "What keeps groups together over a long period of time?" may be considered as the central theme in all society, Simmel's discussion of the *self-preservation of groups*[47] may be regarded as a testing ground of his contributions to theoretical sociology. Simmel refers here to those groupings which ordinarily last much longer than the life-span of their individual members and therefore assume, from the point of view of the individual, a relative permanence of existence.

The first problem which arises is that of the continued identity of the group, in spite of change in its membership composition.[48] The continuity of the group as an identical unit is effected, in the first place, by the persistence of the locality or territory in which it exists, in so far as in many—though not in all—groups the sentiments and intellectual contents are definitely related to a certain special unit, to the domestic "soil" or the "fatherland."[49]

In this connection Simmel presents a most important principle, that "the sociological characters of relationships otherwise perfectly alike, will be significantly differentiated on account of the notions of their different duration that are effective in them."[50]

The second condition of group persistence is the physiological connection of the generations and the web of kinship relations in general. The connection of the generations is of such great importance for the preservation of the larger groups, because the replacement of one generation by the next does not occur all at once, but step by step, so that at any moment those who have already belonged to the group for some time will always be in the overwhelming majority. This permits the conservation and transmission of the objective culture which has been developed and is characteristic of the group.

The same process of gradual replacement of membership occurs in other organized groups, even where no biological relation exists between the generations, e.g., in the Roman Catholic clergy. The gradualness of the change in membership composition serves to preserve the identity of the group, even where, after a long period, the entire culture of the group has changed.

Sometimes a group, originally not based on kinship, will resort to closing its ranks against persons not related to the present members in order to preserve its existence, e.g., the guilds in their late stages or the Russian clergy, who, by contrast to the Roman Catholic clergy, developed into an inbred caste.

Simmel points out that the transmission of the objective spirit of a group through "ordination" and co-optation is superior to the system of heredity of social positions.[51] Gradualness and slowness in the turnover of membership is, thus, a condition of the immortality of groups.[52] Therefore, it is necessary to provide special precautions in such groups whose existence is essentially dependent on the life of a single leading or ruling individual.[53] The main device used in such cases is the objectification of the ruler's position, that is, the development of the idea that the individual ruler is merely the personification of a supra-personal spirit or principle attached to the "office," together with the hereditariness of the ruler's position.[54]

Most essential, however, for the continuity of any group is organization. All associations exist "originally" in immediate interaction between individuals, in their roles as group members through organization; the functions which affect the unity of the group are transferred to officials or functionaries; the direct interaction between members is replaced by interaction between members and these organs. The interrelation of individuals, which, in nonorganized groups, is purely functional, acquires through organization a separate objective existence. Originally merely interaction, the group is now represented by a particular structure.[55]

In addition, there are the well-known technical reasons which make an organized group more resistant to dangers from without or within than an unorganized group.[56] On the whole, this discussion may be taken as a strong plea in favor of the rational forms of association. Nevertheless, Simmel makes the interesting remark that a group which in a crisis can fall back on the unorganized interaction of the rank and file of its members has a better chance to survive than a group that cannot dispose of the functions of specialized organs or offices.[57]

This leads to the further observation that, in some cases, a variability of structure is desirable for the preservation of the group,[58] as evidenced by the history of the Jews.[59] This, however, presupposes a high degree of homogeneity. In groups consisting of heterogeneous elements in latent or open conflict, greater stability of structure and conservatism with respect to changes in institutions and regulations are advisable, for in such situations any change is likely to arouse opposition in some quarters.

It is, therefore, understandable that ruling groups which are on the defensive avoid progressive changes;[60] if they agree to reforms, they do so not because they want the change but because they want, by minor concessions, to preserve their own essential traits—a policy especially noticeable in decaying aristocracies.[61]

Conservatism is, however, also characteristic of groups that are determined in their structure not by a dominating minority but by the broadest social stratum. This is most conspicuously the case in agrarian societies composed of freeholders. The farmer wants security more than change. Where, however, the urban middle class determines the structure, there will be change, for the continuity of such society depends on the chances for individuals to rise to higher social positions. Thus the form or structure of societies is determined by the nature of the social interests.[62] Again, the ambiguity of social situations is apparent—stability and elasticity can both contribute to the chances of group preservation, depending on several other variables, both of structural and of substantial nature.

While the main discussion is kept within the framework of structure analysis, the psychic factors involved are dealt with in a long note on loyalty and gratitude.[63] The structural phenomenon of group persistence after disappearance of the original purposes or motivations is one of the essential principles of sociology. Loyalty is that psychic disposition which produces this phenomenon. It is obvious that "without this phenomenon of loyalty society could not in the actually observed way exist over any length of time."[64]

Gratitude is another essential psychic factor, since all social interaction rests on the scheme of gift-receiving and equivalent giving. The latter can be obtained by compulsion in only certain cases.[65] Gratitude, therefore, is an indispensable complementary element in the maintenance of social interaction.

Every individual belongs as a social being to a variety of social circles which are partly overlapping[66] and, from a different point of view, can be thought of as concentrically arranged. The narrower the circle, the less the individuality for the individual; the circle itself, however, will be something individual, sharply distinct from other circles. If the circle within which one acts expands, the margin for individuality development increases, but the circle itself, as a social whole, will show less individuality.[67]

Simmel explains that this theorem is not meant as a sociological law but merely as an attempt to summarize by a "phenomenological formula," without any reference to causality, the uniform effects of what may be very heterogeneous "causes" in each case.[68] If he offers a psychological explanation, he does so merely as a "heuristic principle."[69]

It seems as though the individual was dominated by a dual urge: to differentiate himself from the social circle to which he belongs and at the same time to differentiate himself as a member of this circle from those who do not belong to it. The more the urge for differentiation from the fellow group members is satisfied, the less will the group itself be differentiated.[70]

Certain kinds of groups assume under this aspect an intermediate position. It seems that the most unreserved emotional attachment is directed only to the most narrow and to the largest circles,[71] not to the intermediate ones. One is willing to sacrifice one's self for one's country and for one's family, but not for the township in which one lives.[72] While this is primarily a static principle, it lends itself obviously to application with regard to social evolution.

C. THE SOCIAL IMPLICATIONS OF A MONEY ECONOMY

Although Simmel's *Soziologie* is chiefly concerned with logicosystematical inquiry into structure elements of society in general, it also contains rather definite ideas on the main social changes in contemporary Western society. Moreover, the *Philosophy of Money* represents in the second, synthetic part, in a more organized form, his ideas on this matter.[73] Simmel accepts here the basic notions of historical materialism or, as he suggests it should be called, "historical sensualism." His position is, however, that this theory has to be modified, in so far as the concrete economic forms are, in their turn, conditioned by profounder evaluations and by psychological, as well as metaphysical, "currents," which, again, are conditioned by profounder economic factors and so on.[74] The main changes resulting from money as an all-pervading institution in modern society can be summarized as follows:

1. An increase of freedom of the partners in any kind of social relations: landlord and peasant, employer and employee. When contractual social relations become possible on a basis of compensation in money rather than in services and kind, they can become depersonalized, in the sense that every moral consideration or interaction process extraneous to the specific kind of relation tends to be eliminated.[75] This gives a freer choice of action to all persons concerned, especially so far as the choice of partners is concerned and also with regard to the place of residence of each partner. There can be no doubt that the general tendency is to make man, on the one side, dependent on the services of more and more people, but, on the other hand, to make him more and more independent of the serving personalities as such.[76]

2. The ensuing separation of objects possessed from the person of the owner permits combinations of ownership between otherwise unrelated individuals. The institution of money makes it possible for the individual to associate himself with others for a common purpose,

merely by contributing money, without getting involved and bound with his entire personality—as was characteristic of the medieval corporation.[77]

3. This depersonalization of social relations makes possible associations for limited purposes of individuals not personally attached to one another: the purely purposive voluntary association.

Consequently, the entire *style of life* is changed under the impact of money as one of the main economic institutions. The trend toward rationalistic attitudes is increased through the development, alleviated by money use, of the habit of calculation—a habit that is spreading into all spheres of life. Even time assumes a money value in Western society with the full unfolding of money economy[78]—an idea which, later on, was elaborated by Oswald Spengler. The trend of social change is thus toward greater rationalization and depersonalization of all human relations, that is, toward a form of society in which the individuals, highly specialized in their social functions (divisions of labor), as personally free atoms tend to be related merely by purposive relations in which, again, the kind of interrelation effected by combinations of monetary wealth or by monetary compensation of services tend to become prevalent.

IV. CRITICISM AND EVALUATION

It is clear from these examples that Simmel actually intended more than a mere systematization of social forms. He made it clear enough that the conceptual distinction between "form" and "content" of society was "really nothing but an analogy," that both are "in reality inseparable elements of any social existence and process."[79] In his sociological papers he refers repeatedly to the "meaning" of social "forms." The two questions—"What do the individuals mean by behaving in a certain way?" and "What is the objective meaning of the described action patterns in their lives?"—are constantly suggested, if not expressly put, to the reader.

As already pointed out, the search for the objective meaning leads beyond sociology, in the strict sense, into metaphysical interpretation. The inquiry into the subjective meaning requires the application of psychological knowledge and methods; yet, in its final intention, it does not aim at the regularities (laws) of psychic processes in the individual but at the causal understanding of the social interaction patterns by which individuals are united into groups.

The objects of sociology are psychic processes which can be conceived by psychological categories. These are indispensable for the description of the facts, but they do not enter into the sociological intention which aims at the association process as such—like the intention of a drama, which, although it can be understood only psychologically, is not directed at psychological insights but at those syntheses which the psychic processes form under the points of view of the tragic or of style or symbols of life.[80]

The problems of social psychology are, according to Simmel, merely special problems of individual psychology. Therefore, these arguments also apply to the objection that Simmel's sociology is not clearly distinguished from social psychology.

The nonpsychological character of Simmel's pure sociology can be exemplified by the principle of correlation between individuality and the expansion of the social circle.[81] The principle, as such, does not contain any psychological theorem; it merely states an observable relationship between two elements of group structure.

Here, however, one weakness of Simmel's approach is revealed. Some of the phenomena could be made intelligible, even as evidence of structural principles, only by careful inquiry into psychic attitudes and processes. Simmel, instead, merely applies a rather general psychological hypothesis as "heuristic principle." The result is often mere conjecture rather than a real insight and secure knowledge. Furthermore, one can scarcely escape the impression that Simmel views society as an interplay of structural factors, in which the human beings appear as passive objects rather than as live and willing actors. Frequently, he refers to the inherent regularities of form principles as if these were the real moving forces in social life. Nowhere do we find a systematic analysis of the will-currents, the antagonisms and harmonies of interest and will which determine the course of individual and collective action and on which the very existence of associations depends.

However, the precise determination of the nature of social forms and the skilful application of the idea in Simmel's essays have opened a new angle of perception—a new outlook on social phenomena—which proves very fruitful in the analysis of concrete social situations—if applied with the necessary discretion. Simmel's procedure of staking off a field of

investigation by abstracting a certain aspect (the "form" of social interaction) from the chaos of experienced reality, is not unique, not peculiar
to sociology; rather, it is the principle on which *all* specialization of the
actual sciences has developed.[82] Simmel applied this principle to a field
(sociology) in which, hitherto, the notion had prevailed that its specific
object of cognition was not a new abstraction but, rather, a synthesis of
the insights into social life gained by the existing specialized social
sciences.

Among the critical objections to this idea of pure sociology, those
offered by Hans Freyer deserve special attention because they raise a
question of fundamental importance. Freyer points out that the conception of pure sociology as a sort of geometry of social phenomena may
prove fatal, since it leads sociological thought off on a wrong track;
phenomena that ought to be conceived as historical processes, imbedded
in the context of the more or less unique situation in the flow of time,
become fixed as static structures. Simmel, according to Freyer's criticism,
tried to establish sociology as a *Logos-Wissenschaft,* which Freyer believes to be foreign to the very nature of its subject. Freyer, however,
emphasizes the fact that, in spite of this fundamental error, Simmel's
essays contain "excellent sociology," because, with a fine scientific tact,
Simmel applied his approach only to such subjects as lend themselves
to this kind of treatment, since they are, indeed, "timeless."[83]

The "formal," or, as one might better say, the "structural" or morphological approach, applied even to the apparently most fluid social unions
or groupings, is so widely different from the layman's point of view that
it becomes immensely stimulating and challenging. The student who
is habitually inclined to think in compartments or fixed "contentional"
categories is suddenly forced to draw comparisons between phenomena that seem to be distant in time or space and unrelated in quality,
focusing his attention on the strictly social, that is, interactional, aspects. This, in itself, would be valuable in a propaedeutical sense. In
addition, this approach is carried out with a meticulous casuistry in
analysis. Never is Simmel content with general notions of social types;
always he insists on defining the specific situations in which the phenomenon arises; always he forms, from general concepts, specific type
concepts of well-defined "cases" of the general phenomenon studied.[84]
In this respect, he is perhaps surpassed among his contemporaries only
by Max Weber. Among the generation of his followers, Max Graf zu

Solms and Leopold von Wiese have carried on this work of classification of forms of social interaction.[85]

While this method would finally result in a fruitless play of the mind —and, in fact, this danger zone is often touched in Simmel's essays— Simmel succeeds in making it a meaningful endeavor. This is accomplished by the introduction, into the "form" analysis, of psychological interpretations, often of a very subtle character. Spykman[86] points out that Simmel agreed that pure sociology alone cannot convey a full understanding of society, that it needs supplementing by psychological and "factual" inquiries. As an illustration we may note his observation that conflicts between individuals intimately related by kinship or other close personal ties tend to be more bitter than those between comparatively strange and loosely related individuals. This is in itself a rather common-sense observation. The real value of Simmel's analysis lies in the fine distinctions between various typical constellations and in the sociopsychological explanations or interpretations.[87] The same manifestations of conflict may be due to a wide variation of motivations and may, therefore, be of quite different meaning for the life of the social groups in which they occur. Furthermore, violent conflicts, such as occur in intimate relations (e.g., in marriage), just because of a profound community of values among the partners, without endangering the relation as such, would definitely destroy any relation of less intimate character. Incidentally, these subtle differentiations of configurations (or "forms") and motivations in social relations suggest the necessity of careful theoretical preparation and utmost caution in any quantitative inquiry into social attitudes and processes.

Simmel's interpretation of the trends of social change in contemporary Western society can hardly be said to be original. It is essentially a synthesis of the ideas developed previously by Marx, Tönnies, Durkheim, and others.

On the whole, his sociological interpretations, although extremely intelligent and subtle, do not betray a great deal of firsthand experience and contact with the great social movements and important societal events of his time. This may partly explain the lack of new original insights into the great social questions of the period.[88]

It seems that Simmel's interest in sociology originated not from an immediate concern with the social problems of contemporary society but rather from a philosophic endeavor to clarify its position in a system of sciences. Obviously, Simmel's occupation with problems of ethics and morals (*Moralphilosophie*) also led him into a discussion of norms and values in their relation to social life.

These reservations have to be made in order to arrive at a fair appreciation of Simmel's work. Its real and lasting value lies not so much in the new knowledge of society it conveys as in the contribution to the classification of the purpose and procedure of sociology.

Even his most severe critics acknowledge the significance of Simmel's idea of sociology as a systematic analysis of social forms. "The influence of Simmel's concepts of 'social form' is present in contemporary sociology, even where the idea of Pure Sociology in Simmel's sense is rejected."[89] It is Simmel's method and procedure of analysis rather than the content of his findings which constitute his unique and lasting contribution to the advancement of sociology. Thus we are confronted with the paradox that the philosopher who started out to redefine the subject matter of sociology gained his place among sociologists rather because of his methodological ideas.

The following selected bibliography will indicate the main sociological and philosophical writings of Simmel and the chief commentaries on his work.

I. BOOKS AND ARTICLES BY GEORG SIMMEL

Soziologie: Untersuchungen über die Formen der Vergesellschaftung. Leipzig, 1908.
Grundfragen der Soziologie. Leipzig, 1917.
Die Probleme der Geschichtsphilosophie. Leipzig, 1892.
Einleitung in die Moralwissenschaft. 2 vols. Berlin, 1892–93.
"Moral Deficiencies as Determining Intellectual Functions," *International Journal of Ethics*, III (1893), 490–507.
"The Problems of Sociology," *Annals of the American Academy of Political and Social Science*, VI (1895), 412–23.
"Das Problem der Soziologie," *Jahrbücher für Gesetzgebung, Verwaltung und Volkswirtschaft*, XVII (1894), 1301–7.
"Le Problème de la sociologie," *Revue de métaphysique et de morale*, II (1894), 497–504.
"Superordination and Subordination as Subject-Matter for Sociology" (trans. Albion W. Small), *American Journal of Sociology*, II (1896–97), 167–89, 392–415.
"The Persistence of the Social Group (trans. Albion W. Small), *ibid.*, III (1897–99), 662–98, 829–36; IV (1897–99), 35–50.
"A Chapter in the Philosophy of Value" (trans. Albion W. Small), *ibid.*, V (1898–99), 577–603.
Philosophie des Geldes. Leipzig, 1900.
"Tendencies in German Life and Thought since 1870" (trans. W. D. Briggs), *International Quarterly*, V (1902), 93–111, 166–84.

"The Number of Members as Determining the Sociological Form of the Group" (trans. Albion W. Small), *American Journal of Sociology*, VIII (1902–3), 1–46, 158–96.

"Grossstädte und Geistesleben," in *Die Grossstadt: Vorträge und Aufsätze zur Städteausstellung* (Dresden, 1903), pp. 185–206.

"The Sociology of Conflict," *American Journal of Psychology*, IX (1903–4), 490–525, 672–89, 798–811.

"A Contribution to the Sociology of Religion" (trans. Albion W. Small), *American Journal of Sociology*, XI (1905), 359–76.

Philosophie der Mode. "Moderne Zeitfragen," No. 11. Berlin, 1905.

Die Religion. "Die Gesellschaft, Sammlung sozialpsychologischer Monographien," ed. M. BUBER, No. 2. Frankfurt, 1906.

"The Sociology of Secrecy and of the Secret Society" (trans. Albion W. Small), *American Journal of Sociology*, XI (1905), 441–98.

"The Problem of Sociology" (trans. Albion W. Small), *ibid.*, XV (1909), 289–320.

"How Is Society Possible?" (trans. Albion W. Small), *ibid.*, XVI (1910), 372–91.

"Soziologie der Geselligkeit," in *Schriften der Deutschen Gesellschaft für Soziologie: Verhandlungen des ersten deutschen Soziologen-Tages, 1910* (Tübingen, 1911), pp. 1–16.

Philosophische Kultur: Gesammelte Essais. "Philosophisch-soziologische Bücherei," Vol. XXVII. Leipzig, 1911.

II. CRITICISM AND INTERPRETATION

SPYKMAN, NICHOLAS J. *The Social Theory of Georg Simmel.* Chicago, 1925.

VIERKANDT, A. "Simmel," *Encyclopedia of the Social Sciences.*

FREYER, H. *Soziologie als Wirklichkeitswissenschaft* (Leipzig and Berlin, 1930), pp. 46–57.

BARNES, H. E., and BECKER, H. *Social Thought from Lore to Science* (Boston, 1938), II, 889–91.

WIESE, L. VON, and BECKER, H. *Systematic Sociology.* New York, 1932.

MACIVER, R. M. "Sociology," *Encyclopedia of the Social Sciences.*

ROSENTHAL, ERICH, and OBERLAENDER, KURT. "Books, papers, and essays by Georg Simmel," *American Journal of Sociology*, LI, No. 3 (November, 1945), 238–47.

NOTES

1. Nicholas J. Spykman, *The Social Theory of Georg Simmel* (Chicago, 1925), p. xxvi.
2. P. A. Sorokin, *Contemporary Sociological Theories* (New York, 1928), pp. 497–98. Sorokin thinks that the idea is very old, dating from the Roman jurisconsults.
3. G. Simmel, "The Problem of Sociology," *Annals of the American Academy of Political and Social Science*, VI (1895), 54–55, 63; *Soziologie: Untersuchungen über die Formen der Vergesellschaftung* (Leipzig, 1908), pp. 6–7; and *Grundfragen der Soziologie* (Leipzig, 1917), pp. 28–29.
4. "The Problem of Sociology," *American Journal of Sociology*, XV (1909), 290; see also "The Problem of Sociology," *Annals*, pp. 52–53.
5. "The Problem of Sociology," *American Journal of Sociology*, p. 291.
6. "The Problem of Sociology," *Annals*, p. 53.
7. *Ibid.*, p. 54.
8. *Soziologie*, pp. 9–11; *Grundfragen*, p. 28.

9. *Grundfragen*, p. 11.

10. *Ibid.*, p. 12.

11. *Ibid.*, p. 15. Translations of all quotations from works not published in English are by the author.

12. *Ibid.*, pp. 20–21.

13. *Ibid.*, pp. 12–13, 14.

14. "The Problem of Sociology," *Annals*, p. 59.

15. *Ibid.*, p. 60.

16. *Grundfragen*, pp. 25–28 and chap. ii, which gives an example.

17. *Ibid.*, p. 32.

18. *Ibid.*, pp. 32–33 and chap. iv.

19. "Die Soziologie der Geselligkeit," in *Schriften der Deutschen Gesellschaft für Soziologie: Verhandlungen des ersten deutschen Soziologen-Tages, 1910* (Tübingen, 1911), 1–16; also *Grundfragen*, chap. iii, pp. 50–71. This paper has not been translated into English, nor has it been abstracted by Spykman. The term *Geselligkeit* in this connection designates the kind of more or less formal conviviality characteristic of the middle and upper classes. The title of Simmel's essay might be freely translated as "Sociology of the Drawing-Room."

20. "Die Soziologie der Geselligkeit," p. 14.

21. *Ibid.*, p. 16.

22. *Grundfragen*, p. 12.

23. *Ibid.*, pp. 14–15.

24. *Ibid.*, p. 12.

25. *Ibid.*, p. 14.

26. *Soziologie*, p. 345.

27. *Philosophie des Geldes* (Leipzig, 1900), p. 417.

28. *Soziologie*, p. 102.

29. "Exkurs über den Fremden," *ibid.*, chap. ix, pp. 509–12.

30. "Der Arme," *ibid.*, chap. vii.

31. *Ibid.*, p. 187; also the "Sociology of Conflict," *American Journal of Sociology*, IX (1903–4).

32. *Soziologie*, p. 189.

33. *Ibid.*, p. 191.

34. The term is used here in its original meaning, free of all pejorative connotations, to designate a procedure of analyzing general concepts of social phenomena (like "competition") by stating very specifically the various "cases" which result from a change of variables.

35. *Soziologie*, p. 205. Simmel's discussion, for example, of jealousy in its morphological and sociopsychological aspects is a masterpiece of analysis. The same may be said of the discussion of competition, its forms, limitations, and effects (*ibid.*, p. 213). One observation deserves quotation because it shows the brilliancy of Simmel's formulations: "Jealousy tends to destroy the very relationship for the preservation of which the jealous individual is striving."

36. *Ibid.*, p. 219.

37. Note the influence of Durkheim.

38. *Soziologie*, p. 220. The entire discussion shows the strength but also the weaknesses of the "form" approach. Clearly, Simmel neglects to mention the decisive fact that party antagonism is destructive to the extent that it involves the fundamental values of the group. The existence of the group is not endangered so long as the strife of parties keeps within the sphere of means or minor ends and does not involve the basic ideas on which the group life rests.

39. *Ibid.*, chap. ii; also "The Persistence of the Social Group," *American Journal of Sociology*, III (1897–99), 662–98, 829–36.

40. *Soziologie,* chap. iii; see also "Superordination and Subordination as Subject-Matter for Sociology," *American Journal of Sociology,* II (1896–97), 167–89, 392–415.

41. *Soziologie,* pp. 115–17.

42. Obviously, this principle holds only for a basically liberal regime, in which private and public matters are separable. It has been disproved by the recent phenomenon of totalitarianism. The principle does not consider the possibility of despotic rule over a heterogeneous mass of subjects with the aid of an organized political machine or gang, although Simmel's discussion of the various forms of hierarchic organization in monocracies (*Soziologie,* p. 120) contains some valuable contributions (the function of patronage, of the idea of service, etc.) to a sociology of authoritarian rule.

43. *Ibid.,* p. 131.

44. Simmel, of course, could not foresee that this "law" would be modified through the emergence of quasi-charismatic leadership regimes. The sociological explanation lies in the fact that subordination to an objective principle presupposes consensus of the group members on at least the fundamental issues of social life. It also requires a certain stability of objective social conditions. Where the latter change quickly, frictions arise, and emergency powers will be given to the authority-bearer who represents the objective principle, and if, in addition, the basis of consensus becomes too narrow, a transition to personal leadership may take place.

45. *Soziologie,* p. 174. He also mentions the device (later utilized in the Fascist countries) to appropriate authority in some functions to individuals otherwise subordinated, thus letting the individual alternate in the roles of superordinated and subordinated.

46. *Ibid.,* p. 183.

47. *Ibid.,* chap. viii; and "The Persistence of the Social Group."

48. *Soziologie,* p. 377.

49. *Ibid.,* p. 378; see also "Der Raum und die räumlichen Ordnungen der Gruppe," *ibid.,* chap. ix.

50. *Ibid.,* p. 378; cf. also the excellent discussion on pp. 500–502.

51. *Ibid.,* p. 383.

52. The ways in which entrance to, and exit from, an association are regulated are therefore important for the chance of longevity of the group. Simmel, with mathematical precision, distinguishes four principal possible combinations: (1) entrance and exit equally easy: as in most voluntary organizations; (2) entrance difficult, dependent on conditions—resignation difficult: secret associations, criminal gangs, etc.; (3) entrance easy—resignation difficult: most proselyting associations; (4) entrance difficult—exit easy: aristocratic associations (*ibid.,* p. 401).

53. *Ibid.,* p. 385.

54. *Ibid.,* p. 389, and the "Exkurs über das Erbamt," pp. 391–96.

55. *Ibid.,* p. 409.

56. *Ibid.,* pp. 410–30.

57. *Ibid.,* p. 433.

58. *Ibid.*

59. *Ibid.,* p. 449.

60. *Ibid.*

61. *Ibid.,* p. 450.

62. *Ibid.,* p. 451.

63. *Ibid.,* pp. 439 f.

64. *Ibid.,* p. 439.

65. *Ibid.,* p. 443.

66. Simmel develops in chaps. vi and x of his *Soziologie* the theorem that the chances of personality development increase with the number of circles to which the individual belongs and also with the degree to which the social circle expands.

67. *Ibid.,* pp. 531–33. In one of his illustrations Simmel refers to the structural differences between northern and southern states in the United States. In the South, where

settlement was carried on by highly individualistic adventurers, one finds political life centering in the more abstract, colorless structure of the states, while the more socially regulated settlers in the North tended to more narrow municipalities, which, however, showed strong individual characteristics and enjoyed privileges of autonomy.

68. *Ibid.,* p. 532.

69. *Ibid.,* p. 533.

70. *Ibid.*

71. *Ibid.,* p. 539.

72. The weakness of this theorem is obvious. It is derived mainly from experiences in the age of liberalism and does not take account of the factors of power and compulsion that can be used by the larger social circle to restrict the chances for individuality development.

73. In accordance with Simmel's ideas on the relation between philosophy and the special sciences, the first part of this work deals with problems preceding the actual economic theory of money, that is to say, with the conditions which make a monetary system possible (for a fuller account see Spykman, *op. cit.,* pp. 219 ff.).

74. *Philosophie des Geldes,* p. viii.

75. The ideal partner for money transactions (*Geldgeschäfte*), in which, as the saying goes, *Gemütlichkeit* ceases to exist, is the completely indifferent personality, biased neither for nor against us (*ibid.,* p. 211). On the other hand, for this very reason, one should not engage in money transactions with one's friends or foes.

76. *Ibid.,* p. 293; see also *ibid.,* p. 338, on spatial separation of the owner from his property.

77. *Ibid.,* pp. 351–52.

78. *Ibid.,* p. 546.

79. *Soziologie,* pp. 4, 5; also p. 10.

80. *Ibid.,* pp. 17–19; cf. also the "Exkurs über Sozialpsychologie," *ibid.,* pp. 421–25.

81. Compare with pp. 254 ff., 262, above, where this has already been discussed.

82. Teaching disciplines which are formed for practical purposes may combine several such "sciences," e.g., geography. The field taught in the departments of sociology is, of course, composed of bits from a great many sciences, more or less well integrated by relation to the subject proper of sociology: the types of groups and social processes. Where "theory" is in disrepute, syncretism and a lack of interior, epistemological, and methodological order will be the consequence. Where Simmel's concept of "formal" sociology is adhered to with pedantry, the teaching will very likely lack substance and relevance to the significant problems of contemporary society.

83. Hans Freyer, *Soziologie als Wirklichkeitswissenschaft* (Leipzig and Berlin, 1930), pp. 46 ff., and 56–57. The same may be said of the work of Simmel's followers, especially L. von Wiese, who has attempted to develop systems (or parts of systems) of formal sociology. As long as they deal with phenomena of *universal* significance, especially with simple processes and relations, the approach proves satisfactory. Where, however, complex structures of a historically determined nature like the modern state are subjected to the same treatment, the approach has to be modified, or the resulting insights are of little significance.

84. Compare Simmel's own statement (*Soziologie,* p. 10): "Even an approximate dissolution of societal forms into simple elements [as in geometry] cannot be hoped for in the near future. Consequently, sociological forms if they are to be to some degree definite can be valid only for a relatively small range of phenomena. If one says, for instance, that super- and subordination is a form found in almost any human society, little will be won with such general statement. What is necessary is the consideration of the various ways of super-and subordination, of the special forms of their realization. These will lose in universality of validity the more concretely they are defined."

85. Max Graf zu Solms, *Bau und Gliederung der Menschengruppen,* I. Teil (Karlsruhe, 1929); and *Führerbestellung: Bau und Gliederung der Menschengruppen,* II. Teil (Leipzig, 1932); also L. von Wiese and H. Becker, *Systematic Sociology* (New York, 1932).

86. *Op. Cit.*, p. 74.

87. Simmel, *Soziologie,* pp. 205–10.

88. It seems symptomatic that Simmel's illustrations referring to the labor problem are almost exclusively taken not from German conditions but from the British Labor Movement or from the sphere of the domestic-servant problem, where Simmel had, of course, firsthand experiences. It is, furthermore, symptomatic that the rich sources of socioeconomic surveys, dissertations, and semiofficial inquiries which had resulted from the influence of the historical school in economics in Germany have scarcely been utilized by Simmel, while he gives ample references to ancient and medieval history. The question of the sources of Simmel's knowledge of the social world can, of course, merely be stated, not answered, in the framework of this chapter.

89. Freyer, *op. cit.*, p. 47. The influence of Simmel's ideas on American sociology cannot be traced within the limits of this chapter.

CHAPTER XII

THE SYSTEMATIC SOCIOLOGY OF LEOPOLD VON WIESE: THE ORIGIN AND STRUCTURE OF INTERHUMAN RELATIONS

J. MILTON YINGER, *Ohio Wesleyan University*

J. MILTON YINGER, *Ohio Wesleyan University*

I. THE INTELLECTUAL BACKGROUND AND MAIN SOCIOLOGICAL
WRITINGS OF VON WIESE[1]

LEOPOLD VON WIESE was born in Silesia in 1876, the son of a Prussian cavalry captain. At eight years of age he was sent to an academy for cadets; but, chafing under the severe discipline there, he was always in trouble. At about eighteen he ran away. Though he secured a job with a German exporting house in Bombay, his restlessness continued. He fell in love with a Ceylonese girl—an affair which found literary expression in a novel, *Nava.*

Returning to Germany, Wiese resumed his education, pursuing graduate work in economics. He lined up, in the economic controversies of the time, with the psychological school. In 1905 he joined the faculty of the Cologne School of Commerce and Finance but was not altogether happy there. He was married and divorced several times. In 1918 the Cologne School of Commerce was made a university—one of several municipal schools that were expanded at the time, partly to counteract the rigidities of the old universities. In this more important academic setting, Wiese became the editor of a sociological journal, the *Kölner Vierteljahrshefte für Soziologie,* which carried a great many important articles and published most of the empirical data gathered by Wiese and his students. Later he developed a research institute for social science, which occupied a large share of his attention. *The Kölner Vierteljahrshefte* was last published in 1934, and the institute was closed in 1935. Wiese's position during the period of National Socialism was one of decreasing influence and security. Most of his classes were taken over by men in favor with the party. Since the end of the war, however, he has come back into prominence as president of the newly organized Deutsche Gesellschaft für Soziologie.

Wiese's own statements, as well as basic similarities to the work of several other writers, make it fairly easy to determine the chief sources of influence of his thought. Most important is the influence of Simmel, who, in maintaining that the isolation of the form of social relations is the peculiarly sociological problem, furnished the general pattern for Wiese's system. In emphasizing the dynamic, sociation aspects, however, Wiese approached the problem from a somewhat different point of view. More than most German sociologists, Wiese was influenced by American writers, particularly Ross, whose work directed his attention not only to the systematic arrangement of societal processes but also to many concrete problems. Park and Burgess, who were also influenced by Simmel and were concerned with problems of systematic sociology, should also be mentioned, as well as Thomas and Znaniecki. Waxweiler, a Belgian sociologist and director of an outstanding research institute, emphasized the importance of the processes of interhuman adjustment, through language, as the source of social life. His *Esquisse d'une sociologie* (1906) helped to focus Wiese's attention on the sociation frame of reference.

The trend of Wiese's thought is evident even in his early essay on Spencer,[2] which contrasts Spencer's cosmic scheme with Simmel's detailed studies, much to the advantage of the latter. Although Wiese is often considered to be too unconcerned with factual material, the error of such an interpretation is seen even in this early essay. Emphasizing the need for a natural-science approach to the study of society, Wiese is consistently empirical in his method.

The work on which his fame as a sociologist rests, however, and with which this paper is largely concerned is his *Allgemeine Soziologie*. Part I, the *Beziehungslehre,* appeared in 1924; Part II, the *Gebildelehre,* in 1929.[3] A recent English translation of three papers by Wiese, entitled *Sociology,*[4] furnishes a succinct and relatively complete statement of Wiese's point of view and system. His short essay, *Soziologie: Geschichte und Hauptprobleme,*[5] is also of value in showing his approach to the problems of sociology and his analysis of its history.

II. ESSENTIAL ELEMENTS IN VON WIESE'S SOCIOLOGICAL SYSTEM

Two elements are of greatest importance to Wiese's conception of the nature of sociology, the first of which is his emphasis on sociology as a science. Wiese is in the tradition of scholars who insist that sociology

can begin to make contributions to the understanding of social relationships only when it has profited by the example of the natural sciences,
broken away from speculative social philosophy, freed itself from the
reform efforts, and eliminated value judgments. Unlike most social
scientists in Germany, he was strongly influenced by the Western
natural-science tradition.[6]

Secondly, Wiese's whole work is orientated toward the idea that sociology is a special social science, with a clearly defined and delimited
area of investigation which differentiates it from the other social sciences.
It does not seek to draw together the results of the other social sciences
in order to get a total view of "concrete reality" but makes an abstraction
of its own, from an entirely unique point of view, in order to contribute
to the understanding of social life. The peculiarly sociological abstraction is the isolation of the processes of sociation, of approach and withdrawal, which characterize all social behavior. Moreover, sociology is
interested not in the purposes served by social relations, which are the
concern of the other social sciences, but only in the direction (approach
and avoidance) and the rhythm of sociation. "Rhythm of sociation"
refers to sequences and repetitions of social relations which establish observable patterns. Sociology, then, in brief, is the study of interhuman
relations as such; its special problem is the analysis of the direction and
patterning of sociation of all human behavior which has as its object
other human beings.

The greater part of Wiese's work is devoted to the systematizing of
the processes of sociation and their recurrent patterns. Part I of his
Allgemeine Soziologie, the *Beziehungslehre,* concerns itself with the
theory of interhuman relations, which Wiese divides into association,
dissociation, and mixed processes. Each of the two main processes—
association and dissociation—is analyzed into many subprocesses, which
are situated along a continuum, according to the degree of association
or dissociation which they represent.[7] The first tentative stages of association are included under "advance," a process in which "there always
remains some feeling of hesitation," of reserve; the participants look
upon the association as a kind of "doubtful experiment." Wiese gives
adoring, enticing, consulting, thanking, and the like as examples of
advance.

Indicative of a greater degree of association is the process of "adjustment," which implies the modification of differences among the persons

involved. This adjustment may be one-sided or mutual; the former usually signifies a condition of dependence on the part of the individual who does the adjusting; the latter is the result of reciprocal influence, generally in the pair-relation, which continues the tendencies initiated in the compromise: "Actions which in compromise are unrelated and transitory become incorporated in an on-going, continuous configuration in adjustment."[8] Wiese gives instilling knowledge, agreeing, imitating, and coming to terms as examples of adjustment.

Adjustment " .... does not wipe out feelings of difference .... , although they are usually somewhat less intense..... When once the stage of accordance is reached, however, mutual participation in emotions, memories and habitual attitudes ensues....."[9] Behavior of the participating individuals becomes more and more similar. Deferring to another's judgment, forming a friendship, and mediating are examples of accordance.

Most complete of the processes of association is that of "amalgamation," which, however, in the human sphere never represents complete coalescence. This process is seldom descriptive of association in mobile and anonymous groupings, such as the modern city, which preclude intense attachment to any one plurality pattern, but is more often found in isolated social structures. Amalgamation finds expression in the formation of pairs and other small groups and in the association of a large number of persons for co-operative purposes.

This analysis of the processes of association is not intended, of course, to correspond to empirical reality. One cannot easily classify concrete interhuman relationships in one category or another; they are set up as analytic devices. Three factors lead to association on all the different levels, although their influence becomes continually greater as one moves from advance to amalgamation: emotionally toned urges and sympathetic impulses; "interests which, although emotionally toned in some degree, usually are consciously recognized as conducive to the enhancement of self";[10] and objective factors in the situation which make association almost inevitable. Wiese thus summarizes the processes which flow from these influences: "By advance, we understand the preparatory steps to coming together; by adjustment, association through simultaneous and mutual recognition of differences; by accordance, the attempts to overcome differences; and by amalgamation, the establishment of some association which is conceived as a new state or condition."[11]

Dissociation, the other main process of interhuman relations, is also influenced by the three factors of emotionally toned urges, interests, and objective factors. Wiese insists that in the treatment of the processes of dissociation, value judgments must be checked even more rigorously than usual, for associative tendencies are likely to be regarded as worthy of diligent cultivation, while dissociation is to be avoided. The sociologist, says Wiese, can make no such distinction.

Dissociation as well as association can be expressed in terms of social distance: "....any social process is a sequence of occurrences through which the distance prevailing between human beings....is increased or decreased."[12] The three main processes of dissociation—competition, contravention, and conflict—signify increasing social distance. They also imply a "gradual increase of definitely antagonistic activity."

Competition, the least dissociative of the three processes, "....may be defined as the general social process comprising the dissociative tendencies inseparably connected with efforts on the part of persons or plurality patterns to attain an identical objective."[13] The objects in view are drawn from every field of human activity. The sociological study of competition, however, refers not to the goals but to competition "as an interhuman relation *per se*." It involves not only dissociative elements but many tendencies toward association—sufferance, compromise, advance, or even adjustment—which limit the degree of dissociation.[14] There is also a tendency, however, for competition to pass over into contravention and conflict, where dissociative influences are stronger. The two main varieties of competition are rivalry and striving; the former contains a larger subjective element or reference to the competitor, while the latter arises from a consciousness of scarcity of desired objects.

Contravention[15] is a process of dissociation which contains, on the one hand, more antagonistic elements than competition but includes, on the other hand, more uncertainty over the nature and extent of the antagonism than conflict. Contravention may be fostered by the emotional factors of exasperation, dislike, and resentment and by antagonistic interests, convictions, and temperaments which preclude agreement. These factors operate in contravention between the sexes and between generations and in majority-minority disputes, in all of which there is a strong clash of interests but also many associative traits which inhibit the appearance of overt conflict.

Conflict is the most extreme process of dissociation. It includes, however, a large variation in intensity of antagonism, ranging from that bordering on contravention to open combat. The latter is the most distinct form of dissociation, but by no means is it always reached in conflict processes. It involves, furthermore, an approximate equivalence in the strength of the contending parties. Conflict does not necessarily result in continuing dissociation; it may, in fact, result in well-marked association. "The more equivocal and latent dissociative processes, particularly contravention that never comes to the surface, may be greater barriers to future amalgamation than the most violent forms of open combat."[16] Attacking, persecuting, blaming, lynching, and abhorring are examples of conflict; and dueling, carrying on a feud, and ejecting a rival are examples of its combat phase.

Wiese's first discussion of these main processes of association and dissociation centered about "common-human" relations, that is, relations which are not specifically channelized by a more or less permanent pattern of behavior which delimits or circumscribes them. Other processes, "circumscribed action patterns," may also be analyzed into associative and dissociative, still with the dynamic point of view as the central concept. The only difference in this approach to the problem is the addition of the influence of plurality patterns,[17] which constitute the background of circumscribed processes and tend to condition the direction and intensity of the sociation. "Common-human relations" and "circumscribed action patterns" are, of course, only heuristic terms, not descriptions of empirical reality. All concrete interhuman processes contain both common-human and circumscribed elements, but the proportion varies greatly.

Turning, then, to the analysis of sociation, as it is circumscribed by more or less permanent patterns of behavior, we have the following statement by Wiese:

All circumscribed processes fall in one of two categories, differentiation or integration.... : disparities and uniformities develop; the growth of plurality patterns brings with it stratification .... individuation perpetually takes place; concomitantly, the associative network within plurality patterns becomes increasingly ingrained in the neuropsychic structures of its members, so that the associative bonds which unite them come to be regarded as more or less necessary, desirable, and justifiable, a consequence which renders the term "socialization" applicable..... Accompanying all these processes is the social ascent and descent of various members of the plurality patterns involved; the ensuing domination and submission are inseparable from group life.[18]

We have space here only to outline the processes of differentiation and integration which Wiese discusses with a wealth of detail. Among the differentiating processes are: the genesis of disparities; domination and submission; gradation, stratification, and selection; individuation, separation, and estrangement. These processes of differentiation follow certain channels which are marked out by the patterns of human relations; they are the circumscribed varieties of dissociation.

On the other hand are the integrating processes, the complements to differentiation. Both are always at work, although they do not balance each other. Uniformation; ordination, superordination, and subordination; and socialization are the main processes of integration. Wiese did not attempt to rank the circumscribed relations, as he had the common-human processes, according to the degree of sociation which they represent.

Using the same dichotomy from the point of view of the impact of differentiation and integration on the continuance of existing plurality patterns, one may speak of "constructive" and "destructive" processes. These are not wholly distinct from integration and differentiation. Constructive processes, for instance, "....are simply regarded as those special types of integration that produce new plurality patterns from old. Of course, all integrating processes are in some measure adapted to this end, and we merely select those which experience shows to be particularly adapted to the construction of new plurality patterns....."[19]

The main destructive processes are: exploitation, favoritism, formalism (ossification), radicalization (attack on old patterns without qualification), commercialism (undue subjection to economic criteria), and perversion (substitution of goals). The principal constructive processes are: institutionalization (the ordering of social relations), professionalization, and liberation (abolishing hindering restrictions).

The study of social processes and distances is central in Wiese's systematic sociology. In the *Gebildelehre,* however, he has extended the analysis of sociation to include the systematization of plurality patterns —the relatively continuous social structures which channelize inter-human relations. In harmony with his conception of sociology, Wiese confines his interest in plurality patterns to the investigation of the ways in which they influence association and dissociation. The bases of classification of social structures are (1) relative duration and (2) degrees of abstractness. By means of these criteria the author distinguishes three types of plurality patterns: crowds, groups, and abstract collectivities, which are consecutively less influenced by the behavior and characteristics of the "concrete human being," are consecutively more durable, more highly organized, and more abstract. "Crowds are very much like the empirical individual in his characteristics .... *groups* .... possess an *organization* which prescribes the activity of the individual .... *abstract collectivities* are considered to be supra-personal, and thus removed as far as possible from the empiric individual man."[20] That is, there is a progressive decrease in common-human behavior patterns and a progressive increase in circumscribed behavior patterns as one moves from crowds to abstract collectivities.

The two chief varieties of the crowd are the concrete (visible and temporary) and the abstract (amorphous and of indefinite duration). The former is a type of social grouping which lies between a leaderless aggregation, on the one hand, and the group, on the other. The latter is the transition between the concrete crowd and the abstract collectivity; it corresponds quite closely to what has become known in the United States as the "public." The term "crowd" is used to designate both concrete and abstract groupings because there is a close empirical connection between them: "there would be no concrete crowd if the abstract were not already present, and the abstract is perpetually rebuilt and renewed by the concrete."[21] The group is defined as ".... those interhuman plurality patterns .... which are of such relatively long duration and relative solidarity that the persons therein affiliated come to be regarded as a relatively homogeneous unit."[22] Duration and solidarity clearly distinguish the group from the crowd. In his classification of groups, Wiese uses size as the main criterion and discusses sociation influences in the pair, the triad, and larger groups. The abstract collectivity is distinguished from the crowd and the group by the lack of "affiliative homogeneity of definite, empirical human beings." That is, more attention is given to the organizational structure and less to the particular members.[23] The main types of abstract collectivities are the state and the church.

The analysis of these social structures—the crowd, the group, and the abstract collectivity—reveals the *patterns* of sociation; it defines the interhuman relations that tend to be continued or repeated, and it is therefore a valuable source of knowledge of the processes of sociation, which continues to be the main concern of Wiese's systematic sociology.[24]

III. CRITICAL APPRAISAL OF VON WIESE'S SOCIOLOGY

Wiese's systematization of sociology has received wide attention. Its scientific usefulness therefore needs careful appraisal. It is not necessary to discuss it on any other grounds than those of its scientific validity and utility, for they are the criteria which it is intended to satisfy.

The question that first arises concerns the validity of *any* attempt to systematize a science, to pay specific reference to the conceptual apparatus. Such activity is held by some to be idle armchair philosophizing which entirely contradicts the scientific pretensions under which it is pursued. One who holds such a position will immediately discount Wiese's system. The result of such a position, however, is not to eliminate the process of concept-building but to hide it, allowing implicit and unwarranted concepts to condition the data. The chief value of Wiese's work is precisely that he has contributed to the methodological "self-consciousness" of sociology, its scientific sophistication, by means of which its concept-building becomes explicit and planned with direct reference to its data. This is the central value of his emphasis on sociology as an abstracting science and as a special discipline.

Having said this, however, in regard to the general value of the development of a systematic frame of reference, one must investigate the usefulness of Wiese's specific systematization. The basic concept of sociation is doubtless a useful descriptive device; but for the most part —and here the critics of the system-builders have legitimate cause for complaint—it has preceded too many of the sociological problems with which it is concerned and has not, therefore, developed methodological tools for research. One must consider, in this connection, the concrete studies which have grown out of Wiese's systematization in order to see whether or not the conceptual apparatus which it furnishes has proved to be a valuable scientific tool. Granting that the analysis and prediction of the types and degrees of sociation are valid social scientific problems (whether or not it "is sociology" is unimportant), may one, by using the sociation frame of reference developed by Wiese, go into an agricultural village or ghetto or city and heighten his ability to say: "Given these conditions, these people will associate or dissociate thus—here competition, there accommodation, there conflict"? A scientific study does not simply record instances of a predetermined classification of processes; it seeks to discover relationships.

Many of the studies by both Wiese and his students[25] indicate that the orientation from which they have worked has proved valuable. It is a conceptual "pair of glasses" that sharpened their vision in studying the family, the village, and the ghetto. No startling new relationships have been discovered, to be sure—few theoretical developments force a sharp new orientation—but the sociation concept has been a clear way of analyzing, for instance, many aspects of the community-society dichotomy which has been important in the work of many writers. Its usefulness as a perspective is probably greatest when it refers to direct interhuman relations and least when applied to abstract crowds and abstract collectivities, such as the state.

Usefulness as a tool for certain sociological problems, however, is a long way from an all-embracing sociological system. It is a futile argument, in fact, from the scientific point of view, to try to decide whether or not Wiese's work is an accurate and complete sociological system. The only question is: Is it a useful conceptual tool for analyzing the data to which it refers? In so far as orderly description is of value in this regard, Wiese's system is only to be praised; but, because it is not oriented toward prediction, it has not generally achieved a more rigorous scientific level.

The felt need for *inclosing* a science in some particular systematization is a manifestation of lack of awareness of the function of that systematization in the scientific process. The history of science is the story of old problems attacked with new weapons, of new insights from fresh orientations. A systematization, by focusing attention, may prove to be a source of these new insights. To concentrate on the system itself, however, as Wiese too often does, is to shut off this source.[26] He himself finds it impossible to keep within the sociation frame of reference in his own concrete studies of interhuman relations. This is as it should be—a system is a tool, not a boundary. There is a good deal of truth in Abel's remark, made in a slightly different connection, that the controversy over Wiese's limitation of sociology " .... resolves itself .... into a mere struggle for a name and thus is without foundation."[27]

A further criticism of Wiese can be made in regard to his oft repeated dictum: No value judgments in science. He does not keep sharply enough in mind the distinction between values as biasing factors in research and values as data for the sociologist, although he accepts Max Weber's definition of sociology as one of the "understanding" sciences, which, in their search for predictive power, attempt to understand not only objectively observable behavior but subjectively intended meaning. This "meaning" is not something mysterious; scientists are not even concerned with its "reality"; but it proves to be a useful concept for the analysis of human behavior.[28] Although Wiese accepts this definition, he never uses it. His system is behavioristically (in a narrow sense) inclined. By insisting so strongly that sociology is a science, upon which there is now almost unanimity of opinion among professional sociologists, he is led to avoid, more than is necessary, the dangers that inhere in the idealistic tradition. Because he sees a need for following the work of the natural sciences, he is unable to develop a strictly sociological method devised for the analysis of "meaning."

Furthermore, there is a danger in the absolute denial to value judgments of a place in science. Value judgments make the positive contribution of sensitizing one to certain data and problems; they may be a source of insights. The danger is not so much the holding of a position as the failure to recognize the bias and thus to make allowance for it. If perspectives distort, it is not enough to deny them. Therefore, if the continued emphasis on elimination of value judgments from science tends only to prevent their explicit recognition, it hinders the scientific process. If, however, it stresses the dangers of biasing factors, it is a useful and necessary emphasis.

In sum, Wiese's work, in so far as it attempts to demonstrate what sociology "really is," has failed to established its point, as, indeed, any such effort must fail when tested by scientific criteria; for, to repeat, such a delimitation is not a surveying activity but a tool-building process. Wiese has failed to pay sufficient heed to concrete methodological tools in relation to specific problems. On the other hand, in the elaboration of his system he has, of course, collected a wealth of valuable detail and made valid empirical insights, the value of which is independent of the system itself. Moreover, when properly qualified, his emphasis on the need for explicit theoretical orientation is essential to the scientific quest; and his insistence upon the special nature of scientific sociology —irrespective of whether or not one accepts his definition of that specialty[29]—is fundamental to a nonempiricist, abstracting science.

NOTES

1. The writer wishes to express his thanks to Professor Howard Becker for making available his excellent library of books and documents on Wiese.

2. *Zur Grundlegung der Gesellschaftslehre: Eine kritische Untersuchung von Herbert Spencers System der synthetischen Philosophie* (Jena, 1906).

3. All references to *Allgemeine Soziologie* given below are to the American adaptation by Professor Becker, *Systematic Sociology* (New York, 1932) (cited hereafter as "Wiese-Becker"). It should be noted, however, that this volume is not simply a translation but a thoroughgoing adaptation of Wiese's work in terms of American material. Though there have been no basic shifts, there are different points of emphasis and several additions. In studying Wiese's work from *Systematic Sociology*, therefore, one must take account of these differences.

4. Edited and annotated by Franz H. Mueller (New York, 1941).

5. This appears in English both in Wiese-Becker, *op. cit.*, Part IV, which is a free translation and adaptation, and as a separate volume, *Sociology: Its History and Main Problems* (Hanover, 1928).

6. Some German writers—Sombart, for instance—spoke with great disdain of Wiese's *westlich* ideas.

7. As Abel and Becker have pointed out, this is not a genuine quantification of sociological data, because the essential requirement of quantification—a scale—is lacking. It is only a ranking procedure (cf. Theodore Abel, *Systematic Sociology in Germany* [New York, 1929], pp. 102–7; and Wiese-Becker, *op. cit.*, p. 59).

8. Wiese-Becker, *op. cit.*, p. 198.

9. *Ibid.*, p. 206.

10. *Ibid.*, p. 230.

11. *Sociology*, p. 60.

12. Wiese-Becker, *op. cit.* p. 243.

13. *Ibid.*, p. 248.

14. In the second edition of *Allgemeine Soziologie*, in fact, the author discusses competition as a mixed, not a dissociative, process.

15. Wiese uses the more general term "opposition," which Becker, however, has changed to "contravention" in order to avoid the confusion which surrounds the former term in English (cf. Wiese-Becker, *op. cit.*, pp. 260–61).

16. *Ibid.*, p. 272.

17. This, again, is a free translation of the German term *Gebilde* ("structure"), in an attempt to catch the meaning more exactly.

18. Wiese-Becker, *op. cit.*, pp. 284–85.

19. *Ibid.*, p. 369.

20. Wiese, *Sociology*, p. 72.

21. Wiese-Becker, *op. cit.*, p. 457.

22. *Ibid.*, p. 489.

23. It should be noted here that Wiese explicitly rejects any notion of "social realism." Though the focus of attention may be on the pattern of abstract collectivities, not on the members, that pattern does not constitute a substantive reality: ". . . . Social structures do not exist in space. . . . . If we attribute to them any reality it cannot be the reality of the perceivable but reality in the sense of an active force affecting and influencing life" (Wiese, *Sociology*, p. 39). This quotation also reveals the connection, according to Wiese, between social process and social structure: the latter is but a static picture of the former.

24. The second edition of *Allgemeine Soziologie*, which appeared in 1933, has several minor changes which should be mentioned, since we have drawn on the English adaptation of the first edition. The author gives a greater place to mixed processes of sociation, among which he includes competition; he elaborates his discussion of social distance; and he develops the application of his system to economic and biosociology. In his chapter on

biosociology he denies the Nazi race doctrine and stresses the mixed racial character of the German people.

25. Cf. various chapters in *Allgemeine Soziologie*, those on the dyad and the triad, for example, and numerous studies by Wiese published in the *Kölner Vierteljahrshefte;* cf. also such studies as Willy Gierlichs, "Zwischenmenschliche Probleme der Ghettos," *Kölner Vierteljahrshefte*, X, 3; and Willy Latten, "Die niederrheinische Kleinstadt," *Kölner Vierteljahrshefte*, XIII, 3.

26. It is difficult to estimate how much the emphasis in Germany on the autonomy of sociology was due to the struggle for academic recognition against intrenched disciplines. It was probably an important influence, fostering an overemphasis on academic boundaries and elaborate system-building—from which Wiese's work suffers. In the polemical situation sociologists were at pains to prove that their science encroached on no other domains and hence paid too much attention to boundaries.

27. Abel, *op. cit.*, p. 10. That is not to imply, of course, that, because this unacceptable element is present in Wiese's work, the whole of it is to be dismissed lightly.

28. Note that not all sociologists who hold the discipline to be an understanding science would agree with this statement: some are concerned with "real meaning."

29. As Abel says: "The primary object of v. Wiese's sociological writings so far has been the establishing and justification of sociology as an independent science. His achievement on this point is not invalidated by the criticism which we advanced against his proposals according to which the various tasks of sociology are to be carried out" (*op. cit.*, p. 114).

CHAPTER XIII

MAX WEBER'S SOCIOLOGICAL ANALYSIS OF CAPITALISM AND MODERN INSTITUTIONS

Talcott Parsons, *Harvard University*

I. WEBER'S LIFE AND ACADEMIC CAREER

MAX WEBER was born in Berlin in 1864.[1] His father was a rather prominent man in the politics of the day, being for many years a member of the Reichstag and a leader in the affairs of the National Liberal party. When Max was a young man he met many of the leading political personalities of the time in his own home. At the university Max studied law under the influence of the historical school, which was dominant in the German universities at that time. Among his more important teachers were Theodor Mommsen and Adolf Goldschmidt.

From his earliest period he was marked off as a particularly able student, and he embarked, apparently without question, on the path leading to an academic career. In due course he was made *Privatdozent* in jurisprudence at the University of Berlin and could have been expected to become a professor of law. His career was, however, dramatically changed by his being called, in 1893, to a professorship of economics at the University of Freiburg. This was followed within a few years by a call to one of the most prominent chairs of economics in Germany— Heidelberg—the previous incumbent of which was the well-known historical economist, Karl Knies.

Weber's shift from jurisprudence to economics was not altogether illogical. His legal interests had, from the first, been historically directed, and in this connection he had become increasingly interested in the relations between law and the economic organization and conditions of the societies he studied. His doctor's dissertation on trading companies in the Middle Ages already showed this trend, and he tended to shift more and more from legal history with an economic slant into economic history.

His career in its earlier stages was undoubtedly one of the most brilliant of his day in the German academic world, with advancement to high position and great reputation at an unusually early age. It was, however, in 1900, suddenly interrupted by a severe illness, reported as a "nervous breakdown," which kept him entirely out of work for about four years. His breakdown was so protracted that it enforced his resignation from his professorship; and, since he was never in good health after his resumption of work, he lived for many years in Heidelberg as a private scholar without official position. Only toward the end of his life, in 1918, did he resume teaching. The summer semester of 1918 he spent as a visiting professor at the University of Vienna and from there soon went to a regular professorship in economics at Munich, as successor to Lujo Brentano. There, in only the second semester of his teaching, he died suddenly of pneumonia in 1920, at the age of only fifty-six.

During these intervening years Weber was active not only as a scholar and in the promotion of scholarly enterprises but in politics as well. He was always passionately interested in political affairs and followed them extraordinarily closely. In 1905 he learned to read Russian in an incredibly short time, in order to be able to read the newspapers in connection with the abortive Russian Revolution of that year. He was personally acquainted with many important political figures and gave a good deal of advice behind the scenes. He was one of the first prominent men in Germany to turn against the regime of Kaiser Wilhelm II. During the war he wrote a notable memorandum in opposition to the unrestricted submarine warfare, predicting that it would inevitably bring the United States into the war against Germany. Toward the end of the war he wrote many articles for the *Frankfurter Zeitung,* and, with the revolution, it seemed as though he might emerge as an important political leader. He served as a member of the commission which presented the famous memorandum on German war guilt to the Peace Conference at Versailles and was also a member of the commission which drew up the first draft of the Weimar Constitution. He failed, however, through a political mischance, of election to the Constitutional Assembly, and his death came soon after.

In the academic world, apart from his own scholarly work, Weber was notable for his part in two important enterprises. It was he, more than any other single person, who was the dominant influence in the

Archiv für Sozialwissenschaft und Sozialpolitik and who made it the most notable social-science periodical in Germany. He was also the moving spirit in developing the plan for the great collaborative work, the *Grundriss der Sozialökonomik,* which was to be as near a complete study of the society of the Western world as German scholarship could produce. His own *Wirtschaft und Gesellschaft* was ultimately published as part of this series.

II. THE NATURE OF WEBER'S SOCIOLOGICAL WRITINGS

Though a many-sided individual and to all who knew him apparently a notably impressive personality, Weber's greatest significance undoubtedly lies in his scholarly achievements. In this respect there is an important reorientation which became evident on his partial recovery from the long illness that divided his career into two parts. Almost at the same time, in 1904 and 1905, he embarked on two different series of studies, both of which resulted in some of the most notable developments in modern social science. The first was a series of critical essays on the methodology of social science, which were directed, in the first instance, against the doctrines then current in the historical schools, especially of economics. These essays were not brought together and published during his lifetime but have been collected since his death in the volume entitled *Gesammelte Aufsätze zur Wissenschaftslehre.* The second development was initiated by his now famous essay, *The Protestant Ethic and the Spirit of Capitalism.* This was not the completion of a program but the beginning. It was followed by the series of comparative studies in the sociology of religion,[2] a number of which were published in subsequent years, but was left unfinished at his death.

Not immediately, but within a few years, Weber embarked on a third related, yet distinct, program of work. He apparently more and more felt the need for the systematic conceptual formulation and collection of material, which, organized under a systematic conceptual scheme, was to be brought to bear on the problem of understanding the position of modern Western society in his time. The work he had done along these lines was, so far as it had been completed, published in *Wirtschaft und Gesellschaft,* only a small part of which had been prepared for publication before his death.

Weber's sudden death occurred at just the time that he was beginning to reap systematically the harvest of a lifetime of research and thought.

It is questionable whether he ever intended to publish a systematic work on methodology; but in the fields of the sociology of religion and of the analysis of Western society, he had just begun to bring his material together and publish it in systematic form. Only one volume[3] of the studies of the sociology of religion was prepared for publication by his own hand. Two other volumes[4] were in sufficiently good condition to be published, but the series was very far from being complete. None of *Wirtschaft und Gesellschaft* had been completed beyond the first section, and the editors were left without even an authoritative table of contents to guide their arrangement of the material. He apparently worked on a number of different things simultaneously, and many of the chapters break off suddenly in manuscript. From internal evidence it is also clear that he intended to write on other subjects on which he did not leave even fragments of manuscript.

III. WEBER'S APPROACH TO SOCIAL SCIENCE AND ITS METHODOLOGY

Weber's approach to social science and the change that it underwent during his lifetime should be understood in terms of the particular intellectual situation in Germany. Germany was the home of idealistic philosophy and of the related attempt to draw a particularly sharp methodological distinction between the natural sciences and the disciplines dealing with human action. It had become almost a dogma in Germany that the latter could not be treated in natural-science terms. It was variously thought of as the sphere of free will, of the development of *Geist,* of the unfolding of cultures, and of the intimate understanding of subjective feelings and ideas, but, above all, it came to be held that it was only in the natural sciences that the use of generalized theoretical categories was admissible. As over against this, explanation in the social field was thought to be essentially historical, to consist in the tracing of genetic sequences of motivation and cultural influence.

It was at this point that Weber's critique of the historical schools began. His essential thesis was that it is only by the use of generalized theoretical categories, implicitly or explicitly, that it is logically possible to demonstrate the existence of causal relationships. This view necessitated a radical reconstruction of the logical structure of the social sciences, since it had become essential to pay attention to questions of systematic generalized theory. It was in undertaking this reconstruction that Weber developed his celebrated doctrine of the ideal type. In a word, to Weber, theory in the field of human action consists in systems of ideal types. In developing this, Weber did not pretend to put forward anything new but merely to formulate more precisely than others what social scientists actually did and what logical canons they were subject to when they claimed to prove causal relationships.

As distinguished from concepts current in the natural sciences, the ideal type had, in Weber's view, three primary characteristics. In the first place, it was formulated in terms of subjective categories—that is, in his own phrase, "of the intended meaning" of an action to the actor. This category—in German referred to as *Verstehen*—had played an important part in the discussion of the distinction between the natural and the social sciences. Weber took it over, but he used it quite differently from such other writers as Dilthey and Simmel.

Second, however, the ideal type did not formulate the actual concrete meaning of an action but an extreme limiting case, in which certain elements were stated in their logically pure form and others intentionally neglected. This gave the ideal type a particular character of abstraction in a special direction. Although he did not hold to it consistently in practice, in some of his most important general statements Weber contended that the ideal type should formulate the rational elements of a pattern of action, leaving those not fitting the rational norm to be treated residually as the sources of deviation from the rational pattern of action. This calls attention to an aspect of the peculiar kind of abstraction involved, which Weber himself did not stress. In fact, what is formulated in most of his ideal types is a description not of concrete action but of the normative patterns which may be considered binding on the actors.[5] There are serious difficulties involved in Weber's treatment of the problems of rationality which cannot be gone into in this chapter.[6]

Thirdly, Weber insisted that the formulation of generalized ideal types could not be treated as the goal of social science. Such types were to be formulated only as instruments for the analysis of concrete historical problems. This view was, in part, based on the conviction that anything like a stable and permanent system of theory was impossible in the social field, since the problems investigated, and hence the concepts useful for their solution, were inevitably relative to the particular values involved in the situation and to the scientific interests of the observer. This he formulated in his well-known concept of *Wertbeziehung*.

While Weber's basic insight on this point is undoubtedly correct, it seems to be clear that his position cannot be upheld as he himself formulated it. On the one hand, he neglected elements in the determination of scientific interests and problems other than their relation to the values of the observer. On the other hand, it can be shown that the difference between the natural and the social sciences in this respect is not so great as he thought it to be. Indeed, this doctrine constitutes the principal barrier to the completion of a very far-reaching methodological unification of all the empirical sciences which Weber's own work, starting from the background of the German doctrines, went far to prepare. It should be noted, in this connection, that Weber's critique of both groups of sciences showed, with a clarity remarkable for the time, that their pretensions to a full grasp of concrete reality were entirely unfounded. One of the principal obstacles to a methodological unification has been this naïve empiricist realism on both sides, for which Weber's critique is one of the best available correctives. But, once this empiricism is abandoned, the harmfulness of systematic theory to the legitimate interests of social science largely disappears.

IV. THE SOCIOLOGY OF RELIGION AS AN INSTRUMENT
OF SOCIAL METHODOLOGY

Weber's importance in social science does not, however, rest primarily on his methodological writings as such. Indeed, unlike many German scholars, he did not carry on methodological investigation for its own sake but rather as a means of clarifying the problems encountered in his empirical research. This program of research centers on a very comprehensive attempt to understand some of the most important aspects of the social and economic order of the modern Western world. Undoubtedly, the studies in legal, economic, and social history made before his illness contributed in important ways, but his maturer general conclusions first began to take shape in connection with the study for which he is best known—*The Protestant Ethic and the Spirit of Capitalism*.

Though this study was an essay in historical research, its importance does not by any means lie entirely in its contribution to our understanding of the forces which account for the development of "modern capitalism." At least equally important is Weber's conception of what elements in the modern social structure were particularly distinctive and of central importance to society as a whole. Most economic historians had paid primary attention to the development of a system of profit-making activity, along with the process by which mechanisms facilitating its functioning, such as credit and banking institutions, markets, and the like, had developed. Weber's primary interest was neither in acquisitive activity, as such, nor in the development of such mechanisms, but in the emergence of a distinctive set of institutional patterns, in so far as these regulated the market activities of business itself—not merely their sanctioning of the goal of profit, which was important, but their subjection of such activity to a certain kind of discipline—and its pursuit in terms of a specifically patterned type of institutional role and social organization. Business activity was regarded as a "calling," as a job in which, in an impersonal and specialized function, an individual proved his competence and his primary qualities of character. Weber thought it particularly significant that such roles were organized to a very high degree into complex bureaucratic structures, with individuals subjected not only to the informal ethical discipline of institutional patterns but also to a rigorous system of formally organized hierarchical authority.

Undoubtedly, in the earlier stages of the vast program of research which Weber devoted to these problems, he laid undue stress on the central importance of acquisitive activity for modern society and neglected the central position of such groups as the professions. The most important results of his analysis are, however, applicable to a considerably broader field than that of business life. Similarly, perhaps under the influence of the special conditions in Germany, he also laid undue stress on the significance of large-scale bureaucratic organization, although the phenomena he was talking about are undoubtedly of great prominence throughout the area of highly developed industrialism.

In formulating the problem of historical origins Weber was undoubtedly influenced by the Marxian point of view. For the fully developed system he accepted the Marxian position that the acquisitive activities of the individual businessman were adequately motivated by the pressures of the situation in which he was placed. He felt, however, that this interpretation could not be applied to the process of development of the system and that it was necessary to find patterns of orientation in terms of which this kind of activity was comprehensible—in terms of its own direct value and not merely as a means of survival on various levels of established conditions. Such an orientation he found in the basic ethical attitudes associated with what he calls the "ascetic" branches of Protestantism—namely, Calvinism and the Protestant sects like the Baptists, Quakers, and Methodists, which, though differing in theology, had very similar ethical orientations.

Weber admitted, quite readily, that these religious movements, far from positively sanctioning materialism and acquisitive greed, were fundamentally otherworldly and suspicious of the temptations of the flesh. But it was precisely this otherworldly ascetic orientation which made the specific pattern of activity in a "calling" meaningful. It provided adequate motivation for devoting one's life to a specialized and impersonal task, with the attendant sacrifice of many otherwise legitimate interests and of the sanctity of traditional ways of life. The positive sanction of acquisitiveness was, at least partly, a consequence of partial secularization, whereby prosperity in the affairs of this world came to be interpreted as a sign of grace. Since, however, acquisitive activity was only one of many different acceptable callings, this fact is not the central basis of Weber's thesis but essentially a secondary phenomenon.

Weber most explicitly repudiated any idea that he was developing a monistic religious interpretation of even one great development in history. On the contrary, he always insisted that many mutually independent conditions were necessary in order to make the development of modern capitalism. He did, however, equally definitely maintain that the Protestant ethic was a necessary condition and that, without it, the development would have been radically different. Weber did not, however, stop with this essay. He made it rather the starting-point of a much more extended program of investigation, partly to verify the interpretation of the importance of Protestantism in this particular historical connection, partly to clarify his analysis and place his empirical material in a more adequate perspective.

The course that he took in pursuing these aims is of the greatest significance, particularly in Germany, where the influence of the historical schools was predominant. Even with this background the normal thing, in the face of any uncertainty, would have been to engage in more and more detailed research into the specific historical antecedents of Western culture. Weber was undoubtedly an unusually competent social and economic historian in the relevant fields and could easily have devoted the rest of his scholarly life to completing a great historical study. Instead of this, he turned to radically different sources, embarking on a large-scale program of comparative studies of the relation between religious ethics and social and economic organization in all the great world religions.

Underlying this choice was a profound methodological insight. His problem was not elucidation of the specific facts of historical sequence but, rather, the definite isolation of the most important variable elements and the demonstration of their causal significance by studying their operation under variant conditions. The comparative method, as Weber used it, is the direct methodological equivalent of experimentation in the laboratory sciences. Only by studying cases which are similar in some respects but different in others would it be possible to arrive at a judgment of the causal influence of any factor. It was a consequence of his criticism of the logic underlying the historical school of economics that he saw that his problem could not be solved by further elaboration of a single historical process. Though he did not say so directly, he must have realized that the same fundamental criticism is applicable to the Marxian analysis of history. In order to achieve determinate results, it is essential to focus attention on a small number of factors.

To Weber the problem was that of the order of influence which can be attributed to what he called a "religious ethic." It was this which he treated as a variable factor. The broad conclusion to which he came was that a critical significance could be attributed to the variations in this factor in the process of the *differentiation* of the institutional structures of the great civilizations from each other. The ranges of variations in which he was interested were precisely those defined by the dominant characteristics of "modern capitalism," as they have been outlined above. He was particularly interested in the conditions favoring a rational orientation, as opposed to traditionalism, a prominent position for functionally specific roles, and, finally, elements of universalism not merely in personal ethics but in the institutionalized definitions of situations.

Weber isolated the influence of the religious ethic by a rough but, for his broadest purposes, adequate method. What he attempted to do was to judge whether, at the time preceding the emergence of the religious movement in question, the general character of the social structure, apart from religion, was more or less "favorable" to the development of the institutional patterns characteristic of the modern Western world. In the two cases most fully worked out—namely, China and India—his conclusion was that at comparable stages, that is, comparable to Europe on the eve of the Reformation, the situation was, in all the relevant respects at least, as favorable as it was in western Europe.

The problems involved in this judgment are too detailed and technical to review here. The religious movements—namely, Confucianism, Hinduism, and Protestantism—however, which came to dominate in these three cultural areas were radically different from one another. If these differences had any influence, it could not have been in the direction of assimilating the three societies to a common institutional pattern. Moreover, in broad terms, in each of the three cases the institutional structure which emerged was of a kind which would have been expected, had the basic attitudes toward social life inherent in each of the three great religious movements exerted a decisive influence.

The case of India is, perhaps, the most obvious because the contrast of attitude with our own is sharpest. Not only were the basic goals of religion in India, as in all such cases, transcendental, but the situation was defined in such a way that these goals could be meaningfully pursued only by turning one's back on everyday social interests and responsibilities, by engaging in mystical contemplation or otherworldly asceticism. The pursuit of salvation in this radical sense was, to be sure, not traditional; but in the nature of the case it was a goal accessible only to a small minority. For the great majority, Hinduism resulted in the most radical sanction of the existing traditional order and ways of doing things that has ever been developed anywhere. In the caste system the only form of virtuous behavior consisted in the conscientious performance of the traditional obligations, especially the ritual obligations, of the station in life in which one was born. Only by such faithfulness to tradition was there any prospect of improvement of one's fundamental religious status by being reborn in a higher caste position.

Though the Indian case is the more obvious, that of China is even more telling, because on a certain level there seems to be a striking resemblance between the typical Chinese and Western attitudes. At least in the Confucian tradition the Chinese have been notable for their shrewd practical worldliness. They have been contemptuous of metaphysical speculation, of mysticism, of transcendentalism. Far from being averse to acquisitiveness, they have been a people who have notably valued the good things of this life with money conspicuously placed among them. What, then, is the difference? It is precisely, as Weber succinctly puts it, "that, while Calvinism was a doctrine of rational *mastery over* the world, Confucianism was a doctrine of rational *adaptation to* the world."

The notable feature of the Chinese social structure is not only its complete failure to root out traditionalism but a sanctification of tradition, second only to that of India. The attitude that the classics, which were the subject of education of every scholar, could never be improved upon is to be contrasted with the inherently dynamic character of Western science. In addition, in China there is a notable absence of any sanction for impersonal specialized functions. The educated man is never the technical specialist but rather the well-rounded cultivated gentleman. Finally, there is also a notable absence of universalism in Confucian ethics. Loyalty to one's own kinship group and one's own particular friends and associates supersedes all generalized obligations as to honesty, truth, and so on.

It is important, in this connection, that, though Weber never came to formulate the results of his comparative studies in any single systematic statement, there is discernible in the later development of the studies and in relevant parts of *Wirtschaft und Gesellschaft* a certain shift of perspective. The problem of accounting for adequate motivation of acquisitive activity, even in the special forms described above, becomes considerably less important, and a broader contrast between the institutional structures of the modern Western world and of China and India becomes more prominent. It is not the existence of a business economy but of patterns which underlie not only business but many other equally important features of our world, such as science and learning, the professions, and governmental administration.

At the same time, there is a certain shift in the perspective on Protestantism itself. In the earlier essay Weber was particularly concerned with the contrast between "ascetic" Protestantism and Catholicism. Comparison with the religions of China and India considerably reduces the significance of this contrast. From the latter point of view the Calvinistic pattern is to be regarded as the most complete realization of possibilities in one particular direction. Catholicism, from this point of view, considerably mitigates the rigor of the Calvinist doctrine; but, by contrast with Confucianism and Hinduism, all branches of Christianity are seen to have much in common.

So far only the "religious ethic" has been mentioned as an object of Weber's analysis. It is this aspect of a great religious tradition which impinges most closely on concrete social activities in the secular sphere. Weber, however, went much further to analyze the structure of a religious tradition itself and to explain the deeper motives underlying the particular attitudes central to the religious ethic in question.

The essential feature of this analysis is a theory of the relation in his own terms between ideas and religious interests.[7] As he repeatedly said, it is not ideas but religious interests which motivate action. The function of ideas is, to borrow W. I. Thomas' term, to "define the situation." At least on the level in which Weber was concerned with the problem, the interest in salvation can be regarded as a constant, in particular as sharing common features between India and the Western world. But pursuing such an interest as salvation is a matter of action, a matter of doing something about an intolerable situation. Unlike the solution of technological problems, the question of *what* to do cannot be answered by merely observing empirical facts. What it will make sense to do will depend upon the cognitive interpretation of the meaning of salvation and the possible paths to its attainment. On the basis of Brahman philosophy, salvation in a radical sense could only mean "escape from the wheel of Karma"; but this goal could not possibly be attained by excelling others in worldly accomplishments of any sort. It could be accomplished only by complete dissociation from all worldly interests and immersion in communication with the Absolute. It furnished, as Weber says, no motive for any positive interest in secular goals.

In Christianity, on the other hand, from the very beginning, salvation has meant fundamentally an act of grace on the part of a transcendental deity; and the deity has often attached specific conditions to the granting of grace. In some branches, good works—that is, the fulfilment of positive ethical norms in secular activity—have been a direct means to the attainment of salvation. In strict Calvinism this was not so. The state of grace was predetermined, which might seem to favor a fatalistic attitude, but at least two factors have operated in the opposite direction. The very doctrine of predestination emphasized more sharply than any other version of Christian thought the complete dependence of man on the will of God, and, since it was His will that man should work in the building of His kingdom, any person with sufficient faith to accept pre-destination would be bound to take seriously his religious duties to fulfil God's commandments. Beyond that, however, for the serious Protestant the doctrine of predestination left him in a state of extreme emotional ten-sion relative to his state of grace. Though he could not by his own action earn salvation, he could prove to himself that he was worthy of it and hence, in all probability, was one of the elect, for "a good tree cannot bear evil fruit." And there was no question about it—God's will was that man should build a Christian society in this world as well as in the next.

The difference between Weber's analysis of motivation on this level and his agreement with Marx as to the automatic enforcement of disci-pline in a developed capitalistic society is, in one sense, not so great as it appears at first sight. To be sure, the devout Calvinist is not explained mainly in terms of external sanctions, but two things may be said. In so far as his interest in religious salvation is a genuinely powerful emo-tional force, external sanctions become unnecessary. There is probably far more of this disinterested attachment to secular activity than most utilitarian thinkers have understood. The addition of external sanctions is not primarily the result of the fact that, to Marx, the interests are acquisitive rather than religious but of the fact that the definitions of the situation have become institutionalized. Comparative study, to which Weber made a great contribution, has shown conclusively that particular goals, when they have become institutionalized, universally become at-tached to a widespread variety of different interests—that is, of deeper-lying elements of motivation. Indeed, almost any goal, provided it is integrated with a meaningful definition of the situation and institu-tionalized, can become a focus not only of economic interests but of a very wide variety of interests. Indeed, one of the most important conse-quences of Weber's work is to suggest that what we talk about as "eco-nomic" interest is not an ultimate category of motivation but is, rather, a consequence of the institutionalization of whatever patterns may be dominant in any given social system.

V. THE CHARACTER OF WEBER'S GENERALIZED SYSTEM OF SOCIAL THEORY

It has also been pointed out that Weber did not believe in the possi-bility or desirability of attempting to formulate a permanent generalized system of social theory. At the same time, there is, especially in his later work, much which constitutes systematic theoretical construction, though he was probably himself unaware of the full theoretical significance of what he was doing.

So far as Weber could be said to have formulated a generalized system of theory, it is most completely stated in the early part of *Wirtschaft und Gesellschaft*.[8] On the explicit level this took the form of a classification of ideal types of social action and relationships. Weber started off by distinguishing four basic types of action. The first two are characterized by certain modes of rationality. In the case of one, *Zweckrationalität,* action is conceived as rationally oriented to the maximum attainment of a plurality of ends which are weighed against one another, and in the choice of means not merely technical efficiency but also cost is considered. In the second case, that of *Wertrationalität,* a given clearly formulated value is put into practice by the most effective available means, regardless of cost or bearing on other values. The other two constitute residual categories in different directions. In the one case, that of traditional action, the departure from rationality consists in the absence of calculation in terms of efficiency or effectiveness and in the adherence to established patterns without further question. The fourth type, affectual action, consists in any mode of orientation which is neither rational nor traditional but motivated in terms of feeling, emotion, sentiment, and so on. There is no point in attempting to specify the meaning of these terms, since the category is, for Weber, residual and its content is not specifically clarified.

Weber employs these concepts throughout his work in a variety of different ways. Systematically, however, the next step is to attempt to work out their various possible permutations and combinations in the structure of more and more complex systems of social relationships. Though Weber does proceed to systematize his types on the relationship level, he nowhere attempts to follow out the logic of this procedure systematically. What he does is, rather, to select among the many logical possibilities a relatively small number which he finds to be of particularly great significance. In certain directions, however, the classifications trail off into endless subdivisions in such a way that it becomes quite arbitrary as to where the process is halted.

Since the mere logical possibility of combinations is not adequate to determine the direction that his systemization takes, we must look for other principles of selection. These it would seem are to be found in two principal directions, which are roughly, though by no means fully, integrated with each other. On the more abstract level, Weber seems to have developed, largely implicitly, a scheme of the generalized structure of systems of social action.[9] The basic categories of this scheme are not types of action but are structural elements which underlie any classification on the type level.

The starting-point for this scheme is clearly the rational means-ends analysis. When this is followed through to a certain point, it becomes necessary to differentiate ultimate goals or ends from those elements of the means-ends system which are primarily significant as means to other ends. The role of ultimate values as the direct goals of chains of action is completely clear in Weber's work. Furthermore, in complex systems the intermediate factors of the means-ends chains are not undifferentiated but involve a series of analytical distinctions which come out clearly in his work. The most important of these is that between the technological and the economic aspects, on the one hand, and between economic allocation and the employment of authority and coercion, on the other.

This direct analysis of means-ends systems, however, is far from exhausting this aspect of Weber's systematic thinking. Action is not oriented merely toward specific goals but also in social systems to an order which defines, within certain limits, the conditions under which goals may be pursued. The systems of order which are of greatest significance in social life Weber found to be characterized by one peculiarly important feature: they are treated as "legitimate." Though conformity with them is generally enforced by various forms of the mechanism of reward and punishment, they are also supported by common moral sentiments, so that conformity is widely treated as a moral obligation and is exacted on the part of those in authority as a morally legitimized right. The element of legitimacy underlying forms of order Weber connects closely with the basic values which enter into means-ends systems. Both of these are derived from the basic ethical orientations of the members of social groups.

These ethical orientations are not isolated phenomena. They always stand in close relation to those aspects of cognitive and affective orientation which we generally call "religious." The typical attitude of respect for moral authority and moral obligation which is the distinguishing feature of legitimacy is closely related to the respect for "sacred," or, in Weber's term, "charismatic," persons and things. For an order to be legitimized and ultimate values to be justified, they must, as a matter of empirical generalization, be closely integrated with man's orientation toward the problems of meaning and the world of sacred entities and symbols. Just as, in Durkheim's work, moral authority in the secular sphere is integrated with sacredness in the religious, so in Weber's is legitimacy bound up with patterns of charismatic prestige and authority. In the concepts of the means-ends system, of ultimate values, legitimacy, charisma, and systems of religious ideas is contained a systematic outline of the generalized structure of systems of action. It is from these that the structural relationships of Weber's more concrete ideal types are derived, so that they constitute a structurally integrated system rather than a mere elaborate spinning-out of logical possibilities.

There is, however, a second aspect of Weber's theoretical systematization. In addition to the comparative studies in the sociology of religion, which have been reviewed above, and closely connected with them, Weber carried out for many years a program of study in comparative institutional structures primarily in the fields of economic and political organization. This interest grew out of his early studies in comparative law and in economic and social history and was extended and refined as his systematic thinking developed. It is this material which forms the main substantive content of his greatest systematic work, *Wirtschaft und Gesellschaft,* unfinished though it remained to his death.

In this context he pursued the same fundamental interests in the forms of, and deviations from, rationality in social affairs which had been basic to his studies in the sociology of religion. Hence he was particularly preoccupied with the status and institutional peculiarities of rationalized patterns, particularly in three most important fields; the system of market exchange and money accounting, the rationalized formal-legal procedure and administration, and the structure of bureaucratic administrative organization with legal control.

In all three of these fields he attributed great importance to patterns of what he called "formal rationality," which in each case came into inevitable conflict with considerations of "substantive rationality." In the case of money and capital accounting, the formal perfection in a free-exchange economy inevitably results in deviations from substantive standards of the satisfactory provisions for the economic wants of a population, as well as in deviations from standards of distributive justice and the like. In the legal sphere formal rational procedure results in conflict with the moral sentiments of substantive justice; and in the sphere of the exercise of authority in administrative procedure strict adherence to formal bureaucratic patterns results in corresponding strains in relation to important interests and sentiments.

Thus in all three spheres a high level of formal rationality is particularly unstable and can be maintained only by overcoming formidable resistance. These three types of formal rationality Weber considered the most distinctive institutional features of modern Western society. He attempted to throw light on the conditions necessary for their development and maintenance in terms of a comparative analysis which showed the most important patterns by which, in each case, they could become transformed by imperceptible degrees into radically different institutional patterns.

In the economic sphere Weber tended to contrast the pattern of free-market economy with a maximization of the use of money and of accounting in money terms with situations in which the orientation of economic activity was, on the one hand, forced to calculate in terms of qualitative comparisons of heterogeneous goods and services and, on the other hand, to take account of considerations not of direct economic significance and not expressible in terms of a numerical unit. He did not in this field develop a specific type classification but devoted much effort to showing the precariousness of the modern market system and the fact that deviation from it tended in the direction of the traditional stabilizing of economic relations through their entanglement in structures of primarily noneconomic significance, such as relations of loyalty between superiors and subordinates in an organization, political, religious, or otherwise. Though his judgment may have been faulty in detail, Weber presented important evidence that the shift to a large-scale planned economy would probably give powerful impetus to the tendency to traditional stereotyping of the economic system.

A second field of analysis is that of property relations. There Weber showed that the modern market economy and many other features of modern society rest on a particular combination in the structure of property rights which he characterized as the full appropriation of the nonhuman factors in production by owners and the complete lack of appropriation of human factors by owners—that is, full private property of natural resources and goods and complete absence of property rights in human beings or their services.

This particular combination is unique and subject to deviant tendencies in very important respects. There are tendencies, on the one hand, to place limitations on full property rights of owners and, on the other, to limit the freedom of the human agents in production. In particular, Weber maintained that, while the tendency of workers to appropriate rights in their jobs and in the means of production and the tendency of employers to appropriate property rights in the services of the workers were formally antithetical, there is a fundamental tendency for them both to lead into the same general consequences—restrictions on the formal rationality of the economy and tying both worker and the material means of production to a traditionally stereotyped system of relationships. Though any such formula is subject to numerous qualifications, one may say that for Weber the basic alternative to our system of free property and free labor was a feudal type of organization of economic life in which the freedom of the worker was traded for a combination of security and dependency; and the employer, though receiving a kind of right over his workers which is now prohibited, would be restricted in the freedom of disposal both of his workers through discharge and of material property. In terms of Weber's more general scheme on both these levels, the alternative to formal rationality in economic life as a stable routine economy is traditionalism.

In the field of the institutionalization of authority, Weber's analysis runs somewhat parallel. There, however, he distinguishes three basic types: rational-legal, traditional, and charismatic. In the case of rational-legal authority, authority is exercised by virtue of incumbency of office under a system of generalized rules. The sources of legitimacy do not lie in the personal prestige of the individual but in the authority of the rules under which he holds office. By the same token, its scope is limited to that which is specifically authorized by the terms of the system of rules. There is a fundamental separation between the individual's sphere of official authority and that outside it, in which he is a private individual. In a complex system such authority tends to be organized hierarchically, with a system of higher and lower authorities, each specifically limited by the terms defining the official role. This type is closely integrated with the property system and the monetary economy, in that there is a rigid distinction between property over which the individual has control in his official capacity—that Weber calls the "means of administration"—and the private income and possessions of the individual. Similarly, the ideal form of remuneration is fixed money salary in such a way that the organization has no control of the specific channels of expenditure.

In the case of traditional authority, authority is not exercised by virtue of an office but of a traditionally sanctioned status. This status is defined in terms of a traditional order which both legitimizes the assumption of authority and, in certain respects, defines its scope. But outside the provisions of the traditional order there is a sphere of arbitrary will in which the individual exercises authority by virtue of his personal prestige and status. There is no clear separation of the sphere of office and the capacity of the incumbent as an individual. Nor does there tend to be a clear segregation between means of administration and personal property. Provision both for expenses of the function and for personal expenditure are met from benefices—that is, handing over to the individual property rights in sources of income over which the organization has command. Just as rational-legal authority is closely correlated with the formal rationality of economic life, so is traditional authority unfavorable to it and correlated to a traditionalized economic order, with a limitation both on full private property in goods and on personal freedom, at least for the more dependent elements of the population.

The third category is that of charismatic authority. This Weber defines as not a form of stable routine organization at all but as a pattern taken by movements of change as such. The charismatic leader claims legitimacy for his demands upon other people by virtue of a personal authority which is in specific conflict with any established order; this is neither an office nor a traditional legitimized status but is, in some respects, in overt conflict with either or both. In contrast to the other two, the charismatic leader claims obedience as a matter of personal devotion to him and his cause. There is, again, no clear separation between his sphere of office and that of private life, or between official property and private resources.

Charismatic authority is not, like the others, linked to a specific form of economic organization, because Weber treats economic organization as a phenomenon of settled routine. The effect of a charismatic movement is to upset whatever settled economic conditions exist; but, like any other social movement, it is bound to economic conditions, and this forms one of many fundamental reasons why the charismatic phase is inherently temporary. There are two typical forms of charismatic provision with means—gifts and booty, that is, resources acquired by coercive methods, whether by force or not. But, once the position of authority becomes established, these must be transformed into regular sources of income which take the form of acquiring segregated property or of granting benefices in the traditional form. According to circumstances, the authority structure of the charismatic movement may change in either a traditional or a rational-legal direction.

This scheme of comparative institutional analysis is by no means complete in Weber's work but nonetheless forms a set of tools of analysis which fits into his generalized analysis of social action and has also been built up in the direct treatment of empirical problems of very wide scope. In a sense in which it has rarely been attempted or even partially achieved, Weber undertook to diagnose certain of the basic institutional features of the social situation of the modern Western world in terms of a comparative perspective of exceedingly broad scope. His emphasis throughout was on the uniqueness and the relative instability of the most important institutional features of our society. It is a diagnosis which, in many respects, has been verified by events since his death and is one of the most impressive demonstrations of the power of careful logical discrimination, combined with extensive and accurate empirical knowledge, in understanding social phenomena on a grand scale.

BIBLIOGRAPHY

A. WORKS OF WEBER

Essays on Sociology. Translated and edited by H. H. GERTH and C. WRIGHT MILLS. New York, 1946.

General Economic History. Translated by F. H. KNIGHT. London: George Allen & Unwin, Ltd., 1927.

Gesammelte Aufsätze zur Religionssoziologie. 3 vols. Tübingen: J. C. B. Mohr (P. Siebeck), 1920–21.

Gesammelte Aufsätze zur Sozial- und Wirtschaftsgeschichte. Tübingen: J. C. B. Mohr (P. Siebeck), 1924.

Gesammelte Aufsätze zur Soziologie und Sozialpolitik. Tübingen: J. C. B. Mohr (P. Siebeck), 1924.

Gesammelte Aufsätze zur Wissenschaftslehre. Tübingen: J. C. B. Mohr (P. Siebeck), 1922.

Gesammelte politische Schriften. Munich: Drei Masken Verlag, 1921.

Grundriss der Sozialökonomik, Part III: *Wirtschaft und Gesellschaft.* 2 vols. Tübingen: J. C. B. Mohr (P. Siebeck), 1925.

The Protestant Ethic and the Spirit of Capitalism. Translated by TALCOTT PARSONS. London: George Allen & Unwin, Ltd., 1930.

The Theory of Social and Economic Organization. Translated by TALCOTT PARSONS. London: Hodge & Co., Ltd. New York, 1947.

Wirtschaftsgeschichte. Edited by S. HELLMAN and M. PALYI. Munich: Duncker & Humblot, 1923.

B. SECONDARY SOURCES

ABEL, THEODORE F. *Systematic Sociology in Germany.* ("Studies in History, Economics, and Public Law," edited by the FACULTY OF POLITICAL SCIENCE OF COLUMBIA UNIVERSITY, No. 310 [New York: Columbia University Press, 1929].)

BARKER, ERNEST. *Church, State, and Study.* London: Methuen & Co., Ltd., 1930.

BENNION, L. L. *Max Weber's Methodology.* Dissertation, University of Strasbourg. Paris: Les Presses modernes, 1933.

FREYER, HANS. *Soziologie als Wirklichkeitswissenschaft.* Leipzig: B. G. Teubner, 1930.

HALBWACHS, MAURICE. "Max Weber, un homme, une œuvre," *Annales d'histoire économique et sociale,* I (January, 1929), 81–88.

——— "Les Origines puritaines du capitalisme moderne," *Revue d'histoire et philosophie réligieuses,* V (1925), 132–34.

JASPERS, KARL. *Max Weber: Deutsches Wesen im politischen Denken, im Forschen und Philosophieren.* Oldenburg: G. Stalling, 1932.

MERTON, R. K. *Science and Society in Seventeenth Century England.* ("Osiris: History of Science Monographs," Vol. IV, edited by GEORGE SARTON [Cambridge, Mass.].)

MISES, L. VON. "Soziologie und Geschichte," *Archiv für Sozialwissenschaft und Sozialpolitik,* LXI (1929), 465–512 (on Weber, pp. 470–97).

PARSONS, TALCOTT. "H. M. Robertson on Max Weber and His School," *Journal of Political Economy,* XLIII (1935), 688–96.

ROBERTSON, HECTOR M. *Aspects of the Rise of Economic Individualism: A Criticism of Max Weber and His School.* Cambridge, England: At the University Press (John Wilson & Son, Inc.), 1933.

SALOMON, ALBERT. "Max Weber's Methodology," *Social Research,* XI (1934), 147–68.

———. "Max Weber's Political Ideas," *ibid.,* II (1935), 368–84.

———. "Max Weber's Sociology," *ibid.,* pp. 60–73.

SCHELTING, ALEXANDER VON. "Die logische Theorie der historischen Kulturwissenschaften von Max Weber und im besonderen sein Begriff des Idealtypus," *Archiv für Sozialwissenschaft und Sozialpolitik.*

———. *Max Weber's Wissenschaftslehre.* Tübingen: J. C. B. Mohr (P. Siebeck), 1934.

SCHÜTZ, ALFRED. *Der sinnhafte Aufbau der sozialen Welt.* Vienna: Julius Springer, 1932.

SPANN, OTTMAR. *Tote und lebendige Wissenschaft.* 2d ed. Jena: Gustav Fischer, 1925.

TAWNEY, RICHARD H. *Religion and the Rise of Capitalism.* New York: Harcourt, Brace & Co., 1926. 2d ed., 1929.

TROELTSCH, ERNST. "Max Weber," in his *Deutscher Geist und Westeuropa.* Tübingen: J. C. B. Mohr (P. Siebeck), 1925.

TROELTSCH, ERNST. *The Social Teaching of the Christian Churches.* Translated by OLIVE WYON. 2 vols. New York: Macmillan Co., 1931.

WEBER, MARIANNE. *Max Weber: Ein Lebensbild.* Tübingen: J. C. B. Mohr (P. Siebeck), 1926.

NOTES

1. On Weber's life see the excellent biography by his widow, Marianne Weber, *Max Weber: Ein Lebensbild.* This also contains a complete bibliography of his writings.

2. *Gesammelte Aufsätze zur Religionssoziologie* (3 vols.; Tübingen, 1920–21).

3. Containing a revision of the essay on the Protestant Ethic, some introductory and interstitial material, and the study of Confucianism and Taoism.

4. Containing, respectively, the studies of Hinduism and Buddhism and Ancient Judaism.

5. Weber himself was always careful to point out that this did not imply that a given norm was considered binding by the observer. He left room for an important range of cultural relativity, which was yet consistent with the view that action was best understood in terms of orientation to normative patterns, whatever their particular content happened to be in a given case.

6. See the Introduction to the author's translation of Part I of *Wirtschaft und Gesellschaft.*

7. Cf. the author's article, "The Role of Ideas in Social Action," *American Sociological Review,* October, 1938.

8. Soon to appear in English translation under the title "The Theory of Social and Economic Organization," translated by A. M. Henderson and Talcott Parsons, and to be published by Hodge & Co., Ltd., London, and Oxford University Press, New York.

9. In the author's *Structure of Social Action* (New York: McGraw-Hill Book Co., 1937), chap. xvii.

CHAPTER XIV

THE SOCIOLOGY OF RELIGION
OF ERNST TROELTSCH

J. Milton Yinger, *Ohio Wesleyan University*

I. TROELTSCH'S TRAINING, INTERESTS, AND WRITINGS

ERNST TROELTSCH was born in Augsburg in 1865, the son of a physician and ardent scientist, who hoped his son would study medicine. With that in view, he introduced him at an early age to the natural sciences; but Troeltsch's preferences moved toward history, philosophy, and religion. As a student of philosophy he came under the direction of Gustav Class, who introduced him to the Kantian tradition, to Hegel, Fichte, and Schleiermacher. Troeltsch was also influenced by Lotze and by the work of his teachers, Harnack, Ritschl, and Lagarde.

He began his teaching career as a lecturer in Göttingen in 1891; after a year he moved to Bonn as professor of theology, 1892–94; and then to Heidelberg, where he taught for twenty-one years. In 1915 he became professor of philosophy at Berlin. He concerned himself there not only with teaching but with politics, was elected to the Prussian Diet in 1919, and served as parliamentary undersecretary to the Prussian minister of education. He died in 1923.[1]

Troeltsch's chief writings, extending over many years, have been published together in his *Gesammelte Schriften,*[2] Volumes I and III of which particularly have established him as a scholar of the first rank. Volume I, translated into English as *The Social Teaching of the Christian Churches,*[3] first appeared in German in 1912. It represents the fruits of many years of research and, it might be added, of invaluable association at Heidelberg with Max Weber, who was at least partially responsible for the shift of Troeltsch's main interest from theology to the philosophy and sociology of religion.

Volume III of the collected works, *Der Historismus und seine Probleme,* was first published in 1922. There is general agreement with

Mannheim's statement that this book "....belongs among the foremost contributions to the history of German philosophical ideas."[4] In it one finds the finest expression of Troeltsch's philosophy of history which, although it lies outside the subject of this paper, may be characterized briefly. It was strongly influenced by Dilthey. Troeltsch held that one cannot understand the life of the "human spirit" by the methods of natural science, for science is unable to reveal the unique and individual character of any event. The historian's understanding of a situation is different from the naturalist's precisely because he attempts to discover the individuality, the "quality" of a particular event, not to develop general laws of human behavior.[5]

Among Troeltsch's important writings one should also mention *Zur religiösen Lage, Religionsphilosophie und Ethik* (1913), *Aufsätze zur Geistesgeschichte und Religionssoziologie* (1925), which compromise Volumes II and IV of his collected works; and *Die Bedeutung des Protestantismus für die Entstehung der modernen Welt* (1906).[6]

II. THE SOCIOLOGICAL STUDY OF RELIGIONS AND THEIR EVOLUTION

As a sociologist of religion, Troeltsch continually posed this problem: To what extent are the various elements of a society conditioned by religious beliefs and organizations and to what extent are they entirely independent of such an influence; and, on the other hand, how far are religious beliefs an outgrowth of purely nonreligious factors, and how much do they have their own independent inner dialectic? In his search for an answer to this extremely difficult and tenuous problem, Troeltsch has brought together an amazing amount of historical detail, which allows him to see a situation in all its complexity. Unlike Weber, who also had at his command an enormous amount of empirical material but who, by means of "mental experiments," attempted to control certain interacting factors in order to focus on some specifically defined problem, Troeltsch, for the most part, sought to trace the whole range of interacting factors in order to discover the precise place of religious groups in the total setting.

In his masterful *The Social Teaching of the Christian Churches*, Troeltsch sets himself the task, as Mannheim says, "....of solving the problem of how far the origin, growth and modifications of Christianity as well as the arrest of that growth in modern times were sociologically determined."[7] But he also sought to discover the reciprocal influence of the churches on the other aspects of social organization. Thus, for example, after tracing the importance of many influences in shaping the medieval church, he says that we must now inquire "....to what extent the Christian ideal determined the social development of the Middle Ages after it had itself been effectively and even decisively influenced in its development of a social philosophy by the actual conditions of the life of the day."[8]

The primitive Christian movement was, Troeltsch declared, a purely religious upsurge, conditioned, to be sure, by the social crises of the time but focused not on the demand for reform and justice in this world but on equality before God. This does not mean, however, that the secular order was not affected by its appearance, for the Christian ethic has a dual impact: It contains not only this thoroughgoing religious asceticism, emphasizing the universalism of love, but also an ethical-prophetic strain, with a radical individualism. Although the former element is dominant, the latter is never eliminated and continues as a latent challenge to the existing order which comes to the fore in times of crisis. During the period of a unified church civilization, both elements were included in the church organization, the radical force being drained off, for the most part, into the monasteries. With the breakup of this unity, however, two distinct types of religious groups emerged: the churches (the successors to the religious world unity) and the sects (which contain the explosive elements). Troeltsch uses this distinction, the methodological importance of which was first suggested to him by Weber, to great advantage in analyzing the place of religious groups in the historical process. The analysis of religious organizations into sociological types is, in fact, crucial to an understanding of their various roles and in Troeltsch's work, even more than in Weber's, is of the utmost importance.[9]

As ideal types,[10] the church and the sect are thus described by Troeltsch: The church is built upon development and compromise; it accepts the secular order but claims universal dominion over it; it is mobile and adaptive. The church is the great educator; "it dominates the world and is therefore dominated by the world." The sect, on the other hand, is usually associated only with the lower classes; it stresses radicalism and literal obedience of the Synoptic Gospels; it has voluntary membership, is small, lacks continuity. The sect rejects compromise with the world and the church's conception of relative natural law.

It is lay religion, free from worldly authority, able therefore, on the one hand, to forget the world in asceticism or, on the other, to fight it in radicalism.[11]

The Social Teaching traces the history of the churches and sects up to the eighteenth century, when, as Troeltsch says, the church civilization was finally replaced by a secular order. The sociological analysis of religious groups is extended to the modern scene in *Protestantism and Progress,* which, although published earlier than the longer work, is a complement to it and attacks the same fundamental problems. In this essay Troeltsch attempts to analyze the complex interacting factors at work in contemporary civilization, to discover ".... how much the Modern Spirit actually owes to Protestantism." The author concludes that ".... Protestantism cannot be supposed to have directly paved the way for the modern world. On the contrary, it appears at first, in spite of all its great new ideas, as a revival and reinforcement of the ideal of authoritatively imposed Church-civilisation, of a complete reaction to medieval thinking, which sweeps away such beginnings of a free and secular civilisation as had already been toilsomely established."[12]

The impact of Protestantism on the modern world was ".... mainly in indirect and unconsciously produced effects, nay, even in accidental side-influences, or again in influences produced against its will....."[13] The indirect influence which has received most attention concerns the importance of Protestantism for the modern economic system. In his study Troeltsch was led inevitably to the problem which Weber had highlighted in *The Protestant Ethic and the Spirit of Capitalism.* There is no question, says Troeltsch, of Protestantism having created capitalism. Can one discover, however, in its economic ethic (especially in Calvinism) the kind of rigorous, this-worldly asceticism which indirectly (and generally against the will of its adherents) encourages the severely rational economic action which typifies modern capitalism? Troeltsch accepts, with some modifications, Weber's thesis that Calvinism was an important influence[14] in the early stages of capitalism:

> Weber has, in my opinion, completely proved his case; though perhaps it ought to be more strongly emphasized that the special character of Reformed asceticism was partly determined by the special conditions of the commercial situation in the Western countries, and more especially by the exclusion of Dissent from political life, with its opportunities and responsibilities, just as, on the other hand, the traditional Lutheran view became emphasized during the economic decline of Germany.[15]

This emphasis is a sharper criticism against Weber's thesis than Troeltsch seemed to realize, for Weber's point was precisely that, *in the beginning,* religious movements have importance for economic systems. Even Marx could agree that religious doctrines, after they have been selectively modified, reinforce the system which modified them. In another place, when Troeltsch says, "I would rate still higher the difference which *Weber* emphasizes between Calvin and Calvinism ....,"[16] he again underestimates the importance of his criticism of Weber, who did not stress the difference between Calvin and Calvinism nearly enough. These statements by Troeltsch require drastic modifications of Weber's thesis—and the present writer considers them to be necessary modifications—but Troeltsch was not fully enough aware of the sharpness of his criticism.

Having denied any direct and initiating power to Protestantism in creating capitalism and secularism, Troeltsch does not, however, consider it to be uninfluential in the contemporary world. He says:

.... We must not allow ourselves to be deceived by all the hostility to the churches and to Christianity, by all the naturalistic or aesthetic pantheism, which prevail at the present day. The present-day world does not live by logical consistency, any more than any other; spiritual forces can exercise a dominant influence even where they are avowedly opposed. Were it not for the religious Personalism which we have had ingrained into us by prophetism and Christianity, individual autonomy, the belief in progress , the all-embracing community of mental outlook, the indestructibility and strength of our confidence in life and of our impulse to work, would be impossible.[17]

The chief influence of Protestantism, however, the unique and immediate influence, is to be found, says Troeltsch, in the purely religious domain which is its central concern.[18] This point is in harmony with his insistence that religion has its own inner dialetic, an intrinsic element which cannot be reduced to other sociological factors.

III. APPRAISAL OF TROELTSCH'S SOCIOLOGICAL STUDY OF RELIGION

Troeltsch's importance for the development of a sociology of religion derives from his great ability to take into account so many of the interacting factors in a complex situation, an ability which enables him to escape a one-sided interpretation of any social movement. He had at his command a vast amount of historical detail, both through his own research and through a thorough acquaintance with the work of others in the field. His religious preconceptions were never denied, but, because he was explicitly aware of them, they did not condition his historical and sociological writings. Troeltsch's work, in fact, is an outstanding example of the possibility of scholarly research stimulated, rather than obscured, by judgments of value, provided only that one is thoroughly self-conscious in regard to those judgments.

The chief value of Troeltsch's work to the student of the sociology of religion, however, is that of a mine, not of a tool. His own work is a model of undogmatic and scholarly research and an invaluable source of information on the whole field of interaction of the Christian churches. But the questions he poses are more often historical than sociological. He asks himself: How must one describe the complete interaction which took place here? The sociological question—What does this situation reveal in regard to general laws of interaction between religious teachings and other life conditions?—is not his central concern. His elaboration of the church-sect dichotomy is a notable exception to this statement, for this has proved to be an important analytic tool for predicting the behavior of religious groups.[19] For the most part, however, Troeltsch is not concerned, as is Weber, with the development of a scientific methodology for the investigation of stated hypotheses. The importance of his work rests, rather, upon the exhaustive treatment that he has made of the complex history of Christianity—a complete and penetrating "intellectual history" which interprets the development of the church in terms of its total cultural setting.

NOTES

1. Cf. Albert Dietrich, "Ernst Troeltsch," *Deutsches biographisches Jahrbuch*, Vol. V: *Das Jahr 1923* (Berlin, 1930), 349–68.

2. Tübingen, 1912–25.

3. Translated by Olive Wyon (New York, 1931).

4. *The Encyclopaedia of the Social Sciences*, XV, 106. (It should be noted that this article seems to refer to Troeltsch's brief essays, *Der Historismus und seine Überwindung*, translated into English, by several authors, as *Christianity: Its History and Application* (London, 1923). This is probably an error, inasmuch as the more important work, *Der Historismus und seine Probleme*, is not mentioned). Dietrich says of this volume: ". . . . in the great definitive work of his life . . . . 'Historismus und seine Probleme' . . . . he has thrown a final and great illumination on German idealism and romanticism, from the point of view of the philosophy of history, of intellectual development and the dialectic, above all the work of Hegel" (*op. cit.*, pp. 357–58).

5. On Troeltsch's philosophy of history cf. Eugene Lyman, "Ernst Troeltsch's Philosophy of History," *Philosophical Review*, XLI (September, 1932), 443–65; H. E. Barnes and Howard Becker, *Social Thought from Lore to Science* (Boston, 1938), I, 767–68; and F. A. Christie, "Spiritual Values in the Work of Ernst Troeltsch," in *Methods in Social Science*, ed. Stuart A. Rice (Chicago, 1931), p. 416.

6. Translated into English by W. Montgomery under the title *Protestantism and Progress* (New York, 1912).

7. *Op. cit.,* p. 106.

8. Troeltsch, *The Social Teaching of the Christian Churches,* pp. 323–24.

9. Howard Becker has expanded the dichotomy of church sect into a fourfold classification—ecclesia, sect, denomination, cult—which is a valuable addition to the usefulness of the type concept as applied to religious groups (cf. Leopold von Wiese, *Systematic Sociology,* adapted and amplified by Howard Becker [New York, 1932], pp. 624–42). J. M. Yinger has also developed a more detailed classification in *Religion in the Struggle for Power* (Durham, 1946).

10. It is perhaps no longer necessary to say that an "ideal type" is not a "desirable type" but a conceptual tool, ideal only in the sense of not corresponding to empirical reality.

11. Cf. *The Social Teaching,* pp. 331–49.

12. *Protestantism and Progress,* pp. 85–86; on this point, cf. also Barnes and Becker, *op. cit.,* pp. 319–30.

13. *Protestantism and Progress,* p. 87.

14. Owing to frequent misunderstandings, one should perhaps stress the point that Weber, as well as Troeltsch, was thoroughly aware of the other very important influences in the development of capitalism. His only point was that Calvinism must also, along with economic and political factors, be given a place. It must be added, however, that he was careless, at some points, in his discussion of the interacting factors.

15. *Protestantism and Progress,* p. 138.

16. *The Social Teaching,* p. 894 n.

17. *Protestantism and Progress,* pp. 38–39.

18. Cf. also on this point A. C. McGiffert, *Protestant Thought before Kant* (New York, 1911).

19. Cf. H. Richard Niebuhr, *The Social Sources of Denominationalism* (New York, 1929), which, in addition to being an important work in its own right, has also made excellent use of Troeltsch's material and method. Cf. also Yinger, *op. cit.*

CHAPTER XV

THE SOCIAL AND ECONOMIC PHILOSOPHY OF WERNER SOMBART: THE SOCIOLOGY OF CAPITALISM

F. X. Sutton, *Society of Fellows, Harvard University*

I. SOMBART'S LIFE AND WRITINGS

WERNER SOMBART was born on January 19, 1863, at Ermsleben-am-Harz, a small town near Madgeburg. His ancestors were of French and Dutch origin, largely Calvinists. Anton Ludwig Sombart, his father, was a liberal, self-made landowner, who took an active part in the social and political affairs of his day, becoming a member of the Prussian Diet in 1861 and a member of the Reichstag in 1867. After 1875 he moved to Berlin, in order to devote the whole of his time to his political activities. The young Sombart was thus early transported from his rural life on his father's estates to the intellectual and cultural surroundings of the capital. Here he pursued his education until graduation from the University of Berlin in 1885, when his health induced him to seek the warmer climate of Italy. Two years were spent in Pisa preparing his dissertation, *Die Römische Campagna* (1888), a study of Italian agricultural conditions which reflected his father's intense concern with agricultural problems. Returning to Germany, he took his degree at the University of Berlin (1888), where he remained until his first academic appointment at Breslau in 1890.

During this early period of his life, Sombart was subjected to the impact of the social problems of late nineteenth-century Germany. While he never took the active part in politics that his father did, he did not hold aloof from the controversial issues of his day. His socialist sympathies early became known and acquired for him a considerable reputation. A series of lectures on socialism, given in 1896 at Zurich, were published in the same year under the title *Sozialismus und soziale Bewegung,* a work which went through many editions and was translated into more than twenty languages. This work established him as a sympathizer with the socialist movement and apparently satisfied all but extreme Marxists; indeed, he was regarded by many as a coming socialist leader. It seems very probable that this sympathy retarded his academic advancement; it was not until 1906 that he left the "exile" of Breslau to accept a post at the newly created Handelshochschule in Berlin. Only in 1917 was he finally called to the University of Berlin to fill the chair in economics vacated by Adolf Wagner.

After his dissertation was completed, Sombart turned his attention from agricultural problems to the wider problems of modern capitalism, which became his lifework. The first edition of his magnum opus, *Der moderne Kapitalismus,* was published in 1902 and was subjected to severe criticism, which stimulated him to a thoroughgoing revision of the work. A series of studies appeared during the next decade, which were in a sense preparatory, special studies for this revision. Important among these were *Die Juden und das Wirtschaftsleben* (1911), *Luxus und Kapitalismus* (1912), *Krieg und Kapitalismus* (1912), and *Der Bourgeois* (1913). Gathering together the fruits of these studies and a vast amount of other material, he published the second edition of *Der moderne Kapitalismus,* the first two sections appearing in 1916–17, the concluding section somewhat later, in 1927.[1]

Paralleling this lifelong preoccupation with the problems of modern capitalism was a continued interest in the problems of socialism. Through successive editions the treatise on socialism grew from the little booklet of 1896 to the pair of large volumes in the ninth edition of 1918. After World War I, Sombart underwent a definite change, revealed in the tenth edition of this work, which appeared under the new title *Der proletarische Sozialismus* (1924). The change of title was symbolic of a complete change of attitude, from one of sympathy with the movement to strong antipathy and bitter denunciation. From an admittedly "convinced Marxist" he had come to a bitter retraction of the beliefs for which he had given enormous effort and delayed his academic advancement. In 1934, with the publication of *Deutscher Sozialismus* (translated into English by K. F. Geiser, under the title *A New Social Philosophy*) the transition became complete in a pledge of allegiance to the new regime in Germany. Further evidence of Sombart's new trends under the Third Reich are to be found in the work *Vom Menschen* (1938), which is subtitled *Versuch einer geistwissenschaftlichen Anthropologie.* This work, an "anthropology" in a sense unfamiliar to American readers, is representative of considerable German literature which attempted to analyze the essential nature of man; it is a treatise more philosophic than scientific and certainly not free from Sombart's particular Weltanschauung.

One more important work remains to be mentioned. In various scattered articles and remarks in his works on capitalism, Sombart set forth his views on methodology; but it was not until his scientific work was essentially complete that he wrote extensively on the subject in his *Die drei nationalökonomien* (1929). This involved and difficult book has been the subject of much controversy because its frequent obscurity and the general diffuseness of Sombart's style in this work invite varied interpretations.

In all his work Sombart reveals a great erudition, and his writings speak of the energy necessary to its acquisition. He frequently expressed dislike for the heavy and unbending seriousness of German scholarly writing and offers in his own works a flowing and vigorous style which has been universally commended. Until his death on May 19, 1941, his prolific pen continued to add more items to a bibliography already of imposing length.[2]

II. SOMBART'S METHODOLOGY AND LEADING CONCEPTS

To those immersed in the traditions of Anglo-American thought the understanding of Sombart's work presents very considerable difficulties. While insisting that his work on modern capitalism is not merely historical but theoretical as well, he adopts a negative attitude toward the great bulk of classical economic theory and hence presumably utilizes some theoretical system of a different nature. To elucidate this theoretical background of his work it will be necessary to examine his views on the nature and methodology of economic research in some detail.

For Sombart the field of economic research is that range of concrete human activity which arises from the fact of environmental resistance to the satisfaction of human needs; as he is fond of saying, it is concerned with the fact that man must obtain the means of his subsistence by the sweat of his brow. The basic methods by which this range of phenomena may be studied are conceived to be three, namely, (1) the evaluative and metaphysical, (2) the natural scientific, and (3) the *geistwissenschaftlich*.

The first of these methods, exemplified by Aristotle, the Scholastics, Adam Mueller, Spann, and a host of others, is concerned less with detached analysis than with the formulation of doctrines as to how human economic activity should proceed. When this program is carried through to its ultimate implications, it inevitably leads into metaphysical or religious systems. The relativity and individuality of such systems make them objectionable, if we are seeking widely acceptable systems of valid knowledge about this or other ranges of empirical fact. Hence we must turn to the nonevaluative methods of study wherein this objectionable regression into metaphysics or theology may be avoided. Concerning the possibility of such a study of social phenomena independent of one's value-judgments, Sombart has written frequently, arguing stoutly in the affirmative.[3]

The other two methods of economic research, which Sombart calls the *ordnend* and the *verstehend,* correspond to his conception of a fundamental distinction between two classes of sciences, the natural sciences and the *Geistwissenschaften.*[4] This distinction, popularized by Rickert and Dilthey, is widely accepted in German social science.[5] It is conceived to involve distinctions of a logical, as well as of a substantive, order. For Sombart this takes the form of characterizing the method of the natural sciences as an "external" ordering of phenomena, ultimately to the end of forming laws of nature (*Naturgesetze*), which he apparently conceives as empirical generalizations. This method (*ordnend*), proper to the natural sciences and supposedly most typically found in their supreme representative, physics, may be applied to the data of the social sciences but is much less productive than a method proper to these data.[6] This, the so-called *verstehend* method, is described as a "grasping of meanings" (*Sinnerfassen*). The scientific study of phenomena by this method consists in relating them to a system of known relationships in such a way that they make sense in terms of this system.[7] It particularly demands the use of subjective categories. The contrast between the type of knowledge which we possess of the formation of wild geese flying and the orderly movement of a military parade is emphasized. The latter case is *verstehbar,* in that the subjects of the scientist's observation are in some sense like himself and may be assigned motives for acting as they do, these motives finding their place in a meaningful complex in the soldier's subjective experience.

In the former case no such ready penetration of the meaning of the formation seems possible.

While admitting the importance of such analysis for the interpretation of human action, it may be seriously contended that, logically, there are no grounds for concluding that the process of *Verstehen* (as Sombart formulates it) is foreign to the natural sciences. Such a conclusion, obviously most damaging to Sombart's position, is supported by the fact that the elaboration of complexes of meanings (*Sinnzusammenhängen*) is one of the most important products of the process of *Verstehen;* inasmuch as no place is left for the development of such systems by other means, we must conclude that mathematics falls under the rubric of the *Geistwissenschaften.* This Sombart explicitly admits.[8] Physics, utilizing mathematical systems, then seems paradoxically close to the *Geistwissenschaften.* In particular, it is difficult to see how Sombart can conceive classical mechanics to be a part of the natural sciences as he understands them, since it certainly does not consist of a body of empirical generalizations. The distinction thus seems to be clearly untenable.

This apparent misconception of the nature of the natural sciences would not entail serious consequences for the development of social science were it not coupled with an empiricist interpretation of the system of meanings to be developed by the *verstehend* method. It has been characteristic of much German economic thought that the abstractness of the great bulk of economic theory has not been recognized. Interpreting the "laws" of economic theory as purporting to be determinant of concrete action, this tradition has rejected them both on the ground of empirical inadequacies and on the philosophic ground of the supposed rigorous subjection of human action to general laws. This methodological difficulty has been described by Professor Talcott Parsons as "idealistic empiricism."[9] It has the expected consequences in Sombart's work.

He begins by emphasizing the organic character of any system of meanings, hence the essential uniqueness of any complex system. This does not mean that a *verstehend* economics must be devoid of "laws" but that these can only be internal to a given system or purely formal characteristic of such systems in general. The so-called "laws of orthodox theoretical economics" have a heuristic value as aids to the process of *Verstehen* but are accorded the status of fictions. Clearly, from the empiricist standpoint, this view of the fictional character of these laws is inevitable. They are not admitted to the respectable status of scientific laws, whatever their heuristic worth. Moreover, they are applicable only within a given system of meanings.[10] Thus he is led to the curious position that classical economics is applicable in this sense only to the capitalistic system, not because of restricted empirical adequacy but because of logical necessity. This fictional status is assigned to rational schema in general, wherein the implications of completely rational action on the part of given actors are traced out; they are a scaffolding and no part of the final building. This does not, of course, exclude rationality as an important distinguishing characteristic of economic systems.

The contrast between the types of knowledge of human action that one can obtain, admitting the accessibility of the subjective aspect and the "externality" of knowledge concerning nonhuman objects, leads Sombart to the conception that this former type of knowledge is ultimate—is knowledge of the essence of things. "Behind the phenomena that we 'understand' there is nothing."[11] This dubious epistemological proposition leads to the position that the fundamental conceptions used in the formulation of a *verstehend* social theory are not arbitrary in any sense but are determined through the character of the phenomena in hand. It is not through mere convenience or adequacy for explanation that the fundamental concepts are chosen; they are forced upon the scientist by their very ultimateness. Sombart has noted in several places[12] the precarious position of the *Geistwissenschaften* between the natural sciences, on the one hand, and metaphysics, on the other; the tendency of the whole system to depart from the canons of general scientific methodology into metaphysics should be evident from this view of the role of general theoretical concepts. While certain basic metaphysical assumptions are necessary to any scientific research, it may be said that in Sombart's formulation of the *verstehend* method there is an objectionable intrusion of unnecessary metaphysics.

The implications of such a general position for an attack on the problems presented by modern capitalism should be reasonably clear. Insofar as it represents self-conscious use of theory, it will not be an application of general theoretical systems, such as, for example, one makes of the classical mechanics in studying the solar system. Sombart is emphatic that his treatment of capitalism is both theoretical and historical,[13] but enough has been said to show that the "theory" involved does not, in his conception at least, transcend the particular economic system which is under consideration. It involves essentially a tracing-out of the possibilities, probabilities, and "necessities" in a given economic system.[14] Always theory is to be subordinated in importance to the understanding of the particular historical individual under consideration. Sombart's interest is not in developing a general analytical social theory; for him only so much theory should be developed as is of apparent use in the study of particular economic systems.

From his earliest days, Sombart rejected the sharp separation of theory and empirical research represented in the famous *Methodenstreit* between Schmoller and Menger. While a student at Berlin, he divided his attention between Wagner and Schmoller, the local representatives of the controversy, and continued throughout his later life to proclaim the necessity of a union of theory and empirical study. What he brought forth from his union we may observe in his study of modern capitalism.

III. THE NATURE AND EVOLUTION OF CAPITALISM

Capitalism, for Sombart, is a unique historical phenomenon, a particular economic system. While it characterizes a particular period in the development of Western civilization, it is not merely the totality of "economic life" during this period. Nor is it conceived as a particular step in the process of economic or, more generally, social evolution. Unlike Weber, Sombart does not regard capitalism as of more general occurrence than is the case in the modern Western world; the emphasis is on the individuality and peculiarity of the system.

The study of this unique historical phenomenon has been Sombart's lifework and is represented most fully in the large volumes of *Der moderne Kapitalismus*. This work falls roughly into three parts. The first is concerned with setting the background for the emergence of modern capitalism in depicting two contrasting economic systems, the self-sufficient (*Eigenwirtschaft*) and the handicraft systems; the second treats the early stages of the capitalistic system; and the third, capitalism in full bloom.

Essential to any economic system are three elements: (1) a system of economic value-attitudes (*Wirtschaftsgesinnung*), i.e., a set of basic goals and rules of economic conduct; (2) an economic order given in some objective organization of economically significant activity; and (3) a technique. Each economic system is characterized by a particular form and combination of these elements. The key differences between the possible forms of the *Wirtschaftsgesinnung* are those between the principle of satisfaction of relatively fixed needs (*Bedarfsdeckungs-prinzip*) and the principle of unlimited acquisition (*Erwerbsprinzip*), on the one hand, and that between traditionalism and rationalism, on the other.[15] The former elements in these pairs characterize the pre-capitalistic forms of economic activity. In these systems, economic activity is directly tied to obtaining the means for satisfying stable, traditional needs. In this aspect of the system, there is no significant distinction between the self-sustaining economy and the handicraft economy. Such distinctions as exist must be sought in the organization of economic life. The self-sustaining economy, characterized by the villages and manors of the Middle Ages, was gradually supplanted in the thirteenth and fourteenth centuries by the development of exchange in many branches of economic life. This development, stimulated by the increase in the supply of money and the growth of cities, resulted in the appearance of a new system—the handicraft economy. It was a distinct economic system but remained characterized by traditionalism and production for the satisfaction of existing needs. Like the earlier self-sustaining economy, its technology remains traditional, empirical, and largely bound to organic natural resources. In the late Middle Ages, according to Sombart, this was the dominant economic system, and it continued in control until the emergence of the capitalistic system. The similarity of these two systems is evident, and it is difficult to see why Sombart distinguished between them, apparently on the same level as he distinguished them from the capitalistic system. Perhaps his curious predilection for classification in triads is responsible.[16]

Against the earlier systems, the capitalistic system stands in sharp contrast. It is characterized as a system based on exchange, in which normally two different groups are involved: (1) the possessors of the means of production, who, at the same time, control the economic unit, and (2) the propertyless workers. These groups are bound together through the market. The economic spirit is that of unlimited acquisition (*Erwerbsprinzip*), and rationality is dominant economically and technologically.[17] This system first made its appearance in Italy in the thirteenth century and remained in faint beginnings for over two centuries. In the sixteenth and seventeenth centuries it definitely emerged in the form of early capitalism and passed into full-blown capitalism near the end of the latter century.

It is quickly apparent what is to become the central element for Sombart in characterizing this system. A new economic spirit had arisen, which was to create and characterize capitalism. In this new spirit there are two main elements, the spirit of enterprise and the bourgeois spirit. The former of these, the dynamic element, is the same restless Faustian spirit which has created the modern state, modern science, and technology. It is a spirit of unlimited worldly striving. Interwoven with this is the calculating bourgeois spirit, which provides the element of rationality.[18]

These contrasting economic systems which Sombart sets up do not correspond to clear-cut historical periods. In any given period characteristics of all three systems may be, and, indeed, are, present.[19] The empirical systems, thus dissected out, may exist simultaneously, differing in relative importance through successive stages of historical development. That period during which some part at least of economic activity is in recognizable conformity with a given system is called an "economic epoch." In any given period, there may or may not be effective dominance of any one system; thus in the period of early capitalism the capitalistic system had not arisen to sufficient prominence to give a characteristic stamp to the period, as it did later in the age of high capitalism. While Sombart's systems divide the historical development of Western economic life into radically distinct units, this does not imply a sharp division of concrete historical periods. Actually, between the periods of dominance of the various systems there is a shading-off of one into the other.

To the emergence of the capitalistic system, which for Sombart is the product of the capitalistic spirit,[20] certain conditions were necessary. Outstanding among these were the development of the modern state, certain technological advances, and the discovery of increased supplies of precious metals. The coincidence of these elements made possible the accumulation of wealth in cities, with a subsequent transformation of the demand for goods. The age of early capitalism thus ushered in bears many characteristics of the new capitalistic system but also involves a considerable heritage from the previous system. The new spirit of enterprise, directed toward profit alone, slowly makes its appearance. The beginnings of modern double-entry bookkeeping make possible an accurate accounting of profits and losses and encourage the separation of the funds of business enterprise from private funds. New forms of business association develop, which increase the depersonalization of economic activity. Technology moves from its traditional ways but remains empirical, i.e., based on rules discovered through experience and deprived of the rational understanding that science was later to supply. The formation of demand still rests with the ultimate consumers, but harbingers of the formative influence of capitalistic enterprise appear.

Conditions hampering the full development of capitalism are still, however, in evidence.[21] The drive to unlimited acquisition was not yet fully evident, and the tendency to abandon business enterprise to become inactive landowners dissipated the forces aiming toward high capitalism. In addition, there were political and religious restrictions, technical inadequacies, and the fortuitous adversities of war and pestilence. Indeed, the exhaustion of the wood supply threatened the whole development.[22] It was not until the latter half of the eighteenth century that conditions necessary to the full unfolding of capitalism were in evidence; after 1760 the age of high capitalism had begun.

In the age of high capitalism, which Sombart delimits by the first application of a coking process in 1760 and the outbreak of World War II in 1939, the capitalistic system was realized in a very notable degree and took its place as the clearly dominant economic system. The objectification of acquisition through the depersonalization of business enterprise gave the system its mechanical compulsive character, which Marx, before Sombart, had stressed. The growth of credit structures released the energies of impecunious enterprising spirits like Solvay, Rathenau, and Ford. Rationality, already gained on an empirical level in technology, was immensely furthered by the wedding of science and technology; this same rational spirit pervades the whole system. In short, the conditions which had fettered the capitalistic spirit fell away, and it attained to full expression, patterning economic life in its own image.

This brief sketch gives only the barest account of a vast canvas on which Sombart has lavished enormous energy and erudition. It is, of course, impossible here to criticize the work in detail, but certain aspects of it may be noted in their importance for the problems of general sociology and the particular problem of modern capitalism.

We have seen that the spirit of capitalism stands at the center of Sombart's scheme; he states quite simply that it has created capitalism. The status of this spirit, for all its central importance, is not completely clear. In one aspect, it seems clearly related to the *Wirtschaftsgesinnung* and thus may be interpreted as a complex of value-elements.[23] The realization of the spirit of capitalism may then be interpreted as the effective patterning of action in terms of these value-elements. On the other hand, this realization comes to be closely identified with the realization of an "idea" of capitalism, much in the Hegelian fashion.

If we accept this latter conception in its most innocuous form, i.e., regard it as the emergence of a definite pattern in modern economic life, the reason for its close association with the realization of the spirit of capitalism in the former sense is not far to seek. For Sombart the driving forces in the development of any economic system and of capitalism in particular must be found in the value-attitudes of some group of actors in the system. This group of prime movers may change radically in the course of development of a system, as it did during the movement of capitalism from the early to the mature stages, but in some form it is always present. To the effective formation of economic activity in accordance with a particular spirit, certain situational conditions are necessary. We have had occasion to note some of these conditions. However crucial they may be, they remain necessary and not sufficient conditions. Sombart criticizes Marx on just this score. While he admits and, indeed, strongly emphasizes the compulsive power of the capitalistic system, it is so only after the capitalistic spirit has been sufficiently realized to permit the system to run under its own power. Technological development, increase in population, and the like are not in themselves capable of providing a dynamic element in the capitalistic system, any more than is the "reproductive tendency of capital," of which Marx made so much.

The emphasis for Sombart is thus on the value-elements in action rather than on the situational conditions—a placing of emphasis quite opposed to that common in the positivistic tradition. Since it has produced capitalism, Sombart concluded that this spirit must have preceded the development of the system. Whence, then, this all-important spirit of capitalism? Sombart can be said to give no satisfactory answer to this problem. In *Der Bourgeois* he argued that Weber's famous association of the spirit of capitalism with the Protestant ethic was unacceptable, but he offered nothing substantial in its place. We are left with a description of its embodiment in certain groups, but otherwise it hovers unexplained as a mysteriously potent force behind the development of capitalism.

Whatever the uncertainty of the provenance of this capitalistic spirit, its prominent position in Sombart's account of capitalism serves to emphasize the peculiarity of the system in a way which has been unfortunately neglected in much discussion of capitalism. In making the action of the capitalistic entrepreneur an expression of a unique spirit, he avoids the plaguing tendency to see acquisitiveness in our economic system as instinctively determined. Sombart inherited from Marx the insight that, whatever may be the ultimate aims of the capitalistic entrepreneur, he must make a profit as a necessary prerequisite to the attainment of these aims. The unlimited character of acquisitiveness in a capitalistic system, wherein the goal is not merely the attainment of an income appropriate to a given status but rather its maximization, is derived from two sources. One is the result of rationalization of business enterprise in money terms. The wide and indeterminate applicability of money profits as a means to further ends makes them particularly prone to take the character of unlimited desirability. Moreover, the dynamic spirit of enterprise, which is one major part of Sombart's capitalistic spirit, is expressed in a competitive preoccupation with business enterprise as a source of power and enhanced status through "success." In short, Sombart's position leads him to a recognition of what may be called the "institutionalization of self-interest" in the modern capitalistic system. His description of the progressive emancipation of capitalistic economic activity from considerations other than the maximization of profit is thoroughgoing and fascinating.[24] In particular, one sees clearly the progressive autonomy of modern capitalistic enterprise from involvement in any particularistic consideration of individuals.[25]

It may now be seriously questioned whether Sombart's emphasis on the peculiarity of the modern capitalistic system is justified. This splitting of the course of development of Western society into distinct units, each characterized by its own special spirit, has been a source of much criticism of Sombart's work. It seems unquestionable that this criticism is justified, inasmuch as he has gone too far in reacting from the Marxian conception of progressive development through necessarily related stages.

This can be seen most clearly in the treatment of technology. As noted above, the technologies of Sombart's systems possess special characteristics. The traditionalism of the precapitalistic era gives way to empirical rationality in the age of early capitalism and, finally, to scientific rationality in the age of high capitalism. Certainly, Sombart makes out a good case for the accuracy of these designations as empirical descriptions, but it seems much more satisfactory to regard the process roughly as one continuous development than as the expression of at least two distinct spirits.

Certain other features of Sombart's general scheme may possibly be traceable to polemical overcompensations. It has already been noted that his first two systems are not very clearly differentiated, notably in the all-important spirit. On the other hand, the periods of early capitalism and high capitalism are distinct in very important characteristics, notably in the role of the state and the character of technology; the spirit, while capitalistic in both cases, is described as "bound" in the one case and "free" in the other.[26] Sombart's strong reaction against those who would find the beginnings of capitalism in eighteenth-century English inventions and his consequent desire to exhibit typically capitalistic characteristics in previous periods may account for this delineation of the system. In any case there seems to be good reason for distinguishing two systems since the Middle Ages, rather than one.[27]

Sombart's ethical attitude toward the subject of his life's work is negative and pessimistic. For all of Marx's revolutionary antipathy to capitalism, Marx saw in it a necessary and proximate stage on the way to a better society. What for Marx should be honored as a mother, bearing a savior in her womb, becomes for Sombart a sterile monster, from which nothing can be expected. Man must seek salvation through other means than capitalism.

This antipathy has been fairly constant through Sombart's intellectual development, and hence it is not accurate to say, as sometimes has been done, that after World War I he transferred the source of all evils from capitalism to socialism and, in particular, Marxism. Nonetheless, after the first World War he abandoned a long-held sympathy for socialism and heaped much responsibility for the miseries of the world onto it. Essentially, it was a reaction similar to that against capitalism.[28] He found in the materialism of socialism the same inadequacies as he had found in the dehumanizing mechanical monster of capitalism. A transition took place, now grown familiar among intellectuals of our time, in which he became definitely religious and insistent on spiritual values. Coupled with this was a growing nationalism, which had begun with his patriotic wartime writings and maintained its strength during Germany's travail of the twenties. Against this background it is evident that his pledge of allegiance to the Third Reich in the *Deutscher Sozialismus* was not merely an accommodation to a new state of affairs. His renunciation of Marxian socialism contained therein is scarcely more complete than it is in the much earlier *Proletarische Sozialismus,* written under the Republic, a work in which he endeavored to show that none of the socialist leaders were true Germans. In *Deutscher Sozialismus,* "the eternal German spirit" replaces the spirit of capitalism as the dominant element in Sombart's thinking. The book is unquestionably a sincere presentation of the beliefs of Sombart, the man and the patriot. As such, we cannot here quarrel with him, except when he intimates that his discussion is within the bounds of science; such vagaries are difficult to accept from one who argued so stoutly for the *Wertfreiheit* of science.[29]

Fortunately, this dissatisfaction with capitalism and its social products did not keep Sombart from giving an objective account of its development. *Der moderne Kapitalismus* is a highly individual work, and, though its accuracy in detail has been attacked by historians, it stands as the most vivid and comprehensive picture of the growth of capitalism which we possess. In concentrating attention on capitalism, it does not do full justice to other equally distinctive features of the organization of economic activity in our society, notably those centering around the professions.[30] The tendency is thus to give capitalism too exclusive importance in characterizing modern Western economic life. Proper adjustment of perspective in this respect is one of the promising tasks for social scientists of our time.

IV. SOMBART AND GENERAL SOCIAL THEORY

In summary, we may briefly consider the significance of Sombart's work for social theory. His own conclusions as to the possibility and utility of general social theory we have seen to be negative. In general, his own work supports his contention for the type of theory he uses. The individuality of his system offers little encouragement to those convinced of the fruitfulness of comparative institutional studies. It may be that the organic complexity of a system like capitalism is so great that its emergent properties make it, in a high degree, incommensurable with other systems of possible use in comparative work. That this is not entirely the case may be argued from the patent fruitfulness of Weber's comparative studies in support of his thesis that the Protestant ethic was a necessary condition to the emergence of capitalism. Sombart's treatment of capitalism seems, further, to involve a personal element, akin to an artistic production, which makes it difficult for subsequent workers to add more than criticism or commentary. This is consonant with Sombart's conception of the nature of the *Geistwissenschaften*. In these sciences it is not possible for a generation of scholars to stand on the shoulders of their predecessors, as it is in the natural sciences. Understanding social systems for Sombart is not a matter of successive approximations to the goal of complete understanding but an irregular process, dependent on the appearance of individual genius. Whatever may be said for such a point of view on other grounds, it is unattractive to those preoccupied with the task of building a body of general theory in the social sciences. To these latter, whatever his own theory in the matter, Sombart's work offers much that is suggestive for this ambitious building. In this respect, we may apply to him his own remark on Taine: He was better than his theory.[31]

NOTES

1. A translation of *Der moderne Kapitalismus* by K. F. Geiser has been promised. A condensed form of this work has been published in English by F. L. Nussbaum, under the title *A History of the Economic Institutions of Europe* (New York, 1933). *Die Juden und das Wirtschaftsleben* and *Der Bourgeois* have been translated by M. Epstein under the respective titles *The Jews and Modern Capitalism* (London, 1913), and *The Quintessence of Capitalism* (London, 1915). The later work, *Deutscher Sozialismus,* has been translated by K. F. Geiser under the title *A New Social Philosophy* (Princeton, N.J., 1937).

2. Biographical material and a bibliography may be found in M. J. Plotnik, *Werner Sombart and His Type of Economics* (New York, 1937).

3. See *Die drei Nationalökonomien* (Munich, 1930), pp. 288–91. His position in these matters is similar to Weber's, with whom he participated in historic discussions of the problem. For Weber's position see Talcott Parsons, *Structure of Social Action* (New York, 1937), pp. 591–601.

4. *Die drei Nationalökonomien, passim.*

5. For a brief summary of this position as presented by Rickert and Dilthey see the article of Alexander Goldenweiser in H. E. Barnes, H. Becker, and F. B. Becker, *Contemporary Social Theory* (New York, 1940), pp. 93–109.

6. In particular, *Die drei Nationalökonomien,* pp. 125–37.

7. In no place does Sombart give a clear statement of his position (see *ibid.,* chap. xiii, "Das Verstehen").

8. *Ibid.,* pp. 174–75.

9. Parsons, *op. cit.*, pp. 476–77. My debt to Professor Parsons in all these matters is profound (see also the paper in Barnes, Becker, and Becker, *op. cit.*, pp. 620–27).

10. *Die drei Nationalökonomien*, p. 301.

11. *Ibid.*, p. 196.

12. See, e.g., *Vom Menschen*, p. xxi.

13. *Der moderne Kapitalismus*, I, xi–xii. All references are to the 2d ed.

14. *Die drein Nationalökonomien*, pp. 299–300.

15. *Der moderne Kapitalismus*, I, 13 ff.

16. This tendency is especially marked in *Die drei Nationalökonomien*, which is literally a hierarchy of triads and strongly suggests artificial organization.

17. *Der moderne Kapitalismus* I. 319.

18. *Ibid.*, pp. 327 ff.

19. See, e.g., *ibid.*, III, 951 ff., where he traces the persistence of the self-sustaining and handicraft economies into the heyday of capitalism.

20. *Ibid.*, I, 329.

21. *Ibid.*, II, 1111 ff.

22. *Ibid.*, pp. 1137 ff.

23. For this aspect see especially *Der Bourgeois*, pp. 441 ff.

24. Especially *Der moderne Kapitalismus*, II, 99–173.

25. These matters are discussed in T. Parsons, "Capitalism in Recent German Literature," *Journal of Political Economy* (1928), XXXVI, 641–61.

26. *Der Bourgeois*, p. 461.

27. Parsons, "Capitalism," pp. 656–58.

28. See R. Michels, *Bedeutende Männer* (Leipzig, 1927), pp. 140 ff.

29. For a highly critical appraisal of *Deutscher Sozialismus*, see Paul K. Crosser, "Werner Sombart's Philosophy of National-Socialism," *Journal of Social Philosophy*, April, 1941, pp. 263 ff.

30. See Talcott Parsons, "Professions and Social Structure," *Social Forces*, XVII (1939), 457–67.

31. *Vom Menschen*, p. 98.

CHAPTER XVI

THE SOCIOLOGICAL DOCTRINES OF FRANZ OPPENHEIMER: AN AGRARIAN PHILOSOPHY OF HISTORY AND SOCIAL REFORM

PAUL HONIGSHEIM, *Michigan State College*

I. OPPENHEIMER'S LIFE AND THE MAIN CURRENTS OF THOUGHT IN GERMANY AT THAT TIME

THE problems raised by Oppenheimer and the answers that he gives are, to a large extent, conditioned by the socioeconomico-political and intellectual trends in Germany before the first World War and by his own personal experiences. Therefore, an introductory consideration of these two, so far as they have influenced his system, is indispensable.

In pre-war Germany the Junker class of eastern Germany had a virtual monopoly on the leading positions in administration and in the army. They were owners of baronial estates, dependent on the labor of very poorly paid agricultural workers, partly seasonal workers of Polish origin. They treated the relatively few middle-class farmers living near their estates as dependent clients. As a result, the younger sons of these middle-class farmers and, to an even greater degree, the agricultural workers themselves migrated to the cities, where they swelled the numbers of industrial workers until the supply exceeded the demand to such an extent that there was no alternative for them but to accept the wages and working hours imposed by the ascendant class of industrialists. There they lived in rookeries owned by middle-class citizens with moderate liberal views. They also organized themselves into moderate socialist or Catholic labor unions.

The intellectual life of that epoch was characterized by a decrease in the importance of religion and the restriction of philosophy to the history of philosophy, experimental psychology, and epistemology—with a few exceptions, such as Driesch, Husserl, Scheler, and Nelson. In the field of epistemology a position of primary importance was held by the so-called "Neo-Kantian school," represented by Jellinek, Rickert, Max Weber, and Troeltsch, who worked on the problems raised by their assumption of a qualitative difference existing between statements of fact and value-judgments and between history and the natural sciences. On the other hand, the prestige of the natural sciences was at that time so great that the demand was raised for other sciences to adopt their methods. This actually took place, for example, in anthropology, which spread the doctrine of the parallel development of the social and cultural phenomena in all parts of the world—conceived by Adolf Bastian and his followers in an optimistic sense of progress, but in a pessimistic sense by Gumplowicz, who saw only cyclical periods without progress and the perpetual use of violence which accomplished nothing permanent. A movement of protest against these ideas as being mechanistic appeared only later, at the beginning of the twentieth century; the protest came from the anthropologists, in the rediscovery of the Mother-right theory of the forgotten Romantic mysticist, Bachofen, and in the emphasis given to diffusion and migration in primitive civilization by the schools of Gräbner and Father Schmidt. In opposition to these predominant tendencies in anthropology, the historical school of Ranke and Treitschke, which enjoyed tacit official recognition, dealt almost entirely with the foreign relations of great and powerful states, said to be under the exclusive direction of so-called great men, such as Bismarck. This school ridiculed anyone interested in hypotheses concerning the relation between history based on written sources, on the one hand, and prehistory and ethnology, on the other, or anyone interested in historical laws or comparative cultural and economic history. This other tendency found more response among Catholics and also among economists.

The economists were not much interested in pure theory or the use of deductive methods, in the manner of the so-called "classical" school, except for Adolf Wagner and the so-called "marginal-utility" school, the followers of the rediscovered Gossen; however, this group taught primarily in Austria. In spite of the fact that this group claimed to be liberal, the belief in pure laissez faire diminished; the demand for state interference could be heard on every side, especially from the so-called "historical" school of Schmoller, long tacitly recognized as the official school. They investigated socioeconomic history, primarily the history of urban handicraft and industry, and claimed to supply the scientific background for the political programs of state-supported welfare work. More or less independently of that dominant group or even in opposition to it, the history of the beginnings of horticulture and animal husbandry was investigated by Eduard Hahn; the history of the medieval co-operatives and their suppression through the reintroduction of Roman law, by Gierke; and the history of agriculture and rural social life, by Knapp, Meitzen, Gothein, Lamprecht, Von der Goltz, Max Weber, and the Austrian Catholic, Dopsch. Some of these were also sociologists.

There were a few other sociologists, as, for example, Tönnies, who was primarily responsible for working out the distinction between "community" (*Gemeinschaft*), conceived as the primary contact group, and society in the strict sense of the word (*Gesellschaft*), conceived as the secondary group, and who also analyzed the replacement of the former by the latter in modern times. These circles of sociologists, anthropologists, and economic historians studied the works of some foreign sociologists, such as Comte, Herbert Spencer, Ward, Giddings, Small, and Ross; but, generally speaking, sociology was a stranger in the German universities at that time. The universities also excluded the following school of socioeconomic theory: the decreasing numbers of Marxians under the leadership of Kautsky; the increasing numbers of so-called "Revisionists" under the leadership of Eduard Bernstein, who rejected Marxian economic determinism and recommended the use of parliamentarian methods and other practical means to improve the social and economic condition of the lower classes; a few so-called "liberal socialists," such as Dühring, who advocated, among other things, maintenance of private property and enterprise to some extent, going back, in part, to the Saint-Simonists and Proudhon; the so-called "land-nationalizers," such as Wehberg, Flürscheim, Hertzka, and Stamm, going back, in part, to Henry George and to some earlier English writers; and the few so-called "federalists," adherents of Constantin Frantz—a critic of Bismarck, who was almost completely unnoticed outside the circle of his immediate followers. This last group attached great importance to the political, economic, and cultural autonomy of professional, local, and provincial associations and of the various districts of Germany, such as Hanover, Bavaria, etc., and to the reunion with Austria.

Such were the main currents of thought in Germany when Franz Oppenheimer began to study. He was born on March 30, 1864, the son of a poor liberal Jewish rabbi in a suburb of Berlin. Having little chance, owing to his family background, of becoming a high-school teacher, much less a university professor, he studied medicine and for many years was a practicing physician in Berlin. Here he had occasion to become aware of the connection between the problems of disease and moral decline, on the one hand, and housing and ground rent, on the other. He, therefore, began to read socioeconomic literature and became personally acquainted with adherents of many of the above-mentioned movements. Dissatisfied with all of them, he felt himself obliged to seek the truth, first, by systematically studying economics. To this end he abandoned his medical practice and supported his wife and child by writing articles. His first books made him known in the scientific world, and in 1909 he became *Privatdozent* of economics at the University of Berlin, i.e., an unsalaried lecturer, receiving only the students' fees; he still had to support himself by his publications. During the first World War he was employed as economic counselor in the war office, and in 1919 he became *Ordinarius,* i.e., full professor, of sociology and economic theory at the University of Frankfurt, where he wrote down his system in much larger and more universal form than in his earlier books. In 1929 ill-health caused him to retire earlier than he was obliged by law, and he took up residence in one of the rural settlement co-operatives he had founded before the first World War in conformance with his own principles. After 1933 he was a guest lecturer, from time to time, in Paris, Palestine, and the United States of America.[1] His death occurred in Los Angeles, September 30, 1943.

II. OPPENHEIMER'S SYSTEM OF SOCIOLOGY

A. EPISTEMOLOGY AND THE SOCIAL AND PHILOSOPHICAL BASIS OF JUSTICE

Although the sciences, in so far as they are distinct from philosophy, have to be based on factual data and have to use inductive methods, it is, nevertheless, possible and also necessary to combine inductive with deductive methods.[2] It is in the so-called "general sciences" that the use of deductive methods is necessary. These are sciences of a class of phenomena, considered in its entirety. Such a science is possible, according to the theory of the Americans, Ward and Giddings, which Oppenheimer accepts, on one condition: The "general science" must deal with attributes of the class that are common to all of its subclasses and not with the particular attributes of any subclass.[3] Here, as in every special science, personal bias played a role, especially in evaluation, but it must, so far as possible, be eliminated.[4] In fact, not all evaluations are based on personal bias; there exist scientific evaluations which can be objectively justified.[5] Of course, there is a difference between statements of fact and value-judgments, but the latter need not be eliminated from all parts of the scientific system as radically as the Neo-Kantians require. Indeed, the limits within which their use is justifiable are different in each branch of science. We shall see in a moment how this affects sociology. The various branches of science are likewise different, not only with regard to their subject matter and type of procedure between the historian, on the one side, and the natural scientist, on the other, but also because the former does not therefore need to be limited, as Rickert demands, to the statement of the unique—that which occurs but once and does not come under general laws—for, on the one hand, the unique also can come under general laws, and, on the other hand, it is both possible and obligatory for the science of history to observe the regularities in recurrent phenomena.[6] It is on such statements of historical regularities, among other things, that sociology is based.

Sociology is one of the general sciences in the above-mentioned sense; it is not a natural science, nor is it a synthesis of all the social sciences; it is a new combination of the results of the investigation of society, considered as an organism, and of the social process; its investigations are made from a point of view different from that of psychology, anthropology, economics (and a number of other sciences), to all of which it is, nevertheless, related. It is necessary to investigate from a sociological point of view all the psychological, economic, juridical, and political phenomena of the past and the present.[7] On the basis of this material, sociology is able to form not only judgments in the form of statements of fact and general laws but also judgments of another character; for, society being an organism, its "normality" can be fixed with sufficient scientific exactitude, that is to say, it can be stated which social status is the normal one. By considerations based on the conclusions of both the social sciences and the philosophy of Right, the normal status of the social organism can be shown to be that status which is regulated and dominated by justice.[8] From history and social psychology we know how the sense of justice originated and developed. Just as there are in human nature, on the one hand, factors favoring conflicts and, on the other hand, instincts for mutual help, so there exists independently of these two—as the American sociologist Ross, in particular, has demonstrated—the sense of justice. The sense of justice is based neither on instincts nor on intellectual considerations about the rights of others, but it originates in the pressure brought to bear on conflicting persons or groups by third persons or groups, primarily not themselves concerned with the conflict in question.[9] But this and many similar statements of a sociopsychological character concern the origin, strength, and content of the sense of justice of a particular group; these are sociopsychological facts important in determining the methods whereby the social structure can be changed. But the essence and content of justice in itself will never be grasped in that way. It can be recognized, being in character identical with the essence and content of natural law, only by pure philosophical perception, following a deductive method and not depending on any factual data. Thus it must be conceived and defined as the limitation of the sphere of liberty of the individual, made necessary in practice by the reciprocal interaction of individuals. This limitation is so essential that, even where something valuable exists in a social situation, this value has to recede if it is in conflict with the demands of justice. Conformance to this principle, which is obligatory on all groups, especially institutionalized groups and, above all, the state, constitutes the realization of the ideal of justice.[10]

If we combine these two considerations, we arrive at the following conclusion: On the one hand, sociology is a general science based on the factual data obtained by the specialized sciences of anthropology, history, and psychology. On the other hand, on purely philosophical grounds, the normal status of the social organism is conceived as the status which is dominated by justice; the essence of a status in which justice is dominant is defined as one in which a limitation on the sphere of liberty of the individual is imposed by the reciprocal interaction of individuals. Thus sociology, having a knowledge of all kinds of society, past and present, is able to compare every known form of social structure with the norm, that is to say, with the status where justice is dominant. On the basis of such a comparison, it is able to make judgments about the deviation of any given social structure from the normal status of the social organism. This is the value-judgment which sociology is able to formulate and which we had in mind when we referred above to the possibility of value-judgments in sociology. Moreover, sociology, being based on factual data obtained by the sciences of anthropology, history, and psychology, is also able to formulate the following two kinds of judgment in the nature of statements of fact. In the first place, based on the knowledge of the particular causes of every particular case of deviation from the norm, sociology is able to establish the causal connection existing regularly between a factor A of social, economic, or political character and the form B of the deviation from the norm. Second, again on the basis of the factual data furnished by anthropology, history, and psychology, sociology is able to determine the means of a social, economic, and political character which have to be used in order to eliminate the causes of the deviation itself, and so to realize the normal status of the social organism.[11]

Since the ideal which has to be realized has, by virtue of the considerations outlined in the first section of our explanation of Oppenheimer's system, been recognized to be the society dominated by justice, we have to deal in Section B with the general causal laws which sociology has formulated, and, finally, in Section C with the practical implications of these laws, i.e., with the means which have to be used in order to realize the ideal—the society dominated by justice.

B. THE FUNDAMENTAL LAWS OF SOCIOLOGY

One of the fundamental pillars of Oppenheimer's system is the law of systematic uniformity in the origin and development of the state, state law, social classes, private property, monopoly, and surplus value. This law was put forward by Dühring, though the first suggestions of it go back to the Saint-Simonists and Proudhon. Its essential content is as follows: Economic activity consists not in the satisfaction of economic needs but in the attainment of any end through the use of economic means. But these are not the only, or even the most important, means of attaining an end.

In particular, where the social structure is involved, the means to a given end are often not exclusively or even primarily economic in character; there may be a simultaneous, or even exclusive, use of political means, such as territorial conquest and the subjugation of other peoples. This is, in fact, the way that primitive economic inequality arose, not as the theory of so-called "primitive accumulation" would have us believe. The theory of "primitive accumulation" was held by the adherents of the idea of natural law and natural rights; these doctrines were advanced by the Stoics in antiquity and in modern times by the thinkers of the eighteenth-century Enlightenment, by the liberals of the nineteenth century, by the "classical" school of economics, and even, in a disguised form, by Karl Marx. All these thinkers shared the following conception of the origin of economic inequality: In the prestate period, a relatively large measure of economic and social equality among the members of the same group existed. Then some were able to become wealthier than others. Thus they laid the foundation for the subsequent reduction of their former equals in the tribe to a condition of economic dependence on them. They were able to do so, according to the majority of the thinkers just mentioned, because they had greater intelligence and ability than their fellows; but according to Rousseau and Marx, because they were more cruel, fraudulent, and antisocial. Yet both these explanations are wrong; for in that period members of a tribe never used means of an economic character to obtain the social objective of having others work for them; rather, one group used the political means of conquering land and subjugating the inhabitants for the purpose of acquiring wealth based on the labor of others. The ruling class then introduced a uniform pattern of institutionalization to guarantee the permanence of the new social situation to which they had so long aspired—the state was founded and a system of laws established.[12]

But the most important and effective measure undertaken for the same purpose was the seizure of the land by this group and the denial of land to the rest, particularly to the subjugated peoples—in other words, the introduction of land monopoly. This is the universal background and cause of the development of all other monopolies, as well as class stratification and surplus value. This is shown by the following reasoning: Those who do not live by the labor of others must work the land in order to obtain the means of livelihood. But, given the existence of private landownership, the relatively few landowners do not need to alienate the land or the right of its usufruct just because the landless persons need access to the land. Therefore, the owners have a monopoly, and thus they have the opportunity to require a monopoly tribute. This is paid by the semidependent tenants in the form of rent; by the almost completely dependent rural workers in the form of money deducted from their wages and retained by the landlord; and by the completely dependent slaves in the form of the totality of the economic value of their labor minus the cost of their maintenance.[13]

The existence of land monopoly and of the resulting monopolies in all other departments of life has further social consequences. First, it follows from the preceding analysis that complete competition never did exist, since the monopolists have always occupied a privileged position. Second, since free competition never has existed, it can in no sense be considered as one, much less the only, cause of any social or economic phenomenon that has appeared since the prestate period or that still exists in the present. Third, because of the existence of land monopoly and other monopolies, there exists one kind of property which is not based on the proprietor's own labor, thus is not in conformance with natural law and justice and therefore is not justifiable—in contrast to property acquired by individual labor, which does conform to natural law and justice and therefore is justifiable.[14]

The consequences of the existence of land monopoly which have just been enumerated are important, but there are others as well. However, they are to be understood only in connection with a group of other laws of an economico-psychological character, which we must deal with first.

This second group of laws concerns the uniformity governing seemingly subjective valuations of economic goods. The assertion of the existence of this regularity is made possible by the theory of so-called "marginal utility" as developed by Gossen, but with a decided emphasis on its objectivistic side, in contradistinction to the subjectivism of some outstanding Austrian adherents of that school. Its main assertions, in so far as they concern Oppenheimer's sociological system, are as follows: The satisfaction derived from consumption decreases with each additional unit of a given commodity until it reaches zero or the point of satiety. From this psychological law of decreasing satisfaction there follows the law of decreasing economic value: Commodities are valued not on the basis of their general importance but in terms of small units in the available supply. All these units of a given commodity being alike, that unit which is set aside for use in the most important category of consumption is interchangeable with the unit set aside for the least important use, and an equal value must attach to both. Hence the effective use-value of any good decreases rapidly as the supply increases.

This and some similar general laws of an economico-psychological character were applied to the theory of wages, as well as to some other problems. Applied to the theory of wages, it led to the following formulation: The amount of the wage is determined by the value attached to the least useful worker whom it is necessary to employ in production, the enterprise in which he is employed being constituent of the sum total of production, even if it is the least important one.[15] This application of marginal utility to the theory of wages will become especially important when combined with two other theories: the first is the above-mentioned theory of the systematic uniformity in the origin and development of the state, private property, and land monopoly; the second is the fundamental law of the ratio between the quantity of emigrating rural population and the distribution of rural property. This law may be stated as follows: The quantity of emigrating rural population is in direct proportion to the amount of land owned by the landed gentry and organized in large estates but is in inverse proportion to the amount of land owned by peasants and worked by the peasant himself and his family. The truth of this law—first discovered by Von der Goltz —can be shown by the following considerations. Where the population is increasing, the profit rate of industrial products regularly rises, while that of agricultural products regularly falls. This phenomenon is compensated for by the emigration of rural population to the cities. This influx to the cities intensifies competition and brings down prices of industrial products. Simultaneously, the increased demand for rural products raises the prices of the latter. This is the general law.

However, this general law is subject to modifications, depending upon the special form of distribution of the rural property. Where the land is predominantly in the hands of peasant proprietors, the surplus income created by the rise of prices of the primary products is distributed among the entire population. The reason for this is that in that situation a reduction in the wages of the urban workers takes place simultaneously with a rise in the income of the rural producers. But, in a country where large estates owned by landed gentry predominate, the land monopolists, as explained above, are powerful enough to prevent a rise in the wages of the agricultural workers. It is particularly easy for them to do so if it is possible, as it was for the Junkers of eastern Germany, to import seasonal agricultural workers from foreign countries who are accustomed to a lower standard of living and the lowest possible wages. Thus the whole of the profit obtained from the increase in prices of primary products brought about by the decrease in prices of industrial products accrues to the holders of large estates in the form of increased ground rent. Under such circumstances the phenomenon observable in countries where peasant proprietors predominate fails to appear—that is to say, the simultaneous fall in the wages of the urban workers and rise in the income of the rural producers. Instead, another form of reaction against the economic pressures of the situation is worked out. The rural population emigrates in larger numbers than in the former case, though not large enough, and goes either to the industrial towns of their own country, where they become factory workers, or overseas, where they settle as pioneers or likewise become urban factory workers.

The difference in the distribution of landownership in the two cases —in the first case, among a large number of independent peasant proprietors and, in the second case, among a small number of landed gentry —is the cause of the difference in the amount of emigrating rural population.

Once this law is established, we are able to determine the cause of the increase in the supply of urban factory workers in excess of the demand, one of the factors bringing about the decline in the wages of this group. All the many earlier theories which attempted an explanation of this phenomenon are incorrect, for the explanation lies not, as is held by the classical school of economics from Malthus to Mill, in the overproduction of children among the working class. Neither does it lie, as is held by Karl Marx, in the displacement of workers by the machine; on the contrary, a great deal of emigration occurs often from countries and in periods in which no machinery was imported for use in rural districts, as in Ireland in the middle of the nineteenth century, which differs from other countries in this respect. Finally, the explanation does not lie in the overpopulation of the rural districts in question; on the contrary, emigration often occurs on a large scale from the less densely populated districts. Thus all these attempts at an explanation of the phenomenon under discussion—the increase in the supply of factory workers in excess of the demand as a causal factor in the decline in wages of the urban factory workers—are seen to be wrong. The true cause of this phenomenon and also of the migration from the rural districts to the city is the fact that the land is not in the hands of peasant proprietors but in those of owners of large estates, i.e., a land monopoly exists.

The coherence of this analysis will become especially evident if we combine Goltz's law of the ratio existing between the amount of emigrating rural population and the distribution of the different kinds of rural properties and forms of rural management with the special application of the marginal-utility theory to the theory of wages, which was discussed previously. According to the latter, as we saw above, the amount of the wage is determined by the value attached to the least useful worker whom it is necessary to employ in production, the enterprise in which he is employed being a necessary constituent of the sum total of production, even if it is the least important constituent.

By applying this general law to the special case of emigration from countries where large estates are the predominant form of rural property, we are justified in making the following inference: The lowest level of wages paid to the lowest type of agricultural worker on the least important establishments of the feudal landlords of eastern Europe—e.g., Russia, Rumania, Hungary, and eastern Germany—determines the amount of the existing supply of urban factory workers and is the cause of the excess of that supply over the demand. Consequently, it is the cause of the low wages paid to the urban factory workers, not only in the industrial countries of Europe but elsewhere also. A further consequence is, as explained above, the emigration of part of the rural workers not to the industrial towns of their own countries but overseas, where, in so far as pioneer farming is not open to them, they, too, become factory workers and thus form an essential element of the sweatshop labor in the overseas industrial centers. But the low wage level of the agricultural workers on the feudal estates of eastern Europe is the result of the existence of a land monopoly. This, in turn, is caused by the use of political means to obtain and maintain an unjustifiable kind of property. Thus land monopoly—this unjustifiable system of distribution and organization of landownership—is the ultimate cause of the existence of a proletariat and of the absence of justice, everywhere in the world, both in the present and in the past;[16] for the truth of this system —as was stated at the beginning of Section II—can likewise be proved by an anthropologico-historical survey of the course of human development.

In analyzing historical development and the relations existing between different historical phenomena, there are two considerations of a general character which we must bear in mind. First, it is possible for cultural gains to be lost, and interpretations of seemingly primitive phenomena must allow for this possibility. Second, all the similarities appearing in different parts of the world need not be interpreted as the result of independent parallel development exclusively, as attempted by the evolutionary school of Adolf Bastian and by Gumplowicz; or as a result of migration and diffusion exclusively, as attempted by Gräbner and by the diffusionistic school of Father Schmidt. In any particular case these two possibilities must be considered before a definite decision is reached.[17] In the light of these two considerations, the following conception of world history emerges:

Primitive hunters, likewise totemistic hunters, as well as neolithic horticulturists of the matrilinear type, lived in a state of relatively broad economic equality and, in particular, knew nothing of land monopoly, conquest, social classes, and private property.[18] The last three institutions were introduced in the Bronze Age by pastoral nomads. In addition to the original pastoral nomads, there were former horticulturists who had adopted the culture of the cattle-breeders with whom they had been in contact.[19] These nomads subjugated other groups with a culture similar to their own, as well as horticulturists of the neolithic type, forced them to work for their new rulers, and introduced the institutions of land monopoly and the state—in the area of the Andes, China, Hindustan, Mesopotamia, Egypt, and the Mediterranean countries.[20]

Confining ourselves henceforth to Occidental civilization, we find a particularly clear example in ancient Rome. There we see the results of the management of land not by peasant proprietors but by a landed aristocracy, who used slaves and farm tenants—viz., famine, proletarianization, depopulation, and ultimate destruction at the hands of the peoples of Germanic origin.[21] These Germanic tribes, like the Celts and, on the whole, the majority of the peoples of Indo-European language-group, were secondary herdsmen—i.e., they had adopted the way of life of pastoral nomads with whom they had been in contact. After conquering other Germanic tribes, they had developed into semi-feudal landlords over these conquered peoples; in the provinces of the Roman Empire they established states whose territory was divided into large landholdings.[22] In these states the condition of the peasants was not the same in all places and at all times; but from the eleventh century on, it became in some countries relatively tolerable. This was primarily due to the fact that the peasants were relatively independent and organized in associations of a co-operative character and because the payments to the landlords were made in kind and were of a relatively low and fixed amount. Hence, while formerly the peasant had to produce in his own home all the goods needed by himself and his family, such as clothes, he was now able to buy these at the markets in the cities, where they were produced by specialized urban handicraftsmen. Thus the economic and cultural flowering of the towns in the great period of medieval civilization depended to a large extent upon the prosperity of the peasant and his relatively large measure of independence from the feudal landlord.[23] Later the Slavic peoples of eastern Europe were subjected to political conquest, the land was divided into large estates, and the peasants were reduced to the position of serfs. A similar situation arose in some parts of central and western Europe. Simultaneously, Roman law was reintroduced, rural community life and co-operatives of a primary contact character disappeared and, with them, the economic basis not only of the cities but of medieval society as a whole.[24] The new absolutistic state took away from the feudality its predominance in some political spheres and replaced it by state employees, bureaucratically organized and receiving salaries not in kind but in money. Nevertheless, the absolutistic state was unable to remove the antagonism existing between the landed gentry and the peasant, and the French Revolution was the result of its failure to do so.[25] In spite of the important role in the nineteenth and twentieth centuries of new social forces, such as the industrialists and financiers, land monopoly still existed and continued to produce its inevitable effects, as we saw at the conclusion of our theoretical analysis.[26]

Thus this anthropologico-historical survey confirms the conclusions reached in the theoretical analysis, namely, the failure of the social organism to realize the ideal of justice and the reasons for that failure. In conformance with the plan developed at the end of our first section, sociology must now indicate the remedies to be applied in order to eliminate the disease and establish a society regulated by the principles of justice.

C. A PROGRAM OF SOCIAL REFORM

The co-operative satisfies all the conditions of a solution to the problem. But there are various types of co-operatives: Consumer co-operatives may be good, but they do not achieve the essential aim; urban producer co-operatives either become stock companies or collapse.[27]

The essential type is the rural producer co-operative, and its ideal form is the rural settlement producer co-operative. It has the following advantages over the urban industrial producer co-operative: It does not involve personal credit but credit on real estate mortgages. Its situation is that of the urban consumer and not that of the urban producer, for it does not and cannot have the urban producer's tendency to eliminate competitors from the market, and, on the other hand, it cannot itself be destroyed by a more powerful competitor, such as an industrial corporation or trust. Furthermore, the continuance of its prosperity does not depend upon the market price of one commodity or even of a few.

Last but not least, it is much easier in a rural producer co-operative than in an urban industrial one to maintain psychological harmony between the co-operative and its members and, simultaneously, among the latter themselves, without resort to coercion; for in the urban industrial co-operative the larger it grows and the more its membership increases, the greater is the necessity for bureaucratization and specialization of the mechanical work of each member, whereas in the rural co-operative, even if it increases in size, each member retains to some extent his economic individuality. Thus a maintenance of individualism in the collectivity is assured. Moreover, if, by the statutes governing landholdings, the individual right to sell and bequeath the allotment is granted by the co-operative, it surpasses in quantity and quality of its products all other kinds of rural management. In consequence of this superiority, the landed proprietor will not be able, in the long run, to compete with the co-operative, in spite of the low wages that he pays his hired workers, since these workers, for the very reason that their standard of living is low, are unwilling and unable to work intensively. In this situation the landed proprietor may be glad to sell his estate to a co-operative cheaply.

Moreover, every rural co-operative keeps more people in productive labor than any other kind of rural management. As a result, in spite of the fact that the individual's freedom of choosing his domicile remains untouched, migration to the industrial cities of the home country or overseas will fall off rapidly. Consequently, the possibility is opened that the supply of industrial workers will fall short of the demand; then the factory-owner will be obliged to pay as high wages as his enterprise can afford. This enables the factory worker to buy goods on the market, which is still maintained as a free institution; this, in turn, giving a further impetus to agricultural and industrial production. On the other hand, the power of the factory owner, like that of the landed proprietor, is continuously diminished in the process.[28] There will be a continuous shift of power in favor of the rural producer association and similar urban professional groups. The higher boards of the co-operative movement must be and will be formed on the basis of federal representation and co-operation between all component groups; the logical climax of the whole is the peaceful federation of all the co-operatives of the world. In such a world federation there would be a synthesis of individualism and collectivism, in which the peculiar genius of every nation would be absorbed.[29]

III. OPPENHEIMER'S DEBT TO PRECEDING THINKERS

We shall be able to determine Oppenheimer's place in the history of social thought if taking note of the indications that Oppenheimer himself gives as to the writers who influenced him, we compare the content of Section I with that of Section II, eliminating minor details and avoiding, as hitherto, any attempt at evaluation.[30] Oppenheimer accepted, without essential modification, the concept of "general science" of Ward and Giddings;[31] the theory of the origin of the state and private property of Dühring and Gumplowicz, which goes back in part to the Saint-Simonists and Proudhon;[32] the theory of primitive hunter economy, totemism, and matrilinear horticulture of Schmidt and Koppers;[33] the analysis of the social history of antiquity and the early Middle Ages of Max Weber, Dopsch, and Gierke;[34] and the concept of a federated social structure of Constantin Frantz.[35]

Oppenheimer accepted, but only with essential modifications or additions, the Neo-Kantian epistemological dichotomies of statements of fact and value-judgment, historical sciences and natural sciences;[36] Ross's theory of the sociopsychological foundation of the sense of justice, which he modified by reducing the importance of the intellectualistic factor;[37] the marginal-utility law, which he developed in a more objectivistic direction; the Goltz law, which he amplified by combining with it the theory that, in general, the amount of emigrating population does not depend on the density of the population; the theory held by a number of advocates of nationalization of the land that land monopoly is the ultimate cause of all other monopolies, to which he added new explanatory elements;[38] and, finally, elements of Schmidt and Koppers and of Eduard Hahn are combined in his subdivision of primitive pastoral culture into two types.[39]

In the philosophy of Right, Oppenheimer and Nelson both developed independently the definition of justice as the necessary limitation of the liberty of the individual.[40]

The following are Oppenheimer's own original doctrines, arrived at quite independently: Pure competition never existed and can, therefore, not be considered as the cause of any social phenomenon; the economic and social conditions of the rural areas of eastern Europe modify indirectly the economic and social condition of the urban industrial population of Europe and overseas; urban producer associations either fail altogether or else become joint stock companies; rural co-operatives follow a separate pattern of development; and the establishment of such rural co-operatives modifies indirectly all spheres of economic life. Equally original in the field of historical analysis is his conception of the Indo-European language-group of peoples, including the Celts and Germans, as secondary herdsmen; his conception of the independent social condition of the peasants in the great period of medieval civilization as the cause of the prosperity of the medieval town; his conception of the theory of so-called "primitive accumulation" as originating in the theory of natural law; and the inclusion of Marx in the tradition of this school of thought.

Finally, Oppenheimer's system represents a new synthesis, or at least a combination in a new form, of certain elements formerly considered incompatible or even diametrically opposed to one another. In economic theory he combines the inductive method of the "historical" school with the deductive method of the "classical" school; in social theory he combines a philosophy of Right with a sociologico-economic system; in anthropology he combines the theory of independent parallel development of Bastian and Gumplowicz with the diffusionist theory of Schmidt and Koppers.[41] He makes a synthesis of the history of preliterate epochs and the history based on written sources; of the history of agriculture and the history of urban civilization; of the marginal-utility theory, the Goltz law, and the theory of the origin of the state and of monopoly based on conquest; and, last but not least, of individualism and collectivism.

APPENDIX

To avoid misunderstanding, it may be added that the author of this chapter does not accept—among other theories of Oppenheimer—his concept of value-judgments, justice, primary and secondary herdsmen; of the relation existing between rural and urban life during the Middle Ages; of the dependence of all other monopolies on land monopoly; and of the unique importance of rural producer associations. On the other hand, he agrees completely with Oppenheimer on the differentiation of political and economic means, on the importance of pastoral nomadism, on the role of forcible conquest in the historical origin of the state and of land monopoly, and on the necessity of establishing a synthesis between individualism and collectivism in the economic field, and the need for a federated superstructure embracing different national states.

NOTES

1. The most important publications of Franz Oppenheimer are the following:

    1. *System der Soziologie,* Vols. I–IV (Jena, 1922–29). This is his chief work; Vol. II is an enlarged edition of the earlier book *Der Staat;* Vol. III, a new revised edition of the earlier book, *Theorie der reinen und politischen Oekonomie;* these two will therefore not be cited in their former separate editions. The *System* will be cited in the footnotes to this chapter by volume, indicated by Roman numerals, and page, without mention of the title. The pagination continues straight through the second part of each volume.
    2. *The State,* authorized translation by John M. Gitterman (Indianapolis, 1914). A translation of *Der Staat,* mentioned above; cited as *"State."*
    3. *Die Siedlungsgenossenschaft* (3d. ed.; Jena, 1922). A history and critique of earlier co-operatives and a program for building up rural settlement co-operatives; cited as *"Siedlung."*
    4. *Wege zur Gemeinschaft* (München, 1924). A collection of earlier articles: cited as *"Wege,"* after mention of the special title of each article.
    5. "Pseudoprobleme der Wirtschaftspolitik," *Die Wirtschaftswissenschaft nach dem Kriege: Festgabe für Lujo Brentano zum 80. Geburtstag* (München, 1925), I, 321–47. A history and critique of the so-called law of "primitive accumulation"; cited as "Pseudoprobleme."
    6. "Die Wanderung, vorwiegend vom universalhistorischen und ökonomischen Gesichtspunkte," *Verhandlungen des 6. Deutschen Soziologentages* (Tübingen, 1929), pp. 149–72. An application of the so-called "Goltz Law" to Oppenheimer's own theories; cited as "Wanderung."
    7. "Mein Wissenschaftlicher Weg," *Die Volkswirtschaftslehre der Gegenwart in Selbdarstellungen,* II (Leipzig, 1929), 69–116. An autobiography with bibliography, which, incidentally, has been used in the preceding survey of Oppenheimer's life.
    8. "Ein neues sozialistisches System der Rechtslehre und Politik," *Archiv für die Geschichte des Sozialismus und der Arbeiterbewegung,* XII (Leipzig, 1925), 69–114. An exposition and critique of Leonard Nelson's philosophy of Right; cited as "Rechtslehre."
    9. "Gesellschaft und Staat," *Archiv für Sozialwissenschaft und Sozialpolitik,* LVIII, No. 1 (Tübingen, 1927), 179–85. A polemical discussion of the terms "economic means," "political means," and some others; cited as "Gesellschaft."
    10. Vorwort—Preface to the German translation of Charles Gide and Charles Rist under the title *Geschichte der volkswirtschaftlichen Lehrmeinungen,* Deutsch

von R. W. Horn (Jena, 1913), pp. 13–18. An exposition of the importance and the methodology of the history of ideas; cited as "Vorwort."

11. Einführung—Introduction to Ludwig Gumplowicz, *Ausgewählte Werke* (Innsbruck, 1926), pp. vii–xxiv. An exposition of Oppenheimer's own relation to Gumplowicz and his concepts of violence, independent parallel development, and the theory of historical cycles; cited as "Einführung."

2. "Wanderung," p. 154; Vorwort, p. xvi.

3. I, 149.

4. I, 681–95; III, 159–61.

5. I, 435, 537; "Wissen und Werten," *Wege,* pp. 2–3.

6. I, 171, 182, n. 3.

7. I, xix, 445; II, 207 f.

8. "Rechtslehre," pp. 253 f.

9. I, 294–98.

10. "Rechtslehre," pp. 253 f.

11. "Wissen und Werten," *Wege,* pp. 2–4; "Pseudoprobleme," pp. 323 f.

12. II, 44–85, 212–50, 259–303, 323, and III, 46, 146–52; *State,* pp. 6–10, 15; Pseudoprobleme," pp. 333–42; "Gesellschaft," p. 184.

13. II, 278; *State,* p. 15; "Das Bodenmonopol," *Wege,* pp. 16 f.

14. II, 689; III, 409; *Siedlung,* pp. 261, 559 f.; "Physiologie und Pathologie des sozialen Körpers," *Wege, p.* 49.

15. III, 100–119; "Die soziale Bedeutung der Genossenschaft," *Wege,* pp. 66 f.

16. "Wanderung," pp. 147–60; *Siedlung,* p. 218; "Zur Geschichte und Theorie der landwirtschaftlichen Produktivgenossenschaft," *Wege,* p. 238; "Die soziale Bedeutung der Genossenschaft," *ibid.,* p. 67.

17. I, 769, 877 (n. 1), 1015.

18. IV, 1–8; *State,* pp. 28–33.

19. II, 264; IV, 10–25.

20. II, 308–546; IV, 8–62; *State,* pp. 33–228.

21. IV, 325–407; *State,* pp. 172 f.

22. IV, 137–44, 225–47, 294–325; *State,* pp. 209–12.

23. III, 153; *State,* p. 286; *Siedlung,* pp. 179 f.; "Die Utopie als Tatsache," *Wege,* pp. 497 f.

24. II, 537; *State,* p. 206; *Siedlung,* pp. 195–98; "Gemeineigentum und Privateigentum an Grund und Boden," *Wege,* p. 198.

25. II, 590–616; *State,* pp. 243–46.

26. III, 215 f., 549–55; *State,* pp. 282–84.

27. *Siedlung,* pp. 16, 22, 33, 89; "Die soziale Bedeutung der Genossenschaft," *Wege,* pp. 61 f.

28. I, 673–76; *Siedlung,* pp. 318 f., 362–69, 381, 517, 559; "Die soziale Bedeutung der Genossenschaft," *Wege,* pp. 76–83; "Gemeineigentum und Privateigentum an Grund und Boden," *ibid.,* p. 203; "Zur Geschichte und Theorie der landwirtschaftlichen Produktivgenossenschaft," *ibid.,* pp. 228, 239 f.

29. II, 793–811; "Rechtslehre," pp. 262, 266; "Einführung," pp. xxi f.

30. Citations of passages by or about Oppenheimer's predecessors are made only when relevant to an analysis of his indebtedness and originality. Where the original editions are not readily available, more recent selections are sometimes cited. For more detailed information on the general subject, the reader is referred to the following works: *"Encyclopaedia of the Social Sciences* (New York, 1930–35), especially the sections "Marginal Utility" and "Historical School" in the article "Economics"; *Handwörterbuch der Staatswissenschaften* (4th ed.; Jena, 1923–29), especially the articles "Bodenbesitzreform" and "Grenznutzen"; Harry Elmer Barnes and Howard Becker, *Social Thought from Lore to Science* (Boston, 1938), I, 716, 719–21, 726, 730, 741, 769–71, and II, 800, 830, 880, 921, 963–73, 976, 978, 983; Pitirim Sorokin, *Contemporary Sociological*

Theories (New York, 1928), pp. 353, 480 f., 491, 508–13, 640–42, 670–72; Charles A. Ellwood, *A History of Social Philosophy* (New York, 1938), pp. 481–88, 546–48; Charles Gide and Charles Rist, *A History of Economic Doctrines* (2d ed.; Boston, 1915), pp. 385–407, 521–28, 570–78; Lewis H. Haney, *History of Economic Thought* (New York, 1922), pp. 493–95, 530–41, 574–78.

31. Lester F. Ward, *Pure Sociology* (New York, 1903), p. 191; Franklin Henry Giddings, *The Principles of Sociology* (New York, 1923), p. 31.

32. *Doctrine de Saint-Simon, Exposition, 1. année 1829,* New ed. by C. Bouglé et Élie Halévy (Paris, 1924), pp. 163, 246, 317; C. Bouglé, *Proudhon* ("Réformateurs sociaux, collection de textes" [Paris, 1930]), pp. 122, 123, 126, 131, and *La Sociologie de Proudhon* (Paris, 1911), pp. 41, 43, 51; Ludwig Gumplowicz, *Ausgewählte Werke* (Innsbruck, 1926), II, 94–105, IV, 225–27. The passages in question of Eugene Dühring are reprinted in Friedrich Engel, *Herrn Eugen Dührings Umwälzung der Wissenschaft* (Stuttgart, 1919), pp. 161, 163, 166, 172, 181, 186, 196, 199.

33. Wilhelm Schmidt and Wilhelm Koppers, *Der Mensch aller Zeiten,* Vol. III: *Gesellschaft und Wirtschaft der Völker* (Regensburg, 1924), pp. 158–93, 225–84, 396–501, 539–89.

34. Max Weber, *Gesammelte Aufsätze zur Sozial- und Wirtschaftsgeschichte* (Tübingen, 1924), pp. 227–78, and *Wirtschaftsgeschichte* (München, 1923), pp. 59–109; Alfons Dopsch, *Wirtschaftsliche und soziale Grundlagen der europäischen Kulturentwickelung* (Wien, 1920–23), I, 94–413, II, 291–393, and *Die Wirtschaftsentwickelung der Karolingerzeit* (Weimar, 1912), pp. 269–369; Otto Gierke, *Das deutsche Genossenschaftsrecht* (Berlin, 1868–1914), I, 14–249, 531–637, 658–96; II, 134–525; 829–976; III, 186–238, 351–416, 645–826; see also Paul Honigsheim, "Max Weber as Historian of Agriculture," in *Agricultural History,* forthcoming soon.

35. Constantin Frantz, *Deutschland und der Föderalismus* (Stuttgart, 1921), pp. 175, 185; Eugen Stamm, *Constantin Frantz* (Stuttgart, 1930), p. 168.

36. Georg Jellinek, *Allgemeine Staatslehre* (2d ed.; Berlin, 1905), Book I, chap. ii, No. 2, pp. 26–40; Heinrich Rickert, *Die Grenzen der naturwissenschaftlichen Begriffsbildung* (Tübingen, 1902), chaps. iii and iv, pp. 226–599; Ernst Troeltsch, *Der Historismus und seine Probleme* (Tübingen, 1922), pp. 83–110, 200–220; Max Weber, *Gesammelte Aufsätze zur Wissenschaftslehre* (Tübingen, 1922), pp. 146–214, 451–523; see also Paul Honigsheim, "Max Weber als Soziologe," in *Kölner Vierteljahrshefte für Soziologie,* I (München, 1921), 32–41; and "Max Weber as Rural Sociologist," *Rural Sociology,* XI (1946), 208–9.

37. Edward Alsworth Ross, *Social Control* (New York, 1916), pp. 11–16, 36–38.

38. Henry George, *Progress and Poverty* (New York, 1931), Book III, chaps. iv, v, vi, pp. 189–217; Book V, pp. 263–96; Book VI, chap. ii, pp. 328–30; Adolf Damaschke, *Geschichte der Nationalökonomie* (12th ed.; Jena, 1920), chap. x, pp. 305–10 (very partial); Hans Wehberg, "Ein deutscher Vorkämpfer für internationale Verständigung," *Die Friedenswarte,* XXXVII, No. 6 (Zürich, 1937), 232–36.

39. Schmidt and Koppers, *op. cit.,* pp. 194–224, 304–51, 502–38, 590–624; Eduard Hahn, "Waren die Menschen der Urzeit zwischen der Jägerstufe und der Stufe der ackerbauer Nomaden?" *Ausland,* LXIV (1891), 482–87; *Demeter und Baubo* (Lübeck, 1896), pp. 14–17, 24–28, 31, 37, 47; "Zur Theorie der Entstehung des Ackerbaues," *Globus,* LXXV (1899), 98, 283; *Das Alter der wirtschaftlichen Kultur* (Heidelberg, 1905), pp. 12, 17, 20, 28, 33, 59, 91, 97, 122, 131, 145, 148, 151; "Die Hirtenvölker in Asien und Afrika," *Geographische Zeitschrift,* XIX (Leipzig, 1913), 311, 380 (see Paul Honigsheim, "Eduard Hahn," *Anthropos,* XXIV [1929], 597–99, with bibliography). A detailed criticism of the special anthropological theories of Oppenheimer can be found in Paul Honigsheim, "Viehzüchternomadismus, Bodenrente, Reichtumsbildung, Staatsgründung," *Kölner Vierteljahrshefte,* IX (1932), 84 ff.

40. Leonard Nelson, *Kritik der praktischen Vernunft* (Leipzig, 1910), secs. 65, 66, 76, 87, 278, 282; *System der philosophischen Rechtslehre und Politik* (Leipzig, 1924), pp. 40, 50 ff., 64, 96, 144; *Die Reformation der Gesinnung* (Leipzig, 1924), *passim; Vom*

Staatenbund (Leipzig, 1918), *passim; Demokratie und Führerschaft* (Stuttgart, 1927), *passim.*

41. Adolf Bastian, *Der Mensch in der Geschichte* (Leipzig, 1860), *passim; Das Beständige in den Menschenrassen* (Berlin, 1863), p. 151; *Die Völker des östlichen Asiens,* V (Jena, 1869), v; *Der Papua* (Berlin, 1885), p. 294; *Ideale Welten* (Berlin, 1892), p. 254; Gumplowicz, *op. cit.,* IV, 178 f.; Fritz Gräbner, *Die Methode der Ethnologie* (Heidelberg, 1911), pp. 91–170; "Ethnologie," in *Die Kultur der Gegenwart,* Part III, subsec. 5 (Leipzig and Berlin, 1923), pp. 444–47; Schmidt and Koppers, *op. cit.,* pp. 63–111 (see Paul Honigsheim, "Die geistesgeschichtliche Stellung der Anthropologie, Ethnologie und Urgeschichte," in *Festschrift: Publication d'hommage offerte au P. W. Schmidt* [Wien, 1928], pp. 851–54, 862–64); "Adolf Bastian und die Entwickelung der ethnologischen Soziologie," *Kölner Vierteljahrshefte,* VI, No. 1 (1926), 66–69; "Soziologische Fragestellungen in der gegenwärtigen prähistorischen und ethnologischen Literatur," *ibid.,* VII, No. 3 (1928), 331–43, and No. 4 (1929), 427–46; "The Problem of Diffusion and Parallel Evolution with Special Reference to American Indians," *Papers of the Michigan Academy of Science, Arts and Letters,* XXXVII (Ann Arbor, 1942), 515–24; "The Philosophical Background of European Anthropology," *American Anthropologist,* XLIV, (1942), 376–87.

CHAPTER XVII

ALFRED WEBER'S CONCEPTION OF HISTORICOCULTURAL SOCIOLOGY

SIGMUND NEUMANN, *Wesleyan University*

I. THE INSTITUTIONAL AND INTELLECTUAL BACKGROUND OF WEBER'S WORK

THE life and the work of Alfred Weber reflect the great qualities, as well as the tragic tensions, of the social sciences in Germany. A clear evaluation of his place in modern sociology must, therefore, begin with an examination of the spiritual climate which has surrounded him. The methods of a modern sociology of knowledge are especially appropriate to Weber, since the whole tenor of his work is inextricably tied up with his era. Original thinker though he is, Alfred Weber is not an esoteric scientist.

Born in 1868 at Erfurt in central Germany, Alfred Weber grew up in the Bismarckian and early Wilhelminic empire. Germany was worlds apart from the evenly tempered British atmosphere which had nourished Herbert Spencer and John Stuart Mill and from an American open-class society which had been the background of William G. Sumner and Lester F. Ward.

The German middle class was twice defeated in its fight for political power: in the premature revolution of 1848 and during the struggle between Bismarck and the Prussian parliament over the control of the army in the sixties. Bismarck's empire, the creation of his victories on the battlefields of three wars, represented a working compromise between the Junkers and the *bourgeoisie*. Recognizing the vital importance of the capitalist middle class in economics, the Reich still left political control entirely in the hands of the old conservative ruling classes. They, in return, promised to win for an expanding capitalism colonial markets abroad and protection against growing proletarian unrest at home. The middle classes relinquished their influence upon internal affairs. The

353

Constitution was retained in name only. The burgher was deprived of all sense of political responsibility in Germany, while in Great Britain a Victorian compromise had merged the middle class with a ruling aristocracy, which, from now on, complied with middle-class standards. In the Reich the social concepts of the traditional ruling classes were generally accepted. A "feudalization" of the German burgher was the result, although it was only after World War I that the serious consequences of this fact became evident. With these developments a decisive change took place in the middle classes themselves, characterized by the substitution of a solely economic *bourgeoisie* for politically minded "burghers."

The conflict between state and society, between the traditional political order and the social reality of newly emerging forces—this crucial issue of the nineteenth century—did not find a genuine solution in Germany and finally led to the breakdown of the empire. In fact, Bismarck's formula, while enthusiastically embraced by the "National Liberal" industrialists, was not at all shared by the whole *bourgeoisie*. The progressive, commercial class lined up with the socialist proletariat and with Catholic Germany—an opposition which foreshadowed the later coalition of the Weimar Republic. Weber's family background definitely put him in the midst of these tensions that split the German *bourgeoisie* of the Reich. His father had actively participated in politics as city councillor in Berlin and in the German Reichstag as a member of the National Liberal party, the champion of unification. The deep political antagonism of the young German middle class shaped Alfred Weber's concepts as a social scientist.

"State and society," as a matter of course, constituted the central theme of the science of the crisis of society, sociology. No doubt, there were numerous academicians who saw in Bismarck's empire the coming of the "social kingdom," as predicted by one of the originators of German sociology, Lorenz von Stein. Solving the social question from above was a natural expectation of a nation whose capitalism had been largely bureaucratic from the outset. The social policies of Bismarck were hailed by social reformers around the Verein für Sozialpolitik. Alfred Weber, though a student of these reformers' most ardent spokesman, Gustav Schmoller, could not share such an optimism.

Neither could Weber accept the radical criticism of the capitalist order by Karl Marx. In fact, opposition to Marxism not only as an economic system but even more as a politico-metaphysical creed became the mainspring in Alfred Weber's own social philosophy.[1]

There was, of course, always the possibility of resigning altogether from an unwanted reality into the ivory tower of the university halls. Such a decision could easily encourage flight into a world of meaningless fact-collection or monstrous abstractions—an accusation often raised against German social scientists. Even if carried through with the intellectual fervor, scientific integrity, and original grasp of a Max Weber, such an approach brought about "nonpolitical," unfortunate consequences and unwholesome tensions.

In fact, Max Weber's clear-cut separation between politics and scientific work, free from preconceived ideas (*wertfreie Wissenschaft*), was only an expedient for a person who was genuinely concerned about politics, yet did not find a place for active participation in the Wilhelminic empire.

Despite the fact that Alfred always regarded Max, four years his elder, with admiration as his ideal in life and science, so much so that he followed closely his brother's pattern of training and development, first studying jurisprudence and political economy, then equally taking up a legal career as a Gerichts-Assessor in Berlin, and, finally, repeating his turn toward sociology—despite such obvious similarities, the younger Weber's whole mental outlook and scientific purpose sprang from different sources. Overshadowed by his more renowned brother—perhaps in his own estimation and most certainly in the judgment of many social scientists—Alfred Weber represents a genuine contribution in his own right. Though his writings may seem to lack the precision and universality of his brother's concepts, they often reflect a greater human intensity and concreteness. His approach, in many respects, opens avenues of more vital significance to his generation. It is safe to state that he will rise in stature as time goes on. At the base of Alfred Weber's work and personality is the concept of social responsibility. Throughout all his writings he rejects a sociology which is *lebensfremd* and which does not answer the needs of the time. For this reason he attacked strongly a "formal sociology" which satisfies nobody (*die niemand satt macht*).

For the same reason he could never accept the political and moral defeat of the German middle class from Bismarck to Hitler. Throughout all his life he had fought the tragic impasse of the German intelligentsia. In spite of the fact that few nations had given as many really great Europeans to the world as Germany had done—Lessing, Beethoven, Goethe, Kant, Ranke, to mention only a few among the thousands—there was hardly any significant country on the Continent which, as a whole, stood so much apart from Europe. The German intelligentsia, symbol though it was to Europe and recognized as such by the whole world, lived essentially separated from the German people, who did not understand their language, did not know their problems, and did not share their experiences. This tragic isolation—so different from the position of the French *hommes de lettres*—was partly due to the deep antagonism which prevailed between *Macht* and *Geist,* a tension which the Weimar Republic tried in vain to eliminate.

National Socialism—the great revolt against the West and against all for which historic Europe stands—by no mere accident concentrated its major attacks on the intelligentsia, that is, on those forces which, by fate and tradition, had become the chief prototypes of this very Europe.

Alfred Weber has always been such a great European. The Huguenot vein in his family and certainly the parental atmosphere had laid such foundations. Early in his academic career, which he started as a lecturer in political economy at the University of Berlin, he accepted a call to the University of Prague. Here he came into close contact with another great European, Masaryk, then professor of sociology and later the first president of the newly created republic of Czechoslovakia.

Even during the first World War, when the nationalistic fever rose to a high pitch everywhere, Weber insisted on the European mission of Germany. His war correspondence, collected in a little volume, *Gedanken zur deutschen Sendung,* gives a vivid testimony—full of contradictions, yet always circumspect and sincere—of Weber's vision of a responsible place for Germany in the midst of European civilization.

When he returned to Heidelberg, where he held a professorship from 1908 until his resignation at the rise of the Third Reich in 1933, he made his Institute of Social Sciences a center of political and social thought for republican Germany and a mecca for social scientists all over the world. Together with Prince Rohan and his Kulturbund, Weber attempted to give sound foundations to European understanding by an appeal to the common historical heritage of the European nations. With the breakdown of the Third Reich, he emerged as the outstanding social scientist of Germany—uncompromised, unbroken, unrelenting in his fight for a new beginning.

The significance of Alfred Weber as a social scientist can be fully appreciated only if it is seen against this historical panorama. Only then will the weight of his specific contributions to sociology be clearly evaluated.

II. THE CARDINAL POINTS IN WEBER'S APPROACH
TO HISTORICAL SOCIOLOGY

While Alfred Weber's approach points to the discrepancies of German society, his works reveal the specific contributions of German sociology: systematic and historical analysis. In fact, throughout all his writings he shows the rare combination of both a fruitful systematization of concepts and a concrete understanding of historical processes. The result is neither philosophy of history nor *Universalgeschichte* (though it is something of both), but culture-sociology.

Since his earliest years, Alfred Weber has showed a deep interest in archeology and history. The dream of his boyhood days was to write a history of Hellenism. Theodor Mommsen, the great historian, was his scholarly ideal. Such an explicit statement weighs doubly when coming from a thoroughly independent thinker who has not recognized too many masters in his intellectual development. His studies under Dove and Lamprecht, pathfinders of cultural and universal history, undoubtedly also left their mark on young Weber; so did his close contact with Gustav Schmoller, leading economic historian of the Bismarckian era. Alfred Weber's Ph.D. thesis on the sweat system of the clothing industry follows the well-known patterns of the Schmoller school. Yet it was probably the great liberal political economist, Lujo Brentano, whose rare merging of exacting criticism and passionate political will exemplified best Alfred Weber's aim and direction for a responsible social science.

After his early study on the theory of the location of industry (*Standortstheorie*), which proved his ability to do exacting work in the field of economics, Weber soon turned to a comprehensive study of the "whole status of our Occidental culture, in order to establish our present position in the general movement of history." His many years' endeavors were crowned in his monumental *Kulturgeschichte als Kultursoziologie*.

In this study he clearly states that, having only *one* life to live, he had to choose between comprehensive case studies of specific cultures and the systematic analysis of the totality of history. It is the latter which has always attracted him, though his studies of Egyptian culture have shown no less his finesse in concrete analysis, on a par with Max Weber's classic studies on ancient agriculture and the city. In fact, Alfred Weber has applied to perfection in his own studies his brother's famous concept of the ideal-type.

Alfred Weber's main endeavor has been directed at the problem of sociological generalization. At the very outset he rejects the naturalistic method. Sociology, according to Weber, is a cultural, not a natural, science. Life is a constant stream of "vital aggregations." It is only with great caution that history in its unique manifestations may be put into the frame of general concepts. A sociology of history and culture which tries to do so must show respect for the concrete. It must, in fact, accept the maxims of Leopold von Ranke, who set for historical science the task of revealing the past, *wie es eigentlich gewesen* ("as it actually and peculiarly happened"). Each historical entity has its own unique essence. Weber equally concurs with the more profound view of Dilthey's concept of the historical character of life and of "understanding" as a key to historical interpretation. Even Meinecke's modern historicism is somewhat reflected in Weber's notion of the characteristic life-attitude and unity of style of every period. Yet as a sociologist he naturally cannot accept an extreme historicism, which denies the existence of any general patterns in history's "unique" manifestations.

While Alfred Weber can justifiably claim to be in full accord with the founders of sociology—Saint-Simon, Comte, Marx, and Spencer—in his own attempt at a systematic sociology he strongly rejects the dogmatic presuppositions of these early schools. In its first conscious appearance sociology was tied up with a philosophical revolution. Positivism in France, the turn from a philosophical idealism to a philosophical naturalism in Germany, and the Anglo-Saxon theory of evolution and progress forced the young social science into an abstract rationalism and a dogmatic philosophy of history. In fact, Alfred Weber's culture-sociology must be regarded essentially as a strong reaction against any philosophical determinism which suppresses the diversity and spontaneity of life.

To steer between the Scylla of extreme historicism and the Charybdis of abstract generalization has been Weber's main task since he first represented his sociological concept of culture more than thirty years ago.[2]

Such a purpose is served by a most fruitful differentiation of the totality of historical reality into three spheres: society, civilization, and culture. Such a distinction leads Weber to his fundamental concepts: the social process, the process of civilization, and the culture movement. Yet, from the very outset, Weber clearly indicates that these three processes, though theoretically well separated, are, in reality, closely interrelated.

The *social process* is visible in the great historical entities of nations and peoples, from primitive societies to the societies of the Mediterranean and the West. Every significant society develops its own specific culture, conditioned by human instincts and volition, by historical fate, and by geographical and climatic influences. There is no continuous process of the totality of human society. Despite some interdependence and factual relations between these entities, they follow their own characteristic life-attitude and their immanent development. Still, typical forms and stages can be detected, a limited variety and specific sequence of social organization, which recurs throughout history and thus invites comparative studies and even indicates general social trends.

The *civilizational process* is concerned with the material development of society. Continuous progress is undeniable in this sphere of rational and systematic conquest of the forces of nature. This is the domain of natural sciences and of techniques. Their knowledge and discoveries are transferable. In fact, Alfred Weber sees in this human mastery over nature an irreversible process which will finally lead to a unitary civilization and generally accepted ideas. It is this side of social existence which has been unjustifiably overemphasized by the early sociologists and which has misled them into the belief in a society of rationality and continuous progress. Those thinkers disregarded a third sphere of human life, probably its most essential component.

The *culture* movement is diametrically different from that of civilization. Culture is not simply transferable from one historical entity to another. It is imbedded in a unique situation. Even a so-called "renaissance" is a new creation, though it may take over external forms and similar aims from other cultures. All emanations of culture are peculiar to their creator because they are creations springing from the inner sources of man. Culture is laden with history and can only be conceived historically. There are no generally valid laws and trends in the world of culture. There is no progress. Spengler's somber prediction of a "decline of the West," in accordance with his grandiose morphology, is metaphysical dogmatism, just as are the promises of a progressive evolution of mankind in its cultural aspects.

Culture derives from the creativeness and spontaneity of man. True, it must be understood in its close connection with the processes of society and civilization. Man is not anarchic; he is a social individual who has to recognize his place in time and society. This is an essential part of his self-realization. Yet there is freedom because there is a great elasticity and tension of human life. Every "primary constellation" of a historical situation, such as a great national crisis, can be answered differently and creatively.

Such thoughts, as a matter of course, recall the basic concepts of "challenge and response," as recently presented by Arnold J. Toynbee in his monumental *Study of History*. They are comrades-in-arms in their fight against a mechanical interpretation of life and society, especially significant in the era of the machine and great technique. In a recent little essay on Ernst Jünger, spokesman of a machine-obsessed generation, Weber brilliantly pointed at the basic pessimism which underlies the "heroic realism" of Ernst Jünger and his many followers among the German youth and elsewhere. Alfred Weber, a great academic teacher for a whole generation, lives by different concepts—above all, by personal courage and independence of mind, intellectual intensity, and human warmth.

During his recent years of forced retirement from active duty and painful contemplation of his nation's political and moral degradation, he has come back to the basic question: "What is man?" His answer may surprise one in these days; yet it reflects all the courage and optimism of this great social thinker: "Heroic sacrifice," he says, "may be found among animals, but no goodness. This belongs to man."

BIBLIOGRAPHY

WORKS BY ALFRED WEBER

Hausindustrielle Gesetzgebung und Sweating-System in der Konfektionsindustrie. Diss. Leipzig, 1897.

"Die volkswirtschaftliche Lage der Hausindustrie," *Schmollers Jahrbuch,* Vol. XXVI (1902).

Die gemeinsamen wirtschaftlichen Interessen Deutschlands und Österreichs (1902).

Über den Standort der Industrien. 1st ed., 1909; 2d ed., 1922. Translated and edited by CARL JOACHIM FRIEDRICH, under the title, *Theory of the Location of Industries.* Chicago, 1929.

"Der soziologische Kulturbegriff," *Verhandlungen des 2. deutschen Soziologentages.* Tübingen, 1913.

Gedanken zur deutschen Sendung. Berlin, 1915.

"Principielles zur Kultursoziologie," *Archiv für Sozialwissenschaft und Sozialpolitik,* Vol. XLVII (1920–21). Translated by G. H. WELTNER and C. F. HIRSCHMAN under the title, *Fundamentals of Culture-Sociology.* New York, 1939.

Die Not der geistigen Arbeiter. Munich, 1923.

Deutschland und die europäische Kulturkrise. Berlin, 1924.

Die Krise des modernen Staatsgedankens in Europa. Stuttgart, 1925.

"Kultursoziologische Versuche," *Archiv für Sozialwissenschaft,* Vol. LV (1926).

Ideen zur Staats- und Kultursoziologie. Karlsruhe, 1927.

"Kultursoziologie," *Handwörterbuch der Soziologie.* Stuttgart, 1931.

Kulturgeschichte als Kultursoziologie. Leyden, 1935.

"Was ist der Mensch?" *Neue Rundschau,* September, 1938.

Das Tragische und die Geschichte. Hamburg, 1943.

Freier Sozialismus. In collaboration with ALEXANDER MITSCHERLICH. Heidelberg, 1946.

Abschied von der Bisherigen Geschichte. 1946.

COMMENTARIES

H. E. BARNES and HOWARD BECKER. *Social Thought from Lore to Science* (New York, 1938), Vol. I, esp. chap. xx.

———. *Contemporary Social Theory* (New York, 1940), chap. xv, "Historical Sociology."

ALBERT SALOMON. "The Place of Alfred Weber's Kultursoziologie in Social Thought," *Social Research,* III (November, 1936), 494–500.

HANS FREYER. *Soziologie als Wirklichkeitswissenschaft* (Leipzig, 1930), esp. pp. 135–45.

EMIL LEDERER. "Aufgaben einer Kultursoziologie," *Hauptprobleme der Soziologie: Erinnerungsgabe für Max Weber.* Edited by MELCHIOR PALYI. München, 1923.

MAX SCHELER. *Die Wissensformen und die Gesellschaft.* Leipzig, 1926.

NOTES

1. If Weber explicitly accepts socialism now, as he does in his latest book, it is a "free socialism" which demands nationalization wherever and whenever it serves the purpose of liberating the individual, who, in return, regards himself as an integral part of the collective. It is the concept of the social individual, as suggested by MacIver and others, that underlies Weber's turn to socialism. Fight against totalitarian control, not class struggle and minority suppression, constitutes to Weber the primary issue of the day—an attitude only too natural to a social scientist who has never compromised with dictatorship of any color.

2. *Der soziologische Kulturbegriff* (Tübingen, 1913).

CHAPTER XVIII

THE SOCIOLOGICAL THEORIES OF HANS FREYER

SOCIOLOGY AS A NATIONALISTIC PROGRAM OF SOCIAL ACTION

Ernest Manheim, *University of Kansas City*

I. THE INTELLECTUAL AND METHODOLOGICAL BACKGROUND OF FREYER'S SOCIOLOGY

THE rapid political and industrial growth of Germany during the nineteenth century and the peculiar social crisis which accompanied it accentuated two European trends of thought on social and political affairs. One accepts an inclusive philosophy of the state with its supremacy over all human organizations. Drawing on the eighteenth-century tradition of the Cameralists, the craftsmen, and theorists of the German absolute state, this point of view gained momentum and influence particularly among Germans who envisaged an ambitious and bold foreign policy, with the essential and inevitable concentration of political power in the domestic sphere as well. At the same time, the very historical process which led to a uniquely German exaltation of the state also gave birth to the second trend: a social and political radicalism of the most methodical type.

These sharp dogmatic polarizations inspired, as well as obstructed, the development of sociology in Germany. From its very start German sociology was flanked by them, both equally intolerant of sociology as an academic and relatively independent science. It is this precarious and, in many ways, defensive middle position which is partly responsible for a good deal of the methodological self-consciousness that is characteristic of certain portions of German sociological literature, including Hans Freyer's own contributions.

The latent social crisis and the sharp political controversies have, on the other hand, stimulated a sociological interest both in social dynamics, the mutability and historical aspect of institutions, and in the study of inclusive social structures, such as classes, domination, and the distri-

362

bution of power. Max and Alfred Weber, Tönnies, Oppenheimer, Scheler, and Karl Mannheim among the more recent sociologists, Lorenz von Stein, Gumplowicz, and Ratzenhofer from among the older school may be cited as illustrative cases in point.

Hans Freyer's interest in both social dynamics and structural sociology is even more pronounced than in any of the writers quoted. His program is a provocative exposition of sociology conceived free of its present methodological limitations. His concern is not how to maintain objectivity in this controversial field but how to make sociology a meaningful account of the trends and aspirations which are inherent in the social crisis of our epoch.

To him, sociology is not merely a method but a point of view rooted in the present period of social transformation and confined to it. Sociology, the product of the social crisis which the industrial revolution inaugurated in Europe after 1750, is the systematic quest for a new social order. In fact, sociology is the reflection of society upon itself in this period of crisis. The sociologist is both the student and the spokesman of social change. Hence objectivity and restraint from evaluation do not constitute imperatives for the sociologist. On the contrary, to Freyer it is the very act of volition which brings the object of this science into focus and makes social reality intelligible. In short, Freyer presents a theory that is political from the start, historical in its orientation, and systematic in its conceptual apparatus.

II. FREYER'S LIFE AND MAIN WRITINGS

The son of a civil servant, Freyer was born in Burgstadt, a Saxonian town, in 1887. He belongs to the generation that gave birth to the German youth movement, a social current which cannot directly be compared with any parallel phenomenon outside Germany. The German *Jugendbewegung* was a spontaneous rising of German youth, initially in protest against an older form of domestic authority. In an amazingly short time this movement spread over the Reich and left its imprint on German mores.[1] It contributed its share toward discrediting the traditions of the nineteenth century, the conventions of the bureaucratic regime, the beer-drinking petty bourgeois, and the German version of the self-satisfied gentleman. Above all, it was a romantic movement, with exalted, though inarticulate, ideals and a cult of medieval traditions, German folklore, and pagan symbolism.

Freyer's youth was bound up with this movement. Its effects are reflected in his early poetic-philosophical publications: *Anthäus: Grundlegung einer Ethik des bewussten Lebens* (1918), and *Prometheus: Ideen zu einer Philosophie der Kultur* (1922). Both publications were widely read by the first and second generations of the *Jugendbewegung*. The effect of the youth movement on Freyer is also noticeable to some extent in his *Der Staat* (1925).

During the first World War, Freyer was wounded several times and decorated. In 1920 he returned to his academic interests, this time as a lecturer in philosophy at his university (Leipzig). His professorial thesis, *Die Bewertung der Wirtschaft im philosophischen Denken des 19. Jahrhunderts* (1921), is remarkable for its concise and objective presentation, a trait which is characteristic of all Freyer's interpretive and polemic writings. In his *Theorie des objektiven Geistes* (1922) Freyer presents a framework of concepts for the philosophy of culture. In 1922, Freyer joined the faculty of the University of Kiel as professor of philosophy for a period of three years. In 1925 he returned to the University of Leipzig, as head of its newly established Institute of Sociology.

From this time on, Freyer's political views, always implicit in his earlier publications, became increasingly articulate. His main contribution to sociology is embodied in his *Soziologie als Wirklichkeitswissenschaft* (1930) and in his booklet *Einleitung in die Soziologie* (1931). His first explicitly political confession, *Revolution von Rechts* (1931), was a bombshell among sociologists, who traditionally did not stray too far from the political center. Subsequent publications, such as *Herrschaft und Planung* (1933), *Das politische Semester* (1933), and a series of articles, show a growing preoccupation with political topics. The same year, 1933, the year of the Nazi revolution, brought both climax and anticlimax into Freyer's career: his appointment as director of the famous Institut für Kultur und Universalgeschichte ("Institute of Cultural and Universal History") at the University of Leipzig, founded in 1909 by the historian Karl Lamprecht, and the closing of the Institute of Sociology. After 1938, Freyer acted as an exchange professor at the University of Budapest.

In his rather consistent mental and professional development Freyer has absorbed a variety of influences that were operative in pre-war and postwar Germany. Nietzsche's literary disenchantment with the world of the second German Reich and his philosophy of living dangerously struck fertile ground among the literati of the youth movement. Hegel's exaltation of the state and his adaptable concept of historical consciousness, Fichte's nationalistic philosophy of history, and Marx's dialectical system contributed greatly to Freyer's historical orientation, so basic to his sociology. He has acknowledged major or minor intellectual debts to his academic teachers—Lamprecht, the psychologizing historian; Ernst Troeltsch, the philosopher of history and religion; and Georg Simmel, the versatile artist of subtle sociological analyses. Last, but not least, Spengler's influence must be mentioned.

Spengler's effect on German postwar nationalism can hardly be overestimated.[2] To a generation of intellectuals, brought up on Nietzsche and the dream of Pan-Germany, Spengler proved prophetic. His bewildering and brilliant *Decline of the West* not only gave the intellectual wing of German nationalism its political metaphysics and its cosmology, as it were, but provided it with a concrete time prognosis and an implicit program of action. His natural history of cultural cycles, his theory of a creative aristocracy, and his diagnosis of our age as a period of struggles for world domination have become cornerstones of Freyer's sociology.

III. LEADING ITEMS IN FREYER'S SOCIOLOGICAL THEORIES

A. SOCIOLOGY AS AN INSTRUMENT OF SOCIAL RECONSTRUCTION

In Freyer's opinion, the nineteenth-century systems of sociology represent not merely an advanced phase of social thinking but the beginning of an entirely new science and a new perspective, born of the industrial revolution. The bourgeois revolutions of the new age have produced the point of view of sociology and suggested its ultimate object—a rational industrial society. Bourgeois society is not a new order but a process of perpetual readjustment. To Freyer, it is a historical interim between two social orders, one which has been decaying since the eighteenth century, and another which is forming within the framework of present society. It is the primary calling of the sociologist to describe and to interpret that process.

Historical perspective, Freyer holds, must be the basic frame of reference of sociology, as it was to its founders, Adam Ferguson, Johannes Müller, Turgot, Condorcet, Saint-Simon, Comte, and Marx. They all conceived of industrial society as a historical process, as a period of transition; and to them observation and analysis were subordinate to prognostication. They all had some conception of *negative* and *positive* periods of history. Positive periods are those in which a social order and its underlying system of values, as expressed in cosmology, law, religion, and art, form the unquestioned and binding universe of man. Such epochs need and produce no sociology. When, as in such periods, the standards by which men live are identified with the natural order and the premises of the existing social and moral universe are beyond the reach of critical reflection, sociology has no function to perform. In negative periods, however, sociology is a positive and constructive force, pointing to a new social order, be that construed as Saint-Simon's "new Christianity," Comte's "positive period," Lorenz von Stein's "social monarchy," or Marx's "free association." This impulse to social reconstruction gives sociological inquiry its focus; and, to Freyer, this was true not only of the utopians of the nineteenth century but of every genuinely scientific sociology of the twentieth century. Only the critic of present society and the pioneer of a new social order can hope to gain a realistic perspective on our industrial era.

B. SOCIOLOGY AND HISTORY

According to Freyer, the greater part of modern sociology has sought a generalizing procedure which has yielded returns in the natural sciences but which is sterile when applied to a dynamic society. To be meaningful, sociological concepts must have a historical connotation. History is an irreversible process; each of its phases is unique. It is true that revolutions or slavery, for instance, reappear in a number of cultures and phases of history, but, so construed, they are abstractions from their concrete social setting. Notions such as the industrial revolution or Greek slavery, on the other hand, designate unique constellations which occur only once and cannot be projected into any other time or place. Concrete concepts of sociology are implicitly historical, because they deal with complex situations sufficiently inclusive to establish their identity in time and space.

Sociology, however, is not historiography. The difference is variable and may become less as historians move increasingly toward the point of view and interests of the sociologist, but attainments in the two fields will rarely duplicate each other. The historian, his selective point of view notwithstanding, may take a detached view of his subject. The sociologist, on the other hand, must, in good faith, apply to his object the yardstick of relevancy. His primary interest is with contemporary issues. Phenomena of another society and another age are relevant to him only in so far as they give perspective to the acute questions of our times.

More important, however, is Freyer's second distinction between the historical and the sociological approach. The historian who is worth his salt is not satisfied with a mere demonstration of the uniqueness of his particular subject. He will present as rich a body of descriptive material as the scope of his problem and the relevancy of the available detail will warrant. The sociologist proceeds more architecturally, as it were; he outlines social structures. It is these structural concepts which, according to Freyer, are the real units of sociological generalization, as distinguished from the direct and concrete interest which the historian takes in the temporal continuity of change.

C. THE NATURE OF SOCIOLOGICAL GENERALIZATIONS

Structural concepts, such as theocracy, feudalism, caste, and class, are capable of general and independent application. They are sufficiently general to exist in more than one historical constellation and to make different phases of history commensurable. The necessary minimum of traits which constitute feudalism are present in ancient Greece, in Persia, in fourteenth-century England, and in eighteenth-century Japan. Middle classes existed in contemporary America, in Elizabethan England, and in the Roman Republic. Yet these terms do not transcend history; they are meaningless unless they are placed in their proper historical context. Sociology is not a generalizing science. Sociological generalizations are valid only within a given historical frame of reference. They are by-products of investigation rather than its aim. The scientific formula, "If conditions A to X are present, Y will result," applies to sociology with this modification: "In historical situation Z, conditions A to X tend to produce Y."

More particularly, two types of generalizations can have meaning for the sociologist. The first is confined to phenomena within a single stream of history. Thus: "The observation in postwar Germany that Y results in the presence of conditions A to X is also true of modern industrial society in general." In generalizations of this type the frame of reference (postwar Germany) of an observation is extended to a more inclusive structure (modern industrial society), which is identified with a wider epoch (a century and a half) of the same stream of history (Occidental).

A second type of generalization is based on the theory of culture cycles, which Freyer partially shares with Spengler. A brief exposition of this will be necessary. The great civilizations (*Hochkulturen*) are, according to this theory, the matrix of history. Universal history is an after-thought, as is "mankind," a mere generic term. Each of the quasi-organisms of history—China, Arabia, western Europe, Rome, and so on—has its phases of growth and expansion, its climax and decay, unless its evolution is arrested in an early stage. The historical cycles of cultures move in a similar rhythm through corresponding phases of political and religious integration. The correspondence of these cycles and their like rhythm make the history of civilizations commensurable. Thus history can be a science as well as an art.

This is the concept of history which Freyer has in mind when he demands that every structural concept of sociology bear a time index and be so used. The time in question is Spengler's "historical" time, and it has reference to the particular life-cycle of a given historical organism. If Spengler's natural history of culture cycles is valid, then evidently customs, social movements, kinship systems, and political organiza-tions assume a historical meaning which cannot adequately be under-stood on the plane of human interaction. A type of community organi-zation, for example, may, in one phase of history, be diagnosed as a sign of "morbidity" and decay and, in another, as a symptom of "health," according to its particular place in the life-cycle of a culture.

This conception of history opens another field for sociological generali-zations. They are relative to corresponding phases of different streams of history. Thus, the observation of phenomenon A made in phase B of civilization C may be found to be pertinent to the same phase B of civi-lizations E and F. For example, the "nobility" as a distinct social group emerges in a particular phase of all civilizations. The social structure of this élite is typical and recurrent in the corresponding periods of nearly all civilizations. Again, imperialism, in certain "late" phases of history, is typically associated with particular forms of social organization. Gen-eralizations of this type, however, pertain only to corresponding periods.

D. FORMAL VERSUS HISTORICAL SOCIOLOGY ILLUSTRATED BY CONFLICTING INTERPRETATIONS OF COMMUNITY AND SOCIETY

Eager to raise their science above partisanship, Georg Simmel and more recent sociologists, such as Von Wiese, have taken their recipe for an objective sociology from biology and geometry. The resulting *formal* type of sociology has become a logically unassailable science of classes of human relationships, first isolated from their complex human setting and then catalogued and juxtaposed under a variety of extraneous aspects.

Freyer's analysis of the concepts *Gemeinschaft* ("community") and *Gesellschaft* ("society") will demonstrate his distinction between formal and concrete types of sociology.

Formal sociologists, such as Ferdinand Tönnies, Leopold von Wiese, Vierkandt, and Max Weber, would describe the two types as manifestations of universal tendencies which are potential in any human aggregation. "Community" is the more restricted, more intimate, and lasting group, while "society" typifies associations of a more mobile personnel for limited ends. Described in terms of social psychology, participation in "society" is based on rational motives, as against the spontaneous sentiments of solidarity and congeniality which are predominant in "community."

To Freyer this formal treatment obscures significant aspects of the matter. Community, as a specific type, represents an early historical phase which invariably preceded periods of "societal" organization. This genuine and primordial type of community is not the same as such intimate and personal associations as the neighborhood and the sect, which have community-like features but are incident to more complex social structures. As a genuine structure, community is a homogeneous ethnic collectivity, a we-group of common understandings, without institutional rule and classes and without social distance. Such collectivities have a timeless existence and no history, for they undergo no important structural and social changes. Indeed, the phrase that "community represents an early phase of history" is, actually, a designation in retrospect.

History, properly conceived, begins with the rise of "societal" structures. Society, as a genuine historical type and not as a sporadic relationship, such as may be incident to any other structure, is a stratified organization which integrates heterogeneous groups into a single fabric. Such structures grow out of interethnic conflicts, usurpation, conquest, and ultimate domination. Domination alone, however, does not in itself establish a new society. A society comes into being only when the conquerors succeed in establishing a caste hierarchy (*Ständeordnung*) and a tradition of acquiescence in the supremacy of the ruling group. With an increasing stabilization of rule, its original ethnic character first becomes blurred and eventually is supplanted by a functional hierarchy.

Societal orders are intrinsically historical. Being built on inequality and domination, they carry the germs of internal conflicts and revolutions. Marx's statement that all past history is a history of class struggles is also true in reverse: wherever classes clash, history is in the making.

To Freyer, aristocracies (*ständische Gesellschaften*) characterize positive and constructive periods of history. They represent the highest type of social and moral integration and the most creative organization of men. All higher civilizations arise from an aristocratic basis. The continued existence of such a civilization, however, depends on the perpetual vigilance of the ruling caste and its ability to forestall revolts and to assert itself forcefully.

Opposition to an aristocratic order usually begins as a democratic movement. Successful democratic revolutions do not abolish domination but change its character, class rule taking the place of caste rule. With this change a period of latent or actual revolutions begins. Castes and ranks are constituted from above—classes always rise from below. Conflicts between castes are accidental and intermittent, while class conflicts tend to become permanent. Opposition in an aristocratic society is not revolutionary but partial and localized. It is directed against usurpation, against impingement upon acquired privileges or against abuses of the system. Class oppositions are latent revolutions directed against the existing order. Every genuine class is a potential claimant to universal power and the right to reorganize society on its own terms. The auspicious statement of the French revolutionary, the Abbé Sieyès, that "the third estate is nothing at present but is potentially everything" is symbolic of the opening period of European revolutions.

In summary, to Freyer, community, society, caste (*Stand*), and class signify irreversible sequences in a *genetic system* of social types and sociological concepts. Each of these terms stands for a genuine social structure, which is preponderant in a corresponding phase of history. The formal and purely typological conception of class or of caste, for example, is inadequate and misleading, because it misses the essential characteristic of these structures—their position and value in a genetic system of categories.

IV. AN EVALUATION OF FREYER'S SOCIOLOGICAL DOCTRINES

In his *Soziologie als Wirklichkeitswissenschaft* Freyer emphatically avows that not only the sociologist as an individual but sociology as a point of view cannot maintain an aloof and impartial position in the essential controversies of our time. The rejection of political and social liberalism is an inescapable conclusion from the historical premises of sociology. Freyer's political manifesto, *Revolution von Rechts,* is more than an expression of personal preference. It represents Freyer's sociology in action. The revolution from the right is announced as an uprising of the people against the paralyzed neutral state of liberal society, as a restoration of the sovereign power of the state to act and to decide in the present era of crucial decisions.

This is not merely and not primarily a social scheme but the social implementation of a broad program of political action. It would, then, be easy, and perhaps not contrary to Freyer's expressed intentions, to say that his design of a sociology is the expression of a particular understanding of the needs of a particular country and, therefore, is neither an article for exportation nor a subject of scientific controversy across frontiers of political geography and creed. To dismiss his views so cheaply would, however, be inappropriate. Besides being one of the most consistent attempts to establish an intrinsically nationalistic theory of social action, Freyer's sociology raises problems which merit critical reflection.

First, the contention that the sociologist must visualize his objects in their specific historical setting and that sociological concepts derive their meaning from their place in a genetic system of structural types calls for qualifications.

Sociological generalizations have a specific range of validity, that is, they refer to a given set of circumstances. These qualifying circumstances can be stated in definite sociological terms of human interaction. The proposition, for example, that extensive landholding is a source of feudal power is valid only under conditions of a predominantly rural and self-sufficient household economy, irrespective of time and place. It is only in cases of incomplete analysis or lack of adequate data about the underlying human constellation that qualifications other than sociological will have to be substituted to make the proposition valid. Then, in place of the restriction "under conditions of a predominantly rural and self-sufficient household economy," historical or geographical qualifications may be necessary, such as "twelfth-century England," "eighteenth-century Japan," "nineteenth-century Java." In other words, the situational frame of reference of a proposition will have to be historically indexed if it cannot be stated solely in terms of structure and interaction. The historical reference itself does not complete the analysis; it only substitutes for it.

Second, a program of sociology which is oriented toward a definite trend of action is open to scientific consideration so long as the value-preferences expressed and the suggested line of action are presented as conclusions from premises about which understandings exist or can be reached among students in the field. A reverse program, which would proceed from values and goals about which there is no present understanding, is tantamount to a virtual renunciation of a common ground of discourse among sociologists. Parts of Freyer's presentation support the second procedure. Large sections of *Soziologie als Wirklichkeitswissenschaft* and of *Revolution von Rechts,* to say nothing of later publications, are addressed to a German public and conceived in terms of its political experience. Hence the discussion must take account of those elements of the German situation which make their axiomatic appearance in Freyer's sociology.

One of the important facts in the history of modern Germany was the lack of social integration and the relative absence of an effective social élite which could count on general acceptance. In fact, the political unification of Germany as a modern entity was accomplished neither by the middle classes nor by the industrial or landed upper classes but by the "state," that is, the army and the civil service. These two organizations enjoyed a status in Germany which none of the other strata could claim.

While German society was politically paralyzed and torn by class antagonisms and caste jealousies, the civil service and the army gave it unity and more than the needed initiative. Hegel's exaltation of the state as the incarnation of freedom on earth, as opposed to society, the scene of unmitigated group egoism, is an involuntary expression of modern Germany's political predicament. The basic phenomenon, the lack of social cohesiveness, has not fundamentally changed since Hegel's days, and neither has the political pessimism, as reflected in the perennial dichotomy of state and society, disappeared from German sociological theory. It runs through the essays of Lorenz von Stein, Rodbertus, Lassalle, and others, as it also pervades Freyer's theory.

Freyer, too, attributes to the state the unqualified capacity to resolve the perennial social crisis of his country. In fact, he considers the state the symbol of a positive epoch of promise and fulfilment. There lies the objective toward which, in Freyer's vision, any relevant sociology should point. The period of liberalism he diagnosis as an intermezzo, a period of disintegration.

Freyer's program of sociology is not of the Nazi hue. It has not played the role in Germany which Pareto's assumed in Fascist Italy. While Pareto accepted Fascist honors and left unrefuted the official designation of a father of Fascist theory, Freyer's sociology found no official place in the ideology of Naziism. Neither, for that matter, has any other sociology found favor with the Nazi party. Freyer himself spent the better part of the war abroad in what may be called a voluntary exile with official blessing.

NOTES

1. Richard Thurnwald, *Die deutsche Jugendbewegung* ("Forschungen zur Völkerpsychologie und Soziologie," Vol. V, [Leipzig, 1927]); Hertha Siemering, *Die deutschen Jugendverbände* (Berlin, 1931); Paul Kosok, *Modern Germany* (Chicago, 1933); O. Staehlin, *Die deutsche Jugenbewegung* (2d ed.; Leipzig, 1930).

2. For further details consult Oswald Spengler, *Decline of the West* (New York, 1926–28), Vol. I, chap. ii and Introd.; Vol. II, chaps. i and iv.

CHAPTER XIX

GUSTAV RATZENHOFER: SOCIOLOGICAL POSITIVISM AND THE THEORY OF SOCIAL INTERESTS

ROBERT SCHMID, *Vanderbilt University*

I. RATZENHOFER'S LIFE AND WRITINGS

THE personal history of Gustav Ratzenhofer is essential to an understanding of his work,[1] not because he was a child of his times, for that cliché applies to everyone, but because his particular life-pattern—that of a high-ranking military man—was so atypical. That a man of the cloth or a philosopher should turn to sociology is reasonable enough; but one wonders, at first, at the combination of sword and social analysis.

Austria was his homeland—Austria of the dual monarchy and the seething ethnic disharmony which preys on all culturally heterogeneous political units. Ratzenhofer was born in Vienna, in 1842. Chapin's living-room scale would have rated the Ratzenhofer family as definitely lower middle class, and the future sociologist's early home and family life was neither comfortable nor serene. His father was a watchmaker, who earned a very modest income and whose early death left the family in economic straits, forcing Ratzenhofer, after a very brief period of formal education, to seek remunerative employment. His experiences as an apprentice watchmaker were not satisfactory, however; and in 1858, owing to a complex chain of circumstances involving family difficulties, economic pressure, and impatience with his petit bourgeois role in society, he joined the Austrian army. His brother, in discussing this period, refers to the moral and intellectual dangers which beset a young cadet in those days, and it is suggested that Ratzenhofer was not immune to these forces. At any rate, he participated in a number of duels, precipitated by youthful quarrels over politics and women; and in one of these affairs of honor he received a severe wound, one which caused considerable discomfort throughout his life and finally led to his death.

He rose rapidly in rank in the Austrian army. He became a lieutenant in 1864 and saw active service in several campaigns, deciding finally to devote his life to military training and service. After four years in an advanced military academy, he was promoted to a responsible position on the general staff in 1872. In 1878 he was put in charge of the army archives, and it was while thus assigned that he began his systematic writing and research on military subjects. In 1898, as field marshal-lieutenant and president of the military supreme court in Vienna, he reached the peak of the army hierarchy. However, the inconsistent and arbitrary nature of much of his work with the military tribunal was contrary to his ways of thinking, and he retired from active army service in 1901, after forty-two years in uniform. His death came in 1904 on the return trip from a visit to the United States, where he had delivered an address on "Sociology and Its Problems"[2] at the Congress of Arts and Sciences held during the great exposition at St. Louis.

As has been seen, Ratzenhofer's formal schooling was extremely limited, and he may justifiably be termed a "self-made" man, as far as intellectual training is concerned. His position in the Austrian government gave him an unusual opportunity to apply his philosophic and scientific insight, gained painfully through many hours of self-directed reading, to the sociopolitical problems of an empire in war and in peace. As the fruit of many years of observation and inquiry, his first theoretical work in sociology was published in 1893. It was called *Wesen und Zweck der Politik* ("The Nature and Purpose of Politics"), but its theoretical framework was sociological rather than political; indeed, he presents in the introductory chapters of this work the thesis that sociological knowledge must be the starting-point for *all* investigations in the social sciences. *Soziologische Erkenntnis* ("Sociological Knowledge") was his second and most important work, published in 1898, and his *Soziologie* was published posthumously by his son in 1908. The latter volume was compiled from an unfinished manuscript and contains little which had not been previously published.

Because he studied at no great university, was connected with no "school" of sociological thought, and was intimately associated with no eminent teacher or scholar of his time, Ratzenhofer remains an enigma so far as the early influence on his thought is concerned. He refers in his works to Gumplowicz, Mill, and Spencer, but especially to Comte; indeed, the similarities between the systematic writing of the Frenchman and the Austrian are so strong as to warrant the classification of Ratzenhofer as the first of the German Positivists, a disciple of Comte.

Ratzenhofer's claim to distinction as a systematic sociologist rests on two important contributions. The first of these is the only one referred to in the conventional histories of social thought, namely, the famous "interests" theory of human behavior, with its elaboration into a hypothesis of social origins which has caused him to be classed frequently with the so-called "conflict school" on the Continent. The second and frequently overlooked contribution of Ratzenhofer is his working epistemology, his total conception of the nature and function of scientific knowledge in the social and the "natural" realm. In the opinion of the present writer the Austrian militarist's incisive thinking—or speculation, if you prefer—on the purpose and promise of scientific sociology will eventually prove to have been a more lasting contribution to the discipline than his interests theory or his social-Darwinism-with-reservations.

II. "INTERESTS" AND THE PRIMEVAL PUSH

At this juncture it will be helpful to consider in barest outline the profile of Ratzenhofer's general intellectual framework, without which no full understanding of his specific theories would be possible. It should be remembered that he lived and worked during that period of bubbling intellectual confusion which followed the bombshell of Darwinism and the evolutionary Weltanschauung. Man needed no longer to be regarded as a mysterious half-god, half-devil, but could be described merely as a splendid animal. The main problem remaining was thought to be that of determining how man came to be such a splendid animal. Where, in the evolutionary process, did the human animal abandon the purely instinctive and begin to cultivate the ability to write a critique rather than bash a skull? Ratzenhofer's approach to this situation was based on a single unifying principle of thought and action, namely, that *lawfulness (Gesetzmässigkeit)* is the one great universal characteristic of observable phenomena and that the behavior of human beings is ultimately as predictable as the behavior of apples swaying on a wind-swept tree. Just as there are forces—wind, rain, and gravity—playing upon the apple, so there are social forces impinging upon man, channeling his behavior; and the task of sociology is the calculation of the laws or regularities in this social process. The simplest way to take up this study

according to Ratzenhofer, is to begin with those aspects of social behavior which have been studied most intensively, namely, the nearly
physicochemical instinctive behavior of man and animals.

But Ratzenhofer was not content to start with the instincts as a "given"
fact; he felt the need to "account" for them before he used them, and
this led him to posit as the ultimate matrix of social behavior a "Primeval
Force" (*Urkraft*) which originates, sustains, and, in a sense, "explains"
life itself: "The concept of the Primeval Force is indispensable for the
understanding of the world. It is the basic property of all being .... the
ultimate oneness of knowledge, the substance of the world which supports the Monistic philosophy and at the same time refutes dualism,
that source of all error."[3]

It is neither necessary nor advisable to follow out the metaphysical
implications of this statement, despite its intriguing similarity, on the
surface at least, to certain other concepts now current, notably the late
Henri Bergson's *élan vital*. Ratzenhofer himself prefers to pass rapidly
from the mere statement of this basic principle of force to the elaborations and rationalizations of it which characterize *homo sapiens*.

In man, Ratzenhofer believes, this *Urkraft* is expressed in the form of
inherent interests (*angeborene Interesse*) which become differentiated
into the following forms:

1. *The procreative interest.*—Based upon the physiological impulses
involved in sexual behavior, this interest is the foundation for social
structures like family, tribe, or race. It insures the perpetuation of the
species and is expressed most dramatically and drastically in the organic
world in the case of many insects "which, with the consummation of
the procreative desire, also end their lives."[4]

2. *The physiological interest.*—This interest centers in the process of
metabolism and the search for, and assimilation of, food. "In this interest
both life and the procreative interest are fulfilled, since growth and development would be impossible without this drive towards food and its
assimilation."[5] It is the interest of self-preservation.

3. *The individual interest.*—Similar to the physiological interest and
based upon physical needs, the individual interest is the social extension
of the purely biological to the total complex of self-centered behavior
patterns of the organism.

4. *The social interest.*—The process of individualization, which is
rooted in the individual interest, gradually expands because of the pro-

creative interest, which necessitates social interaction, and results, finally, in the establishment of the blood bond through consanguinity. Through this expansion of the individual interest the social interest is first approximated, then finally realized.

5. *The transcendental interest.*—Finally, as a precipitant of the ceaseless struggle between individual interest and social interest, "inner restlessness" develops concerning the individual's relation to the total universe, to the infinite. Expressed through various forms of religion, this interest stands the furthest removed from naked food- and sex-interests and is the surest index of advanced socialization.[6]

The meaning of "interest" which Ratzenhofer intended to convey apparently lies somewhere between pure physiological instinct and rationalized purpose or "excuse." He makes a clear distinction between "need" (*Bedürfnis*) and awareness or consciousness of that need: "The need as it appears in our consciousness is not a direct insight into the demands of our .... nature; rather, it is an interest .... every such interest arises as the *expression* of a need through the awareness of [the need's] necessity .... [*Notwendigkeit*]."[7]

As Philip Jacobs expresses it: "Back of interest, for Ratzenhofer, stands necessity. An interest is nothing else than the formulation of a necessity."[8]

This theory of interests has been exploited in the United States by Albion W. Small, long head of the Department of Sociology at the University of Chicago. Small translated several of Ratzenhofer's writings and incorporated many of the German writer's ideas in his book, *General Sociology*. On the basis of the five major interests enumerated above, Small constructed his famous sextet of interests: health, wealth, sociability, knowledge, beauty, rightness. These interests and the elaborations, modifications, and extremes of them which turn up in each society are the touchstone of sociological analysis: "The latest word of sociology is that human experience yields the most and the deepest meaning when read from first to last in terms of the evolution, expression, and accommodation of interests."[9]

Although Ratzenhofer (and Small) would have denied that the interests theory is merely a veiled instinct theory, a careful examination of the German theorist's works sustains that criticism. In Ratzenhofer's own "epitome" of his work he shows clearly that instinct-theory is important:

The sustentation and multiplication of man are the sources of all social contact. .... In social interaction these forces appear as the instinct of self-preservation [rivalry for food—*Brotneid*] and the sexual instinct [blood-bond—*Blutliebe*]; all possible motives toward social contact are modifications or evolutionary forms of these natural drives in the same sense that the various forms of interests, controlling the individual, are variants or evolutionary derivatives of the inborn interest.[10]

Here we see clearly the basic trend in the Austrian's thinking. Interests are not instincts, but they are based upon needs (*Notwendigkeiten*) which are instinctive, and they stem from an "inherent interest." To the present writer this aspect of Ratzenhofer's thinking is as indefensible as the circumlocutionary evasion in Allport's "Master Motives"; modern research in social psychology leaves less and less room for the "explanation" of social behavior by means of universal "mainsprings," arbitrarily inserted into a man in order to account for his movements. Biology, anthropology, and ethnology have conspired to demonstrate rather conclusively that social experiences can modify significantly even those bedrock, biologically rooted "needs," "drives," and "prepotent reflexes" which were formerly believed to shove men about, irrespective of *les faits sociales*.

III. THE SOCIAL PROCESS AND THE EVOLUTION OF THE STATE

Ratzenhofer's theory of "interests" led him directly to a dynamic, "rational" theory of society. Society is not an entity, according to this writer; rather, society exists only in the "social process," which is simply the sum total of the reciprocal social relationships existing between a number of individuals, these relationships being based on the web of interest-seeking behavior which motivates all social action.[11] Society, then, becomes a kind of abstraction, similar to a geometrical figure in which the points (individuals) exist only with reference to the lines (relationships) which connect them. More dynamically, society is the social process, not a being, but a "becoming,"[12] a moving complex of reciprocal relationships.

In this respect Ratzenhofer is significantly different from his contemporary, Ludwig Gumplowicz, for Ratzenhofer considered social data from the point of view of social behavior *within* the group, that is, interpersonal relationships, as circumscribed by the total configuration. Gumplowicz, on the other hand, was interested in the impact of group upon group, necessitating a much more static conception of the group itself. It is difficult, indeed, to theorize about intergroup relationships when the interacting elements are as mobile, even gelatinous, as Ratzen-hofer described them. Hence, *intra*group, not *inter*group relations were the focus of his thought.

Human beings, then, motivated by a complex of inherited and acquired interests, associate by means of social relationships, which, considered in their totality, form the social process, or society. From these factors Ratzenhofer derives in easy steps the origins of the state.

In a state of nature, Ratzenhofer claims, the struggle for existence imposes upon each individual, in the pursuit of his inborn interests, the necessity for absolute hostility to all his fellow-men.[13] Co-operative community economic life eases this man-to-man hostility, when the community is based on kinship or the blood bond; but the appearance of a rival community, alien to the clan, is the signal for a battle which ends only when one group has overcome the other. However, when, instead of destroying the vanquished group, the victor enslaves it, in order to make use of its services, man has entered upon a ".... higher stage of the social process, in which the social structure is no longer dependent upon the blood-bond, but upon culture, and a system of domination. Subordination by means of rulers is the beginning of social organization and of the state."[14]

The state functions as a kind of balance of power in Ratzenhofer's thinking, mediating between the process of individualization (*Differenzierung*) and the process of socialization (*Vergesellschaftung*). The state, in its early forms, is a *conquest state,* based upon subjugation and force; social evolution later brings the *culture state:* "The predominance of peaceful interest on the basis of a community pattern made secure by conquest introduces the culture-state; this state seeks to combine the necessity for subordination with creative culture freedom."[15]

Beyond this stage of statehood, where political exigencies and cultural strivings are balanced and compromised, Ratzenhofer does not venture to predict. However, he leaves the definite impression that the evolution of state forms has not ceased and that the future may hold new patterns in store:

The social order is an organization of the struggle for existence for the purpose of assuring sustenance and the propagation of healthy generations. It is therefore sensible to assume as the end of social evolution a situation in which in spite of the multiplicity of occupationally-differentiated individuals, a cultural, political, and social equality of mankind may enter, under the leadership of an intellectual-moral elite. Under this system of social control by moral and intellectual authority, social evolution may be possible without the degeneration of inborn and acquired interests; but such equality for a long time will be modified by inequality and by changes in the basic conditions of life.[16]

Gottfried Salomon has admirably summarized Ratzenhofer's conception of social and political evolution:

Ratzenhofer regarded conflict as the fundamental social process and in common with Gumplowicz saw the genesis of the state in the struggle of races. According to his evolutionary scheme all primitive social organizations were based upon kinship; as population expanded territorially, racial differentiation occurred. In the resultant conflict between various races over the food supply, subjugation of one group by another led to a higher step in the social process in which the social structure no longer rested principally on blood relationships but upon the state as a system of social control.

There followed a differentiation of social structures based on commerce, alternating with socialization which arose from social necessity and expressed itself in voluntary submission for the sake of social interest or in forcible subjugation under an alien interest. In the course of the evolutionary development of the social structure from simple to complex the state, based on conquest, gave way to the culture state, which attempts to control conquered peoples in harmony with creative freedom by maintaining order in social affairs through compromise of opposing interests.

Ratzenhofer held that struggle and war continue to consolidate the social structure and are thus sources of political power, while culture and commerce weaken the social bond; the universal extension of the socialization process tends to produce concord of interests through the increasing perfection of the social organization, but the basis of social conflict remains.[17]

IV. POSITIVISM IN SOCIAL SCIENCE

Ratzenhofer worked not so much with data as with "hunches," based on casual personal experiences and the ethnology of the day, which consisted for the most part of colorful travelers' tales. Consequently, a realistic appraisal of his importance to contemporary social science must recognize that, for the most part, controlled observation of human behavior is taking the place of the old spontaneous-combustion technique in arriving at generalizations, and hence a large proportion of Ratzenhofer's work must be considered as definitely dated. However, there is an area in the field of sociology where the disciplined imagination is still the primary method of transportation, and it is in this half-metaphysical periphery that Ratzenhofer may still be considered a living force. I refer to that universe of discourse variously referred to as the philosophy of science, epistemology, or perhaps the sociology of knowledge, where able men of all faiths are struggling to survey the unexplored boundaries of scientific effort and to define the direction, scope, and meaning of disinterested inquiry.

On this point Ratzenhofer was unequivocal and, considering the pleistocenic nature of social science at the time that he was writing, his suggestions are remarkably acute. "Positive monism" is the term given by Ratzenhofer to his views, summarized in the following quotation:

> Social life can be scientifically understood only on the basis of a monistic view of the world; that is, in the light of a philosophy which subordinates all phenomena to a unifying principle..... Without this positive monism a sociological regularity is impossible.
> The fundamental problem of sociology is to demonstrate the *peculiar* sociological regularity and to distinguish it from the regularity of the phenomenal world in general.[18]

As suggested earlier, the idea of the lawfulness of the universe supplied this unifying principle. Ratzenhofer believed the social actions of men to be as much governed by laws (regularities) as are the paths of the planets. Particularly incisive were his criticisms of theories which posited "free will" or some other arbitrary element as a motivating agent.[19] In his St. Louis speech he pointed to the problem of volition as a major field for investigation. To what extent, he asked, may the human will affect "the inevitable"?

The central position of the blood-bond in Ratzenhofer's theory led naturally to a sustained interest in racial problems. On this subject Ratzenhofer differed widely from Gumplowicz; for many years the latter held the view that the races of mankind are of polygenetic origin, the myriad strains merging as civilization spread. Ratzenhofer vigorously denied this, upholding the theory of the common origin of contemporary racial stocks. In his St. Louis address he summarized the race problem in the following questions:

1. Is the origin of the human race such that it can be regarded as a unity?
2. What differences of value are to be attributed to the *pure races*, which have developed the permanent forms of racial mixtures through in-and-in breeding, and what values are to be assigned to the *mixed* races, with fluctuating traits?
3. What *value* has the race-concept for social evolution in general and in particular in given times and places?
4. What consequences for social development follow from the fact of *race difference*, and of the *variety* of *inherited talents*, as products of biological development, of history, of locality, of environment, and of prevailing ideas?[20]

Here again Ratzenhofer presents a type of thinking which was good enough for his day but must be modified in the light of empirical research in anthropology and biology. Ratzenhofer's monism led him to place heavy emphasis on the "natural" sciences: ".... the physical laws of the world are the foundation of social phenomena, and chemistry has important teachings for the understanding of the social process."[21] The most important of these teachings from the physical sciences was this: that real sociological assurance lies in the careful observation of the empirical, living *present!* Sociologists are fools, Ratzenhofer says, when they confine their interests to the dead past or to the examination of the atypical—namely, the inhabitants of jails and asylums or the primitives in remote corners of the earth. His warning presages Earnest A. Hooton's more recent statement to the effect that our case record files bulge with information concerning mental and physical deviants, at the same time that we neglect to collect a single complete case study of a normal person.

In line with his eagerness to learn from the physical sciences, there appears in his thought the further notion that control and prediction should be made the goal of sociological research: "From the standpoint of sociology men will learn to recognize as scientific no research until, as is always the case with the natural sciences, it strives after future control of the phenomena."[22] This statement projects an attitude toward scientific sociology which is only beginning to be appreciated today.

Gustav Ratzenhofer's efforts to give dignity to the struggling new sociological discipline—and in Germany sociology's fight for academic status was a bitter one—are being paralleled in the United States today by an equally vigorous group of sociological loyalists, who face the same threat of extinction at the hands of the impatient natural sciences, on the one hand, and sociology's methodologically virginal "pure empiricists," on the other. Ratzenhofer's contribution to this campaign will probably be recorded as his culminating intellectual achievement.

NOTES

1. The most complete biographical account of Ratzenhofer is contained in his posthumous work, *Soziologie* (Leipzig, 1908), which was edited by his son.

2. This essay, Ratzenhofer's last work, has been translated by Albion W. Small in "The Problems of Sociology," *American Journal of Sociology*, X (September, 1904), 177 ff.

3. *Soziologische Erkenntnis* (Leipzig, 1898), p. 24.

4. *Ibid.*, p. 56.

5. *Ibid.*, p. 57.

6. *Ibid.*, p. 253.

7. *Ibid.*, p. 252.

8. P. P. Jacobs, *German Sociology* (New York; privately printed, 1909).

9. A. W. Small, *General Sociology* (Chicago, 1905), p. 282.

10. *Soziologische Erkenntnis*, sec. 22, pp. 244–45. This epitome was translated by Small and appears in his *General Sociology*, pp. 189–95.

11. *Soziologische Erkenntnis*, pp. 3, 227.

12. Jacobs, *op. cit.*, p. 32.

13. The following synopsis is taken from *Soziologische Erkenntnis*, Sec. 22.

14. *Ibid.*, p. 246.

15. *Ibid.*, p. 248.

16. *Ibid.*, p. 250.

17. Article "Gustav Ratzenhofer," *Encyclopaedia of the Social Sciences*, XIII, 121.

18. Small, "The Problems of Sociology," pp. 177–88.

19. *Soziologische Erkenntnis*, p. 306.

20. Cf. Small's translation of the speech in *American Journal of Sociology*, X (September, 1904), 177–88.

21. *Soziologische Erkenntnis*, p. 81. George Lundberg's recent book, *Foundations of Sociology* (New York, 1939), has raised some of these issues again, and the ensuing *Streit um Lundberg* is amusing to watch, particularly when one views it in the light of the antiquity of the argument.

22. Cf. Small's translation of the speech, *op. cit.*, p. 183.

CHAPTER XX

THE UNIVERSALISTIC THEORY OF SOCIETY OF OTHMAR SPANN AND HIS SCHOOL

BARTHOLOMEW LANDHEER

I. PRECURSORS OF THE UNIVERSALISTIC THEORY OF SOCIETY

THE theory which claims to see society and its interrelations in their broad cosmic significance was called "universalism" by the Austrian social philosopher, Professor Othmar Spann, who first developed it. Spann does not, however, pretend to have discovered anything entirely new. The Universalistic theory is based upon ancient philosophical and religious beliefs. As an ardent lover of Germanic culture, Spann saw in his theory the rediscovery of German doctrines which had been lost sight of in the hectic civilization of our machine age.

After the completion of the first books in which he outlined his doctrines, Spann discovered by accident the works of Adam Müller (1779–1829). In Adam Müller's writings he found exactly the same basic principles which underlay his own theories. After pursuing further the history of this trend, he gave to his ideas the name of "neo-romanticism," on account of their affinity with the philosophy of the Romantic period. Strangely enough, romanticism has been regarded mainly as a movement in the realm of art and literature, though it has been quite as productive in the contemplation of the nature of the community.

The most remarkable philosopher dealing with this subject was Johann Gottlieb Fichte (1762–1814). Fichte did not belong to the Romantic school in his early period, but in his thinking he soon lost the connection with French rationalism by which he had been influenced when a young man. The same change occurred in other thinkers of this period, such as Karl Wilhelm Friedrich von Schlegel and Johann Joseph von Görres. They all underwent the influence of rationalism until the French Revolution demonstrated the logical outcome of these doctrines and made these thinkers more conservative.

In his *Reden an die deutsche Nation,* Fichte broke very decisively with rationalism and cosmopolitanism and proclaimed the idea of a national culture. He saw the nation as the spiritual unit, which he considers the *conditio sine qua non* of a real culture. He laid the reason for the breakdown of his country to the egotism of the rulers and to the absence of a rich community life. To overcome this destructive situation, he advocated a rigorous education on a national basis. Fichte considered the community to be of divine origin, and for this reason its cultivation and development is the main duty of the human being. This same idea is expressed in his philosophy in the famous sentence: *Das Ich setzt im Ich das Nicht-ich* ("The individual creates the other through himself").[1] The human being cannot be thought of as a single individual, but only as living in a community as a part of the whole. This is his natural destiny. The abstract individual of English and French rationalism is a pure fiction in Fichte's eyes.

Similar to these thoughts of Fichte were the ideas of the other philosophers of the Romantic school. Among them were Karl Wilhelm Friedrich von Schlegel (1772–1829); Johann Joseph von Görres (1776–1848); Friedrich W. J. von Schelling (1775–1854), who has been called "the Plato of the Germans"; and Franz Xaver von Baader (1765–1841). They all had similar tendencies in their social philosophy. In all of them we find the conception of the state as a higher order of institution. Often this idea is developed in a mystic or pantheistic way.

The fundamental sociological work of the Romantic period, however, was *Die Elemente der Staatskunst* ("Elements of the Art of Governing") by Adam Müller. In this book the social philosophy of romanticism was outlined in the most complete fashion, not only dealing with the state and community but also presenting new views about the economic system.

Adam Müller considered the state and community to be one and the same thing. He did not see any community life outside the state. His basic idea in interpreting the life of communities is the principle of differentiality (*Lehre vom Gegensatz*). The differences between individuals arise through the influence they have on one another, the movement of life. Not only the persons who constitute the present state are a part of it but also the generations which came before them. In the same way he extends this idea to all living human beings outside the community. Both these groups—the living and the dead—though they do not actually belong to the community, do influence its life through their ideas and conceptions. People are dependent not only upon each other but also upon nature through their material wants. Therefore, they are also united in the economic system in their struggle to exploit the material world.

This idea of interdependence is one of the main conceptions of Müller's social philosophy. The final unit of the community is not the individual but the family. The order of old and young, men and women, which is observed in nature, ought to be realized in the community. Müller, consequently, did not cherish the ideal of equality; he believed in a pattern of groups, such as clergy, traders, artists, and nobility. His state was not a democratic association of individuals but a system of unequal groups. He repudiated any utilitarian conception of the state. In the state he saw the highest manifestation of human life. He considered the state to be an eternal institution which we can trace back to the beginnings of history. The state is the most essential tie of the spiritual and physical forces of human beings, the condition for the existence and well-being of a nation.

Most clearly is his view expressed in the following sentence: *Der Staat ist die Totalität der menschlichen Angelegenheiten, ihre Verbindung zu einem lebendigen Ganzen* ("The state is the totality of all human affairs, their unification in a living whole").[2]

The economic system has the function of serving the nation. It has to deal not only with material goods but also with spiritual ones. Müller's theory of money accords with this view. Money is the tie which binds the community together. Its material substance is of no importance. The amount of money, in the form of coin, paper, or credit, ought to be increased or decreased according to the needs of the community. This theory of money, which sounds relatively modern, was one of Müller's greatest contributions to economic science.

In the last period of his life Adam Müller became a member of the Catholic church and developed his ideas further in a theological and mystic direction.

II. FUNDAMENTAL NOTIONS IN SPANN'S UNIVERSALISTIC INTERPRETATION OF SOCIETY

After this short treatment of the ideas of the Romantic[3] period, we shall understand more readily the universalistic theories of Othmar

Spann (1878———) and his school. Spann was already struck, in his first investigation when he was a *Privatdozent* at the University at Brünn, by the idea that social phenomena can be regarded in two ways: genetically, according to their origin, or functionally, according to their consequences in society.[4] This led him to make the distinction between the "individualistic" and the "universalistic" theory of society. The individualistic doctrines, based on the principles of the exact sciences, consider society of secondary value; the individual is something existing by himself and can reach his highest development without being interfered with by others. Social control has to be limited to a minimum to safeguard these rights of the individual.

The clearest example of this theory is found in the philosophy of Hobbes, who postulated a primitive condition of nature to explain state and society. In this stateless condition men lived as solitary beings, each sufficient to himself and in constant war against the others. To end this unbearable condition the individuals bound themselves together in a state. They formed the state by entering into a social contract. This shows clearly how the individualist thinks of the individual as something self-sufficient and how society is based on a secondary and external consideration.

Other examples of this individualistic theory are anarchism, which claims absolute freedom for the individual, and Machiavellianism, the doctrine of the state as an institution of brute power. More important, however, and of much greater historical influence, is the above-mentioned contract theory, according to which the individual deliberately gives up his freedom to secure a safer and more peaceful life. This, however, gives society a merely utilitarian function. This theory played a large role in the period of Sophistic philosophy, and later on in the *jus naturale* of Hobbes, Grotius, Locke, Pufendorf, Spinoza, and other seventeenth-century philosophers. As special forms of the contract theory the schools of "laisser faire, laisser passer" and English liberalism dominated historical trends from the end of the seventeenth century until the present day. Politically, it created our modern democracies and the other liberal forms of government.

In all these theories the basic assumption is the absolute freedom of the individual, the belief that the individual as a spiritual entity can exist entirely by himself. This view was created under the influence of the physical sciences, which dominated the period.

This basic principle of individualism is flatly denied by Spann.[5] Spann believes that society is the core and essence of human life. Only as a member of society is the individual real and able to develop his spirituality. Spann frequently refers to the saying of Aristotle: "For the whole necessarily precedes the part."[6] This does not mean temporal but logical priority: the recognition of the individual as an indispensable part of society.

From this it follows that the human being cannot develop out of himself but only in spiritual community with others, in mutuality or in polarity. Spann calls this mutuality *Gezweiung,* using an old German word. This conception is necessary in order to understand that the world is an intelligible whole, where nothing exists without relation to something else and where not blind chance but purpose governs as the final cause. Whereas the existence of others is a mere accident for individualism, it is of the utmost necessity in the Universalistic conception.

Spann gives many examples—friendship, love, sociability, the family, education, and so on—to show how the human mind comes to full expression only in close relationship to other minds. He shows that we cannot understand the human mind as a spontaneous growth. It is created and stimulated into existence, as *lumen de lumine,* where only others' minds are always the igniting torch, the beaming light out of darkness, the midwife of the mind, to use a Socratic figure. All psychic vitality exists through the being of others, in the same way as parts of the organism are organs through their relation to other members—outside this relation they are not organs but only masses of matter. Psychic life and spiritual existence mean self-existence through existence in others. For universalism the mind is mere potentiality which can realize itself only in a psychical community. As potentiality, the individual is outside society; potentiality is prior to reality, and therefore to society. The creative realization of the individual comes about through mutual creative stimulation in associated mental life. The final factor in this awakening of potentialities is the uniqueness of the individual. The awakening activity of society is not general or abstract, but always special and concrete. The creation of individuality takes place through the impress of mutuality in a unique and peculiar form.

It is clear that the conception of society as a spiritual community leads to very different consequences from the implications of the individualistic view.

Spann considers the "organic" theory of society as partly Universalistic. It is based, however, on a biological principle and therefore has a tendency to become materialistic. The same can be said about the *milieu* theory and historic materialism. They both have a Universalistic trend in their social theories, but their basic philosophy is materialistic. This applies also to all theories which define society as the result of social instincts. They, too, deny the spirituality of the human being and mean a degradation of personality.

More than any of these theories, universalism has a strong resemblance to the Platonic conception of the state. Plato's philosophy of ideas had a tendency to become too rigid in its application to reality. Spann tries to avoid this through his conception of potentiality. This gives his philosophy a dynamic aspect. The totality which gives existence to the members of society, the individuals, is not something static and absolute but something which is in a state of constant development, which always changes and exists in continuous creation—which is Life. Spann calls this theory, to underline this tendency, "kinetic universalism."

The totality of society exists through life in the members. The life of the whole is possible only through the life of the parts. Society emerges and is expressed in partial wholes, such as science, art, religion, philosophy, etc. They are the subtotalities in which the spiritual totality becomes manifest. They are the "objectification systems." Society never exists in its absolute form but in always changing subtotalities. The formal conception of society is: "Society is spiritual and acting totality" (*Gesellschaft ist geistige und handelnde Ganzheit*).[7] Materially, society is totality, realized in concrete subtotalities.[8] In what specific partial totalities society will express itself is a question not to be answered a priori by pure deduction but through an investigation of the facts.

Sociology, therefore, becomes, first, the theory of all the partial totalities of society and, second, the general theory of the main principles of all the special social sciences. The basic concepts of the special social sciences are identical, for they are all taken from general sociology. For some of the partial totalities, such as science, art, religion, and social organization, a general sociology is the only treatment available; for others there are special sciences, such as economics, ethnology, political science, history, etc.

The last two principles on which Spann bases his analysis of society are emotion and action. That which is realized emotionally becomes purpose for action. The mind, being conscious of the emotions, guides all action. Both elements have their own mode of connection. In love, friendship, religion, art, etc., we find the connection of spirituality. As previously outlined, this connection with others is essential to personal development.

We also find connection of actions. Spann believes that the connection of actions produces only external relationships. Both types of connection taken together build up the structure of society.

To make possible a constant mutuality of interaction between society and the individual and between social groups, we need means like language, printing, writing, etc. To obtain a certain continuity in the realm of action we use organization (*Veranstaltung*). Organization builds structures like clubs, groups, churches, etc.

Besides organizing, such groups need planning and guiding. This is done through politics or state activity. They are "structures of higher order" (*Hilfsgebilde höherer Ordnung*). A community also needs material goods, but they are secondary as elements of society. They have reality and value in so far as they are used as means for social purposes. This gives them a functional nature. Their social function is the only thing which brings them within the realm of society.

Besides the elements for the immediate construction of a society, we need education and population to project it toward the future and to insure self-maintenance and perpetuation.

Race and talent are the elements which are realized in different degrees and ways in the various types of society. They limit the possible realization of potentiality. For a theory of society they are basic elements. The relation between action and the necessary means gives us the conception of technique.

The connection of spirituality produces the following totalities: science, art, religion, and philosophy. Morals and law define the spiritual values, in so far as they become purpose for action.

In the realm of action we find both co-operative and antagonistic actions. Co-operative action can be found in the economic system, in the creation of groups, and so on. Examples of antagonistic action are war, revolution, competition, etc.

It would lead too far to follow Spann's precise and detailed distinctions. It may be repeated that the whole structure of society is based on the ultimate elements: emotion and action.

It is evident that in his treatment of the totalities of art, science, etc., we always find his universalistic and antimaterialistic philosophy. The final totality is not dealt with in his *Gesellschaftslehre.* It is the main subject, however, of the theory of categories. The final totality, the *Urganzheit,* is the creator of all life. We shall not go into this metaphysical part of Spann's theories, but shall return to the philosophy of society.

III. UNDERLYING CONCEPTS OF THE UNIVERSALISTIC COMMUNITY

We have outlined the main tenets of Spann's social philosophy, so that we may now deal with the type of society which represents most adequately the requirements of a universalistic view.[9]

The basic principle of a universalistic community is justice instead of freedom, which is the ideal of liberalism. According to the ideal of assigning individuals their real place as members of the whole of society, absolute freedom cannot be the goal. Justice, on the contrary, is a constructive conception aiming at correlation between the parts. Justice has not the meaning of equality, but of *suum cuique,* the distributive justice of Aristotle. This idea that everyone has to perform a certain function which defines his position in the community provides the organic aspect of society. The performance by the individual of the task for which he is best fitted gives the highest possible degree of vitality and efficiency to society. In the same way as, in the body, the function of the heart is more important than the one of the hand, so in society we have to give to every function its place and status in the whole. The inequality of the functions produces the structure of society. Society cannot afford to neglect the existing differences among mankind and social functions, because it should be a true representation of the nature of man. The commutative justice, as it is called by Aristotle, which requires that everyone receive as much as he gives, is antiuniversalistic and cruel in its egotism. This conception of "an eye for an eye, and a tooth for a tooth" is the dominating principle of the modern economy. Strangely enough, it was not understood as the denial of Christian philosophy, though it is such in reality. The recognition of the human being as a spiritual entity forbids such a restricted conception of social life.

Freedom, in the individualistic sense, means the liberty to be free from others. For universalism this desire for freedom is not essential; the human being is a *socius,* needing for his very life the company of others. Therefore, we should desire not a minimum of society but a maximum. Freedom is valuable only as providing a possibility of following the path which gives direction and growth to the individual, not as securing isolation. Freedom in the individualistic sense causes spiritual underdevelopment; it is one of the reasons, according to Spann, for the lack of adequate community life of our modern day.

Another conception which has little structural value is "equality." The ideal of equality has caused the atomistic form of our modern communities, where millions live together without any real relationship among them. In nature we do not discover equality, every part of an organism has its special function. Society as a conglomeration of individuals has no real function; it becomes almost senseless.

The danger of the principle of equality is evident in our modern systems of voting: they give equal power to individuals of very different ability and value in society. It is undeniable that human beings vary greatly in character and abilities; every theory or doctrine denying these differences is, in Spann's opinion, a serious danger for a well-established community life. To believe that these differences can be abolished through education is a noble ideal, but one can bring forward very little evidence to justify it. It is clear that, even in the most nearly perfect democracy, no such thing as entire equality has ever been realized. There are always children, criminals, and other individuals who are outside the political community.

Besides the fact that equality cannot be realized, it is not even desirable according to a universalistic doctrine of society. The true structural laws of society are equality among equals and the obedience of the spiritually less developed toward the spiritually higher-developed individuals.

IV. THE FUNCTIONAL HIERARCHY OF THE UNIVERSALISTIC SOCIETY

On these two basic principles Spann builds his "ideal" state. This gives society an organic structure, which assigns to every individual and to every social group a certain function. Between the different parts there has to be a certain balance, which is best realized through a hierarchical structure of society. Every individual is placed according to his value: the hero is of higher value than the criminal. As Spann believes man to be a spiritual being, it is evident that his hierarchy is built up according to a scale of spiritual values.

Every individual belongs to a certain group. Every group has its place in the whole of society. This creates a structure of ranks in which each is given its place.

Since all groups are based on spiritual mutuality, they have to be small, and their members require a certain similarity of ability, though equality is not necessarily demanded. Every society has its own structural laws, which are created by the dominating philosophy of the period.

Every group of society is characterized by its spiritual nature and through its relationship toward other groups in society. The best form of society is the one which brings the best elements to leadership. The leadership of the best means the leadership of the spiritually and mentally highly developed individuals. Spann believes social organization from the top to be the only justifiable procedure. How these "best" members of society are to be chosen or identified is not quite clear from his arguments. He wishes, however, to keep social groups open by admitting capable individuals to higher education.

Spann distinguishes the following ranks as elements of an ideal society listed from the bottom to the top of the functional ladder: (1) workers—their function is to procure the material means of the community; (2) skilled workers in the realm of techniques (artisans) and intellectual workers of the repetitive type; (3) industrial and business leaders—their function is organization of life; (4) leaders of state, army, and church; (5) spiritual leaders and creators.

As spiritual communities, they are to be evaluated according to this classification. The community life of the first group is realized through club life and visits to movies, parties, shows, etc. The second group contains those engaged in the decorative arts, building, and construction, as their work involves repetitive, acting knowledge, etc. The community life of this group is demonstrated in a more cultured form of daily life and through increased interest in art, science, etc.

The leaders of business and industry deserve their place in society through their function in the realm of action. Qualitatively, they need energy and initiative but not the higher spiritual qualities.

About on the same functional level are the leaders of state and army. They deal with establishing a more permanent and higher social order, which justifies their high position. The same is true for the leaders of church life.

The fifth group, the spiritual leaders, are hardly ever recognized as a social group. First of all, no one would recognize them as social leaders; second, they may themselves prefer to be free from community life. It is the tragedy of the genius that he generally does not succeed in finding a stable place in a community. This is caused by his role as creator of new things or thoughts.

Each of the groups ought to have specialized education in the realm of its own function. The workers ought to teach the younger ones; the artisans, their apprentices; etc.

In the hierarchical structure of social ranks, both a horizontal and a vertical division can be made. The vertical division is the one of grades within each rank; the horizontal division comprises different ranks on the same level of (*a*) spirituality, (*b*) action, or (*c*) organization.

V. THE UNIVERSALISTIC SOCIETY

In the realm of means—the economic system—we get a different division. Spann uses the old distinction of agriculture, manufacture, and commerce. Adam Müller traced this division back to the difference in character of these occupations: agriculture being more conservative and manufacture and commerce more progressive.

It is evident that, in the hierarchy which Spann advocates, the economic system will be stabilized. Property will be allotted in the way of feudal tenure, as in the Middle Ages. Private property will remain, but its use will be regulated by law, as is already done today in some European countries. Objects of importance for the community, like big machines, etc., will be loaned to the individual by the community. This development will give the material means their place in serving higher purposes.

Group ownership would also check egotism and develop the more altruistic attitude which is a necessity for every higher type of culture. Spann regards the guilds of the Middle Ages as ideal in this regard. The general principle regulating these relationships would be this: the greater the limitation of private ownership and individualism, the more essential the group is for the community. A group which performs a very important function in society ought to be subject to severe regulation to curb individualism and the pursuit of private interests. As the mentally highly developed individuals would get the higher positions, there would be no hardship in this system, because they are by nature inclined to live more in a spiritual atmosphere.

Spann does not believe that the industrial concentration, which Marx foresaw, will, in reality, develop. Only where strong common interest exists, can concentration on a large scale be possible. It could never be a trend in all realms of economic activity.

An organization of the economic system could take place through the labor unions, on one side, and the employers' organizations, on the other. Collective bargaining already demonstrates the beginning of a fundamental change in the individualistic system. The system of collective bargaining binds the employers and workers into a closed social group. As a proof, one can be referred to the punishment of workers or employers who do not abide by the regulations. Such agreements, which have begun to fix wages, might easily be extended to regulate the whole economic procedure. In this way organic groups would be formed which would shape the life of the community. In every industry a system of representation of workers and employers ought to be built up which could be united in a central body. Trade and industrial unions ought to be combined according to necessity. It is clear that this will complicate matters, compared to the simple guild system of the Middle Ages, but an intrinsic organization would overcome this. The organizations of workers and employers ought to be developed into corporations to buy raw materials, to fix standards, etc. They could have their own banks and savings institutions.

This development would have a tendency to decrease trade, banking, and stock-market activities and to stimulate the more directly productive activities of the economic system. This would destroy a good number of the parasites which inevitably feed on the individualistic system. It is very natural that planning would increase prosperity. Has this ever been denied to be true for a single company?

Depressions cannot, of course, be entirely abolished—the movement of life always takes place in waves—but they would be less under a system of regulation and stabilization.

Civic activities, which now are largely handed over to special authorities, could be transferred to these social groups. All decisions about the legal problems of their industry ought to be intrusted to them. Special courts for the separate industries would develop their own codes. This would create a very wholesome decentralizing tendency. At the same time, it would cause a much greater consciousness of civic duties. The financial regulation of the life of the industries ought also to be given to them. As modern war is highly technical, every industry could supply the branch of the army with which it would be most closely connected. This would not abolish the existing army but only complete and perfect it in case of war. All this together would develop the life of the community to much greater richness than our present system is able to produce.

A well-organized form of society would give the feeling of safety and security which is now entirely lacking. Increase of enterprises of small size and revival of the pride of workmanship would have the same influence.

All the different organizations of employers and workers of agriculture, industry, and trade ought to be united in one general representative body (*Ständehaus*). For the state, only the control of cultural activities, such as religion, education, and law, ought to be reserved.

Spann does not indicate clearly the relation between the state and the *Ständehaus,* leaving this problem open to be solved in the future.

Spann believes that the rich community life which would develop in a hierarchical system of corporations would solve the problems from which individualistic society—or competitive order—suffers. The increased spiritual development would overcome our present difficulties, which are all caused by the egotism of individuals. This egotism has been fostered by the system of liberalism and the individualistic philosophy on which it was based.

The science of society reveals this conflict of social interests very clearly and, therefore, is able to contribute to the creation of a better type of society. An objective study demonstrates that an individualistic doctrine could interpret only a type of society which is based on material wants and the mere necessities of life. Even to explain such a situation, individualism remains a mere abstraction. Since the last decades have indicated that the world is again moving toward an organized type of society, individualism becomes hard to understand or to defend, even as a doctrine. Only the overdevelopment of the exact sciences and the concentration of mankind on economic pursuits can account for its existence and popularity. Rationally, we may still understand the arguments of individualism; but how wrong they are in practice has been proved by the course of history. Othmar Spann believes that he has opened the way for a new vision of the nature and problems of society and underlined the spirituality of the human being. A materialistic conception of human affairs could, in his opinion, never contribute anything to the study of the problems of the community.[10]

Spann also applied his universalistic principles to economics and built up a very closely reasoned system, based on the functions which the economic means perform for cultural purposes.[11]

This, together with his purely philosophical works, completes his system in the structure as it stands today.

While Spann formulated his general social philosophy in pre–Guild Socialist and pre-Fascist days, it bears a close resemblance to the Guild Socialist idea of self-government for functional groups and the corporative state of the Fascists. Indeed, Spann is probably more respected by Fascist sociologists than is any other pre-Fascist social thinker except Pareto. Taken as a whole, Spann's views constitute a synthesis of the Platonic and Aristotelian notion of government by the élite, medieval notions of economic ethics, the spiritual organicism of the Romantic philosophers, Syndicalist and Guild Socialist notions of functional self-government, and the Fascist idea of the corporative state and of national and folk culture. But his restriction of the state merely to the control of general cultural interests and activities can hardly be harmonized with the totalitarian view of the omnipotence of the state.[12]

Perhaps Spann should be understood as an artistic nature who revolted against the harshness of modern society. By looking backward he created a system that has the merit of pointing out the weaknesses of an unbalanced, overindividualistic society; but his analysis did not go deep enough to evaluate the fundamental trends of modern civilization and to arrive at the belief that an international community might solve the problems which the national state could not answer but for which the solution certainly cannot be found in a return to the past.[13]

NOTES

1. Fichte, *Grundlage der gesammten Wissenschaftslehre* (ed. "Medikus"), I, 285.

2. Cf. Adam Müller, *Elemente der Staatskunst* (Jena, 1922), I, 37.

3. Compare on this period: J. Baxa, *Einführung in die Romantische Staatswissenschaft* (Sammlung, "Die Herdflamme" [Jena, 1931]), and *Gesellschaft und Staat: Ein Spiegel deutscher Romantik* (Jena, 1924).

4. Othmar Spann, *Kategorienlehre* (Jena, 1924), p. 6.

5. Spann developed his theory for the first time in "Zur Logik der socialwissenschaftlichen Begriffsbildung," *Festgaben für Friedrich Jul. Neumann* (Tübingen, 1905).

Further in his main works: *Haupttheorien der Volkswirtschaftslehre* (20th ed.; Jena, 1930), which appeared as *History of Economic Thought*, translated by Eden and Cedar Paul (New York, 1929); *Fundament der Volkswirtschaftslehre* (4th ed.; Leipzig, 1930); *Gesellschaftslehre* (3d ed.; Leipzig, 1930); *Gesellschafts-Geistes* (Jena, 1928); and others.

6. Aristotle *Pol.* i. 1, par. 11 (German translation by Susemihl).

7. *Gesellschaftslehre*, p. 507.

8. To make this clear, it may be mentioned again that "totality" is the final category of Spann and means "spirituality." Spirituality is final substance.

9. Spann develops his ideas on this point in *Der wahre Staat* (3d ed.; Jena, 1930).

10. Spann's universalistic doctrines have been taken up and further developed by others. We mention W. Andreae (Graz) (translation of Plato in "Herdflamme," Vols. V, VI, XIII), *Bausteine einer universalistischer Steuerlehre* (Jena, 1927), *Grundlegung einer neuen Staatswirtschaftslehre* (Jena, 1930); J. Baxa (Vienna) *Geschichte der Produktivitätstheorie* (Jena, 1926), *Gesellschaftslehre* (Leipzig, 1928); Karl Faigl (Brünn), *Ganzheit und Zahl* (Jena, 1926); Walter Heinrich (Vienna), *Grundlagen einer universalistischen Krisenlehre* (Jena, 1928), *Die Staats- und Wirtschaftsverfassung des Faschismus* (Berlin, 1930); J. Sauter, edition of Baader in the collection "Herdflamme"; and others. Rather close to universalistic philosophy are Alfred Ammonn von Below, "Zum Streit um das Wesen der Sociologie," *Jahrbücher für Nationalökonomie*, Vol. CXXIV (Jena, 1926); J. Dunkmann, *Der Kampf um Othmar Spann* (Leipzig, 1928); Wolfgang Heller, *Theoretische Volkswirtschaftslehre* (Leipzig, 1926); E. J. Jung, *Die Herrschaft der Minderwertigen* (Berlin, 1930); and E. Salin, Egon Scheffer, and Suranyi-Unger.

11. In *Fundament der Volkswirtschaftslehre* (4th ed.; Jena, 1929).

12. It is reported that Spann was held under careful observation by the Nazis after the annexation of Austria.

13. The author of this article gave a survey of Spann's thinking in "Othmar Spann's Social Theories," *Journal of Political Economy*, XXXIX (1931), 239–48. Some of the aspects of Spann's philosophy are mentioned in the author's *Der Gesellschafts- und Staatsbegriff Platons* (Rotterdam, 1930). Cf. also his "Presupposition in Social Sciences," *American Journal of Sociology*, Vol. XXXVII, No. 4 (1932), and "Industrie en Cultuur," *Tijdschrift voor Wijsbegeerte*, Vol. XXVII, No. 5 (1934).

CHAPTER XXI

THE SOCIAL AND POLITICAL THEORIES OF
LUDWIG STEIN: A PHILOSOPHY OF SOCIAL
PROGRESS AND POLITICAL REFORM

HARRY ELMER BARNES

I. GENERAL NATURE OF STEIN'S SOCIOLOGICAL THEORY

LUDWIG STEIN (1859–1930) was the most cosmopolitan of the Germanic sociologists. He was born in Hungary of Jewish parents, was educated in Holland and at the University of Berlin, was for years professor of philosophy at the University of Bern, returned to teach at Berlin, took a prominent part in German social science and journalism, and acted as a mediator between the German and the British governments. Few other sociologists in any country have taken so active a part in public life. In 1923–24 he lectured extensively in the United States.

Stein's most distinguished work was done in the field of the history of social philosophy. His major work was his *Die soziale Frage im Lichte der Philosophie: Vorlesungen über Sozialphilosophie und ihre Geschichte.* First published in 1897 and revised and enlarged in an edition of 1923, Part II of this book was for a generation the most competent history of social thought. Its theoretical portions were published in French in 1900 as *La Question sociale.* This is the most readily accessible summary of his sociological views. Other important works by him on sociological topics were *Wesen und Aufgabe der Soziologie: Eine Kritik der organischen Methode in der Soziologie* (1898); *Der soziale Optimismus* (1905); *Die Anfänge der menschlichen Kultur* (1906); *Philosophische Strömungen der Gegenwart* (1908); *Einführung in die Soziologie* (1921); and *Evolution and Optimism* (1926). His last work was designed as an answer to the pessimism with respect to Western culture expressed in Oswald Spengler's *The Decline of the West.*

As might naturally be expected from a professor of philosophy interested in sociology, Stein held that sociology is the unifying philosophy of the special social sciences, in the same way that general philosophy is the unifying element in all knowledge. As he put it in the London *Sociological Papers,* in 1904: "Sociology is social philosophy, a department of the whole philosophy which systematizes and brings into the most complete formulae the unity of the different kinds of relations of men which are investigated separately by the respective specialisms."

This is essentially the view that was held by Schaeffle, Barth, and Ratzenhofer in Germany, and by Albion W. Small in America; it was sharply opposed by Professor Giddings and his followers and, in general, by the statistical school of sociologists. In his general approach to sociology and in his notions of its problems and methods, Stein was most directly influenced by the writings of Comte, Spencer, Morgan, and Lester F. Ward.

The three main tasks of sociology, according to Stein, are: (1) the investigation of the history of social institutions; (2) the tracing of the development of social theories; and (3) the formulation of rules and ideals to guide the social development of the future. This outline of what he believed to be the proper scope of a system of sociology was strictly adhered to in his *Die soziale Frage im Lichte der Philosophie.*

The fundamental principles of Stein's social philosophy are those of causality, teleology, and continuity. Social causality is manifested in the universal tendency of social institutions to change with alterations in the fundamental economic and psychological foundations of society. The best illustration of this principle of causality in society is to be seen in the vast changes in political and social institutions which have taken place since the economic foundations of society have been transformed by the commercial and industrial revolutions. The principle of teleology in society is to be discovered in the changes which have been effected in laws and institutions by the conscious action of society—in other words, the attempt of society to improve its own condition. Finally, the element of continuity is to be discerned in the mutual interrelationships and linkage of different stages of social evolution, in the principle of gradual development, and in the almost invariable failure of any attempt suddenly to change the nature of social institutions by revolutions or direct legislation, unguided by social science.

The basic principle of Stein's interpretation of the phenomenon of human association is the old Aristotelian dictum of the instinctive basis of elemental social groupings, i.e., communities. Stein's rather peculiar and arbitrary definition of society, however, precludes the possibility of his regarding organized society as an instinctive product. Like Ferdinand Tönnies, he distinguishes sharply between "community" and "society." Community life is an instinctive product. The period of community domination in social existence was found in the era when primitive social groups, like the family and the horde, held sway. Here the social bonds were consanguinity, contiguity, the sexual instinct, and common intellectual interests. The economic and intellectual bonds in community life prepared the way for the development of society out of the previous stage of community.

Society, according to Stein, is a more advanced form of social grouping than community. It presupposes, besides contiguity and association, the additional element of conscious co-operative activities. Human groupings do not reach the stage which can accurately be called "society" until they become purposive organizations. Stein's distinction between community and society is, of course, very similar to the differentiation made by Professor Giddings between component and constituent societies or between instinctive and rational societies or, again, that maintained by Durkheim between segmentary and functional types of society.

Stein attempted, in not too convincing fashion, to combine a theory of cultural determinism with the doctrine of the hegemony of the white race. He contended that the cultural environment is of primary importance in shaping social life and the course of history. Yet, at the same time, he held that the operation of the evolutionary process made it inevitable that the white race would gain dominion over the planet.

In harmony with his view of the proper scope of sociology, Stein made a sociological study of the evolution of the family, property, society, the state, language, law, and religion (*Die soziale Frage,* Part I). He next presented his famous history of social philosophy (*Die soziale Frage,* Part II), and concluded his main work with an exposition of his program for the solution of the outstanding social problems of the present (*Die soziale Frage,* Part III).

Stein was an optimist and believed that civilization is improving and is capable of a high degree of further development through the conscious self-direction of society, when guided by the laws reached inductively by sociology. Indeed, as we have noted, his last important work, his *Evolution and Optimism,* was a brief but eloquent effort to combat the pessimism of Spengler.

Stein's original work of 1897, when dealing with the problems of social evolution, while well abreast of the average sociological treatments of these subjects, is now antiquated, as it was based upon the generalizations of the classical anthropologists, such as Lubbock, Spencer, Morgan, Tylor, Post, Max Müller, Letourneau, Lippert, and Grosse. When the volume was printed, however, some fifty years ago, these writers were the "authorities" upon the subject of historical sociology, and to question their conclusions was held to be almost a sacrilege. It is a sad commentary upon the lack of scientific alertness on the part of some sociologists that these very works are often quoted in contemporary sociological writings with the same degree of reverential credulity which was accorded them half a century ago.[1] In his last work, the *Einführung in die Soziologie*, and in the revised edition of *Die soziale Frage*, however, Stein showed decent familiarity with recent anthropological literature and makes many references to the work of Franz Boas.

II. SPECIFIC DOCTRINES REGARDING SOCIAL AND POLITICAL PROBLEMS

A. FUNDAMENTAL CONCEPTS AND DEFINITIONS

It has already been shown that Stein considers sociology to be the general unifying philosophy of the special social sciences. Therefore, political science is regarded by Stein as one of those subordinate specialisms, the results of which are used by sociology as the basis of its final survey and unitary arrangement of social data.

Stein analyzes in detail the essential relations and differences between society and the state. Society may be regarded as the organization of the co-operative activities of individuals for the purpose of regulating their reciprocal relations. The state is a social institution designed to secure the protection of the persons and property of its citizens.

Society is thus the most fundamental organization of humanity and prepared the way for the later development of the state. Though society is prior to the state, it is not, in the opinion of Stein, the most elementary type of association. Society developed gradually out of the more primitive and basic stage of "community." Community, tribal society, the territorial state, and modern international society are the chronological stages in social evolution. Looked at from another point of view, society is voluntary, though conscious, in character and is the chief agency in promoting the interests of the individual. The state is a coercive organ which is mainly concerned with the interests of the political community as a whole. Again, society is a much more all-inclusive organization of individuals and is much more flexible and plastic than the state. After viewing the problem from these various standpoints, Stein formulates his final definition of the state as follows:

We may behold in the State, especially in the modern civilized State, the substantial organization of the inevitable subordination and superposition of the individuals and associated groups within it, with the aim of establishing an equilibrium of interests between the legitimate personal necessities of individuals and the interests of the nation and humanity as a whole which are frequently in conflict with individual interests.[2]

In contrast to his lengthy discussion of the distinctions between the state and society, Stein devoted little attention in his earlier books to the equally important matter of the differences between the state, the government, and the nation. The term "state" was employed by him both in the strict usage of political science and in the popular sense as synonymous with "government." At the same time, he often made the state include the attributes which are usually assigned to the nation. There can be little doubt that Stein's failure to differentiate carefully between the state and the government and his subordination of nationality to the state were the result of his Swiss political environment, where, in many of the cantons the state and the government are practically identical and where a common nationality does not exist, the state being the only unifying agency. In his *Einführung in die Soziologie* his differentiations are much clearer, and he accepts the scientific distinction between the state and the nation.

B. THE ORIGIN OF SOCIAL AND POLITICAL INSTITUTIONS

Stein's theory of the origin of social organization and the state is a qualified combination of Morgan's theory of social evolution with a moderate version of Gumplowicz' doctrine of the conflict of social groups. The first stage of social evolution was the period of community, which was based on the bond of unorganized or undifferentiated blood relationship. In this period the only types of social organization were extremely crude groups, such as the primitive family and the horde. In his theory of the evolution of the family, Stein roughly follows the scheme of development postulated by Morgan, but he considers Westermarck's objections.

The next stage of human evolution—the period of the beginnings of conscious social relations, according to Stein's use of the term "social"—came with the development of the gentile organization of society. While this stage brought a system of regulation of social relations which was, on the whole, adequate to the demands of the time, gentile society was a period of idyllic democracy as compared to the present. Stein's representation of the Iroquois as free from the burden of conventionality and custom which oppresses the modern man strongly resembles the Rousseauean variety of anthropology when viewed in the light of the later researches of Hewitt, Parker, and Goldenweiser. The alleged universality of the gentile organization of primitive society has been disproved by critical ethnologists; and even in those places where it did exist it could hardly be deemed the most primitive type of society, unless one accepts Stein's arbitrary definition of society.

Though the *gens* marked the origin of society, the series of social and technological changes which brought the state into being began with the development of agriculture. Like many writers from Rousseau to Morgan, Loria, and Oppenheimer, Stein holds that private property in land broke up primitive felicity and paved the way for the immediate development of the state. Agriculture created a need for slave labor, and the ensuing raids upon neighboring bands to secure slaves produced the earliest wars and brought about the origin of the warrior class. The danger of attacks from others led to a differentiation of the population of each group into the two fundamental classes of warriors or protectors and laborers or producers. Either offensive or defensive warfare, if successful, required an effective centralization of power; and, when the *gens* conferred upon the leader the power to compel the group to bow to his will, the essence of the state had appeared. Primitive democratic communism was then well on its way to transformation into absolute monarchy. The increased wealth of the chief made it possible for him to render his power more secure and enabled him to assume new functions. As industry and social relations developed, conflicting interests appeared within society, particularly between the servile class and its masters. The state was able to extend its influence here by adjusting the differences between the contending parties which threatened to disrupt the integrity of society. It became an umpire of social conflict.

This period of conquest and the integration of groups was an essential stage in the development of social and political institutions. Tribal communities and small nations have always been doomed to perpetual warfare and arrested development. Only by means of large-scale warfare could a sufficient degree of integration be effected so that a compact and powerful state could be formed. Paradoxical as it may seem, centuries of warfare were required as a preparation for any final cessation of war. Besides this, war provided a valuable discipline for the race.

War being thus the most dynamic agency in the integration of states and the discipline of society and the human mind, the more vigorous the warfare, the more rapidly this bloody but necessary stage in social evolution could be completed. Therefore, the great conquerors of history, while morally little more than assassins on a large and picturesque scale, really rendered a great service to the progress of civilization without being aware of the fact.

While Stein thus practically agrees with Gumplowicz, Ratzenhofer, and Ward in regard to the process through which the state originated, he does not hold with Gumplowicz that progress must always be a result of the conflict of groups. In facing the future he stood, rather, with Novicow. The formation of large and compact states by war was but the necessary preparatory period for the gradual cessation of war and the achievement of progress through the clash of cultural interests, the development of co-operative activities, the division of labor, and legislation based upon the sound principles of sociology. In this respect, the attitude of Stein greatly resembles the position taken by Lester F. Ward. Both emphasize the teleological nature of future progress.

The national territorial state is not, however, the last stage in social evolution. Already modern society, international in most of its interests and activities, has become more powerful and important than the national state. Man's voluntary activities, which are distinct from the activities of the state, are now preponderant. The national state will be followed by the socialized state and a federation of states.

C. SOVEREIGNTY AND THE PRINCIPLE OF AUTHORITY
IN HUMAN SOCIETY

In an interesting article, "Die Träger der autoritätiven Gewalt,"[3] Stein analyzes the nature and value of the principle of authority in society and traces the changes in the nature, sources, and organs of authority throughout history. The principle of authority is as important for the maintenance of the race as the principle of self-preservation is for the

individual. Those who wield authority in society are the instrumentality
for the education and discipline of the social will.

Stein finds that the organs of social authority have been successively:
"1. die elterliche, 2. die göttliche, 3. die priesterliche, 4. die königliche,
5. die staatlich-militärische, 6. die rechtliche, 7. die Schulautorität, 8. die
Wissenschaftsautorität." Stein further maintains (1) that, in the course
of the historic changes in the sources and organs of social authority, institutions have displaced persons as the bearer of authority in society;
(2) that, whereas originally authority was imposed by individuals upon
the community, now the group imposes its authority upon individuals;
and (3), finally, that, while in the past, authority was wielded for the
selfish interest of the individuals in power, at present it is being consciously employed by the community for the purpose of securing social
discipline and the steady improvement of the welfare of the group
The changes in the nature, sources, organs, and conceptions of social
authority have been correlated with successive stages of social development and the different types of civilization.

While Stein nowhere analyzes in detail the nature and importance of
sovereignty, considered in the technical or conventional connotation of
political science, he devotes very considerable space to the treatment of
the principle of authority as manifested in society. As a part of this
general analysis he touches by implication upon the specific problem
of sovereignty. His treatment of the subject is to be found in *Die soziale
Frage* (pp. 460–80), in the article on "Die Träger der autoritätiven
Gewalt," and in another entitled, "Autorität, ihr Ursprung, ihre
Begründung und ihre Grenzen."[4] He gives us a representative sociological approach to the problem of sovereignty.

Authority, Stein holds, is the basis of order in the social organism,
corresponding to the dominance of law in the mechanism of nature.
The development of authoritative control over social groups was the
indispensable prerequisite for the passage from unorganized communal
life to the stage of organized society. This development of authoritative
control in society goes back in its origins to groups of animals, where
it had its beginnings in force and the imitative instinct. Among men,
authority begins in the power of the heads of families and of the leaders
in war. Authority was the force which domesticated man and made him
fit for society. Civilization has never developed except as a result of the
previous establishment of the principle of authority in society.

The type of social authority which is to be found in any particular group depends upon the stage of civilization and the character of the composition of the group. The more fierce and uncivilized the group, the more severe must be the type of authority. Force was thus the first basis of authority. Faith and credulity are the foundation of the second type of authority. Ancient and medieval priests and emperors exercised their control because the masses believed them superior and actually vested with the natural and supernatural powers which they claimed. Beginning with the French Revolution, there has developed a higher form of authority—that based upon intelligence.

Though authority is indispensable in the evolution and functioning of society, it should not exceed its legitimate scope. When it has reached the point where it obstructs and restrains cultural development instead of advancing it, authority is to that extent an undesirable evil. Egypt in antiquity, the Byzantine Empire in the Middle Ages, and Spain in modern times have been "horrible examples" of how an excess of authority can obstruct progress.

Reviving the Hegelian myth, Stein maintains that the Germans have solved for future civilizations the age-long problem of the reconciliation of liberty and authority. *Vernünftige Einsicht und öffentliches Wohl* ("rational intelligence and public welfare") has been the formula followed by them in making this notable contribution, and it is interesting to learn that the main personal agent in grounding the Germans in this principle was no other than Frederick the Great.

D. LIBERTY AND AUTHORITY

Stein, in his treatment of the abstract question of liberty and authority, takes the sensible view that liberty can be secured only through the protection of the interests of the individual by the state. The anarchistic ideal of absolute liberty is a pure chimera. Liberty, while important, is not the sole goal of social effort or of evolution. Equal in importance are a just reward for labor, the intellectual development of the race, and the raising of the standard of living for every stratum of society.

As a substitute for that liberty which is the ideal of the individualists, Stein offers that of the "socialization of law" (*droit*). By this, he says, "we mean the juridicial protection of the economically weak; the conscious subordination of individual interests to those of the State, but ultimately and fundamentally to those of mankind as a whole."[5] In the case of a writer who is so favorably inclined as Stein was toward the socialization of the activity of the state, the abstract question of individual liberty could be regarded only as a minor consideration, when compared with the benefits which might accrue from reform legislation Stein agrees with Priestley and Bentham that "the greatest happiness for the greatest number" is about as satisfactory a formula for the guidance of the social reformer as has ever been devised, in spite of the difficulties involved in both its metaphysical interpretation and its practical application.

E. THE FORMS OF THE STATE AND THE GOVERNMENT

Stein makes little attempt to provide us with a comprehensive treatment of the different forms of the state and the government. He merely touches upon the subject in dealing with other topics. In a republic and a constitutional monarchy, sovereignty is vested in the whole body of the people, while in a despotism the ruler possesses sovereign power.

While he had great confidence in the Swiss democracy, Stein showed no patience with the view that all men are created equal. He maintains that it is one of the primary principles of sociology that men are of unequal ability. While the state may adjust itself to these inequalities, it cannot hope to eliminate them. Equality before the law is the only sense in which men can be held to be equal. Democracy is founded on an aristocracy of ability just as much as a monarchy is. At the same time, the masses in a democracy are not so entirely devoid of reason, as Gustave Le Bon would have us believe. Democracy does not necessarily mean mob rule.

In general, while Stein seems to regard the Swiss democracy as the most advanced type of modern government, he had very high admiration for the efficient German bureaucracy of the Empire. This admiration for the Germany polity of the Hohenzollern Empire, evident in Stein's writings, was somewhat stimulated by his German residence after leaving Bern. His more recent work, the *Einführung in die Soziologie,* however, is notable for the moderation of tone, the absence of chauvinism, and the frank recognition of the inadequacy of the modern national state system.

F. THE DESIRABLE SCOPE OF STATE ACTIVITY

In regard to the question of the proper scope of state activity, Stein lays down the preliminary proposition that the range of legitimate action on the part of the state must necessarily vary with the degree of civilization. The higher the development of society, the greater the number of interests which it is the duty of the state to protect and harmonize.

It is the prime duty of the state to preserve and protect the equilibrium of interests which are represented in its citizens. Only the state is able to harmonize the interests of the individual and the race. This achievement is the real goal of social evolution.

After these few preliminary observations, Stein sketches what he believes to be the desirable activities to be undertaken by the state. He says at the outset that he intends only to suggest the general outlines and will leave the details to be worked out by specialists. While he denies that he can correctly be designated as a socialist, Stein proposes a program of state activity which more nearly coincides with the views of the socialistic group than with the doctrine of extreme individualists, such as Herbert Spencer. He says that his theory of state activity is a wise synthesis of the programs of the socialists and the individualists "qui nous assure les avantages d'un mode de production collectiviste, sans abandonner l'émail incomparable de ce qui est intimement personnel, le parfum enchanteur de l'individualité."[6] Stein makes the very pertinent observation that the amount of successful state activity which is possible depends upon the morale and efficiency of the existing governments.

Stein enumerates a considerable list of activities and industries which should be taken over by the state. This list includes the postal service; the telegraph and telephone service; the railroads, distilleries, mines; the salt, match, and tobacco industries; and all dangerous occupations. Further, the state should assume all insurance business within its boundaries. The state must guarantee to its citizens the right to live, which, under normal circumstances, means the right to work. If the industries mentioned above are not sufficient to employ all who cannot secure private employment, it is the duty of the state to enter into other lines of industrial activity for which it is specially adapted, so that it may furnish the necessary opportunity for employment. Moreover, the state should protect the interests of its prospective citizens who are yet unborn through "the taking over by the state of all the underground natural resources which have not been discovered, of all water power which the technology of the future will exploit for industrial purposes, as well as the exploitation by the state of the most important inventions of the future."[7]

Stein holds that the state should control all the important inventions made by its citizens and should reward the inventors by salaries and official honors which will make the incentive to invent much greater than it is at present. He believes that when the state has taken up the role of the enterpriser to the extent that he has indicated, it will be able to fix and equalize prices and will be strong enough to make private capital follow its lead.

Aside from this direct participation in industry, Stein believes that the state should establish agencies to adjust or eliminate the struggles between capital and labor and to prevent the exploitation of the citizens by monopolistic combinations. As to the practical application of his program for the extension of state activities, Stein points with a considerable amount of justifiable pride to the fact that Switzerland may serve as a school of social reform for the rest of Europe. Stein contrasts his program with that of the socialists in the following paragraph:

The Social Democrats demand the extinction of the modern capitalistic State; we demand its conscious perfection; they desire a fraternal and international alliance of the proletariat of the world; we desire, first of all, a fraternal national alliance of all classes and producers of all levels; they demand the elimination of all private property and of the private ownership of the means of production, and the abolition of all wage employment; we demand the maintenance of an economy of private property under a socialized form, a mixed type of industry divided in control between the State and private enterprise, which would not entirely extinguish labor for wages, but would soften its repulsive harshness; they demand at once a socialized state, or, in fact, a "society," in order that they may build from within it a polity; we demand, on the contrary, first of all, a socialized law and polity from which there will naturally proceed, like ripened fruit, the socialized state.[8]

G. THE STATE AND SOCIAL PROGRESS

Stein maintains that the evolution of political and judicial institutions must keep pace with the general course of social evolution. If the political and legal machinery is not adjusted to the needs of the time, it must submit to a radical reform in order to make it competent to deal with the present situation. It is desirable that political evolution should move along gradually and peacefully so that a revolution may be avoided. It was to avert the necessity of a political and legal revolution in the future that Stein formulated his program for the socialization of law.

Like Lester F. Ward, Stein holds that the progress of the future should be primarily teleological. Legislation must be based upon the accepted doctrines of sociology. The state will not disappear in the future, but, reformed and socialized, it will become an increasingly important organ in achieving social progress. It is folly to expect that the course of evolution will be reversed and that society will return to primitive anarchy and communism. Stein, then, stands with Comte, Ward, Dewey, Small, and Hobhouse as an exponent of "social telesis."

H. THE STATE AND INTERNATIONAL RELATIONS

In regard to the question of international relations, Stein, before the first World War, took the position of the majority of sociologists, namely, that, whereas war has in the past made important contributions to the advance of civilization, its mission has been fulfilled, and it should give way to economic and psychic modes of competition. He believed that an alliance of European states would be brought about in the near future and that international disputes would tend more and more to be settled by arbitration.

Europe could not, however, afford to disarm even after the consummation of an international alliance or after it agreed to settle its disputes by arbitration. The danger of an oriental invasion would render it necessary to keep large standing armies, but this expense would find compensation in the moral and cultural value of military discipline.

While Stein, at the turn of the century, believed that war would ultimately be banished from Europe, he expressed the fear, which later events proved to be well founded, that war would not be eliminated in Europe until after a last great conflict. But though there may ultimately be a cessation of war between states, a continuation of the conflict of interests within the state is inevitable and desirable. Competition, within certain reasonable bounds, is indispensable to progress. Here Stein agreed with Ratzenhofer and Novicow.

Not only was Stein a believer in internationalism; he also worked hard to prevent the coming of the European war, which finally broke out in 1914. He was especially interested in promoting an understanding between Germany and England in order to avert hostilities. He supplemented his writings on this subject in learned treatises and in newspapers by much personal activity. He acted as a mediator between the central European powers and the Allies, both before, during, and after the first World War.

In his postwar book, the *Einführung in die Soziologie,* Stein developed still further his theories on the subject of war and international relations, particularly as they had been formulated as a result of the first World War. His doctrine is an ingenious combination of the Marxian and Hegelian types of determinism. He takes the position that the wars of today are caused primarily by economic factors—by the struggle for raw materials. As man earlier fought for pasture lands, so today he struggles for ore, coal, potash, and petroleum. Yet ultimate world peace, internationalism, and a league of nations are inevitably to be produced by the "immanent logic of history" acting in the service of the *Weltgeist*. At the same time, this manifestation of the *Weltgeist*—internationalism and a league of nations—can be realized in practice only through creating an international organization with power to control and equalize the economic resources of the earth. The following paragraphs best summarize Stein's final views on international relations and a league of nations:

The political and social struggles of the human race can be ended only through a league of nations, of which we have now the first groping manifestations. If authority means essentially and primarily a focus of power, the league of nations will represent just as much authority as it has power. By power, I mean not merely an international army, such as was proposed two decades ago by von Vollenhoven but, above all, economic power—a tribunal of economic authorities for the purpose of settling the world-wide battle between capital and labor. Let us not deceive ourselves about this: The political wars are in their ultimate causes economic wars, and the longer they last the more pronounced this economic aspect becomes. The battle for fuel, for coal and petroleum, especially the struggle between capital and labor, dominated the present war far more thoroughly than was the case in the earlier religious wars or the dynastic wars of succession. A purely political league of nations, without the economic foundations for the purpose of regulating the economic intercourse of the world, will be futile. A rump league of nations without the United States of America, Germany, and Russia is a torso.

The alliances and ententes, which characterized the political situation before the war, have furthered the idea of settling by jury such differences as do not involve vital issues between nations. The two conferences at The Hague, the Red Cross, the Fourteen Points of Wilson, the embryonic Institute of the League of Nations in Geneva, Harding's Conference in Washington in November, 1921, are plain evidences that the idea of the league of nations, as proclaimed by the prophets of the old covenant and the *stoa*, has made more progress in the last three centuries than in the preceding three thousand years of history. One would have deliberately to close one's eyes to these impressive facts not to recognize that they reveal an inner logic of history. One need only review these symptoms to convince even those who are opposed to this idea on principle that the logic of social evolution tends to the final goal of a peaceful adjustment among the civilized nations and that it does this according to immanent laws, tenaciously and unswervingly, even if only slowly and seemingly by circuitous routes.

It is for the sociologist to interpret this immanent logic of the historical process. Statesmen make history, sociologists explain it. Great men, says Hegel, are the instruments of the *Weltgeist*, which avails itself of all the human passions as motive power in order to accomplish the goal of human improvement all the more easily and swiftly. The statesmen believe they are pushing, but in reality they are forced by the immanent logic of history to steer a course that the *Weltgeist* needs.

There was originally opposition to obligatory trial by jury, yet how gladly was it recognized by 1908 that there was the Hague Tribunal as a permanent institution, and that in 1913 it had a fixed home. For history is not the crazy dream of a sleeping Deity, but it reveals in large outlines purpose and plan, and reason and continuity. This continuity was first sensed in the stories and fairy tales, the legends and mythologies of our prehistoric ancestors, in a kind of proto-philosophy, as Wundt termed it. The religious myths are, in fact, a low kind of metaphysics, that is, metaphysics in a popular edition, in the phrase of Schopenhauer. The philosophic metaphysics, on the other hand, is meant for the intellectual élite of the human race: it is, so to speak, a dialectical pocket edition of the old mythologies, in the form of logical conceptual processes. After that come the augurs, seers, and visionaries, the star-gazers and astrologers, and they proclaim the future of humanity. All science, says Comte, has this tendency: *voir pour prevoir,* "to understand, in order to predict." And thus arises the task for the sociologist, to interpret the evident processes of history.

The theory of social articulation and institutions developed in these pages, is no mere abstraction of the study room, no speculation in the sense of Hegel, whose Triadic rhythm has been wittily parodied by Fortlage in remarking that it suffered from articular disease. But my sociology keeps closely in touch with the actual course of history. I use the facts of history only in order to explain its causes, in the words of Bacon: *Vere scire est per causas scire.* For that reason I see in cosmopolitanism, on the one hand, the historical stepping-stone to the idea of nationality, and, on the other hand, also the stepping-stone to the league of nations. Nationalism is the antithesis of cosmopolitanism, internationalism is the synthesis of cosmopolitanism and nationalism on a higher plan of consciousness. Internationalism realizes that section of the mutual interests of all civilized and nationally united people which demands a uniform regulation of their common interests and, therefore, accomplishes it by means of a conscious international convention. This regulation of the economy of the world by means of a kind of economic clearing-house is the basic function of the league of nations. Cosmopolitanism is the longing for, nationalism is the limitation upon, and the league of nations of the future the fulfilment of, the idea of unity within the scope of what it is historically possible to realize. Cosmopolitanism is the dream stage of the idea of humanity, nationalism is the waking of the idea of national unity, and internationalism, finally, as it is to be embodied in the league of nations, is the waking stage of the idea of international unity, inasmuch as it deliberately, i.e., by contract, puts together the common interests of all civilized nations.

Wherever, among civilized nations, there exist, in addition to vital national interests, which must be preserved first of all and most certainly, common interests and compromises of interests, international treaties will have to be made. The radically changed international intercourse, which brings to the fore the problem of a world economy, has smashed the dogma of the isolated national state. The goal of history is the league of nations, in accordance with the words of the New Testament: "Peace on earth and good will toward men."[9]

I. EXTRA LEGAL PHASES OF POLITICAL CONTROL

Stein offers some pertinent observations regarding the extra-legal aspects of social control. Man, he says, is in modern society the slave of custom and convention. A society of the modern type can hardly be said to exist where there is not a well-developed public opinion. In the highly developed states of modern times, society, in its most general sense, is more powerful than the state. Laws are not valid or enforcible unless they are supported by public opinion, and, conversely, the state cannot successfully refuse legislation which is persistently demanded by the organized opinion of the body politic. The organ through which public opinion is molded and society is enabled to exercise its control is the press, taken in its most comprehensive sense.[10] This was written by a sociological journalist before the days of the radio and the movies.

J. POLITICAL THEORY AND THE SOCIAL ENVIRONMENT

Stein devotes about a third of his major work to a discussion of the history of social and political theories and the manner in which they reflect their contemporary environment. Stein's own social and political doctrines in many ways reflect his Swiss environment. In the matter of abstract political theory, his identification of the state and the government, and his emphasis upon the state rather than upon the nation as the most important political concept, are tendencies which might well be natural to a teacher long resident in the Swiss republic. His ideal of the socialization of law and the extension of state activities are in full accord with Swiss practice. He invites the attention of Le Bon to the success of democracy in Switzerland and holds that Switzerland might well serve for the model for Europe, both in regard to advanced social legislation and with respect to the formation of a successful and lasting alliance between the European nations. Likewise, his emphasis on the sociopolitical function of authority and the assertion that the Germans alone have succeeded fully in reconciling it with liberty, reflect Stein's German education, experience, and affiliations.[11]

While significant as a social and political theorist, it must be admitted that Stein excelled as a critical expositor and historian of sociological and philosophical doctrines rather than as an original thinker.[12]

NOTES

1. As evidence of the general anachronism of much historical sociology, compare the prevailing theories with the excellent synthesis of the newer point of view in R. H. Lowie's

Primitive Society (New York, 1920); and Alexander Goldenweiser's *Anthropology* (New York, 1937). See also my paper on "The Development of Historical Sociology," *Publications of the American Sociological Society* (1921); R. H. Lowie, *The History of Ethnological Theory* (New York, 1937); and H. E. Barnes and Howard Becker, *Contemporary Social Theory* (New York, 1940), chap. xv.

2. *La Question sociale* (Paris, 1900), p. 230; *Die soziale Frage* (Stuttgart, 1923), pp. 432–33. Translations from Stein's writings in this chapter are the author's.

3. Published in the *Archiv für Rechts- und Wirtschaftsphilosophie*, October, 1907, pp. 44–65; cf. also, *Die soziale Frage*, pp. 460 ff.; and *Einführung in die Soziologie* (Munich, 1921), pp. 288 ff.

4. Published in Schmoller's *Jahrbuch für Gesetzgebung, Verwaltung und Volkwirtschaft in deutschen Reich*, No. 3, 1902, pp. 1–30. These two articles are revised and reprinted in the *Philosophische Strömungen der Gegenwart* (Stuttgart, 1908), chap. xv; cf. *Einführung in die Soziologie*, pp. 388–452.

5. *La Question sociale*, p. 304; see also, *Der soziale Optimismus* (Jena, 1905), chap. vii; cf. Roscoe Pound, "A Theory of Social Interests," *Publications of the American Sociological Society*, 1920.

6. *La Question sociale*, pp. 267.

7. *Ibid.*, p. 283.

8. *Ibid.*, p. 351.

9. *Einführung in die Soziologie*, pp. 449–54.

10. *La Question sociale*, pp. 220–21; cf. *Einführung in die Soziologie*, pp. 51 ff.

11. *La Question sociale*, pp. 215, 292, 459.

12. For a good appraisal of Stein's sociological thought see Franz Oppenheimer, "Ludwig Stein und die deutsche Soziologie," *Neue Rundschau*, 1922, pp. 888–901; and the article on Stein by Gottfried Salomon in the *Encyclopaedia of the Social Sciences*, Vol. XIV. My chapter, in much the same form that it appears here, was read and criticized by Stein before his death. For more elaborate bibliography and references on Stein see my article on Stein in the *Open Court*, May, 1924.

PART IV

CONTINENTAL EUROPEAN SOCIOLOGY IN
NON-GERMANIC COUNTRIES

CHAPTER XXII

THE SOCIOLOGICAL DOCTRINES OF JACQUES NOVICOW: A SOCIOLOGICAL CRITICISM OF WAR AND MILITARISM

HARRY ELMER BARNES

I. GENERAL NATURE OF NOVICOW'S SOCIOLOGICAL SYSTEM AND A DESCRIPTIVE LIST OF HIS CHIEF WRITINGS

AS WAS pointed out in a preceding chapter on Gumplowicz, the chief immediate influence of Darwinism upon sociology, aside from stimulating research into the early history of mankind, consisted in leading many writers to attempt to construct systems of sociology on the foundation of the Darwinian formula, carried over into the realm of social phenomena without a proper modification. There thus arose a pseudo-Darwinian sociology, bristling with misleading dogmas, though in some instances emphasizing very important social processes which had hitherto been neglected. Among the sociologists of this type, Gumplowicz and his followers were the most conspicuous, and allied with them were certain statesmen and political scientists, who used the pseudo-Darwinism as a cloak for their militaristic dagger. While some biological writers, particularly Wallace, Huxley, and Pearson, had pointed out the fallacies involved in a direct transference of the Darwinian biological terminology into the field of sociological investigation, the Russian writer, Jacques Novicow (1849–1912), was the first avowed sociologist to devote his life and system of sociology to a refutation of the doctrine that an unmitigated physical struggle for existence is the chief factor in the social process and the mainspring of human progress.

The experiences of Novicow's own life doubtless did much to determine the nature of his sociological and political theories. His own cosmopolitanism must have had an important influence upon his fundamental doctrines regarding the value of a federation of nations and the necessity for the cultural assimilation of peoples before attempting to make them a part of any political group. Coming to France as a young man, Novicow used the French language as a medium of expression, and many of his ideas reflect the influence of the western European environment. This is particularly apparent in his antimilitaristic doctrines and his frequent attacks upon Bismarck and the policy of "blood and iron" which the latter represented. The Franco-Prussian War and the seizure of Alsace-Lorraine are constantly utilized, even exaggerated, to illustrate the folly, perfidy, and injustice of militaristic statesmanship. At the same time, his earlier life in Russia left its imprint in making Novicow an implacable enemy of despotism and of all interference with the free and spontaneous development of the human mind and the unhampered spread of ideas. Like Thomas Jefferson, he had apparently sworn "eternal enmity to every form of tyranny over the mind of man." His Russian environment also served to stimulate his emphasis on co-operation and mutual aid as socializing factors.

Novicow's first important work was entitled *La Politique internationale*.[1] According to the opinion of Eugène Véron, who furnished the Introduction to the work, it was the first coherent and comprehensive exposition of a theory of international political organization. Probably this is rather an extreme statement for, as Mr. Darby and others have shown, from the days of Dante onward an occasional writer, from time to time, had set forth the idea of a union of nations; but there can be little doubt that Novicow's work was one of the first scientific modern treatments of the subject.[2] The first portion of the book is devoted to an analysis of the organic theory of society and to a discussion of the nature and mutual relations of the state and the nation. The second part is a prelude to his major work, *Les Luttes entre sociétés humaines,* and states his fundamental contribution to sociology, namely, that, while the struggle for existence is the all-important process in social evolution, this struggle in society is destined to become primarily a cultural, rather than a physical, type of conflict.

The concluding portion, which deals specifically with the problems of international political organization, is based upon this theory of intellectual conflict, since the chief advantage of international federation is that it will make it possible for states to carry on an intellectual struggle, which is beneficial, in the place of the highly detrimental physical conflicts that occur in the form of wars. This work contains the suggestions and theses which were elaborated in *Les Luttes* and further developed afterward in a number of separate volumes.

Novicow's chief work, and the one which embodies all his vital conceptions, is entitled *Les Luttes entre sociétés humaines et leurs phases successives.*[3]

Novicow's basic thesis is that the course of human evolution has been characterized by struggles and alliances which, in a serial succession, have been primarily physiological, economic, political, and intellectual. While all these types of strife must necessarily persist, they constitute a progressive series in which the intellectual struggles are the highest type and are becoming increasing predominant. In fact, even the lower types of strife are tending to come more and more under rational direction. Novicow devotes his first book of *Les Luttes* to a brief survey of the fundamental propositions, the expansion and elaboration of which constitute his sociological system. At its close he summarizes them conveniently as follows:

> The universe is an arena of endless combats and alliances.
> It is impossible to fix any limit to the possible extent of association.
> The struggle for existence is a universal phenomenon. It is in turn and successively chemical, astronomical, biological, and social.
> Between plants and animals the struggle takes two principal phases: elimination and absorption.
> But even among animals we may distinguish economic and mental struggles.
> Alliance does not necessarily exclude the possibility of struggle within groups, but it modifies the nature of the struggle.
> The result of the struggle for existence is adaptation to the environment.
> From the psychological point of view, adaptation to the environment furnishes the most exact formula for comprehending the nature of the universe.
> The struggle for existence, in eliminating those least adapted to the cosmic environment, brings about an increasingly perfect harmony between the subject and the object.
> Pleasure consists in a harmony between the external and the internal world.
> Finally, progress is simply an acceleration of the process of adaptation.[4]

With these general propositions in mind, Novicow's analysis of the chief historic types of human conflict may be examined in greater detail. Each of the four phases of human struggle—physiological, economic, political, and intellectual—appears under two different manifestations— a slow and irrational type and the more advanced, rapid, and rational variety.[5]

The *physiological* struggle has two main modes—elimination and absorption. The processes of the former are self-evident and need not be discussed. The latter is manifested in a slow and irrational manner by the killing of one's own kind for food, as in cannibalism, and in a rapid and rational manner by killing inferior beings for food and by producing food in an artificial manner. In either case the purpose of the physiological struggle is to obtain nourishment.

The *economic* struggle and the more elementary and temporary aspects of the political struggle shade into each other. The purpose is to secure riches, and the slow and irrational type of struggles of this variety takes place by killing or threatening to kill others to secure: (1) the means of subsistence through raids in search of food; (2) private movable goods through raids appropriating personal property and slaves; (3) private immovable goods through the confiscation of lands and dwellings and the reduction of the conquered inhabitants to a condition of bondage and servitude; (4) public movable property through a war tax (5) public immovable wealth by means of a permanent tribute. The rapid and rational manifestation of the economic struggle and of the elementary and temporary political struggle takes the form of (1) more rapid production for a better market than is the case with competitors and (2) good government, resulting in an increase of the revenues of a country.

The higher and permanent *political* struggle has for its object the securing of riches and the satisfaction of national or group vanity. It manifests itself in a slow and irrational manner through killing or threatening to kill or punish others, in order to obtain by conquest a revenue for the conqueror or superior political rights and privileges for the conquering group. The rapid and rational method of carrying on the higher type of the political struggle is through leading foreign states to desire annexation, thereby building up political federations, and by carrying on a propaganda to spread, by persuasion, political conceptions and ideals among the various neighboring nations.

The *intellectual* struggle has for its purpose the securing of mental satisfactions of various sorts. Its slow and irrational manifestation is through killing, threatening to kill or punish, or through granting favors to others, for the purpose of imposing a set of ideas upon a people by religious wars or persecutions or for the purpose of forcing a given type of civilization upon another people by coercive denationalization. Finally, the rapid and rational type of intellectual struggle is seen in promoting the free assimilation of ideas and in stimulating the imitation of the culture, the spread of which is desired.

Novicow formulates certain fundamental deductions and generalizations regarding these four main types of struggles with their various manifestations. He holds that these human struggles in society are but a continuance of the earlier chemical, astronomical, and biological conflicts. These four types of conflict form a logical sequence, and progress consists in increasing the scope and influence of the higher forms and in substituting within each general type of conflict the rational and rapid manifestation for the slow and irrational expression. This progressive transformation is, to a certain extent, brought about automatically by the operation of the universal biological law that all living beings tend to avoid pain and seek pleasure. The lower and more elementary types of conflict are obstructive to progress if introduced into the higher phases of conflict. This explains the folly of any attempt on the part of the state to interfere with the various manifestations of intellectual conflict.

The further development of civilization in the future will not bring about a cessation of conflict but will, rather, tend to produce a greater amount of strife within society. The conflict, however, will become increasingly intellectual in character, and the growth in its volume will thus be beneficial, as social evolution is most rapid in those societies which provide the widest scope for intellectual conflict. Not only will conflict in the future increase in volume and tend to become predominantly intellectual, but it will be accompanied by an increase of justice and sympathy and a decrease of hatred. It will tend toward competition, tempered by mutual esteem and tolerance. This series of struggles tends to bring about the survival of the best individuals, and this survival of the best may be regarded as the essence of justice in its broadest signification. Justice is thus the real goal of the cosmic and social processes, which find their final and most nearly perfect expression in the intellectual struggles of humanity.[6]

The subject of the waste and disorder in modern society, particularly as due to the expenditures in wars and militaristic measures and the bungling interference of the government in economic matters, is discussed by Novicow in his work entitled *Les Gaspillages des sociétés modernes.*[7] The indictment of war and its advocates is carried still further in his *La Guerre et ses prétendus bienfaits.*[8] Here, Novicow examines briefly the physiological, economic, political, intellectual, and moral effects of war. In the concluding portion he develops the thesis that social Darwinism is a theoretical blunder and a misapplication of Darwinian biological theories to social processes. He assails Gumplowicz and Ratzenhofer as the two most conspicuous exponents of this type of sociological theory.[9]

The possibility of a federation of European states and the advantages which would accrue from such a movement—a proposal to be found in all of Novicow's works—is treated in a specific and extended manner in *La Fédération de l'Europe*.[10] The first part of the work is devoted to the economic, political, and general advantages of a federation of European states. In the second portion he finds that the chief obstacles to international federation are: greed for territorial expansion, the prestige of war, the errors of militaristic leaders and theorists, the jealousy of vested militaristic interests, chauvinism and the desire for national expansion, the defiance of the rules of international justice, race hatred, egotistical patriotism or national myopia, the illusions of nationality, the conservative effects and inertia of routine and tradition, and, finally, the lack of constructive imagination. In the third part of the work he discusses the factors which favor federation, such as economic technique and organization, the extension of the mental horizon, ethical and political forces, improved military technique and organization, general European patriotism, and the growing spirit of cosmopolitanism and universalism. In the concluding sections he analyzes the methods by which the federation is to be achieved, the progress which has already been made in this direction, and the probable character of future international federal institutions.

Novicow's most direct and telling attack upon pseudo-Darwinian sociology is embodied in his *La Critique du darwinisme social*.[11] This work is devoted to a relentless criticism of the exponents of the theory that group struggle, on a physical basis, is the chief motive power in social progress. Spencer and Renan are criticized to a certain extent, but Ward and Ratzenhofer receive the brunt of the attack. Gumplowicz, the most flagrant of the offenders in this respect, is for some reason passed over with almost no reference. Aside from a large amount of criticism of individual systems of sociology, the earlier part of the work is devoted to an analysis of the errors of the sociologists in interpreting biological processes and of the logical confusion involved in the direct application of biological formulas to social processes. The latter portion of the work considers the erroneous doctrines and policies which are a result of the elaboration of these systems of pseudo-Darwinian sociology.

While Novicow's criticism is as one-sided as the theories of his opponents and neither school shows an assiduous application to the latest researches in biology, anthropology, and ethnology, no one should attempt to defend the doctrines of the Gumplowicz-Ratzenhofer–Oppenheimer-Ward group without first having considered the objections so skilfully marshaled by Novicow. Particularly satisfactory is Novicow's attack upon what he designates, with a considerable degree of accuracy, as "anthropological romances," namely, the assertions that primitive groups are inherently hostile to one another, that social evolution is the automatic result of physical conflict in society, that industry originated wholly in slavery, and that the state took its origin and development exclusively from the wars of primitive tribal groups.

Novicow's last comprehensive work, *Mécanisme et limites de l'association humaine*,[12] a fitting conclusion and summary of his literary activity, is an elaboration of his oft repeated doctrine that there is no logical or practical limit to the possible extent of human association. He shows that Western society is becoming, in every aspect except that of legal relations, a single unified human association, and he carries further his demonstration of the erroneous nature of the objections offered to the feasibility of international federation. International relations and social progress in all fields depend upon a proper understanding of the mechanism of association.

Exchange is the source of life, while spoliation is the fundamental phenomenon of death. Exchange is the real foundation and source of human association. It involves the exchange of commodities for commodities, of commodities for services, and of services for services. Ultimately, all exchange is based on the increase of personal enjoyments. Not only association but also the division of labor and civilization itself are based on exchange. In modern civilization, with its improved mechanism for transportation and communication, no valid limits can be set to the possible range of exchange. Therefore, one cannot set limits to the development of human association. Exchange not only brings about association and social organization; it also produces the state and justice. The state is essential to the settling of property problems connected with exchange, to the enforcing of rules of exchange, and to the development of the mechanism and technology of transportation and communication. In fact, exchange is far more significant in producing the state than war and conquest, which are so unduly emphasized by Gumplowicz and his followers.

Exchange not only creates the state but is also preparing the way for the federation of states. Most international agreements already made relate in some way to exchange, as, for example, international adjustments relative to waterways, telegraphs, post offices, reciprocity, and the like. Contrary to a general impression, commerce is far more a cause of human solidarity than of social and national conflicts. The true and logical boundaries are those social boundaries based on exchange or on vital circulation. Political boundaries are those which impose limits on lawful spoliation. If it were properly understood that spoliation is not a means of gain but that it ultimately brings about the destruction of the despoiler, as well as his victim—in short, it is a pathological illusion —then political boundaries would tend to approximate basic social boundaries. But it has already been shown that social boundaries, based on exchange, are international. Therefore, the disappearance of the "spoliation illusion" will naturally be followed by international federation and the extinction of the irrational phases of class struggle within human society. International anarchy and social oppression require for their elimination only a proper education of the world as to the dangerous fallacy involved in the doctrine of spoliation, and Novicow's own work constitutes the dedication of a lifetime of literary activity to that laudable end.

Next to his criticism of war and militarism and his resultant defense of international arbitration and federation, the most important of Novicow's contributions to social theory was the sociopsychological contention in his organic theory of society that the élite constitute the brain of the social organism and that they are the source of the ideas and attitudes which exercise control over society. He set forth this conception most forcefully in his *Conscience et volonté sociales,* which was published in 1897. He thus divided with Gaetano Mosca the distinction of having launched the contemporary sociological version of the dominion of the élite in society, a notion which had been common among publicists from Plato and Aristotle to Jefferson and Calhoun.

II. SPECIFIC SOCIOLOGICAL AND POLITICAL DOCTRINES

A. THE NATURE AND SCOPE OF SOCIOLOGY

According to Novicow, sociology is the general and all-inclusive science of society, of which the special social sciences are subordinate branches. It is based upon the laws of biology and psychology and has, for its main subdivisions, economics, political science, and jurisprudence. Sociology is still in the metaphysical stage of a priori dogmatism. It cannot reach a state of high development until it has been based upon the concrete, exact, and inductive methods of the natural sciences. When it has arrived at the status of a true science of society, it will be the indispensable guide for the conduct of political activities.

B. FUNDAMENTAL DEFINITIONS AND CONCEPTS

Novicow's differentiation between the concepts "society," "state," and "nation" is clear and accurate. He admits that it is hard to determine just where society begins in the world of phenomena, even though it is not difficult to decide upon the attributes of a society. The mere contact or contiguity of a number of objects does not constitute a society; in addition to continuity, there must be reciprocal action and relations among the different units. But this reciprocal action begins among the chemical elements in the inorganic world and passes by degrees of intensity up through the cells of organic matter and the mutual relations of individual animals and men to the division of labor between groups of men. In fact, it is as difficult to determine where a society ends as it is to discover just where it begins. From a morphological point of view, a society may be defined as "a group of living beings among whom each individual is easily distinguishable and is separated from the other members of the group in a manner equally discernible."[13] From the functional standpoint, "society implies the bringing together of certain individuals, between whom vital relationships have been established."[14] From the psychological point of view, a group may be said to be transformed into a society "from the moment in which the members are conscious of the solidarity which links them to those of their kind."[15] The close resemblance of this last definition to Professor Giddings' conception of the "consciousness of kind" as the distinguishing mark of a society is readily apparent.

The state is a special type of society—one which possesses an organization designed to defend its citizens and its material possessions. The nation differs from the state primarily in that it is founded mainly upon psychic traits and cultural possessions rather than upon material wealth and interests. The nation is, thus, a higher product of social evolution than the state and need not be identical in extent with the state. While there has been a tendency in European history to attempt to make the state identical with the nation, there are many instances both in the past and at the present of one nationality distributed among a number of states and of one state comprehending several different nationalities.[16]

As no other sociologist has given more careful attention to the problem of nationality than has Novicow, it might be well to describe more in detail his conception of the attributes of nationality. He examines, in turn, the various criteria which have been proposed as tests of nationality, including territorial unity, racial homogeneity, a common language, a similar religious system, like legal institutions, resemblance of manners and customs, and identity of historic destiny. He concludes that neither any one of these criteria nor all taken together can be regarded as constituting the essence of nationality. They are all important elements of nationality, and a common language is an indispensable prerequisite for national development, but to them must be added the element of sympathy or psychic affinity and solidarity.

Nationality is not a sudden acquisition. Rather it is the product of a long period of evolution, in the course of which a group passes from the bonds of a constraining political solidarity, through the attachment of mutual material interests, to a psychic solidarity. This very fact that a nation is the product of a long developmental period and is based upon common psychic traits that can be produced only through a long-continued period of assimilation and interaction demonstrates the folly of attempting to reduce different peoples to a common nationality in a short period of time by compulsory and often brutally repressive measures. Not only is the nation a higher product of social evolution than the state, but it is also a more important agency in social progress. The state is at best a clumsy and expensive collective policeman; progress and initiative have their roots in the nation.

The important distinction between the state and the government is not clearly defined or consistently maintained by Novicow. As to the attributes of the state, at least of the state as it exists at present, Novicow is in accord with the general consensus among the best writers on political science. He holds that its four fundamental attributes are territory, popu-

lation, sovereign power, and governmental organization. While Novicow admits that absolute sovereign power within its boundaries is at
present regarded as an indispensable mark of the state, he believes that
such a power is more metaphysical than real and is, moreover, most
detrimental in its implications and results. The conventional view of
absolute sovereignty is the chief obstacle to the consummation of
European federation. He would allow the state nothing but administrative authority and would confer sovereign authority upon the future
federation of states.

Much more important for political theory is Novicow's discussion of
the psychological and economic factors in the state, but, as these subjects
are dealt with in other sections of the chapter, they may be passed over
briefly here. Particularly important are his emphasis on the significance
of intellectual competition as the chief dynamic force in cultural progress,
his contention that the intellectual artistocracy and not the state are the
real brain of the social organism, and his doctrine that economic phenomena and factors, especially those of exchange, were the chief causes
of the origin and development of the state and the most potent force
which is determining both its present characteristics and its future
changes.

C. THE ORIGIN OF POLITICAL INSTITUTIONS

In regard to the problem of the origin of the state and government,
Novicow's opinions show a considerable variation as between his earliest
and his later views. This change in attitude can best be understood by
examining his opinion on this subject as expressed in *Les Luttes* and
the modification of this theory as found in his latest view of the subject
in *La Critique du darwinisme social* and *Mécanisme et limites de
l'association humaine.*

The account, as presented in *Les Luttes,* may be briefly summarized
in the following manner: Man originally lived as a nomad, and the
primitive social groups were held together by bonds of real kinship.
In other words, the first social bond was biological. These primitive
groups of nomadic kinsmen multiplied and subdivided with each new
generation, and the new groups united with the original bands in larger
kinship groups, such as gentes and tribes. The next type of social grouping—the territorial state—grew up as a result of conflict between these
primordial kinship groups. These bands of kinsmen were wont to carry
on pillaging expeditions against their neighbors, and the successful exe-

cution of such enterprises called for an effective organization for concerted activity. At the same time, as each group was exposed to reciprocal attacks from other pillaging bands, it was compelled to develop an organization for collective defense. Out of this twofold organization for collective activity—offensive and defensive—there grew by degrees the political entity known as the "territorial state." Property also played an important part in the origin of the state. After a chief had conquered a neighboring group and levied a tribute, he was compelled to protect this tribute-paying group, not from humanitarian reasons but to preserve his source of revenue from being appropriated by some rival chieftain. As land was the main type of property in primitive times, the most important booty of these early pillaging groups was the territory of the conquered groups, which was distributed among the followers of the successful chieftain. Of course, history affords instances of pillaging groups, like the German *comitatus,* which were not based upon kinship but, rather, were created by voluntary agreement. Such cases, however, were the exception rather than the rule.

Though the state may have had twofold origin in organization for both offense and defense, the latter purpose has been by far the most important element in its survival. The state has persisted as a social institution, after a long period of evolution, because it has proved its ability to confer advantages upon its citizens, particularly in regard to the security of life and property. Along with this establishment of political institutions on a firm territorial basis, there went a widespread transformation of social institutions in general. Agriculture was improved. Commerce, the development of money and capital, the division of labor and other important progressive steps in social functioning made their appearance. The growing security aided in the production of wealth, and legal institutions had to be improved in order to regulate these increasingly complex industrial and commercial relations.

The first type of territorial state was the small city-state, so characteristic of antiquity and the Middle Ages. It was normally small enough so that all the citizens could participate personally in the political life. The process of war continued to flourish at the expense of those that were loosely or ineffectively organized. In this manner there arose the empires of antiquity and the national monarchies of early modern times. Homogeneity has always been a very important factor in the organization of the state and, consequently, in its expansion. Other things being equal, the more homogeneous a state, the more effective its organization and the more rapid and permanent its expansion. If the expanding state did not take steps to assimilate its additions and keep homogeneity moving apace with aggrandizement, it constantly faced the danger of disruption, and many of the ancient empires perished from this very cause. This homogeneity, taken in all its manifold aspects, including the sentiment of solidarity, constitutes the principle of nationality. For this reason there has been a natural tendency in political expansion to attempt to make the state identical with the nation and forcibly to assimilate conquered peoples. But, at present, this principle of forcible assimilation is no longer justifiable, whatever may have been its value at more remote periods; and the only rational modern procedure is to let the people decide to what state they desire to attach themselves. Political frontiers should be decided by the will of the peoples concerned. The only commendable type of political expansion at present is an attempt at peaceable assimilation of a neighboring group through leading them to imitate and thus adopt the culture of the more powerful state. Annexation should follow and never precede assimilation and should come only as a result of a proposal on the part of the annexed population.

The national state of modern times cannot be regarded as the final stage in political evolution or the limit of human association. Already, neighboring nationalities are forming cultural groups held together by intellectual and economic bonds. Western Europe is, in fact if not in law, one common civilization. The next logical step will be to give the existing condition legal recognition by forming a European federation. This will put an end to the wars on that continent, terminate the almost equally disastrous system of armed preparedness, and leave the revenue of the component nations free to be used for intellectual improvement and the increase of material comforts. This European federation will have for its primary function the maintaining of peace and security among its members. It will not interfere with political subdivision and decentralization within each nation. When statesmen and citizens grasp the fundamental truth that the nation and not the state is the important factor in social evolution and when they understand that nationality will maintain itself best without political interference, then and only then will the state tend to become what it should be in modern times—a convenient administrative unit. Nationalities will subdivide themselves into a number of different states, in accordance with the principle of adaptability to administrative convenience and efficiency. The political development of the future, then, will be twofold: large-scale federation to preserve peace, and administrative subdivision and decentralization to promote governmental efficiency and popular interest in political affairs.

The main subsequent divergence from this early theory of political evolution is to be found in his later treatment of the subject in *La Critique du darwinisme social,* and it appears chiefly in his revised notion of the origin of the state. He almost completely abandons his earlier theory of the origin of the state, by denying that war, force, or spoliation had any important influence in this process. He labels the theory of the origin of the state through war and the forcible subjugation of groups, as advanced by Ratzenhofer and Ward, "an anthropological romance."[17] He asks the pertinent question, which the group-struggle school has rarely been able to answer without resorting to the grotesque theory of a polygenetic origin of mankind, namely, as to the origin of these contending groups which formed the state through their strife.

In this book Novicow maintains that all available evidence goes to show that the state has normally been the product of the peaceful organization of commerce and industry. Industry had its origin in co-operation, specialization, and the division of labor rather than in slavery, as Ward contends. The foundations of the state were laid in tribal society when nomadism had ceased and a group had permanently occupied a tract of land for agricultural pursuits. The bond of kinship was replaced in the course of time by a territorial organization, in order to secure greater administrative convenience. The state had a peaceful economic origin rather than a warlike derivation. Political organization did not even arise from the attempt to defend a territory, much less from the desire to exploit the lands of another group. It took its origin from the fact that a set of impartial rules was needed to control in an equitable manner the economic processes of co-operation, division of labor, and exchange.

The state was, thus, primarily the product of the organization of industry and commerce and the provision of legal rules to protect property and give security to society. It existed, in fact, long before it had assumed a place in conscious theory. War, far from producing the state, actually delayed its origin in many instances.[18] Though wars may have had an influence upon the later development of states, the type of political evolution accomplished in this manner is slow, irrational, and pathological, compared to the rapid and rational progress achieved as a result of economic motives and intellectual impulses.

It would unquestionably have been wiser for Novicow to have presented his later theory as an unemphasized aspect of his earlier doctrine rather than to have denied completely the validity of his first opinion. This course would have had the double advantage of greater consistency and accuracy. Both warlike and peaceful agencies have had an important part to play in political evolution—a fact emphasized by Professors F. H. Giddings, E. C. Hayes, and others. Novicow would have done better to have attempted to present both sides of the picture without denying the partial validity of each.

In his latest work, *Mécanisme et limites de l'association humaine,* Novicow gives a summary of his final views on the origin of the state and holds firmly to the economic, rather than the military, view of political origins:

Another very important conclusion that arises out of the preceding analysis is that the effects of the economic factors of exchange alone are sufficient for the organization of the state. The theories in vogue at the present day contend that the state can only be formed by coercion. Such theories, however, will not bear the most elementary analysis. A single argument is sufficient to refute them completely; that is, that the chief factors of coercion, such as wars, conquests, etc., usually occur at more or less protracted intervals. Economic factors, on the contrary, are constantly at work. We have had exchanges from the very moment that the simplest division of labor took place among men—and that was hundreds of centuries ago. Moreover, since man cannot live without food, the influence of economic factors in society never wanes for a moment. If economic factors alone, therefore, are sufficient for the formation of the state, and if human life is impossible without the economic factors, the latter necessarily constitute the state, whether or not there is coercion. We can easily imagine human life without brigandage and conquests, but we cannot imagine it without economic production.

We know that some countries have existed many years without invasions. But history does not cite a single fantastic and impossible example of a country that was able to exist a day without economic production and without exchange. Exchange invariably leads to political organization.[19]

The weakness of Novicow's attempt to explain the origins of the state solely on the basis of its relation to exchange is apparent from the vague and indefinite concept of the state which he sets forth in this passage and also from the fact that one could take his statement that exchange has existed for hundreds of centuries and make it the basis for disconcerting query as to why the state did not come into existence until well within historic times.

Novicow's theory regarding the proper scope of state action is strikingly similar to that expressed by Herbert Spencer. He was an exponent of that type of uncompromising individualism which would limit the function of the state to that of performing the duties of a national police department. The sole legitimate function of the state is to maintain security and order or, in other words, to protect the persons and property of its citizens. This theory of the function of the state harmonizes with his sociological theory of justice in its more general sense as the survival of the best in society. Not only is any action of the state beyond this function of protecting life and property futile, but it is also dangerous and operates to delay progress. At the same time, the performance of its proper function by the state is absolutely indispensable to the integrity of society. The enforcement of contracts is the extent of legitimate state activity in the economic field. The state should not interfere in any way whatever in intellectual affairs, in religious matters, or in the relations between the sexes. Novicow was an extreme libertarian in discussing sexual matters. He contended that love rather than legal compulsion must be relied upon to hold the family together. He was also an ardent feminist, vigorously attacked the idea of female inferiority, and enthusiastically defended woman suffrage. These views were embodied in his *L'Affranchissement de la femme,* which was published in 1903.

While Novicow is a sufficiently clear thinker to understand that liberty can exist only in connection with the presence of a political authority sufficiently powerful and active to protect the individual in his person and property through a system of legal rules and immunities, he does not believe that liberty can endure where the conception of absolute political sovereignty or extensive state activity is realized in practice. To him, liberty is, in essence, the abandonment on the part of the state of its irrational and expensive interference with those phases of human interests and activities which can best be settled by the free and unimpeded economic and intellectual competition of individuals.

While Novicow was an extreme political individualist, he was an equally ardent exponent of the value of social co-operation and the extension of the principles of mutual aid and the division of labor. Few sociologists have exceeded him in the vigor with which he has urged the significance and encouragement of social solidarity.

Novicow's criticism of socialism is closely related to his analysis of nationalism and militarism. Our present capitalistic society rests upon the theory and practice of spoliation both within and without a state. The socialistic remedy of expropriation is simply a proposal that proletarian spoliation shall supplant bourgeois exploitation. What is needed is a doctrine of "mutualism," which will discredit the spoliation theory and practice and do away with both capitalistic oppression and its proletarian counterpart, socialism. This view Novicow develops particularly in his last work, *Mécanisme et limites de l'association humaine.* He thus takes a point of view in common with G. D. H. Cole, once the leader of the Guild Socialists, namely, that Marxian socialism is the product of a diseased and oppressive economic and social order.

E. THE RECONSTRUCTION OF INTERNATIONAL RELATIONS

The necessary readjustments in international relations and the scope of legitimate state activity in the field of foreign relations claimed a large amount of Novicow's attention. Since it is the prime function of the state to insure the security of the persons and property of its citizens and inasmuch as this obligation extends to the protection of the citizens against assault and spoliation at the hands of members of other states, it is necessary that the state enter into the domain of international relations. But it is futile to expect that this security can be brought about by wars. Wars never settle any question permanently and are themselves the chief source of danger to the citizen from foreign influences. Even an equilibrium of power is, at best, a temporary and treacherous expedient to assure international security. The only sane, effective, and reliable means of bringing about permanent international peace is through a European federation.

Only through such a federation can the separate states be prevented from making war at will. The absolute sovereignty of each state in the matter of making war is the chief cause of international anarchy; and, once this sovereignty is transferred to the central body of the federation of European states, this most active and persistent cause of war will be removed. The function of this federation, as pointed out above, will be confined to maintaining peace between the component states within the federation. This federation is being prepared by the operation of social, psychological, and economic forces. International scientific and industrial congresses, uniform systems of weights and measures, the improvement of international law, international congresses of European powers, and the growing economic interdependence of nations have all tended to make Europe a unified civilization in everything except a legal recognition of the fact. All that is now needed is to develop enough constructive imagination to legalize the conditions which actually exist and perfect the administrative machinery of the new central governing body of the federation.

Once this European federation is formed, political conceptions and ideals will undergo a transformation. The ideal will no longer be to make the state coextensive with any particular nation but will rather be to make the state an administrative unit of the size desired by any particular people. The principle of secession and the sovereignty of the people, when applied to determining the extent of the state, will adjust this aspect of the problem. Peoples should be allowed to decide to which political group they will belong. The right of secession must be freely accorded to all members of a political organization. The Confederate States of America had an unquestionable legal right to secede from the Union. When the right of secession is recognized, political groups will tend to become based upon the interests and loyalty of the citizens. To extend its boundaries, a state will then be required to have a record for good government which surpasses that of its neighbors.

The unification of modern Italy was the first great historic example of the assertion of the popular right to fix the boundaries of a state. Not only should the state allow political boundaries to be determined by the popular will; it should also allow unrestricted emigration and immigration. The subdivision and decentralization of the modern national state will probably accompany international federation, and such a step will then be safe for the first time. Administrative convenience and popular desire will be the dominating motive in political procedure rather than the ideal of national egoism and expansion.[20]

To be sure, the establishment of a European federation will by no means immediately bring in an era of cosmopolitanism or perpetual and universal peace. Federation will, however, eliminate most of the opportunities for making war and will allow conflict to be turned into beneficial intellectual channels. In fact, it is the fundamental purpose of international federation and the resulting freedom from physical conflict to promote a much greater development of that intellectual conflict between individuals, classes, and nations upon which progress depends.

In his *Mécanisme et limites de l'association humaine* (1912), Novicow discusses the problem of internationalism from another angle. Economic factors produce the state, and law tends to follow in the wake of exchange. Exchange is now becoming international; the national state is therefore breaking down, and the way is being prepared for international federation. This will come in time without conscious human endeavor through the pressure of economic forces on politics and diplomacy. Yet the realization of international federation is being obstructed and delayed through the utterly false notions which now prevail concerning the social and political value of war, conquest, and spoliation. The origin and development of the state have been chiefly a process of continually extending the area within which spoliation has been found unprofitable and undesirable. This process will go on until federation has ruled out all conquest and spoliation. What is needed to hasten this development is a vigorous campaign of education, which will demonstrate to the public and to statesmen that the doctrine of the social, economic, and political value of spoliation is the most deadly illusion that has ever been invented by man. Once this is understood, federation will immediately result, and humanity will be spared the generations of war and misery which would intervene before this result could be produced by automatic evolution.

F. EXTRA-LEGAL PHASES OF SOCIAL AND POLITICAL CONTROL

In view of Novicow's lack of faith in the state as the directive organ in society and as an important factor in social progress, one is not surprised to find that he lays great stress upon the nonpolitical factors in society. There is nothing to be hoped for from the state outside of its police function. When it advances beyond this point, it only brings stagnation, degeneration, and confusion into society. Those sociologists who have referred to the government as the brain of the social organism have been guilty of a serious error. The government is only the motor nerves of the social organism; the élite are the true social brain. It is the élite who shape public opinion and thus give moral tone to society. The state is an ineffective regulator of morality; public opinion is the only force which can regulate morality in an efficient manner.

Political parties are absolutely essential to a proper functioning of constitutional government under a parliamentary system. Under the leadership of the élite, political parties supply a most important mechanism for carrying on intellectual conflict in the field of political activities.

III. SUMMARY APPRAISAL OF NOVICOW'S CONTRIBUTIONS TO SOCIAL THOUGHT

Novicow's important contributions to a better understanding of the biological, psychological, and economic factors which exert so potent an influence on the origin, development, and functioning of political institutions have been analyzed in connection with other topics and need not be repeated in this place. They are in harmony with that tendency to broaden the approach to political theory and analysis which has characterized what Professor William A. Dunning has happily designated the "societarian political theory."

While Novicow, along with Spencer and Sumner, is usually taken as an example of extreme individualism and the exponent of the opposite viewpoint from that of Lester F. Ward, L. T. Hobhouse, and Ludwig Stein, yet his solution of social problems bears one resemblance to that of Ward, namely, the emphasis which he places on education. The one great influence which can solve our national and international problems is a system of education designed to discredit the current obsession as to the virtue and necessity of social, economic, and national spoliation. This change of attitude on the part of society would well-nigh produce a social millennium. The great difference between Novicow and Ward on this point is that Ward believed education in social science to be an indispensable prerequisite to an intelligent statecraft, while Novicow believed that the proper type of education would remove most of the problems which now confront statesmen.

Novicow was fortunate enough to die in 1912; otherwise, he would have been the legitimate leader of the "I told you so" chorus. Since 1914 it has been the popular procedure to hold up the internationalist leaders, such as Novicow and Norman Angell, to derision and scorn.[21] As a matter of fact, the first World War and its aftermath have been the means of furnishing most stupendous and tragic proof of the essential accuracy of their contentions as to the nature and results of militaristic psychology and the imperialistic diplomacy. The future holds in it little hope for the Western world unless their doctrines are more effectively put into practical operation—a fact given additional cogency and emphasis by the appearance of the atomic bomb.

NOTES

1. Published in Paris (1886). For much more elaborate references on Novicow and his works see the writer's article on Novicow in the *Journal of International Relations*, Vol XII, No. 2 (October, 1921).

2. For a brief analysis of the earlier plans for international organization in Europe see S. P. Duggan, *The League of Nations* (Boston, 1919), chap. ii.

3. First published in 1893. Citations in the present chapter are from the second revised edition of 1896. His later works are primarily an expansion of some of the theses partially elaborated in *Les Luttes*. If this work and its successor, *La Guerre et ses prétendus bienfaits* (1894), had been familiar to English readers, Mr. Norman Angell's *The Great Illusion* would have attracted far less attention, as it contained few ideas that had not been developed with great vigor by Novicow a decade and a half before. So far as is known to the writer, the best summary of this major work of Novicow in English is to be found in L. M. Bristol, *Social Adaptation* (Cambridge, Mass., 1915), pp. 268–82.

4. *Les Luttes*, p. 50.

5. *Ibid.*, table opposite p. 403; a translation of this table is reproduced in Bristol, *op. cit.*, p. 278.

6. *Les Luttes*, pp. 481 ff., 485–86, 498. Novicow makes the analysis of justice from this standpoint the subject of a detailed exposition in his work entitled *La Justice et l'expansion de la vie* (Paris, 1905). This work is briefly summarized by J. F. Hecker, *Russian Sociology* (New York, 1915), pp. 277–84.

7. Paris, 1894.

8. Paris, 1894; an English translation of this work by Thomas Seltzer appeared in 1911. The work is reviewed by E. V. D. Robinson, in *American Journal of Sociology*, November, 1898, pp. 408–10.

9. In 1897 Novicow published his *Conscience et volonté sociales*, which ranks next to *Les Luttes* among his contributions to sociological theory (reviewed by G. E. Vincent, *American Journal of Sociology*, January, 1898, pp. 544–45). This work was devoted to an elaboration of his psychological interpretation of society, which is, in turn, based upon a modified version of the organic theory of society. His chief thesis is that the élite of society, and not the government, are the social sensorium—the brain of the social organism. He attempts to compute the numerical proportion of the élite in modern society and to estimate their importance in social progress. Like Le Bon, he finds the English aristocracy to be particularly worthy of the admiration of the sociologist. The latter part of the work is essentially a psychological analysis of European social problems, particularly militarism and socialism, both of which naturally fail to secure from him any enthusiastic support. Novicow's elaboration of the organic theory of society, which is briefly referred to in his *Politique internationale* and his *Conscience et volonté sociales*, is to be found in his contribution to the symposium on the organic theory of society, published in the *Annales de l'institut international de sociologie*, Vol. IV (1898), and in his work, *Théorie organique des sociétés* (Paris, 1898). In general, Novicow's organic theory of society is based upon the proposition that the identity between society and the organism consists chiefly in the fact that both are living entities comprehending a unified and organized system of vital processes. It is among the more acceptable of the classic expositions of the organic theory.

10. Paris, 1901.

11. Paris, 1910.

12. Paris, 1912. An English translation by S. P. Otis and edited by Professor C. A. Ellwood appeared in the *American Journal of Sociology*, November, 1917.

13. *Les Luttes*, p. 8.

14. *La Critique du darwinisme social*, p. 124.

15. *Les Luttes*, p. 8.

16. In his *Politique internationale* Novicow was inclined to favor the attempt to make the state identical with the nation, or, at least, he seems convinced that such is the most desirable arrangement (cf. pp. 90 ff.).

17. *Les Luttes,* pp. 199 ff., 243 ff. For Ward's rejoinder see *American Journal of Sociology,* November, 1907, pp. 294–97.

18. *Les Luttes,* pp. 243–50, 292–309. Novicow had reached the same conclusions regarding the primarily peaceful origin of the state in his *La Justice et l'expansion de la vie,* published some five years before (cf. Hecker, *op. cit.,* pp. 281–82).

19. Novicow, *Mécanisme et limites de l'association humaine,* translated by Sophia Hersch Otis as "The Mechanism and Limits of Human Association: The Foundations of a Sociology of Peace," *American Journal of Sociology,* XXIII, No. 3 (November, 1917), 289–349. The paragraphs cited here appear on p. 306.

20. Novicow does not make it clear just how he can consistently support the doctrine of secession as applied to any particular state and not have the same theory apply with even greater force to his general federation of states. Probably he would declare for expediency rather than consistency.

21. See, e.g., William Stearns Davis, grotesque sally in his *The Roots of the War* (New York, 1918), pp. 468 ff.

CHAPTER XXIII

THE SOCIOLOGICAL THEORIES OF
MAKSIM M. KOVALEVSKY

N. S. TIMASHEFF, *Fordham University*

I. THE BACKGROUND OF KOVALEVSKY'S SOCIOLOGY

RUSSIAN sociology is perhaps the best possible illustration of the fundamental theorem of the sociology of knowledge, according to which scientific thought is looked upon as a function of the total social situation. During the second half of the nineteenth century the upper level of Russian society was divided into two sectors: (1) the ruling bureaucracy (supported by the majority of the gentry) and (2) the "intelligentsia," a social group consisting mainly of academic teachers and professional men but also comprising substantial minorities of the groups which supported the opposite camp—there have always been "liberal bureaucrats" and "social workers" from among the gentry. The first sector developed a conservative ideology expressed in the well-known triad, "autocracy, orthodoxy, and nationality," whereas the second adhered to the Western ideologies of liberalism and socialism. The general structure of Russian culture demanded that both sectors justify their respective positions on a high theoretical level. The result was the rise of numerous sociological systems, all of which had in common the bias of serving political purposes.

The rationalizations used by the conservative sector were derived from the well-known ideology of the Slavophiles, the basic proposition of which was that Russia was a special world completely different from that of the West and therefore not subject to the laws of evolution working there. The most interesting work of this trend was *Russia and Europe* by N. Danilevsky, who formulated most of the propositions which received world-wide attention after they had been repeated by Oswald Spengler.[1] In our day the theory has been brilliantly revived in the works of the so-called "Eurasians."[2]

The sociology of the intelligentsia was many-branched. It may be divided into the following "schools": (1) the subjective school of P. L. Lavrov (1822–1900) and N. K. Mikhailovsky (1842–1904), which anticipated the modern sociology of knowledge in that it recognized that "there are truths which cannot be recognized before certain epochs.... in consequence of the subjective unpreparedness of society to understand the question in its active setting," anticipated Max Weber in his attempts to use in sociology the concept of probability, and anticipated Tarde's doctrine on invention and imitation when studying the role of personality in the social process, but which made the methodological error of considering sociology a normative science; (2) the Marxist school, chiefly represented by the orthodox G. V. Plekhanoff and the heretic V. I. Lenin; (3) the anarchist school of Prince Peter Kropotkin; and (4) the revolutionary school of V. M. Chernoff. All the schools had in common, first, the acceptance of the idea of unilateral progress and, second, the idea that sociology should serve as a guide in the struggle for progress to be carried on against bureaucracy and the conservative groups supporting it. Outside of these subdivisions but within the general school of progress was Professor N. I. Kareyev (1850–1931), the only academic person in the movement, who was the first to publish a Russian text on sociology (1897), which was chiefly an able discussion of the sociological theories of the time.

The acuteness of the conflict between the bureaucracy and the intelligentsia inhibited the rise in Russia of a purely scientific sociology but did not make it impossible. The honor of having overcome the political bias belongs to M. M. Kovalevsky, who was the greatest Russian sociologist of the pre-war period. He completely broke with the Russian tradition and built up his sociological system not on political considerations but on a thorough study of the history of social, political, legal, and economic institutions. The breach with the tradition was so radical that in his works he never mentioned Russian sociologists.[3]

II. KOVALEVSKY'S LIFE AND WRITINGS

M. M. Kovalevsky was born August 27, 1851, in Kharkov, in southern Russia, the son of a rich landowner. After having graduated from one of the high schools of Kharkov (1863) and from the law faculty of the University of Kharkov (1873), he spent about three years in western Europe: in Berlin where he studied with Rudolf Gneist, Heinrich Brunner, and Adolf Wagner; in Paris; and in London, where he made the acquaintance of Sir Henry Maine (whom he called his teacher), Herbert Spencer, and Karl Marx. After having returned to Russia, he obtained his Master's degree (1877) and was immediately appointed professor at the University of Moscow; three years later he acquired his Doctor's degree.[4]

During his years of study outside Russia, Kovalevsky published his first work. It concerned the *Dissolution of Agrarian Communities in the Canton of Vaud* (1876).[5] The topic was symptomatic of the scientific preoccupation of young Kovalevsky, which had been the early history of institutions. His second work was devoted to the *Administration and Judicial Organization of English Counties up to the Death of Edward III* (1877); the next entitled, *Agrarian Communities* (1879), studied the formation and dissolution of that form of land tenure in colonial lands; the next covered *The Social Organization of England in the Later Middle Ages* (1880).

A booklet on the *Comparative Historical Method in Jurisprudence* (1880) led to one of Kovalevsky's most important contributions to the social sciences. In the hope of directly observing vestiges of early "Aryan" law, he spent three summers in the high valleys of the Caucasus; the result was three books: *Modern Custom and Ancient Law* (1886);[6] *Primitive Law* (1886); and *Law and Custom in the Caucasus* (1890).

Before the last-mentioned book was published, a catastrophe interrupted Kovalevsky's academic activity in Russia. Though a liberal (a typical member of the intelligentsia), he never was a revolutionary. His teaching on constitutional law in the university of Moscow was based on the idea of the similarity of political development in all countries and implied the assumption that, in his opinion, a constitutional reform in Russia was unavoidable. This could not be tolerated by the reactionary Ministry of Education of that time,[7] and Kovalevsky was suddenly dismissed from the university.

Because Kovalevsky was rich and independent and had never married, he was unhampered in immediately deciding to leave Russia and to continue his scientific activity in liberal surroundings. The decision was the easier for him as he spoke English, French, German, and Italian fluently. He first delivered a series of lectures in Stockholm[8] and then settled in France. He acquired a beautiful estate in Beaulieu on the shore of the Mediterranean and gradually collected a private library of fifty thousand volumes. There he spent about fifteen years, frequently leaving to lecture as visiting professor (in Brussels, Oxford, and other places) or as a member of the Paris School of Social Sciences, which he created in 1900, or to study various societies and cultures. He twice visited the United States. He became vice-president of the International Sociological Institute in 1895 and its president in 1907 (after his return to Russia) and frequently contributed to the *Revue internationale de sociologie*.

The French years were the most productive period in Kovalevsky's life. Three monumental works were written: *The Economic Growth of Europe up to the Rise of Capitalism*,[9] *The Origin of Modern Democracy*,[10] and *From Immediate to Representative Democracy*.[11]

During the same period he published several works in which he described Russian institutions for the use of non-Russian scientists. Two of these were *Le Régime économique de la Russie* (1898) and *Russian Political Institutions* (1902).

The great political changes which occurred in Russia in 1904-6 permitted Kovalevsky to return to his fatherland and there to resume his academic activity. He became a professor at the University of St. Petersburg and in the Department of Economics of the Polytechnical Institute of the same city. At about the same time, Professor Bekhtereff founded in St. Petersburg the "Psycho-neurological Institute" and created there a chair of sociology, the first in Russia. He offered it to Kovalevsky, who gladly accepted.

The last period of his academic and scientific activity was characterized by very much lecturing and much nonacademic activity. In 1906 he was elected member of the first Duma from his native city of Kharkov; he was defeated in the elections to the second Duma but was almost immediately elected one of the six representatives of Russian universities to the State Council (the upper chamber of Russia). He devoted much time and energy to legislative activity. At the same time he was president of numerous scientific and charitable institutions.

However, Kovalevsky did not abandon scientific activity. During the last period of his life his interest was concentrated on sociology. This was a logical crowning of a scientific life devoted mainly to the study of correlations between different aspects of social life in their historical development. In 1905 he published a book entitled *Contemporary Sociologists*, a fine review of the sociological theories of his time and, in addition to this, a brilliant criticism of all kinds of monism in sociology.

In 1910 he published two volumes of *Sociology* (which were to be followed by others), the first being a discussion of the scope and methods of sociology and of its relation to the special social sciences, and the second, a monograph on *Genetic Sociology*. In 1913 he started editing (in co-operation with P. A. Sorokin and others) a series of monographs on "New Ideas in Sociology," to which he made several contributions.[12]

In the summer of 1914, Kovalevsky was living in Karlsbad, then in Austria, for treatment of heart disease. When the war broke out, he was considered a civil prisoner. His liberation was due only to the intervention of influential friends (among them, President Woodrow Wilson), but his health was definitely broken, and he died on March 23, 1916. His funeral was a national event, for Russia was aware that she had lost one of her greatest men of science. A symposium *In Memoriam of M. M. Kovalevsky* appeared in the next year with contributions by outstanding social scientists.

III. THE SCOPE AND TASKS OF SOCIOLOGY

When Kovalevsky began his scientific activity, sociology was dominated by the theory of unilinear evolution and inevitable progress. During his lifetime the theory was gradually undermined and restated in new forms; Kovalevsky was not only aware of this change but contributed largely to it. However, he never was able to reject completely this theory, which was deeply ingrained in his mind; hence, there is a certain duality in his sociological ideas. On the one hand, he explained by "the unfortunate dominance of the organic theory of society" the tendency of his contemporaries to speak of the unilinear evolution as taking place in a similar way among all peoples and reproducing the different stages in the evolution of an organism; but, at the same time, he said that the basic law of sociology was that of progress[13] and that the similarities so frequently appearing between societies which did not interact or possess common ancestors could be explained only by the principle of "the unity of history," meaning that the evolution of humanity was progressive.[14] He frequently returned to this idea: "The similarity of economic conditions, the similarity of legal relations (closely related to the former), the similarity in the level of knowledge formed the cause of the fact that people of different races and belonging to different epochs began their development from identical stages."[15] This similarity continued in later stages: "Structures and institutions belonging to the *gens* structure, to the tribal duchy, to the estate monarchy can be discovered in the history of people who have nothing in common with each other and who never imitated each other. If the level of knowledge was similar, similar or identical legends evolved."[16]

Kovalevsky's vacillation concerning the very nature of the phenomena to be studied by sociology was reflected in his ideas concerning the scope and the purpose of sociology. In his earlier works he accepted Comte's definition, according to which sociology is the science of social order and of social progress.[17] Toward the end of his life, under the influence of American sociology,[18] Kovalevsky changed his mind and defined sociology as the "science of social organization and social change." "It is impossible to assert," he said, "that evolution always tends to the cure of social diseases and to the increase of public welfare; it is also difficult to assume that every social organization is order; there is no order in Czarist Russia."[19]

Consequently, he assigned to sociology the task of studying the collective mentality of social groups in close connection with their organization and their evolution. Sociology must perform this task by abstracting trends from the mass of concrete facts and pointing out the general tendency; in this way it can discover the causes of social stability and social change.[20]

When sociology is assigned such tasks, a certain difficulty arises concerning the delimitation between its field and that of the special social sciences. Kovalevsky was aware of the difficulty and solved the problem in the following way: Sociology, as a generalizing science, cannot borrow its premises from the special social sciences; it has to elaborate them independently, taking into consideration the variability of human needs and sentiments distributed among the realms of religion, law, economics, politics, aesthetics, etc.[21] The special social sciences, although furnishing sociology with materials for its synthesis, must, at the same time, base their empirical generalizations upon the general laws of coexistence and development which sociology is called upon to establish.[22]

In Kovalevsky's opinion, sociology is related not only to the descriptive social sciences but also to the science of social policy.[23] Only sociology, said he, is able to discover all the causes on which depend the progress of societies and their interrelation.[24] Only sociology is able to teach us the lesson that order is impossible without progress and that progress consists of gradual changes in the social and economic structure, in close connection with the accumulation of knowledge and with the growth of population.[25] Only sociology may yield an objective criterion for estimating the value of positive law.[26]

IV. THE METHODOLOGY TO BE EMPLOYED IN STUDYING SOCIAL CHANGE

Kovalevsky's interest was concentrated on the study of social change. Whereas his great works on the history of economic, political, and legal institutions concerned later stages of development, the quest for the origin of society was never absent from his mind, as testified by numerous early essays, and it became his major preoccupation during the later years when he wrote his sociological works. This subject matter he called "social embryology,"[27] or "genetic sociology"—the title of the second volume of his *Sociology*.

Kovalevsky's methods of studying social change (in regard to earlier and later stages) naturally depended on his fundamental hypothesis. In his opinion it is for genetic sociology to establish, first, the several stages of social evolution and, second, the laws governing it. Laws were understood by him as "necessary correlations of phenomena";[28] they had to reflect the variability of the social nature of man, independent of climate or race.

The laws of this evolution can be discovered by the comparison of a number of parallel evolutions. The simple juxtaposition of phenomena is insufficient, and the use of the comparative historical method is necessary.[29] Being master of that method, Kovalevsky, in his sociological constructions, used materials acquired in his studies of the history of institutions and enlarged the perspective by adding data obtained through ethnology and the study of animal societies. Gradually he elaborated a methodology which may be formulated as follows:

1. Comparative ethnology and the comparative history of institutions must deal only with facts which had been correlated with all the past and present of the peoples among whom they occur, especially with their collective mentality.[30] "It is not sufficient," he said, "to present a large number of data which seem to confirm a hypothesis; it is necessary to show that the phenomenon, the existence of which is hypothetically asserted, was closely connected with the bulk of conditions given on a particular stage of social evolution."

2. Facts analyzed in this way must be studied in respect to their nature; in other words, it should be established whether, in the given

stage of evolution, the fact belongs to the existing social structure or is a survival from the past or, perhaps, the germ of future development.[31]

3. However, the similarity of facts may be based on common descent or on imitation.[32] Therefore, before any conclusion is made regarding natural uniformities, these possibilities must be analyzed.

4. The arrangement of similar facts into systems corresponding to the stages of evolution presupposes the knowledge of these stages. Here arises the problem of the relative primitiveness of social forms. The difficulty is the greater as, according to Kovalevsky, it is impossible to see in contemporary savages a picture of the earliest stages of the evolution of historical peoples. One of the symptoms of primitiveness is analogy with the forms of social life among higher animals.[33] However, there is no human tribe which would be actually analogous to animal societies, for each possesses at least the germs of religion and government.[34] Therefore, those human societies must be considered the most primitive which know no limitation of sexual intercourse except the prohibition of intercourse with the mother; essential also is the recognized connection of the child with the mother only.[35]

5. Another criterion of primitiveness may be found by functional analysis: We cannot consider as primitive an institution which is incompatible with a low mental level and primitive material conditions.[36]

6. But the best guide is the principle of survival. Ethnographic material may yield results concerning the remote past only if there is reason to believe that it comprises survivals;[37] the same is correct in regard to early law.[38]

As has already been mentioned, the belief in the survival method induced Kovalevsky to spend three summers in the Caucasus. He explained his expectations in the following words: "Svanets and Ossets have lived for centuries in high mountains and have not been subjected to foreign influences; therefore, they might have preserved numerous survivals of early institutions." The study did not yield the expected results. Kovalevsky recognized his partial failure: "Not in respect to all problems did the law of the Ossets yield the expected answers. In many cases it proved to lack the intermediary links [for which he was looking], and therefore it frequently had to be interpreted by using data concerning other Aryan peoples."[39] However, he found what he especially wanted: vestiges of the matrilinear family; and this permitted him to make, much later on, the following conclusion: "Semites, Aryans,

Polynesians, and American Indians have known the matrilinear family, the survivals of which have been preserved in ancient law and in the folklore."[40]

7. However, this result was relevant for genetic sociology only, because it was possible to establish many shifts from the matrilinear to the patrilinear family, whereas cases of the opposite development were unknown.[41] An important methodological rule is implied in this statement, a rule involving the use in ethnology of the statistical method, for which, in general, Kovalevsky had no great respect.[42]

8. Great caution is necessary, according to Kovalevsky, in all work with ethnological and comparative historical material. The greatest danger is that of groundless generalization. Thus, for instance, said Kovalevsky, the tendency to see in totemism a common stage of human evolution is refuted by the fact that no vestiges of it can be found in Russia.[43] Another danger is that of interpretation based on pre-established patterns of thought. Kovalevsky gave an illustration of this from personal experience:

> During my travels in the mountains of the Caucasus I frequently saw Christian chapels surrounded by high trees. Svanets have lost almost every recollection of having been Christians; the belief is vivid among them that woods are inhabited by spirits ready to punish anyone entering them. I immediately formulated the hypothesis that I had discovered a survival of ancestor worship in combination with the worship of trees. Fortunately, I did not publish anything on this question.

Further investigation showed that the Svanets had allowed trees to grow around the chapels in order to prevent the plundering of ikons and other valuable objects. The case of Svanet chapels was explained by accidental causes, irrelevant for general conclusions.[44]

9. Finally, Kovalevsky never denied the existence of variations. But in one of his earliest works[45] he stated that the study of the causes of variations must be considered a task for later generations of sociologists, to be carried out after the definite establishment of similarities and their reduction to one general law.

V. THE PATTERN AND NATURE OF SOCIAL EVOLUTION

Using the methods described, Kovalevsky formulated the following propositions concerning the stages of social evolution:[46] The most primitive form of social organization is the horde within which the matrilineal family evolves. The next stage (never reached by many tribes) was that of the gens, which is the primitive horde transformed by means of exogamy, taboo, and the prohibition of blood feud. The only mental link was the worship of common ancestors. The further development was closely related with the shift from the nomadic manner of life to a settled one; the clan became divided into "big families" (cognatic; later on, also agnatic), and these evolved, as the result of internal discord and of the growth of the population, into "small families." On the other hand, the gens was replaced by a more complicated structure which might be called the "feudal order." This has existed among nations widely distributed through time and space (western Europe, Byzantium, Russia, Moslem peoples, Japan): the possession of land and public service unified society as strongly as kinship. The shift from the feudal to the democratic order is the last stage of evolution which we know.[47] During this stage progress is manifested by the shift from inequality to equality and from governmental interference to private and collective initiative.[48]

The evolution from one stage to another is not, in Kovalevsky's opinion, a process imposed on men by destiny (to use a Spenglerian term) represented by any single factor, be it race, economic necessity, or anything else. Kovalevsky's lifetime was characterized by the dominance of monistic theories in sociology; but, having accepted Comte's doctrine about the interdependence of factors, he did his best to combat these theories and to formulate a pluralistic theory of social causation. "To accept the hypothesis of economic monism," he said, "or the opposite hypothesis of Stein and Gneist[49] would be admissible only if they were based, not on the study of one or another nation, but on the study of the total development of mankind; up to the present time this has not been done."[50] Despite his predilection for the study of the demographic factor (cf. below), he also combated demographic monism. When A. Coste explained the total processes of evolution merely by the growth of population, he was, in Kovalevsky's mind, guilty of the same one-sidedness as the Marxists.[51]

Kovalevsky's personal views on the subject have been expressed in two frequently quoted passages:

> Sociology will gain much if the attempt to find a first cause is eliminated from the number of its immediate problems and if it limits itself, in accordance with the complexity of social phenomena, to showing the simultaneous and parallel action and reaction of many causes.[52]

To talk about a central fact which would determine all others, is to me the same as to talk about the drops of water of a river which by their movement condition its current. I think that in the future the problem will not be solved, but simply suppressed. I explain the importance attributed to the problem in modern sociology by the desire to find a way out of the chaos of innumerable actions and reactions of which the social process consists.[53]

Kovalevsky's deep insight into the mutual interdependence of factors was largely based on his historical monographs, in which just this question was discussed. The central thesis of the *Economic Growth of Europe* was the connection between the growth of the population and the forms of economic life. The work entitled *From Immediate to Representative Democracy* was devoted to the study of the correlation between the political structure and the political ideals. The *Origin of Modern Democracy* stressed the interdependence between the economic structure, the political structure, and the political doctrine. In a number of cases Kovalevsky discussed the principle of interdependence in regard to particular factors. Thus, for instance, he denied that political and legal institutions would be more closely related to economic phenomena than to the accumulation of knowledge.[54] It is not always, said he, the richest man who becomes the boss; in many cases it is the strongest or the wisest.[55] It would be a great mistake to ignore the influence of the conflict of tribes and nations (political factor) on the creation of estates or classes, independent of the division of labor and the accumulation of riches (economic factor).[56]

Very stimulating was Kovalevsky's analysis of the problem of the apparent dominance of different factors in different epochs. All human needs, said he, are in constant interaction, which sometimes becomes partial antagonism. Temporarily, one or another need may become dominant.[57] In the times of Alexander of Macedonia, of the invasions of barbarians, of Napoleon, the political factor dominated; in the period of the struggle of the popes and the emperors or of the Reformation, as well as in certain periods of Chinese history, the religious factor played the major part; during the period of the shift from servitude to free labor the economic factor was of chief importance. However, deeper analysis shows that always every aspect of social life was subjected to important changes, naturally in close connection with changes in the dominant factor. The social process never stops, though at some times it is more, and at others less, apparent.[58]

The acceptance of the principle of plural causation creates well-known difficulties. Kovalevsky solved the problem by using patterns which might be considered analogous to those of "indeterminate equations": every situation is submitted to simultaneous influences in various directions and may evolve not in one, but in many, ways, though not at random: "It is impossible to explain all social phenomena," said he, "by applying abstract laws. In every concrete *milieu* these laws act simultaneously with a number of particular causes which partly accelerate, but partly inhibit, their influences."[59] Applying these general ideas to one of his favorite objects of study—the evolution of agrarian communities under the influence of the growth of population—he said:

> A social event may be the result of the summation or the subtraction of causes. Assume that the growth of population forces people to shift from the three-crop rotation to more complicated systems of agriculture. To do so men must abolish the system of hereditary leases and the scattering of allotments. What will be the actual course of events? Will not one factor check another? .... We have no possibility of determining the magnitude of the convergent or divergent causes and deciding whether their action should be calculated in terms of arithmetic or geometric proportion.[60]

VI. THE STUDY OF POPULATION AND POPULATION CHANGES

The full understanding of the plural character of social causation did not prevent Kovalevsky from choosing one such cause for close study. This was that of the growth of population and of its density, which seemed to him to give the most constant impulse to economic development. He wrote:

> In my Brussels lectures on the history of the economic development of Europe, as well as in my large work on the same subject, I have attempted to determine the influence of the density of population on the changes in the organization of production and exchange and on the structure of property. This factor has been responsible for the transition from a stage of hunters and fishermen to one of agriculture, and from a primitive system of agriculture to a more intensive one, with corresponding changes in the system of land ownership and land possession..... The substitution of a manufacturing system of production in industry for a domestic one is due to the same factor..... Thus, the simple fact of the growth of population called forth a division of labor, a social differentiation into castes, orders and classes, and the evolution of the technique of production, as well as that of the economic regime.[61]

Illustrating this basic proposition, he showed that even in the thirteenth century the process of the emancipation of serfs had substantially advanced. But the Black Death of 1348 reduced the population by half, and the resultant rise in the cost of labor caused a legislative check on the processes of emancipation.[62] He maintained that the economic development of colonial lands also largely depended on the demographic factor:

The economic process which had started in the mother countries continued in the colonies at a much slower rate, however, because of the lesser density of population and of the additional action of two secondary causes: (1) the necessity of using the labor forces of culturally backward races, and (2) the necessity of spending a part of the social forces for aggressive or defensive operations.[63]

However, Kovalevsky never exaggerated the role of the demographic factor and was never guilty of demographic monism.[64] In the first place, he always asserted that only economic evolution was directly influenced by the demographic factor, and this especially in the earlier stages: "Is it advisable," he asked, "to go further and to ascribe changes in state and church, the accumulation of technical knowledge, perhaps also of theoretical ideas, to the influence of the same factor? I do not think so."[65]

Second, he always stressed the fact that the demographic factor never worked alone. The growth of population (primarily a biological factor) increases or decreases its influence on social evolution in relation to numerous purely social causes: devastating wars, progress or regression in social hygiene, birth control (based on religious or moral principles or on individual or class egoism).[66] Incidentally, he mentioned the disturbances created by the settlement of newcomers (peaceful or as result of wars)[67] and by the interference of governments (permission or restriction of emigration).[68]

VII. FACTORS IN SOCIAL CHANGE

"Factors" were never considered by Kovalevsky as directly compelling men to act in a specific way. He elaborated a doctrine of the mechanism of social change in which the role of personality was stressed.[69] Thus, for instance, "when it appears that there is scarcity in food, the mind looks for a solution of the problem and finds it either in emigration, or in the domestication of animals, or in the first attempts to sow nourishing plants."[70] He explains in a similar manner the rise of political leadership (the creation of the political factor): "The necessity of making adjustment to new situations demands the use of additional psychic energy. In such circumstances actions of persons who possess initiative and creative spirit become necessary, whereas the masses are unable to do anything but submit to the leadership of the former."[71]

The process of social change, in Kovalevsky's opinion, may be described in two closely related ways: First, it is a sequence of inventions, imitations, and adjustments (secondary inventions); second, it is a gradual rise and development of rules of behavior.[72] Both aspects are related to each other as follows:

> Personal invention and imitation result in changes in custom and hence in law. In every legal institution it is possible to distinguish both elements. Thus, for instance, the private appropriation of land first appears as a personal invention; imitation and adjustment transform it into the institution of private property.[73]
>
> For a long time new rules lack any sanction and remain on the level of morals. .... They may enter into conflicts with the existing legal order, but this does not prevent them from gradually becoming recognized in judicial decisions and, later on, being included in the system of legal rules.[74]

These ideas were mainly based on the direct observation of social and legal institutions in the Caucasus. This study, by the way, induced Kovalevsky to reject one of the fundamental ideas of the historical school, that of the superiority of custom in building legal codes: "Custom," says Kovalevsky, "frequently is the result of religious fanaticism, of violence and arbitrariness; frequently it is not the source of later law, but, on the contrary, the reflection of earlier law which ceased to comply with the exigencies of life."[75]

VIII. KOVALEVSKY'S INFLUENCE ON SOCIAL SCIENCE

In an article devoted to the memory of Kovalevsky, René Worms wrote: "For French and English science he was the representative of the Russian social science, whereas everybody in Russia recognized that nobody knew better than he did the achievements of Western science. Thus he was a link between two worlds, Western Europe and Russia."

However, it would be difficult to trace his direct influence on Western science. Coste recognized his indebtedness to Kovalevsky for the understanding of the role of the demographic factor. Loria, who, for a certain time, stressed this factor in his works, disputed Kovalevsky's priority. Orthodox Marxists assailed those statements of Kovalevsky in which he denied the all-determining role of the economic factor.

In Russia, Kovalevsky was given the satisfaction of seeing the rise of a younger generation of sociologists directly influenced by him. But he died only eighteen months before the breach of continuity in Russian social science, which was due to the ascent to power of the Communists, which meant the establishment of the monopoly of Marxism. Most of his pupils were given no opportunity to display their talents and to continue his work. One of the most brilliant, N. D. Kondratieff, after a short period of leadership in Russian rural sociology, suddenly disappeared. The most prominent of them was permitted to escape and to become an outstanding American sociologist; this is P. A. Sorokin.[76]

However, theoretical systems exist independently of personalities. What has been the destiny of that of M. M. Kovalevsky?

One of its elements, the doctrine of the unilinear evolution toward progress, has been definitely abandoned. But it has to be remembered that Kovalevsky accepted it only with great reservations and modifications, and his teaching about the possible causes of cultural similarities is just the one that dominates social science in our day, perhaps with the addition of the principle of "the limitation of possibilities."

The other element for which he persistently fought and which, in his lifetime, was accepted only by an insignificant minority has gained a decisive victory; this is the idea of the plurality of social causation or of the interdependence of factors. Many of Kovalevsky's statements could be subscribed to by both followers of Pareto and modern functionalists. The idea certainly forms the foundation of the sociological doctrine of Sorokin.

Kovalevsky never asserted that he had been original on that subject; he recognized his indebtedness to Comte and to his predecessors. His greatest merit has been that of having preserved a sound idea through an age characterized by its almost wholesale rejection and of having accumulated overwhelming evidence in its favor.

In relation to social science as a whole, one may say that Kovalevsky's outstanding contribution was to introduce historical and anthropological concepts and data into sociology and to impress upon historians the importance of reckoning with sociological and anthropological materials. Among social scientists in other countries, those whose work and interests most resemble those of Kovalevsky have been Max and Alfred Weber in Germany, L. T. Hobhouse in England, and Alexander Goldenweiser, James T. Shotwell, Harry Elmer Barnes, and Hutton Webster in the United States.

NOTES

1. As H. E. Barnes and H. Becker correctly say, "the parallelism is too close to be accidental" (*Social Thought from Lore to Science* [Boston, 1938], II, 1032–33).

2. Cf. my article, "Die politische Lehre der Eurasier, *Zeitschrift für Politik*, XVIII (1929), 558–612.

3. This fact was pointed out, with some bitterness, by N. I. Kareyev in his contribution to the symposium *In Memoriam of M. M. Kovalevsky* (Petrograd, 1917).

4. Up to the Communist Revolution, Russia adhered to the French system of academic degrees. A Master's degree was granted after the publication of at least one original monograph and a public disputation before the Faculty; the Doctor's degree was granted after the publication of a second (usually, larger) work and a similar disputation.

5. A German translation appeared the next year in Zürich.

6. French translation in 1893; abridged English translation in 1891.

7. The last two decades of the nineteenth century form a kind of "Dark Age" in the history of Russian education.

8. They were published in French under the following title: *Tableau de l'origine de la famille et de la propriété* (1890); Russian translation (1891); Spanish translation (1913).

9. Three volumes (Moscow, 1898–1903). An enlarged German edition was published in seven volumes, (1901–14).

10. Four volumes, published in Russian (1895–97); large parts have been translated into French and published under different titles.

11. Three volumes in Russian, published in 1906.

12. A complete bibliography of the works of Kovalevsky, comprising eleven pages, is contained in the symposium *In Memoriam*.

13. *Sociology*, pp. 261, 80.

14. *Contemporary Sociologists*, pp. 10–14.

15. *Sociology*, p. 35.

16. *Ibid.*, pp. 33–35.

17. Maintained in *Contemporary Sociologists*, p. 286.

18. With direct reference to an article "Sociology: Its Problems and Its Relations" by Charles Ellwood, *American Journal of Sociology*, XIII (1907), 300.

19. Kovalevsky obviously had in mind order in the "existential," not in the "procedural," meaning.

20. *Sociology*, p. 9.

21. *Contemporary Sociologists*, p. 286.

22. *Sociology*, p. 30.

23. The necessity of creating this science of social policy was vigorously stressed by Kovalevsky's famous contemporary, L. Petrazhitsky (cf. H. Babb, "Petrazhitsky's Science of Legal Policy," *Boston University Law Review*, XVII [1937], 793 ff.).

24. *Sociology*, p. 14.

25. *Ibid.*, p. 59.

26. *Ibid.*, p. 68.

27. *Ibid.*, p. 84.

28. *Ibid.*, p. 33.

29. Many of Kovalevsky's contemporaries considered that method *the* method of sociology. Thus, for instance, Sir. P. Vinogradoff identified the sociology of law and the comparative history of law (cf. his article on "Comparative Jurisprudence" in the *Encyclopaedia Britannica* [11th ed.], Vol. XV).

30. *Sociology*, pp. 104–5.

31. *Ibid.*

32. *Ibid.*, pp. 36, 80.

33. *Genetic Sociology*, p. 18. The existence of such analogies was illustrated by the fact that the relation of hunters to the occupied territory is almost the same as that of a herd of animals or a flock of birds (*ibid.*, p. 125).

34. *Sociology*, p. 85.

35. *Genetic Sociology*, pp. 51, 76.

36. *Ibid.*, p. 19.

37. *Ibid.*, p. 2.

38. *Ibid.*, p. 17.

39. *Modern Custom and Ancient Law*, pp. iv and vi.

40. *Genetic Sociology*, p. 90.

41. *Ibid.*, p. 63.

42. *Sociology*, p. 90.

43. *Ibid.*, pp. 87–89.

44. *Genetic Sociology*, pp. 6–7.

45. *On the Comparative Historical Method in Jurisprudence* (1880). He repeated this statement in *Sociology*, p. 104.

46. In the monograph on the *Primitive Law;* repeated in *Genetic Sociology*, pp. 104 ff.

47. *Sociology*, pp. 44–50.

48. *Ibid.*, p. 58.

49. Both Stein and Gneist considered basic the political factor.

50. *Contemporary Sociologists*, p. 240.

51. *Ibid.*, p. 247.

52. *Ibid.*, chap. xiv.

53. *Ibid.*, chap. viii.

54. *Sociology*, p. 114.

55. *Ibid.*, pp. 102–3.

56. *Genetic Sociology*, p. 19.

57. *Contemporary Sociologists*, p. 286.

58. *Ibid.*, chap. xlv.

59. *Ibid.*, p. 59.

60. *Ibid.*, chap. xl.

61. *Ibid.*, pp. 200–201.

62. *The Economic Growth of Europe*, Vol. II, chaps. x, xiv, xv.

63. *Contemporary Sociologists*, p. 268.

64. In one of his later works he denied the honor of being the originator of the demographic school in sociology: according to him, Mercantilists, Physiocrats, and Comte had already had a full understanding of the importance of the density of population. Being accused by Marxists of having first recognized and then denied the determinant role of the demographic factor, he explained that the one-sidedness of his treatise on the *Economic Growth of Europe* had been voluntary (*Contemporary Sociologists*, p. 291). As explained by Sorokin, in that treatise the demographic factor was already treated as an "independent variable" (methodological procedure), not as "causa efficiens" (*In Memoriam*).

65. *Contemporary Sociologists*, p. 202.

66. *Ibid.*, chap. xiii.

67. *Ibid.*, p. 168.

68. *Ibid.*, p. 246.

69. Perhaps under the influence of the Russian school of sociology.

70. *Sociology*, p. 300.

71. *Genetic Sociology*, pp. 200, 215, with reference to an article by E. Mumford, "The Origin of Leadership," *American Journal of Sociology*, XII (1906), 216 ff.

72. *Contemporary Sociologists*, pp. 138–39.

73. *Sociology*, pp. 63–68.

74. *Contemporary Sociologists*, pp. 138–39.

75. In his work, *Modern Custom and Ancient Law*, Kovalevsky gave a detailed description of harmful customs. For a few illustrations cf. my *Introduction to the Sociology of Law* (Cambridge, Mass., 1939), p. 128.

76. Among other pupils of Kovalevsky should be mentioned E. Kulischer, also a political emigrant, who published (in German) a good book, A. and E. Kulischer, *Kriege- und Wanderzüge* (Berlin, 1932).

INTRODUCTORY NOTE*

MAIN TENDENCIES IN FRENCH SOCIOLOGY

SOCIOLOGISM has clearly been the dominant tradition in French sociology. This body of sociological thought, which Comte—drawing in part on De Maistre, De Bonald, and Saint-Simon—first stated as an integrated system, and to which De Roberty, Izoulet, Draghicesco, and Espinas made important contributions, reached its culmination in the work of Durkheim and the Durkheim school. So great has been the predominance enjoyed by this type of sociology in France that under the Third Republic some of its conclusions were incorporated in the required courses of instruction in the public schools. In fact, the particular doctrines of sociologism were usually accepted by the lay public as virtually identical with "sociology" or "sociological method" in general.

It would be a mistake, nevertheless, to assume that the French contribution to other kinds of sociology has been negligible. Actually, significant contributions have been made, for example, in anthropogeography, biological sociology, psychological sociology, historical sociology, and social economics.

French scholars have made especially important contributions to anthropogeography and the theory of the influence of the physical environment on society. The comprehensive and generalized anthropogeography, as represented by German writers like Karl Ritter and Friedrich Ratzel, was ably and voluminously expounded by Élisée Reclus, a Belgian by birth, who spent much time in Switzerland. Most influential, perhaps, was the work of Frédéric Le Play and his school, which stressed the importance of regionalism, the social survey, and socioeconomic aspects of family life in relation to the physical setting and resources. Le Play's school had an important role in promoting the social-survey technique and the ecological approach to social and urban problems. Henri de Tourville broadened the approach to family evolution and problems, while Edmond Demolins extended Le Play's regionalism to

* By the editor.

458

include a comprehensive study of geographical influences on mankind, with special emphasis on topography and routes of travel. The influence of Le Play and of more precise methodology in geographical studies led to the creation of regional geography in the works of Paul Vidal de la Blache. Scientific anthropogeography has been developed in France and applied to the explanation of social and political evolution by Jean Brunhes, Camille Vallaux, and Lucien Febvre.

Biological sociology has had a number of protagonists in France. The organismic approach, stressing the analogy between the individual organism and society, was cultivated by René Worms and Alfred Espinas, in their earlier writings. Alfred Fouillée tried to put the organismic analogy on a psychological level by his idea of society as a "contractual organism." The relentless social Darwinism of Gumplowicz received slight support from French sociologists, but the "social selectionism," which we associate with such writers as Galton in England and Schallmayer in Germany, was espoused in France by Paul Jacoby and G. Vacher de Lapouge, both of whom believed that civilization and social evolution produce biological deterioration. Lapouge suggested a program of eugenics as the only solution of this problem, if a given civilization wished to preserve its integrity. Considerable attention was given to population problems by French students. Adolphe Coste and Paul Mougeolle held that the progress of civilization is directly related to the growth and increasing density of the population. Émile Levasseur contended that technological developments, which increase man's power of providing food and clothing, will render us immune to Malthus' law that population is bound to press on the means of subsistence. Arsène Dumont suggested a sociopsychological law of population, to the effect that social ambition tends to retard population growth by encouraging families to restrict the birth rate. Those eager to rise in the social scale do not wish to be handicapped by the burdens imposed by a large family.

France has been especially noted for its students of psychological sociology. The old informal social psychology, based on slight technical psychological knowledge, was applied in colorful fashion by Gustave Le Bon to the analysis of nationality, crowds, political parties, social movements, war, peace, and international organization. A few tentative hypotheses were vastly overworked. Gabriel Tarde is best known for his classic exposition of the social influence of imitation, but he really presented a comprehensive system of psychological sociology, involving invention and adaptation as well as imitation. The ablest and most learned of French psychological sociologists was Émile Durkheim, noted for his theory of "collective representation" and of the psychological influence of the group over the individual. Durkheim's scholarly work will be dealt with thoroughly in a later chapter.

Historical sociology and social history have been encouraged by Paul Lacombe, a disciple of Tarde, who held that history should be a genetic science of institutional evolution; by Henri Berr, exponent of historical synthesis and editor of a great history of civilization; and by Georges Renard, author and editor of many books on social history and the history of industry and labor. Among economists with a sociological orientation one should mention Charles Gide and Charles Rist, who have been much interested in economic reform and economic thought, and Émile Levasseur, a leading expert on labor problems and labor evolution. This brief sketch does not include the anthropological or cultural sociologists, historians, psychologists, economists, jurists, linguists, and others who have fallen more or less within, or who have been deeply influenced by, the sociologistic tradition and will be discussed later on.

CHAPTER XXIV

THE SOCIOLOGICAL THEORIES OF
ALFRED FOUILLÉE*

AUGUSTIN GUYAU

Translated and Adapted from the French by
ARTHUR JULIUS NELSON, *Worcester, Massachusetts*

I. THE THEORY OF IDEA-FORCES IN SOCIETY

ALFRED FOUILLÉE, the French social philosopher (1838–1912), is known chiefly for his doctrine of *idées-forces*, by means of which he sought to reconcile metaphysical idealism with the naturalistic and objective standpoint of science. According to this theory, which dominated his whole philosophy and which he developed in all its aspects, ideas, once conceived and desired, are forces which tend to assert themselves in action. He includes in his definition of ideas not only the intellectual elements but also desires, which, in his view, constitute the prime motor agent in human activity.

Ideas, however, are efficacious only when they signify something logically and experimentally, when they correspond to exact relationships. If they can become real, it is because of the amount of "objective possibility" that they contain. It is only that which is true in an idea which gives it its force; it is not the force of the idea which makes it true; the power of realization presupposes elements of truth in the relationships which are realized by its means. Ideas are forces because they are both caused and causative, and they are causative because they produce effects which, in relation to us, may be considered as desired ends.

As Fouillée puts it in the Introduction to his *L'Evolutionisme des idées-forces,* ideas are not inert representations but are dynamic factors which impel to action both individuals and nations: "Everywhere the 'idea' appears as a power which contains in itself the conditions for a change of consciousness and, thanks to a correlation of psychical proc-

---

* From Augustin Guyau, *La Philosophie et la sociologie d'Alfred Fouillée* (Paris, 1913), pp. 132–81.

esses with cerebral movements, the conditions for a change of cerebral processes themselves..... Ideas compose the collective force stored up in an individual; they have their own intellectual heredity which reacts on biological heredity and often, through education, may direct, and sometimes even dominate, it."

The introduction of the theory of idea-forces into the study of human society entitles Fouillée to a place among the founders of modern sociology and social psychology. Emphasizing as it did the dynamic, as against the static, character of the social organism, the theory did not, however, contradict the Positivist and the organic schools of social thought but served, rather, to complement them. In fact, the whole application of Fouillée's theory may be regarded as a remarkable synthesis of some of the main conflicting views in the field of the social sciences.

In 1880 appeared *La Science sociale contemporaine,* in which Fouillée first set forth at length the doctrine of idea-forces as applied to the concept of the social organism. In the Preface to the 1910 edition of this work we find his ideas more maturely clarified. We may include with the above later books: *Les Eléments sociologiques de la morale,* which was published in 1905; *L'Evolutionisme des idées-forces,* that came out in the following year and contains in the Introduction the best summary of his theory of the idea-forces; *La Morale des idées-forces* (1908); and *La Psychologie des idées-forces* (1910).

II. THE NATURE OF THE SOCIAL ORGANISM

According to Fouillée, sociology is the study of the nature, origin, and development of societies under the influence of physical, biological, psychological, and, particularly, social causes. Among the social causes it is essential to include "the idea itself which a society has of its present constitution and its future evolution."[1]

Four theories are advanced by Fouillée to explain the social organism. The first—the theory of the "contractual organism"—endeavors to synthesize the organic theory of Spencer and the social-contract theory of Rousseau. Society is not an organism in the biologic sense, evolving in a purely mechanical way under the influence of external factors; neither is it a contractual relationship in an explicit sense. Society is an organism in the sense that it is a psychological unity, developed through mutual mental action among individuals within the group and between individuals and the group itself. True, an organized society does exhibit all the characteristics of a living organism, such as a common will-to-live; a common direction of tendencies, partly unconscious, toward the preservation and progress of the whole; and adaptation of individuals to each other, of each individual to the whole, and of the whole to the external milieu. An organized society, however, does not react solely to external stimuli, as a vegetable or an animal does; it has an *internal* life of its own, which consists in "creating and realizing ideals." It is, one might say, in a state of continuous "creation of itself by itself" through the force possessed by ideas and feelings. Thus, in place of a social evolution effected mechanically and determined from without, Fouillée substitutes a concept of social evolution "in the process of being effected from within by psychic factors," making for *innovation* and *progress*.

Society is constituted indivisibly by an "ensemble of collective necessities" and by an "individual consent, more or less implicit, to these necessities." There is in the social bond something at once involuntary or unconscious and voluntary or conscious. The individual must have, even though in a most confused way, the feeling and the desire for his union with others in order to make him an integral part of a society. There is no true society without an "internal accord" between the members; without a "desire for unity," more or less conscious; and without a "representation," more or less vague, of the whole to which they belong. This "representation" is the idea-force, which controls the social development.

Again, the individual consciousness is social in origin: "if it has a natural centralization about desire, it has also a natural movement of expansion toward other beings equally sentient and endowed with desire. The representation of another being similar to ourselves is, therefore, as automatic as the sight of our image in the water or in a mirror." Thus the idea of society is an "integral part of our total self," and the idea of self, once formed, becomes an active agent.

While some sociologists have gone too far in stressing the physical analogies between society and the animal organism, others have exaggerated the psychical analogies between society and the individual. Fouillée contends, contrary to Durkheim, that we have no authority for postulating a social self, of which we have no experience.[2] The laws governing social phenomena are to be sought not only in the individual consciousness but also in the "reciprocal action of many consciousnesses" and in the "reaction of the collective consciousness to itself." These laws are partly biological, partly psychological, but they have their own individuality, nevertheless, and constitute laws that are truly social. Social determinism, therefore, especially "social auto-determinism," is a legitimate object of sociological study. Yet it must not be forgotten that the "collective representations" and the social conscience exist only in the individual conscience, which is enlivened and set in action by ideas.

If the social organism is both an "agent" and a "conscious, self-directing agent," it goes without saying that Fouillée disagrees with those who regard society as a "completed entity" and social facts as uniquely "fixed objects" determined by exterior influences. A true social science, says Fouillée, must be careful not to crystallize what is essentially "fluid and moving"; not to treat social facts as things that are "static and dead," as it were; and not to consider as completed what is unceasingly being created by itself while in the process of conceiving and desiring. This state of "perpetually becoming," which marks the social organism, causes an increasing "flexibility of function" and even an increasing "malleability of structure," leading to a perpetual variation, despite the constancy of the essential elements. "The same event does not happen twice in a concrete manner in human societies any more than it does in individual lives."[3] The problem for sociology, then, is: In what manner and by what sort of "activity inherent in consciousness" are social facts produced?

Although Fouillée believes that Tarde pushed too far his concept of society as an "interaction of minds," he gives the latter credit for illuminating the universal role of "imitation" and "invention" and stressing the importance of the individual. Imitation, however, does not appear to Fouillée so fundamental as it does to Tarde. Imitation is a process of the "expansion" of social facts; it does not "create" them. There is a "voluntary" and "rational" element in the participation of an intelligent being in social life, and this "voluntary and rational element is much more truly social than the imitative, which is mechanical and related to the physical machine." Similarly, invention, more properly psychological, is not characteristic of the social order, though it does play a role which should be made evident by the sociologist.

The concept of the "contractual organism" is boldly extended by Fouillée to the entire animate world, which he represents as a "vast society in the process of formation," as a living organism which tends gradually to become conscious of itself, whose ideal is the mutual affection of all its members.

Fouillée's second theory, a corollary of the first, is that of the "quasi-contract" and the "implicit contract." By this he enlarged the concept of solidarity. There exists between the members of the same society not only a quasi-contract but a real contract, although implicit, "the legal sign of which is not a word or a signature, but action."[4] Fouillée insists that, though we are born "despite ourselves" in a society which we ourselves have not created, the very fact that we continue to live in the midst of it, that we accept its benefits, its obligations, its conditions of all kinds, even those which annoy us or which seem to us ill-established, constitutes a quasi-contract—better still, an "implicit contract," by which the individual is bound by act, idea, and sentiment to all the other individuals and to the entire society or, rather, to such a society as enjoys the life of an independent state.[5]

Referring to the solidarity of the present generation with the generations that have gone before, Fouillée introduced his third theory of the social organism, namely, "that we are born collectively charged with a debt of 'reparative justice.' "[6] "According to the rules of contractual justice, every contract involving an exchange, such as a deed of gift, assumes that, with the benefits, one accepts the obligations."[7] Among these obligations is the reparation of injustices arising from the acts of previous generations. "The reparative function, in the social order, cannot fall upon a single individual nor upon a few; it falls upon all the members of society: it belongs to the province of collective action."[8]

Obligated as we are to future generations, we fulfil those obligations chiefly by executing our obligations to the generations that have preceded us. These services which are rendered us and which we, in turn, render to those to come are "collective" and "reversible" by virtue of a "solidarity" which is not individualistic. "If every service were uniquely individual, every debt individual, every duty individual, resting uniquely on a quasi-contract between individuals who render each other service, the best will in the world could not rationally connect future generations with individuals now living or dead."[9]

The theory of reparative justice demands an increasing intervention of society in favor of justice; but it does not confer upon individuals a positive right to "demand" it, either by force or before the law. Reparative justice is a "moral" duty of society. Since one cannot arm the individual with a right of redress against the whole of society, it becomes highly incumbent upon society and upon the state, which is the organ of society, to rectify unremittingly the evils that result from the very fact of living in society in the midst of *nature*. Hence reparative justice is deducible sociologically from the double character of society, which is at once organic and contractual.

The fourth and last theory contained in *La Science sociale contemporaine* aims to provide a rational basis for the doctrine of solidarity. Fouillée accepts the concept of natural solidarity as applied to society but only as "determinism or reciprocal causality, which has nothing moral in it." "The only true solidarity is the moral and social one, and its foundation is the idea-force of justice and the rational bond between individuals." In the final period of social evolution we may expect a complete union between the individual and his society.

III. PSYCHOLOGICAL AND CULTURAL FACTORS IN SOCIAL EVOLUTION

Three books—*Psychologie du peuple français* (1898), *Esquisse psychologique des peuples européens* (1903), and *La France au point de vue moral* (1908)—though philosophical, constitute one of the first truly systematic attempts at a general social psychology in France. They include not only descriptions of mental qualities, with an abundance of historical illustrations, but also a theory of social development, in which racial, environmental, economic, and, particularly, psychic factors are brought together in a brilliant synthesis. Most suggestive is the essay entitled: "The Factors of National Character," in the Introduction to the first of the above-named volumes.

In Fouillée's view, social psychology is primarily national psychology. The concept of nationality is neither purely physiological, ethnographical, nor economic. To Fouillée the most important aspect of nationality is the solidarity established by the mutual dependence of ideas, feelings, and impulses. The more or less reflective ideas of a people on the origin and nature of the universe, as well as on the meaning and value of life, necessarily affect its morality, happiness, and character. Language, religion, philosophy, art, and poetry are, therefore, some of the psychological signs of a particular nationality and are highly important to the social psychologist.

In a certain sense every nation has a consciousness and a will of its own, but Fouillée would not attribute to a nation a "soul," or "ego," as Novicow and Le Bon did. Individuals placed in mutual relation to one another do create specific phenomena and specific laws, but it does not follow that they create a new being. The interaction of individual minds produces a common manner of thinking, feeling, and willing, different from that of isolated minds or of the mere sum of those minds. It is this organization of mutually dependent ideas and feelings which constitutes the consciousness and will of a nation.

Three great forces act in an inverse ratio to create and maintain the constitution and temperament, as well as the psychic character, of a people: first, heredity, which fixes the race; second, adaptation to the the physical milieu; and third, adaptation to the moral and social milieu. "In proportion as a nation approaches the modern type, the action of the social milieu outweighs that of the physical; and, more than that, the physical factors tend themselves to be transformed into social factors."[10] Scientifically speaking, there is no such thing as a pure-blooded race; consequently, racial psychology is faced with extremely difficult problems, on account of extensive crossings. In proportion as civilization advances, racial factors, like the factors of the physical environment, become more and more secondary; conversely, the social and historical milieu assumes increasing importance.

Fouillée believes in natural selection and the survival of the fittest but warns that natural selection does not necessarily mean the survival of types which are most essential to mankind's higher development. Human progress, he holds, is not achieved automatically, through the simple play of natural laws; moral progress calls for individual morality, and social progress requires that societies work out their own destinies rather than depend upon an animal struggle for existence.

Fouillée questions whether some sociologists have not overstressed the importance of the physical environment. The influence of climate, for instance, has been very much exaggerated by writers like Montesquieu and his successors. Although climate has its role in conditioning society, it is only one of the factors of historical evolution, and its action can be understood only when it is combined with other factors, such as race and the social milieu.[11]

The influence of racial heredity and the physical environment was most potent at the beginning of social evolution. The material environment, such as food, clothing, habitation, tools, weapons, and domesticated animals, furnished the essential needs, while the mind at that time was not sufficiently independent to free itself from its external surroundings. Social relationships were not extensive or complex enough to counterbalance the physical influences of race. On a people with their national character already formed, however, like the French, the external milieu now exerts its influence very slowly; on the other hand, the incessant racial crossings dissociate and partly neutralize the hereditary influences and increase those of the social milieu. Ethnical and geographical influences on national character are, therefore, neither the only factors nor the most important ones in social evolution; social factors, such as uniform instruction, education, common beliefs, and customs compensate for the diversities of both ethnic groups and physical surroundings.

To view social evolution as a race struggle in the midst of geographical surroundings, more or less favorable, is to see only one aspect of social evolution, and that a very primitive one. Early human society was not in a state of perpetual warfare and cannibalism, as some anthropologists and sociologists would have us believe. On the contrary, co-operation as a method of producing goods appeared at an early stage in man's development, forcing physical struggles into a secondary position. Consider, for instance, the peaceful tools that prehistoric man manufactured along with his weapons. Co-operation, in fact, did as much, if not more, for progress than armed conflict, which itself is impossible without preliminary co-operation among those who fight.

The Darwinian conception of social relations is inadequate. It accounts for only one factor in national character and for only one of the motivating forces in history. The struggle for material survival is not the whole story. Ideas, sentiments, and desires exist, too, and among them there is a struggle for life and prestige. Certain sentiments, certain ideas, have a superior force, resulting either from their intrinsic truth or from their better adaptation to present conditions—a kind of relative truth. A certain conception of social duty, of property, of the state, of the universe itself and its principles, may constitute an advantage for individuals as well as for nations in their struggle for survival.

With Le Bon's notion that education counts for little in the face of heredity Fouillée does not agree. He believes that there is a progressive adaptation of individuals to the intellectual milieu. Ideas and sentiments are not distributed by races, except in a few instances that are steadily decreasing in number. Imitation, education, customs, legislation, moral codes, religious beliefs, and economic practices play an increasingly important role and gradually fashion in the same pattern individuals of different families or races.

While Fouillée recognizes that economic factors, such as the mode of production, are among the great causative agents in evolution, he does not agree with the Marxists that human nature is merely an outgrowth of these forces. On the contrary, he regards tendencies, instincts, ideas, beliefs, science, morality, and national character as also causative factors in developing the social order. Indeed, to interpret history realistically on the basis of economic needs implies a psychological approach, if one is dealing with social groups. And here national psychology plays an important role.[12]

Can social psychology ever attain to an appreciable degree the power of forecasting possessed by the physical sciences? Comte, John Stuart Mill, Stein, Ward, and Hobhouse believed it could. Fouillée, however, is not so hopeful. Physical science owes its precision to the small number of elements with which it deals and to the relative constancy of these elements. In social psychology the number of possible combinations surpasses calculation and prediction. It would be as reasonable to deduce all the varieties of animals merely from the physiological laws of growth operating under diverse circumstances as it would be to try to deduce the numerous diversities of human character solely from the fundamental laws of psychology.

If we cannot deduce the present from the past, according to Mill's method, then how can we hope to anticipate and shape the future? We cannot foresee the progress of science. New needs are constantly arising. Man is insatiable in his search for scientific truth, and each step uncovers new horizons and produces new and unexpected problems.

In the history of peoples there are two incalculable elements: individual or collective characters, on the one hand, and, on the other, the progressive discovery of universal laws. A social astronomy founded on a priori knowledge of characters strikes Fouillée as fantastic.

"Every society, that ever existed was in its way a living being," concludes Fouillée. Not only must the historian describe it, but he must explain its life. He must show how the organs of a society functioned; that is, he must reveal its laws, its political economy, its religion, philosophy, morals, scientific achievements, art, mental and physical habits, and ideas about life. From this it is clear that the sociological historian ought to study the character of peoples, their physical environment, their intellectual and moral environment, and, finally, their social environment and relations with one another.[13] Such studies will give us a clearer conception of social evolution and social organization and will thus help us to guide the development of society, even if we cannot predict and control the course of future social development in the same rigorous manner that physical scientists can control their data and experiments.

NOTES

1. *Revue de métaphysique et de morale*, May, 1911.
2. Fouillée wrote extensively in his later years in opposing Durkheim's notion of socio-psychological determinism—such ideas as the purely social basis of morality and the overwhelming impression exerted by the group over the individual.
3. Cf. *La Science sociale contemporaine* (1910), Preface.
4. *Ibid.* (1880), p. 11.
5. *Eléments sociologiques de la morale* (Paris, 1905), p. 309.
6. Cf. *La Science sociale contemporaine* (1910), Preface.
7. *Ibid.*, p. 369.
8. *Ibid.*, p. 371.
9. *Ibid.*, p. 511.
10. *Psychologie du peuple français* (Paris, 1898), p. 22.
11. *Ibid.*, p. 37.
12. *Ibid.*, p. 62.
13. *Ibid.*, p. 71.

CHAPTER XXV

THE SOCIAL AND POLITICAL THEORY OF GABRIEL TARDE

Harry Elmer Barnes

I. GENERAL CHARACTERISTICS OF TARDE'S WRITINGS
AND SOCIOLOGICAL SYSTEM

O F ALL French writers on sociology since the time of Comte, probably no other author except Durkheim has been so influential in
shaping the general body of sociological thought as Gabriel Tarde
(1843-1904).[1] Tarde's contributions to sociology mainly center about
the elaboration of the psychological and sociological importance of imitation, though this principle by no means embraces the whole of his
system. There can be no doubt that his interest in imitation was fostered
by his duties during the greater part of his life as a provincial magistrate
and, later, as director of criminal statistics for the Ministry of Justice,
professions well designed to impress upon the mind the significance of
the repetition of similar circumstances and phenomena.[2]

To be sure, the idea of imitation as a socializing force was not new;
a century and a half before Tarde, Hume had emphasized its action in
his brilliant essay upon "National Character," in which he had defended
the idea of imitation as producing those uniformities of culture attributed
by Montesquieu to geographic influences. The emphasis placed upon
imitation by Bagehot and Huxley is also well known. Finally, at about
the same time that Tarde was elaborating his doctrine, similar views
were being put forward by a number of writers, among them Bordier,
Espinas, Baldwin, James, and Royce.[3] But, whatever Tarde may have
lacked in originality, he compensated for in the completeness and thoroughness of his analysis of imitation.

Tarde's analysis of the social aspects and influence of imitation has
not been received without criticism; Graham Wallas criticizes it sharply
for its ambiguity,[4] and Bristol lightly remarks that "indeed his discussion
of suggestion and imitation is *passé.*"[5] The truth seems to be that, on

471

the one hand, Tarde rather exaggerated the influence of imitation and was not averse to straining a point to claim a given process as the product or manifestation of this socializing force and that, on the other hand, certain of his assumptions regarding the psychology of imitation have not stood the test of refined experiments in the psychological laboratory. At the same time, there can be little doubt that his discussion of the sociological role of imitation will render further exploitation of that field extremely unprofitable.

Imitation, however, was only the central theme of Tarde's system of sociology, and it now remains to examine his system as a whole. Tarde's sociology was almost exclusively psychological, though he frankly admitted that there were other legitimate lines of approach. He held that the social process consists fundamentally in the intermental activity of a group of associated individuals. This intermental activity takes place thorough the three fundamental processes of *repetition* (imitation), *opposition,* and *adaptation;* and these, in turn, operate upon the beliefs and desires of individuals and societies.

In other words, beliefs and desires are the raw psychological materials of socialization; intermental activity is the general process through which socialization is achieved;[6] and repetition, opposition, and adaptation are the special processes through which intermental activity accomplishes its work.[7]

It is obvious that, in his triad of repetition, opposition, and adaptation, Tarde was influenced by Hegel (Tarde was, for a time, professor of modern philosophy at the Collège de France) and the Hegelian dialectic of thesis, antithesis, and synthesis. There was a further marked resemblance between Hegel's idea that the synthesis becomes a new thesis and Tarde's notion that inventions are often the product of an adaptation growing out of the clash of conflicting imitations. The Hegelian and similar influences were also mainly responsible for Tarde's refusal to accept fully the bold Spencerian doctrine of cosmic and social evolution. He preferred *transformation* (change or transmutation) to evolution, and his books on the growth of the state and the growth of law were entitled *Les Transformations du pouvoir* and *Les Transformations du droit,* respectively.

Before discussing further the cosmic and social process, as conceived in terms of repetition, opposition, and adaptation, it is desirable to correct a common impression that Tarde regarded repetition or imitation as the all-important factor in social life and development. On the contrary, he looked upon invention as the source of all progress. Imitation, opposition, and adaptation are important chiefly in spreading inventions already made and in producing new ones through conflicting waves of imitation. Tarde regarded invention as any new form of thought or action which gains expression. Inventions may arise from the thoughts and acts of certain individuals who have a high capacity for originality and invention. The other source of inventions is the conflicting imitation of existing inventions, out of which process a new invention may grow and set up a new wave of imitation, as a stone cast into the water stirs up concentric rings.

Tarde finds that these three principles of repetition, opposition, and adaptation will serve as the basis of a cosmic philosophy as well as for the foundation of a system of sociology. They are the three great factors in the development of all sciences and all phenomena.[8] His general thesis is twofold: (1) in the thoughts and observations of men regarding the operation and existence of these three fundamental processes, the historic progress has been from the observation of the large-scale and sometimes fantastic examples of repetition, opposition, and adaptation to the discovery of the minute and fundamental instances which go to make up the greater; (2) in the actual world of phenomena, the repetitions, oppositions, and adaptations proceed in the reverse order, from the minute and fundamental to the great and extensive.[9]

It will be impossible in this place to do more than to summarize the main points which he makes in regard to society and socialization. In the field of social phenomena one may discover the same inversion of order between observation and fact in regard to *repetition* as was noted in regard to phenomena in general. Beginning with the earlier superficial observation of picturesque social repetitions, like the classical theory of the cycles of government or the triads of Vico and Hegel, the scientific sociologist has now come to regard as fundamental the repetitions of two persons in a state of association. In the same way, the reversal of observed and actual progress in repetition is manifested in the fact that social repetitions proceed in a geometrical ratio from the fundamental one of two persons to that of international repetition or imitation.[10]

Since it is under the head of repetition that Tarde treats the fundamental process of imitation, it might be well as this place to interpolate a brief analysis of the mode of action of this principle in social life as developed in his *Laws of Imitation*. Dr. M. M. Davis sums up Tarde's treatment of imitation in the following ingenious and illuminating manner:

I. The source of social action is in individual initiatives expressed in new ideas or procedures called *Inventions*.

II. The essential and socializing act is *Imitation*, by which Inventions become more or less socially accepted and socially influential.

III. The *origin* of an Invention is influenced by:
   a) The inherent difficulty of combining mentally the ideas whose combination *is* the invention;
   b) The grades of innate mental ability in the society;
   c) The social conditions favoring mental alertness and the expression of ability.

IV. The *imitation* of an Invention is affected by:
   a) The *general law* that imitations spread from their initial center in geometrical progression, with regard to the number of persons affected;
   b) *Physical and biological* influences, including race characteristics; the general law being that "Imitations are refracted by their media";
   c) *Social* influences:
      (1) *Logical:* the agreement or disagreement of the new invention with the inventions already more or less socially accepted (imitated). ["Logical causes operate whenever an individual prefers a given imitation to others because he thinks it is more useful or true than others, that is, more in accord than they are with the aims and principles that have already found a place in his mind."[11]]
      (2) *Extra-logical:*
         x) Ideas are transmitted before means; imitation goes *ab interioribus ad exteriora;*
         y) Imitation proceeds from the socially superior to the socially inferior;
         z) Ages of custom, in which the past has peculiar prestige, alternate with ages of fashion, in which prestige is possessed by the novel and the foreign.[12]

In regard to the principle of *opposition* in sociology and society, the earlier oppositions which were observed by students of society were the mythological struggles between the forces of good and evil. Next, there came the idea of the conflicts of races and nations, which was later softened by the economists into the notion of competition. Finally, however, the sociologist has reduced the matter to such precision that he correctly understands that "the really fundamental social opposition must be sought for in the bosom of the social individual himself, whenever he hesitates between adopting or rejecting a new pattern offered to him, whether in the way of phraseology, ritual, concept, canon of art or conduct."[13] The three main types of social opposition are war, competition, and discussion, mentioned in the order of their historic predominance. Each of these forms has tended to develop on a larger scale and thus again verifies the thesis that the order of the progress of phenomena in fact is the reverse of the order of the observation of these phenomena.[14]

With respect to the third great principle, *adaptation,* the sociological observation of this principle was at first confined to the somewhat fantastic ideas of the philosophy of history, whereby the path of history was looked upon as the result of the adaptation or harmonizing of the work of one nation to that of the nation which had preceded or was to follow it, thus making the process of history appear to be a harmonious and teleological whole. The observation of adaptation was gradually made more scientific and exact, until now, according to Tarde, we know that "we must seek the fundamental social adaptation in the brain and individual mind of the inventor"—a harmony among the ideas in the mind of each individual in society is essential to a harmony of the minds of the different members of a society.[15] Following the usual rule, adaptation in social phenomena proceeds from the lesser to the greater—from those in the individual mind to those adaptations between nations upon which must be based the expectations of eliminating war in the future.[16]

In summing up the interrelation of these three principles of repetition, opposition, and adaptation, Tarde says:

These three terms constitute a circular series which is capable of proceeding on and on without ceasing. It is through imitative repetition that invention, the fundamental social adaptation, spreads and is strengthened, and tends, through the encounter of one of its own imitative rays with an imitative ray emanating from some other invention, old or new, either to arouse new struggles, or to yield new and more complex inventions, which soon radiate out imitatively in turn, and so on indefinitely. . . . . Thus of the three terms compared, the first and third surpass the second in height, depth, importance, and possibly also in duration. The only value of the second—opposition—is to provoke a tension of antagonistic forces fitted to arouse inventive genius. . . . .[17]

The mutual relations of our three terms—repetition, opposition, and adaptation—are easily understood when we consider successive repetitions as operating, sometimes in favor of adaptation, which they spread and develop by their own interferences, sometimes in favor of opposition, which they arouse by interferences of another sort.[18]

This indicates in a brief way the main lines of Tarde's approach to the chief problems of sociology. In his political and legal writings he consistently applied the analysis of the workings of repetition, opposition, and adaptation to the fields of political and legal activity.

Tarde's contributions to political theory can hardly be correctly designated as "sociopsychological prolegomena to the study of politics," as is the case with Graham Wallas' contributions, for Tarde's *Les Transformations du pouvoir*[19] is directly concerned with the problems which are usually analyzed by political science. Perhaps the best description of the work would be a "psychological miscellany relative to the explanation of certain political phenomena, particularly the origin and transformation of political authority." The treatment of those problems with which it does deal is, curiously enough, mainly historical or genetic, rather than the analytical approach one would expect from a sociologist of pronounced psychological tendencies. There is no detailed treatment of such fundamental topics as the nature of sovereignty and the state or the scope of state activity. At the same time, there is a brilliant statement and defense of the doctrine that political life and the state are products of social processes, and that political organization and evolution are mainly a by-product of social organization and social evolution, in general. As such, this attitude is an admirable antidote to historians like the late Professor Edward Freeman and political scientists sharing the particular bias of Professor Henry Jones Ford, who held that political activities are primary in society.

Tarde's chief theses in political theory may be summarized as follows: Political authority rests upon the beliefs and desires of society. People wish to be directed and commanded, and they believe that certain leaders are best able to guide and direct them, either from superior ability or from a special dispensation of Providence. These beliefs and desires have their foundations laid in animal society and are disciplined and developed in the family. Mankind is fitted by this family experience to create and develop more extensive forms of social organization. Imitation gives a coherent and logical form to the agencies for maintaining and administering authority. The cause of the shifts in political organization and authority is to be sought in the changes in beliefs and desires which burst through the older patterns of thought designed to satisfy a more primitive type of culture and mental response. People wish to be led in a different manner and believe that a new set of persons is better qualified to fulfil this function.

The beliefs and desires of any given period depend upon the general conditions of social life, particularly upon the type of scientific thought, religion, and industry in vogue at the time. The agency which produces the transformations of beliefs and desires, and, as a consequence, the dependent systems of political authority is invention spread by imitation. At first, inventions give rise to a nobility which monopolize the benefits of their inventions but also become radiant points for the imitation of their discoveries. In time the nobility are superseded by cities, particularly capital cities, as the seat of inventions and radiant points of imitation, and these, in turn, tend to give way to nations as a whole, though in all cases inventions are an individual product. These transformations of political authority are, thus, a "function" of the general social transformation of beliefs and desires, particularly of the changes in the field of religion and industry.

The processes of invention and imitation operate in accordance with the well-known laws developed in Tarde's *Laws of Imitation*. Political phenomena may fruitfully be studied according to their relation to the general scheme of social life organized about the principles of repetition, opposition, and adaptation. Political repetition may be observed not only in regard to the imitation of political inventions as exhibited in the origin of states but also in colonization. Political opposition takes the form of the struggle between parties and classes within the state and struggles between states, as manifested in war and diplomacy. Party strife, while it has many undesirable features and is a very clumsy method of effecting political progress, serves the purpose of creating and spreading political inventions within the state, thus bringing about the general improvement of political administration and organization. It is impossible, however, to regard liberty as the product of the struggle between powers within the state; rather, it is the result of the independence of belief and desire within the individual mind, which prevents desire from dominating belief. External political opposition or war, imperialism, and diplomacy, though accompanied by a vast amount of cruelty and misery, has for its ultimate result that political expansion and consolidation which alone can make possible permanent peace; for war is an inevitable product of many small political entities. Political adaptation, which is essentially identical with political evolution, is the process whereby political repetition and opposition emerge in ever more harmonious political organization and superior types of political institutions.

Since political evolution is the outcome of the various aspects of social evolution, no single simple formula of unilateral evolution can be devised to explain it. The only unilateral formula which will apply is the very general one, obviously drawn from Herbert Spencer, that the course of political evolution is characterized by a transition from an original disorganized confusion to a harmonious adjustment of differences, in both external and internal political relations, through the operation of psychic forces making for an equilibrium. The future is likely to witness an extension both of the scope of state activity and of the personal power of statesmen; but there is little danger in this prospect, owing to the modern development of effective popular control over those in charge of political administration.

In his younger days, Tarde wrote a utopia in which he predicted the termination of opposition in a universal peaceful adjustment of the conflicting interests of mankind. A sense of human brotherhood would replace all external coercion in human relationships. Entitled *Fragment d'histoire future,* it was not published until after Tarde's death in 1904, and was translated the following year as *Underground Man,* emphasizing a phase of the work which may become more relevant in our age of possible atomic bombings.

In the light of Le Bon's somewhat sensational analysis of the crowd and crowd psychology and his tendency to identify the crowd and the public under modern conditions, Tarde's book on *L'Opinion et la foule* ("Opinion and the Crowd")[20] is interesting and suggestive. In this work Tarde sought to differentiate the crowd from the public and to indicate the role of opinion in public beliefs and behavior.

To Tarde a crowd is an assembly of persons who not only have arrived at unified emotions, beliefs, and actions but are also gathered together in a given place at a certain time. Crowd psychology and behavior are primarily produced by physical, as well as mental, contiguity. A public is any number of persons who have sufficient unanimity of belief and emotion to act in a concerted fashion but are separated from each other in space. There have been crowds all through history; but the public, as Tarde views it, is a product of modern times, since the development of the printing-press and especially of the newspaper. Newspapers permit a large group of widely dispersed citizens to read the same news and similar interpretations of the news and in this way to arrive at unity of belief and potential action.

Since the members of a public are, to a certain extent, isolated when they form their opinions, there is more opportunity for deliberation than is to be found in crowds. Yet the simultaneous dissemination of information and the sensational nature of the news tend to produce a mentality in publics ever more like crowd psychology. In this concession Tarde showed some agreement with Le Bon. Had he written after the radio, moving pictures, and television had come into existence, he would probably have gone even further in conceding the approximation of public opinion to crowd attitudes. Opinion, which is the chief instrument that creates the public mind, is emotional and contemporaneous, as contrasted with tradition and reason, which are less important in the content of the public mentality. Opinion is produced by the joint impact of the printed word and personal conversation upon the minds of citizens.

The importance of all this for political theory and practice is apparent. The success of democracy depends greatly upon increasing the amount of reflection and deliberation which the creation of a "public" and a rational public opinion makes possible. If, however, the printed page, notably the daily newspaper, tends to reduce the element of deliberation and to make publics more and more crowd-minded, this bodes evil for the future of democracy and representative government. As we suggested above, had Tarde written after the advent of the radio and moving-picture newsreels, his alarm over the growth of crowd-mindedness would probably have been far greater than it was back at the turn of the century.

Tarde's writings on criminology and penology, which preceded most of his works on psychological sociology, are as highly esteemed by criminologists as are his books on sociology by the sociologists. The most important were *La Criminalité comparée* (1886); *La Philosophie pénale* (1891); and *Études pénales et sociales* (1892). Tarde's work in the field of criminology, aside from emphasizing the potency of imitation in criminality, was chiefly significant as one of the ablest and most influential attacks on the biological theories of Lombroso and his school. Tarde contended, with much learning and many examples, that the overwhelmingly important causes of crime are social rather than physical, though he did not deny the fact of individual responsibility in practical procedure. In his penology, likewise, Tarde contended that the reformation of the criminal, while possible in many cases, must depend primarily on the social influences brought to bear. Tarde's last important work, *La Psychologie économique* (1901) may be regarded as a contribution to institutional economics in its effort to replace abstract a priori theorizing (pecuniary logic) by the study and social interpretation of the facts of economic life.

NOTES

1. The classic exposition of Tarde's sociological system is to be found in M. M. Davis' monograph, *Gabriel Tarde* (New York, 1906), which was incorporated in his later work, *Psychological Interpretations of Society* (New York, 1909). This work is one of the best expositions of a sociological system extant. Other briefer discussions are to be found in G. Tosti's excellent article, "The Sociological Theories of Gabriel Tarde," *Political Science Quarterly*, 1897, pp. 490–511; Giddings' Introduction to Elsie Clews Parsons' translation of Tarde's *Laws of Imitation* (New York, 1903); Bristol's *Social Adaptation*, pp. 185–92; Gault's Introduction and Lindsey's Editorial Preface to Howell's translation of Tarde's *Penal Philosophy* (Boston, 1912); and A. W. Small's review of Tarde's *Social Laws* in *American Journal of Sociology*, IV (1899), 395–400. For an ingenious American adaptation of Tarde's sociological theories see E. A. Ross's *Social Psychology* (New York, 1908); and for the most extended application of similar theories to psychology by an American writer see J. M. Baldwin's *Social and Ethical Interpretations in Mental Development* (New York, 1897).

2. For a brief survey of the salient points connected with Tarde's career see Giddings' Introduction to Parsons, *op. cit.*

3. For the historic antecedents of Tarde's theories and the stages in the development of his system see Davis, *Psychological Interpretations of Society*, chaps. ii, vii.

4. *The Great Society* (New York, 1914), pp. 119–20.

5. *Op. cit.*, p. 191.

6. *La Logique sociale* (Paris, 1905), chap. i; and *Essais et mélanges sociologiques* (Paris, 1895), pp. 156, 268.

7. Cf. *Social Laws*, trans. H. C. Warren (New York, 1899), *passim*. Each of these three great agencies receives its complete analysis in a separate volume. Repetition is analyzed in *Les Lois de l'imitation* (1st ed., Paris, 1890; 3d ed., 1900); opposition in *L'Opposition universelle* (Paris, 1897); and adaptation in *La Logique sociale*. These were epitomized in his *Les Lois sociales* (Paris, 1898), which presented an outline of his whole system of philosophy as well as of his sociology..

8. *Social Laws*, pp. 1–10.

9. *Ibid.*, pp. 11–23.

10. *Ibid.*, pp. 24 ff.

11. *Laws of Imitation*, trans. Elsie Clews Parsons, p. 141.

12. *Psychological Interpretations of Society*, pp. 97–98.

13. *Social Laws*, pp. 81–84.

14. *Ibid.*, pp. 111 ff.

15. *Ibid.*, p. 166.

16. *Ibid.*, pp. 169 ff.

17. *Ibid.*, pp. 135–37.

18. *Ibid.*, pp. 212–13.

19. Paris, 1899.

20. Paris, 1901.

CHAPTER XXVI

THE PSYCHOSOCIOLOGICAL THEORIES
OF GUSTAVE LE BON

Harry Elmer Barnes

I. GENERAL NATURE OF LE BON'S METHOD AND PROCEDURE

OF THE three chief sociologists that France produced—Tarde, Durkheim, and Le Bon (1841–1931)—the latter is the most versatile and by far the most superficial. In fact, Le Bon may be regarded as a popularizer of the more striking ideas of the first two, especially of Tarde's views on imitation and Durkheim's notion of group psychology. The range of Le Bon's interests, however, is certainly remarkable. Trained originally as a physician, he gave up the practice of medicine but contributed several works on physiology and hygiene. Next he was employed by the French government as an archeologist and paleographer in the Orient. In later years he was editor of the *Bibliothèque de philosophie scientifique*. In addition to these activities, he occupied himself by producing a general work on social evolution in two volumes; studies of the chief historic civilizations; several contributions to mathematical chemistry and physics, among them a paper on intra-atomic energy which was published in a number of the leading scientific journals; a statistical study in physical anthropology; a work or two on education; and some half-dozen books on social psychology.[1]

Of course, it is obvious that a man who ranges at will over a dozen fields of research, any one of which could be only partially traversed with thoroughness in a lifetime, is not likely to have mastered any one of them. This is true of Le Bon, whatever his mental powers may have been. Professor G. E. Vincent has thus characterized him in a fairly accurate manner: "M. Le Bon may be described as an intellectual kodak fiend. His books are filled with snapshots at truth, interesting in themselves, but sadly unconnected and out of focus."[2] At the same time, Le Bon's works are all highly interesting, and many of his generalizations sound plausible. His arguments are bolstered up by copious citations of a pertinent nature.

481

Le Bon is one of those writers who exploit their theories in their own works. In discussing crowd psychology, for example, he tells the reader that the sure and certain method to be successful in convincing an audience of the truth of an assertion is to affirm the dogma repeatedly and, at the same time, to be careful to avoid any attempt at thorough analysis or any reference to a possible exception to its applicability. Nothing is more characteristic of Le Bon's own procedure than this very method. Taking a few rather striking psychological postulates which have the virtue of modernity, novelty, and suggestiveness, he applies these conceptions to nearly every phase of contemporary life, in general, and to French social conditions in particular. These theses are repeated and reiterated without detailed analysis or candid statement of exceptions to their application, until even a wary reader is likely to be beguiled by the facile phraseology of the author. Aside from his brilliant but uncritical dogmatism and "cock-sureness," another characteristic of Le Bon's sociopsychological writings should be noted. That is what Herbert Spencer would call his "antipatriotic bias" and his "class bias." At least down to the outbreak of the first World War, Le Bon could see little good in what he alleged to be the characteristics of the modern Romance peoples. Their assumed tendency toward a crowd-psychological condition and their desire to suppress individuality and put into power the incompetent masses held little of promise from his viewpoint. The oft asserted Anglo-Saxon initiative, energy, will power, and individualism attracted him as strongly as the alleged French traits repelled him.

Again, Le Bon finds little to arouse his enthusiasm in the traits of the masses; from his viewpoint, progress and civilization are almost exclusively the contribution of the intellectually élite. There can be no doubt that Le Bon's exaggerations were, in part, due to his generalizations from French conditions, though even these he views in an extreme and exaggerated light. The relation of Le Bon's doctrines to his social environment is not of that subtle type which is likely to escape the attention of the reader but is so prominent in all his works as to make them full of generalizations which are highly inaccurate and distorted, when viewed as sociological propositions of general import. His fundamental doctrines—the idea of national character, the psychology of crowds and revolution, his "antipatriotic" and "class" bias, his continual scenting of impending calamities, and his bitter attacks upon socialism and syndicalism—are all directly and in large part traceable to his reactions to his French "milieu." At the same time, no one can deny that Le Bon has pointed out tendencies, conditions, and psychological trends which had previously been overlooked or undeveloped. When his works are read with the understanding which permits the discounting of his exaggerations and prejudices, they constitute an important contribution to sociological literature. For our purposes the general nature of Le Bon's sociological ideas can be adequately gleaned from a summary of his views on the psychology of (1) social evolution, (2) crowd behavior, and (3) revolutions.

II. THE PSYCHOLOGY OF SOCIAL EVOLUTION

Le Bon's first considerable work in the field of social psychology was the volume entitled, *Lois psychologiques de l'évolution des peuples.*[3] This work purports to be a summary of the main psychological generalizations reached in his earlier books upon social evolution and the history of the civilizations of Asia, Africa, and Europe. It consists mainly of what might be called psychological prolegomena to the study of history, though few historians or psychologists would agree to all the generalizations. Le Bon's main theme is the nature and importance of national character, or "the soul of a race," in the explanation of history and modern social problems.[4]

This all-important "racial soul" is the sum total of the moral and intellectual characteristics that lie at the foundation of the civilization of a race and determine the course of its evolution. The soul of the race finds objective expression in the totality of the civilization which distinguishes the particular race: "The moral and intellectual characteristics, whose association forms the soul of a people, represent the synthesis of its entire past, the inheritance of all its ancestors, the motives of its conduct."[5] In the formation of the racial soul the influence of the dead is preponderant. The racial soul is primarily unconscious; it underlies the rational phases of national thought and is, on that account, much more dominating in its influence. It is over these unconscious motives of conduct that the influence of the dead is particularly potent: "A people is guided far more by its dead than by its living members. It is by its dead, and by its dead alone, that a race is founded. Century after century our departed ancestors have fashioned our ideas and sentiments, and in consequence all the motives of our conduct."[6] These psychological

characteristics which go to make up the soul of a race are composed
of a relatively few fundamental ideas which are very permanent in
character and are changed only very slowly, except through the effect
of racial intermixture. Only the more superficial and secondary characteristics of a race are modifiable with any degree of rapidity.

Le Bon contends that races may be classified psychologically as well
as anatomically. There are primitive races, or "those in which no trace
of culture is met with," made up of people like the Fuegians; inferior
races composed mainly of Negroes; average races represented by the
Mongolians; and superior races, mainly exemplified by the Indo-European peoples. The higher the race, the more highly differentiated it is
psychologically, and the more superior minds it contains. Though there
may be a vast difference in the intelligence of the different individuals
that go to make up a superior race, nevertheless, the race is practically
uniform in those fundamental psychological factors which determine
its character. This explains why it is that national character and not
intelligence is the dominant factor in social evolution, why the English
can hold in subjection the millions in India who equal or surpass the
English in pure intelligence. Even the most superior races cannot change
the fundamental elements of their civilization with any facility. Cross-
breeding of racial stocks is the only process which can produce a rapid
and fundamental change in national character. Social and physical environment have little strength as compared to physical heredity and
cultural inheritance: "The history of civilizations is thus composed of
slow adaptations, of slight transformations. If these latter appear to us
to be sudden and considerable, it is because, as in geology, we suppress
the intermediate phases and only consider the extreme phases."[7] According to Le Bon's view, therefore, history is little more than a product
of racial character:

History in its main lines may be regarded as the mere statement of the results
engendered by the psychological constitution of races. It is determined by this constitution, just as the respiratory organs of fish are determined by their aquatic life.
In the absence of a preliminary knowledge of the mental constitution of a people, its
history appears a chaos of events governed by hazard. On the contrary, when we
are acquainted with the soul of a people, its life is seen to be the regular and inevitable consequence of its psychological characteristics. In all the manifestations
of the life of a people, we always find the unchangeable soul of the race weaving
itself its own destiny.

The idea that institutions can remedy the defects of societies, that national
progress is the consequence of the improvement of institutions and governments,

and that social changes can be effected by decrees—this idea, I say, is still generally accepted..... The most continuous experience has been unsuccessful in shaking this grave delusion..... A nation does not choose its institutions at will any more than it chooses the color of its hair or its eyes..... Centuries are required to form a political system and centuries needed to change it. Institutions have no intrinsic virtue: in themselves they are neither good nor bad. Those which are good at any given moment for a given people may be harmful in the extreme for another nation..... To lose time in the manufacture of cut-and-dried constitutions is, in consequence, a puerile task, the useless labor of an ignorant rhetorician..... The conclusion to be drawn from what precedes is, that it is not in institutions that the means is to be sought of profoundly influencing the genius of the masses. Peoples are governed by their character, and all the institutions which are not intimately modelled on that character merely represent a borrowed garment, a transitory disguise.[8]

The soul of a race is very visibly and strikingly manifested in its political institutions. Applying this idea to French conditions, he finds that all the French parties, whatever their name, pursue the identical end of attempting to absorb the individual in the state and destroy individual initiative. In England and the United States, however, a different type of racial soul leads all parties to favor individual initiative at the expense of state activity. All this goes to prove that, in reality, forms of government and political institutions, in general, count for very little in comparison with the psychological characteristics of a race. The great historical importance of the psychological traits of a race is well illustrated by the conspicuous success and expansion of Anglo-Saxon colonization and political institutions in America and the equally apparent failure of the Spanish in this respect.[9]

Because of the very fact that cross-breeding is the only method by which it is possible rapidly to change the character of a nation, immigration on a large scale, with the consequent interbreeding, has a very important effect upon the destiny of a nation. Roman civilization perished more as a result of the peaceful amalgamation with barbarians than as a consequence of the subsequent military invasions. The same threatening conditions are now to be detected in the wholesale immigration into America; but, thanks to Anglo-Saxon superiority, the Americans may, if they act in time, exterminate these present-day barbarians as Marius did the Cimbri. If action is long delayed, America must sooner or later meet the fate of the Roman Empire and disintegrate into many small and warring nations.

Aside from the drastic changes in national character which may result from wholesale racial intermixture, there may come about a more gradual modification, as a result of the infiltration of new ideas. A new idea always arises in the mind of an individual who attracts a few enthusiastic disciples to aid him in zealously affirming its truth without analysis or discussion. But this soon leads to a wider and wider discussion of the merits of the idea by the public. If it gains ground, it is spread by contagion and imitation throughout the society, and in time the group becomes as obsessed with the new idea as its originator was in the beginning. But, even with successful ideas, this is a very slow process. An idea never becomes a national obsession until, after years of discussion, it has filtered down into the unconscious levels of national character. When the idea has thus become a matter of national dogma or sentiment, it has reached its full degree of effectiveness. On account of the sentimental and dogmatic nature of religious beliefs, which renders them especially amenable to fanatic support, ideas of this type have been the most powerful of all factors in the past history of mankind. To a large degree, they have tended to shape the other types of beliefs and institutions. Despite the absurdities of past religious beliefs, they have played an immense part in social control and in giving solidarity to society. There can be no doubt that the present tendency toward institutional dissolution is partially a result of the decay of the religious beliefs that society has outgrown but that have not been supplanted by a new body of religious thought to provide social discipline.

Only by an application of social psychology can one comprehend the relation of leadership to social progress. While virtually every substantial advance in culture is the result of the services of the élite in any society, they usually do little more than synthesize the latent possibilities and tendencies of the age. Again, the truly élite never bring about any sudden or startling changes; they affect civilization only gradually. The great dramatic changes in history are the work of fanatics:

At the bidding of a Peter the Hermit millions of men hurled themselves against the East; the words of an hallucinated enthusiast such as Mahomet created a force capable of triumphing over the Greco-Roman world; an obscure monk like Luther bathed Europe in blood. The voice of a Galileo or a Newton will never have the least echo among the masses. The inventors of genius hasten the march of civilization. The fanatics and the hallucinated create history.[10]

As nations are built up by the formation of a national character, so they perish with its breakdown. As an organism decays when it no longer functions, so a nation disintegrates when it has lost its character. Le Bon finds many symptoms of the decay of national character among the Latin peoples of Europe, among which socialism, or the cult of state worship, is the most menacing.

Stated with bold dogmatism and unobscured by being buried beneath a mass of erudition, these propositions of Le Bon sound rather novel and startling, but they are by no means new. His idea of national character as a vital reality, his belief in the superiority of certain races, and even his faith in the supremacy of the Anglo-Saxon or Germanic peoples is virtually identical with the doctrine preached in the works of Burke, and the "Romanticists"; of Freeman, Kemble, and Stubbs in England; and of Waitz, Sybel, Droysen, and Treitschke in Germany. Further, his doctrine of the predominant importance of the ideas and beliefs of a people in their historic development is but an exaggerated statement of the conception of history as a sociopsychic process, stated by Lamprecht in Germany and championed in America by Professor James Harvey Robinson and likely to be one of the most fruitful lines of historical investigation for years to come. He makes wide use of Tarde's ideas of invention, imitation, and contagion. This work on the "psychology of peoples" illustrates the main characteristic of Le Bon's sociological writings—an overworking of a very few basic ideas, some sound and others bordering on the fantastic.

It is diverting and instructive to note that, as a result of the first World War, Le Bon completely reversed his interpretation of the psychic traits of the Latins and the Teutons (see his *Enseignements psychologiques de la guerre européenne* [Paris, 1916]). The Latins were suddenly endowed with unique political genius and became wholeheartedly devoted to political individualism, while the Teutons were portrayed as decadent and degenerate devotees of state socialism. Le Bon thus proved that, so far as he was concerned, his idea of the primacy of emotional factors over the intellectual held true.

III. THE PSYCHOLOGY OF THE CROWD

Le Bon's second excursion into the field of social psychology was embodied in his most popular and best-known work, *La Psychologie des foules.*[11] The ideas of this work, combined with the theories expressed in his *Psychology of Peoples,* constitute all the really important sociopsychological conceptions developed by Le Bon. His other and later works are but the reiteration of familiar doctrines and an application of them in greater detail to specific historic, social, economic, or educational problems. His fundamental doctrines are derived in part from Tarde's notions of imitation and Durkheim's views of the impression of the group on the individual.

Le Bon introduces the reader to his second work by a reiteration of the main thesis of the earlier book, namely, that the really significant historic changes are to be discovered in the modifications of human thought: "The only important changes whence the renewal of civilization results, affect ideas, conceptions, and beliefs. The memorable events of history are the visible effects of the invisible changes of human thought."[12] Many intelligent historians would agree with the statement, however much they might dissent from some of Le Bon's exaggerated applications of the doctrine.

The present era is a critical period, inasmuch as it is characterized by far-reaching transformations of human thought. The social, religious, and political beliefs upon which our civilization has rested are giving way before the growth of modern science and industry. The coming age seems destined to be the era of crowds, as a result of the growth of cities, the extension of the suffrage, and the improvement in communication: "The divine right of the masses is about to replace the divine right of kings." This prospect does not promise well for the future, for crowds are mainly given to violent action and are little adapted to producing careful and accurate thought. Civilizations have always been created by a small intellectual aristocracy, while the rule of crowds has ever characterized periods of decline and disintegration. There is no longer any hope of being able to overcome the rule of the masses. The popular movement has gone beyond the point where it might have been arrested. The only practicable method of meeting the inevitable tendency is for statesmen to acquire a knowledge of crowd psychology and thus be able to reduce the attendant evils as much as possible through a scientific mastery of the situation. Le Bon modestly suggests that it is the purpose of his treatise to make this much-needed information available for the first time.

In defining what he means by a crowd, Le Bon makes it clear that he does not regard a crowd as a mere group of individuals assembled in physical contiguity but, rather, such an organized aggregation that a

collective mind is formed and the conscious individuality of the assembled persons is virtually lost. Not only may some aggregations fail
to constitute a crowd, but, on the other hand, a whole nation may, with
proper facilities for communication and a proper degree of psychic
stimulation, assume all the essential characteristics of a crowd.

Le Bon proceeds to enumerate the main psychic traits which, in general, characterize crowds. A crowd possesses a collective mind and a
psychic unity which alter the normal emotions, thoughts, and conduct
of the individual to a considerable degree. The crowd mind is not the
average mind of its members but is, rather, a complex of new traits
which arise from the combination. The subconscious mind plays the
predominant role in the psychic activity of crowds. Since the subconscious is mainly charged with highly emotional qualities, with the archaic
mental inheritance of the race, and with the more instinctive content of
the mind, these very qualities are brought to the front in the mental
operations of crowds. In a crowd, therefore, the individual members
are assimilated to a common mediocrity, and the crowd is never capable
of engaging in activities requiring a high degree of intellectual effort.

These new psychic traits which arise in the individual, as a result of
his participation in a crowd, are brought about by several factors. In a
crowd an individual feels a sense of invincible power quite absent in his
normal isolated state. His susceptibility to suggestion is very greatly increased, and, as a result of this, the sentiments of a crowd are ultra-
contagious. The net result of these factors is that in a crowd the individual behaves in a sort of half-conscious and hypnotic manner:

> We see, then, that the disappearance of the conscious personality, the predom-
> inance of the unconscious personality, the turning, by means of suggestion and
> contagion, of feelings and ideas in an identical direction, the tendency to im-
> mediately transform the suggested ideas into acts; these we see, are the principal
> characteristics of the individual forming part of a crowd. He is no longer himself
> but has become an automaton who has ceased to be guided by his will.

At the same time, however, the action of a crowd under certain conditions may not be of an inferior sort. Owing to its tendency to act swiftly
in response to a vigorous suggestion, it may perform a heroic act if
the suggestion it receives is of the type to promote such activity.

After thus analyzing the general psychic characteristics of crowds,
Le Bon practically exhausts the list of descriptive adjectives in enumer-
ating the special psychic traits of crowds. He finds that they are im-

pulsive, mobile, irritable, suggestible, credulous, ingenuous, prone to exaggeration, intolerant, dictatorial, conservative, capable of entertaining contradictory ideas, characterized by inferior reasoning powers, possessed of an abnormally sensitive imagination, religiously tenacious of a conviction, and likely to hold fundamental convictions with great firmness while exchanging superficial opinions with amazing alacrity.

Le Bon's chapter on "The Leaders of Crowds and Their Means of Persuasion" is of interest as bearing upon his later discussion of the methods of modern political leaders. He finds that the leaders of crowds are almost uniformly rhetoricians or agitators obsessed by an idea, rather than careful thinkers, and that they tend to be very despotic in their methods of control. The successful leader gets the crowd to accept his belief by constant, dogmatic, and repeated affirmation of his conviction without any attempt at reasoned analysis. Once an idea is accepted by a crowd, it spreads with great rapidity by contagion and imitation. Leaders of crowds maintain their control by their prestige, which is either acquired by wealth or position or is a gift of nature. Napoleon possessed the quality of natural prestige to such a degree that it was sufficient to make an emperor out of his obscure and mediocre nephew, nearly half a century after his glory had passed.

Le Bon then proceeds to apply his theory of crowd leadership to an explanation of the partisan persuasion of crowds. In the first place, the candidate must possess sufficient prestige, as a result of ability, reputation, or wealth, so as to be able to force himself upon the electorate without any question or discussion of his lack of merit. Next, he should vigorously affirm, without attempting to prove, that his opponent is a scoundrel, having been guilty of several crimes. Then he should flatter the electorate without any limit, making wide use of sonorous phrases, condemning the wealthy and powerful and praising the virtues of the masses. While a candidate's written platform should be rather vague and moderate, he may make the most extravagant verbal promises, for the electorate always forgets them after the election. The voter forms no independent opinions but has them forced upon him ready-made by the party leaders and orators. The guidance of the masses is a vital factor in modern civilization, for there is no longer any hope of destroying the doctrine of the sovereignty of the masses which has become wellnigh a religious dogma. Even if it were possible to restrict the suffrage to the intellectual aristocracy, there would be no reason to expect any decided improvement, since, by the laws of the psychology of crowds, assembled individuals tend to be ruled by their emotions and not by the intellectual faculties, and the emotional traits of the most erudite do not differ materially from those of the average individual: "In a crowd men always tend to the same level, and, on general questions, a vote recorded by forty academicians is no better than that of forty water-carriers."[13]

Parliamentary assemblies are another example of modern political phenomena which can be explained only by an application of the laws of social psychology. The whole system rests on the erroneous assumption that large numbers of individuals are more likely to arrive at an accurate solution of a public problem than a small group. Parliamentary assemblies normally manifest most of the characteristics of a crowd: "The general characteristics of crowds are to be met with in parliamentary assemblies: intellectual simplicity, irritability, suggestibility, the exaggeration of the sentiments, and the preponderating influence of a few leaders." Perhaps the most significant special characteristic in the procedure of assemblies is their almost invariable tendency to attempt to solve the complicated problems of public policy by a few simple formulas and by direct legislation. On questions of local or personal interest legislators have fixed and unalterable opinions. On general questions of policy and procedure, however, they are wide open to the suggestions of leaders; and if these leaders happen to be of about equal power but represent different opinions, the legislature will be conspicuous for its indecision and inconsistency, as it will waver in its response to the powerful sources of suggestion. The leaders possess their power as a result of their prestige or ability to arouse enthusiasm and not on account of the logic or profundity of their arguments. Most great parliamentary leaders have been vigorous men, possessed of the gift of florid oratory but with relatively little breadth of mind or intellectual capacity.

If the action of a parliamentary assembly is normally on a little higher plane than that of the ordinary crowd, in times of excitement it degenerates into a mob, as in the case of the assemblies of the French Revolution. The sole salvation of parliamentary government lies in the fact that the laws are usually drafted by specialists and experts, and legislators merely vote for laws rather than frame them.

Despite these shortcomings, Le Bon concludes that, after all, parliamentary government is the best which has yet been devised. Its chief evils, in addition to the presence of the crowd-psychological situation, are two—financial waste, resulting from the fear that legislators have of opposing financial bills lest they lose their influence and the local appropriations, and the restriction of individual liberty, due to the worship of state activity and the faith in the efficacy of the state to solve all social and economic problems. Le Bon finds that an excessive trust in the state is a symptom of national decline and thus ends this work in the same vein as the conclusion of the *Psychology of Peoples,* namely, that the Latin peoples, who put their trust in the state, are beginning their period of final decay, an idea which, as we have seen, Le Bon vehemently repudiated as soon as the first World War broke out.

There is little that needs to be added in the way of comment on Le Bon's doctrines regarding the psychic traits of crowds. His general observations are, in the main, correct but are highly colored and overworked. His treatment is doubtless inadequate, as he is guilty of the same faults that he finds in legislators, namely, of trying to solve a complex problem by a few simple phrases and formulas. As Professor C. H. Cooley very well said on this point:

> The psychology of crowds has been treated at length by Sighele, Le Bon, and other authors who, having made a specialty of the man in the throng, are perhaps somewhat inclined to exaggerate the degree in which he departs from ordinary personality. The crowd mind is not, as is sometimes said, a quite different thing from that of the individual (unless by the individual is meant the higher self), but is merely a collective mind of a low order which stimulates and unifies the cruder impulses of its members.[14]

IV. THE PSYCHOLOGY OF REVOLUTIONS

Le Bon's reflections on the psychology of revolutions, which are more or less present in all his works, are brought together and expanded in the volume entitled *La Révolution française et la psychologie des révolutions.*[15] He introduces this work with a brief discussion of what he calls "the psychological revision of history." His thesis is that the seeming difficulties of historical interpretation vanish as soon as one recognizes that the irrational and often involuntary beliefs, and not the rational and intellectual factors, have been the dominating influences throughout history:

> The solution of the historical difficulties which had so long been sought was thenceforth obvious. I arrived at the conclusion that besides the rational logic

which conditions thought, and was formerly regarded as our sole guide, there exist very different forms of logic: affective logic, collective logic, and mystic logic, which usually overrule the reason and engender the generative impulses of our conduct.[16]

In discussing the psychology of revolutions, Le Bon first proceeds to classify and characterize them. A revolution is any sudden, or apparently sudden, transformation of beliefs, ideas, and doctrines. The real and enduring revolutions are those that transform the character of a people; but such transformations are normally so slow a process that the word "evolution" is more accurately descriptive of them than the term "revolution." The most important of all revolutions are the scientific. They alone are accomplished by rational factors, and they are the only type which really advances civilization. Nevertheless, their gradual and undramatic character has caused their significance to be overlooked by the conventional type of historian. Political and religious revolutions, which, from their dramatic nature, attract the attention of historians, are not derived from rational influences but from affective and mystic forces. This gives them their dynamic power but also renders them likely to be violent, absurd, and futile. Religious revolutions are even more violent than political revolutions. In religious revolutions the participants cannot be disillusioned by the results, because the truth or falsity of their principles can be demonstrated only in another world. Religious revolutions also have the more important results of the two, for, while they do little or nothing to advance the intellectual factors of a civilization, they are the most influential agency in transforming the sentiments of a people. Religion, particularly when intensified during a revolution, gives a people a moral unity and cohesion which could be obtained in no other manner.

Le Bon next analyzes the role that governments and the people play in revolutions. Governments are usually very feeble in opposing a revolution, giving way immediately and with little resistance. A wise and efficient government, however, may check a revolution by following a sagacious policy. The menacing Russian revolution after the Russo-Japanese War was thwarted by the action of the government in temporarily conciliating the discontented masses and then exterminating or exiling the fanatical leaders. Governments may at times attempt to produce a revolution by their own action, but they are rarely successful unless the national character is not yet sufficiently developed to render an effective resistance to the change of institutions, as was the case with the revolutionary reforms in Russian under Peter the Great. Yet, however profound may be the apparent change in the system of government, such a revolution rarely has a serious effect upon the mental characteristics of a nation: "To create a revolution is easy, but to change the soul of a people is difficult indeed."[17]

The mental characteristics of a people play a prominent part in determining the nature of its revolutions. The more stable the mind and institutions of a nation in normal times, the more violent are its revolutions, for such people are not adapted to making gradual nonrevolutionary changes. A nation with a flexible, adaptable mind may not escape revolutions, but those which it experiences are usually slight and only the final stage in a long period of gradual changes. France is a good example of the former type of nation, England of the latter. Contrary to the belief of many historians, the people, strictly considered, never conceive or direct a revolution. They simply obey the dictates of leaders, though they give the aspect of violence to the movement. To be strictly accurate, the people must be differentiated when one attempts to describe the part played by masses in revolutions. The great body of peasants, tradesmen, and honest artisans, who form the solid and substantial element in the masses, take little part in the violence of revolutions. Those who are guilty of violence, under the guidance of obsessed leaders, are the "degenerates of alcoholism and poverty, thieves, beggars, destitute 'casuals,' indifferent workers without employment—these constitute the dangerous bulk of the armies of insurrection."[18]

Le Bon finds that there are several special varieties of mentality prevalent during revolutions. Each individual may have different traits of character, made more prominent at various times because of changes in the stimulation from the social environment. In revolutions the sentiments of hatred, fear, ambition, envy, variety, and enthusiasm, which are normally more or less suppressed, are given full vent. One of the most prominent types of mentality developed by revolution is what Le Bon calls the "mystic mentality." This is characterized by the attribution of a mysterious power to superior beings or forces, which are incarnated in the form of "idols, fetiches, words, or formulae." It is at the bottom of all religious and most political beliefs and is especially important during revolutionary periods. Another influential type of mentality which is conspicuous in revolutions is the "Jacobin mentality."

This is based upon the mystic mentality, to which are added feeble reasoning powers and strong passions. The typical "revolutionary mentality" adds to the mystic and Jacobin traits chronic restlessness and discontent—the spirit of perpetual rebellion. Finally, there is the "criminal mentality," which characterizes the degenerate antisocial class which is normally restrained by the hand of the law. This element constitutes the majority of the savage and violent elements in revolutionary mobs. If one concedes that revolutions are conducted under the combined direction and impulse of mystic, Jacobin, revolutionary, and criminal mentalities, one can be little surprised at their violent nature, their absurd direction, or their ephemeral results.

Le Bon concludes his introductory and general treatment of revolution by a repetition of his overworked views regarding the psychology of peoples, crowds, assemblies, and leadership. In the second part of his treatise he applies these already venerable conceptions to an interpretation of the French Revolution. While this analysis is at times most brilliant and suggestive, his method of procedure is open to the most severe criticism. He apparently reached certain general conclusions regarding revolutions from a study of the French Revolution and then reapplied these views to an interpretation of this very period. Of course, this gives a high degree of apparent plausibility and concrete substantiation to his theories but quite fails to impress the critical reader. He concludes that the general result of the French Revolution, in France, at least, was to substitute the tyranny of the state for the oppression of individual monarchs.[19]

In the concluding portion of his treatise Le Bon discusses the after-effects of the French Revolution, particularly in regard to the development of democratic ideas. The Revolution produced a crop of idealizers and theorizers who planned the complete democratization of society. The ideal of "equality," rather than the shibboleths of "liberty" and "fraternity," has received the greatest emphasis and is at present the pivotal doctrine of socialism.

Le Bon finds that there are two distinct conceptions of democracy. One is that of an intellectual aristocracy under democratic forms; the other is the popular notion of democracy, based upon the ideal of equality or, perhaps better, upon the hatred of superiority. This latter variety is in direct opposition to nature's principle of inequality and has rarely received the support of great minds. Though the popular ideal of democracy is an illusion, it has great vogue because it is a belief. The Jacobin mentality has become general in Latin countries, as evidenced by the growth of anarchy, syndicalism, the hatred of superiority and restraint, and the socialist craving for the extension of state activity. The distinctly new element in the modern situation is the struggle between capital and labor, which is an outgrowth of the industrial revolution. The vicissitudes, uncertainties, conflicts, and extension of duties in modern political life have compelled most states to develop an elaborate administrative system which constitutes the real government and threatens society with the tyranny of a caste of functionaries—the bureaucracy.

V. SUMMARY OF LE BON'S BASIC THEORIES ON SOCIAL PSYCHOLOGY

Le Bon's salient doctrines may be summarized as follows: Every race possesses certain definite psychic traits, built up by the slow accumulations of experience and perpetuated by tradition. These psychic traits, rather than institutions, are the determining factors in civilization, the latter being simply an objective expression of the former. Among these psychic traits which constitute national character, or the soul of the race, the affective, mystic, and unconscious factors are the most powerful, quite overshadowing the conscious, rational, and intellectual elements, though it is to the influence of the latter that progress is due. Without a coherent and unified group of psychic traits constituting the soul of the race, the civilization of that race cannot develop or be perpetuated. It is futile to attempt to change these fundamental psychic traits by a revolutionary or any other artificial transformation of institutions. Therefore, an excessive degree of state activity is worse than useless; lawmaking power should be confined to the codification of well-established and persistent customs; and government, in general, should be limited to that minimum of activity which is necessary to preserve order and secure the proper degree of mental discipline for the individual citizen. Both socialism and syndicalism are, thus, dangerous movements, the former wishing to produce excessive state activity and the latter desiring to abolish the state altogether. Owing to such results of the industrial revolution as the growth of cities and the consequent concentration of population, the improvements in communication, and the extension of the suffrage, modern political life has tended to become dominated by crowds. The crowd is abnormal in its psychological characteristics, being highly emotional, exceptionally weak intellectually, and exceedingly susceptible to suggestion. It is easily guided, however, by leaders possessing prestige, who, to be successful, make use of those principles of affirmation, repetition, contagion, and imitation, whereby a crowd may be persuaded and convinced. Therefore, it is highly essential that society shall assure the highest quality of leadership for crowds, and thus be able to direct their dynamic energy into activities which are conducive to the public welfare. If this is not done and crowds are left to the exploitation of shortsighted and selfish demagogues, they must continue to be a constant menace to the integrity, well-being, and even the existence of modern society.[20]

NOTES

1. For a list of Le Bon's contributions see the article on Le Bon in *La grande encyclopédie* for his earlier works, and the biographical note in the *New International Encyclopedia* for a list of his main works. Another list of his works is given in the French biographical publication, *Qui êtes-vous?* His productivity is perhaps exceeded only by that of his fellow-countryman, Solomon Reinach, who can hardly boast an equal breadth of interests.

2. In review of Le Bon's *The Psychology of Peoples,* in *American Journal of Sociology,* January, 1899, p. 555.

3. Paris, 1895; English trans., *The Psychology of Peoples* (New York, 1898), reviewed by Professor Vincent, *ibid.* Cf. also Bristol, *Social Adaptation* (Cambridge, Mass., 1915), pp. 133–38.

4. Le Bon's notions of social evolution and of the contrasting characteristics of the French and Anglo-Saxon peoples are but a holdover of the doctrines of the "Romanticists," given a modern dress through a dash of psychology.

5. *The Psychology of Peoples,* pp. 63–64.

6. *Ibid.,* pp. 11, 15–16, 51 ff. Le Bon admits that it is practically impossible to find a pure race at the present time in the sense of anatomical purity and states that what he refers to are "historical races"—a product of psychological, rather than physical, evolution. A historic race is produced when two or more not too dissimilar peoples are brought together in fairly equal numbers and subjected to the same environmental conditions for a very long period of time. The apparent confusion which might arise from identifying the soul of a race with national character he explains by taking the ground that nations are normally subdivisions of some well-defined historical race and thus partake of the general characteristics of the race of which they form a part.

7. *Ibid.,* p. 96.

8. *Ibid.,* pp. 129–30; *The Crowd,* pp. 97–101; cf. L. F. Ward, *Pure Sociology* (New York, 1903), pp. 184–93, 544–75; *Applied Sociology* (Boston, 1904), pp. 13–17.

9. *The Psychology of Peoples,* pp. 130 ff. "This terrible decadence of the Latin race, left to itself, compared with the prosperity of the English race in a neighboring country, is one of the most sombre, the saddest, and, at the same time, the most instructive experiences that can be cited in support of the psychological laws that I have enunciated" (*ibid.,* p. 152).

10. *Ibid.,* pp. 204, 211 ff., 219 ff.

11. Paris, 1895; trans. with the title, *The Crowd* (London, 1896); reviewed by A. F. Bentley in *American Journal of Sociology,* January, 1897, pp. 612–14. This book went through twenty-nine editions and was translated again in 1922. I have used the 1913 edition because it best expresses Le Bon's ideas on the crowd before they were distorted by the war and postwar hysteria, which befogged Le Bon's subsequent thinking.

12. *The Crowd* (8th ed.; London, 1913), pp. 13–14.

13. *Ibid.*, pp. 202–12.

14. *Social Organization* (New York, 1909), pp. 149–50. Le Bon's whole treatment of social psychology should be tempered by a reading of pp. 61–205 of this work.

15. Paris, 1912. English translation, *The Psychology of Revolution*, by Bernard Miall (New York, 1913).

16. *Ibid.*, p. 15.

17. *Ibid.*, pp. 49–59.

18. *Ibid.*, pp. 60–74.

19. *Ibid.*, p. 286. For his general summary of the psychology of the French Revolution see pp. 326–30.

20. Le Bon summarized his pre-war theories in a little volume entitled *Aphorismes du temps présent* (Paris, 1913). For a more complete account of Le Bon's other works on social psychology, see H. E. Barnes, "A Psychological Interpretation of Modern Social Problems and of Contemporary History: A Survey of the Contributions of Gustave Le Bon to Social Psychology," *American Journal of Psychology*, XXXI (1920), 333–69.

CHAPTER XXVII

THE SOCIOLOGISM OF ÉMILE DURKHEIM
AND HIS SCHOOL

EMILE BENOIT-SMULLYAN
Associated Colleges of Upper New York

I. DURKHEIM'S PREDECESSORS

SOCIOLOGISM, as we use the term here, is a synthesis of a positivistic methodology[1] with a particular set of substantive theories, for which we have invented the name "agelecism" (from ἀγέλη, meaning "group").[2] By "agelecism" we mean the general sociological doctrine which maintains the reality *sui generis* or the causal priority of the social group *qua* group. Agelecism in its modern form was introduced into the stream of French social thought by De Bonald and De Maistre, who maintained that the social group precedes and constitutes the individual, that it is the source of culture and all the higher values, and that social states and changes are not produced by, and cannot be directly affected or modified by, the desires and volitions of individuals.

Positivism, the doctrine that the social sciences should adopt the methods or schemas of the physical sciences, was first given self-conscious development by Saint-Simon, who sketched a program for a "social physics" or "social physiology" which would search for the "necessary" laws of social development. He laid the basis for a sociologistic theory of morals by treating morals as relative to group structure and pointing out the analogy between an applied science of morals and medicine or hygiene. This synthesis of agelecism and positivism was further elaborated and systematized by Comte. By reviving Bonald's criticism of introspective psychology and by omitting psychology from his classification of the sciences, he introduced an important antipsychologistic bias into the methodology of sociologism. His strongly anti-individualistic program of social control, his theory of social consensus, his conception of society as a "Great Being," and his emphasis on the family as the true social unit all contributed elements to the development of a comprehensive theory of agelecism. De Roberty, who, although a Russian, has figured prominently in the evolution of French sociologistic thought, contributed the biosocial hypothesis which viewed psychology as a concrete and dependent science derived from biology and sociology and explained culture and the higher faculties of the human mind as the product of human interaction and the group situation. The latter doctrine was later echoed and elaborated by Izoulet and Draghicesco. Finally, the biologistic theorist, Espinas, working under the inspiration of Comtean positivism, proclaimed that the individual was only a society of cells and, conversely, that society might legitimately be considered a kind of superindividual possessing a collective consciousness.

The essential dependence of Durkheim on this particular stream of thought would be difficult to deny.[3] Durkheim disagrees with Comte's law of the three stages and with his conception of humanity as composing a single society; and he disagrees with Espinas's biologistic assumptions. But he is profoundly in sympathy with the particular combination of methodological positivism and agelecism which constitutes the essence of the sociologistic tradition as here defined. Durkheim's achievement may be summed up under three heads: first, his brilliant synthesis of positivism and agelecism into a single theoretical structure; second, his investigation and analysis of a number of empirical problems in terms of this theoretical scheme; third, the founding and editing of the *Année sociologique* and, in connection with it, the guidance of an enthusiastic group of collaborators and disciples in a wide but unified program of empirical research.

The purpose of the present chapter is to present a brief exposition and analysis of the Durkheimian sociology conceived as a single integrated system of thought. We shall not, except incidentally, concern ourselves with the historical problem of the succession of Durkheim's ideas and their process of development. Nor will there be any attempt to present a detailed or adequate criticism, although the notes will contain brief criticisms on a few major points.[4] It goes without saying that only the most salient features of the Durkheimian sociology can be treated at all within the confines of a single chapter.

II. METHODOLOGY IN DURKHEIM'S SOCIOLOGY

Some students of Durkheim have maintained that Durkheim's whole sociological system rests at bottom on a few methodological intuitions.[5] There can be no doubt at least that methodological preconceptions played a very important role in shaping the Durkheimian sociology. Our first task, accordingly, is to analyze the essential elements in the Durkheim methodology and to trace their derivation from the positivistic faith with which Durkheim was inspired.[6] Durkheim's continuity with the main Positivist tradition is immediately evidenced in his stand on the relation between sociology and philosophy. He begins by rejecting the assumption that sociology needs to rest on any philosophic presuppositions whatever. Sociology is to be completely independent of philosophy; yet this independence is not reciprocal, for an adequate philosophy will, of necessity, incorporate important elements contributed by sociology, especially an understanding of the basic processes of association. This is clearly in line with the essential element in the positivistic philosophy, namely, the rejection of the main philosophic traditions as unscientific, together with the attempt to erect a new philosophy by generalizing scientific conclusions or by utilizing scientific methods to tackle such theoretical questions as still appear to be meaningful. Like Comte, Durkheim expects the renovation of philosophy to be based particularly on the results of the new science of society.[7] His blueprints for methodological reform in this new science we now propose to examine.

According to his own statement, Durkheim's most basic methodological postulate is that we should "treat social facts as things."[8] The intended meaning of this formula has never been clear, because Durkheim used the term "thing" in four different and not closely related senses, viz., (1) an entity possessing certain definite characteristics which are independent of human observation; (2) an entity which can be known only a posteriori (as opposed, for example, to a mathematical relation); (3) an entity, the existence of which is independent of human volition; (4) an entity which can be known only through "external" observation (as, for example, the sensory observation of the behavior or physiological states of others, in psychology) and not by introspection.

The meaning of the prescription that we ought to treat social facts as things varies with the sense of the word "thing," taken as intended. In the first sense of the word, the prescription means little more than that the sociologist has a real subject matter. In the second sense it means that social facts can be known only through *some type* of experience, and not by an a priori insight. These two contentions would be admitted by virtually all sociologists. In the third and fourth meanings the prescription becomes more controversial. In the third sense it seems to require the assumption of determinism in interhuman relations.[9] In the fourth sense it limits us to external observation of social facts and forbids the use of introspective evidence even if it is selected and checked with scientific caution.

The classical sociological systems of Comte and Spencer, as well as virtually the whole body of jurisprudence, economics, and the theory of morals, are all vitiated, Durkheim feels, by an excessive dependence upon deductive reasoning and by a normative or evaluative approach. Both these errors spring from the same source: a failure to treat social facts as things; for, if social facts are things, then they must be empirically observed at every stage and not merely deduced from certain initial asumptions; and, moreover, we must strive merely to know them and adapt ourselves to them. Valuation is irrelevant. To insure scientific objectivity, the sociologist must begin not with concepts but with sensory data. These will supply the elements of his definitions.[10] The sociologist must find some "objective" set of sensory data, the variations of which will measure the variations in the internal life of society, just as the oscillations of the thermometer provide an objective index to replace the subjective sensory data of temperature. There are three such orders of facts which Durkheim accepts as possessing this objectivity and, at the same time, as being collective rather than individual. They are legal codes, social statistics, and religious dogmas.[11]

Durkheim's basic rules of sociological explanation are, first, that the social fact should always be viewed as mechanically determined and, second, that it should be explained in terms of another social fact, never by a fact of a lower order (e.g., a biological or psychological cause). In his discussion of this topic[12] Durkheim attacks two opponents simultaneously: psychologism and individualism—as well as that particular mixture of the two which constitutes utilitarianism. The common procedure of explaining a social fact in terms of its utility or in terms of the satisfaction it yields to individuals is, Durkheim maintains, entirely fallacious, since our needs do not of themselves create conditions which satisfy those needs; and only an explanation in terms of efficient causation is scientifically acceptable. Furthermore, if we supposed the cause of the social fact to lie within the individual, we should be unable to explain the constraint which the social fact, by definition, exerts over the individual. Hence "the determining cause of a social fact must be sought for among the antecedent social facts..... The function of a social fact must always be sought in its relationship to some social end."[13]

There still remains the question as to which particular order of social facts is to provide the ultimate explanatory principle. Durkheim reasons that, since social facts arise out of the act of association, they must vary in accordance with the forms of this association, "that is to say, according to the manner in which the constituent parts of the society are grouped." Thus "the ultimate origin of all social processes of any importance must be sought in the constitution of the internal social milieu."[14]

This internal social milieu, to which Durkheim elsewhere refers as the social "substratum"[15] is comprised of such morphological elements as: the number of people in the group, the degree of their proximity, the evenness with which they are diffused over a given area, the number and dispositions of the paths of communication and transport, etc. It is, therefore, essentially a matter of the spatial distribution of physical entities (even persons are here considered in their physical aspect). The asserted ultimacy of this factor has caused Durkheim to be taxed, by several writers, with sociological materialism.[16] This criticism Durkheim attempts to avoid by maintaining that it is not simply the number of people in a given area (the "material density") which is important, but the number of people who have established effective *moral* relations ("dynamic density"). However, by introducing this nonmaterialistic element into the concept, Durkheim sacrifices much of its operational value, since the degree of its applicability can no longer be determined by wholly external observations.[17]

An interesting phase of Durkheim's positivism is his program for an applied sociology to formulate rules for social guidance.[18] This science not only would advise us as to the best way in which to achieve social objectives but also would select the ends which a given society ought to pursue, and would do so entirely on the basis of scientific observation of empirical data. This can be accomplished, Durkheim claims, by finding an objective criterion of social health and social pathology. Once in possession of such a criterion, social science can apply the general laws of sociology to the preservation of social health, just as the science of medicine applies the laws of physiology to the preservation of the health of the individual organism.[19]

Durkheim is quick to dismiss the criterion of utility, as requiring an appeal to the subjective states of individuals and, hence, as lacking in scientific objectivity. Instead, he defines health in terms of "normality" and adopts *generality* as the criterion of "normality." The socially health-ful is that which is normal; and as "the normal type is identical with the average type . . . . every deviation from this standard is a pathological phenomenon."[20] In the application of this criterion Durkheim is led to paradoxical conclusions. Since crime is prevalent in all or most societies, it must be considered normal and as an element in social health. On the other hand, certain phenomena which have been common in all the societies of Western civilization for the last century, such as a rising suicide rate, a weakening in the moral condemnation of suicide, and certain types of economic maladjustments, are all classified by Durk-heim as pathological.[21] Critics have pointed out also that this criterion of normality leads to an ultra-conservative morality of sheer social con-formism, since every deviation from what is general in a society is classi-fied as pathological.[22] An implicit concession to this criticism is perhaps apparent in Durkheim's admission that, in periods of great social change (like the present), phenomena which are general may have only an "appearance of normality"; and some phenomena which are excep-tional may be normal because they are closely bound up with the con-ditions of social existence.[23]

III. DURKHEIM'S SUBSTANTIVE THEORIES
A. THE SOCIAL FACT

Durkheim places great emphasis on his definition of the social fact in terms of constraint and exteriority. Unfortunately, the precise mean-ing of these criteria has never been clear. From his fundamental method-ological postulate that we must treat social facts as things, Durkheim infers that the social fact must possess two important characteristics of a thing: it must be *exterior* to (in the sense of not identical with) the idea in the mind of the scientist, and it must impose a certain constraint on the scientist (in the sense of possessing independent characters not influenced by the scientist's volition, to which the scientific theory must conform, or which it must express, if it is to be true). By shifting the center of reference from the *scientist* who *studies* social facts to the acting *individual* who *lives* in an environment of social facts, Durkheim is able to endow the criteria of exteriority and constraint with a new and purely substantive set of meanings. To the acting individual the social fact is exterior in the sense that it is experienced as an independent reality which neither he nor any other individual created and which literally forms a part of his objective environment. In the same way the social fact possesses the characteristic of constraint in that it does not conform to the volitions of individuals but, on the contrary, imposes itself upon individuals, regulating their behavior and even their volitions.

The substantive doctrine of the exteriority of the social fact is thus identical with what we have called "agelic realism." It asserts that society is a reality *sui generis,* above and apart from the individuals. The evidence adduced by Durkheim in defense of this doctrine is of four main types. The first is the alleged heterogeneity of individual and collective states of mind. Thus it is asserted that in a time of national danger the intensity of the collective feeling of patriotism is much greater than that of any individual feeling and society's willingness to sacrifice individuals is greater than the willingness of individuals to sacrifice themselves. Similarly, the individual's hesitant and vague condemnation of dishonesty is said to stand in marked contrast to the "unreserved, explicit, and categorical disgrace with which society strikes at theft in all its forms."[24] A second type of argument, which in one form or another is to be found in practically all Durkheim's writings, stresses the difference in individual attitudes and behavior which results from the group situation. When in a crowd the individual thinks, feels, and acts in a different fashion. It follows, thinks Durkheim, that a new reality must be created by the association of individuals and that this reality reacts upon the sentiments and behavior of the individuals and changes them. A third type of evidence is supplied by the uniformities of social statistics. Many types of social facts, like crimes, marriages, and suicides, show a surprising degree of numerical consistency from year to year, either remaining virtually unchanged or maintaining a uniform rate of change. Such uniformity, Durkheim argues, could not derive from the personal motives or characteristics of individuals, which are so variable as to comprise what is practically a random distribution. Nor can they be satisfactorily explained, Durkheim attempts to prove, by physical, biological, or psychological uniformities. The only remaining explanation is to be found in the influence of certain real social currents which form a (hitherto undetected) part of the individual's environment.[25] A fourth line of argument is based on analogy and on the philosophical theory of emergence.[26] Just as the phenomenon of life is not to be explained by the physicochemical properties of the molecules which form the cell, but by a particular association of molecules, and just as the phenomenon of consciousness resides not in the physiological nature of the cell but in a particular mode of molecular association, so we must assume that society is not reducible to the properties of individual minds but that it constitutes a reality *sui generis* which emerges out of the collocation and interaction of individual minds.

The other characteristic of the social fact, the "constraint" which it exercises over the individual, may be viewed as a simple corollary of its externality. Since the social fact is both real and external, it forms part of the individual's environment and, like the physical and biological parts of his environment, exerts upon him a certain constraint; for the hallmark of an independent reality is the resistance it opposes to our volitions and the counterpressure it exerts on our behavior. Moreover, the fact of social constraint enters into the direct experience of the individual. Legal and moral rules (which are the most typical orders of social facts) cannot be flouted by the individual without his experiencing the tangible evidences of social disapprobation. But if constraint is such an essential element in legal and moral rules, it cannot be wholly absent in other types of social facts.[27]

B. THE DIVISION OF LABOR

The principal problems treated by Durkheim in his book on the division of labor, *De la division du travail social,* concern the nature and the cause of social evolution.[28] Durkheim agreed with Spencer and the Utilitarians that one important aspect of the change from primitive to civilized modes of social existence was to be found in the increase in the amount of division of labor, or specialization. But he felt that the Utilitarians in their description of social evolution unduly emphasized the economic changes and misunderstood or neglected the far more important moral and legal changes. As Durkheim sees it, the fundamental difference between primitive and civilized societies is in the type of morals or social solidarity,[29] which is, in turn, reflected in the type of legal codes.

In primitive society, where division of labor is rudimentary, individuals are relatively homogeneous and bound together by a "mechanical" solidarity characterized by blind acquiescence to the dictates of public opinion and tradition. The legal system is designed primarily to

punish those who violate the collective will and offend collective sentiments and to restore by this punishment a moral equilibrium. In such
a society, moral and legal responsibility is collective, social status tends
to be hereditarily fixed, and a relatively small part of social life is ordered
by the contractual principle. In civilized societies, where division of labor
is well developed, individuals have diverse personalities, experiences, and
functions, and they are bound together by an "organic" solidarity rooted
in their need for each other's services. The primary purpose of the legal
system is to restore to the individual that which has been wrongfully
taken away from him. In this sort of society individualism is the dominant morality, but individualism in a very special sense. Individualism,
as a conscious moral attitude appropriate for our type of society, is
not a claim for the unlimited right of the individual to pursue his immediate desires; it is, rather, an obligation laid upon him to individualize
himself by intensive specialization in order to make his distinctive contribution to social welfare. It is a stern injunction to avoid the delights
of dilettantism and to further the division of labor.[30] Durkheim is intensely concerned to demonstrate that a purely egoistic and hedonistic
individualism could never produce social solidarity or serve as a basis
for social cohesion. He is at pains to point out that peaceful and beneficial contractual relations can exist only in the framework of a legal
and moral order which limits the types of contracts that are valid, gives
the definitive interpretation as to the obligations arising out of the contracts, and enforces their performance.[31]

Still more sharply does Durkheim disagree with the Utilitarians as
to the *causes* of social evolution. They had assumed that the division of
labor and the resulting gains in economic productivity and material
civilization derived, quite simply, from the desires of individuals for
greater wealth and higher planes of living. Durkheim makes this a test
case in his war against the explanation of social facts in terms of the
motives of individuals and the tendencies of human nature. The general
line of the argument is as follows.[32] Human beings have only a limited
and moderate capacity to enjoy economic goods, and therefore they
would long ago have stopped increasing their wealth if happiness had
been the motive for increased production. Happiness is connected with
social health, which is imperiled by excesses of every sort, including a
superabundance of material luxuries. Great social changes which disrupt settled habits create much suffering, and it could not be a desire

for happiness which would lead a whole generation to make such sacrifices in order to produce luxuries which it did not consciously desire and
from which only succeeding generations would profit. Finally, there
is no evidence that material progress and civilization make men any
happier. In fact, the apparent contentment in primitive society and the
relative infrequency of suicides and neuroses reveal a far higher degree
of average happiness than that in contemporary civilizations. Therefore, it is not the desire for happiness which created civilization.[33]

Having disposed of the psychologistic and individualistic explanations of the division of labor, Durkheim now turns to his own morphological explanation, which accords very well with the requirements
set forth in the *Règles de la méthode sociologique*. Division of labor is
due to changes in social structure arising out of an increase in material
and moral density. The increase in population intensifies competition
and thus forces individuals to specialize, in order to survive. Thus Durkheim, rather reluctantly, comes to rest his entire explanation upon the
factor of an assumed natural increase in population. This is obviously
a biologistic rather than a sociologistic type of explanation and comes
closer to an outright materialism than anything in Durkheim's later
work.[34]

C. SUICIDE

Durkheim's intensive study of suicide[35] is more than an interesting
statistical analysis of an important empirical topic. As usual, Durkheim
is vitally concerned to show how the empirical data support a theoretical
doctrine, in this case the exteriority and constraining power of a given
order of social facts.

He begins by refusing to define suicide as an intentional act of self-
destruction, because intentions are not externally observable and are too
variable to define a single order of phenomena. He then proceeds to an
ingenious statistical refutation of theories which explain suicide in terms
of various climatic, geographic, biological, or psychological factors. As
an alternative he proposes a conception of suicide as a social fact, expli-
cable in terms of social causes. The social, superindividual nature of suicide is supported by the observation that the rate of suicide (or its rate
of change) in a given society is remarkably constant from year to year.
Durkheim argues that such constancy woud be inexplicable if the suicide
rate depended on the highly variable and practically random traits of
individual personality and volition. He infers that suicide must emanate

from a single type of causal factor which preserves a uniform strength from year to year. Since climatic, geographic, biological, and psychological factors have been excluded by his statistical demonstrations, he concludes that only in the social realm can a comprehensive explanatory factor be found.

The social factors influencing the rate of suicide are revealed by the correlation of suicide rates with group affiliations and with important collective processes. Thus Durkheim uncovers evidence to prove that free thinkers have the highest suicide rates and Protestants the next highest; that Catholics have low rates, and Jews the lowest of all. The essential difference here, according to Durkheim, is not in the religious beliefs themselves but in the degree of integration of the religious group. Protestantism involves a higher degree of religious individualism than Catholicism, and the religious group is less integrated by uniformities of belief, while Judaism, because of its heritage of persecution, strongly binds its members together to face a hostile environment. Durkheim infers that one important type of suicide ("egoistic") is caused by an insufficient participation by the individual in the life of a group. The individual in himself is of little value; it is only what he derives from participation in a social group that can give his private existence purpose and significance. Hence the individual who remains aloof from strongly integrated social groups, who pursues his own personal ends exclusively, is more liable than others to be overcome with ennui and to find no reason for continuing his existence.

Another important type of suicide described by Durkheim is *"suicide anomique,"* or "normless" suicide. He observes that bachelors have much higher suicide rates than married men and that the general suicide rate decreases in time of war and increases in times both of sharp economic depression and of exceptional prosperity.[36] Durkheim supposes that the individual's desires are in themselves boundless and insatiable and that mental health and contentment require that fixed limits be placed by society on the individual's expectation of personal gratification. During a period of exceptional prosperity, customary standards of living are easily surpassed, and no new norms or appropriate living standards are established. But unlimited expectations must sooner or later engender disappointments, which may easily prove fatal to the individual lacking a strong moral constitution. Similarly, the bachelor, who is less restricted in his sexual life than the married man, is easily disenchanted and disgusted with life. The degree of integration of the society is important, because upon it rests the capacity of the society to discipline the individual. Thus in wartime, when there is normally a strong unification of the society in response to an external threat, it imposes a firmer discipline on the individual and thereby preserves him against suicide. A serious depression, on the other hand, involves social disorganization, and the suffering which this disorganization produces in the social mind is reflected in the minds of individuals, a greater number of whom commit suicide.[37]

The conclusion to which Durkheim comes is that there exist "suicidal currents" produced by the varying states of social organization, which act mechanically upon individuals and force a certain number of them to commit suicide. These suicidal currents are just as real and just as much external to the individual as are the physical and biological forces which produce death by disease. The suicidal current, like the biological epidemic, has a predetermined number of victims, selected from those who can offer the least resistance. There is an individual factor in suicide, just as there is in disease; but it determines who in particular will succumb and not the number of deaths.[38] The individual may appear to himself and to others to be committing suicide from personal motives, but in reality he is being impelled to commit the act by impersonal forces, of which (unless he is a sociologist!) he is presumably unaware. Perhaps nowhere in the literature of sociologism has the doctrine of agelic fatalism been given a more dramatic application![39]

D. AGELIC TRANSCENDENTALISM

Around 1898, Durkheim entered on a new and distinct phase of his work. It is characterized, in the first place, by a more idealistic conception of the social group, with more emphasis on "collective representations" and less on the internal social milieu; and, in the second place, by adventurous speculation concerning the social origin of morals, values, religion, and knowledge. The social group is successively endowed by Durkheim with the characteristics of hyperspirituality, personality, creativity, and transcendence. The inception of this phase is marked by the publication of Durkheim's paper on individual and collective representations.[40]

The chief conclusion of this paper is that there exist collective mental states which are no more reducible to the mental states of individuals than the mental states of individuals are reducible to the physiological states of independent brain cells. The association of individuals gives rise to an emergent reality—society—which is relatively independent of the properties of the constituent individuals. Collective representations are undoubtedly influenced in their formation by the conditions of the material substratum; but, once formed, they are partially autonomous realities, which combine according to their own natural affinities and which are not closely determined by the character of the milieu in which they originated.[41] This conception of social facts as constituting an independent reality is very far from materialism, says Durkheim. If the individual mind is a spiritual reality, social facts must be granted the attribute of "hyperspirituality."

The second major step in the development of a transcendental theory of the social group was taken by Durkheim in connection with the development of a sociologistic theory of morals.[42] To begin with, he holds that the moral fact presents a peculiar duality. The moral rule inspires us with respect and with a feeling of obligation which is quite independent of its content; but, on the other hand, we must assume that this content is good and desirable (even if it does not at the moment correspond with our personal desires).[43]

Now if we seek for the origin of the moral rule, we perceive immediately that it cannot emanate from the individual, since no act has ever been called "moral" which had as its exclusive end the conservation or self-development of the individual. If the agent in himself cannot be a source of moral obligation, neither can *other* individuals, for they are not essentially different from the agent. But disinterestedness and devotion are essential characters of the moral act, and these sentiments are meaningless or impossible unless we subordinate ourselves to another conscious being (preferably of higher moral value than ourselves). If, however, all human beings are excluded, there are only two further alternatives: there is God, and there is society. At bottom these two alternatives are the same, for God is only society "transfigured and conceived symbolically."[44] Thus, if the moral life is to have any meaning, we must assume that society itself is a true moral person, formed by a synthesis of individuals and qualitatively distinct from all the individuals taken distributively.

This solution accounts for the dual character of the moral fact. It is obligatory because it is the command of society, and society so infinitely surpasses the individual, both materially and morally, that its commands carry sufficient authority to produce unquestioning obedience. But, on the other hand, it seems good and desirable, because society is the source of all the higher values of civilization and the creator of that element in the individual which raises him above the animal level. Without society, language would not exist; and without language, the higher mental processes would be impossible. Without science, which is a social product, man would be helpless before the blind forces of nature. So it is to society that the individual owes his real liberty. "We cannot wish to leave society without wishing to cease to be men."[45]

Durkheim ends by drawing certain important relativistic conclusions. Moral rules are always the product of particular social factors, and every moral system is closely dependent upon the social structure of the society in which it exists. There is no single moral system which would be moral for every society, and diversity of morals among different societies is not to be explained by ignorance or perversity. Each society has the moral system it needs, and any other morality would be injurious to it. The social scientist may sometimes help society by showing what moral judgments are truly consistent with the actual state of social organization, but this is as far as anyone can go. "To wish for a different moral system from the one which is implied in the nature of society is to deny society, and consequently to deny oneself."[46]

F. AGELIC CREATIONISM AND THE THEORY OF VALUES

The final stage in the completion of a doctrine of agelic transcendentalism was reached in 1911 with the elaboration of a general theory of value, which portrayed the social group as the transcendental creator of *all,* not merely of all moral, values.[47] As his point of departure, Durkheim calls attention to the apparent objectivity of value-judgments. Assertions that Beethoven's music has aesthetic value, that honest behavior has moral value, that a diamond has economic value, are not intended as mere expressions of personal preference but as characterizations of an external reality.

They cannot, therefore, be supposed to refer to the personal likes and dislikes of myself or any other *individual,* or even of a majority of individuals. Since value-judgments do not refer to any individual's preference, they must express the hierarchy of preferences which society has established—and the fact that it is society which has established and imposed them gives them their objectivity.

The basic problem, however, concerns the source of the whole realm of values. How is it possible that man, who lives in a world of merely factual existence, should conceive and refer to an ideal world of values? How can we pass from what is to what ought to be?

According to Durkheim, the only natural forces which could suffice to account for the emergence of an ideal realm of values are those which are liberated by the association of individuals in the social group. When individuals come together and have vigorous mental interaction, "there emerges from their synthesis a psychic life of a new sort."[48] It is in such periods of effervescence and collective enthusiasm, when gatherings and assemblages are more frequent and the exchange of ideas more intense, that the great ideals of civilization have been formed. Examples are offered by the student movement in Paris in the twelfth and thirteenth centuries, the Reformation, the Renaissance, the French Revolution, and the socialist upheavals in the nineteenth century. In such periods the individual lives a higher life, almost completely devoid of egoistic and vulgar considerations. Then, for a time, the ideal seems to coalesce with the real, and it almost seems as if the Kingdom of Heaven were about to be achieved on earth. However, this illusion cannot last, because the exaltation is too exhausting to be maintained indefinitely. "Once the critical moment has passed, the social network relaxes, the intellectual intercourse slows down, and the individuals fall back to their ordinary level."[49] What is left behind is only a memory, a group of *ideas,* which would soon evaporate if they were not revivified from time to time by celebrations, public ceremonies, sermons, artistic and dramatic performances, and other forms of group concentration and social integration.

Society must be conceived as a mind composed of collective ideas, but these ideas are not simply cognitive representations. They are strongly imbued with sentiment and have important motor elements, i.e., they are stimulants to action. They are the expression of forces which are both natural and ideal at the same time. This is possible because society has a dual character: it comes out of nature, but it synthesizes natural forces to produce a result which is richer, more complex, and more powerful than these forces. "It is nature which has risen to the highest point in its development and which concentrates all its energies in order, in some fashion, to transcend itself."[50]

It must be noted that Durkheim has arrived here at a definitely ambivalent conception of society. On the one hand, it is a transcendental reality, which can plausibly be considered the source of all the transcendent elements in human experience; and, on the other hand, it is still a natural phenomenon (a number of individuals in spatial proximity). An increase in the proximity of the members of the group provides a "naturalistic" explanation for the creation of the transcendental elements in experience, and a decrease in proximity provides an equally naturalistic explanation for the nontranscendent, secular, *alltäglich* element in experience. With the further assumption that the life of the group goes through a natural and necessary rhythm of concentration and dispersion, the doctrine of agelic fatalism becomes practically omnipotent as an explanatory hypothesis.[51]

G. THE THEORY OF RELIGION

As is generally known, the fundamental idea of Durkheim's *Les Formes élémentaires de la vie religieuse*[52] is that religion is entirely a "social thing." This involves two distinct theses: first, that religious ideas and practices refer to or symbolize the social group and, second, that association is the generating source, or efficient cause, of the religious experience. As usual, Durkheim begins with the careful framing of an *ad hoc* definition of the object of investigation.[53]

The next step is the elimination of the chief individualistic and psychologistic theories of religion, especially the animistic theories of Sir Edward B. Tylor and Spencer and the naturistic theory of Müller. The chief objections brought against these theories are that they are unable to account for more than a part of the whole body of religious phenomena; that they fail to explain the radical heterogeneity between the sacred and the secular, which is the essential characteristic of religion; and, finally, that they "explain religion away" by interpreting it as an illusion without any basis in the real world.

Durkheim proceeds next to an examination of the totemic practices of the Aruntas in Australia. The assumption is that this society is about the most primitive society in existence and that its religious practices will therefore exhibit in its simplest form the original nature of religion.[54] The fundamental characteristic of totemism is that the clan takes the name of, claims descent from, and exercises certain ritual restraints toward, some object in the environment, usually an animal or plant. According to Durkheim's analysis, the most fundamental belief implicit in totemism is the belief in a mysterious and sacred force or principle which animates the totem, provides a physical sanction for violation of the totemic taboo, and inculcates moral responsibilities. Now the strong emotions of awe and reverence for the totem can hardly have been derived from the physical properties of the totem itself, since this latter is usually some harmless and insignificant animal or plant. The totem must therefore be considered as a symbol. It symbolizes, first, the sacred totemic principle or god and, second, the clan itself, with which the totem is closely identified. Durkheim infers from this that the totemic divinity and the clan are really the same thing and, more generally, that God is only a symbolic expression of society.[55]

The next problem concerns the origin of the religious experience; and Durkheim's explanation runs as follows:[56] The life of the Arunta is divided into two phases. In the first, or secular, phase the clan is scattered in small groups of individuals pursuing their private economic objectives and living a life which is "uniform, languishing, and dull." In the second, or religious, phase the clan gathers together, and "the very fact of the concentration acts as an exceptionally powerful stimulant." A sort of electricity or collective euphoria is generated, which soon lifts the individuals to miraculous states of exaltation. The effervescence is so intense that delirious behavior and altogether exceptional actions (like violations of the most well-established taboos) are common. It is in these periods of intense agelic concentration and violent interaction that religious sentiments and ideas are born, and it is the sharp contrast between these periods and the dull and languishing periods of group dispersion which explains the radical heterogeneity between the sacred and the profane.

These general conclusions are reinforced by certain considerations concerning the similarity of our attitudes toward society and toward God.[57] Society, it is asserted, is quite capable of inspiring the sensation of divinity in the minds of its members because of its power over them. The individual's feeling of perpetual dependence is alike in each case. Society, like God, possesses moral authority and can inspire disinterested devotion and self-sacrifice. It is also capable of endowing the individual with exceptional powers and is the source of all that is highest and best in human personality. Therefore, the religious man, who feels a dependence upon some external moral power, is not the victim of a hallucination. There is such a power: society. Of course, he may be mistaken in supposing that the religious forces emanate from some particular object (like a totem), but this is simply a mistake in the "letter of the symbol." Behind this symbol there is a reality which does have the ascribed properties.[58]

H. THE THEORY OF KNOWLEDGE

In recent years one major development in sociology has been the elaboration of a "sociology of knowledge," an explanation of knowledge itself as a product of social conditions. In this field Durkheim must rank as one of the most important pioneers. Going beyond the generalities of his predecessors (to the effect that thought depends upon language, and language upon society), he tries to show in detail how both the forms of classification and the basic categories of cognition have been produced by society.

The problem of classification is treated in a monograph on primitive forms of classification (written in collaboration with M. Mauss).[59] The present concept of a "class," we are told, does not go back beyond Aristotle; and our contemporary forms of classification (in terms of class and subclass, species and genus, etc.) are not innate but based upon "a hierarchical order for which neither the sensory world nor our own minds offer us a model."[60] If we observe the classifications of primitive peoples, however, we discover that these classifications closely reflect the social organization of the tribe. The first "classes" were classes of men, and the classification of physical objects was simply an extension of previously established social classifications, since all the animals and objects in the environment were classified as belonging to this or that clan, phratry, or other kinship group. The hierarchy of type and subtype in logical classification reflects the hierarchical character of earlier forms of social structure. The imagery in which, even today, logical relations are expressed, reveals their social origin: things which are alike "belong to the same family"; an entity "possesses" certain characteristics; and one concept is "dependent upon or subordinate to" another.

Primitive classification is not primarily conceptual but is based largely on emotion and social sensibility. Scientific classification emerges when social sentiment becomes less important and when individual observation and speculation have more freedom. But the very framework of classification—the mental habits by which we organize facts in groups (themselves hierarchically related)—bears the indelible mark of a social genesis.[61]

The last and most daring of Durkheim's speculative flights is a sociologistic explanation of the categories of thought and the forms of intuition.[62] As usual, he begins with a criticism of existing theories. Empiricism, he holds, cannot account for the universality and necessity of the categories (i.e., why it is that the individual cannot "think away" or alter essentially his conceptions of space, time, substance, cause, etc.). The aprioristic point of view does not explain where these ideas originate and how it is that we can arrive at knowledge of objective relationships transcending our personal sensory experience. A theological explanation is not "experimental" and cannot account for the variation of the categories in different societies.

Durkheim's own explanation is that the categories are collective representations. As such, they are imposed upon the individual and create in him the impression of being universal and necessary. The uniformity of the categories within a given society is easily explained by the fact that agreement about such fundamental modes of thought as the categories is absolutely essential for social co-operation and thus for the very existence of society. In the interest of self-preservation, the society must impose a minimum of logical conformity. Our obligation to think in terms of space, time, cause and effect, etc., is "a special form of moral necessity which is to the intellect what moral obligation is to the will."[63]

But the categories are not only imposed by society; they reflect its most general characters, and they are in this sense a social creation. The sense of time was derived from the rhythms of group life; "the territory occupied by the society furnished the material for the category of space"; and the power of the social group gave rise to the idea of an efficient force, upon which the category of causality depends.[64] From his own limited temporal and spatial intuitions the individual could never derive the idea of space or time in general. It was necessary, first, to have the concept of totality, and only society, "which includes all things," could give rise to the concept of totality.[65] With the world "inside of society," however, the space occupied by society becomes identified with space in general. Similarly, social rhythms, based on the concentration and dispersion of the social group, supply the generalized notion of time. The divisions of time into days, weeks, months, and years corresponds to the periodic recurrence of social functions; the calendar both expresses the rhythm of social life and assures its regularity.

The dependence of our conception of space on the regions occupied by the society is shown by the following:

> There are societies in Australia and North America where space is conceived in the form of an immense circle, because the camp has a circular form; and this spatial circle is divided up exactly like the tribal circle, and is in its image. There are as many regions distinguished as there are clans in the tribe, and it is the place occupied by the clans inside the encampment which has determined the orientation of these regions. Each region is defined by the totem of the clan to which it is assigned.[66]

Durkheim even hopes that evidence may yet be found to show conclusively that the principle of contradiction itself is a function of a given social system. He thinks that it has already been shown that the extent to which this principle has influenced human minds has varied historically from one society to another.[67]

I. DURKHEIM'S ETHICAL AND POLITICAL ORIENTATION

In the history of thought, agelecism has usually been accompanied by anti-individualism in ethics and conservatism in politics. This combination of elements is well exemplified in many phases of Durkheim's work. His sociology is primarily concerned with the problem of social control and is negatively disposed toward individual deviation from accepted social norms. Both the reality and the value of individual invention are systematically denied. It is a sociology of a static and monistic type, with no adequate explanation for social change.[68] Moreover, it displays a remarkable lack of interest in those structures and processes of group life which are connected with internal division and conflict. There is little concern with social classes, with the clash of interest groups, or with processes of revolution and war.[69]

It is not surprising, therefore, that Durkheim's diagnosis of our social ills and his therapeutic program of social reform should have assumed a pronounced anti-individualistic character. The prevalence of suicide, nervous disorders, and other pathological symptoms were due, he thought, to the fact that the individual was no longer sufficiently restrained by a social group. With the decline in the influence of the neighborhood, the religious group, and the extended kin group and with the increase in the size of the state and its impersonality and distance from the individual, there was no group left which could successfully impose a wholesome moral discipline on the individual. To remedy this deficiency, Durkheim proposed the creation of a type of corporatism which would endow the trade-union or professional association with sufficient authority to enter actively into the regulation and direction of the personal lives of its members.[70] This program bears some resemblances (the importance of which should not, however, be exaggerated) to the corporatism established by Fascist regimes.[71]

Yet, if we would do justice to Durkheim's thought, we must admit a complexity which baffles any simple interpretative pattern. Scattered throughout his work, but especially in the *Division of Labor* and in the *Suicide,* are numerous passages of praise for individualism. In his politics, moreover, he was regarded as a liberal. Certain biographical facts are of considerable relevance here. Durkheim was born in 1857 and came to intellectual maturity in a period when France was exerting enormous efforts to recover from the effects of the Franco-Prussian War. The unification and reintegration of the French nation was considered by most intellectuals of the period to be of the utmost urgency. An intense sentiment of nationalism provided the emotional background for Durkheim's belief in the transcendental reality of the social group (which, ordinarily, he implicitly identifies with the nation) and for his unvarying emphasis on the problems of social control. But the intellectuals were hopelessly divided in their opinions as to the proper *basis* of that social reintegration, the necessity of which they uniformly conceded. On the one hand, the conservatives urged a reversion to Catholicism, royalism, and traditionalism. On the other hand, the intellectuals who most staunchly supported the Third Republic hoped for a secular basis of integration, resulting from the growth and diffusion of scientific information. Durkheim's position was naturally with the latter group. As a social scientist of the positivistic persuasion, he could not fail to support the position that science could provide a new and quite adequate basis of social organization. As a scientific rationalist, he was necessarily distrustful of those *mystiques* which the traditionalists were offering as a substitute. Two other factors inclined him in the direction of liberal individualism: his own struggle against race prejudice, and the strong influence upon him of Renouvier's moral personalism.

What is truly distinctive, however, about Durkheim's individualism is that it is supported by entirely agelic arguments. The individual is sacred, it is claimed, because he bears within himself that culture which has been created by the group; and in doing violence to him we should be indirectly attacking the group. Moreover, the ideals of individualism and liberalism need no metaphysical justification: their rightness *for us* is guaranteed by the fact that they are implicit in our whole contemporary social organization (based on division of labor and specialization). We cannot restore this or that institution characteristic of an earlier civilization, because individualism and liberalism offer the only *possible* basis for integration in a society of our type.[72]

The adequacy of this relativistic and pragmatic defense of individualism is highly questionable. It is not based on any appreciation of the intrinsic value and creative potentialities of the individual in himself but upon the assumed inevitability of individualism at a given stage in the fixed evolutionary pattern of social change. In Durkheim's system, it appears as a paradoxical rationalization of an ideal which he found useful and which he wished to defend but which was, at bottom, incompatible with his fundamental sociological beliefs. The reversion, in recent years, of several civilized nations to a more barbaric principle of law and social organization dramatically illustrates the unsoundness of the doctrine of linear evolution. It may be true that individualism and liberalism are necessarily bound up with our present type of society, but Durkheim, who died too soon to see a Fascist revolution, apparently never realized that a society may actually change over—and quite rapidly—from a more to a less individualistic and liberal type. His relativistic defense of liberal individualism gives us no basis for deciding which of the two *types* is preferable.

IV. THE DURKHEIM SCHOOL IN FRENCH SOCIOLOGY

Durkheim's enormous influence in French sociology arose not only from his research and publications but very largely from his teaching and from his exceptional ability to guide and co-ordinate the research of others. In his position as editor of that remarkable sociological journal, *L'Année sociologique* (1896–1913) he gathered around him most of the best sociologists in France, as well as a considerable number of specialists in other fields (ethnology, law, economics, statistics, history, comparative languages, etc.), who were interested in the sociological aspects of their special fields. The work of this group has been described by Mauss in the following words:

> The *Année* was not only a publication..... Around it was formed .... a "group" in the full sense of the word. Under the authority of Durkheim at the outbreak of the war, it was a sort of society fully developed both on the intellectual and on the spiritual side. A great number of investigations and ideas were being elaborated. .... We practised a true division of labor.[73]

The history of the Durkheim school bears eloquent testimony to the destructiveness of modern war. In 1914 the group was shattered by the necessary suspension of all scholarly activity and by the loss of almost all the promising young men upon whose expected contributions the pre-eminence of the school and of French sociology largely depended.[74]

After the war and Durkheim's death (possibly hastened by the loss of his son), Marcel Mauss, a relative and intimate disciple of Durkheim, bent all his efforts toward the maintenance of the tradition. He edited several of the posthumously published works of Durkheim and of the younger members of the school; and in 1923 he made a valiant, but financially unsuccessful, attempt to revive *L'Année sociologique* (published only during 1923 and the first part of 1924). In 1934, under a new board of editors and with a more flexible organization, it was launched again under the name *Annales sociologiques*. With the approach of another war, the work was again discontinued.[75]

The most orthodox of the followers of Durkheim have been Marcel Mauss, Georges Davy, and Paul Fauconnet. On the theoretical side they have done little more than to expound, rephrase, and defend against various critics the fundamental views of the master. Mauss has been much interested in methodological problems, such as the organization of the special divisions within sociology[76] and the relation of sociology to psychology. He has not hesitated to tell psychologists that sociology is, for the most part, entirely independent of psychology and that, even in the field of collective representations, sociology contributes more to psychology than it derives therefrom.[77] His chief contribution, however, probably lies in his numerous ethnological monographs, which often succeed in illuminating important social processes.[78] Of these, the monograph on the Eskimos is probably the most celebrated. It tries to prove that the intensity of Eskimo social and religious life is directly correlated with the degree of concentration of the social group. The fundamental pattern of this monograph was later used by Durkheim in his studies on value and on religion.

Georges Davy, for many years Dean of the Faculty of Letters at Dijon, has loyally and eloquently defended the Durkheimian position.[79] As a contributor to the great co-operative *Traité* of Georges Dumas, he has given forceful and unqualified expression to the sociologistic point of view in psychology. In the chapter devoted to "Sociology" he defends quite unequivocally the theses of agelic realism and agelic creationism.[80] In a statement on "the moral and the social sentiments," he reaffirms Durkheim's stand that moral obligation is first experienced as an external social constraint which is only gradually interiorized, and that the moral and the social sentiments can therefore never be entirely separated from each other. Each is the product of social organization; consequently, they cannot be explained adequately in terms of biological or psychological forces.[81]

Davy's chief empirical investigation, *La Foi jurée* (1922) is an important contribution to juristic sociology, offering, as it does, a completely sociologistic theory of contract. The attempt is to show that the institution of the legal contract grew originally out of familial relations and obligations and has only gradually assumed an individualistic character. In his study of the origins of Egyptian civilization (in which he collaborated with the eminent Egyptologist, A. Moret), Davy finds evidence to support Durkheim's position on the primacy of the totemic over either the familial or the political group, as well as to corroborate the Durkheimian explanation of the incest taboo.[82] However, he does concede the existence in religion of nonsocial elements.[83]

Paul Fauconnet, who took over Durkheim's chair of pedagogy and sociology at the Sorbonne in 1921, had collaborated with him earlier on a methodological article concerning the relation of sociology to the other social sciences;[84] and he later collaborated with Mauss in an article, "Sociologie," for the *Grande Encyclopédie,* which is perhaps the most authoritative brief statement of the fundamental position of the Durkheim school. His empirical investigations have been concerned mainly with the subject of responsibility.[85] Starting with Durkheim's conception of crime as an act which offends strong and well-defined states of the collective conscience, and of punishment as the result of the need for a restoration of emotional equilibrium, he tries to show that the function of "responsibility" is simply to provide a focus for the application of punishment. In former times children, the insane, and even physical objects have been held responsible and have been punished; and only by a gradual process of social evolution has there emerged the modern conception of responsibility as limited to the free and rational agent.

Maurice Halbwachs, for many years professor at the University of Strasbourg, but more recently at the Sorbonne, has been one of the most eminent and productive of the Durkheim group. He ranks, moreover, as the most able statistician among contemporary French sociologists. His first major work attempted a sociologistic explanation of social classes and standards of living[86] and filled an important lacuna in the Durkheimian sociology. He maintains that social classes are based on differences in the intensity of social existence. In our society the proletarian is desocialized by the mental isolation in which he works and by his low income. This lack of sociality is reflected in the disproportionately small share of his income spent on rent.

An important contribution to the sociology of knowledge is contained in Halbwachs' brilliant, but daring, monograph on "the collective framework of memory."[87] Beginning with the assertions that we never remember in our dreams and that it is in our dreams that we are furthest from the influence of society, he infers that personal memory depends on the objective structure of memories common to the social group. This is further evidenced by the fact that, in order to localize our memories, we customarily relate them to important episodes in group life—episodes such as births, marriages, deaths, holidays, festivals, etc. The rhythm of group life, as expressed in the calendar, provides an objective framework, in the absence of which the individual would be unable to remember. Furthermore, families, social classes, and other social groups all have their own memories, which serve as an indispensable principle of integration and coherence.

Halbwachs' treatment of suicide[88] brings up to date Durkheim's work on this topic and introduces some very significant concessions and modifications. While insisting that "the sentiment of a definitive and irremediable solitude is the unique cause of suicide"[89] and that this sentiment is always at least partially a social product, he admits that the individual motive (even if socially generated) plays a necessary part in the causation of suicide, which therefore always involves a psychological, as well as a social, element. He thinks that the increasing rate of suicide characteristic of the last century is now leveling off and that this rate was caused chiefly by a rapid urbanization, which exposed the individual to more shocks and rebuffs and to frequent feelings of maladaptation.[90]

Célestin Bouglé, from 1927 until his death a director of the Ecole Normale Supérieure, was a balanced and eclectic thinker who actively collaborated in the work of the Durkheim school but who remained highly critical of many of the assumptions upon which it was based. On various occasions he explicitly rejected the doctrine of the independence and externality of the *conscience sociale,* the sociologistic theory of knowledge, the identification of the pathological with the abnormal, the sociologistic derivation of values, and the methodological exclusion of motivation and other psychological data from sociology.[91] His own interests were very largely centered around the problems of equality and democracy. In an early study he clearly formulated a conception of social equality as the provision of equal opportunities for self-development by the elimination of nongenetic hereditary advantages.[92] He tried to show that equality in this sense was a natural and inevitable product of the intensification of such morphological processes as population growth, mobility, centralization, urbanization, and social complication. However, although he succeeded (in his interesting treatment of the caste system) in *describing* the social structure of India in primarily morphological terms, he did not deny that this structure is very largely sustained by ideological forces (particularly the Hindu beliefs in reincarnation and in the peculiar holiness of the Brahmin caste).[93] A defense of the democratic ideals from the attacks of the social biologists is the subject matter of another important monograph.[94] It is urged that the biological processes of differentiation and natural selection cannot be transposed to the social plane except metaphorically; that on the social level it is not the differentiation of hereditary castes but the diversification of individuals in accordance with their different capacities and interests that is to be desired; and that the inheritance of property and privilege falsifies the whole conception of natural selection in the social world, since it no longer follows that the biologically fit survive.[95]

Two eminent French sociologists who are not members of the Durkheim school deserve mention because of their peculiar relation to it. The first, Gaston Richard, was an associate of Durkheim at Bordeaux and played a not inconspicuous role in the early history of *L'Année soci-*

ologique. However, he found himself unable to accept most of the chief sociologistic doctrines and was genuinely shocked by the Durkheimian theory of religion; so that he became, by stages, one of the most explicit and relentless critics of the school.[96] Quite a different case is presented by René Maunier, the genial and eclectic professor of colonial sociology at the University of Paris; he has continued to co-operate with the school,[97] although his own theoretical position combines elements from both Durkheim and Tarde and is far from sociologistic orthodoxy. The social fact is defined as one which is repeated and common in a given society (which accords with Tarde's definition in terms of imitation) but which is also "traditional" and "obligatory for the individual" (which thus conforms to Durkheim's definition as well).[98] Maunier is a sober empiricist, who shares with the Durkheimians a great interest in the morphological type of explanation but who has not found the theory of collective representations a useful hypothesis.[99]

It is necessary, before concluding, to give brief mention to the many specialists in related fields who have been directly influenced by, or who have been more or less associated with, the Durkheim school. Lucien Lévy-Bruhl, the philosopher of neo-Comtian positivism, was never a member of the Durkheim school and has been subjected to criticism by its members on certain points; but between his work and that of the school there is an important parallelism, if not an actual convergence. In *La Morale et la science des mœurs,* he takes the position, closely resembling Durkheim's, that an empirical science of morals can and should be constructed and that this science, by an objective study of existing moral attitudes and practices, will provide a scientific basis for social guidance.[100] Moreover, in his numerous and well-known studies on the thought-processes of primitive peoples, he has tried to show that their mentalities are "pre-logical" and essentially different from our own, because they are dominated by "collective representations."[101] The precise role of morphological factors in the creation of these alleged differences has not been sufficiently examined to satisfy M. Mauss and other orthodox Durkheimians, who, moreover, have preferred to stress the evolutionary continuity between primitive and civilized thought forms rather than their heterogeneity. On the whole, however, these researches of Lévy-Bruhl have been taken as additional corroboration of Durkheim's contention that the fundamental forms of thought are not uniform and universal but are variable because they are socially conditioned.

Charles Blondel, the eminent psychologist of the University of Strasbourg, was much interested in the collective elements in mental life and showed clearly the influence of the sociologistic point of view. According to his analysis, the chief cause of insanity is a desocialization and progressive isolation of the individual mind.[102] Volition reduces to little more than individual obedience to collective imperatives. Both will and reason are gifts which we derive from society ready-made and which for most men involve no more than the application of accepted ideas and rules (collective representations) to their daily experience.[103] In his *Introduction à la psychologie collective,* Blondel comes to the conclusion that, although psychic facts exist only in the individual mind, they are, in large part, of a collective character; that only collective psychology (which studies the collective element in the individual mind) can explain the higher mental functions (intellectual, affective, and volitional); and that a sound psychology of the individual must be based upon the conclusions of psychophysiology and collective psychology.[104]

Two other French psychologists who have shown an active sympathy for the sociologistic point of view are Georges Dumas and Henri Wallon. Dumas, in his monumental treatises, *Traité de psychologie* and *Nouveau traité de psychologie,* has invited Georges Davy to express the Durkheimian position and has himself asserted that collective patterns largely determine the emotional life of the individual, even when the individual is in a state of isolation.[105] Wallon has given us an analysis of child mentality, which is markedly similar in certain respects to Lévy-Bruhl's study of pre-logical thinking in primitive societies.[106]

Among the historians, the one who comes closest to sharing the Durkheimian point of view is the eminent Sinologist, Marcel Granet; he takes a definitely sociologistic approach to the study of Chinese civilization.[107] In particular, his treatment of the influence of group structure on the basic modes of thought in China constitutes the most impressive attempt thus far made at a detailed substantiation of the sociologistic theory of knowledge.[108] Henri Berr, another outstanding French historian, has sponsored a type of synthetic history which lays considerable, but not exclusive, emphasis upon social factors.[109]

François Simiand, one of France's leading economists, was from the beginning an active participant in the work of the Durkheim school. He was an able critic of the orthodox conceptions of economics; his own approach resembled somewhat that of the American Institutionalists.[110] Beginning with the assumption that economic phenomena are primarily an expression of collective judgments of social value, he did several exhaustive statistical studies of wages and prices.[111] Among the jurists who have been influenced by sociologistic theory, the most outstanding have been Léon Duguit, Emmanuel Lévy, and Paul Huvelin. Duguit's "positive" theory of law probably owes something to Durkheim's positivistic methodology and certainly owes much to his doctrine of organic solidarity, which, in Duguit's hands, becomes the objective basis of modern law.[112] Emmanuel Lévy was one of the original collaborators of the *L'Année sociologique,* and he consistently maintained the position that law rests on beliefs which emanate from the *conscience collective.* Paul Huvelin, the jurist and legal historian, was one of Durkheim's first pupils. He emphasized the role of magic in the origin of private law and the influence of social structure on the evolution of commercial law.[113]

Finally, the science of comparative linguistics in France has shown the influence of Durkheim to a remarkable degree. To all appearances, no other order of social phenomena depends less on individual creation or better illustrates the imposition of collective patterns of behavior on the individual. From the beginning, *L'Année sociologique* had the active co-operation of the great and highly revered philologist, Antoine Meillet, who contributed to it a now classic monograph on the influence of social groups in bringing about changes in the meanings of words.[114] In his monumental *Histoire de la langue française* and in his systematic discussion of the relation of thought to language, [115] Ferdinand Brunot has frequent recourse to a sociological (though not always a clearly sociologistic) point of view. But the philologist who shows the influence of Durkheim most clearly is Jacques Vendryes, who has been intensely concerned to prove that linguistic innovations by individuals are only apparent and that all linguistic changes are, at bottom, of social origin.[116]

NOTES

1. We wish to distinguish carefully between *substantive* theories, which attempt to tell the truth about the actual object of scientific investigation in a general field, and *methodological* doctrines, which analyze and evaluate the cognitive processes by which the object is studied.

2. The adjectival form of the term "agelecism" is "agelic." "Agelic realism" asserts that the group is a real entity outside of, and apart from, its members. "Agelic personalism" asserts that the group is, or must be considered, a mind, soul, person, or moral agent. "Agelic transcendentalism" asserts that the social group is a hyperspiritual, ideal, or supernatural entity. "Agelic creationism" maintains that values, culture, and all the higher elements of human personality are of collective origin and that the individual is therefore, in a radical sense, a group product. "Agelic fatalism" asserts that the individual is power-less to influence the course of social change, since the group is bound by necessary laws emanating from its own structure which determine its evolution.

3. Durkheim freely acknowledged his indebtedness to Comte and Espinas (cf. S. Deploige, *Le Conflit de la morale et de la sociologie* [2d ed.; Paris, 1912], pp. 393–413). And Durkheim's disciples and close associates consider him "le véritable héritier d'Auguste Comte sur le terrain de la recherche scientifique" (C. Bouglé, *Bilan de la sociologie française contemporaine* [Paris, 1935], p. 2). See also G. Davy, *Sociologues d'hier et d'aujourd'hui* (Paris 1931), p. 2. For a comprehensive Durkheim bibliography and a survey of the sources of Durkheim's sociological thought see Harry Alpert, *Émile Durkheim and His Sociology* (New York, 1939).

4. The reader interested in a more detailed analysis and criticism of Durkheim's system is referred to the author's unpublished doctoral dissertation, "The Development of French Sociologism and Its Critics in France" (Widener Library, Harvard University) (also avail-able on microfilm from the Library of the University of Wisconsin).

5. Roger Lacombe, Daniel Essertier, Célestin Bouglé, among others. This is probably an overstatement, since important elements of agelecism are to be found in the tradition from which Durkheim springs, and these are apparent in his earliest work. However, the term "methodological" is used by Lacombe *et al.* in a broader sense than that in which we use it.

6. Durkheim rejected the appellation of "Positivist" as applied to himself, probably because he took it as denoting an unreserved adherent of the system of Comte.

7. Durkheim's attempt to "renovate the problems of philosophy" and his preoccupation with problems of morals, values, religion, and epistomology in his later work have been mistakenly criticized by Gaston Richard (in *La Sociologie générale* [Paris, 1912], pp. 364–65) and others, as involving the abandonment of his early positivistic program and his announced separation of science and philosophy. This criticism rests on a mistaken conception of the *kind* of separation between science and philosophy which positivism envisages. In fact, Durkheim made it quite clear in his earlier period that sociology, when developed, would have important philosophical *implications*, though it would never have any necessary philosophical *presuppositions* (cf. *Les Règles de la méthode sociologique* [3d ed.; Paris, 1904], pp. 172–75). (Hereafter cited as *"Règles."*)

8. *Règles*, Preface to 2d ed., p. x.

9. In his Latin thesis on Montesquieu, Durkheim made it quite clear that treating social facts as things required the abandonment of the assumption of free will in favor of a uni-versal determinism. Montesquieu is praised for abandoning occasionally the older concep-tion "that social facts depend entirely on the will of man and that consequently they are not true things" (Durkheim, *Montesquieu: sa part dans la fondation des sciences politiques et de la science des sociétés, Quid secundatus politicae scientiae institundae contulerit* [Bordeaux, 1892]; translated into French by F. Alengry in the *Revue d'histoire politique et constitutionnelle*, I, No. 3 [July–September, 1937], 410).

10. *Règles*, p. 54.

11. It is interesting to note that Durkheim's three empirical studies rely almost entirely upon these types of data: *De la division du travail social* (Paris, 1893), mainly upon law codes; *Le suicide* (Paris, 1897), upon social statistics; and *Les Formes élémentaires de la vie religieuse* (Paris, 1912), upon religious dogmas, myths, and rites.

12. *Règles*, chap. v.

13. *Ibid.*, p. 135.

14. *Ibid.*, p. 138.

15. "Morphologie sociale," Introduction, *Année sociologique*, II (1899), 520.

16. By P. Barth, R. Worms, G. Richard, and R. Lacombe, among others.

17. Durkheim is inclined to hedge on the causal ultimacy of even this attenuated morphological factor, stating that *no* factor is truly ultimate for science and that morphological facts are themselves influenced by other types of social changes (*Règles*, p. 142).

18. Durkheim was bitterly opposed to the introduction of practical considerations and problems into sociology itself, but, on the other hand, he expected sociology to have important practical *applications*. In fact, he states, "we would not consider our scientific labors worth an hour's trouble if they were to have only a speculative interest" (*Division du travail*).

19. *Règles*, pp. 61 ff. This recourse to the analogy of the science of medicine is characteristic of the sociologistic tradition and is found in Saint-Simon, Comte, Roberty, and Espinas. Durkheim, however, is the first one to give serious consideration to the difficulties involved in this conception.

20. *Ibid.*, p. 70.

21. Halbwachs, a follower and close student of Durkheim, maintains that, on the basis of his own criterion, Durkheim should have judged the rising suicide rate to be normal. It seems apparent that the ascription of normality or abnormality is not an entirely objective and mechanical procedure but that it rests upon certain concealed and relatively subjective standards of value.

22. Among the able critics of Durkheim's theory of social pathology may be mentioned G. Tarde, R. Lacombe, G. Belot, C. Bouglé, G. Richard, G. Cantécor, and A. Fouillée.

23. *Règles*, p. 76. This seems to make survival or utility the ultimate criterion.

24. *Le Suicide: étude de sociologie* (new ed.; Paris, 1930), p. 357.

25. *Ibid.*, pp. 346 ff.

26. It is most fully expounded in Durkheim's "Représentations individuelles et représentations collectives," *Revue de métaphysique et de morale*, Vol. VI, (May, 1898). Reprinted in Durkheim's *Sociologie et philosophie* (Paris, 1924), chap. i, pp. 1–48.

27. One of the chief difficulties in understanding Durkheim arises out of the great (and probably unwarranted) extension given to the meaning of the term "constraint." The writer has distinguished *seven* distinct senses in which this term is used by Durkheim, as illustrated by the following cases, all of which are offered by Durkheim as examples of social constraint: (1) A law compels an individual's obedience by penal sanctions. (2) A moral rule is observed by an individual through fear of public opinion. (3) An ideal or value which an individual may have imbibed from his culture influences him to act in a certain way. (4) An inhabitant of France is forced to speak French if he wishes to be understood; similarly, a merchant must pay prevailing rates of interest and wages if he is to continue in business. (5) The paths of transportation and communication influence the course of migrations and the diffusion of culture. (6) The individual in a crowd is led to act in ways in which he would not act when alone. (7) Education or inculcation produces an acceptance of the truth of certain doctrines.

In the writer's opinion, only the first and second cases are true examples of collective constraint. In general, Durkheim fails to note the important distinctions between: (1) *collective constraint*, where the *group* deliberately represses certain types of actions which individuals would like to commit; (2) *cultural determination*, where ideas, values, and action patterns passed on by education and imitation influence what people believe and the way they *want* to act; (3) *physical determination*, where the topography or the material culture influences the unfolding of various social processes; and (4) *psychological compulsion*, where the crowd situation provides certain unusual psychological stimuli, which produce strong emotional reactions and aberrant behavior.

28. Durkheim, *De la division du travail social: étude sur l'organization des sociétés supérieures* (Paris, 1893).

29. As we shall see, individual morality and social solidarity are so closely connected in Durkheim's mind as to form virtually a single entity.

30. *Division du travail,* pp. 450–52.

31. *Ibid.,* pp. 230 ff.

32. *Ibid.,* pp. 256 ff.

33. *Ibid.,* pp. 269 ff. This has often been pointed out as an amazing non sequitur. G. Belot remarked that one might as well say of a bankrupt merchant that he could not have been motivated by the hope of profits. Moreover, the whole argument rests on premises which are inadmissible by Durkheim's own methodological criteria. His discussion about man's capacity for happiness or about the different degrees of happiness enjoyed by primitive and civilized peoples unfortunately relies upon arbitrary and subjective psychological intuitions which Durkheim elsewhere condemns as *prénotions.* Moreover, the conception of human nature as essentially static, and easily satisfied in its desires, appears just as unrealistic as the diametrically opposite, but equally one-sided, conception of human nature which Durkheim elaborates in *Le Suicide* (cf. below, p. 509).

34. Since Durkheim's day, there has been much anthropological evidence to show that in primitive society an increase of population is an exceptional rather than a normal phenomenon and that the size of the population is itself determined by numerous social and cultural factors (see Carr-Saunders, *Population Problem* [Oxford, 1922]). It should, moreover, have been apparent to Durkheim that an increase of population, where it did occur, might have been met by emigration or war and that, where division of labor was selected as a preferable alternative, individual motivation and consideration of personal or collective welfare must have been influential in bringing about a decision. Hence the causation could not have been completely "mechanical."

35. Durkheim, *Le Suicide* (Paris, 1897).

36. The observed increase in suicides during periods of exceptional prosperity has not been corroborated by further investigation.

37. A third type of suicide ("altruistic suicide") is explained by Durkheim as resulting from an excess of social integration. Unfortunately, the nature of this type of suicide is far from clear. Durkheim so defines it as to include apparently the willing sacrifice of life for the benefit of another (as by a soldier to save his comrades or by a mother for her child). Yet, as Halbwachs subsequently pointed out, these are not considered by society to be suicides; and this is therefore not a good sociologistic definition. Moreover, it is curious to note that Durkheim himself forgets about "altruistic suicide" in important parts of his study. Thus he uses the ordinary statistics of suicide in estimating the total number of suicides, entirely overlooking the fact that most of his "altruistic suicides" are not commonly considered to be suicides and do not enter into the official suicide statistics. This error is particularly glaring when he asserts that the total number of suicides decreases during a war. If cases of deliberate self-sacrifice were included, the rate might be vastly increased. He also seems to have forgotten "altruistic suicide" in his blanket condemnation of suicide as a moral evil.

38. *Le Suicide* pp. 366 ff.

39. Two of the chief lines of criticism which we feel might well be brought against the Durkheimian theory of suicide are: (1) Durkheim hypostatizes a statistical average. The uniformity of the suicide rate might arise from the uniform strength from year to year of a great number of suicide-producing factors. (2) Where factors of group composition, social integration, etc., are influential, they probably act on the suicide rate by influencing the motives of individuals; and these form an indispensable link in the causal chain. Society's influence on the suicide rate is not so much a matter of collective compulsion as of cultural determination. Thus, e.g., the suicide of individuals who have lost their money in a depression is to be explained largely by the fact that they have acquired from their culture certain value-judgments stressing the unconditional desirability of maintaining their socio economic status.

40. Durkheim, "Représentations individuelles et représentations collectives," *Sociologie et philosophie* (Paris, 1924), chap. i, pp. 1–48.

41. This constitutes a major breaking-away from the position adopted in the *Règles*— that the sociologist should explain all social changes in terms of changes in the internal social milieu.

42. This theory was first presented by Durkheim in 1906 at two meetings of the Société Française de Philosophie, held on February 11 and March 22. The paper and subsequent discussion are reported in the *Bulletin de la Société Française de Philosophie*, VI (Paris, 1906), 113 ff.

43. *Ibid.*, pp. 121 ff. Durkheim also notes that the same duality is to be found in the notion of sacredness, which is both forbidden and inspiring. He maintains that there is a very close relation, both logically and historically, between religion and morality.

44. "Now in the world of experience, I know of only one subject which possesses a moral reality which is richer and more complex than our own: it is the collectivity. No, I am mistaken; there is another being who could play the same role: namely, the divinity. Between God and society we must make our choice. I will not here examine the reasons which could militate in favor of one or the other solution. Both solutions are, moreover, perfectly compatible. I will add that from my point of view this choice is a matter of indifference, for I do not see in the divinity anything more than society transfigured and conceived symbolically" (*ibid.*, p. 129). Note how clearly this anticipates the fundamental idea of Durkheim's study of religion.

45. *Ibid.*, p. 132.

46. *Ibid.*, p. 116. The *chief* defects in Durkheim's theory of morals, as they appear to the writer, may be summarily stated as follows: (1) Other individuals may legitimately be the object of moral behavior and may properly inspire moral devotion. It is not that they are *better* than we are but that they are *other* than we; and this quality of "otherness" makes possible an element of devotion which no narrowly egoistic objective can inspire. Besides, it is by no means certain that the individual's desire to improve or develop himself is completely lacking in moral content. It is therefore not necessary to postulate that society is a person. (2) The social group conserves culture, but it has not yet been shown that it *creates* culture. Our devotion to culture and to civilization does not necessarily require us to be loyal to the particular group with which we happen to be associated. If that group betrays or inhibits culture, we may be justified in abandoning it or in trying to bring about a radical reorganization. In short, our devotion to the social group is conditional upon *its* loyalty to the fundamental values transmitted by culture. (3) The extreme relativism of Durkheim's theory makes it impossible to criticize an existing moral system "from the outside," in terms of wider and more general standards. If every society has the moral system it needs, there is no basis for fundamental moral criticism and no possibility of moral progress. Mere conservation is not for society, as it is not for the individual, a completely adequate moral objective. The individual may willingly sacrifice his personal existence for a moral end, and a society is similarly dedicated to ends beyond its own mere existence.

47. Durkheim, "Jugements de valeur et jugements de réalité: communication faite au Congrès international de philosophie de Boulogne, 6 avril, 1911," published in *Revue de métaphysique et de morale*, July 3, 1911, pp. 436–53; reprinted in *Sociologie et philosophie*, chap. iv, pp. 117 ff. Our references will be to this reprint.

48. *Ibid.*, p. 133.

49. *Ibid.*, p. 135.

50. *Ibid.*, pp. 141–42.

51. Such universal explanations are obviously of small scientific value. In further criticism the writer would maintain that *mental* interaction is only slightly dependent upon physical contiguity and that it is *mental* interaction which is important in the development of new ideals or values. Durkheim has presented very little evidence that the increase in physical

proximity (as in crowds) plays an important part in the *creation* of ideals. It is probably much more important in creating emotional attitudes favorable for their rapid diffusion.

52. Paris, 1912. References are to the excellent English translation by J. W. Swain, *The Elementary Forms of the Religious Life* (London, 1915).

53. "A religion is a unified system of beliefs and practices relative to sacred things, that is to say, things set apart and forbidden—beliefs and practices which unite into one single moral community called a Church, all those who adhere to them" (*ibid.*, p. 47). The *ad hoc* nature of this definition is implicitly admitted by Durkheim when he writes: "The second element which thus finds a place in our definition is no less essential than the first; for by showing that the idea of religion is inseparable from that of the Church, it makes it clear that religion should be an eminently collective thing" (*ibid.*).

54. This evolutionary approach to the problem of social origins exposes Durkheim to many serious criticisms. For example, some authorities have claimed that other peoples (as, e.g., the African pygmies, who are alleged to be monotheistic) are more primitive than the Aruntas. Moreover, Sir James Frazer, who first revealed to Durkheim the religious nature of totemism, later changed his mind and decided that totemism is not really a religion at all. Perhaps the most serious objections, however, concern the validity of the whole evolutionary approach in sociology. Do primitive peoples represent an earlier phase of our own evolution, or are they end-products of a long and largely independent line of evolution? Can primitiveness be equated with simplicity? Will the essential characteristics of religion be more clearly revealed in a primitive society, where religion is closely bound up with many other phases of social life (kinship groups, tribal patriotism, technological procedures, etc.) or in a highly civilized society, in which all the institutions have been to a much higher degree differentiated and purged of extrinsic elements?

55. ". . . . If it is at once the symbol of the god and of society, is not that because the god and the society are only one? How could the emblem of the group have been able to become the figure of this quasi-divinity, if the group and the divinity were two distinct realities? The god of the clan, the totemic principle, can therefore be nothing else than the clan itself, personified and represented to the imagination under the visible form of the animal or vegetable which serves as totem" (*ibid.*, p. 206).

56. *Ibid.*, pp. 214–16.

57. *Ibid.*, pp. 206 ff.

58. Three of the many possible criticisms of the Durkheimian theory of religion may be briefly indicated here: (1) The group always remains a purely secular and existential reality. It is difficult to see how it could give rise to the ideal and the sacred merely by an increase of density. Crowd excitement is not necessarily of a religious character; and the intense states of excitement aroused in an Australian *corrobori* or in a revival meeting may be very largely nonreligious in origin and nature. We must also remember that many of the most intense and authentic religious experiences occur in solitude. (2) Our attitudes toward God and toward society are not nearly so similar as Durkheim tries to make out, especially if we distinguish between the social group and the culture—which is, in large part, borrowed from other groups. And such similarity, if established, would by no means prove that God and the society are the same entity. (3) Since Durkheim's theory of religion deeply shocks the sentiments of religious people (cf. G. Richard, "L'Athéisme dogmatique en sociologie religieuse," *Revue d'histoire et de philosophie religieuse*, 1923), it seems likely that his theory, no less than the theories he criticizes, portrays religion as resting on an illusion. The religious believer does not consciously worship society, and to say that the entity he worships is only a symbol of society is to accuse him of a gross error if he does not *understand* its symbolic character. If its symbolic character *were* understood, few religionists would continue to worship, because they would not recognize in the empirical reality—society—an adequate substitute for God, unless they had, like Durkheim, begun by deifying society.

59. Durkheim and Mauss, "De quelques formes primitives de classification," *Année sociologique*, VI (1901–2), 1–72.

60. *Ibid.*, p. 6.

61. Perhaps the chief criticism of this theory of classification is implicitly contained in a footnote in which Durkheim admits: "It is probable that from the beginning man has always more or less clearly classified his sources of food" (*ibid.*, p. 66). But if primitive man could always classify his foodstuffs (and, in general, the technological elements in the situation), then the logical powers of classification were already his, anterior to and independent of the classificatory powers derived from the structure of the group. If nature or the structure of his own mind could create a classification in one field, why could it not also create classifications in other fields; and what could prevent classificatory habits exercised in one field from being extended gradually to others? Durkheim's assumption that contemporary scientific classification has its source in the emotional, mythological classifications based on collective representations seems very arbitrary, since our contemporary scientific classification seems logically and "temperamentally" much closer to the utilitarian technological classifications by means of which primitive man was able to exercise some slight degree of prediction and control over the material conditions of his existence. From another point of view, we may also ask whether, if individuals did not already possess at least a general power of classification, they could recognize human beings as constituting a class distinct from the animals or could arrive at such notions as a clan, phratry, or family.

62. This subject is treated in the Introduction and in the Conclusion of *The Elementary Forms of the Religious Life* (see esp. pp. 10 ff. and 440 ff.).

63. *Ibid.*, p. 18.

64. *Ibid.*, p. 440.

65. Here Durkheim lapses into language which brings him very close to an absolute idealism, with society as the Absolute. "Since the universe does not exist except insofar as it is thought of, and since it is not completely thought of except by society, it becomes a part of society's interior life, while this is the totality, outside of which nothing exists" (*ibid.*, pp. 441–42). One puzzling aspect of the situation is that, while the Absolute Idealists believe in only *one* Absolute, Durkheim, as a sociological relativist, insists that there are *many* societies and that they are radically heterogeneous. The simultaneous existence of several societies *each* of which contains the whole universe reminds one of a congress of philosophical solipsists!

66. *Ibid.*, pp. 11–12.

67. There are many points of view from which Durkheim's theory of knowledge can be (and has been) criticized. From the point of view of empiricism, the following objections will appear pertinent: Extension, duration, etc., are real properties of the physical world, not something created by the social mind. It is absurd to say that society imposes categories of space and time on individuals in order that they may meet at a given place and time and otherwise co-operate; for, if the world were not already spatial and temporal, there could not be any problem of "meeting." The rhythm of group life is superimposed upon, and measured by, astronomical time (days, months, seasons, etc.), and the spatial formations which a social group assumes is simply a particular distribution of its members and their possessions over the earth's surface, which possesses fixed spatial properties independent of any society. In the example given, it is not the *society* which is circular, but the camp site; and *its* circularity could be perceived by the individual if the site were uninhabited. The primary function of the categories is to enable us to adapt ourselves to the physical world; and, if they simply reflected the organization of a particular society, they would not so well fit the physical world or enable members of *different* societies to co-operate. The apriorist would urge the following type of objection: If the individual mind did not naturally receive its experience in a spatial and temporal order, society could not possibly impose such an order on the individual minds. The *meaning* of time would be quite incommunicable to one who initially lacked all sense of time. To perceive the rhythm of social processes or the pattern of a camp site, we must first be able to experience temporality and spatiality. Society may influence the conventional methods of dividing or

describing space and time, but it could not give us the fundamental forms of intuition. The same may be said for such categories as cause, substance, etc.

68. The only serious attempt to find an explanation of social changes occurs in the book on the division of labor, and this attempt is generally conceded to have been unsuccessful (see above, p. 508 and nn. 33 and 34).

69. Durkheim's interest in socialism appears to have been chiefly in the history of its ideology. He indicates that, while he has considerable sympathy for its ideal of justice as a principle whereby excessive individual demands may be regulated (he calls this principle "communism" as distinct from socialism), he is opposed to that type of socialism which is interested chiefly in raising the standard of living and which favors collectivism as a more efficient type of economic organization for the creation and distribution of wealth (*Le Socialisme, sa définition, ses débuts, la doctrine Saint-Simonienne*, ed. M. Mauss [Paris, 1928]).

70. This program is presented in an Introduction to the second edition of *De la division du travail social*, written in 1902. Further treatment of the problems of social pathology is to be found in the *Règles*, in the *Suicide*, in *L'Education morale* (Paris, 1925), and in the articles "La Morale," *Revue philosophique*, LXXXIX (1920), 81–97), and "Morale professionnelle," *Revue de métaphysique et de morale*, XLIV (1937), 527–44, 711–38). The last three titles were published, after Durkheim's death, by Marcel Mauss.

71. Under fascism the professional associations are not really autonomous and are simply an additional instrument for bringing the ubiquitous power of the state to bear on the individual. Durkheim's scheme, in contrast to totalitarianism, involves no increase in state power but proposes a decentralization of authority by means of an increase in the powers of vocational associations.

72. It was this type of argument which he adopted against the traditionalists at the time of the Dreyfus trials ("Individualisme et les intellectuels," *Revue Bleu*, X (1898), 7–13).

73. Marcel Mauss, "In Memoriam," *Année sociologique* (new. ser.), Vol. I.

74. Among those lost may be mentioned: Robert Herz, Maxim David, Antoine Bianconi, Jean Raynier, R. Gelly, and André Durkheim, son of Émile Durkheim.

75. By 1939 a new generation of scholars had grown up and entered the group. In general, they adopted a less doctrinaire line and were moving in the direction of the abandonment or modification of agelecism. Among them were included such promising younger men as Raymond Aron, Robert Marjolin, and Raymond Polin.

76. "Divisions et proportions des divisions de la sociologie," *Année sociologique*, Vol. II (new ser.; 1924–25). "Fragment d'un plan de sociologie générale descriptive," *Annales sociologiques*, ser. A, Fasc. 1, 1934.

77. "Rapports réls et pratiques de la psychologie et de la sociologie," *Journal de psychologie*, Vol. XXI (December 15, 1924); see also "L'Expression obligatoire des sentiments," *ibid.*, 1921.

78. Such, e.g., are his studies on the seasonal variations in Eskimo religious life (*Année sociologique*, Vol. IX, in collaboration with H. Beuchat); on primitive forms of classification (*ibid.*, Vol. II, in collaboration with Durkheim); on the nature and function of sacrifice (*ibid.*, Vol. II, in collaboration with H. Hubert); on the general theory of magic (*ibid.*, Vol. III, in collaboration with H. Hubert); and on the gift as an archaic form of exchange (*ibid.*, [new ser.], Vol. I). Note also the following studies in the *Revue de l'histoire des religions:* (1896–97) "La Religion et les origines du droit pénal"; (1901) "Leçon d'ouverture du cours d'histoire des religions, etc."; see also "L'Arte et le mythe, d'après Wundt," *Revue philosophique*, 1909; "L'Origine de la notion de mana," *Anthropologie*, 1914; and "L'Ethnographie en France et à l'étranger," *Revue de Paris*, 1913.

79. *Durkheim: Introduction et morceaux choisis* (Paris, 1911); "Emile Durkheim: l'homme et l'œuvre," *Revue de métaphysique et de morale*, 1919, 1920; and *Sociologues d'hier et d'aujourd'hui*.

80. G. Davy, "La Sociologie," in G. Dumas, *Traité de psychologie*, Vol. II (Paris, 1924).

81. In G. Dumas, *Nouveau traité de psychologie,* Vol. VI (Paris, 1939).

82. Davy and Moret, *Des clans aux empires* (Paris, 1924). Davy has made other contributions in juristic and educational sociology.

83. *Le Droit, l'idéalisme et l'expérience* (Paris, 1922); *Eleménts de sociologie appliquée à la morale et à l'éducation,* Vol. I: *Sociologie politique* (1924).

84. "Sociologie et sciences sociales," *Revue philosophique,* 1903.

85. *La Responsibilité* (Paris, 1920).

86. *La Classe ouvrière et les niveaux de vie: recherches sur le hiérarchie des besoins dans les sociétés industrielles contemporaines* (Paris, 1913).

87. *Les Cadres sociaux de la mémoire* (Paris, 1925).

88. *Les Causes du suicide* (Paris, 1930).

89. *Ibid.,* p. 425.

90. Other important publications of Halbwachs are: "La Doctrine d'Émile Durkheim," *Revue philosophique,* 1918; *Le Calcul des probabilités à la portée de tous* (in collaboration with M. Frechet) (Paris, 1923); and "Matière et société," *Revue philosophique,* July–August, 1920, pp. 120–22; also, "La Nuptialité en France, pendant et depuis la guerre," *Année sociologique,* ser. E, Fasc. 1, 1935.

91. Cf. particularly *Les Sciences sociales en Allemagne, les methodes actuelles* (Paris, 1896), pp. 147 ff.

92. *Les Idées égalitaires* (Paris, 1899).

93. *Essais sur le régime des castes* (Paris, 1908).

94. *La Démocratie devant la science: études critiques sur l'hérédité, le concurrence et la différenciation* (Paris, 1903); 3d ed. with a Preface on "La Sociologie monarchiste" (1923). Some of this material was first presented in two brilliant articles devoted to a criticism of the biologistic sociology: "La Sociologie biologique," *Revue philosophique,* 1900; and "Le Procès de la sociologie biologique," *ibid.,* 1901.

95. Bouglé has also made numerous contributions in the fields of sociological pedagogy and the history of social thought. Under the former heading we may list the following books: *Qu'est-ce que la sociologie?* (Paris, 1907) (an excellent introductory statement); *Guide de l'étudiant en sociologie* (in collaboration with Déat) (Paris, 1921); *Eléments de sociologie* (a source book, edited in collaboration with J. Raffault (Paris, 1926); Bouglé's work on the history of social thought has dealt mainly with socialists and social reformers: *Chez les prophètes socialistes* (Paris, 1918); *La Sociologie de Proudhon* (Paris, 1911); *La Doctrine de Saint-Simon* (in collaboration with Élie Halévy) (Paris, 1924); *L'Oeuvre d'Henri de Saint-Simon* (selected passages) (Paris, 1925); *Proudhon* (Paris, 1929). He has also proved himself a keen and well-balanced commentator on the development of academic sociology (cf. *Les Sciences sociales en Allemagne, les méthodes actuelles* (Paris, 1896); "Un Sociologue individualiste: G. Tarde," *Revue de Paris,* 1905; "Individualisme et sociologie," *Revue bleu,* November, 1905; "La Sociologie et le droit comparé," *Revue de l'enseignement français hors de France,* 1926; "Sociologie et psychologie," *ibid.,* 1927. Especially notable is his useful outline of modern French sociology, *Le Bilan de la sociologie française contemporaine.* We must also make mention of an interesting series of lectures entitled *Leçons sur l'évolution des valeurs* (Paris, 1922), which was translated into English by Helen S. Sellars in 1926 as *The Evolution of Values,* which takes only a moderately agelic point of view with respect to the nature and origin of social values. Bouglé has also written numerous articles and pamphlets on problems of politics and social policy.

96. G. Richard, *La Sociologie générale* (Paris, 1912); "Nouvelles tendences sociologiques en France," *Revue internationale de sociologie,* XXXVI, 648 ff.; "A. Comte et E. Durkheim," *ibid.,* XL, 603 ff.; "La Pathologie sociale d'Émile Durkheim, *ibid.,* XXXVIII, 119 ff.; "Le Conflit de la morale et de la sociologie," *Revue philosophique,* 1911; "L'Athéisme dogmatique en sociologie religieuse," *Revue d'histoire et de philosophie religieuse,* 1923.

97. He has been a collaborator both on *L'Année sociologique,* to which he contributed a monograph on the rituals of exchange in North Africa (Vol. II [new ser., 1924]), and

on *L'Annales sociologiques,* in which he published an important memoire on "Interest Groups and the Idea of Contract in North Africa" (ser. C, Fasc. 2, 1937).

98. Cf. René Maunier, *Introduction à la sociologie* (Paris, 1929), pp. 15 ff.

99. Other important publications of Maunier are: *L'Economie politique et sociologie* (Paris, 1910); *L'Origine et la fonction économique des villes* (Paris, 1910); *La Construction de la maison en Kabylie* (Paris, 1926); and *Essais sur les groupements sociaux* (Paris, 1929).

100. Paris, 1903, and many later editions. Albert Bayet has pushed this view even further in: *La Morale scientifique* (Paris, 1905); and *La Science des faits moraux* (Paris, 1925). In *Le Suicide et la morale* (Paris, 1922), he has carried out his methodological program by a voluminous and painstaking investigation of the history of moral judgments and attitudes bearing on a specific act.

101. Lévy-Bruhl, *Les Fonctions mentales dans les sociétés primitives* (1923); *La Mentalité primitive* (1925); *L'Ame primitive* (1927); *Le Surnaturel et la nature dans la mentalité primitive* (1931); *La Mythologie primitive* (1935); and *L'Expérience mystique et les symboles chez les primitifs* (1938). These are all issued by Alcan in Paris; and the first four have been felicitously translated into English by Lilian A. Clare under the following titles: *How Natives Think* (New York, 1927); *Primitive Mentality* (New York, 1923); *The "Soul" of the Primitive* (New York, 1928); and *Primitives and the Supernatural* (New York, 1935).

102. *La Conscience morbide: essai de psychopathologie générale* (Paris, 1913).

103. Blondel, "Les Volitions," in G. Dumas, *Traité de psychologie* (Paris, 1924), II, 333–425.

104. Blondel, *Introduction à la psychologie collective* (Paris, 1928). However, Blondel has criticized Durkheim's theories of knowledge and of religion (*ibid.,* pp. 96 ff.); and in a more recent work (*Le Suicide* [Strasbourg, 1933]) he presents a formidable criticism of the sociologistic explanation of suicide, emphasizing for his own part the psychophysiological, and particularly the psychopathic, elements in this phenomenon.

105. G. Dumas, "L'Expression des émotions," in his *Traité de psychologie,* I, 641. However, he has seriously criticized an exclusively sociologistic explanation of the mental life (*ibid.,* II, 1150–53).

106. *L'Enfant turbulent* (Paris, 1925); also "La Mentalité primitive et celle de l'enfant," *Revue philosophique,* 1928.

107. Cf. Granet, *Fêtes et danses anciennes de la Chine* (Paris, 1919); *La Polygynie sororale et le sororat dans la Chine féodale* (Paris, 1920); *La Religion des Chinois* (Paris, 1922); *Danses et légendes de la Chine ancienne,* Travaux de *l'Année sociologique* (2 vols.; Paris, 1926); *La Civilisation chinoise,* "La Vie publique et la vie privée," "L'Evolution de l'humanité" (Paris, 1929).

108. *La Pensée chinoise* (Paris 1934). Cf. the author's critical review in the *American Sociological Review,* I, 487–92.

109. Henri Berr, *La Synthèse en histoire* (Paris, 1911). Berr is also the founder and editor of *La Synthèse historique,* and of the series, Bibliothèque de synthèse historique."

110. Cf. *La Méthode positive en science économique* (Paris, 1912); *Statistique et expérience: remarques de méthode* (Paris, 1922); "Méthode historique et science sociale," *Revue de synthèse historique,* 1903; and "La causalité en histoire," *Bullétin de la Société française de philosophie,* 1907.

111. *Salaire des ouvriers des mines de charbon en France* (Paris, 1907); and *La Formation et les fluctuations des prix du charbon en France pendant vingt-cinq ans, 1887–1912* (Paris, 1925). Simiand has had an important influence on Halbwachs.

112. Cf., among other works, *Traité de droit constitutionnel* (1911); *Le Droit social, le droit individuel et la transformation de l'état* (Paris, 1911); *Les Transformation générales du droit privé* (1912); and *Les Transformations du droit public* (1913).

113. "Magie et droit individuel," *Année sociologique*, Vol. X (1907); and *Histoire du droit commercial* (Paris, 1904).

114. Meillet, "Comment les mots changent de sens," *Année sociologique*, Vol. IX 1905–6). A similar sociologistic emphasis is found in his *Les Langues dans l'Europe nouvelle* (Paris, 1918); in *Linguistique historique et linguistique générale* (Paris, 1921); and in many articles.

115. *La Pensée et la langue* (Paris, 1922).

116. "Le Caractère social du langage," *Journal de psychologie* (1921); and "Le Progrès du langage, *Bulletin de la Société française de philosophie*, 1922. Also, *Le Langage: introduction linguistique à l'histoire* ("Bibliothèque de synthèse historique" [1922]).

CHAPTER XXVIII

THE DOCTRINES OF GUILLAUME DE GREEF
SYNDICALISM AND SOCIAL REFORM IN THE
GUISE OF A CLASSIFICATORY SOCIOLOGY

DOROTHY W. DOUGLAS, *Smith College*

I. GENERAL TRAITS OF SOCIOLOGY IN BELGIUM

SOCIOLOGY got off to a good start in Belgium in the nineteenth century as a result of the prestige of the towering figure of Adolphe Quételet (1796–1874), father of the quantitative method in sociology and of statistical analysis in the social sciences. Quételet, as a citizen of the buffer-state of Belgium, was also interested in international relations, and he enunciated a doctrine of international equilibration through a process of social and cultural oscillation. This was taken up and developed more thoroughly by Belgium's foremost sociologist, Guillaume de Greef, whose life and works are the subject matter of this chapter.

Owing, however, to the radical cast of De Greef's sociological doctrines and to the grip of the older special social sciences upon Belgian intellectual life, the later development of sociology in Belgium has been slight and disappointing. Indeed, aside from De Greef, there has been only one other important sociologist in Belgium, Émile Waxweiler (1867–1916), director of the Institut de Sociologie Solvay in Brussels, which was founded in 1901 by Ernest Solvay, a liberal Belgian industrialist. Waxweiler's chief work, *Esquisse d'une sociologie,* published in 1906, was a penetrating quasi-biological analysis of the process of adjustment between personalities in social relationships. Rejecting the organic analogy, Waxweiler adopted a behavoristic social psychology which anticipated the behaviorism of Giddings and Watson by more than a decade.

The Solvay Institute is a well-endowed and well-equipped sociological research organization, carrying on work in social investigation, urban sociology, social surveys, and the like. It directly forwards the ecological movement in sociology.

538

Belgium has produced a number of eminent criminologists, among whom the most distinguished was Adolphe Prins (1845–1919), who gained international repute as a critic of the doctrines of Lombroso and Ferri.

But the one name in general Belgian sociology which stands out above all others is that Guillaume de Greef, to whose career and doctrines we may now turn our attention.

II. DE GREEF'S LIFE

Guillaume de Greef (1842–1924) is a sociologist whose formal theory can best be understood in the light of his practical program of social reform. His life plainly shows the mingling of the two currents of interest.

Born in Brussels in 1842, the son of a well-to-do musician of Flemish stock, De Greef early followed the family bent of free thought, eagerly read Voltaire and the other philosophers who affected the French Revolution, went on in his university years to absorb the then novel French Utopian socialists—Saint-Simon and Fourier—and presently fell under the influence of the greatest leader of youth of the day, the proto-Syndicalist, Proudhon, a radical intellectual with anarchistic leanings, then an exile from France in the Belgian capital.

From Proudhon, De Greef and his fellows learned the theory of "mutualism," that all exchange between individuals should be on a basis of mutual equality, and that the salvation of mankind lies in the establishment of free credit through a network of self-sufficient *syndicats,* at once trade-unions and producers' co-operatives, to be bound together by a new system of interest-free credit furnished by a "Bank of Exchange."

While still a student in the law course of the university, De Greef dedicated himself to the cause of the working class, then in a great state of misery in Belgium, and, with his classmate, Hector Denis, began editing various radical journals, most notably the arch-Proudhonian organ, *La Liberté.*

To Proudhon's idea of free-credit groups, De Greef and Denis added the idea of occupational representation—that the members of the free-credit groups were to be organized, trade by trade, in each locality, not only to carry on their ordinary union activities but to take over what were formerly the functions of the political state itself. In other words, more than a generation before the idea had been reborn in modern French syndicalism with Sorel, or in British guild socialism with Orage and Cole, De Greef and his friends were preaching a Syndicalist society.

In the late 1860's, De Greef appears to have drawn up the program of the Belgian delegates to the International Workingmen's Association. This program (strictly Proudhonian—free-credit and no strong state) not only was defeated in the International by Marx, with his doctrine of the class struggle and the necessity of the proletarian state, but gradually lost ground in Belgium itself. As Marxism steadily increased in power, De Greef found it more and more impossible to serve effectively in the labor movement, although for a number of years he defended labor cases in the law courts.

He turned, then, to more academic writing and published his first work in theoretical sociology, the *Introduction à la sociologie,* in 1886–89. This was so well received that De Greef was appointed to the first chair in sociology at the University of Brussels. When the eminent geographer and philosophical anarchist, Elisée Réclus, was dismissed from the university because of popular agitation, De Greef and Denis, in indignation, led an exodus of other professors and students from the university. These men founded a new institution, L'Université Nouvelle, devoted to the social sciences, freedom of thought, and close co-operation with the workers' educational movement. There De Greef taught quietly for the rest of his life. However, he continued to publish books on his reform schemes, and in 1913 and again in 1919 he appeared before legislative commissions to argue for occupational representation. He died in 1924 at the age of eighty-two.[1]

III. DE GREEF'S WORKS

Easily the most important of De Greef's works, after the *Introduction* —indeed, far ahead of it for freshness of content—is the three-volume *Structure général des sociétés,* published in 1908. This contains his interesting theory of frontiers. His many other theoretical writings contain practically nothing foreign to these two; and none adequately summarizes the *Structure,* although some of the briefer ones, notably the little *Lois sociologiques,* are more convenient for the general reader.

In order to gain a fair perspective of De Greef's theory, however, it is necessary to see it against the background of some of his applied works. The *Ouvrière dentellière,* ("The Women Lace-Makers"), the *Rachat*

des charbonnages ("The Repurchase of the Coal Mines"), and the subsequently republished *Régime représentatif* ("How Government May
Be Made Representative") give a vivid picture of the Proudhonian Syndicalist state, toward which he is determined that all the institutions of
society shall head. It is his belief that his own "system" scientifically
proves the validity of that hope.

Indeed, it is interesting to note that we find De Greef, near the end
of his life, remarking in his autobiography (as yet unpublished): "These
two little brochures [the *Rachat* and the *Ouvrière*] have given me a
satisfaction as great as—in fact greater than—the most substantial of
my theoretical works."

IV. DE GREEF'S PROPOSED SOCIAL REFORMS

The practical program set forth in De Greef's applied works rests, first,
upon a transformation of the credit system and, next, upon the setting
up of collective bargaining on a national scale as a basis for occupational
representation in parliament. Both require the building up of strong
trade-unions.

In the case of the credit system, De Greef proposes the issuance of
what is practically fiat money—notes not redeemable in specie—by the
National Bank, alongside its existing issue of redeemable money. The
fiat notes would represent commercial and industrial transactions under
way. They would carry no interest above the nominal charge for over-
head and risk and would, with various safeguards against inflation, be
apportioned among member-institutions—workingmen's associations, so
far as possible—which would, in turn, supervise the applications for
credit by their members and apportion the notes to them. With credit
thus readily accessible to productive enterprises, De Greef hoped to
see *syndicats* rapidly form and take over collective contracts for work.
Thus idle capital would gradually be absorbed by them, and the
capitalist employer be dispossessed.

In the case of the political system, De Greef proposes that, without
waiting for the *syndicats* gradually to grow up from below, voting may
at once be reformed by having all persons register at the polls by trades
instead of by mere geographic divisions, workers and management being
in every case represented separately and equally. It does not matter, says
De Greef, if this results in an overwhelming inequality of representation:

Equality is not personal, but functional. . . . . Suppose there were formed a nation-wide trust of all coal mines . . . . in the hands of a dozen . . . . large capitalists. These twelve . . . . could have a representation equal to that of the 144,000 workmen! . . . . well, I do not recoil before this abominable situation. Why? Because . . . . I prefer a truthful representation to one which is fictitiously and deceptively democratic. What matters it if the mirror that reflects our social system gives back an ugly image? Is it the fault of the mirror that society is not beautiful, and should we in anger throw down and break the mirror?[2]

It will be time enough to represent labor more amply when labor fills a more predominant economic function. Meanwhile, the local groups of employers and workers in allied trades would be formed into joint industrial councils to preside over trade-interests, grievances, and conditions of work.

Thus, at one stroke, De Greef seeks to build up a system that not only would bring what he considered to be the vital social functions to the political surface of parliament but would, at the same time, hasten the inner reconstruction of those functions in the direction of labor control, through the educational effect of a nation-wide system of collective bargaining. Ultimately, as we have said before, he expected to see the *syndicats,* in a form very like the "guilds" of the late British Guild Socialist school, absorb the employing function and exercise all that remains of political power.

V. THE FRAMEWORK OF DEGREEF'S SOCIOLOGICAL THEORY

De Greef's conception of sociology is that it is "the general philosophy of the special social sciences" and, hence, the crown of all the sciences. Its subject matter is not only man and his social relationships but these viewed and studied in connection with their physical environment: "Society continues and contains all nature."

De Greef contended that his sociology contained the best in the systems of Comte, Spencer, and Quételet. It combined an improvement on Comte's classification of the sciences; Spencer's conception of social evolution, conceived in terms of an increasing organic differentiation and co-ordination; and Quételet's statistical or quantitative method, which De Greef regarded as the only valid approach to social science. Statistics is to sociology what laboratory analysis is to the organic sciences. Indeed, De Greef claimed to have effected an even more comprehensive synthesis. He fused not only Comte, Spencer, and Quételet, but socialism, as well. As he put it, "Sociology is scientific socialism." But his socialism was inspired by Proudhon, not by Marx.

De Greef's "pure" theory contains two parts, a classificatory and a psychological. On the classificatory side (in the theory of "the seven social factors"), De Greef sets out to show that economic factors are always basic in social change and social control; and on the psychological side (in the theory of frontiers) he illustrates this truth from the sphere of group contacts. At the same time (in the theory of "contractualism"), he emphasizes the tendency toward freer and freer groupings.

De Greef builds his system upon the framework of Comte's classification of the sciences. It will be recalled that Auguste Comte had ranged all human knowledge in its abstract aspect on an ascending scale of complexity, with mathematics at the foot and "sociology," or general social theory, at the head. While De Greef accepted Comte's general notion of the classification of the sciences, he added to this his own classification of the social sciences in an order that he regarded as extending from the lower and simpler to the higher and more complex activities of man. It ran as follows:

1. Economics, or the science of social nutrition
2. Genetics, or the science of population, socially organized
3. Aesthetics
4. Collective psychology: religion, metaphysics, positive philosophy
5. Ethics
6. Law
7. Politics

This hierarchical classification is of vital significance, since, according to De Greef, it reveals the natural growth of all man's social life.

Comte maintained that the successive sciences along his scale had developed serially in point of time and that each had to progress through three stages of thought: from the theological through the metaphysical up to the "positive" or scientific.[3]

De Greef will have nothing to do with Comte's "law of the three stages" or with his belief that "ideas rule the world or throw it into chaos." Proudhon and the whole socialist school had made him impatient with such "ideology." But he does take over bodily Comte's belief in a necessary and irreversible serial development of the sciences, and he says his own originality lies in projecting that series over the social field. De Greef has discovered that not the mere thoughts but the activities—what he calls the *"factors"*—of social life themselves have developed serially, with the more complex always dependent upon the less complex.

The series—the seven categories of social factors—as constituted by De Greef thus runs: (1) economic phenomena, (2) genetic, (3) aesthetic, (4) psycho-collective, (5) moral, (6) juridical, (7) political. While he is not always consistent in his doctrine, De Greef holds that reforms must move up the hierarchy of the social factors, beginning with reforms in the economic field and ending with those in the political field. A given improvement in, let us say, political machinery, will be ineffectual unless it is backed up by a sufficient development in the "lower centers of co-ordination," most particularly, the economic, and so on.

De Greef breaks down his general theory of progress into the goals of evolution in the case of each of the factors of social life. The goal of economic life is socialization along Syndicalist lines. The goal of the family is a purely contractual civil marriage. Art is to attain unfettered embodiment of social aspirations, growing out of close touch with the people and independent of all patronage and censorship. Science will progress toward profound and dispassionate analysis, which cannot be expected in a society controlled by either church or state. Religion is to develop toward ultimate extinction, as a result of the undermining influence of science. The goal of morality is the responsible, but perfectly free, individual. In the perfected society, man will serve his neighbors without compulsion or constraint. Legal progress will move toward a complete realization of contractual relationships and a restriction of the severity of criminal law. In the field of government the goal is the elimination of political sovereignty and the increased importance of the natural occupational groups appropriate to a Syndicalist dispensation. In attaining these goals the ideal must be attained, or marked progress made toward its attainment, in serial fashion. That is, economic improvement must take place before perfection can be achieved in the family, and family perfection must be attained before we can expect artistic freedom, and so on along the line. In the case of regression the opposite order is followed, namely, political decline will take place before the legal, and legal regression before moral decline, and so on.

Why De Greef should have chosen the aforementioned seven factors or categories for his series does not matter, though it may be noted that they accord perfectly with his hierarchy of the social sciences, which reflect the social experience of man. The significant thing is the way he uses his series when once it is set up. Although, nominally, social influences are supposed to travel from one link to another along the entire chain of the hierarchy, actually, it is, in practically every case, the effect of economic activities upon every other field in the series that De Greef describes and illustrates. Whatever point he begins with, he always ends there; and the effects he cites are almost always described in terms of "good" or "bad," that is, as heading toward or away from his ideal Syndicalist world state.

Next to economic activities, it is the activities at the other end of the scale—political activities—that receive the most attention from De Greef, again quite naturally if we accept the Syndicalist explanation. Political activities would necessarily be put last in the series, since De Greef considers government a very superficial sphere of activity—one to be minimized as rapidly as possible as society progresses. His system really revolves upon the axis of the interrelationship of these two—economics and politics.

Together with Comte's principle of the classification of social activities, De Greef uses Spencer's formula of their evolution. Herbert Spencer had maintained that all forms of life, including social organization, are evolving from a less to a more complex and more "highly organized" form. De Greef adopts this formula and then proceeds to apply it, not to social "organization" in any literal sense but to Proudhon's kind of voluntary, contractual organization. This shift of meaning makes it possible for him to "prove" the "higher" organization of almost anything. For instance, when he tells us that the Japanese won the Russo-Japanese War because they were "better organized" than the Russians, we may take the comparison in either sense.

Translated into ordinary language, De Greef's theory of progress would seem to be: (1) that an evolutionary change in the forms of human association is generally observable; (2) that, as a rule, it consists, first, in growing complexity of structure with increasing formal control, then gradually in growing autonomy of the differentiated parts; (3) that in any given society the different forms of association will, however, show a time lag, the one behind the other; and (4) that, so close is their interdependence and so predominant the influence of the economic factor upon all the rest, it is hopeless to attempt to push the others far in advance of economic organization. The remedy for Belgium's troubles, De Greef thinks, is to concentrate upon those economic reforms that will make autonomy in other spheres safe.

VI. CONTRACTUALISM AND "DÉBAT" (HIGGLING)—THE GOAL
OF SOCIAL EVOLUTION

Even more important than De Greef's theory of the seven social factors and their progress is his concept of the final goal of that progress—the contractual state itself. "Contractualism" for De Greef means more than for Proudhon. Where Proudhon had used the term to designate the freedom of the individual from social constraint, De Greef deliberately uses it to designate the free give-and-take of interest-groups. He, too, desires equal human dignity for individuals, but his real interest is in the corporate method of getting it. It is upon the process of "contractualization" that he fixes; and he finds the process to consist essentially of a higgling, a *débat,* a balancing and weighing of opposing forces in a sort of social market-place or, to use his own figure, "courtroom" of the interests.

The great fault of political, and so of all civil, life, as he sees it, is that the real interests of men are obscured and twisted to fit the artificial boundaries of unreal affiliations of the seven social "functions" with all their subdivisions. As these become more and more complex, the *débat* within them rises slowly to the level of consciousness, becomes rational and methodical. At any given time some features of the group's life will be in the full focal light of consciousness; others will not yet have reached it; others, again, will already have passed beyond it into the sphere of social habit. Thus, stamping and posting a letter—really an act of unconscious social "contract"—becomes unconscious by virtue of repetition. In time of war or revolution, when the safety of the mails becomes a matter of moment, the "contract" may again grow explicit.

In every case the occasion for the rise of an act into social consciousness is some sort of crisis. So long as things move in their accustomed course, *débat* is unnecessary. It is the unexpected that brings "contractualism" to the surface. In the present age "contractualism" in all spheres is speeding up, and it becomes, therefore, doubly important to have the proper contractual machinery always at hand for the effective handling of new crises as they arise.

VII. A SOCIAL THEORY OF FRONTIERS

If De Greef's scheme of classification is derived largely from Comte; his formula of evolution from Spencer; and his theory of the goal of progress in "contractualism" from Proudhon, his theory of the method of progress, or the "theory of frontiers," is due in great part to his own compatriot, the statistician Quételet. Adolphe Quételet had been as much of an internationalist in his way as Proudhon, although his approach was totally different. He was deeply interested in the problems of Belgium as a buffer-state. Quételet saw the differences of human kind in terms of variation from an abstract "average man." This held true not only of man's physical traits but of his mental and social reactions as well. It was Quételet's belief that, with increasing social contacts as well as with the actual commingling of racial stocks, men's differences would multiply in number but diminish in intensity. He usually speaks of the tendency in terms of a growing equilibrium, a balance of forces. In his own words, civilization "more and more contracts the limits within which the different elements relating to man oscillate."

De Greef takes Quételet's underlying conception of the process of "oscillation," or equilibration, that makes the progressive leveling-off of human differences possible and, once more, applies it to groups rather than merely to individuals.

In terms of international relations, De Greef uses the concept of a moving equilibrium of forces to show that the political boundaries of peoples are the least important thing to know about them. They are only secondary and derived—the momentary result of the real thrusts and resistances within. Frontiers, De Greef insists, are never primarily geographic; they are social and equilibrative, the point at which the social forces of one group strike a momentary balance with those of another. No matter how strong a "natural" barrier may lie in the way, it will be penetrated if social conditions demand it. Thus, in the case of Arabia:

What admirable natural frontiers were .... there! .... And yet, but a little while after the death of the Prophet, the Arabs spread northward outside of their peninsula, and in spite of the mountains they conquered Syria, and in spite of the rivers, Egypt and Persia..... It was internal social conditions which originally made for unity within the peninsula, and it was internal conditions which, developing, drove the Arabs beyond it .... and when the inundation finally halted, it was because it had exhausted its own powers and because, besides, it had been arrested by other social forces that were relatively stronger.[4]

Moreover, whatever effect geographic features do have upon group structure is never constant: it varies with the stage of the culture of the group. The same "natural" boundaries that at one time served as bar-

riers—for example, large rivers—will at another be the most powerful agencies of communication.

The commonest frontiers of all times, indeed, have not been physical
obstacles at all but have been shifting and symbolic, from the sacred
trees and signposts of the ancient Mexicans to the zones of latitude of the
United States and Canada.

The social significance of the frontier is very great. In primitive times
the frontier is normally not a mere line but a zone, made neutral frequently by a desert waste, either natural or artificial. But before long, as a
rule, this desert waste becomes peopled by traders, marauders, government outposts, and incorrigible pioneers of all sorts with their hangers-
on. Once settled, it commonly becomes the place of the community's in-
tensest life, just because it is the place of its most critical contacts. It
resembles in this respect the outer envelope in primordial organic life:
it is the point not only of attack and defense but also of ingestion: "There
are the sensitive spots of each group as regards relations with the external world, thither its attention is always being attracted, there its
power is focused for .... protection and also for pacific agreement."[5]

It is the frontier that commonly stamps social life with its familiar
double aspect of political separatism and economic expansiveness, for
it is at the frontier that military power has to be most concentrated and
most tyrannical, and also there that peaceful social contacts are the most
inevitable. It is the frontier community that makes the first sporadic
economic exchanges with other peoples and that presently becomes the
group's normal center of commerce and trade, binding it to adjacent
territories in ever closer relationships. In modern times it is the great
commercial metropolises of the world that should be the leaders of
international peace.

Again, the buffer-states of the present day may be said to be descended
from the neutral zone of primitive times. The concept of neutrality has
slowly developed out of a *de facto* situation wherein some safety zone
between rivals of growing strength has appeared more and more essential to their survival, especially when that zone was itself desirable com-
mercially. From this selfish beginning, however, a real internationalism
may well arise. When once the leading nations have begun to be reor-
ganized internally, they will see that all the great zones of transit of the
world must be made neutral. And ultimately, banded together, these
should form the beginning of the pacific international world state.

The internal reorganization of each nation, however, must precede any such future, and it is to this internal reorganization as an integral part of his theory of frontiers that De Greef continually recurs.

VIII. RELATION OF THE THEORY OF FRONTIERS TO SOCIAL INTEREST-GROUPS

The expanding social forces to which De Greef looks for the breaking down of political barriers, he, of course, sees embodied in the seven familiar "factors" of his hierarchy. Each "factor" he pictures as having a "frontier" of its own, that is, a limit to its sphere of activity or membership. This figurative "frontier" may or may not coincide with the geographic frontier of the state. More commonly it does not. First, the economic factor will cross the political boundary, then (supposedly in order) the genetic, aesthetic, etc. Finally, the political factor is itself ready for a new adjustment. There is normally a time lag between the adjustment of the successive boundaries, so that the political is always in a state of being behindhand. Moreover, once the more immaterial factors begin crossing over after the economic, they may penetrate into foreign territory much farther than it does. The economic frontier is only "their center of gravity." The whole scheme thus becomes very complicated. However, when De Greef is pinned down to actual illustrations, they are usually quite simple and concrete, showing either the priority of the economic factor or the time lag of the political.

The trend of his discussion shows quite plainly what De Greef thinks of the nature of the "factors" themselves. They are essentially *interest-groupings with a group consciousness sufficiently strong to give them a definite organization*. De Greef chooses to call these subsidiary groupings "societies," in the equivocal sense possible only in French. Thus every religious sect, he tells us, every learned society, every trade-union, is a full-fledged society. The characteristics of a "full-fledged society" are that it shall have "headquarters, a membership, a code of group behavior, a system of group .... control ....," and, most important of all, that each is limited in its activity by other activities and other centers.

It is by perfecting the internal organization of each of these "societies," with their inevitable foreign affiliations, that the structure of the super-society—the state—will become meaningless. It will become for the citizen only one among many of the possible centers of solidarity.

The trend of De Greef's discussion also shows unmistakably by what means these lesser societies are to weaken the state. They are to become organized more and more, "contractually," i.e., voluntaristically, or syndicalistically, until they take over so many of the present positive functions of government that the state, in the old sense of the word, becomes superfluous:

> The formation of occupational *syndicats* has created a host of intermediate powers between the state and the individual......*Esprit de corps,* as an exclusive authoritarian thing, wanes at the same time that the sentiment of solidarity is strengthened.[6]
> The labor unions and the associations of commerce, of agriculture, and of industry, at present sacrificed to our political assemblies which represent nothing save the domination of one class and the anarchy of all, will, with their permanent bureaux of statistics, serve as the organs....of the life of relation between each of the categories of human activity.[7]

We shall have "new groupings in a new world."

To his theory of frontiers De Greef attaches a "theory of social classes," but it is not well worked out. He holds that existing class divisions on the basis of property mark but a temporary stage between ancient castes and future occupational divisions: "Occupational proliferations distend the class envelope until it bursts." The Marxian belief in a growing separation between capital and labor can hold true only in a regressive society. Actually, the trend of industry is rapidly making "capital" and "labor" mere abstractions. Or rather, they are but the end-terms of an extremely long series of occupation grades. In support of this belief De Greef does little more than cite a mass of statistics showing increasing division of labor. He does not demonstrate that the new occupations fall any nearer the center of the hypothetical "capital-and-labor" scale.

However, from his general treatment it is evident that what De Greef is pinning his faith to is, once more, not merely his original "law," taken from Quételet, of the "diminishing amplitude of social oscillations," but the very practical hope that the new occupational gradings may give rise to a larger and larger number of special *syndicats*. De Greef expects that within each trade, the workers—manual and mental together— will more and more take over the functions of business management, and on the ownership side, meanwhile, gradually absorb the functions of finance through their credit associations. In a word, De Greef hopes that the separatist interests of the special trade-groups as producers will presently outweigh, in importance for them, their more widely homogeneous class interests as workers over against owners. At least, he hopes that they will outweigh them sufficiently to permit the setting-up, without a class war, of the trade-machinery that will, in the end, level out the acute class differences themselves.

IX. SUMMARY

Looking over De Greef's work in perspective, it is easy to see the unity of it all. At the base lies the essentially Syndicalist conception that economic activities dwarf the political and that "natural" economic divisions according to function are the logical seats of future power.

De Greef took this leading idea of Proudhon's in the industrial field, coupling with it Proudhon's originally anarchistic conception of "contract" in the political field; added his own experience of the growth and decay of opposed groups through "frontier" contacts, his own faith in the possibilities of mutual understanding and good sense between them, given favorable conditions, and his own experience in the law courts of the actual process of interest adjustment through judicial procedure; and emerged with a new and enlarged view of "contractualism." Its core henceforth was the essentially judicial—or psychological—process of *débat,* and its machinery was group, not individual, pressure.

What if, in the end, De Greef sought to buttress his theory with a "system" composed of all Comte's hierarchy and Spencer's elaborate formula of evolution thrown in? The core remains essentially his own, an interpretation by a participant of the processes of group pressure and accommodation in his own land.

Just as Tarde, with his "laws of imitation," is seeking to interpret the close-knit society of middle-class France; Gumplowicz, with his "race struggle," the conflict situation of imperial Austria; and Giddings, with his "consciousness of kind," the melting-pot of nineteenth-century America, so De Greef, with his syndicalistic internationalism, his theory of "contract" and frontiers, neatly represents the hopes and fears of a section of Belgium, once the buffer-state of Europe and the center of a highly class-conscious and interdependent economic life.

NOTES

1. For a fuller treatment of De Greef's life and works see the writer's *Guillaume De Greef: The Social Theory of an Early Syndicalist* (New York, 1925). For a full list of De Greef's books and articles see *ibid.,* pp. 385–86.

2. *Régime représentatif* (Brussels, 1920), p. 293.

3. Comte believed that, once the study of society itself had become truly scientific, the present disorganization of human life would cease and everything would proceed according to reason and love.

4. *Structure générale des sociétés* (3 vols.; Paris, 1908), II, 126.

5. *Ibid.*, pp. 10–11.

6. *Ibid.*, pp. 111, 177, 181.

7. *L'Ouvrière dentellière* (Brussels, 1886), chap. xiv.

CHAPTER XXIX

REPRESENTATIVE ITALIAN CONTRIBUTIONS
TO SOCIOLOGY: PARETO, LORIA,
VACCARO, GINI, AND SIGHELE

W. REX CRAWFORD, *University of Pennsylvania*

I. THE RETARDATION OF SOCIOLOGY IN ITALY

ONE might suppose that sociology would have had a specially warm reception in Italy and would be extensively cultivated there, for no other country had a more promising tradition in this area of thought. Vico is regarded by many as the real father of sociology; Beccaria was one of the most influential sociological writers of the eighteenth century; Gaetano Filangieri, in the latter part of the eighteenth century, was regarded as the continuator of Montesquieu and a leader of rational social thought. A generation later, Gian Romagnosi joined with Henri de Saint-Simon in calling for a synthetic social science to guide legislation. In the second third of the nineteenth century, Giuseppe Ferrari, deeply influenced by Vico, offered a sociological theory of revolutions and charted the alleged states of social progress. Italy was the home of criminal anthropology and sociology, as expounded by Lombroso, Ferri, and Garofalo.

But the early promise of enthusiastic cultivation of systematic sociology in Italy was not borne out in later experience. In many circles sociology was identified with the positivism of Comte, owing, in part, to the prestige of the sociological writings of Roberto Ardigò (1828–1920), the great Italian Positivist. This helped to discredit it, on the ground that it was old and outmoded and also because this type of philosophy offended the dominant Italian philosophers, like Croce and Gentile, who were under the spell of neo-Hegelianism and neoidealism. Moreover, the philosophy of law is an old and powerful academic vested interest in Italy, and its custodians feel that all that is really valid in sociology is covered by this discipline. Italian economists and political scientists feel much the same way about sociology, holding that they

553

offer all of value in the subject incidental to their teaching in their chosen field. Sociology in Italy is, thus, at best a sort of academic step-child. As a result, the best-known Italian sociologists, such as Roberto Michels, Corrado Gini, Alfredo Niceforo, and Giovanni Lorenzoni, have to sneak in their sociology as incidental to other lines of teaching. For example, Lorenzoni, a really able sociologist, is compelled to devote himself mainly to agricultural economics in the Instituto Cesare Alfiere at Florence.

Fascism in Italy increased the difficulties under which sociology had to operate in Italy. Work in the field of social psychology had to be limited mainly to fascistic adulation of the spirit of the nation and sup-port of a folk culture. The Fascist stress on population increase rendered impossible any scientific and critical approach to population problems. Gini's widely known work on the population question arrives at con-clusions so beautifully suited to the teachings of the Fascist regime that its objectivity seems dubious to an American observer. It is not to be wondered that, along with Gini, the Italian sociological writers most esteemed during the Fascist regime were a naturalized foreigner, Roberto Michels, who contended that democracy always ends in oligarchy, and Vilfredo Pareto, an Italian, who never taught in Italy and whose social theories vindicate the Fascist doctrine of the rule of the élite.

There is, of course, no dearth of sociological writings in special fields in Italy. The influence of the criminal sociologists is still strong. Eman-uele Sella astutely analyzed the process of competition; Michelangelo Vaccaro produced the most thorough study of social adaptation; Nice-foro worked out a biological theory of class stratification; Giuseppe Gergo exploited genetics to buttress aristocratic social theories; Achille Loria produced a classic doctrine of economic determinism; Scipio Sig-hele and Pasquale Rossi brought out two of the best books on the psychology of the crowd, comparable to Le Bon's studies in France; Fausto Squillace wrote what was, a generation ago, the best brief history of sociology and edited an encyclopedia of sociology. But Pareto is the only Italian whose work can qualify as anything like systematic sociology.

In our presentation of Italian sociology we shall limit ourselves to five men—Pareto, Loria, Vaccaro, Gini, and Sighele—as representative of leading trends in Italian sociology. For a summary survey of Italian sociology the reader is referred to chapter xxv of Barnes and Becker's *Social Thought from Lore to Science.*

II. VILFREDO PARETO: RESIDUES, DERIVATIONS, AND THE ÉLITE

A. GENERAL CHARACTER OF PARETO'S SOCIOLOGICAL INTERESTS AND WRITINGS

If education is in some sense a progressive disillusionment, the work of Vilfredo Pareto must crown all preceding sociological theory, for he is the most disillusioned of all the great system-builders. Faith in the legends of the past is entirely lacking in him; he criticizes savagely our pretty hopes for progress and reform in the future; even that last refuge of a modern mind, faith in science, is thrown overboard, for, while scientific method has had no more ardent defender, he possesses none of the usual belief that the scientific truth will make us free or good or produce any social utility. Society may thrive on lies, and the verified truth of science, which he will always follow, may lead us to hell instead of to heaven.

If in disillusionment Pareto may be allowed to have the last word, in another sense his work is the swan song of an era that will never return, for the day of system-builders in social thought is over, and specialized research is prone to look back upon it very critically. Yet it must be remembered that even a man whose system is as a whole an ambitious but unacceptable failure, failing even in some of the phases he emphasized most, may have much influence. Aldous Huxley avows this influence upon his thought; one suspects its presence, though not directly avowed, in James Harvey Robinson and other writers in English; and some are impressed by the fact that Mussolini in his Lausanne days may have heard the lectures of Pareto. This is to say that the direct academic influence of the method of Pareto has been great; in fact, one Italian economist assured the writer that in his country it had been both small and pernicious. The greatness of our author is the man rather than the method. Certain of his ideas are vital and meaningful, but the system as a whole seems fruitless. No one would today go to Thorstein Veblen for an answer to all the problems of economics; but once read him, and you will never forget certain things: in innumerable situations of your own life his theories will jump into your mind, while Marshall and Taussig are forgotten. Pareto is like that. In spite of all the difficulty of language and form, there is something about Pareto that comes home to men's business and bosoms. He is best approached as a valuable adjunct to your newspaper, the political speeches that spout from your radio, the sermons you hear. Treat him not as something to be studied but as a help to understanding the life that all of us lead. His book is no mere monument of historical erudition—though much of it will be over the heads of those who do not know their Greek and Roman history and their French and Italian parliamentary history. Remember that the author of the formidable *Trattato di sociologia generale,* whose appearance may remind you vaguely of someone, whom upon reflection you discover to be Michelangelo's "Moses," boasted the best wine cellar in Switzerland.

Vilfredo Pareto was born in Paris, July 15, 1848, the son of an exiled Genovese nobleman and a French mother. The family returned to Italy when he was ten; and his education, partly classical, partly mathematical and scientific, was completed at Turin. As an engineer he held several important positions in the Italian railways. His advocacy of free trade brought him into sharp conflict with the policies of the Italian government. He was studying constantly and eventually came under the influence of Leon Walras, whose theory of economic equilibrium he was to perfect. Pareto's intention to retire and devote himself to science made his appointment at the University of Lausanne in 1893 very acceptable to him. His major works are those of a man over fifty. In fact, the *Trattato,* English translation, *The Mind and Society*—we shall not be concerned with his economics—was published only between 1915 and 1919. Pareto's death occurred on August 19, 1923.

It is hard to bring out the greatness and originality of Pareto's work, because it is, as all commentators agree, one of the worst-arranged books in the world. The student who approaches the *Trattato* today is fortunate in having at his disposal what has been called with much justification "the finest translation of any sociological work ever made," the magnificent four-volume *The Mind and Society,* edited by Arthur Livingston. This is without doubt an improvement on both the Italian original and the French translation, which had the benefit of Pareto's advice; it is both more correct and more readable, and it has taken no unwarranted liberties with the original, retaining, for instance, Pareto's arrangement by numbered paragraphs, to which all references are made in the present discussion. An airplane view of the enormous territory reveals some outstanding features which we shall meet again and again as we explore it on foot. Pareto's aim is nothing less than the high one of writing a sociology which is a science. The facts of sociology are human actions, and, with human nature what it is, most of such actions are bound to be illogical and sentimental, the outgrowth of a need in human nature to act in such and such a way (residues) rather than the result of the petty reasonings (derivations), elaborate but specious, by which we justify our acts. What these residues and derivations are, in what proportion they exist in different parts of society and in the same society at different times—this is the key to the form of society and to the shifts and changes chronicled by history.

Pareto proposed to take only experience and observation as his guides, presupposing nothing and hoping only to achieve ever closer approximations to the truth. It may be that he here assumes rather uncritically that there is a pot of gold at the end of his rainbow, for truth can be most satisfactorily defined as that which we approach by successive readings, i.e., that with which we are satisfied just because we have sworn to ourselves that that is the sort of thing we would be satisfied with. But most readers will find Pareto quite skeptical enough, so much so that he speaks of skepticism itself as a metaphysical a priori theory and of materialism as practically a religion; like Rémy de Gourmont, he is so free a thinker that he rejects the label "free thinker." Humanitarian or Christian sociology is as absurd to Pareto as Christian chemistry or Marxist physics; his most insistent plea is that this science, like any other worthy of the name, must pursue, regardless of consequences, the logicoexperimental method. If there is a realm within which such a method has no application, Pareto resolutely avoids it. This procedure from concrete cases to general principles may not lead us to the origin of phenomena or to their metaphysical essence, and it may not—contrary to the common illusion—even produce anything socially or individually useful, but it is the only method by which we may attain those highest degrees of probability we know as truth.

If all this talk of objectivity—the ruling-out of the author's feelings—this anxiety to separate a knowledge of the uniformities observable in human society from the attempt to remold that society nearer to the heart's desire, has a somewhat familiar ring, it must be admitted that Pareto has illustrated it endlessly and insisted upon it with unexampled and perhaps unscientific vehemence. There are some who are not to be convinced by logicoexperimental methods, but the main thing we must guard against is the pseudo-experimental and pseudo-logical; all religions, including Pareto's *bêtes noires*—solidarity and humanitarianism—offer us pseudo-scientific proofs, which will have no part in the social sciences when these have become really scientific. We must start with no a priori principles to be held and defended at all costs but only with facts and hypotheses, repeatedly checked by facts. Principles must be subordinated to facts.

Like others who despise philosophy, Pareto seems naïvely sure that he will know a fact when he sees one. Valuable is his observation that beliefs, superstitions, religions, whether true or false, are social facts. In paragraph 69 (Pareto numbered his treatise by paragraphs and desired all references to be made to these numbers), he summarizes his procedure, a procedure designed to yield logicoexperimental truth in sociology. The results may or may not be socially useful, i.e., he rejects the a priori principle that experimental truth and social utility always coincide.

There follow in the *Trattato* many protestations of the purity of his scientific intentions and claims that predecessors have written only sentimental ethics. The great thing is to distinguish between theories subject to experimental verification and those that are not; such a distinction is much more fundamental than the usual one between inductive and deductive methods.

Progress in science means greater and greater precision, precision in language and quantitative expression of social facts wherever possible; these will lead us to theories which are increasingly satisfactory, i.e., which account for larger and larger proportions of the facts. So, setting aside those sins that so easily beset us, our sentiments and the words that evoke them, we shall begin with the classification of social facts.

B. THE DOCTRINE OF LOGICAL AND NONLOGICAL ACTION IN SOCIETY

Pareto envisages his problem as one of finding divisions among human actions which are analogous to those in botany. He considers the most useful classification one into logical (which fit the means to the end in view) and nonlogical actions. Subjectively, of course, an action may seem logical without being so objectively. The most important outcome of observation of human actions is the conclusion that everywhere and at all times nonlogical actions have played a tremendously important role. Acts which come not from reasoning but from a certain psychic state are bolstered up and justified by reasoning—"rationalization" is a term, invented by Ernest Jones, which Pareto seems not to have known. The late Professor Max Handman summarizes the whole process: "For

Pareto, the whole phenomenon of social life becomes a series of equations in which ineluctable sentiments mask their inescapable push by a series of accidental manifestations frantically trying to conform their non-logical character to an equally ineluctable necessity to appear logical to themselves as well as to others.....The history of mankind is therefore a succession of efforts to appear logical."[1]

Reasoning has so little force as motive power that one might almost say it must be changed into sentiment in order effectively to determine conduct (par. 168). Behavior (B) depends upon the unknown psychic state (A) but is justified by a theory (C), which is usually not strictly logical in its connection with (B). Magic in the ancient and Christian eras provides many examples of entirely nonlogical action, for which sometimes theological, sometimes logicoexperimental, explanations are provided. Such examples show a kernel of acts and words more or less constant, while the logical interpretations tacked onto them are quite secondary and change with fads in thinking (par. 217).

Pareto finds traces of the nonlogical even in the various theories or descriptions of social facts. The importance of nonlogical action has been minimized or seen through a glass darkly by the theorists of the past, who have found it simpler to construct theories of logical action than to arrive at a theory that covered all the complex facts of nonlogical action. One may legitimately question here whether Pareto's assumption of the relative complexity of the two fields is justifiable. Are not McDougall's instinctivism or dogmatic Freudianism, in spite of their emphasis upon the nonrational, quite too simple, much simpler than many a logical edifice of scholasticism?

The body of Pareto's treatment of this subject is a very acute exposure of the logical failures of certain celebrated writers. Fustel de Coulanges, Polybius, Maine—even Aristotle and Plato—are castigated. Comte, Spencer, and Mill had glimpses of the importance of sentiments, but they, with Condorcet, Montesquieu, and Voltaire, failed to attain a well-balanced attitude toward the nonlogical in human action. It is an error to think of such action as merely absurd and pathological (par. 309) or as artifices by which, for instance, a priestly caste foists a religion useful to themselves upon the people (par. 314). Real precision is also lacking in the forerunners and founders of sociology and is of singularly little value as a description of social phenomena; it deserves our study as a horrible example of the way the human mind works. Moreover, the tremendous influence of some logically negligible theories is very instructive to the student of social psychology.

An infinity of examples demonstrates that even supposedly rigorous reasoning abounds in meaningless affirmation, sentiment, introduction of the terms "ought" or "must," which correspond to no objective reality. Again we must affirm that sociology should seek only the relations which experience shows; for there is no other principle higher than repeated experiment. Authority and introspection are offered as proofs of religion, but neither has logicoexperimental validity, and Pareto feels that no faith is more scientific than another, although some or all of them may be of supreme social utility.

C. THE CORE OF PARETO'S SOCIOLOGY: RESIDUES AND DERIVATIONS

Pareto next turns to examine theories which make a real pretense of logicoexperimental methods, theories in which a nonexperimental part is hidden or implicit. Cases in which we know both a legend and the corresponding—but different—fact enable us to confront the a priori with the experimental. This is the only valid method, for clinging to what does not *seem* to us as critics to be fabulous gives us merely verisimilitude, not truth. Such a procedure shows us that legends form like crystals around a grain of sand, which is just the concrete expression of a sentiment (par. 675). Our author illustrates a series of ways in which legends may be built up: by poor etymology, by fortuitous association of ideas, by false deductions from real facts, by twisting of the facts in the process of translation from primitive languages. At this point the critique of diffusionist theories and erroneous interpretations of the beliefs and practices of past civilization occupies some scores of pages without advancing us very far toward our author's own contribution, which really begins with Volume II of the Italian edition.

The way has been prepared for our recognition that there is a kernel or core that is a constant part of, let us say, purification ceremonies, and a variable part, which comprises the detailed methods used and the reason advanced for their efficacy. The constant part Pareto calls the "residue," the variable part "derivation." Pareto admits in *Fatti e teorie* that these names are merely convenient, shorthand labels and that any others would do as well. As explanation of such constants in human behavior as he calls "residues," Pareto gives us nothing better than the phrase that they are "manifestations of sentiments," to be studied further by the psychologist but to be accepted as data by the sociologist. Premises for rigorous reasoning they cannot be, but they are as valuable data for sociology as the illogical forms of language for philology.

Residues have been sought unconsciously by sociologists in the past, for they are the forces which explain social equilibrium. Pareto discusses some fifty residues, but they fall into the following six classes (we add the paragraphs in which each is discussed):

    I. Residues of combination (889–990)
   II. Residues of the persistence of aggregates (991–1088)
  III. Residues (or needs) of the manifestation of sentiments through overt acts (1089–1112)
  IV. Residues in regard to sociability (1113–1206)
   V. Residues of the integrity of the individual (1207–1323)
  VI. Sexual residues (1324–96)

Although the strength and proportions of these residues vary from time to time and from social group to social group, they are the constant elements of any social system.

The first class of residues results in our combining certain things, usually for no logical reason, although we seek to give logical reasons for the faith we have in them. Thus we believe that dreams reveal useful information about winning numbers in a number game, that certain days are lucky or unlucky, that certain plants are curative in their properties, without any logicoexperimental ground for our belief. The similarity which makes the combination plausible may be most fantastic; magic furnishes innumerable examples, as do prophecies and presages attending the birth of heroes and divinities. What we say about such beliefs is only a dress or veil for the reality, which is the operation of a residue. Modern beliefs that good is always associated with progress, democracy, universal suffrage, and the people are no more logical to Pareto's way of thinking than such obvious examples of magic. Powerful and widespread sentiments which link mysterious remedies with mysterious diseases and certain numbers with nobility or perfection still exert their influence and must be invoked to explain current social phenomena. Humanitarianism and solidarity are no more than combinations of all that pleases the sentimentality of our intellectuals, covered with a varnish of logic. It is, to be sure, difficult to distinguish a combination of elements A and B, which is proved experimentally, from one believed in as a matter of sentiment; there is, in Pareto's homely illustration (par. 981), an apparent similarity between the propositions that a rooster with hens produces eggs and chickens and that a rooster crowing at midnight means a death, for many instances can be adduced to prove the truth of the latter.

The second class of residues, those of persistence of aggregates, implies that, by a sort of inertia, aggregates once constituted or personified tend to persist; as Rémy de Gourmont pointed out in his *Dissociations des idées,* attempts at their disunion encounter powerful opposition. All the survivals of customs persisting after their causes have disappeared illustrate residues of this class, as does the persecution of sexual "heretics," which is a manifestation of attitudes similar to those of the Inquisition. The cult of the family, city, or country and the myth of Nordic superiority are essentially the persistence of an aggregate comprising a man and other men or places. Similarly, the relation between the dead and the living, or between the dead and their belongings, is only a manifestation of this residue, however much we may dress it up in "derivations." Even abstractions like progress, socialism, or pacifism are dynamic aggregates, lacking only personification. As the residues of Class I may be said to account for innovation, so these of Class II account for the conservation of things as they are.

Both these classes of residues are criticized by Carli (*Teorie sociologiche*) as being merely tautologous. Why, he asks, forsake behaviorism by adding an unseen, and unseeable, residue to the observed fact of combining? A less valuable criticism is that Pareto forces diverse data into the Procrustean bed of his scheme. Pareto might reply that it is just the merit of his social theory to have pointed out the hidden force behind apparently unlike phenomena and that Newton and others of our greater scientists have been doing just that.

An illustration in point may be found in the seventh chapter, which begins with the discussion of residues of Class I. Shamanism and revivalism may seem to have only the remotest of connections with a dog's wagging his tail, but our author sees them both as results of a need for manifesting sentiments in external acts. Shamanism and the religious exaltation of modern civilization are alike in essence, although differing in the derivations imagined in order to explain the facts.

Those residues which make man a social being are grouped in Class IV. The conduct to which they lead may be seen in the necessity of being just like everybody else which a style imposes and in every sort of standardization, making individuals take the mold of some social group, large or small, to which they belong. Pity and cruelty and neophobia, or the fear of innovations as upsetting established uniformity, are discussed in this connection. One of the most interesting subdivisions is asceticism, a sort of renunciation characterized by great intensity and slight social utility and found far beyond the limits of medieval Christianity, for Christian doctrine is only one of the (plausible) derivations employed to give a color of reasonableness to this class of residues. The social processes which take place are unfortunately slighted by Pareto, just as he pays too little attention to custom, tradition, and what we should now generally call "cultural" factors in human behavior. In spite of the name given to these residues of sociability, there is some justification for the charge that thus far Pareto is writing only individual psychology.

Complementary to the preceding class are residues of Class V, which manifest those sentiments opposed to alteration of the social equilibrium. Pareto's name for these is "residues of integrity of the individual and of his dependents." Most of us do not talk in terms of integrity, equilibrium, or residues, but the terms "just" and "unjust," which we do use, really refer to the maintenance or disturbance of an equilibrium. Powerful sentiments rather than good reasoning lead us to resent every attack on ourselves as individuals or on the society of which we are part and to attempt to restore the moral status quo, although the thing done is nonlogical or pseudo-logical. Lynching of the wrong person, which has occasionally happened, is logically absurd but satisfies our sentiments; *something* has been done.

The analysis of the sexual residue in Class VI concludes the long section devoted to the constant elements that underlie the varying theories and ideologies observable in human history. It should be noted that various residues often unite in complex forms, such as the union of asceticism with the sexual residue, which gives us a "sexual religion," with taboos that are never observed and which in their rigidity serve to generate perversion and hypocrisy. As Walter Lippmann, has remarked, one of our troubles in America is that Americans "desire to do so many things that they also desire to prohibit." It is present (he would agree with Freud here) even where repugnance or hate for the union of the sexes is most vehemently protested. Certainly, there would be little of European literature without the sexual residue.

Pareto next turns to the ways in which men dissimulate, change, and explain the true character of their acts, namely, to the derivations, whether they are logical or sophistical arguments, whether their premises accord with experience, or whether they have social utility. Contrary to the common opinion, which mistakes them for logicoexperimental science, they are only nonlogicalexperimental manifestations of our need to reason and are of quite secondary importance. As syllogisms, derivations frequently err by dropping out the weakest term. Our task is, however, more than the logician's discovery of error; we are interested in why the error is accepted as truth by so many. Disregarding minor subdivisions, the classes of derivations are (with the paragraphs in which they are analyzed) as follows:

I. Affirmations (1420–23)
II. Authority (1434–63)
III. Accord with sentiment or principles (1464–1542)
IV. Verbal proofs (1543–1686)

By derivations of Class I, Pareto means simple affirmations or statements, not subordinate to experience as science is, although real or imaginary facts may be cited in support of the derivation. Such taboos without sanction play a diminishing role in modern times. The language of the affirmation or the fact that it appears in print makes it more acceptable.

Authority also persuades and is accepted as demonstration, although the competence of the authorities in the field in question may or may not be experimentally supported. Those who are skeptical in religion may accept the poorest of authorities on the effect of alcohol. The authority of the past, as embodied in tradition and custom, has tremendous power, as has the Divine Will, impossible as it is to ascertain it.

The residues of sociability lend strength to derivations which appeal to the consensus of people, although history shows the opinion of the majority to have been wrong often enough. Allied to these derivations are those arguments that sophistically would persuade us that conduct for the benefit of others is really to our own interests. The attempts of Bentham, Kant, and others to reconcile the logically antagonistic egoistic and altruistic principles are relentlessly criticized.

An entire chapter, concluding Volume II of the *Trattato,* is devoted to the limitless complexities of derivations of the type called "verbal proofs." Such derivations are usually joined to the other types and may have several different residues underlying them. The chief source of error is the use of terms that do not correspond exactly to things. Thus everyone gets out of the terms "liberty" and "solidarity" just what he wants. Or the adjectives "true," "right," "real," or "scientific" are prefixed to "liberty," "love," "religion," "science," or the "sales tax"; in such instances truth means agreement with your sentiments, not with the facts. Rousseau, careless of facts, took from modern society all he disliked and called the remainder "Nature." Metaphorical and allegorical arguments, as used by dozens of authors, offer a mass of material for Pareto's mordant analysis. Such criticism may expose logical absurdities but leave social utility untouched; mythologies are not real, but they may be useful.

Paragraphs 1687–2059 of the *Trattato* constitute the lengthy discussion of the properties of residues and derivations. How do they operate to produce a given type of society? The common opinion errs in thinking derivations the causes of human actions. Pareto finds the explanation of the movements of social phenomena rather in the varying strength of residues, pointing out that the residues of Class I vary little and slowly, those of Class V scarcely at all, but some of the other subgenera vary considerably. The best index of the social state of a people is the proportion of the various classes of residues. Within any given society the residues differ in the many strata of that society, for they vary with occupation, physical environment, and social class, since facts influence the residue as well as vice versa.

Other relations of interdependence are the action of residues on other residues or of derivations on residues and other derivations. The influence of derivations upon residues may be illustrated by newspapers, for their arguments are few and logically not good, yet they do influence sentiments. When a derivation is in fashion, others like it spring up by a process of imitation.

From the wealth of illustration and diagrammatic representation of interrelations of residues and derivations we cull only Pareto's acute observation that the majority of strong residues cannot be contrary to the welfare of society, or it would cease to exist. These residues and the precepts which are based upon them will best be followed if individuals are made to believe that they conduce to their own happiness. Hence no society can exist without some morals, some religion. As a maxim for statesmen, Pareto proposes: Talk about eternal justice, but act as if there were none. It is useful that people should believe that the gods fight for them. This subject serves to introduce Machiavelli, about whom Pareto asks the now commonplace question: Shall we call him immoral merely because he described facts?

D. THE ÉLITE, SOCIAL CLASSES, AND SOCIAL PROGRESS

Pareto gives us an acute discussion of the circulation of the élite classes in society. Although the discussion of the form of society and social equilibrium occupies relatively little space in the *Trattato*, the whole work is pointed toward it, and it is in this connection that we meet Pareto's theory of the cyclical movement of social phenomena, the most clearly sociological part of his writing. History is a cemetery of aristocracies (par. 2052), for the social equilibrium is constantly being disturbed by the accumulation of inferiors in the upper class or superiors in the lower. Evolution finally comes when the upper classes do not have the residues adapted for governing and the lower classes do.

Pareto concluded his work with a discussion of the general form of society and with historical illustrations of the principles involved. To determine entirely the state of society it would be necessary to know the physical environment, the influence of other societies and of earlier states of the one in question, as well as the internal factors of which the residues are only one. These and a few like statements, made as briefly by Pareto as they are here, show that he was not unaware of the complexity of social phenomena when he chose to write of one or a few aspects only.

The molecules of society are individuals, in whom exist sentiments manifested by residues, which, in turn, are manifested in derivations. Unfortunately, only derivations are known to us, and they are not exact in their correspondence to the residues.

How may society move in the direction of the goals it sets itself? What is the relation of utility (which measures our progress) to the residues and derivations? Pareto maintains that no society can maintain itself by reason; it lacks the necessary data. Every society, past and present, uses force instead of reason; all countries are governed by oligarchies using force. The convenience of these theories to the Fascist philosophy of government is obvious. When the governing class loses the capacity or willingness to use force, it is desirable that the governed use it and that the government pass into their hands.

Among the various factors that help to determine the type of society that Pareto thinks the most important to which he can direct our attention is a division of society into two classes: *S* (*Speculators*), whose income is variable and depends on their sagacity, and *R* (*Rentiers*), whose income is fixed or nearly so and is nonspeculative. In the former, residues of Class I predominate; in the latter, residues of Class II. Now the most prosperous society is the one in which the most important residues are found in such proportion that, while the residues of Class I are strong enough to lead the nation to innovate, those of Class II are also strong enough to secure for it all the advantages that may be derived from the new combinations. It is to be desired that the leaders should be strong in residues of combination, the followers in residues of the persistence of aggregates.

Leaders maintain themselves in power by various combinations of force and artful use of existing sentiments and residues. Characteristically modern are the prevalence of interests (economic), the intensity of circulation of the élite, bringing into the governing class those who produce wealth, and the recruiting to this class by offering them chances to acquire wealth of individuals who might prove dangerous to the governing group. If such recruiting does not take place, in the absence of a free use of force, sooner or later there will be an uprising and inversion of classes.

E. A SUMMARY EVALUATION OF PARETO'S SOCIAL THOUGHT

Implicit in all the individual objections that may be made to Pareto's sociology is one all-embracing criticism—it is not science, there is no way of demonstrating it; Pareto has illustrated his theory endlessly, after the manner of Spencer or Frazer, but another might accept his general framework and yet arrive at an entirely different series of residues and derivations, might find, back of a given derivation, an entirely different residue from the one Pareto discovers, and yet neither could be proved to be wrong. It is as hopeless as the Freudians and their symbols, their latent dream content. It suffers the general imperfection of instinctivist theories; they put something into human beings and then explain all conduct by what they have put in. Pareto claims to have discovered uniformities in human conduct; has he found them, or has he made and selected them himself? Perhaps, as Handman concludes, the work is "monumental because of that very passion for a scientific approach which it does not reach and for the terrific blows it gives to the numerous preconceptions different from its own." The general attitude of the work has a fructifying influence; but, specifically, it has pointed out a road that is yet to be followed and, in our opinion, is unlikely ever to be very productive. We are more distrustful than Pareto of large historical generalizations, less willing to rest content with a superficial psychological analysis. The most imposing product of any mind in recent sociological writing, his work is likely to remain a monument rather than a stepping-stone.

III. ACHILLE LORIA: A SOCIOLOGICAL THEORY OF ECONOMIC DETERMINISM

Achille Loria, born in 1857, taught economics successively at Siena, Padua, and Turin. His long career as author and teacher earned him the reputation of being Italy's leading economist and secured an appointment as senator. It is pathetic to think that so much brilliance, so many books, should end only in a footnote to history; we may remind ourselves that it is only one man in a million who merits even the footnote.

He is the author of a long series of works, many issued in repeated editions and translated into European languages and Japanese. No attempt will be made here to treat them exhaustively, for they are, for the most part, economic rather than sociological and, in spite of Loria's pleas that he is as modern as anyone, they speak a language that is old-fashioned today. Moreover, the central idea, while it is endlessly embroidered, applied, and supported, is one which can be briefly stated. The broad outlines of social development are determined by economic considerations, and of these the basic thing is land appropriation. Appropriation ended the regime of free land which obtained in primitive society and began a regime of associative labor under the coercion of the landholders. When their power is abolished, we shall return, at a higher social level, to a regime of free land and associative labor without the whip of the slave-driver. The theory has decided resemblances to that of Henry George, but it is probable that when their early works were written neither knew of the other. Loria's solution is not the same as George's; he would eliminate rent and profit, instead of appropriating rent for the state. The system of landownership which Loria saw around him in Italy molds his statement of the situation. There is little doubt that absolute ownership by a few did entail widespread social misery.

Loria's sensitive and sympathetic nature led him to seek a way out and to picture a utopia in which associative labor, freed from coercive control, should produce and enjoy in common the surplus which association renders possible.

Much of his work is a learned and ingenious attack upon orthodox political economy, for Loria recognized that his own rather peculiar and original system had little chance to gain acceptance before the ground was cleared of the others, which have, according to him, the common weakness of failing to see the very vital part played in all human history by man's relation to the land. This critical work is to be found in his *Analisi* (1889) and in *Il Capitalismo e la scienza* (1901). His own ideas are expounded in his *La Proprietà fondiaria e la questione Sociale* (1897) and in *La Sintesi economica* (1909) (translated and abridged by Paul as *The Economic Synthesis* [1914]). He applies his theory to the explanation of war in *Les Bases économiques de la justice internationale* (1912), translated, with supplementary chapter on the World War, in 1918 (cf. his *Aspetti sociali ed economichi della guerra mondiale* ["Economic Causes of the War"]). Collected essays, entitled *Verso la giustizia sociale* (3d ed., 1916), have a section which he thought of as sociological.

But if only one of his works is to be read, the student of sociology should choose *The Economic Foundations of Society* (translated into English from the 2d French ed., 1899). It elaborates and defends the thesis that our social institutions, particularly those which most directly control our thinking, i.e., morality, law, and politics, are organic products of the capitalistic system, which, in turn, depends upon the appropriation of land by the strong. Thus law is merely the means by which property is protected, the political system is an organization of property holders, and the morality they teach us all is their subtlest defense against attack.

This volume—the most clearly sociological of the series that Loria gave to the world—begins with the fundamental fact which no observer of Western civilization can fail to see, that our society falls into two classes, those who live without working and those who work without living, at least without living a life which one can call "human." Why do we find this condition? It is not an unavoidable outcome of the workings of human nature but, rather, the result of historical causes and destined to disappear in the final stage of social evolution.

The historical causes that have produced this outstanding characteristic of modern life become clear when we reflect that capitalism is impossible with free land and begins only when the mass of the people
are, by slavery, serfdom, or the mere fact that a dense population has
already appropriated the land, prevented from access to what should
be a God-given right.

When all the land is taken up, the worker loses the freedom of choice
which was his defense against the usurpations of capital and has no other
means of livelihood than to sell his labor to a capitalist for a price fixed
by the latter. He is forced to abandon to the capitalist the best part of
his product, which constitutes the profit of the latter. As time passes, the
profit-making mechanism becomes automatic and no longer needs the
violent methods of early slavery. The fact that the lowest possible wages
are paid is enough to prevent the workers' saving to acquire the land,
which is now held at high prices, or to migrate to countries where free
land still exists.

So the basis of capitalist property is always the same—the suppression
of free land, the exclusion of the worker from the land by various
methods from slavery to the simple fact that all the land is held by the
capitalist class. Meanwhile, labor, forced by the capitalist bosses to work
co-operatively, has enormously increased its output, although not so
much as if its association in labor were free and uncoerced. Of course,
it does not enjoy the full benefit of this increased power of production.

Capitalist property needs also, in order to maintain itself, a series of
connective institutions, which are able to guarantee it against all reaction
on the part of those excluded from possession of the land and to insure
the acquiescence of the victims. The chief of these are morals, law, and
the political constitution of society. All are organic products of capitalist
property.

Why do the workers not revolt to destroy the economic system which
holds them in thrall? The arrangements adopted by the capitalist class
are clever. It takes some unproductive laborers, pays them well for
doing nothing but standing ready to defend the status quo, while proportionately weakening the numerical power of the workers. More
than that, a morality which makes the workers fear revolt and endure
the dominance of the capitalist class and which, at the same time, restrains the capitalists from going too far and provoking insurrection
is inculcated from childhood.

The methods used to induce conformity and overcome the dictates of enlightened selfishness are terror, religion, and public opinion. Under slavery, terror is the principal form of moral coercion. Under serfdom, it is no longer dread of present punishment but the sanction of the future life which is the principal means employed. Christianity enjoys a clear superiority to other religions from this point of view. Throughout the feudal period it may be seen imposing upon both classes actions contrary to their real interests. Under modern industrial conditions, however, the same role is played by public opinion, exercising a despotic control over our attitudes and actions.

If morality is not able by its perversion of egoism fully to persuade all to act against their own interests, law steps in, absolutely to prohibit acts in accord with our real interests or to add to their commission penalities so severe that they cease to be dictated by enlightened self-interest. Other writers have, to be sure, vaguely understood this characteristic of law, but they have been hindered by ignorance of the economic element. The power of that element is shown, for instance, by the fact that law changes as economic relations change, and changes little if the object of its control is not closely related to economic life.

To carry the influence of economic arrangements one step further, we observe that in all the various historical forms of capitalism the owners of wealth appropriate political power. The economically dominant class is always the exclusive holder of political power.

Such are the basic ideas expounded in Loria's *Economic Foundations of Society*. They are supported by a wealth of historical illustration and impassioned attacks upon competing theories.

As for the immediate present and the future, Loria ventures the belief that an observant science can today discover the symptoms of decay in our society and can render easier the transition to a new society in which the peace and justice of the primitive age shall be recovered.

"Remarkable," "fascinating," and "learned" are all adjectives which these books deserve. But they leave even their best readers a bit uncertain as to whether they have been perusing one of the great economic masterpieces or merely a literary masterpiece expressing crank ideas. Probably we must reach the conclusion we commonly adopt in the fact of something that overwhelms us but that we neither understand nor like very well: "Brilliant, but unsound." Loria has drawn our attention to a neglected factor, but in detail the claims he makes are indefensible, the solution he proposes, vague and visionary.

IV. MICHELANGELO VACCARO: ADAPTATION AS THE FUNDAMENTAL SOCIAL PROCESS

Michelangelo Vaccaro, a distinguished lawyer of Rome, born in 1854, was the author of several eminently respectable, but scarcely exciting, works. One of his early books was an essay on the positive school of criminology,[2] in which Vaccaro attempted to reconcile the anthropological data, upon which Lombroso relied so heavily, with social data on crime and its causes. The struggle of society against crime and criminals can, with the progress of time, assume ever milder forms, like other aspects of the struggle for existence, and severe punishments tend to give place to reformation and prevention as penological ideals.

Vaccaro's reputation rests, however, chiefly upon studies in social Darwinism, which develop more fully the theories sketched in the volume on *Genesi e funzioni delle legge penali* (1908). One of these volumes, *La Lotta per l'esistenza e i suoi effetti nell'umanità,* reached a fifth edition in 1920. The other, which we shall use as source, since it is the mature expression of his sociological theory, was revised for the French translation which appeared in 1898 under the title, *Les Bases sociologiques du droit et de l'état.*[3] Both works are concerned with the struggle for existence; both seek support in nature and in history for the author's pious wish that the struggle shall in time be more and more disguised, assume ever more innocuous forms, and contribute more to progress through the better adaptation which is its fruit.

Sociology, Vaccaro maintains, is the crowning achievement of modern thought. It has enemies: (1) the conservative representatives of official science, sleeping in the heavy atmosphere of metaphysics and barring the doors of universities to the newcomer, and (2) the half-baked, superficial writers who like to call themselves sociologists but who have no valid claim to be considered scientists. Sociology will overcome this opposition and misrepresentation and solve its own problems. There is room for doubt as to its methodology and the value of its conclusions thus far, but none as to the fact that its field is human social phenomena and its aim the discovery of general social laws.

Such a general law—the supreme one which all history obeys—Vaccaro thinks he has found. Other authors have had glimpses of it, but no more. In the Introduction written for the French edition, Vaccaro pays his respects to them—Comte, Tarde, Gumplowicz, and especially Spencer. Even the latter, for all his emphasis upon adaptation, fails to treat the subject adequately, for he did not appreciate the true nature of groups and group interaction. His atomic individualism prevented his understanding the human plural and led him to confuse sociology with biology.

The fundamental social law, if you will let Vaccaro define "fundamental" to suit himself, is that of *adaptation*. The concept rests, to be sure, upon a biological foundation, and Vaccaro's biology is not only Darwinian but Lamarckian. Lamarck alone sufficiently emphasized the fact that the chief factors in the process of evolution are: (1) the influence of the environment as the cause of organic modification and (2) the hereditary transmission of these modifications. Add the thesis that the struggle for existence, selecting only the most fit for survival, leads organic life to adapt itself better and better to the environment in which it lives, and you have the biology upon which Vaccaro erects the superstructure of his sociological theory.

The method and the conclusion of Vaccaro's work may be briefly stated. Vaccaro examines adaptation between man and the cosmic forces, between man and the vegetable world, between man and other animals, and, finally, between human groups. Projecting the trends which all history reveals, we can, he believes, confidently prophesy the developments of the future. And, of course, his theory, centering around the idea of adaptation, explains to him better than any other the facts of social life, past and present. We shall not discuss the shaky biological foundation of his theory, for it is well known that biologists have abandoned Lamarckianism, or at any rate its cruder forms. Does Vaccaro's appealing concept fit the facts in his own field, that of social life?

All life is a process of adaptation of internal relations to external relations. Pleasure and pain are the natural means which bring it about, the inevitable teachers of human beings and animals alike.

Man, fortunately, can adapt himself to environment not only by being the passive raw material of selection, the object of nature's experiments, but also in a way which Bristol was later to call "active adaptation." Today, we should phrase it by saying that our culture is our mode of adaptation to our environment. No longer changing or being changed in our biological characteristics, we achieve the end of adaptation by the changed ideas in our heads and by the new tools in our hands. This latter process is less costly of human life and vastly more rapid than passive adaptation. Vaccaro saw clearly that adaptation is governed by its own laws and cannot fruitfully be studied as a mere branch of biology. He was, however, too eager to find applications of his pet idea to develop what would now be called the true "cultural approach" to sociology and history.

In the earliest days, man's struggle to reach terms on which he might live with nature and with other animals was unbearably difficult and often bloody, as is the struggle for existence among animals.[4] As mankind acquired artificial—cultural—means of adaptation, this conflict has assumed milder and milder forms.

Among men themselves the struggle for existence originally took the form of direct elimination of competitors, but it gradually became transformed into indirect elimination. How far this is from many facts of primitive life, Elliott Smith's *Human History* will have convinced readers who may not have examined the similar, but less partial, statistics of Hobhouse, Wheeler, and Ginsberg on the peaceable character of the simpler cultures.

A career of war and conquest, Vaccaro contends, becomes ever more difficult and profitless, adaptation more complete, and the forms of the struggle for existence less direct and sanguinary. Within political groups the military control of the conquered by the conquerors is replaced by more and more complete democracy. Unfinished though humanity's onward march may be, it is along a road on which all the signposts read: "To peace, to plenty, and to fellowship." No brutal instincts, no harsh necessities, will mar the beauty of the truly human civilization that will finally be achieved.

Perhaps Vaccaro has been given rope enough with which to hang himself. Comment seems almost superfluous. A little knowledge of the world in the years since Vaccaro wrote is the best commentary; for it does not appear that fighting has given way to voting or that voting always achieves adaptation or that there is an ever growing tendency toward democracy. On the contrary, it appears that Vaccaro's work may best be regarded as rationalization and wishful thinking, as a well-intentioned and doubtless unconscious distortion of biological and historical fact by his tender-mindedness—a distortion in the direction of the better and more peaceful world which he desired no more earnestly than do many of us who are more disillusioned about its speedy achievement.

V. CORRADO GINI: A BIOLOGICAL INTERPRETATION OF
HISTORY AND SOCIETY

Corrado Gini, born in 1884, professor of statistics in the University of Rome, is best known as a demographer. He has also contributed studies of the statistical aspects of war and of war materials. Various articles written by him between 1915 and 1920 are collected in his *Problemi sociologici della guerra.*[5] The principal topics discussed are the causes, effects, costs, and other statistics of the first World War.

His population theories are to be found in his *Nascita, evoluzione, e morte delle nazioni*[6] or in their English dress as part of a volume entitled *Population,* and consisting of the Harris Lectures at the University of Chicago, by Gini and others, and published by the Press of that university in 1930. The three lectures not only summarize Gini's thoughts on population to date but include a bibliography of his previous writings on the subject and copious notes on the literature both in support of and against his theory. While one American student of population, Professor H. G. Duncan, dismisses Gini as a borrower from other current population theories, "interspersed with puerile arguments based on antiquated biological and psychological theories," we feel that he merits attention.

In choosing his general title, "The Cyclical Rise and Fall of Populations," Gini is not thinking of world population but in terms of nations; he insists, somewhat in the face of general informed opinion, on considering nations as biological entities. The very title indicates Gini's rejection of the theory of a persistent geometric increase in population in any society. The facts, he finds, do not support that theory: the wealthy, who are not hindered by lack of the means of subsistence, notoriously have a low birth rate. It is not a valid objection to point to psychological considerations as the reason for that low birth rate; psychological controls are an essential factor in any statement of the population problem, not a mere extraneous factor "interfering" with the operation of a law. Moreover, primitive people often decline in number, even independently of contact with advanced civilization, and when their situation is not economically so bad as to force the decline. The so-called "geometric theory" is unsatisfactory, and Gini believes that many considerations favor a cyclical theory. Full proof of it we do not have at present; but, if our statistical knowledge were fuller, we should find evidence of a cycle and of the fact that human nature, rather than environmental factors, accounts for it.

The curve describing the population tendencies of any nation is a parabola. Families as well as peoples describe such curves in their history; in all classes of society, not only among the wealthy, they show vigorous growth followed by rapid exhaustion. Indeed, the very *Drosophila* and bacteria in our laboratories grow weary of reproducing, and their history may be told in their stages, corresponding to the youth, adult age, and senility of the single organism. In the earlier phases of population growth "each generation consists in a greater degree than its predecessor of the descendants of prolific individuals, so that the average fecundity of the population becomes higher." For a while this tendency just balances that toward exhaustion of the germinal cells, but finally the latter prevails.

In elaborating and applying this theory to the evolution of nations, Professor Gini concludes that "three-quarters of the generation which survives descends from a . . . . small fraction, varying from one-third to one-eighth per cent [*sic*] of the generation which is disappearing." This characteristic of population growth is the background of interesting social changes. If the upper classes are to maintain their numerical relation to the population as a whole, a current must flow to them from the middle classes, and, similarly, one from the lower to the middle classes. This phenomenon, obviously reminiscent of social capillarity, social mobility, and Pareto's *circulation des élites,* Gini prefers to call "demographic metabolism." It is a phenomenon which in the earlier phases of national evolution is feeble; hence during this period the lower classes must pour out their superfluous numbers in war and emigration. This and nothing else is the basis of national expansion. Later, in the period of maturity, the upper classes "absorb all or almost all of the individuals rising from the lower classes, who in their turn, have lost their most prolific elements through wars and emigration, and whose birth-rate has therefore already declined." "But as economic disparity increases and the reproductivity of the upper classes declines still farther, the rising current, although it grows, is, on the one hand, found to be insufficient, unless supplemented by emigration, to fill worthily the ever-widening gaps left by the governing classes; while on the other hand, the numbers of the low classes are reduced to an extent which interferes with the proper equilibrium of social functions."

Temporary checks account for distortions of this neat picture of what happens everywhere and at all times. Thus in England industrial expansion provided such magnificent opportunities for the upper classes that they continued to reproduce rapidly, while sanitary evils kept the death rate of the lower classes at a conveniently high level.

It remains to be added that the parabolic changes in rate of reproduction take place, first, in the upper classes. There is, it appears, a sort of providential mechanism for the elimination of "those family stocks which have fulfilled the cycle of their evolution." Soon the wealthy, the upper, classes are discovered to be desiring only small families, wherein Gini sees a "wise provision by which nature reconciles psychic tendencies with the physiological capacities of those classes who have advanced farthest along the parabola of their evolution." Birth control is not responsible; if the truth were known, it is that the urge of the genetic instincts has ceased. "The primary cause of the evolution of nations must be sought in biological factors."

Providence seems also to have arranged matters kindly so that an Italian statistician's demographic theory should accord with Italy's current aims and future glory. In young, strong nations, young people, optimistic and constructive, prevail; industry hums, arms conquer, poets sing, and historians chronicle their people's achievements. Every nation has its day and must use it to the best advantage.

To be sure, a caste system like that of India slows up the process of demographic metabolism; it encourages reproduction in the upper classes and insures a long, peaceful life to the nation. Gini, however, prefers the briefer but more intense life of our Western nations, which comes from freedom of circulation.

It will be seen that thus far Gini has provided a more or less plausible account of phases of demographic history but no explanation of the whole cyclical movement. Indeed, one is often at a loss to know of what length period or phase he is speaking; are these things that happen in three generations or a thousand years?

A nation has died, and a new one has been born. How? Can final decay ever be avoided and the instinct for reproduction revivified? A neighboring prolific stock of lower culture may offer itself as a drawer of water and hewer of wood and thus insinuate itself into a population, first, into the lower classes, then, as acculturation proceeds, into the middle and upper classes. New blood has entered into the old culture, or civilization has been transmitted to a younger sister-nation almost before anyone knows what is going on. And it should be thus; interference with nature's way does lead to sterility and decay. America refuses Italian immigrants at her peril, one reads between the lines. If many have already left Italy, taking their force and aggressiveness to the new world, Italy is only the gainer, for her homogeneity is increased by sloughing off the maladjusted. Cross-breeding or its variants, the abandonment of an artificial caste system or of an unfortunate regionalism, are the origin of new nations or the new greatness of old nations. Thus it is the magnificent centralization of government in Italy which is breaking down regionalism and providing the crossing of human stock, which is the biological backbone of Italy's greatness.

Gini returns to one topic on which his evidence is meager. How do we know that the decline of births is biological rather than Malthusian and that people do not have children because they cannot? The reason, it appears, is that the fruit of conception in the first three months of marriage has decreased, and Gini knows that there is no practice of contraception in the early months of marriage.

Much of Gini's general sociological theory has come out in the course of this survey of his population theory. He believes that nations are like individuals and that their history is a similar passing from youth spent in rapid growth to maturity and an age of eventual decay and death. He classes his theory "neo-organicism,"[7] and he insists that societies are like organisms in that they have powers of self-preservation and re-equilibration. They oscillate from their courses but are never immobile. What is valid in this theory seems both old and vague; what is new is unconvincing.

VI. SCIPIO SIGHELE[8]

We have now reviewed the doctrines of four typical Italian sociologists: Pareto the methodologist; Loria the economic determinist; Vaccaro, who combined economic and biological interpretations; and Gini, a sociobiologist. It seems natural to select, as a sample of Italian social psychology, Scipio Sighele, who is frequently joined with Tarde and Le Bon as one of the three leading pioneers in that subject in Romance countries.

Scipio Sighele was born on June 24, 1868, in Brescia and died in Florence on October 21, 1913. In his forty-five years or, rather, in the latter half of them, he wrote some twenty-five books, besides scattered smaller contributions in the form of articles, speeches, reviews, and pamphlets. It is not merely the quantity of his contribution to sociological literature that calls for comment; although he was decidedly a child of his age, there is enough that is individual and different about him to warrant brief examination and appraisal even today.

Sighele, who in several of his books was a collaborator with Enrico Ferri and whose works were called *belli e profondi* by Tarde, was, above all, a criminologist and social psychologist; but he was also a prolific writer on questions of sex and feminism, taking some contemporary event or book as a jumping-off place; an acute commentator on literature from the social and psychiatric point of view; and an ardent advocate of Italian nationalism. It is the interweaving of these themes and the peculiar character of his interest in them that constitute the attraction of Sighele to the student of the history of social theory.

Sighele thought of himself as a Positivist, in general, and especially in criminology, and was loyal in his enthusiastic adherence to the founder of his school, Cesare Lombroso. In an address delivered in Florence a month after Lombroso's death, he eulogized him as a genius and asserted that, whatever errors of detail time may reveal in his work, they would not invalidate its merit as an example of positive or scientific method in psychology and anthropology. Society is, he added, the debtor of the Italian school of criminology for insisting on the prophylaxis of crime, on the necessity of social defense through prevention as well as punishment.

It must be admitted that his scientific aspirations did not prevent Sighele in most of his writings from descending to the discursive, to the level of the impressionistic essay, to commentaries on newspaper accounts of sensational crimes, and a general "Doctor Looks at the World" attitude.

This is true even where Sighele's principal contribution was concerned. In social psychology, in crime, in sex relations, and in political processes, it was suggestion and suggestibility, the nonrational ascendancy of one person over another or over the group that impressed Sighele. It is by the narration of selected cases and by his unaided intuition that he chiefly supported his dictum that, as in love one person is more the lover and the other more the beloved, so in crime one is more the instigator, even if not the active agent, in committing the crime which seeks to eliminate inconvenient third and fourth parties.

It is only a step from the dour-faced and strong-minded French and Italian females that look at us from the pages of Sighele, the women who persuaded their weak or moral lovers to use the ax on the unwanted husband to *La Folla delinquente* and the less rigorously scientific, but equally characteristic, book on *L'Intelligenzia della folla*. It is in the former, which grew out of his thesis, translated later, like so many of his books, into various other languages, that Sighele evidently considered himself to have made his most original contribution. Criminology and social psychology meet here, since the crowd is a frequent criminal, just because it is highly emotional and suggestible. Sighele, no extreme democrat, seems to identify aristocracy with rationality and, therefore, to look down on the mob for being the easy prey of demagoguery and its own base instincts. He does, it is true, admit that one can find examples of a kind of collective virtue on the part of the vicious, the homage they pay at least verbally to the mores under which they live.

Crowds are, for Sighele, essentially impulsive and violent; the more diffused public is less so. He permitted himself to differ from Gabriel Tarde, who had called his time the era of publics, and to say that it is the epoch of crowds, only to retract in part later and maintain that both he and Tarde are correct. Le Bon, with whose name that of Sighele is often linked, he accused, in spite of his important contributions, of confusing collective, or crowd, psychology, which deals with temporary aggregates, with the psychology of peoples, or dynamic social psychology, which is, for Sighele, practically synonymous with sociology.

It is interesting and illuminating to note the names that Sighele mentions most frequently. The two just cited are, of course, among them, and Spencer and Taine are there, too. A well-informed scholar, even though he called himself to the end an "obscure student," Sighele knew many others, and when he wrote a manual on the social sciences he mentioned them; but not even there do we meet the names of American pioneers in sociology or any except the briefest mention of American social conditions or legislation. Instead, we find repeated and often lengthy studies of Tolstoy, Ibsen, Dostoevski, Bourget, Zola, Sue, and D'Annunzio. In addition to his interest in their intuitive and subtle observations in the field of criminal anthropology, psychiatry, and interpersonal (especially sexual) relations and his curiosity as to whether what we read may not contribute to the patterns of criminal conduct, Sighele was here operating frankly as the widely read and intelligent man who claims a right to be his own literary critic. If one were to seek in Sighele a model to follow, this concern of his with the relations between the literary and the scientific method might have something to offer to an American sociology that has barely begun to think through the problems of the sociology of art. Neither here nor anywhere, in the opinion of the writer, was Sighele particularly profound, but he does examine the case of Ingres's "Odalisque," to conclude that she is no worse for her extra four vertebrae, whatever the anatomist may say, and to extend the analogy to literature. At least implicitly, here is a theory of the proper activity of scientist and artist and of what we may expect from each.

Since the central theme of much of his thinking was complicity, with its team-mate, suggestibility, it was natural for Sighele to go on from the couple to the crowd, which for him is impulsive and violent and frequently identified with the masses in a disparaging sense, and thence to the criminal association and to what he calls the sect. "Crowd" is a term that he uses loosely as meaning the first degree of association, as is evident from his statement that the barbarians were the great crowds of antiquity, and workingmen the great crowd of today. In criticizing Tarde he shows that he is conscious of the necessity of distinguishing between crowds and publics, but the attraction of a single term for low-grade association is too powerful to be resisted. The sect, in his terminology, however, marks an advance in the scale, for it has a common faith, a shared ideal, and is a step toward the relative permanence of such sociological phenomena as caste, class, and state. It is more static than the crowd, but still violent, still suggestible. It will be apparent why he did not adopt the term "collective crime," which would have seemed altogether too general. Note that it is crime and, in general, the low morality of the group that he stresses. The collectivity is something to be welcomed by the social psychologist as an object of study, proving that he has a right to exist, along with other types of scientists, but that does not for a moment imply that Sighele likes or admires its crowd-like activities. We become more criminal, less intelligent, more emotional, in crowds; and Sighele is too much the intellectual, the aristocrat, to submit willingly to the process. He will admit (cf. Maurice Parmelee's "evolutive criminal") that the conduct of a sect, with its dissident faith, may be regarded as criminal at the time by those in power but may turn out in the long run to be progressive. Sighele held that, since our self-control is automatically and unintentionally reduced in crowd situations, this fact should be taken into account in fixing the penalty for crimes committed under the influence of crowd psychology.

What has been said may give a hint of Sighele's practical attitudes, but they demand further comment.

As a social psychologist and a patriot, he could not help wondering why Italians, individually so able and admirable, have a poor reputation as a nation, why they lack a collective soul worthy of them, why their crime rate—and for such crimes!—is so high. When he studied the chronicles of Italian crime it was in order to document an aspect of Italian social life. On the positive side, he became propagandist and exhorter, urging Italy to make her contribution to the world by being a greater nation, backing ardently the ideas of Crispi. He anticipated current discussion by insisting that Trieste must eventually be Italian, and many other places as well. A democrat can be, he insisted, an imperialist. He certainly was, and held exactly opposite ideas on the subject from, for instance, Nehru. Part of Italy's problem is to *far figli* ("beget sons"), and he woud apparently have sympathized with the abrupt disappearance from Italian railroad stations of little booklets on how not to beget them, which coincided with the trumph of fascism. Fascism would also have been congenial to him from another point of view, though he calls himself a democrat. His essay on parliamentarianism, published in *Morale privata e morale politica,* leaves no doubt as to his low opinion of that political pattern, for the now familiar reason that a parliament is a kind of crowd, its members acting inevitably on even a lower level than their individual capacity. Congressmen are elected by the crowd phenomena of oratory and newspapers. Imposture and immorality are inescapable in politics. A parliament is, in a sense, a woman, and a hysterical one at that. The whole system is created to worsen men and politics, not to improve them.

If we were to list Sighele as a feminist, it would have to be with much the same qualifications as surround his "democracy." He was interested in love, sex, and modern women, to be sure. But he said openly that career women are so unattractive that men can be trusted not to marry them. He would be willing to see divorces granted for insanity, and he would like to diminish the social distance between mistresses and servants, but certainly not to the point reached in present-day society.

In many ways an attractive figure, Sighele seems both out of style and uncongenial to our best contemporary orthodoxies of thought. Among the greatest contributions to the progress of the world, he says, we must list the "sword of the great captains." Other examples besides this civilian, rhetorical militarism have been given. Perhaps, however, it is just because his is not the voice of the here and now that we need to be reminded of Sighele and to turn once more to see if he had anything to offer the social scientist of today.

SELECTED REFERENCES ON PARETO

BOOKS

BARNES, H. E., and BECKER, HOWARD. *Social Thought from Lore to Science* (2 vols.; Boston, 1938), II, 1013–23.

BORKENAU, FRANZ. *Pareto.* New York, 1936.

BOUSQUET, G. H. *The Work of Pareto.* Hanover, N.H., 1928.

HANDMAN, M. S. "The Sociological Method of Vilfredo Pareto," in S. A. RICE, *Methods in Social Sscience—a Case Book* (Chicago, 1931), pp. 139–53.

HENDERSON, LAWRENCE. *Pareto's Sociology: A Physiologist's Interpretation.* Cambridge, Mass., 1935.

HOMANS, G. C., and CURTIS, C. P. *An Introduction to Pareto: His Sociology.* New York, 1934.

PARETO, VILFREDO. *Mind and Society.* Translated and edited by ARTHUR LIVINGSTON. 4 vols. New York, 1935.

SOROKIN, PITIRIM. *Contemporary Sociological Theories* (New York, 1928), pp. 37–62.

ARTICLES

ASCOLI, MAX. "Pareto's Sociology," *Social Research,* Vol. III (February, 1936).

BONGIORNO, ANDREW. "A Study of Pareto's Treatise of General Sociology," *American Journal of Sociology,* XXXVI (November, 1930), 349–70.

GINSBERG, MORRIS. "Pareto's General Sociology," *Sociological Review,* Vol. XXVIII (July, 1936), 221–45.

NOTES

1. In *Methods in Social Science—a Case Book,* ed. Stuart A. Rice (Chicago, 1931), p. 121.
2. *Genesi e funzione delle leggi penali* (Rome, 1889).
3. Published in Paris.
4. Kropotkin had not then written to upset this old-fashioned view of life in the animal world; neither had still later writers come along to make Kropotkin old-fashioned and paint Nature's teeth and claws a fresh vermilion.
5. Bologna, 1921.
6. Rome, 1930.

7. See *Il Neo-organicismo, prolusione al corso di sociologia* (University of Rome, 1927) (Catania, 1927).

8. The following list of Sighele's works gives the most important publications: *La Folla delinquente* (1891); *La Coppia criminale* (1892); *La Teorica positiva della complicità* (1893); *Mondo criminale italiano* (1893); *Mondo criminale italiano* (2d ser.; 1895); *Cronache criminali italiane* (3d ser.; 1896); *La Delinquenza settaria* (1897) (last ed. entitled *Morale privata e morale politica*); *La Donna nova* (1898); *La mala vita a Roma* (1899); *Mentre il secolo muore* (1899) (last ed. entitled *Idee e problemi de un positivista*); *L'Intelligenza della folla* (1903); *Le Scienze sociale* (1903); *Per l'università italiana a Trieste* (1904); *Per Francesco Bonmartini* (1906); *Letteratura tragica* (1906); *Cesare Lombroso* (1910); *Eva moderna* (1910); *Pagine nazionaliste* (1910); *Nell'arte e nella scienza* (1911); *Il Nazionalismo e i partiti politici* (1911); *La Crisi dell'infanzia* (1911); *Ultime pagine nazionaliste* (1912); *La Donna e l'amore* (1913); (repeats in part *Eva moderna*); *Letteratura e sociologia* (1914) (posthumous).

CHAPTER XXX

ADOLFO POSADA: THE "LESTER F. WARD" OF SPANISH SOCIOLOGY

Rex D. Hopper, *Brooklyn College*

I. SOCIOLOGY IN SPAIN

AMONG American students it is customary to assume that sociology has had no significant development in Spain. That this is true is evidenced by the fact that a knowledge of Spanish is not considered to be a necessary part of the research equipment of a sociologist.

Within limits and in a certain sense, the assumption is sound, and it is not my present purpose to challenge it. I am inclined to believe, however, that the effort to explain the retardation of Spanish social thought by using the "Catholic church" and "Latin temperament" as theoretical scapegoats is altogether too simple and represents a type of explanation resorted to by students whose linguistic shortcomings have prevented them from knowing what Spanish social theorists were really doing. Unfortunately, since events occurring in a peninsular appendage of Europe have never seemed important enough to demand overcoming the handicap, the explanation has been permitted to stand. Under the circumstances, therefore, another suggestion may not be altogether out of place.

It should occur to more sociologists than apparently it does that sociology itself is not so much the product of intellectual curiosity as it is the result of social necessity; that is, no less than every other form of human activity, the sociology of any given place or period comes right up out of the general conditions of that place and period. Furthermore, the particular emphasis at a given time is determined by the same conditions. All of us know, though at times some of us seem to forget, that "fact-gathering" (research) and "hypothesis-construction" (theorizing) are supplementary rather than antagonistic forms of scientific endeavor, the emphasis given the one or the other being determined by the social milieu. It is here suggested that in periods of relative stability and slow social change fact-gathering is emphasized and, the current

585

theoretical assumptions being taken for granted, hypothesis-construction is pushed into the background. Conversely, in periods of instability and rapid social change, hypothesis-construction comes to the foreground, and social theorists begin to examine the nature of the assumptions that determine the "facts" which they see.[1]

If what has just been said is valid, the explanation of what the American student calls the "retardation" of social thought in Spain is rather evident. Spain has always been plagued by social instability. Geographically peripheral to the great centers of revolutionary upheaval in the eighteenth and nineteenth centuries, the country was sufficiently influenced by the movement to be thrown into internal confusion and to suffer the loss of her colonial empire. However, the main currents of the development passed her by, and the present finds her still fighting the ideological battles of the nineteenth century. Her political and social instability, born of incomplete assimilation into the revolutionary movement that swept over the rest of the Continent, explains why social thought in Spain has always been philosophical and moralistic rather than experimental and fact-finding. It is for this reason that it has usually been viewed as "retarded."

In the light of this usual point of view, it is interesting to note that social thought in Spain got off to a good start as early as the sixteenth century, with the surprisingly modern work of such men as Juan Luis Vives and Francisco de Vitoria.[2]

As a result of the work of these and other pioneers, social thought in Spain appeared to be launched on a course quite similar to that which was charted in Europe generally. That might have been the case if developments in Spain had kept pace with events in other areas of Europe. Two factors, however, caused the route taken by Spain to diverge from the broad highway down which the rest of Europe was rushing toward the revolutionary movements of the eighteenth and nineteenth centuries.

The first of these influences is found in the fact that the Protestant Reformation, though for a time threatening to take root in Spain, was finally effectively stifled by the Counter Reformation.[3] In consequence, social thought was largely prostituted to the task of rationalizing the respective roles of church and state as they then functioned.

The second factor serving to cause Spain to swerve from the main course of development was her glaring success in the application of

Mercantilist doctrines to the administration of her colonial empire. In her effort to do this she was not, of course, in any sense peculiar; all the great European powers were undertaking to do likewise. But in the extent to which she was able to apply these theories she was the envy of her partners in crime. As a result of her success, social thought was debased to the function of providing intellectual justification for the colonial policy of "strict supervision and monopolistic control" through which Spain sought to keep her tottering internal economy from complete collapse by draining off the resources of her colonies.

Thus, in Spain the entire colonial period (1500–1800) was marked by the efforts of an absolutistic monarchy to build and keep in repair the intellectual dikes needed as protection against the floodwaters of the revolutionary storm gathering to the north. Though the very success with which Spain shut herself off from the rest of Europe spelled her eventual downfall, her policy did result in the effective throttling of significant social thought.

A temporary intellectual "shot-in-the-arm" was provided by the reaction of Charles III to ideological currents in France. The cooling breezes of French Physiocratic thought began to blow through the passes of the Pyrenees and influenced the emperor to inaugurate a program of reform which earned for him the title of "enlightened despot." However, the program came too late. The storm of the French Revolution caught the ship of the Spanish revival in mid-passage; and, though it might conceivably have weathered the gale had it not been for the death of Charles III, his successor was a ne'er-do-well son, who promptly wrecked the ship of state on the rocks of ideological conservatism, and Spain began to turn her back to what was happening elsewhere all over Europe. By 1814 the liberal movement of 1812 had been stifled, Ferdinand VII was back on the throne as the defender of absolutism, and Spanish social thought had settled into a pattern from which it has not yet escaped.

From that day to this, Spain has been the battleground of a fundamental ideological clash, which has been excellently described by José Ingenieros in his *Evolución de las ideas argentinas*[4] and which is best understood today by comparing it with the present conflict between totalitarianism and democracy. What Barnes and Becker have to say regarding the first twenty years following the restoration of Ferdinand VII is just as valid for the entire course of Spanish history: "The next twenty-odd years were characterized by confused struggles between liberals and the adherents of the old order, pretenders to the throne and the ruling dynasty."[5] While the rest of Western social thought embraced positivism and moved on toward the development of what we are pleased to call "scientific sociology," Spain continued to philosophize about the fundamental ideological problems posed by the revolution. While the rest of Western social thought accepted the postulates of modern science and moved on to research and the production of monographic studies, Spain paused to ponder the problem of the very bases of social thought.

The result has been a "polarization" of social theory, with all writers "lining up" on one or the other side of the debate between "liberalism" and "conservatism."[6] Within this framework all the events usually stressed as significant in the development of the social sciences in Spain (the emergence of a group of Krausist disciples, the widespread and earnest acceptance of positivism, the Revolution of 1868, and the reaction of the country to the Spanish-American War in 1898) are but aspects of the fundamental struggle which, since the opening of the century, has served as the point of departure for most significant social thought[7] and in terms of which both these factors and the resultant social thought must be understood.

It would seem, therefore, that Spain's present significance for the study of sociology consists rather largely in two things. In the first place, she constitutes a sort of "laboratory" in which the process of interaction between social theory and social milieu has been "fixated," so to speak, thus enabling present-day students to investigate at firsthand a situation through which most of the countries of the Western world were passing at the close of the nineteenth century. In the second place, Spain dramatizes the fact that in the first wave of enthusiastic desire to develop a "science of man" after the model of the so-called "natural sciences," certain basic issues with reference to theoretical assumptions and methodological procedures were assumed to be settled and so were put away in "theoretical pigeonholes" by the social theorists of the more "advanced" countries. Now, in consequence of the violent social instability into which the Western world was plunged by World Wars I and II and under the proddings of the resultant contemporary emphasis on theory, we are beginning to suspect that we were a bit premature in our easy acceptance of the proposition that the metaphysical assumptions and the methodological techniques of physics, chemistry, and biology were adequate for the investigation of social data.[8] Spain has never been guilty of such complete conversion to the dogmas of nineteenth-century science and so has much less to take back. What we have regarded as "solved" she has carried as "problematical," this basic attitude being reflected in the thinking and writing of all her leading theorists. The subject of this chapter, Adolfo Posada, is but an example of what is typical of Spanish thought.[9]

II. ADOLFO POSADA: THE "LESTER F. WARD" OF SPANISH SOCIOLOGY

It seems to me that the most apt way to indicate the role played by Adolfo Posada (1860–1944) is to designate him the "Lester F. Ward" of Spanish sociology. That he was deeply influenced by Ward is suggested by the fact that Ward is favorably mentioned in 144 citations in Posada's *Principios de sociología*. No other writer has a comparable record, though Comte, Spencer, Durkheim, and Giddings are also frequently cited. However, his use of Comte is quite incidental, and his reaction to Spencer is strongly negative, though he recognizes Spencer's contribution; in contrast, his sociological soul was nourished by the doctrines of Ward, Giddings, and to a somewhat lesser degree, Durkheim.[10]

However, this comparison with Ward must not be taken too literally. It is intended only as a means of identifying Posada functionally as playing a role in Spanish sociology quite comparable to the place Ward holds in American sociology. Both built on the works of others, mostly foreigners; and both served as sociological prophets, crying out in a theoretical wilderness in an effort to call attention to the need for an adequate sociology. Ideologically, Posada seems closer to Cooley, and this in spite of the fact that he refers to Cooley but four times in his *Principios*.

Posada's significance in Spanish sociology is most accurately indicated by his relation to the fundamental ideological cleavage already mentioned. In this basic "polarization" of thought he belongs to the liberal group, which drew its inspiration from the Revolution of 1868 and derived its intellectual diet from German idealism, and more especially from the teachings of Karl Christian Friedrich Krause.[11]

Posada's close connection with this stream of thought is further indicated by the fact that he was an ardent disciple of Francisco Giner de los Ríos and an associate of Gumersindo de Azcárate, with whom he worked in the Instituto de Reformas Sociales for twenty years. De los Ríos was a student of Julian Sanz del Río, the man who was sent to Germany by one of the short-lived liberal regimes in Spain for the express purpose of studying the teachings of Krause. Exiled for his Krausist leanings by a subsequent conservative government, Sanz del Río's work was successfully carried forward by Giner de los Ríos, founder of the Institución Libre de Enseñanza, in which Posada completed his training under the leadership of Giner and Azcárate. Barnes and Becker are quite correct, therefore, when they suggest that Posada definitely belongs in the Krausist tradition.[12]

A final insight into the work of Posada is afforded by the suggestion that he is an excellent example of the effect of social instability on social thought, as that relationship was discussed at the beginning of this paper. For Posada is a "theorist" who is also a "man of affairs," a "philosopher" who also wanted to "do something about it." While writing voluminously in the field of political science from the sociological point of view, he also found time to hold various important academic appointments.[13] In spare moments, so to speak, he was also active in political affairs. A Socialist, he has had a share in the preparation of almost all the labor legislation enacted in Spain. He participated in the initiation of the reform movement led by Manuel Pedregal and G. de Azcárate. He served as city councilman for his home city of Oviedo, as well as several terms as senator for the province of the same name. Not content with this, he made two trips to South America in 1910 and 1921, lecturing in the universities of various republics, and one trip to Washington, D.C., in 1919 as official delegate to the League of Nations' International Labour Conference.

This, then, was the man who, in the midst of an unusually busy life, somehow or other found time to produce an unbelievably formidable list of serious works in the fields of political science and sociology.[14]

III. KEY IDEAS IN POSADA'S SOCIAL THOUGHT

A. POSADA NOT A "SYSTEMATIZER"

The first thing to be noted about the social thought of Posada is the fact that he is not a "systematizer." In view of what has already been said about the functional interdependence of social theory and social milieu, this is not surprising. On the contrary, it is to be expected. Given the conditions that obtained in Spain throughout Posada's productive period, we should expect him to be "eclectic" rather than "systematic," "interpretative" rather than "creative."[15] Though the careful student could systematize what Posada has written but never troubled to organize into a sociological system, it will not be our purpose in what follows to construct a system where none explicitly exists. Rather, it is our intention to present the central ideas in Posada's thought, the conceptual keys that will open the door to his basic ideas regarding the nature and function of sociology.

B. THE DATA OF SOCIOLOGY

Posada's conception of the data of sociology is basic to everything else and is worthy of careful examination. In his belief that a sociology is necessary because there is a field of data to be investigated, he would be considered a bit "old-fashioned" by those American sociologists, who are somewhat inclined to define a science in terms of its methods and conceptual "lingo." In this he is rather closely akin to Znaniecki, of whom he appears not to have heard.[16] For Posada, then, sociology is the science which undertakes to study an objective body of data which he refers to as "the social" or "social reality."[17]

In the light of a somewhat current attitude toward the data of the social sciences, it is significant that Posada considers these data to be "real" not "fictitious." That is, philosophically, he is a "realist" rather than a "nominalist."[18] It is also worthy of note that Posada is a "pluralist" not a "unilateralist." He is not, however, an "omnibus" sociologist. For him, sociology is not the study of all conceivable factors that influence human behavior. Quite to the contrary, sociology is the study of the specifically social, but the factors influencing the social processes are recognized to be plural.[19]

Furthermore, Posada is careful to point out that *the social* is not a substantive entity. He hews a straight line between the effort to make sociology a "natural science" and thus annihilate its data and the tendency so to reify social reality as to elevate it to the status of a "being." Thus, though he focuses attention on social reality as the data of sociology, he avoids the extreme of considering it to be an "organism" in either the Comtian or the Spencerian sense.[20]

Again, for Posada, *the social* is not an order of reality that is limited to human relationships. He refers to social life among the animals and talks of an "animal sociology."[21]

Finally, his conception of *the social* is essentially, though only implicitly, dynamic and implies what we would today refer to as the "processual" approach. Posada himself, however, never quite gets around to discussing this matter save in a few explicit references to "processes."[22]

C. BASIC ASSUMPTIONS

This fundamentally important conception of the data of sociology results in what Posada terms the "basic suppositions" of the science. Freely translated, these may be expressed as follows:

1. Social reality presents itself to us in a manner similar to any other reality. Moreover, it is an order of reality that envelopes and includes us. We live in it, we are in it, perhaps it is better to say that we *are* it![23]

2. The person is a social product. The genesis and development of the social go on parallel with the genesis and development of the person.

3. The fact that personality is a social product does not make it possible to deny the subjective character of the social as a function of the self.[24]

4. It would seem that scientific knowledge of social reality will only result from an approach to the problem which recognizes that the objective social reality under analysis is a product of the interaction of the subjective elements called selves. Furthermore, it is necessary to remember that the analysis itself (in this case, sociology) is the product of such selves.[25]

5. Finally, sociology must be based upon a realization of the methodological value of the study of the self, understood to be the synthetic expression of a universal social evolution, this evolution itself, in turn, being susceptible to interpretation as the result of the interaction of such selves.[26]

D. THE NATURE OF THE PERSON

Just as Posada's conception of the data of sociology determined the five fundamental postulates which he formulated, these in their turn constitute the foundation for Posada's ideas regarding the nature of the person. The point of view represented by the assumptions just outlined might be summarized thus—"the social" results from the interaction of "selves" such as we are. We are *selves* rather than just animals because we possess *consciousness*. Consciousness is composed of such elements as *sentiments, emotions, necessities, desires,* and *instincts.* Thus Posada apparently holds that the emergence of the social process and the development of social reality are to be explained in terms of the psychological nature of the constituent elements of human groupings.

In the elaboration of this point of view, the concept "consciousness" (*conciencia*) is of basic importance.[27] Here, again, there is no great mystery surrounding what Posada has in mind when he employs the term. By "consciousness," "psychical being," or "rational spirit" he evidently means, as, indeed, he repeatedly states, the quality that drives us to seek to understand, interpret, and adjust to the universe in which we live. This individual consciousness and its constituent elements, interacting with other conscious beings, produces the social, the object matter of sociology. He makes no further use of the concepts which are introduced to explain the contents of consciousness.

All this suggests that Posada occupies a position very similar to that of Cooley, on whom he draws in his discussion of this problem. He sensed the fact that the "individual" and "society" were aspects of the same process, but he was never able to describe how and in what sense this was true. He gets the social process started by endowing men with "consciousness" and its elements, though not by recourse to a crudely naïve biological determinism. He himself refers to his conception of "consciousness" as psychological, leaving the reader altogether in the dark as to the sources of "consciousness." He apparently was never able to achieve what would now be called a "social theory of motivation." This is his greatest weakness.

E. THE METHODOLOGY OF SOCIOLOGY

All the foregoing enters into Posada's ideas with reference to the methodology of sociology. To the question of "the problem of method in sociology" he devotes an entire chapter in his *Principios*.[28] The basically important position here is his conviction that *the methods of sociology must be determined by and adjusted to the data under investigation.* This is a refreshing position, in view of the fact that American sociology, out of slavish loyalty to the physical and natural sciences, has frequently so limited itself methodologically as almost to annihilate its data. Posada would argue that the important consideration is the recognition of the fact that there are data to be studied and would argue that we should busy ourselves with the "cultivation of our own garden."[29]

The nature of these data leads Posada to the position that the sociological method par excellence is what he terms "psychological analysis," by which he means a method adequate to the study of "consciousness" in both its individual and its social manifestations.[30] He recognizes, of course, that this is not the only method, and he insists that other methods are necessary if we are adequately to interpret social reality.

Statistic, monographic studies, and surveys are all discussed as important methods in gathering facts, but he argues that they must be supplemented by the historical and comparative methods if the facts are ever to "come alive."[31]

In summary, then, it can be pointed out that Posada urged the development of a methodology adequate to comprehend the data presented to the student; that he felt psychological analysis to be the basic method; but that he recognized the need for many supplementary procedures and techniques.

IV. SUMMARY

In this all-too-brief survey of the social thought of Adolfo Posada two facts stand out as central. The first is his insistence on the "reality" and "objectivity" of the data of sociology; the second is his plea for the development of a methodology adequate to the task of interpreting these data. While there is nothing startlingly new in these ideas, they do represent an emphasis that is greatly needed. Posada is not embarrassed by the nature of his data; he does not feel it incumbent upon him to permit the philosophical assumptions of other scientific disciplines to dictate what he is supposed to observe when he approaches "social reality"; therefore, the study of his point of view will certainly serve to remind the student that the need for some agreement as to the basic field of data to be explored by sociology is still urgent. Accepting as he does the proposition that the data constitute the point of departure in the construction of a sociology, Posada insists on the need for a more adequate methodology. He would appear to be correct in reminding us of the extent to which we have gone astray in our attempts to imitate the physical and natural sciences rather than in experimentally developing our own methodology in the light of the demands of our data. Both the lack of consensus regarding the data and our methodological inadequacies are frequently obscured by the fact that we seldom question the fundamental assumptions upon which the older sciences rest. Posada, and with him most of the leaders of social thought in Spain and Latin America, have never ceased to ponder the problems posed by the breakup of scholasticism and the emergence of the "scientific world-view." From this point of view, it may be said that the reopening of basic theoretical questions represented by the work of such men as Talcott Parsons, L. G. Brown, George Lundberg, and others indicates that the young men of American sociology are picking up the job at the point where Posada, the old man, had to lay it down.[32]

SELECTED BIBLIOGRAPHY OF POSADA'S PUBLISHED WORKS

SOCIOLOGY

Literatura y problemas de la sociología. 1 vol. Barcelona, 1902.
Principios de sociología. 2 vols. Madrid, 1908, 1929.
Sociología contemporánea. 1 vol. Barcelona, n.d.
Sociología general. 1 vol. 1903.

LAW

Tratado de derecho político. 2 vols. Madrid, 1935.
Guía para el estudio y aplicación del derecho constitucional de Europa y América. 1 vol. Madrid, 1894.
Principios de derecho político. 1 vol. Madrid, 1884.
Estudios sobre el régimen parlamentario en España. 1 vol. Madrid, 1891.
La Idea del estado y la guerra europa. 1 vol. Madrid, 1915.
El Régimen municipal de la ciudad moderna. 1 vol. 3d ed. Madrid, n.d.
Evolución legislativa del régimen local en España. 1 vol. Madrid, 1910.
Ciencia política.
Teorías políticas. 1 vol. Madrid, n.d.
Tratado de derecho administrativo. 1 vol. Madrid, 1897.
Instituciones políticas de los pueblos hispano-americanos. 1 vol. Madrid, 1900.
Programa de elementos de derecho político y administrativo español. 1 vol. Madrid, 1883.
La Enseñanza del derecho en las universidades . . . . en España.
Introducción al derecho administrativo y organización administrativo española.
La Administración política y la administración social. 1 vol. Madrid, n.d.
Teoría social y jurídica del estado. 1 vol. Buenos Aires, 1922.
La Política.

MISCELLANEOUS

La Sociedad de las naciones. Madrid, 1925.
Actitud ética ante la guerra y la paz.
España en crisis.
La República argentina. Madrid, 1912.
Femenismo. Madrid, 1899.
La República del Paraguay. 1911.
El Sufragio. 1898.
Ideas y ideales.
Socialismo y reforma social. Madrid, 1904.
Política y enseñanza. Madrid, 1904.
Pedagogía. Madrid, 1892.
Autores y libros. Valencia, 1909.
Para América: desde España.
En América: una campaña. Madrid, 1911.
El Parlamentarismo: tres conferencias.
Ideas de pedagógicas modernas. Madrid, 1892.
El Amor y el sexo: cartas sobre la educación de la mujer.
Pueblos y campos argentinos. Madrid, n.d.

TRANSLATIONS

La Lucha por el derecho. By R. von Ihering. 1881.
La Quinta esencia del socialismo. By Albert Schäffle. 1885.
Principios de política. By Franz von Holtzendorff. 1888.
Teoría de la posesión. By R. von Ihering.
La Criminalidad comparativa. By Gabriel Tarde.
Las transformaciones del derecho. By Gabriel Tarde.
Prehistorias de los indoeuropeos. By R. von Ihering.
El Derecho civil y los pobres. By A. Menger.
La Declaración de los derechos del hombre y del ciudadano. By George Jellinek.
La Transformación del estado. By L. Dugitt.
El Estado. By Woodrow Wilson.
Compendio de sociología. By Lester F. Ward. 3d ed. Madrid, 1939.
La Interpretación económica de la historia. By E. R. A. Seligman.
Principios de sociología. By F. H. Giddings. Madrid.
La Ciencia social contemporánea. By Alfred Fouillée. Madrid.
La Educación y la herencia. By J. M. Guyau. Madrid.
La Justicia y las instituciones eclesiásticas. By Herbert Spencer. Madrid.
Interpretaciones sociales y éticas del desenvolvimiento mental. By James M. Baldwin. Madrid, 1926.

NOTES

1. It should be noted that the reference here is to *social* change. *Fundamental social* change is always "attitudinal": that is, change that is socially significant must affect the attitude-value structure of the group. Thus a given period might be marked by rapid *technological* change of such a character as to leave the *social* structure relatively untouched.

2. Vives has been characterized as a "daring social worker" because of his interest in social reform. The *soundness* of his thinking is suggested by his advocacy of a "whole system of charity organization and relief work," in which he placed the emphasis on the prevention of delinquency and insisted that the state should control all relief work. His *daring* is indicated by his "radical proposal that all immovable property, particularly land, should be taken away from private owners and redistributed under the control of the state, which would retain title, giving only the use of the property to individuals."

Vitoria, an "internationalist in a nationalist world," is of interest because he was so "out of place." Today his "condemnation of the resort to force in settling disputes between nations" and his denunciation of all the ways of military leaders are understandable even though his position may again appear somewhat quixotic in a world overrun by war lords. It is nothing short of remarkable to find him advancing such ideas in his own time.

For a summary treatment of the work of these men see H. E. Barnes and Howard Becker, *Social Thought from Lore to Science* (2 vols.; New York, 1938), II, 1103–5. Their work also includes a bibliography of more basic sources.

3. *Ibid.*, p. 1105. See this book also for a discussion of some of the writers of this period.

4. Though writing with reference to Argentina, the analysis is equally valid for all Latin America and Spain (Buenos Aires, 1937).

5. *Op. cit.*, II, 1108.

6. As Fernando de los Ríos puts it: ".... this struggle stimulated the doctrinal polarization of the social sciences in Spain, giving rise to what may be considered the two schools of Spanish thought around which the name of principal social scientists may be grouped. On the one hand the traditional Catholic school was re-vivified with the sap of Christian socialism and gave place in our day to Christian democracy with its well-known influence in the life and legislation of the country. In this group the profound ideas of Donoso Cortes

.... have ceased to hold sway and have been superseded by the social doctrines of Leo VIII; representative of this trend are Sanz Escantin, Azmar, Sangro and Ros de Olano, Burgos Mazo and Ruiz del Castillo. On the other hand the liberal spirit of the Revolution of 1868 has descended upon the school that upholds the doctrine of the social organism as an ethical entity. The doctrine was inspired by German idealism, especially by Krause, and was expounded and spread by Julian Sanz del Río, professor at the University of Madrid. The real founder of this school was Francisco Giner de los Ríos .... who founded the Institución Libre..... Giner left a profound impression on Altamira, Costa, Dorado, Montero, Buylla, Bernardo de Quiros, and Posada. Positivism also found representatives in Sales y Ferrer and the criminologist Salillas" (see the article by Fernando de los Ríos in the *Encyclopaedia of the Social Sciences*, I, 295–300).

7. A good summary treatment of the influence of these four factors is found in Barnes and Becker, *op. cit.*, II, 1107–18; and in the *Encyclopaedia of the Social Sciences*, I, 295–300.

8. Note the significance in this connection of such divergent schools of thought as McKenzie's ecological approach, Parson's "voluntarism," Lundberg's "logical positivism," and Znaniecki's "sociology of social actions," not to mention "institutional economics."

9. On this point see Posada's *Literatura y problemas de la sociología* (1902), pp. 208–9.

10. See Posada, *Principios de sociología* (2d ed., 1929), I, 45, for evidence on the point, also pp. vii–ix.

11. For a summary treatment of the work of Krause see Barnes and Becker, *op. cit.*, II, 1108–11.

12. For the details of the influence of Krause, Giner, and Azcárate on the work of Posada, consult *ibid.*, pp. 1108–15; *Encyclopaedia of the Social Sciences*, I, 295–300; and *La Enciclopedia universal ilustrada*, XXVI, 671–72. For evidence that Posada, though influenced by Krause through the teachings of Giner, did not consider himself a Krausist see his *Literatura y problemas de la sociología*, IV, 11–12; also *Principios*, I, chap. x, 211–17.

13. At twenty-two years of age Posada was professor of political and administrative law in the university of Oviedo. Later, he helped organize the Instituto del Trabajo. When this venture failed after two years, he served for twenty years as the director of the departments of legislation, bibliography, and social action of the Instituto de Reformas Sociales. In 1910 he was named professor of comparative municipal law in the Central University and professor of political law in the Law School in Madrid.

14. For a selected bibliography of Posada's work see the list at the end of this chapter.

15. As an excellent example of the sense of urgency under which his work must have been done and for a suggestion regarding the role he conceived of himself as playing see his *Principios*, I, 285; see also the Editorial Preface to his *Literatura y problemas de la sociología*.

16. For a fine statement of the intensity of his feeling that a sociology is demanded because of the need to understand "social reality" see his *Principios*, I, 327.

17. There is nothing particularly mysterious in his use of these terms. He means by them just about what we are accustomed to mean when we employ them in sociological discourse, and he has just about the same degree of difficulty in "defining" them. In one passage he says that "*the social,* abstractly defined, consists in the relations of consciousness with consciousness, relationships that are intermental and superpsychical." In another connection he writes as follows: "*The social* is the living work of a spontaneous movement, resulting from a distinct kind of 'irritability' existent in conscious beings by virtue of which such beings interact with others of their kind, establishing thereby an emotional, intellectual, and reflective communication, creating thereby a new world, and producing thereby an order of superpsychical currents because of the fact that these currents transcend the experience of any single consciousness. The relationships thus established are preserved in history in the form of habits, customs, and institutions" (*Principios*, II, 317–20).

18. At first blush, this observation would seem to be altogether insignificant and· unimportant. On the contrary, the present writer would argue that American sociology, particularly, has permitted itself to be jockeyed into a philosophical and methodological posi-

tion which logically results in "apologies" for the very data that the social sciences undertake to study. Whatever may be the nature of "reality," little progress in the understanding of what Posada calls "social reality" can come from a position that refers to the data as "fictitious."

19. For his discussion of this point see his *Principios*, I, 3.

20. *Ibid.*, pp. 175–96 and 217.

21. Whatever may be the general validity of this point of view, it is clear that in the case of Posada the extension of social life to the animal level is a by-product of a philosophical necessity on his part to rationalize certain human values by discovering their foundations in animal life. For evidence on this point see his *Tratado de derecho político*, I, 185, 210; see also his essay on "La Idea de justicia en el reino animal, in *Literatura y problemas de la sociología*, pp. 282–97.

22. See, e.g., his *Principios*, II, 183. Posada stops just short of the significant work of Park and Burgess and of Thomas and Znaniecki. This failure to give adequate consideration to this school of thought is probably due to age. Posada was sixty-one when Park and Burgess published their *Introduction to the Science of Society*, and *The Polish Peasant* was released three years earlier. Allowing some lag before these works became known in Spain, Posada could not have known very much about them or made very great use of them. Evidence that these works had little influence is suggested by the fact that, though he mentions Thomas, the reference is to his *Source Book for Social Origins* (Boston, 1909). Park and Burgess are cited five times but never in connection with any discussion of the concepts that have come to be so fundamental in the "ecological" and "social" approaches. Ross suffers a similar fate. Though an entire chapter is devoted to him in the *Principios*, no mention is made of his treatment of the social processes. Posada's focus of attention was elsewhere!

23. The full meaning of what Posada is saying here is suggested by his deliberate use of words. He uses the Spanish verb *estar* to express the idea that we are surrounded by social reality; he employs the verb *ser* to indicate that persons and social reality are one and the same reality.

24. Posada employs the Spanish *yo* and the Latin *ego* to refer to what is herein termed the "self." It is not our present purpose to discuss what seems to us to be an evident weakness of this postulate. In so far as that is undertaken at all in this paper, it will be done in connection with the discussion of Posada's theory of motivation. At this juncture it is enough to point out that Posada conceives of the social as resulting from "selves" that are thought of as endowed with "sentiments, emotions, necessities, desires, and instincts," all of which are the constituent elements of "consciousness." He believes this psychological foundation to be the "substratum" of social laws, just as inanimate mechanical bodies form the substratum of physical laws.

25. Posada is here involved in an all-too-well-known difficulty. What he says seems to assign priority to such "selves" as the active agents in the social process. This leaves him without any satisfactory theory of the origin of human nature. This difficulty he attempts to avoid by indicating that the "social" and the "individual" are not in sequential, but in interactional, relationship, quoting Cooley in support of the position. This position is understandable but still leaves the basic theoretical issue unsettled, though Posada does recognize it as "the capital problem in Sociology" (*Principios*, II, 98).

26. For Posada's discussion of these postulates see his *Principios*, II, 301–5.

27. The word employed by Posada is *conciencia*, which, translated literally, means "conscience." That he means "consciousness" rather than "conscience" is indicated by the fact that he employs the same word to translate Giddings' concept, "consciousness of kind." The word is not very satisfactory, but Spanish offers no better substitute (see *Principios*, II, 315).

28. II, chap. xix, 297–329.

29. *Ibid.*, pp. 197.

30. *Ibid.,* pp. 312–16. This emphasis relates him rather closely with the "attitude-value" type of analysis in this country, though he does not use these concepts.

31. Several pages are devoted to a consideration of the comparative method. The essence of his position is that comparison is a fundamental psychological necessity of the human spirit, in which we must inevitably engage. This being so, it is better that we do it carefully and systematically. Furthermore, in his view, comparison is the principal substitute for the "experimental" method of the older sciences. He justifies the position he assigns to this method by pointing out that Tarde's emphasis on imitation presupposes that comparison has already gone on, and he insists that previous use of the method warrants his judgment of its importance. He again recognizes that it is not the *only* method.

32. If space had permitted, many other interesting aspects of Posada's work might have been mentioned. For example, his surprisingly modern "public welfare theory" of the functions of the state would delight a "New Dealer" (*Literatura y problemas de la sociología,* p. 10); or "the ecological theory" implicit in his essay on "The Sociology of Local Life" (*ibid.,* pp. 255–82); or the soundness of his skepticism regarding the theories of the "primitivity of primitive man" (*Tratado de derecho político,* I, 209); or, finally, his interesting conception of what he calls "el flúido ético," by which he appears to mean a sort of "sociopsychological energy" deemed to be operative in social reality (*Tratado de derecho político,* I, 50, 279; also his article on "L'Etat et le gouvernement," in which he develops this idea in some detail).

PART V

ENGLISH SOCIOLOGISTS SINCE
HERBERT SPENCER

INTRODUCTORY NOTE*

ENGLISH SOCIOLOGY SINCE SPENCER

DESPITE the extensive writings and great influence of Herbert Spencer, there has been little systematic sociology and little formal sociological instruction in England. There have been only two outstanding figures in contemporary English sociology, Leonard T. Hobhouse and Patrick Geddes, and the former was primarily a metaphysician and philosopher and the latter a biologist. There is only one professional chair of sociology in all the English universities today, the Martin White Professorship at the University of London, previously occupied by Hobhouse and Westermarck and now held by Morris Ginsberg. Even the sociological movement in England got under way outside the universities, much like natural science in England in the mid-seventeenth century. It was launched chiefly by Patrick Geddes and Victor Branford under the impact of the Le Play school and the social-survey movement in France.

There are a number of reasons for this. Spencer's agnosticism and Comte's positivism repelled most of the English social philosophers, who were under the spell of Hegel or Kant. The older English universities are notoriously reactionary in their conception of the curriculum, in general, and in their attitude toward the social sciences, in particular. Then, there was a large amount of work on the border line of sociology and in the special social sciences that absorbed much of the mental energy and professional effort which, in some other countries, have gone into systematic sociology.

There has, however, been no lack of work in England which is grist for the sociological mill. There have been a number of able geographers who were interested in the relation of the physical environment to man and society, such as Andrew Reid Cowan, James Fairgrieve, and H. J. Mackinder. Regional geography was introduced by A. J. Hebertson, Alexander Farquharson, Herbert J. Fleure, and H. J. Mill, similar to that promoted on the Continent by such geographers as Ferdinand von

* By the editor.

603

Richthofen, Camille Vallaux, and Jean Brunhes. Interest in human and social ecology and the social survey has been cultivated by Patrick Geddes, Victor Branford, and Charles Booth. The impulse here came from the Le Play school in France, and Geddes far outshone his master in his breadth of knowledge, tireless energy, and the scope of his work.

Biological sociology has been extensively cultivated in England and the British Isles. J. S. Mackenzie transformed Spencer's organicism into the conception of society as a "moral organism." Eugenics and social selectionism had their effective birth in England under the impulse from Sir Francis Galton and his disciple, Karl Pearson. The latter did more than anybody else to promote and popularize the statistical treatment of genetics and social problems. The population problem has attracted special interest in England, owing, in part, to the Malthusian tradition. Neo-Malthusianism and the birth-control movement received support from George and C. R. Drysdale, Charles Bradlaugh, Annie Besant, and Marie Stopes. Alexander M. Carr-Saunders is one of the sanest students of the population problem, a subject which has also interested Harold Wright, James Swinburne, and Harold Cox.

England has been especially prolific in producing anthropologists interested in the early history of man and human culture. There have been the classical anthropologists—Sir E. B. Tylor, Sir James G. Frazer, Lord Avebury, and others—and more critical successors, such as R. R. Marett and W. H. R. Rivers. Sir Arthur Keith, W. L. H. Duckworth, and Grafton Elliot Smith have been leaders in physical anthropology and the reconstruction of the physical past of mankind.

Social psychology really got under way in England in the famous work of Walter Bagehot on *Physics and Politics,* and the field has been fruitfully cultivated since that time by Graham Wallas, William McDougall, Wilfred Trotter, and A. G. Tansley.

No country has produced more or better students of the economic basis of social problems than England. Here we find such distinguished social economists as J. A. Hobson, Sidney and Beatrice Webb, J. L. and Barbara Hammond, R. H. Tawney, Henry Clay, A. G. Pigou, and G. D. H. Cole, to mention only outstanding figures. A sociological interest in politics was promoted by F. W. Maitland and J. N. Figgis, disciples of Otto von Gierke in Germany. This tradition has been continued by Harold J. Laski. Social historians, interested in the evolution of human culture and institutions, are represented by such names as

Arnold J. Toynbee, Gilbert Slater, A. F. Pollard, J. L. Myres, F. S. Marvin, and others; and this quest was given vast popularity by H. G. Wells's *Outline of History*.

Despite all this, sociology as a systematic discipline has been virtually ignored in Britain, and we could, if we wished to be at all technical, ignore all British writers except Hobhouse in a book formally dedicated to systematic sociologists. But we have chosen to include as representative of the closest approach to systematic sociology in Britain, not only Hobhouse but Benjamin Kidd, who is the outstanding example of the antirationalist reaction against Spencerianism; Edward Westermarck and Robert Briffault, as representative of ethnographic contributions to sociology; Geddes and Branford, who were responsible for launching the sociological movement in Britain and have done more than anyone else to apply sociological investigation and concepts to social welfare, especially in regional and urban planning; Graham Wallas, perhaps England's leading social psychologist and sociological student of political processes; and Arnold J. Toynbee, whose voluminous work, *A Study of History,* has lately aroused much interest in both England and America and is regarded by some as an important contribution to the culture case-study method in historical sociology.

CHAPTER XXXI

THE SUPRARATIONAL SOCIAL PHILOSOPHY
OF BENJAMIN KIDD

Harry Elmer Barnes

I. NATURE OF KIDD'S FUNDAMENTAL ASSUMPTIONS

WALTER BAGEHOT was one of the first writers to apply the new biological formulas to an interpretation of the cultural and psychological development of mankind. He held that the social group had, in the earlier stages of social evolution, dominated the individual through the operation of custom. But the individual was gradually freed from this constraint through the evolution of free discussion.

Twenty years later, in his *Social Evolution* (1894), Benjamin Kidd (1858–1916), the first important English sociological writer after Herbert Spencer, attempted to indicate the more important psychological factors and processes involved in the development of society. Instead of agreeing with Bagehot that the domination of the group over the individual is merely a necessary primordial discipline for the race, Kidd maintained that group constraint is the basic mainspring of social progress, while freedom of individual initiative is a highly corrosive and disintegrating force, which has always endangered the very existence of society. Social evolution is primarily the product of the struggle between the individual, following the dictates of reason, and those socializing forces upon which social organization and progress depend. Since it is essential for the social principle to prevail over the individual, this conquest must be made at the expense of reason, and the governing force in human development must be suprarational in character.

This suprarational principle, Kidd, in common with Vico and Schleiermacher before him, found to reside in religion. Kidd's doctrines, then, constitute one of the more notable examples of that reaction against recognizing the importance of reason in social processes and social development which L. T. Hobhouse vigorously criticized.

Kidd proceeds to explain how religion, operating in opposition to reason, promotes social progress. A severe and brutal struggle for existence is necessary to produce progress. Now the dictates of reason would encourage mankind to prevent or lessen the struggle for existence and the suffering thereby entailed. But religion encourages the growth of population and other factors which intensify the struggle for existence, and in this way religion not only assures but speeds up social progress.

II. THE NECESSITY OF A SUPRARATIONAL BASIS AND SANCTION FOR SOCIAL INSTITUTIONS

Kidd begins with the Darwinian doctrine and the neo-Darwinian revision of that theory by Weismann, to the effect that progress comes only through natural selection, which results from the struggle for existence, and that, if progress does not take place, not only stagnation but also actual retrogression will set in.[1] But his most important assumption is that there is no rational sanction for the development of the social organism.[2] In other words, there is a basic and eternal struggle between the interests of the individual and those of the social organism; progress comes only in proportion as the former are subordinated to the latter.[3] Likewise, the social structures and situations of any given time, as a manifestation of the progressive development of humanity, are without any foundation in reason. In short, reason and all its implications and consequences are antisocial and retrogressive. Kidd says in one typical sentence: "While our evolution is in the first place preeminently a social evolution, the most profoundly individualistic, antisocial, and anti-evolutionary of all human qualities is one which, all other things being equal, tended to be progressively developed in the race, namely, reason."[4] This is, indeed, far removed from the political theory of those philosophers who, for two centuries, had sought to deduce all principles of social progress and conduct from the "dictates of pure reason."

If reason has not guided the progressive development of society, what has been responsible for this process? Mr. Kidd is prompt and dogmatic with his answer; it is neither reason nor the automatic working of evolutionary laws; it is religion which furnishes an "ultra-rational sanction" for those modes of human conduct which are conducive to progress and opposed to reason.[5] Nor can this religion be of the type proposed by

Comte—a rational doctrine of social duties. It must be suprarational. As a matter of fact, no religion can be rational, since such an assumption is a mere contradiction of terms. He sums up the matter as follows: "A religion is a form of belief, providing an ultra-rational sanction for that large class of conduct in the individual where his interests and the interests of the social organism are antagonistic, and by which the former are rendered subordinate to the latter in the general interests of the evolution which the race is undergoing."[6] The social organism, then, according to Kidd, is a religious organism comprehending not a single society or generation but an entire type of civilization. Indeed, as we shall point out more thoroughly later on, Kidd regarded any existing generation or any existing society as of relatively trivial significance compared to the future of the human race and the social organism.

Having reached these conclusions in an a priori manner, Kidd attempts to verify them through an appeal to the concrete facts of history, which he treats with the same easy legerdemain that he had already employed in dealing with epistemology, psychology, and biology. He examines the development of Europe, which he characterizes as "Western civilization."[7] In general, he accepts Spencer's differentiation between military and industrial society, as well as his characterization of both types.[8] The nations of antiquity, Greece and Rome, were military states; and, by their monarchical or aristocratic systems, their sumptuary regulation of life, and their reliance upon the institution of slavery, they stifled the action of social selection and passed into decay.

Civilization was thus gravely threatened when Christianity appeared with the two necessary characteristics for rapid social progress—a strong ultra-rational sanction for conduct and an altruistic ethical system. The task of "Western civilization," as directed by Christianity, was to break down the military systems of antiquity and, by emancipating and enfranchising the masses, to raise the selective struggle from a crude intergroup warfare to the more efficient strife between equals within society.

The culmination of the first stage of Christian influence was the all-powerful Catholic theocracy of the fourteenth century. The second stage, which really revolutionized society, began with the Reformation; and this period, which was actually an era of political opportunism on the part of Protestant princes, the substitution of one set of dogmas and authorities for another, and an economic revolt of the rising middle class, is hailed by Kidd as a movement characterized by the liberation of a vast flood of previously repressed and misdirected altruism.

During this second stage of Christian influence, slavery and serfdom were abolished, and political and social rights were granted to the hitherto disfranchised and exploited masses. The entire Protestant movement was furthered by the growth of altruism. Not only were the masses desirous of obtaining their political, economic, and social rights, but the governing and wealthy classes were so filled with this growing spirit of altruism that they could no longer behold with equanimity the injustice done to the mass of the people. He says:

> It must be observed that the fact of most significance is the extent to which this deepening and softening of character has progressed *among the power-holding class*. This class is even more affected than the opposing party. The result is peculiar. It is thereby rendered incapable of utilizing its own strength, and consequently of making any effective resistance to the movement which is undermining its position. All heart is, in fact, taken out of its opposition; men's minds have become so sensitive to suffering, misery, wrong, and degradation of every kind, that it cannot help itself.[9]

Even political minorities are now safe, thanks to "this extreme sensitiveness of the public conscience to wrong or unfairness."

This idealistic picture is fantastic when one compares it with the actual conditions under which the reform legislation was accomplished, as the result of bitter struggles between opposed classes and interests; and the alleged tender conscience of political majorities was not less inconspicuous as an observed fact.[10] Altruism is, however, according to Kidd, merely an expression of the underlying force—religion. This is the vital impulse and guiding force in social evolution.

Turning to the economic basis of society, Marxian socialism is examined as a means of achieving social justice and progress. While Kidd admits the accuracy of the Marxian criticism of the existing social and economic injustice, he condemns its remedy as tending to eliminate that struggle for existence and natural selection which is essential to progress. State regulation of industry in the future, he thinks, will help to secure fair and real competition rather than suspend its operation.

Finally, lest the reader might still be inclined to believe with Buckle and his school that progress is due to intellectual factors, Kidd turns from history to statistics and anthropology to get support for his doctrine. Mr. Galton is brought in to support that venerable superstitition as to the vast intellectual superiority of the "mythical Greek," who is alleged to have differed almost in kind from the modern man. Again, Mr. Gladstone is cited in support of the superior intellects of the sixteenth century. Neither, says Kidd, can anthropology justify the pride of modern man in his intellectual superiority, for Kidd quotes De Quatrefages as upholding the doctrine of the superior cranial capacity of the cave man. Again, the French nation, which is so prominent in intellectual achievement, is gradually becoming a second-rate nation because of a falling birth-rate. From all types of evidence, therefore, Kidd holds: "It would appear that when man became a social creature his progress ceased to be primarily in the direction of the development of his intellect. Thenceforward, in the conditions under which natural selection has operated, his interests as an individual were no longer paramount; they became subordinate to the distinct and widely different interests of the longer-lived social organism to which he for the time being belonged."[11]

In his concluding chapter Mr. Kidd rephrases the Benthamite ethical formula in terms of his own theory, so that "the greatest number" is made identical with the social organism; and he predicts the dominant tendencies of the twentieth century. These he thinks will be: (1) the completion of the social emancipation of the masses; (2) the filling-up of the habitable sections of the temperate zones; and (3) the extension of the altruism of "Western civilization" to the "tropics" through their political control by the nations of the temperate zones. He fails to mention whether this extension of altruism will be through the medium of that "bottled altruism" which has so often been the entering wedge for the Europeans into the tropics or through such "benevolent" political and industrial systems as King Leopold established in the Belgian Congo district.

Having set forth Kidd's most important sociological concept, namely, the idea that suprarational, or ultrarational, factors are of predominant importance in society and that religion is the chief instrument of the suprarational, we may now examine briefly Kidd's conception of what he calls the "law of projected efficiency," which means that current social situations and efforts are of importance primarily as they bear on the future of the human race. He derived this idea from, or at least tries to justify it by, an exaggeration and distortion of Weismann's idea that the struggle for existence is primarily a struggle between species rather than between individuals within the species. We have already noted that Kidd identifies the greatest good for the greatest number with the greatest good for the social organism, and he conceives of the social organism as made up mainly of future generations. Kidd thus summarizes this law of projected efficiency:

> What we are now brought to see is that the overwhelming weight of numbers as of interests, in the evolutionary process, is never in the present. It is always in the future.....We are, in other words, brought face to face with the fact that, in the scientific formula of the life of any existing type of social order destined to maintain its place in the future, the interests of these existing individuals, with which we have been so preoccupied, possess no meaning, except so far as they are included in, and are subordinate to, the interests of a developing system of social order, the overwhelming proportion of whose members are still in the future.[12]

Therefore, while we may superficially sympathize with the plight of the downtrodden and exploited classes of today, with their misery and suffering, we must rejoice in this misery and suffering, in so far as it intensifies the struggle for existence and assures a better social organism for future generations. It is religion, as the suprarational force, which enables the sufferers to bear their suffering and makes it possible for those who are better off to view the sufferings of the less fortunate with complacency and satisfaction. Just how Kidd harmonizes this attitude with his argument that the Renaissance and Reformation made people's consciences so tender, due to the upsurge of altruism, that they could scarcely contemplate any suffering without shuddering is not made clear in Kidd's books. The most cogent criticism of the whole idea is that offered by Professor L. M. Bristol in his *Social Adaptation:* "Mr. Kidd's chief error is in conceiving that a quality can be of advantage to the species which is not at the same time of advantage to the great majority of the individuals that compose it at any one time. 'Species' is but a class term and a species can survive only through the survival of individuals."

It is obvious that Kidd's thesis could scarcely please anybody who understood it. The rationalistic scientists were naturally greatly displeased with the elevation of what they, for good reasons, considered the chief obstacle to progress; and the ecclesiastics were no better pleased to find religion characterized as inherently irrational. Consequently, one is not surprised to hear Kidd's theory variously described as "a curious obscurantism" and as "a trap for clergymen."[13]

The valid criticisms to which the theory is open are so obvious that one need hardly take time to point them out. Among the most obtrusive errors are his arbitrary definition of reason; his utter failure to look for historic facts which run counter to his theories; his omission of artificial selection, or what Professor Keller calls "rational selection" and "counter-selection";[14] his neglect to lay stress upon the importance of co-operation in evolution, a subject so eloquently described by Kropotkin; and, finally, the disproportionate influence ascribed to religion as a civilizing and progressive factor. Though no one single factor can be relied upon to unravel historic processes, few informed historians would deny science and industry the primal place in the evolution of "Western civilization."[15]

Other works amplified some of the ideas which Kidd expressed in his *Social Evolution*, but they added no new thoughts of any great significance. In his *Principles of Western Civilization* (1902), Kidd appealed to history to vindicate the theory of civilization and social progress set forth in his *Social Evolution*. While suggestive and provocative, the book is a classic example of the manhandling and juggling of historical facts to support a sociophilosophical theory. It was in this book that he elaborated his notion of the law of projected efficiency. In his *Science of Power*, published posthumously in 1918, Kidd shifted his argument to a position which reminds one of Comte's later emphasis on the dominant influence of woman on social progress. He contended that our man-made policies have headed the world toward ruin because they have been built upon a rationalistic science of force. Women, however, worship the ideal and encourage that emotional attitude toward idealism which gives the latter its dynamic power in society and enables the individual to sacrifice his present interests in behalf of the future of the group and the race. The key to the "science of power" which will produce social progress in the future is, thus, to be found in woman's stimulation of "the emotion of the ideal."

Kidd's book, *The Control of the Tropics* (1898), was a sociological defense of British imperialism, comparable to F. H. Giddings' *Democracy and Empire* as an apology for American imperialism. It emphasized in realistic fashion the importance of imperialism for the future of Western civilization and of the control of the tropics by the white race as a vital factor in imperialism and human progress. The terrible suffering and the exploitation of native peoples by white conquerors and proprietors took on a benevolent cast with Kidd, in the light of his law of projected efficiency. It all helps to produce a better human race in the future by intensifying the struggle for existence. Like Ludwig Stein and Giddings, Kidd was a sociological exponent of the "white man's burden." The book had no little influence on the imperialistic policies of Joseph Chamberlain and other British imperialists. In his views on imperialism Kidd stood at the opposite pole from his contemporary, the English sociologist, L. T. Hobhouse, whose opinions on the subject we shall examine presently.

NOTES

1. *Social Evolution* (New York, 1894), chap. ii, particularly p. 37. For a criticism of the doctrine of Weismann on this point see Robert Mackintosh, *From Comte to Benjamin Kidd* (New York, 1899), chaps. xviii–xix. Kidd's position is briefly but concisely refuted by A. A. Tenney, *Social Democracy and Population* (New York, 1907), chap. iv.

2. *Social Evolution* pp. 77–79 and *passim*. Kidd's interpretation of reason, however, is very arbitrary, since he makes it practically synonymous with selfish egotism.

3. *Ibid.*, pp. 65, 286. This view is, of course, a direct contradiction of the basic thesis of the political and social philosophy of Herbert Spencer.

4. *Ibid.*, p. 293.

5. *Ibid.*, pp. 99–100; see also Lester F. Ward, *Pure Sociology* (New York, 1903), pp. 134, 265, 419 f.

6. *Social Evolution*, p. 103.

7. Referring particularly to the postclassical phase (*ibid.*, p. 121; see also his *Principles of Western Civilization* (New York, 1902), pp. 246–343.

8. *Social Evolution*, pp. 132–89.

9. *Ibid.*, p. 179. An excellent discussion of the true nature of this ruling-class "altruism" is to be found in J. L. and B. Hammond's *The Village Labourer* (London, 1911) and *The Town Labourer* (London, 1917); and in the *Report of Interchurch World Movement on the Steel Strike of 1919* (New York, 1920).

10. Cf. H. de B. Gibbins, *English Social Reformers* (New York, 1902), chap. iv; F. A. Ogg, *Economic Dvelopment of Modern Europe* (New York, 1916), chap. xvii; Thorstein Veblen, *The Theory of the Leisure Class* (New York, 1899), and *The Vested Interests* (New York, 1920).

11. *Social Evolution*, pp. 285–86.

12. *Principles of Western Civilization* (New York, 1902), p. 4.

13. One amusing instance of how a clergyman scented the danger in Kidd's work is to be seen in F. M. Sprague's *Laws of Social Evolution* (London, 1895).

14. *Societal Evolution* (New York, 1915), chaps. iv–vi.

15. But better than any specific criticism as an antidote for Kidd's theories is the general attitude of mind and array of information to be obtained from a careful reading of such books as W. E. H. Lecky, *History of Rationalism* (2 vols.; New York, 1910); H. T. Buckle, *History of Civilization in England* (2 vols.; New York, 1873); Andrew D. White, *Warfare of Science with Theology* (2 vols., New York, 1896); F. S. Marvin, *The Living Past* (Oxford, 1917), and *The Century of Hope* (Oxford, 1918); L. T. Hobhouse, *Social Evolution and Political Theory* (New York, 1913); and the writer's *History of Western Civilization* (2 vols.; New York, 1935), and *Intellectual and Cultural History of the Western World* (New York, 1941).

CHAPTER XXXII

LEONARD TRELAWNEY HOBHOUSE: EVOLUTIONARY PHILOSOPHY IN THE SERVICE OF DEMOCRACY AND SOCIAL REFORM

Harry Elmer Barnes

I. GENERAL NATURE OF HOBHOUSE'S WORKS AND OF HIS SYSTEM OF THOUGHT

A. HOBHOUSE AND SPENCER

IT MIGHT seem unusual that England, the country of Herbert Spencer, should, in the five decades following the publication of the first volumes of his *Principles of Sociology,* have produced but one scholar whose writings are of a sufficiently high order to mark him as the worthy successor of England's great philosopher and sociologist.[1] This writer was Professor Leonard Trelawney Hobhouse (1864–1929).[2]

Like Spencer, Hobhouse developed his sociological system as a part of a general philosophy of evolution. There is a still closer similarity between the two systems, in that Spencer conceived of the evolutionary process as one of progressive differentiation and better adjustment, and Hobhouse viewed it as a growth in correlation and harmony, and both looked upon society as an organic unity. But here the resemblance ceases. Spencer held that the course of evolution moves on automatically, regardless of the interference of man. He believed that the latter could, at best, have only an indifferent effect and was extremely likely to hinder the process. Hobhouse claimed, on the contrary, that, however much the evolutionary process may depend upon automatically working factors, such as the struggle for existence, social evolution has come to rest more and more upon conscious control by the human mind. From our period onward, progress will depend primarily upon the conscious direction of the social process by the social mind. Again, while Spencer's conception of the organic nature of society rested upon a wide use of the biological analogy, Hobhouse eschewed the use of technical biological terms and only implied the essential unity and interdependence of social life.

While both were avowed Liberals in English politics, Spencer's liberalism was of the "mid-Victorian" individualistic brand of Cobden and Bright, while Hobhouse was a supporter of that newer liberalism of Asquith and Lloyd George which abandoned most of the laissez faire tenets of the earlier period. It was the growth of this modern phase of liberalism which compelled Spencer in his later years to find himself more inclined to favor the policies of the Conservative party.[3]

One thus finds in Hobhouse the interesting combination of a writer who approaches the problems of society from the standpoint of a philosopher of evolution of a most thorough and recent type, of a sociologist unsurpassed in any country for breadth and profundity of learning, and of a liberal democrat in politics. From a writer who thus combined some of the best elements of sociological thought, one can look for a fair sample of what the sociologists have to contribute to a theory of society and the state.

B. THE FOUNDATION OF HOBHOUSE'S SOCIAL PHILOSOPHY

Attention may now be turned to a brief summary of the main propositions in Hobhouse's general philosophical system which he consistently carried over into his explanation of social phenomena.

In the first place, Hobhouse lays down the premise that any valid body of thought must rest upon the methods and discoveries of the most recent scientific endeavor. Its truth must be ascertained by testing it out through a study of experience, carried on according to scientific principles. Since evolution is the basis of all modern science, it may rationally be assumed to be the cornerstone of any modern system of social thought. As a philosopher, Hobhouse may, therefore, be classed as an evolutionist and an empiricist. He sums up his position on these points as follows: "In the meantime, I was convinced that a philosophy that was to possess more than a speculative interest must rest on a synthesis of experience as interpreted by science, and that to such a synthesis the general conception of evolution offered a key."[4]

The contradictions in the evolutionary theory as applied to human progress, which were so strikingly pointed out by Huxley, were due to the attempts of extreme exponents of evolution and pseudo-Darwinian writers to reduce all mental and social processes to one common level of interpretation and to ignore or deny any real differences of kind between biological and social processes. The real solution of the difficulty lies in an impartial and dispassionate study of mental and social evolution to see what has really been its course.[5]

The process of evolution may have been mainly automatic in the development of the animal kingdom prior to man, and even among primitive men. But there is an increasingly conscious control of the mind over material factors, and, at a certain stage in the development of humanity, the whole process becomes predominantly dependent for its future course upon rational control by the collective mind of society. Hence human progress cannot be assumed to be either inevitable or automatic. The struggle for existence and natural selection predominated in evolution until the gradual development of the human mind was able to produce sufficient mental advantages and compensations to overcome physical handicaps.

Until these mental advantages were sufficient to compensate for weaker physical powers, a stronger and more brutal civilization was likely to wipe out a more cultivated one. Such danger was averted only when mental evolution had reached such a stage that it could control all the vital conditions of human life: "Now it seemed to me that it is precisely on this line that modern civilization has made its chief advance, that through science it is beginning to control the physical conditions of life, and that on the side of ethics and religion it is forming those ideas of the unity of the race, and of the subordination of law, morals, and social constitutions generally to the need of human development which are the conditions of the control that is required."[6]

The similarity of this thesis to Lester F. Ward's main contribution to sociology is obvious, but Hobhouse's originality is vindicated by his divergence from Ward on many points and by the numerous scholarly volumes in which he develops this doctrine in detail. Morever, Hobhouse's far greater command of the data of social and cultural evolution allowed him to speak with greater exactness and authority than did Ward.

Evolution, thus, according to Hobhouse, may be viewed as the stages in the development of consciousness and self-consciousness and the resultant control of mind over the conditions of life.[7] Hobhouse admits the broad similarity of this doctrine to that of Hegel and holds that he accepts the element of truth advanced by Hegel, while rejecting his metaphysical vagaries and his contention that reality is entirely spiritual.[8] His system may, then, be regarded as an attempt to harmonize the valuable parts of the systems of Spencer and Hegel, in other words, to effect a scientific reconciliation of evolutionary materialism and metaphysical idealism. Spencer's attempt to explain reality by a purely mechanical and materialistic system and Hegel's insistence upon spiritual reality are rejected, while Spencer's conception of evolution as a synthesis is combined with Hegel's doctrine of the development of consciousness and purpose as the vital factor in human progress.

If the growth of conscious control over the conditions of life is the essential element in the evolutionary process, then some method must be provided for measuring the growth of consciousness, if the investigation is to have any scientific interest or validity. This standard of measurement Hobhouse finds in the principle of correlation: "I came to take the correlation which is effected in consciousness between different portions of our experience or between different acts and purposes as the basis of classification.....It is by correlation that the mind introduces order and establishes control."[9] The principle of correlation is particularly useful, since it will serve for measuring the elementary mental states of lower organisms, as well as the higher mental processes of man, the evolution of social structures, and the progress of civilization. There is a broad correlation between the growth of mental range and control and the development of human culture, which, in turn, provides an evolutionary basis for a sound sociological ethics.

As a result both of a detailed inductive study of the evolutionary process, taking the growth of consciousness as measured by correlation as the central theme, and of a philosophical analysis of the conception of evolution, thus considered, Hobhouse was led to accept the view of evolution as a purposive process: "It is submitted as a sound working hypothesis that the evolutionary process can best be understood as the effect of a purpose slowly working itself out under the limiting conditions which it brings successively under control."[10]

While at first opposed to the teleological view of the evolutionary process, Hobhouse was compelled by his detailed empirical studies to accept this conclusion. This purposive element, thus revealed, may be summarized as "a development of organic harmony through the extension of control by mind operating under mechanical conditions which it comes by degrees to master.....[11] In the higher organisms the work of establishing new correlations, and therefore in particular the work of adapting the organism to a higher synthesis, is the function of the mind, and in particular of that union of mind-functions which constitutes consciousness. The *growth of harmony* becomes, if not from the first, identical with the growth of mind."[12]

This vital principle of harmony, which reveals the universal purpose, he defines briefly as "mutual support between two or more elements of a whole."[13] A *harmonious system* is, then, one in which the parts work in coherence and co-operation. Progress may be regarded as the evolution of harmony, demonstrated by the increased co-ordination and correlation between the parts of the whole. As Morris Ginsberg puts it, Hobhouse conceived of development as "consisting in the extension of harmony through a series of syntheses, effected by the liberation of elements originally in conflict and the building up of structures of varying degrees of plasticity, scale and coherence."

In the development of this harmoniously organized system, which is the essence of the evolutionary process, reason comes to play a dominating part. Hobhouse thus takes a stand against the anti-intellectualistic attitude of some present-day psychological sociology. He says:

Reason is a principle of harmony pervading experience and working it into an organic whole. So understood, reason is supreme in the mind simply as that which embraces every element of experience, interconnects every feeling and thought, takes account impartially of every suggestion and every impulse, and weaves of them all a tissue which is never ossified but always plastic and recipient. It is the conscious expression of that impulse to harmony which dominates the entire evolution of mind, and the rationality of the process is the best guaranty of its ultimate success.[14]

While Hobhouse lays stress upon mental development as the most vital aspect of the evolutionary process, he disclaims any support of a spiritualistic monism. He simply maintains that the mental element becomes increasingly prominent as evolution proceeds: "There is a spiritual element integral to the structure and movement of reality, and evolution is the process by which this principle makes itself master of the residual conditions which at first dominate its life and thwart its efforts."[15] To put it concisely, mind provides the principle of orderly growth within reality.

Professor Hobhouse first developed this system of thought in four large and scholarly works which consumed twenty-six years in preparation. They form successive stages in the development of his system.

The foundations and presuppositions requisite for the construction of a valid system of thought were laid down in *The Theory of Knowledge*, published in 1896. The evolution of animal consciousness and the transition to human mentality were set forth in *Mind in Evolution*, published in 1901. The evolution of human and social consciousness is analyzed at length in *Morals in Evolution*, first published in 1906.[16] Finally, the results of the empirical studies carried on in *Mind in Evolution* and *Morals in Evolution* were reconciled with the philosophical implications of the process of evolution in *Development and Purpose*, published in 1913. In that work the process of evolution is set forth as a purposive development expressing itself in the working-out of a harmonious and rational system of mental processes and social relationship.

While the writer could by no means assume to pass competent technical judgment on any of these works, with the exception of *Morals in Evolution*, the almost unanimous praise of their high quality by a large number of specialists whose reviews have been consulted, as well as their comprehensive scope, would seem to accord Hobhouse the supreme place as a constructive philosopher among modern sociologists. Of course, his rank at present as a systematic sociologist would be much lower. Morris Ginsberg pays Hobhouse the following tribute in his article on Hobhouse in the *Encyclopaedia of the Social Sciences:*

> The range of Hobhouse's work was encyclopaedic. He was one of the pioneers of comparative psychology; he developed a technique for the handling of the vast and chaotic data of anthropology; he laid the foundations of a scientific sociology; in ethics and social philosophy he gave a penetrating and fruitful restatement of rationalism; and he attempted a synthesis of his scientific and philosophical studies on a scale which must win for him a high place among the systematic thinkers of the world.

Hobhouse re-wrote, condensed, and clarified his social philosophy in four brief books, *The Metaphysical Theory of the State* (1918), *The Rational Good* (1921), *Elements of Social Justice* (1921), and *Social Development: Its Nature and Conditions* (1924).

The Metaphysical Theory of the State was primarily a war product and represented Hobhouse's revulsion against the notion of political omnipotence and *Realpolitik* in the political writings of Hegel and the German idealistic philosophers. It is comparable to John Dewey's book on *German Philosophy and Politics*. It is valuable as a corrective but is the least calm and philosophical of Hobhouse's writings.

The Rational Good is an expansion of the basic theme in Hobhouse's writings, to the effect that the true social good consists in the triumph of harmony, co-ordination, and adjustment in society. This principle of harmony is the key to Hobhouse's system of social ethics. The *Elements of Social Justice* repeats this notion and works out Hobhouse's theory of social ethics in such practical fields as rights and duties, liberty and freedom, justice, property, the redistribution of wealth, and the realization of democracy. *Social Development* is the final statement of Hobhouse's conception of the principle of correlation as the measure of mental and social development. It is combined in this book with the notion of harmony and adjustment, as emphasized by a reasonable interpretation of the organic theory of society. This volume is the condensed synthesis of Hobhouse's social philosophy, combining his basic doctrines of evolution with his interpretation of social ethics. He ends on the theme of how far social science may formulate social laws to guide the quest for social justice and the common weal.

While these books cannot be ignored by the student of Hobhouse's social thought, they do not supersede the fuller and richer treatment of most of these topics in his earlier writings.

In any survey of Hobhouse's writings one must include one of his latest products, written just before his death, his magisterial article on "Christianity" in the *Encyclopaedia of the Social Sciences*. This is one of the ablest sympathetic interpretations of Christianity from the rationalistic point of view ever written. Hobhouse found the essence of Christianity to conform to his view of harmony and adjustment as the basis of social ethics. He concludes that the essence of the social teachings of Christianity "must be absorbed into anything that can call itself a rational reorganization of society."

C. THE GENERAL NATURE OF HOBHOUSE'S SOCIAL PHILOSOPHY

Hobhouse consistently carried over his general evolutionary doctrines into his sociological system as a means of interpreting social processes. His sociological doctrines are summarized in his suggestive little work on *Social Evolution and Political Theory,* which may be said to stand in much the same relation to Spencer's *Study of Sociology* that Hobhouse's volumes on the philosophy of evolution do to the *Synthetic Philosophy*. The *Social Evolution and Political Theory* epitomizes the sociological generalizations developed in Hobhouse's works dealing with his evolutionary system, as well as those put forth in two other works on political theory—*Democracy and Reaction* and *Liberalism*.

In the first place, as to the general field or scope of sociology, Hobhouse holds that it may be regarded chiefly as the science of human progress. He says:

> To form by a philosophic analysis a just conception of human progress, to trace this progress in its manifold complexity in the course of history, to test its reality by careful classification and searching comparisons, to ascertain its conditions, and if possible to forecast the future—this is the comprehensive problem towards which all sociological science converges and on the solution of which reasoned sociological effort must finally depend.[17]

The basic element in the social process, as well as the central subject of social evolution, is the interplay of human motives and the interaction of individuals: "The interplay of human motives and the interaction of human beings is the *fundamental fact of social life,* and the influence which it exercises upon the individuals who take part in it constitutes the fundamental fact of social evolution."[18]

Social progress, which is the prime object of sociological study, is not identical with social evolution. The latter term is the more comprehensive and may include retrogression as well as advance: "By evolution I mean any sort of growth; by social progress, the growth of social life in respect of those qualities to which human beings attach or can rationally attach value."[19] Nor is social progress primarily dependent upon biological factors. It is a cultural item and is chiefly a result of psychological and social forces:

> That is to say, there is progress just where the factor of social tradition comes into play and just so far as its influence extends. If the tradition is broken, the race begins again where it stood before the tradition was formed. We may infer that while the race has been relatively stagnant, society has rapidly developed, and we must conclude that, whether for good or for evil, social changes are mainly determined, not by alterations of racial type, but by modifications of traditions due to the interactions of social causes. Progress is not racial, but social.[20]

> So far as the eugenic principle advocates the substitution of rational for natural selection, it is, in the abstract, upon firm ground. Where it can be clearly established that a stock is tainted with a hereditary blemish so great as to outweigh its merits, it is desirable that the stock should not be perpetuated.....On the other hand, the use of eugenic arguments against legislation designed to replace the struggle for existence by ordered social coöperation is at bottom a misapplication of the principle. It rests on the survival of the older ideas of natural selection under a new form, in a new terminology.[21]

Social progress, in the last analysis, Hobhouse regards as an increase in the harmonious adjustment of man to society, of the different types of social organization to each other, and of society as a whole to its environment: "Social progress may be regarded as the development of the principle of union, order, cooperation, harmony, among human beings."[22] The ideal society, toward which social progress should lead, is one in which this harmony is realized: "The ideal society is conceived as a whole which lives and flourishes by the harmonious growth of its parts, each of which in developing on its own lines and in accordance with its own nature tends on the whole to further the development of others."[23]

This growth of harmonious adjustment in society, which is the essence of social progress, is not solely the result of automatically working factors; it can be completely achieved only by the conscious action of will and intelligence: "But in all its meaning harmony, as already hinted, is something which does not come of itself, but is achieved in greater or less degree by effort, that is to say, by intelligence and will."[24] The growth of rational social control over the conditions of life may thus be taken as the test of social progress: "We may therefore take the growth of social mind and its control over the conditions of life as the measure of progress."[25]

The most significant fact in the modern stage of civilization is that it has now reached the point where the social mind has obtained control over the external conditions of life: "The distinguishing characteristics of our time are that civilization for the first time has the upper hand, that the physical conditions of life have come and are rapidly coming more and more within human control, and that at least the foundations have been laid of a social order which would render possible a permanent and unbroken development."[26]

D. THE NATURE OF HOBHOUSE'S POLITICAL WRITINGS

Professor Hobhouse's political writings, the chief conclusions of which are summed up in *Social Evolution and Political Theory*, are in the main contained in three works—*Democracy and Reaction* (1905), *Liberalism* (1912), and *The Metaphysical Theory of the State* (1918). The first two are devoted to an exposition of the principles of English liberalism and, to a less degree, of the general sociological foundations of democracy. *Democracy and Reaction*, which is the most vigorously phrased of the three works, deals mainly with an elucidation of those liberal and sociological principles which are opposed to nationalistic imperialism and to the doctrine that progress comes from a physical struggle for existence. It is one of the keenest indictments of imperialism and national egoism and was written to combat the imperialistic Unionists, led by Joseph Chamberlain, the party which Hobhouse believed was attempting to deprive England of all the social gains she had made during the last half of the nineteenth century. The *Liberalism* is less polemic in character and is unrivaled by any other work as a brief historical and analytical exposition of the growth of, and changes in, British Liberal policy.[27]

Hobhouse's political doctrines clearly reflect the conditions under which they were written. They are a reaction against: (1) the dominant anti-intellectualism, based upon the mistaken interpretation of biological factors of evolution, which led to a fatalistic trust in natural selection; (2) the imperialistic program, which he demonstrates to be an offshoot of this theory; (3) all one-sided and hasty attempts at social reform, so common in contemporary society; and (4) metaphysical adulation of an absolute state.

II. SPECIFIC CONTRIBUTIONS TO SOCIAL AND POLITICAL THEORY

A. GENERAL CONCEPTS AND DEFINITIONS

In discussing the question of the relation of sociology to political science, Hobhouse holds that the latter is one of the specialisms which grow out of the basic method of general sociology, namely, that specialism which studies the state as a political organization within society. The older discipline of political philosophy, which was in vogue from Aristotle to Bentham, was wider than either. It included what is now known as "sociology," in a rough way, as well as political science and moral philosophy.[28]

Hobhouse apparently looks upon sociology as neither the basic and elemental science of society, as maintained by Professor Giddings, nor the synthetic social science, as held by Professor Small. Rather, he regards it as a broad method of approach to social problems—a view very similar to that held by Professor Durkheim. Not that he holds it to be simply a method but rather that its scope is determined primarily by its method. He says on this point:

Properly considered general sociology is neither a separate science complete in itself before specialism begins, nor is it a mere synthesis of the social sciences consisting in a mechanical juxtaposition of their results. It is rather a vitalizing principle that runs through all social investigation, nourishing and nourished by it in turn, stimulating inquiry, correcting results, exhibiting the life of the whole in the parts, and returning from a study of the parts to a fuller comprehension of the whole.[29]

His conception of the subject matter of sociology as consisting chiefly of a study of social progress in its broadest aspects has already been pointed out above.

Professor Hobhouse's view of the nature of the state is particularly sane and up-to-date, and his distinction of the state from society, government, and the nation is clear. Society, he holds to be a plural number of interacting individuals held together by mutual interest—a product of physical and psychological forces resulting from the "interaction of individuals under the conditions imposed by their physical environment."[30] Society is, thus, the broadest and most comprehensive type of human grouping.

The state is that form of human association which is distinguished by the possession and use of coercive power. Of course, other forms of association have and exercise coercive power, but the members can escape from the coercion of a voluntary form of association by leaving it. In the case of the state, however, the citizen cannot escape from this power unless he leaves the territory under the jurisdiction of the state, and even this avenue of escape is not always open: "The state is one form of association among others, distinguished by its use of coercive power, by its supremacy, and by its claim to control all who dwell within its geographical limits."[31] The state is, however, only one of the associations, among many, which are striving for the maintenance and improvement of group life, and it has no claim to be viewed in the Hegelian spirit of adulation as an ineffable and mystic entity:

The State is an association of human beings—with the exception of the great world churches the greatest of all associations. It has no mystic sanctity or authority rendering it superior to morality or emancipating it from the laws by which transgression brings its own retribution in the lowering of character. It is an association which has its own special constitution and circumstances, and in the concrete its duties and rights, like the duties and rights of every other association and every individual, must be judged in relation to this constitution and to these circumstances.[32]

In his *Metaphysical Theory of the State,* Hobhouse makes a devastating attack upon the Hegelian theory of the state, as set forth by Hegel himself and by such English disciples as Bosanquet. He contrasts in the following manner the Hegelian theory of the state and the modern democratic conception of the state:

> Herein lies the issue between these two views of the state. In the democratic or humanitarian view it is a means. In the metaphysical view it is an end. In the democratic view it is the servant of humanity in the double sense that it is to be judged by what it does for the lives of its members and by the part that it plays in the society of humankind. In the metaphysical view it is itself the sole guardian of moral worth. In the democratic view the sovereign state is already doomed, destined to subordination in a community of the world. In the metaphysical view it is the supreme achievement of human organization.[33]

Hobhouse calls attention to the fact that, while the Hegelian theory of the state has long been familiar to students of political philosophy, its practical significance has scarcely been recognized, and it has been passed over as the creation of a detached metaphysician:

> In older days we passed by the Hegelian exaltation of the state as the rhapsodical utterances of a metaphysical dreamer. It was a mistake. The whole conception is deeply interwoven with the most sinister developments in the history of Europe. It is fashionable to conceive German militarism as a product of the reaction against a beautiful sentimental idealism that reigned in the pre-Bismarckian era. Nothing could be more false. The political reaction began with Hegel, whose school has from the first to last provided by far the most serious opposition to the democratic and humanitarian conceptions emanating from eighteenth century France, sixteenth century Holland, and seventeenth century England. It was the Hegelian conception of the state which was designed to turn the edge of the principle of freedom by identifying freedom with law; of equality, by substituting the conception of discipline; of personality itself, by merging the individual in the state; of humanity, by creating the state as the supreme and final form of human association.[34]

Hobhouse believes that the Hegelian view of the state is not only a generally dangerous and pernicious doctrine but that it also specifically encouraged that view of international relations which produced the first World War.

As to the relation between the state and the government, Hobhouse agrees with the general consensus in modern political science and sociology, namely, that the government is the agent to which the state delegates the practical function of political control: "Government is conceived not as itself the source of unquestioned authority, but as a function which certain individuals are delegated to perform as servants, 'ministers' of the public as a whole."[35]

Hobhouse distinguishes in an equally clear manner between the state and the nation. Logically speaking, the concept of a nation is quite different from either the state or a race. Nationality is primarily a psychic and cultural matter—a sentiment of unity which is apparently a direct heritage or an expansion of the older sentiment of unity based upon the kinship which existed in tribal society:

> Nationality, indeed, is not properly a matter of race. Most of the bodies of people which feel themselves to be nations are of highly complex racial origin. Yet the sentiment of nationality is confessedly analogous to that of kinship: it is a natural unity stronger in the fact than in the logical analysis, a composite effect of language, tradition, religion, and manners which make a certain people feel themselves at one with each other and apart from the rest of the world. Pride and self-respect are closely bound up with it, and to destroy a nationality is in a degree to wound the pride and lower the manhood of those who adhere to it.[36]

Yet, however different the state and nation may be as logical concepts, their practical relation is most intimate and important. If a state happens to embrace a unified nation, the difficulties of political administration are much less than is the case when political sovereignty is extended over a heterogeneous assemblage of different nations:

> Analyze it away as we may, it [nationality] remains a great force, and those states which are rooted in national unity have in them a great living power which will carry them through much adversity. But few states are fortunate enough to be one in nationality, and the problem of dealing with the minority nation is the hardest that statesmen have to solve.....[37]

> Analyze the difference as you will, and explain it as you may, the State which is also a nation will have a different life from the State which is a fortuitous concourse of atoms, or the mechanical aggregation of a series of conquests. To ignore the difference is to leave a huge sunken rock unmarked on the chart of political prophecy.[38]

To the generally agreed-upon attributes of the state—territory, population, and sovereign power—Hobhouse would, as has been pointed out, add that the state should be looked upon as primarily a product of social conditions and as the public form of association for advancing the collective interests of mankind. Like most sociologists, Hobhouse regards the state as originating out of the matrix of society and not as prior to other forms of association.

B. THE HISTORICAL EVOLUTION OF SOCIAL AND POLITICAL INSTITUTIONS

Professor Hobhouse's survey of the origin and historic development of the state is one of the best summaries of that subject to be found in any language. In any account of the origin of the state which purports to conform to historic accuracy, one must start with the assumption of mankind as already socially organized. The doctrine that the political bond was the first which held men together in groups finds no support in either history or psychology. The cohesive principle which formed the foundation of human association was mutual interest and sympathy, corresponding in a broad way to the schedule of vital human interests suggested by Professor Small, combined with Professor Giddings' theory of the "consciousness of kind."

This social bond is resolvable into many components, such as sympathy, interest in one's fellows, altruism, and combination for mutual defense against enemies and for the advantages of industrial co-operation. In addition to this general basis of human association, one may find in each period of social evolution some dominating social bond. While not so fundamental as that of mutual interest, it is more direct and apparent and serves to "give character to the society as a whole." The history of social organization has revealed three such characteristic social bonds—kinship, authority, and citizenship.[39]

The principle of kinship is the dominant social bond in primitive society. The crudest type of social organization among primitive peoples is that of the endogamous horde, but its form is rather exceptional among existing human societies. The most characteristic primitive group is the exogamous clan based on blood relationship, real and fictitious. The clan is, roughly speaking, an enlarged family, living in a group and held together by ties of descent through either male or female ancestors. If the descent is traced through the male, the clan is paternal; if traced through the female, maternal.

Hobhouse wisely refrains from committing himself to the view that the horde, the maternal clan, and the paternal clan represent an invariable serial sequence in the history of institutions, thus avoiding the chief pitfall of those historical sociologists who base their generalizations upon the work of the early evolutionary ethnologists and sociologists.

The larger groups of primitive society were normally the local community, usually composed of a number of contiguous exogamous clans, and the larger tribal union, which included several of these local communities.

In describing the form and degree of government found in this kinship stage of society, Hobhouse makes use of the statistical data gathered in his *Material Culture and Social Institutions of the Simpler Peoples,* written with Ginsberg and Wheeler. He finds that those groups that possess no effective government, aside from the household, constitute about one-half of the lower hunters, one-tenth of the agricultural and pastoral peoples, and are practically absent among the higher agricultural grades. Those which have a recognized governmental organization make up from one-quarter to one-third of the hunting peoples, about one-half of the agricultural and pastoral peoples, and over three-fourths of the higher agricultural peoples, often developing an embryonic kingdom in the latter type. These kinship associations "have much vital force, compactness, and endurance, but they are narrow and in proportion to their strength tend to be hard, self-contained, and mutually hostile. They are, moreover, adapted only to rude economic conditions and a rudimentary condition of the arts of life. Hence, they yield with advancing civilization to the rule of force, by which, in the guise of kingly authority far larger aggregations of men can be held together and a more regular order can be maintained."[40]

The very limitations of the kinship principle thus naturally led to that type of political organization which is first based upon force but is later transmuted into the principle of *authority*. This transition usually comes when a strongly organized paternal clan, for one reason or another, starts on a career of conquest. In this transitional process, personal liberty has usually been forfeited by both conquerors and conquered. The conquerors, in order to preserve the coherence and discipline essential to success, were compelled to confer almost unlimited authority upon the chief, while the conquered peoples, though sometimes slaughtered, were usually reduced to a condition of slavery or serfdom. The conquest usually increased the power of the victorious chief, who became converted into a king, with a religious sanction for his superiority.

There thus came into existence a political society, based upon despotism and reinforced by religion. This new type of political order could not long be based upon force alone, but had to develop a theoretical justification for its existence: "The simple but comprehensive code of despotism merely lays down that one man is divinely appointed to determine what is best for all others, and therewith transmutes arbitrary power into righteous authority and slavish subjection into loyal service."[41] Hobhouse sums up the characteristics and contributions of this type of political order as follows:

To sum up the results which the despotic principle—whether we regard it as authority resting ultimately upon force or as force transmuted into authority—has given us:

1st. as to the form of Society, we have—

(a) The Absolute Monarchy, where the king is divine and lord without restraint of the persons or properties of his subjects. This form has most vitality in relatively small and barbaric communities.

(b) The Feudal Monarchy, suited to wider areas where power is delegated, and the governing class form a hierarchy.

(c) The Empire, founded by the aggregation of kingdoms, overstepping national boundaries and exihibiting very varying degrees of unity and local freedom.

2nd. as to the nature of Government, the conception of a moral duty to the governed develops in proportion to the degree of unity achieved, but throughout law is conceived as based upon authority and the social system upon the subordination of class to class. For this order a religious sanction is found, generally in the special association of the ruler with the deity, often also in the semi-divine character of the ruling race, or caste, or finally, in the belief in their conquering and civilizing mission.

If, finally, we may endeavor to sum up in a sentence the function of this principle in human evolution, we may say that it belongs to the epochs of expansion in culture and improvement in the arts of life. It is one method by which large communities can be formed with greater facilities for self-government and for the maintenance of internal order than the primitive clan or village community can enjoy.[42]

The third type of political order is that which is based upon the bond of *citizenship* and which seeks to secure the recognition of personal rights and the advancement of the common good. The two fundamental features of any state based upon citizenship are "the responsible individual fully seized of civic rights and obligations, and the responsible government expressing the will of the whole society in law and administration."[43] In this third type of political order the relations between the governed and the governing, as compared with conditions in the previous stage of authority and force, are reversed. Government is no longer the source of final or sovereign authority, but merely the delegated agent of the people as whole. Law is no longer the ordinance of a despot, but the will of the people expressed through their elected agents: "The subjects of a government have now become citizens of a state, and the citizen has rights which are no less important than his duties. These rights hold good against the government just as they hold against other individuals, for it is a prime characteristic of the state based upon citizenship that it establishes the reign of law, and subjects its officers to this impersonal sovereign."[44]

This type of political organization, based upon citizenship, first came into being among the Greeks of Athens, where civic idealism probably reached the highest level in all history. At the same time there were inherent weaknesses in the Greek system that rendered its perpetuation impossible. The so-called "democratic" Athenian state included a large slave class, and the lack of unified action in the administration of government, together with petty jealousies among the separate city-states, prevented the formation of that large-scale political federation which was essential to self-preservation.

The Roman system degenerated into a political order based upon authority rather than citizenship. The Roman system of republican city-state government could not adapt its administrative mechanism to territorial expansion with speed or success; and, by the time that the idea of federation had made headway, the Roman republic had passed away.

The medieval city-states escaped the blight of slavery, which had been a curse to the Greeks and Romans, but their internal dissensions and their spirit of local isolation and exclusiveness were, if anything, more extreme than among the Greeks.

Because of these earlier failures, the experiment of founding a political system on the principle of citizenship had to be tried over again in the rise and development of democracy and the national state. In this last experiment there have been two stages—the period of absolutism, bringing political concentration and territorial aggression comparable to that during the earlier domination of the authoritative principle, and the period of the democratic reaction against absolutism. As a result of this latter struggle, which has occupied the greater part of modern history,

government has come to recognize that its position is only justified by its function in serving public order and the general happiness. .... The principle of personality has won the successive recognition of one right after another—the right to the protection of the tribunals or immunity from arbitrary punishment, freedom in religious matters, first freedom of conscience, afterwards freedom of expression and public worship, the right to discuss and criticize the acts of government, the right of meeting and association, ultimately the political right to secure these liberties by an indirect share in the government of the country—all the rights which, when taken together, make the modern state what it is.[45]

Hobhouse recognizes that the evolution of the modern state, based on the principle of nationality, has been an important progressive step in the history of human liberty, but he is also alive to the menace of nationalistic aggression:

Nationality is a Janus. It looks both ways—towards freedom and towards aggression. The struggles of subject nationalities with oppressors and conquerors have filled a great chapter in the history of freedom. Yet nationalities that have become free have often gone on to enslave others..... Hence the rise of nationality, essential in its first stages to political liberty, is also a permanent menace to peace and order.[46]

Yet the emancipation of suppressed nations is the indispensable preliminary prerequisite of a permanent and enduring internationalism: "In proportion as political unity can be brought into accord with national sentiment the chances of international union are improved."[47]

The national territorial state is not likely, however, to be the final stage in political development, on account of one inherent weakness. The military ambition, which is based upon nationalism, is incompatible with the development of internal liberty and social harmony within the state itself. The growth of imperialism, with its double code of political ethics—one for home government and another for dependencies—has already seriously threatened the existence of liberal and democratic institutions.

Hobhouse maintains, as Kant and others had a century before, that the political prospects of the future depend upon the development of a spirit of internationalism, which will put an end to national aggression, with its wasting of the national resources and its encouragement of political despotism, and will allow a nation peacefully to devote itself to the settlement of its internal problems and the realization of social justice:

The future of the State is bound up with Internationalism. If the rivalries and jealousies of the civilized nations can be so far overcome as to admit of combined action in the cause of peace, there is every reason to expect that within each nation the rule of right will be maintained and developed. If, on the contrary, wars are to give way only to periods of armed peace, each country alike must gradually relapse into the rule of a dictatorship. The country state, therefore, can hardly be the final word of politics, but if progress continues it must consist in the quickening into active life of those germs of internationalism which the best statesmen of the nineteenth century helped to bring into a precarious existence.[48]

Federalism, as a principle, has suggested a method of reconciling the ideas of empire and democracy, while international arbitration is an equally effective agent for settling international disputes, if its aid were only more frequently and universally invoked.

In concluding the discussion of political evolution, Hobhouse makes it clear that he does not imply that these three broad stages in the development of the state have always followed one another in a uniform sequence in all cases. He simply holds that they are the dominant features of political evolution: "It follows that we cannot say that any of these forms succeeds another in serial form as we ascend the scale of culture. The history of society unfortunately is not so simple. All that we can say with certainty is that the three principles can be distinguished and the forms of social union arising out of them predominate at successive stages in the order named."[49]

Hobhouse's masterly excursion into historical and comparative jurisprudence cannot be analyzed in this discussion, but it might be mentioned in passing that nothing to equal it exists in any language within the same number of pages. He summarizes the main conclusions in the following paragraphs:

Briefly to resume the main phases in the evolution of public justice, we find that at the outset the community interferes mainly on what we may call supernatural grounds only with actions which are regarded as endangering its existence. Otherwise justice, as we know it, in the sense of an impartial upholding of rights and an impartial punishment of wrong-doing, is unknown. In the place of that we have at the outset purely private and personal retaliation. This develops into systematized blood-feuds of consolidated families and clans. At this stage, responsibility is collective, redress is collective, intention is ignored, and there is no question of assessing punishment according to the merit of the individual. When retaliation is mitigated by the introduction of money payments no change in ethical principle occurs. It is only as social order evolves an independent organ for the adjustment of disputes and the prevention of crime that the ethical idea becomes separated from the husk, and step by step the individual is separated from his family, and his intentions are taken into account, his formal rectitude or want of rectitude is thrown into the background by the essential justice of the case, appeals to magical practices are abandoned, and the law sets before itself the aim of discovering the facts and maintaining right or punishing wrong accordingly.

The rise of public justice proper necessitates the gradual abandonment of the whole conception of the trial as a struggle between two parties, and substitutes the idea of ascertaining the actual truth in order that justice may be done. That is at first carried out by supernatural means, viz., by the Ordeal and the Oath. These in turn give way to a true judicial inquiry by evidence and rational proof. The transition occurred in England mainly during the thirteenth century, the turning-point being marked by the prohibition of the ordeal by Innocent III in 1215. The early stages of public justice administered by the recently developed central power led to excessive barbarity in discovery and punishment of crime. It took some more centuries to prove to the world that efficacy in these relations could be reconciled with humanity and a rational consideration of the best means of getting at the truth. By so long and round-about a process is a result, so simple and obvious to our minds, obtained.[50]

C. THE FORMS OF GOVERNMENT AND THE PROBLEMS OF DEMOCRACY

With respect to the various forms of government, Professor Hobhouse had little to say about any type except democracy. His discussion of the nature, value, and limitations of democracy is extensive and illuminating.

First, as to the meaning of democracy, Hobhouse correctly points out that the term may be used in two different senses. It may mean the direct participation of the mass of the people in the affairs of government. Democracy in this sense—as a form of government—is, however, no longer practicable. The affairs of government have become so complex and multifarious that the citizens have neither the training nor the time to handle the business of government. Even in America, the land which has most cherished this conception of democracy, it has been recognized that it is a forlorn ideal, and a specialized and trained civil service has developed.

The other conception of democracy is that which is based on the idea of ultimate popular sovereignty—the idea of a democratic state as contrasted with democratic government, though Hobhouse does not make this vital distinction explicit. The successful operation of democracy, even in this second sense, is difficult, though not impossible. This is due to the complexity and remoteness of most political issues and agencies which cannot attract a high degree of interest on the part of the average voter. The problem is increased by that confusion of issues which is partially the result of deliberate obfuscation and evasion by party organizations and leads the voter to despair of intelligent action. Hobhouse agrees with Graham Wallas that one of the most essential steps which need to be taken to clarify issues and awaken a sense of interest and responsibility on the part of the mass of the voters in the affairs of government is to revive the vitality of local self-government.

That which may be reasonably expected of the mass of the citizens under a regime of popular sovereignty is that they will give their assent to those measures which will promote the common welfare. They cannot be expected to make independent investigations into the merits of every public question, but a successful democracy presupposes that there will be able leaders to enlighten the people and that the people, on their part, will be sufficiently interested to give heed to this advice of the leaders. Democracy need not be assumed to give a more efficient government than monarchy or bureaucracy, but it may be justly claimed that, by interesting and informing the people, democracy can develop the individual personality to a greater extent than any other type of government. If the people cannot be induced to study public questions, then the time is not yet ripe for democracy. Hobhouse sums up the advantages of democracy in the following paragraph:

> Self-government, with all its defects, implies a recognition of the duties of government and the rights of the people; it postulates a measure of personal freedom and of equal consideration for all classes. It is the natural instrument of a growing sense of social solidarity, and the appropriate organ of a stirring national life. In a word, it is the political expression of the idea of Right on which the modern State rests, and if there be any other mode of government which would maintain that idea equally well, it has yet to be produced.[51]

If democracy is as important as this, it is worth while to examine some of the difficulties which it faces and to suggest some of the improvements needed to make its operation more effective in the future.

Hobhouse devotes the majority of his work on *Democracy and Reaction* to a substantiation of the thesis that nationalistic imperialism, with the resulting despotic government of inferior races, is incompatible with the existence or success of democratic self-government at home. It is impossible to develop an arrogant and overbearing bureaucracy to deal with foreign administration without suffering from a reaction of the same principle upon domestic affairs. On the other hand, there is no necessary conflict between democracy and an extension of imperial federation, which permits local self-government within the larger units. But, on the whole, internationalism rather than imperialism is the ally of democracy.

There is, again, the serious handicap, already pointed out, of the "dilution" of responsibility and of the complexity and confusion of issues in a modern democracy: "All that the ordinary voter feels about a given act of government, then, is that it is an act of men to whose return to power he contributed one vote out of some two million or more it may be three or four years ago, when probably quite other questions were under discussion, and whom he will not be able to dislodge until perhaps two or three years more have passed, by which time again other questions have come up."[52] One remedy that he suggests for this difficulty—an increase of the vitality of local self-government—has already been pointed out.

Another of the difficulties of democracy is to provide adequate leaders. No form of government is more dependent upon able statesmen for its success than democracy, yet it must be admitted that democracy is not well adapted to produce such men. A certain amount of brazenness is required of any man who puts himself forward as a public leader in a democracy, and this is a quality which few great men possess, while it is a quality which the politician possesses in an egregious degree. Therefore, while democracy is particularly in need of men who can guide public opinion with wisdom and discretion, this form of government makes it especially easy for quite the opposite type of person to assume the function of political guidance:

Finally, every form of government must be held responsible for the type of man whom it tends to bring to the front, and he who would weigh the merits and defects of democracy must take into account the character of the democratic leader. He must measure the power of brazen self-assertion and unblushing advertisement to bring a man to the front in a society like ours; he must allow that the capacity of gaining power depends more on the effective use of the rapier or the bludgeon in debate than on any proof of capacity to serve the country, while the art of maintaining power resolves itself into the art of so keeping up appearances as always to maintain the show of success for the moment, trusting to the levity of the public and the shortness of political memories to let the real final reckoning go by without close inquiry. A popular leader is not wont to take long views. He seldom looks farther than the next General Election. It would sometimes seem that he looks no farther than the next Parliamentary division, and as long as he keeps his majority, recks little of the effect his words may produce—it may be, on the future of a historic party; it may be on the broad interests of the nation; it may be in deepening the wretchedness of some persecuted people in a distant land. If sufficiently endowed with sophistical skill and debating readiness, a democratic ruler may become a very irresponsible being.[53]

Then, on the psychological side, democracy has to make assumptions which render its position precarious in proportion as they are not verified by experience. Democracy, of all forms of government, assumes the existence of a common or public will. Without such an organization of the will of the community, the democratic system must fall flat or degenerate into mere forms to which the real substance of democracy is foreign. Since it is well-nigh impossible for the mass of the people to study in detail the issues at stake, arrive at a common opinion, and manifest a united interest in public matters, it is particularly necessary that they be instructed by the press, "but the bulk of the press will lay before the public nothing that will not be popular. Its business is to tickle its master's vanity, to tell him solemnly that his duty lies there whither his prejudices already lead him, and to cover up and hide away all things done in his name which might be hurtful to his self-esteem. The few who persist in telling the truth share the traditional fate of the honest counsellor at the hands of the mob of courtiers."[54]

Finally, there are the problems of majority rule, including the protection of the minority and the avoidance of precipitate legislation. This problem has usually been looked upon from the standpoint of preventing radical legislation, and the aristocratic and conservative second house has been hit upon as a device to prevent undue haste in progressive measures. Hobhouse quite rightly points out that there is another side to be considered. At present, the restraints are all placed upon progressive tendencies and none on reactionary movements. There is nothing to frustrate extreme measures proposed by a conservative majority, while a liberal majority has to face the aristocratic upper chamber, the bench, and the conservative tendencies in society, in general, which are now usually upheld by minorities. Hobhouse, of course, wrote these passages several years before the Parliament Act of 1911 had shorn the House of Lords of its veto power.

A way to make the protection of the minority operate impartially, Hobhouse suggests in his proposal for an impartial second chamber, without the power to overthrow the government but with the right to refer appropriate measures to the vote of the people. He thus advocates a limited use of the referendum but stipulates that financial measures and others affecting only certain interests or localities should be eliminated from this sort of procedure.

Hobhouse points out how the English experience has disproved at least one common charge against democracy, namely, that it plays into the hands of the rabble. No sooner had the people finally been enfranchised in England in 1867 and 1884 than they put the Conservative party back into power and kept it there most of the time for two decades: "The first act of the new British democracy was to install the Conservatives in power, and to maintain them with but partial exceptions for nearly twenty years. Never were the fears or hopes of either side more signally disappointed."[55]

Hobhouse considers the question as to whether an efficient bureaucracy or a partially bungling democracy should be preferred. He believes that, with all its faults, the latter promises more for the future of mankind. Bureaucracy provides an excellent means for efficient administration but is very poorly adapted for determining policy on a large scale. It is "the means to an end rather than the means for determining an end." Again, a bureaucracy tends to become mechanical in its action and makes no provision for the development of the individual personality: "When administrative efficiency is made the supreme end, personal liberty, and religious and national divergencies become secondary and subordinate matters. There is not much consideration for the weaker brother, nor much patience with the offender. The grinding of the machine wears away these graces of humanity."[56]

Hobhouse makes it clear how, in the last analysis, the future of democracy is involved in the general progress of civilization and in the development of a socialized theory of politics. No people is fully enjoying political liberty when its industrial conditions are such as sap the vitality of the people or when its international affairs are in such a condition that armed preparedness is necessary: "We may fairly conclude that the ideas of democratic government, personal liberty, the supremacy of law as against arbitrary rule, national rights, the wrongfulness of aggression, racial and class equality are in principle and in practice closely interwoven."[57]

D. SOVEREIGNTY, LIBERTY, AND NATURAL RIGHTS

Hobhouse's use of the term "sovereignty" is hardly clear or consistent. It seems that in most cases he uses it to mean the lawmaking and enforcing power, though at times he appears to mean by it the ultimate power behind the constitution, which in democratic countries resides in the mass of the people. While this is essentially Dicey's distinction between legal and political sovereignty, Hobhouse does not explain explicitly which use he has in mind at different times.

In his *Morals in Evolution* he states that the distinguishing characteristic of the state based upon citizenship is the fact that law is now the embodiment of popular will and that government is subjected to the sovereignty of law. Again he asserts that the federal system in the United States is characterized by the division of sovereignty between the states and the nation. Of course, it is a cardinal quality of sovereignty, in the generally accepted sense, that it cannot be divided; but here Professor Hobhouse seems to refer to governmental power. Then, in his work on *Liberalism*,[58] he contends that "the old doctrine of absolute sovereignty is dead. The greater states of the day exhibit a complex system of government within government, authority limited by authority." Here, again, he must mean by "sovereignty" governmental power, for in no important modern state is actual sovereign power divided and distributed.

In his *Democracy and Reaction,* in discussing the possibility of an international state or of an enforcement of international agreements, he argues that law may be enforced without any sovereign power behind it if the customary precedent for the enforcement of law is strong enough. But he refers in many places to the conception of ultimate popular sovereignty as the indirect control of the government by the people—the ultimate power of the electorate to determine questions of law and political policy. In spite of these seeming inconsistencies, however, it need not be assumed that he does not have clear and definite conceptions about the nature of sovereignty, since nothing more than casual references to the term occur in his works and nowhere does he attempt a formal definition and interpretation of the concept.

Hobhouse's discussion of liberty and its reconciliation with authority is particularly clear and satisfactory. Liberty he defines in its most general sense as "the condition of mental and moral expansion, and of all forms of associated as well as personal life that rest for their value on spontaneous feeling and the sincere response of the intellect and of the will."[59] Practically, however, liberty means the freedom of individual conduct along those lines of activity which do not interfere with the similar privileges of all other normal members of society. Hence liberty, by definition, implies the presence of restraints, and, as a matter of fact, the task of realizing liberty in a society resolves itself into the problem of successfully organizing a system of restraints within the group. The old tradition of the antithesis between liberty and authority therefore vanishes—the former cannot exist as a universally realized ideal without the existence of the latter: "The function of State coercion is to override individual coercion, and, of course, coercion exercised by any association of individuals within the State. It is by this means that it maintains liberty of expression, security of person and property, genuine freedom of contract, the rights of public meeting and association, and finally its own power to carry out common objects undefeated by the recalcitrance of individual members."[60]

Hobhouse resolves liberty into its various aspects—civil, fiscal, personal, social, economic, domestic, local, racial, national, international, and political. By pointing out the degree and quality of freedom which each implies, as well as the corresponding restraints which are required, he gives a high degree of concreteness to a discussion which is otherwise wont to run into metaphysical generalities.

The question of liberty and the restraints which it involves, both upon individuals and upon society as a whole, naturally leads to the question of what justification there is for restraints. This justification is usually found in the so-called rights of individuals, and Hobhouse devoted his attention to an analysis of just what these "rights" actually mean and imply from a sociological viewpoint. A right, in its most general sense, he finds to be an expectation which will appeal to an impartial person as being adapted to the promotion of the general welfare of the community. There can be no right of the individual which conflicts with the common good of the community or is independent of society. Hence, there can be no "natural rights" in the older metaphysical and juristic sense, according to which man was assumed to possess rights antecedent to, and independent of, society and government. Yet if one conceives of the harmonious functioning of an evolving society as something natural, then one may readily discern natural rights in a sociological sense. Such natural rights would be those indispensable liberties and immunities which society would guarantee to the individual in order to secure proper adjustment between the welfare of society as a whole and the good of its constituent members:

> The rights of man are those expectations which the common good justify him in entertaining, and we may even admit that there are natural rights of man if we conceive the common good as resting upon certain elementary conditions affecting the life of society, which hold good whether people recognize them or not. Natural rights, in that case, are those expectations which it would be well for a society to guarantee to its members, whether it does or does not actually guarantee them. If this view is accorded, the more developed the conception of the common good the more completely will a society guarantee the natural rights of its individual members.[61]

Therefore, a right is virtually only a condition of social welfare, and there must be many such rights; it is the "problem of social philosophy to define in principle, and of statesmanship to adjust in practice the bearing of these several conditions."[62]

Liberty is, thus, a social conception which involves such a degree of restraint upon individual and group conduct as will insure the maximum freedom for society and for its component members. This restraint is, in turn, justified by the rights of individuals, which are the essential conditions of public welfare. Both liberty and rights are, thus, social in origin and justification, and liberty is reconciled with authority by a demonstration that it is really dependent upon authority for its origin, existence, and maintenance.

E. THE PROPER SCOPE OF STATE ACTIVITY

In handling crucial problems in every theory of the state—the function and sphere of political action and the reconciliation of authority and liberty—Hobhouse's treatment is among the best to be found in sociological literature. In the first place, he lays down the general rule that it is useless to try to define the sphere of legitimate state activity in specific terms, and at the same time hope to make that definition valid for every society. The scope of state activity is dependent upon the fundamental social conditions existing in any society. If the society is highly homogeneous, the state may successfully develop a considerable degree of activity and interference, while a similar program would cause a revolution in a society made up of many different nationalities with diversified customs and ideals. To give the problem a mathematical statement, the scope of state activity is a function of the composition, progress, and organization of the society under consideration: "The legitimate functions of the state must depend upon the whole circumstances of the society which is under consideration. The kind of compulsion that is necessary, the degree of success with which compulsion can be applied, and the reflex consequences of its employment upon the general life of society will depend essentially upon the composition of the community and the relation of the government to its subjects."[63]

But this does not mean that it is impossible to define in general terms the proper scope of state activity which will apply to any society. It may be stated, as a general principle, that the proper sphere of state activity lies in carrying out those lines of activity in which uniformity and concerted activity on the part of the society is necessary:

This function of state activity may now be defined in general terms as that of securing the best conditions for the common life, (a) so far as these are best obtained by the use of public resources and governmental machinery, (b) so far as such conditions are only obtainable by the use of compulsion; that is to say, where action is frustrated if not universal, and again where in the absence of regulation one man can directly or indirectly constrain another, infringe his rights, obstruct his rational choice, or take advantage of his weakness or ignorance.[64]

The state is an association for dealing with men in mass and with highly generalized matters and hence cannot possess that plasticity in administration which is essential in handling the higher aspects of social life or those questions in which variations of opinion and action are desirable. Its function is primarily to deal with the fundamental commonplace foundations of social welfare, which will allow the superstructure of voluntary effort and activity to function in safety and harmony:

> The life of the state is crystallized into the form of definite institutions, its ordinances have to be incorporated in laws and rules of universal application, and it must deal with men in masses and with problems in accordance with what is general and not with what is particular. Hence it is with difficulty adapted to the individuality of life; it is a clumsy instrument, as it were, for handling human variation. It is inadequate, to adapt Bacon's phrase, to the subtlety of human nature. Its sphere is the normal, the prosaic, the commonplace; its business is to solidify the sub-structure of society rather than to pursue its adornment. It can handle the matters upon which ordinary people agree rather than those upon which there is a variety of opinion.[65]

This conception is, indeed, far removed from Hegel's conception of the state as "perfected rationality," but it is probably far closer to the truth.

Hobhouse thus established in general terms the sphere of legitimate state activity as that which is primarily concerned with producing a coercively secured uniformity where necessary; with promoting the conditions which make possible an organic and harmonious development of society and of the individual; and, finally, with handling commonplace and routine affairs. He then turns to analyze more in detail some of the specific activities which the state might undertake within this general sphere of justifiable activity.

First, as to the desirable attitude of the state toward private property, he tries to steer a middle course between the antiquated metaphysical and legalistic theory of an inherent natural right of property and the socialistic view, which so far emphasizes the social basis of property that it ignores the psychological importance of the element of personal possession. The foundations of property are essentially social, for, without protection through the organized force of the community, the property of the individual would be very insecure and, without the co-operative industry of society, the production of wealth would be very small indeed:

> In spite of all criticism many people still seem to speak of the rights of property as though they were conferred by Nature or by Providence upon certain fortunate individuals, and as though these individuals had an unlimited right to command

the State, as their servant, to secure them by the free use of the machinery of law in the undisturbed enjoyment of their possessions. They forget that without the organized force of society their rights are not worth a week's purchase.[66]

On the other hand, one must not ignore the value of individual property rights in stimulating effort. Without this personal initiative, society would function as inefficiently as it would if the social basis of economic life were left insecure: "To maintain and stimulate this personal effort is a necessity of good economic organization, and without asking here whether any particular conception of Socialism would or would not meet this need we may lay down with confidence that no form of Socialism which should ignore it could possibly enjoy enduring success."[67]

The proper solution of the problem of property lies in allowing to individual effort a reward which will insure its efficient functioning and putting the remaining wealth at the disposal of society for the furthering of the collective welfare:

> The central point of Liberal economics, then, is the equation of equal service and reward. This is the principle that every function of social value requires such remuneration as serves to stimulate and maintain its effective performance; that every one who performs such a function has the right, in the strict ethical sense of that term, to such remuneration and to no more; that the residue of existing wealth should be at the disposal of the community for social purposes.[68]

The method which Hobhouse recommends for dealing with the large fortunes of today, which represent a control of property and of politics quite out of proportion to the services of the individual possessor of wealth, is a progressive scheme for taxing inherited wealth, socially created forms of individual wealth, and excessively large incomes: "The true function of taxation is to secure to society the element in wealth that is of social origin, or, more broadly, all that does not owe its origin to the efforts of living individuals."[69]

Had Hobhouse lived to the present day, he would have seen his ominous predictions as to the disastrous effects of imperialism and war and his proposals as to drastic taxation of the very rich borne out with dramatic and drastic thoroughness. The second World War transformed the British Empire from a creditor to a debtor state and shattered its prosperity and solvency. The burdens thus entailed brought about a tax schedule so crushing that, in the fiscal year ending March 31, 1947, less than fifty persons out of a total population of about fifty millions retained an income of over $24,000 after payment of taxes.

Society must try, as far as possible, to discriminate between earned and unearned incomes. It should levy a very considerable tax upon the unearned type and a sufficiently high one upon the earned incomes so as to prevent their rising unduly above what the receiver of the income contributes to society. Hobhouse admits that it would be hard to determine just what amount a great genius contributes to society, but he contends that this is never a practical question, "for the man of genius is forced by his own cravings to give and the only reward he asks from society is to be let alone and have some quiet and fresh air."[70]

This social appropriation of unearned incomes raises the question of what is to be done with the revenue thus obtained. This by no means so difficult a problem as it is to provide a method whereby society will be able to get a just reward for its share in the creation of wealth. The opportunities for fruitful expenditure in the realms of public education and sanitation have by no means been exhausted. Then there is the ever present question of improving the lot of the poor. Hobhouse points out the fallacy in the argument against the taxation of the rich for this purpose, which is expressed in the phrase of "robbing Peter to pay Paul." He shows how this charge is groundless, since, in the first place, to allow a person to absorb more wealth than he creates is to allow him to rob society and, in the second place, the fulfilment of the requirement of an organic and harmonious social life requires that no one be allowed to suffer from the lack of adequate physical comforts. He believes, further, that the proper method of handling the question of poverty is to aim at socialized prevention rather than the mere relief of individual destitution. Old age pensions and social insurance are steps in the right direction.

The discussion of the sphere of the state in regard to poverty naturally leads to an analysis of what the general attitude of the state should be in regard to labor. The basis of the legitimate interference of the state in problems of labor is twofold. In the first place, it is the duty of the state to control industrial contracts which are made under conditions in which one party is at a distinct advantage. It is perfectly obvious that the individual laborer is at a disadvantage in bargaining with his employer. Out of the recognition of this duty has grown the legislation that resulted, first, in the regulation of laboring conditions among women and children and then, gradually, an extension of the supervision of the state over the condition of adult male laborers. The second justification

of state interference with labor is to be found in the duty of the state
to provide for the normal functioning of the life of the mass of its citizens:

> If we grant, in accordance with the idea with which we have been working all
> along, that it is demanded of all sane adult men and women that they should live
> as civilized beings, as industrious workers, as good parents, as orderly and efficient
> citizens, it is, on the other side, the function of the economic organization of society
> to secure them the material means of living such a life, and the immediate duty of
> society is to mark the points at which such means fail and to make good the
> deficiency. Thus the conditions of social efficiency mark the minimum of industrial
> remuneration, and if they are not secured without the deliberate action of the State
> they must be secured by means of the deliberate action of the State.[71]

Furthermore, there is the problem of how far the state may rightfully
interfere in family affairs, and in matters of religion and education. The
state is justified in interfering in the affairs of the family in preventing
it from interfering with the liberty of individuals and on "the basis of
the rights of the child, of his protection against parental neglect, of the
equality of opportunity which he may claim as a future citizen and of
his training to fill his place as a grownup person in the social system."[72]
In the matters of religion, the state should refrain from any attempt to
prescribe a specific form of worship, but at the same time it should prevent such religious practices as contravene the welfare of society: "It is
open to a man to preach the principles of Torquemada or the religion
of Mahomet. It is not open to men to practice such of their precepts as
would violate the rights of others or cause a breach of the peace."[73] With
respect to education, the whole theory of the harmonious adjustment
of the individual to society and of the organic functioning of society,
which is the basis of Hobhouse's social theories, demands that the individual shall be fitted for an active participation in social life. Hence the
state cannot neglect the duty of providing adequate education for its
future citizens without being guilty of the gravest inconsistency.

Hobhouse agrees with the position taken a century earlier by Kant,
to the effect that the improvement and perfection of the internal arrangements of a political society are inseparably bound up with the provision
of external security. Throughout his *Democracy and Reaction* and in
his books written during the first World War, Hobhouse shows with
great clarity the fundamental antithesis between socialized democracy
at home and militarism and imperialism in foreign policy: "The supporter of the League of Nations finds in the requirement for internal

reform nothing but a pious platitude as long as security against external disturbance is not guaranteed."[74]

F. IS SOCIAL PROGRESS TO BE ACHIEVED BY CONSCIOUS EFFORT?

In his discussion of political and social reform Hobhouse emphasizes two of his fundamental theses—the idea of progress as an ever more successful achievement of social harmony and the doctrine that Western society has now reached the stage where it can achieve further development by the deliberate action of the social mind. In the first place, the old Spencerian and pseudo-Darwinian conception of "continuous, automatic, inevitable progress" must be given up, since social evolution is more or less distinct from biological evolution and its elements are quite different in their operation from the biological factors in organic evolution. Though, in the earlier stages of human development, consciously and deliberately planned legislation to achieve social progress was uncommon, if not unknown, society has now come to the point where it can, if it will, control the direction and degree of its own development. Here Hobhouse gives his assent to Ward's major thesis: "The turning-point in the evolution of thought, as I conceive it, is reached when the conception of the development of humanity enters into explicit consciousness as the directing principle of human endeavor, and, in proportion as the phrase is adequately understood, is seen to include within it the sum of human purpose in all its manifold variety.....Progress has consisted in the realization of the conditions of full social co-operation and in the extension of the rational control of life."[75]

Not only should progressive measures be brought under the deliberative control of the social mind; they must also be synthetic in outlook and designed to promote the harmonious development of society, for this is the essence of progress. This is where the danger enters from narrow-minded agitation for social reform that takes into account only one need for, or one method of, improvement. No plan for social reform can be permanently successful unless it recognizes the necessity for the harmonious and organic development of all society. What is needed to make this synthetic view possible is a comprehensive and well-balanced science of society.

G. THE SOCIOLOGY OF INTERNATIONAL RELATIONS

In treating international relations, Hobhouse was one of the most uncompromising critics of modern nationalism and imperialism. He stood firmly as a foe of manifest destiny, of the idea of the necessity of war to promote social progress, and of the notion that foreign affairs are a field where the ethics of personal relations do not apply. This was, of course, in keeping with the Liberal tradition established by Cobden and perpetuated by Gladstone. In a splendid paragraph he exposes the basic hypocrisy of the imperialistic apology for territorial aggression at the expense of a weaker people:

Of course in every case of aggression some excellent reason has been forthcoming. We were invariably on the defensive. We had no intention of going to war. Having gone to war we had no intention of occupying the country. Having occupied the country provisionally, we were still determined not to annex it. Having annexed it, we were convinced that the whole process was inevitable from the first to the last. On each several occasion we acted purely on the defensive, and on each several occasion we ended by occupying the land of our aggressive neighbors. Such is the fiction still solemnly maintained. The naked fact is that we are maintaining a distinct policy of aggressive warfare on a large scale and with great persistence, and the only result of attempting constantly to blink that fact is to have introduced an atmosphere of self-sophistication or in one syllable, of cant, into our politics which is perhaps more corrupting than the unblushing denial of right.[76]

Of course, each imperialistic country suffers at home for its crushing of the rights of others. As has been pointed out above, Hobhouse holds that imperialism and democracy are mutually exclusive and that the pursuing of an imperialistic program abroad reacts at home in destroying the reform program of a democratic regime. Along with the unfortunate general reaction of imperialism upon democracy, it diverts the attention of the people from the need for improvement at home and causes the revenues of the state to flow into costly armaments rather than into channels for the improvement of domestic social conditions.

As a remedy for the problem of imperialism, Hobhouse suggests an extension of the accepted code of individual ethics to the conduct of one nation with another. He believes that each nation should devote itself to the improvement of its internal conditions and leave other nations free to do the same. If there is ever any excuse for the voluntary interference of one nation with another, it must be on purely humanitarian grounds. He recognizes "that the nation which would endeavour to follow a lofty standard of duty and honour would, in the present state of international morality, be in the position of a man who should carry Christian principles into effect upon the Stock Exchange, or of a Quaker who should adhere to the strict tenets of his religion in the company of highwaymen."[77] Nevertheless, he feels that if each nation stopped short at insisting on the maintenance of its own rights, it would find its neighbors much more willing to co-operate in this respect. Finally, he believes that, in spite of the absence of an international sovereign to enforce the enactments of international law, the force of custom and the fear of ostracism would be entirely adequate to secure the enforcement of international law if the nations would co-operate heartily and sincerely in submitting their difficulties to arbitration.[78]

As might have been expected of an alert and thoughtful student of human relations, Professor Hobhouse was deeply interested in the fundamental sociological problems involved in the first World War, its causes, and probable results. These he briefly analyzes in his little book entitled *The World in Conflict.* He finds that, at just the time when the old European alliances and concerts were disintegrating from moral dry rot and were leaving Europe without any international guaranty against aggressive militarism, a very dangerous philosophy of force and *Realpolitik* was being developed out of a perversion of the biological formula of the survival of the fittest:

> The biological theory of evolution which was the crowning glory of nineteenth century science could be interpreted as a justification of force and self-assertion. It then became a theory of revolt against law and morals, and more particularly against the morals of Christianity..... The idea of violence was in the air, then, in the years before the war; and it was not merely the violence that comes naturally from despair of all legal remedy. There was a deliberate theory of force. Men were being taught not to look too far ahead, not to wait till they could see where they were going, not to follow deliberately a reasoned policy, but rather to throw themselves on instinct, to strike a blow which would smash something and make an echo in the world even if they did not quite know what they were breaking or what would follow.[79]

This doctrine, which was fairly general in the Western world before 1914, was intensified and exaggerated in Germany through the addition of certain associated obsessions of recent origin: "Hegel's divine State, Treitschke's power, Nietzsche's contempt of restraint are fused together in the faith which animates the governing classes of Germany, political, military and academic—fused in the medium of some misty conception of the progress of mankind through competition and the fated superiority of the German race."[80]

In the latter part of this work and in the concluding chapter of his *Questions of War and Peace,* Hobhouse deals with the question of the necessary reconstruction of international relations which should follow the war if there was to be any hope that the world would be henceforth free from such calamities as the cataclysm of 1914–18.

Hobhouse sees two alternatives facing the states of the world—a continuance of militarism, preparedness, more wars, and the cumulative self-destruction of Western civilization, on the one hand, and the provision of "some orderly mode of governing the intercourse of nations," on the other.[81] The old cosmopolitanism, based on humanitarianism and free trade, died with Cobden. There is no longer any hope of reviving cosmopolitanism; only an internationalism based upon the recognition of both the independence and the interdependence of national states can serve as an adequate foundation for the international relations of the future. Hobhouse regards as insufficient guaranties of future peace such proposed solutions as the Hague Tribunal and arbitration agreements, union against an aggressive state which violates international law, and the economic boycott of offenders against the law of nations. "I am forced, therefore," he says, "to the conclusion that we must either go further or not attempt to move at all, and I should agree with my friend, Mr. Hobson, that there is no formal guarantee of a permanent peace except in the formation of an international state."[82] Hobhouse believes that the most practicable method of erecting a world state consists in developing a federation out of the Entente Alliance of 1914–18, then uniting this with a federation of neutrals, and finally taking in Germany, when it becomes certain that the pacific elements dominate that country. The following paragraph briefly summarizes his plan: "I would look forward, then, to the conversion of the existing Alliance into a permanent League or Federation, with a regular constitution and definite functions, which should include some measure of control over the production of munitions of war. But from the outset I would contemplate the extension of the League by the free entry of new members.....This would at once transform it from an ordinary alliance into something approaching a world-federation."[83]

There is little doubt that the events and outcome of the peace conference at Paris in 1919 disillusioned Mr. Hobhouse, as it did so many other hopeful liberals, on the matter of the adaptability of the Entente Alliance to furnishing the foundation of a just and durable league of nations.[84] No one can doubt, however, that the moral collapse of the peace conference and the events since that time have substantiated, rather than discredited, Hobhouse's thesis that some kind of world organization had to be provided if peace was to endure longer than was necessary for the European nations to recover from the losses sustained in the first world conflict.

H. EXTRA-LEGAL FORMS OF SOCIAL CONTROL

Of Hobhouse's detailed discussions of the origin and growth of those extra-legal forms of social control exerted by society over the individual, available space forbids more than a casual mention. In substance, he demonstrates how great a part of human conduct is the result of the more or less unconscious coercive power of social customs and traditions, which are often more tyrannical in their domination than the coercion of the codified law but are less odious to the individual because he accepts them as a matter of course or quite unconsciously bends to their sway:

> The greater part of each man's personal experience is made up out of his inter-action with others in the multifarious relations of life, and these relations, from the earliest known phases of human society, are controlled by customs which arise out of the needs of social life and are maintained by the social tradition. Through this tradition society exerts a continuous control over the individual, of which avowed and obvious coercion is the least important element. The vital fact is that from infancy upwards the social *milieu* into which he is born interpenetrates his thought and will, and turns his individuality into a creation of the time and place of his life.[85]

In conclusion, Hobhouse points out at length how the political and social theory of a period is a reflection of the social and intellectual conditions at the time that it is produced. He traces this in detail in regard to the development of the political creed of the English Liberals.[86]

I. CONCLUSION

To sum up very briefly the nature of his writings and the contributions of Professor Hobhouse to social and political theory, it might be said that his method of presentation is characteristically English. Like most English social scientists, he steers clear of abstract metaphysical questions in his strictly social theories and is eminently practical, concrete, and matter-of-fact in his analyses.

His insistence upon the necessity of harmonious social development as the proper goal of social evolution and upon the desirability of applying the best constructive thought to this problem, thus making it an artificially directed movement, cannot be too highly commended.

Again, his candid analysis of democracy, in which he makes plain its many defects and yet demonstrates with equal clarity that no adequate alternative for it has yet been discovered, is one which is likely to startle the complacent apologists of democracy but is equally designed to give courage to those who are seeking to eliminate its defects and to save its virtues for the benefit of humanity. Moreover, he clearly outlines what so many writers have ignored, namely, the very intimate relation and interdependence between social, economic, and political democracy.

He is also one of those clear-headed thinkers who understand that the modern state is not an isolated unit but is dependent for its internal prosperity and progress upon security against external aggression and upon freedom from the paralyzing expense of providing extensive armament for potential wars and imperialism. He therefore lent the weight of this authority as a student of social science to the support of those who are working to secure a stable and pacific international order.

NOTES

1. For Professor Small's explanation see *American Journal of Sociology*, XVIII (1912–13), 206–7. The best analysis of the social philosophy of Hobhouse is Hugh Carter, *The Social Theories of L. T. Hobhouse* (Chapel Hill, N.C., 1927).

2. Martin White Professor of Sociology in the University of London (1907–29) and first editor of the *Sociological Review*. Of course, this statement refers to sociologists in the strictest sense of the term and thus excludes the many brilliant English ethnologists, social psychologists, political scientists, moralists, eugenists, and metaphysical students of social phenomena.

3. Hobhouse's little volume, *Liberalism* (New York, 1911), is probably the best analysis of this fundamental transition in British liberalism.

4. *Development and Purpose* (New York, 1913), Introd. p. xviii. On Hobhouse's general philosophical approach to social issues and problems see Carter, *op. cit.*, chaps. i, iv, vii.

5. *Development and Purpose*, p. xix; *Social Evolution and Political Theory* (New York, 1913), chaps. i–ii.

6. *Development and Purpose*, Introd., pp. xx–xxii; cf. *Social Evolution and Political Theory*, chaps. ii, iv, vii; *Democracy and Reaction* (London, 1904), chap. iv; *Morals in Evolution* (New York, 1915), p. 637; see also *Social Development: Its Nature and Conditions* (New York, 1924), chaps. iv–x.

7. *Development and Purpose*, Introd., pp. xix–xxiii, and 364.

8. *Ibid.*, pp. xxvii, 154–55. Hobhouse's qualified acceptance of Hegel's evolutionary formula does not by any means imply that he accepts the Hegelian theory of the state. This he repudiates and severely criticizes (see *The Metaphysical Theory of the State* [New York, 1918], pp. 6, 23–24, 137).

9. *Development and Purpose*, Introd., p. xxiii; see also *Social Development*, pp. 301 ff.

10. *Development and Purpose*, p. xxvi.

11. *Ibid.*, p. 372.

12. *Ibid.*, p. 364.

13. *Ibid.*, p. 284.

14. *Ibid.*, p. xxix; cf. also *Democracy and Reaction*, chap. iii.

15. *Development and Purpose,* Introd. p. xxvii.

16. Third and revised edition (1915). Reviewed by Norman Wilde in the *Journal of Philosophy, Psychology, and Scientific Methods,* 1907; pp. 183–86, and by James Seth in *International Journal of Ethics,* 1907–8, pp. 375–81. This work is one of the most notable single contributions to the study of the mental and cultural evolution of humanity. This estimate is made in full knowledge of the bulky volumes of Frazer's *Golden Bough* and Westermarck's *Origin and Development of the Moral Ideas.* The former is no longer taken seriously in its theoretical aspects by any scientific student of ethnology, and the latter, while infinitely better, partakes of many of the faults of classical anthropology and manifests a far less subtle insight into the nature of human cultural evolution than Hobhouse's volumes (see Carter, *op. cit.,* chap. iii).

17. Editorial Introd. to the *Sociological Review,* I, ii.

18. *Social Evolution and Political Theory,* p. 33.

19. *Ibid.,* p. 8.

20. *Ibid.,* p. 39.

21. *Ibid.,* pp. 75–76; cf. also *Democracy and Reaction,* chap. iv.

22. *Social Evolution and Political Theory,* p. 127, cf. also p. 185. For a more complete treatment of harmony as the essence of social well-being see *Elements of Social Justice* (London, 1921), chap. i; and *The Rational Good* (London, 1921), chaps. iv–vi.

23. *Liberalism,* p. 136; cf. also *Social Evolution and Political Theory,* pp. 87, 92–93, 204–5; and *Social Development,* chap. iii.

24. *Social Evolution and Political Theory,* p. 93; cf. also pp. 162 ff.

25. *Ibid.,* p. 101.

26. *Ibid.,* p. 163. Contrast this view with that expressed by Graham Wallas, *The Great Society* (New York, 1914), p. 323, where he maintains that the distinctive characteristic of the present state of society is that, for the first time, society has allowed the conditions of its collective life to get beyond its control.

27. Mention might also be made of Hobhouse's remaining works, *The Labor Movement* (3d ed.; London, 1912), an analysis of the labor movement in England and its economic limitations and justification; *The Material Culture and Social Institutions of the Simpler Peoples* (London, 1915), a pioneer treatise in the extension of statistical methods to the study of comparative ethnology; *The World in Conflict* (London, 1915), a brief but penetrating analysis of the sociological causes and implications of the world war; and *Questions of War and Peace* (London, 1916), a profound dialogue on the causes, progress, and issues of the war, with a final chapter on the future of international relations. For a good account of the career and literary activity of Hobhouse see J. A. Hobson and Morris Ginsberg, *L. T. Hobhouse: His Life and Works* (London, 1931). On Hobhouse as a metaphysician and philosopher see J. A. Nicholson, *Some Aspects of the Philosophy of L. T. Hobhouse* (Urbana, Ill., 1928). The best summaries of Hobhouse's social philosophy are J. S. Burgess, "Certain Concepts and Contributions in the Social Science and Social Philosophy of L. T. Hobhouse," *Chinese Social and Political Science Review,* XIII (1929), 119–43; and Carter, *op. cit.* (see pp. 133 ff. of the latter for a bibliography of Hobhouse's writings and of comments on Hobhouse's contributions to philosophy and social science).

28. "Editorial Article" in the *Sociological Review,* I (1908), 4–9.

29. *Ibid.,* p. 8.

30. *Social Evolution and Political Theory,* pp. 29–30, 127–28; see also *Social Development,* chap. ii.

31. *Liberalism,* p. 133.

32. *Democracy and Reaction,* p. 207.

33. P. 137.

34. *Ibid.,* pp. 23–24. Hobhouse calls attention to Mr. Clarke's famous article in the *Contemporary Review* for January, 1899, pointing out the relation between the Hegelian philosophy and the Bismarckian policy.

35. *Morals in Evolution* (3d ed., 1915), p. 60; cf. also *Democracy and Reaction*, p. 221.

36. *Social Evolution and Political Theory*, p. 146; cf. also *Democracy and Reaction*, pp. 158 ff.

37. *Social Evolution and Political Theory*, p. 146.

38. *Democracy and Reaction*, p. 160.

39. *Ibid.*, p. 128; *Morals in Evolution* (3d ed., 1915), pp. 42–43; cf. also *Social Development*, chap. xi. For Hobhouse's handling of the problems of social evolution through a discreet use of the comparative method see Carter, *op. cit.*, chap. iii.

40. *Social Evolution and Political Theory*, p. 147.

41. *Morals in Evolution*, pp. 57–58.

42. *Ibid.*, pp. 59–60; cf. also *Social Evolution and Political Theory*, pp. 138–39.

43. *Morals in Evolution*, p. 63; cf. also *Social Evolution and Political Theory*, p. 140.

44. *Morals in Evolution*, p. 60.

45. *Ibid.*, p. 67; cf. *Liberalism*, chaps. ii–iii.

46. *The World in Conflict*, p. 63.

47. *Ibid.*, p. 86.

48. *Morals in Evolution*, p. 68.

49. *Ibid.*, p. 69; cf. also *Social Evolution and Political Theory*, p. 148.

50. *Morals in Evolution*, pp. 130–31.

51. *Democracy and Reaction*, pp. 186–87; for Hobhouse's final estimate of democracy see *Elements of Social Justice*, chap. xi.

52. *Democracy and Reaction*, pp. 182–83.

53. *Ibid.*, pp. 184–85.

54. *Liberalism*, pp. 183–84.

55. *Democracy and Reaction*, p. 50.

56. *Ibid.*, pp. 119–24.

57. *Ibid.*, p. 166; cf. also *Liberalism*, *pp.* 248–51.

58. P. 238.

59. *Social Evolution and Political Theory*, p. 200; cf. also *Elements of Social Justice*, chaps. iii–iv.

60. *Liberalism*, pp. 146–47.

61. *Social Evolution and Political Theory*, p. 198; cf. also *Elements of Social Justice*, chap. ii.

62. *Social Evolution and Political Theory*, pp. 198–99; cf. also *Liberalism*, p. 127, and *Democracy and Reaction*, pp. 131–37.

63. *Social Evolution and Political Theory*, p. 188.

64. *Ibid.*, pp. 200–201; for Hobhouse's detailed analysis of social and political justice see *Elements of Social Justice*, *chaps.* v–vi.

65. *Social Evolution and Political Theory*, pp. 186–87. This is practically identical with Durkheim's view.

66. *Liberalism*, p. 189; on Hobhouse's notions of property see, further, *Elements of Social Justice*, chaps. viii–ix; and Charles Gore (ed.), *Property: Its Rights and Duties* (New York, 1922), chap. i.

67. *Liberalism*, p. 191.

68. *Ibid.*, p. 209; cf. also *Elements of Social Justice*, chap. ix. Probably Professor Hobhouse would agree that this generalization is a good summary statement of the problem rather than its practical solution.

69. *Liberalism*, p. 202.

70. *Ibid.*, pp. 195–202.

71. *Ibid.*, pp. 204–5; cf. also pp. 163–64, 185–86.

72. *Ibid.*, pp. 39–40.

73. *Ibid.*, pp. 29–31; cf. also *Social Evolution and Political Theory*, pp. 181–82.

74. *Metaphysical Theory of the State*, p. 106; cf. also *Democracy and Reaction*, pp. 49 ff.

75. *Social Evolution and Political Theory*, pp. 155–56; cf. also *Development and Purpose*, pp. 281 ff.

76. *Democracy and Reaction*, pp. 28–29; for an excellent treatment of Hobhouse's application of sociological principles to world affairs see Carter, *op. cit.*, chap. v.

77. *Democracy and Reaction*, pp. 204–5.

78. These arguments are summarized in *Democracy and Reaction*, chap. viii. In the 1915 edition of his *Morals in Evolution*, Hobhouse mentions in a footnote that his statement that the future of democracy and social progress was bound up with the progress of internationalism was written before the outbreak of the first World War.

79. *The World in Conflict*, pp. 38, 50.

80. *Ibid.*, p. 56.

81. *Questions of War and Peace*, pp. 183–86.

82. *Ibid.*, pp. 192–99.

83. *The World in Conflict*, p. 94.

84. See J. M. Keynes, *Economic Consequences of the Peace* (New York, 1920), for the most trenchant analysis of the manner in which the old diplomacy and international policies dominated the Paris conference.

85. *Social Evolution and Political Theory*, p. 94; cf. also *Morals in Evolution*, Part II.

86. Cf. *Liberalism, passim*, particularly chap. iii; and *Democracy and Reaction*, chaps. i–ii, ix.

CHAPTER XXXIII

EDWARD ALEXANDER WESTERMARCK AND THE APPLICATION OF ETHNOGRAPHIC METHODS TO MARRIAGE AND MORALS

C. Wright Mills, *Columbia University*

I. THE LIFE AND WORKS OF WESTERMARCK

IT DEPENDS on the definition into which the tally is made, but, not counting hillbillies, peasants, and folk-societies, there are something under one hundred major cultural types of nonliterate people on the globe today. Since the eighteenth century they have been "data" for social thinkers. Exhausting work, good minds, and a lot of money have been spent in exploiting them. Many of their languages have been learned. Detailed graphs have been constructed of their family and social organization. They have been lived among. Thin, mensurative instruments have been pushed around their heads. Their very existence, as well as the details of their lives and minds, have been the object of many theories. They have been much explained, and they have been used in various and imaginative explanations of the development of mankind.

If we conceive of the history of intellectual doctrine as a series of learned conversations, we may designate Westermarck as one given to monologues. Twice he monopolized the round table—on two topics: (1) the origin and history of kinship structures and rules and (2) the character and history of moral ideas.[1] He also spoke on ethics,[2] but the philosophers could not believe it, and the ethnologists, although respectful, were not interested in "philosophy."

Most of his traveling was to the British Museum and in shuttling between London and Finland, but he left the round table occasionally and went to Morocco and came back with three collections which had only a small audience.[3] A triangle with points in London, Finland, and Morocco encompasses the major movements of Westermarck's life. He was close to academic contexts by antecedents and location. Born in Helsingfors, in 1862, he breathed out a sickly childhood, being barred

654

from the romp and game of associates of his own age. As an under-graduate he took a strong dislike to German metaphysics, was attracted greatly to English empiricism, and became an agnostic. He remained an agnostic, being quietly but firmly hostile to religion all his life.

He must have conceived of the marriage study around 1887; in that year he came to the British Museum for library materials. Fourteen years later the book appeared. In the meantime, as a professor of moral philosophy he taught at Helsingfors, escaping these duties in 1893 and 1897 for periods of work in London. He met and was associated with such men as Shand, Tylor, Marett, Branford, and the Maecenas, J. Martin White, who was instrumental in securing for him a university lectureship in sociology at the University of London in 1907. At the same time he held the chair of moral philosophy at Helsingfors and spent his summers in field work in Morocco. Intermittently, he was active in Finnish politics. But his life was filled mostly with scholar-ship up to the last days. He died on September 3, 1939.[4]

II. THE ORIGINS, EVOLUTIONS, AND FORMS OF MARRIAGE

The "conversation" into which Westermarck plumped his monu-mentally sized tomes on marriage and the family had been going on for some time. Since many of the logically possible positions concerning the origin and early forms of marriage had already been taken, it is to be expected that Westermarck had antecedents. There were those who were upholding and those who were contraverting theories similar to those with which Westermarck's name was to be connected. Sir Henry Maine (*Ancient Law* [1861]) had held the primordial cell of social development to be the patriarchal family and had voiced other views similar to those that Westermarck was to enunciate. However, Maine had not supported his notion with primitive materials; his sources were largely Roman. Bachofen (*Das Mutterrecht* [1861]), using Greek data primarily, had challenged the notion of the patriarchate as the first form of the family. Tylor, in his review of *The History of Human Marriage,* made it clear that Westermarck was not the first to reject primitive promiscuity; Tylor himself had never sponsored it.[5]

The primary objective of those who have studied family organiza-tions and marriage rules among primitive peoples has been the recon-struction of the sequence of forms which are antecedent to those now existent. Taking existent types as the end-product, other forms have been scaled according to their degrees of difference and similarity to them; various features of contemporary culture have been treated as survivals from, putatively, earlier stages that no longer exist; also the mating behavior of anthropoids have been used analogously.

Perhaps the prevailing views on the topic were those of the classical evolutionists, represented by such men as Post, McLennan, Lubbock, and Morgan. Using the comparative method and positing certain stages to have been universally followed, the evolutionists set forth the following scheme:

In the beginning was promiscuity. "Society" was without form; chaos prevailed and unregulated sex intercourse. Then groups of women, related or not, were looked upon as wives of groups of men, related or not. But the clans came forth: tribes were divided into these hereditary social units, and these were composed of blood relatives and also of some who were not so related. Thus social organization became more clearly formed. At first, and dominantly, this form was maternal in principle: the children belonged to the clan of their mothers. Later the gens developed: the children belonged to the gentes of their fathers. Finally, after all this had passed, the monogamous family (and the village) became the basic units of organization.

It was against this view that Westermarck formulated what impressed many as a definitive and adequate counterstatement. He did not think mankind had to go through so much to reach monogamy. Man was originally monogamous. Rejecting primitive promiscuity in the first well-rounded attack on that notion, Westermarck asserted that a paternalistic family was the earliest, and universal, social unit. It was present in the most primitive tribes, in those having no clan structure; and it persisted among all those which had acquired such structures of kinship. Westermarck attempted to refute the precedence of matrilineal over patrilineal descent. He set forth alternative explanations for observed social forms which had been explained by the evolutionists as survivals of group marriages and promiscuity.

His evidence was gathered, as seems to have been a custom of the day, illustratively; it was of two kinds—ethnographic and from the anthropoids, which he indicated as being given to pair arrangements of some permanence. In both cases his evidence has been strongly imputed to have been selected for the theory. He profusely illustrated the alleged fact that hunters and fishers, whom the classical evolutionists considered "most primitive" economically, were, in the main, monogamous. He set forth many detailed cases around which argument over the question could swirl.

Besides these two modes of proof there was another: Westermarck grounded the idea of a universal and original monogamous patriarchate in the realm of Darwinian biology and in what passed (and "still passes") for a psychology. He supported the Darwinian view of the family, bottomed on male possessiveness and jealousy, with monopoly by force later becoming enshrined in custom. He argued from supposedly universal "psychological causes" to social forms. He accepted "mere instincts" as playing a "very important part in the origin of social institutions."[6] This mode of proof supported and was supported by the evidence from the anthropoids. I shall comment later upon the psychological inadequacy of Westermarck's thinking.

How do present-day American ethnologists stand on the question of the origin and sequence of marriage forms? In so far as they permit themselves an opinion on such a large question, they are, as a group, closer to Westermarck than to the Morgan type of evolutionist. But their reasons are not his. Such men as Boas, Kroeber, Lowie, and Malinowski hold that the biosocial unit of the monogamous family seems to be a very fundamental and prevailing one in existent preliterate societies. However, properly speaking, we know of no such institution as *"the* primitive family"; there are many and diverse types of organization among primitive peoples, some quite similar to "modern" forms, some not. At the "lowest levels" of society, family life is quite varied. There seems to be no thoroughly acceptable evidence that a "stage" of promiscuity ever existed. The father, the mother, the child, and their net of relationships are primary. By various types of extension their interrelationships have grown into such (often complex) groupings as the clan and into such arrangements as group marriage. The latter occurs but rarely and then as an outgrowth of previous conditions of individual marriage. The family and village groupings are near-universal units of social organization; they extend "from the beginning"; they persist through all the other forms.

But, in the main, modern ethnologists have not answered the sort of questions and topics which formed the theme of the evolutionists' and Westermarck's work on marriage and family structures. They have dropped the questions. They have given up the search for origins.

They no longer seek all over the world, albeit via libraries, for "the fundamentally primitive" condition. It is a methodological refusal to ask a question whose answer presumably would rest upon evidence that is not available. And, more important, the quest for origins is a significant and compulsive problem only within a framework which assumes the fundamental conception of evolutionism: a universal uniformity of development through stages. The legitimacy and the significance of the origin hunt died with the evolutionists.

From present elements found in nonliterate cultures, modern ethnologists do not *readily* infer into a constructed past, certainly not into a "stage" arbitrarily postulated as previously existent. Such an element is studied functionally in a context that is seen; it is not interpreted as evidence for an affiliated context supposed to have been there but which is now forever vanished.

III. ON METHOD AND COMPILATION

In a growing science it is often over questions of method that arguments hover; and it is through this sphere that individuals really shape deeply and lastingly the contour of their science. If you spread out the histories of various sciences, you see that compilations of fact are not important unless they are logically connected with sharp theory and incisive method. Theory, fact, and method are the inseparable rungs of the ladder to scientific fame. Methodology is what others can take away from an individual's work and use themselves. You will learn very little, save industry, from Westermarck as methodologist.

The model of thought which informed the classical evolutionists was not the paradigm drawn from physics of Descartes; nor was it the scheme of Hegel. It was Spencer's, and back of Spencer lay the geology and biology of the early nineteenth century, and alongside of him sat Darwin. Among others, Comte had used a comparative method. Spencer used it more generously, and it was from Spencer that the classical evolutionists derived their way of thinking. Like them, Westermarck used the comparative method, but with this scheme and method he dug out of the British Museum, and presented to the round table, an alternative sequence of the forms of marriages and families and of kinship structures in general.

Unlike the classical evolutionists, Westermarck rejected *in toto* the small interpretative trick with which any kind of rabbit can be made to appear from anybody's sleeve of abstractions: the theory of survivals. He thought it was based on speculation, that it took unfair advantage of empirical materials. And in this he has been vindicated.

But the concrete way of work utilized by Westermarck was the famous little-slips-of-paper-piled-topically-and-write-it-up-method.[7] It was the encyclopedic and comparative method. The data so collected suffer in general in that they are not oriented so as to be crucial empirical evidence in the solution of carefully defined problems. In ethnological work this method has been rejected for a more specialized reason: it dislocates particular phases and bits of a "total culture" and tears societal features from their contexts.[8] Given the present ethnographic norms for the determination of whole facts, the result is plain and simple inaccuracy.[9] Also, since the cultural world is a big place with a lot in it, such grab-bag methods are bound to result in ethnographic inadequacy, for even encyclopedias are selective. A severe appraisal of Westermarck's method, sources, and work has been written by R. Lowie. After commenting on the profusion of documents used in an amazingly uncritical way, he states: "Not only are there inconsistencies .... but bad, good, and indifferent sources are cited indiscriminately .... even good sources are abused..... Westermarck neither appraises his evidence discriminatively nor becomes absorbed in his cultural phenomena; and while his views on early family life largely coincide with current doctrines, we are not able to discover any signal advancement of ethnology due to his writings."[10] Yet, in so far as ethnography in its quest for facts and more facts around the turn of this century implemented a concretizing of social science, Westermarck's Darwinian ethnography helped. He did live with the Moors for nine years.

For many ethnologists, however, Lowie has carved an epitaph that cannot easily be rubbed off the tomes of Westermarck with their six to twelve footnotes per page.[11]

IV. THE NATURAL HISTORY OF SOCIAL INSTITUTIONS

But other thinkers with other interests sat at the round table of intellectual history. Some of them listened to Westermarck's monologue and took away certain influences and certain models of thought. By some sociologists, Westermarck is remembered as among the first to shift the focus from old-fashioned history to the "natural history of social institutions." If a sociological standpoint occurs when historical studies become studies of the regular growth of institutions, then Wester-marck's *History of Human Marriage* is one of the earliest wholesale sociological studies. The book may be viewed as a large-scale natural history of a social institution. In this connection Westermarck writes:

Like the phenomena of physical and psychical life those of social life should be classified into certain groups and each group investigated with regard to its origin and development. Only when treated in this way can history lay claim to the rank of a science in the highest sense of the term, as forming an important part of Sociology, the youngest of the principal branches of learning. Descriptive his-toriography has no higher object than that of offering materials to this science.[12]

The sociological interest in historical and ethnological materials was greatly augmented by Darwinian doctrine, and Westermarck's work is dominated by the Darwinism of *The Descent of Man*. The direct translation of Darwinian principles into social interpretation imagina-tively ran itself to a brief end in such men as Gumplowicz. The other line of development was the classical evolutionist and, following in partial reaction to it, the historical and institutional evolutionism of such men as Westermarck.

England was one of the several places where idiographic facts got caught up in a level of abstraction. In England, history and ethnography were used as stuffing for natural histories. In so far as English thinkers have imprinted patterns upon American sociology, it is by means of this notion of the natural history of social institutions. And Westermarck was a big man among them.

His view of sociology is indicated clearly in the above quotation. He had no systematic view of the scope of the discipline; it was synthetic, a collection of studies dealing with all aspects of social life. His own interest was in the comparative study of social institutions, which he thought of as sets of social relations regulated and sanctioned by "society." In American publications he is also classed as a forerunner of folk, or, more usually, of "cultural," sociology. In this connection, W. I. Thomas, in his influential course on social origins, told his classes that *The Origin and Development of Moral Ideas* was an important book to pur-chase, but, he added, "because of the wealth of material rather than for theory."[13]

Ward and Giddings and their generation knew Westermarck at firsthand, and he seems to have influenced Cooley in his formulation of the importance of primary groups, although how much or in what way, we do not know. Cooley writes: "The best comparative studies of the family, such as those of Westermarck or Howard, show us .... a universal institution ..... as more alike the world over than .... an earlier school had led us to suppose."[14] Cooley also cites him as rendering evidence for Cooley's cherished primary ideal of "the universality of kindness and the kindly ideal."[15] Yet it cannot be denied that Westermarck has not been, and is not now, of any focal importance in the actual work of American sociologists.

V. THE PSYCHOLOGICAL MODE OF EXPLANATION AND BIOLOGICAL METAPHYSICS

Closely tied in with the comparative method but also standing weakly by itself, there is in the recorded thinking of Westermarck an instinctivist psychology. This psychology is linked to a model of causal explanation, and both are determined by the Darwinian notion of survival value. Westermarck used "cause" interchangeably with "origin." By these terms he meant the *biological* condition which determined a phenomenon or which lent to it a biological survival value. Thus the cause and origin of marriage lie in the need of prolonged parental care and protection. Mammals, including human beings, with such instinctive proclivities are favored by processes of natural selection. Upon such instincts (in 1936 Westermarck called them "primeval habits," and "feelings"[16]) rests the origin and persistence through various kinship vicissitudes of the family grouping. The basic explanatory apparatus upon which rests the application of causal analysis is, for Westermarck, the Darwinian theory of natural selection. This theory is used in accounting for the "psychological" tendencies and structures of men. Such tendencies and structures are the causes and lead to the motives underlying social groups and relationships. Hence, "in the last analysis," the *real* hub of the wheel of social life is found to be biological conditions. This was the metaphysical bent which underlay the psychology of the day.

It is because the "instincts and sentiments" underneath it are deep in the universal organic makeup of man as animal[17] that the family existed "from the beginning" and will probably continue to exist in times not yet here. Any reconstruction or explanation of social institutions must be based on "the fundamental causes" which Westermarck took to be biological and psychological in nature. "I put particular stress," he says, "upon the psychological causes .... and more especially I believe that the mere instincts have played a very important part in the origin of social institutions and rules."[18]

Thus, although Westermarck treated his ethnographic data in terms of the concept of social institution, he relied for their ultimate explanation upon psychobiological theory. Robertson Smith[19] criticized his *History of Human Marriage* on two related grounds: It is not "natural" history, for an institution is "controlled by public opinion and regulated by law." Second, to treat the study as a *natural* history of pairing involves the assumption that "the laws of society are at bottom mere formulated instincts, and this assumption really underlies all our author's theories. His fundamental position compels him . . . . to hold that every institution connection with marriage that has universal validity, or forms an integral part of the main line of development is rooted in instinct, and that institutions which are not based on instinct are necessarily exceptional and unimportant for scientific history."

Such a writer as Sir Edward B. Tylor considered that Westermarck had executed a valuable attempt to work out the biological and cultural sides of anthropology into a connected scheme.[20] But today, when one of the major emphases in ethnology is sociological psychology, it is not necessary to detail the reasons why Westermarck's formulation and assumptions are outmoded and otiose. The Durkheim school and also Rivers[21] criticized him for "explaining" social phenomena on a "psychological" basis, told him to watch it, but he shook them off.

VI. THE SOCIOLOGY OF MORALS AND THE THEORY OF ETHICS

Perhaps the ground tone of all Westermarck's writing is a persistent interest in moral codes and in ethical theories. The initial problem which led to the three volumes on marriage was that of sexual modesty. Later this concern expanded to include all relations between the sexes.

This drive toward a sociology of morals is one component of Westermarck's work which I believe could, but probably will not, influence the direction of American sociological interests. A sociology of morals, worthy of the name, cannot be said to exist among American social thinkers. Their intellectual tradition harbors certain hard phrases, distinctions, and many logical knots, which hang by the neck any attempt really to analyze moral phenomena. The theoretically inadequate work of Sumner is still for most the last word. An adequate social psychology of moral rules and judgments has not yet been written.

But if a sociology of morals were to be developed, Westermarck[22] would be written of as *one type* of its "forerunners." His voluminous synthesis of ethnographic material[23] was one of the pioneering books that placed the *historical* and *grossly empirical* aspect of ethics on a much more secure foundation. He documents moral variability; he presents data on the evolution of ethical behavior; his collection of facts shows a "connection" of custom with morals.[24] He shows morals as an early religious function.[25] One comes from his books with an absorbed realization of the *factual*[26] relativity of moral ideas. In his books the divine-origin view of morals is bathed in a lethal bath of facts. His name must be placed on the list of those who helped hammer out a naturalistic view of morals, even though *its* theoretical basis was mistaken. There is in Westermarck much timber that was growing in his time and that must be cleared from his work by a sociology of morals. Perhaps the utilization of his large body of anthropological materials in reconstructing the evolution of morals is vitiated by an uncontrolled comparative method. But the generic weakness in his thought on morals, as in his thought on kinship, lies in its psychological foundations.

His data show custom to be related to morals. It may be said that Westermarck misstates the point of these data: although he recognizes a certain objectivity and distinterestedness[27] as a characteristic of custom, he is so dominated by a subjective psychology that he is able to write: "Custom is a moral rule only on account of the indignation called forth by its transgression . . . . it is nothing but a generalization of emotional tendencies."[28]

The ultimate basis of moral judgments is individual and emotional. Moral concepts are generalizations of emotions that are within us. In certain cases specific emotions underpin certain moral concepts. Moral disapproval is a form of resentment, and moral approval is a form of retributive kindly emotion.[29] These two are distinctly *moral emotions*. Psychologically, Westermarck is not a bad bedfellow for McDougall, and certainly he would not fail to welcome Adam Smith if he had brought his "sentiments" with him.[30] Moral judgments spring from the individual's "own moral consciousness; they are judgments of other's conduct from one's own point of view and in accordance with one's own feelings and opinions about right and wrong." Although relative, they are not arbitrary, for we approve and disapprove "because we cannot do otherwise; our moral consciousness belongs to our mental constitution which we cannot change as we please."[31]

Yet, factually, "there is no absolute standard in morality."[32] Hence Westermarck must posit innate emotional differences to account for the ethnographic fact of a variety of moral judgments. He falls back upon the notion of an innate "emotional constitution."[33] The basic moral factor in evolution springs not from social relations but from individual sentiments of praise and blame. Westermarck evolutionized the Adam Smith of the "Moral Sentiments."

He speaks of "the evolution of the moral consciousness" which to "a large extent consists in its development from the unreflecting to the reflecting, from the unenlightened to the enlightened."[34]

Although, as I have indicated, the excessively psychological and subjective interpretation given by Westermarck to his data makes it necessary to give us the explanatory structure of his thought, the gross data are still valuable for certain purposes and there are also scattered inklings which a sociology of morals would wish to consider carefully and possibly to develop.

VII. THE MORAL

The younger generation of American ethnologists and sociologists do not know Westermarck at firsthand. It is possible to receive gracefully the Ph.D. degree in ethnology, and certainly in sociology, without ever opening any one of his books. In diluted fashion his effort lives in passages in histories of social thought and in the chapters of symposiums.[35] But he is not a direct determinant of the working day of American social scientists.

Searching the pages of contemporary texts, monographs, and symposiums you will find few references to Westermarck. You do find scattered bits of information ("In Java, among the ...."), with his name footnoted, or references to, or paragraph summaries of, his theories of incest and ornament and the monogamic family.

Why is this? Why did this man have his best time in other times and then drop from the running in the operative, the pivotal, footnotes of fresh writing? Many general and perhaps some social reasons could be given, but I think there are two more or less specific ones.[36]

One reason is that between Westermarck and us there stands a modern sociological psychology which comprises a new view of the role of biological elements in social systems and which excludes the psychological as explanatory, making physiological science a strict counterpart and a parallel endeavor to work within a sociological perspective. With varying degrees of adequacy, ethnologists are grasping and using this view; it forms one of the more fruitful trends of interest in modern American ethnology. The past is written and used in terms of the present, and Westermarck does not contribute to this trend.

The other reason is the changed status of "fact" within the accepted models of inquiry. Westermarck got hold of a lot of "facts," but he used them either in a kind of planless empiricism or like a philosopher illustrating his feelings in the grand manner. His facts do not now appear to be crucial. They are not caught up in a firm mesh of theory, which they prove or disprove. The comparative method and the evolutionist theory, within which his facts make sense, have been overthrown for new models of inquiry and new and perhaps more modest theory. That is the history of the changing content of science. And so his books bore us a little because their masses of fact seem irrelevant to our theoretic directions. Encyclopedic compilation prevails over analytic theory, and he is heavy with obsolete problems. The undisturbed dust on his volumes is an object lesson in method and in the ways of setting up problems.

These things might have been forgiven if he had possessed the synoptic mind that can squeeze from masses of data the analytically characterizing sentence. But Westermarck did not write such sentences. Maybe he made some of the men at the intellectual round table get up and thenceforth look to their facts. But he does not give us anything to look to them through; he sat at some other round table with other chairmen.

NOTES

1. *The History of Human Marriage* (London, 1901). The major propositions of these three volumes are to be found in a one-volume edition, *A Short History of Marriage* (New York, 1926); and in *The Origin and Development of Moral Ideas* (2 vols.; London, 1906). He also considered *The Future of Marriage in Western Civilization* (New York, 1936).

2. *Ethical Relativity* (New York, 1932).

3. *Marriage Ceremonies in Morocco* (London, 1914); *Ritual and Belief in Morocco* (2 vols.; London, 1926); *Wit and Wisdom in Morocco: A Study of Native Proverbs* (London, 1930); see also "The Belief in Spirits in Morocco," *Acta academiae Aboensis, Humaniora,* I (Helsingfors, 1920), 1–167.

4. The best life-history in brief compass is to be found in M. Ginsberg's "The Life and Work of Edward Westermarck," *Sociological Review* (Eng.), January–April, 1940; see

also, for self-told account, Westermarck's *Memories of My Life* (New York, 1929), trans. A. Barnewl.

5. *Academy*, XL (October 3, 1891), 288 ff.

6. *History of Human Marriage*, p. 5.

7. See Westermarck, *Memories of My Life*.

8. It is interesting to note the way in which museum arrangements reflect ethnological theory and vice versa. Westermarck's books are arranged like the museums set up by Pitt-Rivers. Both reflect evolutionist theory. The present method of arrangement is "regional," and the corresponding theory incorporates such notions as "cultural area" and the necessity for contextual work.

9. There is a remarkable criticism of Westermarck written in 1900 by Karl Pearson (*Grammar of Science*). After criticizing the "obscurity attaching to the use of the words force and cause" (p. 132), he adds that "to find sequences of facts . . . . we must follow the changes of one tribe or people at a time. We cannot trace the successive stages of social life except by minute investigation of facts relating to one social unit" (p. 359).

10. *The History of Ethnological Theory* (New York, 1937), p. 98–99.

11. Before leaving Westermarck as ethnologist, however, it must be recorded that the common idea of him as merely an armchair librarian is mistaken. Those who hold such a view are sentenced to thirty days with the very flat idiographic descriptions in *Ritual and Belief in Morocco* and the ethnographic pages of "The Belief in Spirits in Morocco." These works show that Westermarck knew what a campstool felt like; they do not harbour any conclusions, and they have not entered into the stream of American social science. Although the bulk of *Wit and Wisdom in Morocco* consists of a mere compilation of proverbs (with full Arabic texts), there is a 63-page Introductory Essay (embodying the Frazer lecture of 1928), which contains a neat set of characterizing criteria for *proverbs*, an empiric taxonomic scheme, and notes on their societal function. It should also be mentioned that two of Westermarck's more specific theories still run through writers on these topics (see the *Encyclopaedia of the Social Sciences*, articles by Reo Fortune on "Incest" [VII, 621] and by Ruth Bunzel on "Ornament" [XI, 496]).

12. *The History of Human Marriage*, p. 1.

13. *Source Book for Social Origins* (Boston, 1909), p. 911 and 869.

14. *Social Organization* (New York, 1909), p. 24.

15. *Ibid.*, p. 40.

16. *The Future of Marriage in Western Civilization*, pp. 5, 264.

17. Hence, given the biologistic premises, the relevance of the mating habits of the cognate species of anthropoid.

18. *The History of Human Marriage*, p. 5.

19. *Nature*, XLIV, 270 (cited by Park and Burgess, *An Introduction to the Science of Sociology*, pp. 16–17).

20. Tylor, *op. cit.*, pp. 288 f.

21. See the critical reviews in *Revue philosophique*, 1907, pp. 409 ff.; *L'Année sociologique*, X, 283 ff., XI, 274 ff.; W. H. R. Rivers, "Survival in Sociology," *Sociological Review*, VI, 304 ff., and "Sociology and Psychology," *ibid.*, IX, 3 ff.

22. Along with Hobhouse, *Morals in Evolution* (London, 1906); Sumner, *Folkways* (Boston, 1906); and Spencer, *The Data of Ethics* (New York, 1879).

23. *The Origin and Development of Moral Ideas* (2 vols.; London, 1906).

24. But see below.

25. *Op. cit.*, II, 745.

26. But, as we shall see, in his interpretation of moral phenomena and in his ethics it is clear that moral ideas are relative to "the emotions they express" and not to social factors, e.g., custom (see *Ethical Relativity*, p. 289).

27. See, e.g., *Origin and Development of Moral Ideas*, I, 120–21; cf. also A. Smith's notion of the "impartial spectator" and "sympathetic resentment."

28. *Ibid.*, I, 121.

29. *Ethical Relativity*, p. 89.

30. *Ibid.*, see p. 71 for laudatory references to *The Theory of Moral Sentiments*.

31. *Ethical Relativity*, pp. 58–59.

32. *Ibid.*, p. 59.

33. *Moral Ideas*, I, 11: "The emotional constitution of man [which underlies moral phenomena] does not present the same uniformity as the human intellect." The very engaging manner in which Westermarck uses his very pliable psychology to account for what he considers to be another fact should be noted: "The general uniformity of human nature accounts for the great similarities which characterize the moral ideas of mankind. . . . . But at the same time these ideas also represent racial differences" (*ibid.*, II, 742). Although "different external conditions" and "different measures of knowledge" [*Ethical Relativity*, p. 187] may also be reasons for these variations, "the most common differences of moral estimates have undoubtedly a psychical origin [ultimately 'emotional']" (*Moral Ideas*, II, 742).

34. *Moral Ideas*, I, 10.

35. See H. E. Barnes and Howard Becker, *Social Thought from Lore to Science* (Boston, 1938), and *Contemporary Social Theory* (New York, 1940).

36. I am here concerned *only* with immanent reasons, not those, if any, to be found by a sociological analysis of his work in its various societal contexts. See V. F. Calverton's ideological imputations, "The Compulsive Basis of Social Thought," *American Journal of Sociology*, March, 1931; also Westermarck's reply (*ibid.*, March, 1936).

CHAPTER XXXIV

ROBERT BRIFFAULT AND THE REHABILITATION OF THE MATRIARCHAL THEORY

HUNTINGTON CAIRNS, *National Gallery of Art, Washington, D.C.*

I. BRIFFAULT'S LIFE AND WRITINGS

ROBERT BRIFFAULT, the author of *The Mothers*, was born in London in 1876. His mother was Scottish, his father French. His father, Frédéric Briffault, served in the French diplomatic service, but, after involvement in some of the Louis Napoléon plots, he became a British national. Briffault's early years and youth were spent on the Continent, where he was educated privately, in Florence and Germany and later at Liverpool. He began medical studies in London, graduating as a Bachelor of Medicine and a Bachelor of Surgery from the University of London. At the age of eighteen he went to New Zealand as a practicing surgeon. During his stay there he was president of the Auckland branch of the New Zealand Institute. The war of 1914–18 brought him again to Europe, and he served with the Fifth York and Lancaster Battalion at Gallipoli, in Flanders, and in France. At Nieuport he was severely gassed, which disabled him for active pursuits for some years. The Military Cross was twice awarded him for conspicuous bravery. After the war he retired permanently from medical practice and took up a career in literature. His first writings appeared in the *English Review*, but not until he was past thirty; and his first book, published in 1919 when he was forty-three, was *The Making of Humanity*. Upon completion of *The Mothers* he spent some years in the United States but eventually settled permanently in Paris, where he was living at the outbreak of World War II. He has regarded himself primarily as a psychologist and philosopher, his interest in anthropology being secondary with him and only a part of his general philosophical outlook.

The Making of Humanity, which arose out of disgust at Benjamin Kidd's *Social Evolution*, was largely written in the trenches. It is an attempt to answer the question: By what means has human progress been effected? He recognizes elements of worth in the attempts to solve the problem in the past on the basis of race, geography, and economics, but, as he correctly observes, no one of them is broad enough to encompass the whole field. "Progress" he defines as "increased control over the conditions of life"; he assigns an ethical value to the process, upon the grounds that whatsoever promotes the efficiency of the expansion of that control is good, whatsoever frustrates and vitiates it is bad. He himself believes that this desired control over the conditions of life is realized by what he terms the process of "rational causation." This process is the utilization by the organism of past experience in dealing with present and future conditions. It is the method customarily regarded as that of trial and error. The moth, repeatedly throwing itself against the chimney of the oil lamp, persists until it finds the opening leading to the object of its desire; the child, having once been burned, does not touch the hot poker. The first is the method of trial and error, the second the process of rational causation. If the moth escapes with singed wings, the next lamp will attract it as before. There is no line of demarcation between trial and error and rational causation; the one merges with the other. Briffault's explanation, it is apparent, answers the question by putting it back one step; he describes the process but does not account for it. With this theory as a foundation, Briffault summarizes in a capital manner the apparent development of civilization from the primitive inhabitants of the alluvial plains of Asia and North Africa to the European power states of the present day. A rewritten edition of *The Making of Humanity* was published in 1930 under the title *Rational Evolution.*

Psyche's Lamp, which appeared in 1921, was composed in its entirety in a ship's cabin. The book raises the perplexing question of the reality of individuality. Bishop Berkeley attempted to show the impossibility of a rigorous proof of the existence of the external world of the thinker; Briffault clasps hands with him and challenges the conception of individuality. He repudiates Descartes's magical formula, *cogito ergo sum,* which purported to establish the reality of the Ego, as being illusory. He argues that the ultimate residuum of matter is motion. Analyze matter to its final point, and there is nothing but vibration. Grammatically, we are compelled to say, if we do not demand a subject for our verb, that it is "pure motion," that is, that nothing is moving but motion. We can take a further step and ask the cause of the motion, but that is outside the problem. We have reached the point in the analysis that transcends our experience and beyond which we cannot go. Language or symbolism, our only tool, has failed us. We are compelled to think of motion in terms of the system of which it is a part. Analyze the subject, and we have nothing left. The same process holds when we analyze the subject of psychology. The "thinker" or the "doer" is a concept we can handle when it is a part of the whole; but, analyze the organism to its ultimate configuration, and the "thinker" vanishes as does the subject in an analysis of matter. There is no "thinker" over and above that complex whole which we term the "organism." The "doer" is the summation of the forces of the organism. Dissolve the forces, and the "doer" ceases to be. Thus individuality is a myth, and everything must be viewed as part of the "continuous life stream." The life-stream had its source in the inorganic world, and the organism is a measured portion of energy, as is the stone upon the beach. This raises the question of the proper attitude of man in the extra-individualistic, impersonal, impenetrable universe. Briffault answers that we can trust the universe; that the order of nature is above the callous indifference of our individual morality; and that it will take account of, and punish ruthlessly, inadaptations, unveracities, and evolutionary crimes and misdemeanors obstructing the course of life. This is the main point of the book, which is more metaphysical than psychological. "I am one of the few who still believe in metaphysics," he writes; and his arguments are, in the main, metaphysical arguments.

He is also the author of various other works: *Sin and Sex* (1931), a critique of the supposed supernatural origins of morals and an analysis of some of their contemporary manifestations; *Breakdown* (1932), an attempt, written during the period of enthusiastic communism of the early 1930's, to show that "traditional civilization," which he said is based on class divisions, was collapsing and that the signs of that breakdown were everywhere evident; *Reasons for Anger* (1936), a collection of essays; *The Decline and Fall of the British Empire* (1938), a bitter analysis of British social conditions and policy; *Les Troubadours et le sentiment romanesque* (1945), an amplification of his study of troubadour poetry in *The Mothers;* and four novels—*Europa* (1935), *Europa in Limbo* (1937), *Fandango* (1940), and *New Life of Mr. Martin* (1947).

II. THE MATERNAL ASCENDANCY IN EARLY SOCIETY

The Mothers, which appeared in 1927, is a huge work of more than two thousand pages, with a bibliography of some five thousand titles. It was composed under the most adverse conditions. Five years in straitened circumstances and broken health were consumed in writing it; and during that time he suffered a series of family disasters, losing his wife, his eldest daughter, and his dearest friend all within a few months. He worked single-handed, amassing the thousands upon thousands of references and sparing himself no drudgery. The flight, he says, that began with still youthful buoyancy was brought to a conclusion on broken wings. The personal mishaps, however, that occurred during his years of labor are reflected nowhere in the book. He brought to his task an immense knowledge and a fine talent for the clear and orderly presentation of his material.

He is concerned to show that the human mind in all that distinguishes it from the mind of animals is a social product and not a biological product and that the social characters of the human mind are determined exclusively by the operation of the maternal instinct. He holds that the mind has a twofold derivation—the biological and the traditional. The traditional inheritance is the stored-up social development which each individual has to acquire anew. If the traditional inheritance is eliminated, the human individual is indistinguishable from the animal. There are no innate ideas, moral, intellectual, or emotional. The characters that distinguish human beings from animals are all a part of the social inheritance; and, if the individual were placed in a position, whether through environment or because of organic defects, such as deaf-mutism, so that the traditional inheritance were closed to him, his actions would be entirely animalistic and devoid of all the so-called "human" qualities. This theory, which has long been discussed by psychologists, is the foundation of his main investigation—the supposed origin and development of the social characters of the human mind.

The social characters of the human mind, the characters which distinguish it from the mind of animals, could have originated only in a process whereby the accumulated knowledge of the individual was imparted to its offspring. This process Briffault traces to the function of maternity. As we advance from the lower to the higher mammals, the length of the period of gestation increases, and the period of immaturity is prolonged. The length of the period of care for the immature offspring depends upon the operations of the maternal functions. If those functions are absent and the offspring is left to shift for itself soon after birth, the occasion to impart individual education will not exist, and the organism will possess only the biologically inherited mind. Accepting education as a fundamentally feminine function, Briffault is led to an examination of the facts of social anthropology, and he believes that women have uniformly played a predominating part in the shaping of social institutions. He concludes that "the social characters of the human mind are, one and all, traceable to the operations of instincts that are related to the functions of the female and not to those of the male."

Upon the basis of this approach Briffault develops his main argument—the validity of the matriarchal theory. His position on this controversial subject is far from being the extreme one that it is frequently represented to be. Indeed, his approach to what is admittedly one of the most complex questions confronting historical anthropology is marked by a caution and understatement not characteristic of a number of his opponents. He recognizes explicitly that the achievements which constitute what, in the best sense, we term "civilization" have taken place in societies organized on patriarchal principles; that is to say, those achievements are, for the most part, the work of men. That assumption, he points out, appears justified by a survey of human societies during historical times. Early investigators, however, such as Sir Henry Maine, in spite of their great ability, were largely confined to speculation; their materials were restricted to classical history and the picture of patriarchal society in the Old Testament. Briffault assumes that the pioneer labors of Morgan, McLennan, Tylor, W. Robertson Smith, and the anthropologists of the last fifty years have removed the problem from the sphere of abstract speculation to that of inductive inference. He believes that two generalizations have emerged from the scattered facts of the reports of savage peoples, which are particularly important in promoting the growth of our knowledge of the origins of human society. He thinks that it is now clear that primitive social organization has as its most fundamental unit not the state or the family but a group of kinsmen, having generally an animal or a plant for its badge. He thinks also that the part played in primitive society by women and their influence differs markedly from that which their place in civilized societies during historical times has assigned to them.

It is the latter conclusion which is generally described as the "matriarchal theory," a term devised by McLennan in opposition to the theory of his time, which attributed social origins to a patriarchal age similar to that represented in the biblical descriptions of early Hebrew nomads. Briffault points out that the term has been loosely employed to denote a status of women in primitive society, which ranged within wide limits from the mere reckoning of descent in the female, instead of in the male, line to gynaecocracy, that is, the exercise of supreme authority by women. The numerous objections advanced against Briffault's position generally proceed upon the assumption that the matriarchy he describes is, in substance, a gynaecocracy. He has been extremely careful, however, to use, in a relative sense, the term "matriarchy," which is established by usage but which he recognizes as open to objection and in opposition to the term "patriarchy." In his volumes "matriarchy" refers to a state of society in which the interests and sentiments that are directly connected with the instincts of the women play a more important part than is the rule in the civilized societies with which we are most familiar. He explicitly repudiates the notion that the constitution of matriarchal societies is a matter of the domination of one sex over the other. In his view what is significant is that almost every variety and degree of feminine influence and power is to be found in the lower cultures; sometimes it is considerable, as where superstition has invested the women with the imaginary monopoly of magical and supernatural powers; sometimes it amounts to little more than a status of social equality with the men. Whether the women do or do not enjoy power in a matriarchy, their status is not, in such a society, defined by the specific disabilities which mark their position in a patriarchally constituted social order.

Having found that early societies were matriarchies, Briffault next proceeds to examine a wide variety of sentiments and institutions from the standpoint of that position and with a view to discovering their origins. His initial hypothesis largely determined the outcome of this procedure; that is to say, the role of the female in the origins of sentiments and institutions was found to be predominant. This is merely an assertion of a principle that social science has neglected, namely, that first assumptions decide the view that we are to take of facts, and even the facts for which we are to search. Westermarck, assuming a patriarchal point of view, found the origin of the family in the activity of masculine jealousy and possessiveness, the male exhibiting anger if faced with loss, or fear of loss, of his exclusive rights. Briffault, assuming an original matriarchy, finds the origin of the family in the biological group formed by the mother and her offspring, a group economically self-contained through the co-operation of clan-brothers and clan-sisters, of which the sexual partner is not a member. Similarly, he deduces the rule of exogamy from the jealousy of the mother, and he deduces the origin of taboo from the biological functions of the female. His investigations are supported by an almost overwhelming citation of authority; and, though the volumes are of exceptional length, they are sustained by a brilliance of writing rarely encountered in their field.

III. CRITICAL APPRAISAL OF BRIFFAULT'S MATERNAL THEORY

Criticism of Briffault's undertaking falls into two classes: (1) criticism of such studies in general, their methodology, and their consequences or, rather, lack of consequences and (2) criticism of Briffault's work in particular. As to the first, it is asserted that the quest for social origins is a vain one. This may be taken in two principal senses: first, that social origins are hopelessly lost and, therefore, their quest is fruitless. This assertion, of course, begs the question, since it is Briffault's object to show that the origins of some institutions and sentiments are not lost. Inasmuch as no demonstration has yet been offered on a priori grounds of the fruitlessness of the quest, Briffault's explanation of social origins must be met by an examination of the soundness of the evidence which he has brought forward in support of his position and the inferences he has drawn from it. Until that task has been accomplished, the question of the soundness of the quest for social origins remains an open one. It is also argued that social origins can never be discovered, because social institutions of the more fundamental sort do not have a beginning, or even an end, in time. It is admitted that, while there was a time when there was no state, yet the state had no beginning in time; it had no specific moment of creation but only an emergence; there are germs of state organization in all societies long prior to the appearance of what we today term the "state." This argument represents an application of the doctrine of social evolution, a theory itself as much under attack as Briffault's own exposition of matriarchal origins and need not, therefore, detain us.

Briffault throughout his study has employed the so-called "comparative method," which has been subjected to severe criticism in recent years. Here, again, the only a priori demonstration of its inherent invalidity, aside from the philosophic and mathematical infirmities to which induction is subject generally, is in connection with its use to establish a unilinear developmental series. Other applications of the method do not appear to have been successfully impugned, and in Briffault's particular case the only point open is the trustworthiness of his source material and the inferences which he made. Finally, it is maintained that, even if Briffault's matriarchal position is established, the theory is barren. This criticism, of course, is a reflection of the thought of a utilitarian age. If the matriarchal theory is established, it becomes, if not history, at least the equivalent of history, and it is justified by whatever considerations support the study of history itself. Briffault himself has been careful to point out that the theory bears only indirectly upon problems of today.

Of the criticism of the work itself, the most damaging point that has been brought against it is the unreliability of its authorities. It is charged that the authorities are dubious; that they do not stand for the point on which they are cited; that they stand for the opposite point; or that their position is otherwise misrepresented. The most thorough effort to establish this criticism was undertaken by Westermarck (*Three Essays on Sex and Marriage* [1934]), who examined the references that Briffault cited in refutation of Westermarck's position. A random sampling of a dozen citations relied upon by both Westermarck and Briffault indicates that Westermarck's criticism of the authorities which he analyzed is justified; at the same time, a score of Briffault's citations sampled at random were found to be accurate. A one-volume edition of *The Mothers,* re-written for popular use and devoted merely to an exposition of the main thesis, was published in 1931 and takes account of the criticism that had appeared up to that time. Westermarck's criticism, moreover, does not go to the main thesis of the book, since he was concerned only with criticism directed at his own position. Furthermore, both Briffault and Westermarck share many views in common.

Both the patriarchal and the matriarchal theories may be placed together today in the same category by the Scotch verdict, "Not proven."
Undoubtedly, the most patient attempt to establish the latter theory is
Briffault's *The Mothers,* and it will no doubt remain so for many years
to come. It is the most closely reasoned and exhaustive study ever made
of the subject; its views as a whole, when its length and the multitude
of theories it embraces are considered, are remarkably coherent. At the
very least, it is a work which cannot be safely ignored by those who
venture into its field.

CHAPTER XXXV

PATRICK GEDDES, VICTOR BRANFORD, AND APPLIED SOCIOLOGY IN ENGLAND: THE SOCIAL SURVEY, REGIONALISM, AND URBAN PLANNING

Lewis Mumford, *Amenia, New York*

I. INTRODUCTORY REMARKS

NOTWITHSTANDING the fact that Patrick Geddes (1854–1932) and Victor Branford (1864–1930) devoted a good part of their lifetimes to the advancement of sociology, their contributions are scarcely known. What accounts for that fact? Three things: the originality of their thought, the completeness of their presentation, and their use of schemata and diagrams and other forms of graphic notation that are still relatively unfamiliar in sociology—particularly among the more literary and philosophical schools.

In one sense it is still too early to judge their life-work or render an adequate account of it. Sir Patrick Geddes, who was the older man and the more profoundly creative mind, left behind him an enormous mass of unpublished material: lectures, unfinished books, and diurnal notes —great heaps of them—some of which have been sorted and put in order at the Outlook Tower in Edinburgh, to be published when sufficient aid is forthcoming. These notes and papers are comparable to the notebooks that Leonardo da Vinci left behind: indeed, Geddes possibly bears the same relation to the biotechnical period which he anticipated that Leonardo now plainly bears to the mechanical and scientific developments whose growth after the seventeenth century was finally to outstrip Leonardo's boldest dreams. At all events, the notes outweigh Geddes' published work in bulk and probably in importance. In the meanwhile, however, it may be useful to sum up Geddes' life work and make a preliminary appraisal of his contributions both to sociology proper and to social philosophy.

Patrick Geddes was born in Perth, Scotland, in 1854. After showing an adolescent interest in chemistry and physics, which never came back with any force until he wrote his biography of the Indian bio-physicist, Jaghadis Chandra Bose, Geddes became a student of biology. In the seventies he studied under Huxley at South Kensington, where he occasionally met Darwin; and after that he studied under Lacaze-Duthiers in Paris and Haeckel in Jena. His early connections with France never weakened. France, as with so many Scotch thinkers, even before Hume and Adam Smith, was his second home. Le Play, Demolins, Reclus, Durkheim, to say nothing of the French town-planners, historians, and philosophers (Bergson especially), all made contributions to his thought. At the end of his life he founded a students' hostel, which he called the Collège des Ecossais, on the outskirts of Montpellier, the birthplace of that other great sociologist, Auguste Comte, whose essential contributions to historical sociology he sought, among other things, to continue.

Thanks to Huxley and Haeckel, Geddes received an early initiation into ecology; and he passed beyond Huxley's neat morphological studies, with their emphasis upon the dead and the mechanical, to a biology concerned with living organisms reacting upon one another and upon their various environments. The central motif of biology for Geddes was precisely this functioning of the organism in its environment. This led to an early appreciation of Frédéric Le Play, whose formula, *lieu, travail, et famille,* was—Geddes perceived—the equivalent of "environment, function, and organism," as used by the biologist. So, while Geddes rejected the easy metaphorical comparisons of society with an organism, which Spencer and later sociologists pushed to absurdity, he regarded social life in man as continuous with the life of other organisms, and the realities of *organism, function, environment* were translated, in a slightly broader conception than Le Play's, as *folk, work, place.*

Returning to Edinburgh after his studies, Geddes took up a university career by becoming a lecturer in zoölogy at the School of Medicine. Throughout his life his interest in the biological sciences was a deep and central one: indeed, the chair of professor of botany at Dundee, which he held for many years, he did not relinquish until the end of the first World War. One of Geddes' earliest books, on the *Fvolution*

of Sex, written with his pupil, J. Arthur Thomson, became a pioneer
classic on the subject; and the two men published a number of books,
Sex, Evolution, and *Biology,* in the "Home University Series." In all
these collaborations, Geddes' contributions are easily identified by reason
of his compact style, with an irregular rhythm and various characteristic elisions and manufactured words—prose, in other words, with a
touch of Meredith and Carlyle in it, and at times something of their
epigrammatic concentration, as in his description of "good form" as
"shamming dead," or in his characterization of specialized knowledge
as "knowing more and more about less and less." As for his neologisms,
he was as prolific here as was Jeremy Bentham, whose utilitarian limitations Geddes so heartily despised: "paleotechnic," "neotechnic," "geo-
technic," "eutopian," "eupsychic," "bio-psychosis," "dis-specialism,"
"verbalistic empaperment," "biotechnic," were but a few of them.

While Geddes himself was pre-eminently a botanist, if one can pick
out a single subject among the many of which he made himself master,
he regarded the mathematical and physical sciences as basic to further
work in biology or sociology. In the eighties the concept of energy was
making its way into the physical sciences, and Geddes was quick to
perceive its importance and to trace out its implications in society itself.
His earliest contributions to sociology were, in fact, two papers, one on
"The Classification of Statistics" and the other on the "Principles of
Economics." In these papers he applied the doctrines of energetics to
the tabulations of the census-taker and to the formal concepts of official
political science. These papers antedated Ostwald's *Energetische Grundlagen der Kulturwissenschaften* by almost a generation, and they anticipated the views and methods of Frederick Soddy by an even longer
period.

Meanwhile, Geddes' interest as a naturalist in the society about him
was deepening. From his vantage point—a top-floor flat in a renovated
tenement in the old town of Edinburgh, later in a new co-operative
apartment house just below the Castle esplanade—he became conscious
of the social world about him. The historic mile from the Holyrood
to the Castle is a veritable mine of social and cultural history; and Geddes
became more and more aware of the city itself as the special environment created by man for the transmission of his social heritage.

By the middle of the nineteenth century the city had all but dropped
out of consciousness as a subject of thought. Here and there, in Paris

and Vienna, a little of the traditional baroque planning was still being done in a grandiose way. But the new factory towns were mere agglomerations of mean hovels, cut through by railway yards and chopped up by dirty factories, disorderly storage yards and slag heaps, and smoky factory districts. The new city had become a by-product of the factory in its most antisocial phase: it exhibited neither technical competence nor social co-operation. And the city had dropped out of political thought. Legally, it was looked upon as a mere creature of the state; and in the new sociologies the city was nonexistent. The individual, the class, and the state were, in general, the only realities recognized.

Geddes was perhaps the first modern sociologist to appreciate the role of the city in the development and continuation of the social heritage. Fustel de Coulanges had in effect demonstrated this in his treatise on *La Cité antique;* but Geddes generalized that approach and carried it further. At the Outlook Tower, which he founded in 1892 as a civic and regional museum and as a sociological laboratory, he carried on a systematic study of the city, beginning with that which was immediately around him. While Geddes' survey of Edinburgh was contemporary with Booth's massive survey of London, Geddes' superior equipment in history and sociology enabled him to give the survey a more useful form. It was he who formulated the procedure—survey before action— as the basis for civic and social planning, and it was from the Outlook Tower that this idea was brought back to America in the nineties, partly through Charles Zueblin, of Chicago, to form the basis of the survey movement.

Through summer meetings that were held at the Outlook Tower, Geddes began in the nineties the assimilation of the best thought on the Continent, repeating in his day what another Scotchman, Carlyle, had done sixty or more years before. Élisée Reclus, the world geographer, and Peter Kropotkin, the brilliant author of *Mutual Aid* and *Fields, Factories, and Workshops* were among the lecturers at the summer school, and Geddes started to weave another thread into his sociology—that of geography. The concept of the human region, as developed by the French human geographers, became an essential part of his thought. Here the two poles of nature, nature as given and nature as modified by human action—to use G. P. Marsh's phrase—are brought together. Geddes, by the way, greatly valued G. P. Marsh's pioneering work on human geography and geotechnics; and he kept his memory alive while Marsh's own countrymen permitted his work to slide into oblivion. A pupil of Geddes', Herbertson, became the exponent of the new regional geography in Great Britain; and out of this came the Oxford School of Geography.

During the 1900's, Geddes began to spend a good part of his time in London. With his pupil and colleague, Victor Branford, he busied himself in 1903 with the foundation of the Sociological Society; and in the years immediately after—as again toward the end of both men's lives—Geddes was an active contributor to the *Sociological Review,* as well as a frequent lecturer at the society. From this London sojourn dates a series of important university extension lectures, whose syllabuses, even today, are vivid and stimulating. Among these are a course on "Country and Town," another on "Contemporary Social Evolution," a third on "Cities," and a fourth on the "Evolution of Occupations: Introduction to the Sociology of Labour."

This career as a professing sociologist was at first abortive: the Martin White professorship at the University of London, originally intended for Geddes, went, by some unhappy accident connected with Geddes' original lecture, to the philosophic liberal, Leonard T. Hobhouse. But in 1920, Geddes was called to a professorship in civics and sociology at the University of Bombay, a post which he held for four years. By this time, unfortunately, Geddes' encyclopedic range of learning and his extensive systematization had taken on such huge proportions that he could scarcely handle them. He cried aloud for a collaborator capable of living with the same intensity, working with the same terrific energy, and writing on the same heroic scale as he himself lived and worked and thought. The collaborator did not appear: those who had the mind had not the strength and stamina, and those who had the necessary capacity for sacrifice and self-annihilation alas! did not have sufficient mind. And while Branford remained closer to Geddes in sociology than any other disciple, it remains true that Branford's best works were those he wrote by himself.

Meanwhile, Geddes had brought to scientific sociology an intellectual equipment and a practical experience that few sociologists could boast. As a biologist, he remained an active student, if not an experimenter, to the end of his days; and he was, incidentally, coplanner with his son-in-law, Frank Mears, of one of the best of the new naturalistic zoos

after the pioneer but overrated example of Hamburg—that at Edinburgh. As an educator and civic administrator, Geddes had cleaned up
some of the filthiest slums of Edinburgh, had instituted the gardening
of leftover open spaces, had built a series of university student halls,
and had planned and developed the Outlook Tower. From 1914 to
1924 he surveyed and planned fifty cities in India and Palestine. Among
other things, he selected the site for the University of Jerusalem and,
with Mears, did the early planning of its buildings. His two-volume
Report on Indore includes a magnificent critique of the modern university: it is in every way a classic. In short, Geddes knew "cities, climates,
councils, governments" as no one since Aristotle had known them.
Although a prodigious reader and scholar, no one relied less upon books
than he did, unless they had been personally verified by observation
and experience.

So much for what went into Geddes' sociology. Let me now try to
outline its main points of approach and the particular orientation of his
social philosophy. But, before I can do this, I must say a word about
Branford, who was Geddes' collaborator in a whole series of undertakings, beginning with the Sociological Society itself and going on
to the series of books on the "Making of the Future."

III. THE PERSONALITY AND CONTRIBUTIONS OF VICTOR BRANFORD

Victor Branford was Geddes' junior, and, like Geddes, he began as
a student of biology. But family circumstances cut him off from his
natural career as teacher, and he became a certified accountant and
financier. In the latter capacity his work brought him to South America,
where he had interests in a Paraguayan railroad, and to the United
States, where Geddes had preceded him and had, in Chicago, discovered Veblen.

Victor Branford was a remarkable man and a pregnant thinker;
but, because he was out of the fashion of his time, he was scarcely
known in America, and in England, where he led an active, indefatigable life, he was hardly better appreciated, although he had a wide
circle of acquaintances and moved freely among financiers and scholars.

Victor Branford was a unique combination of the man of affairs and
the speculative thinker, a type England has so often produced from
the time of Sir Walter Raleigh and Sir Francis Bacon. By profession
he belonged to the abstemious guild of certified accountants, the medi-

cal diagnosticians, as he used to say, of business; by interest and attainment, he was a sociologist, a historian, and a philosopher; and in his character were mingled a wordly shrewdness, an ability to appraise all the mischief and madness of his fellows, with a wild devotion to losing causes and remote ideals.

Victor Branford's first book of importance was his *Interpretations and Forecasts,* which was published by Mitchell Kennerley in America on the eve of the first World War; and the book that sums up his observations and his philosophy of art and science and religion and life is *Science and Sanctity*—a treatise whose audacious title is in itself a volume. By indefatigable effort he founded the Sociological Society in London, and by continuous preaching and practice he did his utmost to carry on the substantial tradition of Auguste Comte and Frédéric Le Play, endeavoring to make sociology a true observational science, dealing not with abstractions, such as the "herd instinct" or the "common will," but with the actual processes and functions of definite regional societies. This method has been independently developed and fruitfully used by the American school of anthropologists in dealing with primitive peoples; but because of their original bias, the anthropologists have until recently been reluctant to take over more complex societies, particularly contemporary ones; and in their isolation of the concept of culture, they originally too complacently ignored the data of geography and psychology.

Unlike the American sociologists, who have at last adopted the notion of the survey as an instrument of exact thought in sociology, Victor Branford did not confine the survey to the purely spatial society of the present, without reference to its complex historical filiation, its heritage of mores, customs, laws, ideas, and ideals. Outdoor observation was for him an essential of both life and thought; a sociology of the chair was little better than so much stuffed upholstery for the mind; and Branford invented many ingenious ways of seeing the country, one of them, as I remember, from the top of a moving van—a useful expedient in the days before the double-decker bus began to ply the English roads.

Walking with Branford through Westminster or Oxford or the New Forest was one of the liveliest pleasures in the world; every stone came to life, and the very advertisements on the hoardings became pregnant commentaries upon our venal and life-starved civilization. His conversation had something that his books lacked: a certain spice of worldly observation that might have become cynicism in a less generous soul or have led to despair in a less hopeful one. He would gleefully point out some sinister exhibition of the social process, as in the combination of a bank with a meeting hall in the Methodist center in Westminster, or the juxtaposition of the bust of Cecil Rhodes with the new examination buildings in Oxford, which sorted out the brains of an imperial bureaucracy.

Acquainted with the statistical predictions of that remarkable prophet of modern warfare, Jean Bloch, and himself a keen observer in the financial centers of Europe, Branford was perhaps less surprised by the outbreak of the European War than were any of his contemporaries. As early as 1911, in collaboration with Geddes, he circulated a memorandum among his intellectual associates, pointing out that, unless there was a decisive reversal in policy, the nations of Europe would be at each other's throats by 1915. He proposed, therefore, to issue a series of books which would analyze the economic and spiritual causes of the approaching conflict—the lack of vital economy, the competition of rival megalopolies, the debauchery of all ideal values in a slavish financial and bureaucratic and military regime—and would, before the actual conflict broke out, lay down a positive program of reconstruction which might either help avert the disaster or salvage the ruins.

This proposal sounded so fantastic even to watchful, sober minds in 1911 that Branford and Geddes were forced to drop it; but they had the sad triumph of seeing their prophecy come true; and toward the end of the war, in the midst of the intellectual helterskelter, Branford began to publish—with the advice and help of his colleague Geddes—a series of books called "The Making of the Future," in which he and his contributors sought to embody a more adequate conception of life, economics, and polity. It is interesting to note, by the way, that in the original memorandum, Thorstein Veblen figured as one of the possible contributors.

Neither these books nor Branford's series of postwar pamphlets, called "Papers for the Present," received the attention they deserved; although, if I am not mistaken, his pamphlet, *The Drift to Revolution,* has a fairly wide circulation. In that pamphlet Branford analyzed the historic aims and programs of the "party of order" and the "party of revolution." He showed how one tended to beget the other—hence an oscillation of ferocious dictatorships and a deadlock in the fulfilment of all that was positive in their programs. He suggested a composition of forces, not a compromise, which would achieve nothing that either party sought, but a disinterested effort to get beyond the regime of power into one which would depend more completely upon the verified knowledge of science and that nonpartisan good will which is latent in all the arts and professions. This he called the "party of the Third Alternative," differing from the other two in that its emphasis was not upon abstract shibboleths but upon definite, concrete, realizable aims: reforestation, better houses, more adequately designed towns, co-operative agriculture, socialized credit, regenerated schools. The radical New Towns policy of Britain today, which has both Tory and Labour sponsorship, is an admirable example of Branford's "Third Alternative"—and a confirmation of his political realism.

An expert in finance, he proposed to substitute insurance, plus a definite charge for actual service, for the haphazard and often extortionate incidence of interest. He had no doubt that finance and industry could bring forth disinterested minds, quite as much as medicine and science could—indeed, he was one of them; and, though he had much in common with Thorstein Veblen, whose genius he was one of the first in Europe to recognize and hail, he was far from placing his hopes for a more vital and better-integrated society in the ministrations of some single class, such as the engineers. He knew that social counterpoint was a more complex matter, and his ideal figure for a fine society was that of a symphony orchestra.

The deeper that Branford's feet sank into the muddy slough of finance, the more passionately he longed for social deliverance. So that there is, in Branford's writings, a recurrent note of almost apocalyptic yearning for a grand conversion which would alter all the dominant values of imperialist society, even as Christianity had transformed those of Rome. In consequence the orderly pattern of Branford's thought is sometimes broken by an unexpected emotional eruption, not always justified by the immediate context or the general train of his argument. This defect, which makes some of his writing seem obscure and wilful, is, however, associated with a real quality. Both he and Geddes looked upon thought as an organic process. Instead of ejecting feeling and sentiment, they sought to integrate them in rational thinking, so that the subjective element, eliminated by the Cartesian methods inherited from seventeenth-century science and thereafter discarded as "unreal,"

should not come back again in a perverse and morbid form. Hence the
paradoxical title of perhaps the best of Branford's books, *Science and
Sanctity,* is a clue to his whole philosophy. The synthesis of facts and
values, of the sciences and the arts, of the practical and the poetic, was
his leading interest as a philosopher. Geddes went further than Branford in expressing this synthesis systematically by means of his brilliant diagrams; but Branford was the more active in translating these
ideas into literary form.

In 1903, as we have noted, Branford and Geddes were the leading
figures in the group that founded the Sociological Society in London,
with Spencer's papal blessing and with Galton as the first president
and a host of distinguished names in social science and politics on
the Council. During the first five years of its existence the society had
a healthy growth and showed a stir of intellectual activity. After this
the absence for long periods, first of Branford, then of Geddes, and
the hiatus of the war interfered with its development. At the end of
the war, Branford, by assuming the financial responsibilities for its life
and supplying it with a house in Westminster (Le Play House), attempted to resuscitate it and put it on its feet.

Unfortunately, personal rivalries and doctrinal divisions had broken
up the original consensus. Neither Branford nor Geddes suffered fools,
particularly academic fools, very gladly, nor were they sparing in their
criticism of the verbalistic, fragmentary, and unscientific work that
often passed for sociology or the social sciences in the established schools.
They sought to create a coherent framework that would make possible
a co-ordinated attack on the whole sociological front. But those who
needed their rigorous discipline most were least ready to receive it.
Sociology remained, for most of their opponents, another name for
social philosophy; and there were as many schools of this as there were
philosophers.

What influence the Sociological Society and the *Sociological Review*
exercised was a personal influence. It had brilliant contributors, like
Christopher Dawson, the Catholic historian; and, besides Geddes' and
Branford's work, it published some notable regional surveys, done under
the guidance of Alexander Farquharson; but the core of the review
was the contributions of Branford and Geddes. One real victory, however, both Geddes and Branford had, even in their own lifetimes. The
method of civic and regional survey, first developed by Geddes at Edin-

burgh, took on in the schools and exercised a positive influence on the teaching of history, civics, geography, and nature study in the elementary and secondary schools of Great Britain. The incomparable city-development reports of Sir Patrick Abercrombie and his school have their source in Geddes' teaching and example. The land-utilization survey of England was another direct outcome of his work. In the universities, Fleure at Aberystwith and Marett at Oxford, like J. L. Myres, remained natural allies, though not disciples. Other one-time students, like Marcel Hardy and C. C. Fagg, have carried the Geddesian doctrines into geography.

Branford's main contribution, perhaps, was as an expositor and continuator of the Geddesian outlook and vision of life. But the two men, in association with Branford's partner, John Ross, were pioneers in still another department. Following up Ernest Solvay's effort to arrive at a system of social accountancy to replace the pecuniary accountancy of capitalism, they did a series of studies on the nature of modern finance. Branford, out of his vast experience and sharp insight, wrote a number of papers upon banking and credit which were published in the afore-mentioned series of postwar pamphlets issued from Le Play House, called "Papers for the Present."

As sociologist, Branford's mature point of view is perhaps best expressed in the two articles on sociology which he wrote, respectively, for the recent edition of *Chambers' Encyclopaedia* and for the fourteenth edition of the *Encyclopaedia Britannica*.

For Branford the tradition of modern sociology has a double origin. On one side, it begins with Vico's conception of the philosophy of history as expressed in the *New Science* and runs through Herder and Condorcet, until finally it is systematized and set in order by Comte. On the other side, it begins with Montesquieu and the Physiocrats and the cultivators of the special social sciences, and in turn it is synthesized by Le Play in his threefold study of work, place, and people. From this point of view the adequate systematization of sociology in its temporal and spatial aspects would put an end to that abortive series of "systems of sociology" which have succeeded each other since the middle of the nineteenth century. Branford states his point of view succinctly in the *Britannica* article as follows:

From the foregoing psychological approaches collectively there is growing up a doctrine of society, its structure, functions, origins, and purposes which, in popular estimation, probably outranges any sociological presentation yet made. Similarly, the anthropologists are in course of creating a sociology of their own. Ignoring the vast and profound labors of Comte in establishing and elaborating the concept of the Social Inheritance as the essential subject-matter of sociology, those anthropologists who emphasize and work out the idea of cultural diffusion are in danger of substituting a biased particularism for the synthetic generality which a genuine sociology demands. And the same criticism could be levelled against the more generalizing exponents in each of the many specialized sub-sciences found within the social field. Since these specialisms began under the influence of the evolutionary spirit to orient themselves in a sociological direction .... they have collectively accumulated a body of more or less verified knowledge which today must be held to constitute the main corpus of sociology, if that word be taken in a scientific rather than in a philosophic sense. But this body of specialized science suffers several grave defects. It is (a) unsystematized, and therefore, since lacking in real unity, is ill-adapted to the concerted activity on which assured progress depends; (b) uninformed by the master concepts on which the scientific foundations of sociology were originally laid; (c) inadequately related to biology and the other established sciences which, preliminary to sociology, compose an essential part of the equipment needed for the culminating study of society in evolution.

IV. THE CONTRIBUTION OF PATRICK GEDDES TO SOCIOLOGY
AND SOCIAL RECONSTRUCTION

We are now ready to go back to Geddes. His prime sociological contribution came, first, through his concrete and many-sided study of actual groups and communities. In this study, practice alternated with theoretical development. Second and not less important was his attempt to systematize and order these experiences by creating a framework which would not merely contain his own material but serve equally as a focus for studies, both generalized and specialized, that might be made by others. He attempted nothing less than the art of ideological cartography. Like the work of the pre-Columbian map-makers, it was to lead to new explorations and conquests in the actual world.

I cannot attempt in this short study to explain and comment upon all Geddes' diagrams, or even to present adequately the most significant ones. It is important, however, to outline the general method that he used, which others may revamp and develop.

Perhaps the largest part of Geddes' thinking was done on squared paper, which he folded rather than ruled; and the major categories on his intellectual maps were arranged in triads, in which a subject and an object were connected by a third category indicating action or function—therefore often a verb. Take the simplest of these triads:

from organism, functioning, and environment Geddes went on to the sociological equivalent of folk, working, and place. From this point of view it was important never to think of these categories as separate, except as a momentary convenience of thought. By using an intellectual map it was possible to keep them present simultaneously to the eye and to the mind—hence his occasional reference to this type of operation as "simultaneous thinking."

But these categories are neither separate nor inert. Hence if they are drawn on a diagonal in the middle of nine squares, the remaining boxes can be used to show their possible forms of interaction. Instead of picking activities and ideas at random, Geddes first evolves them from their fundamental logical categories as these categories are derived from experience. What is the outcome of this method? The outcome of using it is that one becomes aware of facts and relations that may not immediately be given in either observation or experience—just as, when the periodic table was first formulated, the unfilled spaces called attention to elements that were not yet discovered but whose general characteristics could be predicted from their position in the table.

If place, work, and folk are the fundamental categories of any society, then geography, economics, and anthropology, considered in their broadest sense, are the fundamental sciences of sociology. But the factor of time and the accumulation of the social heritage modify this simple scheme. The human group not merely is influenced by its environment but learns to dominate it; by improving its tools and weapons it creates a store of free energy that is available for art and thought and religion and play; and it criticizes its laws and customs and modifies its social heritage by deliberate selection. Hence human society comprehends polity, culture, and art, as well as work, folk, and place. If the concept of determinism applies usefully to life on the lower level, the concept of creative freedom applies to its upper levels. Holland made the Dutch; but the Dutch, with their dikes and their windmills and their land reclamation, also made Holland.

The fake dilemma of determinism versus free will Geddes rejects in sociology as he had rejected it previously in biology. Life, as he puts it, is not merely a matter of environment working on the passive organism but also a matter of the organism, in insurgent mood, working on the environment. In fact, even in its most passive state, it modifies the environment, as the animal does by inhaling air and giving out a larger amount of carbon dioxide. Both reactions are given in experience. In other words,

$$\text{Life} = \frac{OFE}{EFO} \ .$$

Approaching society from the level of choice and creative activity—that is, essentially from the level of the city—Geddes sees through Comte's eyes the division of all social groups into spiritual and temporal powers and into active and passive members. But, as a social philosopher, Geddes saw the weakness not merely of earlier social orders but of Comte's too rigid classification of their systems, particularly as expressed in the medieval polity. These functional elements—chiefs and people, intellectuals and emotionals—have a way of hardening into castes. The function becomes isolated and specialized; in the course of transmission it becomes stereotyped, and finally it fails to express its original content. The "chief" whose opinions are deservedly respected in the motor works becomes the arbiter of education as well, whereas, functionally, with respect to education he is merely one of the "people." So the man of the people may remain a day laborer all his life, through lack of opportunity, whereas functionally, like Burns, he may be a poet. In short, Geddes turned Comte's static divisions of society into dynamic ones, for, to him, each functioning social group had its appropriate regrouping of chiefs, people, emotionals, and intellectuals. He was always, however, dissatisfied with this terminology; perhaps the best substitute that he achieved was "leaders, workers, energizers, and initiators."

If Geddes' central diagram of thirty-six squares is an attempt to chart the field of social life, his bookcase diagram is a map of the biological and social sciences, by means of which this life is more clearly presented and integrated in thought.

This diagram is divided into an upper and a lower department: the upper deals with the group, the lower with the individual. With respect to time, four vertical compartments are divided into three sections: at the extreme left, the past; at the extreme right, the future or the possible; and the middle two, the present. These sections again are divided into the static and the dynamic. Giving these squares their proper values in biology, one has the following:

Paleontology	Taxonomy	Ecology	Phylogeny
Embryology	Anatomy	Physiology	Ontogeny

Is there the same sort of parallel between the essential sciences of biology and those of sociology as there is in society between organism, function, and environment and folk, work, and place? Geddes' answer to this is clear:

History and Archeology	Ethnography	Economics (and Politics)	Philosophy of History
Biography	Anthropography	Economics (detailed)	Biography (critical)

Only with great reluctance and with due caution may one substitute other categories from those which Geddes himself used. Nevertheless, the diagram will perhaps gain wider assent if one takes as the individual unit of sociology the group instead of the individual, and for the collective unit a whole society with its congeries of groups. Again, instead of the old terms "economics" and "politics," which are too limited, one might substitute social ecology, and for the individual aspect the functional study of component institutions.

It will be noted that this diagram gives a place to social philosophy, from Plato and Aristotle down to Karl Marx and John Dewey. But, instead of supposing that social philosophy or dialectic thinking can be a substitute for social science in the study of society, it limits philosophy to the possible. At the same time, by introducing the future and the possible as, so to speak, a legally bounded terrain in social thought, Geddes breaks with the nineteenth-century notion that valid thought must concern itself solely with the past and with those aspects of reality that do not imply either revaluation or action. Indeed, for Geddes, as for Dewey, thought was incomplete until it had passed back again into life and modified it. The weakness of the sociological precursors was that their "possible" rested on insufficient scientific data as to the past and the present. The weakness of the so-called "scientific" school today is that what it calls the future—when it chooses to consider that dimension of time—is in reality the past, since no allowance is made for chance, creative thoughts, and plans and for those emergent elements that are never clearly definable within the past social complex. Geddes' conception of man and society allowed not merely for outwardly conditioned responses but also for those that had an origin *within* the personality or the group; and, like Lloyd Morgan, whose work he valued, he knew the importance of "prospective reference" and anticipatory responses.

For the reader who wishes to go further with Geddes' social logic, I would refer to Amelia Defries' description of Geddes in *The Interpreter Geddes,* where he will find a complete layout of the "36," and to the series of diagrams Geddes included in two of the books he wrote with J. Arthur Thomson, *Biology* and *Life: Outlines of Biology.* It was Geddes' mission to restore, on a modern level, the essential structure of Greek thought as described by George Santayana—"physics" and "dialectics." He was one of the few non-Marxian scientists, outside the mathematical disciplines, who realized the importance of dialectic thinking and who, in the very act of acknowledging his debt to Comte, broke outside the narrow positivism of Victorian science.

This systematization of knowledge was, I must repeat, an important part of Geddes' life-work. His aim was to effect a passage from the dispersed, specialized, one-sided, narrowly pragmatic thinking that has dominated the last three hundred years to a synthetic, organic, and related mode of thinking—and thus of acting. It was not that he rejected, or failed to esteem, the separate results of highly specialized research. What he rejected was the notion that the separate compartments of thought or life could be kept separate. There was no guaranty that the accumulation of such separate particles of knowledge was bound—like the individualistic profit-seeking of the Victorian era—to produce a wealth of knowledge for the community. He saw that, on the contrary, knowledge became infertile and impoverished to the extent that it was, as he put it, "dis-specialized": becoming divorced from life, it failed to produce interesting hypotheses or to reflect vital dilemmas. For a specialism to be valid, it must be capable of reciprocal interaction with the entire body of thought that surrounds it. It needed, however, more than a metaphysical intuition to create this new wholeness. Hence, while Geddes appreciated the philosophic approach of both Jan Smuts and, still more, Whitehead, he believed that synthesis required a method as well as a formula: to live the life was a vital part of knowing the doctrine.

One turns finally to Patrick Geddes as a social philosopher. Beyond his ideological synthesis was the living example of the man himself. He was, above all, the philosopher of life. Though full of admiration for our technical triumphs, his life was dedicated to turning men away from the worship of things, from preoccupation with the impedimenta of existence, to the service of life itself. The paleotechnic period that began in the eighteenth century and devoted itself to mass production and power expansion and the general quantification of existence—was for Geddes a period of vital starvation: the peasant and the North Sea fisherman were for him higher biological types than the successful cockneys who looted a railroad system or cornered the grain market. In his work on city development, from the early report on Dunfermline to his final reports on Indore and Jerusalem University, he sought to reintroduce into Western civilization a balanced and life-maintaining environment. The nurture of children and the care of gardens, the mating of lovers and the building of homes, were for him the central tasks of civilization. The whole masculine world of machines, with its rigors and strenuous efforts and asceticisms, had meaning only to the extent that it furthered the elemental needs of life and afforded an opportunity for those higher growths of art and culture that spring out of a communal effort. Similarly, while Geddes acknowledged the many acute contributions of the urban mind, he looked forward to a new cycle of thought and activity when the more rustic types would come to the fore again; hence one of the acute problems in planning was to provide for the effective interaction of town and country on every level, from the growth of food to the propagation of thought.

Filled with awe and wonder and delight over the fact of life itself, Geddes rejected none of its manifestations; abstract thought was for him as real as an orgasm, and the hygiene of the digestive tract and the movement of the bowels were as important for clear thinking as the refinements of logic. So, too, he rejected those partial visions of life that sum themselves up in this or that philosophy or religion, or, rather, he accepted everything about them except their partiality. He could learn from the streetsweeper as well as from Bergson; the Hindu Brahmin had a glimpse of life not vouchsafed to the disciple of Marx; and, wherever Geddes encountered the living touch of experience and feeling, he seized it. This omnivorousness, this inclusiveness, this tremendous appetite for so many diverse parts of reality, which had been achieved on an emotional level by Walt Whitman, was attained on a more intellectual plane by Geddes. In weaker minds with less capacity to appropriate and assimilate, the process would be described as "eclecticism"; but in Geddes one feels that there is a beginning of that deeper world-wide understanding which is necessary for our intellectual health and our social salvation.

As a social philosopher Geddes was against the absolute state and *for* the functional organizations of cities and regions; against bureaucracy and militarism and *for* the voluntary action of groups; against mass regimentation and *for* the gradual leavening of action by education and example; against sessile aristocracies and ignorant democracies and *for* that aristodemocracy which he saw arising in the Scandinavian countries; against a verbalistic and pecuniary culture with the sham education of the three *R*'s in their crude form and their recent disguises and *for* a vital culture which combined the three *H*'s—head, heart, and hand. As for the positive movements that he started, one can only say that what is sound in regional planning, regionalism, and city development today either owes a direct debt to Geddes or was anticipated by his own earlier thought. Geddes the social philosopher rounds out the work of Geddes the systematic sociologist. And it may be that in the century to come Geddes will have an effect upon the ordering of our civilization even more powerful than that which Rousseau and Marx have successively exercised. If that turns out to be true, it will be partly, perhaps, because he was a better sociologist.

BIBLIOGRAPHY

BOOKS AND ARTICLES BY PATRICK GEDDES

The Classification of Statistics. Edinburgh, 1881.

An Analysis of the Principles of Economics. Edinburgh, 1885.

Civic Survey of Edinburgh. Edinburgh, 1911.

City Development: A Study of Parks, Gardens, and Culture Institutes. Edinburgh, 1904.

The Masque of Learning. Edinburgh, 1912.

Cities in Evolution. London, 1915.

Ideas at War. Lectures given with GILBERT SLATER, some of whose material was incorporated in the manuscript. London, 1917.

Report to the Durbar of Indore. 2 vols. London, 1920. The most exhaustive and the most important of Geddes' city-planning reports.

John Ruskin, Economist. "Round Table Series." Edinburgh, 1886.

Autobiographical papers: "Talks from My Outlook Tower," *Survey Graphic,* February–September, 1925.

Sociological papers in the series "Publications of the Sociological Society." London, 1905, 1906, 1907.

"Essentials of Sociology in Relation to Economics," *Indian Journal of Economics,* III, Part III (1922).

BOOKS BY PATRICK GEDDES AND J. ARTHUR THOMSON

The Evolution of Sex. 2 vols. London, 1888.
Evolution. New York, 1912.
Sex. New York, 1914.
Biology. New York, 1925.
Life: Outlines of Biology. New York, 1931.

BOOKS BY PATRICK GEDDES AND VICTOR BRANFORD

The Coming Polity. London, 1917.
Our Social Inheritance. London, 1918.
The Coal Crisis and the Future: A Symposium. Edited by VICTOR BRANFORD. London, 1926.
Coal—Ways to Reconstruction. Supplement to *The Coal Crisis.* London, 1926.

BOOKS BY VICTOR BRANFORD

St. Columba. Edinburgh, 1912.
Interpretations and Forecasts. New York, 1914.
Science and Sanctity. London, 1923.
Living Religions. London, 1925.
The following pamphlets in "Papers for the Present" series: *A Citizen Soldier, The Banker's Part in Reconstruction, The Modern Midas, The Drift to Revolution, A Rustic View of War and Peace.* London, 1917–20.
Articles on sociology in *Chambers' Encyclopaedia* (1928) and *Encyclopaedia Britannica* (14th ed.).

For a comprehensive study of the life and work of Geddes, see PHILIP BOARDMAN, *Patrick Geddes: Maker of the Future.* Chapel Hill, N.C., 1944.

CHAPTER XXXVI

GRAHAM WALLAS AND THE SOCIOPSYCHOLOGICAL BASIS OF POLITICS AND SOCIAL RECONSTRUCTION

Harry Elmer Barnes

I. THE NATURE AND SCOPE OF THE WRITINGS OF GRAHAM WALLAS

AN EXCEEDINGLY suggestive attempt by an Englishman to apply sociology and psychology to the treatment of public problems is to be found in the works of Graham Wallas (1858–1932), late professor of political science in the University of London. Wallas, like Bagehot, was a happy combination of the student and the practical man of affairs —something that is distressingly rare in America but need not be so if Wallas' suggestions are carried out in the near future. This healthy juncture of the scholar and the observer of practical affairs gives to his works that intellectual flavor so remote from the writings of the agitator and that concreteness and grasp of actual conditions which are so conspicuously absent from most of the academic works upon social and political science.

Wallas entered the field of political literature as one of the authors of the famous *Fabian Essays* of 1888. His first extended work, however, was the splendid biography of Francis Place, published in 1897. The works which contain his chief social and political theories are *Human Nature in Politics,* published in 1908; *The Great Society,* published in 1914; and his American lectures, *Our Social Heritage,* published in 1921. As these works will be analyzed below, all that need be mentioned in this place are some of the outstanding general characteristics of his writings.

In the first place, his early training as a classical scholar gave him a thorough grasp of the Platonic and Aristotelian social theories, to which he often recurs for example and comparison. His connections with the Fabian Society generated a rational and conscientious desire for sound social reform. Finally, his interest in that modern functional psychology, of which William James was the first important exponent, led him to think along psychological lines in both his academic studies and his practical relations to political problems and encouraged him to apply psychological principles consistently in formulating plans for social and political betterment.

Important in Wallas' political psychology is his emphasis upon the instinctive and subconscious processes of the mind as important factors in determining conduct. In this regard, he mentions his indebtedness to the suggestive essays of Dr. Trotter. While this is a step in the right direction, it is to be regretted that his first work presents no acknowledged acquaintance with the vast development of this field by psychiatrists like Morton Prince and Boris Sidis, or Sigmund Freud, Karl Jung, and the psychoanalysts. Wallas seems to have reached empirically many of their fundamental doctrines, and in his later books he specifically acknowledges his indebtedness to their conceptions. Yet, despite a courageous attempt to modernize political psychology, some critics have complained that Wallas had not entirely freed himself from some vestiges of the older psychology and logic. Ernest Barker, for example, in discussing *Human Nature in Politics,* has summarized some of these possible defects:

Many lines of criticism occur. Something could be said of its sensationalist premises; something of its nominalist philosophy; something of that tendency to explain the higher in terms of the lower, which leads to the explanation of civilised life by the conditions of life in prehistoric times and to the repeated coupling of man with "the other animals." We might urge that reason is none the less reason when it is not conscious inference, and that it is a fallacy to derationalize political society because it is not an explicit organization of conscious reason. Better however than to criticise is to emphasise the truths which Mr. Graham Wallas suggests.[1]

II. THE IRRATIONAL NATURE OF POLITICAL THOUGHT AND BEHAVIOR

In his *Human Nature in Politics,*[2] Wallas criticizes the defects in the modern psychological interpretations of political processes, outlines a rational method of remedying these defects, and suggests the main improvements which may be hoped for from such procedure. His main thesis is that psychology either is wholly omitted in the modern treatment of politics or, if employed at all, is the old, erroneous hyperintellectual hedonism, coming down from Bentham, which deals with man as a calculating machine, undisturbed by emotion, custom, tradition, and the like. The following passage well indicates the general line of his argument on this point: "For the moment, therefore, nearly all students of politics analyze institutions and avoid the analysis of man. The study of human nature by the psychologists has, it is true, advanced enormously since the discovery of human evolution, but it has advanced without affecting or being affected by the study of politics."[3] Wallas points out the domination of the old-fashioned views about human nature by referring to certain passages by Professors Ostrogorski, Bryce, and Merivale as good examples:

> Apparently Merivale means the same thing by "abstract" political philosophy that Mr. Bryce means by "ideal" democracy. Both refer to a conception of human nature constructed in all good faith by certain eighteenth-century philosophers, which is now no longer exactly believed in, but which, because nothing else has taken its place, still exercises a kind of shadowy authority in a hypothetical universe.....[4]

> If so, the passage [by Mr. Bryce] is a good instance of the effect of our traditional course of study in politics. No doctor would now begin a medical treatise by saying "the ideal man requires no food, and is impervious to the action of bacteria, but this ideal is far removed from the actualities of any known population." No modern treatise on pedagogy begins with the statement that "the ideal boy knows things without being taught them, and his sole wish is the advancement of science, but no boys like this have ever existed.....[5]

> This essay of mine is offered as a plea that a corresponding change [i.e., corresponding to the revolution of modern criminology and pedagogy by psychology] in the conditions of political science is possible. In the great University whose constituent colleges are the universities of the world, there is a steadily growing body of professors and students of politics who give the whole day to their work. I cannot but think that, as the years go on, more of them will call to their aid that study of mankind which is the ancient ally of the moral sciences.[6]

The fundamental basis of political behavior is to be found in the mental organization of the individual, acted upon by the stimuli of the political environment. The individual is, psychologically considered, a bundle of impulses and potential responses to external stimulation. These impulses are the product of the mental evolution of the race; and the effective functioning of the individual in political society depends upon an adequate stimulation of these impulses and predispositions to thought and action. In analyzing the foundations of individual and social behavior, the first prerequisite is that we give up the old psychology, which maintained that human acts are deliberately calculated means to a preconceived end, and recognize that the majority of human mental processes are subconscious or half-conscious—the result of instinctive or habitual impulses: "Whoever sets himself to base his political thinking on a re-examination of human nature must begin by trying to overcome his own tendency to exaggerate the intellectuality of mankind."[7]

The chief personal impulses which Wallas emphasizes are affection, fear, ridicule, desire for property, pugnacity, suspicion, curiosity, and the desire to excel. Each of these impulses is most effective to the extent that it acts without competition with other impulses, arises from direct stimulation, and results from an appeal to an instinct formed early in the evolution of the race. For this reason the artificial and recently developed stimulation of books and newspapers is superficial and transient in its effect, while the emotions caused by the bodily presence and personal traits and behavior of a political candidate are much more stirring and lasting than reading about politics or an appeal to abstract principles. Political campaigns are planned for the purpose of creating an impulsive personal affection for a candidate rather than a reasoned conclusion as to his personal merits or the excellence of his platform. In contrast to Le Bon, Wallas holds that the frequent repetition of a subject tends to create an impression of unreality upon both speaker and audience; therefore, the successful political leader must vary his appeal. Since the conditions of human evolution have required a mixture of privacy and social intercourse, the individual in modern life thrives best when this proper proportion of both is maintained. But such a pattern of life is difficult for the politician, who is called upon to be in almost perpetual association with his party workers. Finally, all political impulses are likely to be greatly intensified if they are stimulated when individuals are assembled in a crowd. This psychic instability of crowds may result from the fact that a stampede of the primitive social groups was the surest way to safety.

The political environment, as the stimulus which operates upon the impulsive dispositions of men, differs from these dispositions in that it is far more variable. Human nature has apparently changed but little since the beginning of the historic era. Therefore, any great reforms must be based upon the improvement of the political environment rather than upon any hope of a fundamental revolution of human nature. But, even though no considerable change in human nature may be looked for, an understanding of its characteristics and behavior may be able to produce a real transformation in conduct, quite aside from changes in the environment. Now the most significant thing about the political environment is that the great political entities which stimulate mankind are mainly recognized by the human mind through symbols. Some of the most important symbolized political entities are parties, nations, justice, authority, freedom, rights, etc. The mind does not, as a rule, comprehend the whole complex of ideas involved in a political entity but associates this complex with some aspect, image, or interpretation of it which serves as a symbol for the whole. For example, the royal scepter or other insignia of office tend to symbolize the institution of royalty, and the individual is content to let it stop with this rather than proceed to analyze the whole history and psychology of kingship. Even language itself is mainly intelligible to us through its symbolic nature and content, and the reception and interpretation of the symbols which words represent will naturally differ among individuals according to the experiences of their past life. The farther back the origin of the complex of ideas which are thus symbolized, the greater the emotional value that will attach to the symbol. A good example of the necessity for having a deep emotional association for a symbol is to be seen in the difficulty of creating loyalty to a newly constructed nation, dynasty, or aristocracy.

Of all modern political entities which stimulate our individual impulses, the political party is the most important and powerful. While the party may have an intellectual origin and be designed to achieve a definite end, it will have little strength or duration unless it secures sufficient emotional values for its symbols, such as party colors, tunes, names, and the like. A skilful party uses its symbols in the same way that a commercial concern employs its trade-marks and advertisements. The nature and validity of the thing symbolized may vary considerably, but that is not so important to the success of the party as that a high emotional response to the symbol be provided and sustained. If a candidate is not properly symbolized by his party, he has no chance of success. The most insignificant nonentity, properly associated with the party symbols, is much more likely to be successful in an election than the strongest personality in a country, if the latter cuts himself off from all party connections and makes an appeal solely to the intelligence of the voters. The instances of a man's forming a successful political entity in himself are rare. Even in such cases a man must adhere for a long time to a given set of principles, so that his followers may attach a high emotional value to them. This same continuity in doctrine must be observed by every newspaper that desires to be the successful organ of a party.

Wallas next makes a specific inquiry as to the extent to which reason enters into political action. His conclusion is essentially the same as that presented by Benjamin Kidd, namely, that reason plays only a small part in political life. The process by which he reaches this conclusion is quite different, however, from that employed by Kidd. Instead of arbitrary definitions and a priori assumptions, Wallas bases his judgment on an acute psychological analysis of human conduct. While it is difficult to say at just what point instinctive and habitual actions end and reasoned action begins, it is certain that there is a very large range for subconscious, nonrational inference in our mental processes, and it is equally obvious that the majority of our political opinions are reached in a nonrational manner. Men seem to attach greater emotional significance to the opinions which are reached intuitively than to those which are the result of reasoned conclusions. While subconscious impulses may be a fairly satisfactory guide for general affairs, since they are usually the result of several convergent suggestions, such is not the case in the field of our political thoughts and actions. It is the primary purpose of the political art deliberately to exploit our tendency to reach our opinions in a subconscious manner, and it aims so to stimulate our subconscious mind that we will automatically agree with the position taken by the party.

Yet, after all, reasoning in politics may better be described as extremely difficult rather than impossible. The difficulty is twofold. In the first place, man has to create the political entities about which he reasons, and these are, in turn, represented to the mind through symbols, largely subconscious in their psychic operation. In the second place, while reasoning in pure science is based upon the comparison of concrete similar objects or of objects alike in certain abstract qualities, political psychology has never found a satisfactory standard for comparing men. Neither Platonic idealism, Locke's theological ethics, Rousseauan natural rights, or Benthamite hedonism is able to furnish this standard for comparison. As a substitute for the failures of political psychology in the past, Wallas offers a synthetic program for the scientific study of political phenomena which will make reasoning in politics possible. The whole problem is to obtain, arrange, and study as many facts about man as are available. The beginning of this study should be a thorough acquaintance with the facts about human behavior which can be gained from the latest developments in psychology. Little or nothing can be hoped for from the pursuit of formal political science, based upon analyses of constitutions and unreal intellectualistic presuppositions. The only way to get any idea of the human type, with its infinite variations in thought and action, is to measure these variations by the statistical method and thus obtain some conception of the modal type and the nature and extent of the variations from this type. One must get into the habit of thinking in terms of statistical curves. Finally, the environment, natural and social, must be studied in the same manner, with a view to discovering the interaction between the individual and the environment. Most real statesmen now think quantitatively but only roughly and automatically. What is needed is such a cultivation of the scientific method as will enable one to start in political life with that exact quantitative knowledge which is now crudely and subconsciously acquired only after long experience. Wallas finds an indication of a step in the right direction in the present employment of statistics in the governmental bureaus and in the taking of censuses. The information thus compiled enables the citizens to check somewhat upon the wild statements of politicians designed to stir emotions but based on false assumptions and inaccurate information.

Wallas next takes up a consideration of the results which may be expected from the application of his proposed methods of study of political processes. In the first place, the faulty intellectualistic conceptions of political conduct would be abandoned, and the knowledge of actual political methods would provide citizens with the ability to fortify themselves against exploitation by masters of the art of political manipulation and would help them to curb the evils in the present methods of political parties. As soon as men are made conscious of the nature and genesis of the political thoughts and actions which have hitherto been subconscious, they will be able to handle the situation with greater realism and intelligence. In fact, Wallas advocates a sort of general political psychotherapy analogous to developments in psychiatry. He holds that a pathological political system may be reformed if the mass of the citizens are made fully conscious of the actual nature of their malady. Certain half-conscious progress in this direction may be seen in the growing use of such terms as "spellbinder" and "sensational," which make men a little less susceptible to the mental influences thus designated. The extension of this knowledge must, however, be deliberate and vigorous if it is to keep ahead of the constantly improving art of political exploitation and propaganda. While this extension of political knowledge may be aided by intellectual appeals through preaching and teaching, it can never succeed on a large scale until it is given an emotional background. That there may sometime be a co-ordination of thought and feeling, leading to a reformed and purified political system, is indicated by the action of the Japanese as revealed to the world in their struggle with Russia.

The next question that arises is the relation of the foregoing suggestions to the improvement of representative government and democracy, which, while by no means an entire success, may be regarded as the most satisfactory political system yet devised. While the consent of the governed may be accepted as an essential condition of a democratic government, what is most needed at present is a reform in the electoral system—the modern method of registering consent. It is useless to attempt to create a superior governing class which will live apart from the emotions of the world; what is really urgent is to make a political election similar to an English jury trial, namely, designed to obtain the facts in the circumstances and render an intelligent verdict. The pressing need is to improve the methods by which political opinions are formed rather than merely expressed. Encouraging steps have been taken in the English laws against bribery and inordinate expenditures in election. The old tendency to attempt to solve the problem through purely intellectual devices reappears in the proposal of Mill for public voting and that of Lord Courtney for proportional representation. Much more desirable are an abolition of the elements of mob suggestion and intimidation in elections; the spread of education in political methods; and the increase in the number of persons actively interested in the political life of the nation. The greatest improvement in political administration in the nineteenth century was the establishment of a permanent and efficient civil service in England and America. This branch of the government is the really effective "Second Chamber," for the information which it collects leads to the discrediting of the emotional appeals of a political orator which are based upon gross ignorance of facts. A consistent improvement and extension of the civil service is one of the most promising methods of moving toward a better political system.

International politics, like domestic policies, may greatly improve if subjected to a psychological reconstruction: "The future peace of the world turns largely on the question whether we have, as is sometimes said and often assumed, an instinctive affection for those human beings whose features and color are like our own, combined with an instinctive hatred for those who are unlike us." Since the days of Aristotle there has been a great change in the conception of the possible extent of a state. The modern state can no longer be a thing comprehended by direct personal observation; it can exist only as a mental entity, symbol, or abstraction. It was the thesis of Mazzini and Bismarck that no state could be successful unless composed of homogeneous peoples. This view has since been weakened because diverse nationalities have prospered within single successful states, and modern imperialism and colonization have tended politically to unite European and non-European types. What is now most to be desired is not national or imperial egoism but a recognition of the value of national differences. This stage of political thought might have been reached already if it had not been for the misinterpretation of Darwinism, which represented war as the chief source of progress. A healthy sign is the present tendency among biologists and sociologists to represent progress as the result of co-operation quite as much as the outcome of struggle:

> No one now expects an immediate, or prophesies with certainty an ultimate Federation of the Globe; but the consciousness of a common purpose in mankind, or even the acknowledgment that such a common purpose is possible, would alter the face of world politics at once. The discussion at the Hague of a halt in the race of armaments would no longer seem utopian, and the strenuous profession by the colonizing powers that they have no selfish ends in view might be transformed from a sordid and useless hypocrisy into a fact to which each nation might adjust its policy. The irrational race hatred which breaks out from time to time on the fringes of empire, would have little effect in world politics when opposed by a consistent conception of the future of human progress.[8]

The main importance of Wallas' *Human Nature in Politics* for social and political theory is that it worked a veritable revolution in political psychology among informed and thoughtful students of the subject. It constituted the *reductio ad absurdum* of the Benthamite felicific calculus, which had dominated political thought from the days of the Utilitarian political philosophers to those of Bryce and Ostrogorski and had affected the thinking of Marx and the radicals as well as that of the liberals. This theory had held that man's political behavior is founded upon rationality, clear perception of individual interests, and deliberate calculation of results. Wallas revealed the far more fundamental importance of irrational traits and emotional forces in behavior, without resorting to any fanciful mysticism or illogical flights, such as those manifested by Kidd.[9]

III. THE SOCIOPSYCHOLOGICAL TRAITS OF THE GREAT SOCIETY

When Wallas' second work, *The Great Society,* appeared, several new and interesting developments in his general sociological thinking came to light.[10] His first work, while stating that a sound psychology of society and politics must rest upon a consideration of both individual traits and the social environment which stimulates them, had been devoted primarily to an investigation of the manner in which personal traits operate in political life. *The Great Society* is logically devoted mainly to a consideration of the social and political environment and of the desirable methods whereby it can be so reconstructed as to provide a more complete set of stimuli for the individual personality. It seems that Wallas may have been affected by the afterthought that he had done his work too well in his earlier book. His clear and convincing demonstration that modern political activities are based upon a distressingly small amount of intelligent action on the part of anyone except the leaders in party exploitation seemed to trouble him. While he had emphatically stated in his *Human Nature in Politics* that our only hope lies in increasing the deliberate and intelligent analysis of political institutions and activities, he apparently felt that a better case should be made out for the position and function of rational thought.

The scope of Wallas' second work is considerably broader than that of the first. Instead of devoting his attention primarily to the problems of contemporary politics, he makes a psychological analysis of our modern civilization which has grown up since the industrial revolution. This civilization he designates as "The Great Society." His avowed aim is to suggest a new type of social organization which would produce more of a harmony between human nature and the new material conditions produced by industrialization and urbanization. As, in his first book, he found representative democracy to be an experiment which was not entirely successful, so he discovers in *The Great Society* that our modern civilization has developed serious problems. They were, for the most part, unforeseen by the majority of those who witnessed the transformation but are threatening enough to render the question of the ultimate success of urban industrialism problematical rather than assured. To the consideration of these grave problems Wallas brings the same broad conception of psychology that distinguished his earlier work, even improved at certain points. It is particularly refreshing to find an author who attempts an analysis of society upon the basis of modernized dynamic psychology.[11] In *The Great Society* Wallas' psychology combines the introspective and the behavioristic theories; he had enriched his knowledge of the unconscious processes in the individual mind by a study of the discoveries made by modern abnormal psychology; and, finally, his social psychology rejects all one-sided explanations and is based upon the broad conception of the reactions of the individual organism to the complex of stimuli from the environment. Again, he has now become an avowed "sociologist." The word was mentioned but once in his earlier book, but now all his analyses are made from the "sociological viewpoint." All in all, it is a more valuable sociological study than *Human Nature in Politics.*

The society of the present day is to be traced to the great mechanical inventions of the industrial revolution, which gave the material basis for our civilization. The social transformation has been as far-reaching as the industrial and far less happy in its attendant circumstances. Instead of a social system based upon local association and personal relationships, we now have one founded upon world-wide, impersonal, and almost mechanical relations. Those great scientific discoveries, which have made the technical changes in industry possible, have not been accompanied by a parallel and proportionate development of a science of social relationships. Psychological knowledge has been diffused only among a small class of experts and has not permeated society in a manner comparable to the knowledge of technical processes in industry.

It is Wallas' aim to supply this need and to discover how far a realistic psychology of social processes can go toward discovering a way out of our present social dilemma through formulating the outlines of a satisfactory form of social organization for our times. To achieve an acceptable theory of social psychology upon which to base an analysis of our society, Wallas contends that one must accept the doctrine that the type forms of human conduct are the result of both inherited and acquired dispositions to act in a certain manner, stimulated by the experiences of the organism within its environment. The two especially important complex dispositions in mankind are instinct and intelligence, and Wallas, somewhat in opposition to the position taken in his previous work, insists that man is as naturally disposed to thought as he is to instinctive action. But human dispositions, either instinctive or intellectual, cannot function properly unless they are acted upon by the "appropriate stimuli" in the environment. Unstimulated dispositions develop into what he designates as "balked dispositions," or what modern dynamic psychologists would call "repressed complexes." These balked dispositions cause that nervous and mental instability so prevalent in our modern civilization. This has no basis in organic defects of the nervous system, but it is the fundamental pathological characteristic of modern society.[12] The reason for the prevalence of balked dispositions in modern society is that our hereditary natural makeup has changed but little for ages, while the environment which stimulates that nature has been completely revolutionized in the last century. While no one can hope to revive exactly the same set of stimuli as operated in an earlier type of culture, it is the task of modern social reorganization to discover and supply equivalent stimuli to release that repressed energy which has been dammed up by our balked dispositions and make a happy and efficient life once more possible for the majority of the race.

On the basis of such a conception of social psychology Wallas finds that those theories which emphasize but one subjective aspect of the psychology of social processes are inadequate and unsatisfactory. Among the theories of this type which he rejects are those based upon habit, fear, hedonism, love, hatred, and the various psychologies of the crowd, founded on imitation, sympathy, and suggestion. The problems of modern society can be solved only by the application of carefully reasoned thought; and, while thought may have a subconscious basis, it is highly essential that society shall do all in its power to improve and increase those aspects of thought which are amenable to deliberate and conscious operations.

Since all human activities are an expression of thought, will, and emotion, efficient social organization must make provision for bringing all these aspects of human activity into play in an effective and well-balanced manner. The organized activity of society in this direction, however, has thus far been distressingly inadequate. The old method of stimulating thought by oral discussion has been largely displaced in modern society by mechanical devices for imparting information, which, while they are much more efficient in distributing printed or oral information are greatly inferior in originating new thought. Particularly difficult is it for the average workingman to develop any independent or fruitful thought on public affairs, because of the destruction of the close personal relationships that formerly existed in small groups of workmen, and the efforts of the vested interests, political and economic, to exploit the workingman's ignorance by perversions and distortions of the truth in the printed journals that reach the working class. The attempt to create a condition of effective thinking by discussion in modern legislatures has all too often degenerated into a burlesque which makes the members good-natured cynics. This travesty reaches its height in the speeches of American congressmen, written by their secretaries and published, without being delivered, in the *Congressional Record*.

The effective organization of the social will is equally deficient in modern society. The three contending varieties of will organization—individualism, based on the institution of private property; socialism, founded upon the proposition to extend the functions of the democratic state; and syndicalism, demanding a government on the basis of representation by occupations—all possess certain advantages but are equally inadequate when taken alone. The next essential step in political invention is to find by experiment the correct combination of these three contending principles.

As to the organization of society to promote human happiness through a richer emotional life, it seems that, while modern industrialism has tremendously increased the technical devices for producing commodities for human comfort and convenience, it is equally true that the process has failed proportionately to increase the sum total of human happiness. The great advances have been made with the aim of increasing the production of wealth rather than with the aim of securing a greater amount of satisfaction in its consumption. One of the most alarming aspects of the modern social transformation is that society had allowed the process to gain such momentum, before it awakened to what was going on, that the new developments have begun to get beyond the control of society: "That which chiefly angers and excites us now, as we contemplate the society in which we live, is not a conviction that the world is a worse place than it has ever been, but the feeling that we have lost grip over the course of events, and are stupidly wasting the power over nature which might make the world infinitely better."[13]

It will be the test of the success of modern society if it is able to make up by future efforts what it has lost through its lethargy and apathy in the past. The laboring class has been especially unfortunate in this transition. The impersonal, monotonous, large-scale, and highly sub-divided and standardized industry of today has destroyed the pleasure of manual labor, and the conditions of urban life among the working classes have made it difficult for them to achieve happiness outside of working hours.

The conclusion of Wallas' work—its constructive program—is its most unsatisfactory part. In his proposals as to how to reorganize society to attain happiness, he mixes many fertile suggestions as to diversifying interests and economizing effort with Aristotle's metaphysical concep-tion of the "mean" as the ideal, and he ends by practically throwing up his hands and passing the problem over to philosophy. As R. M. MacIver well observes: "His discussion of the type of social organization which would bring a new harmony of life and environment did not advance much beyond some luminous suggestions as to the need for it." For-tunately, he had already provided his readers with enough suggestions as to a more practical and promising program so that they need not assent to his conclusions or regret their lack of coherence and precision.

IV. RECONSTRUCTING OUR SOCIAL HERITAGE

Wallas' third sociological treatise—and the logical completion of his body of social theory—was presented in a series of lectures delivered at the New School for Social Research and at Yale University. It was pub-lished in 1921, under the title *Our Social Heritage*. Each of his books seems to have proceeded naturally out of the shortcomings which Wallas recognized in its predecessor. His *Human Nature in Politics* attacked the current intellectualism in political, social, and economic theory. His *Great Society,* while assuming the dominance of subconscious and emotional elements, insisted that improvement could come only through rational thought and conscious effort. But, when it came to showing how rational thought and conscious effort might create a new and more satisfactory social organization, Wallas proved rather feeble and incon-clusive. *Our Social Heritage* is a well-reasoned analysis of important factors involved in any sound program for the conscious improvement of society. It deals with "the ideas, habits, and institutions directly con-cerned in the political, economic, and social organization of those modern communities which constitute 'The Great Society.' " It had an immediate pragmatic and remedial purpose, for he believed that, without an adequate understanding of our "socially inherited ways of living and thinking" and a determination to adjust them more closely to the needs of the day, humanity will speedily be confronted with greater disasters than the first World War.

Wallas takes as his starting-point the essential distinction between "nature" and "nurture." Man's nature, or his physiological and neurological equipment, has not changed for thousands of years. Indeed, man may be said to have become "biologically parasitic on his social heritage." The other animals can thrive without a social heritage, but man would soon become extinct without its support. "Nurture," upon which man must depend for his present existence and for his future progress, includes both personal acquisitions and those which come to the individual from society, past and present. The cultural supremacy of man has been primarily, if not wholly, a product of his social heritage, or nurture. Likewise, any hope of future improvement depends upon a better understanding and utilization of our socially inherited culture and institutions. Yet this problem is becoming progressively more difficult, for the great increase of pertinent information is making it more difficult to find the means for an adequate transmission of our social heritage, and the rapid technological changes are necessitating a constant social readjustment.[14]

Any adequate utilization and reconstruction of our social heritage involves sustained muscular and mental effort. Impulses must be to some extent replaced by conscious effort. There must come into being a self-conscious will for improvement. It is not easy, however, to sustain conscious effort. Physiological reactions and instincts have been evolved to meet continuous needs. Higher conscious activity has been produced to serve only occasional wants. Therefore, conscious effort brings a high degree of fatigue. It is doubtful whether either conscious mental or muscular effort can function with great efficiency or persistence unless it is accompanied by a free play of the emotions and the force of the "artistic drive." Conscious intellectual effort has been most successful in pure science and technology and least so in the social sciences; but the improvement of our social heritage depends upon a more scientific and pragmatic social science.[15]

In a very real sense, social reconstruction and the reorganization of our social heritage depend upon devising better ways for the development and organization of various types of co-operation—group, national, and international. There are several forms of co-operation exhibited in the biological world—the leaderless and unorganized co-operation of the ants, the co-operation of cattle under a single leader, and the co-operation of a wolf pack, in which each member is affected by instincts of both leadership and obedience. Mankind exemplifies this last, or wolf, type of the co-operation of a "loosely and intermittently gregarious animal." Man is capable of consciously organized and directed co-operation, but this requires unusual effort and produces an excessive amount of fatigue. Conscious group co-operation has been as yet only imperfectly attained by mankind and tends to break down in times of stress, as proved by the disasters of the British Dardanelles and Mesopotamian expeditions during the first World War.

National co-operation is far more artificial than group co-operation and depends to a much greater extent on socially inherited knowledge and conscious effort. Group co-operation rests to a considerable extent upon personal knowledge and contacts, but "a modern civilized man can never see or hear the nation of which he is a member, and, if he thinks or feels about it, he must do so by employing some acquired entity of the mind." An accurate idea of the nation, then, is essential if we are to have any "reliable stimulus to large-scale coöperative emotion and coöperative action." The average citizen, however, has no systematic method for building up his "idea of the nation." It is the unconscious and carelessly acquired product of his daily experiences. Much of it is due to conscious propaganda by the vested interests, for, though the average citizen may be aimless, careless, and thoughtless, "the controllers of newspapers, especially of the sinister American or British journals whose writers are apparently encouraged to 'color the news' as well as their comments on the news, in accordance with the will of a multi-millionaire proprietor, know pretty exactly what they are doing." Hence, if we are to have any solid basis for national co-operation, we must work out a more scientific method of acquiring our idea of a nation and its accompanying emotions.

Wallas submits some interesting and thoughtful suggestions toward this end. We should start with a Cartesian skepticism and proceed by critical reasoning. Our conclusions must be based upon a careful and patient observation of our fellow-citizens, their type, actions, and aspirations.

Such scrutiny of our countrymen will convince us of the wide divergence and variety of type, fitness, tastes, and capacity which exist. The fallacious notion of the uniformity of men has been the curse of modern politics and economics. Yet we can never have a stable national organization or effective national co-operation without a greater degree of common consent to the existing social and economic order than that which now prevails. The problem will probably best be solved by recognizing this diversity of taste and capacity and providing an equality of opportunity for the diversified population to realize their aspirations according to their differing capacities. The better adjustment of individual tasks and responsibilities to individual differences between human beings must become "the conscious, organized and effective purpose of modern civilization."

World co-operation is even more difficult of achievement than national co-operation. If one is to approach intelligently the problem of international relations, he must make the initial admission that "the change of scale from national coöperation to world-coöperation involves a change in the form and character of the coöperative process. It is a change of kind as well as degree." Many of those very instinctive and emotional forces which produce group and national co-operation automatically impel us to hate aliens and induce a combative attitude toward them. Yet world co-operation in certain phases of economic and commercial activity has become a basic fact in modern life, and it is futile to retain Cobden's dream that we can enjoy commercial intercourse without involving political relations. There is little hope of building up a sound internationalism on a purely instinctive or emotional basis. It must be founded on conscious thought and reasoned calculation of results. Especially must we learn to calculate the disastrous results of a world war and obtain therefrom an impulse to avoid war and a willingness to take those steps which are necessary to prevent its recurrence. Woodrow Wilson's "Fourteen Points" once seemed destined to provide a basis for rational international co-operation, but the opportunity was ingloriously lost at Paris in 1919. Certain improvements in international thinking must be made if we are to have any effective world co-operation. We must abandon generalizations about an abstract state which will not apply to any concrete state; we must study history, government, law, and biology from the new problem attitude of world co-operation; **we** must work out a control of the press which will make it impotent to debase statesmanship and arouse unnecessary international hatred and will make journalism a real force for sound international education; we must reconsider liberty, independence, nationality, and equality from an international point of view and also give them greater recognition at home; we must stimulate political invention, so as to adapt national institutions to supernational needs; and we must co-operate in every way in any procedure which will produce an international outlook. It would even be worth while to send representatives to the League of Nations meeting at Geneva, if only to co-operate in an international survey of the heavens.[16]

Since the first World War there have been many appeals from representatives of organized Christianity, and especially from those who come from the more conservative religious circles, to make religion the basis of world union and co-operation. Wallas suggests that it would be most pertinent to inquire what organized religion had contributed during the ten years preceding 1921 to make good its claim to fitness to assume leadership in world unity. His examination of the evidence constitutes an overwhelming indictment of the role of organized Christianity in world affairs. Without notable exceptions, the church has aligned itself with the reactionary and vicious elements in the international situation. The German Lutherans supported Prussian militarism and the invasion of Belgium. The Austrian Catholics were the leaders in the anti-Serbian movement. The Anglican church vigorously favored crushing peace terms for Germany and condoned the Irish policy of the government and the massacres in India. The French Catholic elements have supported the peace of revenge and French postwar diplomacy. Above all, sacramental Christianity lacks the essential ethical element which is necessary for social reconstruction. No group accepts the sacraments with more reverence and enthusiasm than the Spanish brigands. Wallas concludes:

> The special task of our generation might be so to work and think as to be able to hand on to the boys and girls who, fifty years hence, at some other turning-point of world history, may gather in the schools, the heritage of a world-outlook deeper and wider and more helpful than that of modern Christendom.[17]

Science also needs to be revamped before it can be of much assistance in world co-operation. It has been of great aid in technology, but it is indispensable that science be socialized and moralized and that these revamped and broader scientific methods be adopted more rapidly in the moral and social sciences.

In this manner Wallas makes a plea for conscious, rational, and "telic" progress, which entitles him to a place with Comte, Lester F. Ward, Ludwig Stein, and L. T. Hobhouse among social philosophers.

The above summary of the more salient points in Wallas' *Social Heritage* gives but a faint impression of the content of the book, with its wealth of concrete illustrative material, but it will probably justify Harold Laski's contention that it is the product of "sober wisdom."[18]

After finishing *Our Social Heritage,* Wallas appears once more to have had misgivings about the adequacy of a published book, especially about the vagueness of his suggestions concerning the type of education needed to lead society into a more rational form of organization and to put an end to war. At any rate, Wallas produced two later books which revolved around the problem of "how far the knowledge accumulated by modern psychology can be made useful for the improvement of the thought-processes of a working thinker." These books were *The Art of Thought* (1926) and the posthumous volume, *Social Judgment* (1935).

In these books Wallas argued the theme, already familiar to readers of *The Great Society* and *Our Social Heritage,* that, while we have greatly increased our power over nature, we have failed to guide and utilize this control over nature through a social organization harmonious with an age of applied science and technological efficiency. He stresses the point made in *Our Social Heritage,* that, while we can wage war ever more effectively, we seem as impotent as ever in preventing war. Wallas agrees with Ward that the only way to assure the type of social program needed to adjust man to an industrial age and to curb war is to create a realistic educational setup. He goes on from there to criticize the archaic content and faulty methods of contemporary education and to suggest how scientific psychology might be exploited to effect a salutary revolution in both pedagogy and the technique of social reconstruction. While Wallas comes out with the same general "telic" philosophy as Ward, his emphasis is more on the methods of education than upon its content and social objectives.

The book on *Social Judgment,* as published, was an unfinished torso, embodying only the first and introductory portion of what might have been Wallas' most mature and complete contribution to social and political theory. What was published is chiefly prolegomena to systematic theory—wise but rather discursive homilies on history, morals, philosophy, psychology, and education. The unfinished portion was to be the systematic section of the work. As his daughter, who edited the book, tells us: "It appears from his notes and raw material which were among his papers that Part II would have opened with a long chapter on Government, dealing in the main with the problems and institutions of democratic government in the modern world, and that the later chapters would have included one on Private Property and one on International Organization."

Even this brief and inadequate summary of Wallas' works will suffice to convince the reader of their importance. If, as A. A. Tenney once said, the prime end of sociology is a rational criticism of public policy, then few writers have acquitted themselves of the responsibility imposed by their subject in so efficient a manner as has Graham Wallas.

His works represent, in a general way, the best that sociology has to offer in the way of suggestions to political science and practice. He insists that, first of all, political science must be modernized, both in subject matter and in method. It must take account of the vast changes in civilization since the time of Aristotle, or even of Montesquieu and Burke, and must deal effectively with the new problems which these changes have produced. It can no longer afford to concern itself with metaphysical questions about society or with unreal conceptions of human nature but must deal with actual conditions of the present, and deal with them scientifically. By this "scientific" treatment he means that political science must base its generalizations upon the fundamental laws of human psychology, as revealed by careful empirical observation of human conduct, not only in political groupings but in wider forms of association.

To be sure, there are many defects in his books. The professional psychologist would quarrel with him over many points of detail, and he gives little evidence of having read widely in the strictly sociological literature of recent times, but these defects are more than compensated for by the abundance of illuminating concrete illustrations of his main propositions, which a keenly observant and reflective mind had drawn from close contact with many phases of English life in a half-century of active connection with academic and political affairs.

Until students of political science turn their attention from a preponderant concern with formal treatises on their subject, from Pufendorf to Burgess, and deal seriously with those defects in their subject which Wallas has so clearly revealed, there can be little hope that academic political science will have any considerable leavening effect upon modern political life. Likewise, practical democratic politics are likely to go on the rocks unless some method of rational control over political emotionalism and propaganda can be assured. Further, the problem before us is not only that of introducing rationality into democracy; we must also have a democratic program of social reconstruction which will readjust our ways of living and thinking to the realities of the post–industrial revolution age. Such a program must rest upon an up-to-date educational system, not only inspired by realistic social objectives but also guided by the expert techniques which have been provided by scientific psychology.

NOTES

1. *Political Thought in England from Herbert Spencer to the Present Day* (New York, 1915), p. 156.

2. This work is well reviewed by another leader in English political thought, J. A. Hobson, in the *Sociological Review,* 1909, pp. 293–94. See also Barker's excellent analysis, *op. cit.,* pp. 153–57.

3. *Human Nature in Politics,* p. 14.

4. *Ibid.,* p. 128.

5. *Ibid.,* p. 127.

6. *Ibid.,* p. 18.

7. *Ibid.,* p. 21.

8. *Ibid.,* pp. 294–95.

9. Cf. W. C. Mitchell, "Bentham's Felicific Calculus," *Political Science Quarterly,* June, 1918.

10. This book is reviewed by E. L. Talbert in the *American Journal of Sociology,* March, 1915, pp. 708–11; and by A. B. Wolfe in the *American Economic Review,* June, 1915, pp. 311 ff. The latter is especially to be commended.

11. A good analysis of Wallas' psychology is to be found in W. C. Mitchell, "Human Behavior and Economics," *Quarterly Journal of Economics,* November, 1914, pp. 12–18.

12. *The Great Society,* pp. 63 ff.

13. *Ibid.,* p. 323.

14. *Our Social Heritage,* chap. i.

15. *Ibid.,* chap. ii.

16. *Ibid.,* chaps. iii–iv, ix, xi–xii.

17. *Ibid.,* p. 291.

18. It is especially gratifying to note that Wallas apparently escaped the effects of the war hysteria which distorted the writings of so many sociologists and publicists. Yet he relies to a distressing degree upon English data and illustrations, a procedure which is all the more unpardonable in an author with an extensive knowledge of the United States.

CHAPTER XXXVII

ARNOLD JOSEPH TOYNBEE: OROSIUS AND AUGUSTINE IN MODERN DRESS

HARRY ELMER BARNES

I. TOYNBEE'S TRAINING AND INTERESTS

NO OTHER publication in the field of history since the appearance of H. G. Wells's *Outline of History* and Oswald Spengler's *The Decline of the West* has attracted so much interest, received such extensive and diversified adulation, or collected so large and influential a following as Arnold J. Toynbee's *A Study of History*. And neither Wells nor Spengler developed a cult, which Toynbee is already on the high road to assembling and leading. Indeed, his book has created a stir comparable to the appearance of Voltaire's *Essai*, H. T. Buckle's *History of Civilization*, J. W. Draper's *History of the Intellectual Development of Europe*, Andrew D. White's *History of the Warfare of Science with Theology*, Brooks Adams' *Law of Civilization and Decay*, and the aforementioned books of Wells and Spengler. Since Toynbee's work is usually referred to as sociological history or historical and comparative sociology, it deserves analysis in this History of Sociology.

Toynbee was born in 1889, received a classical training at Oxford, and went into archeological work. But the first World War turned his interests to public affairs, and ever since he has combined historical writing, especially on international politics and the contemporary history of the Near East, with activity in public life. He joined the British Foreign Office in 1918 and was an adviser at the Paris Peace Conference of 1919. He wrote his first, and an able, book on *Nationality and the War,* dealing with the relation of nationality to the first World War. In the period between the two world wars, much of his intellectual activity was devoted to editing and writing the *Survey of International Affairs,* published by the Royal (British) Institute of International Affairs. He also wrote excellent books on contemporary Greece and Turkey, and traveled fairly extensively in both the Old World and the New. He served temporarily as adviser to the Council of Foreign Ministers in Paris in the summer of 1946.

During this period he also began his studies of world civilizations, which have appeared in his famed *A Study of History*. The first instalment of this work was published in three volumes in 1933.[1] They were devoted primarily to a statement of the problem of the growth and decline of civilizations, the historical principles to be observed in their study, and the processes involved in the genesis of civilizations. Three more volumes came out in 1939.[2] These were given over chiefly to a description of the maturity, decline, and disintegration of civilizations. Three more volumes are promised, and it is announced that these volumes to come will treat of the contacts and rhythms of civilizations, the outlook for Western civilization, the sources of inspiration for historians, and the lesson of the whole enterprise for mankind today.

The sudden and extensive interest generated in Toynbee's ideas after the second World War led to the preparation and publication of an abridgment by D. C. Somervell of the first six volumes.[3] This abridgment is a great improvement for the general reader, since it prunes away the vast mass of confusing, and often tiresome and dubious, detail and gives all the essentials of the story and the argument.

In addition to finishing *A Study of History,* Toynbee has now engaged to edit a vast subsidized history of the second World War, financed by the Royal Institute of International Affairs and the Rockefeller Foundation. It is evident from all this that Toynbee believes that the historian should both be a man of affairs and also put his learning and energy at the disposal of his country and the world. In this sense, he resembles his eminent British predecessor, Lord Bryce. But the similarity ceases at this point. Bryce was a freethinker who put his faith for the future in better government, especially better democratic government. Toynbee is a devout Christian mystic who sees all hope for the salvation of mankind in the possibility that Western civilization may grasp in time the implications and inspiration residing in Christ's Incarnation.

II. THE CHRISTIAN EPIC REVIVED: NEO-AUGUSTINIANISM

Few books have been more misunderstood or misinterpreted than Toynbee's *A Study of History*. This has been due to the fact that readers, commentators, and reviewers have been prone to regard it as a serious exercise in secular history—a sincere and straightforward effort to find out just what the course of history has been and how civilizations really grow and decline. It has been viewed as history, after the fashion of Leopold von Ranke—scientific history, written just as things actually were—only painted on a far vaster canvas than Von Ranke ever conceived, even in his unfinished world history. Unfortunately, to understand Toynbee's project and aim one must have a competent grasp upon both intellectual history and historiography. When one views it against such a background of knowledge, the book appears as something quite different, perhaps greater, but not the same. As Howard Becker well expresses the matter, it is "a Theodicy" rather than straight history or scientific sociology. The dictionary defines a theodicy as the "vindication of divine justice in permitting evil in the world." In Toynbee's terms, this came about when man moved from the beatific condition of passivity in the state of *Yin* into the creative, but doomed, ordeal involved in his participation in the state of *Yang*.

A Study of History is really a grandiose and majestic revival of what George Santayana has called "the Christian Epic," as expounded by Augustine and his associates. The epic is reinstated on a magnificent and planetary scale and elaborated in terms of wide and varied knowledge and of twentieth-century ideas and experiences. To unfold the drama of the past damnation and possible ultimate salvation of humanity, not sober and direct historical exposition, is the primary aim of Toynbee. To use his own terminology, he is, as it were, the John the Baptist of the second and, presumably, final "challenge" of the Incarnation.

Like Henry Osborn Taylor, Toynbee resolutely believes in the dominant role of God in history. God is the most active force in history, and the Kingdom of God is the goal of the historical development of mankind. The Incarnation of Jesus is the central fact of human history. The birth of which the Angels sang at Bethlehem "was not a rebirth of Hellas nor a new birth of other societies of the Hellenic species. It was the birth in the flesh of the King of the Kingdom of God."[4]

In his main formula of historical evolution—"Challenge and Response"—Toynbee introduces a mystical and apocalyptic element: each nascent civilization is destined to fulfil the role that God intended for it. While Toynbee vigorously rejects any idea of materialistic determinism in history, his whole work is a majestic effort to establish the reality of creative, spiritual determination. The role of the Savior is a powerful factor in history, and, of all the historic saviors, Christ was unique. Toynbee himself appears to his own cult in the role of the "Creative Genius as the Savior." As George Catlin has written, Toynbee presses "to an issue the question of the significance of Christianity, redemption and original sin in its application to 'the world' of force." To Toynbee, the historical process is chiefly a spiritual matter. Faith in the divine order of the universe and in God's control of man's destiny is what produces that spiritual creativity which Toynbee regards as the dynamic factor in human development. As Hajo Holborn puts it, Toynbee construes "the birth, life and death of civilizations as a struggle in the human soul." Toynbee is far closer to Plotinus than to Marx in his genetic ideology. With him, neither reason nor material factors play any determining role in history.

When Augustine worked out his classic and powerful statement of the Christian epic in his *City of God,* he was able to have the historical perspective supplied by his disciple, Paulus Orosius, in the latter's *Seven Books of History against the Pagans.* But Toynbee provides both the dolorous history of the pagans and the pattern of God's plan for mankind under Christian auspices.

Augustine and Orosius were alarmed by the breakdown of society in the western Roman Empire and the incursion of the barbarians. They inquired into God's will and the divine plan in it all. This they found in the Fall of Man in Eden, and they discerned the hope of the future in the vicarious sacrifice of Jesus. As Orosius pointed out, the pagans were all condemned by God's wrath, and their cultures had all decayed and passed away or were on their way to oblivion. A new era had arisen, and there was a new hope in Jesus, the Savior of mankind. All this is duplicated on a far grander scale in Toynbee. He was dismayed by the destruction wrought by the first World War, by the decline of the power and prosperity of the British Empire, by the threat of more wars, and by the rise of new "barbarians" in the East. The core of the great drama of mankind is the same with Toynbee as with Augustine—the struggle of good and evil. It is once more the conflict between God and the devil, as symbolized by the ominous fate of man in leaving the perfect condition of divine perfection and passivity in the state of *Yin* and entering the creative ordeal of the state of *Yang,* in which pagan societies were doomed to extinction after many centuries of effort and tribulation.

Augustine and Orosius limited themselves to the Western world and to one fall of man. Toynbee ranges from Korea to Yucatan, and he describes not one but twenty "falls." If Western civilization does not soon respond to the challenge of Jesus and salvation, there will be twenty-one "falls," or as many as there have been civilizations in human experience. Each historic civilization fulfilled the destiny which God had laid out for it, and this destiny has always been ultimate collapse—a gigantic and ominous warning of the penalty for having lived before Jesus' time or for having rejected him, either totally or in spirit. The Orthodox-Byzantine and Orthodox-Russian civilizations knew Christ's teaching, but they never entered into its real spirit, sacrificing saving principles to organization and ecclesiastical politics. Further, they were never able to sheath the sword and permanently establish the Peace of God.

Toynbee's work is devoted to showing how civilizations which could not know Jesus or which rejected his saving mission came to grief. While there were some differences in matters of detail, the general pattern of rise, maturity, decline, and collapse has been the same in all places and at all times. The processes and stages through which societies have perished without the True Faith constitute both the theory and the action of *A Study of History,* and to this we may now turn our attention.

III. THE THEODICEAN DRAMA OF DAMNED CIVILIZATIONS

As a professional historian and publicist, Toynbee is primarily a specialist on the modern history of the Near East, particularly contemporary Greece. This is a source both of strength and of weakness for his larger study. Knowing all Hellenic civilization thoroughly, from the Mycenaean Age to the ELAS, Toynbee's account of the rise and vicissitudes of Hellenic civilization is especially expert. But he uses Hellenic civilization as the type or pattern for the formulation of his general theory of the rise, growth, and decline of all civilizations, thus frequently having to squeeze his facts into a pattern and framework which they do not always fit. There were, obviously, many departures, even in kind, from basic Hellenic experience in the twenty other civilizations which Toynbee studies. The main defect of Toynbee's work, aside from its fundamentally theological purpose and orientation, lies in the fact that he had reached his main conclusions before he had got past his synthesis of Hellenic historical experience and had really begun his survey of the twenty-one civilizations that he formally examines.

As we shall see later on, Toynbee regards the wars between parochial states within a civilization as one of the great problems or challenges of a society. This was suggested to him by the wars between Greek city-states. These wars were ended by Roman conquests, so the rise of the Roman Empire gave him the idea of the foundation of a Universal State as a means of curbing parochial warfare. Then the decline of the Roman Empire furnished him with most of the facts and generalizations about the decay of civilization which he later sought to apply to the analysis of the life-history of the twenty-one civilizations. When we add to the Hellenic historical cycle, within which Toynbee includes Roman history, a devout acceptance of the Christian epic, we have all the main items in his philosophy of history and historical formulas.

One of Toynbee's sound, basic procedures is the fact that he takes, as his unit for historical theory, societies not states, civilizations not nations. It may be fairly pointed out that Toynbee did not dodge the problem of nations through lack of competence, since he is the author of a masterly book on the relation of nationality to the first World War. He rejects the national pattern because he believes that no culture is purely national; hence a study of civilizations cannot be based on a national frame of reference or circumscribed by national boundaries. He holds that nationalism, operating through what he calls "the parochial sovereign state," has stultified and endangered our modern Western civilization.

This eschewing of nations as the unit of historical study by Toynbee is not, however, as important or significant as it might seem at first glance. There were no nations, strictly speaking, until modern times, and Toynbee thus far devotes little space to modern history. Even the old-fashioned historians were wont to study *civilizations* in the period before the breakup of feudalism is western Europe—Egyptian, Mesopotamian, Hellenic, Roman, and medieval civilization. Therefore, there is nothing especially unique about Toynbee's concentration on civilizations, so far as the volumes that have appeared are concerned. Further, since Toynbee regards each of his twenty-one civilizations as essentially self-contained, with little significant contact and cultural interaction, his treatment of the evolution of civilizations is about as "parochial" and narrow as the former handling of nations. As one commentator has observed, Toynbee's civilizations are only "nations writ large." There is no real universalism in Toynbee's perspective in this respect.

Taking as his unit of investigation the origin and destiny of specific civilizations, Toynbee finds that there have been some twenty-one altogether in the course of history, along with certain peripheral cultures, which never attained a creative civilization. He first lists nineteen such civilizations: the Egyptiac, Sumeric, Babylonic, Hittite, Syriac, Minoan, Hellenic, Iranic, Arabic, Hindu, Indic, Sinic, Far Eastern, Andean, Yucatec, Mayan, Mexic, Orthodox Christian, and Western. He gets his twenty-one by dividing the Orthodox Christian into Orthodox Byzantine and Orthodox Russian; and Far Eastern into Chinese and Korean-Japanese.

During the course of recorded history the "civilizational" process has disposed of all but seven of these world *civilizations:* the Orthodox Christian, the Orthodox Russian, the Islamic (which combines the old Iranic and Arabic civilizations of the original list), the Hindu, the Chinese, the Korean-Japanese, and the Western (western Europe, the British Commonwealth, the United States, and Latin America).

All except Western civilization are now in their terminal stages and have already fallen into the orbit of Western civilization. Their period of basic breakdown runs from 977 for Orthodox Christianity to 1500 for Islamic civilization. Even the outcome for Western civilization is highly uncertain, and it may turn out that its period of breakdown is to be located in the Conciliar Movement of the fifteenth century or the Religious Wars of the sixteenth. The main assurance of escape from impending doom for Western civilization resides in two facts: (1) we have not yet reached the period of the "Universal State," which always portends inevitable dissolution; and (2) we may have the good sense and inspiration to recognize in time the destiny for which God has intended us and rise to claim our divine heritage. The chief hope for the second possible avenue of salvation lies in a great revival of Christian faith and zeal. In the case of every doomed civilization, the period of breakdown came prior to the era which is usually regarded as the height of that civilization; therefore, the "golden ages" of all civilizations are invariably periods of "Indian summer."

We may now summarize Toynbee's conception of what the late Albion W. Small would call the "process" of civilization—its rise, maturity, and decline. He rejects racial factors as valid forces in the growth and character of civilization. While physical environment plays its role in the evolution of civilization, it is not sufficient, in itself, to account for the rise of cultures. The great historical formula to explain not only the rise of civilizations but also their decline Toynbee finds in what he calls "Challenge and Response," which, as Howard Becker has pointed out, is very similar to the sociopsychic mechanism of "Crisis," as used by W. I. Thomas. There is little likelihood, however, that Toynbee was at all influenced by Thomas, for there is no indication that he is familiar with American sociological literature. It has been suggested that he may have derived his basic formula of challenge and response from Winwood Reade's once highly popular book on *The Martyrdom of Man,* first published in 1872 and reprinted in numerous editions.

At the outset, this challenge is chiefly presented by the physical environment, and the response is society's effort to meet this challenge and conquer it. The ideal initial challenge is one which will call forth the greatest possible efforts of mankind but is not overwhelming enough to exhaust all human energy in meeting it. If the challenge is too severe, the response will deplete human energy and initiative sufficiently to produce an arrested civilization like that of the Eskimo. If the challenge is too slight, mankind will linger comfortably and slothfully on the borders of civilization and never create a high culture.

The first great pattern or complex of challenges and responses were those involved in the conquest of the physical and social environment in the period of the rise of civilizations. After civilization has been attained, the second main pattern of challenges and responses arises. This new complex is most directly related, not to the physical environment, but to the problems involved in successfully conducting the civilization which has been produced—in other words, to social problems and public life. The gravest of these problems—challenges—which a mature civilization has to face are the perpetuation of adequate spiritual creativity in the leaders and the prevention of wars between what Toynbee calls the "parochial states" which make up each civilization.

If the institutions and social policies which have been created by the struggle to attain civilization are not in accord with those later essential to master the challenge of social relationships in a mature culture, the second series of responses is likely to fail, and the breakdown of civilization ensues. This is often followed, however, by what is commonly regarded as the period of maximum splendor of that civilization, but it is a splendor which contains the fatal seeds and symptoms of decay. Civilizations always break down because of internal weaknesses rather than on account of external attacks. The disintegration of civilizations may be temporarily held in check by the regeneration of leaders through what Toynbee calls "Withdrawal-and-Return," which is his second great formula in explaining historical development and will be described shortly.

Toynbee's portrayal of the main stages and traits in the life-history of a typical civilization runs as follows: In the earlier and growing period of civilization—when mankind is responding to the first great pattern of challenges from the physical or natural environment—the historic process is guided by what Toynbee calls a "Creative Minority," among whom great religious leaders are the most important and influential element. The masses follow this creative minority willingly and unquestioningly because of spontaneous admiration and trust. Toynbee espouses the "Great Man" theory of history with gusto and consistency.

When a civilization has become well established, a trend invariably seems to set in which constitutes the universal and persistent cause of the decline of all civilizations: the creative minority, which had led mankind from primitivism to civilization, loses its spiritual potential and creative vigor—at least loses enough of its guiding and inspiring élan so that it can no longer keep society moving steadily ahead to higher levels. As a result of this loss of spiritual creativity, the creative minority becomes transformed into what Toynbee designates as the "Dominant Minority." This dominant minority tends to maintain itself by the use of force of one kind or another, since it lacks the spiritual vigor, inspiration, and inventiveness to continue to keep the masses in a state of awe and admiration, as the creative minority had earlier done. Toynbee has no objection to minority rule, but he holds that valid minority rule must rest upon charm and the capacity to ingratiate, which are, to him, the outward and visible signs of creativity. Whatever the many and sundry other causes of the hitherto inevitable decay of all civilizations, the fundamental fact is the loss of creativity in the minority.

When the creative minority is supplanted by the dominant minority, as a result of the loss of spiritual creativity on the part of the leaders, what Toynbee calls the "Time of Troubles" arrives in the civilization. These "troubles" take the form of class struggles and parochial conflicts within the society and of wars between the society or civilization and one or more of its neighboring civilizations. But the most serious of these troubles is what Toynbee described as wars between the "parochial states" within the civilization. The wars of the Greek city-states are the best example of what he means here.

Despite all the "troubles," there still seems to be a chance to save the civilization through what Toynbee denominates "Withdrawal-and-Return" and the resulting "Etherialization" of leaders. There still remain creative geniuses, and they withdraw from the masses to gain spiritual regeneration through communion with God, the contemplation of the Absolute, and the searching of their own souls. The resulting spiritual rebirth, renewal of grace, and moral convictions are the product of what Toynbee calls "etherialization." These regenerated leaders then return to inspire the masses, as the creative minority had done in the period of the origin of civilization. Examples of such withdrawal-and-return are Moses' ascent of Mount Sinai, Caesar's Gallic Wars, Christ's fast in the Wilderness, Paul's withdrawal into the desert of Arabia, Gautama's seven-year renunciation of the world, Mohammed's experience of fifteen years as a caravan trader, and Peter the Great's visit to western Europe. Nevertheless, this regenerated leadership has never been able to save a civilization from ultimate decline and extinction— unless, as the exception that proves the rule, we of the Western world accept Christ's message before it is too late. All other civilizations are already extinct or doomed.

As we have pointed out, the greatest public challenge in the second series—during the time of troubles—is that of wars between parochial states within the civilization. The response of the dominant minority to this challenge is the creation of what Toynbee calls a "Universal State," though it is never literally universal—what he means is a great political empire, such as that which Rome built up to check the wars between the parochial states of Hellenic civilization. The remedy, however, turns out to be as bad as the disease, for the creation of a Universal State, so-called, invariably heralds the doom of every civilization which installs it.

The attempt of the dominant minority to rule by force rather than by awe-inspiring creativity leads to a cleavage between the masses and their minority of leaders. The masses fall into two groups: the "Internal Proletariat," or the body of citizens within the society, and the "External Proletariat," or the "barbarians at or within the gates." Toynbee appears to have derived this conception of the internal and external proletariat from the great Russian social historian, Michael I. Rostovtzev. To combat the forceful dominion of the dominant minority, the internal proletariat embraces a universal religion and creates a "Universal Church" to oppose the Universal State controlled by the now noncreative leaders. The external proletariat seeks to inject its foreign ideas and ways of life into the civilization. The conflict terminates in the dissolution of the Universal State when the dominant minority accepts the universal religion of the internal proletariat and takes over the manners and arts of the external proletariat. The doomed civilization then goes into gradual but inescapable decline through a series of "routs" and "rallies," in the course of which each rout becomes more devastating and each rally more feeble.

The period of "troubles" and decline brings in its wake schisms in the body politic and in the souls of the citizens. The former take the form of class struggles and foreign conflicts. The schisms of the soul manifest themselves in mental conflicts, split personalities, personal demoralization and degeneration (cf. Nordau), and divided loyalties.

This is the time for saviors to appear to rescue man from his trials and tribulations. There are many types of saviors: creative geniuses from the dominant minority; saviors with the sword—great warrior-conquerors; saviors with the Time-Machine, or vendors of utopias; saviors in the guise of Plato's philosopher-kings, such as Marcus Aurelius; and saviors who pretend to be God incarnate, of whom there has been only one whose pretensions were genuine, Jesus Christ. In the past all these saviors have failed to save. The hope of Western civilization depends upon our ability to grasp the opportunity which lies in Jesus' divinity and to stage a great religious revival which will bring "peace on earth, good-will to men."

IV. AN APPRAISAL OF TOYNBEE'S "A STUDY OF HISTORY"

Because of its peculiar character, few books are harder to appraise than Toynbee's *A Study of History*. Since wholly in purpose, and partly in execution, the work is primarily neither history nor sociology, it cannot be assessed fairly or fully in terms of either of these subjects.

It may be freely conceded that these six volumes are the most impressive example of the impact of religious faith upon historical writing in the case of a single author since the origin of writing. And the more volumes that appear, the more impressive will be the result. They also represent the most voluminous influence of Christianity upon comparative sociology and the culture case-study method in sociology, with the possible exception of Pitirim Sorokin's *Social and Cultural Dynamics* and related volumes by the same author. If Toynbee is the Augustine of historical writing, so is Sorokin the Augustine of contemporary sociology. Sorokin's historical condemnation of sensate culture and his plea for the adoption of an ideational and spiritual civilization, through a return to God and the Absolute, are only the sociological abstraction of Toynbee's more direct and personal appeal to exploit the uniqueness of Christ's Incarnation.

Of the accuracy and validity of Toynbee's theological and poetical excursion into theodicy and apocalypse and into the divine purpose in the universe and human experience, only God himself could be an adequate judge. It may or may not be the last book of its kind, in this sense, but it is surely the most impressive to date. Whether or not the historian is ever to succeed in portraying the heavy and wrathful hand of God in history, Toynbee has surely made the most magnificent effort.

To leave this inscrutable and imponderable field for the more mundane and secular areas of history and sociology, we can get on firmer ground. We may here pass over as lesser blemishes the peculiar jargon; the bizarre terminology of *Yin* and *Yang,* and the like; the frequent strained and dubious analogies; the mystical motif; and the religious overtones and terminal crescendo.

As social history, Toynbee's work is strong in taking for its theme the rise and fall of civilizations rather than the course of national and dynastic history. In Toynbee's treatment of the history of the civilizations studied in the course of the work, there are many brilliant and illuminating sections, especially in the case of those which Toynbee knows best, such as Hellenic history and the history of western Europe. His account of the manner in which the potential blessings of our modern industrial age and democratic society have been distorted and wasted by nationalism and warfare is something which needs constant emphasis both in understanding our age and in working for a better era.

Toynbee's preconceptions prevent him, however, from always giving a fair picture of the historical data he knows best. His assumption of the transcendent importance of faith and spiritual creativity leads him to minimize the great achievements of Greek rationalism in the age of Pericles and the vital contributions of Rome in creating a great system of law and bringing peace and unity to the Western world. Toynbee includes the Roman Empire as a phase of Hellenic civilization—its decadent phase as a universal state—and many of his general theories of the decline of civilization are obviously based on the course of Roman disintegration. But here he displays a very incomplete knowledge of the more vital factors or passes them over because they do not fit into his spiritual interpretation of history.

As sociology, Toynbee's contribution lies chiefly in what the sociologists now call "culture case-study," and Howard Becker declares that "Toynbee has given to sociologists a magnificent example of the possibilities of culture case-study in historical sociology."[5] Further, Toynbee's work, as a whole, is, from the viewpoint of sociology, a vast excursion into comparative sociology, differing chiefly from the earlier studies by the classical anthropologists and historical sociologists in that it is devoted mainly to historic civilizations rather than being confined primarily to primitive societies.

The defects of Toynbee's work as strictly history lie chiefly in the fact that his interests in truly scientific history are only incidental. Despite the title of the book, it is not primarily a history, or a "study of history." It is not objective, or even interpretative, *history*. It is theology, employing selected facts of history to illustrate the will of God, as the medieval bestiaries utilized biological fantasies to achieve the same results. Toynbee's work differs from that of Orosius and Augustine chiefly in that he makes relatively more use of the deeds of men than of divine figures to prove the same case. Toynbee's vast materials throw far more light upon the processes of Toynbee's mind than upon the actual processes of history.

Not only is Toynbee's aim and motivation divergent from those of the historian of civilization, but he has little technical preparation to execute a vast comparative history of civilization. He is a mystic, a classicist, a capable *political* historian, and a publicist. And he has oceans of that charm which he regards as the source and sign of creativity. But he does not possess the indispensable command of the techniques and subject matter of cultural anthropology, historical sociology, and social history, which, whatever else may be said against him, Sorokin does possess. Many commentators have stressed Toynbee's great erudition and industry and his command of many languages. This may be freely, almost enviously, conceded. But the vital point here is not how much one can read or in how many languages, but whether or not he has read the "right things"—the indispensable materials for the task in hand. Here it must be said that Toynbee fails to measure up to the test. It would have been far better if he had read the relevant literature which exists in the English language alone. This failure to command the essential techniques has made it impossible for Toynbee to make the most competent use of what he has read, which is vast and immense. His theological orientation and motif lead to a definite pattern of selection and interpretation of historical materials. He writes history as he thinks it should be to further the cause of salvation, rather than as it has really been.

Even without this theological distortion, it would have been difficult for Toynbee to compose a great history of civilization because of his lack of the genetic perspective which comes from an acquaintance with cultural anthropology, historical sociology, and social history. This is devastatingly illustrated by his basic thesis that all civilizations have been essentially contemporaneous because they have all sprung up within the last six thousand years or so. He ignores the fact that greater changes in human life and institutions have taken place in the last six thousand years than in the previous million—and that the transformations of the last two centuries are greater than those which occurred in the previous five thousand years. To try to compare the civilizations of pre- and post–industrial revolution times, in any literal and exact sense, is a flagrant defiance of true historicity. And to minimize or overlook the influence of reason, science, and technology in history is to lose sight of the most dynamic factors in human development—those which have created modern civilization and have produced the contemporary problems which it is a main purpose of history to help us to understand and solve.

Toynbee's treatment and arrangement of historical facts are carried out chiefly in such a manner as to suit the needs of his comparative program and his particular scheme of case study. They are sought and presented in such a fashion as to vindicate his theodicean drama and not necessarily in keeping with the full sequence of actual development in the twenty-one civilizations studied. No one of his histories of various civilizations can be accepted as a full and literal history of that civilization. We cannot always feel sure whether the civilizations treated actually declined for the reasons given and in the manner described or whether they "fall" in the book in the way which suits Toynbee's prearranged plan for them to decay and disappear.

Toynbee's conception of the fall of civilizations runs counter to a growing tendency on the part of social historians to doubt or minimize the element of "fall" or collapse. For example, we are now told that Rome never fell but that Roman civilization in the West passed on gradually to that of medieval Europe, as Alfons Dopsch has shown with great learning. The civilization of Hellenistic Egypt was more magnificent than that of any period of Pharaonic Egypt. Likewise, neither Sargon, Nebuchadnezzar, nor Darius knew anything equal to the splendors of Muslim civilization at Bagdad under Harun al-Rashid, and so on.

Nations and dynasties may pass away, and the domination of particular races may shift, but the civilization may endure, despite all this. If so, this is the important item, by Toynbee's own standard of historical values and realities, since he eschews nations, dynasties, and races as primary historical factors. Further, there may be a bit of Western arrogance in the assumption that all these Eastern civilizations have actually "fallen." Mustapha Kemal showed what Islamic civilization can do when modernized. If China and India ever achieve political union, internal peace, and mechanization, they are likely to leave Western civilization far behind in power and prosperity. Spengler may have been more nearly correct in prophesying the future ascendancy of the Far East.

There happens to exist one historical work which has done just what Toynbee's admirers imagine he has done. This is Ralph E. Turner's *The Great Cultural Traditions*.[6] Nothing could be more edifying and illuminating in the case at issue than to read and compare these two books. Turner had the preparation to write a real history of civilization and was willing to leave theology to the theologians.

Similarly, as a contribution to culture case-study in sociology, Toynbee's work is reduced in value by the fact that he usually has formulated his "case" before he starts to study it and he builds it up to suit his program. When compared with the work of great masters in culture case-study, such as Émile Durkheim and Max Weber, Toynbee's case-studies of civilizations appear to be of the "rule-of-thumb" type which is the inevitable result of failure to master the principles of cultural anthropology and sociology as a preparation for this type of investigation and synthesis.

As comparative historical sociology, the work labors under the same defective methodology that vitiated a large part of the work of the older classical, comparative, or evolutionary anthropologists and historical sociologists and has been so clearly exposed by Boas, Lowie, and Goldenweiser. Like the classical anthropologists, Toynbee assumes the universality of a social type or historical pattern and then seeks data from history to vindicate it. It is not unfair to say that he is more in error than evolutionary anthropologists like Lewis Henry Morgan, who held firmly and steadfastly to natural, evolutionary forces and did not invoke the hand of God in their behalf. Morgan is as far ahead of Toynbee here as Herbert Spencer's *First Principles* was of Augustine's *City of God*. If one wishes to get some notion of Toynbee's status as a historical sociologist, there would be no better exercise than to compare his book with William Christie MacLeod's *Origin and History of Politics*.[7]

The comparative method is valid only when the things compared are comparable. To equate and compare the process of civilization in all periods of history, without making adequate allowance for differences in technology, institutions, and ideas is completely unhistorical. Toynbee freely admits differences in detail but avers that the basic process is the same everywhere and at all times. This is akin to the popular effort to find warnings for modern America in the trials and tribulations of ancient Rome. It may be protested by some that at least human nature is the same, whether in China in 3000 B.C. or in the United States in 1947; but human nurture is vastly different, and that is what counts, as witness Toynbee's own rejection of the factor of race as a decisive force in history. There is no validity whatever in comparing the processes of civilization in a period of antique agrarian supernaturalism with those in an age of secular and urban industrialism.

Even Toynbee's conception of challenge and response, while valid as a general principle, is frequently based on dubious interpretations of historical facts and a shaky anthropogeography. New ideas, born of technological changes, institutional shifts, class changes, and the contact of cultures, go further to explain the rise of reform programs than the "withdrawal-and-return" of great men and heroes. One might ask the source of the new ideas which Peter the Great withdrew to study. One may also question the necessity of the complexity of much of Toynbee's analysis. As Huxley once said, the simpler the explanation, the more likely it is to be true, provided it is adequate. Spencer's "dead-hand" and Ogburn's "cultural lag" will explain many of the changes and conflicts which Toynbee obscures in complicated verbiage and theological vagaries. And one may doubt the propriety and relevance of a philosophy of spiritual predestination and revivalism in an era in which secularism has triumphed.

One reason why Toynbee's analysis is impressive is that most of his readers have read little or no sociology. In many ways Toynbee's work is not so up-to-date and satisfactory as even Comte's *Principles of a Positive Polity*. Certainly, Comte's "Religion of Humanity" should have more appeal to intellectuals today than neo-Augustinianism. Compared with Max Weber's studies of the civilizations of the East and West, Toynbee's handling of sociohistorical data often seems naïve and amateurish.

For the excessive adulation of his work and the fantastically extreme estimates of its nature and significance, it is unfair to blame Mr. Toynbee. From my friends who know him well personally, I gather that he is a simple and modest man, mainly bent on doing good in the world. It is surely an exaggeration to regard Toynbee as the "Copernicus" or the "Einstein" of historiography. It is even more grotesque to hold that, from now on, historical writing must be designated as "B.T." and "A.T." (before and after Toynbee). If his attitude and approach are to set the pattern for historical writing in the future, then we may expect current and future crops of histories after the fashion of twentieth-century versions of Otto of Freising and John Zonoras. It is improbable that many historians will follow the pattern of Toynbee because nobody else is likely to be able to do this kind of work as well or as thoroughly as he has, if for no other reason. And there is no need for another book of its kind.

V. SOME REASONS FOR THE POPULARITY OF TOYNBEE'S WORKS

The question may cogently be raised as to why Toynbee should be so widely and ecstatically acclaimed at any time, and especially in 1947. His first three volumes appeared fourteen years earlier, and they contained most of his basic ideas. The second three came out in 1939—eight years ago. Some might say that it is because a one-volume digest had just been made available, but this is not the answer. The clamor of the growing Toynbee cult was what suggested the condensation. There would seem to be at least five groups to whom the work make a special and timely appeal—and that particularly in our chaotic postwar epoch.

To understand the source of interest on the part of the largest element in the host of Toynbee's devoted followers, one would have to turn back for a precedent to the intellectual fears, consternation, and "loss of nerve" on the part of the literate population in the days of the breakup of the Roman Empire in the west, which has been described by Gilbert Murray. In those years of groping and yearning, Orosius' *Seven Books of History against the Pagans* and, above all, Augustine's *City of God* provided the alarmed and disconsolate with a historical perspective, a cosmic philosophy, and a faith to which they might cling. Toynbee has done for our period of institutional disintegration what Augustine and Orosius did for that earlier era of chaos and transition.

Another group of Toynbee followers are those who have eventually become flabbergasted by the sorry state of the world which has resulted from actually applying the policies which they urged upon us for a decade or more. They have now come to the "mourners' bench" and seek to expiate their sins and get assurance of better times to come. Clifton Fadiman has warmly indorsed Toynbee's work.

Then there is a host of literary figures and journalists who have been fascinated and "bowled over" by the book, partly because they know little history, historiography, or sociology. Some have obviously been "tipped off" by their employers, others have been given assignments, and some have jumped on the "bandwagon" because they scented the possibility of "good copy." Alone of this type of adulator, Granville Hicks has shown a saving spirit of qualification and skepticism in a very friendly exposition of Toynbee's ideas for the general reader.[8]

Fourth, there are those whose emotional yearning is always ministered to by an unintelligible jargon, a strange terminology, and a mystical air, which seem to them wise to the extent that they are inscrutable. This was a large part of the source of the power of Mrs. Eddy's *Science and Health*. James T. Shotwell once said that the essence of the religious and mystical thrill lies in a thing apprehended but not comprehended. Toynbee's work partakes of this nature to many. As Charles Austin Beard observes: "Some fragments of imaginative metaphysics underlie the structures of his chapters, but it is scarcely possible to make a system of these fragments; nor does it appear that the author has made up his own mind on the point of the ultimate design of the universe about which he is speaking at great length. His erudition and his metaphysics, combined with his metaphorical language and use of analogies, give a peculiar and elusive character to the whole."[9] Or, as Howard Becker puts it: "By the end of the third volume the mystical motif becomes so loud that it almost drowns out the systematic-empirical theme."[10]

Fifth, a large number of readers of Toynbee's work are intrigued in these postwar days by his enthusiastic internationalism and "one-world" political philosophy, to which he brings an almost religious devotion, despite the fact that he points out that the establishment of even incomplete universal states in the past has been the almost invariable symptom and signal of impending social disintegration.

In addition to those who follow Toynbee devoutly and sincerely, even if mistakenly in some cases, there is also a deliberate effort under way to build him up as the greatest historical figure of our generation. He has been commissioned and lavishly subsidized to supervise and help write the official Anglo-American history of World War II. To the extent that he can be made to seem omniscient and infallible, it will be difficult for the "wicked" revisionists to attack his findings and conclusions.

Of course, all the members of the Toynbee cult are immensely impressed with the size of the work—six volumes by 1939, and at least three more to come. No fair commentator would deny Toynbee great learning or prodigious industry, but the size of his treatise has a special explanation. The complete edition is not a polished and well-organized literary masterpiece, but it is, in part, a collection of studies and notes. Had a man like James Westfall Thompson, our great medievalist, done the same thing with all his lecture and seminar notes, the results would not have been six or nine volumes, but perhaps nineteen. Further, no other method of work in history and sociology enables one to pile up pages so rapidly as does the comparative method in which one has formulated his program in advance and seeks data to confirm it. Witness the extensive works of the classical anthropologists, Westermarck's many volumes on marriage and morals, Herbert Spencer's *Principles of Sociology,* or, above all, the vast bulk of Sir James G. Frazer's *The Golden Bough* and the interminable volumes of Charles Letourneau.

Yet Mr. Toynbee can no more be blamed for his cult than for the laurels they have cast upon him. Whatever the merits or defects of *A Study of History*, Mr. Toynbee is a genuine article; only his cult is a fraud and a "phony." Granville Hicks has well characterized his opus as an "epic—a great imaginative thrust .... the achievement of a poetic imagination." Unfortunately, that great imagination is primarily centered on the Second Coming of the Lord under Anglican auspices. An eminent historical novelist has crisply summarized Toynbee's achievement in these words: "Toynbee buries the universe in an Anglican churchyard."

NOTES

1. *A Study of History* (Amer. ed.; New York, 1934), Vols. I–III.
2. *Ibid.*, Vols. IV–VI (New York, 1939).
3. *A Study of History* (abridgment of Vols. I–VI by D. C. Somervell) (New York, 1947).
4. Somervell abridgement, p. 532.
5. H. E. Barnes and Howard Becker, *Contemporary Social Theory* (New York, 1940), p. 513.
6. 2 vols.; New York, 1941.
7. New York, 1931.
8. *Harper's Magazine*, February, 1947.
9. *American Historical Review*, April, 1940, p. 593.
10. Barnes and Becker, *op. cit.*, p. 512.

PART VI

SOCIOLOGICAL THEORY IN AMERICA

INTRODUCTORY NOTE

THE GENERAL CHARACTER OF
AMERICAN SOCIOLOGY*

THERE is little doubt that sociology has been more enthusiastically received and more extensively cultivated in the United States than elsewhere in the civilized world. We have already presented the doctrines of early pioneers in American sociology, such as Sumner, Ward, and Morgan. In this section we shall survey the views of other American systematic sociologists. Some of them, such as Giddings and Small, might well have been included among the pioneers. But it has seemed most logical to present them here, along with later systematizers, some of whom were their students. By some, Cooley, Ross, and Ellwood are regarded more as psychological sociologists than as systematizers of the whole field of sociological knowledge, but each of these men has reached out further than the field of psychological sociology. Their interests, achievements, and prestige entitle them to inclusion in this book.

The selection of sociologists for extended treatment here need not be taken as implying that the editor believes their work or rank to be of greater importance than that of several other sociologists who are not dealt with. The scope of this book provides the test for selection. The work of the specialists in various fields of sociological work has been amply appraised and credited in other books, especially those edited by the present writer in co-operation with Howard Becker.

While we shall in the following chapters deal with the outstanding systematic sociologists in this country, we may well point out that the subject has now passed from the earlier stage of magisterial systematization under Ward, Small, Giddings, Stuckenberg, Cooley, Ross, Hayes, and Ellwood to various types of specialization. The day of the system-builders is past, though Pitirim Sorokin, of Harvard, has recently produced an impressive effort at systematization. So rapidly is specialization being forced upon us that some have even prophesied that the field will be pre-empted eventually by the special social disciplines. Certainly, there

---

* By the editor.

is now such an increase in the materials available for social research that the sociologist is compelled to specialize. As he does so, he inevitably tends to align his work with biology, psychology, anthropology, history, economics, ethics, or law.

Meanwhile, historical sociology in the United States, has now advanced far beyond the state reached thirty years ago in Giddings' justly famous *Principles of Sociology*. What has been achieved here has been mainly the contributions of the cultural anthropologists in the study of primitive cultures and institutions, along with the work of social historians, primarily Shotwell, Turner, Beard, and their students, in surveying the institutional development of Europe and America. Sorokin's *Social and Cultural Dynamics* is the most extensive contribution to the field by an American sociologist, and Howard Becker has been the most active of the sociologists in outlining the methodology and principles to be followed in sound historical sociology.

In the study of the geographic factors in society little independent work has been done by the professional sociologists. The cultivation of human geography has been carried on chiefly by the geographers, particularly by Ratzel's disciple, Miss Ellen Churchill Semple; by the brilliant theorizer, Ellsworth Huntington; and by the able student of regional geography, J. Russell Smith. The critical anthropologists, led by Boas and his disciples, have attempted to evaluate in a discriminating fashion the accumulated mass of anthropogeographical data. But Franklin Thomas has been the only sociologist who has made an effort to digest and expound this work for sociology.

Anthropogeography has been, at least indirectly, linked up with sociology through social ecology, forwarded by such sociologists as R. E. Park, R. D. McKenzie, James A. Quinn, Nels Anderson, E. W. Burgess, Clifford Shaw, Milla Alihan, and others. It has, in particular, revolutionized the study of urban sociology.

In biological sociology, some excellent work has been done by men who have, in general, abandoned the old voluminous speculations about the similarity between society and the biological organism. W. F. Willcox, A. B. Wolfe, W. S. Thompson, E. B. Reuter, H. P. Fairchild, L. I. Dublin, Frank Lorimer, Frederick Osborn, F. W. Notestein, J. A. Field, and others have studied population problems in the light of the developments since Malthus. F. H. Hankins, Carl Kelsey, and others have studied the application of the laws of heredity to social problems. Then there have been notable contributions to eugenics and the racial history of man by such social biologists as C. B. Davenport, Raymond Pearl, E. G. Conklin, H. H. Goddard, E. A. Hooton, and S. J. Holmes. Some biologists, such as E. M. East, have also made additions to our knowledge of population problems. The problems of race have been studied scientifically by F. H. Hankins, by Franz Boas and his students, and by R. B. Dixon and C. S. Coon, of Harvard. Hankins has done more than any other American sociologist to synthesize and evaluate the whole range of biological contributions to scientific sociology.

In psychological sociology there has been much progress beyond the philosophical, descriptive, and systematizing stage of Cooley, Ross, and Giddings and toward a specialized application of psychological principles to social processes by such writers as L. L. Bernard, F. H. Allport, T. D. Eliot, E. R. Groves, E. D. Martin, and Kimball Young. C. A. Ellwood and E. S. Bogardus occupy a position intermediate between the older philosophical systematizers and the inductive students of scientific psychology as applied to society.

A relatively recent approach to social problems, based on the analysis of cultural processes and institutional growth, has been forwarded chiefly by the cultural anthropologists of the Boas school and a few others, notably, A. M. Tozzer, of Harvard. The only sociologists to devote serious attention to this mode of social analysis have been W. I. Thomas and W. F. Ogburn and his followers, most of whom have derived their stimulus from the Boas school of anthropologists. The ethnographic method of Lippert and Sumner has been preserved and extended by A. G. Keller; and Leslie A. White has enthusiastically rehabilitated Morgan's social evolutionism.

Probably the largest group of sociologists are what are usually called "social economists" or "practical sociologists," namely, those chiefly interested in social work and amelioration. In this group well-known personalities have been E. T. Devine, S. M. Lindsay, Jane Addams, Graham Taylor, Edith Abbott, Mary van Kleeck, Mary E. Richmond, Jessica Peixotto, Robert Woods, James Ford, Porter Lee, R. M. MacIver, J. L. Gillin, Paul U. Kellogg, Philip Klein, R. W. Kelso, S. A. Queen, J. S. Burgess, P. A. Parsons, and D. M. Schneider. Here the emphasis has been progressively shifted from amelioration to prevention, though the "uplift" attitude is still strong in many quarters.

An important field of practical sociology which has been most extensively cultivated by American sociologists in recent years is criminology and penology, which deal with the causes, consequences, treatment, and prevention of delinquency. Here some of the leading writers have been E. H. Sutherland, J. L. Gillin, P. A. Parsons, Sanford Bates, Thorsten Sellin, Nathaniel Cantor, Frank Tannenbaum, William Healy, R. H. Gault, F. E. Haynes, D. R. Taft, Blake McKelvey, N. K. Teeters, J. P. Shalloo, L. N. Robinson, W. C. Reckless, A. E. Wood, J. B. Waite, L. E. Lawes, and Maurice Parmelee.

Family and divorce problems have also claimed much interest on the part of practical sociologists in the United States, among them A. W. Calhoun, J. P. Lichtenberger, R. E. Baber, E. W. Burgess, L. S. Cottrell, Willystine Goodsell, Willard Waller, E. R. Groves, G. E. Howard, C. C. Zimmerman, B. J. Stern, Ruth Reed, M. F. Nimkoff, E. R. Mowrer, G. V. Hamilton, M. C. Elmer, R. S. Cavan, and Jessie Bernard.

Especially notable has been the development of the quantitative method in sociology not only in the special branch of social statistics but also in the general approach to sociology. In forwarding this method, Giddings must be assigned the primary place as the "herald," which is conventionally given to Francis Bacon in the history of scientific thought in general, even if Giddings' actual contributions to statistical method are comparable only to Bacon's slight scientific achievement in his *Sylvae sylvarum*. Of Giddings' students, W. F. Ogburn, R. E. Chaddock, and Stuart A. Rice have been the most enthusiastic in promoting the quantitative method. In George A. Lundberg's *Foundations of Sociology* and in S. C. Dodd's *Dimensions of Society*, attempts have been made to re-write general sociology from the quantitative point of view.

As to the periodicals dealing with sociological problems in this country, there are several devoted specifically to the subject—the *American Sociological Review*, the organ of the American Sociological Society; the *American Journal of Sociology*, published at the University of Chicago, and founded and long edited by Albion W. Small; the *Journal of Social Forces*, published at the University of North Carolina, under the editorship of H. W. Odum; and the *Journal of Applied Sociology*, now called *Sociology and Social Research*, published at the University of Southern California, and edited by E. S. Bogardus.

Of these, the *American Journal of Sociology* carries, perhaps, the best array of relatively long monographic articles; but its former excellent book-review section has now degenerated into brief notices, though its bibliographic classification is very helpful. A very wide range of topics is dealt with in the *Journal of Social Forces*. The *American Sociological Review* is the only one in which adequate attention is given to the reviewing of current sociological literature.

Other journals publish material closely related to sociology, among them the *American Anthropologist,* the *Journal of Abnormal and Social Psychology,* the *Political Science Quarterly,* and *Mental Hygiene.* Of these, the most important and valuable for sociologists is the last mentioned. This is a comprehensive and substantial quarterly, published by the National Committee for Mental Hygiene. It contains valuable articles in each issue on the applications of modern psychology and biology to social problems.

The diverse interests and products involved in sociological specialization are comprehensively assembled, presented, and appraised in H. E. Barnes and Howard Becker, *Contemporary Social Theory* (1940).

CHAPTER XXXVIII

THE SOCIOLOGICAL THEORIES OF FRANKLIN HENRY GIDDINGS: CONSCIOUSNESS OF KIND, PLURALISTIC BEHAVIOR, AND STATISTICAL METHOD

CLARENCE H. NORTHCOTT, *York, England*

I. DISCURSIVE AND EVOLUTIONARY CHARACTER OF GIDDINGS' WRITINGS

IN ATTEMPTING to give an outline of the sociological theories of Professor Franklin Henry Giddings,[1] one is beset by the difficulty of finding them in any complete and final form. His writings are scattered over a period of more than thirty years.[2] Each book is, to a certain extent, complementary to all others in the series, so that a study of them in chronological order gives a realistic impression of the open mind and analytic power of the author, without affording anything that even he would claim to be a completed system of sociological theory. The absence of revision and co-ordination also bewilders the student as to what part, if any, Giddings accepted or rejected at the end of his life and what he would have modified. Moreover, personal contact with him in the lecture-room does not help one greatly. His custom of applying his analytical mind to any pressing question of immediate import, whether suggested by the publication of a new book, the exposition of a new theory, or the application of some political policy, and his habit of injecting the results of his analysis as new wine into old bottles shatter the outline and symmetry of any tentative system. Nevertheless, the fundamental theories on which his sociological system is built are so clearly stated that an attempt may reasonably be made to synthesize them.

While Giddings was a man of great mental originality, his sociological system and ideas were also based on a wide reading of his sociological predecessors and contemporaries. From Auguste Comte he derived the idea of the need for a basic or fundamental social science. As Giddings once forcefully expressed this conviction: "To teach ethnology, the philosophy of history, political economy, and the theory of the state, to men who have not learned the first principles of sociology, is like teaching astronomy or thermodynamics to men who have not learned the Newtonian laws of motion." From Comte's *Positive Polity* he drew his outline of the main stages in the history of civilization. He also fully adopted Comte's repudiation of theological and metaphysical thinking about society and upheld the contention that sociology must always be an empirical science, worthy of our scientific age. From Darwin and Herbert Spencer he learned that scientific social thinking, in turn, must be evolutionary thought, and he held tenaciously throughout his life to a stalwart evolutionary naturalism. Giddings' earlier sociological system was essentially an adaptation and elaboration of Spencer's system, as stated in the latter part of *First Principles*. From Lester F. Ward he took over the notion that a main purpose of sociology is to furnish scientific guidance for civic reform and social betterment. His conception of the "consciousness of kind" was derived mainly from Adam Smith's notion of reflective sympathy. He leaned heavily on Tarde for some of his social psychology, and his views of social constraint were affected by the conceptions of Darwin, Durkheim, and Sumner. His psychology of social values was in part derived from a reading of the economic theories of the Austrian school and John Bates Clark. Finally, Giddings' ideas of scientific method and social statistics were taken over mainly from John Stuart Mill, Stanley Jevons, Leon Walras, and Karl Pearson.

II. THE ORIGIN AND EVOLUTION OF HUMAN SOCIETY

To Giddings there are four general problems for the sociologist to study: (1) the origin and evolution of society; (2) social constraint and the conformation of behavior and character to type as the immediate and general function of society; (3) the effect of social constraint upon selection; and (4) the final consequence of social constraint, conceived of as an amount or rate of progress. The greater bulk of his own thought has been devoted to the first problem, though he has given many significant sidelights in his later works upon all the others.

Society, which in his later writings he distinguishes from all swarms, herds, and packs of animals, he regards as a product of association, which he is at pains to differentiate from gregariousness. All these phenomena —namely, gregariousness and the herd, association and society—are products, as he contends, of a collective or pluralistic mode of the struggle for existence. Pluralistic behavior is the behavior of a "plural," that is, many creatures (animals or human beings) in one place at one time, played upon by the same set of circumstances and acting and reacting upon one another. Behavior is affected by the material environment, which supplies "an infinitely differentiated group of stimuli."[3] These play upon beings who have held together from birth or have assembled under the stress of the struggle for existence. The multiplication of offspring not only aids the collective life but insures a mutuality of needs and capacities for either attainment or resistance. A given habitat will include a number of groups of this kind, whose points of resemblance will measure the degree of their similarity.

Their most important similarities will be found in their behavior. The primary activity of the living organism is to adapt the environment to itself in order to satisfy its primary needs of safety and food. In the human being these adaptations are the basis of appreciation, that is, a change in consciousness describable as the attaching of more interest or value to one thing than to another. Appreciation arises out of those reactions, which are, first, instinctive, then habitual, and later on are rationalized. When, at length, man finds the limits which restrict the adaptation of the environment to himself, he begins the reverse process of the adjustment of himself to the environment. His interest is attached to the behavior of his fellows, who, by reason of their biological relationship and the pressure of a common environment, are at the same time interested in his behavior. His reactions and those of his fellows tend to be alike, and there arises a perception of the likeness of external stimuli to self-stimuli. This is co-ordinated with the adjustment of one organism to the like behavior of similar organisms, a process furthered by imitation and reflective sympathy. This interstimulation produces dramatic behavior: "In the presence of fellow-beings action becomes acting."[4] When language arises, such behavior is conversationalized: it is talked about, and differences and similarities among objects, activities, behavior, and persons are felt and perceived. Out of this arises a consciousness of kind, compounded of "organic sympathy, the perception of resemblance, conscious or reflective sympathy, affection, and the desire for recognition."[5] There is a distinct stimulus in "kind," a direct reaction to it, and presently a discriminating awareness of it. Natural selection works upon this; and, since competition and the struggle for survival lead to co-operation and preferential association, there is produced that collective behavior with which social organization begins. So it comes about that talk and the consciousness of kind convert gregariousness into association and the herd or pack into society.

Among the most elementary similarities of behavior are habits of toleration. Individuals living in a group necessarily come to tolerate one another. Conflict is natural in a group, since, by reason of original differences of nature and habit, the imitation involved in consciousness of kind is never perfect, and because of the drive toward domination and conquest: "Antagonism, however, is self-limiting; it necessarily terminates in the equilibrium of toleration."[6] Individual members of the group prove to be too evenly matched to make fighting worth while. Thus primal natural rights, in the sense of the immunities and liberties of toleration, come to be enjoyed long before they get conscious recognition. Soon, under the pressure of a common danger or a common opportunity, these similarities of behavior develop unconsciously into spontaneous collective action. This effect is produced under the stimulus of communication, imitation, suggestion, and, later, leadership and subordination. The group which acts collectively represents an assembling and economizing of effort. The assembled effort of the group becomes co-operation, that is, conscious practical agreement for the better realization of common purposes.

The organizing force or influence whereby this type of social organization is launched is to be found in an analysis of the degrees of reaction. Some individuals react more promptly, some more effectively, some more persistently. The first type of reaction is mainly one of sensation and emotion, which practically all share. Some, fewer in number, will examine, inquire, think, and discuss, while the remainder, forming the minority, will initiate action. In so doing they create new situations to which others must adapt themselves. The protocracy, or the nucleus of the ruling minority, seek the co-operation of the group which has given them power and authority, and the latter must either co-operate or oppose. But the protocracy is in a position to see opportunities of wealth and power before others and to dispense patronage on a definite understanding of loyalty and allegiance. Where the protocracy does not actually rule, it dominates by virtue of ability, integrity, or beneficent purpose. Thus, "in terms of like or of unlike, of prompt or of slow, of persistent or of intermittent response, all the phenomena of natural grouping and of collective behavior can be stated and interpreted."[7]

Social organization began with the few exercising rule or domination; later, collective choices or decisions were made, and concerted volition came into existence. The concert of wills, of which this consists, is of various degrees of completeness, according to the proportion of individuals who are instinctive, sympathetic, dogmatic, or deliberate. Many fewer persons share in approving a collective deliberative decision than in one requiring an instinctive or sympathetic attitude. From this arises a law of concerted volition, that "in a normal population, the percentage number of individuals participating in a collective decision diminishes as the intellectual quality of the decision rises."[8] With increasing necessity for collective action, social organization tends to develop internal complexity and to assume a hierarchical form.

From one point of view these grades represent the divisions which the collective struggle and the reactions of the majority and minority upon one another create. Through conquest, the assertion of privilege and authority, and the use of the *commendatio,* there are produced within the social organization groups that may be privileged and closed, selectively open, or indiscriminately open:

> Eligibility to membership in a privileged and closed group is governed by consideration of source. Descent from members of the group in a former generation is one of the oldest and best-known requirements. Membership in an antecedent group or category may be the requirement. Eligibility to membership in a selectively open group is determined by the functioning value of members individually for the functioning of the group collectively. In the indiscriminately open group there are no eligibility tests.[9]
>
> In the historical evolution of social organization, intragroup conflict develops between closed and open groups.[10]

The group based on ethnic unity or kinship is replaced by one based on civil unity. The alien is admitted to the privileges of the folk and to the obligations of tax-paying and military service. This mutuality of obligation and opportunity is the basis of civilization, which may, therefore be defined as "modally and characteristically a substitution of the open for the closed group in politics, religion, trade, and education."[11]

Through the organization of relations within the open group and the establishment of co-operation, the protocracy acquires political power or sovereignty. This can never be an unconditional power to compel obedience but is finite and conditional, dependent on the balance and composition of forces. In social evolution, sovereignty has assumed four distinct modes. The personal sovereign, the strong personality, commands obedience but cannot compel it. The class—aristocracy, capitalists, or labor—can inspire obedience, if mentally and morally superior, or exact it through the control of wealth. In mass sovereignty the majority has the power to compel a large measure of obedience for a time through numbers or the potentialities of superior force. Finally, an organized, enlightened, and deliberative community may evoke obedience through a rational appeal to intelligence and moral sense.[12]

When the supreme will of society is organized for requiring and directing obedience, government comes into existence and, like sovereignty, is determined by the prevailing conditions of the social mind and the degree of circumstantial pressure. In times of chaos and insecurity the forceful personality crushes his competitors and, with the active co-operation of the community born of their dislike of anarchy, sets up an absolute government. Where there is much spontaneous co-operation and more like-mindedness than difference and antagonism, with a fair resistance to arbitrary power, government takes the form of limited minority rule. Where revolutionary conditions exist, whether political or industrial, absolute majority rule tends to be found as a product of the revolt. Finally, in a community that is, on the whole, homogeneous and composed of individuals approximately equal in ability and condition, limited majority rule is the form of government.[13] In the latter form, constitutional limitations are stated to insure the rightful balance between the coercion through which government as a form of social control operates and the liberty associated with that full development of personality that is the purpose of social organization.[14]

But liberty, says Professor Giddings, is not guaranteed by a written constitution; it is determined by the composition of sovereignty, which is the real constitution. The bond by which the most democratic form of sovereignty is held together is the agreement to abide by the decision of the majority. The conditions implied in this form of organization of majority rule are twofold: (1) the majority may not and does not override certain rights agreed on by the majority and most of the minority, and thereby guaranteed to all the minority. These rights must be set forth in a constitution, which is necessary for minorities and for democracies generally. The defense and the safeguard of liberty, however, does not lie in this constitution but in the maintenance of this condition and the establishment of a second. (2) Minorities must have freedom of speech, of the press, of meeting, and of orderly and peaceful agitation, to the end that they may be able to turn their minority into a majority. The repression of minorities throws society back onto lower planes of organization, where patriotism and various forms of lordships are the chief characteristics.[15]

III. THE NATURE OF SOCIAL ORGANIZATION

With this as an inadequate presentation of the account that Giddings has given of the processes involved in the genesis and evolution of human society, let us now attempt to summarize his analysis of social organization. In a community there are two forms of organization: one called the "social composition," combining those who dwell together in one specified place; the other, a constituent society, combining those who are desirous of carrying on special forms of activity or of maintaining particular interests. Each group in the social composition may be called a "component society." The earlier tribal forms of component societies were brought together by genetic aggregation, while the later civil component societies are the product, in addition, of congregation. Tribal societies insist on kinship as the bond of association; civil societies have broken that bond of ethnic unity. The path of development toward a civil organization of society, where kinship is of less value, has lain in the transition from the loosely knit, even segregative, matronymic group, generally the more primitive, to the more compact and powerful patronymic group, in the establishment of a barbaric and pastoral feudalism and in the effect of migration and settlement in producing a varied demotic composition in which the bond of kinship is no longer adequate. With the establishment of male descent and ancestor worship, clan headships and tribal chieftainships tended to become hereditary in certain families. Barbaric feudalism arose as the chief became wealthy in cattle and land, which he received as rewards from his tribe. It became his duty to protect the borders of his land, and for this purpose he used the broken and ruined men, the landless and the refugees from other clans, and bound them to him as feudal dependents in a bond of uncritical and unquestioning obedience. The development of this form of organization and a synchronous development of agriculture led to civil society, based on neighborhood, mutual interest, and co-operation.

In civil society, constituent societies wherein membership is not an incident of birth became possible. Constituent societies grow out of, and are differentiated from, component societies through a specialization of function; they are voluntarily formed purposive associations.

Their chief characteristics are co-ordination, mutual aid, and division of labor.[16] The chief of these purposive organizations in civil society is the state, through which the social mind operates to achieve the co-ordination and domination of the whole community and its lesser purposive associations. Its functions are coextensive with human interests, for its primary purpose is to perfect social integration. In so doing, it is carried into economic activities and cultural functions. Yet equally vital to social organization are the various private and voluntary associations which arise, duplicating in many cases the functions of the state: "The state, so far from being the only political organization, could not exist in a free or republican form, were there not voluntary and private political associations."[17] It follows, therefore, since the compulsory state and the voluntary association are both vital and essential, that "whatever belittles the state or destroys belief in its power to perform any kind of social service, whatever impairs the popular habit of achieving ends by private initiative and voluntary organization, endangers society and prevents the full realization of its ends."[18]

IV. SOCIAL CONTROL AND SOCIAL CONSTRAINT

Turning, now, to the second problem which Giddings enunciates as facing the sociologist, that of social constraint, we find him defining his point of view thus:

> We make the initial assumption that the institutions of human society and all the events of history, including the migrations of men from place to place, the great enthusiasms, the intellectual awakenings, the wars and the revolutions, may be regarded as responses to varying stimuli, and that they are governed by certain laws of combination or by certain facts of resemblance or of difference among the minds responding.[19]

That is, social constraint and the conformity of behavior and character to type are functions of the operation of the social mind. This social mind is no abstraction, nor, on the other hand, is it a mere summation of individual minds. It is an integration of them, born of their interaction: "The social mind is the phenomenon of many individual minds in interaction, so playing upon one another that they simultaneously feel the same sensation or emotion, arrive at one judgment and perhaps act in concert."[20] It is to be explained in terms of response to stimulation, of consciousness of kind, and of concerted volition.[21] From like response spring the phenomena of agreement and co-operation; from differences of response in kind, degree, and completeness come the innumerable phenomena of unlike interest, antagonism, conflict, rivalry, and competition.[22] The process of interstimulation is carried on by suggestion, impression, example, and imitation, with conflict as a co-efficient, and with forms of expansive association, such as travel, commerce, diplomacy, and war, as further determinants. With the accumulation, through the advance of socialization, of innumerable conditions, events, relations, acts, ideas, beliefs, plans, and ideals, there are created large classes of secondary stimuli which, in modern social life, play a greater role in the formation of the social mind than do the primary stimuli: "The very arrangements under which we live, the groupings of human beings, their ideas and purposes, their aims, their ideals, their laws and institutions are ever-present, ever-potent causes of continuing collective action."[23] These secondary stimuli are divisible into four classes: the ideomotor, directly inciting the motor system; the ideo-emotional, awakening chiefly emotional reactions; the dogmatic-emotional, appealing to emotion and belief; and the critically intellectual, appealing to the higher intellectual processes. Corresponding to these stimuli are classifications of like-mindedness, according to whether the individuals are swayed by feeling, emotion, belief, or reason, respectively. A correlation can be established between these psychic traits and the extent of the forms of like-mindedness. This correlation is expressed in the law: "More individuals agree in feeling than agree in belief. More agree in belief than concur in reasoned opinion. Sympathetic like-mindedness is more extensive than dogmatic like-mindedness, and dogmatic like-mindedness more extensive than deliberate like-mindedness."

This movement of the social mind may also be viewed from the standpoint of the modes of activity of the individual, the types of character that shape it, and the motives and ideals that are indorsed. The modes of activity of the individual are fourfold. There is, first, *appreciation,* the seizing of the facts of experience and their organization into knowledge, preference, and values. Next comes *utilization,* the turning to use of the objects of the external world. Then the conscious individual adapts himself to his situation, to the opportunities and activities possible to him, which constitute the process of *characterization.* Finally, conscious individuals adapt themselves to one another in the process of *socialization.*[24] Parallel with the complex of psychic states involved in appreciation are the motor, emotional, and intellectual types spoken of above. Parallel, in the same way, with the four degrees in which utilization is carried out are four types of disposition—the aggressive, the instigative, the domineering, and the creative. Thus, also, four types of character come into existence in the process of characterization—the forceful, the convivial, the austere, and the rationally conscientious. The former emphasizes the qualities of courage and power; the convivial is of the pleasure-loving type; the austere is the product of reaction against the excesses of convivial indulgence; while the last is a product of the reaction against and progress beyond the austere type.[25]

Correlated with the phenomena of the social mind and the form and degree of social constraint is the type of human rational society. Of this there are eight subdivisions: (1) A homogeneous community of blood relatives, among whom the chief social bond is sympathy—the *sympathetic* type. (2) The *congenial* type, made up of like spirits drawn together by similarity of nature and agreement in ideas. Illustrations of this type are found in the Mayflower band, the Latter-Day Saints, partisan political colonies, and communistic brotherhoods. (3) The *approbational* type, a community of miscellaneous and sometimes lawless elements drawn together by economic opportunity, where a general approbation of qualities and conduct is practically the only social bond. (4) The *despotic* type, where the social bonds are despotic power and a fear-inspired obedience. (5) The *authoritative* type, where the arbitrary power has identified itself with tradition and religion, and reverence for authority is the social bond. (6) The *conspirital* type, where intrigue and conspiracy are the social bonds. (7) The *contractual* type, such as the league of the Iroquois and the confederation of American commonwealths in 1778, where the social bond is a covenant or contract. (8) The *idealistic* social type, where a population collectively responds to certain great ideals, where the social bonds are comprehension of mind, confidence, fidelity, and an altruistic spirit of social service.[26]

The genetic standpoint from which Giddings approached sociology prompted him to lay slight stress upon the modes and forms of social control. He gives little space to the tribe in primitive society, the state and municipality in civil society, or the instruments of social control therein adopted. Only brief sketches are devoted to the influence of custom, law, the church, parental authority, and various voluntary associations.

Social control is compared with that of natural selection: it is control of variations from type. In the organic struggle for existence "there is

an environmental constraint compelling conformity of organic structure and of life to certain adapted or adaptable types, from which variation is possible only within somewhat definite limits."[27] In group life
"human beings, instinctively, by habit, and rationally, manifest a dominant antipathy to those variations from type which attract attention."[28]
Among savages and barbarians such persons are killed or abandoned.
In civilized societies they are suspected or avoided, guarded or restrained.
In savage and barbarian communities a considerable degree of uniformity of conduct is obtained: "by the conscious coöperation of elders
in directing the rearing of children by young parents, by organized initiation ceremonies, by clan and tribal councils, each new generation is
remorselessly trained in those beliefs, habits and loyalties which the
group regards as vital to its existence." While in civilized communities,
such "restraints, inculcations and obedience-compelling devices" are so
greatly interlaced as to be difficult to distinguish, they are found, when
stripped of all adventitious features, to be means to the same end, to
"determine, limit, and control variation from type, now extending its
range, now narrowing it and compelling a closer conformity."[29]

The method of constraint may be summed up in the one word "discipline." The methods are described in greater detail in the following
sentence: "By praise and blame, by avoidance and rebuke, by indulgence
and license, by penance and fine, by suspension and expulsion, by
corporal punishment and maiming, by imprisonment and execution,
men are forced to desist, to obey, to help; their conduct is educated into
habits; their efforts are stimulated or goaded to acceptable degrees of
intensity and persistence; their characters are moulded to approved
types."[30] These particular methods are employed in the "conviction that
such conformity to kind or type or standard is essential to security and
to coöperative efficiency."[31]

Social constraint is affected by environmental pressure and by the
composition and the degree of homogeneity of the population. The
character of the environment "determines the composition of a population as more or less heterogeneous, more or less compound," while "the
composition of the population determines the character, the complexity
and the range of its reactions to stimulation,"[32] including its mental
characteristics, its potentialities of co-operation, its capacity for progress,
its ideals, and the degree of its democratic organization. Environments
are either poorly or richly endowed, and each is either accessible or iso-

lated. The poor and isolated environment is filled with a sparse, relatively simple, and homogeneous population, where the struggle for existence causes a large proportion of the people to fall into the "middle age frequencies." A poor country, easy of egress, contains an equally homogeneous population, but one which, under the attraction of more favorable lands, suffers from the emigration of its more virile members. A rich land, but relatively isolated, like several of the South Sea island groups, carries a dense population in which every inequality of energy or ability counts. From this more favored land, under the pressure of the food supply, vigorous elements go forth to conquer new homes. Or, where a stronger race can do so, distant populations come to invade and exploit these rich natural resources. The bountiful and accessible environments furnished, for instance, by the great river valleys of the world form the seats of composite and varied populations, welded into an amalgam by conquest, immigration, and intermarriage.

The composition of the population limits the vigor and adaptiveness of its reactions to stimulation. A vigorous reaction is characteristic of adolescence and maturity; adaptation is difficult to the old. The ethnic composition of a population determines whether its total reaction to stimulation will be relatively simple or complex. A homogeneous population may be expected to show a reaction uncomplicated by conflicts between differing groups. A heterogeneous population will react to a greater number of stimuli; it will have a wider circle of interests. In the more heterogeneous populations, stimulation must be stronger before like behavior will result.

Social pressure generates countless forms of co-operation that can most appropriately be called "folkways." When these folkways have been affected by emotion, belief, reflection, and conscious inculcation and are to some extent socially enforced, they become "mores." Usage, custom, fashion, manners, ceremonies, ritual, morals—all these indefinable and flexible forms of social pressure operate upon the individual chiefly through penalties of disapprobation and ostracism.[33] More important mores, such as religion and justice, which apply social pressure through "boycotting, outlawry, and other social dooms, including death,"[34] are called "themistes."

On the third problem, the effect of social constraint upon selection, Giddings recognizes that association, though involving scarcely anything beyond involuntary social control, gives advantage in survival. It assists in perpetuating the race, in diminishing the expenditure and waste of energy, and in favoring the growth of intelligence. He holds a view differing in a measure from that of Fiske in regard to the relation of prolonged infancy to social development. He contends that association stimulated conceptual thought, which, in turn, reacted upon mental activity until it became man's dominant interest. A slower development of the individual and a longer infancy resulted.[35] Association favors survival by providing greater power of defense for the group, by affording a longer and more certain food supply, and by making maturity and reproduction of the race more certain. It makes variation more fruitful and gives survival-value to such social characteristics as toleration, sympathy, and compassion.

By emphasis upon the value of toleration, social constraint modifies selection. In the conflict which preceded the establishment of toleration "the very strong kill off the weak. Then the very strong in turn are overborne by the numerical superiority of the individuals of average power. The majority then left is composed of those that are too nearly equal in strength for one to hope to vanquish another, and they are obliged to live on terms of toleration that make possible the reassertion and renewed activity of the socializing motives."[36] Along with these objective conditions go subjective consequences, the chief of which is an idea of toleration, finding expression in rules of custom, formulating "those enjoyments and immunities that are habitually allowed."[37]

Society is a selective agent, for social selection converts survival of the fit into survival of the better. This is both an individual and a social matter: "Social conditions determine for each individual what elements of his personality shall be played upon by the influences that strengthen or weaken; what suggestions shall consciously or unconsciously give direction to his thoughts, quality to his feeling and so, at length, determination to his will."[38] The aim of society is to carry on the process of individuation without endangering race survival. The function of social control is "to increase the practical effectiveness of society as an instrumentality for the protection and improvement of life."[39] The social discipline in which it consists secures the extermination or restraint of the antisocial and the selection for survival and encouragement of the sympathetic, the intelligent, and the self-controlled. But social pressure, being mainly repressive and destructive, has distinct limits of utility. It curtails variation, limits differentiation, checks spontaneity, restricts individuality, and tends toward rigidity of social organization. There must, therefore, be a balance between the restraint that it imposes upon the antisocial and the freedom that it gives to the elements adapted to a social life. If it offers opportunity for the development of individuation without endangering race survival, it has turned the selective struggle of evolution into progress. For "race maintenance and evolution with diminishing cost of individual life, with increasing freedom, power and happiness of the individual person—is progress."[40]

V. CO-OPERATION, SOCIAL DISCIPLINE, AND SOCIAL INSTITUTIONS

The fourth problem, the final consequences of social constraint, conceived of as an amount or rate of progress, has much more attention given to it. Social constraint, which is, to Giddings, a form of concerted volition, co-operation, and discipline, is a chief factor in the organization of society. Organized society, in contrast to any of those imaginary states where every man's hand was against his neighbor, has become a mutually beneficial association for attaining security, opportunity, enjoyments, or improvements: "Society is a means to a definite end—namely, the survival and improvement of men through a continuing selection of intelligence and sympathy."[41] The development of community life meant more than the establishment of social order; it meant greater security, a social and economic surplus, more definite rights for the individuals, and the definition of those rights in codes of law interpreted and applied by specialized talents and institutions. Administrative agencies came to shape activities of society and were, in turn, reacted upon by the collective organization. Civil society gave opportunities and problems to intelligence and, in application and reaction to the economic, cultural, and political environment, produced a civilization that stands for the vast complex wealth of an intelligent humanity.

After this general statement we turn to an analysis of the policies whereby this co-operation was effected. Such policies are formed "through deliberation upon the composition, the character, and the circumstances of the community."[42] They are of two types, internal and external. The former have for their object the achievement of certain relations of unity, liberty, and equality within the group; the latter aim to achieve policies of subjugation, exploitation, and assistance between one group and another. Policies of unity aim to perfect the cohesion, the homogeneity, and the solidarity to the group through control of amalgamation and assimilation, of language and religion, of law and conduct. Policies of liberty are reactions against the restraints of excessive unification. They depend for their origin upon diversity of social composition, incomplete assimilation, and freedom of communication: "No scheme of unification ever quite destroys the restless individualism of the rational mind." Hence, when unifying policies have produced administrative order, and in part set the mind free for, and in part instigated it to, public agitation, destructive criticism, and even overt rebellion, an ideal of liberty arises, becoming actualized in the establishment and protection of individual liberty by forms of constitutional law. Policies of equality are reactions against the abuse of liberty and a limitation of it, so as to procure equality of liberty and opportunity. These policies include political and legal equality, the abolition of state-created privileges in economic activities, equality of educational opportunities, and socially remedial measures.

Policies of subjugation result in the integration of small ethnic groups into larger tribal systems and in the consolidation of small civil states into great political systems. Race struggles and class conflicts have also been, to a great extent, expressions of consciously formulated policies of subjugation. In policies of exploitation the economic motive has become ascendant. In most advanced modern civilizations both these policies tend to be superseded, in part, by policies of assistance, where "the powerful and prosperous classes of the relatively strong people extend educational advantages, relief of acute distress, and, to some extent, economic opportunity to the wage-earning classes, to inferior races and to dependent peoples."[43] It is of interest here to trace the connection that Giddings establishes between surplus energy and the policies of assistance.[44] Certain organisms develop surplus energy, which enables them to survive under the circumstances that cripple other organisms and to transmit to posterity a rich legacy of ability or to give their own generation much socially beneficial help. In the social sphere America, which has developed this surplus energy, has been able to extend assistance to Europe and the Orient:

Of all the modes of socially distributed surplus energy, the most important are sympathy and its allied elements in the consciousness of kind. Given this force, the transformations of the weak by the strong necessarily become to some extent an uplifting instead of an exploitation. Given the equilibration of energy through uplifting, there is a necessary growth of equality and an increasing possibility of successful democracy of the liberal type.[45]

In the development of these policies the internal and external varieties come to be combined in highly complex schemes. Thus internal policies of unification become combined with external policies of subjugation to produce militarism. Prior to attack, unity and cohesion are demanded in the attacking state, and to a great extent the organization of society becomes coercive. After the conquest and the establishment of a heterogeneous people, policies of unification again come into play, to secure uniformity in language, religion, and conduct, through criminal law, sumptuary administration, and isolation. Successful militarism prepares the way for exploitation and stimulates it; but in the long run militarism works out its own destruction. With the downfall of militarism, much administrative energy hitherto devoted to political integration, much economic activity hitherto diverted, and much intellectual energy hitherto suppressed are freed, and the result is a growth of liberalism. Diversity of peoples, laws, manners, and customs in the heterogeneous nation has a stimulating effect. Physical and mental plasticity results. The investigating, critical, and philosophical spirit arises. The nation becomes liberal and progressive and has to face the problem of pursuing policies that will maintain unity and stability and yet guarantee liberty and equality. To solve this problem it must perfect legal and rational methods of government and procedure.

The political ideas which come to guide this latter form of social development are transformed and converted into highly complex social values. Subjectively considered, these are judgments of the "utility, or goodness, or dignity, or importance, of any object, act or relation."[46] Socially considered, they are "the social estimates of things that are socially important."[47] First among these social values comes the type of conscious life characteristic of the society; next comes social cohesion; third, the distinctive possessions and properties of the community, such as territory, sacred places, national heroes, ceremonies, laws, worship, and amusements. Last in order of evolution are the "values attaching to certain abstract conditions that are favorable to social integrity and development, and to certain modes of effort that are intended to extend or to perfect the social type. The conditions are liberty, equality, and fraternity."[48] Social value, in the singular, means "regard or esteem for any social habit, relation, or institution which makes men cherish and defend it."[49]

What is the relation of this form of social valuation to progress? To this Giddings makes two answers, which differ only in their point of view: (1) "The rational improvement of society proceeds through a criticism of social values."[50] Society must accurately estimate the utility of every institution or custom and the cost and sacrifice involved not only in defending the old but also in renovating it and making possible developments along new lines. By this criticism the foundations of a rational social choice will be secured. (2) Social conduct is the resultant of a certain combination of social values, determined by rational choice. Group the social values in a certain way, and a certain form of social conduct will follow in obedience to the unchanging relations embodied in the laws of social choice. Progress then is dependent on (a) the formulation of the laws of rational social choice and (b) the combination of social values.

The laws of social choice may be formulated under two heads: (1) the law of preferences among ends to be achieved and (2) the law of the relation between interests and social choices.[51] These two laws, first sketched in the *Principles,* receive fuller statement in *Descriptive and Historical Sociology.*[52] The first one in full runs:

> In all social choice, the most influential ideals are those of the forceful man, the powerful community, of virtue in the primitive sense of the word; second in influence are ideals of the convivial man, the prosperous and pleasure-loving community, the utilitarian or hedonistic virtues; third in influence are ideals of the austere man, the righteous or just community, the Stoic or Puritan virtues of self-restraint; fourth in influence are the ideals of the rationally conscientious man, of the liberal and enlightened community, of the virtues of reasonableness, broad-mindedness and charity [but, if mental and moral evolution are to continue], the higher ideals [must] become increasingly influential.

The second law is formulated in terms of interests, that is, of "the elements, modes and means of good." Varied experiences and manifold interests lead any distinct section of society to "choose, select or decide, strictly in accordance with the mental characteristics that these different experiences have developed."[53] The law runs:

> A population that has only a few interests, which, however, are harmoniously combined, is conservative in its choices. A population that has varied interests, which are as yet inharmoniously combined, is radical in its choices. Only the population that has many, varied and harmoniously combined interests is consistently progressive in its choices.[54]

Functionally, therefore, progress depends upon the establishment, step by step, of the higher ideals named in the first law and the creation of the many, varied, and harmoniously combined interests named in the second. To that end certain "public utilities" must be realized. First in functional importance, though often last in genetic order, stands security of life, of territory, and of institutions. This security includes both international peace and domestic peace and order: "To secure and to maintain these, as far as possible, is the supreme function of the political system."[55] Next in functional order comes equity, "a certain compromise and reconciliation of the differing interests and claims of the individuals, the racial elements and the classes, making up the social population." To adjust these differing interests and claims requires some restriction of the liberty of the strong to curtail the liberty of the weak. The only practical method for conserving and extending liberty has been by establishing certain objective modes of equality. Only an approximation to such equality will insure progress in liberty, prosperity, and enlightenment. Springing out of this principle of utility comes public control of the economic system, in the interest of a greater equality of economic opportunity, and a tendency toward complete equality of cultural advantages.[56] To these public utilities, as the functional content of social progress, must be added a formal test of efficiency. The organization must benefit the organized and must be regarded by the members as beneficial.

Considering progress as an end to be attained, these public utilities fall into place as means to an ultimate end, which is "life in its higher developments, especially its moral and intellectual developments.... a social nature, or personality, adapted to social coöperation and enjoyment. This social personality .... is the ultimate end of social organization."[57] The development of the social personality is measured both positively and negatively. Positively it consists in the increase of vitality, sound mentality, morality, and sociality. Negatively it connotes a decrease in the number of the defective, the abnormal, the immoral, and the degraded. Practically it includes a eugenic program, based along its positive side on a "pure and sane family life, which disciplines the welcome and untainted child in the robust virtue of self-control, and in an unswerving allegiance to duty,"[58] and, on the negative side, on a ruthless suppression of the feeble-minded and other dysgenetic stocks.

VI. THE QUANTITATIVE METHOD IN SOCIOLOGY

In handling the descriptive and historical material of sociology, Giddings took a position in which, as a sociologist, he stood almost alone at the time. His evolutionary standpoint enabled him to pass naturally and logically to a statistical treatment of the objective subject matter of sociology. Collective behavior is typical and modal: "To the extent that safety and prosperity depend upon group cohesion and coöperation, they are seen to depend upon such conformity to type as may suffice to insure the cohesion and to fulfil the coöperation."[59] "Sociology is the science of the origin, the process, the extent and the results of type control of variation from itself, within a group of more or less freely associating individuals."[60] "Society is a type, controlling variation from itself for its own survival and further evolution."[61] Therefore it preeminently calls for precise or quantitative study by the statistical method;[62] for the phenomena of type can always be expressed in the statistical terms of "frequency" and "mode." When the full significance of the many statistical reports available today is realized, greater progress will be made in statistical sociology. There may also be needed some development of statistical terminology and methodology, for frequencies of sort, which predominate in our large collections of data in census and other reports, are not held to be so amenable to the present statistical methods as frequencies of size. Rates of births and deaths, of marriage and divorce, are numerical and measurable, being items of number and size. But numbers of illiterates, of foreign- and native-born, of adherents of religious denominations, of delinquents and dependents, and so on are frequencies of sort.

Some of the feasible points of attack have been suggested by Professor Giddings. From an analysis of the statutory enactments of legislative bodies, it is possible to obtain index numbers to measure social pressure.[63] The work of state and municipal commissions could be tested statistically, as also could the struggle for mastery between integral society and the corporations. More important are such problems as the measure of social constraint, the extent of human variation, and the range of socialization and individuation. The first of these affords an instance of the value of a knowledge of normality and of the meaning and significance of variation.

The extent of social mutation, in which the ameliorative effects of social organization are reflected, is obviously a matter for statistical investigation.[64] While measures of such variations and especially of the preferences and characterizations which are called for in many sociological inquiries have not yet been adequately established, the purpose and method of sociology must be to discover "ratios, modalities, coefficients of variation и nd correlations."[65]

The question, how much restraint, how much liberty, how much conformity to type, how much variation from it, are conducive to the general welfare, is the supremely important question in all issues of public policy. The right answer to it turns upon the determination of the previous question, namely, what is normal social constraint in a given community, at a given stage of its evolution, and what at a given moment is the actual range of fluctuation? .... To obtain, then, determinations of normal social constraint for modern communities, including municipalities, commonwealths and nations, and to perfect the methods of measuring fluctuations must, I think, be regarded as the chief object of sociological effort in the immediate future. That that effort will be successful is, I am convinced, a fairly safe prediction.[66]

To sum up, Giddings approaches the social process from the standpoint of a psychologist who is also a statistician and a scientist. In one single sentence he defines the subject matter of the science and determines its method: "Pluralistic behavior is the subject matter of the psychology of society, otherwise called Sociology, a science statistical in method, which attempts, first, to factorize pluralistic behavior, and, second, to explain its genesis, integration, differentiation and functioning by accounting for them in terms of the variables, (1) stimulation, and (2) the resemblance (more or less) to one another of reacting mechanisms."[67] Around these two variables his whole sociological theory revolves.[68]

NOTES

1. Franklin Henry Giddings (1855–1931) was probably the ablest sociologist that the United States has ever produced, and among sociologists abroad perhaps only Durkheim, Hobhouse, and Max Weber would rank with him. He was less impressively erudite than Lester F. Ward, but he had a more penetrating mentality and greater capacity for theoretical formulation and analysis.

Giddings was born in Sherman, Connecticut, in 1855. His father was an orthodox and puritanical Congregationalist minister, and Giddings' strong reaction in mature life against orthodoxy and puritanism can probably be traced mainly to his early surroundings. He received an engineering training at Union College but entered journalism in Springfield, Massachusetts, where he remained for ten years on the *Springfield Republican* and the *Springfield Union*. He succeeded Woodrow Wilson as professor of politics at Bryn Mawr College in 1888 and accepted the newly created chair of sociology at Columbia University in 1894. Here he taught as professor of sociology and the history of civilization until shortly before his death in 1931.

Giddings possessed a most impressive personality and a remarkable gift for both the oral and the written exposition of his thoughts. Had he entered public life he would have been a distinguished political orator. He impressed his students with his personal vigor and gusto, but the more serious and alert among them were disconcerted by the often careless and informal conduct of his classes. No other American sociologist could lecture with the power, conciseness, and organization that Giddings could exhibit when he wished to do so, but he rarely conducted a course systematically, and, at times, a course of lectures might bear little apparent relation to the subject matter announced. This was especially true after 1914. In a certain sense, Giddings was an intellectual "war casualty." He was veritably obsessed with anti-Germanism, which, after 1918, turned into anti-Bolshevism, and for years his lectures were more often diatribes against his pet hates than calm sociological analysis. But, however little they might contribute to sociological clarification, they were always interesting and stimulating.

While of a kindly and sympathetic disposition, Giddings was a markedly dominating personality and very dogmatic in his views. He insisted upon doctrinal loyalty, not to say worship, from his departmental colleagues. For this reason he surrounded himself with satellites rather than equals or professional rivals. In this way he stood at the opposite extreme from the other leading academic sociologist of his day, Dean Albion W. Small, of the University of Chicago, and was prevented thereby from building up anything like the impressive department of sociology which Small created at Chicago. (This biographical material is supplied by the editor and Dr. Northcott has no responsibility for the opinions expressed.)

2. Among Giddings' more important books are the following: *Principles of Sociology* (New York, 1896), far and away his most important work and probably the most important single volume yet to be published in the sociological field; *Elements of Sociology* (New York, 1898), the best brief statement of Giddings' early sociological ideas; *Democracy and Empire* (New York, 1900), the best synthesis of Giddings' views on public questions and a defense of American imperialism; *Inductive Sociology* (New York, 1901), a syllabus of principles and problems, with suggestions for further research; *Descriptive and Historical Sociology* (New York, 1904), a further summary and development of sociological principles, with illustrative readings; *The Responsible State* (Boston, 1918), the application of sociological principles to political science, colored by Giddings' wartime psychology and anti-Germanism; *Studies in the Theory of Human Society* (New York, 1922), the most important restatement of his theoretical sociology since the publication of the *Principle of Sociology; The Scientific Study of Human Society* (Durham, N.C., 1924), the most extended of Giddings' arguments for the inductive and statistical method in sociology; *The Mighty Medicine* (New York, 1930), an application of sociological principles to education and religion; and a posthumous volume, *Civilization and Society* (New York, 1932), summarizing his theories and principles.

For good surveys of Giddings' life and contributions to sociology see J. L. Gillin, in H. W. Odum, *American Masters of Social Science* (New York, 1927), chap. vii; and F. H. Hankins, "Franklin Henry Giddings, 1855–1931: Some Aspects of His Sociological Theory," *American Journal of Sociology*, November, 1931, pp. 349–67. Gillin is strongest on the personal side and Hankins on the theoretical.

3. Cf. *Sociology* (New York, 1911), p. 32.

4. *Theory of Human Society*, p. 259.

5. *Descrptive and Historical Sociology*, p. 289; cf. also the treatment in the *Theory of Human Society, passim.*

6. *Principles of Sociology*, p. 114.

7. *Sociology*, p. 32; cf. also *Theory of Human Society*, pp. 267–68.

8. *Ibid.*, p. 261.

9. *Theory of Human Society*, p. 274.

10. Quoted from unpublished lectures; cf. also *Theory of Human Society*, p. 87.

11. Quoted from unpublished lectures; cf. also *Theory of Human Society*, p. 87.

12. *Descriptive and Historical Sociology*, p. 359; *The Responsible State*, chap. iii.

13. Cf. *Descriptive and Historical Sociology*, p. 373.

14. *Principles of Sociology*, p. 421.

15. Cf. *The Responsible State*, pp. 75–78.

16. *Theory of Human Society*, pp. 269–72.

17. *Inductive Sociology*, p. 217.

18. *Descriptive and Historical Sociology*, p. 515.

19. "Theory of Social Causation," *Publications of the American Economic Association*, 1903, p. 144.

20. *Principles of Sociology*, p. 134; cf. also *Theory of Human Society*, p. 266.

21. *Inductive Sociology*, p. 68.

22. *Descriptive and Historical Sociology*, p. 128.

23. *Ibid.*, p. 176.

24. *Ibid.*, p. 127.

25. *Democracy and Empire*, pp. 317–20.

26. *Descriptive and Historical Sociology*, pp. 11–13.

27. *Theory of Human Society*, chap. xii; cf. also p. 202.

28. *Ibid.*, p. 203.

29. *Ibid.*, p. 204.

30. *Ibid.*, p. 206.

31. *Ibid.*

32. *Ibid.*, p. 147; cf. chap. viii.

33. *Ibid.;* cf. also pp. 192–94, 264.

34. *Ibid.*, p. 264.

35. *Principles of Sociology*, p. 229.

36. *Descriptive and Historical Sociology*, p. 315.

37. *Principles of Sociology*, p. 142.

38. *Ibid.*, p. 380.

39. *Sociology*, p. 34.

40. *Ibid.*, p. 36; cf. also *Theory of Human Society*, pp. 118–19.

41. *Theory of Human Society*, p. 246; cf. also chap. xiv.

42. *Descriptive and Historical Sociology*, pp. 395 ff.; cf. also *Theory of Human Society*. pp. 278–81.

43. *Descriptive and Historical Sociology*, p. 415.

44. *Theory of Human Society*, p. 280.

45. *Descriptive and Historical Sociology*, p. 416.

46. *Ibid.*, p. 393.

47. *Principles of Sociology*, p. 147.

48. *Ibid.*, p. 149.

49. *Democracy and Empire*, p. 59; cf. also *Theory of Human Society*, p. 173.

50. *Democracy and Empire*, p. 59.

51. *Principles of Sociology*, pp. 409–11.

52. P. 351.

53. *Inductive Sociology*, p. 181.

54. *Ibid.*

55. *Descriptive and Historical Sociology*, p. 526.

56. *Ibid.*, pp. 526–28.

57. *Ibid.*, p. 523.

58. *Principles of Sociology*, p. 352.

59. *Political Science Quarterly*, XXIV, 575; see also *Theory of Human Society*, pp. 202, 206–8, 282, 286.

60. *Political Science Quarterly*, XXIV, 578.

61. *Ibid.*, p. 580; cf. also *Theory of Human Society*, pp. 202, 206.

62. For a full discussion see his *Scientific Study of Human Society*.

63. *Quarterly Publications of the American Statistical Association*, March, 1908.

64. *Ibid.*, p. 286.

65. *Ibid.*, p. 300.

66. *Theory of Human Society*, p. 208.

67. *Ibid.*, p. 252.

68. *The Scientific Study of Human Society*, several chapters of which appeared in the *Journal of Social Forces*, 1923–24; and an article, "Stimulation Ranges and Reaction Areas," *Psychological Review*, November, 1924.

CHAPTER XXXIX

ALBION WOODBURY SMALL: PROMOTER OF AMERICAN SOCIOLOGY AND EXPOSITOR OF SOCIAL INTERESTS

Harry Elmer Barnes

I. INTRODUCTION

W E SHALL attempt in the following pages to present an estimate of the work of Albion Woodbury Small (1854–1926), considered in its relation to the history of modern sociology as a whole. An article by Annie Marion MacLean in the *American Journal of Sociology* (July, 1926), and a chapter by Edward Cary Hayes in Odum's *American Masters of Social Science* have described his personal life and academic career, and we shall bring that interesting story into the present chapter only in so far as it is directly related to the nature and influence of Small's sociological doctrines and objectives.

It is also obvious that we cannot in the space available for this article present a summary of all Dean Small's varied and voluminous writings in the field of sociology and social economics. We shall limit ourselves primarily to (1) an analysis of the origins of his sociological interests and doctrines; (2) the leading stages in the progress of his sociological thinking and writing; (3) his chief books, as related to his sociological thought; (4) his fundamental sociological conceptions; and (5) his academic and editorial activities that bear upon the growth of sociology.

II. THE BACKGROUND OF SMALL'S SOCIOLOGICAL INTERESTS AND EQUIPMENT

While Small was, from the standpoint of chronology, influence, and activities, one of the "founders" of sociology, his writings were a sort of transition from the "systematizers," like Comte, Spencer, Ward, Giddings, and Stuckenberg, who dealt with all, or nearly all, the various fields and problems of sociology, to the subsequent generation of specialists who have approached social analysis from the standpoint of

766

methodology, anthropogeography, biology, psychology, cultural analysis, institutional history, social economics, or human betterment. Small soared magisterially at times with the systematizers; at other times he made extremely profound and cogent contributions to social economics; and he always believed himself to be notably furthering the cause of sociological methodology. While, in his later years, he looked upon himself as in large part a specialist, concentrating upon the problems of methodology, he lacked the training to function effectively as a rigorous methodologist. What he meant, for the most part, when speaking of "method" was, in reality, an attitude toward, or the results to be gained from, social analysis. He was, likewise, too much absorbed in his general sociological interests to break away long enough to produce any large amount of specialized writing in the fields in which he was particularly proficient, namely, history, social economics, and social politics.

In the comprehensive summary of the history, problems, and fields of sociology contained in his article on "Sociology" in the *Encyclopedia Americana,* Small points out that, until very recently, the majority of American sociologists were not trained as sociologists from the beginning of their academic careers but were recruited from the fields of theology, history, economics, or political science.

In his own case Small was "recruited" from all these fields. Though he did not serve long as a preacher, he was trained in theology at the Newton Theological Institution from 1876 to 1879. The years 1879–81 Small spent in Germany at the universities of Leipzig and Berlin, where he pursued his studies in the above-mentioned subjects. Particularly important were his courses under the great German social economists, Gustav Schmoller and Adolf Wagner. It was here that he delved deeply into the subject of the conflict of interests and classes in human society and was thoroughly indoctrinated with the constructive German views as to the propriety and effectiveness of state supervision of the social process. These two basic doctrines were the core of Small's thinking in social science and his ablest contributions to sociological thought in America.

After teaching at Colby College for some years, Small attended Johns Hopkins University during the year 1888–89, and here he continued his historical studies. The "Adams School" of historians based their work in part upon the dubious Teutonic and Aryan hypotheses, as

applied to the evolution of political institutions; but they were, nevertheless, primarily interested in that comparative and genetic approach
to historical problems which is of special value to the sociologist as
training in the problems of social genesis. While at Johns Hopkins, Small
produced an important and undeservedly ignored monograph on *The
Origins of American Nationality*. Though his experience at Johns Hopkins helped to impress upon Small the significance of the genetic approach to social institutions, he never forgave the historians for their
narrowness, their provincialism, their perversion of method from a
means into an end itself, and the limited and superficial scope of their
interests. In his discussion of Professor F. H. Giddings' paper on "A
Theory of Social Causation" at the New Orleans meeting in 1903 he
said, in part, of the historians:

> The quarrel of the sociologists with the historians is that the latter have learned
> so much about how to do it that they have forgotten what to do. They have become
> so skilled in finding facts that they have no use for the truths that would make
> the facts worth finding. They have exhausted their magnificent technique in dis-
> covering things that are not worth knowing when they get through with them.
> These discoveries may be taken up by somebody else and brought into their mean-
> ing relations, but history, as it is mostly written today, does not come within sight
> of these relations. The historians are locating cinders on the face of the glacier, but
> they overlook the mountain ranges that carry the glacier.
> When we once start to study human affairs, there is no stoppingplace, on any
> other ground than confession of mental incompetence, till we reach answers to
> these questions: What are the essentials in human relations? In what varieties do
> these essentials appear under different circumstances? How do we account for these
> universals and their accidents? What pointers does this knowledge give us about
> our own conduct?[1]

Economics, political science, and history, in the order named, were
Small's chief stock in trade in his sociological work. To these he added
a broad synthetic aim, with the end in view of diminishing the narrowness and suspicion prevalent among the various branches of social science and of pooling their mutual resources and results in one common
service, namely, that of a clearer and more profound understanding of
the social process as a whole. Small was, however, in no sense a master
of anthropogeography, biology, psychology, or anthropology, which
placed definite limitations upon his efforts to attain a comprehensive
approach to the analysis of the social process. He was also relatively innocent of statistical methods, which was a grave handicap to his ambitious efforts in the field of general sociological methodology.

III. THE GENESIS OF SMALL'S SOCIOLOGICAL THINKING

In his *General Sociology* Small states that the history of sociology may be described as "a gradual shifting of effort from analogical representation of social structures to real analysis of social processes." This characterization also admirably describes the progress of Small's own sociological achievements. Owing to his reading of Schäffle and the other "Organicists," his earliest sociological writings exhibit the influence of this group of writers, whose chief interest lay in the elaboration of the analogies between the individual organism and the social organism. This is particularly evident in Books III and IV of his *Introduction to the Study of Society*. Yet he was never guilty of any of the absurdities of many of these writers in going to grotesque extremes in elaborating such analogies. He used the analogical method in a very sensible and discriminating manner as an effective mode of illuminating his description of social processes and institutions.

His studies with the German economists, especially Schmoller's exposition of the conflict of classes, impressed upon Small the importance of material interests in the social process. His work on the history of economics in the nineteenth century convinced him, however, of the narrowness of the classical economists' view of interests, a conviction which was buttressed by his own theological and religious training and by the fundamentally ethical orientation of his thought from his student days to his death.

This led Small to the conviction that the cataloguing and classification of a broader and more inclusive schedule of human interests and the description of their emergence, conflict, and adjustment in human society constitute the key to any truly dynamic sociology. He worked along this line himself during the last decade of the nineteenth century, and, about 1900, he came upon the leading works of Gustav Ratzenhofer, who had simultaneously developed the same mode of approach to social analysis. Small's *General Sociology* is a synthesis of his own views, independently arrived at, with the contributions of Ratzenhofer. It was his study of the struggle and accommodation of social interests that brought Small to his larger conception of society as a "becoming" or "emerging" process, which constitutes the dynamics of his system.

The conception of the *group* as the core of organized interests and the unit of the social process led Small to what he called his "methodological" studies, namely, his discussions of sociology as primarily a study of man and society viewed in relation to the group basis of life. He never tired of emphasizing this point of view, and almost his last intellectual effort was a circular letter of September 11, 1924, on this subject, brought forth by Professor Malcolm M. Willey's review of his *Origins of Sociology*.

Though the ethical element was never absent from Small's writings and teachings, his interest in social betterment increased as years went on. Indeed, from the first, he held that sociology owed both its origins and its justification to its potential services as a guide to a valid program of social reform. To him ethics was not primarily a matter of sexual purity but an improvement of social institutions and intellectual life. Both the wrecking of a major railroad system, through the predatory manipulation of high finance, and the obstructive stupidities of a bigoted fundamentalism seemed to him worse sins than adultery. He was particularly interested in the mitigation of capitalism and in the substitution of service for profit as the basic motive of economic organization and activity. His general notions in this field were expressed in his *Between Eras: From Capitalism to Democracy,* and much more systematically in his famous university course on "The Conflict of Classes."

There is thus to be seen in the development of Small's sociological interests a logical sequence of doctrinal evolution. An intelligent appreciation of the organic analogy emphasized the primary significance of function as compared with structure. The analysis of function led to his conception of the importance of the manifestation and accommodation of interests in society. This, in turn, created the notion of society as a process of social conflict, ultimately transformed under state control into socialization and co-operative endeavor. The social process was, however, seen to be a group affair, and this made it evident that sociology is primarily an analysis of the group aspects of life. Finally, the understanding of the social process is a purely academic matter unless the information so gathered can be exploited in the service of social betterment, which fact makes it clear that the ultimate purpose of sociology is to initiate and encourage a broader approach to social ethics.

IV. SMALL'S CHIEF WRITINGS AND THEIR PLACE IN
SOCIOLOGICAL LITERATURE

With the possible exception of his *Between Eras,* Small's books all grew out of his classroom lectures and seminar discussions. This accounts in part for the colloquial nature of some of them and the lack of literary and textual finish which characterizes most of them. Tables of contents and extensive excerpts from books analyzed were freely embodied in the text of his books. Even many of his articles published in the *American Journal of Sociology* and subsequently embodied in his books were read in his classes or seminars.

His first publications in the field of sociology were three syllabi for a course in social science in Colby College, the first of these being the earliest printed foundation of a course in sociology in this country. Next came his *Intrcduction to the Study of Society,* in the preparation of which he had the collaboration of his student and colleague, George M. Vincent. This was published in 1894, two years after he went to the University of Chicago to become head of the new department of sociology there. It was a pioneer work in which he endeavored to chart the field of sociology and to present its main problems within the scope of a college manual. It dealt with the province and development of sociology, described the evolution of society from isolated agrarian entities to the modern metropolitan groups, analyzed social structures and functions on the basis of the organic analogy, and risked a highly rudimentary excursion into social psychology. If the work seems an archaic curiosity at the present time, this is only an indication of the progress in social science since 1894, when the book was literally an intellectual adventure.

By all odds the most substantial and enduring of Small's work was his *General Sociology,* published in 1905 and reprinted many times thereafter. The first part of the book is a sketch of representative stages in the history of sociology. Then comes a presentation of Ratzenhofer's conception of sociology as primarily a classification of human interests and an analysis of their significance in the social process. Next follows a detailed discussion of the social process, in which Ratzenhofer's conceptions are extensively supplemented by those of Small. The work concludes with a sociological consideration of ethical problems and methods. This section constitutes a profound and courageous effort to relate the ethical concepts and problems of society to the social process and to provide a positive basis for ethical judgments and social betterment. In many respects the book contains basic contributions to economic and politics that are quite as important as those to sociology itself.

Following the *General Sociology* came the *Adam Smith and Modern Sociology,* published in 1907. Here Small considered Smith a harbinger of modern sociology, on the basis of Smith's economic-ethical doctrines. Giddings had, a decade before, traced at least his own version of sociology to the psychological theory of sympathy in Smith's *Theory of Moral Sentiments*. As Small interpreted Smith, he was very really a forerunner of Small from the standpoint of his analysis of the social process. According to Small, *The Wealth of Nations* was, in reality, a treatise on sociology with a special emphasis on the economic processes of society. As Small says:

> If one were to come upon *The Wealth of Nations* for the first time, with a knowledge of the general sociological way of looking at society, but with no knowledge of economic literature, there would be not the slightest difficulty nor hesitation about classifying the book as an inquiry in a special field of sociology..... Smith set a new standard of inquiry into the economic section of the conditions of life, while life presented itself to him as, on the whole, a moral affair, in which the economic process is logically a detail..... Modern sociology is virtually an attempt to take up the larger program of social analysis and interpretation which was implicit in Adam Smith's moral philosophy, but which was suppressed for a century by prevailing interest in the technique of the production of wealth.[2]

It would be difficult to state more precisely in the same number of words Small's own view of socioeconomic problems or the nature of his major contribution to the science of society. Small's book on Smith is, incidentally, an effective indictment of the tendency of the economists —or "pecuniary logicians"—of the last century to concentrate upon the wealth interest in society, to exaggerate its significance, and to consider it in relative isolation from the other social factors. Small expresses his view on this matter in the following paragraph:

> Applying these generalities to the case in hand, the question which the sociologist is always implicitly asking of the economist is: To what extent are you making your analyses and passing your valuations of economic activities as though they were bounded by the wealth interest alone, and to what extent do your analyses and valuations take account of the whole process of moral evolution within which the wealth interest is an incident? Economic theory, in England and America, throughout the nineteenth century made the wealth interest unduly prominent in the process of moral evolution, and thereby introduced confusion into the whole scale of moral valuation. The present essay makes a beginning of showing this in detail. The principal methodological thesis which the exhibit is to support is that a sufficient interpretation of life to be a reliable basis for social programs must express economic relations at last in terms of the whole moral process. This is true of political economy in so far as it purports to be more than a technology of things. To the degree in which political economy proposes to establish norms for evaluating the activities of persons, it must answer to the whole moral process in which all the activities of persons derive their meaning.[3]

Small's most erudite volume, *The Cameralists,* was the fourth in the list of his publications. This was a thorough study of that type of German social, economic, and political doctrine which was, in a rough way, the analogue of British mercantilism. Small was interested in cameralism, both as a forerunner of the synthetic social science for which he was laboring and as an example of the exploitation of social science to guide public policy and social betterment. He thus explains the interest which led him through this painstaking but thankless compilation:

This system of ideas and of practice had been developing since 1555. It did not correspond in its subdivisions with later academic definitions of the social sciences. It started not as a general theory but as a formulation of administrative expediency. It set forth with the frank purpose of subordinating everything within the control of the state to the state's problem of existence. The central question to which cameralism elaborated answers was: The ruler being all-powerful over his territories and his subjects, what policies, and what details of practice in pursuance of the policies must he adopt, in order to make his rule most secure at home, and in order to provide most abundant means of asserting himself against other rulers? It would require but little reflection to prepare against surprise at what happened. Under the circumstances of the time, this question necessarily led to answers which amounted to prescribed programs covering the entire outward life of the subjects of German rulers. It soon became evident to the advisers of those rulers, and to the administrators of their states, that their problem involved not merely physical factors, but that it was a question of training the whole population for all the different sorts of useful work of which human beings are capable. From generation to generation the men who developed cameralistic theory and practice saw more and more clearly that if the rulers of German states were to command abundant resources, they must rule over resourceful people. This meant that the people must be trained physically, mentally, morally, and technically. In the end, therefore, cameralistic theory covered everything in the lives of the citizens, from farm work to religious worship. The machinery for administering this theory grew more and more complex. In detail its organization differed in one state from that in another. Its main purpose was everywhere the same, viz., to make the people as amenable as possible to all the discipline necessary to insure maximum performance of all the physical, mental, and moral processes tributary to the strength of the ruler.

It need not be pointed out that this program involved dealing from this special point of view, with every sort of activity which has since come under the attention of political science and political economy in their latest forms. In so far as cameralism dealt with economic questions in the later sense, it treated them as matters primarily of the state, not of individuals. German economic theory, therefore, was collectivistic in the highest degree. Only incidentally, and in a wholly subordinate degree, was it individualistic. It was a theory of, for and by the government.[4]

Small's fifth book, *The Meaning of Social Science,* was a telling attack upon the unfortunate tendency to departmentalize the social sciences in the nineteenth century, with the resulting suspicion, jealousy, narrowness, and incomplete analyses of social situations. Small's healthy contempt for the departmental bigotry of the social scientists constitutes a leading thread running through all his writings. It appears as early as his first syllabus prepared in the eighties at Colby College, and in one of his very latest published reviews he came back to the matter with all his old time vigor:

Without essential perversion, the story of the social sciences in the United States during the past generation might be told under the figure of a pack of mongrels foraging for their keep and each snarling at each whenever one found a consumable bite. All the needed reduction of exaggeration in the analogy might be effected by the substitute that until recently the typical American social scientist has acted as though he feared that the supply of truth in the world is not enough to go around, and that his share of its might run short if anybody else went in search of it along any but his own beaten paths. The social scientists have manifested a maximum of short-diametered clannishness each toward his own kind, and a minimum of magnanimity toward everybody else. The result has been stunted and shriveled social scientists and social science.[5]

The major theses defended in *The Meaning of Social Science* are: (1) that knowledge of society must be unified, however much specialization may be needed in different types of investigation; (2) that there can be no adequate social science which does not take into account all phases of human experience and their interaction upon one another; and (3) that the chief purpose of social science is to arrive at a valid appraisal of human values, with the aim of promoting the creation of a more adequate and just social order. Some of his more decisive statements upon these points follow:

Whatever else may be true or false about sociology, its reason for existence is something which does not shut it off nor set it apart from other social sciences. On the contrary, its essence is an assertion which must be the center of all sane social science, namely, that knowledge of human experience cannot at last be many; in the degree in which it approaches reality it must be one knowledge. . . . .

Sociologists declare that the experience bounded by the reactions between men and physical nature, on the one hand, and the reactions of men with one another, on the other, is an interconnected experience, and that we shall have a science of it only in the proportion of our insight into the way and degree in which each item of this experience is affected by every other item of it.[6]

Much the most striking and original of Small's works was his *Between Eras: From Capitalism to Democracy,* published in 1913. This is one of the most outspoken and courageous books yet published in America, but the peculiar nature of the presentation of the material in the form of dialogues prevented any extensive circulation of the work, and it created little stir.

Between Eras is as relentless a criticism of our conventional unmitigated capitalism as can be found in Veblen's *Theory of the Leisure Class, The Theory of Business Enterprise,* and *Absentee Ownership;* in Tawney's *Acquisitive Society;* or in the Webbs' *Decay of Capitalist Civilization.* In arriving at his critical attitude toward capitalism and his unusually frank and capable analysis of capitalistic institutions, Small was greatly influenced by Schäffle, Schmoller, and Veblen, but, beyond all others, by Werner Sombart, whose *Moderne Kapitalismus* came into his hands about 1905.

Small adopted the quasi-socialistic thesis that nature and labor are the sole ultimate factors in productivity. He showed the ethical bankruptcy of the profit economy and thoroughly exposed the wastes, inefficiency, and injustices of capitalistic exploitation. He attacked the whole conception of the inheritance of immense fortunes, carrying with them extensive financial and industrial control. He made clear the fictitious nature of the divine-right theory of unlimited private property, which was the veritable cornerstone of our American *Politik* and economic system. In the place of the profit economy he would substitute the conception of production for human service under state supervision. Inheritance should be severely limited and labor given its just share in the control of industrial enterprise and social policy. As a startling and suggestive work, *Between Eras* can, without exaggeration, be compared with Plato's *Republic,* and its dialogues are much more cogent and relevant for contemporary readers than those contained in the work of the great Greek.

The same line of analysis, in a somewhat more conservative vein, was carried on by Small in one of his last utterances—an article on "The Sociology of Profits," published in the *American Journal of Sociology* for January, 1925. The fundamental principles and positions expounded in *Between Eras* were set forth in much more thorough and formal fashion in Small's famous course on the "Conflict of Classes," and it is a great misfortune that the material in this course was never published systematically in book form.

While it was printed in the *American Journal of Sociology* for May, 1916, Small's "Fifty Years of Sociology in the United States" (1865–1915) was in reality a book.[6a] It is an invaluable source for the history of

American social science, particularly in its academic aspects, and it contains much autobiographical material. It was based upon unique personal reminiscences and careful research. The monograph also contained much upon the development of sociological methods and objectives. It is admirably supplemented by his article on "The Future of Sociology," which appeared in the *Publications of the American Sociological Society* for 1920. He also left unpublished a work on the history of sociological method in the United States which we may hope will ultimately see light.

Small's last work was his *Origins of Sociology,* published in 1924. It is a comprehensive history of outstanding tendencies in German social science during the nineteenth century. Particular attention is given to those Germanic influences which helped to shape American social science between 1800 and 1900. As an authority on the subjects covered in this book, Small was without a rival in the United States.

In this work he selected the following topics to illustrate the development of social science in Germany during the nineteenth century: (1) the Savigny-Thibaut controversy as illustrative of the development of the concept of continuity in the historical and social process; (2) Eichhorn's emphasis on the complexity of social and historical situations; (3) Niebuhr's contributions to the scientific scrutiny and evaluation of historical sources; (4) Leopold von Ranke's insistence upon adequate documentation in historical narrative and generalizations; (5) the organization of source and archival material through the labors of Pertz, Waitz, and the editors of the *Monumenta;* (6) cameralism and the rise of objectivism in the social sciences; (7) the rise of systematic economics with Adam Smith and the classical school; (8) the development of systematic historical methodology by Bernheim; (9) the development of economics along the lines of comparative economic history by Wilhelm Roscher; (10) Karl Menger and presentation of the psychological point of view in economics; (11) Karl Knies and the entry of the ethical factor into economic science; (12) Schäffle, Schmoller, Wagner, and the professorial sociologists, who insisted upon the social and ameliorative point of view in economic and political activity; (13) the Treitschke-Schmoller controversy, which illustrated the clash of the individualistic and social points of view in *Politik;* (14) the contributions of Albert Schäffle in the way of introducing the sociological approach to economics; (15) the work of the Ahrens–Von Mohl group in developing the sociological orientation in German political science; and, finally, (16) the rise of the sociological movement in the United States.

In addition to these books, Small contributed many articles to the *American Journal of Sociology,* though most of them were later reprinted in book form. Whatever the verdict which historians of sociology may pass upon the value of his discussions of methodology and his positive sociological theory, there can be no doubt that Small's written work falls primarily under the heading of the history of social theory, especially Germanic social theory and its influence upon American social science. No other man did so much to make the fundamental contributions of modern German social science available to American readers.

While Small was a man of wide erudition and possessed of a very fertile and alert mind, he lacked almost every quality which goes to make an attractive writer. In part, this was due, as pointed out above, to the fact that his books were mainly the publication of classroom notes and lectures, sometimes admittedly without any alteration or revision. His style was extremely verbose and discursive. There were also endless repetitions of the same thought and phraseology. His major points and contentions were almost always sound and suggestive, but their phrasing was often tortuous and confused, a condition which was intensified by the involved nature of his verbal style.

It is true that Small exercised an influence upon American sociology greater and more salutary than any other individual except, perhaps, Giddings; but he did it chiefly through his intellectual courage and integrity, his great energy as a teacher, his real erudition, his capacity to charm and inspire students by his gracious and kindly manner, and his influence as the editor of the world's foremost sociological journal. We may well wonder what his national and international influence might have been if the cogency and penetration of his thinking had equaled that of Giddings or if his writing had possessed the verve and lucidity of Ross. In a letter of December 11, 1924, to the present writer, commenting on my review of the *Origins of Sociology,* Small, with characteristic candor, admitted these stylistic defects:

As to form, you are of course utterly right. My mother once asked me with a deep sigh, "Why is it that you never publish anything that contains either gospel or entertainment?" I could only admit the soft impeachment, and leave the subject with an unsatisfying answer. I do not remember that I have ever written anything, except things to be spoken, without feeling myself trailed by some coming man who could carry the job nearer to completion. All my life I have felt myself under mandate to get out stuff in the rough, which would be a challenge to somebody to work it over, or to get out more and better stuff of a more ultimate order. I have never been able to address myself to book *readers*, but only to potential book *makers*, and I have already felt that, with them, as makers not of literature but of technical treatises, not form, but substance, and pointers toward more substance. matters.[7]

In fairness to Small, however, it should be pointed out that his stylistic defects are to be found chiefly in his theoretical works. His critical reviews, and especially his treatment of concrete historical materials, as exemplified by his *Beginnings of American Nationality,* often exhibited clarity and directness.

V. DOMINANT POINTS IN SMALL'S SOCIOLOGICAL THEORY

We may now devote our attention to a brief summary of Small's central and dominant contributions to sociology. In the first place, he was thoroughly converted to Lester F. Ward's view that the only adequate guidance in adjusting man to the complex conditions of modern life and in effecting orderly social change must be sought in the social sciences. Small was, however, fully aware of the rudimentary and timid nature of the social sciences at the present time. In his circular letter of September 11, 1924, he frankly admitted this in the following words:

As to the so-called social sciences, on the average and as a rule, they have not passed far out of the homely wisdom stage of development. If we apply the acid test to the total output of what we now call the social sciences, from Herodotus down, and including the 1924 vintage, each social science has consisted of 95 parts *omnium gatherum* of all sorts of pertinent and impertinent selections from the scrap heaps of human experience, promoted in a few later generations by use of bibliographies and card-indexes, combined with five parts of critically authenticated first-hand discovery strictly pertinent to some accurately defined problem. On the whole, every social scientist, whether he preferred to call himself historian, economist, sociologist, or what not, has actually, in ninety-five hundredths of his activities been a rationalizer at large, and only in five percent of his activities has he concentrated upon close investigation of strictly defined problems, by use of an adequate method. I am prepared for correction as to my arithmetical terms. It is conceivable that the ratio may turn out to be 94% general discursiveness and 6% serious science, but that will not fatally affect the principle.[8]

Yet the social sciences are being rapidly improved in their objectivity and quantitative methodology. We shall probably be correct in expecting that they will have reached a status which will make them adequate for social guidance fully as soon as society is ready to accept advice from this quarter. Small devoted his professional life to the advancement of both these programs: the improvement of the social sciences and the increase of their public prestige.

Small's conception of the nature of sociology underwent important modifications along with the general progress of his sociological thinking. In his *Introduction to the Study of Society,* he presented the view that sociology is primarily a general synthetic science, embodying an organization of all the knowledge concerning man which has been accumulated or is being gathered by the special social sciences. Subsequently, he became preoccupied with Ratzenhofer's approach to sociology from the standpoint of the struggles of "interest-groups," and he approved Simmel's notion of sociology as a type of methodology concerned with the nature and forms of social groups. Small, accordingly, developed his later contention that sociology is "a collection of techniques for exposing group relations in human affairs" or, again, "sociology is that variety of study of the common subject-matter of social science which trains attention primarily upon the forms and process of groups." Perhaps the best of his later definitions of sociology is that contained in his *Americana* article:

The sociological technique is that variant among the social science techniques which proceeds from the perception that, after allowing for their purely physical relations, all human phenomena are functions not only of persons, but of persons whose personality on the one hand expresses itself in part through the formation of groups, and on the other hand is in part produced through the influence of groups. In brief, sociology is that technique which approaches knowledge of human experience as a whole through investigation of group-aspects of the phenomena.[9]

Small himself recognized the transformation of his views on this subject and repudiated to some extent his earlier omnibus conception of sociology. In his article on the "Future of Sociology" he admitted:

In proportion as sociology becomes responsibly objective it will leave behind its early ambition for a hegemony over social sciences, and it will realize its destiny of functioning within a federation of scientific activities. With widening and clarifying of social consciousness, it must become progressively evident that a single technique, no matter how penetrating, can at most lay bare only certain constituent aspects of the total social process.[10]

His view of sociology thus passed from a notion of a synthesis of the special social sciences to a notion much more like that of Giddings, namely, that of sociology as the elemental or basic social science. Yet Small never departed from his original healthy notion that the study of society must be a unified and co-operative process, in which sociology and the special sciences should carry on an intelligent and co-ordinated division of labor. Sociology may not legitimately aspire to be an over-science or a complete synthesis of all existing knowledge concerning society. But it must always operate in the closest rapport with the special social sciences and must appropriate the latest contributions from each of the latter which can aid in arriving at a more comprehensive and profound understanding of the group life of man as the core of the social process. To quote once more from Small's letter of September 11, 1924: "I have never been able to admire the ideal of a scientist as a man who should confine his personality within the bounds of his specialty. On the contrary, my conception of the ideal scientist is a consummate technician in his own specialty, or specialties, but over and above that a reliable liaison officer between his specialty and all other divisions of knowledge, including the arts of converting scientific knowledge into human advantage."[11]

The same spirit emerges from the following paragraph, taken from his article on the "Future of Sociology":

We may well congratulate ourselves upon the complete absence from our horizon of signs that the near future of sociology is to be sectarian. Differences of opinion there are among us in plenty. We differ about emphasis, about method, about vocabulary, about choices of immediate programs. All this makes for health. On the other hand, there is nothing among us remotely parallel with the quarrels in the eighteen-eighties between the economists of the "classical," the "historical," and the "Austrian" communions, not to speak of the minor sects. We are not a jangle of party proclamation—"I am of Paul, and I of Apollos, and I of Cephas." Various as our expressions are in outward appearance, we are bound together by common consciousness of a vocation to see that group aspects of human experience receive their dues in all attempts to interpret or to control human affairs.[12]

In his *Americana* article Small recognizes the present trend in sociology away from the older practice of attempting a systematic presentation of the whole field of sociology in one general treatise and toward specialization in what may be called "schools" or "provinces" of the subject. He distinguishes some six fields into which contemporary sociology has been differentiated: (1) methodology, (2) group psychology, (3) social analysis, (4) social survey, (5) social diagnosis and (6) drafting of specific programs for social betterment.

While Small himself wrote and discoursed incessantly during the last fifteen or twenty years of his life concerning "method" and "methodology" in the social sciences, it may be doubted if he used this term in a strictly accurate sense or recognized exactly what "methodology" means. Despite his rather complete divorcement from obscurantism, Small's early training and methods of thought were an almost insuperable handicap to his ambition as a specialist in sociological methodology. His early training was in philosophy and theology, and, despite his subsequent intellectual emancipation, he tended to think and write in a philosophical and metaphysical strain and to deal with imponderable abstractions. His mental patterns were of the prescientific and premethodological stage of social science.

Strictly speaking, sociological method is a combination of the broad, synthetic approach of sociology to human and social problems with the appropriate techniques of investigation and synthesis for the particular field which is to be studied and organized. Most sociologists agree that the methodology of sociology must be the *scientific* method of empirical inquiry; and some, such as Giddings, Ogburn, Lundberg, and others, insist that the scientific method in sociology means the quantitative or statistical method. Professor Ellwood, among others, has vigorously attacked this narrow conception of sociological method, in his book on *Methods in Sociology* (1933), and contends that there are important fields of sociological study for which the strictly statistical method is not suited. Such writers hold that, in social problems, there are necessarily value-judgments which are not comparable to the problems dealt with by the scientific method applicable to the physical sciences. Indeed, Howard Becker contends that sociological problems are primarily qualitative rather than quantitative and, hence, cannot be adequately handled by the statistical approach.

Small possessed almost no knowledge of modern statistics, which prevented him from dealing thoroughly with quantitative sociological methodology. Likewise, of the special fields of sociology, he had a competent command of technical knowledge only in matters of historical, economic, and political analysis, and here he did work of great distinction.

The fact is that what Small was pleased to call "sociological method" was, in reality, a sort of combination of the general sociological approach with what he regarded as the province and objectives of sociology. Methodology, then, was to Small chiefly definitions of sociology and its subdivisions; invention and elucidation of sociological categories; discussions of the province of sociology; and suggestions as to the ultimate ethical objectives of sociology. This is well illustrated by his summary definition of sociological method in his *Meaning of Social Science:* "This method is throughout objective investigation and evaluation of human experience, with the purpose of constructing valuations into more complete realizations."[13] Some may object that the present writer is too narrow or technical in his definition of sociological methodology; but, even if we concede that Small was correct in his conception of methodology, we must admit that, except in the politicoeconomic province, he wrote and talked primarily *about* sociological method instead of indicating just what it is.

The pivotal element in Small's own sociological system was the notion of human interests and their social control. The analysis of the origins, expression, adjustment, and more intelligent direction of human interests constituted the essence of both the analytical and the ethical aspects of his systematic writings.

The concept of interests and interest-groups as the clue to the dynamics of the social process has a long history, going as far back as Aristotle. It was basic in the thought of the "Fathers," from Madison to Calhoun. In modern sociology it took its origins from the ideas of the economists and from the fundamental work of Ludwig Gumplowicz in his elucidation of the essence of the *Rassenkampf.* His disciple, Gustav Ratzenhofer, still further elaborated this formula, and Small constructed his system on the basis of his own views and those of Ratzenhofer. The cardinal importance of this phase of his work Small pointed out as early as 1903 in his discussion of Giddings' paper on "A Theory of Social Causation" at the New Orleans meeting of the American Sociological Society, two years before the publication of the *General Sociology:*

> We need to know, in the concrete, just how human interests have combined with each other in every variety of circumstance within human experience. There has never, to my knowledge, been a fairly successful attempt to schedule efficient human interests in general, till Ratzenhofer did it less than ten years ago in *Das Wesen und Zweck der Politik.* With this work sociology attained its majority. Henceforth, all study of human relations must be rated as provincial, which calculates problems of life with reference to a less comprehensive scheme of interests than his analysis exhibits.[14]

As early as 1893,[15] Small had formulated a schedule of human interests in six groups:[16] (I) the primary or "Health Interest," subdivided into three constituent elements: (1) the "Food Interest," (2) the "Sex Interest," and (3) the "Work Interest"; (II) the "Wealth Interest"; (III) the "Sociability Interest"; IV the "Knowledge Interest"; (V) the "Beauty Interest"; and (VI) the "Rightness Interest."

The emergence of these interests in society, their conflicts and adjustments in the form of group activity, carried on under the mitigating mediation of the state, and the progressive development of ever greater appreciation of the importance of the higher types of interests, constitute the social process, which is the vital subject matter of all dynamic sociology. Small summarizes his views on these critical matters in the following selections, which we have taken from the *General Sociology*:

In a word, then, the energies that have their basis of action in the human animal differentiate into impulses that cause the actions of that animal to radiate. The individual that comes into being through this differentiation is the resultant of the different interests that wrestle with each other in his personality. The career of that individual, and of all individuals combined, is persistent struggle, on the one hand, of the interests in the individual, by virtue of which he is what he is at any moment, and, on the other hand, of the combination of interests in one individual with the combination of interests in all the others.....

So far as I am able to account for the activities of men, they all run back to motives that have their roots in combinations of this health-interest with interests that arrange themselves in five other groups. Men have a distinct interest in controlling the resources of nature, in asserting their individuality among their fellows, in mastering all that can be known, in contemplating what seems to them beautiful, and in realizing what seems to them right. I have not been able to find any human act which requires, for explanation, any motive that cannot be accounted for by specialization and combination of these interests. Each of the groups has subdivisions, more or fewer than those of the first. All men, however, from the most savage to the most highly civilized, act as they do act, first, because of variations in the circumstances of their environment, both physical and social; second, because of variations and permutations of their six elementary interests.....

Without affirming that either conflict or conjunction of interests is the essence of the social process, we may say that, in form, the social process is incessant reaction of persons prompted by interests that in part conflict with the interests of their fellows, and in part comport with the interests of others. The ratio of the conflict and of the harmony is also infinitely variable. The kinds of conflict and harmony are likewise variable. In general, conflict is the obvious phase of association in earlier stages of the social process, while conjunction of interests grows more evident in later stages.....

We must at the outset disarm the prejudice that States are merely political organizations. That notion is parallel with the economic provincialism just noticed. The modern State is both a political organization and an economic system, but it is much more. The State is a microcosm of the whole human process. The State is the co-operation of the citizens for the furtherance of all the interests of which they are conscious.....

Whatever else the State may or may not do, this at least is its constant role, viz.: The State always brings to bear upon the individuals composing it a certain power of constraint to secure from them, in all their struggles with each other, the observance of minimum established limits of struggle. This is not a hypothetical statement of what the State might, could, would, or should do. It is a literal generalization of what every State actually does. It is an objective statement of a cardinal fact in the social process.....

Civic society organized as the State is composed of individual and group factors, each of which has in itself certain elements of political independence..... That is, each has interests seemingly distinct from the interests of the others. Each has some degree of impulse to assert these interests in spite of the others. Thus the State is a union of disunions, a conciliation of conflicts, a harmony of discords. The State is an arrangement of combinations by which mutually repellent forces are brought into some measure of concurrent action.....

At present we may use the terms "socialization" and "civilization" interchangeably. Each is a phase of the other. We have just seen how struggle—i.e., the specialization of interests—unwittingly pays tribute, and become vassal to, socialization. It turns the interests which are antagonists of each other into a common social stock, administered by a group composed of all the previously conflicting groups.....

Civilization, so far as it is bounded by national limits, consists in enlargement of the content of the common spiritual substance, until it approaches inclusion of all interests, so far as they depend upon concerted conduct; leaving scope for independence only in those activities in which free individual movement best realizes the common interests.....

Our whole life—from our eating and sleeping, to our thinking, and trading, and teaching, and playing, and praying, and dying—is a part of the social process. In us the process has its lodgement. In the process we live and move and have our being. Instead of not being concerned with it, nothing else is our concern, so far as we are citizens of the world. We do not know our personal concerns until we see through and through the social process.....

Human experience composes an associational process. The elements of that process are interests lodged in individuals. These interests may be reduced to least common denominators containing relatively simple essentials, but in the conditions of actual life, even at the most primitive stages, the interests express themselves in wants capable of infinite variation and combination. The individuals thus stimulated seek satisfaction of their wants, and efforts to this end bring them into contact with each other. At first these contacts are more evidently collisions; interest clashes with interest. The immediate result is formation of groups for offensive and defensive purposes. These groups in time vary more and more from the primitive animal type. As the variation increases, association becomes an accelerated process of differentiation or permutation of interests within the individuals, of contacts between individuals, of conflict and of co-operation among individuals and the groups into which they combine. Incidental to this pursuit of purposes, and to the process of adjustment between persons which results, individuals enter into certain more or less persistent structural relationships with each other, known in general as "institutions," and into certain more or less permanent directions of effort which we may call the social functions. These social structures and functions are, in the first instance, results of the previous associational process; but they no sooner pass out of the fluid state, into a relatively stable condition, than they become in turn causes of subsequent stages of the associational process, or at least conditions affecting details of the process. There comes a time when some of the individuals in association begin to reflect upon the association itself in a fragmentary way. They think of their family, their clan, their tribe, their nation, as having interests of its own, instead of confining themselves to impulsive action stimulated merely by their individual interests. These men coin and utter thoughts and feelings and purposes which become current in their group. There are thenceforward more or less distinct group-programs co-ordinating the instinctive endeavors of the individuals, and producing a certain mass-movement, in addition to the molecular motions, in the associational process. That is, the groups, as such, entertain purposes, and combine their efforts with some degree of reference to them. With this consummation the associational process is in full swing. All that follows is merely differentiated in detail. Interpretation of specific stages or areas of human experience is consequently a matter of qualitative and quantitative analysis of the experience in terms of these primary factors. History, or our own current experience, records its meaning in the degree in which it discloses the form, the quality, the force, and the proportions with which these various powers of the different elements and conditions of association participate in the given action.[17]

Small held that knowledge is worth while only in so far as it contributes to the betterment of society: "The primary and chief function of science is to act as all men's proxy in finding out all that can be known about what sort of a world this is, and what we can do in it to make life most worth living."[18]

The only valid guide to social change is the scientific knowledge available in the premises, presented by a co-operating group of scientists, representing the various fields of knowledge involved:

The most reliable criterion of human values which science can propose would be the consensus of councils of scientists representing the largest possible variety of human interests, and co-operating to reduce their special judgments to a scale which would render their due to each of the interests in the total calculation.

This declaration of principles, and the program which it implies would not be the abdication of science. It would be science stripped of cant. It would be science with its eyes open. It would be science with its decks cleared for action!

From this outlook there is nothing utopian whatsoever in anticipating the development of institutes of social science, composed not alone of academic men, by any means, but reinforced more and more by scientific men of action functioning as councils of elder statesmen, and focusing all the wisdom within human reach upon the conduct of men's affairs.[19]

Conforming to the above criteria and objectives of useful knowledge in general, sociology is of ultimate importance only in so far as it furnishes the basis for an intelligent and efficient control of the social process and a progressive improvement of human culture and social institutions:

If sociology is profitless, by all means let it alone. Wisdom is justified of her children, but she is always compromised when the unwise claim her maternity.....

Sociology has arrived at the outlook that human experience is the evolution of purposes in men, and of the action and reaction of men upon one another in pursuit of these changing purposes within conditions which are set by the reactions between men and physical nature.....

To do the right thing, except by accident, in any social situation, we must rightly think the situation. We must think it not merely in itself, but in all its connections. Sociology aims to become the lens through which such insight may be possible. There must be credible sociologists in order that there may be far-seeing economists and statesmen and moralists, and that each of us may be an intelligent specialist at his particular post.[20]

Small makes the following constructive and dynamic suggestion as to the social basis of fundamental ethical judgments: it is the function of the social process to increase the sum total of human satisfactions through an ever more perfect realization of vital human interests. The only valid criterion of "good" or "bad" is whether any act or policy speeds up or retards the social process:

If we are justified in drawing any general conclusions whatever from human experience thus far, it is safe to say that the social process tends to put an increasing proportion of individuals in possession of all the goods which have been discovered by the experience of humanity as a whole, and that all social programs should be thought out with a view to promotion of this tendency.....

All the systems of ethics, and all the codes of morals, have been men's gropings toward ability to express this basic judgment: That is good for me or for the world around me, which promotes the on-going of the social process. That is bad, for me or for the world around me, which retards the on-going of the social process.[21]

While Small rightly contended that all worth-while sociology must directly or indirectly contribute in differing degrees to the uplift of humanity, yet he conceded that not all uplift is sociology:

It will continue to be our misfortune if we persist in using the word sociology as an omnibus designation for all the different functions which are performed by the different types of people who in general make desire for human improvement the ostensible motive for their efforts. Instead of designating precision in the judgment of scientific men such indiscriminate use of a term confuses and compromises everything to which it is applied. When Lester F. Ward was spending certain hours of each day contributing to paleo-botany, and certain other hours of the same days wrote *The Psychic Factors of Civilization* he did not ask people to call paleo-botany social psychology nor vice versa. If he had he would simply have furnished an extreme illustration of the fallacy of the sociologists in trying to make terms for functions coincide with the persons functioning.[22]

In spite, however, of his courageous assertion of the ultimate validity of scientific knowledge as the basis for social judgments, Small was never quite able to escape from the religious background of his career and training. This is well brought out in an eloquent paragraph from *The Meaning of Social Science:*

No man has lived his life to the full who is not at last, in one preserve of his personality, a mystic. It is a grub's life not to feel out after the connections of what we can know with what we cannot know; after the fulfillment of what we have been or might have been in what we may be. From the first to last religions have been men's more or less conscious attempts to give finite life its infinite rating. Science can never be an enemy of religion. Stop the stress and strain, the rush and roar, the fuss and bluff of modern life long enough for the deeply human in us to have his chance, and the more science we have the more are we awed and lured by the mystery beyond our ken; the more do the unsatisfied longings in us yearn for larger interpretation.[23]

VI. GENERAL ESTIMATE OF SMALL'S PLACE IN AMERICAN SCIENCE

Briefly to summarize Small's contributions to sociology which are embodied in his books, we should give first place to his work as a historian of sociological thought. Here he was the most voluminous American contributor of his generation. He rendered a real service in interpreting the development of Germanic social science in such a fashion as to be of great utility to American readers. This was an achievement of the highest importance and, in all probability, was one which would not have been performed at all if Small had not executed it.

He was also a tireless worker in promoting the cause of sociology in all his writings. No other American writer devoted so much attention and energy to the program of justifying the existence of sociology as a subject of academic standing and professional importance. He was the leading propagandist of sociology in this country, employing the term "propagandist" in its best sense as a form of highly animated and enthusiastic education.

Small was likewise an indefatigable contributor to the indispensable, if somewhat thankless, field of delimiting and justifying the province of sociology and stating what he believed to be its objectives. If these last two contributions are interpreted, as Small himself interpreted them, to mean an elucidation of the problems of sociological methodology, then he was our most voluminous contributor to this department of sociological endeavor.

In conjunction with the supplementary work of Ratzenhofer, Small excelled any other sociologist writing in the English language in the thoroughness of his elaboration of the interest concept and the group idea as sociological clues. No other American sociologist has rivaled him in the development of the concept of the social process or in his emphasis upon the significance of its dynamic interpretation.

Finally, Small was exceeded only by Lester F. Ward in the persistence and ardor of his contention that sociology is to be justified, if at all, through its potential contributions to the triumph of scientifically guided social betterment. In other words, he always insisted that, in its fundamental goal, sociology is social ethics. He gave to this latter subject a broad foundation which distinguished it from its usual interpretation as the rationalized pseudo-scientific mental operations of the prohibitionist, vice-crusader, and smut-censor. He made it a dynamic and comprehensive agent for the general elevation of society, the deepening of the meaning of human life, and the improvement of social institutions. His writings were an appropriate and genuine outgrowth of his personality. This high ethical import of his writings was consistent with a personal character of real nobility and unusual generosity.

Significant as are the above contributions to sociology through the written word, the writer of this chapter is thoroughly convinced that Small's permanent influence upon sociology through his writings will ultimately prove slight and ephemeral as compared with the impress of his personality and personal activities upon the development of the sociological movement. In other words, Small was a much more significant figure in the campaign to establish sociology as a valid field of academic and professional endeavor than he was in sociological literature, magisterial though his position may be in this latter regard.

First and foremost, in determining Small's place in sociology, the writer would put his methods, ideals, and influence as a teacher. He possessed a singularly gracious personality, combined with an impressive dignity that was never forbidding. He at once secured the confidence of his students, and his many academic duties never led him into carelessness or neglect with respect to the legitimate needs of his classes. He carried a relatively heavy teaching schedule throughout his entire academic career, in spite of the fact that he was not only head of the department of sociology and editor-in-chief of the *American Journal of Sociology* but also dean of the Graduate School of Arts and Literature for nearly twenty years, having been appointed in 1905. He introduced thousands of students to the sociological idea, and he trained many of the professional teachers of sociology who are now expounding the subtle secrets of the science between the Alleghenies and the Pacific.

Particularly significant as an outgrowth of his teaching activities was his direction of the University of Chicago department of sociology for over thirty years. This was for a generation the only adequate and well-balanced faculty of sociology that had yet graced a graduate school in the United States. Small was a man of real tolerance of viewpoint and true catholicity of interests, and this led him to build up a sociology department that represented a great diversity of points of view and specialized interests, e.g., Henderson, Vincent, Thomas, Park, and their successors. This was of particular value to Chicago students, and it also served to disseminate throughout the country a broad conception of the nature of sociology and a wide array of the facts embodied in its subject matter. This was of immensely greater value than the inculcation of the essential elements of any single system of sociology, however impressive that system might be. The divers conceptions of the members of the Chicago department were reflected in the training and equipment of the many students who exposed themselves to the instruction of the Chicago staff and carried the knowledge thus acquired to teaching posts in all parts of the country.

Next to his teaching and departmental supervision, Small's most important work in promoting sociology lay in his founding and editing of the *American Journal of Sociology*. Established in 1895, this has been by all odds the most important sociological journal in the world during the last half-century. While now supplemented by the *Journal of Social Forces* and the *American Sociological Review,* it still carries more important monographic articles than either of the other two and must be reckoned the most significant of the three in respect to the discussion of theoretical issues in the sociological field. The *American Journal of Sociology* has served as a medium of expression for sociologists the world over.

Small's extensive acquaintance with European literature and personalities was of vital importance in securing contributions from the leading European sociologists. It also furnished a place where many ambitious young sociologists risked their first published ventures in the field. Small was never pontifical as an editor, and he encouraged young men to publish their materials in his journal if their contributions were articles of merit. It would be an interesting exercise to ascertain just how many important American sociologists of the present generation first broke ground in a literary way in the *American Journal of Sociology*. In recent years a combination of limitations of space and a great increase in the rate of publication of sociological books have tended to make the reviews in this journal very brief and sometimes casual. Yet for a generation this periodical was almost the only place in which American readers could acquaint themselves with the progress of sociological literature. There cannot be any doubt whatever that Small's service to the development of sociology through his editing of the *American Journal of Sociology* was in itself of greater consequence than all his own books combined.

In addition, Small was a leading figure in the development of modern sociology through his work in connection with the American Sociological Society and its meetings and activities. This society was founded in Baltimore in 1905 and has constituted the chief arena for sociological discussion and for the clarification of sociological opinion since that time. It has also furnished the nucleus for the organization of special committees of sociologists for the promotion of research and teaching. The papers read at the annual meetings have been published with unusual completeness in the so-called annual *Publications* of the society. They constitute an admirable source for the history of sociological opinion in this country, as well as containing much informatin on a great variety of technical and special problems. It will scarcely be denied by anybody that while he lived Small carried more of the burdens associated with the work of the Society than any other three men in the organization, and to him also fell, to a large extent, the task of editing for publication the papers read at the annual meetings. Small was always very active at these annual meetings, promoting discussion both in the formal sessions and in informal gatherings. He was much more in his element here than in the compilation of learned treatises. Moreover, his extensive travels and lecturing in this country and abroad served to promote the exchange of opinions between American and European social scientists. Likewise, he was the means of bringing to Chicago and elsewhere in this country a number of distinguished European social scientists, who left their impress upon this side of the Atlantic.

Further, the writer is going to risk what to many will seem a startling, if not absurd, contention, namely, that in his written work and even more in his teaching, Small's chief contributions were made to the fields of economics, and political science rather than sociology. His *Adam Smith,* his *Between Eras,* his *Cameralists,* and much of his *Origins of Sociology* constitute cardinal contributions to institutional economics. If he had seen fit to put into print the well-organized material from which he gave his famous course on the "Conflict of Classes," he would have produced a work which would have made him a rival of Veblen as an original and courageous economist. His course on Karl Marx and his doctrines and influence were likewise chiefly an exercise in economic dynamics and the history of economic thought.

In the field of political science Small's *General Sociology* may safely be called the most profound book published on the subject in this country between Calhoun's *Disquisition on Government* and A. F. Bentley's *Process of Government,* the latter of which was based upon the contributions of Small and Ratzenhofer.[24] Throughout most of his teaching career he gave a course under various titles which dealt with the sociological basis of the state and civic policy. There is little doubt that, a half-century hence, the historical student of Amerian political theory will find much more of permanent value in Small's writings than in those of a dozen contemporary political scientists of the conventional pattern. Small is likely to have a high place in the history of functional political science in the United States.

In other words, while it was a great gain for sociology that Small devoted his professional life primarily to this subject, it was a real misfortune to Small that he did not occupy himself more specifically with either economics or political science. His mind was better adapted for this type of analysis than for work in the more highly theoretical field of general sociology. Likewise, he would have been a far better stylist in these fields, for in these less theoretical and abstract subjects his thought and expression were much more clear, direct, and precise. In short, his work would have been more profound, articulate, and influential.

Finally, one cannot overlook Small's contributions to ethics. He was truly a pioneer in the foundation of the sociological attitude toward ethics. He powerfully promoted the movement to take the subject out of supernaturalism and metaphysics, as well as to remove it from the narrow conception of a rigid guide for an archaic view of sexual purity. He worked to identify it, instead, with the effort to promote a broader and more comprehensive view of social justice and human happiness.

As a final estimate of Small's place in American sociology the present writer would hold that among the first generation of our sociologists Small's status in advancing the subject matter of sociology was second only to that of Ward and Giddings, while in promoting the professional and academic position of sociology, he was without any close rival.

NOTES

1. *Publications of the American Economic Association, Third Series,* V, No. 2 (1904), 178–79.

2. *Adam Smith and Modern Sociology* (Chicago, 1907), pp. 1, 235, 237. For a bibliography of Small's books, articles, and reviews see *American Journal of Sociology,* July, 1926, pp. 49–58.

3. *Adam Smith and Modern Sociology,* pp. 23–24.

4. Article "Sociology," in *Encyclopedia Americana,* XXV (1920), 209–10.

5. *American Journal of Sociology,* July, 1925, p. 89.

6. *The Meaning of Social Science* (Chicago, 1910), pp. 9, 10, 61.

6a. This was republished in 1947 in the *American Journal of Sociology.*

7. Letter to author, December 11, 1924.

8. P. 3.

9. P. 208.

10. *Publications of the American Sociological Society,* XV (1920), 192.

11. P. 5.

12. P. 193.

13. P. 273.

14. *Publications of the American Economic Association, Third Series,* V, No. 2 (1904), 181.

15. The year in which *Wesen und Zweck der Politik* was published in Leipzig.

16. *General Sociology* (Chicago, 1905), chap. xiv.

17. *Ibid.,* pp. 197–98, 205, 226, 242, 252–53, 363, 472, 551, 619–20.

18. *The Meaning of Social Science,* p. 260.

19. *Ibid.,* pp. 242–43.

20. *General Sociology,* pp. 728–29; *The Meaning of Social Science,* p. 88.

21. *General Sociology,* pp. 522, 676.

22. Open letter to M. M. Willey, September 11, 1924, p. 6.

23. P. 275.

24. The author obviously refers here to Small's contribution to the analysis of the actual processes of government and not to his influence upon formal academic political science. Here he was far less influential than the professional political scientists like Woolsey, Burgess, Willoughby, and Lowell. The writer bases his judgment upon the assumption that it has already become evident that the analysis of political processes is of greater significance than the definition of political terms and concepts.

CHAPTER XL

WILLIAM ISAAC THOMAS: THE FUSION OF PSYCHO-LOGICAL AND CULTURAL SOCIOLOGY

HARRY ELMER BARNES

I. THE PERSONAL AND PROFESSIONAL BACKGROUND OF THOMAS' SOCIOLOGICAL CONCEPTIONS

WILLIAM ISAAC THOMAS (1863——), one of the key members of the great department of sociology set up by Professor Small at the University of Chicago following 1893, is regarded by many students of sociological theory as the most erudite and creative of American social psychologists. In his later years Thomas extended his conceptions and methods to what might be called a "psycho-cultural" approach to social phenomena. Certainly, no other sociologist excels Thomas in his mastery of the subject or in a firm command of the auxiliary sciences essential to the successful exploitation of the field of ethnic and psychological sociology. Unfortunately, Thomas confined his systematic exposition of psychological sociology to his university lectures, which were never published. His published contributions to the subject are relatively few and fragmentary, woven into extensive documentary studies. But his general position and method can be reconstructed and summarized with relative confidence and accuracy.

Few leading sociologists have had a more curious and informal preparation for the cultivation of their subject. Thomas was reared in Tennessee, where he loved to roam in the woods with a gun. As he says: "My own childhood was of a strictly manual, perceptual-motor type, taking the direction of rifle shooting, which was the main sport of mountain people. My zeal for this was fanatical. I reckon that I passed not less than seven years of my youth in the woods alone with a rifle, without a dog, shooting at a mark, and regretting the disappearance of large game and the passing of the Indian and pioneer life."[1]

Ultimately, Thomas attended the University of Tennessee but paid no attention even to such rudiments of the social studies as were then taught. Rather, his main interests were in Greek culture and in biology. His Greek teacher interested him in German scholarship, and his biology professor in Darwinism and evolution, more than a generation before Tennessee discovered the dangers inherent in teaching evolution. For a time after his graduation Thomas taught Greek, Latin, French, German, and English at the University of Tennessee and then went to the University of Berlin to study. At Berlin and later at Göttingen, Thomas concentrated on philology; then he returned to teach English at Oberlin College for three years.

Thomas' first contact with sociology came from reading the reports of the American Bureau of Ethnology while at Tennessee and Spencer's *Principles of Sociology* while at Oberlin. In the spring of 1894 he learned of the establishment of the Department of Sociology at the University of Chicago under Professor Small and noted that attractive courses were offered in sociology and anthropology. Following the drive for new experience, he decided to enroll. But even when he arrived in Chicago to study sociology, most of his attention and interest were bestowed upon courses marginal to sociology, such as physiology with Jacques Loeb and brain anatomy with Adolf Meyer. While respecting them personally, he disclaims any important influence on his thinking by his formal teachers of sociology: "I do not feel that I have been greatly influenced by any of my teachers of sociology. My interests, as I have indicated, were in the marginal fields and not in sociology as it was organized and taught at that time, that is, the historical and methodological approach of Professor Small and the remedial and correctional interests of Professor Henderson." But, during his period of study and early teaching at Chicago, Thomas did arrive at the attitudes and methods which later dominated his professional activities in the field of sociology. He summarizes them as follows:

(1) I never became influenced by philosophy as offering an explanation of reality; (2) I kept notes of reading and classified and reclassified materials so that I eventually had at hand, with exact references, all that interested me in sociological and marginal literature; (3) I read widely and in marginal subjects—biology, psychology, ethnology—and acquired a habit of rapid reading; (4) I explored the city. This last was also largely a matter of curiosity. I remember that Professor Henderson, of sainted memory, once requested me to get him a bit of information from the saloons. He said that he had never himself entered a saloon or tasted beer.

About this same time, or a little later, Thomas developed the idea that more could be gleaned from *inspecting* both literature and social situations than from encyclopedic reading of formal sociological materials. He says that he was led to this conclusion by reading all the existing German theses on a certain sociological theme and deciding that they were so extremely banal and futile that they appeared to have no value or merit save that they were written in a foreign language.

Immediately after he received his Doctor's degree in 1896, Thomas again went to Europe. He traveled about, inspecting and observing, as far as the Volga. On this trip he was struck with the fruitful idea of a comparative study of the European nationalities, which was later to bear fruit in his great work on *The Polish Peasant in Europe and America* (1918–21), with Florian Znaniecki. It was in connection with his book on the Polish peasant that Thomas developed his conception of the importance of the life-history and personal-documentation approach to the study of sociological themes and issues. Thomas later gathered material for a work on immigrant Jews which he expects to publish. Thomas retired from the University of Chicago in 1918, and, except for some casual instruction at the New School for Social Research and at Harvard University, he devoted himself from that time onward to study, travel, and writing.

If Thomas was not greatly affected by his university teachers of sociology, there were several important personal influences on his sociological thinking. He was cordial to John Dewey's instrumentalist philosophy, and George H. Mead and Charles Horton Cooley had some influence upon his thinking with respect to personality, the social mind, and the social process. From Florian Znaniecki he may have gained the impulse to fuse the functional-psychological approach with a consideration of the cultural object or value element in the social situation. Thomas' contact with John B. Watson in the 1920's emphasized the concepts of behavioristic psychology. In his later years he was influenced by his wife, Dorothy Swaine Thomas, which is reflected in his increasing respect for the methods of quantitative investigation in social science. But the influence of others on Thomas has often been exaggerated. His was a singularly original and independent mind. Further, even in the case of most of those who had any real influence on him, Thomas' reciprocal influence upon such associates was fully as great.

As we have noted, Thomas never wrote a systematic work on sociology or social psychology, but he made many important contributions to these fields, though his writings, like his interests, were marginal rather than central to systematic sociology. His anthropological interests led to his monumental *Source-Book for Social Origins* (1909) and his later *Primitive Behavior* (1937). In the former the psychological approach was dominant, in the latter the cultural mode of comparison and analysis. His *Sex and Society* (1907) was a healthy release from the prudery of conventional academic sociologists. Unquestionably, his greatest published work was the five-volume masterpiece on the *Polish Peasant,* in which he developed and combined the life-history, personal-documentation, and culture-value approach and outlined the conception of the "four wishes." This book also put the study of immigrant maladjustment on a sound, scientific basis. Thomas made important contributions to the volume on *Old World Traits Transplanted,* by R. E. Park and H. A. Miller (1921). *The Child in America* (1928) combined his interest in psychology, education, and the social situation. At the time of its publication, no other book even approached it as a discerning and stimulating summary of all the cogent information concerning the psychological and cultural setting of child experience and development in this country.

II. THE DEVELOPMENT OF THOMAS' METHOD OF PSYCHOCULTURAL ANALYSIS OF THE SOCIAL SITUATION

As we have noted, Thomas' methodological principles and leading sociological generalizations have to be drawn from key passages scattered throughout his numerous works, the main body of which tends to be source material or other descriptive data. His views and methods grew gradually over the years and took definite form in the long methodological introduction to the *Polish Peasant.* Thomas' methodological conceptions and his interpretations of personality and society were further developed in his chapter in the symposium on *The Unconscious* (1927); in the *Proceedings of the Second Colloquium on Personality Investigation* (1930); in the Brookings Institution *Essays on Research in the Social Sciences* (1931); in the theoretical portions of *Primitive Behavior;* and in the *Critiques of Research in the Social Sciences* (1939).

In a notable paper read before the Congress of Arts and Sciences at St. Louis in 1904, Thomas presented his views on the province of social psychology, indicating its importance to the social scientist.[1a] He held that social psychology is "an extension of individual psychology to the phenomena of collective life," and he suggested some of the chief problems with which it should concern itself. Among these are: (1) crises and shocks in the experience of the social group, with their results upon culture and social organization; (2) the emergence and influence of great personalities; (3) the results of the contacts of social groups; (4) social organization; (5) the psychology of the temperament of races and social groups; (6) the relation of educational systems to social evolution; and (7) the problem of the parallelism between the mental development of individuals and that of the race.

In 1907, Professor Thomas published his *Sex and Society*, which was, probably, the most important American contribution to the sociology of sex at the time the book appeared. Especially significant are the chapters on "Sex and Primitive Social Control" and "Sex and Social Feeling." On the whole, the author, while indicating significant differences between the sexes, criticizes the tendency to regard woman as an inferior being, properly kept in a subordinate position.

Thomas' long period of study and reflection on primitive society and culture bore fruit in 1909 in his *Source-Book for Social Origins,* an admirable collection of material bearing upon the culture and social life of primitive man.[2] The Introduction to this work included a brief analysis of certain sociopsychic factors as keys to the interpretation of society and culture. Among these concepts he emphasized, in particular, control, attention, habit, and crises. In his idea of "crisis," Thomas anticipated by many years Arnold Toynbee's mechanism of "challenge and response."

Between 1918 and 1921, Thomas, as we have noted, published, in collaboration with Florian Znaniecki, a notable series of volumes on the problem of immigration and adjustment, entitled *The Polish Peasant in Europe and America.* At the beginning of the first volume the authors presented a long Methodological Note, which is regarded by some authorities as the most important American contribution to the methodology of sociological investigation.

Znaniecki participated in the *Polish Peasant* mainly in the role of a translator, but he did contribute the "values" concept, for which Thomas has given him full credit. The greater portion of the Methodological Note was the work of Thomas. Thomas stressed the importance of life-history and personal documentation in research, and his basic idea of the "point-by-point" approach—the idea that science moves ahead from a first "guess" to a second "guess" and so on. This emphasized his funda-mental assumption that any "theoretical" formulation must be regarded as highly temporary and subject to many later modifications and devel-opments. We may now turn to some of the theoretical points offered in the Methodological Note.

Here is to be found a brief review of various attempts to state social theory and social causation in "particularistic," i.e., "single-track," terms. After indicating the inadequacy of these, Thomas goes on to formulate his own social psychology as "precisely the science of attitudes" in refer-ence to object-values.[3] These terms, "attitude" and "value," help us "to understand and to control the process of *becoming*." The *attitude* is indi-vidual—the peculiar response organization, implicit or explicit, of the personality. But attitudes cannot be understood by themselves alone. We must take into account the other term in the equation, namely, "value."[4] Value is the object of the activity of the individual. Any object may become a value by the injection of meaning into it, and meaning is socially determined.[5]

> By a social value we understand any datum having an empirical content accessible to the members of some social group and a meaning with regard to which it is or may be an object of activity. Thus, a foodstuff, an instrument, a coin, a piece of poetry, a university, a myth, a scientific theory, are social values.....
> By attitude we understand a process of individual consciousness which deter-mines real or possible activity of the individual in the social world..... The atti-tude is thus the individual counterpart of the social value; activity, in whatever form, is the bond between them.[6]

The following passages develop thoroughly the distinction between the scope and the province of social psychology and sociology:

> Thus, the field of social psychology practically comprises first of all the attitudes which are more or less generally found among the members of a social group, have a real importance in the life-organization of the individuals who have devel-oped them, and manifest themselves in social activities of these individuals. This field can be indefinitely enlarged in two directions if the concrete problems of social psychology demand it. It may include attitudes which are particular to cer-tain members of the social group or appear in the group only on rare occasions, as soon as they acquire for some reason a social importance; thus, some personal sexual idiosyncrasy will interest social psychology only if it becomes an object of imitation or of indignation to other members of the group or if it helps to an

understanding of more general sexual attitudes. On the other hand, the field of social psychology may be extended to such attitudes as manifest themselves with regard, not to the social, but to the physical, environment of the individual, as soon as they show themselves affected by social culture; for example, the perception of colors would become a socio-psychological problem if it proved to have evolved during the cultural evolution under the influence of decorative arts.

Social psychology has thus to perform the part of a general science of the subjective side of social culture which we have heretofore usually ascribed to individual psychology or to "psychology in general." It may claim to be *the* science of consciousness as manifested in culture, and its function is to render service, as a general auxiliary science, to all the special sciences dealing with various spheres of social values. This does not mean that social psychology can ever supplant individual psychology; the methods and standpoints of these two sciences are too different to permit either of them to fulfil the function of the other, and, if it were not for the traditional use of the term "psychology" for both types of research, it would be even advisable to emphasize this difference by a distinct terminology.

We have seen that social psychology has a central field of interest including the most general and fundamental cultural attitudes found within concrete societies. In the same manner there is a certain domain which constitutes the methodological center of the sociological interest. It includes those rules of behavior which concern more especially the active relations between individual members of the group and between each member and the group as a whole. It is these rules, indeed, manifested as mores, laws, and group ideals and systematized in such institutions as the family, the tribe, the community, the free association, the state, etc., which constitute the central part of social organization and provide through this organization the essential conditions of the existence of a group as a distinct cultural entity and not a mere agglomeration of individuals; and hence all other rules which a given group may develop and treat as obligatory have a secondary sociological importance as compared with these. But this does not mean that sociology should not extend its field of investigation beyond this methodological center of interest. Every social group, particularly on lower stages of cultural evolution, is inclined to control all individual activities, not alone those which attain directly its fundamental institutions. Thus we find social regulations of economic, religious, scientific, artistic activities, even of technique and speech, and the break of these regulations is often treated as affecting the very existence of the group. And we must concede that, though the effect of these regulations on cultural productivity is often more than doubtful, they do contribute as long as they last to the unity of the group, while, on the other hand, the close association which has been formed between these rules and the fundamental social institutions without which the group cannot exist has often the consequence that cultural evolution which destroys the influence of these secondary regulations may actually disorganize the group. Precisely as far as these social rules concerning special cultural activities are in the above-determined way connected with the rules which bear on social relations they acquire an interest for sociology. Of course, it can be determined only *a posteriori* how far the field of sociology should be extended beyond the investigation of fundamental social institutions, and the situation varies from group to group and from period to period. In all civilized societies some part of every cultural activity—religious, economic, scientific, artistic, etc.,—is left outside of social regulation, and another, perhaps even larger, part, though still subjected to social rules, is no longer supposed to affect directly the existence or coherence of society and actually does not affect it.

It is, therefore, a grave methodological error to attempt to include generally in the field of sociology such cultural domains as religion or economics on the ground that in certain social groups religious or economic norms are considered—and in some measure even really are—a part of social organization, for even there the respective values have a content which cannot be completely reduced to social rules of behavior, and their importance for social organization may be very small or even none in other societies or at other periods of evolution.[7]

The fundamental methodological principle, therefore, of both sociology and social psychology—"the principle without which they can never reach scientific explanation"—is this: "The cause of a social or individual phenomenon is never another social or individual phenomenon alone, but always a combination of a social and an individual phenomenon." Or, in more exact terms: "The cause of a value or of an attitude is never an attitude or a value alone, but always a combination of an attitude and a value."[8]

Further, it may be maintained that:

.... a nomothetic social science is possible only if all social becoming is viewed as a product of a continual interaction of individual consciousness and objective social reality. In this connection the human personality is both a continually producing factor and a continually produced result of social evolution, and this double relation expresses itself in every elementary social fact; there can be for social science no change of social reality which is not the common effect of pre-existing social values and individual attitudes acting upon them.[9]

Contrary to the usual practice, Thomas regarded social psychology as a broader social science than sociology.[10] He held that sociology is a "special science of culture," concerned with the "theory of social organization," while social psychology is "the general science of the subjective side of culture." Social psychology studies "the attitudes of the individual towards *all* cultural values of the group." Sociology studies "only one type of these values—social rules—in their relation to individual attitudes."[11]

Quite independent of Freud, Thomas, out of his own investigations, developed a set of fundamental wishes, four in number, which express the principal attitudes that one finds in individuals. The impulses behind these wishes are: (1) the desire for new experience or fresh stimulations; (2) the desire for recognition; (3) the desire for mastery, or the "will to power"; (4) the desire for security.[12]

On the side of the objective reality, there exist "definitions of situations," delimited ways of reacting, which modify and control the four wishes. Moreover, these "definitions" become organized into schemes or rules of action and in this way serve to determine the "run of attention" of the group toward certain values of the group (family, clan, religious body, guild, state, etc.) and the consequent ignoring of others. Conflict arises when the definitions of the situation change too rapidly for the individual, as well as when there exists a hiatus between the fundamental wishes and these definitions in more static societies. These points are illustrated in the study of the Polish peasant both in Europe and in the chaotic industrialism of America.[13]

Thomas elaborated his idea of the four wishes and their sociological implications in his work on *The Unadjusted Girl* (1923). After the publication of this latter book, Thomas abandoned his use of the "wishes" formulation in this phraseology. He was both surprised and somewhat shocked at its popularity. The "wishes" seemed to him to become in too many quarters mere intellectual fetishes which stultified, rather than stimulated, research. The change in his phraseology was evident in his chapter on "The Configurations of Personality," in the symposium on *The Unconscious* (1927), where the wishes appear as "fields" or "classes" of values: (1) new experience; (2) desire for response; (3) desire for recognition; and (4) security.

In addition to the life-history and fundamental-wishes approach to the psychology of the individual personality and the culture-value concept, the third vital element in Thomas' sociological interpretation of individual and social behavior is the notion of the social situation. This he summarizes in the following manner in his *Child in America:*

> The behavioristic or situational approach .... ignores or minimizes instincts and original nature and studies behavior reactions and habit formation in a great variety of situations comparatively. It assumes that whatever can be learned about original nature will be revealed in its reactions to these various situations. We regard this approach as the only one capable of giving a rational basis for the control of behavior.[14]

In his later work on *Primitive Behavior,* Thomas used the social-situation concept as a basic technique for the interpretation of culture and behavior:

> Employing the term "culture" to represent the material and social values of any group of people, whether savage or civilized (their institutions, customs, attitudes, behavior reactions), the structuralization of cultures, their diversification and the direction of their development, the total configuration of the patterns they contain, and the reaction of the personalities to the cultural situation can best be approached in terms of *the definition of the situation.* An adjustive effort of any kind is preceded by a decision to act or not act along a given line, and the decision is itself preceded by a *definition of the situation,* that is to say, an *interpretation* or *point of view,* and eventually a policy and a behavior pattern.[15]

This approach to sociology through a functional-dynamic psychology of the individual personality, on the one hand, coupled with the importance of the culture-object or -value, on the other, constitutes, to the mind of the writer, an extremely important advance over the older theories. Its attempt to integrate the individual with the cultural factors in social causation and the creation of the social situation is outstanding. For instance, Thomas, speaking of the causes of social progress, stresses the following factors: (1) individual initiative, creative ability, and the accompanying outstanding individual attitudes; (2) the level of culture of the group; (3) the "run of attention" in the group, especially of those individuals of capacity, in terms of the "values" which the group culture holds to be valid.[16] This view might, without difficulty, be utilized to harmonize the alleged opposing views of the culture theorists, such as Boas and his school, and those who follow the Galtonian tradition in emphasizing the place of individual initiative and innate capacity for social development and cultural change.[17]

An authoritative epitome of Thomas' comprehensive approach to the study of personality and culture is his own summary, embodied in a notice to the American Sociological Society, of which he was then president, justifying his selection of "The Relation of the Individual to the Group" as the general topic to be discussed at the coming meeting of the society. This brings out well the breadth of his approach to the subject, both as to the divers methods of studying the evolution of the human personality and as to the multiplicity of techniques and sciences essential to a full understanding of personality:

Our conception of the relation of "experience" to the development of the "person" has been undergoing a rapid modification. "Environment" is no longer regarded as a scene of action for the person, but as material out of which the personality itself is built. "Integration" and "conditioning," as first elaborated by Sherrington and Pavlov, have been further developed by the physiologists, neurologists, and psychologists, and have an important position in sociological method. The "Gestalt" psychology has contributed to the concept of integration as a totality of elements, and of meaning as appearing always in a context and upon a background. The sociologists are now producing important studies on "social distance" and "social position." The social psychologists are working out comparisons between the social classes, and between urban and rural populations, from the same standpoint. The anthropologists are taking the same attitude toward the questions of cultural areas and migrations of peoples, and the question of inferiority and superiority of races. The psychiatrists connected with the child-guidance clinics, even those who formerly gave a preponderating importance to the factors of heredity, are being forced by their own case-studies to seek the sources of the behavior difficulties of the child in his relation to the family and the groups with which he comes into contact at his various age-levels.[18]

The conclusions to which his studies had brought him, on the matter of personality, attitudes and values, a decade after the publication of the Methodological Note in the *Polish Peasant,* are well presented in the above-mentioned symposium on *The Unconscious:*

> I am assuming, at least for the initial standpoint for the study of the formation of personality, that there are certain satisfactions, objects of desire, which men always and everywhere want and seek to secure, and we may speak of these satisfactions as values. These values will also be found to fall into classes or fields, corresponding partly with instinctive or unlearned action tendencies and partly with learned or conditioned tendencies. We may speak of the action tendencies as attitudes and of the values as stimuli.
>
> From this standpoint a personality would be regarded as the organization of attitudes, and personalities would be distinguished among themselves by their greater or less tendency to seek their satisfactions, play their rôles, in this or that field of the values.....
>
> Viewed as a configuration, a personality would be a background of attitudes and values common to everybody, upon which certain attitudes and values, or constellations of attitudes and values, assume a prominent or perhaps a dominant position.[19]

In December, 1938, Thomas' *Polish Peasant* was subjected to a critical analysis by leading American social scientists under the auspices of the Social Science Research Council. A long analysis and critique of the book had been prepared in advance by Professor Herbert Blumer, of the University of Chicago, and this critique and the book were then discussed at length at a Round Table presided over by Professor Warren S. Thompson, of Miami University. Thomas and Znaniecki were present to comment. Thomas laid special stress upon the development of his conceptions and methodological principles in the twenty years since the book had been published. In general, he agreed with Blumer's appraisal and critique. A letter from Thomas to Professor Robert E. Park was introduced into the discussion. In this Thomas had outlined his famous "point-by-point" procedure, which he regards as his most important contribution to the methodology and techniques of social science:

> It is my experience that formal methodological studies are relatively unprofitable. They have tended to represent the standpoint developed in philosophy and the history of philosophy. It is my impression that progress in method is made from point to point by setting up objectives, employing certain techniques, then resetting the problems with the introduction of still other objectives and the modification of techniques.....
>
> In all this, there is no formal attention to method but the use of some imagination or mind from point to point. The operator raises the question, at appropriate points, "What if," and prepares a set-up to test this query.....

We move from point to point without necessarily any formidable attempt to rationalize and generalize the process. It is only, in fact, so far as sociology is concerned, since we abandoned the search for standardized methods based largely on the work of dead men, that we have made the beginnings [in truly empirical social science] which I have indicated.[20]

At the close of the Round Table conference, Professor Read Bain, of Miami University, well stated not only the significance of the *Polish Peasant* for methodology in social science but also the contribution which Thomas has made to empirical social science:

The Polish Peasant is a monumental instance of the revolt against "armchair" sociology which began about 1900 and has progressed to such an extent that sociologists increasingly regard themselves as natural scientists. Few present day sociologists fail to give lip-service, at least, to this conception of sociology and they also profess to base their theories upon actual or possible empirical research.[21]

NOTES

1. The biographical material on Dr. Thomas is derived mainly from a personal memorandum prepared by him and supplied to the author of this chapter.

1a. *American Journal of Sociology*, January, 1905, pp. 445–55.

2. Chicago, 1909.

3. *The Polish Peasant in Europe and America* (5 vols.; Chicago, 1918–21), I, 27. Republished in 2 vols. (New York, 1927). See Herbert Blumer's admirable summary of the methodological contributions of *The Polish Peasant* to sociology and social psychology, in *Critiques of Research in the Social Sciences*, I (New York, 1939), 81–82.

4. *The Polish Peasant*, I, 21–26, 45, 48.

5. Thomas would agree in the main with the theory of meaning and social consciousness developed by George H. Mead at Chicago (see his "Social Consciousness and the Consciousness of Meaning," *Psychological Bulletin*, VII [1910], 397 ff.).

6. *The Polish Peasant*, I, 21–22.

7. *Ibid.*, pp. 30–31, 34–35.

8. *Ibid.*, p. 44.

9. *Ibid.*, III, 5.

10. *Ibid.*, I, 33–37.

11. *Ibid.*, p. 33.

12. *Ibid.*, I, 73.

13. Cf. W. Trotter, *Instinct of the Herd* (London, 1918); G. Wallas, *The Great Society* (New York, 1914); and, above all, W. F. Ogburn, *Social Change* (New York, 1922).

14. *Op. cit.*, p. 561.

15. *Op. cit.* (New York, 1937), p. 8. By permission of the McGraw-Hill Book Co.

16. *Source-Book for Social Origins* (Chicago, 1909), Introd., pp. 18–22.

17. Cf. Kimball Young, *Mental Differences in Certain Immigrant Groups* ("University of Oregon Publications," Vol. I, No. 11 [1922]), chap. v, for an attempt to harmonize these opposing views.

The writer desires to express his gratitude to Professor Young, a former student of Professor Thomas, and to Professor Read Bain, for indispensable aid in drawing up this brief formulation of Thomas' contributions.

18. *American Journal of Sociology*, March, 1927, p. 814.

19. *Op. cit.* (New York, 1927), pp. 143–44.

20. *Critiques of Research in the Social Sciences*, I, 166–67.

21. *Ibid.*, p. 192.

CHAPTER XLI

THE SOCIAL AND POLITICAL THEORIES
OF J. H. W. STUCKENBERG

Harry Elmer Barnes

I. GENERAL NATURE OF STUCKENBERG'S WRITINGS

AMONG the American writers on sociology who were not, at the same time, primarily university teachers of the subject, Lester F. Ward was easily first in importance.[1] There is little doubt that second place should be assigned to John Henry Wilburn Stuckenberg (1835–1903). Both Ward and Stuckenberg suffered unmerited obscurity because of their lack of association with sociology in university circles. Ward, however, became better known in later years, especially after his entrance into the professorial ranks. Stuckenberg, on the other hand, has remained more obscure among academicians.

Stuckenberg was born in Hanover, Germany, in 1835. He came to this country as a youth but returned to Germany to complete his education. He was professor of philosophy in Wittenberg College until 1880, when he went to Berlin to be pastor of the American Chapel. Just before Stuckenberg left for Germany, he brought out his *Christian Sociology,* the first book published in the United States to justify such a title. In this book he was a forerunner, by nearly a half-century, of such writers as Ellwood, who later attempted to adapt Christian doctrine to sociological concepts. Stuckenberg elaborated these ideas in his *The Social Problem,* published in 1897, which he regarded as his complete statement of "the philosophy of a Christian society."

Returning to America in 1894, Stuckenberg devoted the remaining years of his life to his sociological writings. His *Introduction to the Study of Sociology* appeared in 1898, and his larger work, *Sociology: The Science of Human Society,* was published in two volumes in 1903, the year of his death.

Stuckenberg's works are characterized by a considerable amount of erudition and mental vigor, a wholesome degree of common sense, and freedom from technicalities. His works stand at the opposite pole from Ward's in many respects. He evidences little of Ward's detailed knowledge of natural science, and his work presents none of those forbidding technical terms with which Ward's *Pure Sociology* bristles. Another distinctive characteristic of Stuckenberg's writings is the extensive acquaintance with German psychological, sociological, and political literature, which came from his prolonged residence in Germany. He was especially impressed and influenced by Wundt and Simmel. The chief criticisms which can be directed against Stuckenberg's work are a tendency toward diffuseness and the lack of careful discrimination in his source material and his bibliographical references—in short, the faults common to writers whose methods have not been developed in the disciplinary atmosphere of academic life.

Stuckenberg's first sociological treatise, *Introduction to the Study of Sociology,* consists chiefly of prolegomena to sociology, such as its nature, scope, province, relationships, and methodology. Except for a lack of critical discrimination in bibliographical details, the work is one of the best early treatments of these rather overworked subjects.[2]

The systematic treatment of social science is embodied in his *Sociology.* After briefly surveying a part of the ground covered by his earlier volume on the nature and province of sociology, Stuckenberg treats in logical sequence the nature of society; the social forces; the causes of social evolution; the stages of social evolution, including an analysis of the consanguine, the political, and the international eras; and sociological ethics, or the social ideal and the means of attaining it. He sums up his view of his sociological system in the following paragraph:

> Our purpose throughout has been to make the interpretation scientific, systematic. Three fundamental and comprehensive problems we found to be involved in this purpose: the inherent nature of society; the manifestation of this nature in the process of development; and what, taking all the social data into account, society ought to become. By omitting either the Nature of Society, Social Evolution, or Sociological Ethics, numerous weighty questions remain unanswered; but in these three divisions, of which each occupies a realm peculiar to itself, a place is found for every legitimate inquiry respecting the science of society.[3]

The only theoretical innovation of any importance which Stuckenberg contributes is the concept of *sociation.* This term is introduced in the attempt to clarify the relation between the individual and society and to describe the nature of association. Men cannot be bodily united in society; neither do their minds coalesce. The individual personality remains and is distinct from the social personality: "This is only another way of saying what was said before, that society does not consist, strictly speaking, of individuals, but only of so much of them as is associated."[4] Stuckenberg invents the term "sociation" to describe this relation between associated individuals. He defines this term as follows: "We use it to designate those personal forces which interact between men; to indicate what men share, what associates. It stands for all that makes society as distinguished from the sum of individuals. Sociation thus gives the essence of society and differentiates it from all other objects."[5]

The value of this bit of terminology will be differently appraised by writers according to their views upon social psychology. Professor C. H. Cooley argued at considerable length that the whole attempt to distinguish between society and the individual, as separate entities, is based upon false psychological premises.

Stuckenberg's main interest in sociology was the amelioration of social ills and the creation of a more just social order. His system of sociology was therefore designed to culminate in a program of sociological ethics, to which he devotes Part II of the second volume of his *Sociology*. He regarded his discussion of sociological ethics as the most original and important item in his sociological writings. Fifty years ago such views were more novel than they are today, and Stuckenberg may be given credit for both pioneering and courage.

At the outset, Stuckenberg attacks the extreme biological doctrine, a phase of social Darwinism, to the effect that sociology is a rigorous sociobiological subject which excludes all concern with ethical interests and problems. But he is equally firm in repudiating the metaphysical ethics of the a priori philosophers and in insisting that he proposes to treat ethics from the social point of view—to trace the social origins and consequences of conduct and ethical principles. He frankly admits that conscience is not a divinely implanted spark but the conditioned product of social experience, and he declares that ethics must reckon with the conception of social evolution. There are no absolute ethical principles, independent of time, space, human nature, and group folkways.

A sound system of sociological ethics must take into account all the principles and factors of social progress. Its fundamental purpose is to determine the nature, and forward the realization, of the social ideal. This is can do only by scientific inquiry into the nature of man, the basis of society, and the course of social evolution. As the result of such scientific study, the sociologist can (1) create the best possible social setting for a rich individual life and (2) prepare the individual for the most successful life in his social surroundings. This successful life must be regarded as adjustment to social institutions and not solely the most enjoyable life from the standpoint of sensual pleasures. The ultimate good is the perfection of society. Stuckenberg's notion of the ethical process is not unlike that of Fichte, namely, a striving after perfection.

Stuckenberg does not try to give any specific account of the ideal social system. Indeed, he recognizes that there can be no static ideal of social perfection. Even the subject of sociological ethics is as much subject to evolutionary action as the evolving society which sociology studies. The broad purpose of sociological ethics—creating the social ideal— may persist unchanged, but the nature and content of both the social ideal and ethical doctrine will undergo evolutionary changes.

Looking at the subject in a large way, Stuckenberg takes the same general position as Hobhouse, in holding that the growth of harmony and co-operative activities in social organization constitutes the soundest test of progress toward the ideal society. There must be efficient social organization, but this must not preclude the existence of all reasonable freedom for the individual. The social interests must be formulated, directed, and improved. Due attention must be given to both the feelings and the intellect. Stuckenberg agrees with Ward that the state must play an important role as the directive agent in the realization of the social ideal. Sociology should determine what is right. The state must support this right by the might of the public will. Might must not prevail over right, but it must give to right both prestige and power.

II. SPECIFIC CONTRIBUTIONS TO SOCIAL AND POLITICAL THEORY
A. FUNDAMENTAL CONCEPTS AND DEFINITIONS

Stuckenberg's distinction between sociology and political science is clear and definite. Sociology is the science of human association in its most general and comprehensive sense: "The subject-matter of sociology is thus made definite—every kind of human association."[6] "The science of politics," on the other hand, "confines itself to the State, explaining its structure and functions, marking the peculiarity of its organization as distinguished from other societies, treating of the relations of the citizens to one another and to the State, and of the government to the governed, the constitution and laws, and all that belongs to the domain of national life."[7] Sociology also studies the state, but from a different standpoint from that of political science. It does not center its attention upon the inner organization and functioning of the state but rather concentrates upon the relation of the state to society in general: "The sociological view considers the place of the State in social evolution and the general influence of the State on human association."[8]

Sociology is not, however, merely the sum or synthesis of the social sciences. It is the elemental social science which furnishes the logical foundation for the more detailed and specialized work of the particular social sciences: "Sociology is therefore the general social science of which the special social sciences are differentiations; it is the genus of which they are the species, the trunk on which they are the branches."[9] Or, again, "the relation of sociology to the special social sciences is similar to that of science to the sciences, of philosophy to the philosophies, of history to the histories, of language to the languages, of literature to the literatures, and of art to the arts."[10]

Stuckenberg distinguishes clearly between the concepts "state" and "society." Society is a group of individuals in a process of psychic interaction and interstimulation. The state is the sovereign organization of society: "The State is the authority of the collectivity, whether that authority be seated in one man as a despot, in a chosen few as noblemen or aristocrats, in the male citizens, or in all the inhabitants of a given age."[11]

Stuckenberg's differentiation between the state and the government is equally definite:

In idea, the State and its Government are distinct; but the Government, including the legislative and judicial, as well as the executive functions, is the political actuality which makes itself visible and felt..... We can say that the State is the sovereign power in the form of a political organization. The Government is the organ of the State for the realization in actual life of the inherent sovereignty.....[12]

The Government is not the State, but only its directive or executive function, the organ through which the state expresses itself. Governments change while the State continues to exist. The State is the concentrated political force of the totality, which force is expressed by the legislative, judicial, and executive powers.[13]

In discussing the relation between the state and the nation, Stuckenberg's general treatment of the subject makes it plain that he regards the nation as identical with the sovereign state. He protests, however, against the views of writers like Ratzel and Morgan, who, he says, overemphasize the territorial basis of the state and hold that territory and property are the essential characteristics of civil society which mark it off from the previous stage of consanguine organization. Stuckenberg maintains that it is the peculiar relation of the sovereign political authority to the inhabitants rather than the territorial and property basis which is the vital criterion of the existence of a state: "The essence of the State is the citizenship, the relation and functions of the inhabitants. The state can be understood only as a truly human and social institution, with man in his varied relations, not property, as the central idea."[14]

B. THE ORIGINS OF POLITICAL INSTITUTIONS

In his theory of the origin of the state, Stuckenberg follows the doctrines of Morgan and Hearn, namely, that the state was a natural development out of the consanguine or kinship stage of society. This was a gradual process in which the growing complexity of economic interests and social relations rendered the kinship basis of society inadequate and obstructive. While he is acquainted with the writings of Ratzenhofer and Gumplowicz, he strangely makes no use of their theories regarding the origin of the state. Stuckenberg envisages three broad stages of social evolution—the consanguine, the political or the period of the national state, and the international.

In the consanguine period the foundations were laid for all future social development, and government originated in family discipline. Stuckenberg's summary of the contributions of the prepolitical period is one of the best in sociological literature:

> With all its disadvantages, that first era has the honour of being the pioneer of the entire course of humanity. The mind we call, probably contemptuously, savage or barbarian, furnished mankind with spoken, and perhaps written language, certainly among the most marvellous achievements of the race. That first era also evolved racial characteristics which were permanent, but not necessarily final; it developed hunters and fishers; taught men to make use of nature and how to make tools; developed pastoral and agricultural life and learned the value of metals; it established important relations among men, founded the family, instituted tribal government and still larger governmental institutions, and was rich in associations from which higher organizations could be evolved; it began art, formulated ethical rules, made religion of some kind universal, and laid a basis for intellectual development. Besides laying a foundation, it left to the second era a vast amount of material with which to build a suitable structure for the growing needs.[15]

He holds that we cannot tell exactly when or how political organization in the form of the state arose, but he maintains that we can be certain regarding the conditions which made its appearance inevitable. These conditions "involved the development of industries, the growth of trade, the mingling, through commerce and otherwise, of peoples of different blood, the establishment of cities where strangers located and formed a community, and the increase of human and social relationships, which physiological connection does not account for."[16] Cities were probably the nuclei of the first states, as they supplied in the highest degree these conditions which created the necessity for a new type of political organization.

The transition from the consanguine to the political type of social evolution was a long and gradual process with numerous intermediate stages, but it was one of the great advances in social evolution: "The transition, though gradual and imperceptible, involved one of the greatest principiant changes in history, a change during which men passed from what nature has instituted biologically to what their developed minds, enlarged personal interests, and the totality of their social relations required."[17]

A theocratic type of organization may have intervened between the consanguine and the political stages in some instances, as was the case with the Hebrews. In view of the fact that the mass of the people are always conservative, the actual institution of the state was probably due "to a few leaders or men in authority, who recognized the new needs and made provision to meet them."[18]

When the new political era was inaugurated, the principle of consanguinity was limited but not extinguished. It was usually accorded recognition and awarded certain privileges in the new order and lingered on for centuries, especially in the matter of property and inheritance.

While the territorial basis of the state is very important, the central feature of the state is the principle of citizenship, which was created in the consanguine period:

Citizenship involves a vast range of relations and interests which could not be provided for in the preceding era. Law substitutes a rule of general application for individual whim, caprice, and passion; it sets up an impartial, impersonal, and universal standard in place of personal prejudice and malice. The State puts a judicial tribunal where formerly blood-feud prevailed. Tradition and custom no longer suffice, because new relations have been entered and new cases for adjudication arise. The state as a law-making and law-executing sovereignty applies rational tests to human relations and actions, instead of letting them be determined by biology. Its laws reveal the State as a higher psychical stage of evolution.[19]

The national state, however, cannot be regarded as the final goal of political evolution. The increased contact of citizens of different states and the growth of international interests and relationships in every sphere of life have created the need for an international type of political organization:

Therefore, we affirm that just as, in the first era, evolution led beyond the family organization as final, so now evolution is leading beyond the State as final. Practically, in the intercourse of States, the second era has already been superseded. The State is not the ultimate form of organization, but a step that leads to something beyond. Statesmen as well as sociologists and other investigators seize the idea of the family of nations and seek to determine what relations and actions are involved in this idea. Not at once can this idea be realized; but every deeper view of the political trend points to a more comprehensive organization than the State as ultimate.[20]

C. FORMS OF THE STATE AND THE GOVERNMENT

Stuckenberg makes no formal attempt to classify or describe the different types of states and governments. He merely discusses in a general way the underlying principles and salient characteristics of republican and monarchical government.

The true basis of republican or popular government is not the fallacious notion that the people ought to govern because they best understand their own interests but, rather, their undoubted right to manage their own affairs—even if badly. The monarchical theory of government is that the people are not competent to govern themselves but must be governed from above. These two different views mark the opposite extremes of political theory and practice, between which there are many possible gradations of both types.

One of the greatest mistakes in political theory is the common belief that the people have a native or inherent ability for self-government. In reality, successful popular government can only be the result of a long period of gradual development and training. Most of the defects of contemporary popular government are those which are inherent in any imperfectly developed institution. The chief weakness of popular government, in its present stage of development, is the difficulty involved in obtaining specialists in the government and in securing united and intelligent action in emergencies. Probably most of these defects will be eliminated by further political experience. The main hope for the future perfection of popular institutions lies in the education, particularly the political education, of the citizens.

"Sovereignty," says Stuckenberg, "means supreme power from which there is no appeal..... Whether the sovereignty be regarded as inherent in the people or as hovering over them, its unconditional authority is regarded as axiomatic—a sovereignty which recognizes no appeal outside of and beyond itself."[21] Sovereignty is an indispensable attribute of the independent state.

Stuckenberg, however, freely admits the difficulties involved in this conception of absolute sovereignty when it is applied to the cases of dependencies, protectorates, and spheres of influence, and especially when extended to the relations between independent sovereign states. He admits with extreme frankness that this view of sovereignty breaks down when applied to foreign relations, whatever may be its validity in regard to domestic or internal affairs:

Sovereignty in foreign affairs is a myth with which fools try to deceive each other.....[22]

The sovereignty of the State received an application in former times which must be abandoned now. The State was regarded as in all respects the final appeal, in external as well as in internal affairs..... This kind of sovereignty has proved itself untenable; it is illogical. If ten States are equally sovereign, then none of them is sovereign. If one State can determine its relation to other States, then all with an equal sovereignty must have the same right. International affairs are, therefore, in a state of chaos.[23]

Stuckenberg's solution of this problem of reconciling sovereignty and international relations is to demand recognition of the sovereign authority of an international court of arbitration for the decision of international disputes. This is based upon the conception "that there are spheres in which no state is sovereign, but that in these the sovereignty resides in several States, or is international."[24] The sovereignty of the state, which is conferred by the people, applies only to internal affairs: "Outside of this all sovereignty is a usurpation which is perpetuated by traditionalism, by fictions, and by might."[25]

In treating the important question of the legitimate scope of state activity, Stuckenberg advances the preliminary proposition that it is impossible to make any dogmatic statements upon this point except of the most general kind. The proper functions of the state depend upon the stage of social evolution and general enlightenment and hence will vary in different periods and regions. One must always, therefore, assume the historical and comparative viewpoint in generalizing upon this question. Stuckenberg maintains, however, that one is safe in making the generalization that, in any period of political or social development, the state should control and administer all matters which pertain to the general or public welfare of the group and cannot be adequately dealt with by private or voluntary organizations:

> Here we come to the function of the State. If it fails to attend to the interests which lie beyond the function of a particular society yet are common to all the societies and necessary for their welfare, it abdicates its authority. On the other hand, it leaves its special sphere and becomes a usurper if it assumes the functions of the particular societies and dictates terms which belong to the freedom of these societies. . . . . The State as an embodiment of the political force of the totality ought to organize and control whatever pertains to the public welfare of the community.[26]

The basic rule that the state should follow in its relation to voluntary private organizations is to lay down the general laws which are to govern the activities and relations of these organizations, in so far as they directly affect the public interest. It should then leave private organizations to their own initiative within the limitations which are imposed for the general good of the community. Under no consideration should the state attempt to control the thoughts as well as the actions of its citizens.

Political institutions in the past "have been chiefly restraining, coercive and punitive forces." In the future their functions will include, to an increasing degree, the reformation, improvement, and exaltation of the people. In general, however, the state has been and is likely to continue to be the indispensable condition of progress rather than the direct cause or chief instrument of social evolution. Its protective and regulative functions allow voluntary organizations "to develop their resources and make the most of their opportunities."

While it is impossible to make any specific prediction as to the future of state activity, it is reasonably certain that, as intelligence increases and the people become better trained in self-control, the direction of social activities by the state will become more restricted and will allow a larger degree of freedom to individual initiative: "As the citizens grow in the ability of self-government, the State will increasingly confine its attention to the general interests of the public. The largeness of the political interests, being commensurate with the extent of human concerns, makes it impossible to forecast the future functions of the State."[27] In any event the improvement of political institutions in the future must depend primarily upon the education of the citizens in statecraft, greater political experience, and the general improvement in intelligence.

The related problem of the reconciliation of state authority with liberty Stuckenberg dismisses with the pertinent observation that true liberty can be obtained only through the protection afforded by the state and that liberty is increased in proportion as political life passes from anarchy to stable and efficient organization. Again, the state promotes the growth of individuation to a far greater degree than the consanguine social organization, thus being favorable to both liberty and individuation.

F. THE STATE AND INTERNATIONAL RELATIONS

Stuckenberg's views on the function of the state with respect to foreign relations have been touched upon in analyzing his opinions about the final or international stage of political evolution and the problem of the relation of sovereignty and international interests. He was, along with Stein and Hobhouse, one of the most ardent advocates among sociological writers of an adequate development of international political machinery, so as to be able to put an end to the anarchical and chaotic condition of international relations. In every aspect, except political organization, social relations have become international in scope:

Everywhere narrow political limits are being burst. In that great trend towards enlarged combinations only the States are behind, each preferring to nourish its own interests and in the larger affairs engage in destructive rivalry and conflict. Capitalism has international organizations in the form of syndicates and trusts. Labour is forming leagues regardless of nationalities; and both socialism and anarchism have international affinities and unions. Religion transcends State bounds and makes the world its kingdom. Learning is rapidly becoming cosmopolitan, the boundlessness of truth being its only limit. A university or academy of science fails in its calling if its influence is not international. Ethics, like religion, makes humanity its sphere.[28]

Humanity, not the state, is regarded as ultimate by sociology. The first step toward the development of internationalism in political organization must be the further development of international law and the practice of international arbitration in matters which involve the interests of more than one state. The ultimate stage in political evolution will probably be a federation of nations: "This seems to be the natural course of revolution: first, a federation of nations having most in common; then,

a federation of all the nations which have relations which require regulation; finally, a federation of all the States of the world."[29]

G. EXTRA-LEGAL PHASES OF SOCIAL AND POLITICAL CONTROL

Stuckenberg emphasizes the importance of the nonpolitical organs of
social control: "Besides the effects wrought by the laws of the State, other
processes are at work to settle social affairs, particularly in the large
spheres not under political control. Tradition and custom prevail, though
they have less power than in the first or consanguine era. Public opinion,
churches, schools, voluntary associations, often determine the course
of the people and may affect the State and its laws. Society changes much
or little, according as the social or non-political institutions are mobile
or fixed."[30]

Not only do these nonpolitical institutions determine the general trend
and rapidity of social evolution, but they also influence political organization and development: "In free states, and even in others, the nonpolitical societies can make moral progress in principle and practice, and
became a leaven of the whole citizenship, and eventually determine
the political course."[31]

It is the prime problem of political theory and practical statesmanship
to arrive at the most perfect adjustment between the political and the
nonpolitical types of organization so as to secure the maximum degree
of initiative and progress in the realm of voluntary activity and, at the
same time, to protect the public against exploitation by selfish private
interests. But the greatest danger from exploitation is to be found in
political parties, which put their interests above the public welfare. Yet,
in the last analysis, in a popular government the people have only
themselves to blame if they suffer from protracted exploitation at the
hands of any party organization.

H. PROBLEMS OF POLITICAL REFORM AND SOCIAL PROGRESS

Stuckenberg's opinions as to the most urgent steps in the matter of
political reform have already been pointed out. In internal or domestic
political administration he urges the development of a more specialized
knowledge for governmental officials, the elimination of the evil phases
of partisan politics, the democratization of political institutions, and
the development of organs for the expression of united and intelligent
political action in emergencies. In the field of international politics he

demands an extension of the principle of international arbitration and, ultimately, the realization of international federation. The chief means of attaining these aims is the improvement of education, both in general matters and, particularly, in sociology, political science, and international law—what we now call the "social studies."

To conclude, one may safely say that, while Stuckenberg sets forth no unique and novel special contribution to social or political theory, his work constitutes as typical, balanced, and generally acceptable an exposition of social philosophy and the sociological theory of the state as can be found in the writings of any modern sociologist and that it was a harbinger of a broader and sounder approach to public problems.

NOTES

1. Ward's more important sociological writings had been published before he went to Brown in 1906. The facts of Stuckenberg's life are well assembled in J. O. Evjen, *The Life of J. H. W. Stuckenberg, Theologian, Philosopher, Sociologist* (Minneapolis, 1938). See also C. T. Pihlblad, "The Sociology of J. H. W. Stuckenberg," *Ohio Sociologist*, Vol. II, No. 2 (1928).

2. It is well reviewed by Professor A. W. Small, *American Journal of Sociology*, May, 1898, pp. 855–59.

3. *Sociology: The Science of Human Society* (2 vols.; New York, 1903), II, 292.

4. *Introduction to the Study of Sociology* (New York, 1898), pp. 126–27.

5. *Ibid.*, p. 127.

6. *Ibid.*, p. 52.

7. *Ibid.*, p. 80.

8. *Sociology*, II, 65.

9. *Introduction to the Study of Sociology*, p. 77.

10. *Sociology*, I, 41. Stuckenberg's discussion of the relation of sociology to political science is one of the most effective answers in print to those archaic political scientists who would make their subject the fundamental and all-inclusive social science (cf. *Introduction to the Study of Sociology*, pp. 78–83; *Sociology*, I, 17–21).

11. *Introduction to the Study of Sociology*, p. 81; cf. also *Sociology*, I, 214.

12. *Sociology*, II, 88–89.

13. *Ibid.*, pp. 85–86.

14. *Ibid.*, pp. 74–76.

15. *Ibid.*, pp. 118–19.

16. *Ibid.*, p. 66.

17. *Ibid.*, pp. 67–68.

18. *Ibid.*, p. 68; cf. also Professor Giddings' theory of "protocracy" in his *Responsible State* (Boston, 1918), pp. 17–20.

19. *Sociology*, II, 78.

20. *Ibid.*, p. 129.

21. *Ibid.*, I, 214.

22. *Ibid.*, II, 127.

23. *Ibid.*, pp. 124–25.

24. *Ibid.*, p. 170.
25. *Ibid.*
26. *Ibid.*, p. 92.
27. *Ibid.*, p. 120.
28. *Ibid.*, p. 151.
29. *Ibid.*, p. 183; cf. also pp. 135–94.
30. *Ibid.*, p. 93; cf. also p. 105.
31. *Ibid.*, p. 113.

CHAPTER XLII

THE SOCIOLOGICAL THEORIES OF
EDWARD ALSWORTH ROSS

WILLIAM L. KOLB, *Newcomb College, Tulane University*

I. THE NATURE OF ROSS'S SOCIOLOGICAL WRITINGS

FEW writers in the field of sociology have been able to put the results of their speculation and research before the reading public in as interesting and vivid a fashion as has the sociologist who is the object of our attention in this chapter. There is little doubt that the reputation which Edward Alsworth Ross (1866——) enjoys in sociological circles today is due in large measure to his ability to present his ideas in a manner which attracts the lay reader as well as the professional sociologist. Although his tendency to popularize has at times led Ross into the pitfalls of overeasy generalization, it must be recognized that sociology owes a great deal to Ross for arousing public interest concerning certain of its problems and methods.

This emphasis on getting ideas across to the general reader seems to be the result of a fusion of a genuine scientific interest in societal phenomena with a strong desire to aid in solving the problems which the peoples of the world have been called upon to face. It is possible to trace the presence of this combination of interests in Ross from his graduate student days at Johns Hopkins through his periods of teaching at Indiana, Cornell, Stanford, Nebraska, and, finally, Wisconsin. As his autobiography reveals, Ross's zeal for social reform has more than once involved him in difficulties with various groups and has been equaled only by his insatiable curiosity concerning the regularities to be found in social life.[1]

No other American sociologist has had so interesting and colorful a life as has Ross. While a voluminous writer on sociological subjects and a conscientious and brilliant university teacher for nearly fifty years, Ross was as much a publicist and social reformer as he was a professional sociologist. A graduate of Coe College, he studied at Berlin and Johns

Hopkins universities and received his doctorate at the latter in 1891. His graduate training was more strictly in the field of economics and finance than in sociology.

Ross accepted a professorship in economics at the University of Indiana in 1891 but remained there only a year, moving to a chair in economics and finance in Cornell in 1892. This was a short stay, also, for he assumed a professorship in sociology at Leland Stanford in 1893. Here he developed a great reputation as a teacher but was dismissed in 1900 for too great frankness in describing the coolie labor used by Leland Stanford in building the Central Pacific Railroad, as well as for other evidences of liberal thought. He then accepted a professorship in sociology at the University of Nebraska in 1901 and remained there until 1906, when he moved to Wisconsin, where he held the chair in sociology until his retirement in 1937. It is pretty generally conceded that Ross was the most dramatic and effective classroom teacher in the history of American sociology. While not a meticulous scholar, he was a man of vast learning and was unrivaled among sociologists in his command of the raw materials of public affairs and world events.

Ross maintained a deep interest in social reform from his youth onward, and he wrote and lectured extensively against the evils of plutocratic society and partisan politics. His *Sin and Society* attracted the attention and received the approval of Theodore Roosevelt. He was an inveterate globe-trotter and studied social change and reform movements at first hand from Mexico to Russia and from India to Sweden. He was, at one and the same time, the incarnation of the sociologist who believed that social sciences should promote social reform and the despair of the cloistered devotees of statistical research and professorial timidity.

The duality of approach—scientific and reformist—shows itself in even more marked form in Ross's writings than it does in other aspects of his life; and, while the fusion of these two attitudes in his personality has prevented his producing any book which subordinates one point of view completely to the other, his writings can be conveniently classified according to the predominance of one or the other standpoint.

Among the more important of his works which were written primarily from the scientific point of view are *Social Control, The Foundations of Sociology, Social Psychology,* and *Principles of Sociology.*[2] The first of these is perhaps the most important and enduring of all Ross's writings. In the author's own words it consists of "a survey of the foundations of order," in which Ross, after dismissing the possibility that a complex society can exist on the basis of what he terms "a natural order," attempts to establish the thesis that social order exists because of the conscious control of the individual on the part of society.[3] The study of social control, according to Ross, is part of the domain of social psychology, which, in turn, is part of the larger field of sociology.[4] In spite of the fact that Ross is handicapped in his analysis by the individual-society contrast and that his division of social psychology into individual and social ascendancy, with social ascendancy, in turn, divided into social influence and social control, serves no particularly useful purpose, this book still stands as one of the best analyses available of the problems involved in social control.

The Foundations of Sociology contains Ross's conception of the field of sociology and its relations to some of the other social sciences. The work consists primarily of a series of constructive criticisms of the writings of other men about such topics as "The Scope and Task of Sociology," "The Sociological Frontier of Economics," "The Unit of Investigation of Sociology," etc. The most striking aspect of the book is that, despite Ross's defining sociology in such a way as to include the other social sciences, the map of the sociological field which he presents in the chapter on "The Unit of Investigation in Sociology" indicates a field for specialized research which does not encroach on the domains of the other social sciences.[5]

In his *Social Psychology* Ross turns his attention to the planes and currents of "feeling, belief, or volition—and hence in action—which are due to the interaction of human beings....."[6] These planes and currents are analyzed in terms of Tarde's concepts of conventionality and custom based on imitation, united with the biological conception of human nature which was prevalent at the time and with some of Le Bon's ideas concerning crowd psychology.

The study of the main body of the phenomena which constitute the subject matter of sociology, i.e., social processes, is to be found in the *Principles of Sociology*. In this work the basic concept of social interaction is broken down. The various processes in which individuals engage and which result in the formation of subjective products, such as the planes and currents mentioned above, and objective products or actual human groupings and social structures are presented and analyzed.

Turning for the moment from Ross's writings, which we have designated as essentially written from the scientific viewpoint, we find that a still greater number of his books have been written as appeals for reform or as popular presentations of specific cultures. One of the earliest of these was his *Sin and Society*, a work written in the spirit of the muck-rackers of the turn of the century, castigating those individuals who are free from personal vice but engage in antisocial conduct which harms others, which Ross designates as sin.[7] Pointing out how the morality of the early twentieth century tended to control vice rather than sin, he pleaded for a reorientation and extension of morality so that sin may be controlled.

Nowhere is Ross's interest in social reform more clearly revealed than in his *Changing America*.[8] The purpose of the book is to bring the citizen's conception of social problems into closer alignment with the actual problems of the day, and in it Ross deals with such matters as women in industry, contemporary commercialism, and capitalist influence over the press. The last few chapters are devoted to a description of social conditions in the Middle West and to the promise which this region holds for American society. While *Changing America* consists of a discussion of several social problems, *The Old World in the New* deals with the specific problem of immigration into the United States.[9] Approaching the problem from a sociological point of view, Ross attempts to point out that unrestricted immigration will result in the fall of the standard of living and the degeneration of some important social institutions.

Almost a decade later Ross brought his discussion of social problems in the United States up to date in his *Social Trend,* and in this popular book is to be found the germ of *Standing Room Only,* which followed in a few years.[10] Although he has been forced to modify the thesis of overpopulation which is presented in this work, owing to the decline of population growth in the western European world since 1920, Ross still feels that the thesis is true of other parts of the world.[11]

Ross showed his customary intellectual alertness by being the first American sociologist to interest himself actively in the Russian revolution of 1917, which he investigated on the spot. His *Russia in Upheaval* (1918), *The Russian Bolshevik Revolution* (1921), and *The Russian Soviet Republic* (1923) were among the best of the early interpretations of that great social transformation. He also studied the social changes in Mexico and in 1923 wrote a book on *The Social Revolution in Mexico*.

He further investigated the social changes taking place in contemporary China and India.

Although the volumes mentioned above are far from completing the list of the books that Ross has written, they are representative of the type of writing which he has done in the spirit of reform. Most of Ross's later works are either of this sort or are popularized treatments of social phenomena in other countries and are written in a much less scientific vein than such books as his *Social Control* or *Principles of Sociology*. While there is little doubt that his popularized works have attracted many people to sociology who would not have been interested otherwise, and with all due regard for the contribution which Ross has made to the cause of sociology in such a manner, the purpose of this chapter directs our attention away from the popularizing function that his writings have performed and turns it toward the contribution he has made to the development of general sociology.

II. THE ESSENTIALS OF ROSS'S SOCIOLOGICAL SYSTEM

Any discussion of the system of sociology that is present in Ross's work must deal with the four books which were mentioned as being written primarily from the scientific point of view: *Social Control, The Foundations of Sociology, Social Psychology,* and *Principles of Sociology*. Although chronology would indicate that the works be taken up in the order listed, a clearer conception of his system can be developed if we start with *The Foundations of Sociology*. The chapter on "The Unit of Investigation in Sociology" presents a comprehensive map of the field of study for the sociologist as Ross conceived it.[12] The basic unit of sociological investigation, although not the sole unit, is the social process:

> The five units so far favorably considered—groups, relations, institutions, imperatives, uniformities—are products. They precede the individual and survive him. To the onlooker they appear as gods or fates, moulding the lives and disposing upon the destinies of ordinary men. Nevertheless, they have all risen at some time out of the actions and interactions of men. To understand their genesis we must ascend to that primordial fact known as the social process.[13]

According to Ross, if we choose any of the other five units as the basis for the investigation of social phenomena, we soon arrive at an impasse that does not permit further exploration, since it is the process that lies behind every other form of sociological data that is of fundamental importance. If, on the other hand, we begin with the social process, we can trace out the development of the phenomena which go to make up the other classes of data. Ross divides the processes involving human interests into three different classes for purposes of analysis: preliminary, social, and reconstructive. The first of these classes is made up of processes which are not strictly social, since they do not involve "the action of man on man," but which render man amenable to the social processes.[14] One illustration of such a process would be the influence of a common occupation in molding people to such an extent that they would be receptive to being drawn into the same society. Once processes of the preliminary variety have operated over a long enough period of time, the actual social processes may come into play, and it is out of the workings of these that groups, institutions, etc., are produced. The processes which disturb these social products, which have grown and solidified over a period of time and prevent them from becoming completely static, are the reconstructive processes.

These processes, of course, do not comprise the whole of the system, since some provision must be made for the analysis of the products of the social processes. The products Ross considers to be either subjective or objective: institutions, uniformities, and imperatives are classified as subjective, while groups and social relations are thought of as objective. The latter are objective in the sense that they "evince themselves in behavior" and can be observed without communicating with the participants. Institutions are subjective, since they are a sanctioned grouping or relation, though the actual grouping may or may not conform to the sanctioned grouping, while imperatives are subjective, because they are sanctioned actions or beliefs. The uniformities are subjective, since they are beliefs and feelings, but they are not binding.[15] Despite the fact that the old dichotomy of objective and subjective is no longer held to be valid, Ross has succeeded in marking off the division which is still widely used to separate social psychology and sociology, and he has, moreover, dealt with the contents of both categories as being the product of social interaction.

The outline presented above is the scaffolding of Ross's system of sociology as it is described in *The Foundations of Sociology,* and for our purposes the rest of his scientific writing must be regarded as an attempt to fill out this framework. Before proceeding to an analysis of his system, it is necessary to discover the foundations upon which Ross builds, i.e., under what conditions does he believe that social processes, the basic units of sociological investigation, occur?

While the phenomena which compose the rest of the system are the products of social interaction, we must look elsewhere for the source of social interaction itself, and Ross finds this source in the "social forces." These social forces are nothing more than the desires which motivate human beings and are blended into the complex patterns of interests "which shape society and make history." Some of these desires have always been present in the form of biological needs and are later modified by the cultural environment, e.g., the appetitive desires such as hunger, thirst, and sex, while others have developed only after man has become a cultural being, e.g., religious, ethical, and intellectual desires.[16]

The difficulty with this theory of the social forces is the same that plagues other theories of the same sort and is one of the centers of controversy in sociology at the present time: the tendency to reify certain classifications of social phenomena and then use the reified classifications as causal factors in the analysis of the rise of the phenomena. If this use of desires and interests on Ross's part is regarded as a convenient classification of the conditions under which social interaction arises, criticism of it must wait for an analysis of the results which Ross has secured with it. This, of course, leads us to consider the manner in which Ross has dealt with the social processes and how he has actually related his concept of social forces to social interaction.

When we turn to Ross's discussion of the social processes, however, we find that the gap between the social forces and social interaction is not bridged in any generalized formulation but only in examples of how specific traits of human nature determine specific social responses. Thus combat reactions are used to infer that man inherits a struggling response, and the struggling response is, in turn, used as a means of explaining combat reaction. Moreover, with a few exceptions, the examples which are used are not carried over into the discussion of the social processes. It must be concluded that the social forces have little to do with the working-out of the system, since the classificatory device which they offer is not used as such.[17]

In his discussion of the social processes in the *Principles of Sociology*, Ross modifies his system to a certain extent. The preliminary processes are broken up into two sections: one an analysis of the environment, in which it is pointed out that environment serves essentially as a limiting factor in the development of society; and the other a discussion of the relationship of occupation to social function. On the other hand, the reconstructive processes are discussed mainly under the heading of "The Social Population," where the effects of population change, urbanization, and the sex ratio are indicated.

The social processes proper are considered under the several different categories. Association, communication, domination, and exploitation are regarded as being the processes which are most intimately tied up with the genesis of society.[18] How association can be regarded as a process in its own right rather than as a symbol denoting the other social processes is not clear in Ross's writing, and the fact that it is not clear indicates that there is little ground for the assumption that he makes. A similar difficulty is encountered in dealing with the process of communication, in that all other processes are carried out largely through the medium of communication, so that it must be considered to be a phenomenon of a different order. Ross's discussion of the forms of domination and exploitation, as being persistent and recurrent processes, is doubtless correct; but why they and not other processes should be regarded as being the most important in the genesis of society is difficult to perceive. This is particularly true, if we regard society as consisting of the network of social relations that are set up by the social processes.

Ross's attempt to deal with the processes of opposition, conflict, competition, and adaptation is hampered severely by his interest in what he considers to be the good and bad effects of these forms of interaction, and the discussion is limited largely to such topics as wholesome opposition, services of economic competition, and antagonistic effort.[19] If, however, it is realized that this interpretation of good and bad can be translated to mean the strengthening or weakening of a particular group, whether that group be good or bad, the description of these processes becomes much more satisfactory. Moreover, the grouping of opposition, competition, and conflict into a single unit reveals an awareness on Ross's part that there is some common element which renders them akin to one another. The nature of this common element is never revealed, with the result that it is left to the reader's own discretion to decide whether or not these processes do belong together. The uniting of the discussion of the processes of co-operation and organization into a single section also bears witness to this tendency to order the processes around a never revealed common element.[20] It should be obvious by this time, however, that the former are grouped together because they are essentially dissociative processes, while the latter are considered in the same section because they are associative.

A different factor serves as the combining element in the classification of the processes of stratification, the rise of gross inequalities, gradation, and segregation under the heading of class and caste.[21] This factor seems to be that, although dissociative, the primary function which these processes serve is that of differentiation. They are the processes by which division of labor and of benefits develops, and they prevent society from showing a dead level of uniformity. If it is thought that this factor does not explain his placing of equalization and social circulation under the same heading as the above, it must be remembered that, just as adaptation is considered as the process which offsets conflict and competition, so the processes of equalization and social circulation are included under the heading of class and caste because they tend to offset the complete dominance of gradation, stratification, etc.

The processes of socialization, estrangement, and liberation are considered in the same class by Ross because he feels that their greatest importance lies in the relationship which they establish between the individual and society, while ossification, decadence, transformation, etc., are considered under the heading of social regress and progress. The heterogeneity of the classification is still further emphasized by the fact that anticipation, simulation, individualization, deterioration, and balance are not considered as social processes at all but are regarded as sociological principles.[22]

Only one conclusion can be reached from the above description of Ross's treatment of the social processes: systematization of the social processes, as such, exists only in incipient form, and then according to diverse, implicit principles. Some of the processes are systematized according to whether or not they are associative or dissociative, and others are classified as contributing to the growing complexity of society; still others are grouped according to their influence on the relationship between the individual and society. Such systematization amounts essentially to no systematization at all, since no relationship is established between the processes which are classified according to one principle and those grouped around a different standard of judgment.

This does not mean that Ross's discussion of each individual process is invalid, but only that no method is set up by means of which we can relate one process to all the other processes in terms of a certain common element, which all represent to a certain degree. Certain predictions can be made concerning the occurrence and the results of the occurrence of each process, but these generalizations cannot be constructed into a systematized body of knowledge. Had any one of the principles by which Ross classified the processes been carried through consistently, the analysis could have been regarded as systematic, and the validity of the system would have depended upon the increased understanding of social phenomena which it made possible. As it is, the material concerning the processes contains some valid analysis of particular processes and some suggestive principles for future classification but cannot itself be regarded as a systematic description of the social processes. The effects of this carry over into the other aspects of Ross's map of the sociological field. They make rather difficult the demonstration of how the phenomena which go to make up the other divisions are produced by social interaction. The latter, of course, is one of the primary duties that Ross laid upon himself when he outlined his system of analysis, and it is the object toward which most of the remainder of our investigation will be directed.

Ross restricts his analysis of the objective products of social interaction to a brief discussion of groups in the *Principles of Sociology,* and even this discussion is limited essentially to those groups which are regarded as being the product of other than the social processes. Moreover, social processes are "group-makers" to the extent that they, like other phenomena, mark "....off certain persons from others, or establish a community of interest....."[23] This limited presentation of the role of the social processes in the formation of groups does not, of course, offer a satisfactory explanation of how social interaction is responsible for the formation of groups.

Social Psychology and *Social Control* deal primarily with the subjective products of social processes, and in these works Ross points out in detail the fashion in which certain phases of individual mentality and action are determined by the society in which the individual lives. Much has been made of the fact that, in the latter work, Ross has attempted to show that a natural order can develop out of the instinctive behavior of man; but it must be remembered that he casts aside this natural order as not being sufficient to support a complex society and then proceeds to point out how order is brought about on a social basis.[24] Although Ross deals to some extent with the agencies of control which are external to the individual controlled, i.e., law and public opinion, he places primary emphasis on those controls which are social in origin but are internalized in the individual and are an essential part of his personality and are subjective products of social interaction in the meaning of Ross's use of the term. Whether or not the control which is exerted is consciously directed toward certain ends or not seems to be a relatively minor matter. Indeed, except for his mentioning it in the Introduction, Ross pays little or no attention to the restriction that he has theoretically placed on himself. It is for these reasons that *Social Control* is still unsurpassed as a listing of the various means of social control and of the types of behavior which these agencies control. The weakness of the work lies where we might expect it: in the explanation of how these subjective products become part of the personality of the individuals who are controlled by them.

It is in Ross's description of the influence of custom that we see this weakness most clearly illustrated. The individual may obey custom because he is afraid of the consequences which are to follow, but Ross points out that custom is largely self-enforcing, meaning that the fear of external factors need not enter the situation. Thus we get a picture which, in almost every way, corresponds to the most sophisticated theories of social control; but Ross then attributes this self-enforcing quality of custom to the power of suggestion and habit:

> The secret of this power must be sought, in the last analysis, in suggestion and habit. The child receives the ideas, precepts, and likings which are to become the organizing factors of its life, because it has no habits, because it is not yet obsessed by other ideas and feelings, because it wants something that may help it to bring order out of the chaotic contents of its mind, and because the hunger of a growing creature makes it greedy for mental aliment. On the other hand, the adult who has passed the suggestible age and emerged from the family chrysalis, allows the early organization of his life to dominate him because habit is strong and the wrench of mental adjustment is painful.[25]

The point must be re-emphasized that Ross sees that a connection exists between social interaction and attitudes, mind, and other so-called "subjective" phenomena but hides the essential element of the problem behind the symbols—suggestion and habit. So again he fails to bridge the gap between one segment of his system and another. This applies not only to his treatment of the factors involved in social control over a long period of time but also to his treatment of the material concerning all psychic planes and currents which are due to social interaction. A good part of the *Social Psychology* is taken up with the phenomenon of suggestibility and the part it plays in transferring to another group the ideas, habits, and attitudes of one group of individuals. It is true that Ross is interested primarily in the broad uniformities of attitudes, ideas, and habits that people possess within a given society rather than in the development of the unique personality in social interaction. But the problem, in so far as it is connected with the process by which these attitudes are internalized, is essentially the same, whether they be the attitudes of a small group or attitudes which are present throughout a whole society. He fails to answer the question as to the conditions under which the social mind develops.[26]

We must conclude, therefore, that that section of Ross's system which deals with the subjective products of social interaction cannot be regarded as being actually systematic. His discussions concerning specific factors in social control and other particular problems, such as crowd behavior and mob mind, are brilliant and useful, but each of them forms a separate and distinct piece of work. There is little relationship demonstrated between the phenomena, since their basic relationship must grow out of the fact that they are products of social interaction, and Ross is unable to show how they are so produced.

III. A CRITICAL APPRAISAL OF ROSS'S SOCIOLOGICAL DOCTRINES

Ross's system as a whole must then be regarded as a map of the sociological field, and a map in which the connection between the various areas is not clearly demonstrated. The map, however, does contain the basic dividing line along which sociology has continued to grow, in that social interaction is the core of systematic sociology, while groups, attitudes, mind, etc., are regarded as products of the social processes. As a system, however, it is definitely unsatisfactory. The two basic requirements of a system of scientific theory are that the relations between the major divisions be demonstrated and that within each major division the various phenomena dealt with be clearly related. Ross's system meets neither of these requirements: the social processes are not successfully related to one another, nor are the products of interaction related to one another. Ross fails to establish his hypothesis that what he calls "social products" are actually produced by social interaction. As has been pointed out before, this does not invalidate the results which Ross has secured in dealing with the problems presented by various individual phenomena; it indicates only that Ross has not successfully erected his findings into a system.

How much influence on systematic sociology Ross's map of the sociological field has had is difficult to determine. Blackmar and Gillin adopted Ross's outline of the social processes, with some modification, and Von Wiese and Becker have utilized Ross's material to some extent.[27] In the latter case, however, it is primarily a use of the specific description of certain processes, since the authors have systematized the processes according to one consistent standard throughout.

The influence which Ross's writing will have in the future will also probably stem from his description of specific problems and processes. Systems superior to Ross's system in consistency and explanatory power have already been developed, and their existence minimizes the possibility that his system as such will ever have a great deal of importance for formal social theory. Future interest in his system must be essentially of a historical nature.

NOTES

1. *Seventy Years of It* (New York, 1936).
2. *Social Control* (New York, 1901); *The Foundations of Sociology* (New York, 1905); *Social Psychology* (New York, 1908); *Principles of Sociology* (2d ed.; New York, 1930).
3. *Social Control*, title-page.
4. *Ibid.*, pp. vii–viii.
5. *Foundations of Sociology*, p. 98.
6. *Social Psychology*, p. 1. It is realized that what has been said here about these books has been said countless times before, and it is included only to set the stage for the more lengthy analysis which is to follow.
7. *Sin and Society* (Boston, 1907). For a survey of Ross's contributions to public problems see the article on Ross by Harry Elmer Barnes, in the English *Sociological Review*, April, 1923.
8. New York, 1914.
9. *The Old World in the New* (New York, 1914).
10. *The Social Trend* (New York, 1922). The first two chapters deal with the problem of population increase and migration; see also *Standing Room Only* (New York, 1927).
11. *Seventy Years of It*, pp. 226–29.
12. *The Foundations of Sociology*, pp. 71–99.
13. *Ibid.*, pp. 90–91.
14. *Ibid.*, pp. 88–90.
15. *Ibid.*
16. *Ibid.*, pp. 149–81.

17. One of the exceptions is his discussion of opposition. Ross points out that interference of interests leads to the processes of opposition, competition, and conflict (*Principles of Sociology*, p. 149).

18. *Ibid.*, pp. 93–146.

19. *Ibid.*, pp. 149–262.

20. *Ibid.*, pp. 265–310.

21. *Ibid.*, pp. 313–71.

22. *Ibid.*, pp. 375–498, 531–85.

23. *Ibid.*, p. 515.

24. *Social Control*, pp. 41–61.

25. *Ibid.*, pp. 184–85. Ross's use of suggestion is similar to his use of the social forces. Suggestion is inferred from the behavior of individuals and then used to explain that behavior. This use of the term prevents a detailed discussion of the conditions under which attitudes, ideas, and habits of others are taken over into the personality in question.

26. Compare this point of view with that of Kimball Young, "Social Psychology," in H. E. Barnes (ed.), *The History and Prospects of the Social Sciences* (New York, 1925), pp. 156–209, and particularly pp. 161–62.

27. F. W. Blackmar and J. L. Gillin, *Outlines of Sociology* (New York, 1915), pp. 296–307; see also G. Lundberg, *Foundations of Sociology* (New York, 1939), p. 248; L. von Wiese and Howard Becker, *Systematic Sociology* (New York, 1932). Consult Index in the latter work for references to Ross.

CHAPTER XLIII

CHARLES HORTON COOLEY: PIONEER IN PSYCHOSOCIOLOGY

RICHARD DEWEY, *University of Illinois*

I. COOLEY'S LIFE AND TRAINING

THE life of this scholarly idealist unfolded its uneventful length almost within the shadows of the university buildings in Ann Arbor. Here he was born in 1864, here he spent his creative years, and here he died in 1929. A troubled childhood, attended by bodily ills and personal misgivings, left Cooley with few pleasant memories of his youth.[1] All was not loss, however, for intellectual interests in the form of reading and introspective interrogation were evidenced in early adolescence.[2] His ill-health persisted until his early twenties, making it necessary to devote seven years to undergraduate college training.

His graduation from the University of Michigan in 1887 was followed by a year's training in mechanical engineering at the same school. In 1888, while working as draftsman at Bay City, he expressed the desire to study for a Master's degree in political economy, with a minor in history.[3] He returned to school in January to begin his studies but, three months later, accepted an assignment in Washington, D.C., with the Civil Service Commission. This, together with a second position with the census bureau, kept him in Washington for two years. He married in 1890 and, after a six months' trip to Europe, returned to the University of Michigan in the fall of 1892 to begin his teaching career.[4]

Except for the time spent in Bay City and Washington, Cooley always made his home in Ann Arbor. Despite numerous invitations to go elsewhere, he refused to leave the University of Michigan.[5] In contrast to the active, public service career of his illustrious jurist father, Thomas M. Cooley, the life of Charles Horton was quiet indeed. Handicapped by partial deafness and a speech impediment, Cooley never was sparkling in his classroom conduct; ". . . . he was quiet, shy, unobtrusive. . . . ."[6]

Unimpressive as an undergraduate teacher,[7] he nevertheless was successful in influencing more mature students.[8]

His interest in sociology was waxing even when he accepted the instructorship in political economy. His first published work, "The Social Significance of Street Railways," which appeared in 1891, was in essence an ecological study.[9] Cooley received his doctorate in 1894 and began teaching sociology in the academic year 1894–95, lecturing three hours per week the first semester on "principles" and, as is so often the procedure today, devoted the second semester to "problems."[10] His early courses on contemporary life were, he records, more concerned with economics than with social psychology.[11] His doctoral thesis, *The Theory of Transportation,* "... an attempt to interpret this function in terms of an organic whole,"[12] furnished material for his early teaching. His treatment of this led him to study other phases of the social process in like manner.

Cooley's readings centered mainly in the works of Emerson, Goethe, Comte, Ward, Spencer, Darwin, Gumplowicz, Quételet, Maine, Morgan, McLennan, Westermarck, Jane Addams, Giddings, and, of course, Tarde, James, and Baldwin. But more time and labor, he tells us, than was spent on any of these "... went to an arduous perusal of the first volume of Schäffle's *Bau und Leben des sozialen Körpers,*" which seemed to him to offer a view of the social system preferable to Spencer's.[13] Regarding Schäffle, it has been said that "at heart he stood closer to Schelling and Hegel than to Darwin, Spencer, or Haeckel. Schäffle's way of thinking followed rather an ethical, teleological conception of the world..... In his view, the gist of a people's life is its civilization; the ideal for society is an increasing socialization."[14] This parallels Cooley's ideal of the extension to all society of primary group characteristics and suggests a significant early influence. Cooley readily accords Darwin and Baldwin source credit for his thinking, and Emerson played a larger part in Cooley's thinking than is apparent on the surface.

Not all Cooley's publications will be discussed here. In addition to the famous trilogy, *Human Nature and the Social Order* (1902; rev. ed. 1922), *Social Organization* (1909), and *Social Process* (1918), attention will be directed to most of the papers collected and published in *Sociological Theory and Social Research* (1930), which includes a complete list of his thirty-one publications on pages 343–45. The Cooley,

Angell, and Carr textbook, *Introductory Sociology,* absorbs a large part of the Cooley hypotheses in relatively unadulterated form.

II. COOLEY'S MAIN SOCIOLOGICAL WRITINGS

Perhaps the two outstanding characteristics of Cooley's writings on sociology are his avoidance of one-sided and particularistic interpretations of social phenomena and the freedom of his generalizations from the dogmatism that is to be found in the works of many sociologists of his generation. While he treated social processes and problems primarily from the psychological standpoint, he accorded full recognition to the value of other modes of approach. In his own specialty of psychological sociology he avoided overemphasizing the importance of a single principle or formula and insisted that the social process is controlled by many factors, all of which must be taken into account in any well-rounded treatment. Indeed, he went so far in this direction that his interpretation of society might, in a fundamental way, be regarded as more of a social philosophy than a social psychology. His interpretation of society is philosophic not only in scope but also in its attitudes and methods.

In reading Cooley's works one can scarcely escape from the conclusion that his generalizations, keen and scholarly as they are, were derived chiefly from books perused thoughtfully in the comfortable setting of the library. His own books draw quite as much upon the great monuments of general literature as upon technical treatments of sociology. Cooley's admiration for Thoreau, whom he quotes more frequently than any other author, may have rested upon a certain degree of psychic affinity with that interesting figure in American literary and philosophic history. By this reserved and idealistic attitude Cooley gained in breadth and sanity of view, in that he escaped from the passionate, but unscientific, enthusiasm of the advocate of social reform, on the one hand, and from the all too frequent narrowness and technicality of the laboratory psychologist and statistical sociologist, on the other. His mastery of the art of dignified expression gave Cooley's writings a high degree of literary merit not only in content but also in the form of expression.

Fundamental to Cooley's broad approach to social phenomena was his comprehensive and practical view of the organic nature of history and society. This was well presented in his comment on Professor F. H.

Giddings' paper on "A Theory of Social Causation," read at New Orleans in 1903:

The organic view of history denies that any factor or factors are more ultimate than others. Indeed it denies that the so-called factors—such as the mind, the various institutions, the physical environment, and so on—have any real existence apart from a total life in which all share in the same way that the members of the body share in the life of the animal organism. It looks upon mind and matter, soil, climate, flora, fauna, thought, language, and institutions as aspects of a single rounded whole, one total growth. We may concentrate attention upon some one of these things, but this concentration should never go so far as to overlook the subordination of each to the whole, or to conceive one as precedent to others.[14a]

As the basis of his general sociological system is the organic view of the social process, so the central theme of Cooley's psychological sociology is the doctrine of the inseparable and complementary nature of society and the individual—the notion of the social creation of the "self." He emphasizes, time and again, that either the individual or society is a mere abstraction when not considered in its natural relation to the other. The elucidation of the interaction and interrelationships of the individual and society furnishes the subject matter of Cooley's books and constitutes a coherent system of social philosophy. We may now turn to a consideration of Cooley's main writings in the field of sociology.

A. "HUMAN NATURE AND THE SOCIAL ORDER" (1902)[15]

"Society and the Individual," states Cooley, is really the subject of this book.[16] Undoubtedly influenced by his good grasp of Darwin and Baldwin, Cooley sought to further the trend already under way, i.e., that of viewing the individual and the group as closely related phenomena. He held that ".... the antithesis, society *versus* the individual, is false and hollow whenever used as a general or philosophical statement of human relations."[17] The position which Cooley regarded as sound is ".... that individuality is neither prior in time nor lower in moral rank than sociality; but that the two have always existed side by side as complementary aspects of the same thing....."[18] He contended that man's psychical equipment is not divisible into social and nonsocial, "but that he is all social .... all a part of the common human life....."[19]

Viewing behavior in this manner, Cooley devotes the rest of the book to discussions of suggestion and choice, sociability and personal ideas, sympathy, the social self, hostility, leadership, conscience, personal degeneration, and freedom.

The now familiar concept of the "looking-glass self" is a small but signal part of chapter v. This self-idea has, according to Cooley, three principal parts: "the imagination of our appearance to the other person; the imagination of his judgment of that appearance, and some sort of self-feeling, such as pride or mortification."[20] The analogy breaks down, he admits, on the second point, which is vital to the acquisition of a self-idea that functions well in society.

In chapter x, "The Social Aspects of Conscience," is evidenced the oft made assertion that Cooley's sociology is oriented toward a normal, midwestern American community.[21] The chapter is, in the words of Mead, ".... an admirable ethical treatise rather than a scientific analysis of the situation within which lie moral judgments and the whole apparatus of impulses."[22]

B. "SOCIAL ORGANIZATION" (1909)

"In this .... [book] the eye is focussed on the enlargement and diversification of intercourse which I have called Social Organization, the individual, though visible, remaining slightly in the background."[23] The emphasis upon the unity of society and the social nature of the self which characterized *Human Nature and the Social Order* is translated into this larger view. Thus we are reminded again that social consciousness is inseparable from self-consciousness, that "self and society are twin born."[24]

In chapter ii, Cooley offers a discussion of the relativity of moral values, a concept still restricted to the world of the social scientist. Reform must be sympathetic, that is, it must afford the offender an explanation for his aberrant behavior.[25] A naturalistic interpretation is a prerequisite to *real* reform.

Chapter iii, the original source of the concept of "primary groups," is the most often quoted of all of Cooley's works.[26] "By primary groups I mean those characterized by intimate face-to-face association and cooperation..... They are primary in several senses, but chiefly in that they are fundamental in forming the social nature and ideals of the individual."[27] The family, the children's play group, and the neighborhood or community of elders are most important.[28] It is in these groups that the individual's human nature is defined.

In discussing the characteristics of this human nature, Cooley introduces a "psychic unity" theme: "Life in the primary group gives rise to social ideals which, as they spring from similar experiences, have much in common throughout the human race."[29] These primary ideals of loyalty, truth, service, lawfulness, freedom, etc., discussed in chapters iv and v, are acquired and transmitted by the primary groups. When social interaction takes place in groups beyond the primary in extent, the failure to provide adequate organization is the essence of our failure to build a moral social order.[30] The mechanism upon which such organization rests is communication, which ".... must be full and quick in order to give that promptness in the give-and-take of suggestions upon which moral unity depends."[31] Forms and customs of rational organization must supplement this communication technique.[32]

The implications for a democratic order are clear in the following statement: "The work of communication in enlarging human nature is partly immediate, through facilitating contact, but even more it is indirect, through favoring the increase of intelligence, the decline of mechanical and arbitrary forms of organization, and the rise of a more humane type of society."[33]

Cooley's faith in democracy is evidenced in the chapters on "The Democratic Mind." The enlargment of consciousness is the "central fact of history, from a psychological point of view,"[34] and the success of democracy is a reflection of this. Public opinion is ".... an organization, a coöperative product of communication and reciprocal influence."[35] Again, this is a bulwark of democracy, and the communication and organization are, of course, successful to the extent that primary ideals are developed and communicated. It is the masses who contribute the sentiment and common sense which are utilized by the leader, whose utterance of these vital tendencies constitutes his main function and gives a claim to seeming originality.[36] Barnes holds that Cooley's faith in the ability of the people to choose competent leaders[37] is probably the weakest phase of Cooley's defense of democracy.[38]

Cooley's ninety-five-page treatment of social classes was one of the first to appear in American sociology. He views heredity as the signal factor in establishing and maintaining castes, while desire to lessen competition is conducive to the formation of classes. It will be observed that he points out in "Personal Competition" that status (the basis of class) reduces competition and vice versa.

Dealing with the growth of capitalistic classes and the organization of the ill-paid, Cooley again broaches the subject of the symmetry of social organization. He makes the interesting point regarding the capitalistic class that men of genius seldom predominate here, since "only a somewhat commonplace mind will give itself whole-heartedly to the commercial ideal."[39]

Cooley feels that a real caste system is a prerequisite to revolution, since a class system permits the more capable of the lower strata to be drawn into the upper. They identify themselves with the moneyed classes and escape from the underprivileged class, not attempting to improve it.[40] This would not be the case were castes part of our social structures; but Cooley feels that the development of castes is a remote possibility here.[41]

Wielding the familiar hypotheses, Cooley pioneered in the theoretical discussion of institutions.[42] Describing institutions as the "organized attitudes of the public mind," he writes that these institutions exist in the individual as "....a habit of mind or action, largely unconscious because largely common to all the group....."[43] In certain individuals the usual institutional control is lessened, and there is set up a habit of change, this unrest being explained by transition in society.[44]

Tradition, as carried by institutions, plays as significant a role in modern society as in medieval times: "It is only that tradition is so intricate and so spread out over the fact of things that its character as tradition is hardly to be discovered."[45]

Formalism, described as an excess of mechanism in society, is undesirable, in that it "....interferes with growth and adaptation, when it suppresses individuality and stupefies or misdirects the energies of human nature."[46]

In the chapters on "Disorganization" Cooley treats of the family, the church, the economic system, education, etc., indicating the operation of special phases of the social process.

In a section entitled "Public Will" Cooley defines public will as "....the deliberate self-direction of any group"[47] and asserts that there is a trend toward the development of an adequate public will.[48] This is integral to his faith in democracy.

The proper sphere of government as expression of the public will is relative to the time and situation.[49] It is essential to attain symmetry of organization, and governmental functions should be adapted to this end; recent extension of governmental influence is only in keeping with the growth of other organizations.[50]

Cooley concludes with an optimistic note in "Some Phases of Larger Will." The "growing efficiency of the intellectual and moral processes as a whole is the reason behind this more effective public will..... The guiding force back of public will, now as ever, is of course human nature itself in its more enduring characteristics, those which find expression in primary groups and which are little affected by institutional changes."[51] Here, once more, is evidence that Cooley's agenda for an adequate society hinges upon the extension of primary group ideals to the whole social order. It is to these that the quest for principles of successful social interaction leads!

c. "SOCIAL PROCESS" (1918)

Contemporary reviewers noted the absence of technical terminology, the avoidance of the "hackneyed and scholastic," in *Social Process*. Perhaps less of a textbook than his other two books, *Social Process* brings to full term the central theme of the other works, i.e., the organic view of society. Here he writes:

> We see around us in the world of men an onward movement of life. There seems to be a vital impulse of unknown origin, that tends to work ahead in innumerable directions and manners, each continuous with something of the same sort in the past. The whole thing appears to be a kind of growth, and we might add that it is an adaptive growth, meaning by this that the forms of life we see—men, associations of men, traditions, institutions, conventions, theories, ideals—are not separate or independent, but that the growth of each takes place in contact and interaction with that of others. Thus any one phase of the movement may be regarded as a series of adaptations to other phases.[52]

Perhaps the best summary of Cooley's idea of the organic nature of society is the following:

> If then we say that society is an organism, we mean, I suppose, that it is a complex of forms or processes each of which is living and growing by interaction with the others, the whole being so unified that what takes place in one part affects all the rest. It is a vast tissue of reciprocal activity, differentiated into innumerable systems, some of them quite distinct, others not readily traceable, and all interwoven to such a degree that you see different systems according to the point of view you take.....
>
> It is the aim of the organic view to "see life whole," or at least as largely as our limitations permit. However, it by no means discredits the study of society from particular standpoints, such as the economic, the political, the military, the religious. This is profitable because the whole is so vast that to get any grasp of it we need to approach it now from one point of view, now from another, fixing our attention upon each phase in turn, and then synthesizing it all as best we can.....
>
> It should be the outcome of the organic view that we embrace specialty with ardor, and yet recognize that it is partial and tentative, needing from time to time

to be reabsorbed and reborn of the whole. The Babel of conflicting particularisms resembles the condition of religious doctrine a century ago, when everyone took it for granted that there could be but one true form of belief, and there were dozens of antagonistic systems claiming to be this form. The organic conception, in any sphere, requires that we pursue our differences in the sense of a larger unity.[53]

Much of the book is recognizable as restatement of previous writings under the division headings of "Personal Aspects of Social Process," "Degeneration," "Group Conflict," "Valuation," etc. It is a very readable book, containing carefully restated aspects of the hypotheses nurtured by Cooley.

D. "SOCIOLOGICAL THEORY AND SOCIAL RESEARCH" (1930)

Cooley selected various articles and monographs which he deemed worthy of publication, and these are included in *Sociological Theory and Social Research*. Not of the group selected by Cooley, but included in this book, is a short paper, largely autobiographical, describing the development of sociology at the University of Michigan. Because of the biographical material given above, this is not included in the list of briefly annotated papers which follow.

1. *"Theory of Transportation."*—This, Cooley's doctoral thesis, was designed to disclose more completely the relationship of transportation facilities to economic and political life. He saw in the growing analysis of society by sociology a basis for his plan; thus a demographic approach to the problem was established. He shows the interactive relationship between social and physical in the determination of transportation lines and the subsequent growth of population centers. His maxim that "population and wealth tend to collect wherever there is a break in transportation" is now classic. His later interest in psychic factors was not evidenced here.

2. *"Genius, Fame, and Comparison of Races."*—Francis Galton's *Hereditary Genius* prompted Cooley's effort to refute the thesis advanced in that work, viz., that fame is generally a sufficient test of genius.[54] Research for this purpose is reflected in the lengthy retort in which, among other things, agronomic analogy, Renaissance Italian painters, and American baseball are garnered to disprove the assertion that biological endowment determines all and that biological groupings, such as Anglo-Saxon, Ancient Greeks, Negroes, and Lowland Scots, etc., are possessed of endowment differentials.[55] Cooley claims no originality for the manner in which he dispatches Galton's stand,[56] i.e., by indi-

cating the fallacy inherent in the particularistic biological position. Looking at the question from a vantage point of a period wherein the relativity of these two factors is taken for granted, today's student is induced to question the need for so thorough a treatment of Galton's position.

3. *"Personal Competition."*—Cooley states that he purposes to discuss personal competition ".... with a view to the part it plays in social life as a whole and to the effect it has upon the character and happiness of men."[57] He treats of this subject under the following headings: (1) *The function of personal competition:* ".... to assign to each individual his place in the system."[58] There is, however, an alternative to competition, which may determine the place of the person in society; this is some form of *status,* usually inherited.[59] (2) *The intensity of competition:* ".... any diminution of the intensity of competition is inevitably accompanied by an advance in the alternative principle of status."[60] As classes form, status gains over competition.[61] Cooley reminds us that there can and must be combinations of the advantages of these alternative principles in society.[62] (3) *The relation of competition to association:* "When the selective process has performed its function, when it has answered the question, what is the fittest, it ought to cease and give place to organization."[63] It is the failure to maintain symmetry between competition and association that causes many, if not most, of the evils of our time.[64] (4) *Conditions of success:* Cooley's conditions are not unusual. (5) *Success and morality:* Success and morality have a community of origin which increases the likelihood of their association. (6) *Competition and sympathy:* competition gains sympathetic understanding for the competitor.[65] (7) *Restlessness, insecurity, and strain:* the zestful, chaotic competition of American life stimulates to heightened action but induces feelings of insecurity where opportunity is not afforded members of society through education and symmetrical social organization. (8) *Individuality, self-reliance, earnestness:* ".... whatever its evils, [competition] .... promotes individuality, self-reliance and earnestness."[66] (9) *The standard of success:* success is whatever men think it is.

4. *"A Study of the Early Use of Self-words by a Child."*—In the manner of Baldwin, Cooley observed and recorded the early self-words used by his children, hoping to throw light on the social conception of the self.[67] This article has reference to Cooley's third child; he had already

made "some scanty observations" of his first two children. The observations were recorded from the second to the twenty-third month, at which time the use of self-words seemed normal.[68]

The correct understanding of "I" and "you," when used by others, which was gained in the middle of the nineteenth month, was followed in the twenty-second by the imitative use of "I," but the "I" was not discriminated from the rest of the phrase.[69] The twenty-third month saw the correct use of "I," with reference not to body but to a *self-assertive feeling*.[70] Cooley holds that the "I" is social in that the ".... very essence of it is the assertion of self-will in a social medium of which the speaker is conscious."[71]

5. *"Political Economy and Social Process."*—Contending that "a social science which is not also, in its central principles, an ethical science is unfaithful to its deepest responsibility, that of functioning in the aid of general progress,"[72] Cooley says that "it would seem that the ingenious but circumscribed science of political economy deals with social process almost wholly in its immediate and somewhat transitory aspects."[73] Is not the spirit of political economy, he asks, for the most part pre-Darwinian?[74]

6. *"Reflections upon the Sociology of Herbert Spencer."*—A brief biographical sketch precedes a discussion of Spencer's personal characteristics, which Cooley feels disqualified Spencer as an observer of society.[75] His deficiency lay certainly not in intellectual ability but in a lack of "sympathetic qualities which are, after all, the only direct source of our knowledge of other people."[76] Cooley's critique of Spencer stems from, and is guided by, this feeling. He points to the analogical character of Spencer's writings and their remoteness from actual life and to the latter's ".... wish to extend over the social field conceptions drawn from physics and biology."[77]

E. ON RESEARCH

Specific works on methodology are not usually associated with Cooley's name.[78] To be sure, the weight of his efforts is lent to the development and elaboration of carefully drawn hypotheses concerning social behavior. Shortly before his death in 1929, Cooley saw fit to supplement the methodological thinking which was implicit in his writings by a series of short articles. These will be briefly discussed below.

The keynote of his thinking on method is clearly stated in *Social Process:* "Knowledge requires both observation and interpretations, neither being more scientific than the other. And each branch of science must be worked out in its own way, which is mainly to be found in the actual search for truth rather than by *a priori* methodology."[79] "The sooner we cease circumscribing and testing ourselves by the canons of physical and physiological science the better."[80] Cooley's special liking for the work of Thomas and Znaniecki and Sumner is indicative of his position on research methods.

In "The Roots of Social Knowledge" Cooley points out the principal dichotomy of the conditions with which the mind has to deal: (1) the material and (2) the human or social.[81] This basic division requires an application of different methods. We gain a sympathetic knowledge of social conditions by living in society.[82] This interactive process (Baldwin's "dialectic of personal growth") affords one an "....understanding of persons, of society and of ourselves."[83] Critical introspection, says Cooley, is more objective than the usual practice of floating upon social currents without attempting to become aware of them."[84]

There is no essential antagonism between statistics and sympathetic observation and interpretation. Social science becomes exact, not through the substitution of statistics for the latter method but through a supplementation of it by the mathematical manipulation of data.[85] In "Case Study of Small Institutions as a Method of Research" Cooley reiterates his principles, illustrating specifically the type of project desired. He also indicates his willingness to employ movies in attempts to gain further advantage in social research.[86]

In "Sumner and Methodology" Cooley asserts that *Folkways* is the "most successful work of research that American sociology has produced[87]—and this despite the fact that it is not quantitative, statistical, psychoanalytical, behavioristic, or yet a case study.[88] It is suggested that the methodological dogmatist should not be taken too seriously[89] and "....that a working methodology is a residue from actual research."[90] Those "....who contributed to it did so unconsciously, by trying to find out something that they ardently wanted to know."[91]

"The Life-Study Method as Applied to Rural Social Research" again sets before the reader Cooley's plea for "....life-like description covering a period of time....," an extension of the case-study method.[92] These

must be based upon "sympathetic or dramatic perceptions," the "....
basis of reality for our knowledge of man."[93] Believing that adequate
models are not available to guide rural sociologists in this descriptive
technique, Cooley sees a need for ".... something new, something that
combines the insight of literatures with the distinterestedness and factual truth of science."[94]

III. COOLEY'S CONTRIBUTION TO SOCIOLOGY

It has been said that Cooley's trilogy remains "....the clearest general
statement of psycho-sociology yet produced in the English language."[95]
"In so far as recent sociological literature is concerned, ... few writers
are as frequently and as confidently quoted in reference to the social-
psychological point of view."[96] The latter statement can readily be verified by an inspection of the indexes of standard works in sociology.
Believing that it might aid in isolating the contributions of Cooley, the
author has made a classification of those of his works to which reference
is most often made.

Cooley himself "....was quite convinced that.... [his] .... concept
of organic growth, with its corollary of non-particularism," was his most
important contribution; but he once said, smiling slightly, that he supposed he would be remembered, if at all, for "primary groups."[97] An
inspection of some twenty standard books in sociology suggest that
Cooley's fears were partly warranted. The most frequent single references were made to the concepts of the "primary group" and the "looking-glass self"—more to the former than to the latter. The fact that his
name is more readily associated with these concepts may well be at-
tributable to our liking for catch-phrases and, of course, to the fact that
he originated them.

Contributions to social thought, however, cannot be assigned only to
originality, and I would agree with Cooley that his signal contribution
to sociology is to be found in the emphasis which he placed upon furthering the concept of organic growth and its corollary, nonparticularism.
As a matter of fact, if the numerous references associated with the
organic-unity idea are considered together, they outnumber those to the
primary-group concept. Cooley's contributions to sociology can easily
be treated under the heading of "Theme and Variations." The organic

theme is the hub upon which all Cooley's works turn, including the concepts of "primary group" and "looking-glass self." The self is a social product, gaining its fundamental characteristics from the primary-group experiences.

A. THE THEME: ORGANIC UNITY

Since the conception of society as an organic whole is *the* recurrent theme in Cooley, it is given priority here. He uses the term "organic" ".... in the sense that influences may be and are transmitted from one part to any other part so that all parts are bound together into an inter-dependent whole."[98] To the reader who has been exposed to modern sociological social-psychology, as represented by Dewey, Mead, Faris, *et al.,* Cooley's works will be viewed as a fair statement of this phase of sociology. Such readers will note the value-laden tenor of the writings and a seemingly needless repetition of the life-a-unified-whole theme. Page after page contains, directly or implicitly, the thesis that a separate individual is an abstraction unknown to experience. However, Cooley was not addressing himself to straw men when he wrote: "Most people not only think of individuals and society as more or less separate and antithetical, but they look upon the former as antecedent to the latter."[99] Nor is the sociological position widely known and accepted today by persons not in the line of inheritance of the Cooley-Mead-Dewey tradition. Much of the confused thinking in the field of social psychology[100] may well be a result of the failure of investigators in this field to see what Cooley and his successors hold to be factual data, empirically known, i.e., the social nature of self and the unity of the group.[101]

For evidence that discussion of this topic of social relativity is not of the "coals to Newcastle" order, instance the unfruitful quests for ir-reducible units of personality, the search for innate motives to explain behavior, the particularistic interpretations still subscribed to by current students of behavior, e.g., the psychoanalysts, extreme Marxists, and many physiological psychologists.

Even a cursory perusal of current sociological works (including social psychological) will reveal a continued use of Cooley's terminology; and, where this is lacking, the essence of the thought begun by late nineteenth-century writers and furthered by Cooley is apparent in the treatment of situational behavior and in variations on the social process, e.g., Ross, Wiese and Becker, Park, and Burgess. As is true in the case of any intellectual tradition, the influence of a particular contributor to this tradition is difficult to establish.

1. *Primary group.*—The shift toward the sociological interpretation of behavior evidenced in the late nineteenth century induced students of individual behavior to investigate the various milieu in which the individual moved. The growing distrust of instincts as an explanation of social behavior and the widening application of the genetic approach to social problems logically led to studies of the early influences on the human organism. J. M. Baldwin's writings[102] preceded Cooley's in this respect, but Cooley approached the subject mainly from the sociological viewpoint, thus supplementing Baldwin's writings.[103] Cooley followed Baldwin in observing his children's progress in acquiring a world in which to live. He correctly pointed to the family, the play group, and the neighborhood as the most influential groups in the individual's life. These groups are of primary importance in the development of the person, and the term "primary groups" is a fortunate one. Cooley's contribution in this respect cannot be accurately measured by the large number of references made to this concept alone; nearly every textbook in sociology or social psychology, especially the introductory texts and those on the family, are indebted for their viewpoint to the tradition of which Cooley's thought is an integral phase.

2. *Self.*—Current social psychological theory concerning the nature and development of the self is the product of varied intellectual efforts. Cooley's thought in this sphere of social psychology is definitely interstitial, and his importance lies in elaborating in a sociological context the thinking of earlier scholars, thus providing subsequent students with a more advantageous point of departure. This is by no means an insignificant contribution.

Assignment of origins in social thought is hazardous in any event, and particularly so in a field as widely ramified as that of the precursors of social psychological thought. For our purpose it will be sufficient to name a few of the representative writings on the subject. It does not seem amiss to indicate that the writings of J. S. Mackenzie[104] on this point are among the earliest. Tarde unsuccessfully attempted to establish imitation as the mechanism whereby personality was developed. At about this time William James made an abortive move in the direction later taken by Cooley *et al.,* defining the "social self" as the recognition which is accorded one by his mates.[105] Could this be the germ of Cooley's "looking-glass self"? Karpf reminds us that James "....made no attempt to follow through consistently the social-psychological aspects of his new approach.....".[106]

Baldwin placed greater emphasis upon the social origin of the self than did James.[107] This emphasis which he introduced runs throughout the modern period of social psychology[108] and is, of course, a cardinal point in Cooley. However, Baldwin was no more successful than Tarde was in his quest for a mechanism with which to explain the development of man's social nature.[109] "The superiority of Cooley's position," says Mead, "lies in his freedom to find in consciousness a social process going on, within which the self and others arise."[110] This establishment of the self and others on the same plane of experience was highly significant for the advancement of social psychological theory.

This is, however, as far as he successfully carried the torch. In viewing the imaginations as the solid facts of society, he veers away from the modified behaviorist view and toward a solipsistic position that is hardly acceptable.[111] The following excerpts from Mead's criticism best sums up the thinking on this score:

> The evidence for this [that selves do belong to objective experience which we distinguish from the psychical] is found in the fact that the human organism, in advance of the psychical experiences to which Cooley refers, assumes the attitude of another which it addresses by vocal gesture, and in this attitude addresses itself, thus giving rise to its own self and to the other. In the process of communication there appears a social world of selves standing on the same level of immediate reality as that of the physical world that surrounds us. It is out of this social world that the inner experiences arise which we term psychical, and they serve largely in interpretation of this social world as psychical sensations and percepts serve to interpret the physical objects of our environment.....If this is true, social groups are not psychical but are immediately given, though inner experiences are essential for their interpretation.[112]

C. SOCIAL DYNAMICS: THE CONCEPT OF CREATIVENESS

Cooley's social dynamics was rooted in a broad and consistent faith in the reality of progress, and he found the basis of progress to reside in the capacity of the individual and society for *creativeness.* As Dr. Samuel M. Levin remarks: "Cooley habitually resorts to the hallmarks of originality or creativeness as a frame of reference."[113] This is akin to Tarde's faith in invention as the great instrument of progress, and Cooley had much respect for Tarde's ideas.

To Cooley, the fresh and original constitute the raw material for both individual and social advancement. Creativeness provides the means of self-expression for both persons and societies. It arises, in the most fundamental sense, from the surplus of biological energy in the individual and manifests itself in the development of novel forms of social ideals and institutions. The masses have a great potential impulse toward creativeness in their sentimental response to such forces as feeling, imagination, sympathy, and impression. But they need leaders to set off, inspire, and direct this mass trend to creation. For this reason Cooley was both a believer in democracy and a keen student of the problems of leadership. His faith in democracy rested upon his conviction that, by and large, the masses possess the ability to discern, respect, and follow the best leaders, though not infallibly so. In our day functional groups are especially important and potent in stimulating and directing creative social action.

Cooley fully recognized that many of our impulses to creativeness are irrational or nonrational; but he contended that in the future we must, more and more, foster and rely upon rational factors and intelligent leadership. This justifies social planning, but the latter must always make place for freedom and liberty. Without these, neither the individual nor society can function effectively in the task of creativeness.

Cooley's significance, then, rests in two closely related spheres: (1) his attention to the development of the social process as a means of unifying the social order and (2) his thinking on the rise and nature of the self. In the latter sphere he prepared the way for Mead's more sophisticated treatment of this problem; regarding the former, one can well agree with Read Bain in his statement that Cooley is the symbol of anti-particularism.[114] It should be noted that, despite Cooley's good analysis of the social processes, it is quite true that his works are devoid of any attempt formally to systematize these processes.[115]

NOTES

1. R. C. Angell, Introd. (p. viii) to C. H. Cooley, *Sociological Theory and Social Research,* (New York, 1930).

2. *Ibid.*

3. *Ibid.,* p. xii.

4. *Ibid.,* p. xiii.

5. Walton H. Hamilton, "Charles Horton Cooley," *Social Forces,* VIII (December, 1930), 186.

6. *Ibid.*, p. 189.

7. Floyd N. House, *Development of Sociology* (New York, 1936), p. 321.

8. See Read Bain, "Cooley, a Great Teacher," *Social Forces*, IX (December, 1930), 160–63; and Hamilton, *op. cit.*

9. Charles H. Cooley, *Sociology and Social Research*, pp. 4–5.

10. *Ibid.*, p. 6.

11. *Ibid.*, p. 7.

12. *Ibid.*

13. *Ibid.*, p. 6.

14. L. von Wiese and Howard Becker, *Systematic Sociology* (New York, 1932), pp. 694–95.

14a. *Publications of the American Economic Association*, V, No. 2 (3d ser., 1904), 18.

15. As an introduction to the revised edition (1922), Cooley included his article, "Heredity and Instinct in Human Life," originally published in *Survey*, XLIX (January 1, 1923), 454–56.

16. *Human Nature and the Social Order* (New York, 1902), p. 1.

17. *Ibid.*, p. 7.

18. *Ibid.*, pp. 10–11.

19. *Ibid.*, p. 12.

20. *Ibid.*, p. 152.

21. Sorokin goes so far as to call Cooley's a "family sociology" (*Contemporary Sociological Theories* [New York, 1928], p. 436).

22. "Cooley's Contribution to American Social Thought," *American Journal of Sociology*, XXXV, No. 5 (March, 1930), 702.

23. Preface, *Social Organization* (New York, 1909).

24. *Ibid.*, p. 5; see Ellsworth Faris' criticism, "The Primary Group: Essence and Accident," *American Journal of Sociology*, XXXVIII (July, 1932), 41.

25. *Social Organization*, pp. 13–14.

26. The term "secondary groups" is often erroneously attributed to Cooley. He does not use it.

27. *Social Organization*, p. 23.

28. *Ibid.*, p. 24.

29. *Ibid.*, p. 32.

30. *Ibid.*, p. 53.

31. *Ibid.*, p. 54.

32. *Ibid.*

33. *Ibid.*, p. 90.

34. *Ibid.*, p. 113.

35. *Ibid.*, p. 121.

36. *Ibid.*, p. 198.

37. *Ibid.*, pp. 143–48.

38. "Charles Horton Cooley," *Sociological Review*, XV (July, 1923), p. 199, n. 7. See this article for more extended discussion of Cooley's thought in political spheres.

39. *Social Organization*, p. 259.

40. *Ibid.*, p. 273.

41. *Ibid.*, p. 276.

42. See House, *op. cit.*, p. 323.

43. *Op. cit.*, p. 319.

44. *Ibid.*, pp. 328–29; see also Harry Elmer Barnes, *Society in Transition* (New York, 1939).

45. *Social Organization*, p. 339.

46. *Ibid.*, p. 342.

47. *Ibid.*, p. 395.

48. *Ibid.*, p. 401.

49. *Ibid.*, p. 403.
50. *Ibid.*, p. 410.
51. *Ibid.*, p. 419.
52. *Social Process,* p. 3.
53. *Ibid.*, pp. 28, 48, 49–50.
54. *Sociological Theory and Social Research,* p. 122.
55. *Ibid.*, p. 144.
56. *Ibid.*, p. 122.
57. *Ibid.*, p. 163.
58. *Ibid.*, p. 164.
59. *Ibid.*, p. 165.
60. *Ibid.*, p. 174.
61. *Ibid.*
62. *Ibid.*
63. *Ibid.*, p. 177.
64. *Ibid.*, p. 178. The similarity of Ogburn's concept of "cultural lag" to that of Cooley's "symmetry" is patent.
65. *Ibid.*, p. 213.
66. *Ibid.*, p. 220.
67. *Ibid.*, p. 229.
68. *Ibid.*, p. 233.
69. *Ibid.*, pp. 230–31.
70. *Ibid.*, p. 231.
71. *Ibid.*, p. 232.
72. *Ibid.*, p. 258.
73. *Ibid.*, p. 259.
74. *Ibid.*
75. *Ibid.*, p. 265.
76. *Ibid.*, p. 266.
77. *Ibid.*, p. 283.
78. Mead says that "evolution was a philosophy and a faith rather than a method" for Cooley (*op. cit.,* p. 703).
79. P. 398.
80. *Social Process,* p. 397.
81. *Sociological Theory and Social Research,* p. 289; see John F. Markey, "Trends in Social Psychology," in Lundberg, Anderson, and Bain, *Trends in American Sociology* (New York, 1929), pp. 145–46, for adverse criticism of this point.
82. *Sociological Theory and Social Research,* p. 293.
83. *Ibid.*
84. *Ibid.*, p. 299.
85. *Ibid.*, p. 304.
86. *Ibid.*, p. 314.
87. *Ibid.*, p. 325.
88. *Ibid.*
89. *Ibid.*, p. 326.
90. *Ibid.*
91. *Ibid.*
92. *Ibid.*, p. 331.
93. *Ibid.*, p. 333.
94. *Ibid.*, p. 335.
95. H. E. Barnes and Howard Becker, *Social Thought from Lore to Science,* II (New York, 1938), 985.
96. Fay Karpf, *American Social Psychology* (New York, 1932).
97. Bain, *op. cit.,* p. 162.

98. *Social Process*, p. 26. Cooley does not mean to imply an analogy to the biological organism in the manner of the Organicists, Lilienfeld, Schäffle, Fouillée, and Worms in their earlier writings. "In England and the United States, the terminology of the organismic school lingers in a general way among writers on social problems, but it is now used mainly as a means of pseudoanalysis . . . ." (Barnes and Becker, *op. cit.*, I, 691, 688–92; Von Wiese and Becker, *op. cit.*, p. 693).

99. *Human Nature and the Social Order*, p. 7.

100. See S. H. Britt, "Social Psychology or Psychological Sociology—Which?" *Journal of Abnormal and Social Psychology*, XXXII (1937), 314 ff.; "Past and Present Trends in Method and Subject Matter of Social Psychology," *Social Forces*, XV (1937), 462 ff.; S. L. Pressey, "Fundamentalism, Isolationism, and Biological Pedantry versus Socio-cultural Orientation in Psychology," *Journal of General Psychology*, XXIII (October, 1940), 343–49.

101. See Gordon Allport, *Personality* (1937), for an example of the logical cul-de-sac resulting from an adherence to the individual-society dichotomy, particularly pp. 257, 287–89, 559.

102. *Mental Development in the Child and the Race* (New York, 1900) and *Ethical Interpretations in Mental Development* (New York, 1913).

103. Karpf, *op. cit.*, p. 291.

104. See Barnes and Becker, *op. cit.*, I, 695.

105. William James, *Principles of Psychology*, I (New York, 1890), 291.

106. *Op. cit.*, p. 253.

107. See Baldwin, *The Individual and Society* (Boston, 1911), pp. 18–29; also Karpf, *op. cit.*, pp. 269–91.

108. Karpf, *op. cit.*, p. 291.

109. Mead, *op. cit.*, p. 699.

110. *Ibid.*, p. 700.

111. Cf. T. V. Smith, *Beyond Conscience* (New York, 1934), pp. 112 ff., 260–63; G. H. Mead, *Mind, Self, and Society* (Chicago, 1934).

112. "Cooley's Contribution to American Social Thought," p. 704.

113. S. M. Levin, "Charles Horton Cooley and the Concept of Creativeness," *Journal of Social Philosophy*, April, 1941, pp. 216–29. This is a full and well-documented study of Cooley's social dynamics as founded upon the idea of creativeness.

114. "Trends in American Sociological Theory," in Lundberg, Anderson, and Bain, *op. cit.*, p. 821.

115. Cf. Sorokin, *op. cit.*, p. 436. For the most complete study of Cooley as a man and sociologist see Edward Jandy, *Charles Horton Cooley: His Life and Social Theory* (New York, 1942).

CHAPTER XLIV

CHARLES ABRAM ELLWOOD: FOUNDER OF SCIENTIFIC PSYCHOLOGICAL SOCIOLOGY

Harry Elmer Barnes

I. ELLWOOD'S LIFE, PROFESSIONAL TRAINING, AND MAIN WRITINGS

CHARLES A. ELLWOOD was born January 20, 1873, on a farm in northern New York, about sixteen miles west of Ogdensburg. He attended the Ogdensburg Free Academy in preparation for Cornell University, which he entered in September, 1892, after having won one of the state scholarships. Even as a high-school student he had become interested in economics and sociology through reading Professor Richard T. Ely's *Introduction to Political Economy*. At Cornell he came under the influence, during his Freshman year, of Professor Edward A. Ross, then a young Ph.D. from Johns Hopkins University. Through the influence of Professor Ross he gave up his plan to study law and undertook to fit himself to become a teacher of sociology. At Cornell he studied under Professor W. F. Willcox and Professor J. W. Jenks, among others. He wrote his Bachelor's thesis, which was then required for graduation at Cornell, under Professor Jenks on the topic "The Social Sciences as a Basis for the Science of Ethics." In this early thesis he took many of the characteristic positions regarding social amelioration which are more or less familiar to those who have read what he has since written along this line.

After graduation from Cornell he went to the University of Chicago in 1896, becoming a graduate student in sociology under Professors Small, Henderson, Vincent, and W. I. Thomas, and in philosophy under Professor John Dewey. Later he had work also under the social psychologist, Professor G. H. Mead. Upon the advice of Professor Small he went to the University of Berlin in the fall of 1897, studying there under such men as Schmoller, Simmel, and Paulsen. From Schmoller he learned more about the historical approach to social problems and from Paulsen, the ethical approach. Simmel also stimulated him, but he regarded his lectures on sociology as outside the field of that science and in the metaphysics of human social relations. Returning to the University of Chicago in 1898 on a fellowship, he took, in June, 1899, his Doctor's degree in sociology and philosophy. His Doctor's dissertation was on "Some Prolegomena to Social Psychology" and was published in the *American Journal of Sociology,* March–November, 1899.

No position seemed to be open in any American university after he had taken his Doctor's degree at the University of Chicago. Accordingly, he was forced to accept, without a stipend, the secretaryship of an insolvent charity organization society in Lincoln, Nebraska, which carried with it a lectureship in sociology in the University of Nebraska. T. H. Tibbles, who later became a candidate for Vice-president on the Populist ticket, assured him that if he would come to Lincoln to accept this position, the society would pay him a salary of $800 a year; but he discovered that he had to raise his own salary and that no stipend would be furnished from the university, though he taught two classes in sociology at the university throughout the year.

In April, 1900, Ellwood was offered a newly established chair in sociology at the University of Missouri at a salary of $1,500 a year. From this point on, for thirty years he was absorbed in developing the department of sociology at the University of Missouri. He began his work with an enrolment of only a little over thirty students in the courses in the department and ended in 1930 with about fifteen hundred. In the course of his thirty years of teaching at the University of Missouri, Ellwood had among his students such later eminent sociologists as E. B. Reuter, Herbert Blumer, C. C. Zimmerman, and L. L. Bernard.

In 1904 Ellwood acted as chairman of the section on social psychology of the Congress of Arts and Sciences held that year at St. Louis in connection with the World's Fair. In 1914–15 he visited England and took lectures under Dr. R. R. Marett at Oxford and Professor L. T. Hobhouse at the University of London, returning to the United States in June, 1915.

The visit to England had a very fundamental influence upon the development of both Ellwood's sociological theories and his practical outlook. In 1912 he had published with the Appleton Company a work entitled *Sociology in Its Psychological Aspects,* in which he insisted that sociology must be based upon a scientific psychology. But through his work under Marett at Oxford he become convinced that a psychological approach to social problems must be supplemented by an anthropological approach. His work under Hobhouse at the University of London in the winter of 1915 fully converted him to the historical-cultural approach to human social problems. Moreover, he became persuaded that Hobhouse's evolutionary philosophy afforded more complete insight into social processes than Dewey's pragmatism. Thereafter he began to reshape his sociology and to give it more of a cultural and anthropological basis.

The war of 1914–18 also had a great influence upon Ellwood's practical outlook. He studied again the whole foundations of democracy, becoming more convinced than ever that any other form of society and government was out of line with the great tendencies of cultural evolution. But the war also convinced him of the futility of intelligence alone as a solution of social problems unless it was supplemented by a high degree of altruistic spirit among the masses of mankind. He became more interested than ever, therefore, in the religious approach to the solution of social problems, and this led him to re-examine the work of Comte and to appreciate more deeply the ideas of Hobhouse.

These changes in his intellectual and practical outlook led him to re-write his *Sociology in Its Psychological Aspects* and to publish it under a new title, *An Introduction to Social Psychology*. In this revision he attempted to re-write his psychological sociology from a cultural viewpoint, without being very successful. His failure led him to attempt still another revision in 1925, which was published by Appleton under the title *The Psychology of Human Society,* though he himself would have preferred the title "The Behavior of Human Groups."

To summarize the main influences which have operated upon Ellwood's thinking, one may say that his deep and abiding interest in social reform, the meliorative undercurrent in all his social philosophy, and his belief in the possibility of rational social progress through education in the social sciences were derived from his reading of Lester F. Ward and Auguste Comte and from the teachings of his mentor, Albion W. Small. His interest in, and command of, functional psychology and his application of it to sociology came mainly from his studies under Dewey and Angell. His later shift to an anthropocultural approach to social problems was due mainly to the influence of L. T. Hobhouse and R. R. Marett. In the reconstruction of his psychological sociology in the twenties, Ellwood was influenced not only by Marett and Hobhouse, but especially by C. H. Cooley. He was particularly impressed by Cooley's synthesis and restatement of his psychological sociology in his *Social Process*.

While at Oxford in 1914, under the stimulus of the first months of the world war, Ellwood had written a brief book on *The Social Problem*, which was essentially an expansion of a paper on the social problem in its relation to the world war which he had read before the British Sociological Society. The book was published under the editorship of Professor Richard T. Ely in the "American Citizen Series" by the Macmillan Company. This book pointed in the direction of social ethics and led him to an attempt to complete a larger work on social ethics which he had already begun in 1912. It was finally completed in 1922 and was published by the Macmillan Company under the title *The Reconstruction of Religion*. As it attempted to give scientific support and confirmation to those religious leaders who wished to give a social interpretation to Christianity, it created considerable attention and had a wide sale. It resulted in Ellwood's being invited to deliver a series of lectures in the fall of 1923 before the Yale Divinity School. These were published by the Macmillan Company under the title *Christianity and Social Science* and were essentially a continuation and elaboration of positions which had already been taken in *The Reconstruction of Religion*. He concluded his religious studies by a book on *The World's Need of Christ*, published in 1940, and the most nearly devout of his religious books.

In 1927, Ellwood published the lectures in cultural anthropology which he had been giving at the University of Missouri for the previous ten years, under the title *Cultural Evolution: A Study of Social Origins and Development*. Perhaps it is in this book that one must seek the clearest statement of his cultural approach to sociology.[1] In 1933, Ellwood brought out his work on *Methods in Sociology*, which is not only a critical appraisal of all the main sociological methods and techniques of operation but especially an argument against the methods of physical science and the statistical technique as adequate and complete modes of approach to the study of social processes.

Because he was suffering from ill health in 1927-28, he sought and obtained sabbatical leave from his duties at the University of Missouri. In September, 1927, he sailed for France and spent practically all the year 1927-28 in France, Italy, and Austria, coming into contact with a great number of the sociological leaders in those three countries. These

contacts resulted in his election to the presidency of the International
Institute of Sociology in 1935-36. By virtue of this office he became automatically president of the International Sociological Congress which
was held at Brussels, Belgium, in connection with the Brussels Universal Exposition in August, 1935.

Ellwood's attitude toward international relations was also greatly
influenced by his two years' residence in Europe and his experience
on two other shorter trips. At first, his attitude might be designated as
"Anglo-Saxon imperialism," for he believed that the English-speaking
world could unite to maintain world peace. But his residence in England in 1914-15 convinced him that this would be a mistake, since several
English friends told him that the only result of such a union of English-
speaking peoples, who comprise only one-tenth of the population of
the earth, would be to unite all the rest of the world against such an
English-speaking union, even though it were most peaceful in intention and methods. Accordingly, he came, in 1914, to indorse the idea
of Aneurin Williams, then a member of Parliament, that the peaceful
nations should form a league to enforce peace. He attended some of
the earliest meetings to forward this movement in London in 1914,
long before it had reached the United States. For several years thereafter he enthusiastically identified himself with the League of Nations
movement; but, when he saw that the League had become an instrument for the enforcement of the vindictive Treaty of Versailles and
was largely dominated by Great Britain and France, he gradually withdrew his support.

In later years Ellwood adopted a more completely pacifist position
and came to the conclusion that only a federation in which all nations
were admitted on a plane of equality and whose methods were thoroughly democratic could expect to do much to help the cause of international peace. He also became more and more convinced that the
peace movement suffered from the same dangers and difficulties from
which the temperance movement and many similar movements suffered, namely, that it had not yet secured sufficient foundations in individual intelligence and character among the masses of mankind. He
also took the same attitude toward the democratic movement, namely,
that its chances of success for a long time to come were slight unless
strong efforts are made in the direction of the social and political education of the masses of the people in Western civilization to fit them to

participate successfully in the work of government. In general, he came to the conclusion that all the higher and more spiritual achievements of our civilization were destined to collapse unless social and political education of the most extensive and intensive character could be extended to the masses in both Europe and America with much greater rapidity than such education had progressed during the preceding fifty years.

In 1930, Ellwood was called to Duke University to start a new department of sociology. He was joined at Duke by Dr. Howard E. Jensen, Dr. Hornell Hart, and Dr. E. T. Thompson. The work of the department in maintaining a high standard of scholarship has received general recognition. While at Duke University, Ellwood helped to train such sociologists as Paul E. Root, Guy V. Price, Austin L. Porterfield, and Leonard Bloom.

In February and March, 1937, while on sabbatical leave, Ellwood took a cruise to South America, which gave him some opportunity to acquaint himself with conditions in Latin America. In general, this confirmed his contention for the need of more, and more rapid, social and political education. Brazil particularly appealed to him as one of the most promising countries in the Western Hemisphere, even though at the present time it is so culturally, educationally, politically, and industrially backward.

Ellwood retired at Duke as professor emeritus of sociology in 1945 and died on September 25, 1946. His last years were his saddest. He was disillusioned by the abandonment of the New Deal reform program for a bellicose foreign policy which possessed greater political potency at the moment. He was opposed to the aggressive and provocative American foreign policy before Pearl Harbor and had little faith in the grandiose promises of President Roosevelt that the second World War would end in a utopia of peace, freedom, and prosperity. But if these years were Ellwood's saddest, owing also to the death of his wife in 1945, they were also his bravest. He valiantly fought war-mongering when it took great courage and opposed peacetime conscription with valor and cogency, both before Pearl Harbor and after V-J Day.

II. ELLWOOD'S SOCIOLOGICAL THEORY IN LARGER PERSPECTIVE

Ellwood's sociological theory is essentially a theory of human social evolution, which he regards as partly a product of nature but even more a result of the development of culture. He does not deny the existence of social behavior and social organization in animal groups below man, but he emphasizes that human social behavior and social organization are mainly products of culture, something which no animal group possesses. There is, therefore, according to his view, a distinct line between animal groups and human groups, even though animal traits, such as inborn hereditary reactions and emotions, are carried over to human groups.[2]

On the whole, human groups have been characterized by accumulating knowledge, skills, and co-operative attitudes, which have made them very distinct from animal groups. The most fundamental factor in this human social development has been methods of communication, both natural and artificial.[3] The web of intercommunication among the individuals of a group, in the form of the social tradition which they accept, controls their social behavior and gives rise to all their customs, institutions, and methods of living together. The animal nature of man merely forms a background for this higher social development that is brought about by culture. As all social traditions and customs have to be learned, there is the possibility of a great variety and of many trends in a multitude of directions. Some human groups, owing to circumstances, will develop superior adjustments, establish them in their traditions, and gradually subject them to refinements. Improvement and progress in human institutions are, thus, theoretically as possible as improvement and progress in the making of physical tools. However, many mistakes will be made, and the process of social development through learned adjustments has thus far proved to be a process of trial and error.[4]

Certain patterns must necessarily be followed by human groups in their development. Some of these have come from nature, some from the innate drives and propensities of human nature, but for the most part they have come from the experiences of group life. These experiences were found originally and primarily in the face-to-face groups of men. As culture is a group trait, there must be human groups which are the special bearers of all the essential cultural patterns. These are especially the "primary groups" or the groups which involve face-to-face relations and intimate personal acquaintance. With C. H. Cooley, Ellwood holds that these groups are the potent agencies for socializing individuals, for the bearing of culture, whether culture be regarded mainly as tradition or as custom, and for the generation of primary social ideals or patterns. In these primary groups intercommunication carries essential group traditions and sets up group attitudes.[5] Both the traditions and the attitudes are, however, learned by individuals. These traditions and attitudes make up the culture of the group and determine its form of organization and its general behavior. Changes in such group behavior are brought about through the use of the processes of intercommunication to make new adjustments. Hence group "discussion" is fundamental in the normal process of group change. Ordinarily, this results in group opinion or a public opinion of the group, which points the way to a new adjustment of the members of the group toward one another, toward other groups, or toward physical nature.[6]

Thus group behavior is subject to scientific analysis and explanation. Group action and group unity are to be explained in terms of the process of interstimulation and response and coadaptation among the members of the group. The historical continuity of the group is likewise to be explained in terms of the process of intercommunication and the resulting growth of group traditions and customs. If changes within the group are not brought about by the normal process of intercommunication, that is, by discussion and the formation of a public opinion, then they are liable to be brought about by violent means, and the group as a whole or sections of the group resort to fighting. This results in violent changes, which are typified in human history by political and social revolutions.[7]

However, Ellwood regards the process of physical conflict between classes within the group as essentially exceptional and abnormal. Conflict between strange groups is probably natural and a survival of the old hunting pattern of primitive times turned toward human enemies. Such conflicts could be avoided in many instances by the development of means of intercommunication, discussion, and control among groups. The political movements toward regional and world federation are therefore in line with all that sociology teaches regarding peace, harmony, and co-operation among individuals or groups. But the success of such a movement on a world-wide scale must wait for the establishment of a firm tradition of understanding, good will, and co-operation among the larger groups of men.[8]

Several obstacles now stand in the way of any world-wide co-ordination or federation of national groups. One of these is the tradition which has been fostered by some biologists as well as by some social scientists, namely, that human nature is necessarily selfish and egoistic and cannot be trusted to make enduring harmonious adjustments either with other individuals or between groups. Such an egoistic theory of human nature favors the view that hostile conflict is normal in human relations and inevitable. Even the family group is said to be an "antagonistic co-operation." The best that can be achieved under such circumstances will be a balance of egoism or of selfish interests. No learning process working with such a human nature could produce enduring peace between individuals, classes, nations, or races. Ellwood holds that this egoistic and militant theory of human nature is not sustained by scientific psychology and is only a social tradition, even though seemingly supported by experience in our present stage of culture.[9]

But a more powerful obstacle to harmonious social adjustment between human groups on a world-wide scale is the tradition that these groups necessarily have only egoistic motives. This tradition especially characterizes the state or the national group and holds that its only end is defense against other groups and power over them. This tradition, Ellwood holds, rests upon a mistaken theory of human nature and also upon the historical fact that the modern state was formed largely for purposes of military defense and military aggression. Ethnocentrism, nationalism, and militarism are simply so many traditions which have come down from a past in which exploitation of the weak, the ruthless egoism of the strong, and a military organization of society grew up because of the mental, social, and cultural immaturity of human populations. In the present human world all these should be considered survivals or lags in our social culture, susceptible of being overcome by a more socialized education of the masses and especially of their leaders.[10]

Ellwood holds, therefore, that social tradition is the fundamental and primary element in determining human social behavior; it conveys the knowledge, beliefs, values, and standards which guide the behavior of human groups and determine the form of their organization. Interpretation of human social life purely in terms of automatic natural forces is therefore a scientific error. It is a greater error in interpreting modern society than in interpreting the life of primitive groups, because the psychic factors just mentioned have accumulated and become preponderant in the human social process. This process is therefore dominantly psychological. It is a process which results in *learned* adjustments. These adjustments will vary according to the tradition, according to what is taught, and according to what is learned. But the forms of human social life may, therefore, vary indefinitely as the tradition which guides society ranges the whole scale from the lowest savages to the most highly cultivated peoples. External conditions affect this process only in so far as they condition it.[11]

All analogies between organic evolution and human social evolution are therefore superficial and misleading. Organic evolution is generally regarded as proceeding by the automatic processes of variation, heredity, and selection. Human social evolution proceeds by invention in the mental and social realm and by the diffusion of inventions from the socially élite down, from the inventor to the user, from the leader to the follower. Thus the human social process proceeds by intercommunication and interlearning and results in collective adjustments. The process of organic evolution by variation and selection only affects it as a framework—hence the conclusion that culture dominates the human social process and that we must expect as great a variety of social behavior as there are possibilities of learned adjustments.[12]

It is obvious that, if social forms and institutions are products of culture and have been made by man, if they are *learned* adjustments, they can be changed within reasonable limits. Human society is neither a conscious contract nor a machine of the gods which works automatically. Since human institutions are built by man under conditions afforded by nature, they may be changed to human advantage. Social progress or improvement through the development of higher social intelligence in the masses and leaders of mankind is not impossible. On the contrary, it is the great possibility or probability held out to mankind by the development of the social sciences. It may indeed, as Turgot said, be regarded in the long run as inevitable, if it is true that man necessarily learns from mistakes and calamities as well as from his successes.[13]

In summary, Ellwood's sociology makes human society preponderantly the creation of the human mind. Its basis is to be found in the purposes of man, all of which are capable of being guided and controlled by human intelligence. The psychic factor, as Lester F. Ward said, is therefore the guiding and controlling factor in human relations. Social institutions and social organizations are products of human culture and involve, no less than physical tools, "the artificial modification of natural phenomena." Sociology, as a practical human science, must deal, therefore, with the artificial rather than with the purely natural.

The culture that controls human groups in their organization and behavior is, however, at first built up largely accidentally and unconsciously by the working-out of the desires and purposes of individuals; but it is capable of being transformed by intelligent collective action. Therefore, there is a possibility of future improvement in human relations, or social progress; but this can be made certain only through the development of the social sciences, and of sociology in particular. To reach some value-judgments as to such improvement in human relations is the end of the social sciences. But such value-judgments, pointing out possible means of amelioration, are relative to the general ends of human society, such as unity, continuity, and rational change.[14]

The method of sociology as a science of culture must be a historical-psychological method, since human society is a historicopsychological product. This does not mean that any one inductive method should be favored at the expense of others, though it does mean that the historical method of studying social behavior, social movements, and social institutions is paramount. There remains plenty of room for statistical studies and cross-section surveys. Moreover, inasmuch as the human mind stands back of all cultural development, there is also room for psychological analysis and for deductions from the probable working of biological factors. In effect, therefore, the method of sociology must be synthetic, making use of all established knowledge for the understanding of social behavior and human relations.[15]

The total outcome of such a sociology must be to establish scientifically a melioristic attitude toward all human problems. The real justification of sociology is, therefore, social reform and the betterment of the lot of mankind, both within national groups and in international relations.[16]

III. ELLWOOD'S PLACE IN AMERICAN SOCIOLOGY

In their general attitude toward sociological problems there are some notable similarities between the writings of Cooley and those of Ellwood. Both have been primarily interested in the psychological phases of sociology, but they readily concede the importance of other modes of approach to the study of social processes and problems. Both lay much stress upon primary groups, social tradition, and the social importance of communication. Further, in their specialty of psychological sociology both have sought to avoid any one-sided interpretation and have presented a synthetic analysis of the psychic processes in society.

In the specific form of their sociological systems there is, however, a marked difference. Cooley presented a series of brilliant and philosophically unified essays dealing with some of the more important social phenomena which can be explained by means of psychology. But he paraded little knowledge of technical psychology, nor did be make much of an effort to assemble a formal, orderly, and systematic exposition of psychological sociology. On the other hand, Ellwood executed far and away the most successful of the early American attempts to link up scientific psychology with systematic sociology. In so doing he showed a wider mastery of the technical literature of psychology and social psychology than any other American sociological writer of his generation.

Other sociologists, such as Tarde, Le Bon, Simmel, Durkheim, Giddings, and Ross, have produced more striking interpretations of society from the psychological point of view. But most of them selected some special psychological factor, such as imitation, impression, suggestion, crowd psychology, and the like. Moreover, few of them had much knowledge of technical psychology but based their generalizations on common sense and rule-of-thumb psychological concepts. Ellwood made no pretense of presenting an "original" or "brilliant" interpretation of society; but he did, for the first time, demonstrate that a coherent and systematic psychology can be projected into a unified and consistent body of sociological theory. Moreover, Ellwood gave evidence of a scholarly acquaintance with psychology as it had been developed down to his time.

Ellwood's works are not characterized by the great powers of sustained abstraction which are evident in the writings of Giddings and Durkheim, the literary charm of Cooley, of the trenchant phraseology of Ross. They are notable, rather, for their logical coherence, their wholesome common sense and practicality, their extensive acquaintance with psychological and sociological literature, and their synthetic comprehensiveness.

In the development of Ellwood's sociological outlook we see what has been a characteristic trend in contemporary sociology, namely, a recognition of the fact that psychological sociology is a branch of cultural sociology—that psychic forces are more of a cultural, than a biological, product. Ellwood's attitude toward culture has been evolutionary. In approaching cultural evolution his thought is in harmony with that of

Comte, Ward, and Hobhouse, namely, that the course of cultural evolution can be brought under the control of the human mind and can be consciously directed in harmony with the teachings of social science.

Ellwood has succeeded Ward as the main protagonist in his generation of the idea that sociology should be a normative and ameliorative social philosophy, justified mainly by its aid in improving society and the well-being of mankind. He has fought valiantly against a sterile "objectivism" in social science.

Ellwood's interest in the ethical side of sociology encouraged his deep interest in religion as a social force. It is in this field that he has exhibited his only notable inconsistencies. There is no incompatibility between sociology and an emancipated humanistic religion. Ellwood is thoroughly aware of the latest studies in the history and psychology of religion, which have undermined even devout modernism, and he seems to approve of these. Yet he adopts an attitude toward Christianity and the teachings of Jesus which would be accepted by the more urbane and better-educated Fundamentalists and is shared by all devout Modernists. It is only another case of trying to have one's cake and eat it, too. But no fair person will quarrel with Ellwood's aim of making religion a dynamic social force, for he is free from all trace of religious bigotry.

Ellwood has been one of those sociologists who recognize that democracy and social justice at home cannot be assured unless we are able to avert world war. Like Kant, he understands that social utopia can come only in a world of peace and that there is little chance of bringing world peace without some form of strong world organization. But Ellwood is sensible enough to expect no miracle. We cannot get world organization until education undermines arrogant nationalism and imperialism. Peace attitudes must be created to get peace organization. A militant internationalism is more dangerous than a militant nationalism because it is more deceptive.

All in all, one may say that, while Ellwood has gained the respect of many able sociologists, he has been more highly esteemed by social reformers, social workers, and Modernist clergymen. His contributions to social amelioration and religion have been given a wider hearing than his sociopsychological doctrines. But even in this latter field he took the lead, not only in creating systematic psychological sociology but also in putting psychological sociology in its logical place within the larger framework of cultural sociology. The summation and essence of Ellwood's social philosophy is well expressed in one of his latest statements, taken from his article on "What's the Matter with Sociology?" in the *American Sociologist,* February, 1943:

Long ago a great teacher taught me that, in final conception, "society is humanity viewed from the standpoint of its reciprocal relationships." Somewhat later I dis covered that Auguste Comte in the later years of his life was driven to this concep tion of society. However, Gumplowicz declared that there was no such entity as humanity, that it could not be the subject of sociological research or thinking, that there were only hostile, warring groups in what is called humanity, with no definite relationship to one another. This, to be sure, is a pure natural-history conception of mankind. But it has broken down even for scientific thinking. Natural science, by revealing new means of communication and transportation, has made the physical interdependence of mankind beyond question. The spiritual inter- dependence of all human societies has been, moreover, strikingly revealed by the war. Those who would limit human relations to the relations which can be ob- served between existing individuals and groups will now have to shut their eyes, or at least deny common sense. Human relations are world-wide, not only in space but in time also. If sociologists are to function in the present world they must think in terms of the spiritual unity of mankind. They cannot afford to overlook any human relationship; the integration not simply of the city, or of the local com- munity, or of the nation, but of the whole human world is their concern. Any sociology that fails to see the functional unity of mankind, and the need of world- wide social adjustments is hardly abreast of developments in our human world. Such problems may be too difficult for scientific solution. That is another question. But they should not be ignored, if we wish sociology to function in the present human world—to have even a little to say about world-wide human relations.

But the spiritual unity of mankind is not simply a matter which concerns the present. Human relations stretch back into the past and project themselves into the future. The social behavior of men, cultural sociology has demonstrated, is largely a matter of the tradition of their groups. These group traditions are obvi- ously now in deadly conflict. Sociology ought to be a systematic procedure for arriving at reasoned value-judgments as to the relative social worth of these tradi- tions. It should expose the facts upon which they are based, and it should critically judge their functioning in human relationships. A sociology which is not a criticism of institutions has hardly any social value. If possible, emotional value-judgments of customs and institutions should be replaced by scientific value-judgments based upon the facts of human experience.

Indeed, in one sense the whole mission of sociology as a science is to bring about a transition from arbitrary and emotional traditions to scientific traditions in guiding social behavior. There need be no fear that the real values in past social traditions will be destroyed by scientific examination and criticism. They may be, to be sure, if social scientists are not aware of the facts of history and the lessons which those facts teach. But at bottom science is not an attempt to destroy any- thing; it is an attempt to understand, to control, and to use for human advantage. A sociology which understands its human mission will undertake this task.

But the continuity of civilization and of civilizing values is, after all, not the main practical problem of scientific students of human relations. What we call civilization has been filled with too many errors, too many value-judgments not based upon all the facts of experience, for sociologists to be over-zealous about the continuity of human cultures. Inevitable questions of intelligent rational changes in human relations will arise. If the social sciences are worth anything, they should afford guidance in the bringing about of rational social changes. The advocates of the use of force in bringing to pass social changes have not only so far won out that they wish to suppress criticism of the institutions of certain groups, but some even talk openly of a war after the present one to settle the relations between classes.

Science is, after all, at bottom, faith in human intelligence, in its capacity to solve problems, if the right method of approach is used. Its faith is in patient study, in the diffusion of knowledge, and in the establishment of reasoned social values based upon the solid facts of human experience. This is as true of the social sciences as it is of the natural sciences; and some of us cannot help but feel that it is something of a disgrace that the students of the social sciences have not seen that this is their work. There is, of course, the excuse that the social sciences have been so neglected, so pushed aside, that they have had no opportunity to make their contribution to a world-wide civilization based upon valid judgments of human experience and recognizing the interdependence of all mankind. But if this war leaves any worth-while sociology surviving, it is surely time that sociologists should recognize the inadequacies of their past efforts and formulate a new program for the future.

NOTES

1. Ellwood's major writings include the following books:
    Sociology and Modern Social Problems (New York, 1910; rev. eds., 1924, 1932, 1935). Over 300,000 copies sold to date; translated into Chinese in 1922.
    Sociology in Its Psychological Aspects (New York, 1912, 1915; rev. ed., 1919). French translation, 1914.
    The Social Problem: A Reconstructive Analysis (New York, 1915; rev. ed., 1919). Translated into Japanese, 1917; into German, 1924; into Chinese, 1922.
    An Introduction to Social Psychology (New York, 1917). Translated into Japanese, 1921; into Chinese, 1923.
    The Reconstruction of Religion (New York, 1922). Translated into German, 1924; into Japanese, 1925.
    Christianity and Social Science (New York, 1923). Translated into Japanese, 1926.
    The Psychology of Human Society: An Introduction to Sociological Theory (New York, 1925). German translation, 1927.
    Cultural Evolution: A Study of Social Origins and Development (New York, 1927).
    Man's Social Destiny in the Light of Science (Nashville, Tenn., 1929).
    Methods in Sociology—a Critical Study (Durham, N.C., 1933).
    A History of Social Philosophy (New York, 1938).
    The World's Need of Christ (New York, 1940).
2. *The Psychology of Human Society* (New York, 1925), chap. ii.
3. *Ibid.*, pp. 219–22, 323–25.
4. *Sociology in Its Psychological Aspects* (New York, 1912), chap. xviii.
5. *The Psychology of Human Society*, chap. iv.
6. *Ibid., chap.* vii.
7. *Sociology in Its Psychological Aspects.*, pp. 163 ff.; and *The Psychology of Human Society*, chap. viii. See also Ellwood's article on "A Psychological Theory of Revolutions" in the *American Journal of Sociology*, July, 1905.
8. *The Psychology of Human Society*, pp. 413 ff.

9. *Methods in Sociology* (Durham, N.C., 1933), chap. iv; *Cultural Evolution* (New York, 1927), chap. ix.

10. *The Social Problem* (New York, 1915), chap. vi.

11. *The Psychology of Human Society*, chaps. vii, xiii–xiv.

12. *Ibid.*, chap. ii.

13. *Cultural Evolution*, chap. xix; *The Social Problem*, chap. vi.

14. *Methods in Sociology*, chaps. ix–xiii.

15. *Ibid.*, chap. vii.

16. *The Social Problem, passim; Sociology and Modern Social Problems* (New York, 1919), *passim*. For a consideration of Ellwood's contributions to social reform and public problems see the article on Ellwood by the author in the English *Sociological Review*, October, 1923.

CHAPTER XLV

THE SOCIOLOGICAL THEORIES OF
EDWARD CARY HAYES

HARRY ELMER BARNES

I. GENERAL NATURE OF HAYES'S SOCIOLOGICAL WRITINGS

PROFESSOR EDWARD CARY HAYES (1868-1928), for a number of years the head of the department of sociology at the University of Illinois, was one of the better known among Dean Albion W. Small's disciples, who, in the main, dominate the sociological thought of the Middle West.[1]

Hayes was originally trained for the ministry and preached for a number of years. It was not until he was over thirty that Small persuaded him to take his Doctor's degree in sociology and turn to education. He not only studied under Small and the Chicago sociologists and the Chicago philosophers, Mead, Dewey, and Tufts, but also spent a year at the University of Berlin at Small's behest, taking work under Schmoller, Wagner, Simmel, and others. Hayes was an alert and active man, a magnetic and virile personality, and an admirable classroom teacher, in which he made ample use of the histrionic talents he had developed in the pulpit. He was always interested in social welfare and took a leading part in all the social projects of the academic and urban communities in which he lived.[2]

Hayes's professional life was spent mainly at the University of Illinois. After being ordained for the ministry in 1893, he spent the next three years in a pastorate at Augusta, Maine. He then entered academic work as Dean of Keuka College, in the Finger Lake area of central New York. He remained here until 1899, when he began his graduate work in sociology. After getting his doctorate in Chicago in 1902, Hayes became professor of sociology at Miami University in Oxford, Ohio, where he built up, during the next five years, a remarkable reputation as a dynamic classroom teacher. In 1907 he accepted a professorship in sociology at the University of Illinois, where he remained until he died

in 1928, while still at the height of his intellectual powers. In addition
to producing his own books, Hayes edited the Lippincott Sociological
Series. Here appeared, among others, such important books as E. H.
Sutherland's *Criminology,* H. A. Miller's *Races, Nations and Classes,*
E. B. Reuter's *Population Problems,* and Seba Eldridge's *Political Action.*

Hayes's first considerable contribution to sociology was embodied in
his enlarged doctoral dissertation, "Sociological Construction Lines."[3]
Here he attempted to lay out, in a general way, the proper lines along
which sociology should be developed, more especially with respect to
general scope and methodology than in regard to specific problems to
be considered. It reflected Small's doctrine that society is to be regarded
primarily as a dynamic process. Hayes was one of the first sociologists
to make consistent use of the term "social process." While not so profound as Giddings' treatment of the problem a decade earlier[4] or so
strikingly original as Small would seem to indicate by his introductory
note, Hayes's initial monograph was one of the clearest and most satisfactory discussions of this now overexploited field that had appeared.
Some of his chief conclusions are summed up in the following paragraph:

> The statement that the objects of sociological study are processes means that the
> students of the existing particular social sciences as well as of branches of social
> investigation that may remain to be worked out, cannot find the object of their
> most fruitful study in phenomena regarded as established, fixed, and static, be they
> never so monumental and institutional, but will find them rather in changes
> and the conditions of change which are often diffused, minute, and fleeting. It
> means also that which is even more fundamental and significant, namely, that
> social phenomena are essentially activities, whether they are constant or whether
> they are changing, and that the most significant social causes are likewise activities.[5]

Many of the suggested lines of development which are discussed in
this work were later expanded at greater length in Hayes's comprehensive work on sociology—his *Introduction to the Study of Sociology,* published in 1915. In the introductory portions of this book Hayes deals with
the nature and province of sociology. In the next part he treats of the
"causes" affecting the social process, such as geographic conditions, technical factors and economic institutions, biological forces and processes,
and psychic factors in social life. Following this comes the theoretical
heart of the book, namely, an analysis of social activities and the social
process. Then Hayes presents his treatment of the evolution of social institutions and human culture, in which he makes a discriminating use
of the comparative method of Spencer, Lippert, Morgan, Tylor, and

others, and gives some place to the stage theory of social evolution.[6] In the last part of the book, he deals with social control in connection with crime and law enforcement, religion, and education. On the basis of the *Introduction,* Hayes's doctoral dissertation, articles published in the *American Journal of Sociology,* especially "The Classification of Social Phenomena" (1911–12), and his work on *Sociology and Ethics,* which we shall discuss later, one may epitomize Hayes's sociological theory.

Hayes was primarily interested in the organization and interpretation of sociological data rather than in esoteric and minute social research. He wished, above all else, to make sociology clear, coherent, and socially useful. In Hayes's opinion, the prime object of sociological study is the social process. This is the product, outgrowth, and final result of social activities. These social activities, rather than the social organism or the social group, should be the center of sociological interest.

Social phenomena fall into two main groups: (1) social activities and (2) the conditioning factors that shape and alter social activities. Sociology is the philosophic synthesis of all knowledge relating to both social activities and their conditioning factors.[7] Social activities always involve social experience, and they have three salient characteristics: (1) they are prevalent, that is, they dominate and give character to any age of social development; (2) they express themselves in speech and writing, namely, they have a symbolic basis; and (3) they are the product of antecedent social activities, in other words, they are socially caused.[8] Hayes holds that the conditioning factors in social phenomena operate as sociopsychic relations rather than as social forces, and he offered a cogent criticism of what he called "the social forces error."[9] These social relations that condition social activities grow out of the geographical environment, the biological traits and behavior of man, economic activities, and such psychic influences as suggestion, sympathy, imitation, inducement, deterrence, accumulation, accommodation, corroboration, emulation, domination, competition, conflict, co-operation, and organization. Small's influence is evident in this list of psychic factors in the social process.

Because the activities which make up the social process are fundamentally sociopsychic, this means that a competent handling of sociological data requires adequate training in scientific psychology and social psychology. The psychic interrelations between individuals in society contain within themselves such social values as exist. To estimate, select, and promote these social values is a primary purpose of scientific sociology, and this need leads sociology directly to the field and problems of social ethics. As Ellwood puts it, Hayes believed that "sociology is a natural science with an ethical purpose or outcome."

The ultimate goal and the educational and public justification of sociology are social ethics. Hayes trenchantly expressed his conviction of the fundamentally ethical objective of sociological study and teaching as follows: "Sociology aims at nothing less than the transfer of ethics from the domain of speculative philosophy to the domain of objective science." Hayes agreed with Ward, Stuckenberg, Small, and Hobhouse that social ethics consist chiefly in the building of a better social order under governmental direction, the latter resting on the rigorous education of public officials in the social sciences and the willingness of government to be guided in its policies by a "brain trust" of social scientists. A sound social ethics can proceed only from a synthetic co-ordination of all available knowledge concerning social activities. The social good must imply social activity, that is, it must be dynamic, and it must rest upon and encourage social experience.

Hayes's most original work was a book entitled *Sociology and Ethics,* published in 1921. It is an effort to formulate a strictly naturalistic and sociological approach to ethics. While Hayes could not entirely escape from his preacher and religious background, the book is a resolute attempt to create a secular analysis of ethical problems. He thus formulates his thesis as to the necessity of founding any valid attitude toward ethics upon sociology and the social point of view:

From the fact of our social nature it results that neither the thought of God nor the thought of participation in the social life inspires us to our best unless that thought is the common property of our group. The weakness of an age of transition is its lack of social agreement. Neither a residuum of faith, purged of anthropomorphism and superstition, nor the contemplation of the social reality can adequately serve the purpose of inspiration and adjustment unless institutionalized, that is to say, rationally adopted as a social agreement. It is reasonable to hope, and experience already justifies the hope, that an adequate recognition of the social reality, of all human life as a participation, and of normal human life as a coöperation, if once it becomes institutionalized, so as to be reflected upon us each from the common life, in literature, in ritual, and by the social atmosphere of suggestion and sympathetic radiation, will serve the essential purposes of religion; that is to say, it will adjust the intricate mechanism of conscious life to attainment of life's highest individual and social fulfillment.....

At this point is illustrated the truth that the intellectual movement called sociology may produce significant results, not only in so far as it brings to light new facts or recondite principles, but by merely looking at familiar facts in a scientific spirit, for we have winced from viewing many of the most familiar facts of life in that open-minded way. If the principles of causation or conditioning which apply to individual and social life should prove in their main outline to be rather simple and obvious as soon as we are willing to look for them, yet to learn to look at them as true principles of causation and to adjust our system of thought and action accordingly, this may be both theoretically and practically one of the most momentous of all results of the scientific spirit and method.

If investigation of sociology's general problem, the problem of social causation, seems to threaten destruction of the accepted world-view, there already is promise that investigation of the special problems of ethics by the sociological method will prove to be constructive of a modified world-view not less adapted to afford guidance, motive, and worth to life, having the incalculable advantage over the old world-view of being impregnable to any attacks by incongruous facts, and requiring no blinking of the clear eyes of intellectual honesty.[10]

Hayes is very insistent that a true sociological ethics must adopt the methods of natural science and abandon any dualistic approach to ethical problems:

Sociology, including sociological ethics, if it is to adopt the scientific method, if it is to proceed, not by a priori speculation but by the investigation of facts, is forced to be a "natural" science, a science, that is to say, that has for its business the explanation of a special class of facts that constitute its problems, by reference to other facts as their causes or conditions. The dualism between what is caused and what is done has vanished, or is vanishing as fast and as far as knowledge advances. Practical endeavor has always been forced to deny that dualism, and even theory, cannot continue to affirm it without self-contradiction and blindness.[11]

Hayes takes a sensible attitude toward the problem of the freedom of the will, holding that an adequate knowledge of the social sciences, acquired through education, may help man to rise superior to the drives of physical nature. But he is wise enough to recognize that such wisdom becomes, in turn, a determining influence over conduct. Hence there can never be any such thing as absolute freedom, divorced from physical impulses and rational knowledge:

This is the conclusion of a natural science view of the world with reference to freedom and responsibility: If freedom means that the acts of man may issue undetermined by the functioning of his cerebroneural mechanism, by the peculiarities of his inborn nature, or by anything in his education or past experience or present surroundings, then no man was ever free. But if freedom means so to function as to attain results chosen by our own reason, then men can be free, and a natural science view of life helps them to achieve freedom. By nature, education and resulting endeavor one may become capable of central control so that his acts are the expression not merely of sense perception appealing to instinct and predisposition but also of the wisdom stored by the experience and reflection of the individual and of the race. Then, knowing which path leads to evil, he will avoid it, and, knowing which leads to good, he will follow it, not driven about by vagrant thoughts and accidental percepts, but by his organized intelligence functioning as the cause of his overt deeds.[12]

Hayes treats at some length the social origin of moral codes. He makes it clear that they are not divinely revealed or absolute but are the relative and temporary products of social experience. In general, he follows Sumner's conception of the mores, though he is somewhat less relentless in his logic and analysis.[13]

In dealing with social values, Hayes insists that they always find a common basis in activity. He holds that there can be no passive social values. He lists five leading social values, each of which he traces and analyzes in some detail:[14]

1. Physical satisfactions
2. Esthetic pleasures
3. Intellectual satisfactions, leading to that rational contemplation which Aristotle eulogized
4. Social contacts and experiences
5. Self-contemplation and personal idealism, emerging in a well-rounded individuality

When he comes to the matter of moral imperatives, Hayes fully recognizes that these are wholly social in their origin and goals. He thus repudiated all the old metaphysical doctrines regarding the categorical imperative.[15]

Hayes's sociological writings were, on the whole, characterized more by a large amount of practical common sense than by special profundity or brilliant powers of generalization. He wrote in a very clear and readable style, and—to compare him with two of his best-known contemporaries in middle western institutions—his work stands midway between the erudition of C. A. Ellwood and the brilliant phraseology of E. A. Ross.

II. SPECIFIC SOCIAL AND POLITICAL THEORIES

A. SOCIOLOGY AND POLITICAL SCIENCE

In the opening chapter of his *Introduction,* on the nature of sociology, Hayes offers no formal definition but rather aims at leading the reader to an understanding of the general characteristics of sociology by an explanation of its chief aims and its method of procedure. He states that it is "the general science of social life" and holds that it must be causal, functional, synthetic, and objective. Again he says that sociology is "an intellectual movement resulting from the insistence of the mind that the methods of science shall be carried out in the realm of human activities."[16] While he nowhere makes the formal distinction, it is plain enough from the context of his discussion that he regards political science as the specialism which devotes itself to a study of political organization, that is, the state, in its most general connotation.[17]

B. SOCIETY AND THE STATE

Hayes conceives the state to be the political organization of society; it is "an independent political society, organized to promote the interests of its members through the exercise of sovereignty."[18] His distinction between society and the state is clear and consistent. Society is a group of associated individuals engaging in a number of important common activities which causally condition each other. The state, as has been pointed out, is society politically organized for the purpose of achieving an effective form of social control through sanctions in the form of coercion.[19] The more refined academic distinctions between the state and the government and between the state and the nation are not made clear. "State" and "government" are used as practically synonymous terms, though perhaps such a procedure was followed in accordance with the purposes of an elementary textbook in order to avoid confusing students by this very essential, but rather abstruse, distinction.

In his earlier work on "Sociological Construction Lines" Hayes presents a clear definition of a nation. Here he says: "A 'nation' is a people that is of one nativity, and that shows the other similarities of custom and culture which usually accompany unity of blood." At the same time, he often seemed to regard the modern state as all but identical with a nation, and he points frequently to the "nation-state" as the most powerful and characteristic of contemporary social groups.[20] He agrees with the usual classification of the essential attributes of the state, which include territory, population, sovereign power, and a governmental organization.[21]

C. ORIGINS OF THE STATE

As to the origin of the state and the government, Hayes believes that the development has been twofold, being based (1) upon the primarily warlike external relations of groups and (2) upon the generally peaceful internal relations between the members of each group. He would thus strike a balance between the theories of Gumplowicz and his followers, who stress the importance of the first process, and those of writers like Sutherland, Kropotkin, and Novicow, who are inclined to emphasize the primary efficacy of the second.

The operation of warlike external elements in the building of the state first appears in the creation of the temporary war chief, who surrenders his authority with the adjustment of the particular struggle in which he was chosen to guide the destinies of the group.[22] Before such an institution as permanent leadership can arise, however, there must be a long preparatory period, during which the tradition of group sanction for such an institution slowly develops:

> The development of such folk-ways and institutions involves: (1) the temporary supremacy over a few immediate followers due to response to emergency; (2) the more lasting prestige engendered by such prowess; (3) a sense of the necessity of military success as a matter of group policy; (4) the instinct of dominance expressed in conduct that suggests and evokes subservience; (5) the habit and custom of obedience; (6) partisanship and the prestige of desire, glorifying leaders; (7) mob reduplication of these sentiments in times of pageant and triumph; (8) specific inventions, due to incident and accident playing upon predispositions and ingenuity, which define the conduct proper to a king and the conduct proper in approaching him; (9) rational approval of the necessity of established group organization. All of these together produce a constitution, unwritten, of course, but imbedded in the minds of the participants in the social process.[23]

The development of the state from the influence of war naturally varies in rapidity and completeness with the frequency of war and the success of the participants. A group which is consistently successful and, as a result, is able to exploit an increasing number of conquered groups will enjoy a political evolution of maximum rapidity.

The other early influence in the development of the state is to be seen in the enforcement of discipline within the group by the elders of the primitive social group. This activity centers around "the enforcement of group customs and taboos regulating food distribution and other matters, the carrying out of ceremonies, particularly the ceremony of initiation, the organization of coöperative hunts, and game round-ups, the direction of the group wanderings, later the distribution of plots of ground, and the settling of disputes and quarrels."[24] Hayes does not, however, explain the interesting process whereby these two phases of political evolution, guided, at first, by different authorities, gradually coalesce into one coherent political organization for the conduct of both external and internal activities.

As to the relative importance of the external, or military, factors and the internal, or economic, social, intellectual, and religious, factors in the development of the state, Hayes is inclined to assign the greater influence to the latter. The romantic interest which has been attached to war has obscured the more important role of peaceful activities. In a letter to the writer, he expressed himself as follows: "I believe that my way of thinking about the theory of the State differs from the usual treatment in that I put relatively greater emphasis upon peaceful activities and their regulation as playing a part in the growth of governmental institutions. Not that I would underestimate the importance of war, conquest, and slavery in the origin of the State, but that I think non-sociological writers have given too exclusive emphasis to this latter class of activities as the main forces in political origins."[25] He might have added, however, that some of the worst offenders in this respect have been avowed sociologists, Gumplowicz having been most prominent in this respect.

Viewed from another standpoint, the evolution of the state may be regarded as the product of the struggle of contending interests within the state. This, of course, is the theory of Ratzenhofer and probably reflects the influence of Small, who was the most ardent of Ratzenhofer's disciples in America. This struggle of interests within the state results in political, as well as social, evolution, (1) because the strength of the social interests corresponds, in a general way, to the importance of the interests concerned; (2) because any society which opposes or suppresses important social interests cannot survive in the struggle for existence with other groups which allow this conflict of interests to go on unimpeded; and (3) because among the conflicting interests there are some which are motivated by sentiments of justice and altruism and thus mitigate the conflict of the more purely selfish interests.[26]

Those followers of Nietzsche and the adherents of pseudo-Darwinian sociology, who look upon social evolution as the result of an unmitigated struggle for survival, are the victims of a misconception of biological processes. The struggle for existence is primarily a struggle between members of different species and groups rather than between members of the same species or the same groups, and the efficiency of each social group rests essentially upon the degree of co-operation and mutual aid which its members have developed.[27]

D. FORMS AND FUNCTIONS OF THE STATE AND GOVERNMENT

Hayes attempts no formal analysis of the various forms of the state or the government. He mentions in various places the well-known classifications of monarchy, aristocracy, and democracy. His sympathies are clearly with democracy, though he does not hesitate to point out the various methods whereby the benefits of democratic forms are nullified in our present society, and he makes many suggestions as to urgent reforms, which are essential to make democracy a working reality.[28]

Hayes holds that there is a close relation between the form of government and the geographical conditions in any state. Regions which are exclusively agricultural tend toward aristocracy, for wealth here depends more upon the peculiar adaptability of land to monopolistic control than upon the ability and enterprise of the individual. Again, agriculture and its folkways favor conservatism and exclusiveness more than commercial pursuits. Commerce, on the other hand, is usually correlated with democracy, since it tends to break down local and national exclusiveness, is dynamic in character, and encourages individual ability and initiative rather than class privilege and monopoly.[29]

Sovereignty, Hayes defines as "that power which no other power within the state can successfully oppose," thus giving it the meaning of political, rather than legal, sovereignty, to use the terminology of Dicey.[30]

Following the example of Bagehot, Hayes draws an important distinction between the written and the unwritten constitution of a state. The unwritten constitution, which is by far the more important of the two, "is not a written document, but an actual situation created by prevalent ideas and sentiments." The English constitution, in so far as it is set down in legal forms, is that of a monarchy, while the constitutions of the Latin-American republics formally declare for a democracy. But, actually, England is one of the most democratic of governments, while the Latin-American republics alternate between anarchy and a dictatorship. Moreover, laws are, in the most fundamental sense, merely the legislative ratification of customs and institutions which have grown up within society and have received the sanction of public opinion.[31]

The primary function of the state, according to Hayes, is to assure an unimpeded and constructive struggle between the various interests within the state: "The primary purpose of law and politics in a democracy is to protect interests against destructive forms of struggle, to the end that all interests may have an equal opportunity to express themselves through governmental action in proportion to their strength as human motives. The worst tyranny is the suppression of the free struggle of interests."[32] Space forbids a discussion of Hayes's concrete proposals as to the proper relation of the government to the questions of property, the family, religion, education, labor, immigration, and international problems, but his views here are those of a liberal democrat.

In discussing the problem of liberty Hayes considers the argument of the two schools of thought regarding the right of the individual to disregard a law which he believes unjust. He cites Jefferson and Emerson as among those in favor of the view that it is not only the privilege but also the duty of a citizen to disregard a law that he believes, after careful consideration, to be an unjust and unwise measure. Hayes is inclined, however, to support passive obedience as the lesser of two evils, at least in the present stage of social evolution.[33]

E. EXTRA-LEGAL FORMS OF SOCIAL CONTROL

In discussing the extra-legal aspects of social control Hayes has some suggestive observations to offer concerning public opinion, the press, and political parties. He believes that public opinion is probably the most important and influential of all types of social control. It is more powerful than law, since the latter depends upon the support of public opinion for its respect and enforcement. Public opinion has an advantage over law, in that it offers rewards as well as punishment and can thus elicit good conduct as well as suppress crimes. Again, it is superior to law, in that it acts freely without any slow and expensive legal formalities:

Public sentiment remains the most original and pervasive and probably also the most powerful of all the agencies of social control by sanction. It is capable of progressive development, as the experience of ages becomes crystallized in definite judgments, incorporated into the "common-sense"; as newly developed possibilities of good and evil become more generally understood; as the general level of personality is raised by the agencies of education; and as the method of organization gives increasing definiteness and publicity to social responsibility.[34]

In modern society the most effective agency in developing public opinion is the press: "The press is as essential to the democratic control of activity in a great nation as nerve fibers to the control of activity in a vertebrate animal. Without it a democracy of a hundred millions would be like a vast jelly-fish, inert and certain to fall to pieces."[35] The press keeps the voters informed regarding the progress of political activity and legislation and thus makes it possible for them to form intelligent opinions. Again, most of the equipment of the individual mind is a product of the stream of impressions which the press pours into it. The press is also an important factor in moral control, in so far as it makes public the reward which comes to virtuous conduct and the punishment which follows transgression. On the other hand, the publication of gross immoralities and the frequent examples in newspaper accounts of how crime goes unpunished and how many attain positions of wealth and importance by illegal or immoral means tends to make the press, to this degree, an aid to social degeneration.[36]

As a consequence of the important role of the press in modern society, the freedom of the press carries with it a high degree of responsibility, and the press should be so controlled as to make its services contribute the maximum amount of good and the least possible amount of evil. To this end Hayes suggests (1) that the newspapers be compelled to make public their actual owners; (2) that there should be endowed nonpartisan periodicals, in the same way that there are endowed schools and colleges; (3) that there should be a greater development of non-partisan municipal newspapers; and (4), finally, that it should become the general editorial policy to publish properly signed articles opposing the particular views advocated by the paper in question.[37]

In his discussion of political parties Hayes adheres to the view of Ratzenhofer and Bentley that a political party is essentially an interest-group. He says: "A party is a self-conscious class whose bond of similarity consists not merely in common ideas and sentiments but in a common practical interest and aim and the activities prompted thereby."[38] The strength of a party depends (1) upon the possibility of communication and organization on the part of its members; (2) upon the possession of sufficient wealth to secure control of the best methods of communication and publicity; (3) upon the ability and prestige of its leaders; and (4), most important of all, upon the possession of "an indefatigable working nucleus."[39]

Our interest-groups are, of course, normally much more numerous than merely those which are conventionally known as the great political parties. This is partly to be explained by the fact that each interest-group supports one or another of the main parties because it is a matter of tradition that its special interest can best be protected by that particular party. This conviction is, however, often a habitual fancy rather than an actual fact. Party loyalty is, in most cases, about as intelligent as adhering to a single grocer, regardless of the services which he renders. The hope of the political future lies in the possibility that the more intelligent members of society will be able to hold the balance of power by nonpartisan support of the best policy, regardless of party: "Perhaps only the more intelligent can escape the bonds of habit, the hypnotism of names and of the glories of the past which each party that has survived a generation is sure to possess in the eyes of its adherents, and overcome the instinctive tendency to take sides, like shouting spectators at a football match, sufficiently to actually select between candidates. If so, it is to be hoped that there will be enough of the more intelligent to hold the balance of power."[40]

The "politicians," in the conventional use of that term, really constitute in themselves a very definite interest-group, whose interest is not the welfare of the public but rather their own profit and preferment, which will result from the victory of their particular organization. In general, the interest of politicians is opposed to that of the public, or it profits at the expense of the public, though, of course, there are some exceptions to the rule. Politicians are the "purveyors" of two very essential commodities—offices and laws; the real evil lies in the fact that they usually offer a rather poor quality of goods and also that the people are prevented by their partisanship from exercising their best judgment in making their selection from the rather slender and shabby stock that is presented to them.[41]

F. THE STATE AND SOCIAL REFORM

In regard to the important matter of social reform, as accomplished through governmental activity, it has already been pointed out that Hayes believes that this process, in a properly functioning society, is realized to a large extent automatically through the struggle and adjustment of conflicting interests.[42] But Hayes did not propose to rely solely upon the automatic working of the social process. In his *Sociology and*

Ethics and in the book which he edited on *Recent Developments in the Social Sciences*[43] he made it thoroughly clear that he regarded it as a function of the state to direct social progress. The knowledge required for this remains to be provided. But it would have to be a type of education which lays far more stress upon the social sciences than our present curriculum does.

Hayes explains the general tendency of governments to remain conservative, on the ground that those who are most prosperous under given conditions and are thus least desirous of change are the persons who usually control the policy of the government: "Since the well-fixed—the rich and the powerful—tend to conservatism, conservatism has the advantage over radicalism in power. The rich, the influential, those who mould opinion and enjoy prestige, who now own great newspapers and who once commanded armed retainers, are mostly conservative. 'The respectable classes' have usually been conservative, and in general it has been decidedly 'bad form' to be otherwise."[44]

Hayes also attempts to account for conservatism and radicalism on the psychophysical basis of differences in temperaments. This savors a little of Hippocrates and Galen. Much more important than any such item as alleged differences in temperament are the different complexes developed in the mind of the individual, owing to the experiences of life, quite irrespective of any organic differences. Hayes admits that his psychophysical explanation of conservatism and radicalism is of less importance than the influence of interests, which will profit either by preserving the present order or by modifying it.[45]

NOTES

1. See Hayes's tribute to Small in H. W. Odum, *American Masters of Social Science* (New York, 1927), chap vi. For an excellent summary of Hayes's training, work, and sociological theories see E. H. Sutherland, "Edward Cary Hayes, 1868–1928," *American Journal of Sociology*, XXXV (July, 1929), 93–99. A bibliography of Hayes's writings is included on pp. 98–99.

2. See Sutherland, *loc. cit.*

3. Published serially in the *American Journal of Sociology*, X (March, 1905—July, 1906). This represents a considerable elaboration of the dissertation as originally presented and accepted.

4. See F. H. Giddings, *A Theory of Social Causation* (New York, 1904); also *Inductive Sociology* (New York, 1901).

5. Hayes, *American Journal of Sociology*, X (May, 1905), 764.

6. *Introduction to the Study of Sociology* (New York, 1915), pp. 463 ff.

7. *Ibid.*, chaps. i–ii.

8. *Ibid.*, pp. 350 ff.
9. "The Social Forces Error," *American Journal of Sociology*, XVI (1910–11), 613–25.
10. E. C. Hayes, *Sociology and Ethics* (New York, 1921), pp. 25–26, 38–39. By permission of the D. Appleton–Century Co.
11. *Ibid.*, p. 51.
12. *Ibid.*, pp. 105–6.
13. *Ibid.*, chap. ix.
14. *Ibid.*, chap. vii.
15. *Ibid.*, chap. xi., and pp. 211, 246, 284–86.
16. *Introduction to the Study of Sociology*, pp. 4–8, 345, 378.
17. *Ibid.*, pp. 6–8, 424–26, 637 ff.
18. *Ibid.*, p. 637.
19. *Ibid.*, pp. 301–5, 417–18, 427, 637.
20. *American Journal of Sociology*, X (March, 1905), 625 ff.
21. *Introduction to the Study of Sociology*, pp. 32–34, 419–22, 637 ff.
22. *Ibid.*, pp. 538–9.
23. *Ibid.*, p. 539.
24. *Ibid.*, p. 540.
25. December 14, 1917.
26. *Introduction to the Study of Sociology*, pp. 646–48.
27. *Ibid.*, pp. 648–51.
28. *Ibid.*, pp. 108–70, 680 ff.; see also "Democracy as a Social Ideal," *Journal of Applied Sociology*, IX (1924–25), 6–10.
29. *Introduction to the Study of Sociology*, pp. 32–34.
30. *Ibid.*, p. 637.
31. *Ibid.*, pp. 637–38.
32. *Ibid.*, pp. 643–44.
33. *Ibid.*, pp. 644–46.
34. *Ibid.*, pp. 636–37.
35. *Ibid.*, p. 680.
36. *Ibid.*, pp. 680–83.
37. *Ibid.*, pp. 683–84.
38. *Ibid.*, p. 428.
39. *Ibid.*, p. 640.
40. *Ibid.*, p. 643.
41. *Ibid.*, pp. 640–44.
42. *Ibid.*, pp. 646 ff.
43. (New York, 1927), Editor's Introduction.
44. *Introduction to the Study of Sociology*, p. 416.
45. *Ibid.*, p. 415.

CHAPTER XLVI

THE SOCIOLOGICAL IDEAS OF PITIRIM ALEXANDROVITCH SOROKIN: "INTEGRALIST" SOCIOLOGY

HANS SPEIER, *New School for Social Research*

I. THE CULTURAL BACKGROUND AND PERSONAL EQUATION IN SOROKIN'S WRITINGS

PITIRIM A. SOROKIN is one of the most prolific writers in contemporary sociology. Because of his broad historical interests, his systematic grasp of factual detail, and his aptitude for facile theoretical reasoning, he occupies a place of distinction among the sociologists of our time. This place would have been his due, even if he had never written the four volumes of *Social and Cultural Dynamics* which are his most spectacular, but not his most important, contribution to sociology.

Sorokin is of Russian origin. His parents were peasants. He was born in Touria in 1889 and studied at the Psycho-neurological Institute and at the University of St. Petersburg, where he received his Doctor's degree in sociology in 1922. From 1914 to 1916 he taught at the Psycho-neurological Institute and from 1917 to 1922 at the University of St. Petersburg and at the Agricultural Academy. In 1917, Sorokin was editor-in-chief of the *Volia Naroda,* a moderately progressive paper. He was also a member of the Executive Committee of the All-Russian Peasant Soviet, of the Council of the Russian Republic, and secretary to Alexander Kerensky, the Russian prime minister in 1917. In 1918 he became a member of the Russian Constitutional Assembly.

Sorokin's experiences during the Russian revolution exerted a profound influence on his political attitudes and on his social theories. His hatred of communism, many of his antiprogressive and reactionary political opinions, and his rejection of the ideals of modern, Western civilization as a whole may be traced to this period of his life.

Sorokin claims that he believed in egalitarian principles at the beginning of the Russian revolution but that his observations of life in Russia during the revolutionary period led him to realize that this belief was untenable.[1] His *Leaves from a Russian Diary 1917–1922*[2] contains many gripping details of the Russian revolution. Apart from being a valuable source for the student of the revolution, this diary offers many clues for understanding the personal background of Sorokin's later works. During the revolution Sorokin completed his *System of Sociology* (2 vols., 1920; in Russian). His Marxian critics found many faults in this work. They criticized, in particular, the author's insistence on the importance of racial homogeneity for sociopolitical unity, on the unchangeable character of the Jewish race, and on the physiological basis of social inequality.[3]

Sorokin was sentenced to death by the Bolshevik authorities in 1922. Former students intervened in his behalf, and the death penalty was converted into banishment from the country. In 1923, Sorokin came to the United States. From 1924 to 1930 he was professor of sociology at the University of Minnesota, and in 1930 he was called to Harvard University.

Sorokin's first sociological book in English, *The Sociology of Revolution*,[4] is not one of his major works. It contains theoretical propositions which he later discarded, such as the theory of social equilibrium.[5] It is not primarily a study of the social conditions and social causes of revolutions but a treatise on the pathology of human behavior. Both the causes and the characteristics of revolutions are interpreted in terms of various conflicting psychologies which are not reconcilable with one another, except for the fact that they all minimize the importance of man's rational conduct. Sorokin's main line of reasoning in this book is derived from psychological doctrines in which the instinctive, "irrational" nature of man is stressed. Under the influence of Pareto, whom Sorokin read when the Russian revolution was in its initial phase, and also under the influence of Freud and Pavlov, Sorokin emphasized the limited power of human reason. Unfortunately, the weakness of reason is implemented by the evil nature of human instincts, which renders man a rather weird being. A revolution occurs when the balance of reason and instinct is suddenly disturbed on a mass scale. Then, man, as a social being, is reduced to an uninhibited, instinctive animal that shakes off the fetters of custom, morals, and law. Revolution is, thus, essentially anarchy and destruction, as instinct is essentially destructive.

Revolution is evil, since man is evil unless he is restrained by fear, force, or faith. Revolution is crime on a mass scale.

While the book contains many interesting facts on mass behavior in the Russian and earlier revolutions, it does not display an understanding of the historical conditions of revolutionary change. In particular, it fails to deal with the ideas that go into the making of revolutions. Because of Sorokin's emotional bias, which pervades both the general structure and the particular statements of the book, *The Sociology of Revolution* does not rank among the outstanding contributions in this field of sociological research; but, for the same reason, the book offers the best revelation of the personal equation in the author's outlook on man and society.

In the third volume of his more recent work, *Social and Cultural Dynamics*,[6] Sorokin returned once more to the analysis of revolutions. There he studied the fluctuations of internal disturbances through time, analyzing 1,622 revolutions and other internal conflicts in the history of Greece, Rome, and Europe as to the social area, the duration, the intensity of the disturbance, and the masses participating in it. This investigation is based on a much broader historical survey than the earlier study of revolution. While Sorokin repeats that the main difference between crime and revolution is one of magnitude only,[7] he does not reiterate his earlier misanthropic psychological doctrines. Instead, he advances a general interpretation of the social conditions of revolutions, viz., that "the main and the indispensable condition for an eruption of internal disturbances is that the social system or the cultural system or both shall be unsettled." One will hardly be inclined to regard this statement as especially illuminating. Sorokin tries, however, to increase the significance of his findings by attacking a number of popular theories to which he takes exception. Thus his curves on the frequency of revolutions show that the twentieth century has been one of the most turbulent periods of history, and he exclaims: "This conclusion will certainly startle all the manufacturers and consumers of the 'sweet applesauce' theories that civilization is progressive through a process of orderly change toward universal peace."[8] Here, as in many other of his polemics, Sorokin neglects to consider that the readers whom he deserves are not quite so naïve as the views which he attacks.

In yet another volume Sorokin discussed revolutions, treating them together with famine, pestilence, and war as one of the four most terrible disasters that befall mankind. *Man and Society in Calamity*[9] is devoted to a study of the effects of these disasters on the human mind, human behavior, the vital processes, social mobility, social organization, and "cultural" activities. There is again a wealth of quotations from historical sources and monographs in this book, but the analytical findings are disappointing by comparison. Sorokin's main thesis is the "law of diversification and polarization of the effects of calamity." It does not seem unfair to regard this law as the elaboration of a commonplace when its meaning is explained as follows: "The effects of a given calamity are not identical—indeed are often opposite—for different individuals and groups of the society concerned."

Sorokin's first major contribution to sociology in English was his *Social Mobility,* published in 1927.[10] In this work, Sorokin analyzed the phenomena of vertical and horizontal mobility, their nature, causes, and consequences. The wealth of quantitative data and the rich historical documentation of the volume have made it an indispensable textbook for anyone interested in social stratification. Sorokin discusses not only social mobility but also certain differential characteristics of social classes which have been studied by earlier sociologists, such as longevity, health and bodily features, intelligence, and character traits. Furthermore, the book contains a brief theoretical discussion of the nature and causes of social stratification. In *Social Mobility* Sorokin's political opinions determine the course of his investigation to a lesser extent than in his *Sociology of Revolution.* They are not entirely suppressed, however, in favor of scientific detachment. In his study of social mobility and stratification he found many of Pareto's ideas suggestive.[11] Specifically, with Pareto and a number of other modern critics of democracy, Sorokin considers it "a matter of necessity" that the leaders of politics and business must be immoral; they are either "lions" or "foxes."[12] At the same time, the "scepticism and destructive criticism" of modern intellectuals is presented as resulting from a deplorable lack of "any firm and sacred convictions," which Sorokin attributes in this work to the mobility of modern society, or, to put it in his own inimitable way: "Intellectuals of our epoch are a mixture of Protagoras, Gorgias, Socrates and Montaigne."[13] He concluded *Social Mobility* with a declaration of personal preference for the mobile type of society, which at that time he liked "too much to prophesy its funeral."[14]

Contemporary Sociological Theories, his next publication,[15] is one of the best introductory texts in the field. It most satisfactorily demonstrates his impressive erudition. By its invariable simplification of the theories presented for review and criticism, by its pedagogically skilful presentation, and by its successful attempt to consider theories in the light of factual findings, the book excels most similar writings on the history of social theory. Its bibliographical usefulness is considerable, since the book contains ample reference to works in five or six different languages.

Sorokin's contributions to rural sociology are embodied in a monumental *Source Book in Rural Sociology,* in three volumes,[16] prepared jointly with Carle C. Zimmerman and Charles J. Galpin under the auspices of the United States Department of Agriculture and the University of Minnesota, and a manual, *Principles of Rural-urban Sociology,* written jointly with Carle C. Zimmerman,[17] which is a concise summary of the *Source Book.* The outstanding value of the *Source Book* consists in the systematic presentation of selected passages from classic investigations of rural life in many different cultures. Data from numerous societies provide the rural sociologist with a wealth of factual material for comparative studies of contemporary rural life in America with that of other civilizations, past and present. Some of the conclusions which Sorokin suggests at the end of his *Principles of Rural-Urban Sociology* are of the same ethos that pervades his main work on social and cultural change. Thus he advocates a "deep spiritual revolution . . . . towards reinforcement and regeneration of the Stoic attitudes towards life instead of the Epicurean."[18] Among other things, this revolution would retard the "progressive extinction of the offspring" of the upper classes and counteract the "progressive impoverishment of the racial fund."[19]

Before turning to Sorokin's main work, mention should be made of another study which he undertook with Clarence Q. Berger on *Time Budgets of Human Behavior.*[20] This work is based on a collection of records which approximately one hundred individuals kept from day to day during a period of four weeks. These individuals were asked to record accurately the kinds of activities in which they engaged during the twenty-four hours of the day and precisely how much time was consumed by each activity. A part of the book is devoted to a factual discussion of human motives on the basis of "motivation schedules." For a period of two weeks the individuals whose time budgets were investigated recorded also the motive or motives for their varied activities. Finally, the authors deal with the problem of the predictability of human behavior and of social processes. One hundred and six individuals were asked to predict their own behavior accurately a day, several days, a week, or a month in advance, "listing exactly all the activities which would occupy them on the stated days from the moment of rising to that of retiring. Any activity with a duration of five minutes had to be listed separately. . . . . ." As was to be expected, the authors found that the errors in prediction were considerable and increased as the prediction extended further into the future. To this result there are added others of equal importance; for example, *"The more stable and routine the social life in which an individual lives and acts, the more clock-like its functioning from day to day, the higher the accuracy of prediction."*[21]

The volume closes with an eloquent chapter devoted to warnings against "reckless" "scientific" forecasting and large-scale social planning. "Perhaps," we are told, "the percentage of right *guesses* compared with wrong ones was rather higher in institutions like the Pythia of Delphi or the famous oracle of Apollo than in the contemporary predictions supposedly based firmly upon science."[22]

Still another book, *Russia and the United States*,[23] was written during the war when American sentiment ran high in praise of the Red Army and the Russian people. Today the volume is interesting mainly for the light it throws upon the conflict between anti-Bolshevik and pro-Russian feelings in the author's heart. The conflict was resolved in favor of the pro-Russian feeling. Sorokin attacked American apprehensions of "Russian communism, atheism, 'imperialism' and 'barbarism,' " regarding them as altogether unfounded. He tried to prove the essentially democratic nature of Russian life before and after the destructive phase of the revolution and found that the United States and Russia exhibited a most extraordinary similarity in moral standards, social institutions, cultural creativeness, etc. The "mutual, cultural and social congeniality of the two nations" held the promise of even closer co-operation between them in the future. "It is refreshing to sense, within the otherwise dark and chaotic maze of events, so beneficent a destiny."[24]

When the merit of this book is assessed in the light of subsequent events, it should not be forgotten that the "vital interests" of the two nations fall, strictly speaking, under the heading of international relations. Sorokin did not really examine these interests anywhere in his book but approached his subject more freely from a "sociocultural" point of view. Instead of talking about Manchuria, China, Korea, or about the Balkans, Germany, Austria, Italy, the Middle East, etc., he pleaded at the time, as an American citizen, for good will toward America's ally.

We have tried to indicate how all Sorokin's major writings are the expressions of a personality with firm convictions, convictions of a kind which are not too popular in modern democracy. Much as Sorokin the scholar tries to control his valuations which have inspired him in all his endeavors, his books are distinguished from many other monographs and textbooks in the social sciences by the evidence of a struggle in the author's soul between political passion and "scientific objectivity," objectivity being an ideal too often proclaimed by those who fail to be inspired by anything. One may justly doubt whether, in Sorokin's publications, this struggle is always resolved in favor of objectivity. Those who disagree with his valuations and preferences will, indeed, be inclined to deny most vigorously that it is so resolved. Some critics have contended that Sorokin's sociological writings are a long and elaborate —almost classic—demonstration of the validity of Max Weber's contention that the interjection of "value-judgments" vitiates sociology as an objective social science.

A more dispassionate answer can be given only after Sorokin's valuations are understood more clearly. Precisely what are his preferences? Are they dogmatic or critical? Do they differ in any way from the reactionary opinions of men who do not devote much time and energy to social philosophy? In short, are they prejudices or ideas? In order to answer these questions, we must turn to Sorokin's main work, which contains the most explicit exposition of his social philosophy.

II. "SOCIAL AND CULTURAL DYNAMICS": ITS THEME AND METHODOLOGY

Social and Cultural Dynamics[25] is a very ambitious study. It covers the history of civilization for the last twenty-five hundred years and contains numerous excursions into the history of many civilizations in order to ascertain the forms and kinds of sociocultural change.

Fundamentally, the work is a gigantic re-examination of the theory of progress which, in popular form, has dominated the philosophical views of many social scientists in the nineteenth century and has exerted a deep influence upon the mores of modern Western society. The theory contained not only the prospect of an ever increasing efficiency of man's control over nature—making for greater safety and comfort—but also of an ever increasing liberation of man from prejudice, ignorance, and destructive passions.

Even in its heydey this doctrine was not uncontested. There have been numerous scientists who tried to prove that the history of cultures resembles organic birth-growth-decline-death cycles, to be compared with recurring cyclical movements rather than a progressively ascending line. Leaving aside various refinements and modifications of these two basic doctrines of historical change, there has also been a much more radical criticism of the theory of progress: it has been denied that certain fundamental tenets of the theory of progress are sound. Briefly, the theory of progress endows different stages of history with significantly varying degrees of moral worth; and implies that the present may shine in the complacency of superiority as long as it lasts. This characteristically "modern" attitude was created by the advance of modern natural science, its marvelously effective application to man's control over nature, and the overwhelming prestige which quantitative methods acquired.[26]

The modern theory of progress is also an outgrowth of the increased *philosophical interest in history,* and it has been shown that this interest, which begins, roughly speaking, with Francis Bacon, emerged with the systematic doubt of the efficacy of rational moral precepts. A radical criticism of the theory of progress and of the ethical notions which it embodies would have to re-examine the relevance of historical investigations for moral considerations, on the one hand, and the adequacy of quantitative methods for dealing with this philosophical problem, on the other hand. Sorokin falls short of this kind of radical criticism. He discusses the philosophical problems which he raises, to a large extent, with the help of quantitative methods, but without ever disentangling the ethical problem of what is good from the essentially meaningless one, namely, how good was man in different periods of history. In other words, Sorokin's study of history is imbued with the spirit of the doctrine that he desires to refute. For this reason the work is an "expression"—or "derivative," to use Pareto's term—of our civilization rather than a critique of our civilization.

Sorokin comes to the conclusion that, viewed in historical perspective, there has not been any progress, nor has there been any cyclical movement. What he finds is *fluctuation:* fluctuation of the basic types of culture, fluctuation of the types of social relationships, fluctuation in the concentration of power, in economic conditions, in the occurrence of conflict—fluctuations everywhere.

The data from which this generalization is derived are taken from an area as varied as civilization itself. The first volume of *Social and Cultural Dynamics* deals with forms of art; the second with systems of truth, ethics, and law; the third with numerous social relationships, groups, and institutions, from the family to the state and from the church to economic conditions. It also contains a monumental study of about one thousand wars and sixteen hundred revolutions, and an inquiry into the relation between culture, personality, and conduct. Thus the research which went into the making of *Social and Cultural Dynamics* is truly enormous. It was undertaken with the help of numerous specialists. Even so, the encyclopedic enterprise would have been impossible had it not been for the fact that the research was confined to investigations which are, strictly speaking, unhistorical. The historical phenomena were not studied in order to understand their specific historical character but rather in order to "grade" them! Works of historians and occasionally also—for example, in the section on law—original documents were used with the single question in view: If all cultural phenomena are divided into a small number of classes, into which of these classes do the phenomena under investigation fall? Are they good, satisfactory, or bad?

The terms designating these classes are, of course, not quite so simple. They vary, in fact, from one cultural domain to another. For example, the opposing categories for classifying the "topics" of painting, sculpture, architecture, music, and literature are *religious* (good) and *secular* (bad); for their styles, *symbolic* (good) and *visual* (bad). The corresponding terms for social relationships are *familistic* (good) and *contractual-compulsory* (bad). Again, all pairs of categories are co-ordinated, since they are derived from a pair of basic values. The names of these basic values are *ideational* and *sensate*.

Once the historical phenomena are thus reduced to a basic index, i.e., subsumed under one of the classes, it becomes possible to compare the frequencies through time of the indices within any given series of phenomena. By doing the same for other series, frequencies in various series can be compared. No matter how heterogeneous the various departments of culture are; no matter how surprising it may appear to compare families with symphonies or states with systems of philosophy, once a common denominator of values—"externalized" in family, symphony, state, or philosophy—is established, the circle is squared.

In many respects Sorokin's sociological approach to history reminds one of the methodology of the old unilateral evolutionists in ethnological theory, who started out with an assumed and prearranged scheme of universal evolution and then searched for materials to round out the skeleton outline and vindicate the evolutionary scheme, having little regard for the cultural context from which they wrenched their data.

This, in brief, is the procedure which Sorokin follows in his attempt to arrive at generalizations about social and cultural change, namely, regarding almost everything in the history of mankind as an index of a strictly limited number of values.

The historian will consider this treatment of historical data, in which the most divergent phenomena are torn from their historical context and put in the same "class," as very strange indeed. He may well wonder what the significance of this cumbersome undertaking can possibly be when, on the highest level of generalization, the period of absolutism in the sixteenth and seventeenth centuries is made to appear *identical* with the period between the two world wars. Nor will he be convinced that the statistical method has been used with proper caution, when, even in its application to economic facts, it leads to such startling results as the following one, in which the understanding of historical circumstances is entirely neglected in favor of drawing a time curve, cutting across the most heterogeneous systems of economic organization: the general economic situation in France was "satisfactory" (rather than "bad" or "excellent," etc.) in the twelve following years, 1115, 1350, 1480, 1585, 1610, 1650, 1685, 1740, 1785, 1800, 1920, and 1925.[27]

Much as the historian may be at a loss to recognize the merit of such procedures and results, the moralist may reserve his judgment until he understands precisely what Sorokin's scale of values is. Unfortunately, Sorokin knows more definitely what is bad than what is good. Everything *sensate* is definitely bad. Contemporary society is bad, because the values externalized in contemporary society are hedonistic, utilitarian, and relativistic. Sorokin likes to dwell on the syndrome of the contemporary crisis of Western civilization in both America and Europe, in order to persuade his readers that they have made a mess of everything noble, decent, and good. His eloquence is that of a professorial Abraham, a Santa Clara.

It should be noticed that in his grandiose historical perspective there is not much difference between America and Europe,[28] nor is there any essential difference between democratically organized societies and non-democratic societies. It is characteristic of sensate "culture mentality" that people take seriously the "slogan," "Give me liberty or give me death," whereas the much superior ideational mentality "is little interested in political and civil rights and declarations, in various political devices to guarantee the liberty of speech, press, convictions, meetings, and overt actions; in the constitution, in free government, and the like."[29] On the other hand, the rise of totalitarianism is also indicative of sensatism; only, it is not "sensate liberation" but "sensate curbing" of the individual.

In any case, we must find our way back to the values of ideationalism, the culture of faith, or to the idealistic types of culture, which is the culture of reason. Unlike Spengler, Sorokin is not a straightforward prophet of doom. To be sure, sensatism will perish; but, after a catharsis, new values, i.e., the old values of idealism or ideationalism, will be once more externalized in society. In the end, then, everything will be well, until the new culture will again reach its "limit" and, by the operation of "immanent change," presumably make room for a new sensatism. In short, there is no final doomsday, there is only condition: a fluctuating prophecy of recurring doomsdays alternating with recurring days of a more fortunate lot of man.

In the fourteenth book of Augustine's *Civitas Dei* we read: "Epicurean philosophers lived after the flesh because they placed man's highest good in *bodily pleasure;* and .... those others do so who have been of opinion that in some form or other bodily good is man's supreme good." According to Augustine, the next higher level of life is represented by the Stoics, "who place the supreme good of man in the soul." Since "both the soul and the flesh, the component parts of man, can be used to signify the whole man," both Epicureans and Stoics (and Platonists) live "according to man." Or one may say that they live according to *reason,* if reason can be divorced from faith. Only the Christian, in his *faith,* lives according to God.

Sorokin's basic distinction between "sensate," "idealistic," and "ideational" bears more than a faint resemblance to the ideas expressed in this quotation from Augustine. Sorokin's basic philosophy may be regarded as a modern vulgarization of early Christian thinking. The distinction between senses, reason, and faith is retained as a universal principle of division of the types of men, cultures, and "systems" within each culture. The hierarchization of these values, however, is blurred. The idea of a supreme good is given up in favor of a relativistic point of view, tempered by eclectic professions of absolute standards. Throughout his work some kind of hierarchy of the three values is implied, as is particularly evident from the expressions of contempt, disgust, and revulsion in which Sorokin indulges whenever he describes the "sensate sewers" of our time. However, it is not the truth of faith which ranks highest, as one might expect from familiarity with the tradition which Sorokin follows in distinguishing the three values. Rather, he "prefers" idealism to ideationalism. Again, ideationalism is constructed as a compromise between sensatism and idealism, which blurs the distinctions further. Finally, the methods used in *Social and Cultural Dynamics* are those of "sensate science," which has induced a malicious critic to remark that the work may be a satire on modern social science.

The three kinds of truth are first distinguished and utilized in classifying philosophical systems, as well as cultural epochs. They are irreducible, and, consequently, Sorokin, the antirelativist, presents an elaborate system of historical relativism. In the fourth volume of his work, however, this relativism is suddenly revoked. In the first three volumes, Sorokin speaks of the three basic "systems of truth," leaving the reader at a loss as to what the author means by "truth," or, rather, plainly admitting a pluralism of three different kinds of truth. In the fourth volume, two new kinds of truth are introduced under the name of *integral truth,* which "embraces" "all three forms of truth,"[30] and *absolute truth,* which is reserved for God. The integral truth is called "three-dimensional" by Sorokin, because its sources are intuition, reason, and the senses. Sorokin claims that his "integralist sociology" has accomplished "a profound revolution" in the social sciences, because "instead of dispensing with anything valuable in the cognitive sense, in any of the systems of truth," the integralist method contains them all and is hence fuller and more adequate than any of them taken separately.[31]

Integral truth resembles the type of "synthetic" thinking which Karl Mannheim invented, in order to rid his "sociology of knowledge" of the epistemological difficulties arising from the "perspectivism" of "situationally determined" types of thinking. Both Sorokin and Mannheim speak of the relative and "partial" truth of the philosophies they reject, and then they emerge from the welter of relativism with a pretentious claim of a "supertruth." Mannheim proposes that his "sociology of knowledge" may serve as a foundation of all social science; Sorokin claims that his integral truth is closer to the absolute truth than any one-sided truth. This claim, characteristic of all those who try to reconcile historicism with philosophy, hardly merits serious refutation. But, as an intellectual curiosity, it may be noted that Sorokin does not hesitate to elevate his own thinking above the one-sidedness of all philosophers of the past whom he regards as representatives of idealitionalism, idealism, or sensatism, respectively: "Hence the greater adequacy of the integral system of truth—compared with partial or one-sided truth .... over each of these systems."[32]

Within the confines of this chapter it is impossible to do justice to the great number of discussions contained in the four volumes of Sorokin's work. Two of them may be singled out for brief analysis, however, since they are especially important for understanding the structure of the work, viz., the problem of cultural integration and the general theory of social change.

Sorokin distinguishes between various meanings of cultural "integration." Cultural elements may be (1) merely adjacent in time or space but independent or contradictory in meaning; (2) associated with one another, because of adaptation to an "external" factor; (3) functionally or causally interdependent; and (4) "internally" or "logico-meaningfully" united.

For two reasons the choice of the term "logico-meaningful" for the highest form of integration is not fortunate. Both functional and external forms of integration are meaningful and not all cases of logico-meaningful integration are logical. For example, the relationship between the motor and the battery in an automobile is functional, that between refrigerators and sun suits and other light clothing is external; yet the fact that the automobile is supposed to move and that both refrigerators and sun suits are related to the prevalence of a warm climate indicate that the integrations are not strictly meaningless in either case. Again, logical integration is claimed not only for certain interrelationships of cultural elements that we encounter in the form of verbal propositions, such as statements in written documents, but also for nonverbal cultural elements, such as monuments and music, and for relationships between different classes of cultural elements, such as a specific family organization, a style of culture, a specific type of personality, and a particular kind of legal code. Sorokin himself admits that many units which he calls logico-meaningful are not logical units in the formal sense of the word "logic."

It appears, therefore, that what is meant by "logico-meaningful integration" is a type of integration which exists with reference to an arbitrarily selected norm, while "causal-functional integration" refers to the structure of the whole whose parts are functionally interdependent. Association due to an external factor is, of course, functional, too; but in this case integration exists only in view of the fact that social data are dependent upon nonsocial facts (climate, natural resources, etc.). By stressing the importance of logico-meaningful integration and by proclaiming it to be the highest form of integration, Sorokin is in a position to reject as insufficient or faulty those theories of culture which take cognizance only of that form of integration which depends on an external factor. Also, by differentiating spatial adjacency and integration in a narrower sense of the term, Sorokin makes allowance for the existence of unintegrated elements in a culture. Such elements are called "congeries." Sorokin repeatedly points out that any empirically given culture contains logico-meaningful systems and, in addition, congeries, although in the historical parts of his work he does not indicate which elements of the culture under investigation fail to be integrated. Sorokin takes exception to all theories of culture which insist on the functional interdependence of *all* cultural elements without admitting the possibility of unintegrated elements. Similarly, he rejects the "atomistic" theories which deny the existence of *any* integration, and in doing so he falsely regards any denial of a philosophy of history as a process with an integral meaning as a denial of the interdependence of various cultural elements in a given period of time.

Sorokin's analysis of culture centers around the logico-meaningful integration, i.e., around integration of culture with reference to norms. External phenomena of culture, such as objects, events, processes, are regarded as "incarnations" or "realizations" of the internal aspect of culture. In its organized form this internal aspect of culture consists of systems of thought which are "woven out of the inner experience" of a culture. Another term frequently used to designate this internal aspect is "culture mentality." External aspects of a culture are taken into account "only as manifestations of its internal aspects. Beyond this, they cease to be a part of an integrated system of culture."[33] This quotation confirms the statement that what is meant by "logico-meaningful integration" is integration with reference to norms. In addition, it indicates the antimaterialistic orientation of Sorokin's sociology. Sorokin's system may indeed be regarded as intellectualistic.

For purposes of analysis the external aspects of culture—say, the state organization or the prevailing family system—can be identified as integrated parts of a culture only if these social institutions can be translated by the analyst into normative terms and if, in addition, these norms are found to be identical, or at least compatible, with the basic values, sensate, idealistic, ideational, and their modifications. Sorokin, however, does not proceed according to this cumbersome method. He takes a short cut which is methodologically ingenious. Instead of investigating the philosophy, the art, the social institutions, the codes, the techniques, and the resources of a given society in order to understand the historical nature of these phenomena before proceeding to an analysis of integration, he takes as a starting-point a series of classifications of the various departments of culture in *all* periods, as has been indicated above. All these classifications are, from the beginning and by definition, compatible with the fundamental types of culture mentality. It is this procedure which renders his historical investigations unhistorical in the strict sense of the term.

In his general theory of social change Sorokin rejects the "externalistic" doctrines, according to which the changes that a cultural "system" undergoes are caused by external, environmental factors, for example, changes in the family structure by industrialization. The logical objection to all these theories is, according to Sorokin, that they postpone rather than solve the problem of change. By explaining a change of (*a*), say the family, by a change of (*b*), say industrialism; and the change of (*b*) by a change of (*c*), say the population structure; and the change of (*c*) by a change of (*d*), say the climate, an unlimited regression is introduced. This regression often involves the further difficulty of explaining transformation in one sphere, where much change occurs, in terms of causes located in another sphere, where less change occurs, as is especially evident in the explanation of social change in terms of climate.

In this case, as rather frequently in his writings, Sorokin does not fairly present the theory that he rejects in its most reasonable form, which is more difficult to criticize than its popular, simplified version.

Thus Sorokin attributes to the "externalistic" theories of social change the presupposition that change rather than "unchangeableness" of a sociocultural system needs explanation, whereas Sorokin himself stresses quite rightly that life is always changing and that unchangeableness rather than change needs explanation.

The occurrence of social change is, indeed, a universal fact, but the inquiry into the reason for this fact is part of the metaphysical problem of what life is. The various "externalistic" theories offer hypotheses regarding the causes of *specific* changes, not of the principle of change itself. Thus it is perfectly sensible to investigate the dependence of social life on climate or geography without investigating the metaphysical problem of change and stagnation, or of life and death. The scientific criticism, as distinguished from the metaphysical one, of such externalistic theories would have to determine whether the proposed causal dependence can be reversed, as, for example: Are climate and geography dependent upon social life? It would have to inquire to what *extent* and *degree* the hypothesis is correct; to what *extent* and *degree* other causal factors have to be introduced into the explanation of specific changes, etc. In short, the externalistic theories are not necessarily incompatible with the principle of *immanent change,* to which Sorokin adheres and to which he devotes a very stimulating discussion.

While it is generally true that "change needs much less explanation than any case of unchangeableness," it also remains true that any specific case of change needs as much explanation as any specific case of unchangeableness. Now Sorokin does recognize "externalistic" causes of social change, in addition to the principle of immanent change, but he attributes only a *subsidiary* significance to the externalistic principles and claims immanent change to be the primary principle. No protagonist of the externalistic doctrines will, however, go so far as to suggest that a state can by any effort of external factors be changed into a night club;[34] all protagonists of the externalistic doctrines will give implicitly more credit to the principle of immanence than Sorokin is inclined to give to intelligence, in the case of his opponents. On the other hand, Sorokin's emphasis on the principle of immanent change leads very easily to an attitude of resignation regarding the scientific explanation of specific changes. If everything changes anyhow and primarily according to the principle of immanent change, why bother much about *explaining* specific social changes? It will be noticed that this logical outcome of Sorokin's doctrine closely corresponds to his skepticism regarding forecasting and social planning. If everything changes anyhow and primarily according to the principle of immanent change, why bother much about *effecting* a specific change in society?

In conclusion, it may be said that Sorokin's main work revives the tradition of the encyclopedic endeavors of the early sociologists like Comte and Spencer. The greatest compliment that can be paid to it is that it invites comparisons with other contemporary attempts to arrive at an integrated philosophical view of human history, such as Spengler's or Toynbee's, or with other contemporary studies of the crisis of our time, such as Huizinga's. In such comparisons, however, Sorokin does not fare too well. Even Spengler excels him in historical judgment, imagination, and taste. H. Leisegang's older study, *Denkformen* (1928), offers a more penetrating analysis of the basic differences between various "types" of thinking than does Sorokin's integralist sociology. With all due respect for the gigantic labor that went into *Social and Cultural Dynamics,* for many stimulating discussions in this work, and especially for Sorokin's courageous attacks on many cherished errors in contemporary social science, one cannot help concluding that the work, as a whole, suffers from the persistent interjection of personal prejudices and that it combines the faults of European and American social science: unclear metaphysics and the application of quantitative techniques to philosophical problems which evade figures and curves.

NOTES

1. Hans Kasspohl in the *Introduction* to the German edition of Pitirim Sorokin's *Sociology of Revolution* (1925): *Die Soziologie der Revolution* (Munich, 1928), p. 18.

2. New York, 1924.

3. Kasspohl, *op. cit.,* p. 16.

4. Philadelphia, 1925.

5. See his criticism of this theory in "Le Concept d'équilibre est-il necessaire aux sciences sociales?" *Revue internationale de sociologie,* September–October, 1936. An abbreviated version of this article is contained in Sorokin's *Social and Cultural Dynamics,* IV (New York, 1941), 677–93.

6. (New York, 1937), pp. 383–508.

7. *Ibid.,* III, 501.

8. *Ibid.,* III, 478.

9. New York, 1943.

10. New York, 1927.

11. *Contemporary Sociological Theories* (New York, 1928), p. 60, n. 83.

12. For the context in which Sorokin uses these terms of Pareto cf. *Social Mobility,* p. 310.

13. *Ibid.*, p. 520.

14. *Ibid.*, p. 544.

15. New York, 1928.

16. Minneapolis, 1930–31.

17. New York, 1929.

18. *Principles of Rural-urban Sociology*, p. 635.

19. *Ibid.*, p. 632.

20. Cambridge, Mass., 1939.

21. *Time Budgets of Human Behavior*, p. 170 (italics Sorokin's and Berger's).

22. *Ibid.*, p. 179.

23. New York, 1944.

24. *Russia and the United States*, p. 209.

25. Vols. I–III (New York, 1937); Vol. IV (1941). A popularization of these four volumes appeared later under the title *The Crisis of Our Age* (New York, 1941). The methodology employed in his main work is discussed and summarized in *Sociocultural Causality, Space, Time* (Durham, N.C., 1943).

26. For two of the most penetrating discussions of this subject, cf. Edmund Husserl, "Die Krisis der europäischen Wissenschaften und die transcendentale Phaenomenologie," *Philosophia*, I (1936), 77–176; and Jacob Klein, "Die griechische Logistik und die Entstehung der Algebra," *Quellen und Studien zur Geschichte der Mathematik*, Abteilung B: *Studien*, II (Berlin, 1934), 18–105, and III (Berlin, 1936), 122–235.

27. *Social and Cultural Dynamics*, III, 236, Fig. 4.

28. See "Socio-cultural Trends in Euro-American Culture during the Last Hundred Years," *A Century of Social Thought* (Durham, N.C., 1939), pp. 96–125. In this essay Sorokin tries to prove that "any contention that American and European cultures are different is wrong." They are "identical . . . . in all essential traits!"

29. *Social and Cultural Dynamics*, III, 167.

30. *Ibid.*, IV, 763.

31. *Sociocultural Causality, Space, Time*, p. 230.

32. *Social and Cultural Dynamics*, IV, 764.

33. *Ibid.*, I, 55.

34. The example is Sorokin's (cf. *ibid.*, IV, 604).

CHAPTER XLVII

THE SYSTEMATIC SOCIOLOGY OF MARIANO H. CORNEJO

L. L. Bernard, *Washington University*

I. GENERAL NATURE AND DEVELOPMENT OF LATIN-AMERICAN SOCIOLOGY

THE development of Latin-American sociology falls into four fairly distinct, but connected, periods. These correspond roughly to (1) the decades of the 1840's; (2) the 1880's, extending into the 1890's; (3) the first decade of the twentieth century; and (4) the decade in which we now find ourselves. The most typical representatives in all these stages were perhaps predominantly from Argentina, although Peru, Brazil, Mexico, Cuba, and Chile have run close seconds to Argentina and all the other republics have honorable representation in one or more of these periods of growth in sociological writing and investigation.

1. The romantic and revolutionary stage may be said to have begun in 1845 with the publication of *Facundo* by the Argentine statesman and sociologist, Domingo Faustino Sarmiento (1811–88), while he was still an exile in Chile. In this work was first stated Sarmiento's fruitful thesis that the great vice of Latin-American culture and politics was traceable to the preponderance of the untutored mixed breeds and frontier elements of the population, who so readily lent themselves to the designs of the *caudillos,* or dictators, who seized the governments in their own interests and sabotaged the early feeble attempts at responsible constitutional government.

The second great contribution to this period of sociological writing was the *Dogma socialista* (1846) of Esteban Echeverría (1809–51), who brought back from an extended residence in France the romantic social idealism of the schools of Comte Henri de Saint-Simon and who became the teacher of the men who later achieved the Argentine revolution of 1852. Besides the *Dogma socialista,* in which he made a dignified appeal for the recognition of the newly stated rights of man in social practice, he described brilliantly the life of the Argentine pampas in *Guitarra* (1842) and wrote *La Insurección del sur* (1849).

The *Bases* (1852), a work in political sociology by Juan B. Alberdi (1810–84), did for the establishment of constitutional government throughout Latin America what the *Dogma socialista* and the *Facundo* had done for the freeing of men's minds in general from the tyranny of the old absolutisms in social and political values and aspirations. Alberdi was perhaps the greatest social philosopher produced by Latin America. After the fall in 1861 of President Urquiza, whose political adviser and diplomatic representative he was, he remained in Europe until his death in 1884. There he came in contact with the advancing thought of the time and wrote his *Ensayos sobre la sociedad* and the masterly *El Crimen de la guerra,* both of which were published after his death.

2. The 1860's and 1870's were periods of political and social unsettlement throughout Latin America, owing to the growing pains accompanying the establishment of constitutional government in those decades. But the decade of the 1880's brought a more settled state of affairs and with it serious reflection upon the problems of democratic social control. In this period Sarmiento brought out his *Conflictos y harmonias de las razas en América* (1883), and J. M. Ramos-Mejia (1849–1914) published his *Neurosis de los hombres celebres en la historia argentina* (1878) and his *Las Multitudes argentinas* (1893). Then also began the publication by Agustin Alvarez (1857–1914) of his series of works dealing with the problems of popular intelligence and control. Alvarez was the legitimate successor of Alberdi and Sarmiento, whose theories he represented and extended, as guide and mentor to Latin-American social thinkers and public men around the turn of the century. His books, of which *South America* (1894), *Manual de patología política* (1899), *Ensayo sobre educacción* (1901), *Adonde vamos* (1904), *La Transformación de las razas en América* (1908), *Historia de las institutiones libres* (1909), and *La Creación del mundo moral* (1912) were the chief, had and continue to have tremendous influence throughout Latin America.

All these writers were Argentineans, but there were many other men in other Latin-American countries who wrote on the same or similar themes with scarcely less distinction.[1] It will be seen that these writings were primarily in the field of racial and collective psychology, following more or less the lead of Walter Bagehot, Henry Maudsley, Gabriel Tarde, and Gustave Le Bon in Europe. The influence of Positivist ideas and of the psychological and historical methodology from Renan and of Taine is also strongly manifest in the writings of this period. The European writers mentioned in this paragraph were the intellectual masters of Latin-American social philosophers in the last quarter of the nineteenth century.

3. It was not until the first decade of the twentieth century that systematic sociology had its real inception in Latin America. A Puerto Rican of distinction, with wide cultural contacts with Europe and with Latin America in general, Eugenio Maria de Hostos (1839–1903), produced the first systematic treatise in the field, publishing his *Tratado de sociología* in 1901. Ernesto Quesada (1858–1931) was perhaps the leading early representative of this new period of sociological writing, although he never produced a systematic treatise on sociology proper and in his later years he became an exponent of Spenglerian doctrines, which he attempted to apply to Latin-American conditions. But as professor of sociology at the University of Buenos Aires in the first decade of the century, he influenced many other young men of ability in the direction of sociological study and writing. Preceding him and in close succession to his term as professor of sociology at the University of Buenos Aires, came Juan Agustin García, with his *La Ciudad indiana* (1900), Alfredo Colmo's *Principios sociológicos* (1905), Enrique Martínez Paz's *Elementos de sociología* (1911), José Ingenieros' *Sociología argentina* (1913), Raúl A. Orgaz' *Estudios de sociología* (1915), José Olivia's *Sociología general* (1924). Not all these men owed their inspiration primarily to Quesada. García, an independent student of Argentine culture and professor of sociology at the University of Buenos Aires, rivaled Quesada as a leader in this field.

After the first decade of the twentieth century, emphasis upon sociology spread widely throughout Latin America. We have already referred to the treatise by De Hostos. Angel M. Paredes' able *Sociología general,* after the European model, appeared in two volumes in Quito in 1924. It was around this time that José de Oliveira Vianna began to publish in Brazil his numerous works on sociology. Of these we may mention *Populações meridionães* (1920), *Pequeños estudios de psicología social* (1921), *Raza e assimilação* (1932), *Formation ethnique du Brasil colonial* (1932), *As novas directrizes da política social* (1939). The chief development of sociology in this period was undoubtedly in Argentina, where courses were introduced into all the leading universities; but Puerto Rico, Brazil, Peru, and Ecuador also made very important contributions to the science. In the third period the ablest and most erudite of all these Latin-American writers on systematic sociology was Mariano H. Cornejo, of Peru, whose work is the main object of emphasis in this chapter. No one in Latin America has yet surpassed his classic contribution on the European model. On the whole and with few exceptions, this third period was not marked by originality. It never grew up to its European models except in the work of Cornejo and possibly that of Paredes, and, as a consequence, the fame of most of its writers was relatively short lived.

4. Beginning early in the 1930's a new and major revival in sociological theory began in Latin America, gathering much momentum around the end of the decade. It probably proceeds from four sources: (1) the intellectual maturing of the generation whose youth fell in the period which produced Quesada, García, Alvarez, De Hostos, Martínez-Paz, Colmo, Cornejo, Oliveira Vianna, Paredes, and Ingenieros. (2) The growing political unrest of Europe spread its unsettlement to Latin America much more than to the United States and challenged the accepted philosophic foundations of social thinking there. (3) The depression which fell upon the world in the second decade following the first World War also presented a similar challenge. (4) Popular and higher education, especially regarding social and political matters, has had a marked growth in Latin America within the last few decades.

Space is lacking for the adequate analysis of the growing volume of sociological writings that is pouring from the Latin-American presses, but we can at least mention, without prejudice to others, a few of the more systematic treatises on sociology which have appeared in these countries in the last decade preceding the second World War. These include *Sociología genética y sistemática*, by Antonio Caso (Mexico); *Tratado de sociología*, by Florentino Menezes (Brazil); *Sociología de la interdependéncia*, by Agustin Venturino (Chile); *Sociología contemporánea*, by José Medina Echavarría (Mexico); *Psicología social*, by Arthur Ramos (Brazil); *Sociología*, by Roberto MacLean y Estenós (Peru); *Fundamentos de sociología*, by A. Carneiro Leão (Brazil); *Epítome de culturología*, by José Imbelloni (Argentina); *Sociologie économique*, by François Dalencourt (Haiti); *Sociología de la autenticidad y simulación*, by Cayetano Betancur (Colombia); and *Sociología de la revolución* and *Sociología como ciéncia de realidad*, both by Alfredo Poviña (Argentina).

Since 1940, sociological production has had a remarkable development throughout Latin America, due in part at least to the stimulus of the late war. The writings in this field are now so numerous that they cannot all be listed. But six recent writers on theoretical sociology appear to deserve special mention. These still follow the European pattern of conceptual speculative discussion more closely than the North American pattern of realistic induction from specific social data. Fernando de Azevedo, professor of sociology in the University of São Paulo, is most typical of this trend in his *Principios de sociología* (3d ed., 1939). Like many other Brazilians, he leans heavily toward the Comtist tradition in this work on the conceptual methodology and historic schools of sociology. Alfredo Poviña, of the University of Cordoba (Argentina), is one of the younger and most active Latin-American sociologists. His *Cursos de sociología* (1945) includes a division on cultural sociology, along with four other parts devoted to systematic conceptual methodology. Raúl A. Orgaz, of the same university, is now at work on his general comprehensive treatise, *Sociología,* and has published Part I (1942), which includes preliminary discussions and a theory of institutionalized groups. This emphasis upon group analysis is a promising departure in the direction of social realism.

Roberto MacLean y Estenós, professor at Lima, is one of the most productive and promising of Latin-American sociologists. His earlier treatise has been mentioned, but in 1945 he brought out his *Sociología integral,* a work of approximately nine hundred pages. About half of this treatise deals with realistic subjects, such as social dynamics, social evolution, social structure, and social forces (including sex—to which much attention is given), social mentality, language, myths, art, law, and morals. There is a long section of approximately three hundred pages dealing with the history and schools of sociology. Roberto Agramonte, dean and professor in the University of Havana, is perhaps closest of all these men to the North American pattern. He is a scholar of great intellectual energy and diverse talents, having written on psychology, psychiatry, social policy, and sociology. His *Sociología* (3d ed., 1940) devotes but a minor portion of its space to verbal methodology and by far the greater space to social forces, social invention, social processes, and social problems. His briefer work, *Introducción a la sociología* (450 pp.) was published in 1944. To these works must be added the writings of José Medina Echavarría, including his *Sociología contem-*

poránea, already referred to, and his *Sociología: teoría y técnica* (1941), *Responsibílidad de la inteligencia* (1943), and *Consideraciones sobre el tema de la paz* (1945). One of his most valuable sociological undertakings has been the promotion of a detailed study of war in its various aspects, causes, and consequences, which was carried through and published in ten monographs by himself and his associates in El Colegio de México, of which he is the sociological research director. Francisco Ayala, a Spanish sociologist now in Argentina, has just published (1947) a *Tratado de sociología* in three volumes, covering the history of sociology, a system of sociology, and a biobibliographical glossary of sociology.

Latin America is the original home and still the chief source of social ecological studies. To Sarmiento's *Facundo* and Ingenieros' *Sociología argentina* have recently been added Luis López de Mesa's *Disertación sociológica* (Bogotá), Roberto MacLean y Estenós' *Sociología peruana* (1942), and many other similar treatises. Educational sociology is also ably represented by Fernando de Azevedo's *Sociología educacional* (1942), Roberto MacLean y Estenós' *Sociología educacional del Perú* (1944), Paul Arbousse-Bastide's *Formando o homem,* and Ernesto Nelson's *El Analfebetismo en la República Argentina* (1944).

Because of characteristic conditions in Latin America, political sociology remains the chief interest there and will doubtless continue to be so for some time. Vallenilla Lanz's *Cesarismo democrático,* apologizing for the Gómez dictatorship in Venezuela, is perhaps the ablest defense of Latin-American fascism. Maximiliano Koberg B's *El Verdadero orden social* (1944) makes a well-reasoned argument for democracy on the basis of a sociological program. This Costa Rican's work is incisive and able. Fernando de Azevedo, in *Velha e nova política* (1943), presents a fundamental discussion of the forces decomposing the old social order and of the lines along which the new social order must be constructed. Among other outstanding works on political ideology may be mentioned *La Evolución de la democrácia* by Luis Bossano (Ecuador) (1944); *Política sindical brasileira,* by Geraldo Bezerra de Menezes; *Los Fundamentos del socialismo en Cuba,* by Blas Roca; and *Influéncia de la industria azucarera en la vida antillaña y sus consecuéncias sociales,* by Francisco M. Zeno, of Puerto Rico.

The work of Luis Lagarrigue of Chile in interpreting in several volumes the moral and religious ideology of positivism should also be mentioned in this connection. Gilberto Freyre has also described the plantation life, slavery, and the church as an institution in Brazil in a series of very able studies after the manner employed by North American investigators. His *Sobrados e mucambas* (1936) may be taken as typical of his studies. Social and collective psychology have also had recent as well as early able representatives in Latin America. Perhaps the work of Arthur Ramos, of Brazil, is most outstanding among current contributors in this field. His *Introducção a psicología social* (1936), *O negro brasileiro* (1934), *O folk-lore negro do Brasil* (1935), and *As culturas negras no novo mundo* (1937) claim special mention. In this connection also should be named *Genio y acción* (1938), by Emeterio S. Santovenia, and *Cervantes y El Quizota* (1945), by José de Armas y Cardenas, both of Cuba, and *Typología do líder* (1942), by Theodor Geiger, of Brazil.

Latin-American sociologists are also interested in the history of their science at home and abroad. *Las grandes escuelas de la sociología* (1941), by Ramón T. Elizando, of Argentina, reviews selected outstanding theories of society from Manu to Condorcet. Alfredo Poviña's *Historia de la sociología en Latino-América* (1941) is the fullest account of this subject yet to be published. Leopoldo Zea's *Apogeo y decadencia del positivismo en México* (1944) is a valuable study of one section of the Comtean influence in America. Mario Lins has an enlightening brief monograph on *Tendéncias de la sociología en el Brasil* (1944). Carlos A. Echánove Trujillo, of Mexico, has prepared a *Diccionario abreviado de sociología* (1944), which is as good as anything of its kind anywhere.

There has been space in this account for examples only of the recent work in sociology in Latin America, a fact which should be kept in mind by the North American reader interested in this subject. There are many other writers in the field who also deserve mention and even analysis, if that were possible. We must conclude our sketch by listing a few of the secondary treatises on theoretical sociology, such as Luis Lagarrigue's *Nociones de sociología* (1926), perhaps the ablest orthodox Comtean treatise on this subject; Felipe López Rosado's *Apuntes de introducción a la sociología* (1942); Georg Nicolai's *Fundamentos reales de la sociología* (1937); Luis Bassano's *Los Problemas de la sociología* (1941); and Romano Barreto and Emilio Willem's *Leituras sociológicas* (1940). The last two authors publish at São Paulo a worthwhile sociological review, *Sociología,* now in its eighth year. The *Revista méxicana de sociología* of Lucio Mendieta y Nuñez, of the University of Mexico, is a large quarterly, also in its eighth year. The *Boletín del Instituto de Sociología* of the University of Buenos Aires, published under the general direction of Ricardo Levene, is an ably edited annual of approximately four hundred large pages. The thing most to be desired for the future development of sociology in Latin America is the establishment of full-time professorships of the subject in all the leading Latin-American universities.

II. GENERALLY BACKWARD CHARACTER OF LATIN-AMERICAN SOCIOLOGY

The work of Cornejo may be taken as the most typical of the Latin-American systems of sociology already completed. It cannot be said, however, that Cornejo has made a strikingly original contribution to systematic sociology. Few Latin Americans since the days of Sarmiento and Alberdi have shown great originality in sociology, although Ingenieros, at least, has left a mark on international sociological thinking, and Echeverría, De Hostos, Alvarez, Colmo, Venturino, Paredes, Agramonte, Orgaz, Poviña, Elizando, Azevedo, Ayala, Mac-Lean y Estenós, among others, have produced works of significant challenge. But few of their general treatises, unless we except that of the last named, may be called truly original, although they are usually constructed in a systematic manner. Among the many causes of this failure of Latin-American sociologists to produce truly original contributions, especially outside the fields of criminology and penology, are the lack of research funds and full-time professorships for sociologists in their universities. Almost without exception, the sociology taught in the Latin-American universities is limited to a single course in the law schools and perhaps another in the faculty of philosophy and letters, when there is such a faculty. These two courses are nearly always taught by different men, whose profession is not teaching but that of law. The teaching of sociology is, thus, practically always an avocation rather than a vocation. It is not surprising that under such circumstances the professor of sociology draws heavily on the European sociologists, adding his own interpretation or a few illustrative local data here or there.[2] This situation is, however, rapidly changing, and the indications are that a great development of sociology is already under way in Latin America.

The most original contributions from Latin-American sociologists have come in the form of their interpretations of the impact of the native culture and the frontier upon the European culture and the struggle between the antagonistic types of civilization arising therefrom. The great work, *Facundo,* by Sarmiento[3] was the first and chief essay in this field, and the theme has been repeatedly emphasized by such writers as Ingenieros,[4] Alvarez,[5] Colmo, and Venturino[6] since the time of the first expositor. The most original sociological work in Latin America, therefore, has been in the fields of culture conflict and human ecology. Where their sociologists have dealt with the ordinary processes of social origins, organization, control, and methodology, they have found these fields already developed by European sociologists, who described more highly matured cultures than their own. As a consequence, they could do little but imitate, adding an idea here and there. Language barriers and the absence of easy contacts with North America have prevented them from profiting adequately from the highly developed science of sociology in the United States. Indeed, few Latin-American sociologists know much about it or suspect its superior achievements.[7]

It is, however, not to be expected that this backwardness of Latin-American sociology will continue indefinitely. The establishment of the *Revista méxicana de sociología,* under the patronage of the Mexican government and with the able leadership of Lic. Lucio Mendieta y Nuñez, started a new era of sociological investigation in that country, which has extended to other Latin-American countries as well. One of the great handicaps to sociological productivity in Latin America has been the lack of adequate journals devoted to the subject. Reviews carrying sociological articles have been started from time to time, but they have rarely survived for long periods. The number of readers in any one country is too small, and until recently there has been no outstanding international journal of this sort in Latin America.

Certain types of problems prevalent in Latin America, such as those of the still surviving frontier, relations between native and imported cultures, culture conflict due to excessive immigration, dictatorships thriving on mass ignorance and race antagonism, geographic and climatic resistance, and European propaganda organization, offer exceptional opportunities to Latin-American sociologists who can find the time and can secure funds for their investigation in order to realize these opportunities. The Latin Americans are so accustomed to follow European leads in thought—partly because of their own cultural immaturity—that they rarely saw opportunities for sociological investigation except through European eyes. Their greatest need in order to stimulate original sociological study in Latin America is to be made to realize that they have situations for original investigation second to none.[8] It was in Argentina that this fact was first and most strongly realized, by such men as Sarmiento, Ingenieros, and Alvarez. But Cornejo either failed to grasp his opportunity or preferred to work after the European pattern of sociology. Later sociologists have begun to exploit indigenous materials and problems. This has been done successfully in a series of monographs edited by José Medina Echavarría, of the Colegio de México.

III. CORNEJO'S LIFE, SOCIOLOGICAL WRITINGS, AND INTELLECTUAL ENVIRONMENT

Mariano H. Cornejo was born in Arequipa, Peru, in 1866. He was educated in the province of Cujo and at the University of San Marcos at Lima, where he took his Ph.D. degree in 1887 and later his doctorate in jurisprudence. He was admitted to the bar in 1889. Elected a deputy to the national house of representatives from Cujo, he soon acquired a reputation for eloquence which is said to have been the greatest in Peru for a hundred years. In 1897 he joined the Democratic party and became one of its leaders. He was made president of the chamber in 1902. In 1903 he was appointed minister plenipotentiary to Ecuador to adjust a boundary dispute and in 1905 to Spain on the same mission, the king of Spain having been chosen as referee. In 1911 he was elected to the national senate. In 1920 he was made minister to France and delegate to the League of Nations. He retired from public office in 1930, when Leguia was deposed in Peru.

In 1914, Cornejo proposed the reform of the constitution of Peru, and he wrote the constitution of 1919. His point of view was that of the naïve democrat who believes that by challenging the people with a great opportunity for self-government it is possible to achieve it. He sought, says his son-in-law, Dr. Luis Ernesto Denegri, professor of economics in the University of San Marcos, to make Peru one of the most highly civilized countries by giving it a parliamentary system similar to that of the English. In this connection Denegri writes:

Cornejo's outlook is essentially democratic and democratic after the French manner, that is to say, declamatory, ideological, and oratorical. In this connection I laugh a bit at the North Americans who praise our democracy without understanding it. Like the Spanish, we are still the later inheritors of the Italian tyrants of the Renaissance. Here democracy exhausts itself with rights and liberties written on paper. Basically it is always a dictatorship. In other countries . . . . it is a plutocracy..... In international politics Dr. Cornejo favored collective security through the Society of Nations. He supported the Allies in 1914 and considered the Treaty of Versailles as an evangel. In spite of his enormous talent, Cornejo did not see that the Treaty of Versailles worked a tremendous injustice..... Cornejo has suffered many disillusionments in his public life, but none equal to that which he today experiences in seeing all the artificial policies of the Society of Nations tumble to earth and the destruction of the French democracy in which he has always believed without perceiving its tremendous corruption. As a sociologist Cornejo is a positivist, but as a politician he has been an incorrigible idealist.[9]

We also quote Denegri's statement regarding Cornejo's standing as a sociologist. Speaking of his systematic treatise, *Sociología general,* Denegri says:

The sociology of Dr. Mariano H. Cornejo is one of the most important books published in Peru, and in Europe and America in the field of Sociology. In Mexico, Ecuador, and Peru it has served for many years as a textbook in the universities. It is my impression that in Mexico and Ecuador it is studied with much interest [in this I can corroborate his opinion]. Here in Peru it is largely forgotten. The new generations know very little of the sociology of Cornejo. Sociological studies are out of fashion here. At the present moment certain spiritualistic criteria, opposed to the positive criterion of Cornejo, prevail in the discussion of social phenomena. In France, Cornejo's treatise has had a generous welcome.[10]

I may add that it is not alone in Peru that positivism has been largely discarded for neo-Hegelian and neo-Kantian metaphysics. I found the same tendency in the universities of Argentina a decade or more ago.

After his retirement from political life in 1930, Cornejo lived in France, where he died in 1942, after enduring many hardships during the German occupation.[11] I met him at the International Sociological Congress at Brussels in 1935, where he appeared on the program. He was still active, a modest and retiring personality, made much of by his friends.

Cornejo's system of sociology is based primarily on Spencer, Wundt, and Lester F. Ward, but he cites nearly one hundred other sociologists and other authorities in his first volume and more than two hundred other sources in the second volume. No other South American sociologist has ever shown so great a familiarity with previous writers in sociology as has Cornejo, and this familiarity extends in some degree to the sociologists of the United States as well as to those of Europe. Most Latin-American sociologists know next to nothing of North American sociology, but this is not true of Cornejo. With Ward and Giddings he was, of course, familiar through their French and Spanish translations; but he also knew something of the work of Ross, Small, Stuckenberg, and others. He is much better acquainted with our anthropologists than with our sociologists, and he cites them frequently, for his knowledge of English enabled him to utilize these sources. His comparative neglect of North American sociologists is probably due to the fact that he wrote primarily for a European reading public even more than for an American audience. The first edition of his work was published in Spain under the patronage of the Spanish sociologist, Doctor José Echegaray, in 1908. The second edition, a French translation by Émile Chauffard with an Introduction by René Worms, appeared in Paris in 1911. In 1924 an American edition was published in Mexico. A revised edition of Volume I appeared in Paris in 1929.

The *Sociología general* must be taken as the chief and almost exclusive source of Cornejo's systematic theories of sociology, although he is also the author of several other volumes, dealing chiefly with political subjects, and of many papers presented before the Institut International de Sociologie and published in sociological journals or as pamphlets. These latter publications make no essential departures from his fundamental principles of sociology, as set forth in the *Sociología general* of 1908. The source of his views cited in this chapter is the French translation of this work, issued in 1911, this being the one most accessible to the majority of our readers.

IV. OUTLINE OF CORNEJO'S SOCIOLOGICAL SYSTEM

Cornejo's chief claim to rank as the most outstanding representative of systematic sociology in Latin America is the remarkable industry that he has shown in assimilating the sociological theory developed before his time and in organizing a well-integrated and intelligible system of his own. The body of this chapter will be devoted to the analysis of Cornejo's sociological system. This system falls into two major divisions. After an adequate Introduction of some thirty pages on the history of sociology, the remainder of the first volume of his *Sociología general* is given over to an analysis of such factors as human evolution, inventions, the growth of group organization and group life, cultural accumulation and social synergy and such other factors as geography, climate, heredity, race, population dynamics, education and the imitation of models, the division of labor, and war. The second volume is devoted to the second major division of his subject—social institutions. Of these he makes seven major subdivisions, as follows: (1) language, (2) myth and religion, (3) art, (4) custom, law, and morals, (5) marriage and the family, (6) the state, and (7) science. Like his chief masters, Spencer and Wundt, Cornejo draws most of the data with which he sustains his conclusions from cultural history rather than from contemporary observation or statistical and documentary sources.

It is reasonable to conclude from this general outline of Cornejo's system that he has been influenced primarily by the cultural and institutional approach to sociology, as set forth in Spencer, Wundt, and Tylor, and secondarily by the students of social dynamics, such as the writers on anthropogeography, technology and invention, population, heredity, and race and the French social psychologists and writers on educational theory. Reference to his documentation confirms this view. Wundt is cited on 62 different pages; Spencer on 45; Frazer on 20; Tarde on 19; Durkheim on 16; Comte, Fouillée, Lazarus, and Steinthal on 12 each; Darwin on 9; Ratzl and Tylor on 8 each; Demolins, Lapouge, Le Dantec, Max Müller, Renan, and Westermarck on 7 each; Bastian, Ripley, and Simmel on 6 each; Schmoller and Ward on 5 each; and Giddings, J. S. Mill, Ribot, and Weismann on 4 each. Kant, Plato, Hegel, and Rousseau are also frequently cited. It is significant that practically no Latin-American sociologists are referred to; nor is the really original work of Sarmiento and Ingenieros given recognition. Although Maudsley is mentioned, the outstanding elaborations of his and Le Bon's interpretations of social pathology made by Ramos Mejia, Alvarez, and Ingenieros are passed over in silence.

As the general background for his system of sociology, Cornejo accepts Comte's law of three stages and makes it the basis of his neopositivist theory of society. He recognizes philosophy—especially in the teleology of Kant, the dialectical growth of Hegel, and the instinctivism of Hartmann—as one of the major sources of sociology; but he considers the philosophy of history as explained by Vico, Montesquieu, and Gibbon as of greater significance in this connection. To Rousseau he attributes the major emphasis upon the basic importance of property and the division of labor for the growth of civilization. To Condorcet he attributes the deepest insight into the nature of social progress. The major defect of Rousseau and of the intellectualists generally is, he contends, that they conceived of society as the product exclusively of human thought and ideals and gave too little emphasis to the blind forces of nature. Comte was the first to see that society is a superorganism, and he set in motion the development of those organismic theories which reached their extreme form in the works of Schäffle and Lilienfeld. Gumplowicz made clear the role of race conflict; and Bastian, Lazarus and Steinthal, Wundt, and Tarde developed the significance of collective behavior. The racial theorists and the anthropogeographers, opposing each other, have nevertheless raised sociology from the metaphysical speculations of the philosophy of history to an inductive basis, while "the theories of Darwin have exercised a decisive influence upon the social sciences." Gumplowicz and Ratzenhofer, following the lead of Darwinism, explained society as the product of racial and social conflict, while Lippert and Bagehot saw it as the result of an increasing collective adaptation of mankind to their environment. The statisticians, such as Quételet, have helped to define and standardize norms in social processes, but "statistical documents may serve to verify a law, but not to discover it." The works of Tarde, Ward, Fouillée, Giddings, Durkheim, Simmel, and Worms especially deserve mention as contributions in their particular fields to the young and developing science of sociology.

V. THE FACTORS CREATING SOCIETY AND SOCIAL ORGANIZATIONS

Turning, now, to Cornejo's analysis of the factors which account for the existence and development of society, we encounter, first of all, a discussion of evolution. Here he follows Spencer primarily and bases his discussion largely upon the theories set forth in the *First Principles* regarding the persistence and transformation of energy within the cosmic, organic, and social orders. Thus he arrives at a position in essential agreement with Haeckel's and Ward's monism. To this he assimilates the Tardean concepts of repetition and rhythm and differentiation of social phenomena. He brings in Henry Adams' application of the law of entropy to society (without mentioning Adams) to explain the resulting process of devolution and ultimate physical and social disintegration. Man's control over the evolutionary process, in so far as it exists, results from the power of the "intelligence, in all its degrees, from the obscure perceptions of the animal up to the generalizations of the savant .... to note, on whatever level, resemblances and differences." He summarizes the significance of the theory of evolution for sociology as follows:

The theory of evolution is extremely important for the study of society since it offers the only possible scientific interpretation of social phenomena. As Schaeffle says, it serves to determine the position of human society in the world. . . . . It views societies as aggregations subject to general laws of antagonism, repetition and equilibrium, which regulate variations of movement. But since in every order of phenomena the internal factors (that is, the energies which form the aggregate), the external factors (that is, the energies which constitute the resistance of environment), and the products (that is, the results of the conflict between the two preceding factors), give rise to a special process, a special science to study this process becomes necessary. Social science has for its object the study of the nature, the causes and the effects of the (evolutionary) process characteristic of society; which, like all groups, represents a complex of continuing relations, although these relations change with the individuals who maintain them. One general phase of this complex study undertakes to determine the nature of the principal forces or factors of social evolution and the forms of coordination established in society among the diverse products and social areas. This general phase constitutes the subject matter of sociology. The special analysis of each factor or of each product or social area is the task of various special sciences known by the name social sciences.[12]

From this point Cornejo begins to apply the general theory of evolution to the development of society. First, he considers the origin and development of primitive man, whom he regards as a savage without material cultural resources or institutions to aid him in the struggle for existence. He holds to a single origin of the human race, but erroneously credits the discovery of an example of *Pithecanthropus* in the province of Santos, Brazil, to Nehring. The human faculties he regards as of the same general type, differing only in degree from those of the lower animals, who also have a social life. Human civilization has developed out of mutual aid and forbearance, family and social affections, the growth of a technology, foresight, and social control. Primitive man lived from hand to mouth and suffered great hardship, but:

It would be a mistake to suppose that the life of primitive men was extremely unhappy, as would be the case with men of our time if they had to live in the midst of constant menaces. They took little thought of the future and their poorly developed intelligence did not permit them to take account of the severity of their destiny. Nor to dwell on what would happen to them when their strength failed them. They took great pleasure in their food. To capture prey marked the height of their joy. . . . . Civilization is not a progress toward happiness. Indeed the perils of savagery have disappeared. But society has created other pains and risks. Many of these have been indispensable to progress. The earliest civilizations became possible solely . . . . when discipline was established under the constraint of iron laws, cruel and unmitigated by compassion. Such discipline was necessary to govern the carnivorous savage of the caves, and such invariably is the character of the earliest customs and the first legislation of all peoples when they arrive at complicated social organization.[13]

This organization was primarily the product of a process of collective adaptation of man to nature. Reasoning somewhat metaphysically and by analogy, Cornejo says: "If the basis of life is nutrition, that is to say, the egoism of the cell, the basis of society should be the egoism of the group, the bond of *solidarity* which maintains the group. And sociology should begin by studying the subjective and objective processes, the internal and external forces, which determine and modify this bond."[14] For the internal bond he accepts Giddings' "consciousness of kind." He distinguishes three kinds of external forces compelling solidarity: (1) voluntary co-operation in the face of an environment which requires communal response; (2) compulsory co-operation or political constraint, imposed either by voluntary consent or by a ruling class or caste (here may be found the reason for the origin of caste systems); (3) peaceful co-operation, based primarily on the economic advantage of the division and specialization of labor. Social solidarity thus advances from compulsory co-operation and caste to contract, and, by a similar token, society evolves from a military to an industrial order. But even with this social transformation, in the acceptance of which Cornejo follows Spencer, external control cannot be dispensed with. Mankind has not yet achieved that degree of social consciousness which would enable co-operation to be carried out by means of individual initiative. Less acceptable to most sociologists of the present may be Cornejo's neoutilitarian conclusion that "desire and its concomitants, pleasure and pain, are the stimulants to both organic and social evolution." This statement reminds one of Ward's *Psychic Factors of Civilization.*

Social solidarity manifests itself in the concrete forms of social organization. The simplest of these is the family, which is a direct product of organic evolution. The whole social process may, indeed, be regarded as directly or indirectly the product of this same type of evolution, since it is "nothing but the organization of the means of satisfying organic needs"; but not all social organization is a direct product of organic adjustment. Cornejo makes a distinction between primary and derivative types of social organization similar to that stated by Cooley[15] and his predecessor, R. J. Wright,[16] according to whether they depend directly or indirectly upon adaptation to the subsistence process. He says: "Social organizations may be divided into two major groups: domestic and political associations; the former based upon a biological process, the latter, upon a social process." Biological groups become social, and political association superimposes itself upon domestic association by a process which, following Ward, he calls "synergy." At first, the domestic or primary groups are in violent conflict. This conflict is natural to the human species, since it is waged for the possession of the means of sustenance. This conflict results in the domestication of animals and the institution of slavery, thus giving the groups successful in the struggle a larger command of natural energy sources. Out of this and later forms of group conflict arise that moral and political discipline which produces voluntary co-operation as a means to social solidarity. Conflict also sharpens the intellectual processes, which, in turn, result in those inventions which promote civilization. The lower animals never achieved either group solidarity, organized conflict, high intellectual development, invention, or civilization. Human conflict, however, by the process of increasing synergy, has expanded until ever larger units of social organization, including states and nationalities, have appeared. In this analysis we find a composite of the theories elsewhere stated by Gumplowicz, Ward, and Cooley, although the statement was written before the publication of Cooley's *Social Organization*.

Both biological and psychological processes enter into society, but neither type of process constitutes society. "The characteristic indication of the social fact is the relation between the collectivity and the individual felt or perceived by him. Acts of cooperation, of subordination or of imitation, whether they are caused mechanically or organically, are never unconscious. They are accompanied by the sense, more or less clear, of their relation or of their dependence upon the collectivity. This recognition inspires them; in it is found their cause and their aim." Social life has an objective existence which cannot be denied. It is, indeed, a superior manifestation of life, although not of a biological organism. It also possesses a personality corresponding in perfection to the superior degree of its organization and integration. This personality is not exclusively psychological, for the social as well as the individual sentiments have an organic base. He says:

The individuality of a society is wholly real, although it lacks a materially centralized brain. The centralization of the nervous system is not necessary, since communication between sentient elements can take place at a distance by means of language. . . . .

The greatest service that biological laws render to sociology is the light they throw upon social dynamics, that is, upon the problem of progress. The idea of progress is essentially a biological idea. . . . . Biological theory represents progress as a development of organization resulting from the antagonism between forces; as a modification of structure resulting from adaptation of functions; as an internal movement of parts and an external movement of the mass which consolidates order by augmenting its elements and its flexibility; and, finally, as one of the general phenomena of life, due to a conflict between the energy accumulated in the synthesis which living matter represents and the resistance of the physical environment.[17]

Progress is not an a priori concept but is arrived at experimentally and through effort, expressed in invention and scientific analysis. Ideals are an effective element in social progress.

While social progress has been initiated and supported by biological and material environmental factors, it has been regulated and guided, at least in its later stages, by collective psychic or psychosocial factors. The recognition of this fact gave rise to such concepts as the "oversoul," the "world soul," and the "social mind." The chief elements in these psychosocial controls are language constructs, such as myths, traditions, the mores, and the like. Modern science, education, and other abstract factors operating, as Lester Ward said, telically are now the most potent aids to social progress. In their most effective form these factors assume the character of social ideals.

In chapter vi of his first volume Cornejo discusses in a conventional manner such external social factors as climate, surface contour, pastoral life, and forests. He concludes by calling attention to the fact that the growth of technology and civilization has diminished the effectiveness of these external factors in their power to mold society. He points out a possible connection between totemism and the origin of domestication. He also shows that Haeckel applied the term "ecology" to certain types of physicosocial relationships.

There need be no surprise that the chapter on heredity is the weakest one in the Sociología general. Not only does it affirm the inheritance of acquired characteristics, mental and social as well as physical, but it falls into the errors of assuming that inbreeding is necessarily disadvantageous, of contending for the inheritance of temperaments and character, of crude atavism, of prenatal influences, and the existence of social and moral instincts. All this may be explained by the fact that the book was written before 1906 and under European influences. He is much interested in social types and discusses many classifications of these and some more of his own, such as primitives, orientals, moderns, Jews, and Yankees. All these discussions are largely invalidated by his failure to distinguish between genuine inheritance and culturally transmitted traits. An uncritical acceptance of the doctrine of the inheritance of acquired characteristics has betrayed him. He concludes with a more acceptable statement to the effect that "social types are created by society on the basis of temperament, provided by heredity, and of character, determined by education."

Cornejo accepts the inheritance of both physical and mental race traits and fails to recognize the fact that race characteristics are merely individual traits that have been generalized in population aggregates. He accepts a threefold classification of races and makes a conventional presentation of race traits. Although he believes that races originally had distinctive psychological and moral traits, he recognizes the fact that these have no fixed correspondence to physical traits. He also declares that there is no Aryan race. Races are now so confused by crossing that no psychology of races can be formulated. Attempts have been made to develop the psychology of peoples instead, but so far little success has attended these efforts, in spite of the work of Taine, Renan, Le Bon, and others. He makes an interesting prophecy which has not proved correct, saying, "that which is called the yellow peril does not exist, since the future expansion of peoples will be economic and not military."

The chapter on population is superior to the two preceding chapters, but he immediately falls into the error so common in the nineteenth century of ignoring the principle of diminishing returns in industry and invention as well as in agriculture and of forgetting that voluntary checks on population are the preventive checks of Malthus. Thus in some measure he misrepresents Malthus. But his discussion of population is much more inclusive than the Malthusian principle. He concludes that natural resources and the cultural factor of opportunity are the chief determinants of the growth of population, while the control of death rates is a major factor in determining its size. He discusses three types of migration: (1) early mass movements due to conquests, (2) voluntary movements of smaller groups, as in colonization, and (3) the modern migration of individuals in search of economic opportunity, political or religious freedom, etc. The last type of migration became possible only with the development of something approaching a common culture internationally. The economic and cultural effects of such movements are, of course, numerous and serious, such as the lowering of the standard of living and disruption of political mores. He discusses also the migration from country to city in a conventional manner and points out the effect of the growth of large urban populations upon health and public and private morals. He sums up the social effects of an increasing population as follows:

The increase of population, whether due to an excess of births over deaths or to immigration, is the result of natural and social conditions which might be regulated by a wisely directed policy. This increase must be considered as a factor of universal and continuous significance in social evolution, since decisive social changes are produced by the augmentation and concentration of population. When the population increases, the social constitution, formed for a given number of individuals, is rent like a dress made too small and must be mended in various ways. The progress of industrial technology and of political organization is affected by these changes. A people incapable of material growth must stand still and decline morally.[18]

Cornejo wisely associates imitation and education and recognizes the fact that education consists largely of transmitting past achievement by imitation to each new generation. He defines imitation in the Tardean sense of social repetition. He locates these factors in the second of two groups of collective factors in social development, which he outlines as follows: (1) language, myth, and morals, which are both social products and social causes, and (2) imitation, education, the division of labor, and war. This second group of collective factors occupies the remainder of the first volume. Most sociologists would consider that he exaggerates the influence of great men. He regards the phenomena of multiple synchronous inventions as proof of the objective and largely imitative character of the inventive process. Social assimilation is based upon imitation (adaptation) and education (transmission). His statement that "imitation rests upon a biological instinct" must be interpreted in terms of the social psychology of 1908, when McDougall's treatise on this subject appeared. He follows Tarde in saying that imitation is determined by logical and extra-logical causes, that is, it is adaptive or subjective and nonadaptive in character. Social progress depends on logical or adaptive imitation.

Education supplements imitation and invention in producing social homogeneity, since by means of education the collectivity transmits its mode of thinking, feeling, and acting to the individual. Moral education is the most difficult, since it deals largely with subconscious attitudes. Education cannot be subject to the law of supply and demand but must be imposed upon the young in order to insure the continuity of culture and the solidarity of society. It should be universal. It should teach the essentials of the culture, as well as prepare individuals for vocations and professions. It should assume absolute neutrality regarding conflicting religions. And it should apply to women as well as to men, only with due recognition of vocational and functional differences. The functions of imitation and education are summarized as follows:

Imitation and education are the two factors which led to adaptation and assimilation of the individual to society. Imitation is the means by which society shares in individual ideas. Education is the social function which enables the individual to utilize the treasure of collective knowledge. But also imitation develops inventive faculties in the individual and education raises the level of society. Civilization is the direct product of the exchange of actions and reactions. Imitation and education complete that ensemble of collective ideas and sentiments which comprise the psychological basis of solidarity.[19]

In treating the division of labor, Cornejo follows Durkheim in the main. He looks upon it as a method of social differentiation in the adaptive process. He recognizes two types: the division of authority among equals or likes and the division of functions in the utilization of materials. The former results in social classes and the latter in occupations. Although the social importance of the division of labor has been recognized since ancient times, its multifold social significance has been made clear only with the development of sociology, beginning with Adam Smith. The fundamental cause of the division of labor has been the growth of population. Among supplementary causes, such factors as physical differences in environment, race and individual differences, and technological development stand out especially. The social consequences are numerous, but the rise of professional, occupational, and economic classes is perhaps the most important. The growth of commerce and finance has produced in some measure exploiter classes, and the liberal professions are in some degree parasitic at the same time that they render social services. Trade, in particular, has been an international and intercommunity socializer. Slavery, the most exploited form of labor, has arisen through conquest. Proletarian labor, although nominally free, is in effect compulsory. Geographic division of labor increases in importance with the advance of civilization and international trade. Agriculture declines in relative importance with the growth of industry. Professions and occupations have definite obligations to society as the result of their specialization.

According to Cornejo, war has its biological basis in an instinct of combativeness. He does not ignore the economic causes of war, but he has not emphasized them adequately. He also makes the mistake of following Spencer in the assertion that economic competition is replacing war, whereas, in reality, war is the grand weapon of economic competition. The chief social effects of war are the creation of greater solidarity in contending groups and a higher degree of discipline and the development of countermovements which work against war. War also results in greater functional differences and antagonisms between groups. In spite of the fact that modern man has become more reflective and less impulsive in the face of war stimuli, war still continues. The main reason for this, says Cornejo, is that collectivities have not yet evolved those rational controls which individuals have developed in their own self-control. Is it possible that Cornejo, himself a senator and an international arbiter, does not know how and in whose interests wars are made?

VI. SOCIAL INSTITUTIONS

In the second volume of the *Sociología general* Cornejo is concerned with the institutions engaged in the function of social control. To the first of these, language, he devotes almost one hundred pages. He makes it clear that sociology is not concerned with phonetics and philology, as such, but with the collective and communicatory aspects of language. He says:

> As a social product, language has sociological interest because of its [social] origin and because it is a form of collective intelligence. From the point of view of relations, it should study the connection between the elements of language, sounds and meanings and psycho-social development; and, as a [social] factor, it is important to see how language influences all the other social products and gives to them a special character which they would not have if collective consciousness could not be objectivated under that ideal form.

Cornejo follows Wundt mainly in his discussion of language, as he does in his treatment of religion and myth, to follow. This discussion constitutes a crowded monograph in itself and cannot be abstracted here, but it contains most of what was known about the sociology of language before 1908. Cornejo shows some insight into the relations between parts of speech and other language and literary forms and thought. He points out, that, because of its great fluidity, the historic past cannot be adequately reconstructed from the language. On the other hand, he makes clear the fact that language is the chief carrier of civilization and the most effective instrument of social progress. He does not believe that there will ever be a universal artificial language, simply because language is, of necessity, a slow cultural growth, holding in solution a great mass of intangible meanings and sentiments which embody its spirit or "soul." Languages change, but only as the people who use them change. The chief distinguishing qualities of nationalities and peoples are imbedded in their languages and literatures. Language both carries and perpetuates the traditions of a people on their passive side and projects and makes articulate their ideals on their active side. Thus language is the basic and most fundamental human institution.

An even longer treatment is given to myth and religion. But this discussion is closely tied up with that of language, for myth is a literary form and religion finds its expression through language. On its intellectual or credal side its language outlet is verbal, while on its emotional side its expression is through both words and pantomime and gesture. Ritual, always a large element in early religions, is primarily pantomimetic and operates on the level of gesture and overt emotional expression. Cornejo, of course, finds magic closely connected with religion; in fact, it is the earliest intellectual content of religion. In this phase of his treatment he appears to follow Frazer, just as in his treatment of myth and folklore in general he takes Wundt as his guide. When he considers the ecclesiastical side of religion, he is closest to Spencer. Speaking of the sociology of religion, he says:

> Ethical religions embody within themselves the history of the collective development of imagination, sentiment and reflection. Thus mythical and religious phenomena manifest the general laws of consciousness and the special influence of nature and of civilization. It is from this standpoint that sociology considers religion. It leaves to the history of mythology and of religions the study of the details characteristic of each tradition and each theogony and studies mythology and religion as the necessary products of collective psychology, as the general relations of thought with reality and life, as universal and preponderant factors of human civilization. This limitation arises from the fact that sociology is especially interested in the production and evolution of psychological phenomena and the habitual forms under which they are manifested. Sociology should not neglect the study of myth and religion, since it is not possible to understand these social phenomena without comprehending the collective psychological motives which result from physical influences or arise from biological processes and serve as the immediate cause of social behavior. Just as in nature the equilibrium of forces compels a belief in mechanism and as in life the adaptation of instincts strongly suggests atavism, so also in society the immanent logic of facts compels a

psycho-collective interpretation. Sociology assumes a positive character only when it passes from uncritical observation to the investigation of the process by which the collective mind is formed as the result of the systematic organization of intellect, sentiment and will as manifested in language, myth and morality.[20]

Among the subjects discussed acceptably in this long chapter are the origin and history of the concept of the soul; the nature and forms of magic; the practice of sorcery as a social technology; the social origins and history of totemism and its decline as the result of a particularization and specialization of personality in the supernatural; survivals of primitive religion and magic in contemporary social systems; the growth of the ethical element in religion; the growth and decline of tradition; the evolution and decline of theologies and theogonies; and the increasing secularization of social controls under the supervision of the social sciences.

The chapter on art is perhaps the least sociological in the book. Its inclusion is justified by the statement that "the development of art reveals it as an essential manifestation of social life. It is both cause and effect of psychic development and in its different aspects and in all degrees it is intimately associated with the traits of the historic milieu and especially, during the period of its early evolution, with mythical and religious phenomena." Cornejo quotes approvingly three conceptions of art stated by Taine (art is the embodiment of environment, race, and incident), Lamprecht (art is the expression of intellectual, social, political, and economic conditions), and Wundt (art is the expression of the imagination) "as together mutually completing and providing the sociological theory of the evolution of art. Art, like every social product, expresses an unbroken development; the present derives from the past; the explanation of a style is in its own history." He distinguishes the sociological from other points of view regarding art as follows:

Sociology looks upon art from a point of view different from that of history or scientific or esthetic criticism. History is concerned with the objects and productions of art. Sociology looks for the principal orientations of the psychic processes in connection with the social influences which determine the art. The products of a completed art have little importance for sociology, since the utilization of the accumulation of mature art forms there available depends primarily upon the personality of the artist who combines and modifies them with the greatest possible independence. On the contrary the early works of art reveal the connection between the social conditions of the time and the progressive development of the imagination, just as the rudimentary forms of life reveal to us the influence of environment and its primitive differentiations better than the highly developed organisms whose individuality has been fixed by heredity can do. Criticism seeks to discover the personal and social factors in any particular work or artistic or literary school, while sociology is interested only in the total phenomena, that which is common, fundamental, permanent, and collectivistic in the artistic work, ... sociology takes into consideration the synthetic development of its psychic and social features.[21]

The forms of art discussed by the author are personal ornamentation, including both tattooing and clothing, ceramics, architecture, sculpture, rhythmic art (including songs, dance, and music), epics, drama, and myths. He distinguishes three historical periods in art: the record or memory aid, the imitative, and the ideal. He makes much of the ideal function of art which inspires new social forms and achievements. This he finds best expressed in drama, especially in the modern social-problem drama. He does not deal with history or philosophy in this connection, but he finds considerable attention given to the ideal in the epic. The dance, of course, is largely ritualistic until modern times and looks back toward the past. In contrasting ancient and modern drama, he says:

The great difference between ancient and modern drama lies in the fact that the latter is concerned with the bourgeoisie and ordinary life, while classical tragedy dealt only with gods and heroes. This democratisation arises wholly from social causes. Antiquity possessed no middle class; that is the product of modern civilization and industrialism and could not have been represented in former times. Drama is to ancient tragedy what the romance is to the epic. It is not a new type of art, but a special form produced by a different type of civilization. In it the realism of the comedy and the idealism of the tragedy are combined to provide subjects and effects more realistic and more human. The diverse dramatic types, like the historical already produced by the romance, and the psychological type of our day, are derived forms which do not concern the sociologist.[22]

The long chapter on custom, law, and morals is properly a continuation of the subject of myth and religion, already treated. The criteria and sanctions of morality are regarded by Cornejo as relative both as to origin and as to purpose or end and grow out of the perceived value of behavior in the adjustment process. Morality is a social concept, concerning which he says:

Sociologically speaking, ethical phenomena, inseparable from the tendencies of the species and the conditions of social life, consists of a mode of adaptation which, taking precedence over individual divergences, determine a pattern of conduct and organize the human will . . . . by means of general synergic formulas which discipline the desires. . . . . The good is defined little by little under the influence of collective experience as a concept drawn from a common adaptive mode of behavior.

We use the concept of the *good* man when referring to his conduct with reference to others in the same sense that we speak of a good hunter or fisherman. The preeminence of the supreme good which we call moral derives from the importance which that sort of perfection possesses for society. Duty is conceived socially, as a thing we would disregard, but which the mandate of past generations and regard for the present and future generations—that is, heredity and education—oblige us to perform.[23]

Like Westermarck,[24] Cornejo bases his theory of ethical development upon the growth of the sentiments of egoism and altruism. Custom, he regards as a formalization of ethical phenomena, a point of view which forces a distinction between collective habit and usage. Many types of custom and taboo are discussed by the author, the most prominent of these being food practices. Law, he conceives, grew not only out of custom but also out of the use of force by the strong to exploit the weak. Punishment had both an emotional and a rational utilitarian origin. Property is a major object of interest to the author, but there is nothing new in his discussion of this subject. His classification of the stages of the growth of ethical ideals and ideas shows much insight. He states them as (1) the *premoral,* in which magical concepts and imperatives are dominant and sorcery is practiced to determine desirable forms of conduct; (2) the *religious,* in which the gods prescribe, by revelation or otherwise, their prescriptions taking form in proverbs and other simple statements of wisdom—here a definite social consciousness arises; and (3) what he calls the *eudemonistic,* in which the criteria of social welfare determine ethical values. The relation of sociology to ethical opinion he states as follows:

Sociology leaves to ethnology and history the task of describing the condition of moral consciousness at different epochs and in diverse groups and to the history of philosophy or of religions the review of the numerous systems composed by the philosophers and theologians. The role of sociology is limited to the examination of the fundamental ideas to which collective psychology attributes an ethical value. In a general way it may be said that the religious influence and the sentiment of sympathy idealize little by little the physiological means and the psychological consequences of action. . . . . . Every human action consists of three aspects: physiological, psychological, and social. When from these three points of view the act is in harmony with the functions, the states and the given conditions of the species of the individual consciousness, and of the society, happiness and welfare result. In other words individual and collective good arise from a harmony of the past and the present, of the parts and the whole, of a well proportioned development of complex energies in equilibrium with the pressures of environment. The two ideas, derived alike from experience, are bound together in the ideal, like two aspects—the subjective and the objective—of the same social phenomenon.[25]

In Cornejo's conception, the ultimate ideal of all custom, law, and morals is the common welfare.

The chapter on marriage and the family is conventional, except perhaps for the acceptance of primitive promiscuity. It approaches its subject matter primarily from the standpoint of primitive peoples. The data were all gathered before 1908, which means that the interpretations begin with Bachofen, MacLennan, Lubbock, Morgan, and Spencer and do not reach beyond Westermarck and Frazer. The chapter on the state also makes large use of anthropological data dealing with the origin, forms, and control of the state. Cornejo holds that the state was originally the product of war, but, with the coming of an industrial organization of society, the old national state may be transformed into a worldwide federation of economic and cultural units. He says:

> If biological factors do not interfere, it is probable that humanity may achieve, under some form which we cannot now foresee, a political organization in which the equilibrium and the flexibility will be superior to any that characterize our present institutions. De Greef believes that this will be realized under the form of a great confederation, the world state, in which political frontiers will be replaced by frontiers of social organization and differentiation. Moreover it is evident that a gigantic state is not necessary to the peaceful union of groups. It is conceivable that in a superior type of ethical and juridical culture political solidarity might cease to rest on a territorial base and be founded on economic interests and intellectual principles. It is certain that the [political] reality of the future will be richer than all our theories. The sociological outlook on this question is necessarily limited.[26]

In Cornejo's opinion, political forms are closely correlated with the environment, or perhaps with man's functional adjustment to environment. The state has always been controlled by classes, ranging from the military and priestly down to the *bourgeoisie* and the working classes. What we call democracy has evidenced much corruption, inefficiency, and exploitation.

A brief final chapter on science makes three major emphases. In the first place, says Cornejo, "science is the most advanced of all social products. It provides exact and systematic knowledge of certain relations within reality. It represents the most perfect possible adaptation of the intelligence to the external world..... Being a phenomenon of adaptation it cannot be otherwise than the result of experience, and being an intellectual phenomenon it is essentially relative." In the second place, science increasingly formulates its principles quantitatively, and this is true of sociological sciences as well as of others. In the third place, sociological science is destined to exercise a preponderant function in the determination of the future. Thus:

We may say, by way of conclusion, that if sociology is in its infancy, it is a robust and well developed infancy. The fundamental principles of the science are fully established; its well determined categories permit the systematization of all its observations. . . . . . Sociology in its present condition acquaints us not only with the forms in which the collective life, the family and the state, are crystallized, but even more the development of the social (?) consciousness. It shows us how, little by little, sentiment and thought are coordinated in the categories of language, myth, and morals. It indicates to us how the principle of universal adaptation controls the ensemble of the collective life, its functions and structures, and how . . . . it leads to a systematic knowledge of reality, that is to say, to science, and to an endeavor to explain and foresee, revise and complete consciously the work of nature and of history.[27]

VII. SUMMARY APPRAISAL OF CORNEJO'S SOCIOLOGY

It may be said that Cornejo's *Sociología general* is a comprehensive and erudite treatise on systematic sociology after the European manner, which assigns major importance to generalizations inductively derived from anthropological data by means of the comparative method. It disregards almost entirely Latin-American research and data. The work is especially well documented, but its sources are naturally prior to the date of publication, 1908. Consequently, some of the biological and psychological theories expressed in the book are out of date. The importance which the author assigns to collective psychological processes is almost as great as those which he attributes to the anthropological. His chief literary sources are French, but the German citations are also numerous, while British and North American sources rank third and fourth. The social processes emphasized are both psychosocial and social-organizational. He devotes major attention in his book to the institutions of language, myth, religion, art, custom, law, and morals. According to the author, all these are intimately connected and serve as a psychosocial basis for the study of the social institutions which take an objective form in social organization. These latter include the family and the state, while the church, the school, industry, and other external institutions are not discussed in detail. This relative lack of emphasis upon the external aspects of institutions is manifestly due to the fact that Cornejo conceives of sociology as essentially a theory of collective behavior expressed in terms of a psychosocial interpretation rather than as a study of administrative organization as such.

NOTES

1. See W. Rex Crawford's *Century of Latin American Thought* (Cambridge, Mass., 1944), for examples of such other writers.

2. L. L. Bernard, "The Social Disciplines in Latin America," *Encyclopaedia of the Social Sciences*, I, 301–20; also "The Development and Present Tendencies of Sociology in Argentina," *Social Forces*, VI (September, 1927), 13–27.

3. *Encyclopaedia of the Social Sciences*, XIII, 543–44.

4. *Ibid.*

5. *Ibid.*, II, 16.

6. *American Sociologist*, II, No. 3 (June, 1940), 1.

7. *Ibid.;* also, L. L. Bernard, "Sociology in Argentina," *American Journal of Sociology*, XXXIII (July, 1927), 110–17.

8. This fact is recognized by Agustin Venturino, who made a spirited appeal for its recognition by Europeans at the International Sociological Congress at Brussels in 1935.

9. From a personal letter from Dr. Denegri to the author, L. L. Bernard.

10. *Ibid.*

11. *Ibid.*

12. *Sociología general*, I, 116–17.

13. *Ibid.*, pp. 140–41.

14. *Ibid.*, p. 146.

15. C. H. Cooley, *Social Organization* (New York, 1909).

16. R. J. Wright, *Principia or Basis of Social Science* (Philadelphia, 1875).

17. *Sociología general*, I, 220, 231–32.

18. *Ibid.*, pp. 414–15.

19. *Ibid.*, p. 462.

20. *Ibid.*, II, 115–16.

21. *Ibid.*, pp. 253–54.

22. *Ibid.*, pp. 304–5.

23. *Ibid.*, p. 314.

24. Edward Westermarck, *The Origin and Development of the Moral Ideas* (2 vols.; London, 1906).

25. *Sociología general*, II, 377–79.

26. *Ibid.*, pp. 462–63.

27. *Ibid.*, pp. 472–73.

INDEXES

INDEX OF NAMES*

Abbott, Edith, 741
Abel, Theodore, 215, 283
Abélard, Pierre, 18
Addams, Jane, 741
Aeneas, Sylvius, 22, 29
Aeschylus, 6
Agobard of Lyons, 17
Agramonte, Roberto, 906
Ahrens, Heinrich, 115
Alberdi, Juan B., 903
Albertus Magnus, 19
Alihan, Milla, 740
Allengry, Franck, 74
Allport, Floyd H., 379, 741
Althusius, Johannes, 24, 32
Alvarez, Agustin, 903
Ammon, Alfred Otto, 211, 215
Anaximander, 6
Anderson, Nels, 740
Angell, Norman, 438
Aquinas, Thomas, 19–20, 31
Arbousse-Bastide, Paul, 907
Ardigo, Roberto, 553
Aristotle, 6, 8–9, 15, 17–20, 23, 24, 30, 34, 35, 60, 83, 86, 89–92, 96, 111, 115, 180, 217, 232, 238, 319, 389, 391, 398, 401, 426, 516, 623, 709, 874
Armas y Cardenas, José de, 908
Augustine, 16, 720, 729, 734, 894
Austin, John, 67, 119
Ayala, Francisco, 907
Azcárate, Gumersindo de, 589–90
Azevedo, Fernando de, 906, 907

Baader, Franz Xavier von, 386
Baber, R. E., 742
Babeuf, François, 45
Bacon, Francis, 39, 43, 47, 414, 742
Bacon, Roger, 39
Bagehot, Walter, 10, 53, 181, 471, 606, 696, 878
Bain, Read, 803, 804
Baldwin, J. M., 847, 848
Barker, Ernest, 119, 697
Barnes, Harry Elmer, 455, 743

Barreto, Romano, 908
Barth, Paul, 213, 401
Bassano, Luis, 908
Bastian, Adolf, 97, 212, 333, 344, 348
Bates, Sanford, 742
Baur, Ferdinand Christian, 60
Beard, Charles Austin, 734, 740
Beccaria, Cesare de, 55, 69, 553
Becker, Howard, 724, 735, 743, 781
Bekhtereff, Wladimir, 444
Benoist, Charles, 202
Bentham, Jeremy, 55–56, 68, 69, 119, 128, 409, 564, 611, 623, 678, 697, 704
Bentley, A. F., 202, 880
Berger, Clarence Q., 888
Bergson, Henri, 377
Berkeley, George, 46, 52
Bernard, Jessie, 742
Bernard, L. L., 741
Bernhardi, Friedrich von, 202
Betancur, Cayetano, 905
Bezerra de Menezes, Geraldo, 907
Bichat, M. François, 96
Bismarck, Otto von, 353, 354, 355, 420
Blackstone, William, 24, 55, 67, 119
Bloch, Jean, 684
Blondel, Charles, 526
Blumenbach, Johann Friedrich, 69
Blumer, Herbert, 803
Boas, Franz, 116, 149, 741
Bodin, Jean, 7, 24, 25, 30, 56, 73
Bogardus, E. S., 741, 742
Bonald, Louis de, 65, 499
Boniface VIII, 21
Bonnet de Mably, Gabriel, 45
Bosanquet, Bernard, 625
Bossano, Louis, 907
Bossuet, Jacques Bénigne, 65, 71
Bouglé, Célestin, 524
Bourdin, J. J. L., 74, 84
Brandt, W. I., 21
Branford, Victor, 603, 677–94
Brentano, Lujo, 288, 357
Briffault, Robert, 71, 668–76
Bristol, L. M., 471, 573, 611
Broca, Pierre Paul, 70
Broussais, F. J. V., 96
Brown, L. G., 594

*This Index was prepared by Charles N. Lurie.

Bryce, James, 56
Buchanan, James, 30
Buckle, Henry Thomas, 24, 62
Buffon, G. L. L., 49
Burgess, E. W., 740, 742
Burgess, J. S., 741
Burgess, John William, 67, 716
Burke, Edmund, 38, 65, 66, 68, 165, 166
Burnham, James, 74, 107
Buxton, Thomas Fowell, 69

Cabanis, Pierre Jean Georges, 96
Caesar, Julius, 13
Calhoun, A. W., 742
Calhoun, John C., 202, 426
Calvin, John, 313
Campanella, Tommaso, 43
Camper, Peter, 70
Cantor, Nathaniel, 742
Carey, Henry C., 116
Carli, F., 562
Carlyle, A. J., 29
Carneiro, Leão A., 905
Carver, T. N., 116
Caso, Antonio, 905
Catlin, George, 720
Cavan, R. S., 742
Chaddock, R. E., 742
Chardin, Jean, 70
Chernoff, V. M., 442
Christ; see Jesus Christ
Cicero, 12
Clark, John Bates, 55, 745
Cole, G. D. H., 435
Colmo, Alfredo, 904
Comte, Auguste, 6, 24, 41, 46, 60, 72–76,
    81–109, 110, 115, 117, 123, 131, 185,
    193, 222, 231, 253, 334, 358, 366, 375,
    401, 412, 414, 446, 450, 455, 458, 469,
    499, 500, 501, 502, 542, 543, 545, 546,
    551, 553, 573, 589, 608, 678, 683, 688,
    690, 692, 714, 733, 744–45, 865, 866,
    906, 908
Comte, Charles, 49
Condorcet, M. J. A. N., 24, 40, 46, 47, 55,
    73, 75, 84, 96, 193, 365
Conklin, E. G., 741
Cooley, Charles Horton, 106, 212, 492,
    589, 593, 660–61, 807, 833–52, 917, 918
Coon, C. S., 741
Cornejo, Mariano H., 902–30
Coste, Adolphe, 454
Cottrell, L. S., 742

Cramb, J. A., 203
Croce, Benedetto, 553

Dalencourt, François, 905
Danilevsky, N., 441
Dante, 20, 21
Darwin, Charles, 111, 139, 140, 157, 468,
    573
Davenport, C. B., 741
Davis, M. M., 474
Davy, Georges, 521, 522, 526
Denegri, Luis Ernesto, 911–12
Denis, Hector, 539
Déroulède, Paul, 203
Descartes, René, 39, 47
Devine, E. T., 741
Dewey, John, 412, 800, 855
Dicey, A. V., 127, 878
Dietrich, John H., 107
Dilthey, Wilhelm, 209, 213, 291, 310, 319,
    358
Dodd, S. C., 742
Dopsch, Alfons, 347, 733
Dublin, L. I., 740
Dubois, Pierre, 18, 20, 21, 23, 32
Du Bois-Reymond, Emil Heinrich, 217
Dühring, Karl Eugen, 338, 347
Duguit, Léon, 202, 527
Dumas, Georges, 522, 526
Dunning, William A., 438
Duplessis-Mornay, Philippe de, 30
Du Pont de Nemours, Pierre Samuel, 61
Durkheim, Émile, 116, 192, 202, 253, 267,
    302, 402, 458, 460, 463, 471, 488, 499–
    537, 589, 623, 662, 731, 864, 922

East, E. M., 741
Echánove Trujillo, Carlos A., 908
Echeverría, Esteban, 902
Eddy, Mary Baker, 734
Ehrenreich, Paul Max, 116
Eichhorn, Karl F., 46
Eliot, T. D., 741
Elizando, Ramón T., 908
Ellwood, Charles Abram, 76, 82, 87, 853–
    68
Elmer, M. C., 742
Engels, Friedrich, 150
Epictetus, 13
Erigena, Johannes Scotus, 17
Espinas, Alfred, 459, 500

Fadiman, Clifton, 734
Fairchild, H. P., 740

Fauconnet, Paul, 521, 522
Fénelon, François, 44
Ferguson, Adam, 24, 38, 46, 49, 53, 57, 60, 66, 181, 365
Ferrari, Giuseppe, 553
Ferri, Enrico, 579
Fichte, Johann Gottlieb, 59, 65, 365, 385–86
Field, J. A., 740
Figgis, John Neville, 32
Filangieri, Gaetano, 553
Filmer, Robert, 33, 35, 36
Fischer, Kuno, 217
Fiske, John, 6, 32, 89, 756
Flint, Robert, 42
Fontenelle, Bernard de, 39, 46, 47
Ford, Henry Jones, 476
Ford, James, 741
Fouillée, Alfred Jules Émile, 106, 461–70
Fourier, Charles, 539
Frantz, Constantin, 347
Frazer, Sir James G., 567, 924
Freeman, Edward, 476
Freyer, Hans, 215, 266, 362–73
Freyre, Gilberto, 907–8
Friedrich, Carl J., 32

Galen, 14
Galileo, 47
Gall, Franz Josef, 74, 83, 92, 96
Galpin, Charles J., 888
Galton, Francis, 841
García, Juan Agustin, 904
Gault, R. H., 742
Geddes, Sir Patrick, 603, 677–94
Geiger, Theodor, 908
Gentile, Giovanni, 553
Gentilis, Alberico, 32
George, Henry, 568
Giddings, Franklin H., 3, 9, 25, 29, 32, 35, 52, 75–76, 87, 106, 107, 114, 168, 177, 199, 239, 334, 335, 347, 401, 402, 427, 433, 538, 551, 589, 623, 627, 660, 740, 742, 744–65, 864, 917
Gierke, Otto von, 24, 32, 347
Gillin, J. L., 741, 742
Giner de los Ríos, Francisco, 589–90
Gini, Corrado, 51, 554, 575–78
Ginsberg, Morris, 574, 603, 618, 619, 628
Gneist, Heinrich R. H. F. von, 450
Goddard, H. H., 741
Godwin, William, 41, 47, 55, 193
Görres, Johann, 385, 386
Goldenweiser, Alexander, 149, 455

Goltz, Kolmar von der, 341, 343, 347, 348
Goncourt, Rémy de, 562
Goodsell, Willystine, 742
Gossen, Hermann Heinrich, 340
Gräbner, Fritz, 344
Granet, Marcel, 526
Greef, Guillaume de, 203, 538–52
Gregory VII, 18
Grotius, Hugo, 24, 32, 34, 388
Groves, E. R., 741–42
Guizot, François Pierre Guillaume, 46
Gumplowicz, Ludwig, 11, 24, 34, 60, 81, 106, 118, 175, 181, 191–206, 211, 214, 333, 344, 347, 348, 363, 375, 379, 381, 382, 404, 406, 419, 424, 425, 426, 459, 551, 573, 660, 866, 876, 877, 918

Haddon, Alfred C., 138
Haeckel, Ernst H., 919
Hahn, Eduard, 348
Halbwachs, Maurice, 523–24
Hall, G. Stanley, 218
Haller, Ludwig von, 65
Hamilton, Alexander, 162
Hamilton, G. V., 742
Handman, M. S., 567
Hankins, F. H., 741
Harrington, James, 44
Harrison, Frederic, 106
Hayes, Edward Carey, 433, 766, 869–83
Haynes, F. E., 742
Healy, William, 742
Heeren, Arnold, 57
Hegel, Georg Wilhelm Friedrich, 24, 56, 58–60, 65, 92, 365, 372, 408, 413, 414, 472, 473, 616–17, 619, 624, 625, 641
Helvétius, Claude Adrien, 38, 40
Herder, Johann Gottfried, 24, 40–41, 46, 49, 58, 75
Herodotus, 6–7, 13
Hertzler, Joyce O., 5
Hesiod, 6, 73
Hicks, Granville, 734, 736
Hincmar of Reims, 17
Hippocrates, 7, 9
Hitler, Adolf, 355
Hobbes, Thomas, 31, 34, 36, 37, 60, 91, 97, 119, 180, 228, 230, 232, 238, 241, 388
Hobhouse, Leonard T., 82, 129, 132, 170, 412, 438, 455, 469, 574, 603, 605, 606, 615–53, 681, 714, 808, 815, 855, 867, 872
Hobson, John Atkinson, 132
Hodgkin, Thomas, 129
Höffding, Harald, 242

Holborn, Hajo, 720
Holmes, S. J., 741
Hooker, Richard, 30, 32, 35
Hooton, Earnest A., 383, 741
Horace, 12
Hostos, Eugenio Maria de, 904
Hotman, François, 30
Howard, G. E., 742
Hubert, Henri, 116
Huizinga, Jan, 900
Humboldt, Alexander von, 49, 83
Humboldt, Wilhelm von, 163 181
Hume, David, 10, 11, 24, 30, 35, 38, 46, 47, 52–54, 60, 74–75, 83, 471
Huntington, Ellsworth, 740
Hutcheson, Francis, 35, 55
Huvelin, Paul, 527
Huxley, Aldous, 555
Huxley, Thomas Henry, 131, 471, 615, 733

Imbelloni, José, 905
Ingenieros, José, 904, 907
Irnerius, 21
Isidore of Seville, 17

Jacobs, Philip, 378
James, William, 697, 847–48
Jarrold, Thomas, 51
Jefferson, Thomas, 101, 161, 420, 426
Jellinek, Georg, 333
Jerusalem, F. W., 210
Jesus Christ, 14–15, 719–21, 727, 728, 865
Jevons, Stanley, 55
Johannes Scotus Erigena; see Erigena
John of Salisbury, 18, 20
Jünger, Ernst, 360
Julius Caesar; see Caesar, Julius
Justi, Johann Heinrich von, 61

Kant, Immanuel, 41, 46, 58, 74, 83, 564, 631, 865
Kareyev, N. I., 442
Karpf, Fay, 848
Keller, A. G., 156, 211, 741
Kellogg, Paul V., 741
Kelsey, Carl, 740
Kelso, R. W., 741
Khaldun, ibn-, 7, 24, 25
Kidd, Benjamin, 56, 168, 606–13, 701
Klein, Philip, 741
Knies, Karl, 287
Knox, John, 30
Koberg B, Maximiliano, 907
Kondratieff, N. D., 455

Koppers, Wilhelm, 347, 348
Kovalevsky, Maksim M., 441–57
Krause, Karl Christian Friedrich, 115, 588–90
Kropotkin, Peter, 442, 612, 680, 876

Lafitau, Joseph François, 71
Lagarrigue, Luis, 907, 908
Lamarck, J. B. P. A., 96, 573
Lamprecht, Karl, 365, 925
Languet, Hubert, 30
Lanz, Vallenilla, 907
Lassalle, Ferdinand, 373
Lavrov, P. L., 442
Lawes, L. E., 742
Lazarus, Moritz, 212
Le Bon, Gustave, 11, 192, 193, 415, 467, 468, 478, 481–98, 554, 578, 580, 699, 821, 864
Lee, Porter, 741
Leibniz, Gottfried Wilhelm von, 217
Leisegang, H., 900
Lenin, V. I., 442
Le Play, Frédéric, 92, 678, 683
Levene, Ricardo, 909
Lévy, Emmanuel, 527
Lévy-Bruhl, Lucien, 98, 525, 526
Lichtenberger, J. P., 742
Lilburne, John, 33
Lilienfeld, Paul von, 82, 106, 210
Lindsay, S. M., 741
Linnaeus, Carolus, 69, 70
Lins, Mario, 908
Linton, Ralph, 150
Lippert, Julius, 157, 211, 741
Lippmann, Walter, 56, 563
Litt, Theodor, 210, 212
Littré, Maximilien Paul Émile, 106
Livingston, Arthur, 556
Locke, John, 36, 37, 41, 52, 66, 67, 127, 388
Lombroso, Cesare, 479, 572, 579
López de Mesa, Luis, 907
López Rosado, Felipe, 908
Lorenzoni, Giovanni, 554
Loria, Achille, 203, 405, 454, 554, 568–72
Lorimer, Frank, 740
Lowie, R. H., 150
Lucretius, 6, 11
Lundberg, George A., 594, 742

Mably, Gabriel Bonnet de, 45
MacCulloch, John Ramsay, 63
MacDougall, William, 213, 663, 921

Machiavelli, Niccolò, 11, 20, 22–23, 34, 193, 200, 201, 566
McIver, R. M., 709, 741
McKelvey, Blake, 742
Mackenzie, J. S., 847
McKenzie, R. D., 740
Mackintosh, Robert, 69
McLean, Annie Marion, 766
Maclean y Estenós, Roberto, 905, 906, 907
MacLeod, William Christie, 732
Mahan, Alfred Thayer, 203
Maine, Sir Henry Sumner, 24, 67, 233, 443, 655, 672
Maistre, Joseph de, 65, 75, 83, 96, 499
Malthus, Thomas Robert, 50–51, 63, 342, 459, 920
Manegold of Lautenbach, 18
Mannheim, Karl, 215, 310, 363, 895
Marcus Aurelius, 13
Marett, Robert Ranulf, 70, 116, 854
Mariana, Juan de, 31
Marsh, G. P., 680–81
Marsiglio of Padua, 18, 20–23
Martin, E. D., 741
Martínez-Paz, Enrique, 904, 905
Marx, Karl, 60, 150, 240–42, 267, 325, 326, 327, 328, 339, 348, 354, 358, 365, 366, 370, 396, 413, 435, 443, 704, 720
Masaryk, Thomas G., 356
Maunier, René, 525
Mauss, Marcel, 116, 516, 521, 522, 525
Mead, George H., 848, 849
Medina Echavarría, José, 905, 906–7
Meinecke, Friedrich, 358
Mendieta y Nuñez, Lucio, 908, 910
Menezes, Florentino, 905
Michel, Henri, 110
Michels, Roberto, 199, 554
Mikhailovsky, N. K., 442
Mill, James, 63
Mill, John Stuart, 110, 342, 353, 375, 469
Milton, John, 33
Mitchell, Wesley C., 56
Moede, Walter, 212
Moltke, Helmuth von, 202
Montaigne, Michel Eyquem de, 39, 47, 64
Montesquieu, Baron de (Charles de Secondat), 25, 46, 48, 53, 57, 58, 60, 63, 66, 67, 69, 70, 73, 75, 84, 161, 467, 471, 553
More, Sir Thomas, 42–43
Morelly, 44–45
Morgan, Lewis Henry, 25, 71, 81, 138–54, 211, 233, 401, 405, 732

Morgan, Lloyd, 691
Mosca, Gaetano, 107, 426
Mowrer, E. R., 742
Mueller, Adam, 319, 385, 395, 386–87
Müller, Johannes, 365
Müller-Lyer, Franz, 212
Murray, Gilbert, 734
Mussolini, Benito, 555

Napoleon I, 68, 490
Napoleon III, 490
Nelson, Ernesto, 907
Nelson, Leonard, 348
Newton, Sir Isaac, 47, 129, 563
Niceforo, Alfredo, 554
Nicholas of Cusa, 18, 22
Nicolai, Georg F., 211, 908
Niebuhr, Barthold G., 46
Nietzsche, Friedrich Wilhelm, 364, 365, 877
Nimkoff, M. F., 742
Nordau, Max, 727
Notestein, F. W., 740
Novicow, Jacques, 184, 203, 406, 412, 419–40, 467, 876

Odum, H. W., 742
Ogburn, William F., 146, 214, 733, 741, 742
Oliveira Vanna, José de, 904
Olivia, José, 904
Oppenheimer, Franz, 203, 210, 214, 215, 332–52, 363, 405, 425
Orgaz, Raúl A., 904, 906
Orosius, Paulus, 720, 729, 734
Osborn, Frederick, 740
Ostwald, Wilhelm, 679

Paine, Thomas, 47, 65
Paredes, Angel M., 904, 905
Pareto, Vilfredo, 107, 373, 398, 455, 554, 555–68, 885, 887
Park, Robert E., 275, 740
Parmelee, Maurice, 742
Parsons, Philip A., 741, 742
Parsons, Talcott, 320, 594
Paul, Saint, 15, 17, 114
Paulsen, Friedrich, 227, 853
Pavlov, Ivan, 885
Pearl, Raymond, 741
Pearson, Karl, 745
Peel, Sir Robert, 69
Peixotto, Jessica, 741
Perrault, Charles, 39

Peschel, Oskar, 210
Peter, Saint, 17, 21
Philip the Fair, 21
Place, Francis, 696
Plato, 6, 7, 18, 23, 43, 86, 92, 101, 115, 214, 390, 398, 426, 775
Plekhanoff, G. V., 442
Plotinus, 13, 720
Polybius, 10, 35, 193
Pope, Alexander, 47
Popes: Boniface VIII, 21; Gregory VII, 18
Posada, Adolfo, 585–99
Potter, Charles Francis, 107
Poviña, Alfredo, 905, 906, 908
Priestley, Joseph, 55, 409
Proudhon, Pierre Joseph, 338, 347, 539, 543, 545, 546, 547, 551
Pufendorf, Samuel von, 34, 36, 388, 715–16

Quatrefages de Bréau, Jean Louis Armand de, 70
Queen, S. A., 741
Quesada, Ernesto, 904
Quételet, Lambert Adolphe Jacques, 6, 538, 542, 547, 550
Quinn, James A., 740

Radcliffe-Brown, A. R., 149, 150
Radin, Paul, 150
Rae, John, 129
Ramos, Arthur, 905, 908
Ramos-Mejia, J. M., 903
Randall, J. H., 19
Ranke, Leopold von, 46, 358
Ratzel, Friedrich, 210
Ratzenhofer, Gustav, 118, 175, 181, 191, 202, 203, 211, 214, 363, 374–84, 401, 406, 412, 424, 425, 432, 769, 771, 779, 782, 877, 880
Raynal, Guillaume Thomas, 71
Reade, Winwood, 724
Reckless, W. C., 742
Reed, Ruth, 742
Renan, Joseph Ernest, 424
Renouvier, Charles Bernard, 519
Retzius, Anders, 70
Reuter, E. B., 740
Rhabanus Maurus, 907
Ricardo, David, 63
Rice, S. A., 742
Richard, Gaston, 524–25
Richmond, Mary E., 741
Richthofen, Ferdinand von, 210

Rickert, Heinrich, 209, 212, 319, 333, 336
Ritchie, D. G., 29, 131
Ritter, Karl, 7, 49, 210
Rivers, W. H. R., 116, 662
Roberts, Lord, 203
Roberty, Eugène de, 106, 499–500
Robinson, James Harvey, 555
Robinson, L. N., 742
Roca, Blas, 907
Rodbertus, Johann Karl, 373
Rohan, Prince, 356
Romagnosi, Gian, 553
Romilly, Sir Samuel, 69
Ross, Edward Alsworth, 106, 107, 275, 334, 337, 347, 820–32, 864
Ross, John, 687
Rostovtzev, Michael I., 727
Rousseau, Jean Jacques, 32, 37–38, 46, 53, 58, 127, 130, 167, 180, 339, 405, 462, 565

Sadler, Michael T., 51–52
Saint-Pierre, Charles Castel de, 40, 41, 72, 73, 75, 84
Saint-Simon, Henri de, 41, 46, 72–75, 82–84, 338, 347, 358, 365, 366, 499, 539, 553, 902
Salomon, Gottfried, 381
Santovenia, Emeterio, 908
Sanz del Río, Julian, 590
Sarmiento, Domingo Faustino, 902, 903, 907
Savigny, Friedrich Karl von, 65, 68
Say, Jean Baptiste, 97
Schäffle, Albert, 82, 106, 210, 214, 215, 401, 769, 775, 834
Schallmayer, Wilhelm, 211
Scheler, Max, 215, 363
Schelling, Friedrich W. J. von, 65, 386
Schlegel, Friedrich Karl Wilhelm von, 385, 386
Schmidt, Wilhelm, 344, 347, 348
Schmoller, Gustav, 354, 357, 767, 769, 775, 853
Schneider, D. M., 741
Schopenhauer, Arthur, 414
Seligman, E. R. A., 42
Sellin, Thorsten, 742
Semple, E. C., 740
Seneca, 12, 15, 16
Senior, Nassau William, 63
Shaftesbury, Earl of, 47
Shalloo, J. P., 742
Shaw, Clifford, 740

Shotwell, James T., 455, 734
Sidney, Algernon, 35–36
Sieyès, E. J., 54–55, 370
Sighele, Scipio, 192, 193, 203, 554, 578–83
Simiand, François, 526–27
Simmel, Georg, 213, 217, 249–73, 275, 291, 365, 368, 779, 806, 853, 864
Sismondi, Jean Charles Leonard Simonde de, 98
Small, Albion Woodbury, 3, 61, 72, 75, 107, 116, 129, 135, 156, 157, 179, 191, 202, 204, 211, 334, 378, 401, 412, 623, 627, 723, 766–92, 872, 877
Smith, Adam, 11, 24, 35, 46, 47, 53, 54, 62–63, 181, 663, 664, 771–72, 922
Smith, G. Elliott, 574
Smith, J. R., 740
Socrates, 4, 7
Soddy, Frederick, 679
Solms, Max Graf zu, 266–67
Solvay, Ernest, 538, 687
Sombart, Werner, 214, 215, 316–31, 775
Sonnenfels, Joseph von, 61
Sorokin, Pitirim Alexandrovitch, 445, 455, 728, 729, 740, 884–901
Spann, Othmar, 214, 319, 385–99
Spencer, Herbert, 6, 52, 56, 71, 75, 81, 82, 85, 87, 103, 104, 106, 107, 110–37, 157, 353, 358, 375, 401, 410, 424, 434, 438, 443, 462, 472, 478, 482, 502, 506, 514, 542, 545, 546, 551, 567, 580, 589, 603, 606, 608, 617, 733, 843, 912, 917, 923, 924
Spengler, Oswald, 11, 215, 264, 359–60, 365, 368, 400, 402, 441, 450, 894, 900, 904
Spinoza, Baruch, 11, 24, 34, 36, 388
Spykman, Nicholas J., 250, 267
Stangeland, Charles E., 50
Stein, Lorenz von, 231, 354, 363, 366, 373
Stein, Ludwig, 60, 129, 215, 400–16, 438, 450, 469, 714, 815
Steinthal, Heymann, 212
Stern, Bernhard J., 150, 742
Stoltenberg, Hans, 212
Stuckenberg, John Henry Wilburn, 805–18, 872
Suárez, Francisco, 31, 32
Sumner, William Graham, 10, 56, 71, 81, 106, 112, 130, 155–72, 184, 211, 353, 438, 662
Sutherland, Alexander, 24, 35, 876
Sutherland, E. H., 742

Tacitus, 13
Taft, D. R., 742
Taine, Hippolyte, 580, 925
Tannenbaum, Frank, 742
Tarde, Gabriel, 20, 53, 192, 203, 441, 459, 464, 471–80, 487, 488, 525, 551, 573, 578, 579, 580, 581, 821, 847, 848, 864, 921
Tawney, R. H., 19, 775
Taylor, Graham, 741
Taylor, Henry Osborn, 719
Teeters, N. K., 742
Tenney, Alvan Alonzo, 33, 715
Theognis, 6
Thibaut, Anton Friedrich Justus, 68
Thomas, Franklin, 740
Thomas, William Isaac, 275, 298, 660, 724, 793–804
Thomas Aquinas; see Aquinas, Thomas
Thompson, James Westfall, 735
Thompson, W. S., 740
Thomson, J. Arthur, 692
Thurnwald, Richard, 212
Tiedemann, Friedrich, 70
Tönnies, Ferdinand, 212, 213, 215, 227–48, 253, 267, 334, 363, 369, 402
Topinard, Paul, 70
Toynbee, Arnold Joseph, 210, 360, 717–36, 797, 900
Tozzer, A. M., 741
Treitschke, Heinrich von, 200
Troeltsch, Ernst, 213, 309–15, 333, 365
Trotter, Wilfred, 192
Turgot, Anne Robert Jacques, 24, 40, 46, 47, 62, 72, 73, 75, 83, 84, 193, 365, 862
Turner, F. J., 740
Turner, Ralph E., 731
Tylor, Sir Edward B., 514, 662

Vaccaro, Michelangelo, 203, 554, 572–75
Van Kleeck, Mary, 741
Veblen, Thorstein Bunde, 56, 556, 682, 684, 685, 775, 791
Vegetius, 14, 20
Venturino, Agustin, 905
Véron, Eugène, 420
Vesalius, Andreas, 69
Vico, Giovanni Battista, 24, 25, 40, 46, 56–57, 73, 75, 83, 93, 193, 473, 553
Vierkandt, Alfred, 212, 213, 215, 369
Vincent, George M., 76, 481, 771
Virchow, Rudolf, 70
Vitoria, Francisco de, 586
Vitruvius, 13–14

Vives, Juan Luis, 586
Voltaire, F. M. Arouet de, 21, 24, 46, 47, 58, 69
Von der Goltz, Kolmar; see Goltz, Kolmar von der.

Wagner, Adolf, 333, 767
Wagner, Alfred, 227, 228, 243
Waite, J. B., 742
Wallas, Graham, 56, 471, 476, 607, 633, 696–716
Waller, Willard, 742
Walras, Leon, 745
Walton, Henri, 526
Ward, Lester Frank, 6, 56, 75, 81, 87, 104, 107, 129, 131, 158, 166, 173–89, 191, 193, 196, 334, 335, 347, 353, 401, 406, 411, 412, 425, 432, 438, 469, 589, 616, 645, 660, 714, 778, 786, 788, 805, 806, 808, 862, 865, 872, 912, 917, 918, 919
Watson, John B., 538, 795
Waxweiler, Émile, 275, 538
Webb, Beatrice and Sidney, 775
Weber, Alfred, 213, 353–61, 363, 455
Weber, Max, 56, 213, 214, 231, 233, 266, 283, 287–88, 309, 310, 311, 312, 313, 314, 322, 326, 329, 333, 334, 347, 355, 363, 369, 441, 455, 731, 733, 890
Webster, Hutton, 455

Westermarck, Edward Alexander, 71, 401, 603, 654–67, 674, 675, 927
Wheeler, G. C., 574, 628
White, Leslie A., 741
Wiese, Leopold von, 242, 267, 274–86, 368, 369
Willcox, O. W., 51
Willcox, W. F., 740
Willem, Emilio, 908
Willey, Malcolm M., 770
Windelband, Wilhelm, 209, 213
Wirth, Louis, 215
Wolfe, A. B., 740
Wood, A. E., 742
Woods, Robert, 741
Worms, René, 82, 106, 107, 454
Wright, R. J., 917
Wundt, Wilhelm, 111, 174, 211, 212, 213, 216–26, 227–28, 414, 806, 912, 923, 924, 925

Young, Kimball, 741, 804

Zea, Leopoldo, 908
Zeller, Eduard, 60
Zeno, 9
Zeno, Francisco M., 907
Zimmerman, Carle C., 742, 888
Znaniecki, Florian, 275, 591, 795

SUBJECT INDEX

Absolution, secular, 23
Accord with sentiment or principles, 564–66
Accordance, 277
"Accumulation, primitive," 338–39
Acquisitiveness, 293, 294, 297, 323, 325, 327
Action
  collective; *see* Co-operation
  and emotion, 390–91
  logical and nonlogical, 558–60
  and relationships, social, 300
"Action patterns, circumscribed," 279
Activities, social, 871
Activity
  economic, 338–39
  human, 318–20
    and general laws, 320–21
  intermental, 472
  state, 640–45
  scope of, 128–34
Actuality, psychic, 219
Adaptation, 472, 826
  to milieu, 467
  to nature, 917–18
  principle of, 475, 573
"Adjustment," 276–77
Adjustments, *learned*, 861–63
Advance; *see* Progress; Reform
"Advance," 276
Affirmations, 564–66
Agelecism, 499, 518
  creationism, 512–14
  fatalism, 510, 514
  personalism, 511–12
  realism, 505
  transcendentalism, 510–11, 512
Aggregates, persistence of, 561, 562
Agrarian philosophy, 332–52
Agreements, international, 426
Aim of sociology, 266
Almsgiving, 16
"Alternative, third," 685
Altruism, 43, 93, 608–10
  and egotism, 564
"Amalgamation," 277
America; *see* United States

American *Journal of Sociology,* 742, 788, 789, 790
American *Sociological Review,* 742, 789
American Sociological Society, 742, 790
Analogies, social and individual, 769
Anarchism, 180, 388, 408
  Godwin's, 55
"Ancient" and modern society, 144–45
Ancients, admiration for, 39
Anglican Church; *see* Church of England
Animism, 94
Année sociologique, 520–21
Antagonisms, 253
Anthropogeography, 49, 57, 210, 458
Anthropologists, classical, 403, 405
Anthropology, 69–70, 121, 142–44
Antievolutionism, 149
Antirational viewpoint, 13
Antithesis, thesis, and synthesis, Hegelian, 59
Apperception and perception, 218–19
Appreciation, individual, 752
"Approach" to sociology, 266
Arbitration, international, 21, 132
Aristocracy, 7, 181, 214, 486–87, 555–58, 566–67, 878
  versus democracy, 148
  government by, 107, 370, 394, 426, 437
  intellectual, 44, 82, 101
Art
  development of, 925–26
  and polity and culture, 689
Aruntas (Australian) 514–15
Asceticism, 296, 297, 311, 312, 563
Assemblages; *see* Gatherings, social
Assimilation, 200
Association, 276, 784–85, 826
  and gregariousness, 745–47
  process of, 265
  and socialization, 191
  see also Society
"Association, free," of Marx, 366
Associationism, 218, 220
Associations, purposive, 750–51
"Associations" (Commonwealth period), 29
Astrology, 9

Astronomy, social, 469
Athens, 630
Atomic bomb, 438
"Atomism," 897
Attitudes, 803
    science of, 798
    social, 829–30
Augustinianism, new, 718–21
Austria-Hungary, 192
Autarchy, 180
Authority, 564–66
    delegated; see Government
    and domination, 258
    institutionalization of, 304–6
    and liberty, 408
    and political and individual liberty, 127
    principle of, 406–9, 628–29
    religious and secular, 302
Autocracy, 181
Autodeterminism, social, 464
"Averarge man," 547

"Bad" and "good," 786
Being, Great, of Comte, 88, 89
Behavior (collective), 745–48, 762, 861–62
    interpretation of, 847
    political, 698–705
    predictability, 889
Behaviorism, 538, 563
Belgium, 538
Bible, the; see Holy Scriptures
Biological elements in social systems, 665
Biological interpretation of society, 115–16,
    210–11
Biological sociology, 459
Biology
    social, 231
    and sociology, 573
Birth control, 577, 888
Birth rate, 51
Bomb, atomic; see Atomic bomb
Boundaries, international and social, 426
    see also Frontiers, theory of
Bourgeoisie; see Middle class
Brahmanism; see Religion
"Brain trust," 185
Bronze Age, 344
Brotherhood of man, 10, 12, 14, 16–17
Budgets, time, 888–89
Bureaucracy, 124, 259, 496, 636, 637
    German, 354
Business, 293
    cycles of, 230
    growth of, 324–25

Calamity, law of, 887
"Calculus, felicific"; see "Felicific calculus"
Calvinism; see Religion
Cameralists, 46, 61, 362, 773
Capacity, industrial and positive, 100
Capital and labor, 496, 550
Capitalism, 63, 98–99, 214, 241, 242, 292–
    94, 312, 316–31, 570, 775, 838–39
    "bound" and "free," 328
    early and high, 328
    "elements, reproductive," 326
    ethic, Protestant, as a condition, 329
    and imperialism, 132
    incommensurability, 328–29
    nature and evolution of, 322–29
    necessity for, 328
    origin of, 339
    and political power, 571
    and religion, 214
    spirit of, 326
Case-study method, 728, 729, 731
Caste
    and class, 827, 838–39
    system of, in India, 296
Categorical imperative, 874
Categories of thought, 517–18
Catholic church; see Religion
Causality, 401
    physical and psychical, 218
Causation
    plural, 451–52
    social, 873
"Cephalic index," 70
"Challenge and Response," 360, 724, 732
    797
Change
    opposition to, 4
    social, 447–49, 896, 898–900
Character, national, 484
    and government, 127
Characterization, individual, 752
Charisma, 302, 305–6
Charity, 16
Chartists, 33–34
Checks and balances in government, 11
Chicago, University of, 789
Chieftainships, 750
Child and mother, 448
Child-guidance, 802–3
China, 4, 296–97, 526
Choice, social, laws of, 760
Christianity; see Religion
Church and churches; see Religion
Church of England, legal system of, 29

Circle, social, 234–35
Cities; *see* Towns
Citizenship, 629–30
  principle of, 811
City of God, 16
City-state, 20, 431
Civil service, 703
Civilization, 784
  development of, 359, 621
  leaders, "etherialization," 726
  origin of, 507–8
  process of, 25, 723–24
Civilizations
  breakdown of, 724–25, 731
  damned, 721–27
  great, 368
  life-history of, 725–26
  study of, 722–23
Civitas and *societas,* 144–45
Clan, the, 627
  and tribe, 145
Class and caste, 827, 838–39
Class struggle (*Klassenkampf*), 107
  origin of, 198
Classes (social), 523, 550, 566–67, 827
  basic, 99–100
  characteristics of, 887
  lower, 41–45
  of Middle Ages, 17
  mutual duties of, 164
  origin of, 122–23, 198
  privileged, 146
  reproduction of, 577
"Classical Economists," 63, 116, 129
Classification, 516–17
Climate and man, 7, 13, 20, 24
Code Napoléon, 68
Codes, legal and moral, 502, 505, 874
Collectives, social, 234–36
Collectivism, 347
Collectivities, abstract, 281
Collectivity; *see* Society
Colonization and discoveries, books on, 71
Combination, aggregates of, 560–61
Command and obedience, 91
Commendatio, 748
Commerce; *see* Trade
Commercial revolution; *see* Revolution, commercial
Commercialism, 63
Commonwealth, ideal; *see* Utopia
Commonwealths; *see* States
Communication, 826, 838, 859, 860

Communism
  Aristotelian arguments against, 8
  of Campanella, 43
  primitive, 228
"Communism in living," 147
Community
  and society, 213, 368–69, 401–2, 403–4
  and state, 386–87
"Community feeling," 120
"Community-law of nature," 238
Community-society, 283
Compact, governmental, 19
Competition; *see* Conflict
"Composition, social," 750
"Compulsion" in social relations, 256
Conation, social, 175, 218
Conduct
  antisocial, 822
  group, 158
Conflict, 279, 472, 826
  class, 370
    origin of, 198
  economic, 340, 378
  group, 747
    and amalgamation, 195–210
    struggle-school, 432
  human, types of, 421–24
  intellectual, 423, 429
  international, 412
  intragroup and intergroup, 860
  personal, 842
  phenomena, 257, 267
  principle of, 474
  social, 770
  in social development, 60, 193, 194–95
  see also War
"Conflict school," 191, 203
Conformism, 301, 504, 517
Confucianism; *see* Religion
Congeries, 897
Congress, 708
Conquest, and society, 349, 369–70
"Conquest state," 204
Consanguine stage; *see* Kinship
Conscience, 807
Consciousness
  growth of, 617–18
  individual and social, 463, 837
Consent of the governed, 36
Conservatism, 4, 16
  economic, 303
  Greek, 6
  and radicalism, 882
Constants in behavior, 560–61

Constitutions, 749, 878
Constraint, social, 505, 522, 745, 750
Continuity in history, 46, 401
Contract
    freedom of, 63
    original, social, error of doctrine, 8
    quasi and implicit, 465
    social, historicity of, 127–28
Contractualism, 543, 544, 545, 546, 550, 551
Contradiction, principle of, 518
Contravention, 278
Control
    extra-legal, 816
    over life-conditions, 669
    social, 5, 10, 24, 29, 388, 751, 820–21, 829–30, 875, 923–29
        extra-legal, 879–80
        and governmental, 22, 437–38
Co-operation, 711–12, 747, 757–61, 917–18
    international, 704
    private and public, 118, 120
    and progress, 468
Co-operatives, 345–47
Corporations, social, 234–36
Corporatism, 519
Correlation, principle of, 617–18
Cosmogony, Christian, 139
"Cosmopolitan" state, 180
Cosmopolitanism, 414, 436, 648
Court, international, 813
Creationism, agelic, 512–14
Creativeness, 848–49
Credit, 541
Crime, 504, 522–23
    and revolution, 886
Criminals, 479, 495
Criminology and penology, 742
"Crisis," 724
Crowd, the, 281, 487–92
    psychology of, 580, 581
    and the public, 478–79
    traits of, 482
Cultural and psychological sociology, 793–804
Culture, 359
    aspects of, internal and external, 220, 897–900
    case-study of, 728, 729, 731
    cycles of, 368
    determinism of, 402
    evolution of, 58, 70–71
    gains in, loss of, 343–44
    and history, sociology of, 358

human, 862–63
idealistic and rational, 894
integration of, 897–98
and personality, 802
and politics and economics, 240–42
and polity and art, 689
primitive, 13, 140
three aspects of, 220
"Culture," 801–2
Culture-object or -value, 802
Culture-sociology, 357
"Culture state," 204
Custom, 562, 829, 927
    and law, 454
    and morals, 663
    theory of, 236–37
    and tradition, 120–21, 829, 927
Cycles
    of business, 230
    in culture, 368
    in history, 11, 38, 193
    in social phenomena, 566

Damnation and salvation, 719
"Dark Ages," the, 17
Darwinism, 419, 424, 660, 704
    social, 24, 106–7, 211, 807
Dead, influence of, 483
"Dead hand," 121
Débat, 546, 551
Deduction and induction, 8, 348
    Greek, 6
    in science, 335
Definitions of sociology, 336, 363, 427, 446, 462, 621, 624, 762, 763, 771, 772, 779, 788, 807, 808, 809
Deism, 21, 47, 61, 128
Democracy, 120, 125, 181, 370, 409, 524, 633–37, 703, 838, 849, 878
    versus aristocracy, 148–49
    fitness and unfitness for, 125–26
    "pure," distrust of, 82
    and republican system, 161–63
    and totalitarianism, 894
    two conceptions of, 495
Democrats, Jacksonian, 34
Demography, 231
Derivations, 555–58, 560–66
Desires, biological and cultural, 824
Despotism, 120, 126
Determinism, 413, 502
    agelic, 510, 514
    cultural, 402
    versus free will, 689–90

materialistic and spiritual, 719–20
philosophical, 358
social, 201, 202, 464
Development; see Evolution
Dialectic, Hegelian, of progress, 59–60
Differentiation, 279–81
and origin of sociology, 75
Discipline
intragroup, 876
moral, 519
social, 754, 757–61
Discoveries and colonization, books on, 71
Disintegration, national, 486–87
"Dispositions, balked," 707
Dissociation, 257, 276, 278, 280
Distribution of functions, 90
Divine right, 31, 33
Division of labor; see Labor
Dogmas, religious; see Religion
Domination, 369–70, 826
and authority, 258
Drama, the, 926
Dreams, 523
Dualism and monism, 377
"Dynamics, social," 23, 73, 84, 86, 174–75

Economic factors in evolution, 469
Economic system, 395–98
Economics
and politics, 545
and politics and culture, 240–42
"Economics, psychological," 55
Economists, Classical, 46, 63, 116, 129, 321, 339, 342
Economy
planned, 396
self-sufficient, and handicraft, 322–23
Education
and heredity, 468
and imitation, 921–22
influence of, 438
and the state, 185–87, 644
theory of Rousseau on, 38
Efficiency, projected, law of, 610–11, 612
Effort, muscular and mental, 710
Efforts, combination of, 91
Egoism; see Individualism
Egypt, 3, 4
Elements, three, of an economic system, 322–23
Elite; see Aristocracy
Emancipation, political, 200
Embryology, social, 447

Emigration, 485, 755
of rural population, 341
Emotion
and action, 390–91
and will and thought, 707–8
Empiricism, 517
"idealistic," 320
Encyclopedists, 47
End, prime, of psychology, 715
Endogamy and exogamy, 627
Ends, heterogeneity of, 219
Ends-means system, 301–2
Energy, surplus, 758
England, 603–6
applied sociology in, 677–94
middle-class, 354
plutocracy in, 149
Poor Law of 1603 in, 16
Enlightenment, the, 60, 66, 339
Enterprise
business, 327
spirit of, 324
Entertainment, social, 253–54
Entities, social, 231, 232, 234–36
Entrepreneurs, 327
Environment, 689–90, 754–55, 824–25
adaptation to, 746
as basis of social theory, 215
functioning and organization of, 689–91
and individual, 705, 706
internal social, 503
in origins of social philosophy, 46
physical, and society, 7, 9, 24–25
social, 105
and historical, 467
and the writer, 3–4
subjection of, to man's mind and will, 177
Epicureanism, 9–12, 894
Epistemology, 335–38
Equality
economic, 339
of men, 162, 393, 409
social, 524
Equalization, 827
Equilibration, 547
Equilibrium, social, 885
"Error, social forces"; see "Social forces error"
Eschatology, 13, 15, 16
Eskimos, 521–22
Estates of a realm, 18–19
Estrangement, 827
"Ethical culture," 242

Ethics, 770, 786, 791, 807, 926–28
  Christian, 311
  and politics, 22, 23
  religious, 295, 298
  social, 872–73
  and the state, 201
  of state, future, 123, 125
  theory of, 662–65
  see also Morality
Ethnocentrism, 861
Ethnography, 157, 211–12
Ethnology, 70–71, 121
Ethnosociology, 212
Eucharist, 15
Eugenics, 7, 459
"Eurasians," 441
Europe, western, federation of, 431, 435
Evaluations, 336
Evil and good, 874
  struggle of, 720
Evolution, 70–71
  activational, 93
  antievolutionism in, 149
  cosmic and social, 176
  cultural, 140–42
  economic factors in, 468
  of family, 142–43
  goals of, 544
  historical, 92–96, 719
    law of, 253
    three stages of, 57
  human, 421
    and organic, 862
  intellectual, 376
  organic
    and human, 862
    and social, 129
  political, 478
    and social, 379–81, 410–12, 423, 432–33
  reason in, 618
  social (institutional) 6, 8, 24, 56–58, 90, 104–5, 121–23, 138, 140–42, 160, 180, 449–52, 468, 481–98, 506–7, 566, 614–19, 745–50, 877–78, 921
    according to Kant, 58
    elimination of war in, 203–4
    and social progress, 621–22
    stage theory of, 871
  sympodial, 174
  technological, 140–42
  theory of, 915–16
  theory and laws of Spencer, 111–16
  unilinear, 445, 455

Evolutionary socialist, first great, 11
Evolutionism, classical, 220
Exchange of goods; see Trade
Exogamy and endogamy, 627, 674
Expansion, national, 431
Expansionism, 167–70
Exploitation, 758, 826
Extra-legal social control, 134–35

Fabian Society, 696
Fact
  and legend, 560
  social, 453–54, 502–3, 504–6
Factor, political, origin of, 453
Factors
  dominant, 451
  external social, 919
Faith and reason, 894
"Fall" of man, 13, 15, 16, 18, 38, 140, 721
Fame, 841–42
  and notoriety, 20
Family
  evolution of, 142–43, 655–56
  and the individual, 89–90
  matrilinear, 448
  patrilinear, 449
  and property, 146
  and religion, 87
  single, origin of society, 24
  as social unit, 499
  state care, 644
Fascism, 519, 554
  see also Italy
Fatalism; see Determinism
Father, descent through, 449
"Fatherland," conception of, 94
Fathers, Christian; see Religion
Fecundity, unfavorable condition for, 116
Federalism, 32, 631
Federation of nations, 857, 860–61, 928
  see also League of Nations
"Feeling of the community," 120
"Felicific calculus," 55
Fetishism, 93–94
Feudalism, 23, 344–45
  origin of, 94–95
Fields of contemporary sociology, 780
Fluctuations, social, 891, 894
Folk, work, and place; see Place, work, and folk
Folk psychology, 220–22
"Folk state," 200

Folkways, 755
  Sumner's theory of, 158–59
Food and population, 50–51
Force
  automatic natural, 862
  as basis of government, 91, 97
  of idea, 461–62
  positive and constructive, of sociology, 366
  social, 99–100, 176, 376, 824
  supernatural, 5
"Force, Primeval," 377
"Forgotten man," the, 130, 164
"Formal school" of sociology, 250
Formalism, 839
Forms
  of government, 181
  of society, 135
    meanings of, 264
  of state and government, 123–27
Foundations, economic, of society, 7
France, 21, 458–60, 519
Freedom; see Liberty
French Revolution; see Revolution, French
Frequencies of size and sort, 762
Freudianism, 567
Friendship, 9, 12
Frontiers, theory of, 540–41, 543, 546–51
Function
  social, and occupation, 825
  and structure, 770
Functionalism, 455
Functioning, organization, and environment, 689–91
Functions
  specialization of, 85–86, 90
  of the state, 62
Future
  and past, 691
  planning for, 72
Future life; see Otherworldliness

Gains, cultural, loss of, 343–44
Games, 253–54
Gatherings, social, 253–55
Gemeinschaft and Gesellschaft, 232–34
Generalization, sociological, 358, 367, 371
Genesis, social, 768
"Genesis"
  and "individuation," 115–16
  and "telesis," 174, 176
Genetic sociology, 447
Genius, 395, 841–42
Gens; see Society

Geographical interpretations, of society, 48
Germany
  breakdown of the empire, 354
  bureaucracy in, 354
  Code, Imperial, of, 68
  contributions of, to sociology, 357, 362
  eastern, pre-war economy in, 332
  history of modern, 372
  Institute of Social Sciences in, 356
  intelligentsia, aloof, 356
  Kulturbund in, 356
  Macht and Geist in, 356
  middle class in, decline of, 353–54, 355–56
  militarism in, 625
  National Socialism in, 356, 373
  nationalism in, 59
  nineteenth-century, 776
  opposition of, to recognition of sociology, 383
  science in, pre-war, 332–34
  Weltgeist, 92
  youth movement (Jugendbewegung), 363
Geselligkeit, 254
Goals of evolution, 544
God
  in history, 719
  and society, 511–12, 515–16
  as source of political authority, 20
"Golden Age," 6, 12, 13, 15, 16, 18, 38, 73
Good, 926–27
  and evil, 786, 874
  struggle of, 720
Government
  abolition of, 55
  abuse of, 183–84
  American, analysis of, 202
  authority, delegated to, 16
  based on force, 91, 97
  character of, national, 127
  compact, 19
  democratic and republican, 161–63
  failures of, 132–33
  force as basis of, 91, 97
  forms of, 161–63, 181, 812
    and functions of, 878–79
  foundations of, philosophical, 67
  "functions" of, 100–103, 878–79
  limitations of, 437–38, 496
  majorities and minorities in, 65, 127, 749
  mixed, 126
  nature of, 88

Government—*continued*
  notions of, false, 184
  origin of, 10, 24, 25, 749
    divine, 15–17, 20
    and nature, 14
    theory of Hume, 53
  by popular consent, 22
  power of, directive, 100–103
  representative, 21, 22, 703
  self-government, 812
  and society, 36, 90
  and state, 37, 119–21, 809, 875
    forms of, 96–97, 123–27
  structure of, triune, 120–21
  types of, three, 120, 125–26
  universal, federation of, 132
Gratitude, 262
Great Being, of Comte, 88, 89
Great Britain; *see* England
"Great Man," in history, 725
"Greatest happiness of the greatest number," 55, 409
Greece, 4–11, 94, 630
  civilization of, ancient, 721–22
Gregariousness and association, 745–47
Group, the, 769–70, 828
  control of activities by, 799
  discipline of, intragroup, 874
  ideals, 840
  and the individual, 499–500, 691
  interest, 881
  matronymic and patronymic, 750
  national, 860
  primary, 837, 845, 847, 859–60
  in society, 748
  see also Society
"Group-struggle" theory, 60, 432
Guild Socialists; *see* Socialism
Gynaecocracy, 173, 176, 673

Habit, 829–30
  group, 158
Hammurabi, Code of, 4
Happiness, elements of, 927
Harmony, 618
Health, social, 503–4
Hebrew codes and teachings, 4
Hedonism, 54
  hyperintellectual, 697
Hellenic civilization; *see* Greece
Heredity, 466, 775, 919–20
  and education, 468
"Heretics, sexual," 562
Heritage, social, 709–16
Heterogeneity of ends, 219

Heuristic principle, 262, 265
Hierarchy in society, 393–95
Hinduism; *see* Religion
Hippocratic doctrine, 25
Historical sociology, 121–22, 769
  of Spencer, 116
Historicism, 358
Historiography, 25, 366
History
  agrarian philosophy of, 332–52
  concepts of, historical, 367
  and culture, sociology of, 358
  cyclical movement in, 193
  economic interpretation of, 241
  evolution of, 93–96
  "Great Man" theory of, 725
  and sociology, 212, 366–67
  philosophy of, 24, 26, 93–96, 231, 252, 475
    Comte's, 85–86
  processes, negative and positive, 366
  and psychology, 221
  purpose and plan in, 414
  sociopsychic, 487
  views of ibn-Khaldun on, 25
Holy Scriptures, 15
Homogeneity in population, 4, 29
  necessity of, 25
Horde, the, 627
Humanism, 107
Humanitarianism, 71, 91–92, 561
Hyperspirituality, 511

Idea-forces, 461–62
Ideal of racial perfection, 808
Ideal types, 290–92
Idealism, 6, 895
Ideals, 919
  of group, 838, 840
Ideas
  categories of, 517–18
  freedom of, 814
  infiltration of, 486
  influence of, 241, 488
  political, 697–705
  social, origins of, 847
Ideationism, 894, 895
Imitation, 847
  and education, 921–22
  and invention, 464
  principle of, 471
  process of, 473–74
  in social process, 20
Immigration, 485, 755, 822

Imperatives, 824
  moral, 874
Imperialism, 157, 161, 167–70, 631, 865
  capitalistic, 132
Improvement, social; see Reform
Impulses, political, 699
Incomes, earned and unearned, 643
India, 4, 296, 298, 524
Individual
  the activity of, modes of, 752–53
  control of, social, 648
  development of, 847
  domination of, by mores, 159
  and environment, 705, 706, 707
  and family, 89–90
  and group, 499–500, 691
    organization of, 391
  in social thinking, 4–5
  ideal of, 463
  nature of, 592–93
  in political society, 698–99
  restraints on, 327, 638–40
  rights of, legal, 128
  social, 360
  social settings and psychology, 220
  and society, 9, 85–86, 252, 253, 258,
    505, 510–11, 513, 517–18, 806–7,
    821, 827, 836–37, 846, 918
    analogy of, 22
  and species, 610–11
  and state, 18–19, 485
    analogy of, 18
  unimportance of, 192
Individualism, 62, 110–37, 163, 1181–82,
  241, 347, 386, 388–89, 391, 397, 408,
  410, 434, 438, 502, 519–20, 563, 578
  and egoism and altruism, 564, 860–61
  racial, 201
Individuality, 669–70
Individuation, 756, 815
  and "genesis," 115–16
Induction and deduction, 8, 348
  Greek, 6
  in science, 335
Industrial revolution; see Revolution, in-
    dustrial
Industrial revolutions, 451
Industrialism, 293, 708
  and militarism, 114, 123–25
Industry
  development of, 95–96, 124
  and government, 90–91
Inequality
  economic, 339

  of man, 393, 409
Infancy, human, prolongation of, 6, 31, 32,
    89
Inheritance
  and property, 145–49
  traditional, 67
  see also Heredity
Initiative, social, 158
Injustice, reparation of, 465
Innovation, social, 175
Insanity, 526
Instinct, 53, 661–62, 847
  and reason, 376–77, 706–7, 885–86
Instinct-theory, 378–79
Institute of Sociology, University of Leipzig,
    364
Institutional patterns, 296, 297, 299, 302
Institutionalists, 527
Institutionalization, origin of, 339
Institutions
  political; see State
  social; see Society
"Integralist" sociology, 884–901
Integration, 279–81
  causal-functional, 897
  cultural, 896–98
    logico-meaningful, 896–98
  of society, 509–10
Intellectualistic conception of society, 10
Intelligence
  and instinct, 376–77, 706–7, 885–86
  social, 862
Interaction, social, 825, 828–31
Intercommunication; see Communication
Interdependence, 386–87
Interests
  and interest-groups, 782–83, 824, 881
  theory of, 376–78
Intermixture, racial, 485–86
International relations, 132, 412–14
International Sociological Congress, 857
International Sociological Institute, 444
Internationalism, 406, 420, 435–37, 438,
    547–49, 712, 812, 815, 865
  and nationalism, 631
Interpretations, mechanical, 360
Invention, 473, 474
  and imitation, 464
  social, 186
Inventions, 410, 411, 921
Isolationism, 414
Italy, 553–84
  fascism in, 107, 373, 398
  unification of, 436

Jacksonian Democrats, 34
Jacobin mentality, 494–95, 496
Jews, 38, 261
Journal of Applied Sociology, 742
Journal of Social Forces, 742, 789
Journalism; *see* Newspapers
Judgments, value; *see* Value-judgments
Jurisprudence, comparative and historical,
    66, 68
Jus naturale, 388
Justice
    commutative, 392
    and freedom, 392
    idea of, origin of, 10
    public, evolution of, 632
    reparative, 465
    social and philosophical basis of, 335–38
    theory of, 434

Karma, 298
"Karyokinesis, social," 175
"Kingdom, social," 354
Kinship (consanguinity), 627, 810–11
    in family, 142, 146
    systems of, 143–44, 151, 222, 260
Klassenkampf, 107
Knowledge, 785
    sociology of, 215, 441
    specialized 692
    theory of, 516–18
    ultimate, 321
Krausism, 588
Kultur, 202

Labor, 304, 643–44
    associative, 568–69
    and capital, 496, 550
    division of, 7, 17, 35, 63, 86, 90, 91, 120,
        264, 506–8, 550, 922
    emancipation of 95
    modern, 709
    and religion, 571
    supply of, increase in, 342
    supply and demand, 343
    "theory of value" in, 63
    thought of, on public affairs, 708
    unemployment of, technological, 342
    unions, 259
    wages, theory of, 340–41
Laissez faire, 46, 47, 62, 107, 130, 134, 156,
    158, 160–61, 163, 165, 179, 181, 182,
    333, 388

Land
    monopoly of, 339–40, 342–43, 570
    ownership of, 146–47, 214, 568
Language, 512, 516, 527, 923–24
    common, in a nationality, 428
    as factor in history, 90
    self-words in, 842
    symbolism in, 700
Latin America, 902–30
Law, 878–80
    codes of, German and French (*Code Na-
        poléon*) 68
    codification of, 68
    "community-law of nature," 238
    criminal, 68–69
    and custom, 454
    evolution and history of, 66–67
    function of, 31
    international, 32
    jurisprudence, comparative and histori-
        cal, 66, 68
    natural, 388
        and human, 7
        in economic world, 61–62, 129
    and order and morality, 236–37
    origin of, 339
    resistance to, 878
    Roman, effect of, on church and state, 21
    socialization in, 408, 411
    theory of, 237–38
Lawfulness, 376, 382
Laws
    fundamental, of sociology, 338–47
    general, and human activity, 320–21
    "iron," of economics, 63
    of universal evolution, Spencer's, 112–13
Lawyers, medieval, 16
Leaders
    in a democracy, 838
    "etherialization" of, 726
Leadership, 876
    of the crowd, 490
    evolution of, 122
    immortal, 887
    views of Machiavelli on, 23
    see also Aristocracy
League of Nations, 413, 425, 426, 429,
    435–36, 648, 857, 912
    European, 431
    factors in, favorable, 424
    obstacles in way of, 424
    views of Kant on, 58
Legend and fact, 560

Legislation
  "attractive," and "speculative," 166, 186
  failure of, 134
  principles of, 48
  struggle for control in, 199
Legislature, sovereignty of, 127
"Legitimacy" in systems of order, 301
"Levelers," 33
Liberalism, 371, 373, 520, 759
  economic, 61
  see also Neoliberals
Liberation, 827
Liberty, 166–67, 178–79, 637–40, 749, 758,
  815
  and authority, 408
  civil, 163–66
  of contract; see Contract
  equal, Spencer's law of, 130
  individual, 434
    consciousness of, 59
    and political authority, 127
    restriction of, 337
  and justice, 392
  political, origin of, 477
  restrictions of, 761
  self-consciousness of, 59
  of thought, 814
  of will, 873
Lieu, travail et famille; see Place, work,
  and folk
Life, formula for, 690
Linguistics; see Language
Logic, 896–98
  various kinds of, 492–93
Logos, divine, 14
"Looking-glass self," 837, 845–47, 848
Loyalty, 262

Machiavellianism, 23, 388
Machinery, effect of, 98
Machtpolitik, 203
Magic, 559
Majority rule; see Government
Malthusianism, 50–51, 116
Man
  "the average," 547
  "the forgotten," 130, 164
  and human nature, 697–98
  "a legal animal," 31
  primitive, 222, 916
  a social being, 8, 360
"Managerial" social philosophy, 74, 107
Mariolatry, 95

Marriage
  and inheritance, 145
  and morals, 654–67
Marxism, 201, 203, 295, 299, 313, 326,
  327–28, 334, 342, 442, 450, 454, 469,
  540, 550, 609
Masses, the; see Crowd, the
Materialism, 294, 390, 398, 508, 511
  evolutionary, 10
  historic, 252, 263
  sociological, 503
Mathematics and social progress, 52
Matriarchy, 196, 668–76
Matronymic groups, 448, 750
Matter and motion, 669–70
Mayflower Compact, 29
"Meaning of sociology," 283–84
  see also Definitions of sociology
Means-end system, 301–2
Mechanical interpretations, 360
Mechanics, social, 174
Medieval period, 16–20
  thought in, dominance of, by Aristotle, 8
Meliorism, 863
Memory, 523
Mentality; see Mind
Mercantilism, 46, 61, 587, 773
Metaphysics, biological, 661–62
Methodology, 289, 290–99, 658, 767, 781–
  82, 797, 799–800, 843–45, 863
  logicoexperimental, 557–58, 560
  scientific, 84–85
  of study, 447–49
Middle Ages; see Medieval period
Middle class, 30, 41, 98, 164, 199–200,
  365
  in Germany, decline of, 353–54, 355–56
  in Great Britain, 354
  origin of, 198
  spirit of, 324
Might and right, 808
Migration, 755, 920–21
Milieu; see Environment
Militarism, 419–40, 631, 759, 861
  and industrialism, 114, 123–25, 169, 201,
  202–3
Mind
  animal and human, 671
  and climate, 7
  "culture," 894, 897–98
  individual and social, 7
  Jacobin, 494–95, 496
  mystic and criminal, 494–95
  "social," 621, 751–52, 830, 919

Minorities, 749–50
Minority
    "creative," 725–26
    "dominant," 725
    and majority, 127
"Misarchists," 184
Mobility, vertical and horizontal, 887
Modern and "ancient" society, 144–45
Monarchies, growth of, 21
Monarchomachs, 30
Monarchy, 31, 33–36, 125, 812, 878
    "social," of Stein, 366
Money, 303
    economy of, 263–64
    theory of, 387
Monism
    demographic, 453
    and dualism, 377
    and pluralism, 450
    "positive," 382, 383
    spiritual, 618
Monogamy, 142, 143, 146, 656–57
Monopolies
    consequences of, 340
    in land, 342–43, 570
    origin of, 339
Monotheism, 93–94
    defensive, 95
    social, 94–95
Morality, 158, 499, 926
    codes of, 874
    and customs, 663
    industrial and social, 98–99
    and marriage, 654–67
    and order and law, 236–37
    origin of, 10
    sociology of, 662–65
    theory of, 511–12
    values of, 837
Mores, 158–59, 755, 874
"Mortmain" ("dead hand"), 112
Mother
    and child, 448
    descent through, 448, 750
        see also Matriarchy;   Matronymic
        groups
Motion and matter, 669–70
Motivation, 299
    mutation of, 219
    "schedules" of, 888–89
Mutation; see Variation
Mutualism, 435, 539
Myth, and religion, 924–25

Nation
    definition of, 118–19, 427, 875
    evolution of, 576
    expansion of, 431
    heterogeneous, 795
    and state, 404, 626, 711, 809–10
National Socialism, 59, 215, 238
"National" stage of development, 180
Nationalism, 20, 60, 371, 386, 446, 722,
        861, 862, 865
    German, 59, 215, 238
    and imperialism, 645–49
    and internationalism, 631
Nationality, 168, 428
    principle of, 431
Nations, League of; see League of Nations
Natural-science tradition, 276
"Naturalism," 129
Naturalistic method, 358
Nature
    adaptation to, 917–18
    "community-law," 238
    human, 837–38, 860–61
    mastery over, 359
    state of, 36, 37
"Nature" and "nurture," 710
Needs; see Interests
Neo-Augustinianism, 718–21
Neo-Kantians, 333, 336, 347
Neoliberals, 132
Neo-Platonism, 13
"Neoromanticism," 385
Neuroses, 508
Neutrality, 548
New Deal, 170
News, dissemination of, 478–79
Newspapers, 711, 712–13, 880
Nonaggression, 132
Nonparticularism, 845
Norms, social, 236–38
Notoriety and fame, 20
"Nurture" and "nature," 710

Obedience and command, 52, 91
Object-values, 798
Objects of sociology, 265, 266, 365
Obligation
    moral, 522
    mutual, 18–19
Obscurantism, 46
Observation, scientific method of, 84
Occupation and social function, 825
Officeholders, 259
Oligarchy, 120, 125

Ontogenetic forces, 176
Opinion, public, 103–4, 134–35, 238–40, 415, 437, 478–79, 879–80
Opposition
  to sociology, 383
  see also Conflict
Optimists, 40
Order
  law and morality and, 236–37
  social; *see* Control
Orders, societal, 370
Organism, 459
  contractual and social, 462–66
  and society, analogy of, 115
Organization, 391
  ecclesiastical; *see* Religion
  functioning of, and environment, 689–91
  nonpolitical, 816
  social; *see* Society
  world, 865
Oriental social thought, 4–5
Origin
  and differentiation of sociology, 75
  of man, polygenesis, 432
  of society; *see* Society
Originality; *see* Creativeness
Origins
  political, 195–201
  social, 674
Oscillations, social, 547, 550
Otherworldliness, 13, 16, 38–39, 294, 296
Overpopulation, 342
Oversoul, 919
Ownership of land; *see* Land

Pacifism, 857
Pair-relation, 277
Pantarchy, 180
Parliaments, 491–92, 582
Parsimony, law of, **174**
Parties, political, 179, 437–38, 700, 880–81
  government by, 202
  rise of, 199
Past and future, 691
Pathology, political, 22
Patriarchy, 33, 142, 196, **672, 673**
Patriotism, 94, 125, 260, 263
  nationalization of, 25
Patristic Christianity, social philosophy of, 14–16
Patronymic groups, 750
Patterns
  institutional, 296, 297, 299, 302
  plurality of, 279, 280–81

Paulinism, 15
Peace
  internal, in building of a state, 875–76
  through arbitration, 72
Penology and criminology, 479, 572, 742
Perception and apperception, 218–19
Perfection, quest for, 59
"Period, positive," of Comte, 366
Periodicals, 742–43
Person; *see* Individual
Personalism
  agelic, 511–12
  moral, 519
Personality, 258
  and culture, **802**
  social, 761
Phenomena
  cultural and historic, 892–93
  social and individual, 388, 800
Philosophes, 61, 129
Philosophy
  agrarian, 332–52
  of history, 24, 26, 252, 475
  social, 82, 691
  and sociology, 501
  synthetic, of Spencer, 113
  "telic," 714
  unifying, of sociology, 400–401
Phylogenetic forces, 176
Physiocracy, 46, 47, 61–63, 72, 129, 181
Place, work, and folk, 678, 688–89
Planning, public, 61, 185
Platonists, 894
Pluralism
  and monism, 450
  political, 32
Plutocracy, 181
  in England, 149
"Police" function of government, **183**
Politarchy, 180
Political authority; *see* Government
Political economy, 843
Political science, 623, 699–705
  and economics, 545
  and ethics, 22–23
  international, 703–4
  opinions, nonrational, 701
  principles of Machiavelli, 23
  psychology of, 701
  sociological theory of, 476–80
  and sociology, 87, 117–18, 177, 808–9, 874–75
Politicians, 166, 881

Politics
  and economics and culture, 240–42
  see also Political science
"Politics, rational," 63
Polity, culture and art, 689
Polygenism, 195–96, 202
Polytheism, 93–94
Poor; see Poverty
Poor Law of 1603, English, 16
Population
  checks on, and increase, 342, 575–78,
    920–21
  composition of, 755
  and food, 50–51
  and population changes, 452–53
  rural, 341
  social, 826
  trends in, Spencer's theory of, 115–16
  and wealth, 841
Positivism, 81–109, 462, 499, 501, 503,
    553
  sociological, 374–84
Possibilities, "limitation" of, 455
Potential, social, 175, 390
Poverty, 643–44
  as part of "divine order," 16
Power
  political; see Sovereignty
  spiritual and temporal, 101
Predestination, 298–99
Predictability of behavior, 889
Premises of sociology, 446
Prepolitical period, 810
Press; see Newspapers
Pride, patriotic, rationalization of, 25
"Priesthood," Positivist, 100–103, 185
Priests, function of, 22
"Primitive" society, 144–45, 448
Primordial state, 7
Principles, form, regularities of, 265
Probability, concept of, 442
Processes
  "constructive" and "destructive," 280
  reconstructive, 826
  social, civilizational, and cultural, 359–
    60, 783–85, 823–24, 827–29, 870–72
  predictability of, 889
  products of, 824, 830
Productivity, factors in, 775
Profit; see Acquisitiveness
Profit economy; see Capitalism
Profit-making, 293
Program of sociology, 372

Progress
  denial of, 192, 193
  dialectic of, Hegelian, 59–60
  intellectual, three stages of, 86–87
  law and theory of, 38, 74
  of man, 140–42, 244
  social, 406, 411, 566–67, 645, 802, 816,
    918–19
    and evolution, 621
  theory of, 544, 890–91
Proletariat, 98
  "internal" and "external," 726–27
Proofs, verbal, 564–66
Property, 303–4, 340, 344
  communal, 146–47
  and inheritance, 145–49
  as prime factor in civilization, 148
  private, 12–13, 36–41, 44–45, 641–42,
    775
  origin of, 147
  taxation of, 642
Protectionism, 124, 125
"Protective" function of government, 183
Protestantism; see Religion
"Protocracy," 199, 747, 748
Psychiatrists and psychoanalysts, 697
Psychological and cultural sociology, 459,
    793–804
Psychologism, 502
Psychology
  dynamic, 706, 707
  economic and social, 469
  folk, 211, 212, 220–22
    and individual, 34, 212, 221, 231, 236,
      265, 698–99, 797
  and history, 221
  influence of Wundt on, 217–18
  instinctivist, 661–62
  mass; see Crowd, the
  national-social, 466
  social, and sociology, 798, 821
Psychosociology, 212, 216–26, 833–52
"Public," the, 281
Public and crowd, 478–79
Punaluan family, 142, 143
Purposes, human, 862

Quantitative method, 742, 761–63

Races, 920
  comparison of, 841–42
  differentiation of, 381
  egoism in, 201

problem of, 382
white, domination by, 402
Radicalism
and conservatism, 312, 882
social, beginning of, 44–45
Rationalism, 13, 54–55, 66–68, 232, 323
growth of, 38
Rationality, 321
"formal" and "substantive," 302–3
Rationalization, 558–59
Reaction, in groups, 747
Realism, agelic, 505
Reality
historical, three spheres, 359
social, 592
Realpolitik, 203
Reason
Absolute, 59
in evolution, 618
and faith, 894
and instinct, 376, 885–16
Rebellion as a sin, 16
Reconstruction, social
Positivist scheme of, 97–103
by sociology, 365–71
Reform, 837
governmental, 185–87, 816
nineteenth-century, 56
social, 41–45, 165, 185–87, 215
agrarian philosophy of, 332–52
plan for, 345–47
and the state, 881–82
through state activity, 163–66
views of Sumner on, 160
Reformation, 608
Regimentation, 124
Regionalism, 92
Regulative institutions, 5
Rehabilitation, national, 215
Relations
"common-human," 279
international, 815
political; *see* Government
social, 234–36
institution, of, 10
and social action, 300
Relativism, historical, 895
Relativity, social, 846
Relief (charity), 16
Religio, 12
Religion, 56, 236–37, 607–8, 611–12, 865
Brahmanism, 298
Calvinism, 297–99, 313

and capitalism, 214
Catholicism, 297
Christianity, 13, 865
cosmogony of, 139
early and patristic, 14–16, 38
ethic, 311
Fathers of the Church, 13–15, 115
medieval, 15
"new," 74
of Saint-Simon, 366
patristic, sociological doctrines of, 15–16
Paulinism, 15
philosophical expression, 19
Protestantism; *see* Religion, Protestantism
Roman Catholic; *see* Religion, Roman Catholic church
in social, philosophy, 13
church, universal, 21
church and state, 14, 17, 18, 21, 644
separation of, 101
views of Aquinas on, 20
churches, 15
Confucianism, 296, 297
decline of, 486
dogmas in, 502
establishment of the church, 95
"ethic," 295, 298
"ethical culture," 242
and family, 87
"fear of the dead" in, 119
Hinduism, 296, 524
humanism, 107
of Humanity, 91–92
in international affairs, 713
and labor, 571
and myth, 924–25
organizations, 311
orientation, 301–2
proofs of, 560
Protestantism, 294, 296, 297, 608–9
influence of, 313
and the modern spirit, 312
rise of, 20
psychological interpretations of, 53–54
Roman Catholic church, 15
attack on, by Marsiglio, 21–22
legal system of, 29
and science, 787
"sexual," 563
sociology of, 289, 290, 292–99
ideas of Troeltsch, 309–15
theocracy, 94, 96, 811

Religion—*continued*
   theology, patristic and medieval, 13
   theory of, 514–16
Renaissance, the, 22–23
Rent, for land, law of, 341–42
Rentiers and speculators, 567
Repetition, social, 472, 921
Representation
   collective, 460, 510–11, 517, 521, 525–26
   territorial, 37
Representative government, 125
Reproduction, class, 577
Republic
   "conservative," 45
   as form of government, 812
Republicanism and democracy, 161–62
Research
   methods of, in social sciences, 803
   rural social, 844–45
   social, 841–45
Residue, sexual, 563
Residues, 555–58, 560–66
Responsibility, social, 355
Restraints on the individual, 638–40
Revolution
   commercial, 30, 47, 57, 401
   and crime, 886
   of 1848, 103
   French, 37–38, 40, 45, 46, 65, 73, 96, 97,
      345, 495
   industrial, 47, 63, 71–72, 97, 130, 363,
      365, 366, 401, 496, 705–6, 730
   from the right, 371
   right of, 33, 35, 36–37, 41, 45
   social, 244
   "Western," 95
Revolutions, 370, 885–87
   psychology of, 492–96
Right
   divine; *see* Divine right
   human (natural), 119, 128, 200, 637–40
   and might, 808
   natural, and chartered, 167
   political, 166–67, 200, 630
Roman Catholic church; *see* Religion
Romanticism, 57, 58, 65, 165, 232, 385
Rome, 94, 630
   economy of, 344–45
   social philosophy in, 11–14
Rule; *see* Government
Ruler
   necessity for, 19
   as physician to the state, 22
Rules; *see* Codes

Rural social research, 844–45, 888
Russia, 441–42, 889
   revolution, 493
   see also Union of Soviet Socialist Re-
      publics

Salvation, 298
   and damnation, 719
   risk to, in social reform, 16
Samtschaft, 234–36
Savior, Divine, 727
Saviors, 720, 727
"Schedules, motivation," 888–89
Scholasticism, 17, 19, 20, 319
"School, formal," of sociology, 250
Science
   in international affairs, 713–14
   modern, vision of R. Bacon, 39
   natural, and social, 47, 209, 319–21,
      383, 512, 785, 867, 928–29
   political; *see* Political science
   and religion, 787
"Science of society," 72
Sciences
   fundamental, of sociology, 689
   hierarchy of, 84–85
   political and other, 73
   social, 543–44
Secession from nation, right of, 436
Security of state, internal and external,
   644–45
Selection
   natural, 755–56
   societal, 158, 459
"Self"; *see* Individual
"Self, looking-glass," 837, 845–46, 848
"Self-consciousness" of sociology, 282
Self-interest, 327
   Epicurean, 10
Self-words, 842
Selfishness, 860–61
Sensatism, 894
Sense-perception, renunciation of, 13
"Sensualism, historical," 263
Sentiment, public; *see* Opinion, public
Setting, social, and individual psychology,
   220
Sex
   "heretics," 562
   morality; *see* Morals
   "religion," 563
   residues, 561, 563
   sociology of, 797–99

Shamanism, 562
Similarities and variations, 449
Single-family origin of society, 24
Single tax; *see* Taxation
Situation, social, 801–2
Skepticism, 13
Slavery
  the "coming," 179
  origin and abolition of, 147, 197
Sociability, 60, 89
"Social forces error," 871
Socialism, 63, 495–96, 708
  criticism of, 435
  Guild, 19, 398, 435
  menace of, 487
  program for, 411
  Spencer's antagonism to, 131
  state, 242
"Socialization," 279, 752, 784, 827
  and association, 191
  of law, 408, 411
Sociation, 275, 276, 279–83, 806–7
Societas and *civitas,* 144–45, 147
"Societies," 549
Society, 281
  ambivalent conception of, 514
  "becoming," or "emerging," 769
  classes, and leaders in, 394–95
  cohesion in, 627
  and community, 213, 368–69, 401–2
  component, and constituent, 750
  conflict and amalgamation in, 195–201
  control in, extra-legal, 415
  definitions of, 427, 624–25, 757
  double nature of, 466
  environment and political theory of, 415
  evolution of, 359, 379–81
  foundations of, philosophical, 67
  genesis of, 826
  "gentile" and aristocratic, 146, 147–48
  and God, 511–12, 515–16
  and government, 36, 90
  gratitude in, 262
  as "Great Being," 499
  group basis of, 24
  group self-preservation in, 259
  groups in, 234–36
  heritage, social, of, 709–16
  hierarchy in, 393–95
  human rational, 753
  identity of groups in, 260
  and individual, 9, 22, 252, 253, 258, 505, 510–11, 513, 517–18, 806–7, 821, 827, 836–37, 846, 918
    organization, 391
    in social thinking, 4–5
  institutions of, 659–61, 757–61, 784–85, 824, 839, 923–29
    evolution of, 121–23
    natural history of, 659–61
  integration of, 509–10
  interactions and relations in, 192, 258–63
  international, 406
  loyalty in, 262
  modern, 706
    organization of, 708
  as natural product, 15
  nature of, 254–57
  organic, 840–41
  and organism, analogy of, 115
  organization of, 690, 750–51, 837, 917–18
    beginning of, 747–48
    "gentile," 405
    group, 261
    nature of, 750–51
    normal, 337
  origin of, 12, 22, 24, 196
    and evolution, 745–50
  and politics, principles of Machiavelli, 23
  relations, 254
  "science" of, 72
  and state, 118, 354, 362, 403–4, 875
    Hegel on, 372
  structure, 258–63, 391
    differentiation, 381
    syngenetic, 176, 192
  theories of, 231, 390
  totality in, 390
  unity and solidarity in, 196
Society-community, 283
"Society, the Great," 705
"Society" and "state," differentiation of, 194–95, 809
Sociocracy, 94, 96, 181–82, 186
Sociogenetic forces, 176, 192
Sociography, 232
Sociolatry, 95
Sociological Review, 686
Sociological Society, 686
Sociologism, 458–60, 499–537
Sociology and Social Research, 742
Solemn League and Covenant, 29
Solidarity, 561
  natural, 466
  social, 917

Solvay Institute, 538
Sophists, 7
Soul
  racial, 483
  world, 919
Sovereignty, 97, 127, 166–67, 178–79,
    406–8, 429, 637–40, 748–49, 878
  attributes of, 67
  definitions of, 24, 813
  limitations of, 813
  origin of, 197
  political, 127
  and wealth, 571
  popular, 14, 16, 18, 30, 31, 33, 37
  principle of, 242
  unlimited, 119
  see also specific entries in the Index; e.g.,
    Monarchy
Soviet Russia; see Union of Soviet Socialist
  Republics
Space, category of, 517–18
Spain, 585–99
Specialization
  of function, 90
    see also Labor, division of
Species and individual, 6, 10–11
Speculators and rentiers, 567
Spheres, three, of sociology, 230–31
Spirit, modern, and Protestantism, 312
Spiritual forces, 176
Spirituality, 391
Spoliation and exchange, 425–27
Stability, state, 6
State
  activities of, 410, 434–35, 640–45
  attributes of, 89, 428–29
  as brain of the social organism, 178
  and church, 14, 17, 18, 21
    views of Aquinas on, 20
  city-state, 430–31
  and community, 386–87
  conquest and culture, 380
  control, 928
  corporative, 398
  definition of, 783–84
  development of; see State, origin of
  and education, 644
  ethics and, 201
  evolution of, 379–81
  expansion of, 200–201
  and family, 644
  "folk," 200
  forms and scope of, 62, 165, 182–84,
    409–11, 812, 813–14, 878–79

functions of
  proper, according to Spencer, 130–31
  restriction of, 163–66
  and government, 37, 118–21, 809, 875
    forms of, 96–97, 123–27
  "ideal," 393–95
  and individual, 18–19, 485
    analogy of, 18
  institutions, 484–85
    origin of, 810–11
  and international relations, 412–14
  as joint-stock company, 130
  modern, 704
  monopolies, 410
  and nation, 404, 626, 711, 809–10
  natural and political, 232–34
  nature of, 88, 194–95
  origin of, 19, 176, 180–81, 197, 339,
    380, 405, 429–30, 810, 875–78
  power of, increase in, 21
  rationalistic, 242
  and religion, 644
  and social reform, 881–82
  and society, 118, 354, 362, 403–4, 875
    Hegel on, 372
  stability of, 6
  struggles in, intrastate, 877
  Sumner's conception of, 161
  supremacy of, 61
  theory of, 236
  universal, 21, 726–27, 928
"State, Universal," 723, 726
"State" and "society," 809
  differentiation between, 194–95
States, parochial, 724
Static outlook; see Conservatism
"Statics, social," 73, 84, 86, 174, 175
Statistics, social, 502, 505, 762
Stimuli, 803
Stoicism, 5, 9–10, 13–15, 338, 894
Stratification; see Classes
Structure and function of society, 770
Structures, institutional, 296, 297, 299, 302
Struggle; see Conflict
Studies, social, 188
Study, comparative, of institutions, 64
Subject matter of sociology, 174
Subjugation, 758
Subordination and superordination, 250,
  258–63
"Substratum," social, 503
Success, 327
  in conformity with mores, 159

Suggestion and suggestibility, 829–30
Suicide, 504, 508–10, 523–24
Superiority, race, 487
Supernatural forces, 5
Superordination and subordination, 250, 258–63
Superstate, need for, 349
Surveys, 680, 683, 686–87
Survival, principle of, 448, 755–56
  struggle for, 468, 877–78
Switzerland, social reform, 411, 415
Symbiosis, 32
Sympathy, 24, 53, 54
  reflective, 11, 35
Sympodial development, 174
Syndicalism, 496, 539–42, 544–45, 550–51, 708
Syndyasmian family, 142
Synergy, social, 173, 174, 175, 179, 918
Syngenism, 196
Synthesis, creative, 173, 217–18
Synthesis, antithesis, and thesis, Hegelian, 59
System
  economic, 395–98
  of sociology, threefold, 232
Systematization of science, 283
  social, modern, 706
  of social processes, 827–28

Taboos, 515, 522, 563, 564, 674
Tasks of sociology, 401
Taxation, 642
  single, on land, 62
Technocracy, 107
Technological unemployment, 342
Technology, 328
Teleology, 401
"Telesis," social, 104, 107, 158, 173, 176, 185, 187, 201, 412
  and "genesis," 174, 176
Tendencies, social, 803
Themistes, 755
Theocracy; see Religion
"Theodicy," 719, 721–27
Theology; see Religion
Theories, evolutionary and organic, 116
Theory
  organic, of society and state, 106, 136
  "societarian political," 438
  sociological, 841–43
  of Spencer, summary of, 114
  system of, 300

Thesis, antithesis, and synthesis, Hegelian, 59
"Thing" of Durkheim, 501
Thought
  and will and emotion, 707–8
  see also Ideas
Time
  budgets, 888–89
  division of, 518
"Time of Troubles," 725–26
Toleration, 747, 756
Totalitarianism, 32, 214, 398
  and democracy, 894
Totality, concept of, 517–18
Totemism, 449, 514, 515, 518, 522
Towns, 679–80
  growth of, 343–44
  urbanization, 705–6
Trade, 426
  exchange, and spoliation, 425-27
  international, 437
Tradition, 839
  and custom, 120–21
  natural-science, 276
  social, 861–62, 866
Traditionalism, 297, 323
Traits, racial, 496, 920
Transcendentalism, agelic, 510–12
Transformation, 42, 472
Transition period, medievalism to modernity, 20–28
Transportation, theory of, 841
Triads
  of Comte and Vico, 93
  of Geddes, 678, 688–89
Tribe, and clan, 145
Truth, 557–58
  three kinds of, 895
Type, formal, of sociology, 368–69
Types
  ideal, 290–92
  social, 370
    variations from, 753–54
Tyrannicide, defense of, 18
Tyranny, and rebellion against, 18

Unemployment; see Labor
Unification, social, 200
Uniformities, 824
Union of Soviet Socialist Republics, 889
Unions, labor; see Labor
United States
  defects in government of, 162–63
  sociology in, 739–44

Unity
  corporate, of society, 65
  human, 866
  organic, 845, 846–48
"Universalism," 214, 385–99
Urbanization; see Towns
Use-value, 340
Utilitarianism, 40, 54, 55, 68, 502, 503–4,
  506, 507, 708
"Utilities, public," 761
"Utility, marginal," 340
Utilization, individual, 752
Utopia, 8–9, 12, 41–45, 92, 188, 201, 393–
  95
  of Plato, 6, 7
  Positivist, 81–109
  theories of, 6

Valuations, subjective, of economic goods,
  340
Value-elements, 326
Value-judgments, 336, 863, 866, 890
  in science, 283
Values, 803
  ideational and sensate, 892
  individual and objective, 800
  moral, 837
  object, 798
  social, 236–38, 759–60, 872, 874
  theory of, 512–14
"Values" concept, 797–98
Variations
  of motives, 219
  from social type, and similarities, 449,
    753–54, 762–63
Volition, 382, 526
  concerted, 7, 748
  free, 382
    and determinism, 689–90, 873
  human, 233
  public, 839–40
  will, emotion, and thought, 707–8

Wages; see Labor
War, 406, 419–40
  arbitration as a substitute for, 132
  in building of a state, 875–76
  cause of, economic, 413
  causes and effects, 477, 923
  economic and physical, 203
  elimination of, 475
    by social evolution, 203–4
  emphasis upon, 877
  interparochial, 722
  as obstacle to progress, 72
  outmoded, 412
  in political development, 202
  see also Conflict
Warrior class, 124
Wealth
  accumulation of, 324
  and population, 841
  social responsibility of, 102
  see also Capitalism
Weltgeist, 92, 413, 414
White race, domination by, 402
Will; see Volition
"Wishes, four," 796, 800–801
"Withdrawal-and-Return," 725–26, 732
Women
  emancipation of, 95
  rule by (gynaecocracy), 173, 176
  see also Matriarchal theory
Work; see Labor
Work, folk, and place; see Place, work, and
  folk
World state, 928
World War I, 647–48
Writer, and social environment, 3–4
Würzburg School, 800

Yang and Yin, 719, 720, 728

"Zoism," 175